EPIC COLLECTION

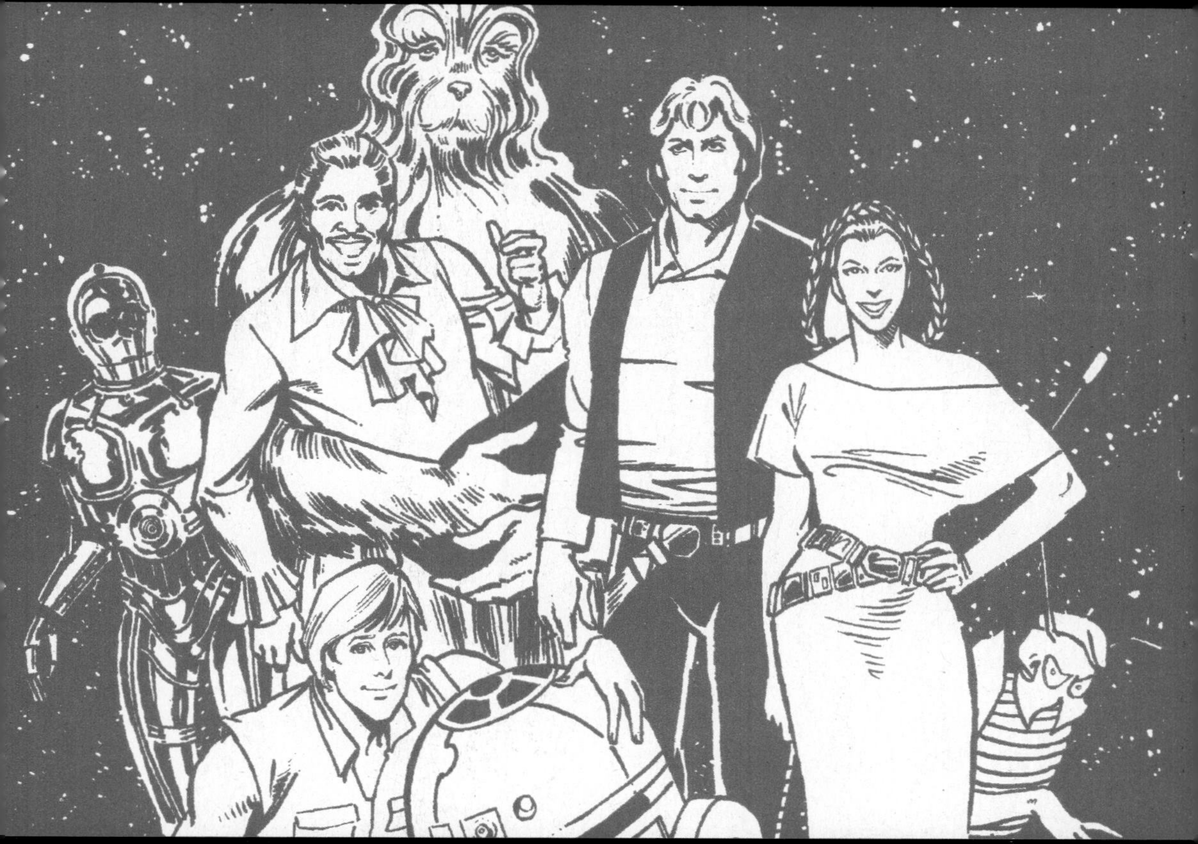

STAR WARS™

THE ORIG
MARVEL YEARS

STAR WARS
LEGENDS

WRITERS:
ANN NOCENTI, JO DUFFY, ARCHIE GOODWIN & MATTHEW ROSENBERG

PENCILERS:
BRET BLEVINS, BOB McLEOD, TONY SALMONS, JAN DUURSEMA, SAL BUSCEMA, CYNTHIA MARTIN, AL WILLIAMSON & RON FRENZ WITH STEVE LEIALOHA, GIUSEPPE CAMUNCOLI, ANDREA BROCCARDO, KERRY GAMMILL, STEFANO LANDINI, LUKE ROSS & LEONARD KIRK

INKERS:
**BRET BLEVINS,
TOM PALMER,
TOM MANDRAKE,
STEVE LEIALOHA,
BOB WIACEK,
ART NICHOLS,
AL WILLIAMSON,
SAM DE LA ROSA,
KEN STEACY,
WHILCE PORTACIO & CO.
WITH CAM SMITH,
ANDREA BROCCARDO,
ZÉ CARLOS,
JAN DUURSEMA,
STEFANO LANDINI,
LUKE ROSS &
LEONARD KIRK**

COLORISTS:
**GLYNIS OLIVER,
BOB SHAREN,
PETRA SCOTESE,
MICHELE WRIGHTSON,
DAINA GRAZIUNAS,
ELAINE LEE &
CHRIS SOTOMAYOR**

LETTERERS:
**JOE ROSEN,
RICK PARKER,
KEN BRUZENAK,
ED KING,
TOM ORZECHOWSKI &
VC's CLAYTON COWLES**

ASSISTANT EDITORS:
**PETER SANDERSON,
TERRY KAVANAGH &
TOM GRONEMAN**

EDITORS:
**LOUISE SIMONSON,
ANN NOCENTI &
MARK PANICCIA**

FRONT COVER ARTISTS:
**CYNTHIA MARTIN &
JOSEF RUBINSTEIN**

BACK COVER ARTIST:
TOM PALMER

COLLECTION EDITOR: **JENNIFER GRÜNWALD**
ASSISTANT EDITOR: **DANIEL KIRCHHOFFER**
ASSISTANT MANAGING EDITOR: **MAIA LOY**
ASSOCIATE MANAGER, TALENT RELATIONS: **LISA MONTALBANO**
ASSOCIATE MANAGER, DIGITAL ASSETS: **JOE HOCHSTEIN**
VP PRODUCTION & SPECIAL PROJECTS: **JEFF YOUNGQUIST**
RESEARCH: **MIKE HANSEN**
BOOK DESIGNER: **SARAH SPADACCINI**

SENIOR DESIGNER: **JAY BOWEN**
SVP PRINT, SALES & MARKETING: **DAVID GABRIEL**
EDITOR IN CHIEF: **C.B. CEBULSKI**
SPECIAL THANKS TO **ROBERT SIMPSON** & **LUCASFILM**
AND **DEIDRE HANSEN**

STAR WARS LEGENDS EPIC COLLECTION: THE ORIGINAL MARVEL YEARS VOL. 6. Contains material originally published in magazine form as STAR WARS (1977) #89-107 and STAR WARS (2019) #108. First printing 2023. ISBN 978-1-302-95158-0. Published by MARVEL WORLDWIDE, INC., a subsidiary of MARVEL ENTERTAINMENT, LLC. OFFICE OF PUBLICATION: 1290 Avenue of the Americas, New York, NY 10104. STAR WARS and related text and illustration are trademarks and/or copyrights, in the United States and other countries, of Lucasfilm Ltd. and/or its affiliates. © & TM Lucasfilm Ltd. No similarity between any of the names, characters, persons, and/or institutions in this book with those of any living or dead person or institution is intended, and any such similarity which may exist is purely coincidental. Marvel and its logos are TM Marvel Characters, Inc. **Printed in Canada.** KEVIN FEIGE, Chief Creative Officer; DAN BUCKLEY, President, Marvel Entertainment; DAVID BOGART, Associate Publisher & SVP of Talent Affairs; TOM BREVOORT, VP, Executive Editor; NICK LOWE, Executive Editor, VP of Content, Digital Publishing; DAVID GABRIEL, VP of Print & Digital Publishing; SVEN LARSEN, VP of Licensed Publishing; MARK ANNUNZIATO, VP of Planning & Forecasting; JEFF YOUNGQUIST, VP of Production & Special Projects; ALEX MORALES, Director of Publishing Operations; DAN EDINGTON, Director of Editorial Operations; RICKEY PURDIN, Director of Talent Relations; JENNIFER GRÜNWALD, Director of Production & Special Projects; SUSAN CRESPI, Production Manager; STAN LEE, Chairman Emeritus. For information regarding advertising in Marvel Comics or on Marvel.com, please contact Vit DeBellis, Custom Solutions & Integrated Advertising Manager, at vdebellis@marvel.com. For Marvel subscription inquiries, please call 888-511-5480. **Manufactured between 3/10/2023 and 4/11/2023 by SOLISCO PRINTERS, SCOTT, QC, CANADA.**

10 9 8 7 6 5 4 3 2 1

THE ORIGINAL MARVEL YEARS — VOLUME 6

THE ORIGINAL MARVEL YEARS
VOL. 6

The Empire is in ruins! The Rebel Alliance has at last defeated the Imperial forces, destroying the second Death Star and saving the galaxy from oppression. Luke Skywalker has become a Jedi Knight, triumphing over the evil Emperor Palpatine and redeeming his father, Anakin Skywalker, who was once Darth Vader.

Rebel General Han Solo has been rescued from the horror of being frozen in carbonite, with the rebel leaders staging a dangerous mission to retrieve him from the clutches of the now-dead gangster Jabba the Hutt.

Despite the Emperor's defeat, the galaxy is still filled with danger. The Rebel Alliance now has a new mission: To spread the word about the Empire's defeat, and build a new alliance of free planets to keep the galaxy safe from terror. Alliance leaders now travel from world to world, in an attempt to stamp out the Empire's reach once and for all — and create a New Republic.

On the planet Herdessa, General Leia Organa and Alliance leader Mon Mothma have led a delegation to negotiate for peaceful trade. However, they soon discover that the planet is actually being run by Imperials and slavers, and lead a rebellion against the oppressors. But the Imperial leader Lumiya, has sworn revenge — and schemes to become new Dark Lord of the Sith....

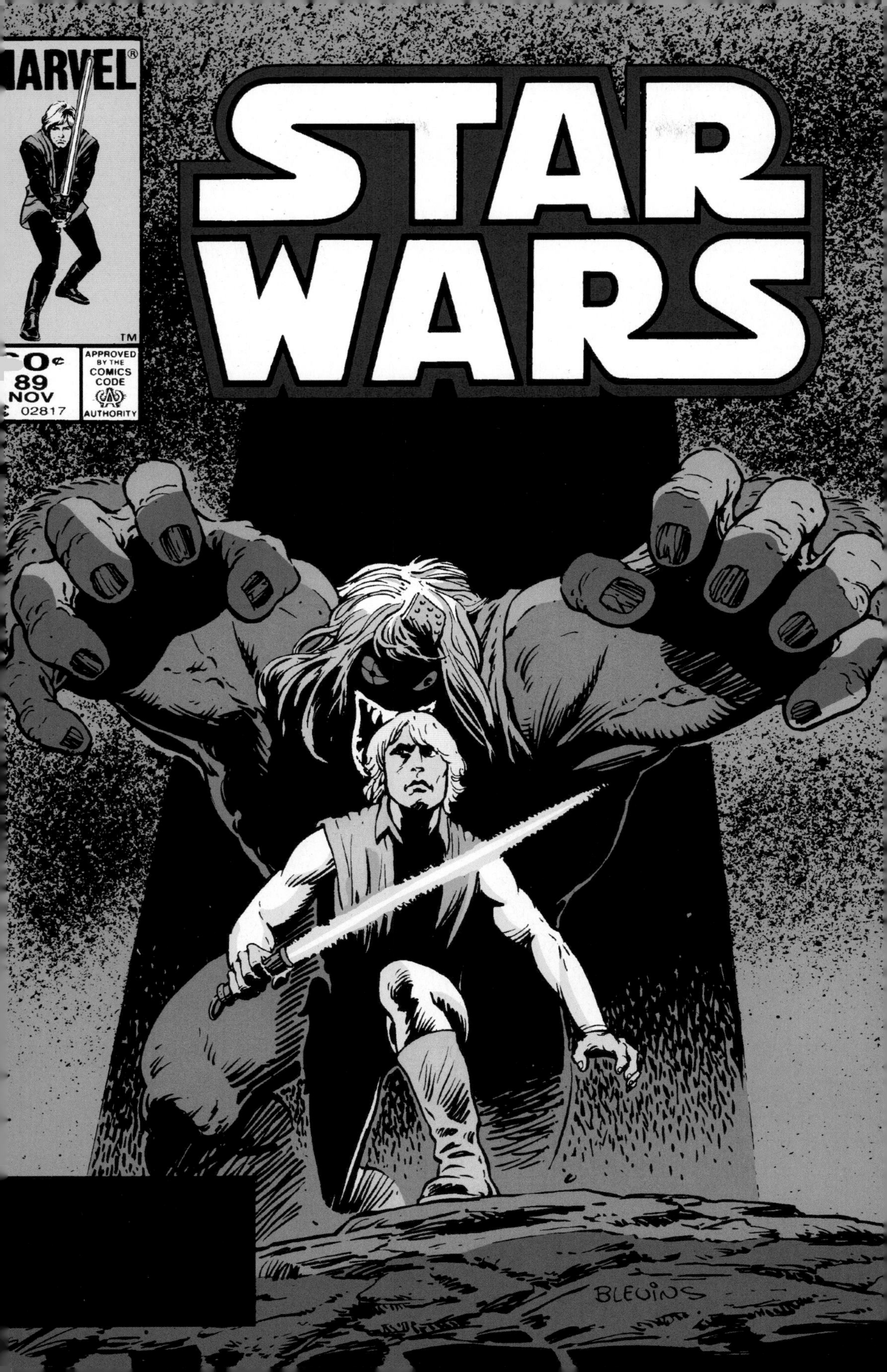
MARVEL®
STAR WARS
TM
89
NOV
02817
APPROVED BY THE COMICS CODE AUTHORITY
BLEVINS

THE EMPEROR IS DEAD! DARTH VADER IS DEAD!

AND AS IT IS WHENEVER *RULERS TOPPLE*--THE COSMOS SHUDDERS WITH REPERCUSSIONS, AND MANY WORLDS BECOME CRACKED WITH *CHAOS!*

THE FRACTURED EMPIRE STRUGGLES TO KEEP ITS STRUCTURE, WHILE THE REBEL ALLIANCE STRUGGLES TO TEAR IT APART!

THE TIMES ARE RIPE FOR *REBELLION!* FREEDOM FIGHTERS YEARN TO STRIKE AT THE EMPIRE'S WEAK POINTS AND TOPPLE THE GIANT!

THE ENTIRE GALAXY IS IN TURMOIL, AND TYPICAL OF THE CHAOS IS *SOLAY,* A BRILLIANT PLANET OF TEN SUNS!

IT'S THE PERFECT PLANET TO VISIT, IF YOU ARE *LUKE SKYWALKER,* AND YOU'RE LOOKING FOR NEW RECRUITS TO JOIN A NEW PEACE-DEDICATED ALLIANCE...

MY TIMING IS PERFECT! I GOT HERE FOR THE FINAL BATTLE! THIS PLANET'S FREEDOM FIGHTERS FINALLY HAVE THE ADVANTAGE! AND THE COURT'S PRO-EMPIRE TROOPS ARE *SCARED,* EVEN WITH ALL THEIR FANCY ARMOR, THEY ARE NO MATCH FOR THE SPIRIT OF FREEDOM! AND THE INSURGENTS ARE LUCKY TO BE LED BY SUCH A COURAGEOUS OLD REBEL--

--*RAGGOLD!* IT IS AN HONOR TO FIGHT BESIDE YOU, AND AMONG SUCH BRAVE MEN!

IT TOOK AN OLD DOG LIKE ME FIFTY YEARS OF REVOLUTION TO CROSS THESE LAST FIFTY YARDS-- WE'RE FINALLY IN THE KING'S COURT! VICTORY IS OURS! I TELL YOU, LUKE--

I'LL SEE YOU IN THE THRONE ROOM!

ANN NOCENTI	BRET BLEVINS	JOE ROSEN	GLYNIS WEIN	LOUISE JONES	JIM SHOOTER
STORY	ART	LETTERS	COLORS	EDITOR	EDITOR-IN-CHIEF

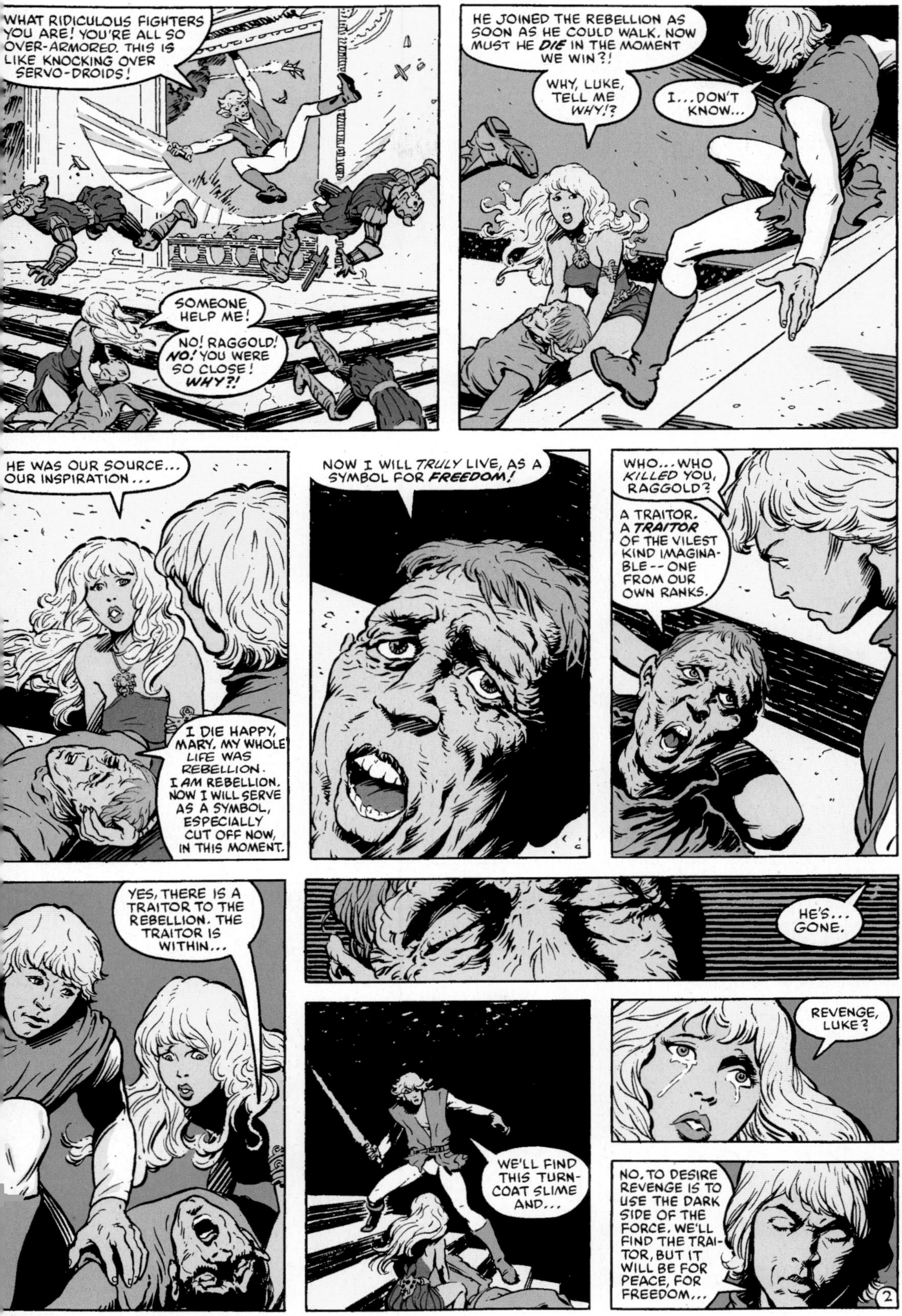
WHAT RIDICULOUS FIGHTERS YOU ARE! YOU'RE ALL SO OVER-ARMORED. THIS IS LIKE KNOCKING OVER SERVO-DROIDS!
SOMEONE HELP ME!
NO! RAGGOLD! NO! YOU WERE SO CLOSE! WHY?!
HE JOINED THE REBELLION AS SOON AS HE COULD WALK. NOW MUST HE DIE IN THE MOMENT WE WIN?!
WHY, LUKE, TELL ME WHY!?
I...DON'T KNOW...
HE WAS OUR SOURCE... OUR INSPIRATION...
I DIE HAPPY, MARY. MY WHOLE LIFE WAS REBELLION. I AM REBELLION. NOW I WILL SERVE AS A SYMBOL, ESPECIALLY CUT OFF NOW, IN THIS MOMENT.
NOW I WILL TRULY LIVE, AS A SYMBOL FOR FREEDOM!
WHO...WHO KILLED YOU, RAGGOLD?
A TRAITOR. A TRAITOR OF THE VILEST KIND IMAGINABLE--ONE FROM OUR OWN RANKS.
YES, THERE IS A TRAITOR TO THE REBELLION. THE TRAITOR IS WITHIN...
HE'S... GONE.
WE'LL FIND THIS TURNCOAT SLIME AND...
REVENGE, LUKE?
NO. TO DESIRE REVENGE IS TO USE THE DARK SIDE OF THE FORCE. WE'LL FIND THE TRAITOR, BUT IT WILL BE FOR PEACE, FOR FREEDOM...
2

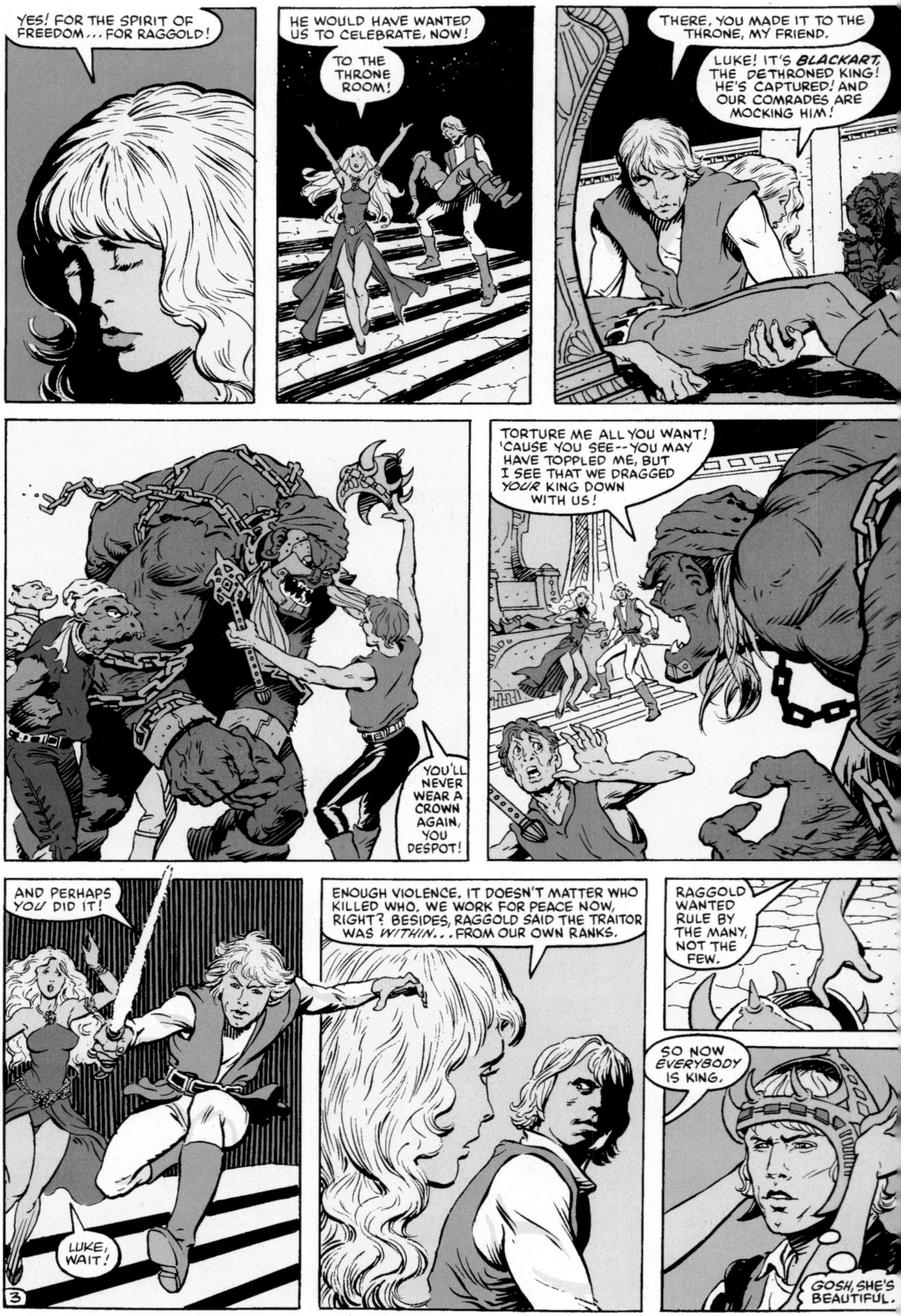
YES! FOR THE SPIRIT OF FREEDOM... FOR RAGGOLD!
HE WOULD HAVE WANTED US TO CELEBRATE, NOW!
TO THE THRONE ROOM!
THERE, YOU MADE IT TO THE THRONE, MY FRIEND.
LUKE! IT'S BLACKART, THE DETHRONED KING! HE'S CAPTURED! AND OUR COMRADES ARE MOCKING HIM!
YOU'LL NEVER WEAR A CROWN AGAIN, YOU DESPOT!
TORTURE ME ALL YOU WANT! 'CAUSE YOU SEE--YOU MAY HAVE TOPPLED ME, BUT I SEE THAT WE DRAGGED YOUR KING DOWN WITH US!
AND PERHAPS YOU DID IT!
LUKE, WAIT!
3
ENOUGH VIOLENCE. IT DOESN'T MATTER WHO KILLED WHO. WE WORK FOR PEACE NOW, RIGHT? BESIDES, RAGGOLD SAID THE TRAITOR WAS WITHIN... FROM OUR OWN RANKS.
RAGGOLD WANTED RULE BY THE MANY, NOT THE FEW.
SO NOW EVERYBODY IS KING.
GOSH, SHE'S BEAUTIFUL.

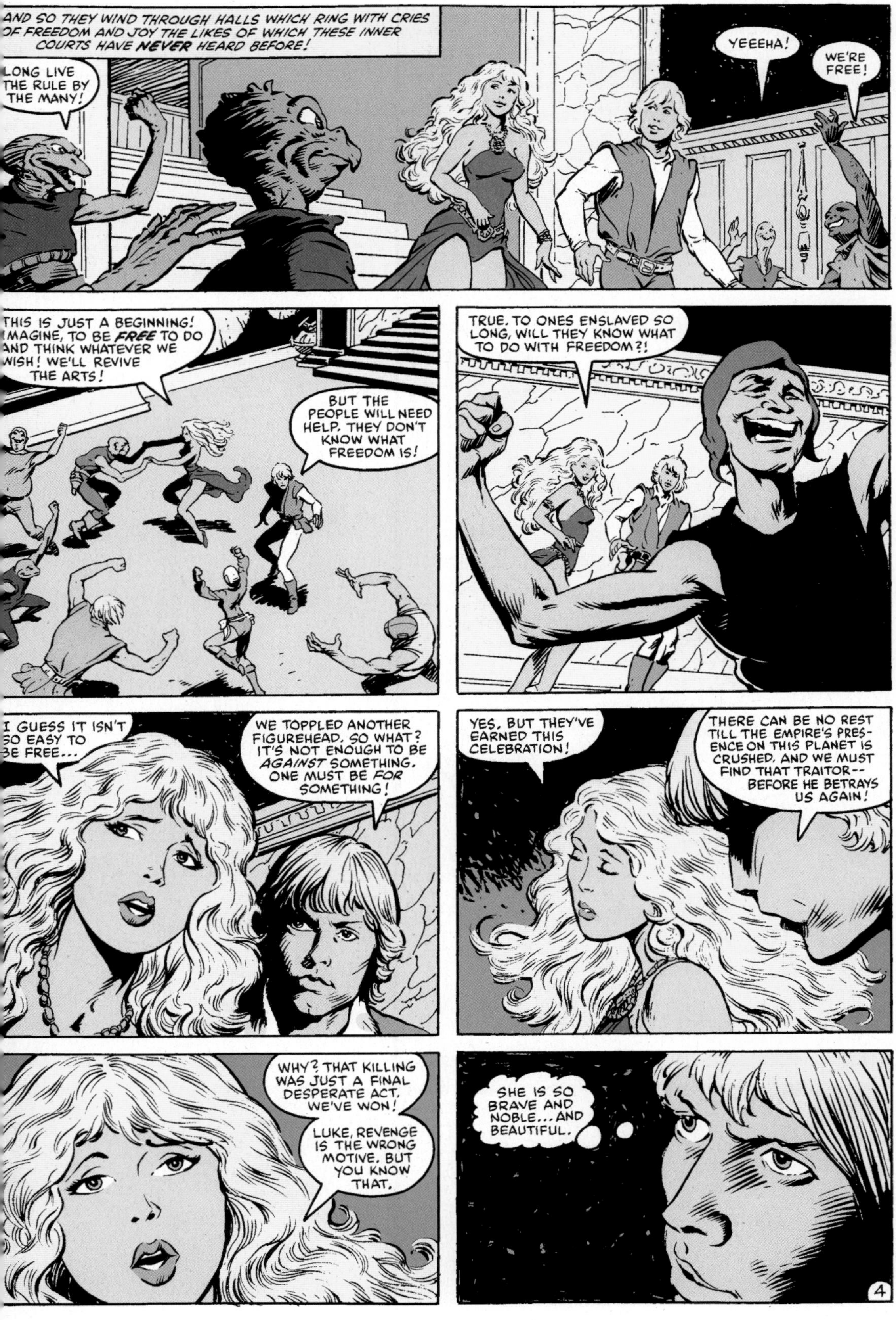
AND SO THEY WIND THROUGH HALLS WHICH RING WITH CRIES OF FREEDOM AND JOY THE LIKES OF WHICH THESE INNER COURTS HAVE NEVER HEARD BEFORE!
LONG LIVE THE RULE BY THE MANY!
YEEEHA!
WE'RE FREE!
THIS IS JUST A BEGINNING! IMAGINE, TO BE FREE TO DO AND THINK WHATEVER WE WISH! WE'LL REVIVE THE ARTS!
BUT THE PEOPLE WILL NEED HELP. THEY DON'T KNOW WHAT FREEDOM IS!
TRUE. TO ONES ENSLAVED SO LONG, WILL THEY KNOW WHAT TO DO WITH FREEDOM?!
I GUESS IT ISN'T SO EASY TO BE FREE...
WE TOPPLED ANOTHER FIGUREHEAD. SO WHAT? IT'S NOT ENOUGH TO BE AGAINST SOMETHING. ONE MUST BE FOR SOMETHING!
YES, BUT THEY'VE EARNED THIS CELEBRATION!
THERE CAN BE NO REST TILL THE EMPIRE'S PRESENCE ON THIS PLANET IS CRUSHED, AND WE MUST FIND THAT TRAITOR-- BEFORE HE BETRAYS US AGAIN!
WHY? THAT KILLING WAS JUST A FINAL DESPERATE ACT. WE'VE WON!
LUKE, REVENGE IS THE WRONG MOTIVE. BUT YOU KNOW THAT.
SHE IS SO BRAVE AND NOBLE... AND BEAUTIFUL.
4

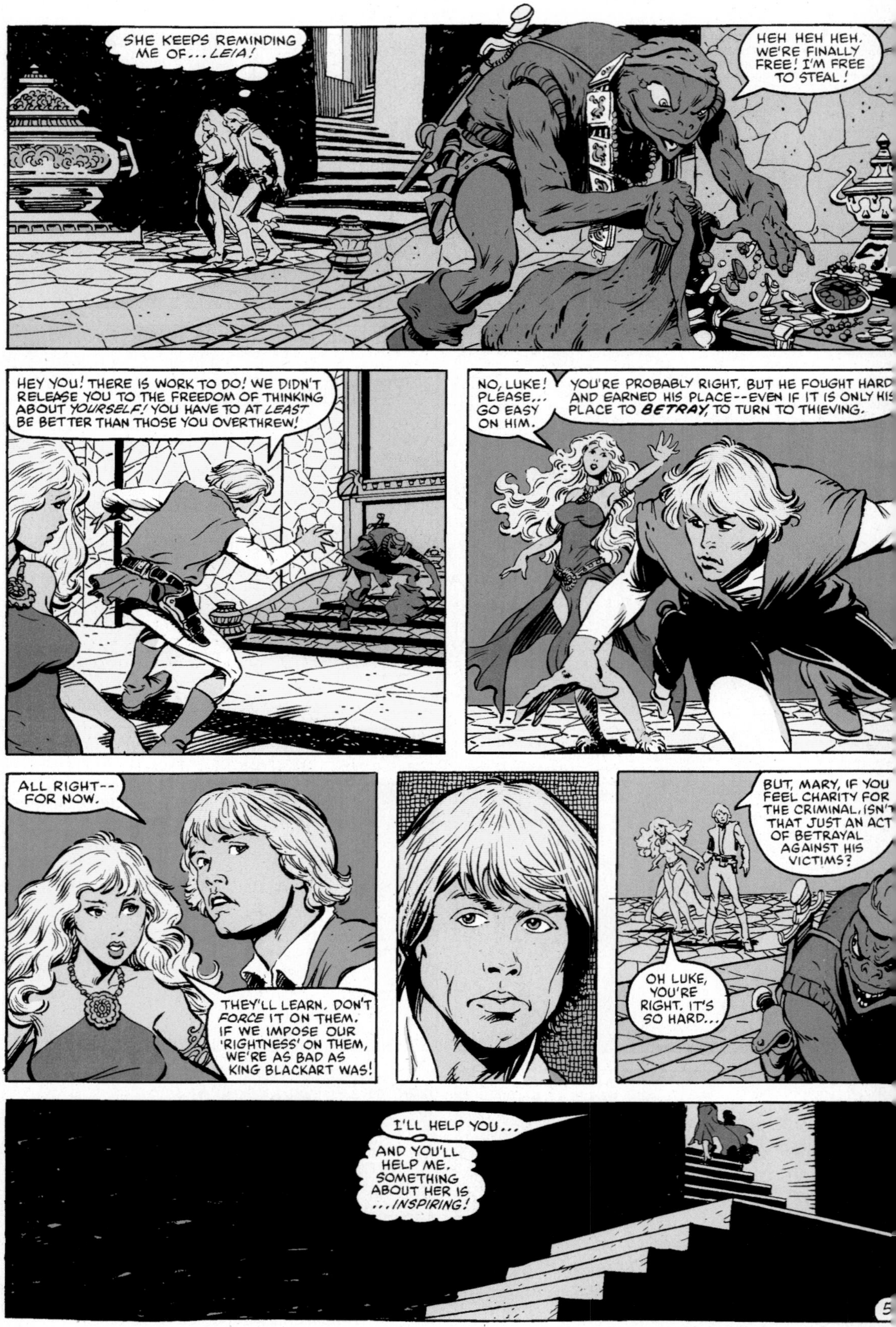

SHE KEEPS REMINDING ME OF... LEIA!
HEH HEH HEH. WE'RE FINALLY FREE! I'M FREE TO STEAL!
HEY YOU! THERE IS WORK TO DO! WE DIDN'T RELEASE YOU TO THE FREEDOM OF THINKING ABOUT YOURSELF! YOU HAVE TO AT LEAST BE BETTER THAN THOSE YOU OVERTHREW!
NO, LUKE! PLEASE... GO EASY ON HIM.
YOU'RE PROBABLY RIGHT. BUT HE FOUGHT HARD AND EARNED HIS PLACE--EVEN IF IT IS ONLY HIS PLACE TO BETRAY, TO TURN TO THIEVING.
ALL RIGHT-- FOR NOW.
THEY'LL LEARN. DON'T FORCE IT ON THEM. IF WE IMPOSE OUR 'RIGHTNESS' ON THEM, WE'RE AS BAD AS KING BLACKART WAS!
BUT, MARY, IF YOU FEEL CHARITY FOR THE CRIMINAL, ISN'T THAT JUST AN ACT OF BETRAYAL AGAINST HIS VICTIMS?
OH LUKE, YOU'RE RIGHT. IT'S SO HARD...
I'LL HELP YOU...
AND YOU'LL HELP ME. SOMETHING ABOUT HER IS ...INSPIRING!
5

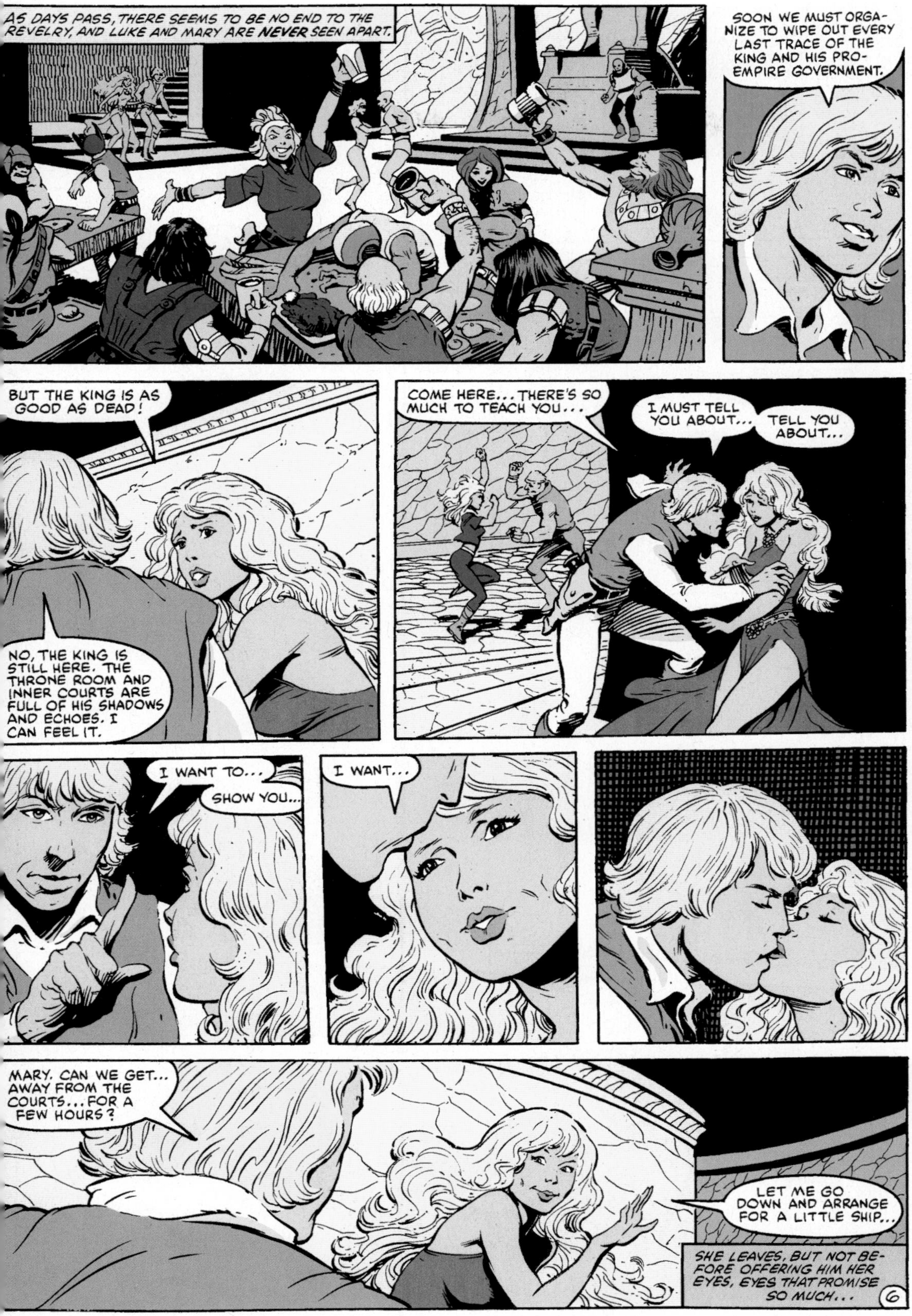
AS DAYS PASS, THERE SEEMS TO BE NO END TO THE REVELRY, AND LUKE AND MARY ARE NEVER SEEN APART.
SOON WE MUST ORGANIZE TO WIPE OUT EVERY LAST TRACE OF THE KING AND HIS PRO-EMPIRE GOVERNMENT.
BUT THE KING IS AS GOOD AS DEAD!
NO, THE KING IS STILL HERE. THE THRONE ROOM AND INNER COURTS ARE FULL OF HIS SHADOWS AND ECHOES. I CAN FEEL IT.
COME HERE... THERE'S SO MUCH TO TEACH YOU...
I MUST TELL YOU ABOUT...
TELL YOU ABOUT...
I WANT TO...
SHOW YOU...
I WANT...
MARY. CAN WE GET... AWAY FROM THE COURTS... FOR A FEW HOURS?
LET ME GO DOWN AND ARRANGE FOR A LITTLE SHIP...
SHE LEAVES, BUT NOT BEFORE OFFERING HIM HER EYES, EYES THAT PROMISE SO MUCH...
6

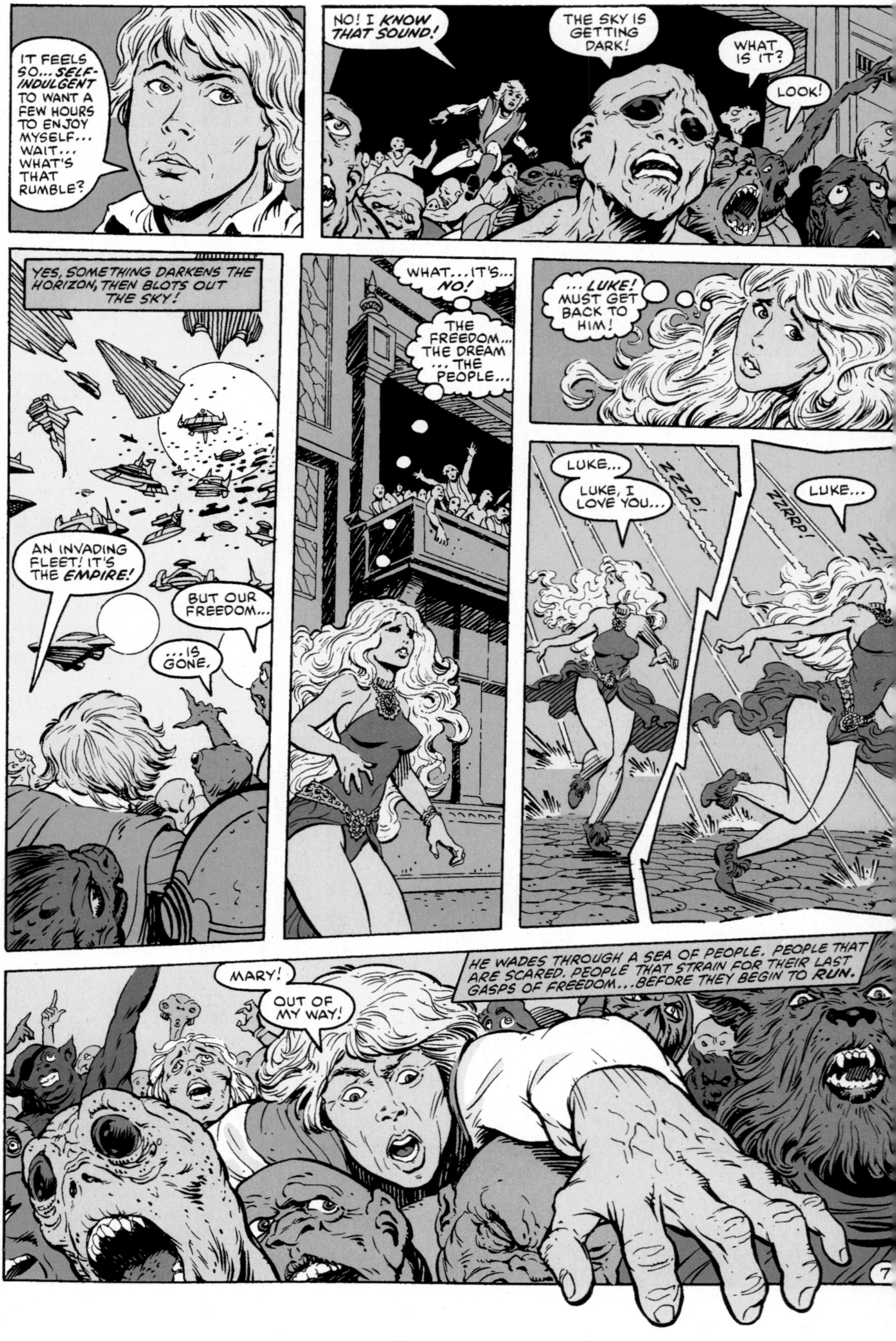
IT FEELS SO... SELF-INDULGENT TO WANT A FEW HOURS TO ENJOY MYSELF... WAIT... WHAT'S THAT RUMBLE?
NO! I KNOW THAT SOUND!
THE SKY IS GETTING DARK!
WHAT IS IT?
LOOK!
YES, SOMETHING DARKENS THE HORIZON, THEN BLOTS OUT THE SKY!
AN INVADING FLEET! IT'S THE EMPIRE!
BUT OUR FREEDOM...
...IS GONE.
WHAT... IT'S... NO!
THE FREEDOM... THE DREAM ... THE PEOPLE...
...LUKE! MUST GET BACK TO HIM!
LUKE...
LUKE, I LOVE YOU...
ZZZP!
ZZRRP!
LUKE...
ZZ!
HE WADES THROUGH A SEA OF PEOPLE. PEOPLE THAT ARE SCARED. PEOPLE THAT STRAIN FOR THEIR LAST GASPS OF FREEDOM... BEFORE THEY BEGIN TO RUN.
MARY!
OUT OF MY WAY!
7

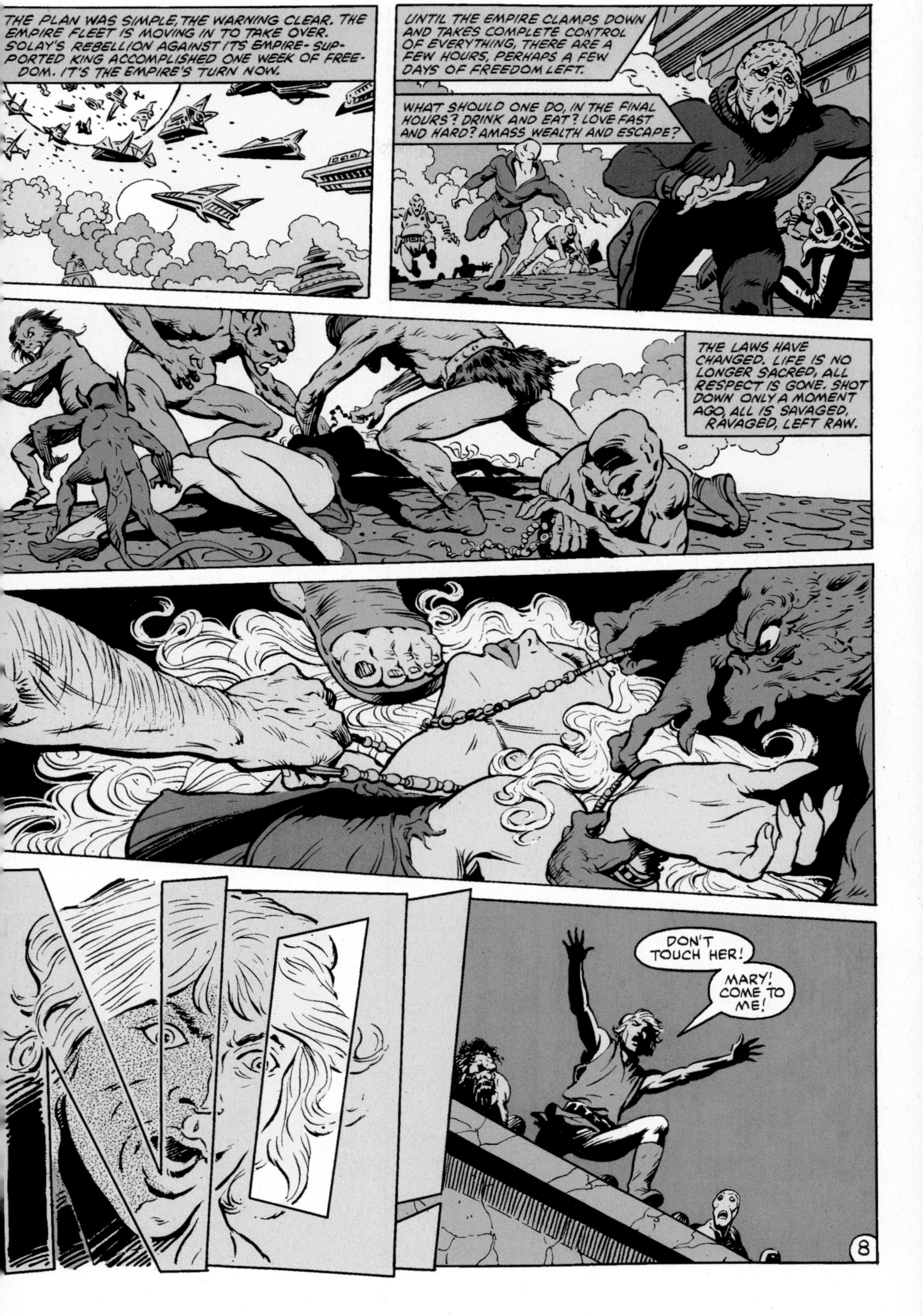
THE PLAN WAS SIMPLE, THE WARNING CLEAR. THE EMPIRE FLEET IS MOVING IN TO TAKE OVER. SOLAY'S REBELLION AGAINST ITS EMPIRE-SUPPORTED KING ACCOMPLISHED ONE WEEK OF FREEDOM. IT'S THE EMPIRE'S TURN NOW.
UNTIL THE EMPIRE CLAMPS DOWN AND TAKES COMPLETE CONTROL OF EVERYTHING, THERE ARE A FEW HOURS, PERHAPS A FEW DAYS OF FREEDOM LEFT.
WHAT SHOULD ONE DO, IN THE FINAL HOURS? DRINK AND EAT? LOVE FAST AND HARD? AMASS WEALTH AND ESCAPE?
THE LAWS HAVE CHANGED. LIFE IS NO LONGER SACRED, ALL RESPECT IS GONE. SHOT DOWN ONLY A MOMENT AGO, ALL IS SAVAGED, RAVAGED, LEFT RAW.
DON'T TOUCH HER!
MARY! COME TO ME!
8

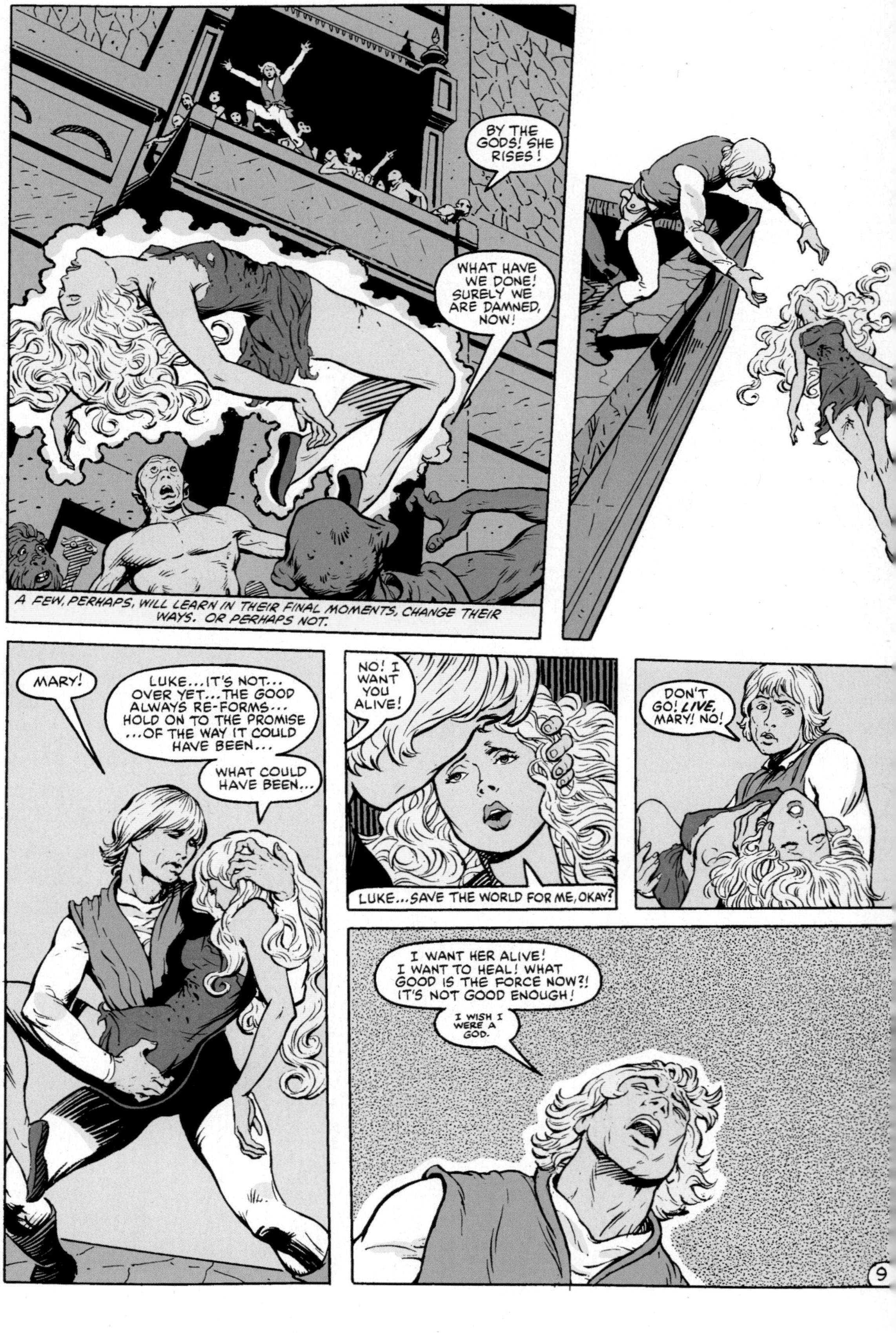
BY THE GODS! SHE RISES!
WHAT HAVE WE DONE! SURELY WE ARE DAMNED, NOW!
A FEW, PERHAPS, WILL LEARN IN THEIR FINAL MOMENTS, CHANGE THEIR WAYS. OR PERHAPS NOT.
MARY!
LUKE... IT'S NOT... OVER YET... THE GOOD ALWAYS RE-FORMS... HOLD ON TO THE PROMISE ...OF THE WAY IT COULD HAVE BEEN...
WHAT COULD HAVE BEEN...
NO! I WANT YOU ALIVE!
LUKE... SAVE THE WORLD FOR ME, OKAY?
DON'T GO! LIVE, MARY! NO!
I WANT HER ALIVE! I WANT TO HEAL! WHAT GOOD IS THE FORCE NOW?! IT'S NOT GOOD ENOUGH!
I WISH I WERE A GOD.
9

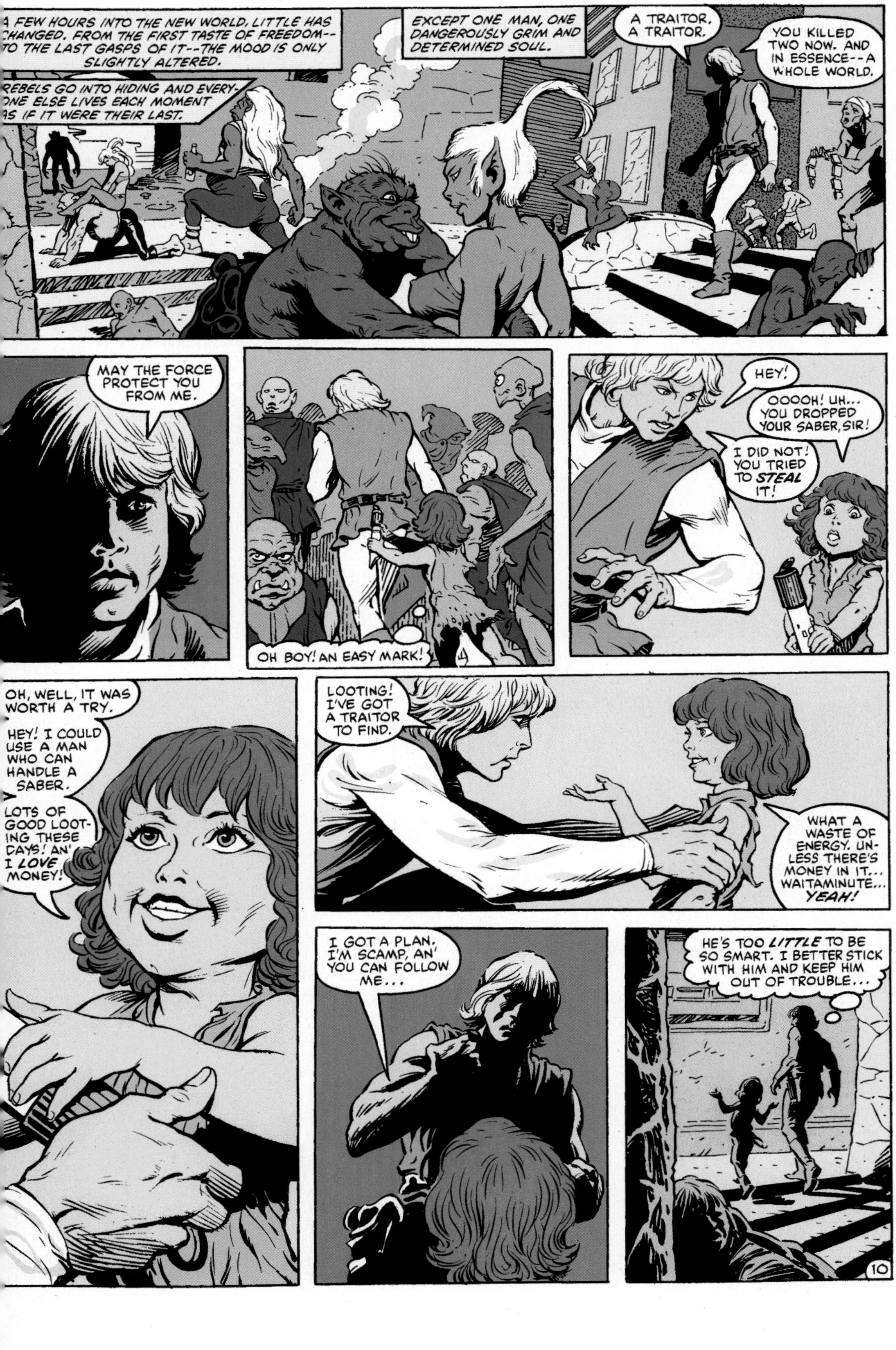
A FEW HOURS INTO THE NEW WORLD, LITTLE HAS CHANGED. FROM THE FIRST TASTE OF FREEDOM-- TO THE LAST GASPS OF IT--THE MOOD IS ONLY SLIGHTLY ALTERED.
REBELS GO INTO HIDING AND EVERYONE ELSE LIVES EACH MOMENT AS IF IT WERE THEIR LAST.
EXCEPT ONE MAN, ONE DANGEROUSLY GRIM AND DETERMINED SOUL.
A TRAITOR. A TRAITOR.
YOU KILLED TWO NOW. AND IN ESSENCE--A WHOLE WORLD.
MAY THE FORCE PROTECT YOU FROM ME.
OH BOY! AN EASY MARK!
HEY!
OOOOH! UH... YOU DROPPED YOUR SABER, SIR!
I DID NOT! YOU TRIED TO STEAL IT!
OH, WELL, IT WAS WORTH A TRY.
HEY! I COULD USE A MAN WHO CAN HANDLE A SABER.
LOTS OF GOOD LOOTING THESE DAYS! AN' I LOVE MONEY!
LOOTING! I'VE GOT A TRAITOR TO FIND.
WHAT A WASTE OF ENERGY. UNLESS THERE'S MONEY IN IT... WAITAMINUTE... YEAH!
I GOT A PLAN. I'M SCAMP, AN' YOU CAN FOLLOW ME...
HE'S TOO LITTLE TO BE SO SMART. I BETTER STICK WITH HIM AND KEEP HIM OUT OF TROUBLE...
10

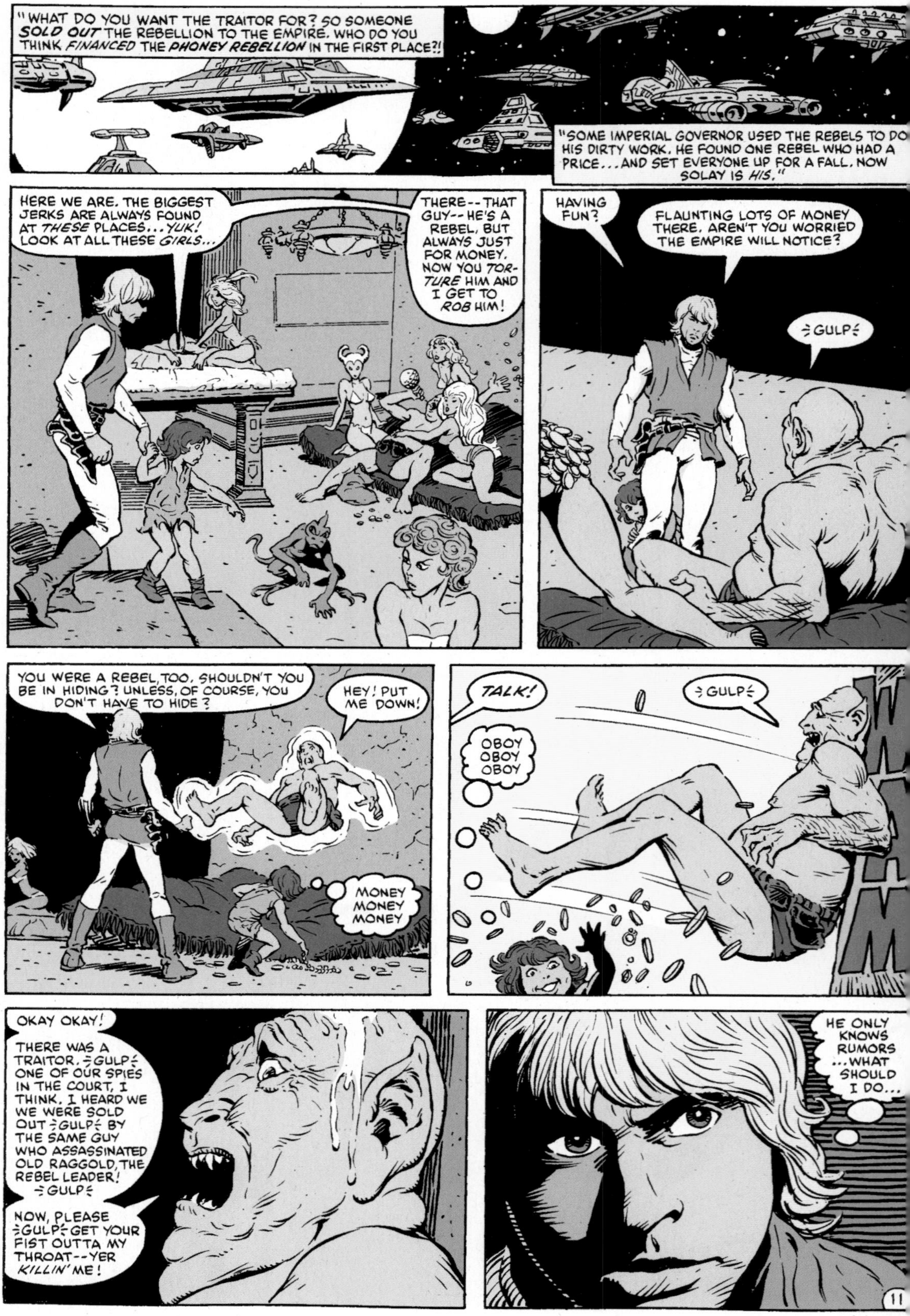
"WHAT DO YOU WANT THE TRAITOR FOR? SO SOMEONE SOLD OUT THE REBELLION TO THE EMPIRE. WHO DO YOU THINK FINANCED THE PHONEY REBELLION IN THE FIRST PLACE?!
"SOME IMPERIAL GOVERNOR USED THE REBELS TO DO HIS DIRTY WORK. HE FOUND ONE REBEL WHO HAD A PRICE... AND SET EVERYONE UP FOR A FALL. NOW SOLAY IS HIS."
HERE WE ARE. THE BIGGEST JERKS ARE ALWAYS FOUND AT THESE PLACES... YUK! LOOK AT ALL THESE GIRLS...
THERE--THAT GUY--HE'S A REBEL, BUT ALWAYS JUST FOR MONEY. NOW YOU TORTURE HIM AND I GET TO ROB HIM!
HAVING FUN?
FLAUNTING LOTS OF MONEY THERE. AREN'T YOU WORRIED THE EMPIRE WILL NOTICE?
GULP
YOU WERE A REBEL, TOO. SHOULDN'T YOU BE IN HIDING? UNLESS, OF COURSE, YOU DON'T HAVE TO HIDE?
HEY! PUT ME DOWN!
MONEY MONEY MONEY
TALK!
GULP
OBOY OBOY OBOY
OKAY OKAY!
THERE WAS A TRAITOR. GULP ONE OF OUR SPIES IN THE COURT, I THINK. I HEARD WE WE WERE SOLD OUT GULP BY THE SAME GUY WHO ASSASSINATED OLD RAGGOLD, THE REBEL LEADER! GULP
NOW, PLEASE GULP GET YOUR FIST OUTTA MY THROAT--YER KILLIN' ME!
HE ONLY KNOWS RUMORS ...WHAT SHOULD I DO...
11

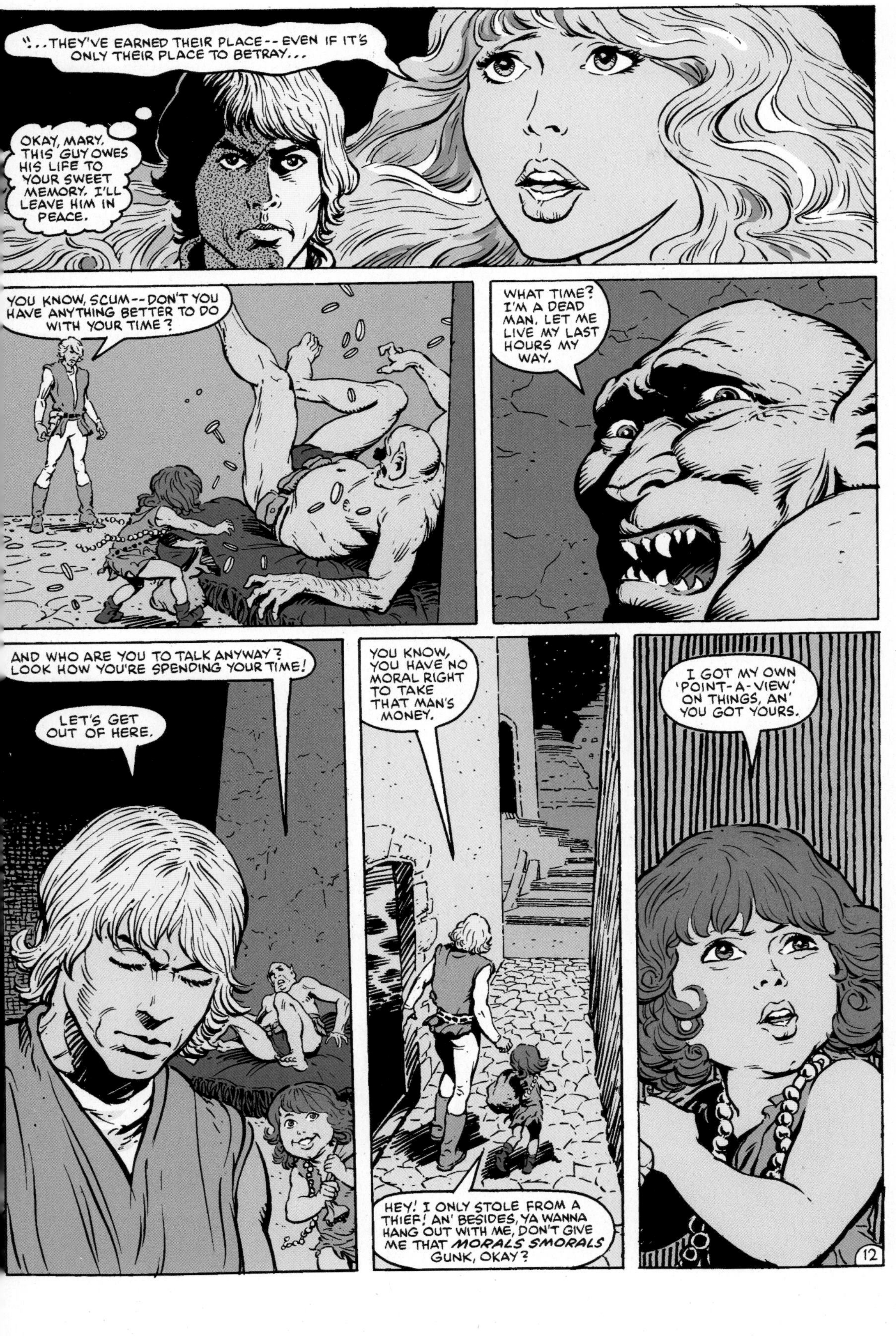
"...THEY'VE EARNED THEIR PLACE -- EVEN IF IT'S ONLY THEIR PLACE TO BETRAY...
OKAY, MARY. THIS GUY OWES HIS LIFE TO YOUR SWEET MEMORY. I'LL LEAVE HIM IN PEACE.
YOU KNOW, SCUM -- DON'T YOU HAVE ANYTHING BETTER TO DO WITH YOUR TIME?
WHAT TIME? I'M A DEAD MAN. LET ME LIVE MY LAST HOURS MY WAY.
AND WHO ARE YOU TO TALK ANYWAY? LOOK HOW YOU'RE SPENDING YOUR TIME!
LET'S GET OUT OF HERE.
YOU KNOW, YOU HAVE NO MORAL RIGHT TO TAKE THAT MAN'S MONEY.
HEY! I ONLY STOLE FROM A THIEF! AN' BESIDES, YA WANNA HANG OUT WITH ME, DON'T GIVE ME THAT MORALS SMORALS GUNK, OKAY?
I GOT MY OWN 'POINT-A-VIEW' ON THINGS, AN' YOU GOT YOURS.
12

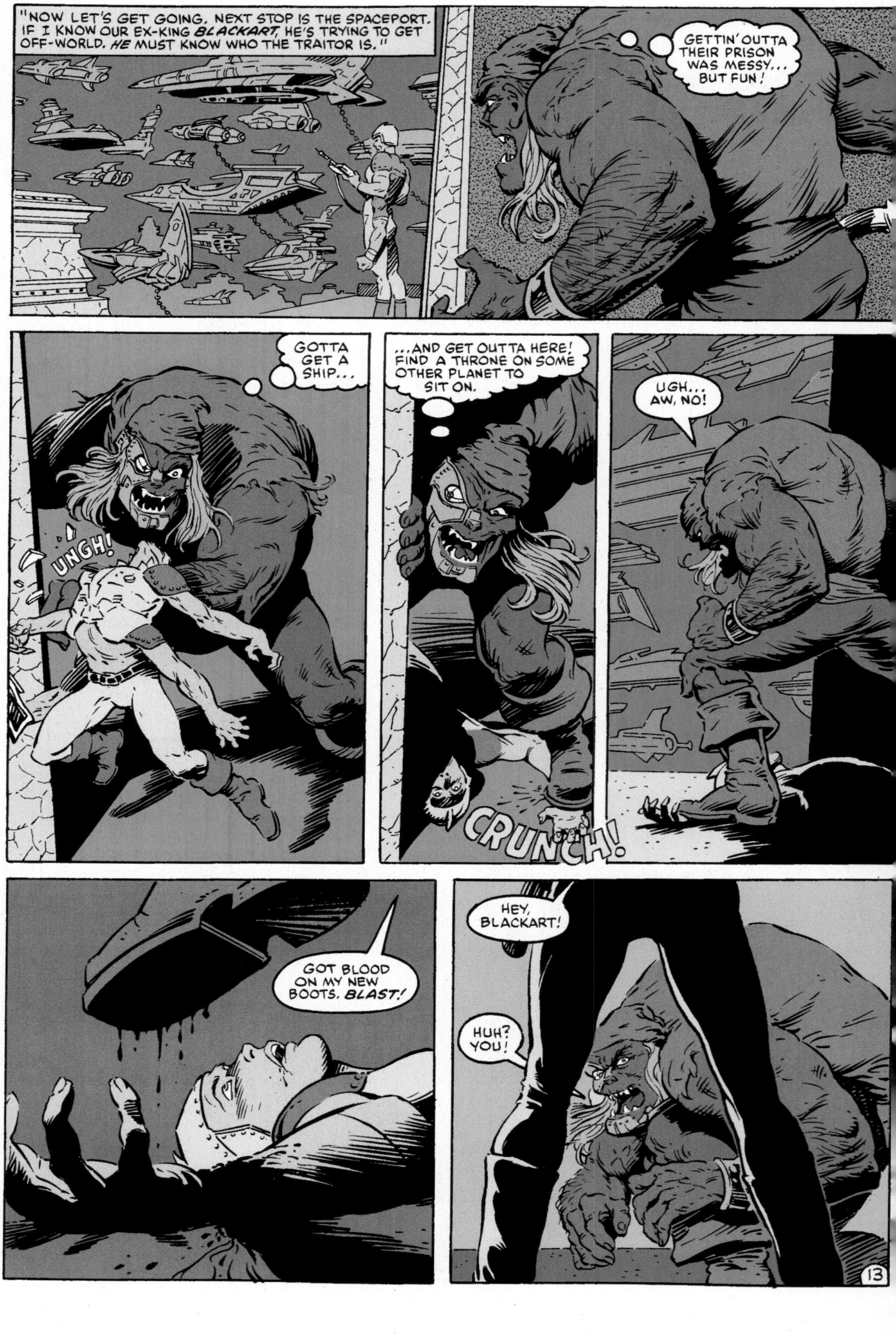
"NOW LET'S GET GOING. NEXT STOP IS THE SPACEPORT. IF I KNOW OUR EX-KING BLACKART, HE'S TRYING TO GET OFF-WORLD. HE MUST KNOW WHO THE TRAITOR IS."
GETTIN' OUTTA THEIR PRISON WAS MESSY... BUT FUN!
GOTTA GET A SHIP...
UNGH!
...AND GET OUTTA HERE! FIND A THRONE ON SOME OTHER PLANET TO SIT ON.
CRUNCH!
UGH... AW, NO!
GOT BLOOD ON MY NEW BOOTS. BLAST!
HEY, BLACKART!
HUH? YOU!
13

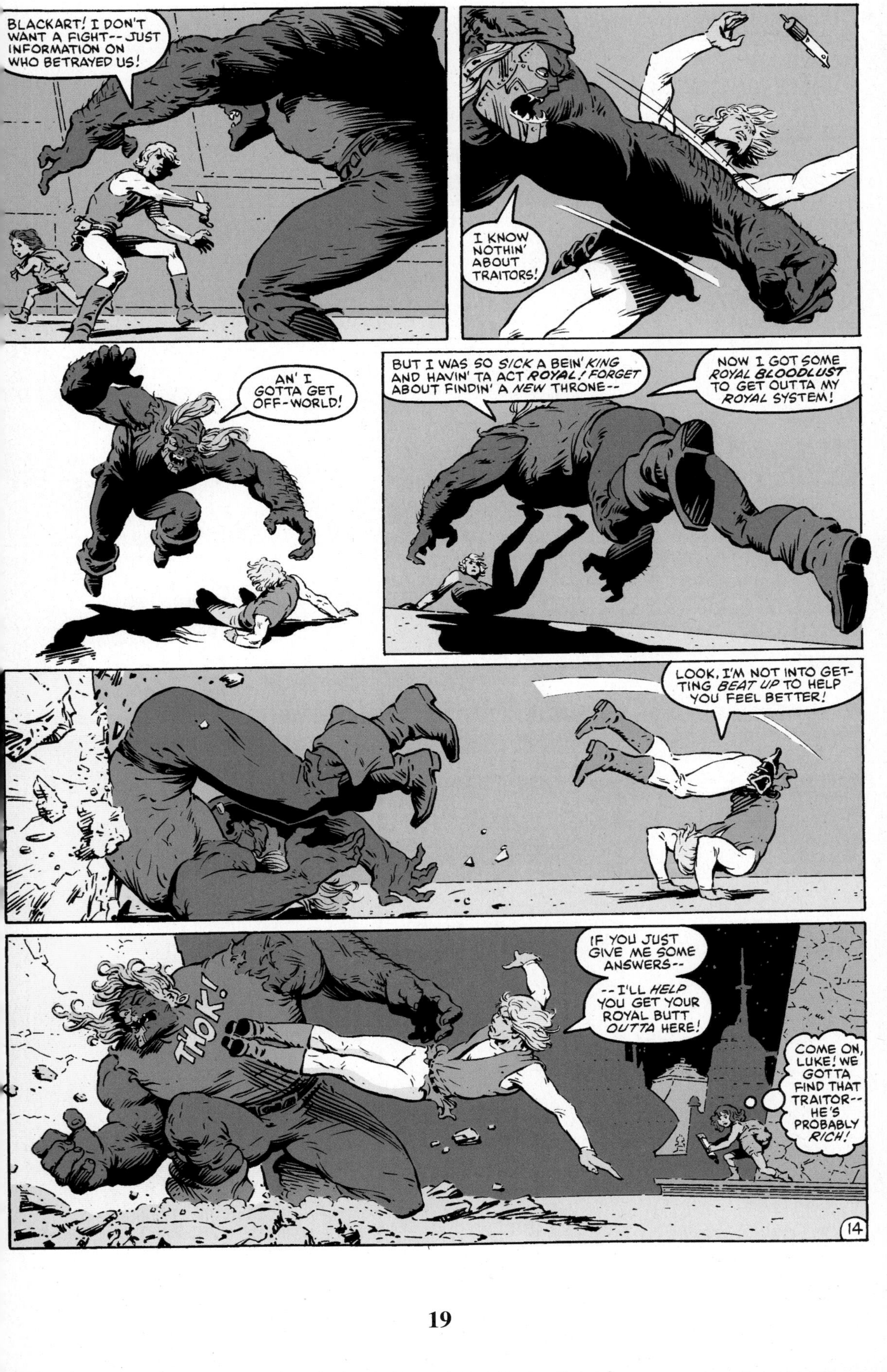
BLACKART! I DON'T WANT A FIGHT-- JUST INFORMATION ON WHO BETRAYED US!
I KNOW NOTHIN' ABOUT TRAITORS!
AN' I GOTTA GET OFF-WORLD!
BUT I WAS SO SICK A BEIN' KING AND HAVIN' TA ACT ROYAL! FORGET ABOUT FINDIN' A NEW THRONE--
NOW I GOT SOME ROYAL BLOODLUST TO GET OUTTA MY ROYAL SYSTEM!
LOOK, I'M NOT INTO GETTING BEAT UP TO HELP YOU FEEL BETTER!
THOK!
IF YOU JUST GIVE ME SOME ANSWERS--
--I'LL HELP YOU GET YOUR ROYAL BUTT OUTTA HERE!
COME ON, LUKE! WE GOTTA FIND THAT TRAITOR-- HE'S PROBABLY RICH!
14

21

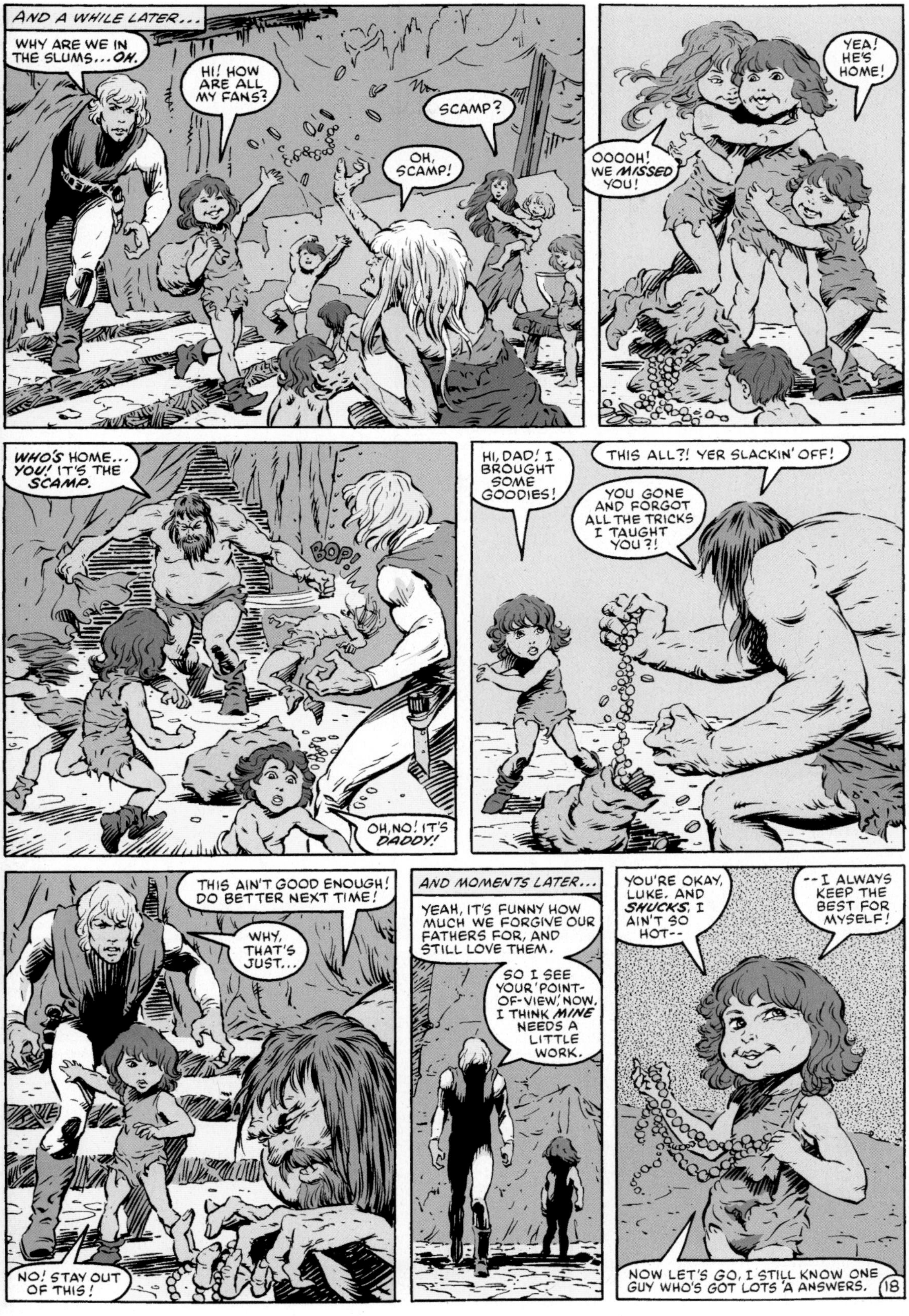
AND A WHILE LATER...
WHY ARE WE IN THE SLUMS... OH.
HI! HOW ARE ALL MY FANS?
SCAMP?
OH, SCAMP!
YEA! HE'S HOME!
OOOOH! WE MISSED YOU!
WHO'S HOME... YOU! IT'S THE SCAMP.
BOP!
OH, NO! IT'S DADDY!
HI, DAD! I BROUGHT SOME GOODIES!
THIS ALL?! YER SLACKIN' OFF!
YOU GONE AND FORGOT ALL THE TRICKS I TAUGHT YOU?!
THIS AIN'T GOOD ENOUGH! DO BETTER NEXT TIME!
WHY, THAT'S JUST...
NO! STAY OUT OF THIS!
AND MOMENTS LATER...
YEAH, IT'S FUNNY HOW MUCH WE FORGIVE OUR FATHERS FOR, AND STILL LOVE THEM.
SO I SEE YOUR 'POINT-OF-VIEW,' NOW. I THINK MINE NEEDS A LITTLE WORK.
YOU'RE OKAY, LUKE. AND SHUCKS, I AIN'T SO HOT--
--I ALWAYS KEEP THE BEST FOR MYSELF!
NOW LET'S GO, I STILL KNOW ONE GUY WHO'S GOT LOTS 'A ANSWERS.
18

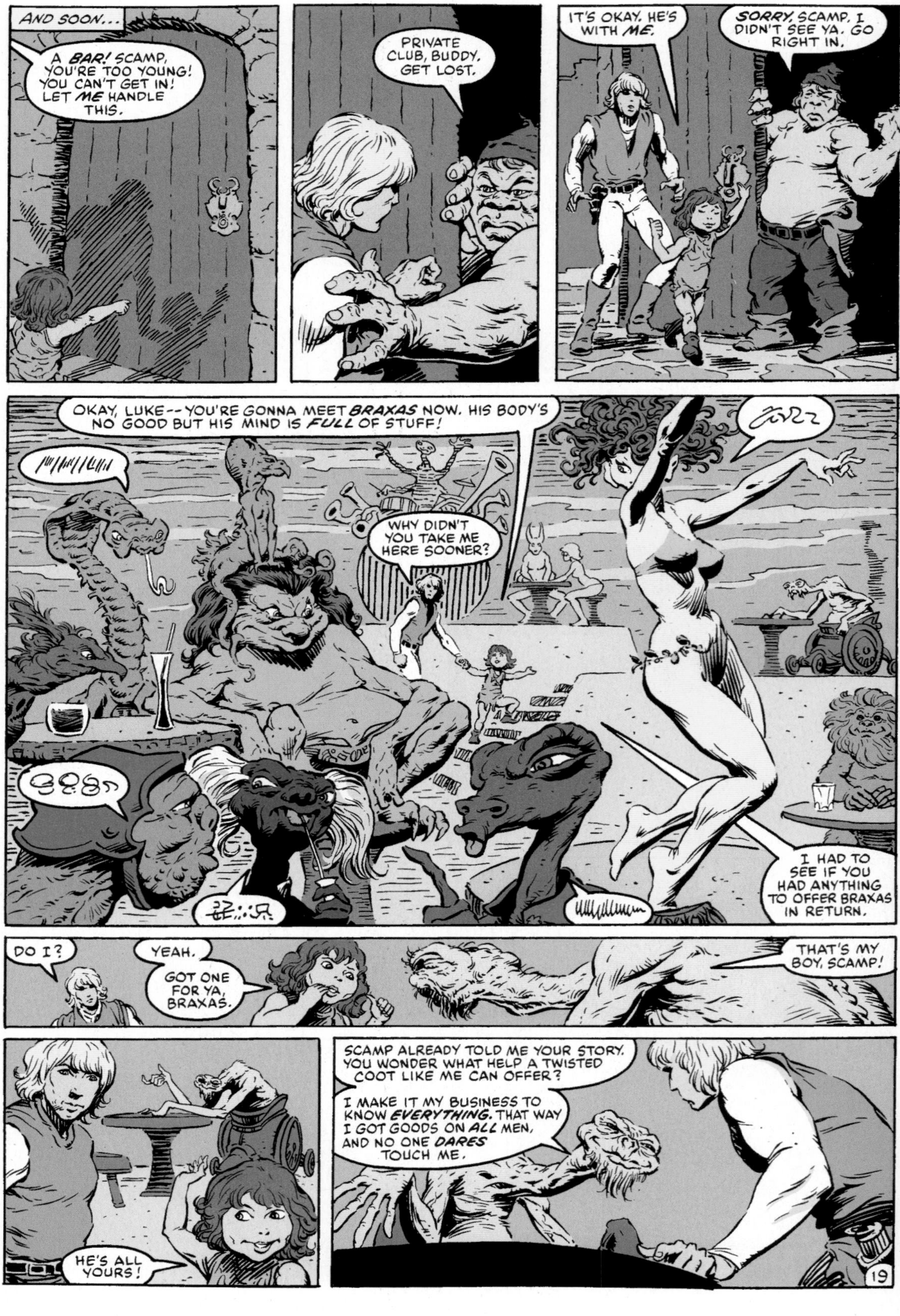

AND SOON...
A BAR! SCAMP, YOU'RE TOO YOUNG! YOU CAN'T GET IN! LET ME HANDLE THIS.
PRIVATE CLUB, BUDDY. GET LOST.
IT'S OKAY. HE'S WITH ME.
SORRY, SCAMP, I DIDN'T SEE YA. GO RIGHT IN.
OKAY, LUKE--YOU'RE GONNA MEET BRAXAS NOW. HIS BODY'S NO GOOD BUT HIS MIND IS FULL OF STUFF!
WHY DIDN'T YOU TAKE ME HERE SOONER?
I HAD TO SEE IF YOU HAD ANYTHING TO OFFER BRAXAS IN RETURN.
DO I?
YEAH. GOT ONE FOR YA, BRAXAS.
THAT'S MY BOY, SCAMP!
HE'S ALL YOURS!
SCAMP ALREADY TOLD ME YOUR STORY. YOU WONDER WHAT HELP A TWISTED COOT LIKE ME CAN OFFER?
I MAKE IT MY BUSINESS TO KNOW EVERYTHING. THAT WAY I GOT GOODS ON ALL MEN, AND NO ONE DARES TOUCH ME.
19

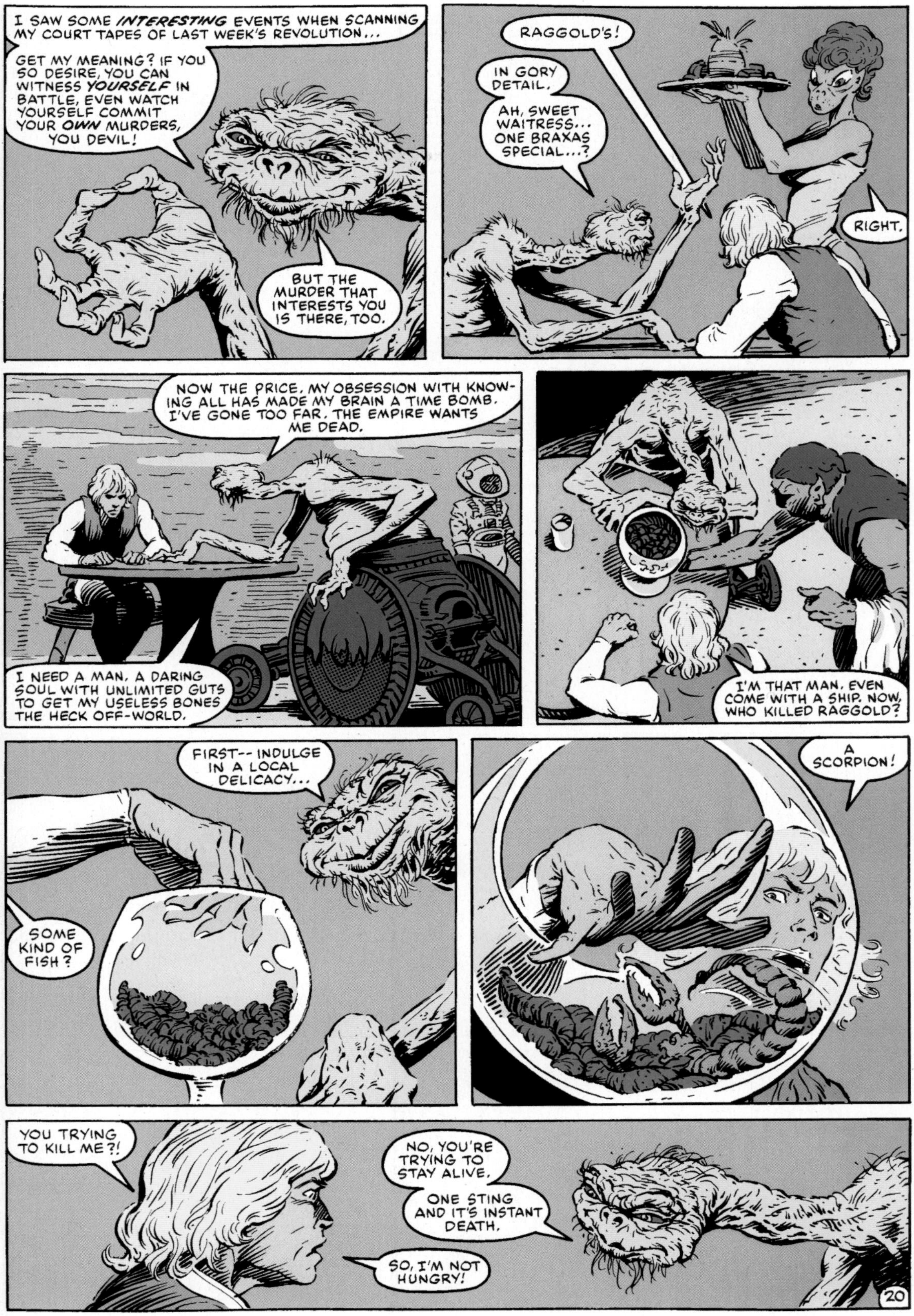
I SAW SOME *INTERESTING* EVENTS WHEN SCANNING MY COURT TAPES OF LAST WEEK'S REVOLUTION...
GET MY MEANING? IF YOU SO DESIRE, YOU CAN WITNESS *YOURSELF* IN BATTLE, EVEN WATCH YOURSELF COMMIT YOUR *OWN* MURDERS, YOU DEVIL!
BUT THE MURDER THAT INTERESTS YOU IS THERE, TOO.
RAGGOLD'S!
IN GORY DETAIL.
AH, SWEET WAITRESS... ONE BRAXAS SPECIAL...?
RIGHT.
NOW THE PRICE. MY OBSESSION WITH KNOWING ALL HAS MADE MY BRAIN A TIME BOMB. I'VE GONE TOO FAR. THE EMPIRE WANTS ME DEAD.
I NEED A MAN. A DARING SOUL WITH UNLIMITED GUTS TO GET MY USELESS BONES THE HECK OFF-WORLD.
I'M THAT MAN. EVEN COME WITH A SHIP. NOW, WHO KILLED RAGGOLD?
FIRST-- INDULGE IN A LOCAL DELICACY...
SOME KIND OF FISH?
A SCORPION!
YOU TRYING TO KILL ME?!
NO, YOU'RE TRYING TO STAY ALIVE.
ONE STING AND IT'S INSTANT DEATH.
SO, I'M NOT HUNGRY!
20

WANT YOUR TAPE?

IT'S AN OLD MAN'S TEST OF GUTS... AND *LUCK.*

FINISH YOUR MEAL, SKY-WALKER.

HUH?! *LEFT* HAND, LUKE, THAT MECHANICAL RIGHT OF YOURS WOULD JUST BREAK HIS LITTLE STINGER.

HOW DID YOU *KNOW!?*

AND A LITTLE *ETI-QUETTE,* PLEASE ...USE *THESE.*

AH, CHOP-STICKS...

SUCH AN ELEGANT UTENSIL.

MAKES THE RITUAL OF EATING SO EXQUISITELY... *EXCITING.*

TRUST IT. TRUST MYSELF.

DON'T TOUCH ME, YOU VERMIN.

FOR YOU, MARY...

FOR MARY ...AND FOR THE FORCE!

MY LOSS OF FAITH IN THE FORCE...I MUST BELIEVE AGAIN!

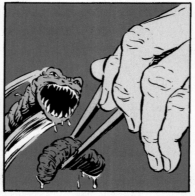

MIND IF I DON'T EAT THIS ONE?

NO... *ANYTHING* FOR MY NEW PILOT!

21

AND SOON...

ON THIS TAPE IS... RAGGOLD'S *MURDERER.*

I DON'T WANT TO SEE THIS...

WHAT AM I AFRAID OF?

WHO COULD IT BE? OR AM I AFRAID THAT ONCE I SEE THE TRAITOR I WON'T BE ABLE TO RESIST KILLING HIM?

RAGGOLD!

WE'VE WON!

AND SO MY ROLE HAS ENDED.

I'VE LED THEM TO VICTORY-- AND SOON THEIR DEATHS. I'VE SERVED THEM UP TO THE EMPIRE, USED THEIR TRUST IN ME. I'VE MURDERED THEM ALL, AND SOON I WILL BE REVEALED.

BUT IN LEADING THESE FINE MEN... I'VE CHANGED.

I TOOK A ROLE, AND THAT ROLE HAS TAKEN ME!

FOR THE REBELLION! FOR FREE-DOM!

BAM!

BY THE FORCE!

IT MAKES SENSE. HE WAS THE TRAITOR-- AND IN THE END HE COULDN'T HANDLE THE CONSEQUENCES OF WHAT HE'D SET UP. RAGGOLD WAS KILLED BY THE SAME THING THAT KILLED MARY-- THE WAR. AND HIMSELF.

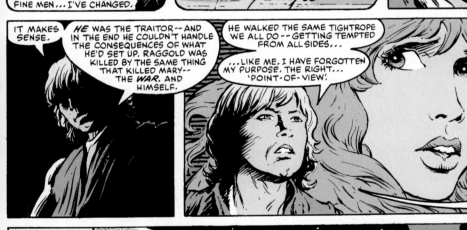

HE WALKED THE SAME TIGHTROPE WE ALL DO-- GETTING TEMPTED FROM ALL SIDES...

...LIKE ME. I HAVE FORGOTTEN MY PURPOSE, THE RIGHT... 'POINT-OF-VIEW'.

FORGET ILLUSIONS, LUKE. THERE'S TOO MUCH *REALITY* OUT THERE.

AND MINUTES LATER...

YOU SAID YOU NEEDED A PILOT WITH GUTS, BRAXAS...

HEH, HEH! ALL THE GUTS IN THE WORLD, GOOD BYE, SOLAY. MAY I NEVER SEE YOUR TEN SUNS AGAIN.

MAYBE NOT YOU, BRAXAS. BUT *I* WILL RETURN SOME DAY... TO CONTINUE WHERE MARY AND *RAGGOLD* LEFT OFF!

END

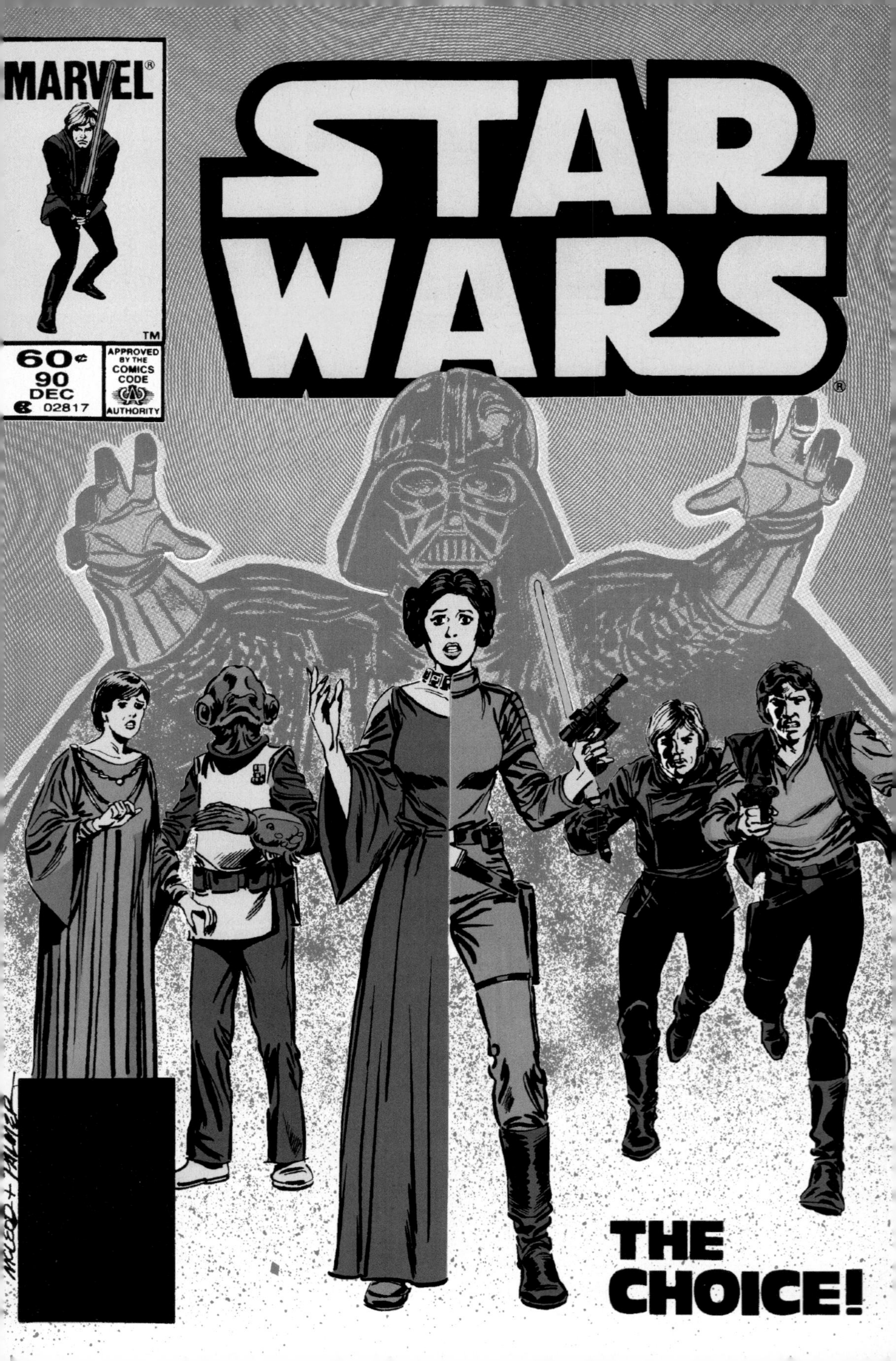

MARVEL®
STAR WARS®
TM
60¢
90
DEC
02817
APPROVED BY THE COMICS CODE AUTHORITY
MCLEOD + PALMER
THE CHOICE!

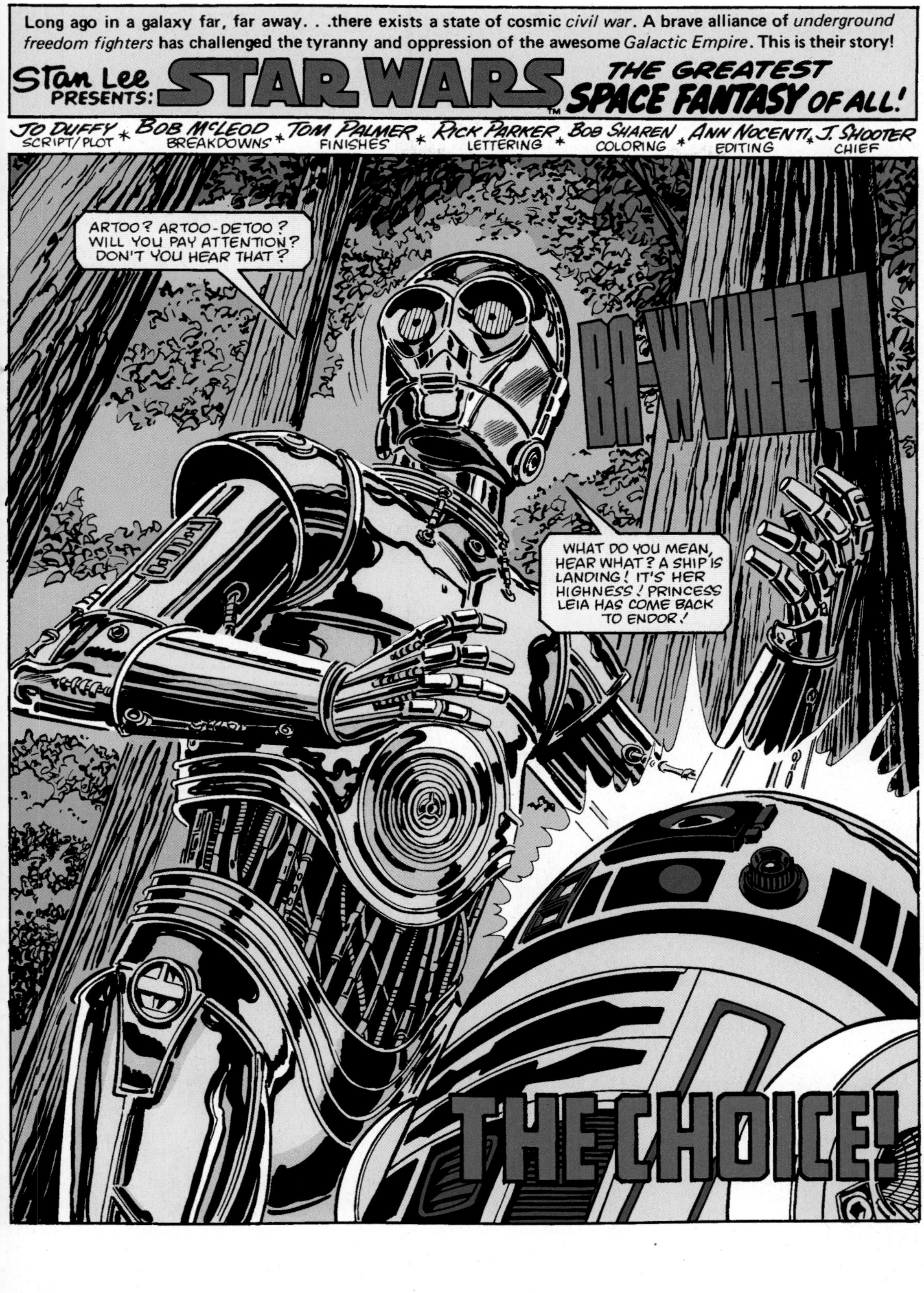

Long ago in a galaxy far, far away. . .there exists a state of cosmic civil war. A brave alliance of underground freedom fighters has challenged the tyranny and oppression of the awesome Galactic Empire. This is their story!
Stan Lee PRESENTS: STAR WARS™ THE GREATEST SPACE FANTASY OF ALL!
JO DUFFY SCRIPT/PLOT * BOB McLEOD BREAKDOWNS * TOM PALMER FINISHES * RICK PARKER LETTERING * BOB SHAREN COLORING * ANN NOCENTI EDITING * J. SHOOTER CHIEF
ARTOO? ARTOO-DETOO? WILL YOU PAY ATTENTION? DON'T YOU HEAR THAT?
BA-WVHEET!
WHAT DO YOU MEAN, HEAR WHAT? A SHIP IS LANDING! IT'S HER HIGHNESS! PRINCESS LEIA HAS COME BACK TO ENDOR!
THE CHOICE!

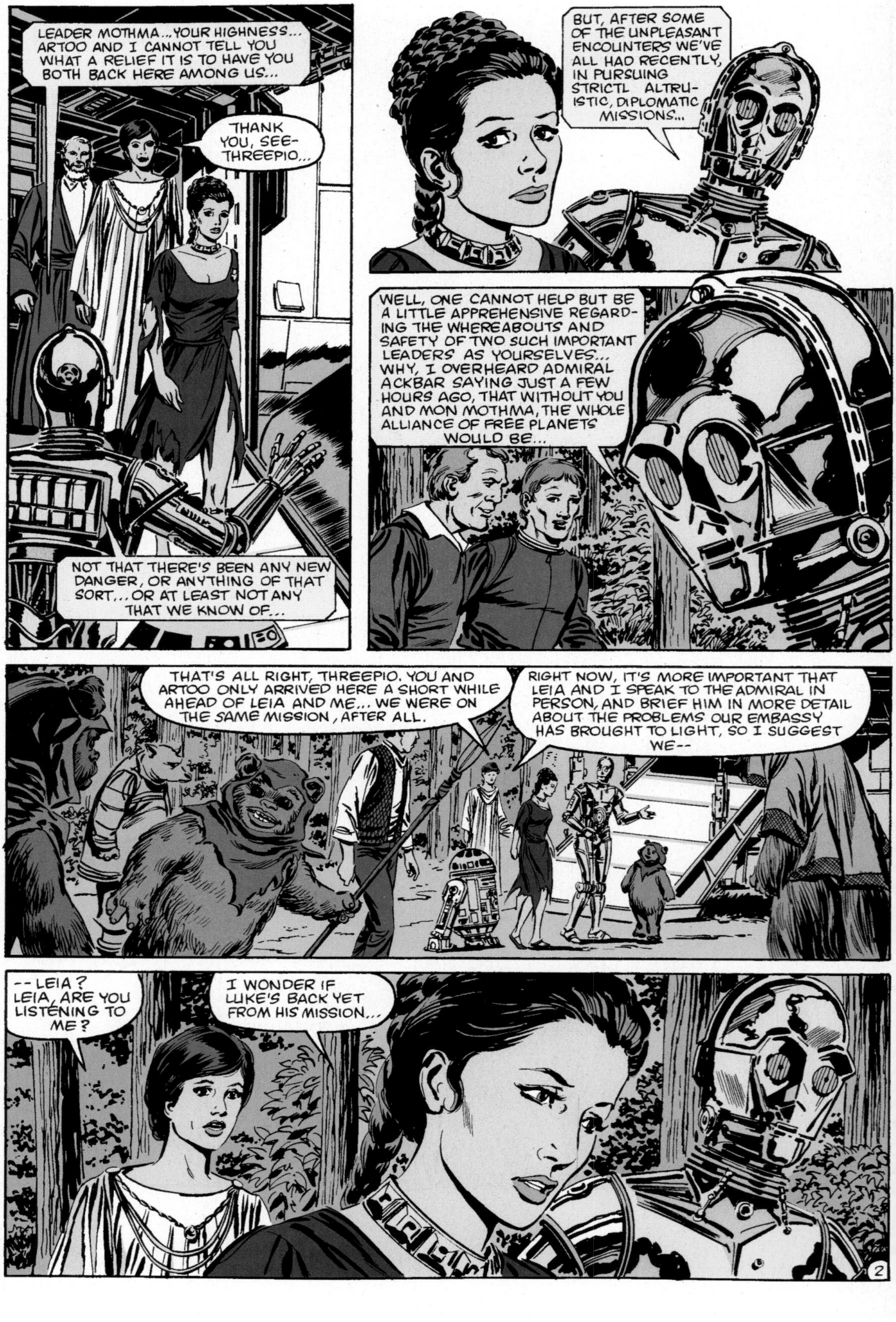
LEADER MOTHMA... YOUR HIGHNESS... ARTOO AND I CANNOT TELL YOU WHAT A RELIEF IT IS TO HAVE YOU BOTH BACK HERE AMONG US...
THANK YOU, SEE-THREEPIO...
NOT THAT THERE'S BEEN ANY NEW DANGER, OR ANYTHING OF THAT SORT... OR AT LEAST NOT ANY THAT WE KNOW OF...
BUT, AFTER SOME OF THE UNPLEASANT ENCOUNTERS WE'VE ALL HAD RECENTLY, IN PURSUING STRICTL ALTRUISTIC, DIPLOMATIC MISSIONS...
WELL, ONE CANNOT HELP BUT BE A LITTLE APPREHENSIVE REGARDING THE WHEREABOUTS AND SAFETY OF TWO SUCH IMPORTANT LEADERS AS YOURSELVES... WHY, I OVERHEARD ADMIRAL ACKBAR SAYING JUST A FEW HOURS AGO, THAT WITHOUT YOU AND MON MOTHMA, THE WHOLE ALLIANCE OF FREE PLANETS WOULD BE...
THAT'S ALL RIGHT, THREEPIO. YOU AND ARTOO ONLY ARRIVED HERE A SHORT WHILE AHEAD OF LEIA AND ME... WE WERE ON THE SAME MISSION, AFTER ALL.
RIGHT NOW, IT'S MORE IMPORTANT THAT LEIA AND I SPEAK TO THE ADMIRAL IN PERSON, AND BRIEF HIM IN MORE DETAIL ABOUT THE PROBLEMS OUR EMBASSY HAS BROUGHT TO LIGHT, SO I SUGGEST WE--
--LEIA? LEIA, ARE YOU LISTENING TO ME?
I WONDER IF LUKE'S BACK YET FROM HIS MISSION...
2

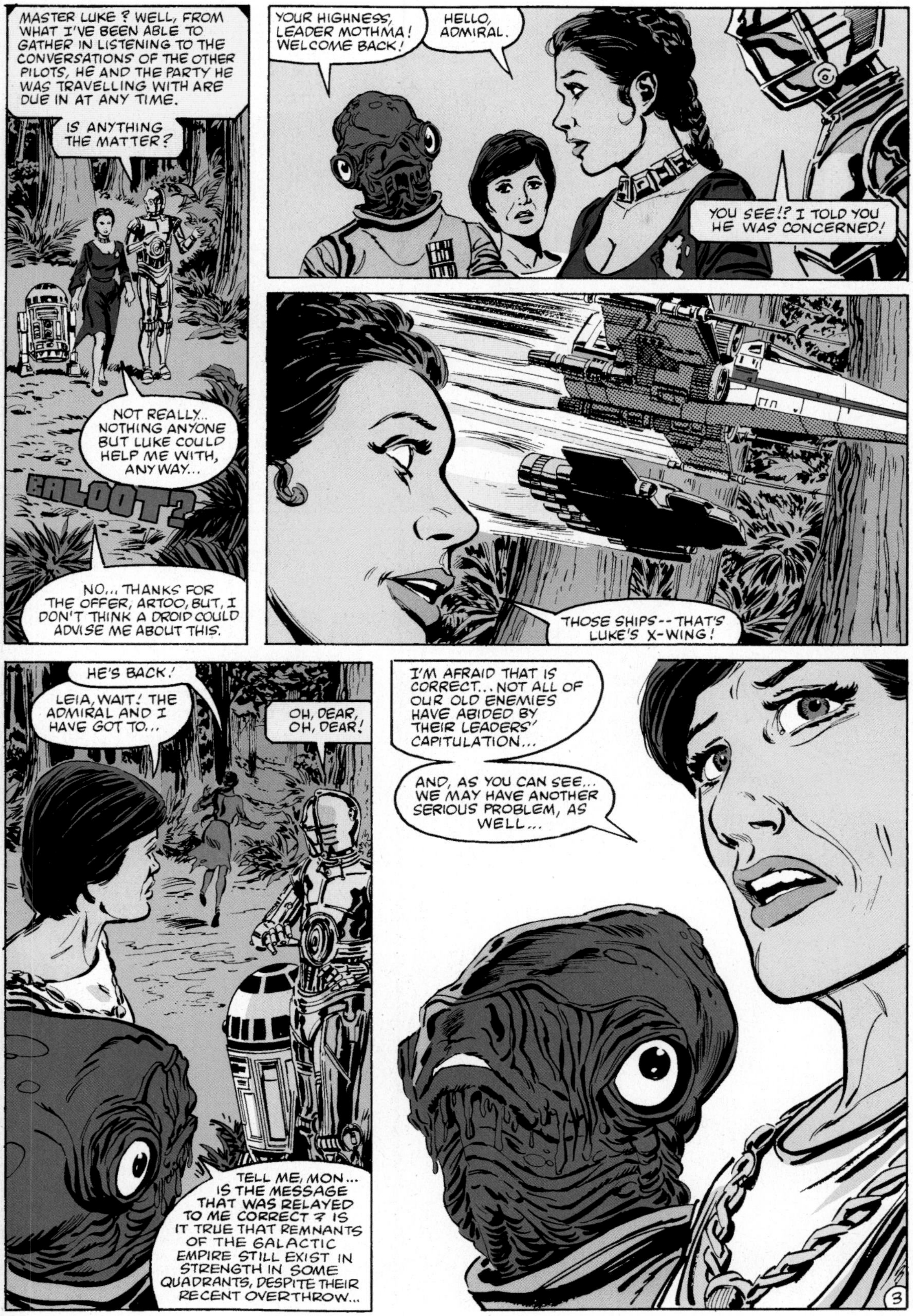
MASTER LUKE? WELL, FROM WHAT I'VE BEEN ABLE TO GATHER IN LISTENING TO THE CONVERSATIONS OF THE OTHER PILOTS, HE AND THE PARTY HE WAS TRAVELLING WITH ARE DUE IN AT ANY TIME.
IS ANYTHING THE MATTER?
NOT REALLY... NOTHING ANYONE BUT LUKE COULD HELP ME WITH, ANYWAY...
BALOOT?
NO... THANKS FOR THE OFFER, ARTOO, BUT, I DON'T THINK A DROID COULD ADVISE ME ABOUT THIS.
YOUR HIGHNESS, LEADER MOTHMA! WELCOME BACK!
HELLO, ADMIRAL.
YOU SEE!? I TOLD YOU HE WAS CONCERNED!
THOSE SHIPS--THAT'S LUKE'S X-WING!
HE'S BACK!
LEIA, WAIT! THE ADMIRAL AND I HAVE GOT TO...
OH, DEAR, OH, DEAR!
TELL ME, MON... IS THE MESSAGE THAT WAS RELAYED TO ME CORRECT? IS IT TRUE THAT REMNANTS OF THE GALACTIC EMPIRE STILL EXIST IN STRENGTH IN SOME QUADRANTS, DESPITE THEIR RECENT OVERTHROW...
I'M AFRAID THAT IS CORRECT... NOT ALL OF OUR OLD ENEMIES HAVE ABIDED BY THEIR LEADERS' CAPITULATION...
AND, AS YOU CAN SEE... WE MAY HAVE ANOTHER SERIOUS PROBLEM, AS WELL...
3

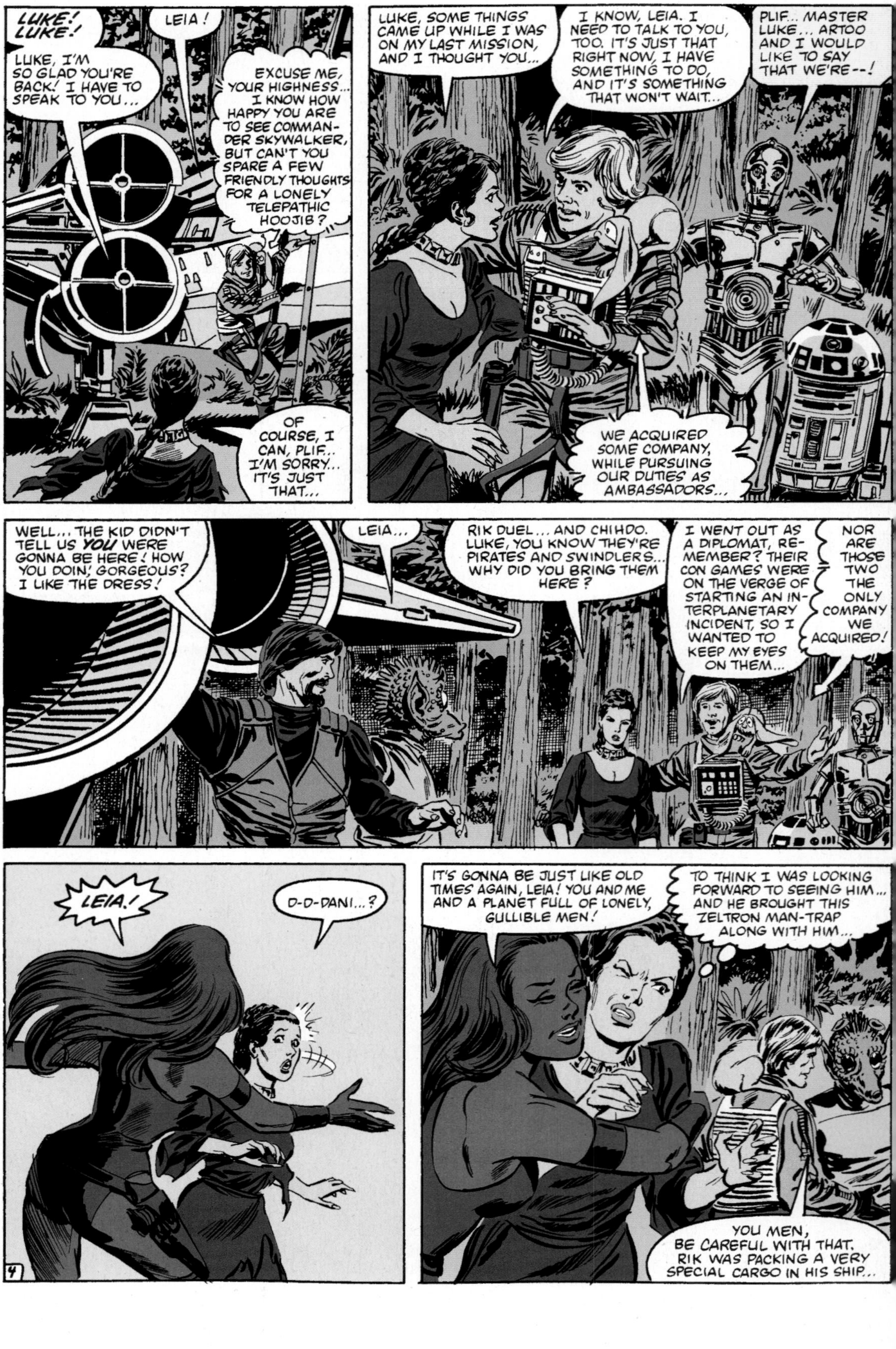
LUKE! LUKE!
LEIA!
LUKE, I'M SO GLAD YOU'RE BACK! I HAVE TO SPEAK TO YOU...
EXCUSE ME, YOUR HIGHNESS... I KNOW HOW HAPPY YOU ARE TO SEE COMMANDER SKYWALKER, BUT CAN'T YOU SPARE A FEW FRIENDLY THOUGHTS FOR A LONELY TELEPATHIC HOOJIB?
OF COURSE, I CAN, PLIF... I'M SORRY... IT'S JUST THAT...
LUKE, SOME THINGS CAME UP WHILE I WAS ON MY LAST MISSION, AND I THOUGHT YOU...
I KNOW, LEIA. I NEED TO TALK TO YOU, TOO. IT'S JUST THAT RIGHT NOW, I HAVE SOMETHING TO DO, AND IT'S SOMETHING THAT WON'T WAIT...
PLIF... MASTER LUKE... ARTOO AND I WOULD LIKE TO SAY THAT WE'RE--!
WE ACQUIRED SOME COMPANY, WHILE PURSUING OUR DUTIES AS AMBASSADORS...
WELL... THE KID DIDN'T TELL US YOU WERE GONNA BE HERE! HOW YOU DOIN', GORGEOUS? I LIKE THE DRESS!
LEIA...
RIK DUEL... AND CHIHDO. LUKE, YOU KNOW THEY'RE PIRATES AND SWINDLERS... WHY DID YOU BRING THEM HERE?
I WENT OUT AS A DIPLOMAT, REMEMBER? THEIR CON GAMES WERE ON THE VERGE OF STARTING AN INTERPLANETARY INCIDENT, SO I WANTED TO KEEP MY EYES ON THEM...
NOR ARE THOSE TWO THE ONLY COMPANY WE ACQUIRED!
LEIA!
D-D-DANI...?
4
IT'S GONNA BE JUST LIKE OLD TIMES AGAIN, LEIA! YOU AND ME AND A PLANET FULL OF LONELY, GULLIBLE MEN!
TO THINK I WAS LOOKING FORWARD TO SEEING HIM... AND HE BROUGHT THIS ZELTRON MAN-TRAP ALONG WITH HIM...
YOU MEN, BE CAREFUL WITH THAT. RIK WAS PACKING A VERY SPECIAL CARGO IN HIS SHIP...

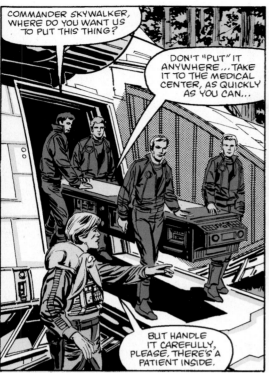

COMMANDER SKYWALKER, WHERE DO YOU WANT US TO PUT THIS THING?

DON'T "PUT" IT ANYWHERE... TAKE IT TO THE MEDICAL CENTER, AS QUICKLY AS YOU CAN...

BUT HANDLE IT CAREFULLY, PLEASE, THERE'S A PATIENT INSIDE.

A PATIENT...? IT'S KIRO!

LUKE, WHAT'S WRONG WITH HIM? IS HE GOING TO BE ALL RIGHT?

I HOPE SO, LEIA.

THAT'S WHY COMMANDER SKYWALKER INSISTED ON BRINGING HIM BACK TO ENDOR, YOUR HIGHNESS... SO THAT HE'D GET THE BEST POSSIBLE MEDICAL CARE...

SHOO...GET AWAY, YOU GUYS...

OOHH?

RRUF

HEY, NOW... YOU CAN'T JUST SHOO THE EWOKS AWAY. THIS IS THEIR HOME PLANET WE'RE ON, AFTER ALL!

AAARROOK?

NO, IT IS NOT SOMETHING GOOD TO EAT. IF YOU'D LOOKED MORE CLOSELY, YOU'D HAVE REALIZED THAT THAT CANISTER CONTAINS A *MAN!* WELL, A MAN OF SORTS, ANYWAY.

5

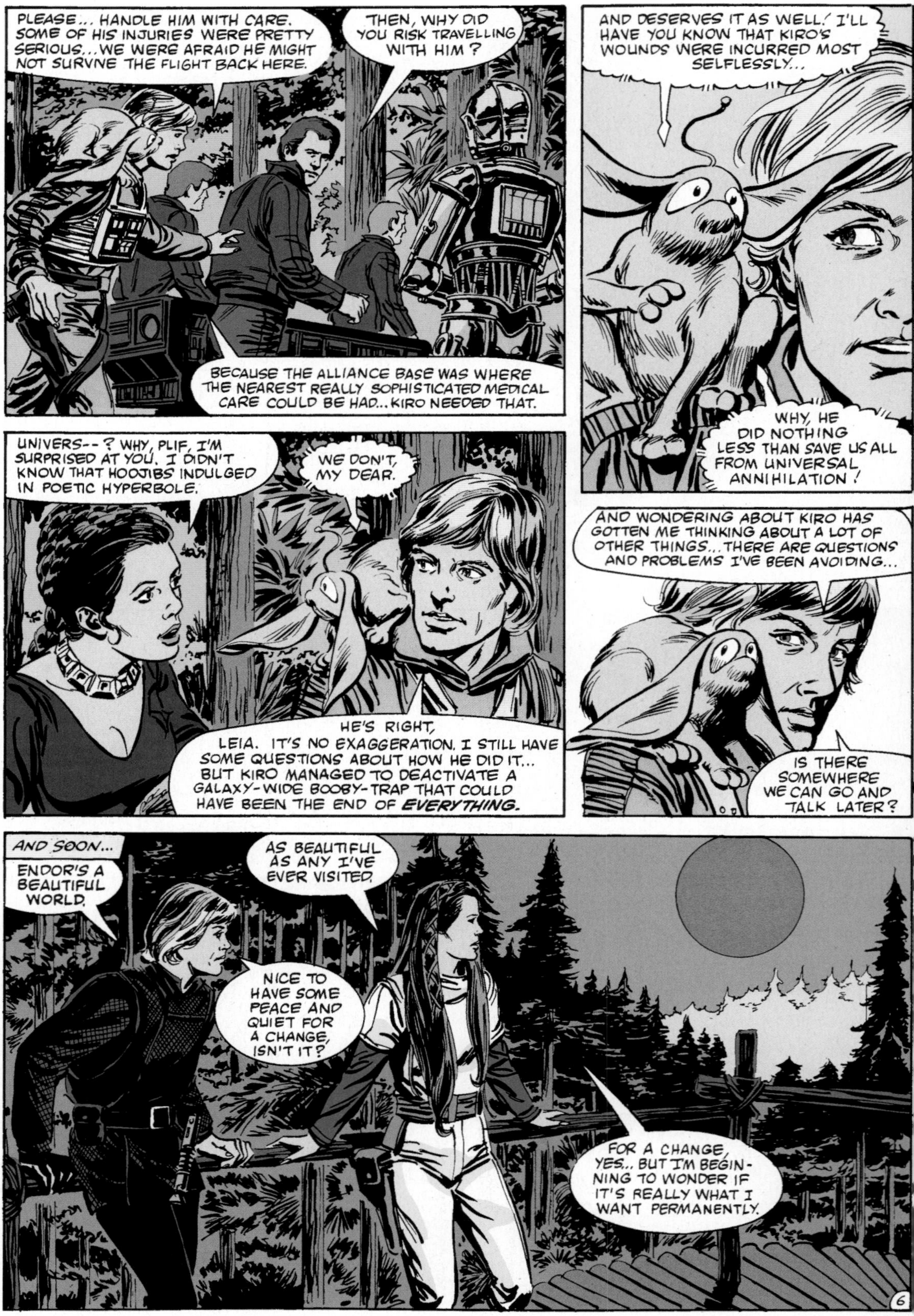
PLEASE... HANDLE HIM WITH CARE. SOME OF HIS INJURIES WERE PRETTY SERIOUS... WE WERE AFRAID HE MIGHT NOT SURVIVE THE FLIGHT BACK HERE.
THEN, WHY DID YOU RISK TRAVELLING WITH HIM?
BECAUSE THE ALLIANCE BASE WAS WHERE THE NEAREST REALLY SOPHISTICATED MEDICAL CARE COULD BE HAD... KIRO NEEDED THAT.
AND DESERVES IT AS WELL! I'LL HAVE YOU KNOW THAT KIRO'S WOUNDS WERE INCURRED MOST SELFLESSLY...
WHY, HE DID NOTHING LESS THAN SAVE US ALL FROM UNIVERSAL ANNIHILATION!
UNIVERS--? WHY, PLIF, I'M SURPRISED AT YOU. I DIDN'T KNOW THAT HOOJIBS INDULGED IN POETIC HYPERBOLE.
WE DON'T, MY DEAR.
HE'S RIGHT, LEIA. IT'S NO EXAGGERATION. I STILL HAVE SOME QUESTIONS ABOUT HOW HE DID IT... BUT KIRO MANAGED TO DEACTIVATE A GALAXY-WIDE BOOBY-TRAP THAT COULD HAVE BEEN THE END OF EVERYTHING.
AND WONDERING ABOUT KIRO HAS GOTTEN ME THINKING ABOUT A LOT OF OTHER THINGS... THERE ARE QUESTIONS AND PROBLEMS I'VE BEEN AVOIDING...
IS THERE SOMEWHERE WE CAN GO AND TALK LATER?
AND SOON...
ENDOR'S A BEAUTIFUL WORLD.
AS BEAUTIFUL AS ANY I'VE EVER VISITED.
NICE TO HAVE SOME PEACE AND QUIET FOR A CHANGE, ISN'T IT?
FOR A CHANGE, YES... BUT I'M BEGINNING TO WONDER IF IT'S REALLY WHAT I WANT PERMANENTLY.
6

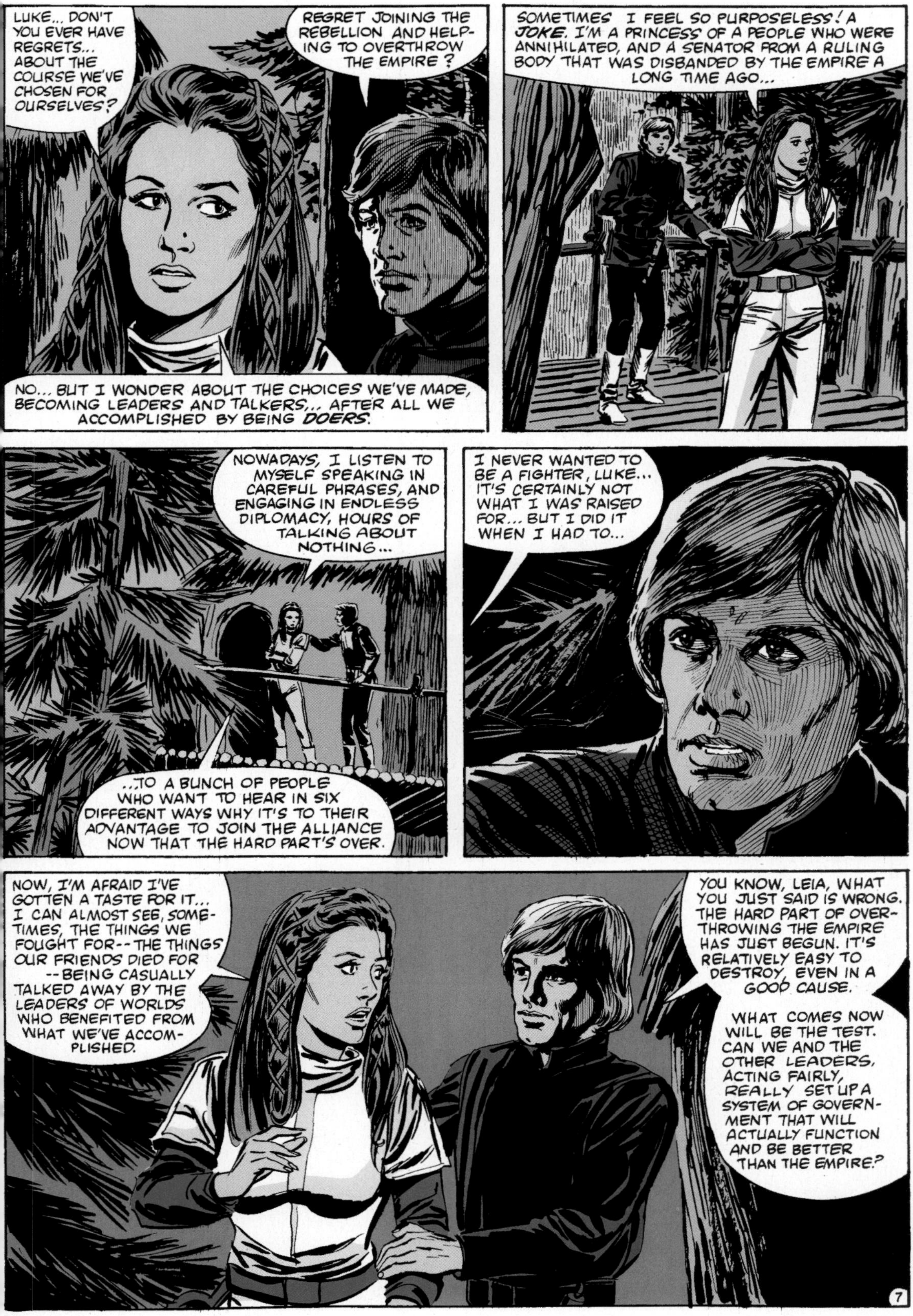

LUKE... DON'T YOU EVER HAVE REGRETS... ABOUT THE COURSE WE'VE CHOSEN FOR OURSELVES?
REGRET JOINING THE REBELLION AND HELPING TO OVERTHROW THE EMPIRE?
NO... BUT I WONDER ABOUT THE CHOICES WE'VE MADE, BECOMING LEADERS AND TALKERS... AFTER ALL WE ACCOMPLISHED BY BEING DOERS.
SOMETIMES I FEEL SO PURPOSELESS! A JOKE. I'M A PRINCESS OF A PEOPLE WHO WERE ANNIHILATED, AND A SENATOR FROM A RULING BODY THAT WAS DISBANDED BY THE EMPIRE A LONG TIME AGO...
NOWADAYS, I LISTEN TO MYSELF SPEAKING IN CAREFUL PHRASES, AND ENGAGING IN ENDLESS DIPLOMACY, HOURS OF TALKING ABOUT NOTHING...
...TO A BUNCH OF PEOPLE WHO WANT TO HEAR IN SIX DIFFERENT WAYS WHY IT'S TO THEIR ADVANTAGE TO JOIN THE ALLIANCE NOW THAT THE HARD PART'S OVER.
I NEVER WANTED TO BE A FIGHTER, LUKE... IT'S CERTAINLY NOT WHAT I WAS RAISED FOR... BUT I DID IT WHEN I HAD TO...
NOW, I'M AFRAID I'VE GOTTEN A TASTE FOR IT... I CAN ALMOST SEE, SOMETIMES, THE THINGS WE FOUGHT FOR--THE THINGS OUR FRIENDS DIED FOR --BEING CASUALLY TALKED AWAY BY THE LEADERS OF WORLDS WHO BENEFITED FROM WHAT WE'VE ACCOMPLISHED.
YOU KNOW, LEIA, WHAT YOU JUST SAID IS WRONG. THE HARD PART OF OVERTHROWING THE EMPIRE HAS JUST BEGUN. IT'S RELATIVELY EASY TO DESTROY, EVEN IN A GOOD CAUSE.
WHAT COMES NOW WILL BE THE TEST. CAN WE AND THE OTHER LEADERS, ACTING FAIRLY, REALLY SET UP A SYSTEM OF GOVERNMENT THAT WILL ACTUALLY FUNCTION AND BE BETTER THAN THE EMPIRE?
7

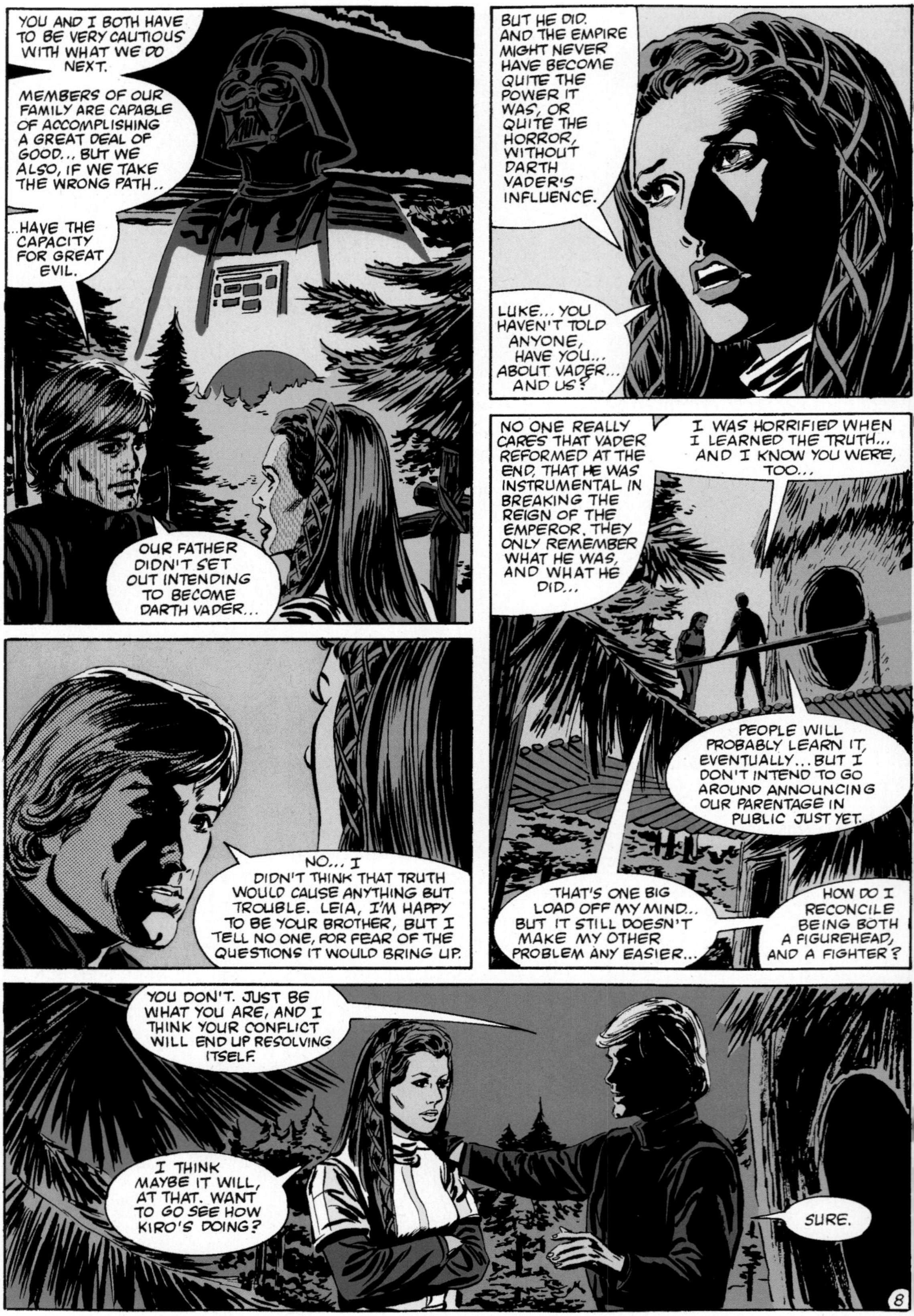
YOU AND I BOTH HAVE TO BE VERY CAUTIOUS WITH WHAT WE DO NEXT.
MEMBERS OF OUR FAMILY ARE CAPABLE OF ACCOMPLISHING A GREAT DEAL OF GOOD... BUT WE ALSO, IF WE TAKE THE WRONG PATH...
...HAVE THE CAPACITY FOR GREAT EVIL.
OUR FATHER DIDN'T SET OUT INTENDING TO BECOME DARTH VADER...
BUT HE DID. AND THE EMPIRE MIGHT NEVER HAVE BECOME QUITE THE POWER IT WAS, OR QUITE THE HORROR, WITHOUT DARTH VADER'S INFLUENCE.
LUKE... YOU HAVEN'T TOLD ANYONE, HAVE YOU... ABOUT VADER... AND US?
NO... I DIDN'T THINK THAT TRUTH WOULD CAUSE ANYTHING BUT TROUBLE. LEIA, I'M HAPPY TO BE YOUR BROTHER, BUT I TELL NO ONE, FOR FEAR OF THE QUESTIONS IT WOULD BRING UP.
NO ONE REALLY CARES THAT VADER REFORMED AT THE END, THAT HE WAS INSTRUMENTAL IN BREAKING THE REIGN OF THE EMPEROR. THEY ONLY REMEMBER WHAT HE WAS, AND WHAT HE DID...
I WAS HORRIFIED WHEN I LEARNED THE TRUTH... AND I KNOW YOU WERE, TOO...
PEOPLE WILL PROBABLY LEARN IT, EVENTUALLY... BUT I DON'T INTEND TO GO AROUND ANNOUNCING OUR PARENTAGE IN PUBLIC JUST YET.
THAT'S ONE BIG LOAD OFF MY MIND... BUT IT STILL DOESN'T MAKE MY OTHER PROBLEM ANY EASIER...
HOW DO I RECONCILE BEING BOTH A FIGUREHEAD, AND A FIGHTER?
YOU DON'T. JUST BE WHAT YOU ARE, AND I THINK YOUR CONFLICT WILL END UP RESOLVING ITSELF.
I THINK MAYBE IT WILL, AT THAT. WANT TO GO SEE HOW KIRO'S DOING?
SURE.
8

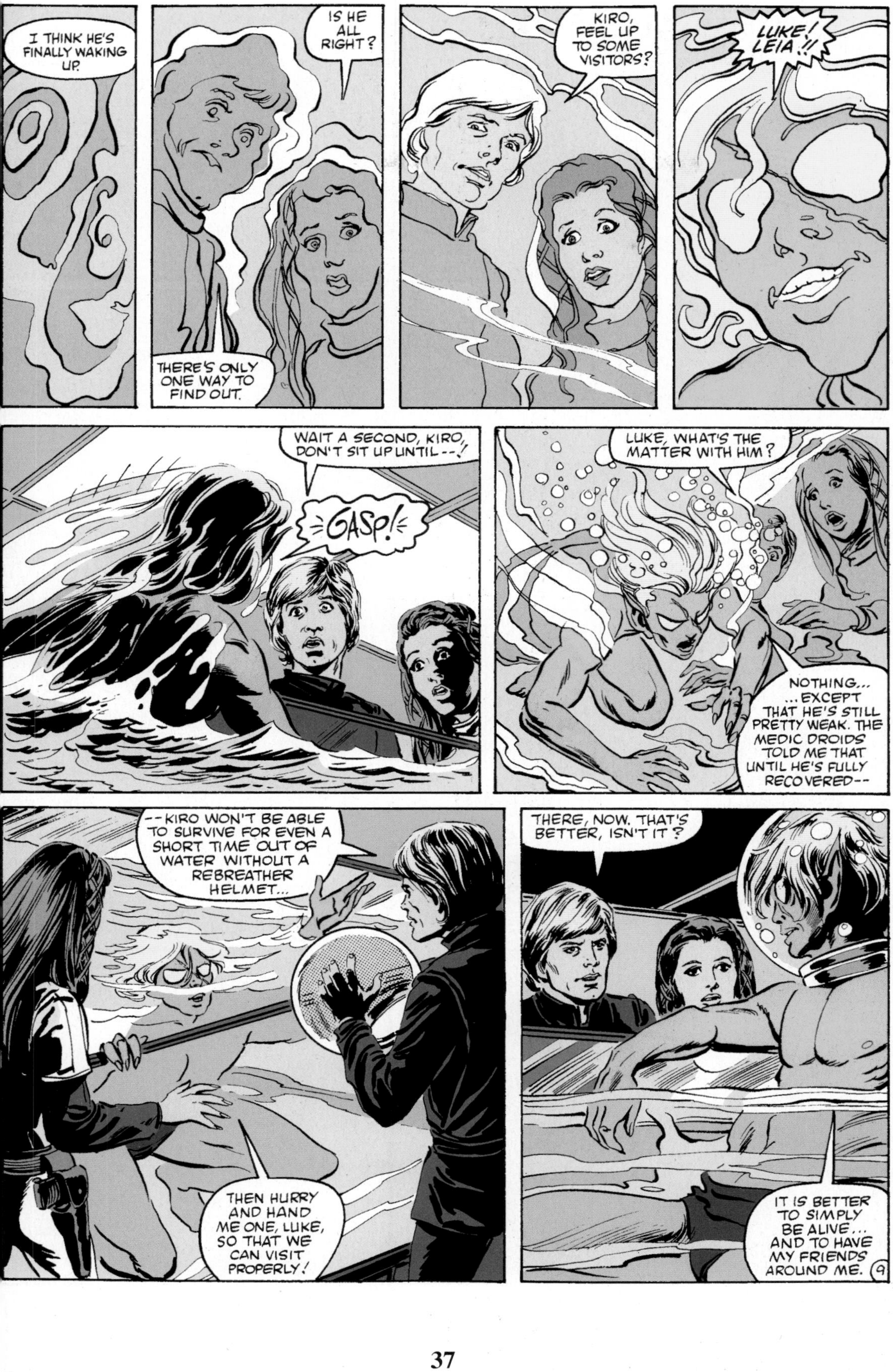
I THINK HE'S FINALLY WAKING UP.
IS HE ALL RIGHT?
THERE'S ONLY ONE WAY TO FIND OUT.
KIRO, FEEL UP TO SOME VISITORS?
LUKE! LEIA!!
WAIT A SECOND, KIRO, DON'T SIT UP UNTIL--!
GASP!
LUKE, WHAT'S THE MATTER WITH HIM?
NOTHING... ...EXCEPT THAT HE'S STILL PRETTY WEAK. THE MEDIC DROIDS TOLD ME THAT UNTIL HE'S FULLY RECOVERED--
--KIRO WON'T BE ABLE TO SURVIVE FOR EVEN A SHORT TIME OUT OF WATER WITHOUT A REBREATHER HELMET...
THEN HURRY AND HAND ME ONE, LUKE, SO THAT WE CAN VISIT PROPERLY!
THERE, NOW. THAT'S BETTER, ISN'T IT?
IT IS BETTER TO SIMPLY BE ALIVE... AND TO HAVE MY FRIENDS AROUND ME.
9

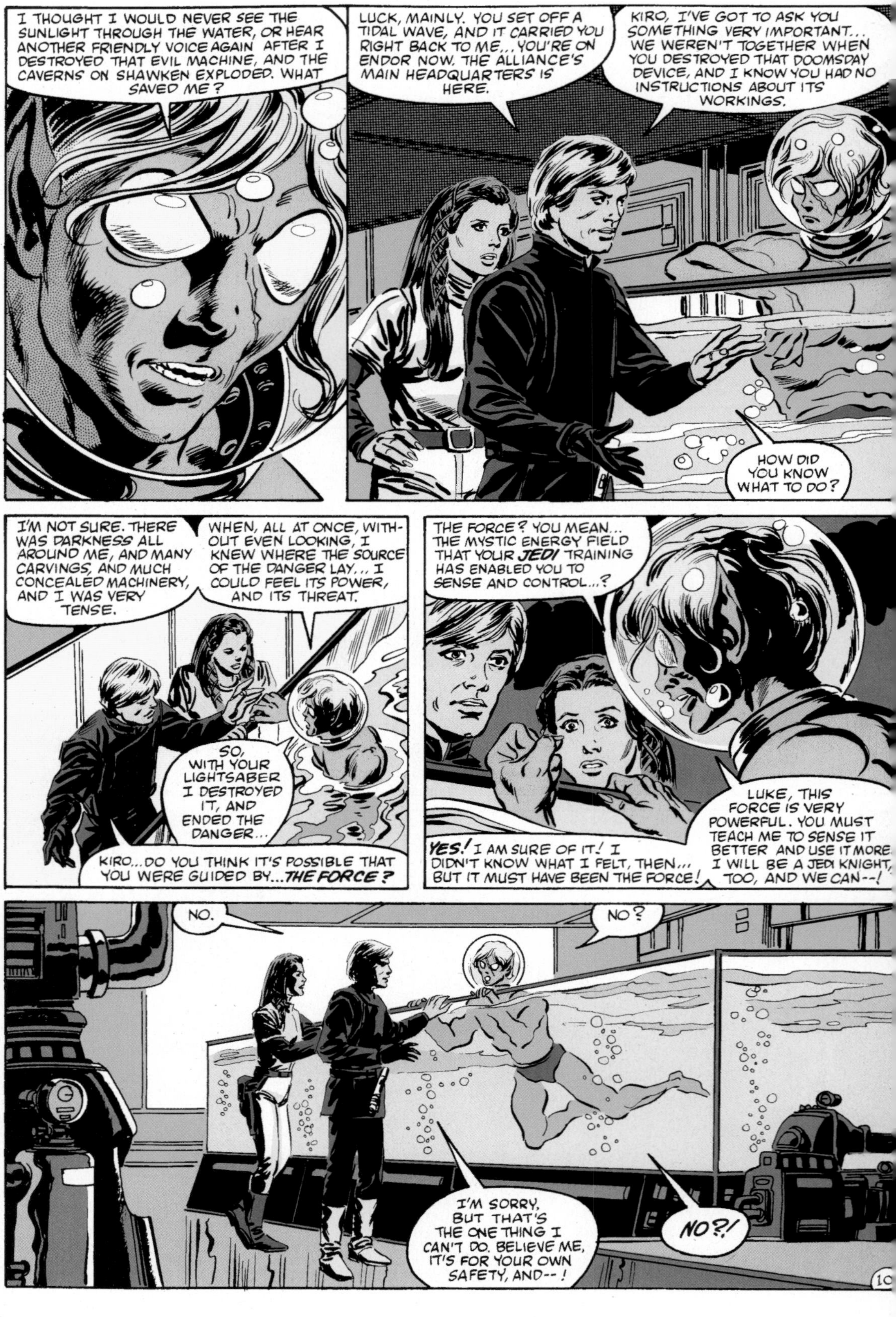
I THOUGHT I WOULD NEVER SEE THE SUNLIGHT THROUGH THE WATER, OR HEAR ANOTHER FRIENDLY VOICE AGAIN AFTER I DESTROYED THAT EVIL MACHINE, AND THE CAVERNS ON SHAWKEN EXPLODED. WHAT SAVED ME?
LUCK, MAINLY. YOU SET OFF A TIDAL WAVE, AND IT CARRIED YOU RIGHT BACK TO ME... YOU'RE ON ENDOR NOW. THE ALLIANCE'S MAIN HEADQUARTERS IS HERE.
KIRO, I'VE GOT TO ASK YOU SOMETHING VERY IMPORTANT... WE WEREN'T TOGETHER WHEN YOU DESTROYED THAT DOOMSDAY DEVICE, AND I KNOW YOU HAD NO INSTRUCTIONS ABOUT ITS WORKINGS.
HOW DID YOU KNOW WHAT TO DO?
I'M NOT SURE. THERE WAS DARKNESS ALL AROUND ME, AND MANY CARVINGS, AND MUCH CONCEALED MACHINERY, AND I WAS VERY TENSE.
WHEN, ALL AT ONCE, WITHOUT EVEN LOOKING, I KNEW WHERE THE SOURCE OF THE DANGER LAY... I COULD FEEL ITS POWER, AND ITS THREAT.
SO, WITH YOUR LIGHTSABER I DESTROYED IT, AND ENDED THE DANGER...
KIRO... DO YOU THINK IT'S POSSIBLE THAT YOU WERE GUIDED BY... THE FORCE?
THE FORCE? YOU MEAN... THE MYSTIC ENERGY FIELD THAT YOUR JEDI TRAINING HAS ENABLED YOU TO SENSE AND CONTROL...?
YES! I AM SURE OF IT! I DIDN'T KNOW WHAT I FELT, THEN... BUT IT MUST HAVE BEEN THE FORCE!
LUKE, THIS FORCE IS VERY POWERFUL. YOU MUST TEACH ME TO SENSE IT BETTER AND USE IT MORE. I WILL BE A JEDI KNIGHT, TOO, AND WE CAN--!
NO.
NO?
I'M SORRY, BUT THAT'S THE ONE THING I CAN'T DO. BELIEVE ME, IT'S FOR YOUR OWN SAFETY, AND--!
NO?!
10

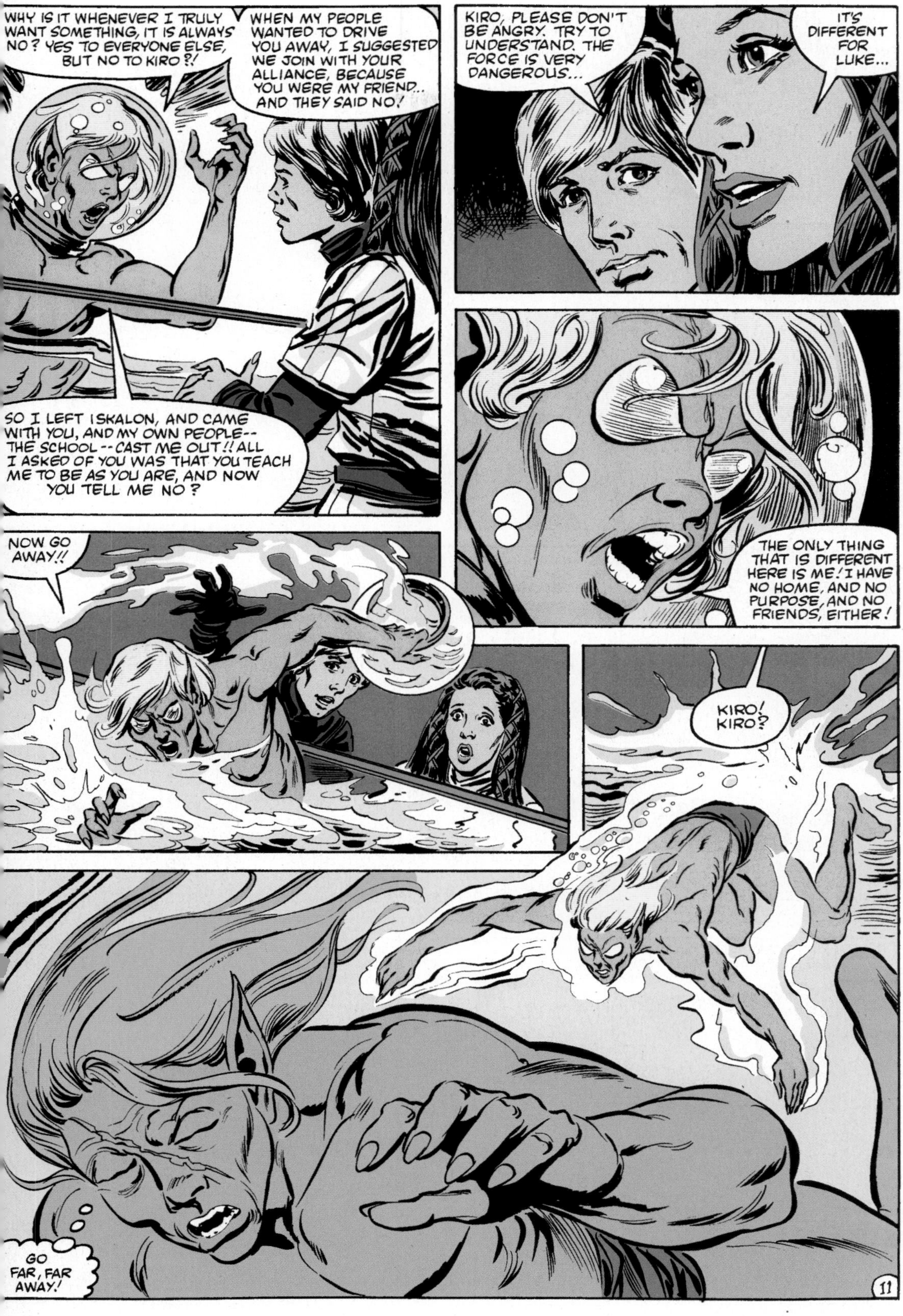
WHY IS IT WHENEVER I TRULY WANT SOMETHING, IT IS ALWAYS NO? YES TO EVERYONE ELSE, BUT NO TO KIRO?!
WHEN MY PEOPLE WANTED TO DRIVE YOU AWAY, I SUGGESTED WE JOIN WITH YOUR ALLIANCE, BECAUSE YOU WERE MY FRIEND... AND THEY SAID NO!
SO I LEFT ISKALON, AND CAME WITH YOU, AND MY OWN PEOPLE-- THE SCHOOL--CAST ME OUT!! ALL I ASKED OF YOU WAS THAT YOU TEACH ME TO BE AS YOU ARE, AND NOW YOU TELL ME NO?
KIRO, PLEASE DON'T BE ANGRY. TRY TO UNDERSTAND. THE FORCE IS VERY DANGEROUS...
IT'S DIFFERENT FOR LUKE...
THE ONLY THING THAT IS DIFFERENT HERE IS ME! I HAVE NO HOME, AND NO PURPOSE, AND NO FRIENDS, EITHER!
NOW GO AWAY!!
KIRO! KIRO?
GO FAR, FAR AWAY!
11

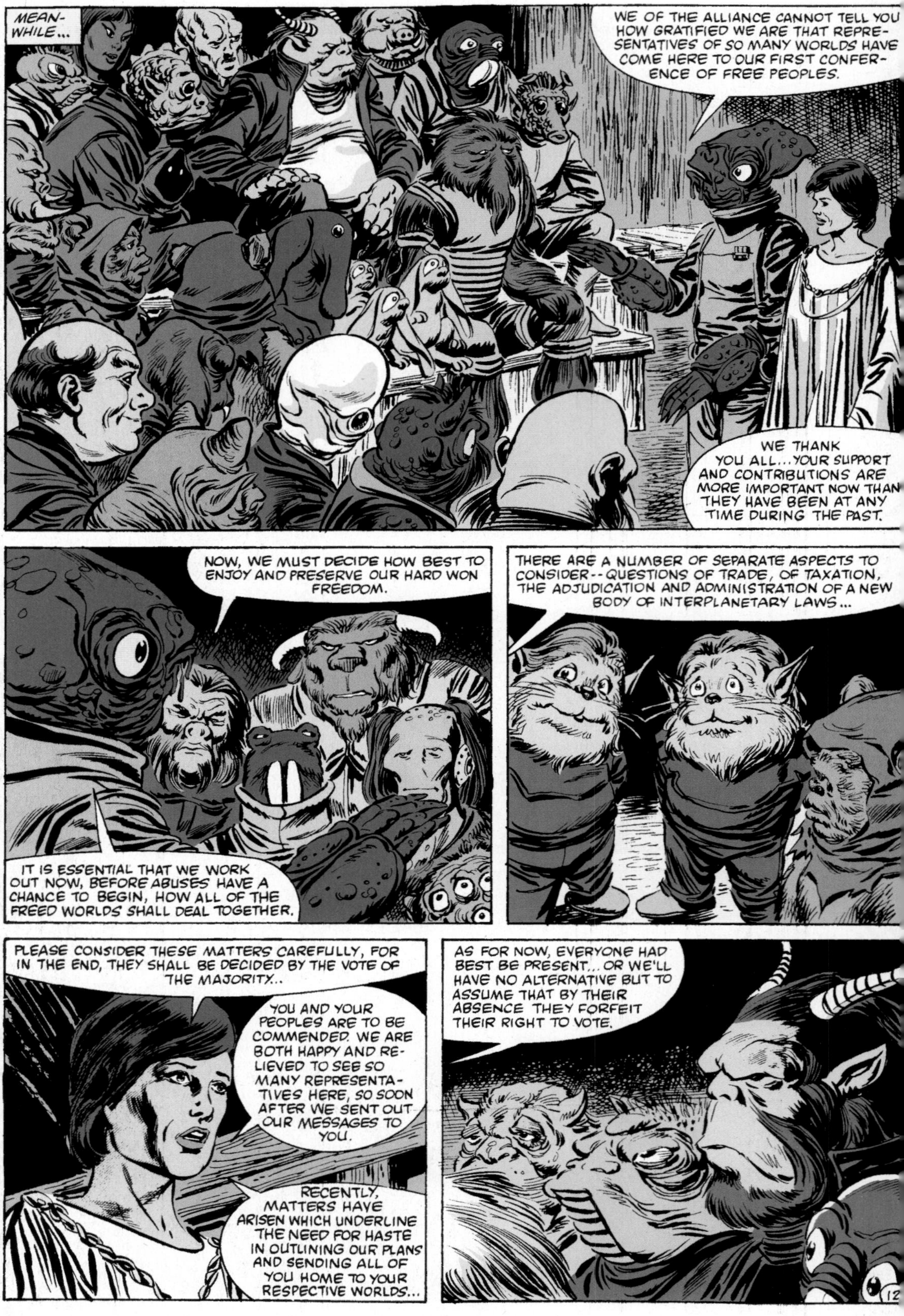
MEAN-WHILE...
WE OF THE ALLIANCE CANNOT TELL YOU HOW GRATIFIED WE ARE THAT REPRESENTATIVES OF SO MANY WORLDS HAVE COME HERE TO OUR FIRST CONFERENCE OF FREE PEOPLES.
WE THANK YOU ALL... YOUR SUPPORT AND CONTRIBUTIONS ARE MORE IMPORTANT NOW THAN THEY HAVE BEEN AT ANY TIME DURING THE PAST.
NOW, WE MUST DECIDE HOW BEST TO ENJOY AND PRESERVE OUR HARD WON FREEDOM.
IT IS ESSENTIAL THAT WE WORK OUT NOW, BEFORE ABUSES HAVE A CHANCE TO BEGIN, HOW ALL OF THE FREED WORLDS SHALL DEAL TOGETHER.
THERE ARE A NUMBER OF SEPARATE ASPECTS TO CONSIDER--QUESTIONS OF TRADE, OF TAXATION, THE ADJUDICATION AND ADMINISTRATION OF A NEW BODY OF INTERPLANETARY LAWS...
PLEASE CONSIDER THESE MATTERS CAREFULLY, FOR IN THE END, THEY SHALL BE DECIDED BY THE VOTE OF THE MAJORITY..
YOU AND YOUR PEOPLES ARE TO BE COMMENDED. WE ARE BOTH HAPPY AND RELIEVED TO SEE SO MANY REPRESENTATIVES HERE, SO SOON AFTER WE SENT OUT OUR MESSAGES TO YOU.
RECENTLY, MATTERS HAVE ARISEN WHICH UNDERLINE THE NEED FOR HASTE IN OUTLINING OUR PLANS AND SENDING ALL OF YOU HOME TO YOUR RESPECTIVE WORLDS...
AS FOR NOW, EVERYONE HAD BEST BE PRESENT... OR WE'LL HAVE NO ALTERNATIVE BUT TO ASSUME THAT BY THEIR ABSENCE THEY FORFEIT THEIR RIGHT TO VOTE.
12

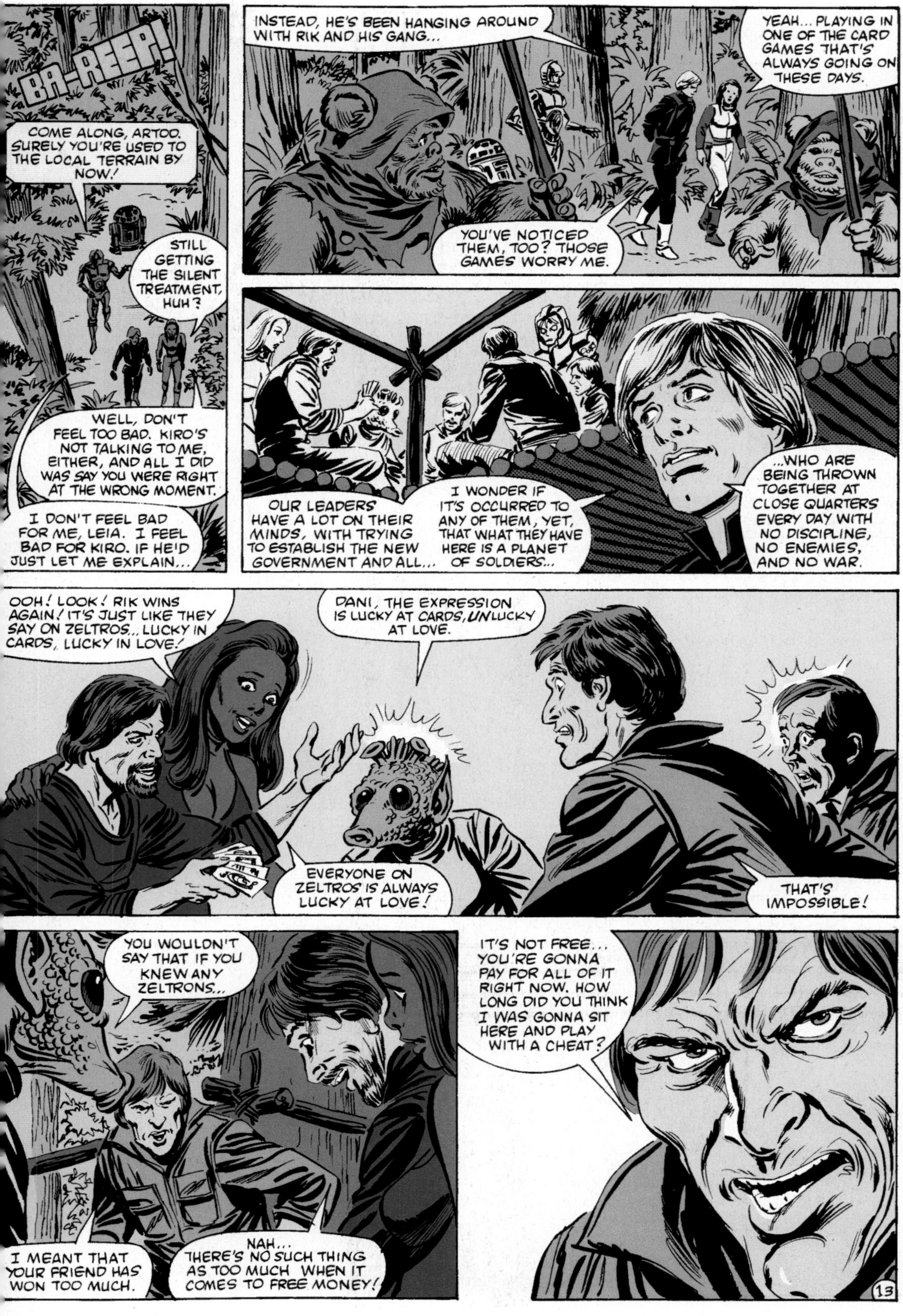
BA-REEP!
COME ALONG, ARTOO. SURELY YOU'RE USED TO THE LOCAL TERRAIN BY NOW!
STILL GETTING THE SILENT TREATMENT, HUH?
WELL, DON'T FEEL TOO BAD. KIRO'S NOT TALKING TO ME, EITHER, AND ALL I DID WAS SAY YOU WERE RIGHT AT THE WRONG MOMENT.
I DON'T FEEL BAD FOR ME, LEIA. I FEEL BAD FOR KIRO. IF HE'D JUST LET ME EXPLAIN...
INSTEAD, HE'S BEEN HANGING AROUND WITH RIK AND HIS GANG...
YEAH... PLAYING IN ONE OF THE CARD GAMES THAT'S ALWAYS GOING ON THESE DAYS.
YOU'VE NOTICED THEM, TOO? THOSE GAMES WORRY ME.
OUR LEADERS HAVE A LOT ON THEIR MINDS, WITH TRYING TO ESTABLISH THE NEW GOVERNMENT AND ALL...
I WONDER IF IT'S OCCURRED TO ANY OF THEM, YET, THAT WHAT THEY HAVE HERE IS A PLANET OF SOLDIERS...
...WHO ARE BEING THROWN TOGETHER AT CLOSE QUARTERS EVERY DAY WITH NO DISCIPLINE, NO ENEMIES, AND NO WAR.
OOH! LOOK! RIK WINS AGAIN! IT'S JUST LIKE THEY SAY ON ZELTROS... LUCKY IN CARDS, LUCKY IN LOVE!
DANI, THE EXPRESSION IS LUCKY AT CARDS, UNLUCKY AT LOVE.
EVERYONE ON ZELTROS IS ALWAYS LUCKY AT LOVE!
THAT'S IMPOSSIBLE!
YOU WOULDN'T SAY THAT IF YOU KNEW ANY ZELTRONS...
I MEANT THAT YOUR FRIEND HAS WON TOO MUCH.
NAH... THERE'S NO SUCH THING AS TOO MUCH WHEN IT COMES TO FREE MONEY!
IT'S NOT FREE... YOU'RE GONNA PAY FOR ALL OF IT RIGHT NOW. HOW LONG DID YOU THINK I WAS GONNA SIT HERE AND PLAY WITH A CHEAT?
13

42

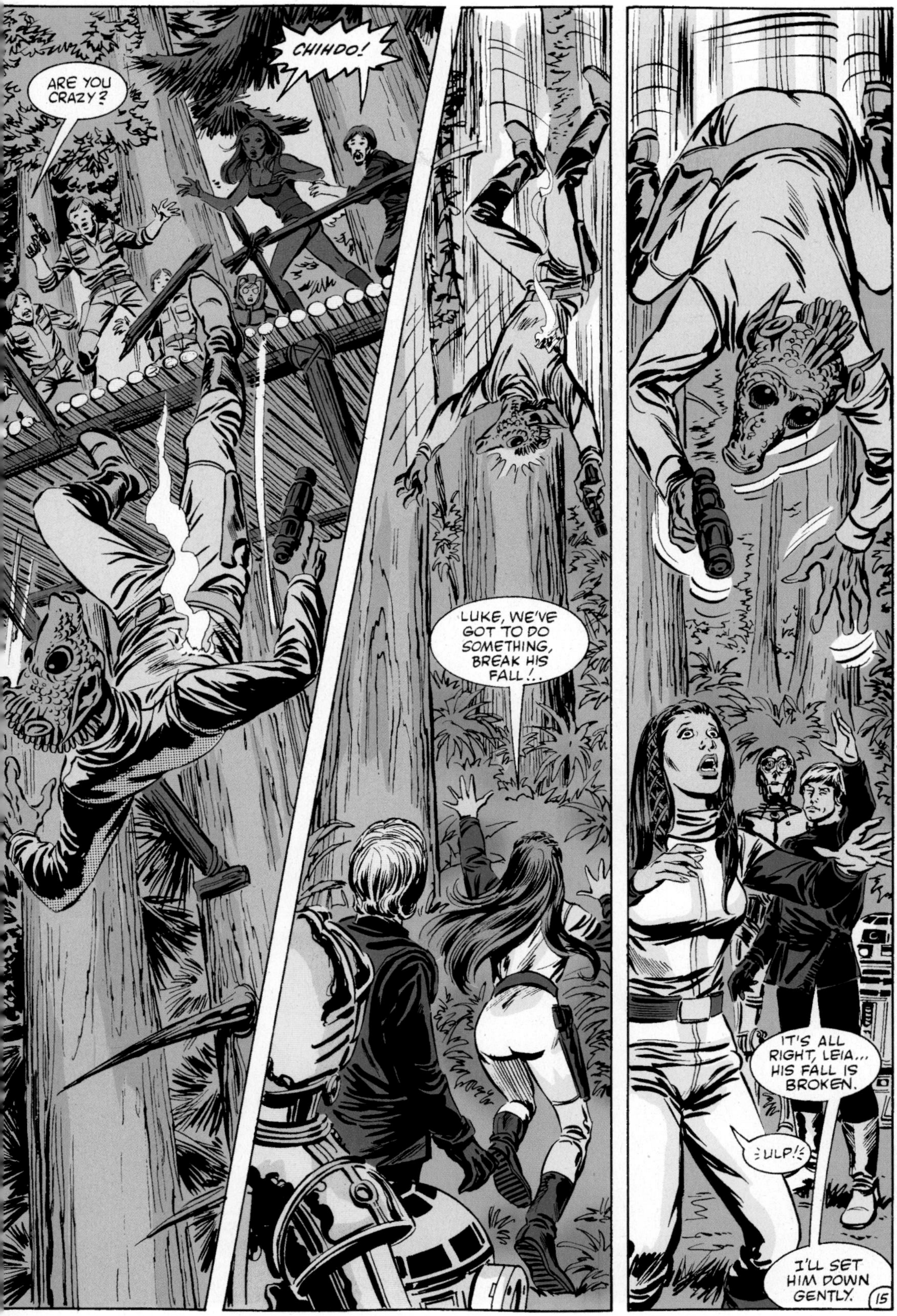
ARE YOU CRAZY?
CHIHDO!
LUKE, WE'VE GOT TO DO SOMETHING, BREAK HIS FALL!..
IT'S ALL RIGHT, LEIA... HIS FALL IS BROKEN.
ULP!
I'LL SET HIM DOWN GENTLY.
15

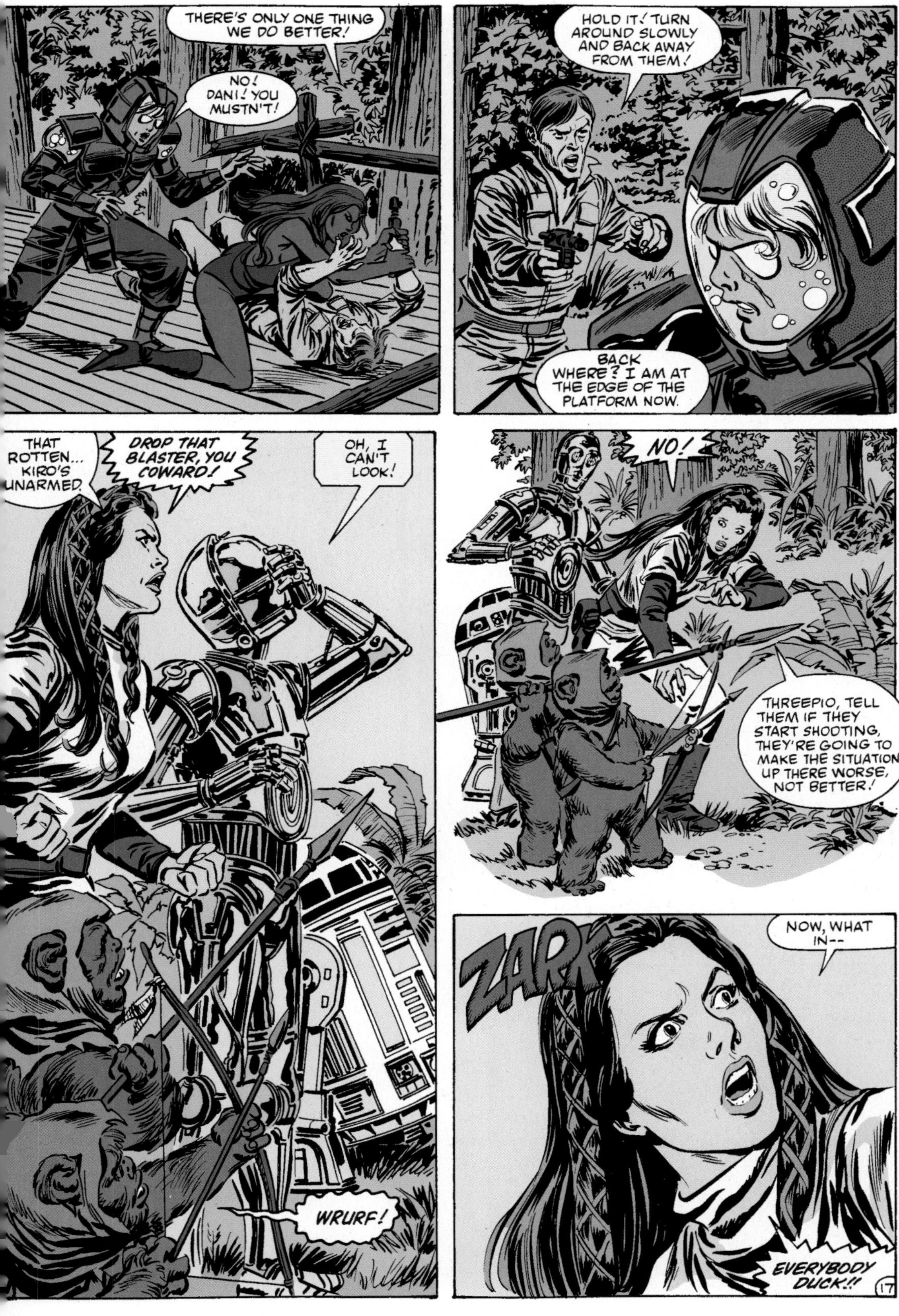
THERE'S ONLY ONE THING WE DO BETTER!
NO! DANI! YOU MUSTN'T!
HOLD IT! TURN AROUND SLOWLY AND BACK AWAY FROM THEM!
BACK WHERE? I AM AT THE EDGE OF THE PLATFORM NOW.
THAT ROTTEN... KIRO'S UNARMED.
DROP THAT BLASTER, YOU COWARD!
OH, I CAN'T LOOK!
WRURF!
NO!
THREEPIO, TELL THEM IF THEY START SHOOTING, THEY'RE GOING TO MAKE THE SITUATION UP THERE WORSE, NOT BETTER!
ZARK
NOW, WHAT IN--
EVERYBODY DUCK!!
17

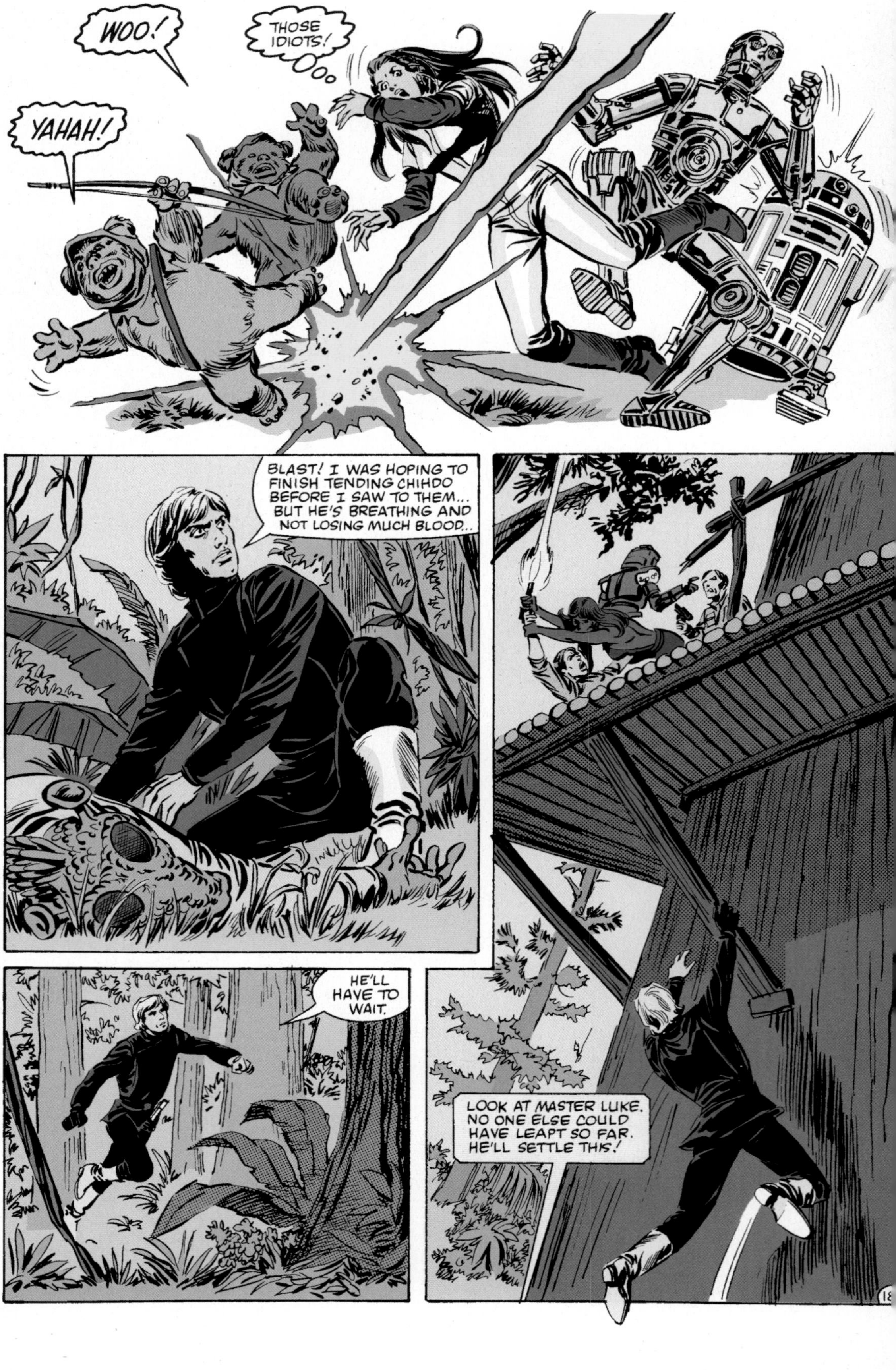
WOO!
THOSE IDIOTS!
YAHAH!
BLAST! I WAS HOPING TO FINISH TENDING CHIHDO BEFORE I SAW TO THEM... BUT HE'S BREATHING AND NOT LOSING MUCH BLOOD..
HE'LL HAVE TO WAIT.
LOOK AT MASTER LUKE. NO ONE ELSE COULD HAVE LEAPT SO FAR. HE'LL SETTLE THIS!
18

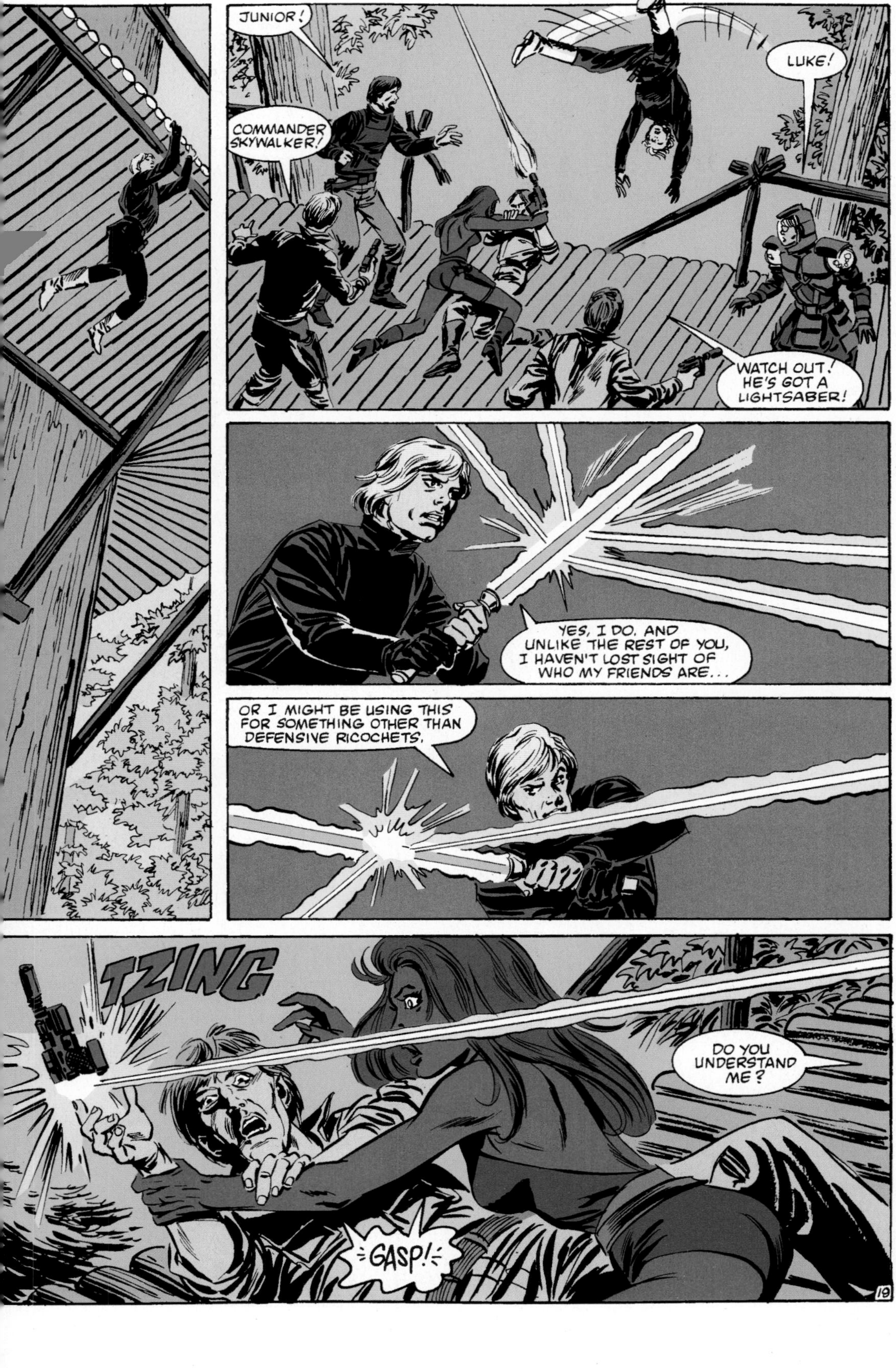
JUNIOR!
COMMANDER SKYWALKER!
LUKE!
WATCH OUT! HE'S GOT A LIGHTSABER!
YES, I DO. AND UNLIKE THE REST OF YOU, I HAVEN'T LOST SIGHT OF WHO MY FRIENDS ARE...
OR I MIGHT BE USING THIS FOR SOMETHING OTHER THAN DEFENSIVE RICOCHETS.
TZING
DO YOU UNDERSTAND ME?
GASP!
19

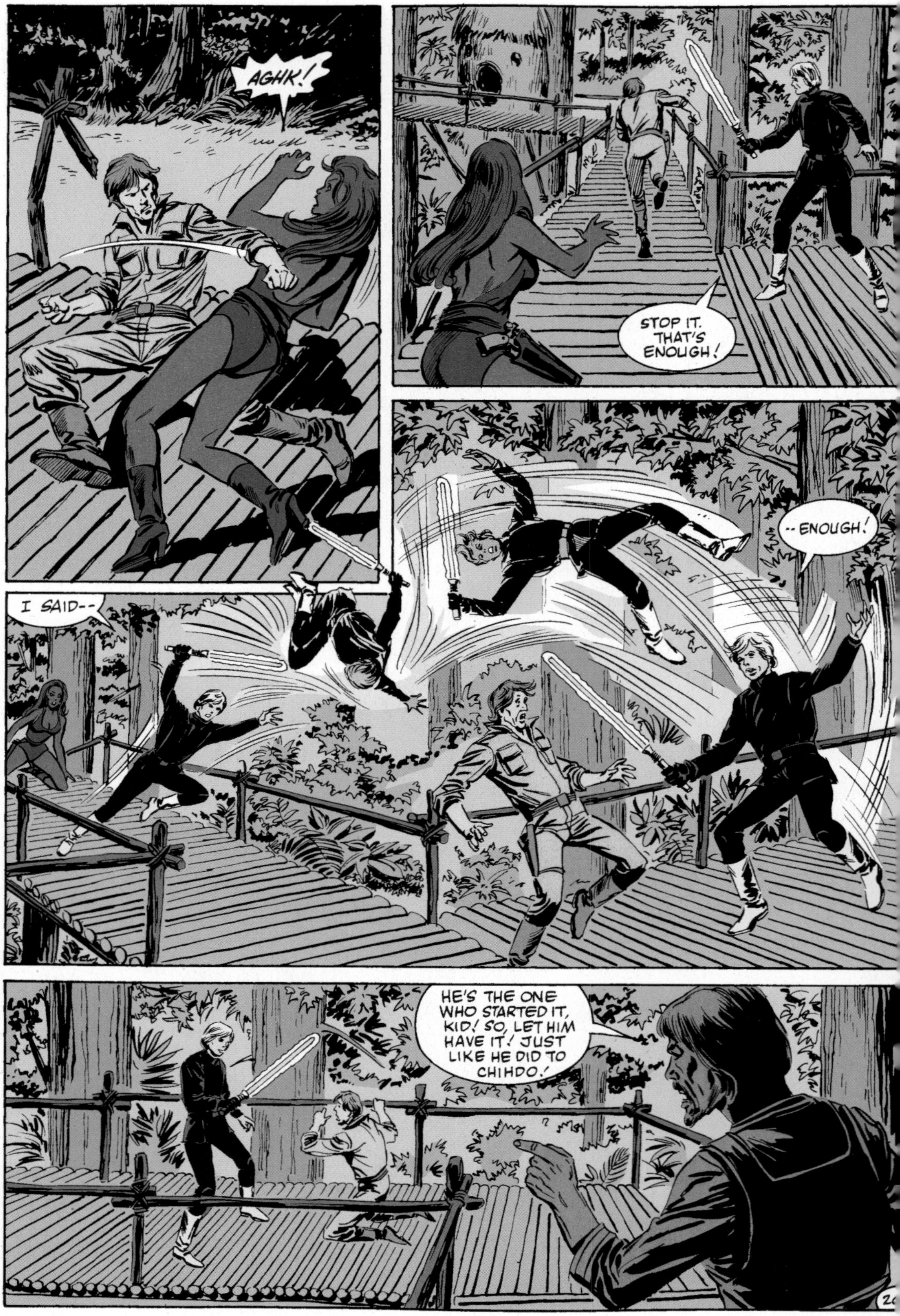
AGHK!
STOP IT. THAT'S ENOUGH!
I SAID--
--ENOUGH!
HE'S THE ONE WHO STARTED IT, KID! SO, LET HIM HAVE IT! JUST LIKE HE DID TO CHIHDO!

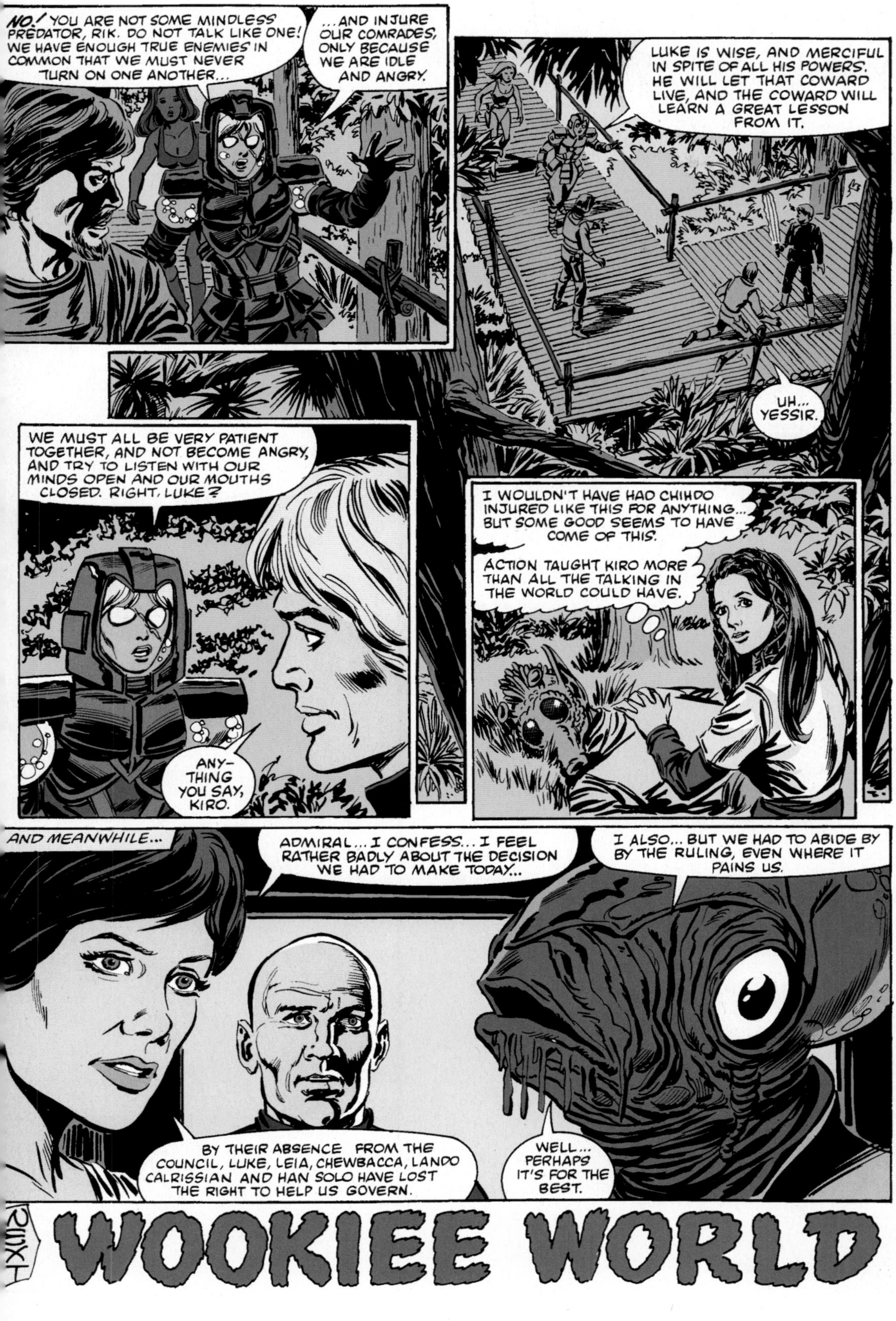
NO! YOU ARE NOT SOME MINDLESS PREDATOR, RIK. DO NOT TALK LIKE ONE! WE HAVE ENOUGH TRUE ENEMIES IN COMMON THAT WE MUST NEVER TURN ON ONE ANOTHER...
...AND INJURE OUR COMRADES, ONLY BECAUSE WE ARE IDLE AND ANGRY.
LUKE IS WISE, AND MERCIFUL IN SPITE OF ALL HIS POWERS. HE WILL LET THAT COWARD LIVE, AND THE COWARD WILL LEARN A GREAT LESSON FROM IT.
UH... YESSIR.
WE MUST ALL BE VERY PATIENT TOGETHER, AND NOT BECOME ANGRY, AND TRY TO LISTEN WITH OUR MINDS OPEN AND OUR MOUTHS CLOSED. RIGHT, LUKE?
ANY-THING YOU SAY, KIRO.
I WOULDN'T HAVE HAD CHIHDO INJURED LIKE THIS FOR ANYTHING... BUT SOME GOOD SEEMS TO HAVE COME OF THIS.
ACTION TAUGHT KIRO MORE THAN ALL THE TALKING IN THE WORLD COULD HAVE.
AND MEANWHILE...
ADMIRAL... I CONFESS... I FEEL RATHER BADLY ABOUT THE DECISION WE HAD TO MAKE TODAY...
I ALSO... BUT WE HAD TO ABIDE BY BY THE RULING, EVEN WHERE IT PAINS US.
BY THEIR ABSENCE FROM THE COUNCIL, LUKE, LEIA, CHEWBACCA, LANDO CALRISSIAN AND HAN SOLO HAVE LOST THE RIGHT TO HELP US GOVERN.
WELL... PERHAPS IT'S FOR THE BEST.
WOOKIEE WORLD

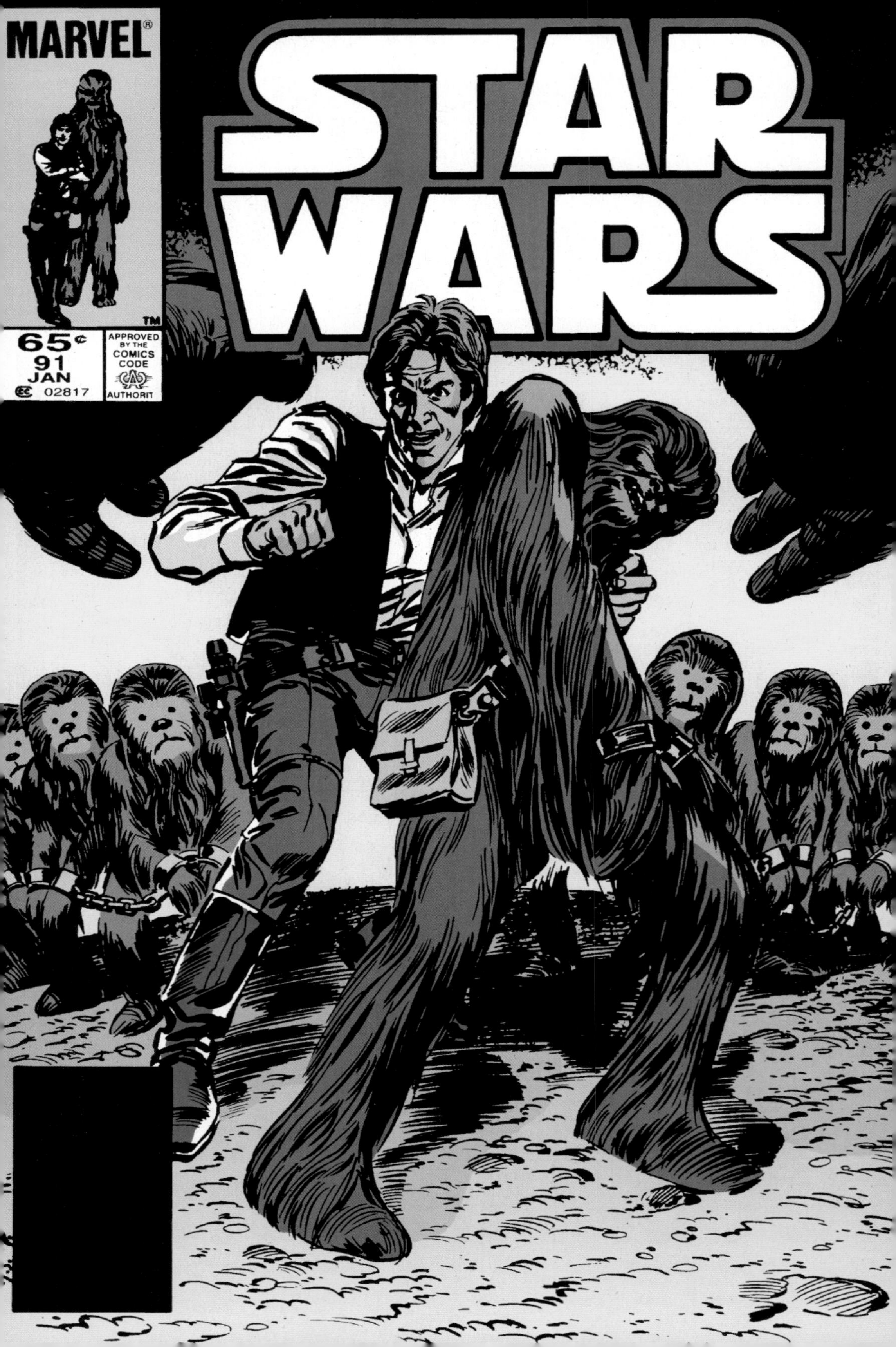
MARVEL®
STAR WARS
TM
65¢
91
JAN
02817
APPROVED BY THE COMICS CODE AUTHORITY

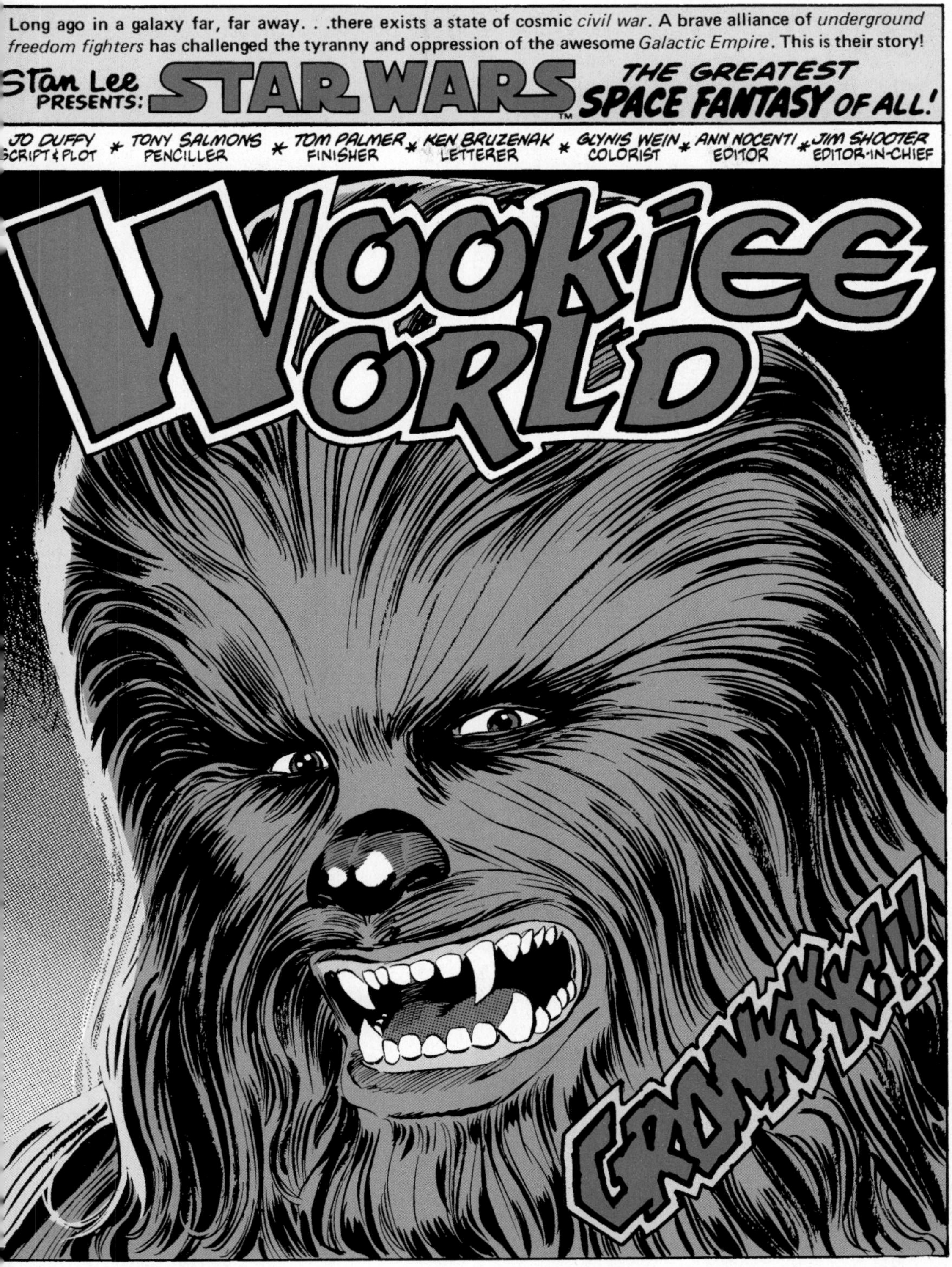

Long ago in a galaxy far, far away. . .there exists a state of cosmic *civil war*. A brave alliance of *underground freedom fighters* has challenged the tyranny and oppression of the awesome *Galactic Empire*. This is their story!
Stan Lee PRESENTS: STAR WARS™ THE GREATEST SPACE FANTASY OF ALL!
JO DUFFY SCRIPT & PLOT * TONY SALMONS PENCILLER * TOM PALMER FINISHER * KEN BRUZENAK LETTERER * GLYNIS WEIN COLORIST * ANN NOCENTI EDITOR * JIM SHOOTER EDITOR-IN-CHIEF
WOOKIEE WORLD
GRONNKK!!

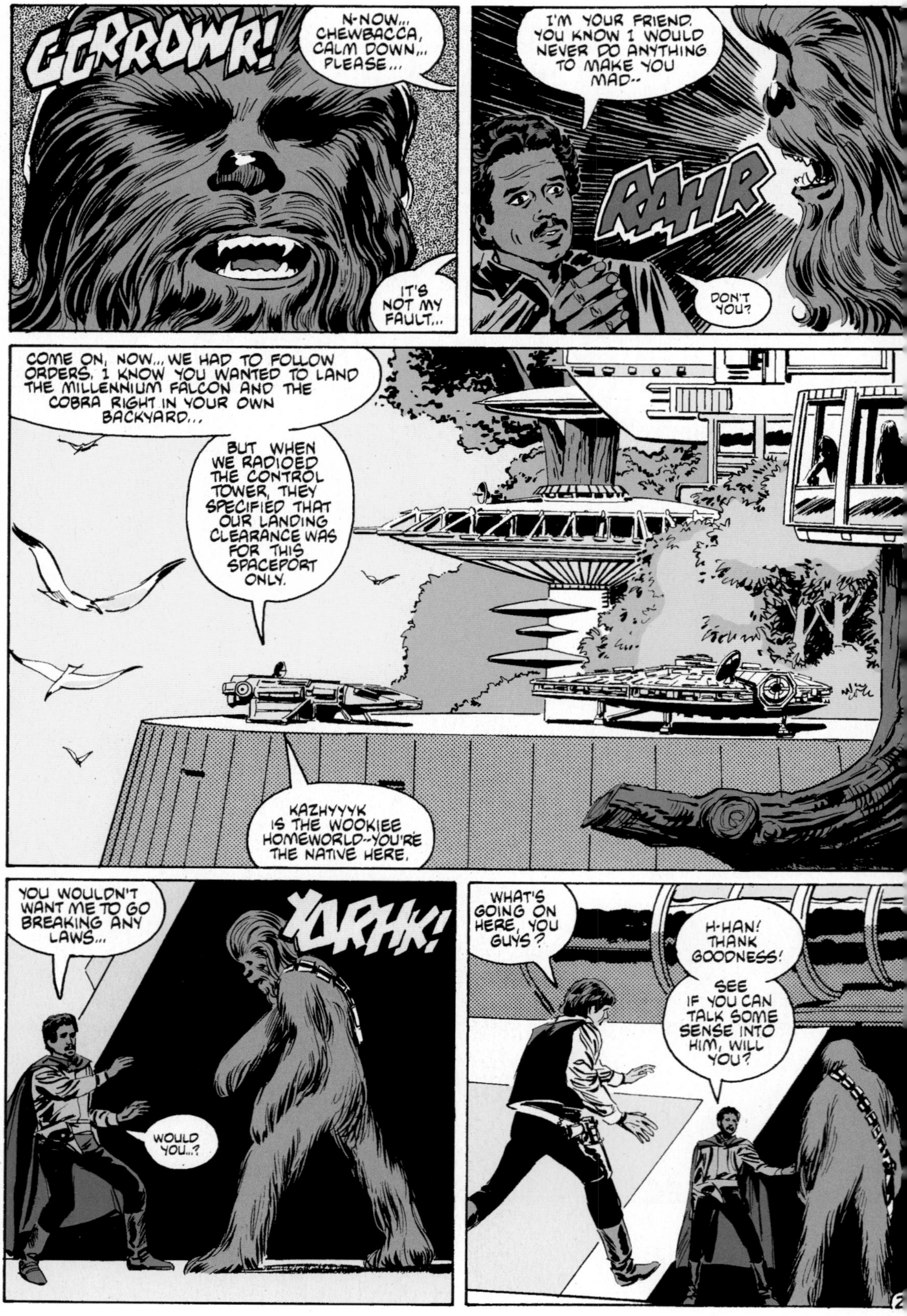
GGRROWR!
N-NOW... CHEWBACCA, CALM DOWN... PLEASE...
IT'S NOT MY FAULT...
I'M YOUR FRIEND. YOU KNOW I WOULD NEVER DO ANYTHING TO MAKE YOU MAD--
RAHR
DON'T YOU?
COME ON, NOW... WE HAD TO FOLLOW ORDERS. I KNOW YOU WANTED TO LAND THE MILLENNIUM FALCON AND THE COBRA RIGHT IN YOUR OWN BACKYARD...
BUT WHEN WE RADIOED THE CONTROL TOWER, THEY SPECIFIED THAT OUR LANDING CLEARANCE WAS FOR THIS SPACEPORT ONLY.
KAZHYYYK IS THE WOOKIEE HOMEWORLD--YOU'RE THE NATIVE HERE.
YOU WOULDN'T WANT ME TO GO BREAKING ANY LAWS...
YARHK!
WOULD YOU...?
WHAT'S GOING ON HERE, YOU GUYS?
H-HAN! THANK GOODNESS!
SEE IF YOU CAN TALK SOME SENSE INTO HIM, WILL YOU?

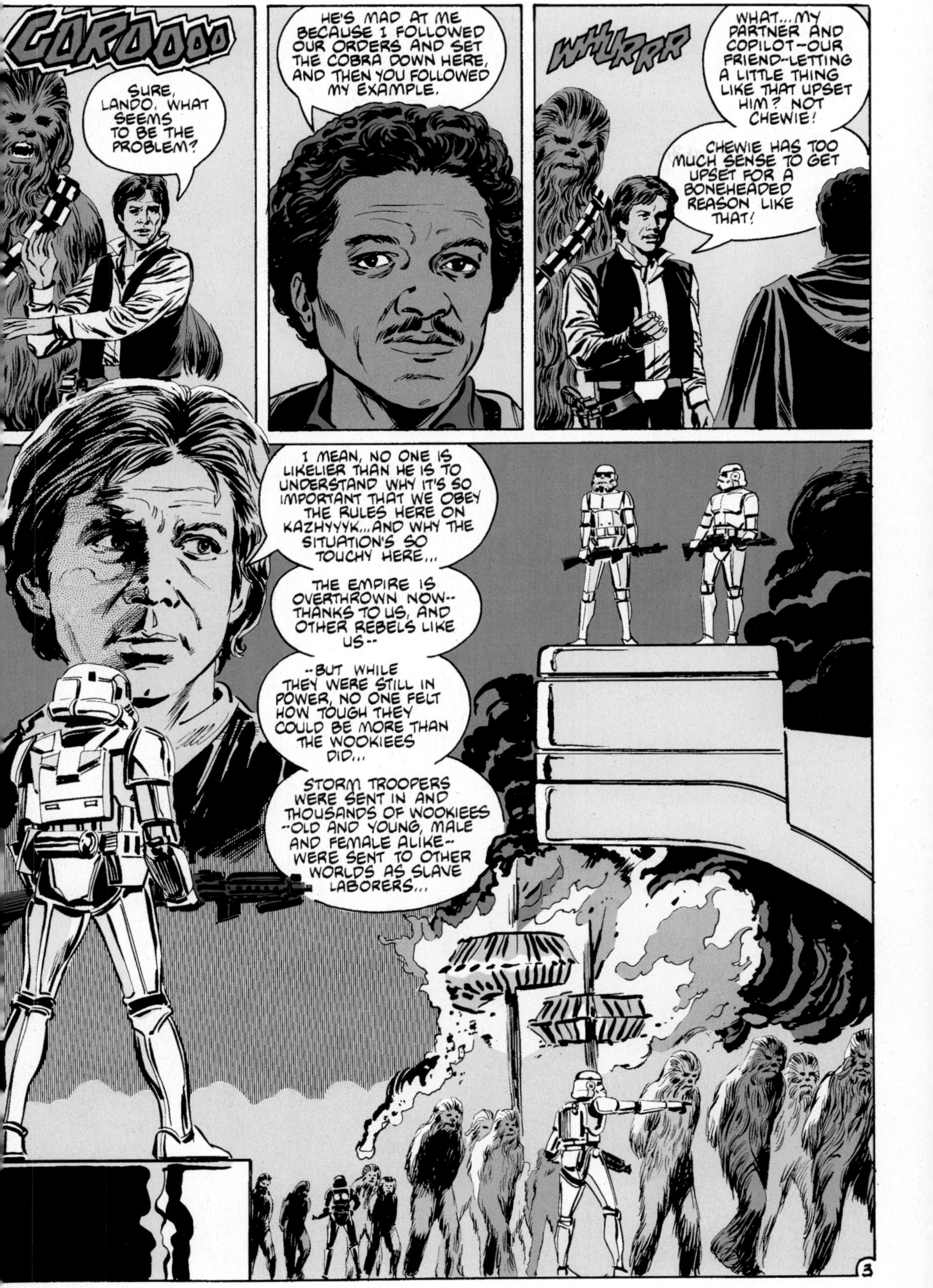
GARDOOO
SURE, LANDO. WHAT SEEMS TO BE THE PROBLEM?
HE'S MAD AT ME BECAUSE I FOLLOWED OUR ORDERS AND SET THE COBRA DOWN HERE, AND THEN YOU FOLLOWED MY EXAMPLE.
WHURRR
WHAT... MY PARTNER AND COPILOT--OUR FRIEND--LETTING A LITTLE THING LIKE THAT UPSET HIM? NOT CHEWIE!
CHEWIE HAS TOO MUCH SENSE TO GET UPSET FOR A BONEHEADED REASON LIKE THAT!
I MEAN, NO ONE IS LIKELIER THAN HE IS TO UNDERSTAND WHY IT'S SO IMPORTANT THAT WE OBEY THE RULES HERE ON KAZHYYYK...AND WHY THE SITUATION'S SO TOUCHY HERE...
THE EMPIRE IS OVERTHROWN NOW-- THANKS TO US, AND OTHER REBELS LIKE US--
--BUT WHILE THEY WERE STILL IN POWER, NO ONE FELT HOW TOUGH THEY COULD BE MORE THAN THE WOOKIEES DID...
STORM TROOPERS WERE SENT IN AND THOUSANDS OF WOOKIEES --OLD AND YOUNG, MALE AND FEMALE ALIKE-- WERE SENT TO OTHER WORLDS AS SLAVE LABORERS...
3

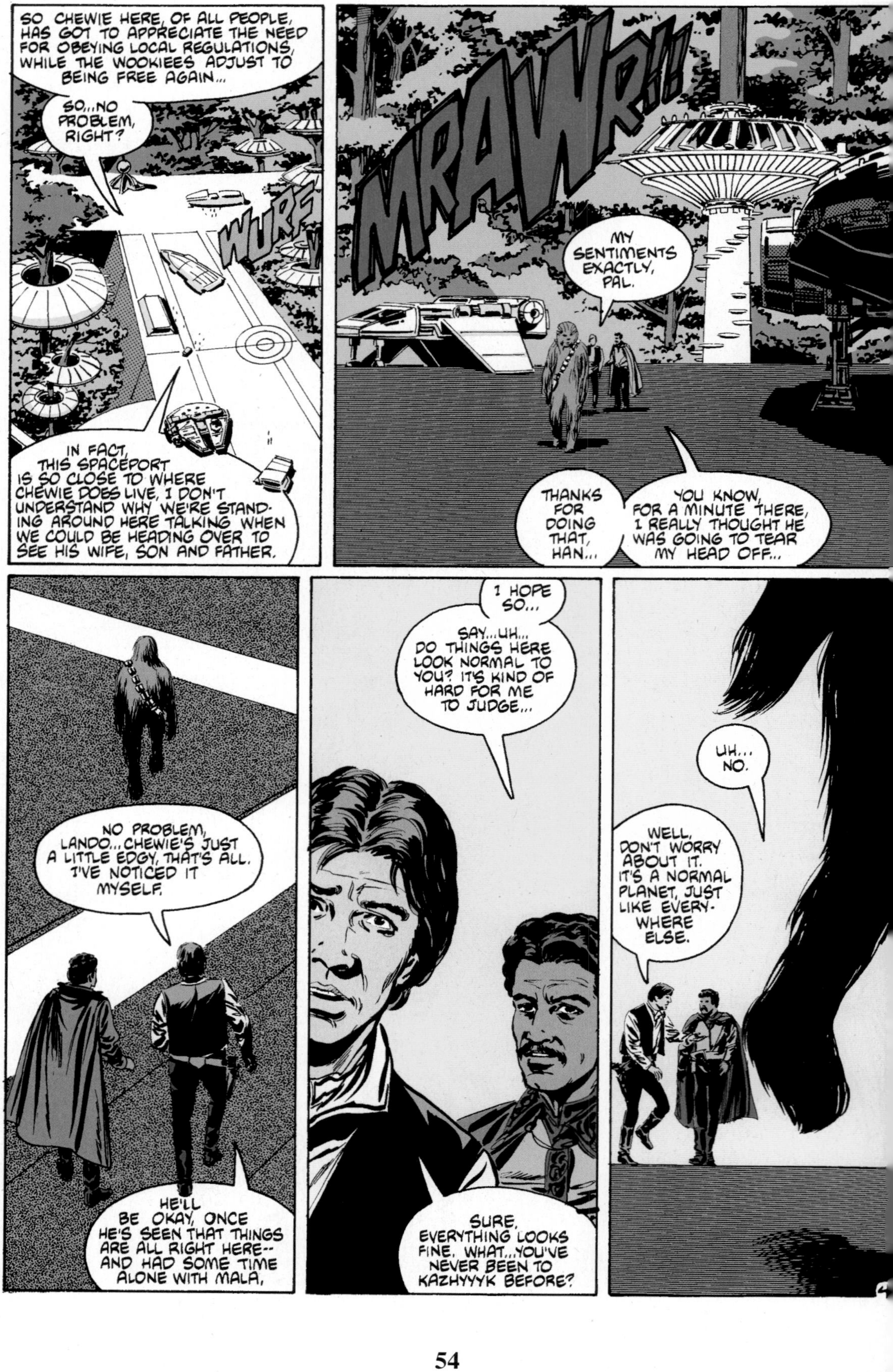

SO CHEWIE HERE, OF ALL PEOPLE, HAS GOT TO APPRECIATE THE NEED FOR OBEYING LOCAL REGULATIONS, WHILE THE WOOKIEES ADJUST TO BEING FREE AGAIN...
SO...NO PROBLEM, RIGHT?
WURF
IN FACT, THIS SPACEPORT IS SO CLOSE TO WHERE CHEWIE DOES LIVE, I DON'T UNDERSTAND WHY WE'RE STANDING AROUND HERE TALKING WHEN WE COULD BE HEADING OVER TO SEE HIS WIFE, SON AND FATHER.
MRAWR!!
MY SENTIMENTS EXACTLY, PAL.
YOU KNOW, FOR A MINUTE THERE, I REALLY THOUGHT HE WAS GOING TO TEAR MY HEAD OFF...
THANKS FOR DOING THAT, HAN...
NO PROBLEM, LANDO...CHEWIE'S JUST A LITTLE EDGY, THAT'S ALL. I'VE NOTICED IT MYSELF.
HE'LL BE OKAY, ONCE HE'S SEEN THAT THINGS ARE ALL RIGHT HERE-- AND HAD SOME TIME ALONE WITH MALA.
I HOPE SO...
SAY...UH... DO THINGS HERE LOOK NORMAL TO YOU? IT'S KIND OF HARD FOR ME TO JUDGE...
SURE, EVERYTHING LOOKS FINE. WHAT...YOU'VE NEVER BEEN TO KAZHYYYK BEFORE?
UH... NO.
WELL, DON'T WORRY ABOUT IT. IT'S A NORMAL PLANET, JUST LIKE EVERYWHERE ELSE.

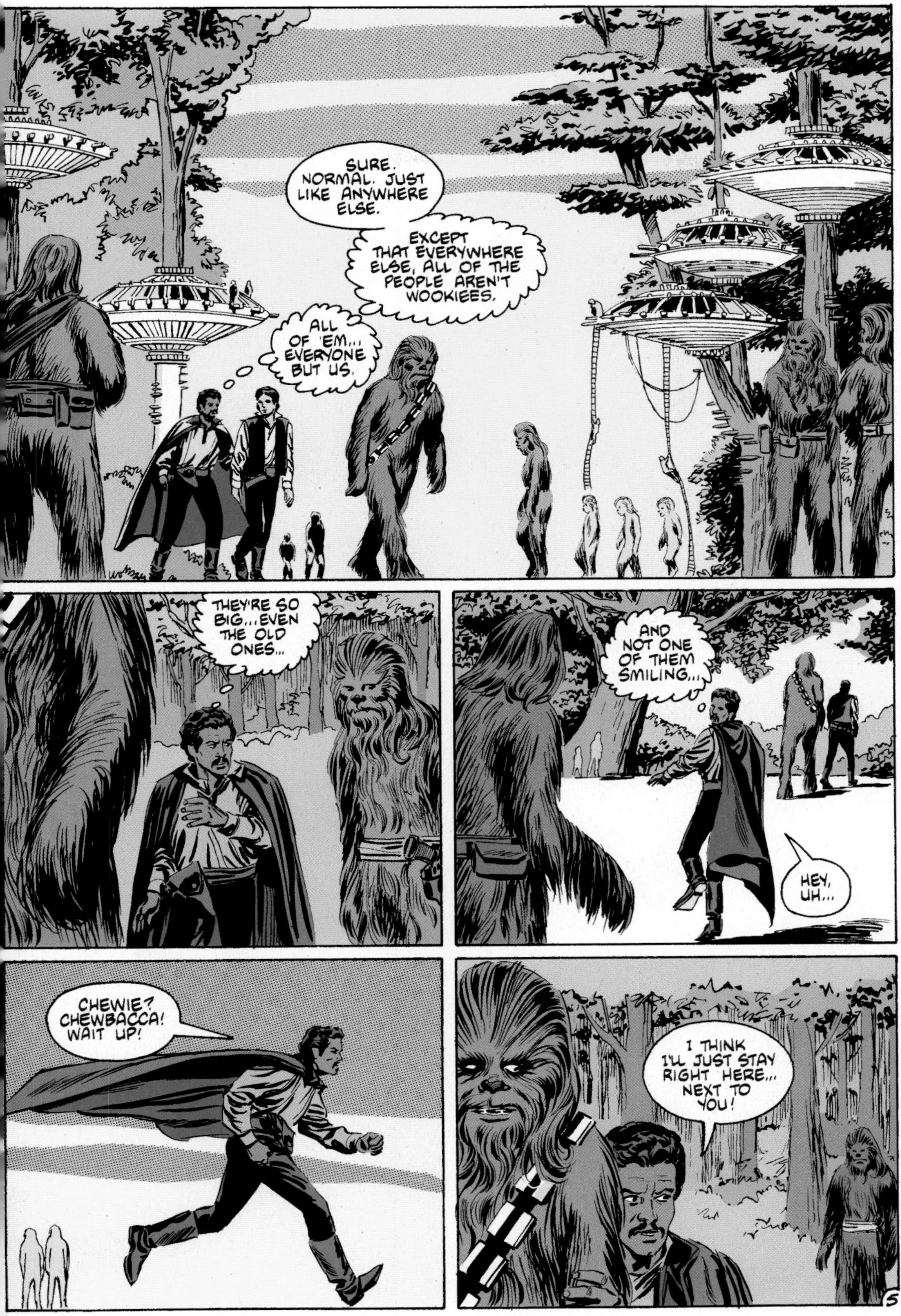
SURE. NORMAL. JUST LIKE ANYWHERE ELSE.
EXCEPT THAT EVERYWHERE ELSE, ALL OF THE PEOPLE AREN'T WOOKIEES.
ALL OF 'EM... EVERYONE BUT US.
THEY'RE SO BIG... EVEN THE OLD ONES...
AND NOT ONE OF THEM SMILING...
HEY, UH...
CHEWIE? CHEWBACCA! WAIT UP!
I THINK I'LL JUST STAY RIGHT HERE... NEXT TO YOU!
5

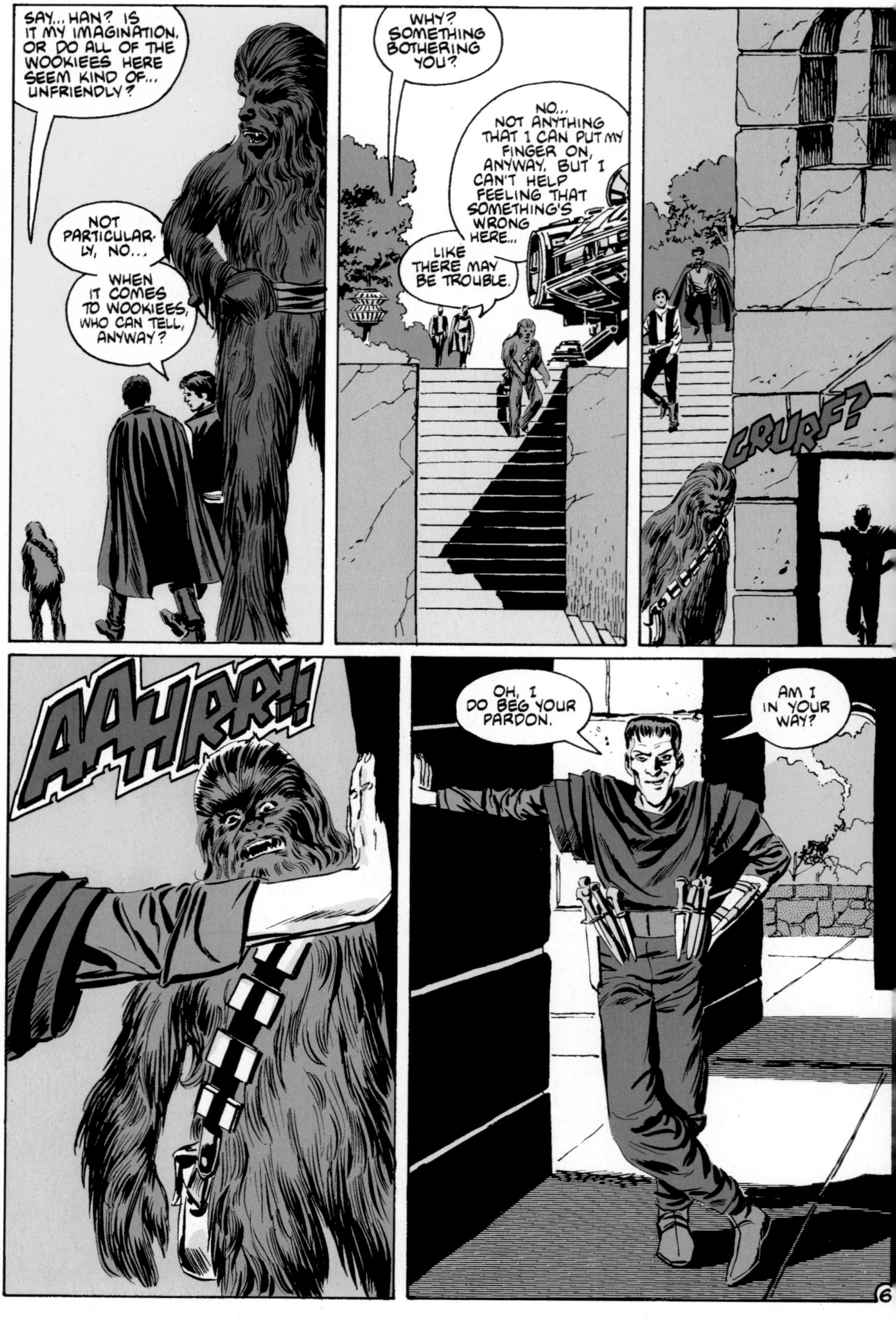
SAY... HAN? IS IT MY IMAGINATION, OR DO ALL OF THE WOOKIEES HERE SEEM KIND OF... UNFRIENDLY?
NOT PARTICULAR-LY, NO...
WHEN IT COMES TO WOOKIEES, WHO CAN TELL, ANYWAY?
WHY? SOMETHING BOTHERING YOU?
NO... NOT ANYTHING THAT I CAN PUT MY FINGER ON, ANYWAY. BUT I CAN'T HELP FEELING THAT SOMETHING'S WRONG HERE...
LIKE THERE MAY BE TROUBLE.
GRURF?
AAHRR!!
OH, I DO BEG YOUR PARDON.
AM I IN YOUR WAY?
6

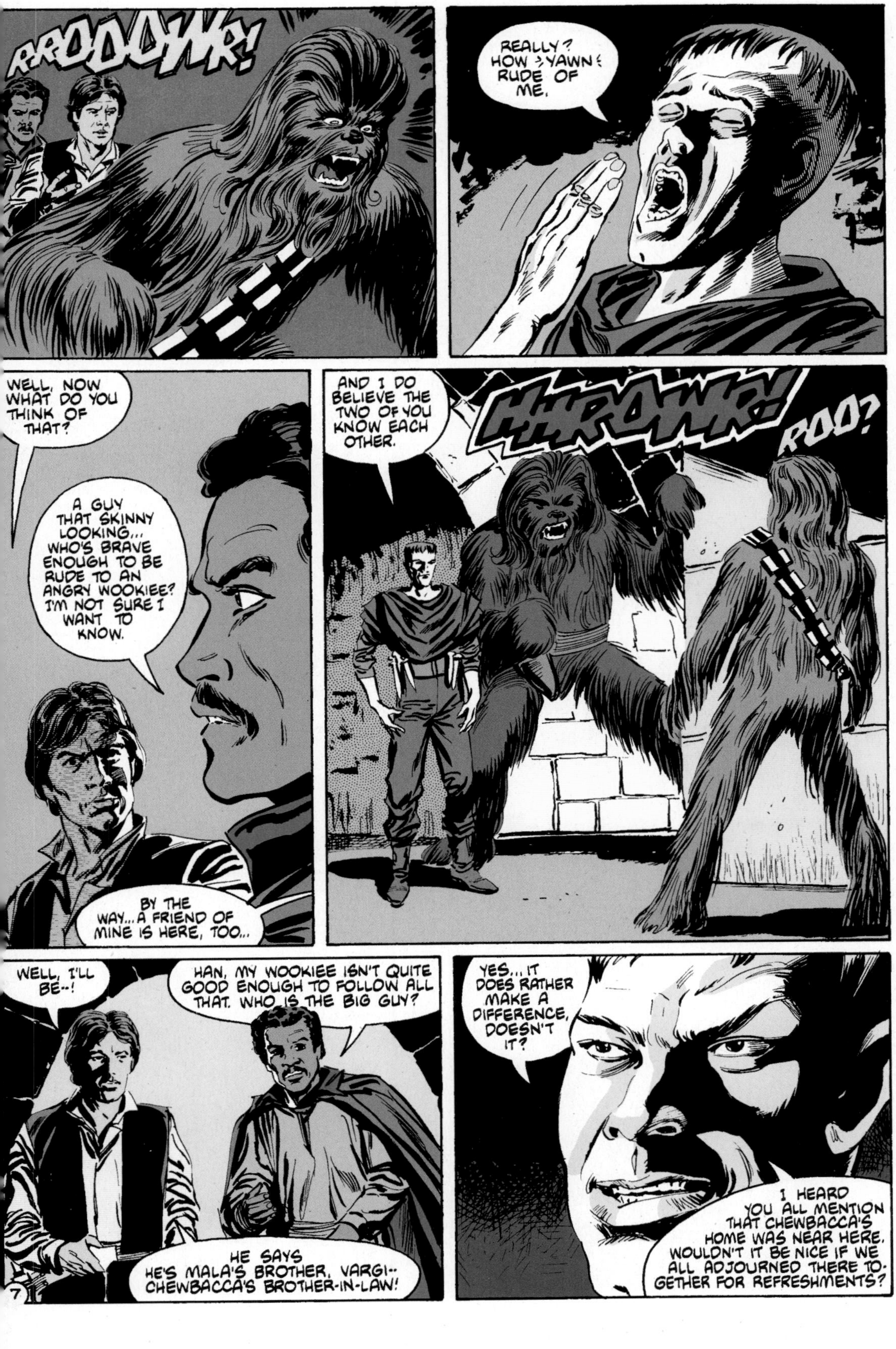
RROOOWR!
REALLY? HOW ⋟YAWN⋞ RUDE OF ME.
WELL, NOW WHAT DO YOU THINK OF THAT?
A GUY THAT SKINNY LOOKING... WHO'S BRAVE ENOUGH TO BE RUDE TO AN ANGRY WOOKIEE? I'M NOT SURE I WANT TO KNOW.
BY THE WAY... A FRIEND OF MINE IS HERE, TOO...
AND I DO BELIEVE THE TWO OF YOU KNOW EACH OTHER.
HHROWR!
ROO?
WELL, I'LL BE--!
HAN, MY WOOKIEE ISN'T QUITE GOOD ENOUGH TO FOLLOW ALL THAT. WHO IS THE BIG GUY?
HE SAYS HE'S MALA'S BROTHER, VARGI-- CHEWBACCA'S BROTHER-IN-LAW!
7
YES... IT DOES RATHER MAKE A DIFFERENCE, DOESN'T IT?
I HEARD YOU ALL MENTION THAT CHEWBACCA'S HOME WAS NEAR HERE. WOULDN'T IT BE NICE IF WE ALL ADJOURNED THERE TOGETHER FOR REFRESHMENTS?

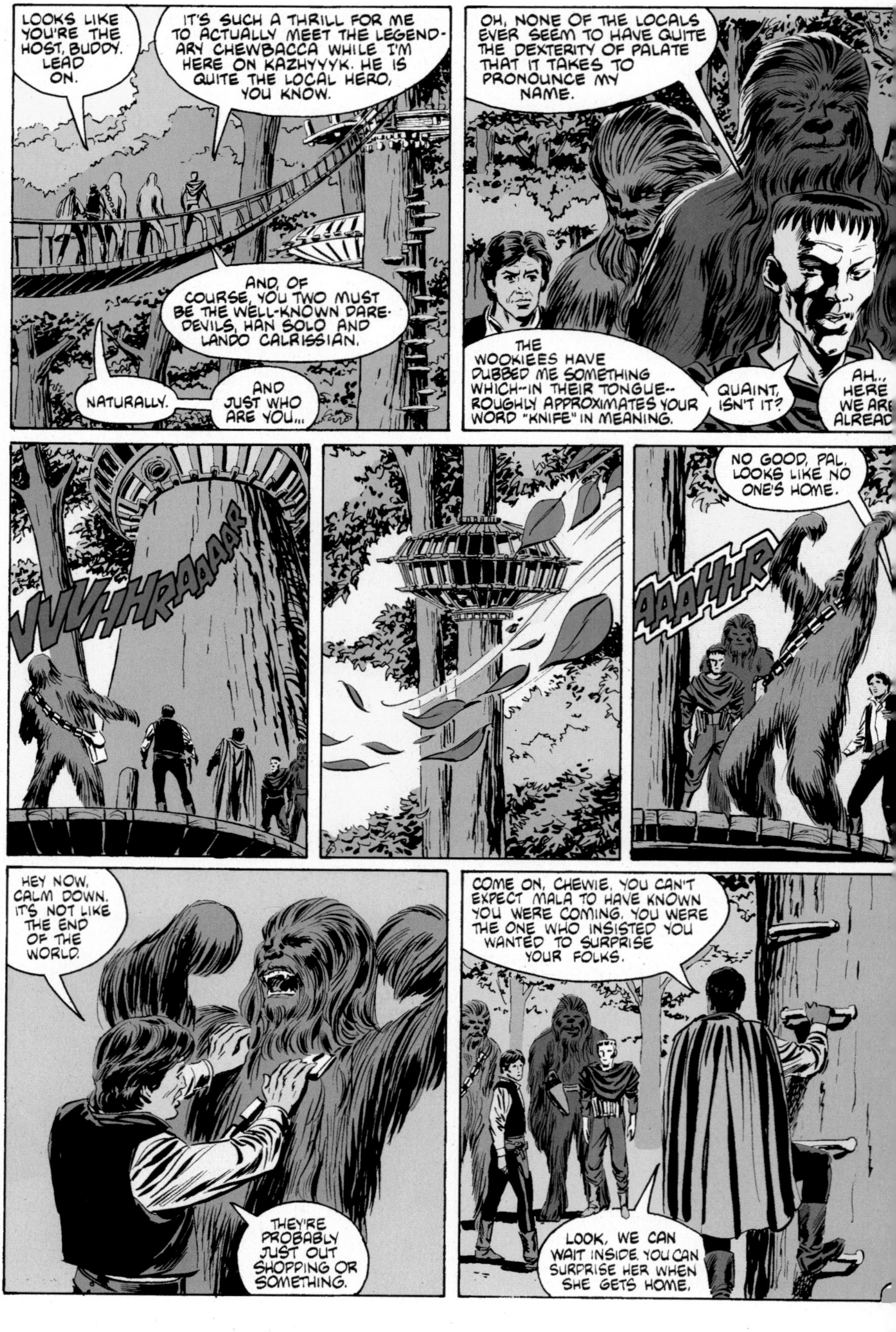
LOOKS LIKE YOU'RE THE HOST, BUDDY. LEAD ON.
IT'S SUCH A THRILL FOR ME TO ACTUALLY MEET THE LEGENDARY CHEWBACCA WHILE I'M HERE ON KAZHYYYK. HE IS QUITE THE LOCAL HERO, YOU KNOW.
AND, OF COURSE, YOU TWO MUST BE THE WELL-KNOWN DAREDEVILS, HAN SOLO AND LANDO CALRISSIAN.
NATURALLY.
AND JUST WHO ARE YOU...
OH, NONE OF THE LOCALS EVER SEEM TO HAVE QUITE THE DEXTERITY OF PALATE THAT IT TAKES TO PRONOUNCE MY NAME.
THE WOOKIEES HAVE DUBBED ME SOMETHING WHICH--IN THEIR TONGUE--ROUGHLY APPROXIMATES YOUR WORD "KNIFE" IN MEANING.
QUAINT, ISN'T IT?
AH... HERE WE ARE ALREAD
VVVHHRAAAAR
AAAHHR
NO GOOD, PAL, LOOKS LIKE NO ONE'S HOME.
HEY NOW, CALM DOWN. IT'S NOT LIKE THE END OF THE WORLD.
THEY'RE PROBABLY JUST OUT SHOPPING OR SOMETHING.
COME ON, CHEWIE. YOU CAN'T EXPECT MALA TO HAVE KNOWN YOU WERE COMING. YOU WERE THE ONE WHO INSISTED YOU WANTED TO SURPRISE YOUR FOLKS.
LOOK, WE CAN WAIT INSIDE. YOU CAN SURPRISE HER WHEN SHE GETS HOME.

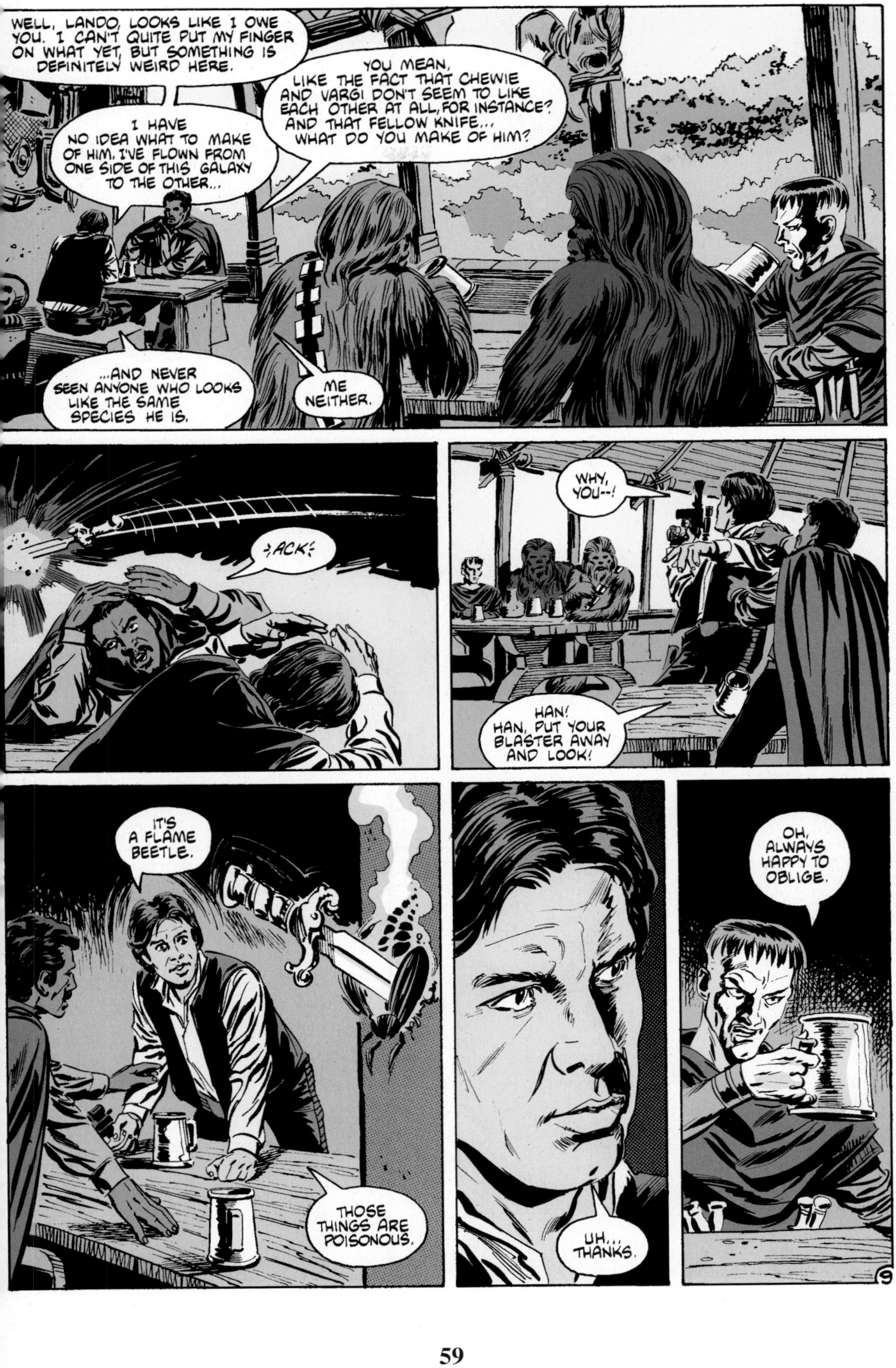
WELL, LANDO, LOOKS LIKE I OWE YOU. I CAN'T QUITE PUT MY FINGER ON WHAT YET, BUT SOMETHING IS DEFINITELY WEIRD HERE.
YOU MEAN, LIKE THE FACT THAT CHEWIE AND VARGI DON'T SEEM TO LIKE EACH OTHER AT ALL, FOR INSTANCE? AND THAT FELLOW KNIFE... WHAT DO YOU MAKE OF HIM?
I HAVE NO IDEA WHAT TO MAKE OF HIM. I'VE FLOWN FROM ONE SIDE OF THIS GALAXY TO THE OTHER...
...AND NEVER SEEN ANYONE WHO LOOKS LIKE THE SAME SPECIES HE IS.
ME NEITHER.
ACK
WHY, YOU--!
HAN! HAN, PUT YOUR BLASTER AWAY AND LOOK!
IT'S A FLAME BEETLE.
THOSE THINGS ARE POISONOUS.
UH... THANKS.
OH, ALWAYS HAPPY TO OBLIGE.
9

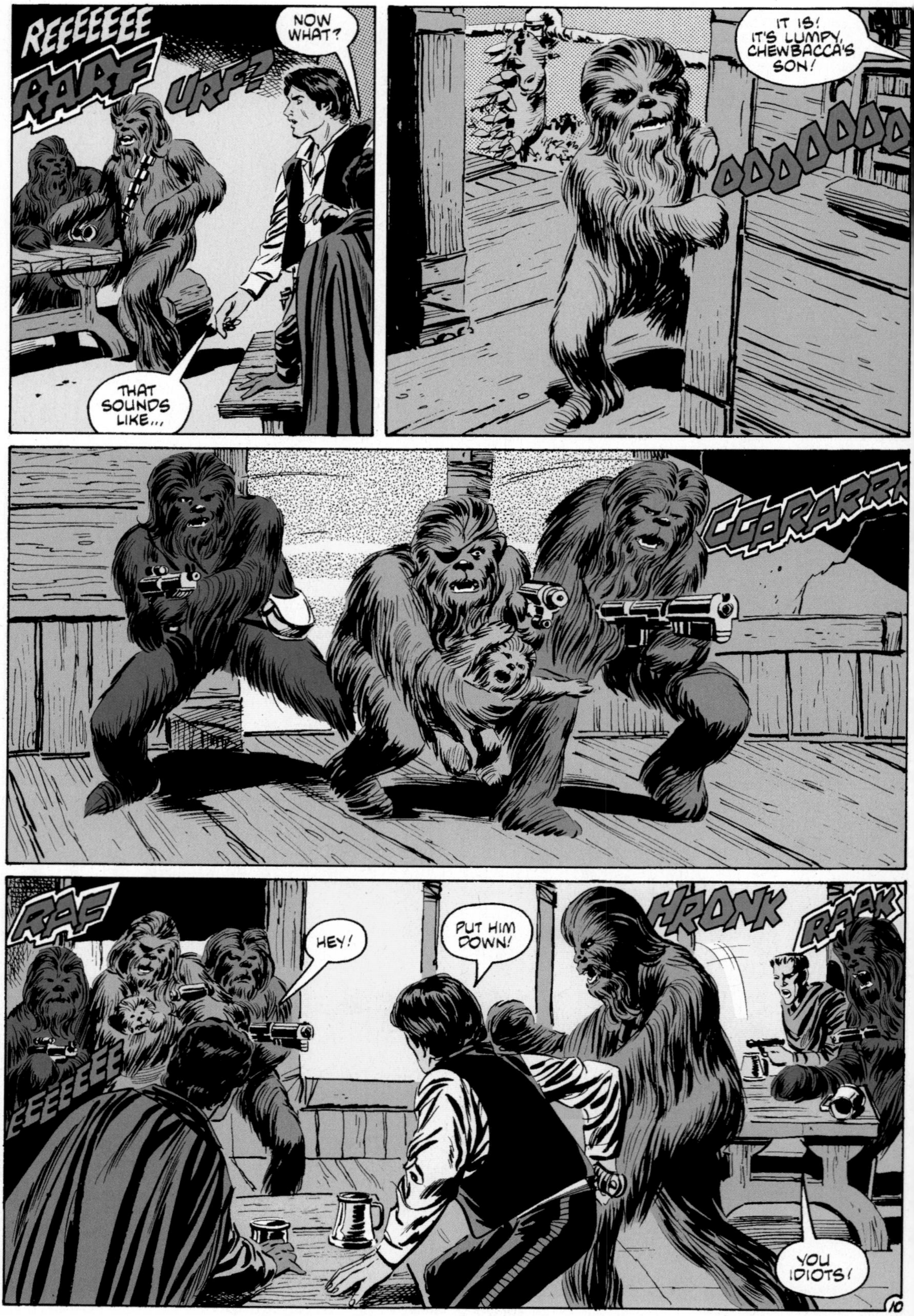
REEEEEEE
RAAF
URF?
NOW WHAT?
THAT SOUNDS LIKE...
IT IS! IT'S LUMPY, CHEWBACCA'S SON!
OOOOOOOO
CGARARRR
RAF
EEEEEEE
HEY!
PUT HIM DOWN!
HRONK
RAAK
YOU IDIOTS!
10

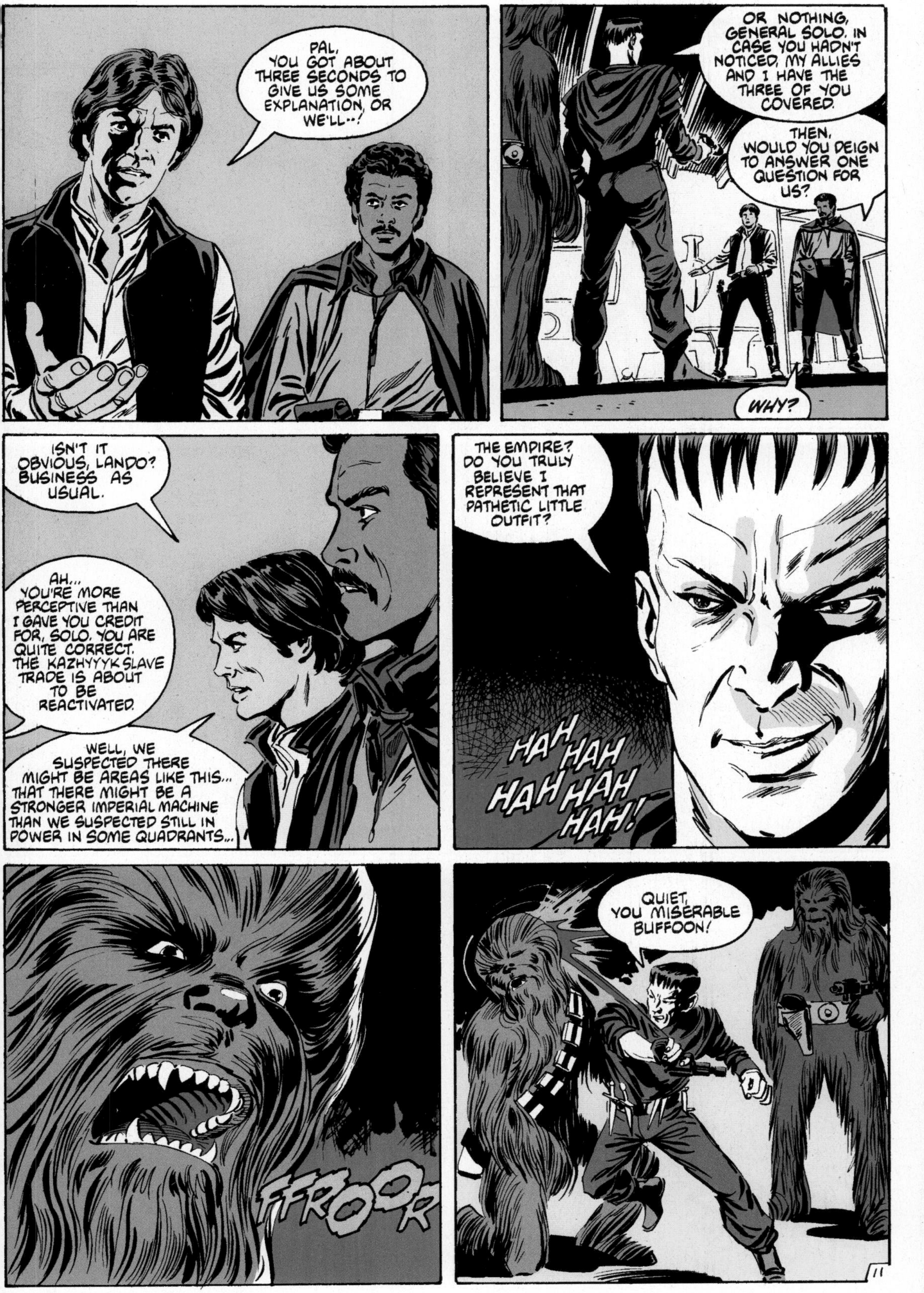
PAL, YOU GOT ABOUT THREE SECONDS TO GIVE US SOME EXPLANATION, OR WE'LL--!
OR NOTHING, GENERAL SOLO. IN CASE YOU HADN'T NOTICED, MY ALLIES AND I HAVE THE THREE OF YOU COVERED.
THEN, WOULD YOU DEIGN TO ANSWER ONE QUESTION FOR US?
WHY?
ISN'T IT OBVIOUS, LANDO? BUSINESS AS USUAL.
AH... YOU'RE MORE PERCEPTIVE THAN I GAVE YOU CREDIT FOR, SOLO. YOU ARE QUITE CORRECT. THE KAZHYYYK SLAVE TRADE IS ABOUT TO BE REACTIVATED.
WELL, WE SUSPECTED THERE MIGHT BE AREAS LIKE THIS... THAT THERE MIGHT BE A STRONGER IMPERIAL MACHINE THAN WE SUSPECTED STILL IN POWER IN SOME QUADRANTS...
THE EMPIRE? DO YOU TRULY BELIEVE I REPRESENT THAT PATHETIC LITTLE OUTFIT?
HAH HAH HAH HAH HAH!
FFROOR
QUIET, YOU MISERABLE BUFFOON!
11

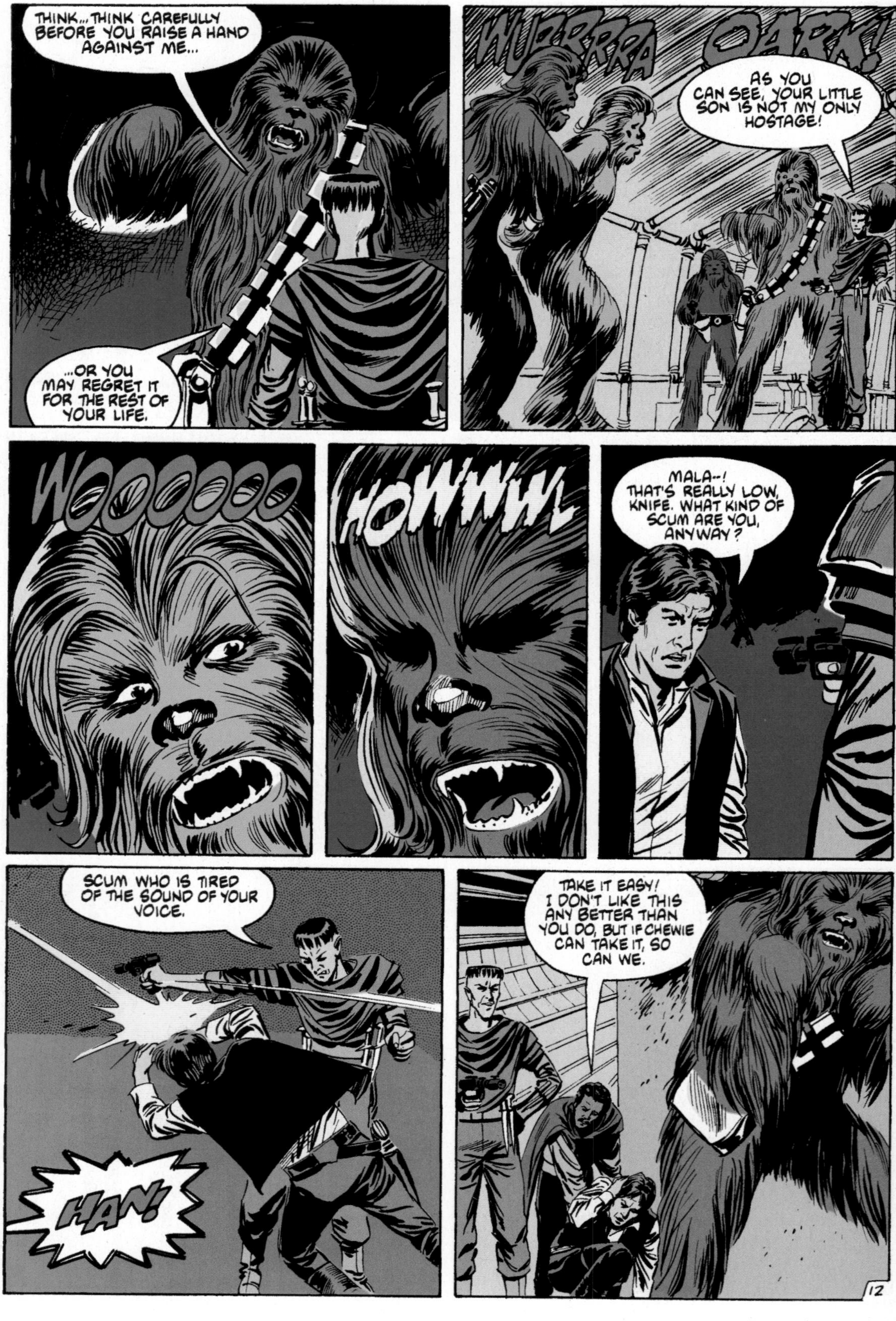
THINK... THINK CAREFULLY BEFORE YOU RAISE A HAND AGAINST ME...
...OR YOU MAY REGRET IT FOR THE REST OF YOUR LIFE.
WURRRRA OARK!
AS YOU CAN SEE, YOUR LITTLE SON IS NOT MY ONLY HOSTAGE!
WOOOOOOO
HOWWWL
MALA--! THAT'S REALLY LOW, KNIFE. WHAT KIND OF SCUM ARE YOU, ANYWAY?
SCUM WHO IS TIRED OF THE SOUND OF YOUR VOICE.
HAN!
TAKE IT EASY! I DON'T LIKE THIS ANY BETTER THAN YOU DO, BUT IF CHEWIE CAN TAKE IT, SO CAN WE.
12

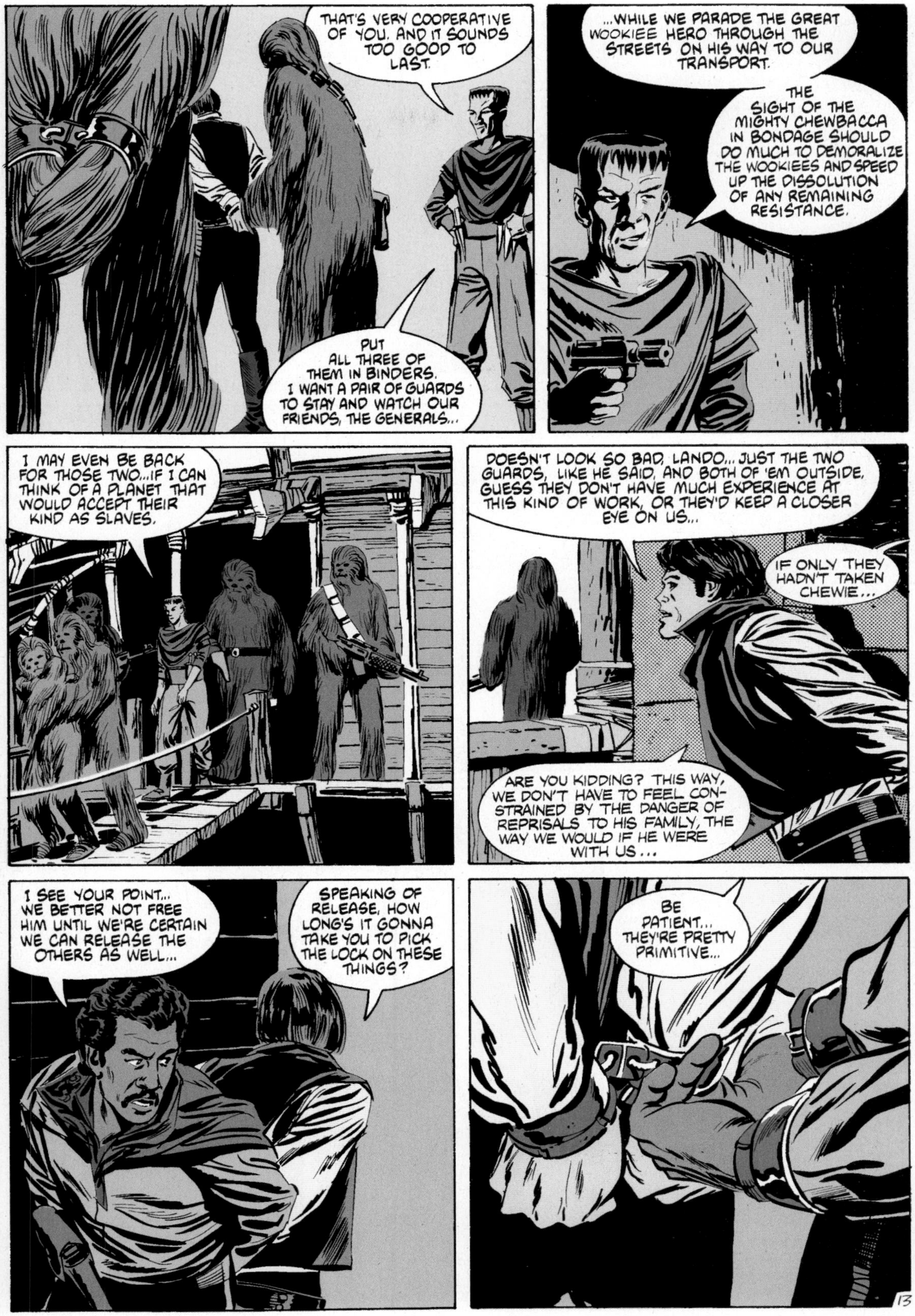
THAT'S VERY COOPERATIVE OF YOU. AND IT SOUNDS TOO GOOD TO LAST.
PUT ALL THREE OF THEM IN BINDERS. I WANT A PAIR OF GUARDS TO STAY AND WATCH OUR FRIENDS, THE GENERALS...
...WHILE WE PARADE THE GREAT WOOKIEE HERO THROUGH THE STREETS ON HIS WAY TO OUR TRANSPORT.
THE SIGHT OF THE MIGHTY CHEWBACCA IN BONDAGE SHOULD DO MUCH TO DEMORALIZE THE WOOKIEES AND SPEED UP THE DISSOLUTION OF ANY REMAINING RESISTANCE.
I MAY EVEN BE BACK FOR THOSE TWO...IF I CAN THINK OF A PLANET THAT WOULD ACCEPT THEIR KIND AS SLAVES.
DOESN'T LOOK SO BAD, LANDO... JUST THE TWO GUARDS, LIKE HE SAID, AND BOTH OF 'EM OUTSIDE. GUESS THEY DON'T HAVE MUCH EXPERIENCE AT THIS KIND OF WORK, OR THEY'D KEEP A CLOSER EYE ON US...
IF ONLY THEY HADN'T TAKEN CHEWIE...
ARE YOU KIDDING? THIS WAY, WE DON'T HAVE TO FEEL CONSTRAINED BY THE DANGER OF REPRISALS TO HIS FAMILY, THE WAY WE WOULD IF HE WERE WITH US...
I SEE YOUR POINT... WE BETTER NOT FREE HIM UNTIL WE'RE CERTAIN WE CAN RELEASE THE OTHERS AS WELL...
SPEAKING OF RELEASE, HOW LONG'S IT GONNA TAKE YOU TO PICK THE LOCK ON THESE THINGS?
BE PATIENT... THEY'RE PRETTY PRIMITIVE...
13

WHAT DO YOU THINK?

I'M NOT SURE ABOUT THIS, HAN... JUST BECAUSE WE CAN'T SPOT KNIFE DOESN'T MEAN HE'S NOT DOWN THERE SOMEWHERE. THESE BRANCHES MAKE IT HARD TO SEE.

AND I STILL DON'T SEE CHEWIE'S FAMILY, EITHER...

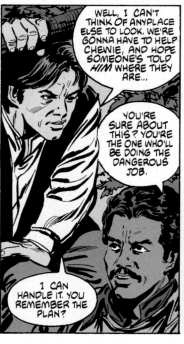

WELL, I CAN'T THINK OF ANYPLACE ELSE TO LOOK, WE'RE GONNA HAVE TO HELP CHEWIE, AND HOPE SOMEONE'S TOLD *HIM* WHERE THEY ARE...

YOU'RE SURE ABOUT THIS? YOU'RE THE ONE WHO'LL BE DOING THE DANGEROUS JOB.

I CAN HANDLE IT. YOU REMEMBER THE PLAN?

YEAH...WHILE YOU'RE GETTING YOURSELF KILLED, I TRY TO GET BACK TO OUR SHIPS, SEND OUT A DISTRESS CALL TO THE ALLIANCE, IF OUR RADIOS ARE STILL WORKING...

...AND PICK UP AS MANY BLASTERS AND OTHER WEAPONRY AS I CAN LAY HANDS ON...

RIGHT. GOOD LUCK.

YOU, TOO.

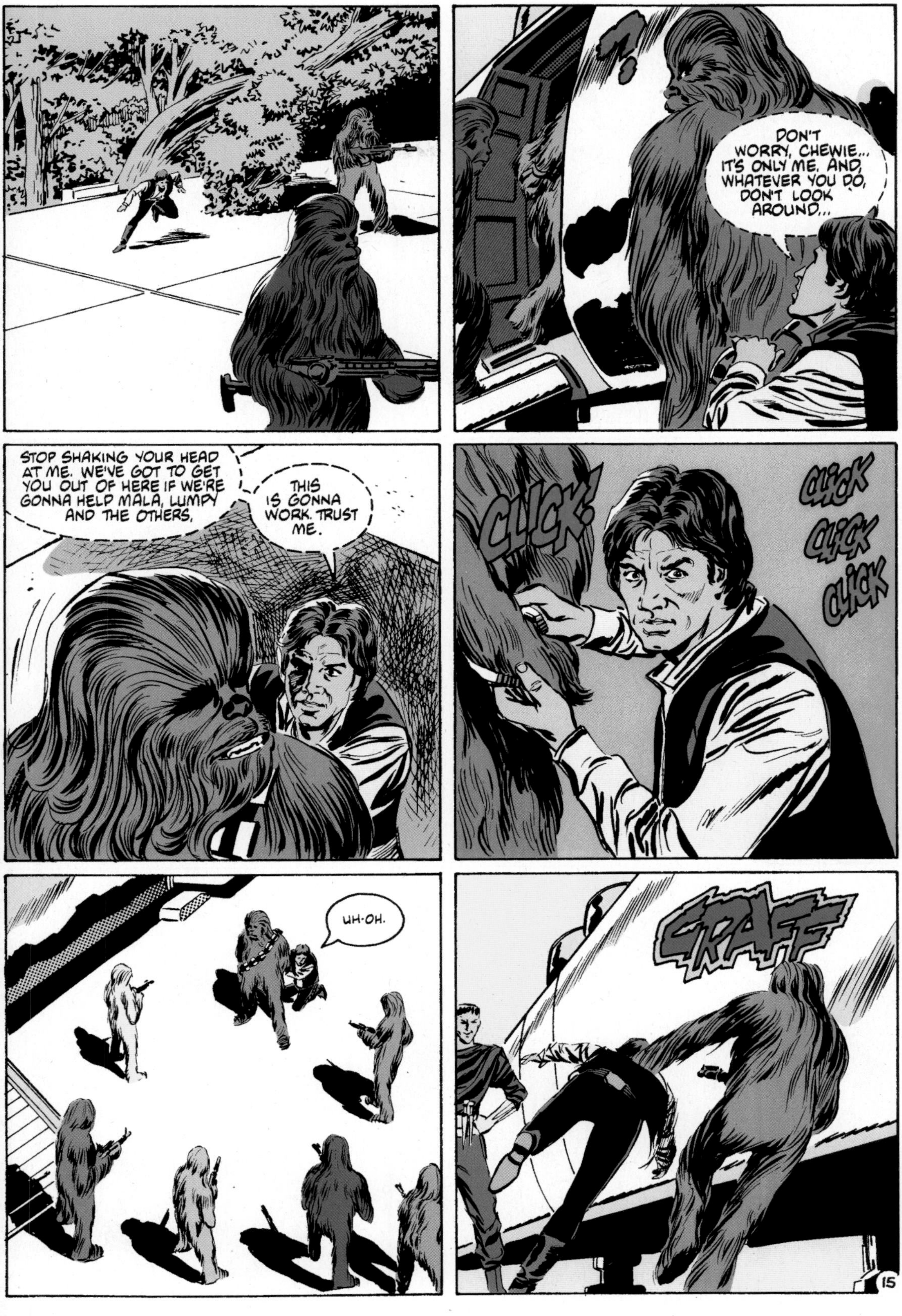
DON'T WORRY, CHEWIE... IT'S ONLY ME. AND, WHATEVER YOU DO, DON'T LOOK AROUND...
STOP SHAKING YOUR HEAD AT ME. WE'VE GOT TO GET YOU OUT OF HERE IF WE'RE GONNA HELP MALA, LUMPY AND THE OTHERS.
THIS IS GONNA WORK. TRUST ME.
CLICK!
CLICK
CLICK
CLICK
UH-OH.
CRAFF
15

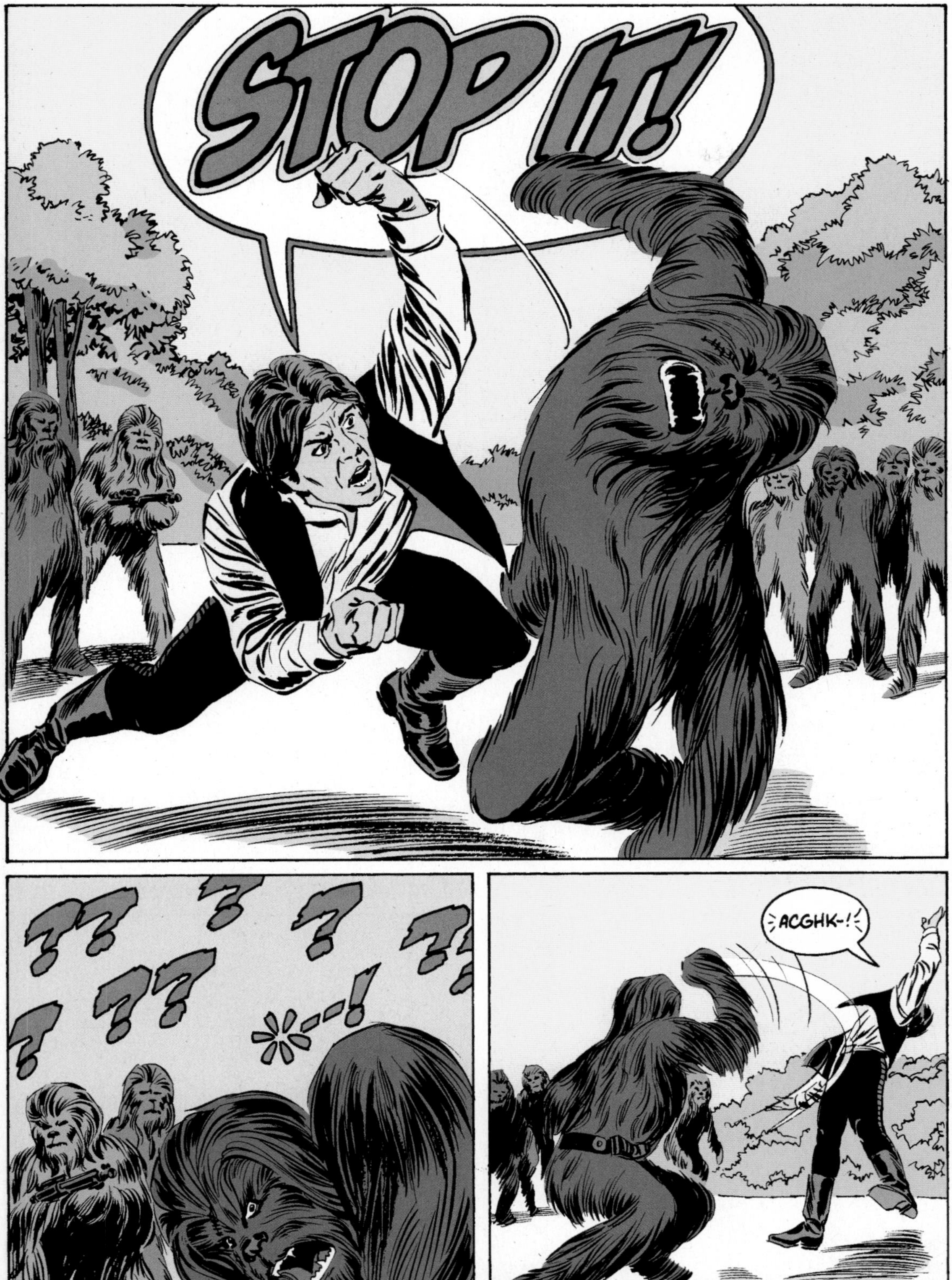
STOP IT!
??
?
?
??
??
*--!
ACGHK-!
17

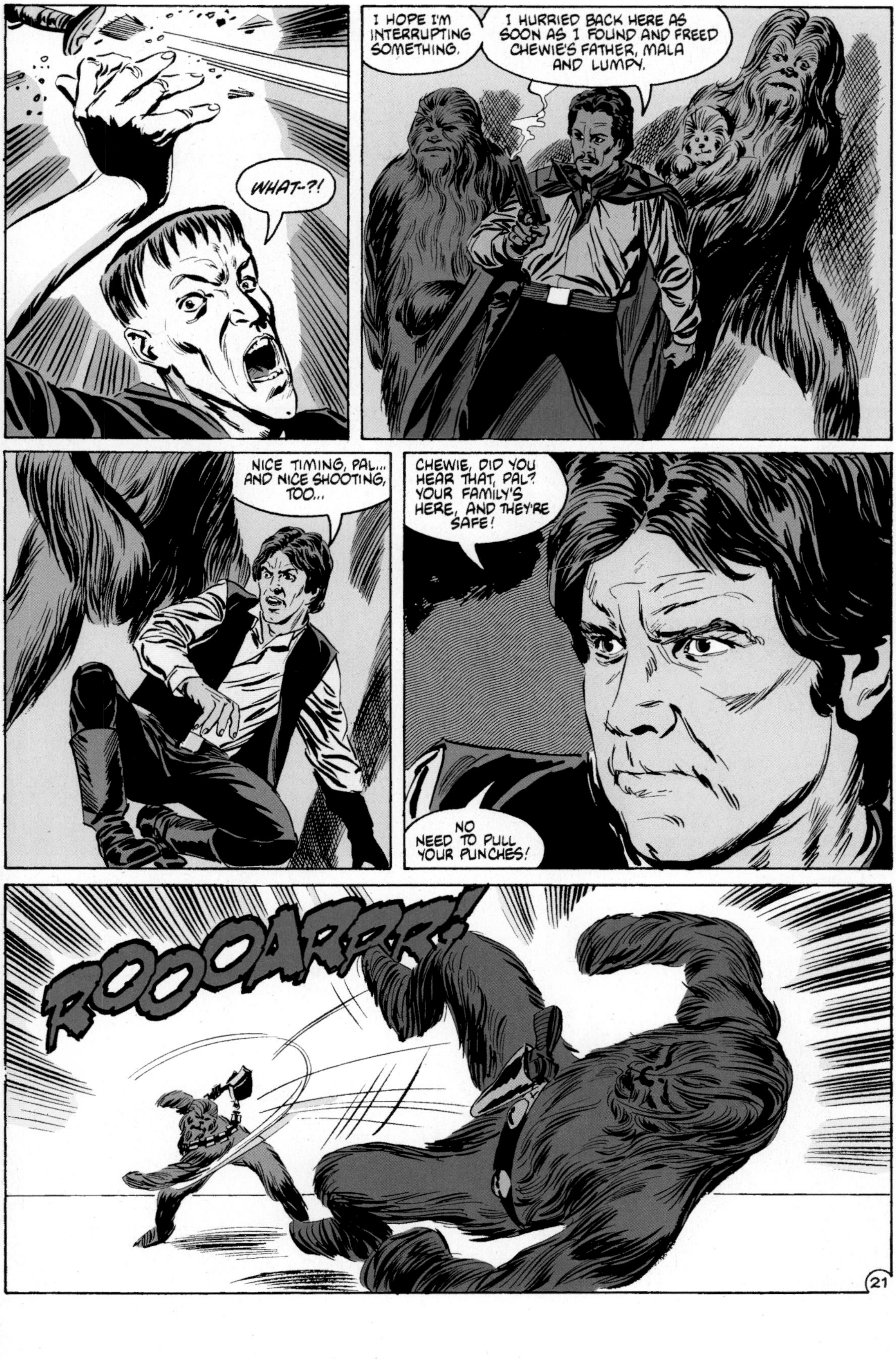
WHAT--?!
I HOPE I'M INTERRUPTING SOMETHING.
I HURRIED BACK HERE AS SOON AS I FOUND AND FREED CHEWIE'S FATHER, MALA AND LUMPY.
NICE TIMING, PAL... AND NICE SHOOTING, TOO...
CHEWIE, DID YOU HEAR THAT, PAL? YOUR FAMILY'S HERE, AND THEY'RE SAFE!
NO NEED TO PULL YOUR PUNCHES!
ROOOARRR!
21

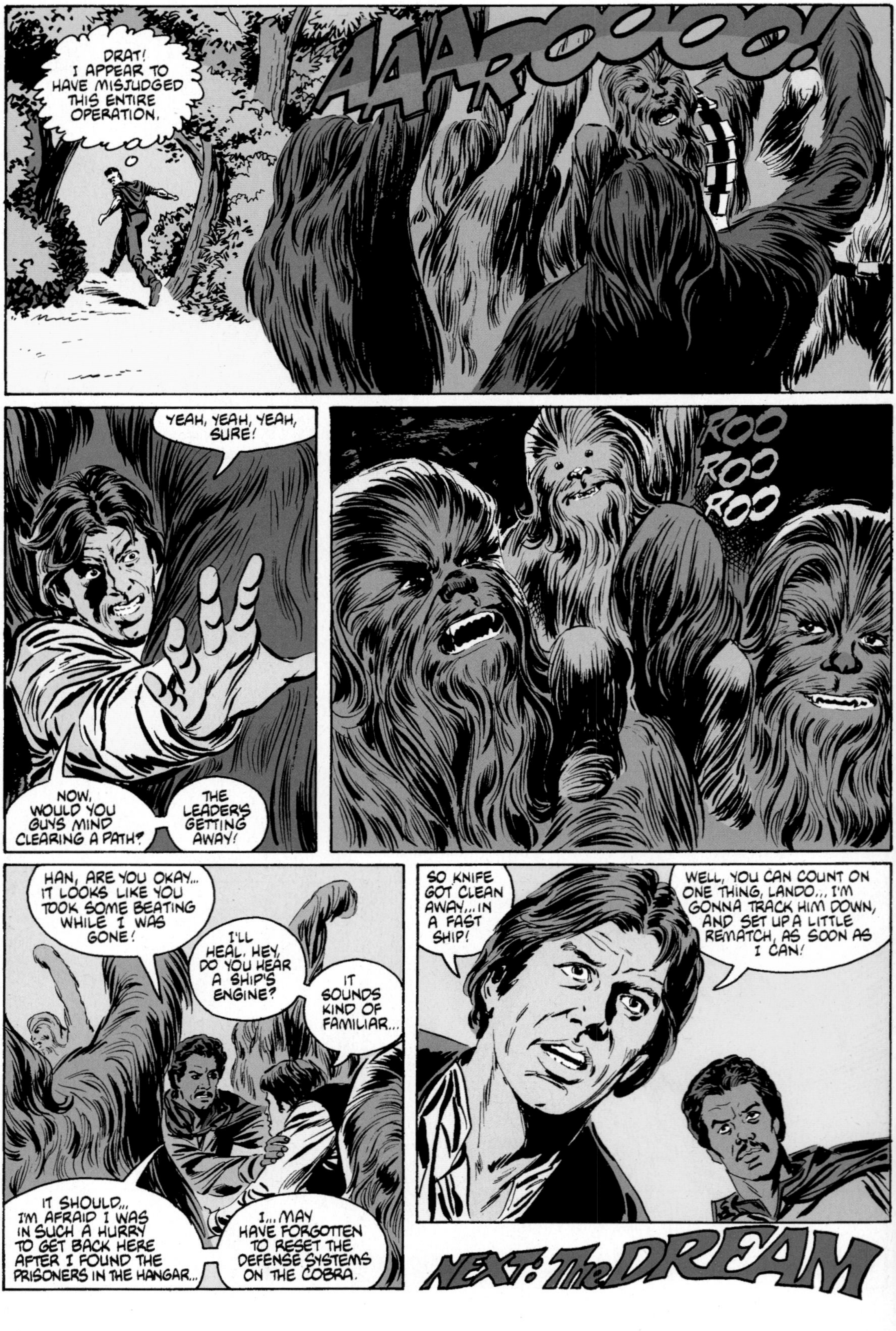
DRAT! I APPEAR TO HAVE MISJUDGED THIS ENTIRE OPERATION.
AAAROOOOO!
YEAH, YEAH, YEAH, SURE!
NOW, WOULD YOU GUYS MIND CLEARING A PATH?
THE LEADER'S GETTING AWAY!
ROO ROO ROO
HAN, ARE YOU OKAY... IT LOOKS LIKE YOU TOOK SOME BEATING WHILE I WAS GONE!
I'LL HEAL. HEY, DO YOU HEAR A SHIP'S ENGINE?
IT SOUNDS KIND OF FAMILIAR...
IT SHOULD... I'M AFRAID I WAS IN SUCH A HURRY TO GET BACK HERE AFTER I FOUND THE PRISONERS IN THE HANGAR...
I... MAY HAVE FORGOTTEN TO RESET THE DEFENSE SYSTEMS ON THE COBRA.
SO KNIFE GOT CLEAN AWAY... IN A FAST SHIP!
WELL, YOU CAN COUNT ON ONE THING, LANDO... I'M GONNA TRACK HIM DOWN, AND SET UP A LITTLE REMATCH, AS SOON AS I CAN!
NEXT: The DREAM

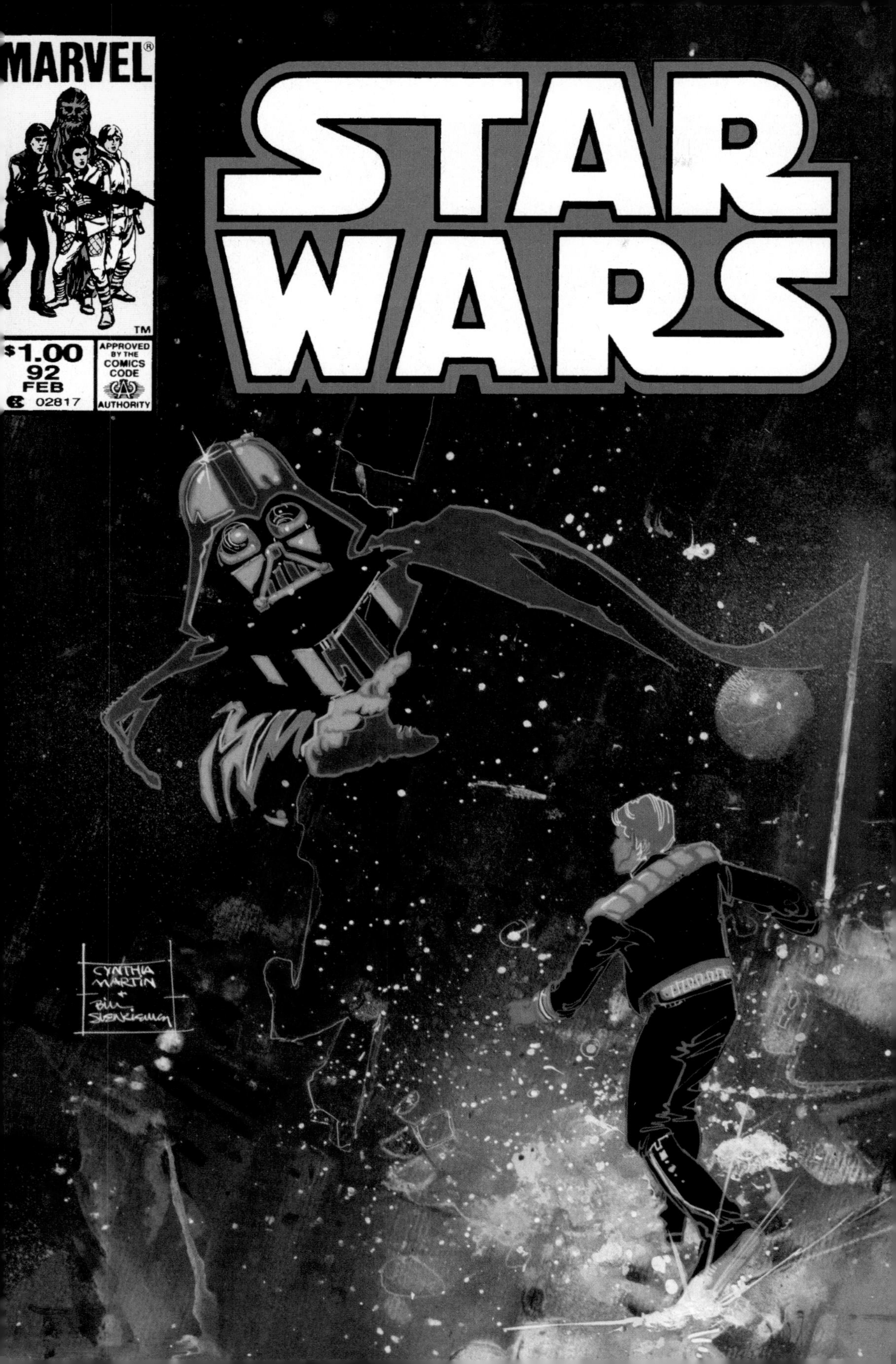
MARVEL®
STAR WARS
TM
$1.00
92
FEB
02817
APPROVED BY THE COMICS CODE AUTHORITY
CYNTHIA MARTIN + BILL SIENKIEWICZ

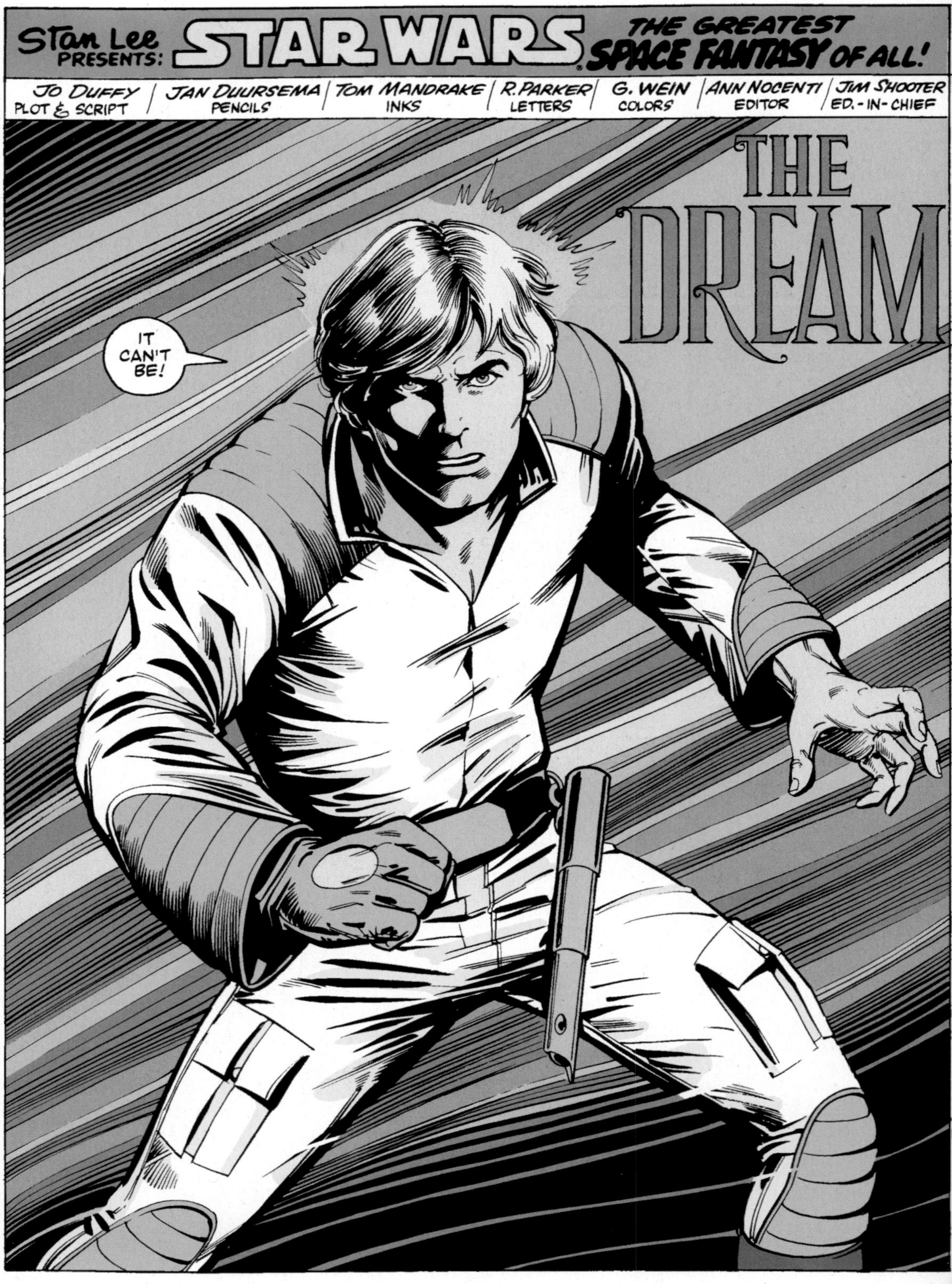
Stan Lee PRESENTS:
STAR WARS
THE GREATEST SPACE FANTASY OF ALL!
JO DUFFY PLOT & SCRIPT
JAN DUURSEMA PENCILS
TOM MANDRAKE INKS
R. PARKER LETTERS
G. WEIN COLORS
ANN NOCENTI EDITOR
JIM SHOOTER ED.-IN-CHIEF
THE DREAM
IT CAN'T BE!

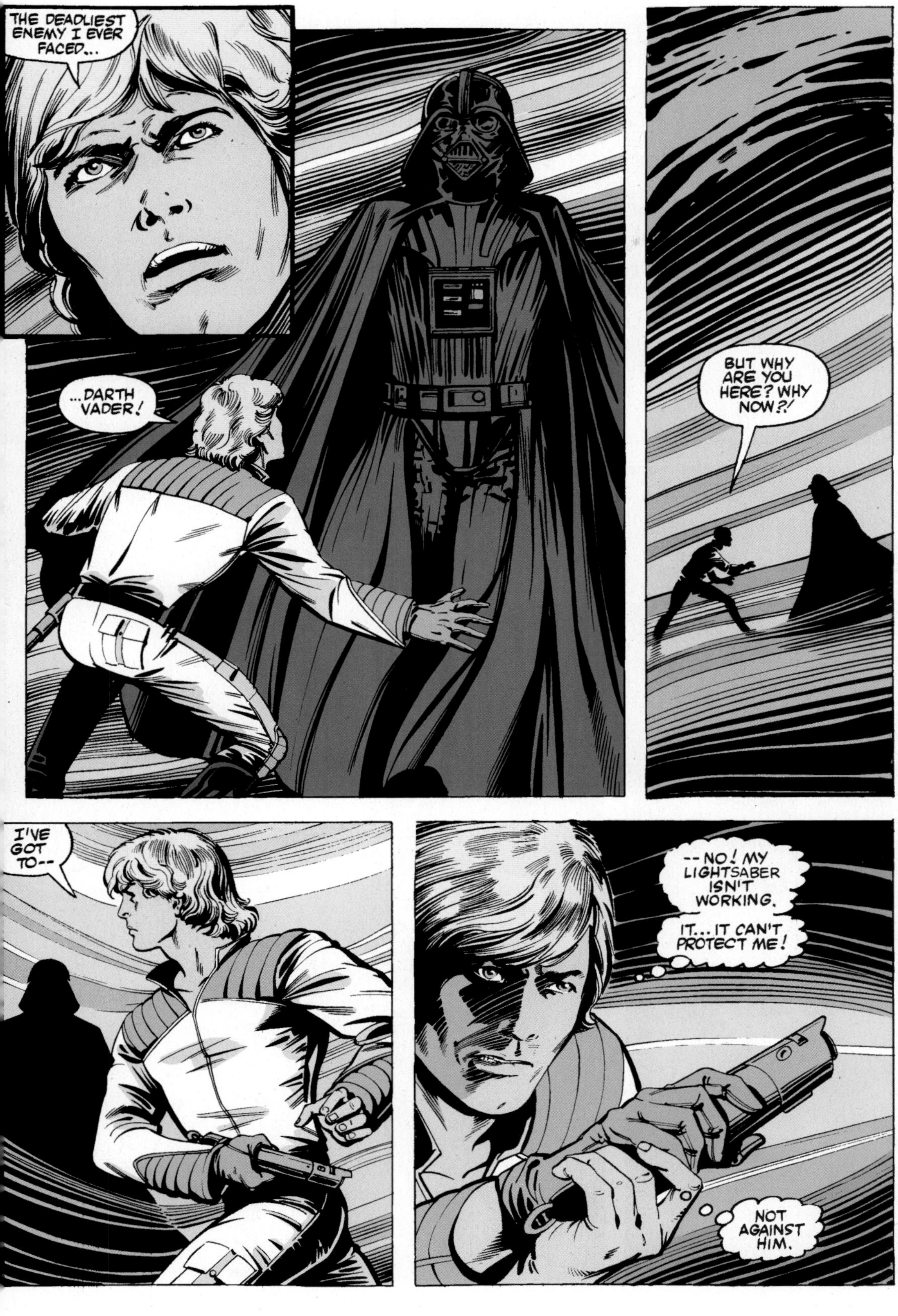
THE DEADLIEST ENEMY I EVER FACED...
...DARTH VADER!
BUT WHY ARE YOU HERE? WHY NOW?!
I'VE GOT TO--
--NO! MY LIGHTSABER ISN'T WORKING.
IT... IT CAN'T PROTECT ME!
NOT AGAINST HIM.

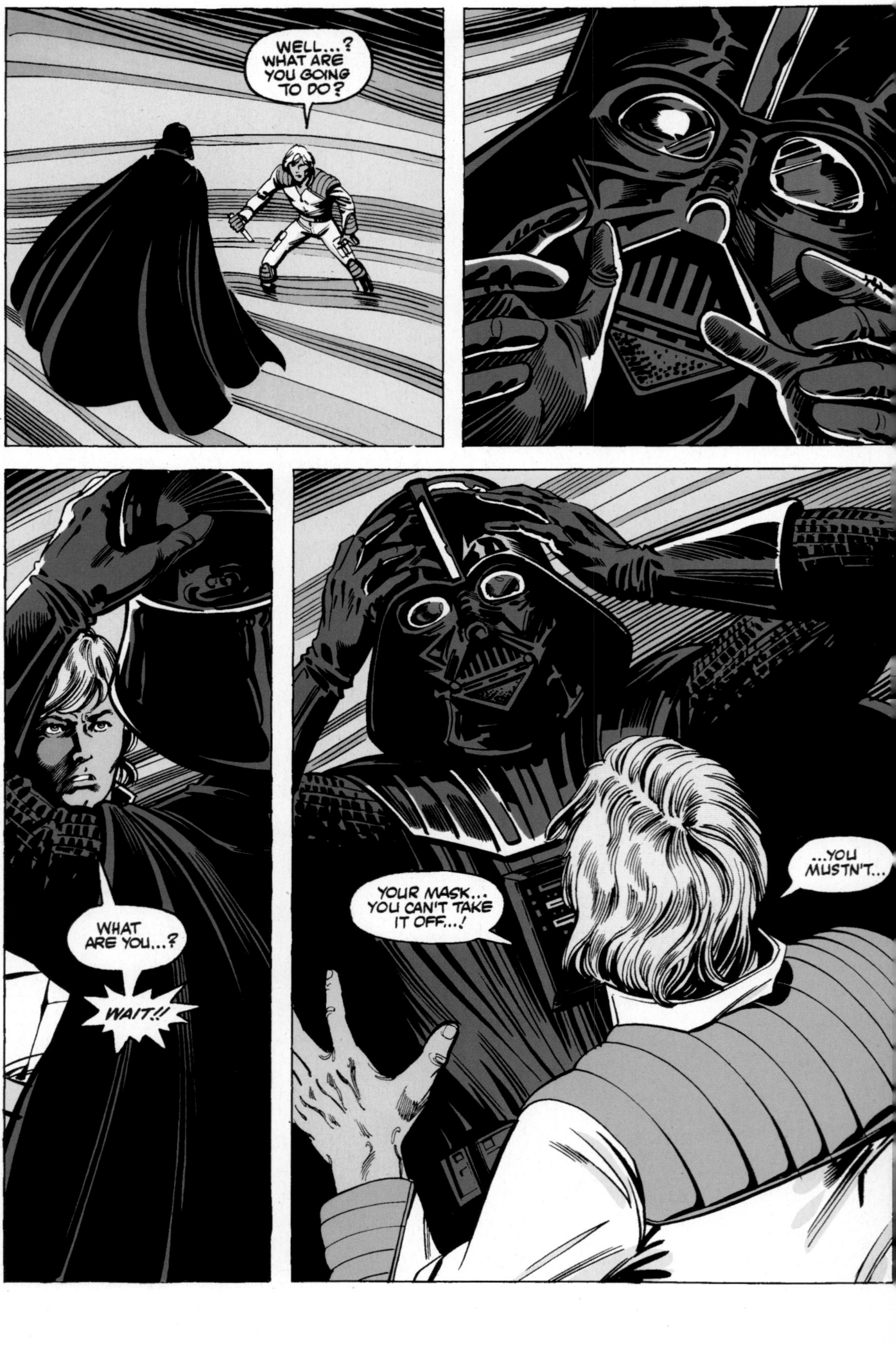
WELL...? WHAT ARE YOU GOING TO DO?
WHAT ARE YOU...?
WAIT!!
YOUR MASK... YOU CAN'T TAKE IT OFF...!
...YOU MUSTN'T...

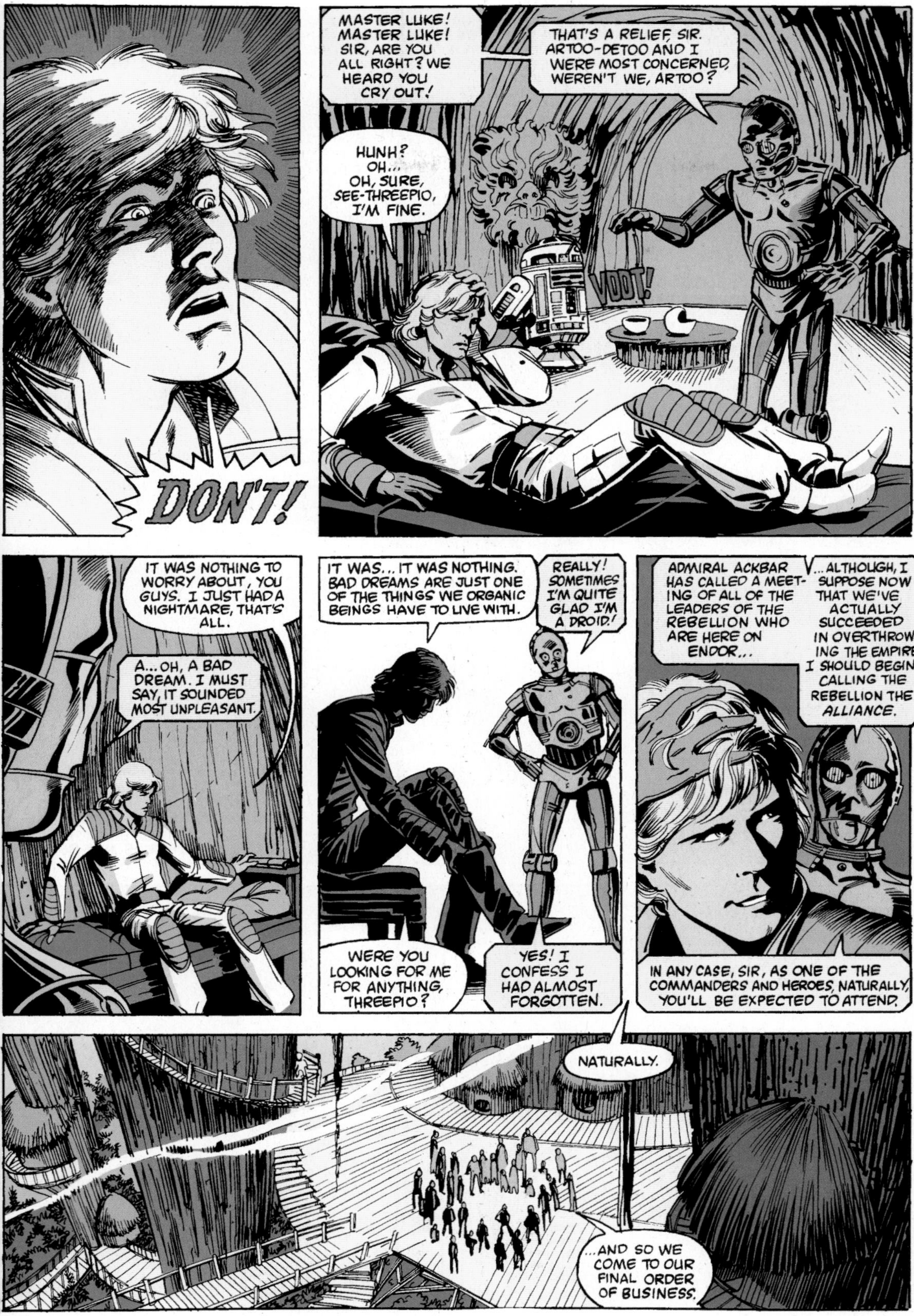
DON'T!
MASTER LUKE! MASTER LUKE! SIR, ARE YOU ALL RIGHT? WE HEARD YOU CRY OUT!
HUNH? OH... OH, SURE, SEE-THREEPIO, I'M FINE.
THAT'S A RELIEF, SIR. ARTOO-DETOO AND I WERE MOST CONCERNED, WEREN'T WE, ARTOO?
VOOT!
IT WAS NOTHING TO WORRY ABOUT, YOU GUYS. I JUST HAD A NIGHTMARE, THAT'S ALL.
A...OH, A BAD DREAM. I MUST SAY, IT SOUNDED MOST UNPLEASANT.
IT WAS... IT WAS NOTHING. BAD DREAMS ARE JUST ONE OF THE THINGS WE ORGANIC BEINGS HAVE TO LIVE WITH.
REALLY! SOMETIMES I'M QUITE GLAD I'M A DROID!
WERE YOU LOOKING FOR ME FOR ANYTHING, THREEPIO?
YES! I CONFESS I HAD ALMOST FORGOTTEN.
ADMIRAL ACKBAR HAS CALLED A MEETING OF ALL OF THE LEADERS OF THE REBELLION WHO ARE HERE ON ENDOR...
...ALTHOUGH, I SUPPOSE NOW THAT WE'VE ACTUALLY SUCCEEDED IN OVERTHROWING THE EMPIRE, I SHOULD BEGIN CALLING THE REBELLION THE ALLIANCE.
IN ANY CASE, SIR, AS ONE OF THE COMMANDERS AND HEROES, NATURALLY, YOU'LL BE EXPECTED TO ATTEND.
NATURALLY.
...AND SO WE COME TO OUR FINAL ORDER OF BUSINESS.

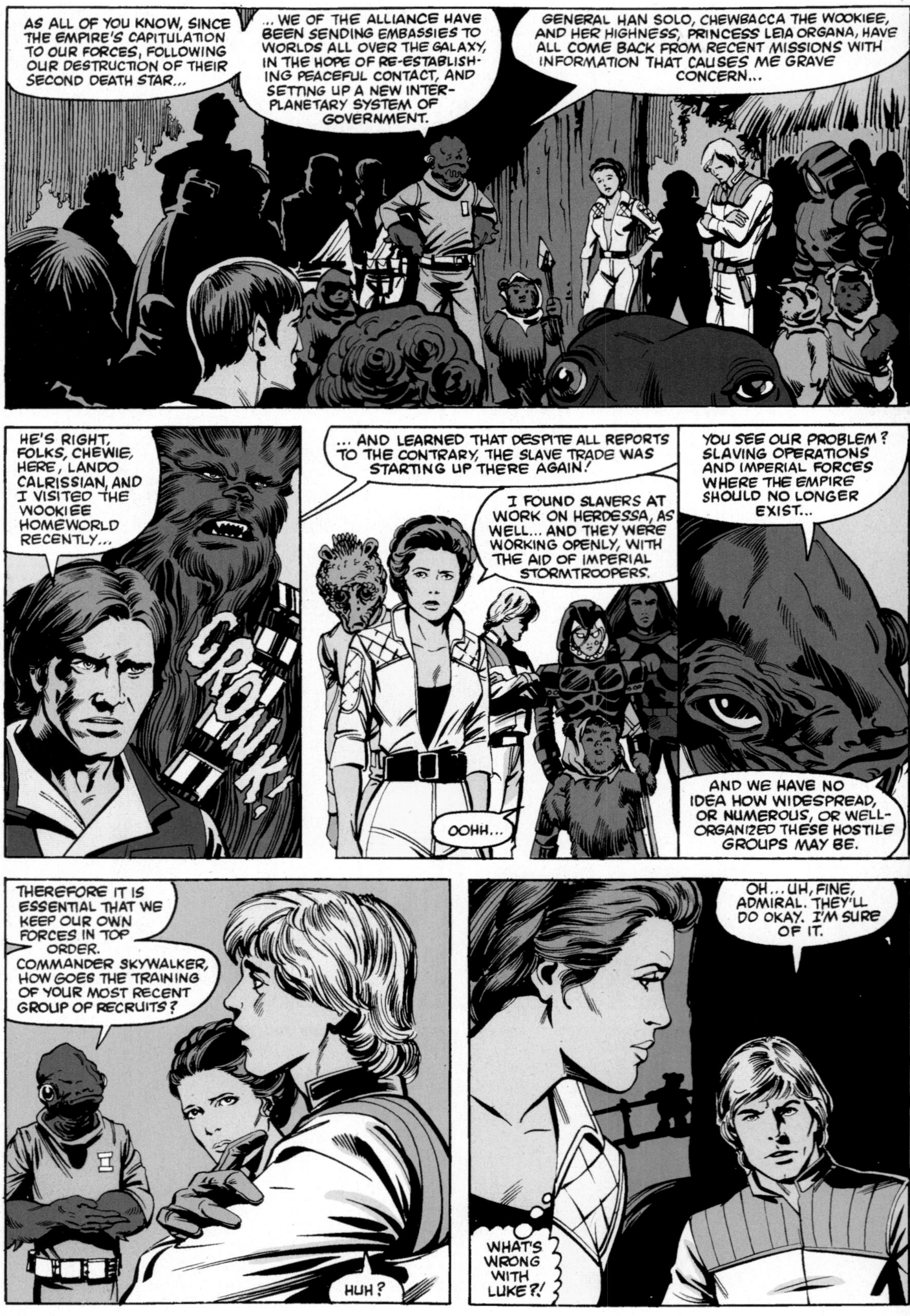
AS ALL OF YOU KNOW, SINCE THE EMPIRE'S CAPITULATION TO OUR FORCES, FOLLOWING OUR DESTRUCTION OF THEIR SECOND DEATH STAR...
... WE OF THE ALLIANCE HAVE BEEN SENDING EMBASSIES TO WORLDS ALL OVER THE GALAXY, IN THE HOPE OF RE-ESTABLISHING PEACEFUL CONTACT, AND SETTING UP A NEW INTER-PLANETARY SYSTEM OF GOVERNMENT.
GENERAL HAN SOLO, CHEWBACCA THE WOOKIEE, AND HER HIGHNESS, PRINCESS LEIA ORGANA, HAVE ALL COME BACK FROM RECENT MISSIONS WITH INFORMATION THAT CAUSES ME GRAVE CONCERN...
HE'S RIGHT, FOLKS. CHEWIE, HERE, LANDO CALRISSIAN, AND I VISITED THE WOOKIEE HOMEWORLD RECENTLY...
CRONK!
... AND LEARNED THAT DESPITE ALL REPORTS TO THE CONTRARY, THE SLAVE TRADE WAS STARTING UP THERE AGAIN!
I FOUND SLAVERS AT WORK ON HERDESSA, AS WELL... AND THEY WERE WORKING OPENLY, WITH THE AID OF IMPERIAL STORMTROOPERS.
OOHH...
YOU SEE OUR PROBLEM? SLAVING OPERATIONS AND IMPERIAL FORCES WHERE THE EMPIRE SHOULD NO LONGER EXIST...
AND WE HAVE NO IDEA HOW WIDESPREAD, OR NUMEROUS, OR WELL-ORGANIZED THESE HOSTILE GROUPS MAY BE.
THEREFORE IT IS ESSENTIAL THAT WE KEEP OUR OWN FORCES IN TOP ORDER. COMMANDER SKYWALKER, HOW GOES THE TRAINING OF YOUR MOST RECENT GROUP OF RECRUITS?
HUH?
OH... UH, FINE, ADMIRAL. THEY'LL DO OKAY. I'M SURE OF IT.
WHAT'S WRONG WITH LUKE?!

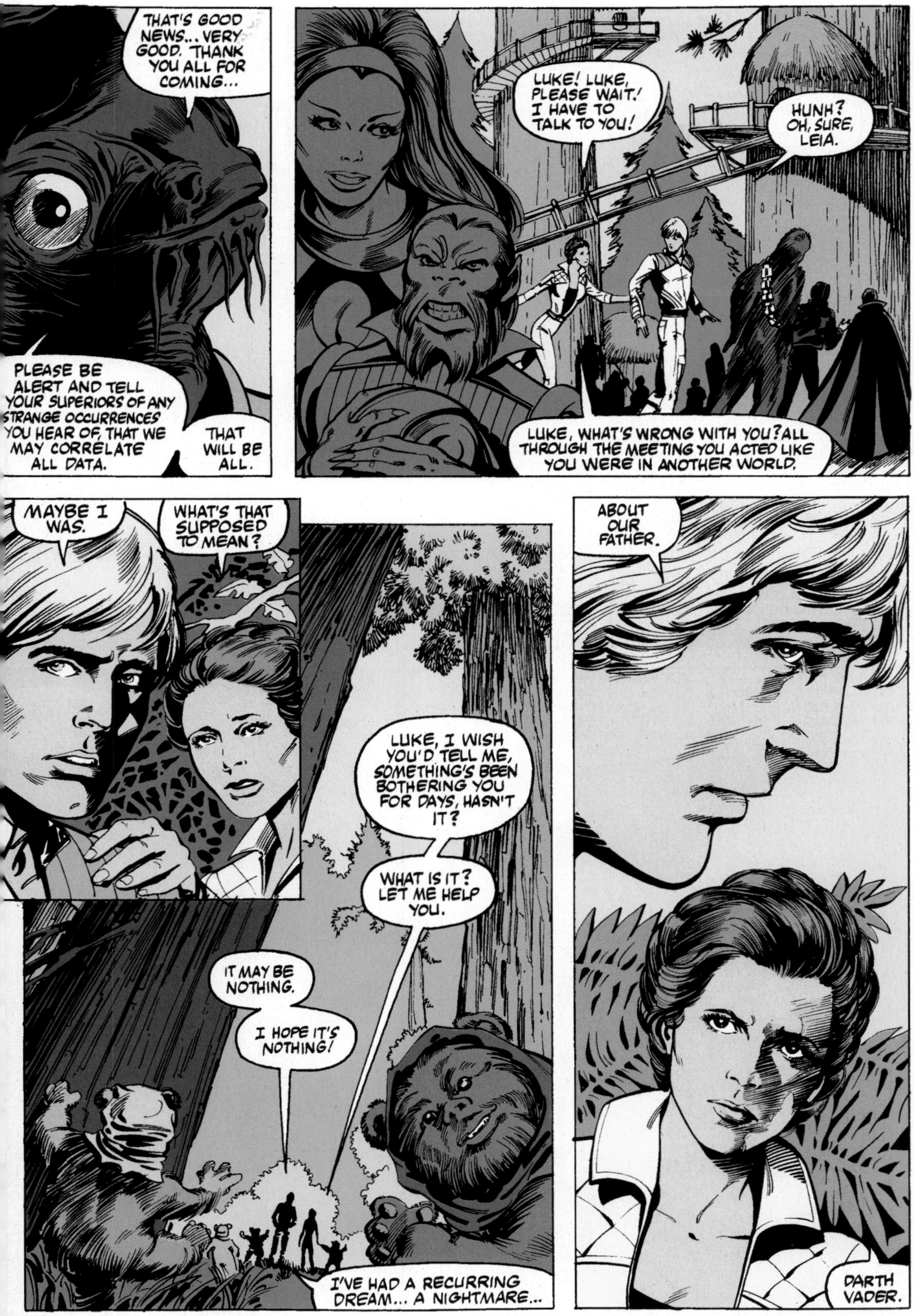
THAT'S GOOD NEWS... VERY GOOD. THANK YOU ALL FOR COMING...
PLEASE BE ALERT AND TELL YOUR SUPERIORS OF ANY STRANGE OCCURRENCES YOU HEAR OF, THAT WE MAY CORRELATE ALL DATA.
THAT WILL BE ALL.
LUKE! LUKE, PLEASE WAIT! I HAVE TO TALK TO YOU!
HUNH? OH, SURE, LEIA.
LUKE, WHAT'S WRONG WITH YOU? ALL THROUGH THE MEETING YOU ACTED LIKE YOU WERE IN ANOTHER WORLD.
MAYBE I WAS.
WHAT'S THAT SUPPOSED TO MEAN?
LUKE, I WISH YOU'D TELL ME. SOMETHING'S BEEN BOTHERING YOU FOR DAYS, HASN'T IT?
WHAT IS IT? LET ME HELP YOU.
IT MAY BE NOTHING.
I HOPE IT'S NOTHING!
I'VE HAD A RECURRING DREAM... A NIGHTMARE...
ABOUT OUR FATHER.
DARTH VADER.

WHAT HAPPENS... IN THE DREAM?

I'M ALL ALONE, IN A PLACE I DON'T RECOGNIZE. AND SUDDENLY, HE'S JUST... *THERE.*

AND I'M TERRIFIED... AND HE COMES TOWARD ME, AND I GET MORE FRIGHTENED BY THE SECOND... AND THEN HE GOES TO TAKE HIS MASK OFF... AND I NEVER LET HIM. AND THEN I FEEL SO GUILTY, LIKE THERE'S SOMETHING TERRIBLY WRONG THERE...

SOMETHING I COULD SET RIGHT, IF I COULD JUST FIGURE OUT HOW.

EVERY TIME I DREAM IT, IT GETS A LITTLE FARTHER ALONG, BEFORE I WAKE UP... SOON, I THINK I'M GOING TO HAVE TO SEE HIS FACE... ...AND I DON'T THINK I CAN BEAR IT, LEIA.

LUKE... HAVE YOU TOLD ANYONE ELSE ABOUT THIS?

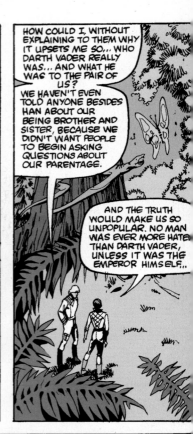

HOW COULD I, WITHOUT EXPLAINING TO THEM WHY IT UPSETS ME SO... WHO DARTH VADER REALLY WAS... AND WHAT HE WAS TO THE PAIR OF US? WE HAVEN'T EVEN TOLD ANYONE BESIDES HAN ABOUT OUR BEING BROTHER AND SISTER, BECAUSE WE DIDN'T WANT PEOPLE TO BEGIN ASKING QUESTIONS ABOUT OUR PARENTAGE.

AND THE TRUTH WOULD MAKE US SO UNPOPULAR. NO MAN WAS EVER MORE HATED THAN DARTH VADER, UNLESS IT WAS THE EMPEROR HIMSELF...

HE WAS THE DARK LORD... THE ONE WHO ALWAYS DID THE EMPEROR'S DIRTY WORK FOR HIM...

BUT LUKE, EVEN IF MOST PEOPLE CHOOSE TO FORGET IT, HE TURNED BACK TO GOOD AT THE END, AND HELPED TOPPLE THE EMPEROR... FOR YOU!

YOU DON'T NEED TO FEEL ASHAMED OF HIM.

I DON'T. BUT IN MY DREAM, I'M AFRAID OF HIM.

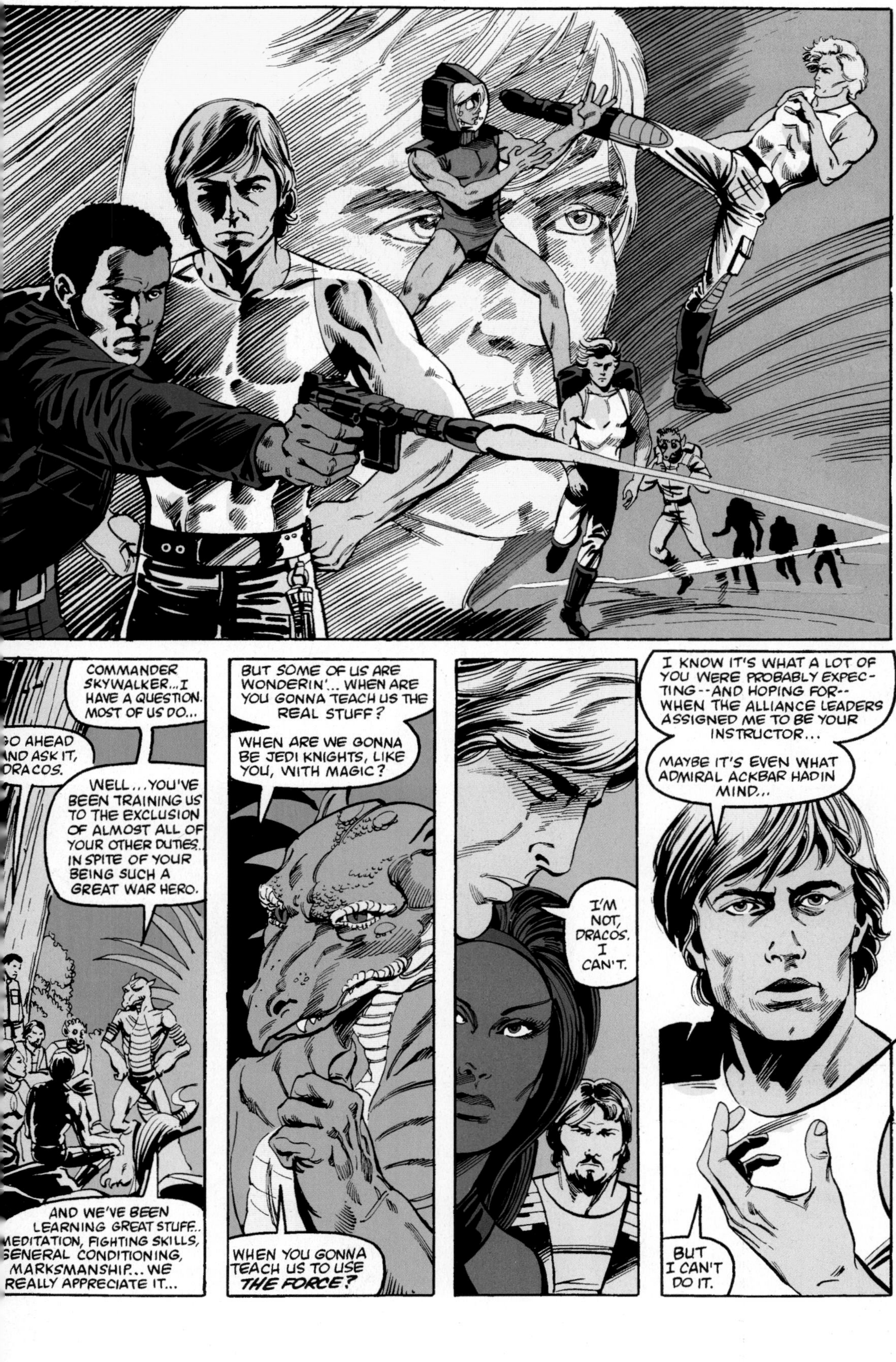
COMMANDER SKYWALKER...I HAVE A QUESTION. MOST OF US DO...
GO AHEAD AND ASK IT, DRACOS.
WELL...YOU'VE BEEN TRAINING US TO THE EXCLUSION OF ALMOST ALL OF YOUR OTHER DUTIES... IN SPITE OF YOUR BEING SUCH A GREAT WAR HERO.
AND WE'VE BEEN LEARNING GREAT STUFF... MEDITATION, FIGHTING SKILLS, GENERAL CONDITIONING, MARKSMANSHIP... WE REALLY APPRECIATE IT...
BUT SOME OF US ARE WONDERIN'... WHEN ARE YOU GONNA TEACH US THE REAL STUFF?
WHEN ARE WE GONNA BE JEDI KNIGHTS, LIKE YOU, WITH MAGIC?
WHEN YOU GONNA TEACH US TO USE *THE FORCE?*
I'M NOT, DRACOS. I CAN'T.
I KNOW IT'S WHAT A LOT OF YOU WERE PROBABLY EXPECTING--AND HOPING FOR--WHEN THE ALLIANCE LEADERS ASSIGNED ME TO BE YOUR INSTRUCTOR...
MAYBE IT'S EVEN WHAT ADMIRAL ACKBAR HAD IN MIND...
BUT I CAN'T DO IT.

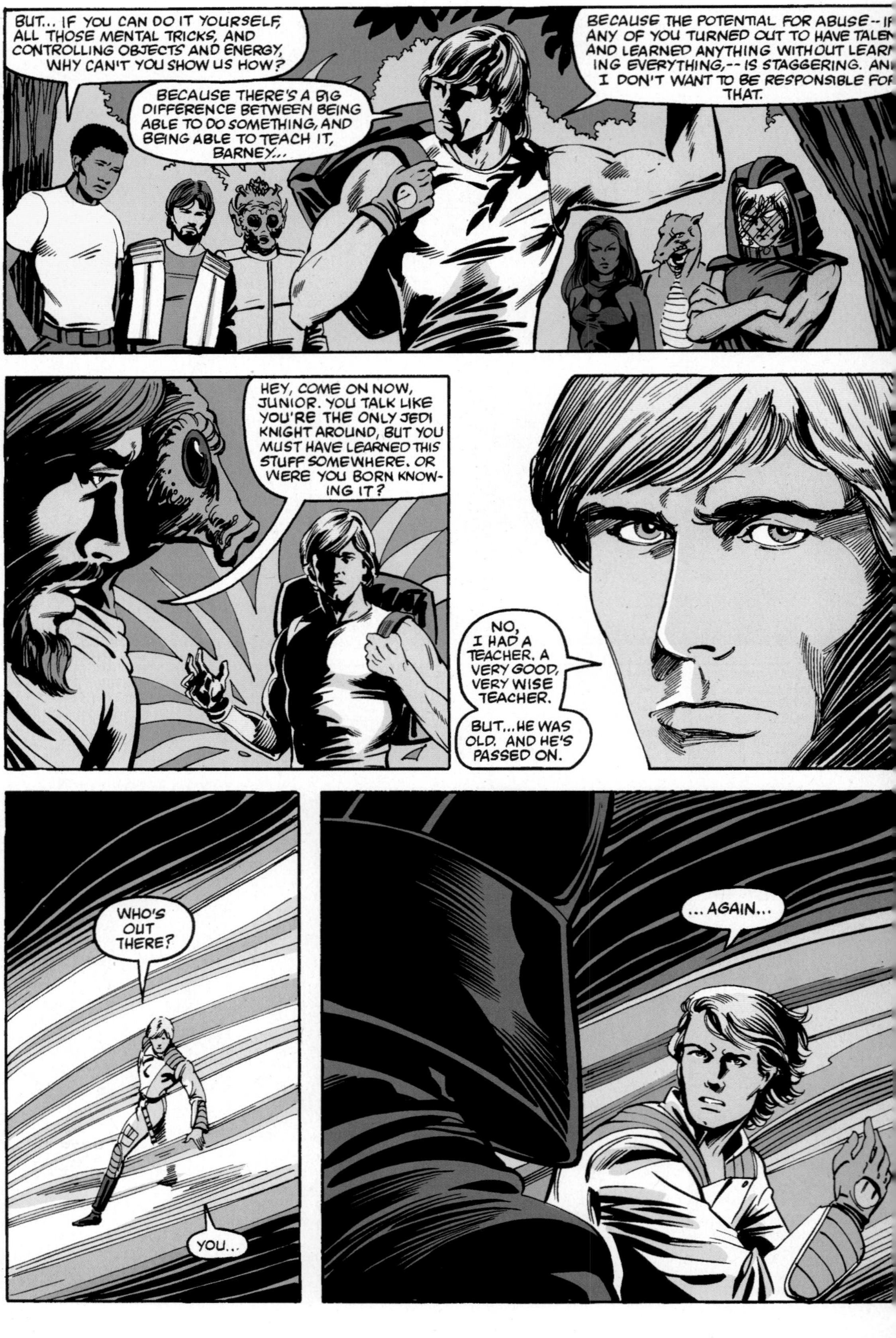
BUT... IF YOU CAN DO IT YOURSELF, ALL THOSE MENTAL TRICKS, AND CONTROLLING OBJECTS AND ENERGY, WHY CAN'T YOU SHOW US HOW?
BECAUSE THERE'S A BIG DIFFERENCE BETWEEN BEING ABLE TO DO SOMETHING, AND BEING ABLE TO TEACH IT, BARNEY...
BECAUSE THE POTENTIAL FOR ABUSE-- IF ANY OF YOU TURNED OUT TO HAVE TALENT AND LEARNED ANYTHING WITHOUT LEARNING EVERYTHING,-- IS STAGGERING. AND I DON'T WANT TO BE RESPONSIBLE FOR THAT.
HEY, COME ON NOW, JUNIOR. YOU TALK LIKE YOU'RE THE ONLY JEDI KNIGHT AROUND, BUT YOU MUST HAVE LEARNED THIS STUFF SOMEWHERE. OR WERE YOU BORN KNOWING IT?
NO, I HAD A TEACHER. A VERY GOOD, VERY WISE TEACHER.
BUT...HE WAS OLD. AND HE'S PASSED ON.
WHO'S OUT THERE?
YOU...
...AGAIN...

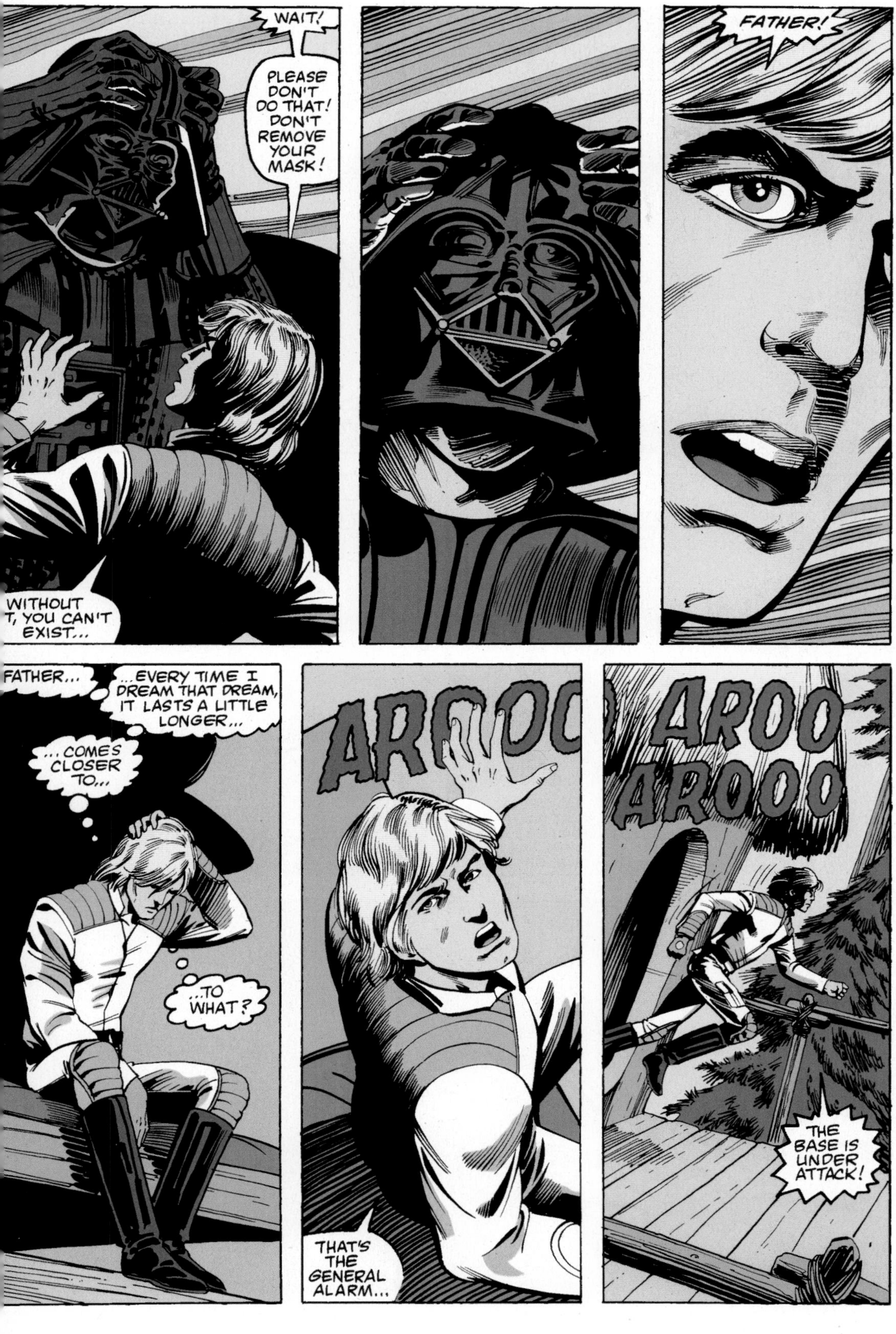
WAIT!
PLEASE DON'T DO THAT! DON'T REMOVE YOUR MASK!
WITHOUT T, YOU CAN'T EXIST...
FATHER!
FATHER...
...EVERY TIME I DREAM THAT DREAM, IT LASTS A LITTLE LONGER...
...COMES CLOSER TO...
...TO WHAT?
AROOO AROO AROOO
THAT'S THE GENERAL ALARM...
THE BASE IS UNDER ATTACK!

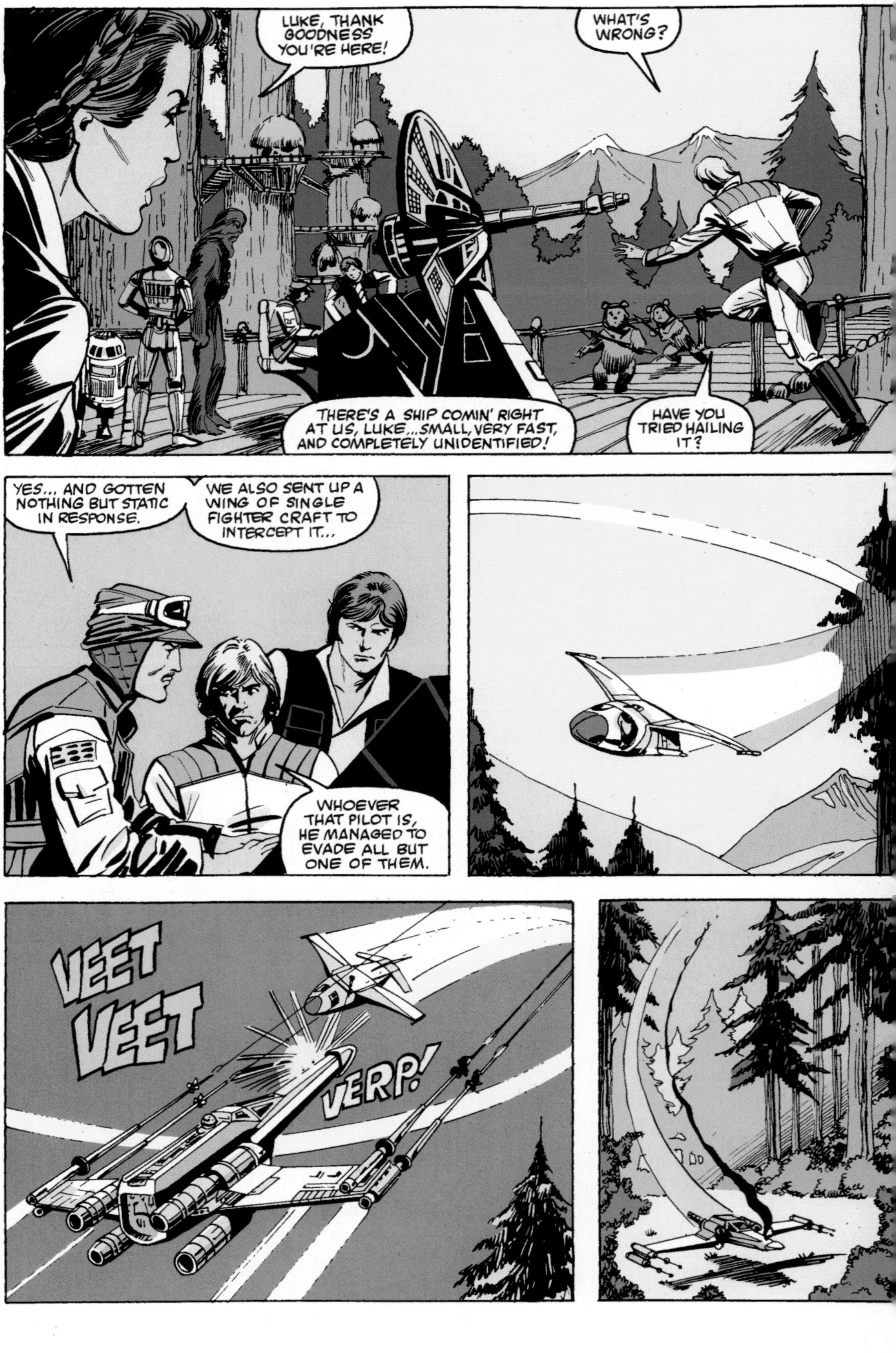
LUKE, THANK GOODNESS YOU'RE HERE!
WHAT'S WRONG?
THERE'S A SHIP COMIN' RIGHT AT US, LUKE...SMALL, VERY FAST, AND COMPLETELY UNIDENTIFIED!
HAVE YOU TRIED HAILING IT?
YES... AND GOTTEN NOTHING BUT STATIC IN RESPONSE.
WE ALSO SENT UP A WING OF SINGLE FIGHTER CRAFT TO INTERCEPT IT...
WHOEVER THAT PILOT IS, HE MANAGED TO EVADE ALL BUT ONE OF THEM.
VEET VEET
VERP!

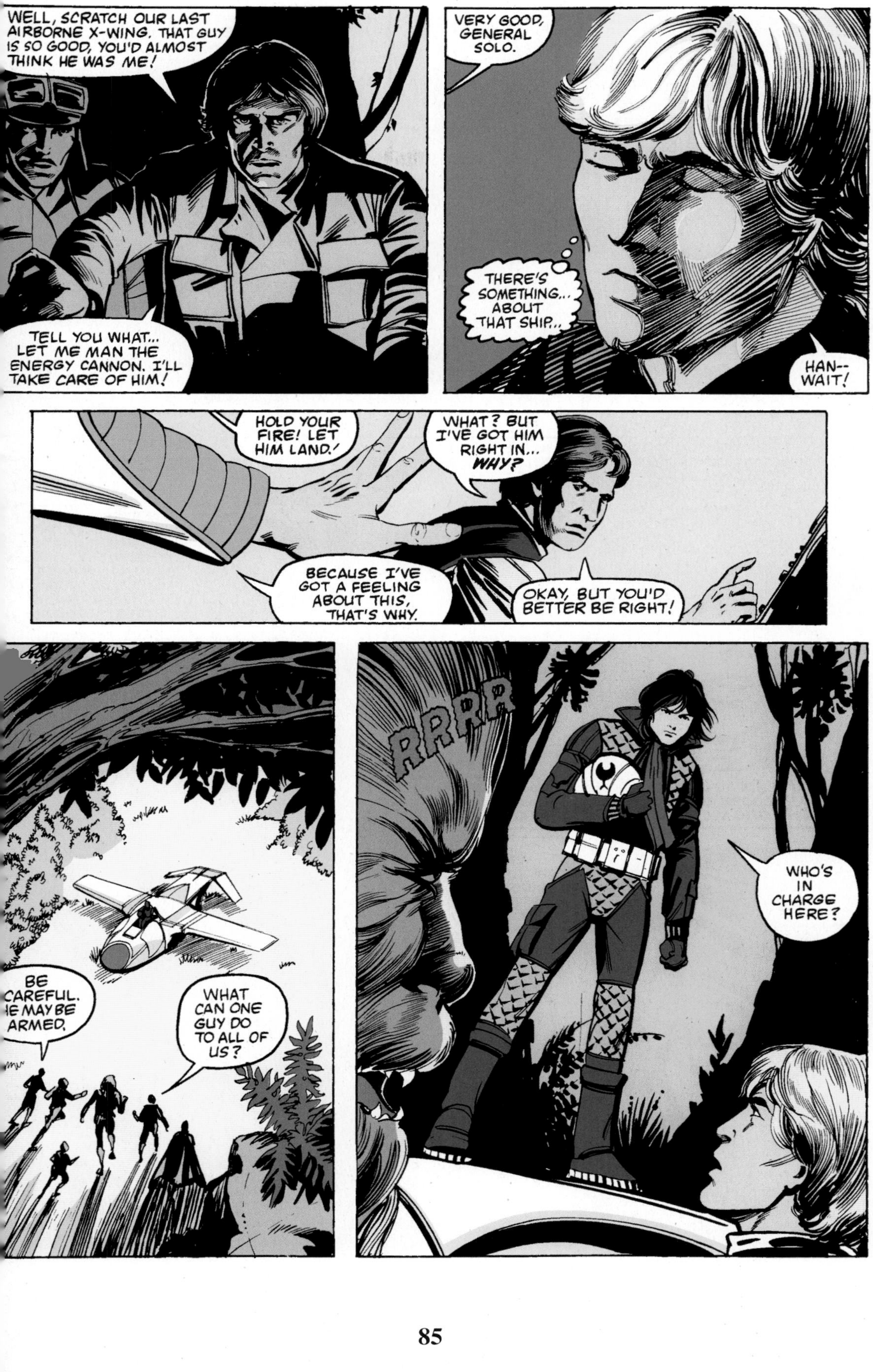
WELL, SCRATCH OUR LAST AIRBORNE X-WING. THAT GUY IS SO GOOD, YOU'D ALMOST THINK HE WAS ME!
TELL YOU WHAT... LET ME MAN THE ENERGY CANNON. I'LL TAKE CARE OF HIM!
VERY GOOD, GENERAL SOLO.
THERE'S SOMETHING... ABOUT THAT SHIP...
HAN-- WAIT!
HOLD YOUR FIRE! LET HIM LAND!
WHAT? BUT I'VE GOT HIM RIGHT IN... WHY?
BECAUSE I'VE GOT A FEELING ABOUT THIS, THAT'S WHY.
OKAY, BUT YOU'D BETTER BE RIGHT!
BE CAREFUL. HE MAY BE ARMED.
WHAT CAN ONE GUY DO TO ALL OF US?
RRRR
WHO'S IN CHARGE HERE?

HEY, HAVEN'T YOU GOT THAT BACKWARDS, PAL? YOU LANDED ON OUR BASE WITHOUT CLEARANCE. *WE'LL* ASK THE QUESTIONS.

IT'S HARD TO GET CLEARANCE WHEN ENEMIES HAVE SHOT OUT YOUR COMMUNICATIONS SYSTEMS...

IS THIS ENDOR? ARE THERE ANY ALLIANCE LEADERS HERE, OR ARE ALL OF YOU JUST WASTING MY TIME?

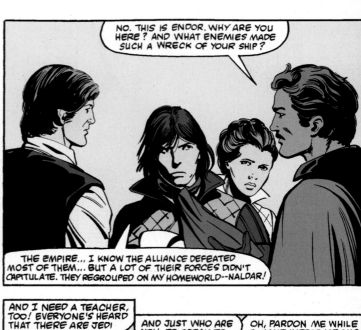

NO. THIS IS ENDOR. WHY ARE YOU HERE? AND WHAT ENEMIES MADE SUCH A WRECK OF YOUR SHIP?

THE EMPIRE... I KNOW THE ALLIANCE DEFEATED MOST OF THEM,... BUT A LOT OF THEIR FORCES DIDN'T CAPITULATE. THEY REGROUPED ON MY HOMEWORLD--NALDAR!

THEY'RE SLAUGHTERING MY PEOPLE... I'M DENIN, THE--THE ONLY SURVIVING CHILD OF NALDAR'S KING.

YOU'VE GOT TO LET ME HAVE TROOPS, TAKE THEM BACK AND SAVE MY WORLD!

AND I NEED A TEACHER, TOO! EVERYONE'S HEARD THAT THERE ARE JEDI AMONG YOU.

I CAN DO MORE, FASTER, IF SOMEONE TEACHES ME TO USE THE FORCE... I KNOW I HAVE AN AFFINITY FOR IT!

AND JUST WHO ARE YOU, TO SPEAK TO ME LIKE THAT?

OH, PARDON ME WHILE I MAKE INTRODUCTIONS.

YOUR ROYAL HIGHNESS, PRINCE DENIN, OF THE CONQUERED PLANET NALDAR, PERMIT ME TO PRESEN HER ROYAL HIGHNESS, PRINCESS LEIA ORGANA, OF THE DESTROYED PLANET ALDERAAN.

YOU'RE VERY FULL OF DEMANDS, FOR SOMEONE WHO'S COME HERE AS A BEGGAR, IN A SHIP THAT'S FULL OF HOLES...

LIKE THAT STORY YOU'RE TELLING.

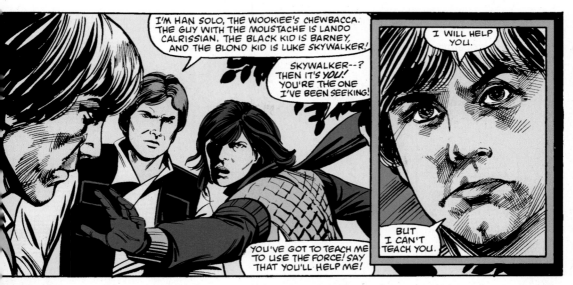

I'M HAN SOLO, THE WOOKIEE'S CHEWBACCA. THE GUY WITH THE MOUSTACHE IS LANDO CALRISSIAN, THE BLACK KID IS BARNEY, AND THE BLOND KID IS LUKE SKYWALKER!

SKYWALKER--? THEN IT'S *YOU*! YOU'RE THE ONE I'VE BEEN SEEKING!

I WILL HELP YOU.

BUT I CAN'T TEACH YOU.

YOU'VE GOT TO TEACH ME TO USE THE FORCE! SAY THAT YOU'LL HELP ME!

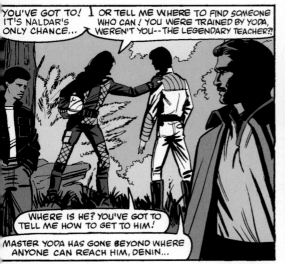

YOU'VE GOT TO! IT'S NALDAR'S ONLY CHANCE...

OR TELL ME WHERE TO FIND SOMEONE WHO CAN! YOU WERE TRAINED BY YODA, WEREN'T YOU--THE LEGENDARY TEACHER?!

WHERE IS HE? YOU'VE GOT TO TELL ME HOW TO GET TO HIM!

MASTER YODA HAS GONE BEYOND WHERE ANYONE CAN REACH HIM, DENIN...

BUT SOMEONE'S GOT TO TEACH ME! THAT'S ALWAYS BEEN MY DREAM...

MAYBE... MAYBE A DREAM ISN'T ENOUGH, DENIN. I'M ONE OF LUKE'S STUDENTS-- HE TEACHES US OTHER GOOD THINGS--

--AND HE EXPLAINED THAT--!

I'M NOT GOING TO GIVE UP!

I'M WARNING YOU, I'M GOING TO STICK WITH YOU UNTIL YOU HAVE TO TEACH ME SOMETHING!

WONDERFUL. AND WERE YOU EXPECTING TO USE THAT SAME BRAND OF PERSUASIVE DIPLOMACY TO CONVINCE ADMIRAL ACKBAR TO SEND AID TO YOUR WORLD?

IF SO, MAYBE YOU'D BETTER LET US MAKE THE REQUEST.

WE'LL SEE TO IT THAT YOU GET A FAIRER HEARING THAN YOU JUST GAVE LUKE.

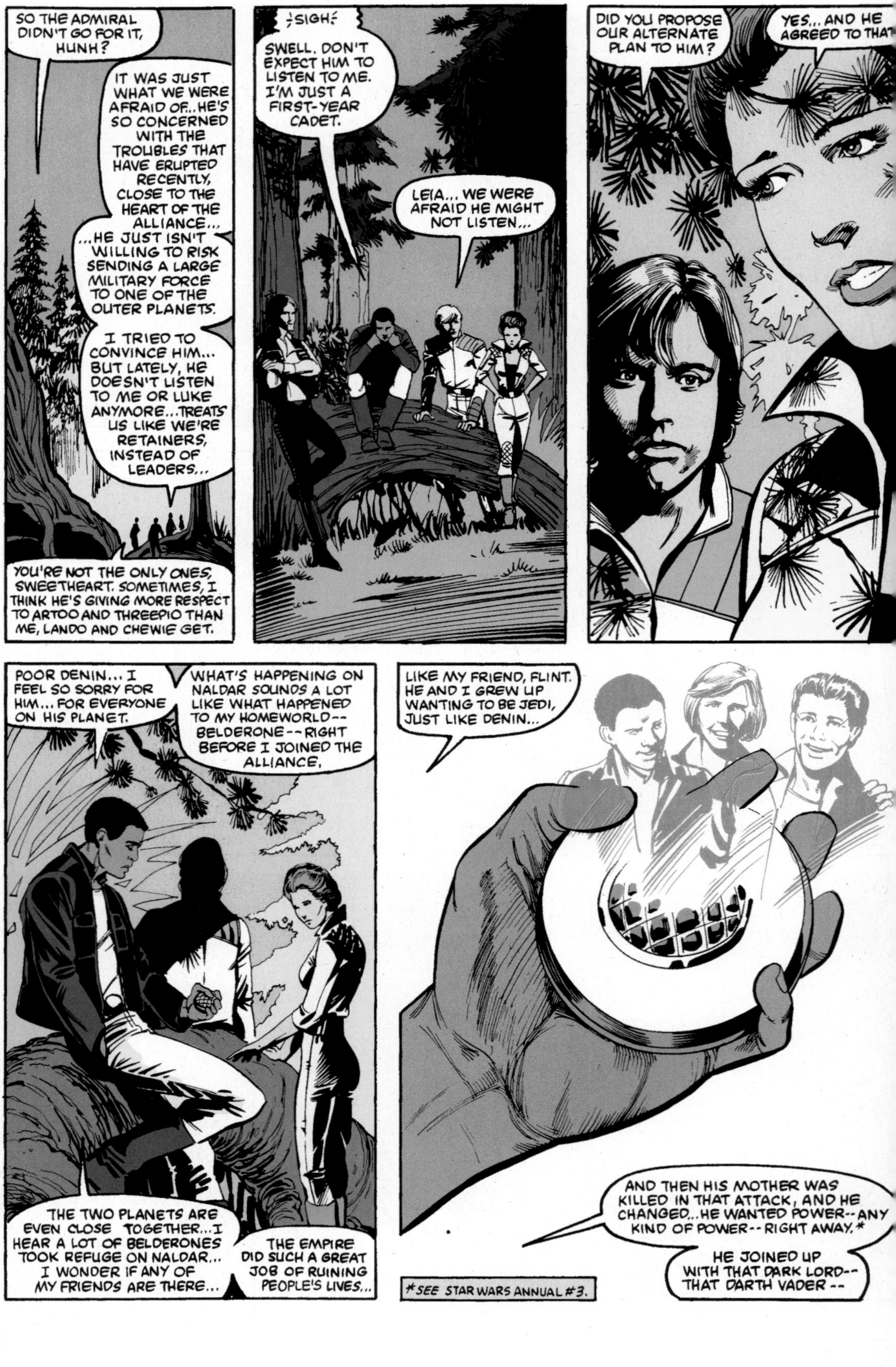
SO THE ADMIRAL DIDN'T GO FOR IT, HUNH?
IT WAS JUST WHAT WE WERE AFRAID OF... HE'S SO CONCERNED WITH THE TROUBLES THAT HAVE ERUPTED RECENTLY, CLOSE TO THE HEART OF THE ALLIANCE...
...HE JUST ISN'T WILLING TO RISK SENDING A LARGE MILITARY FORCE TO ONE OF THE OUTER PLANETS.
I TRIED TO CONVINCE HIM... BUT LATELY, HE DOESN'T LISTEN TO ME OR LUKE ANYMORE... TREATS US LIKE WE'RE RETAINERS, INSTEAD OF LEADERS...
YOU'RE NOT THE ONLY ONES, SWEETHEART. SOMETIMES, I THINK HE'S GIVING MORE RESPECT TO ARTOO AND THREEPIO THAN ME, LANDO AND CHEWIE GET.
SIGH
SWELL. DON'T EXPECT HIM TO LISTEN TO ME. I'M JUST A FIRST-YEAR CADET.
LEIA... WE WERE AFRAID HE MIGHT NOT LISTEN...
DID YOU PROPOSE OUR ALTERNATE PLAN TO HIM?
YES... AND HE AGREED TO THAT
POOR DENIN... I FEEL SO SORRY FOR HIM... FOR EVERYONE ON HIS PLANET.
WHAT'S HAPPENING ON NALDAR SOUNDS A LOT LIKE WHAT HAPPENED TO MY HOMEWORLD-- BELDERONE-- RIGHT BEFORE I JOINED THE ALLIANCE.
THE TWO PLANETS ARE EVEN CLOSE TOGETHER... I HEAR A LOT OF BELDERONES TOOK REFUGE ON NALDAR... I WONDER IF ANY OF MY FRIENDS ARE THERE...
THE EMPIRE DID SUCH A GREAT JOB OF RUINING PEOPLE'S LIVES...
LIKE MY FRIEND, FLINT. HE AND I GREW UP WANTING TO BE JEDI, JUST LIKE DENIN...
AND THEN HIS MOTHER WAS KILLED IN THAT ATTACK, AND HE CHANGED... HE WANTED POWER-- ANY KIND OF POWER-- RIGHT AWAY.*
HE JOINED UP WITH THAT DARK LORD-- THAT DARTH VADER--
*SEE STAR WARS ANNUAL #3.

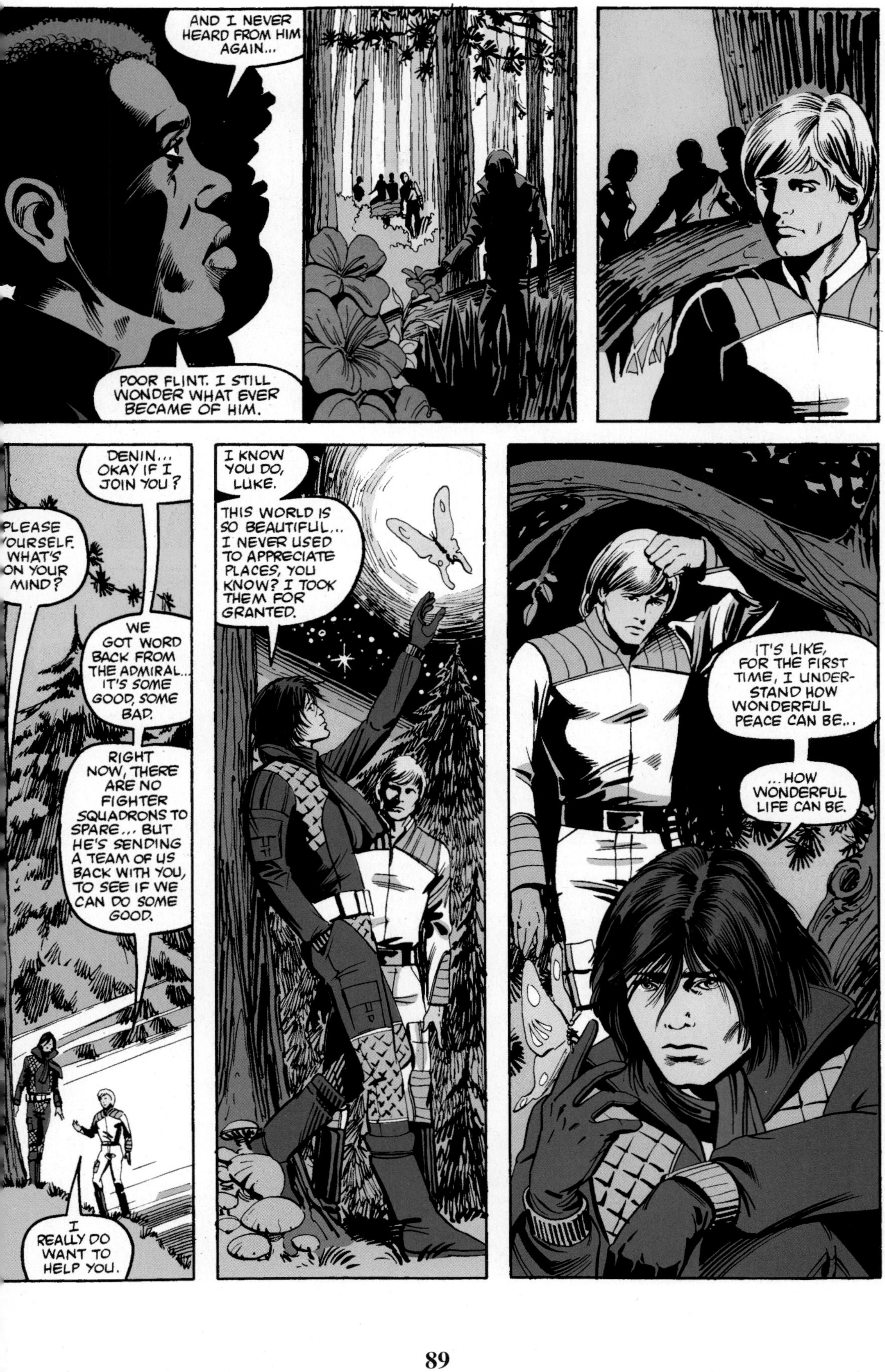
AND I NEVER HEARD FROM HIM AGAIN...
POOR FLINT. I STILL WONDER WHAT EVER BECAME OF HIM.
DENIN... OKAY IF I JOIN YOU?
PLEASE YOURSELF. WHAT'S ON YOUR MIND?
WE GOT WORD BACK FROM THE ADMIRAL... IT'S SOME GOOD, SOME BAD.
RIGHT NOW, THERE ARE NO FIGHTER SQUADRONS TO SPARE... BUT HE'S SENDING A TEAM OF US BACK WITH YOU, TO SEE IF WE CAN DO SOME GOOD.
I REALLY DO WANT TO HELP YOU.
I KNOW YOU DO, LUKE.
THIS WORLD IS SO BEAUTIFUL... I NEVER USED TO APPRECIATE PLACES, YOU KNOW? I TOOK THEM FOR GRANTED.
IT'S LIKE, FOR THE FIRST TIME, I UNDERSTAND HOW WONDERFUL PEACE CAN BE...
...HOW WONDERFUL LIFE CAN BE.

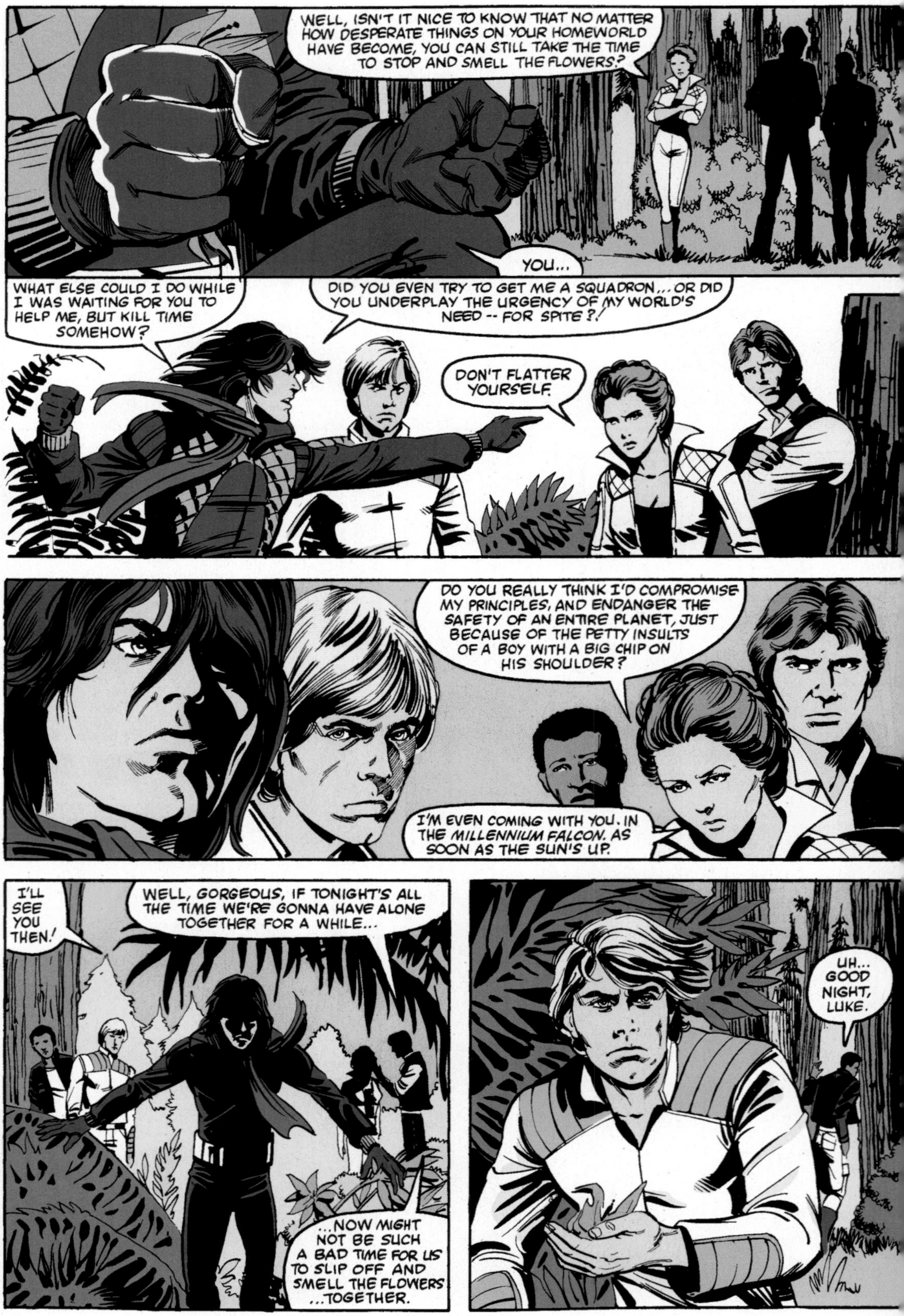
WELL, ISN'T IT NICE TO KNOW THAT NO MATTER HOW DESPERATE THINGS ON YOUR HOMEWORLD HAVE BECOME, YOU CAN STILL TAKE THE TIME TO STOP AND SMELL THE FLOWERS?
YOU...
WHAT ELSE COULD I DO WHILE I WAS WAITING FOR YOU TO HELP ME, BUT KILL TIME SOMEHOW?
DID YOU EVEN TRY TO GET ME A SQUADRON... OR DID YOU UNDERPLAY THE URGENCY OF MY WORLD'S NEED -- FOR SPITE?!
DON'T FLATTER YOURSELF.
DO YOU REALLY THINK I'D COMPROMISE MY PRINCIPLES, AND ENDANGER THE SAFETY OF AN ENTIRE PLANET, JUST BECAUSE OF THE PETTY INSULTS OF A BOY WITH A BIG CHIP ON HIS SHOULDER?
I'M EVEN COMING WITH YOU. IN THE *MILLENNIUM FALCON*. AS SOON AS THE SUN'S UP.
I'LL SEE YOU THEN!
WELL, GORGEOUS, IF TONIGHT'S ALL THE TIME WE'RE GONNA HAVE ALONE TOGETHER FOR A WHILE...
...NOW MIGHT NOT BE SUCH A BAD TIME FOR US TO SLIP OFF AND SMELL THE FLOWERS ...TOGETHER.
UH... GOOD NIGHT, LUKE.

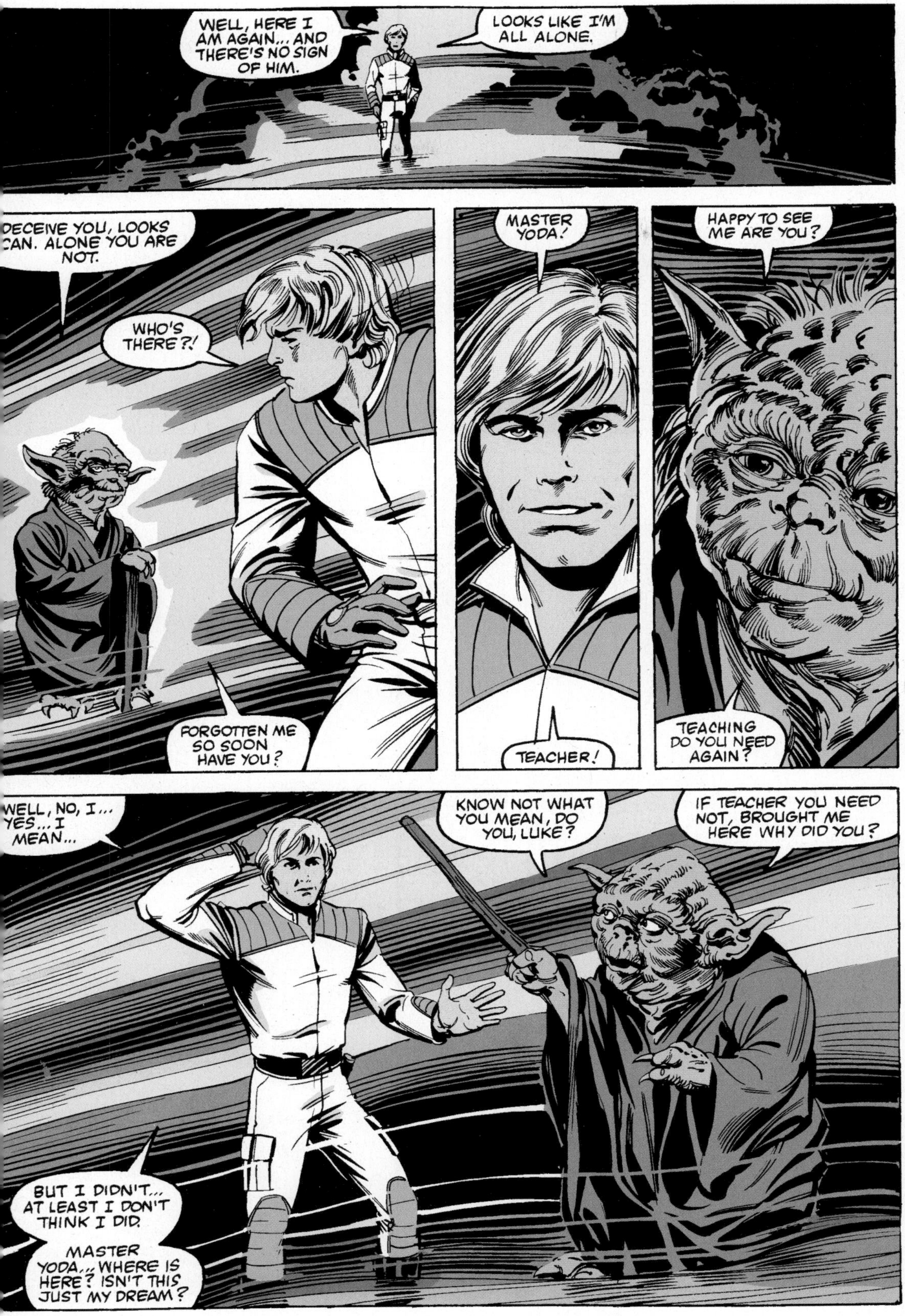
WELL, HERE I AM AGAIN... AND THERE'S NO SIGN OF HIM.
LOOKS LIKE I'M ALL ALONE.
DECEIVE YOU, LOOKS CAN. ALONE YOU ARE NOT.
WHO'S THERE?!
FORGOTTEN ME SO SOON HAVE YOU?
MASTER YODA!
TEACHER!
HAPPY TO SEE ME ARE YOU?
TEACHING DO YOU NEED AGAIN?
WELL, NO, I... YES... I MEAN...
KNOW NOT WHAT YOU MEAN, DO YOU, LUKE?
IF TEACHER YOU NEED NOT, BROUGHT ME HERE WHY DID YOU?
BUT I DIDN'T... AT LEAST I DON'T THINK I DID.
MASTER YODA... WHERE IS HERE? ISN'T THIS JUST MY DREAM?

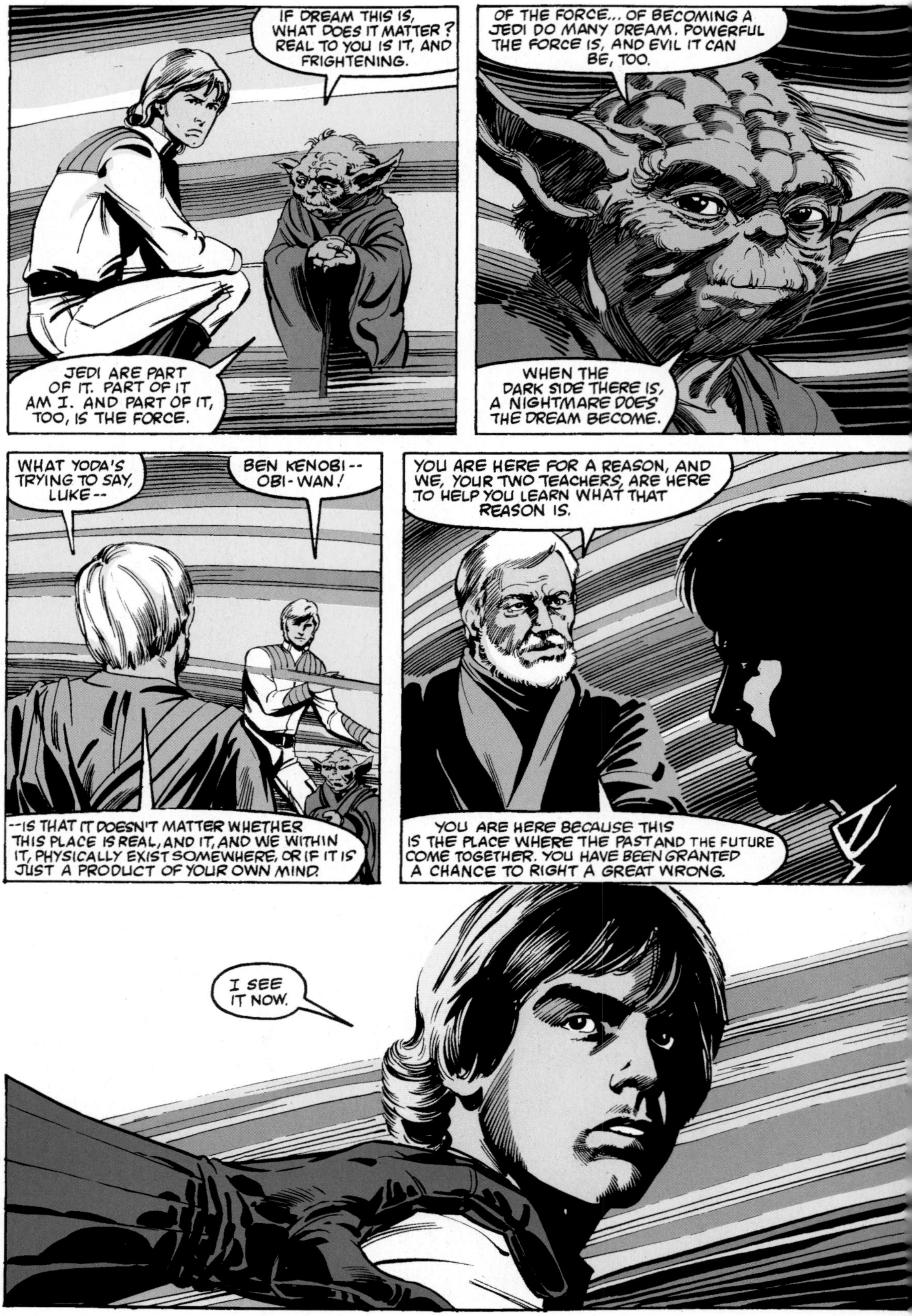
IF DREAM THIS IS, WHAT DOES IT MATTER? REAL TO YOU IS IT, AND FRIGHTENING.
JEDI ARE PART OF IT. PART OF IT AM I. AND PART OF IT, TOO, IS THE FORCE.
OF THE FORCE... OF BECOMING A JEDI DO MANY DREAM. POWERFUL THE FORCE IS, AND EVIL IT CAN BE, TOO.
WHEN THE DARK SIDE THERE IS, A NIGHTMARE DOES THE DREAM BECOME.
WHAT YODA'S TRYING TO SAY, LUKE--
BEN KENOBI-- OBI-WAN!
--IS THAT IT DOESN'T MATTER WHETHER THIS PLACE IS REAL, AND IT, AND WE WITHIN IT, PHYSICALLY EXIST SOMEWHERE, OR IF IT IS JUST A PRODUCT OF YOUR OWN MIND.
YOU ARE HERE FOR A REASON, AND WE, YOUR TWO TEACHERS, ARE HERE TO HELP YOU LEARN WHAT THAT REASON IS.
YOU ARE HERE BECAUSE THIS IS THE PLACE WHERE THE PAST AND THE FUTURE COME TOGETHER. YOU HAVE BEEN GRANTED A CHANCE TO RIGHT A GREAT WRONG.
I SEE IT NOW.

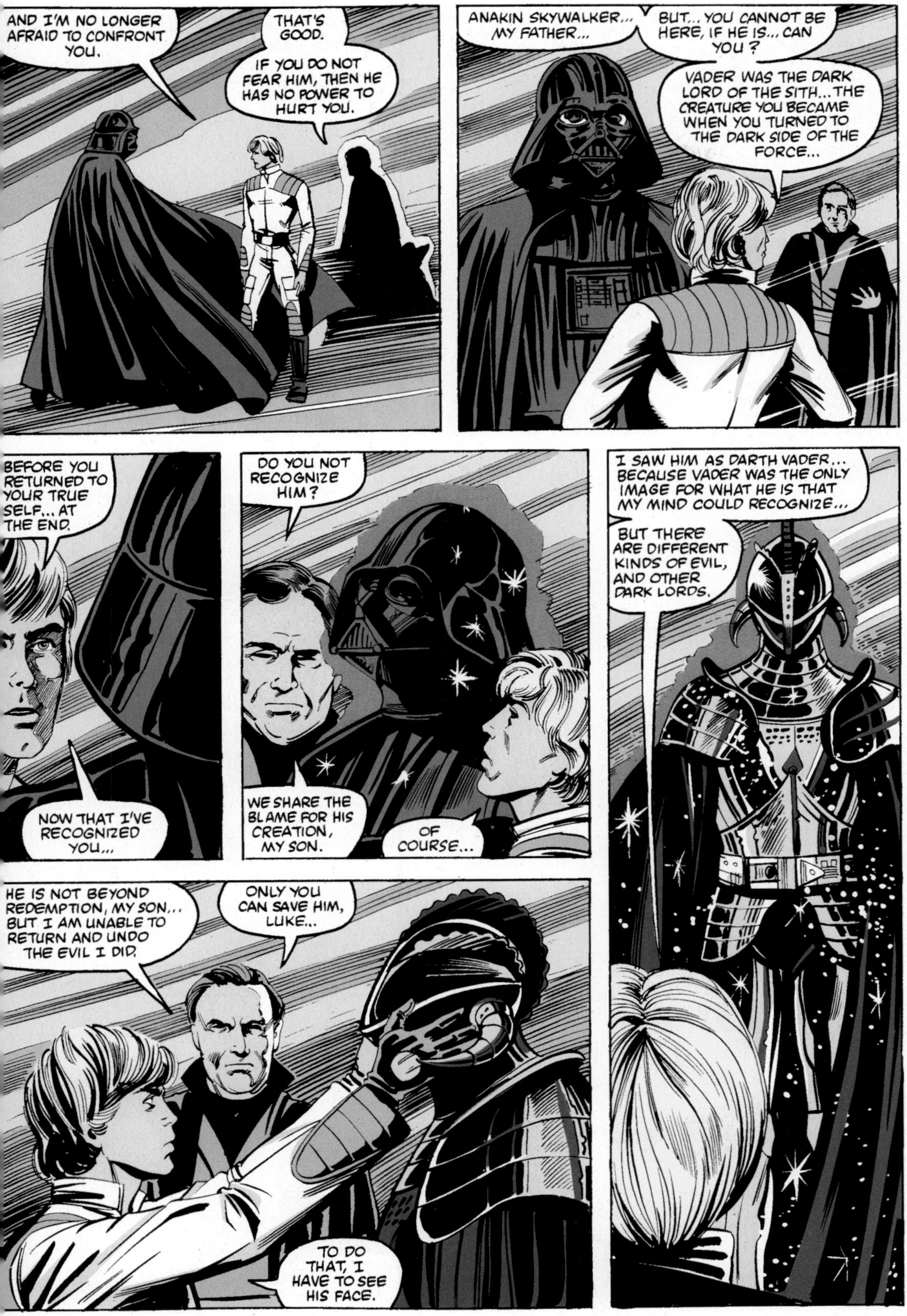
AND I'M NO LONGER AFRAID TO CONFRONT YOU.
THAT'S GOOD.
IF YOU DO NOT FEAR HIM, THEN HE HAS NO POWER TO HURT YOU.
ANAKIN SKYWALKER... MY FATHER...
BUT... YOU CANNOT BE HERE, IF HE IS... CAN YOU?
VADER WAS THE DARK LORD OF THE SITH... THE CREATURE YOU BECAME WHEN YOU TURNED TO THE DARK SIDE OF THE FORCE...
BEFORE YOU RETURNED TO YOUR TRUE SELF... AT THE END.
NOW THAT I'VE RECOGNIZED YOU...
DO YOU NOT RECOGNIZE HIM?
WE SHARE THE BLAME FOR HIS CREATION, MY SON.
OF COURSE...
I SAW HIM AS DARTH VADER... BECAUSE VADER WAS THE ONLY IMAGE FOR WHAT HE IS THAT MY MIND COULD RECOGNIZE...
BUT THERE ARE DIFFERENT KINDS OF EVIL, AND OTHER DARK LORDS.
HE IS NOT BEYOND REDEMPTION, MY SON... BUT I AM UNABLE TO RETURN AND UNDO THE EVIL I DID.
ONLY YOU CAN SAVE HIM, LUKE...
TO DO THAT, I HAVE TO SEE HIS FACE.

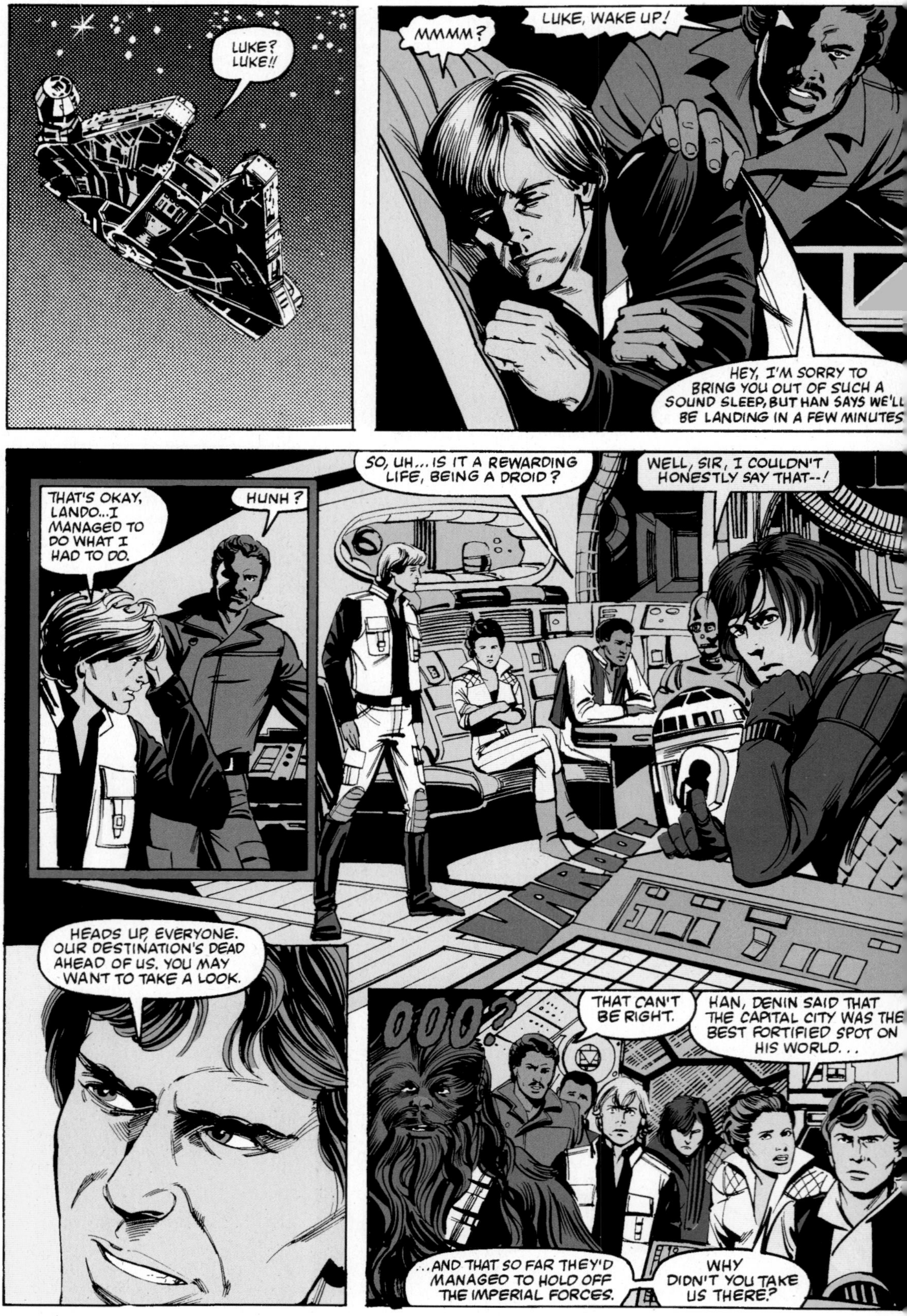
LUKE?
LUKE!!
MMMM?
LUKE, WAKE UP!
HEY, I'M SORRY TO BRING YOU OUT OF SUCH A SOUND SLEEP, BUT HAN SAYS WE'LL BE LANDING IN A FEW MINUTES
THAT'S OKAY, LANDO...I MANAGED TO DO WHAT I HAD TO DO.
HUNH?
SO, UH... IS IT A REWARDING LIFE, BEING A DROID?
WELL, SIR, I COULDN'T HONESTLY SAY THAT--!
VAROOOM
HEADS UP, EVERYONE. OUR DESTINATION'S DEAD AHEAD OF US. YOU MAY WANT TO TAKE A LOOK.
OOO?
THAT CAN'T BE RIGHT.
HAN, DENIN SAID THAT THE CAPITAL CITY WAS THE BEST FORTIFIED SPOT ON HIS WORLD...
...AND THAT SO FAR THEY'D MANAGED TO HOLD OFF THE IMPERIAL FORCES.
WHY DIDN'T YOU TAKE US THERE?

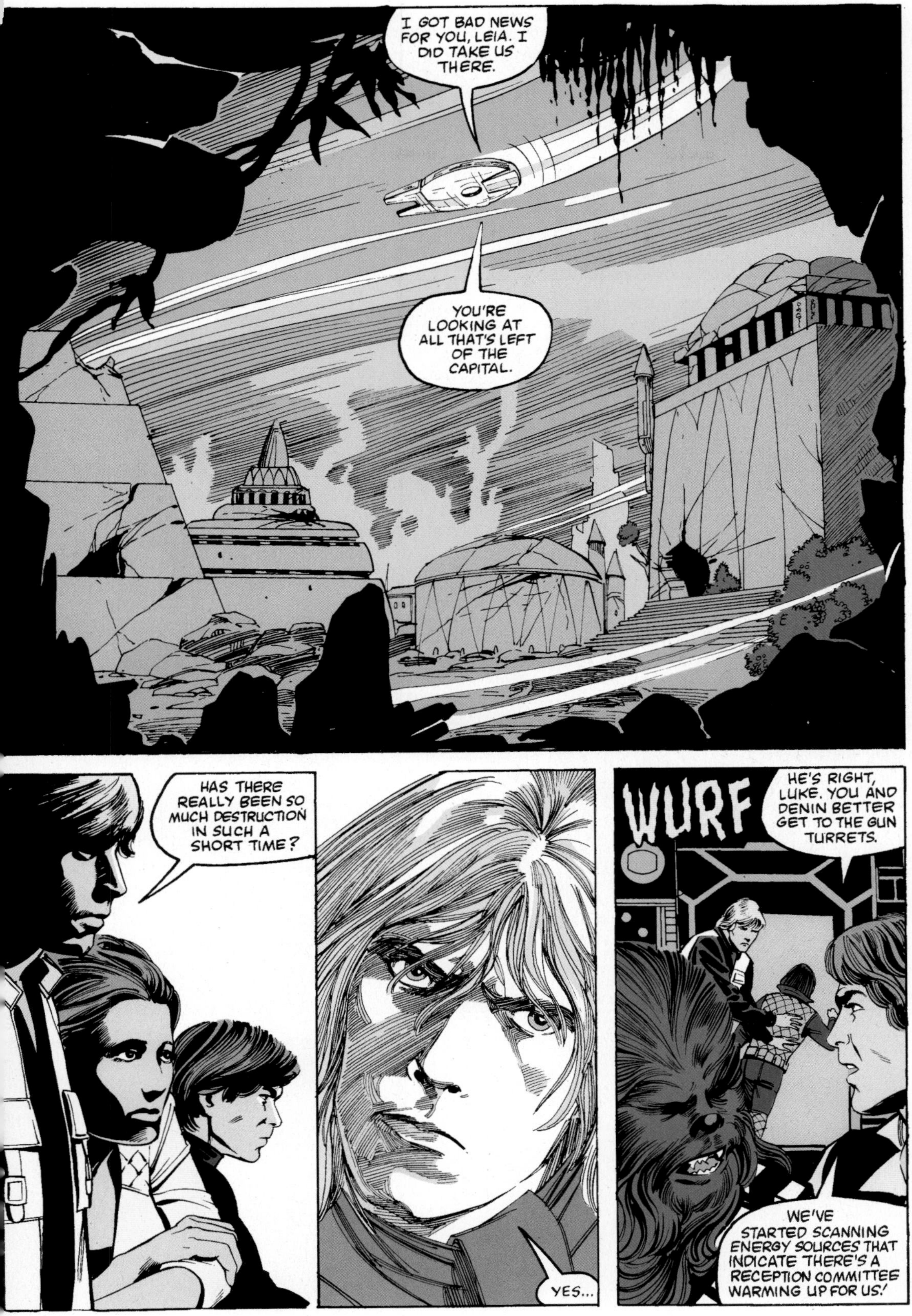
I GOT BAD NEWS FOR YOU, LEIA. I DID TAKE US THERE.
YOU'RE LOOKING AT ALL THAT'S LEFT OF THE CAPITAL.
HAS THERE REALLY BEEN SO MUCH DESTRUCTION IN SUCH A SHORT TIME?
YES...
WURF
HE'S RIGHT, LUKE. YOU AND DENIN BETTER GET TO THE GUN TURRETS.
WE'VE STARTED SCANNING ENERGY SOURCES THAT INDICATE THERE'S A RECEPTION COMMITTEE WARMING UP FOR US!

WHARUMMP!

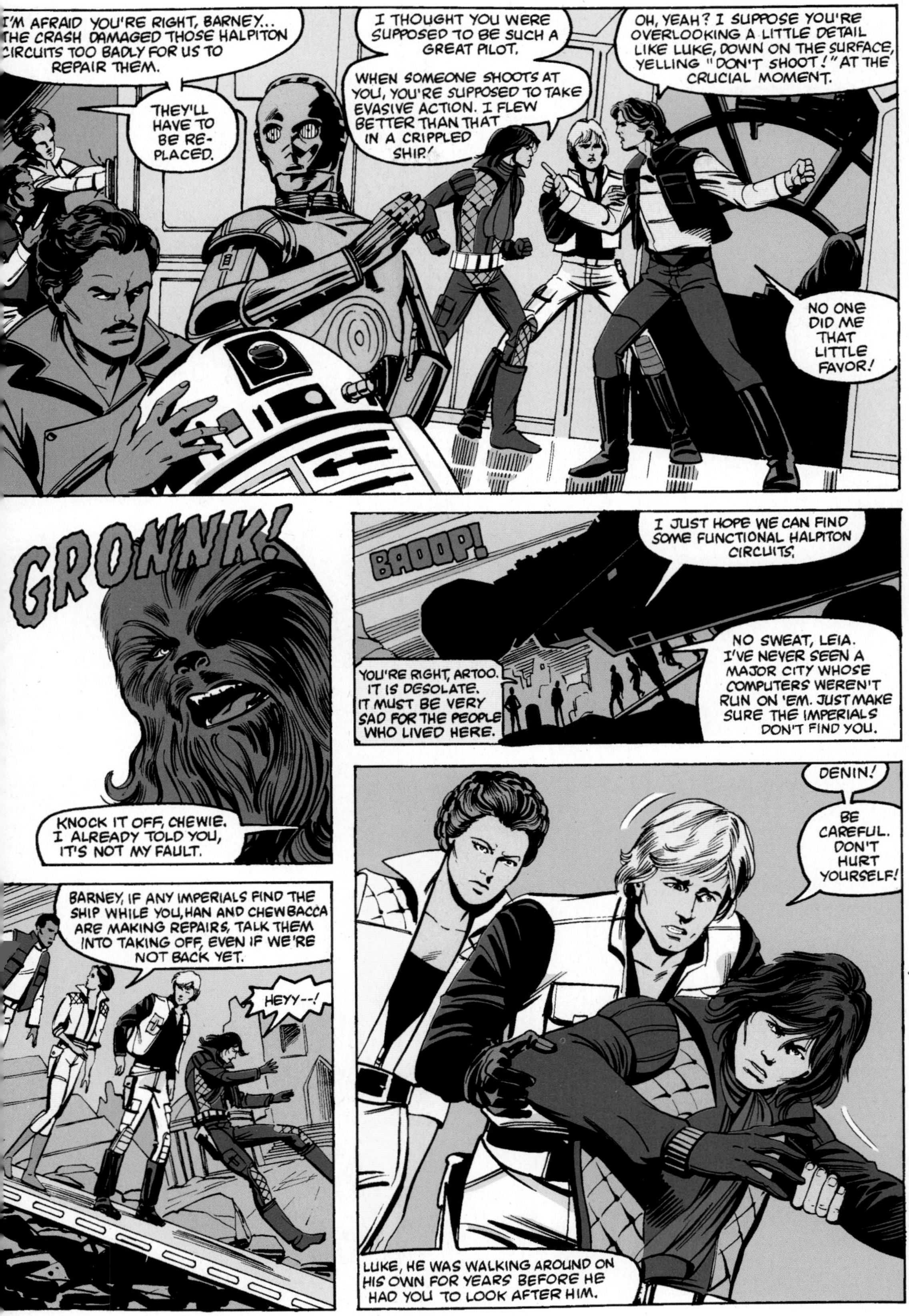
I'M AFRAID YOU'RE RIGHT, BARNEY... THE CRASH DAMAGED THOSE HALPITON CIRCUITS TOO BADLY FOR US TO REPAIR THEM.
THEY'LL HAVE TO BE REPLACED.
I THOUGHT YOU WERE SUPPOSED TO BE SUCH A GREAT PILOT.
WHEN SOMEONE SHOOTS AT YOU, YOU'RE SUPPOSED TO TAKE EVASIVE ACTION. I FLEW BETTER THAN THAT IN A CRIPPLED SHIP!
OH, YEAH? I SUPPOSE YOU'RE OVERLOOKING A LITTLE DETAIL LIKE LUKE, DOWN ON THE SURFACE, YELLING "DON'T SHOOT!" AT THE CRUCIAL MOMENT.
NO ONE DID ME THAT LITTLE FAVOR!
GRONNK!
KNOCK IT OFF, CHEWIE. I ALREADY TOLD YOU, IT'S NOT MY FAULT.
BADOOP!
I JUST HOPE WE CAN FIND SOME FUNCTIONAL HALPITON CIRCUITS.
YOU'RE RIGHT, ARTOO. IT IS DESOLATE. IT MUST BE VERY SAD FOR THE PEOPLE WHO LIVED HERE.
NO SWEAT, LEIA. I'VE NEVER SEEN A MAJOR CITY WHOSE COMPUTERS WEREN'T RUN ON 'EM. JUST MAKE SURE THE IMPERIALS DON'T FIND YOU.
BARNEY, IF ANY IMPERIALS FIND THE SHIP WHILE YOU, HAN AND CHEWBACCA ARE MAKING REPAIRS, TALK THEM INTO TAKING OFF, EVEN IF WE'RE NOT BACK YET.
HEYY--!
DENIN!
BE CAREFUL. DON'T HURT YOURSELF!
LUKE, HE WAS WALKING AROUND ON HIS OWN FOR YEARS BEFORE HE HAD YOU TO LOOK AFTER HIM.

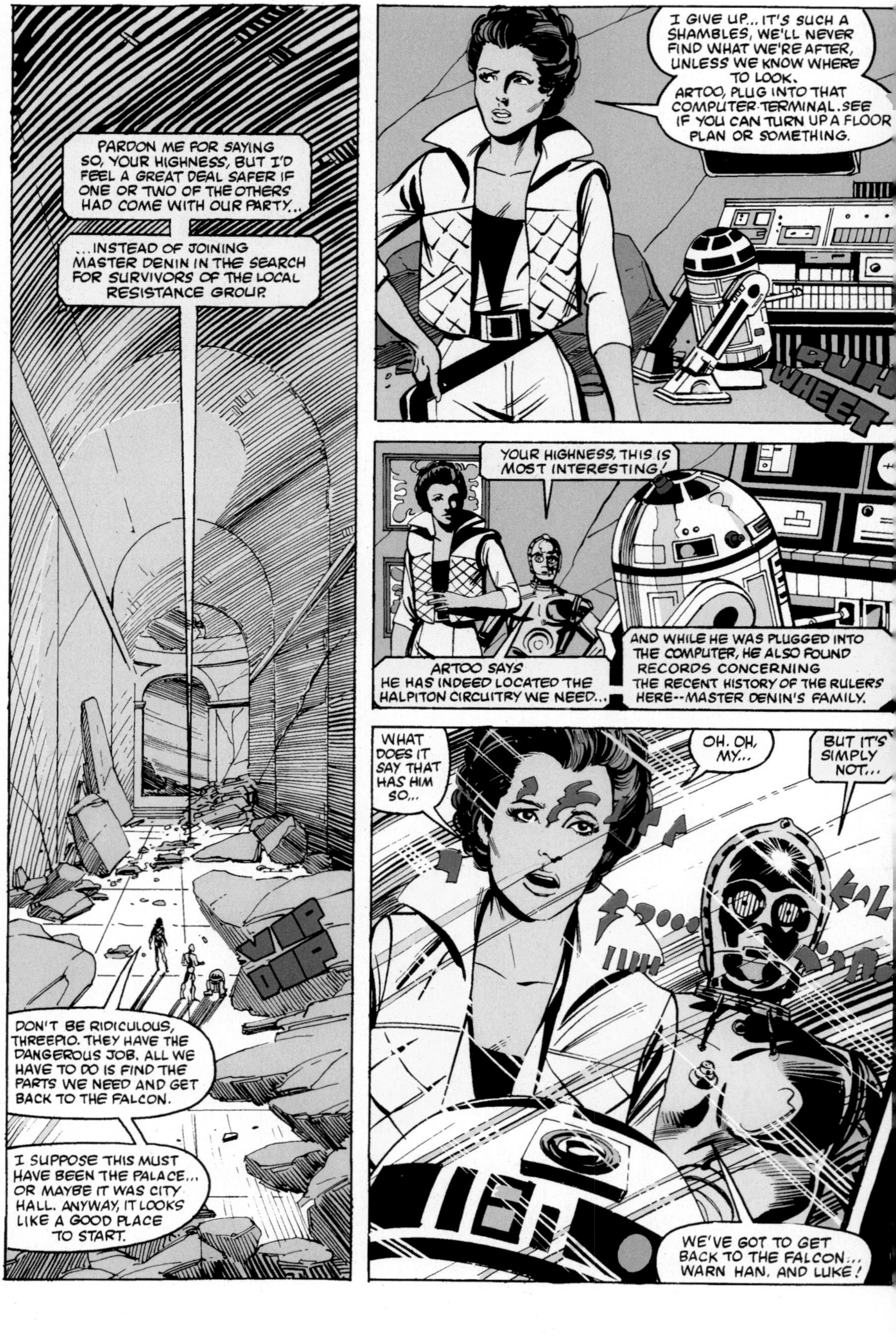
PARDON ME FOR SAYING SO, YOUR HIGHNESS, BUT I'D FEEL A GREAT DEAL SAFER IF ONE OR TWO OF THE OTHERS HAD COME WITH OUR PARTY...
...INSTEAD OF JOINING MASTER DENIN IN THE SEARCH FOR SURVIVORS OF THE LOCAL RESISTANCE GROUP.
VIP DIP
DON'T BE RIDICULOUS, THREEPIO. THEY HAVE THE DANGEROUS JOB. ALL WE HAVE TO DO IS FIND THE PARTS WE NEED AND GET BACK TO THE FALCON.
I SUPPOSE THIS MUST HAVE BEEN THE PALACE... OR MAYBE IT WAS CITY HALL. ANYWAY, IT LOOKS LIKE A GOOD PLACE TO START.
I GIVE UP... IT'S SUCH A SHAMBLES, WE'LL NEVER FIND WHAT WE'RE AFTER, UNLESS WE KNOW WHERE TO LOOK.
ARTOO, PLUG INTO THAT COMPUTER-TERMINAL. SEE IF YOU CAN TURN UP A FLOOR PLAN OR SOMETHING.
PUH WHEET
YOUR HIGHNESS, THIS IS MOST INTERESTING!
ARTOO SAYS HE HAS INDEED LOCATED THE HALPITON CIRCUITRY WE NEED...
AND WHILE HE WAS PLUGGED INTO THE COMPUTER, HE ALSO FOUND RECORDS CONCERNING THE RECENT HISTORY OF THE RULERS HERE--MASTER DENIN'S FAMILY.
WHAT DOES IT SAY THAT HAS HIM SO...
OH. OH, MY...
BUT IT'S SIMPLY NOT...
WE'VE GOT TO GET BACK TO THE FALCON... WARN HAN. AND LUKE!

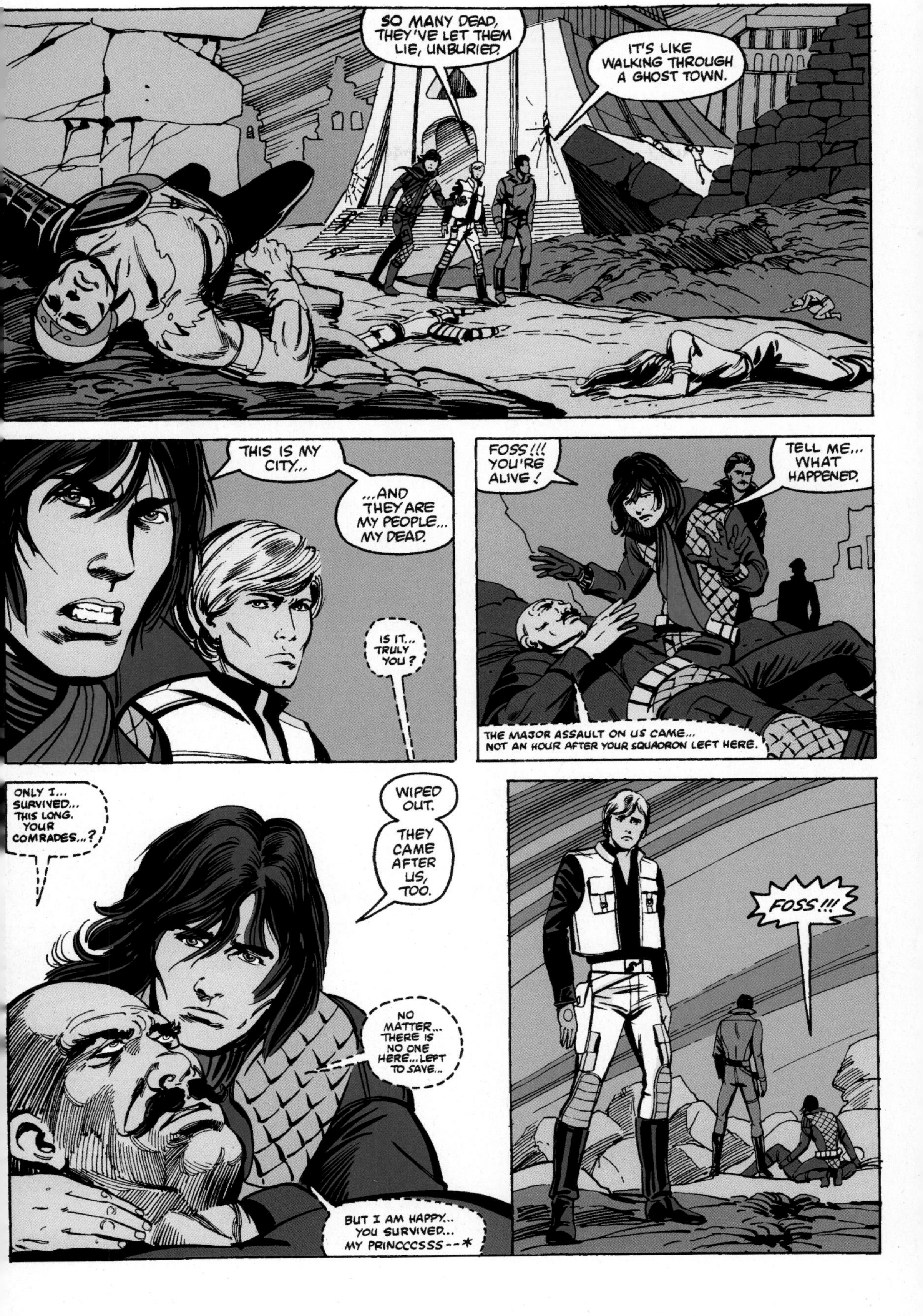
SO MANY DEAD, THEY'VE LET THEM LIE, UNBURIED.
IT'S LIKE WALKING THROUGH A GHOST TOWN.
THIS IS MY CITY...
...AND THEY ARE MY PEOPLE... MY DEAD.
IS IT... TRULY YOU?
FOSS!!! YOU'RE ALIVE!
TELL ME... WHAT HAPPENED.
THE MAJOR ASSAULT ON US CAME... NOT AN HOUR AFTER YOUR SQUADRON LEFT HERE.
ONLY I... SURVIVED... THIS LONG. YOUR COMRADES...?
WIPED OUT.
THEY CAME AFTER US, TOO.
NO MATTER... THERE IS NO ONE HERE... LEFT TO SAVE...
BUT I AM HAPPY... YOU SURVIVED... MY PRINCCCSSS--*
FOSS!!!

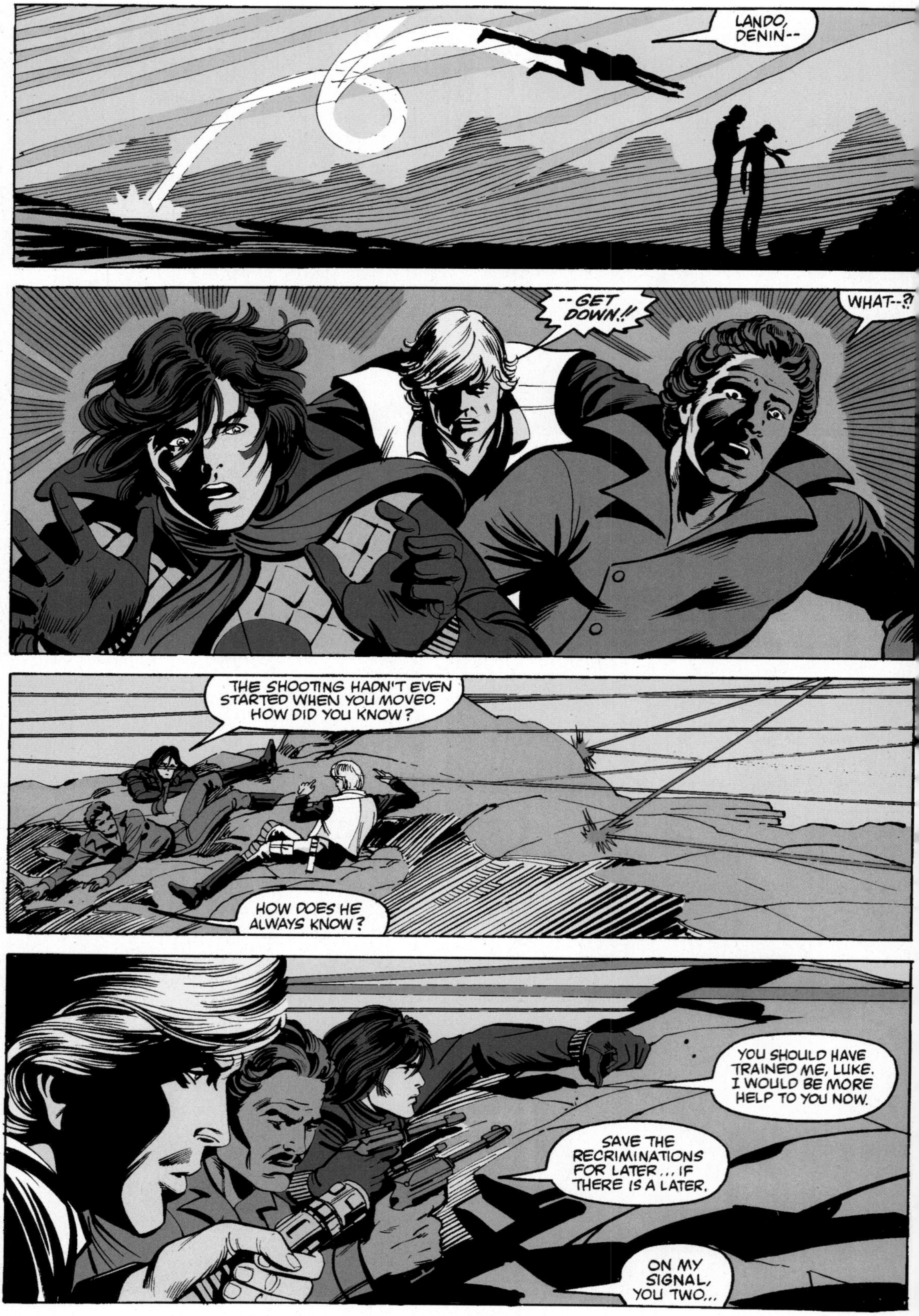
LANDO, DENIN--
--GET DOWN!!
WHAT--?!
THE SHOOTING HADN'T EVEN STARTED WHEN YOU MOVED. HOW DID YOU KNOW?
HOW DOES HE ALWAYS KNOW?
YOU SHOULD HAVE TRAINED ME, LUKE. I WOULD BE MORE HELP TO YOU NOW.
SAVE THE RECRIMINATIONS FOR LATER... IF THERE IS A LATER.
ON MY SIGNAL, YOU TWO...

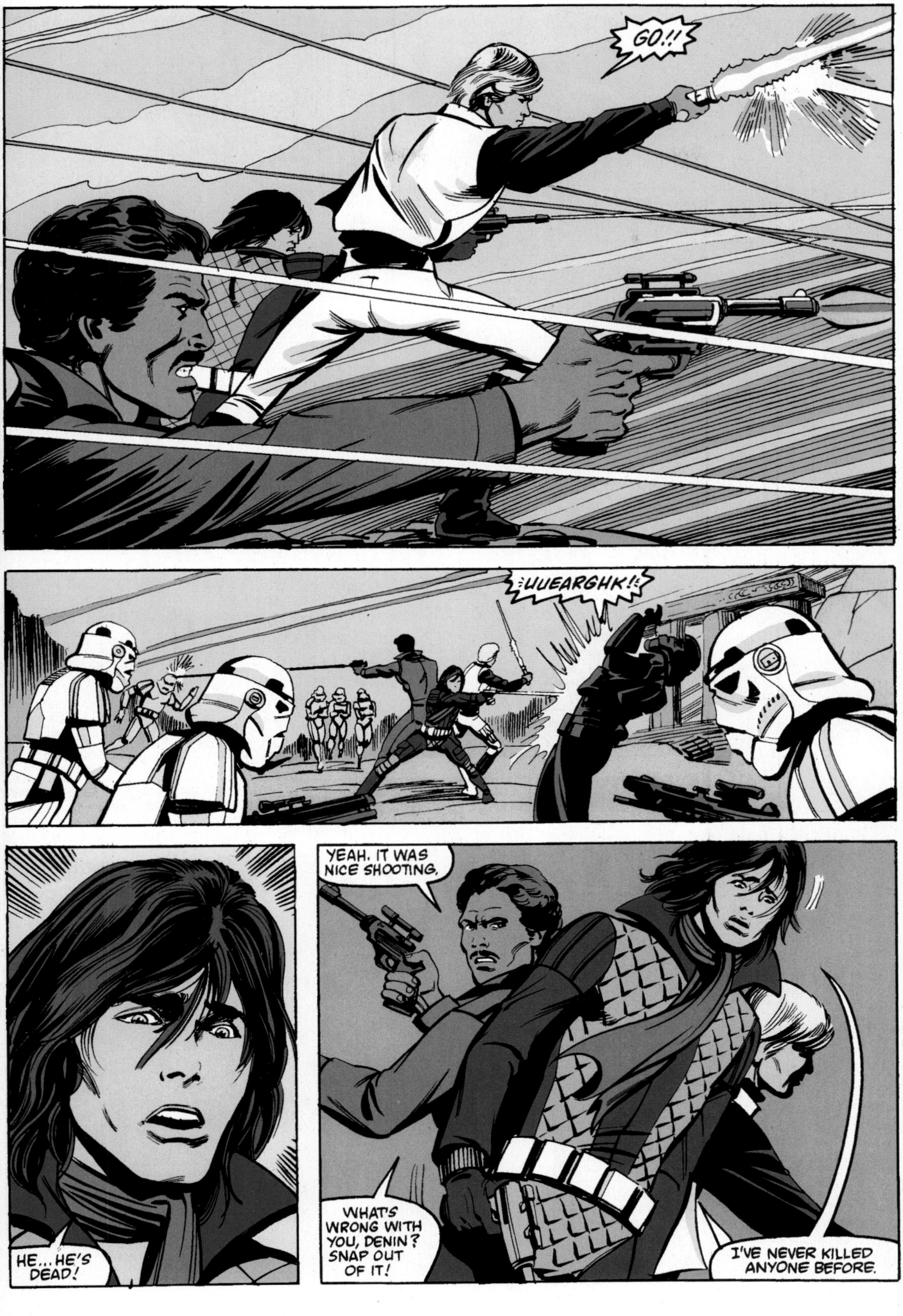
GO!!
UUEARGHK!
HE... HE'S DEAD!
YEAH. IT WAS NICE SHOOTING.
WHAT'S WRONG WITH YOU, DENIN? SNAP OUT OF IT!
I'VE NEVER KILLED ANYONE BEFORE.

BLEET

YOU'RE RIGHT, ARTOO. IT IS A RELIEF TO BE BACK.

HAN? HAN! I HAVE TO TALK TO YOU!

TAKE IT EASY, LEIA. WHAT'S WRONG? YOU'RE ACTING LIKE YOU'VE SEEN A--!

ARE LUKE AND THE OTHERS BACK YET?

NO. SAY, WHAT'S THIS ALL A--?

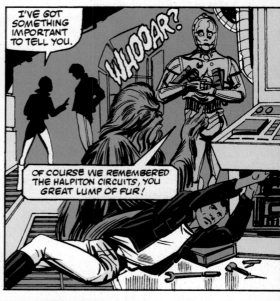

I'VE GOT SOMETHING IMPORTANT TO TELL YOU.

WHOOAR?

OF COURSE WE REMEMBERED THE HALPITON CIRCUITS, YOU GREAT LUMP OF FUR!

WE FOUND THEM IN THE LIBRARY. WHILE WE WERE LOOKING FOR THEM, ARTOO TURNED UP THE MOST RECENT HISTORICAL DATA...

...STORED HOLOGRAPHICALLY BEFORE THE WAR GOT SO BAD, PEOPLE STOPPED KEEPING RECORDS.

THERE WAS A GREAT DEAL OF INFORMATION ON IT ABOUT THE ROYAL FAMILY.

LIKE WHAT?

TWO YEARS AGO, WHILE DEFENDING THE REST OF HIS FAMILY DURING THE EMPIRE'S INITIAL ASSAULT THERE, PRINCE DENIN OF NALDAR WAS KILLED.

102

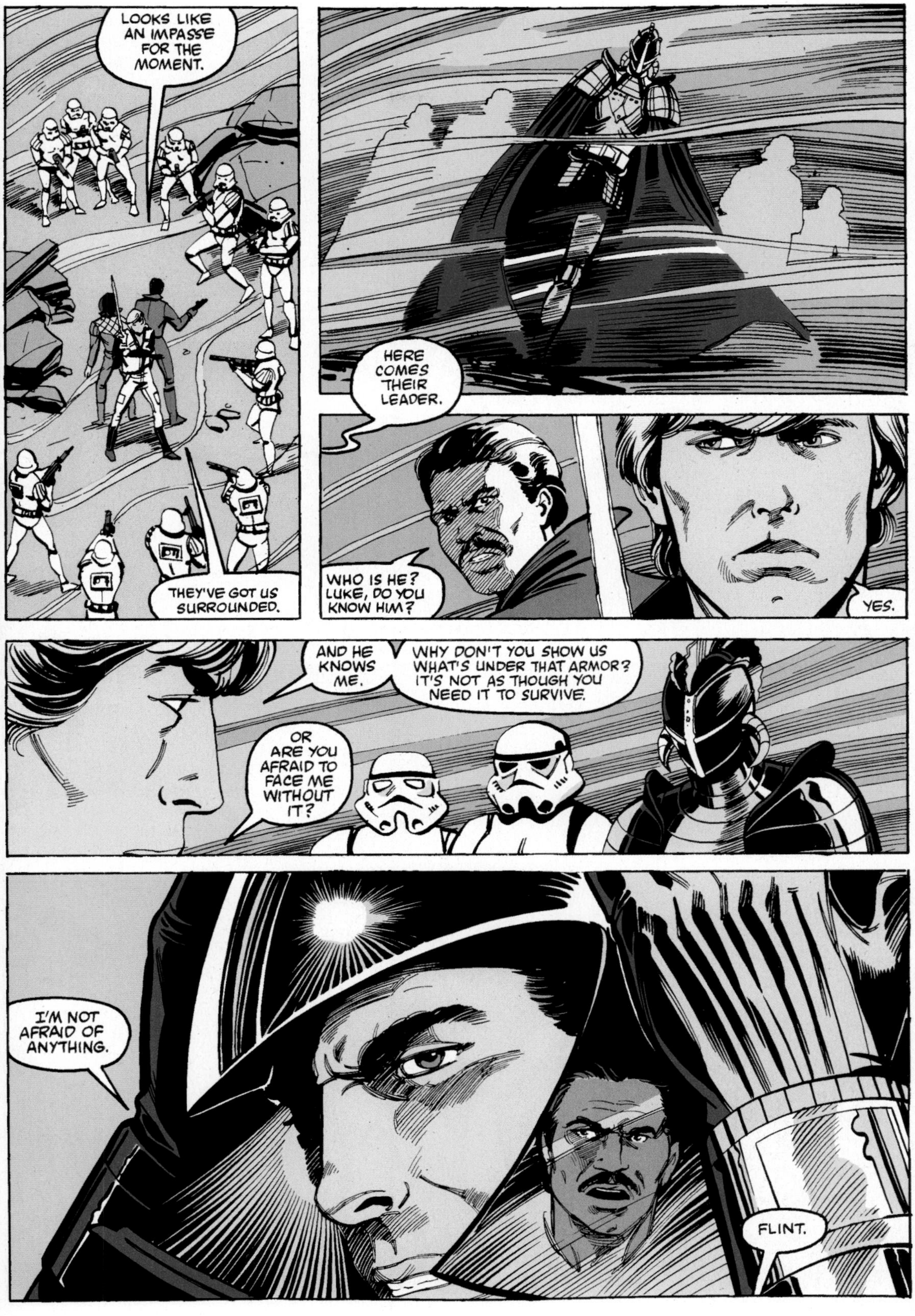
LOOKS LIKE AN IMPASSE FOR THE MOMENT.
THEY'VE GOT US SURROUNDED.
HERE COMES THEIR LEADER.
WHO IS HE? LUKE, DO YOU KNOW HIM?
YES.
AND HE KNOWS ME.
WHY DON'T YOU SHOW US WHAT'S UNDER THAT ARMOR? IT'S NOT AS THOUGH YOU NEED IT TO SURVIVE.
OR ARE YOU AFRAID TO FACE ME WITHOUT IT?
I'M NOT AFRAID OF ANYTHING.
FLINT.

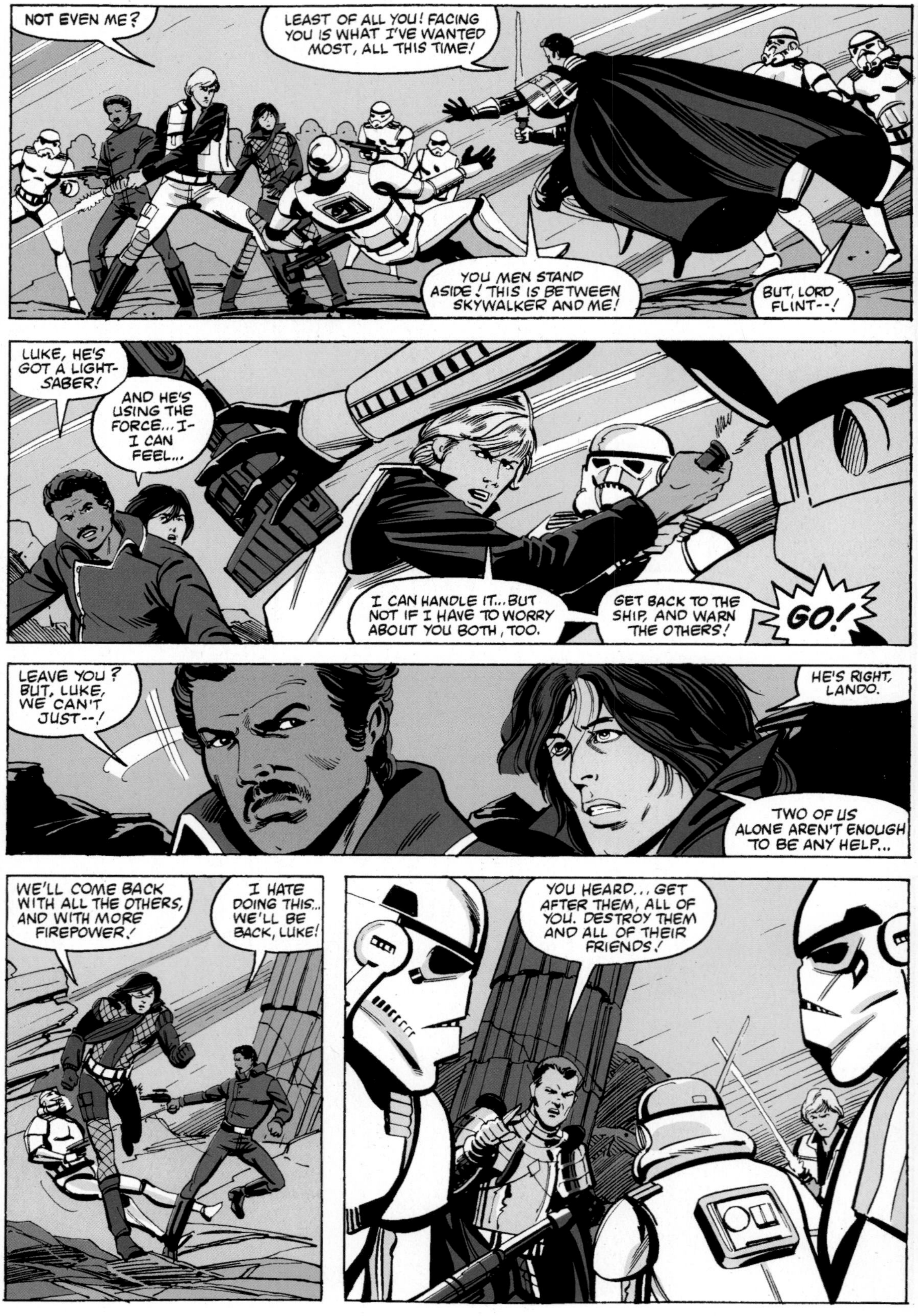
NOT EVEN ME?
LEAST OF ALL YOU! FACING YOU IS WHAT I'VE WANTED MOST, ALL THIS TIME!
YOU MEN STAND ASIDE! THIS IS BETWEEN SKYWALKER AND ME!
BUT, LORD FLINT--!
LUKE, HE'S GOT A LIGHT-SABER!
AND HE'S USING THE FORCE... I-I CAN FEEL...
I CAN HANDLE IT... BUT NOT IF I HAVE TO WORRY ABOUT YOU BOTH, TOO.
GET BACK TO THE SHIP, AND WARN THE OTHERS!
GO!
LEAVE YOU? BUT, LUKE, WE CAN'T JUST--!
HE'S RIGHT, LANDO.
TWO OF US ALONE AREN'T ENOUGH TO BE ANY HELP...
WE'LL COME BACK WITH ALL THE OTHERS, AND WITH MORE FIREPOWER!
I HATE DOING THIS... WE'LL BE BACK, LUKE!
YOU HEARD... GET AFTER THEM, ALL OF YOU. DESTROY THEM AND ALL OF THEIR FRIENDS!

I STILL CAN'T GET OVER HOW FAST YOU LOST THOSE STORM-TROOPERS, DENIN...

THEY'RE JUST INVADERS, LANDO. I GREW UP HERE. IT'S MY WORLD.

HOW MUCH TIME DO YOU THINK YOUR SHORT-CUT BOUGHT US?

NOT ENOUGH...

IT'S US! LET US IN!!

QUICKLY, CLOSE THE DOOR, AND WATCH FOR PURSUIT. THERE'S A BAND OF STORMTROOPERS SEARCHING FOR US!

WE'VE GOT TO GET BACK TO LUKE. WE LEFT HIM ALL ALONE... HE WANTED US TO, BUT WE'VE GOT...

...GOT TO HELP HIM...

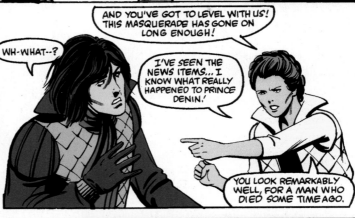

AND YOU'VE GOT TO LEVEL WITH US! THIS MASQUERADE HAS GONE ON LONG ENOUGH!

WH-WHAT--?

I'VE SEEN THE NEWS ITEMS... I KNOW WHAT REALLY HAPPENED TO PRINCE DENIN.'

YOU LOOK REMARKABLY WELL, FOR A MAN WHO DIED SOME TIME AGO.

AND HOW DO I LOOK...FOR A PRINCESS... WHO'S BEEN LIVING HER BROTHER'S LIFE FOR HIM, SINCE HE LOST IT SAVING HERS?

IT WASN'T A MASQUERADE... I DIDN'T DECEIVE YOU FOR FUN... SINCE THE DAY DENIN DIED, I'VE BEEN DENIN.

MY PARENTS HAD TWINS--DENIN, WHO WANTED NOTHING MORE ALL HIS LIFE THAN TO MEET ONE OF THE LEGENDARY TEACHERS AND BECOME A TRUE JEDI KNIGHT--

--AND PRINCESS VILA, WHO DIDN'T KNOW WHAT SHE WANTED, EXCEPT THAT SHE WISHES HER FAMILY, ESPECIALLY HER BROTHER, WERE STILL ALIVE.

LOOK, I'M SURE THIS IS VERY IMPORTANT TO THE BOTH OF YOU, BUT CAN'T IT WAIT?

WE'LL HAVE TIME FOR ALL THE EXPLANATIONS IN THE WORLD, AFTER WE'VE SAVED LUKE.

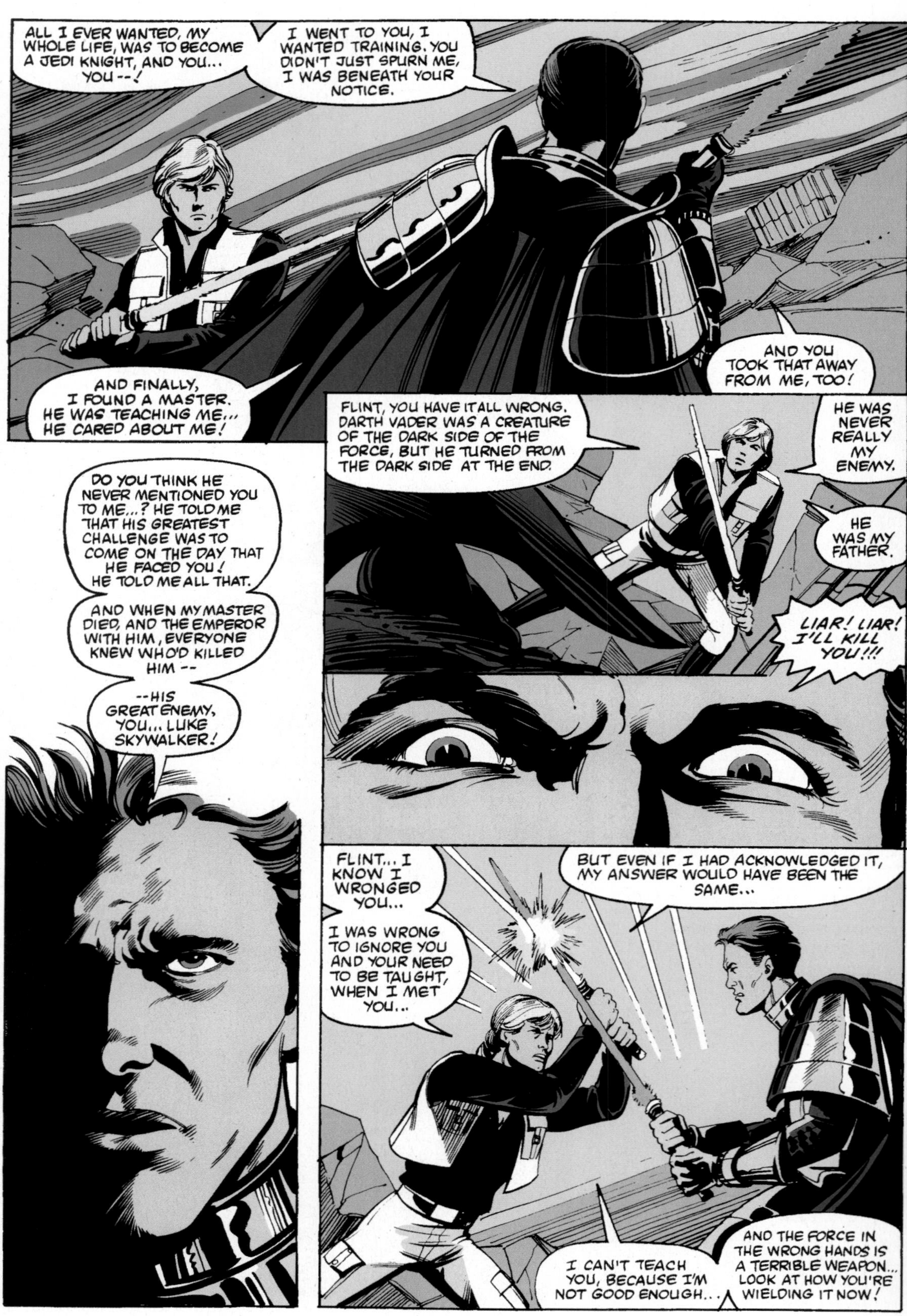

ALL I EVER WANTED, MY WHOLE LIFE, WAS TO BECOME A JEDI KNIGHT, AND YOU... YOU --!
I WENT TO YOU, I WANTED TRAINING. YOU DIDN'T JUST SPURN ME, I WAS BENEATH YOUR NOTICE.
AND FINALLY, I FOUND A MASTER. HE WAS TEACHING ME... HE CARED ABOUT ME!
AND YOU TOOK THAT AWAY FROM ME, TOO!
FLINT, YOU HAVE IT ALL WRONG. DARTH VADER WAS A CREATURE OF THE DARK SIDE OF THE FORCE, BUT HE TURNED FROM THE DARK SIDE AT THE END.
HE WAS NEVER REALLY MY ENEMY.
HE WAS MY FATHER.
LIAR! LIAR! I'LL KILL YOU!!!
DO YOU THINK HE NEVER MENTIONED YOU TO ME...? HE TOLD ME THAT HIS GREATEST CHALLENGE WAS TO COME ON THE DAY THAT HE FACED YOU! HE TOLD ME ALL THAT.
AND WHEN MY MASTER DIED, AND THE EMPEROR WITH HIM, EVERYONE KNEW WHO'D KILLED HIM --
--HIS GREAT ENEMY, YOU... LUKE SKYWALKER!
FLINT... I KNOW I WRONGED YOU...
I WAS WRONG TO IGNORE YOU AND YOUR NEED TO BE TAUGHT, WHEN I MET YOU...
BUT EVEN IF I HAD ACKNOWLEDGED IT, MY ANSWER WOULD HAVE BEEN THE SAME...
I CAN'T TEACH YOU, BECAUSE I'M NOT GOOD ENOUGH...
AND THE FORCE IN THE WRONG HANDS IS A TERRIBLE WEAPON... LOOK AT HOW YOU'RE WIELDING IT NOW!

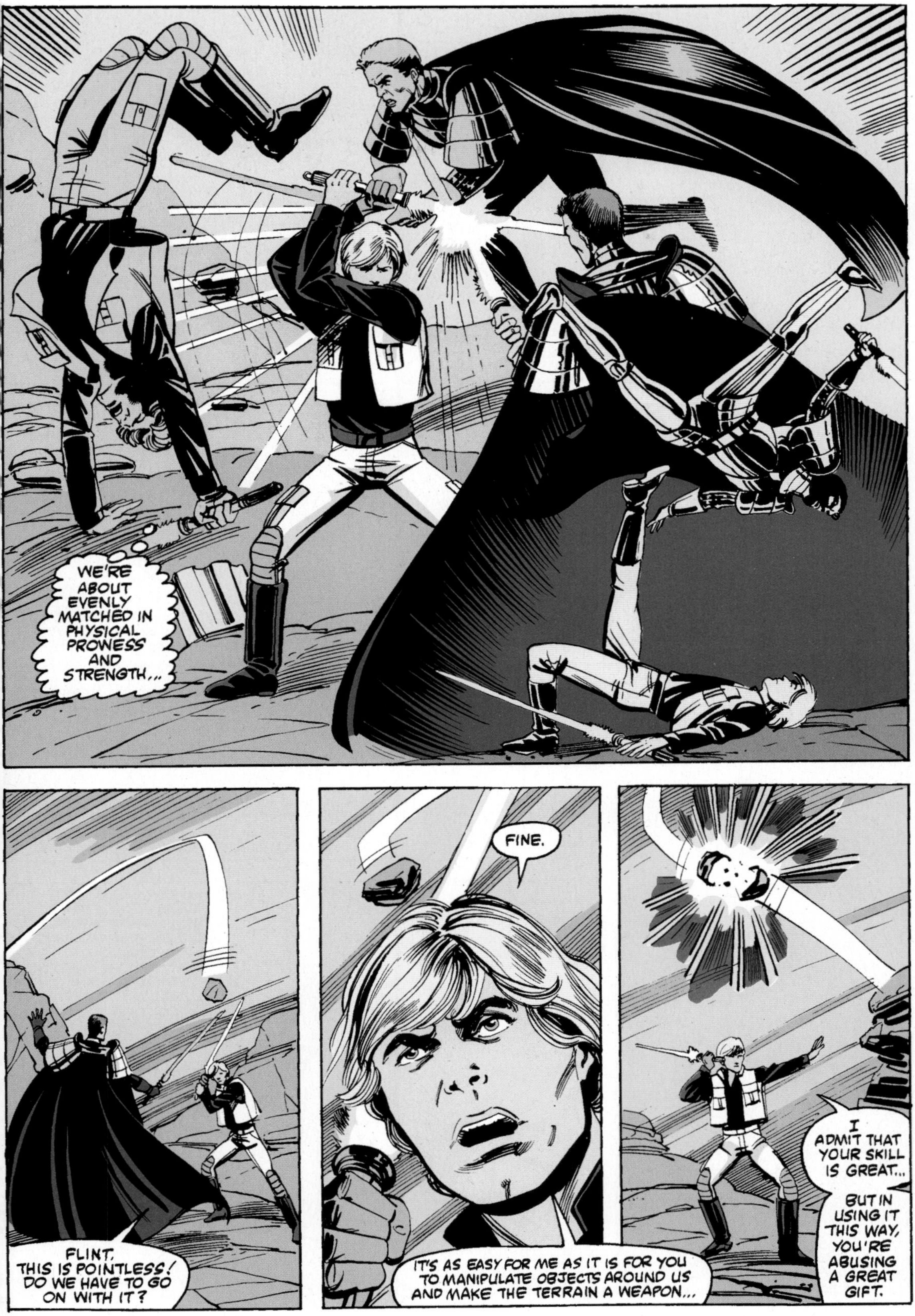
WE'RE ABOUT EVENLY MATCHED IN PHYSICAL PROWESS AND STRENGTH...
FLINT, THIS IS POINTLESS! DO WE HAVE TO GO ON WITH IT?
FINE.
IT'S AS EASY FOR ME AS IT IS FOR YOU TO MANIPULATE OBJECTS AROUND US AND MAKE THE TERRAIN A WEAPON...
I ADMIT THAT YOUR SKILL IS GREAT...
BUT IN USING IT THIS WAY, YOU'RE ABUSING A GREAT GIFT.

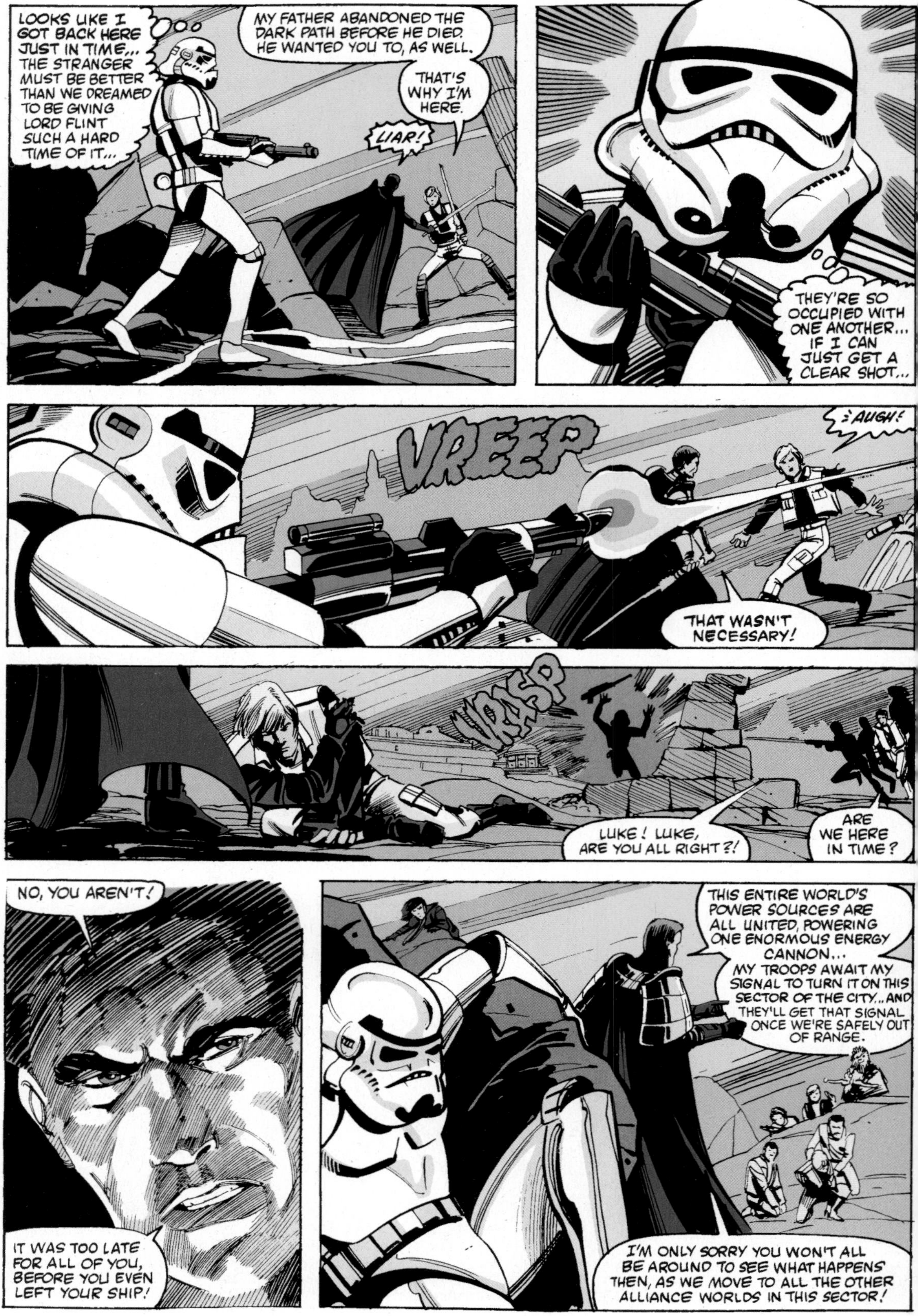

LOOKS LIKE I GOT BACK HERE JUST IN TIME... THE STRANGER MUST BE BETTER THAN WE DREAMED TO BE GIVING LORD FLINT SUCH A HARD TIME OF IT...
MY FATHER ABANDONED THE DARK PATH BEFORE HE DIED. HE WANTED YOU TO, AS WELL.
THAT'S WHY I'M HERE.
LIAR!
THEY'RE SO OCCUPIED WITH ONE ANOTHER... IF I CAN JUST GET A CLEAR SHOT...
VREEP
AUGH!
THAT WASN'T NECESSARY!
VRASP
LUKE! LUKE, ARE YOU ALL RIGHT?!
ARE WE HERE IN TIME?
NO, YOU AREN'T!
IT WAS TOO LATE FOR ALL OF YOU, BEFORE YOU EVEN LEFT YOUR SHIP!
THIS ENTIRE WORLD'S POWER SOURCES ARE ALL UNITED, POWERING ONE ENORMOUS ENERGY CANNON... MY TROOPS AWAIT MY SIGNAL TO TURN IT ON THIS SECTOR OF THE CITY... AND THEY'LL GET THAT SIGNAL ONCE WE'RE SAFELY OUT OF RANGE.
I'M ONLY SORRY YOU WON'T ALL BE AROUND TO SEE WHAT HAPPENS THEN, AS WE MOVE TO ALL THE OTHER ALLIANCE WORLDS IN THIS SECTOR!

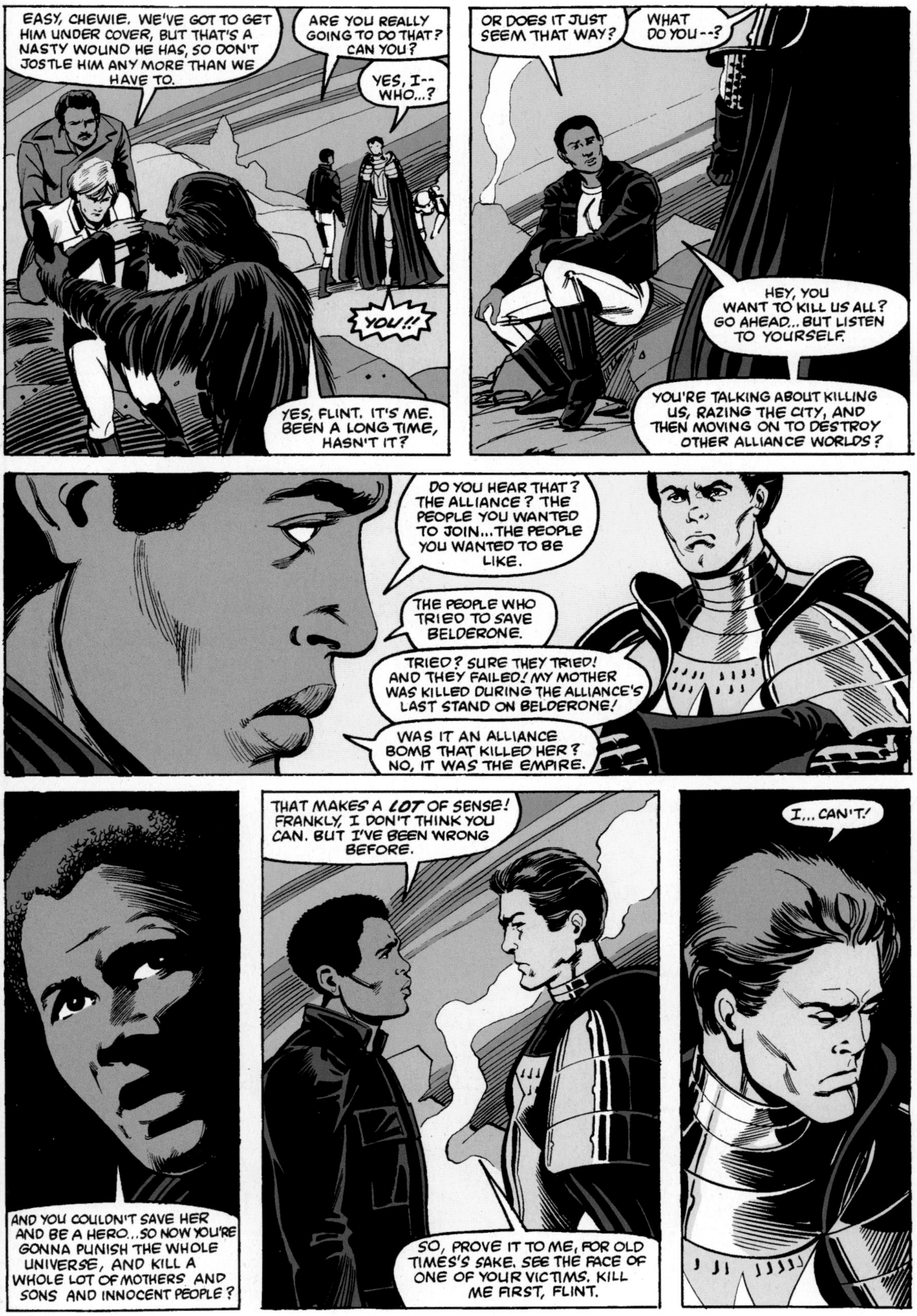

EASY, CHEWIE. WE'VE GOT TO GET HIM UNDER COVER, BUT THAT'S A NASTY WOUND HE HAS, SO DON'T JOSTLE HIM ANY MORE THAN WE HAVE TO.
ARE YOU REALLY GOING TO DO THAT? CAN YOU?
YES, I-- WHO...?
YOU!!
YES, FLINT. IT'S ME. BEEN A LONG TIME, HASN'T IT?
OR DOES IT JUST SEEM THAT WAY?
WHAT DO YOU--?
HEY, YOU WANT TO KILL US ALL? GO AHEAD... BUT LISTEN TO YOURSELF.
YOU'RE TALKING ABOUT KILLING US, RAZING THE CITY, AND THEN MOVING ON TO DESTROY OTHER ALLIANCE WORLDS?
DO YOU HEAR THAT? THE ALLIANCE? THE PEOPLE YOU WANTED TO JOIN... THE PEOPLE YOU WANTED TO BE LIKE.
THE PEOPLE WHO TRIED TO SAVE BELDERONE.
TRIED? SURE THEY TRIED! AND THEY FAILED! MY MOTHER WAS KILLED DURING THE ALLIANCE'S LAST STAND ON BELDERONE!
WAS IT AN ALLIANCE BOMB THAT KILLED HER? NO, IT WAS THE EMPIRE.
AND YOU COULDN'T SAVE HER AND BE A HERO... SO NOW YOU'RE GONNA PUNISH THE WHOLE UNIVERSE, AND KILL A WHOLE LOT OF MOTHERS AND SONS AND INNOCENT PEOPLE?
THAT MAKES A LOT OF SENSE! FRANKLY, I DON'T THINK YOU CAN. BUT I'VE BEEN WRONG BEFORE.
SO, PROVE IT TO ME, FOR OLD TIMES'S SAKE. SEE THE FACE OF ONE OF YOUR VICTIMS. KILL ME FIRST, FLINT.
I... CAN'T!

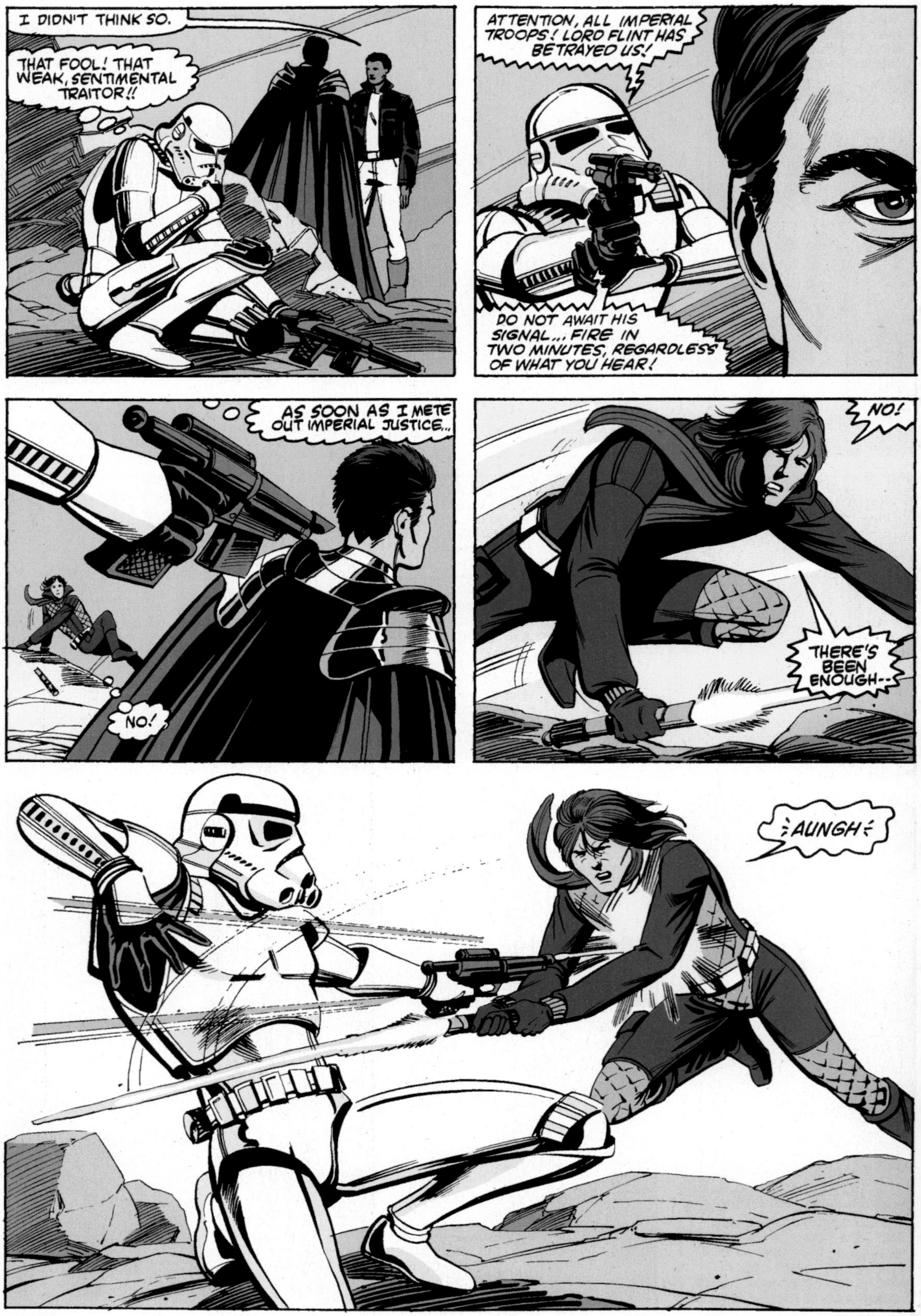
I DIDN'T THINK SO.
THAT FOOL! THAT WEAK, SENTIMENTAL TRAITOR!!
ATTENTION, ALL IMPERIAL TROOPS! LORD FLINT HAS BETRAYED US!
DO NOT AWAIT HIS SIGNAL... FIRE IN TWO MINUTES, REGARDLESS OF WHAT YOU HEAR!
AS SOON AS I METE OUT IMPERIAL JUSTICE...
NO!
NO!
THERE'S BEEN ENOUGH--
AUNGH

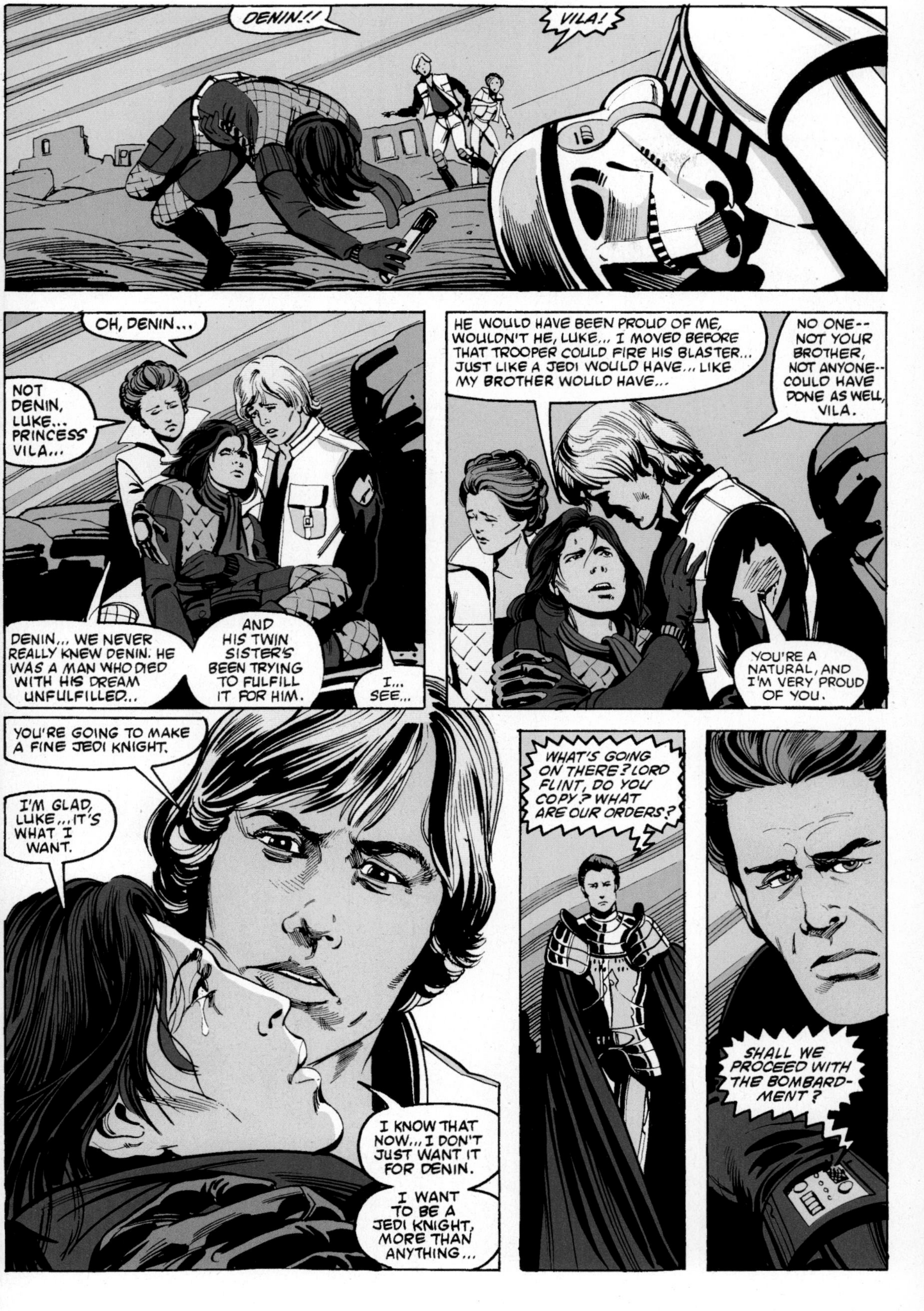
DENIN!!
VILA!
OH, DENIN...
NOT DENIN, LUKE... PRINCESS VILA...
DENIN... WE NEVER REALLY KNEW DENIN. HE WAS A MAN WHO DIED WITH HIS DREAM UNFULFILLED...
AND HIS TWIN SISTER'S BEEN TRYING TO FULFILL IT FOR HIM.
I... SEE...
HE WOULD HAVE BEEN PROUD OF ME, WOULDN'T HE, LUKE... I MOVED BEFORE THAT TROOPER COULD FIRE HIS BLASTER... JUST LIKE A JEDI WOULD HAVE... LIKE MY BROTHER WOULD HAVE...
NO ONE-- NOT YOUR BROTHER, NOT ANYONE-- COULD HAVE DONE AS WELL, VILA.
YOU'RE A NATURAL, AND I'M VERY PROUD OF YOU.
YOU'RE GOING TO MAKE A FINE JEDI KNIGHT.
I'M GLAD, LUKE... IT'S WHAT I WANT.
I KNOW THAT NOW... I DON'T JUST WANT IT FOR DENIN.
I WANT TO BE A JEDI KNIGHT, MORE THAN ANYTHING...
WHAT'S GOING ON THERE? LORD FLINT, DO YOU COPY? WHAT ARE OUR ORDERS?
SHALL WE PROCEED WITH THE BOMBARD- MENT?

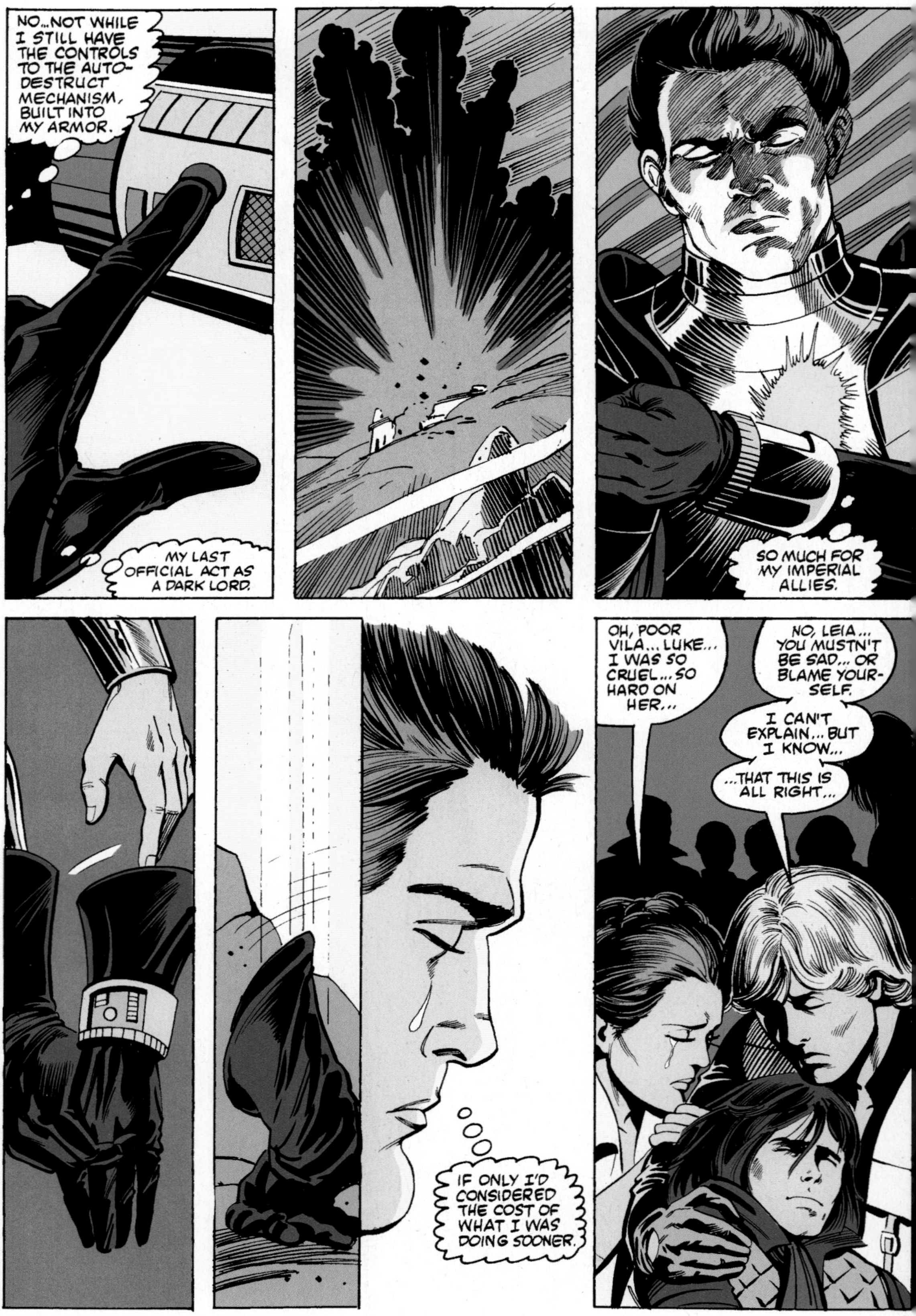
NO...NOT WHILE I STILL HAVE THE CONTROLS TO THE AUTO-DESTRUCT MECHANISM, BUILT INTO MY ARMOR.
MY LAST OFFICIAL ACT AS A DARK LORD.
SO MUCH FOR MY IMPERIAL ALLIES.
IF ONLY I'D CONSIDERED THE COST OF WHAT I WAS DOING SOONER.
OH, POOR VILA... LUKE... I WAS SO CRUEL... SO HARD ON HER...
NO, LEIA... YOU MUSTN'T BE SAD... OR BLAME YOURSELF.
I CAN'T EXPLAIN... BUT I KNOW...
...THAT THIS IS ALL RIGHT...

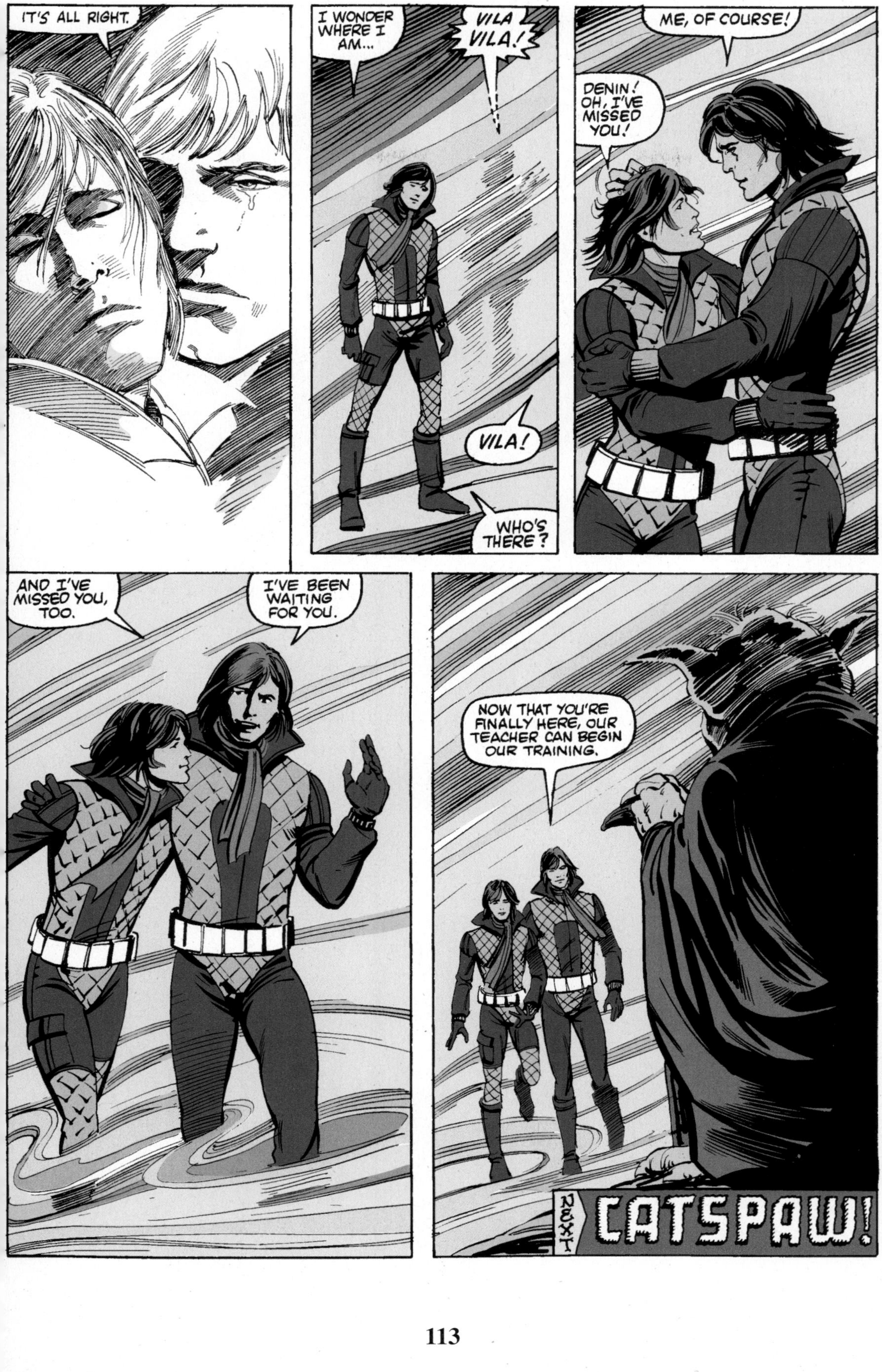
IT'S ALL RIGHT.
I WONDER WHERE I AM...
VILA VILA!
VILA!
WHO'S THERE?
ME, OF COURSE!
DENIN! OH, I'VE MISSED YOU!
AND I'VE MISSED YOU, TOO.
I'VE BEEN WAITING FOR YOU.
NOW THAT YOU'RE FINALLY HERE, OUR TEACHER CAN BEGIN OUR TRAINING.
NEXT CATSPAW!

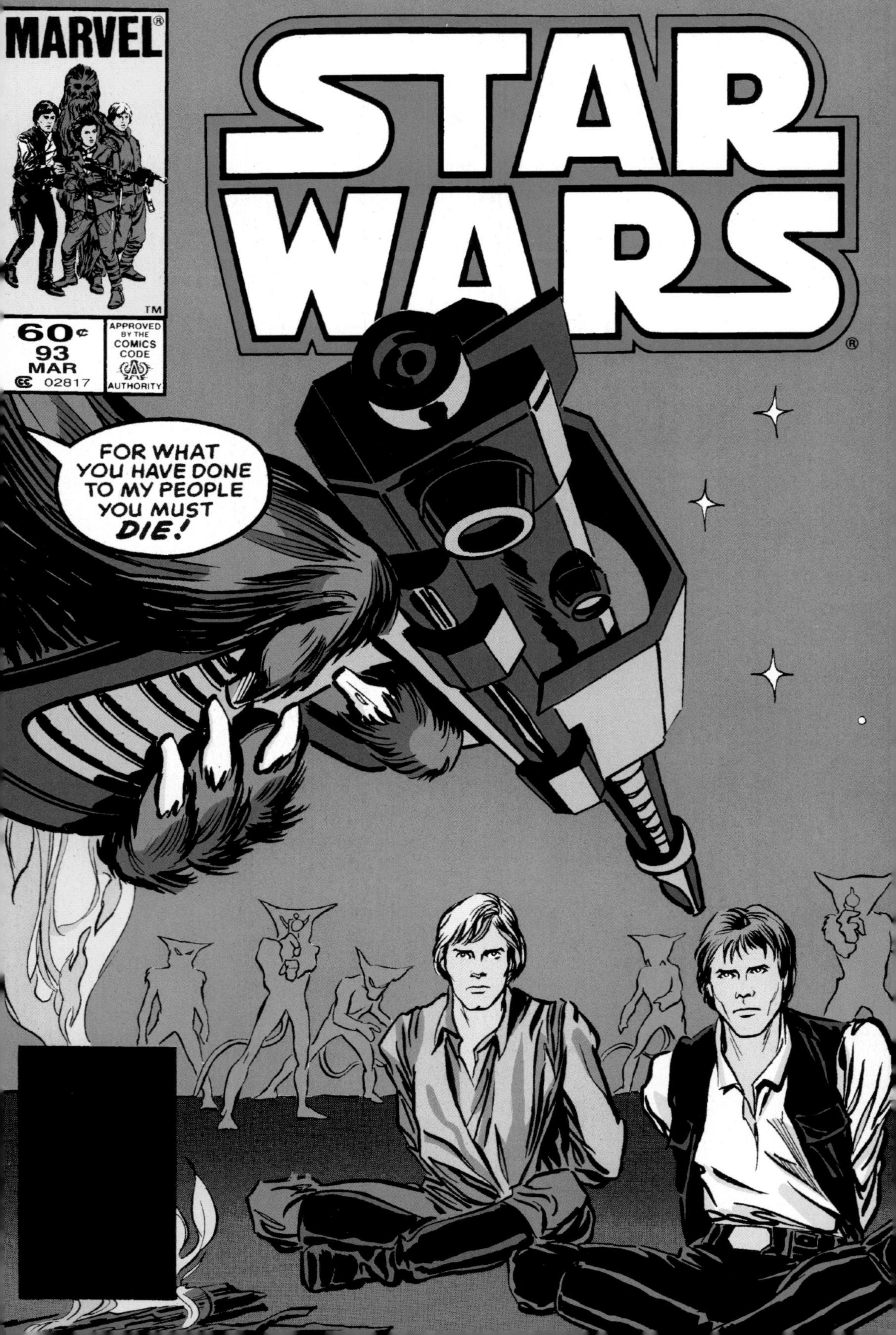
MARVEL®
STAR WARS®
TM
60¢
93
MAR
02817
APPROVED BY THE COMICS CODE AUTHORITY
FOR WHAT YOU HAVE DONE TO MY PEOPLE YOU MUST *DIE!*

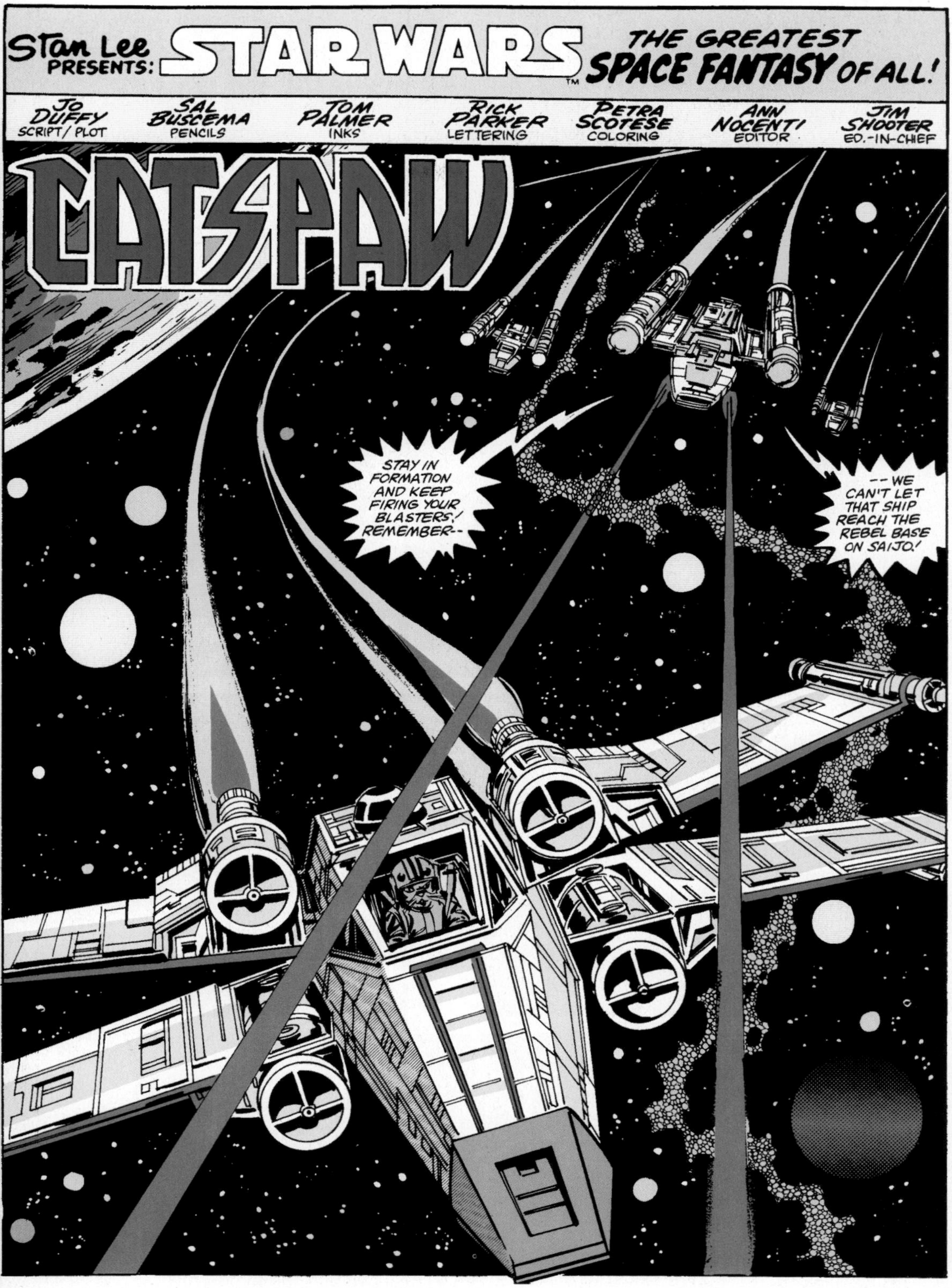
Stan Lee PRESENTS: STAR WARS THE GREATEST SPACE FANTASY OF ALL!
JO DUFFY SCRIPT/ PLOT
SAL BUSCEMA PENCILS
TOM PALMER INKS
RICK PARKER LETTERING
PETRA SCOTESE COLORING
ANN NOCENTI EDITOR
JIM SHOOTER ED.-IN-CHIEF
CATSPAW
STAY IN FORMATION AND KEEP FIRING YOUR BLASTERS! REMEMBER--
--WE CAN'T LET THAT SHIP REACH THE REBEL BASE ON SAIJO!

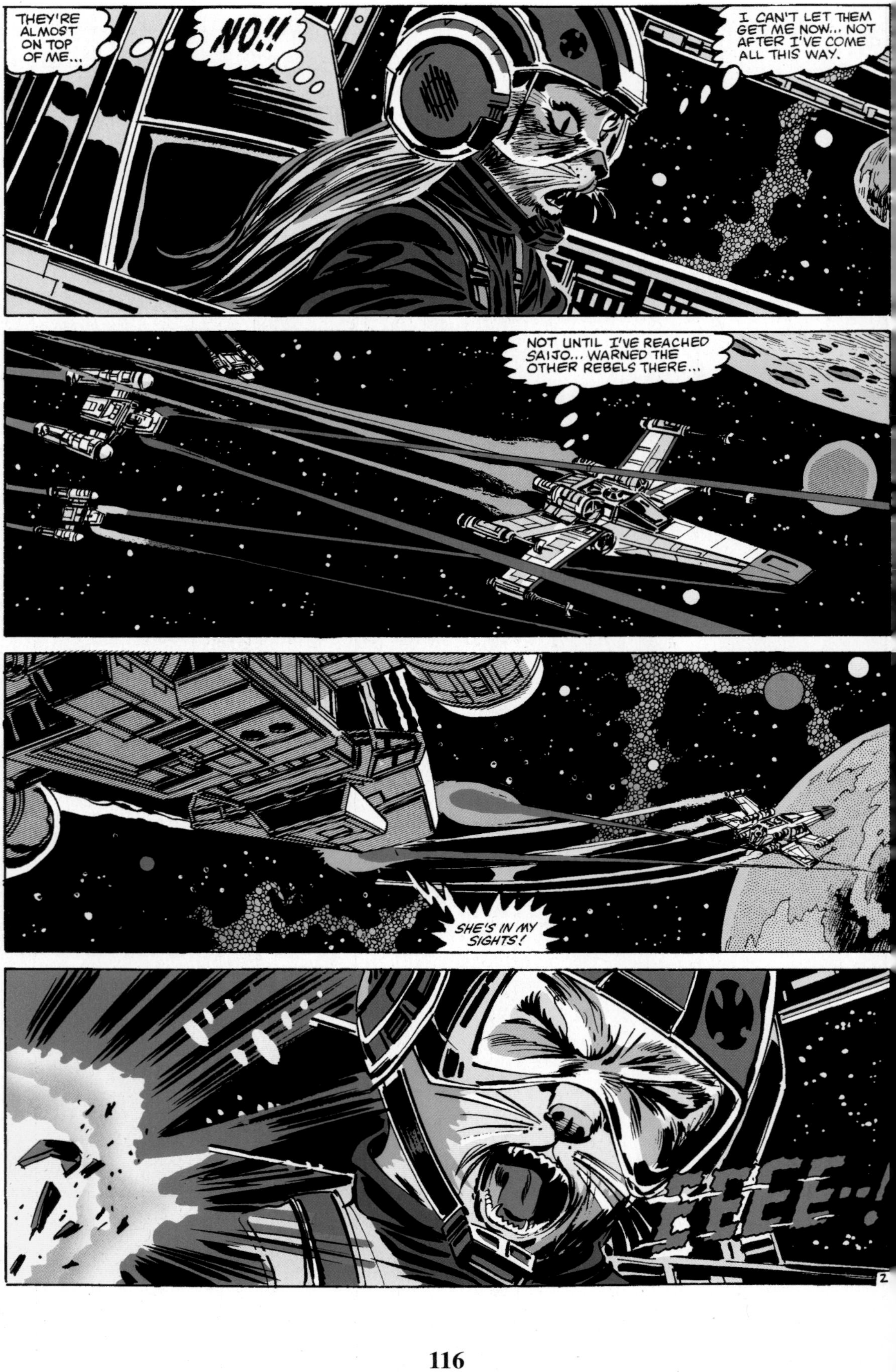
THEY'RE ALMOST ON TOP OF ME...
NO!!
I CAN'T LET THEM GET ME NOW... NOT AFTER I'VE COME ALL THIS WAY.
NOT UNTIL I'VE REACHED SAIJO... WARNED THE OTHER REBELS THERE...
SHE'S IN MY SIGHTS!
EEEE..!
2

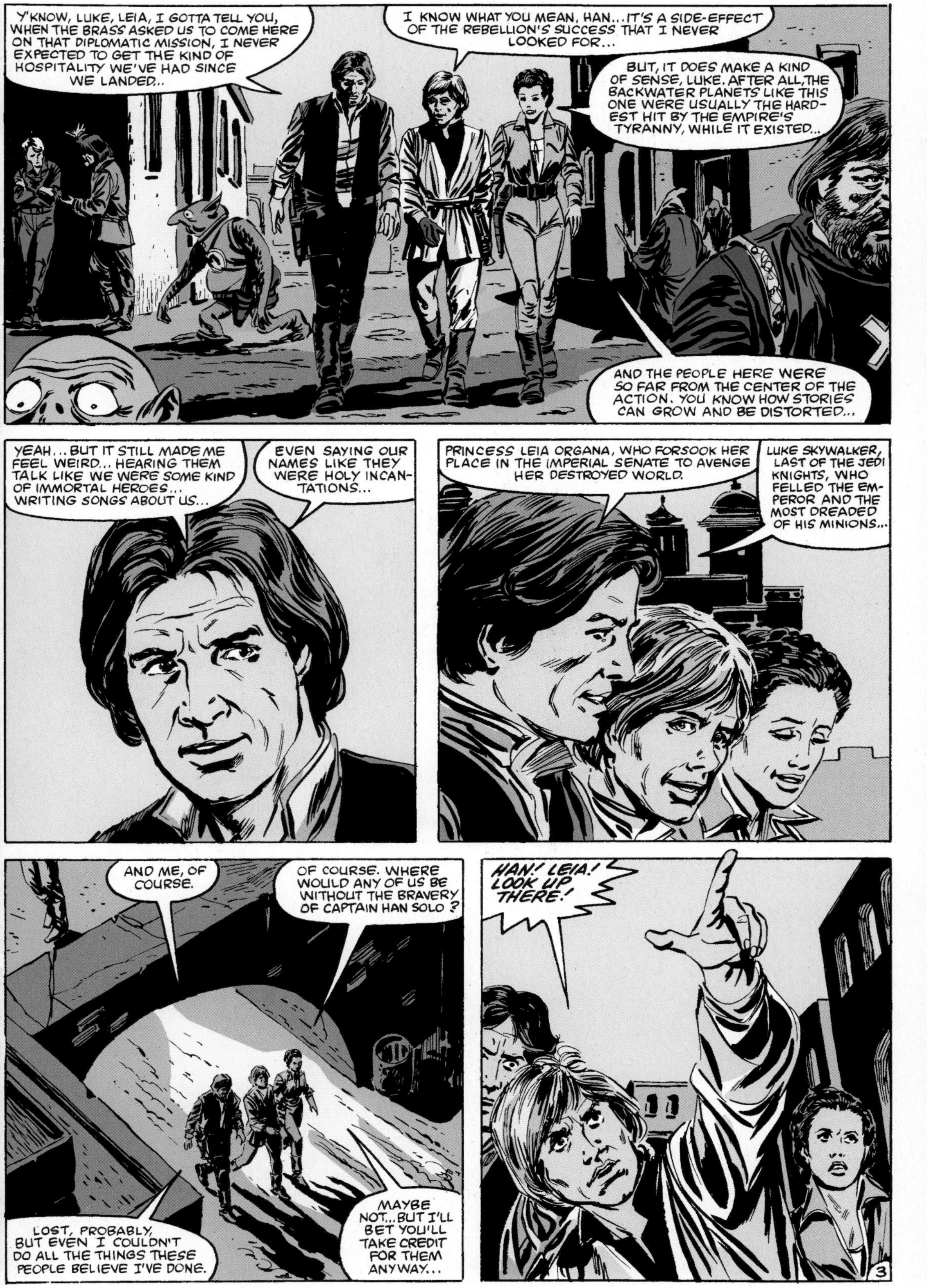
Y'KNOW, LUKE, LEIA, I GOTTA TELL YOU, WHEN THE BRASS ASKED US TO COME HERE ON THAT DIPLOMATIC MISSION, I NEVER EXPECTED TO GET THE KIND OF HOSPITALITY WE'VE HAD SINCE WE LANDED...
I KNOW WHAT YOU MEAN, HAN... IT'S A SIDE-EFFECT OF THE REBELLION'S SUCCESS THAT I NEVER LOOKED FOR...
BUT, IT DOES MAKE A KIND OF SENSE, LUKE. AFTER ALL, THE BACKWATER PLANETS LIKE THIS ONE WERE USUALLY THE HARDEST HIT BY THE EMPIRE'S TYRANNY, WHILE IT EXISTED...
AND THE PEOPLE HERE WERE SO FAR FROM THE CENTER OF THE ACTION. YOU KNOW HOW STORIES CAN GROW AND BE DISTORTED...
YEAH... BUT IT STILL MADE ME FEEL WEIRD... HEARING THEM TALK LIKE WE WERE SOME KIND OF IMMORTAL HEROES... WRITING SONGS ABOUT US...
EVEN SAYING OUR NAMES LIKE THEY WERE HOLY INCANTATIONS...
PRINCESS LEIA ORGANA, WHO FORSOOK HER PLACE IN THE IMPERIAL SENATE TO AVENGE HER DESTROYED WORLD.
LUKE SKYWALKER, LAST OF THE JEDI KNIGHTS, WHO FELLED THE EMPEROR AND THE MOST DREADED OF HIS MINIONS...
AND ME, OF COURSE.
OF COURSE. WHERE WOULD ANY OF US BE WITHOUT THE BRAVERY OF CAPTAIN HAN SOLO?
LOST, PROBABLY, BUT EVEN I COULDN'T DO ALL THE THINGS THESE PEOPLE BELIEVE I'VE DONE.
MAYBE NOT... BUT I'LL BET YOU'LL TAKE CREDIT FOR THEM ANYWAY...
HAN! LEIA! LOOK UP THERE!
3

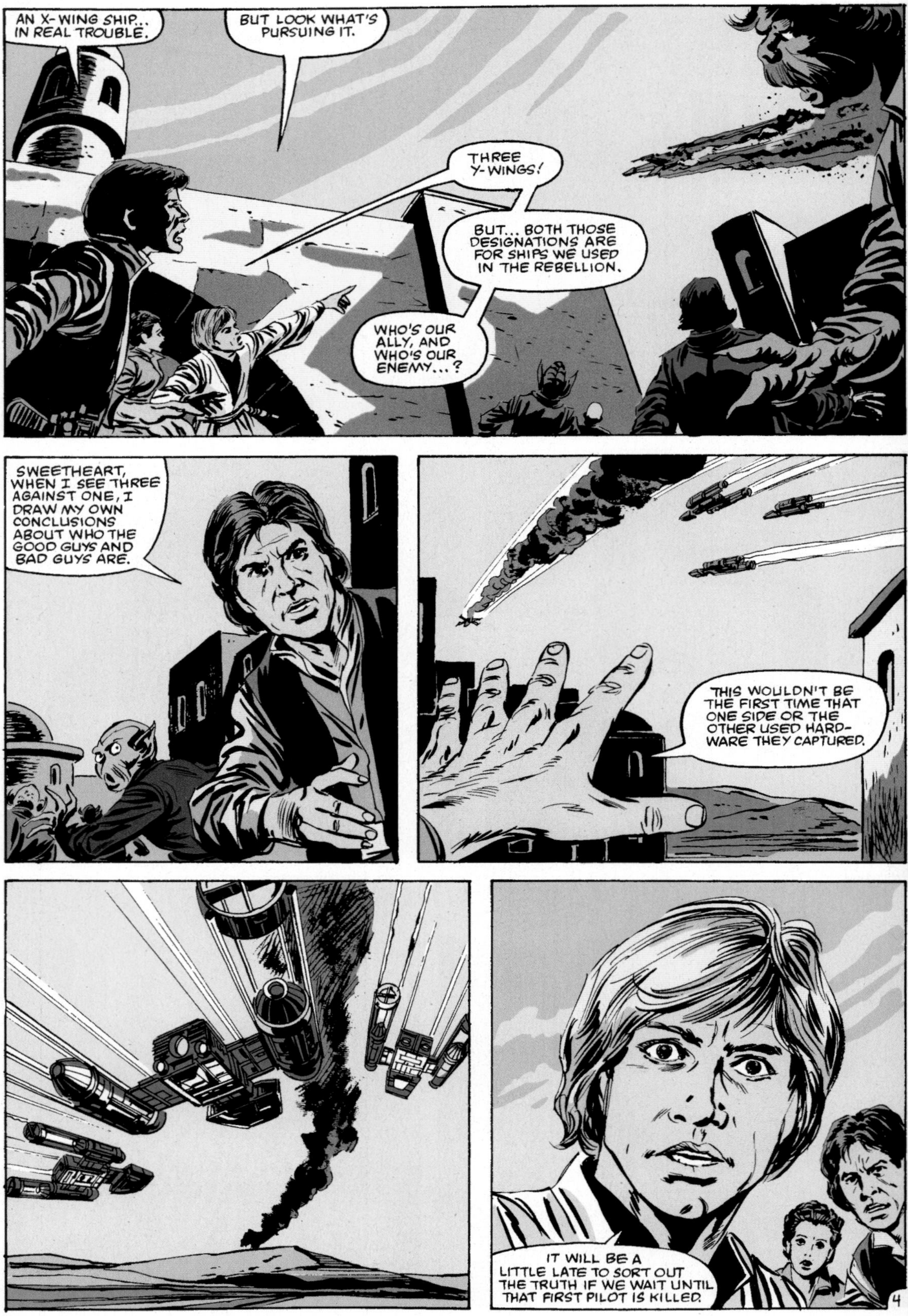
AN X-WING SHIP... IN REAL TROUBLE.
BUT LOOK WHAT'S PURSUING IT.
THREE Y-WINGS!
BUT... BOTH THOSE DESIGNATIONS ARE FOR SHIPS WE USED IN THE REBELLION.
WHO'S OUR ALLY, AND WHO'S OUR ENEMY...?
SWEETHEART, WHEN I SEE THREE AGAINST ONE, I DRAW MY OWN CONCLUSIONS ABOUT WHO THE GOOD GUYS AND BAD GUYS ARE.
THIS WOULDN'T BE THE FIRST TIME THAT ONE SIDE OR THE OTHER USED HARD-WARE THEY CAPTURED.
IT WILL BE A LITTLE LATE TO SORT OUT THE TRUTH IF WE WAIT UNTIL THAT FIRST PILOT IS KILLED.
4

RIGHT. LET'S GET TO THE MILLENNIUM FALCON. YOU TWO STRAP INTO THE GUN TURRETS. I'LL TAKE THE CONTROLS.

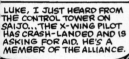

LUKE, I JUST HEARD FROM THE CONTROL TOWER ON SAIJO... THE X-WING PILOT HAS CRASH-LANDED AND IS ASKING FOR AID. HE'S A MEMBER OF THE ALLIANCE.

AND THE OTHER THREE SHIPS AREN'T ANSWERING ANY HAILS...

THAT'S OKAY, HAN. WE KNOW NOW WHAT WE HAVE TO DO.

READY, LEIA?

WHENEVER YOU ARE, LUKE.

THEN LET'S DO IT!

5

119

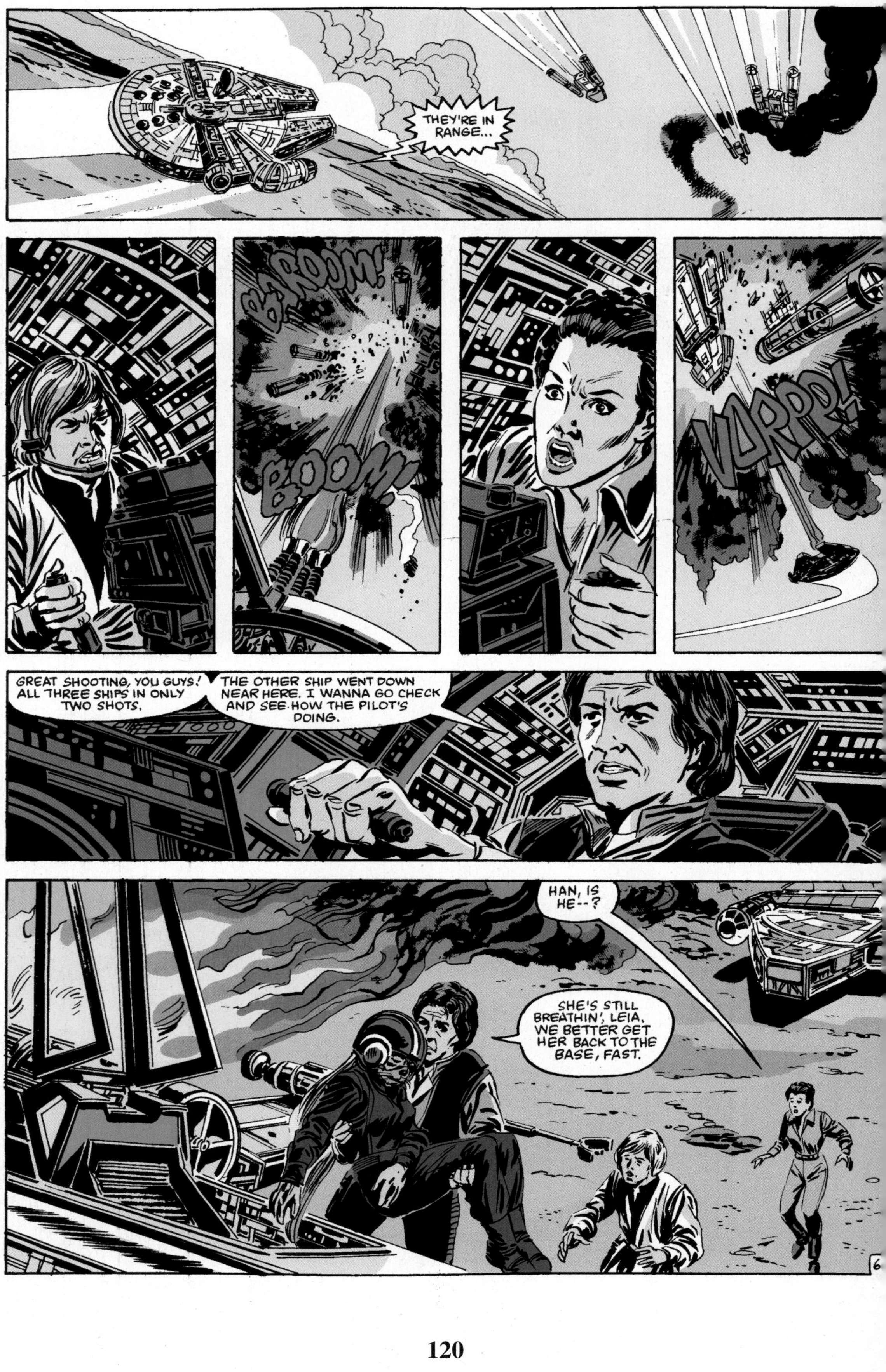
THEY'RE IN RANGE...
BA-ROOM!
BOOM!
VARRR!
GREAT SHOOTING, YOU GUYS! ALL THREE SHIPS IN ONLY TWO SHOTS.
THE OTHER SHIP WENT DOWN NEAR HERE. I WANNA GO CHECK AND SEE HOW THE PILOT'S DOING.
HAN, IS HE--?
SHE'S STILL BREATHIN', LEIA. WE BETTER GET HER BACK TO THE BASE, FAST.
6

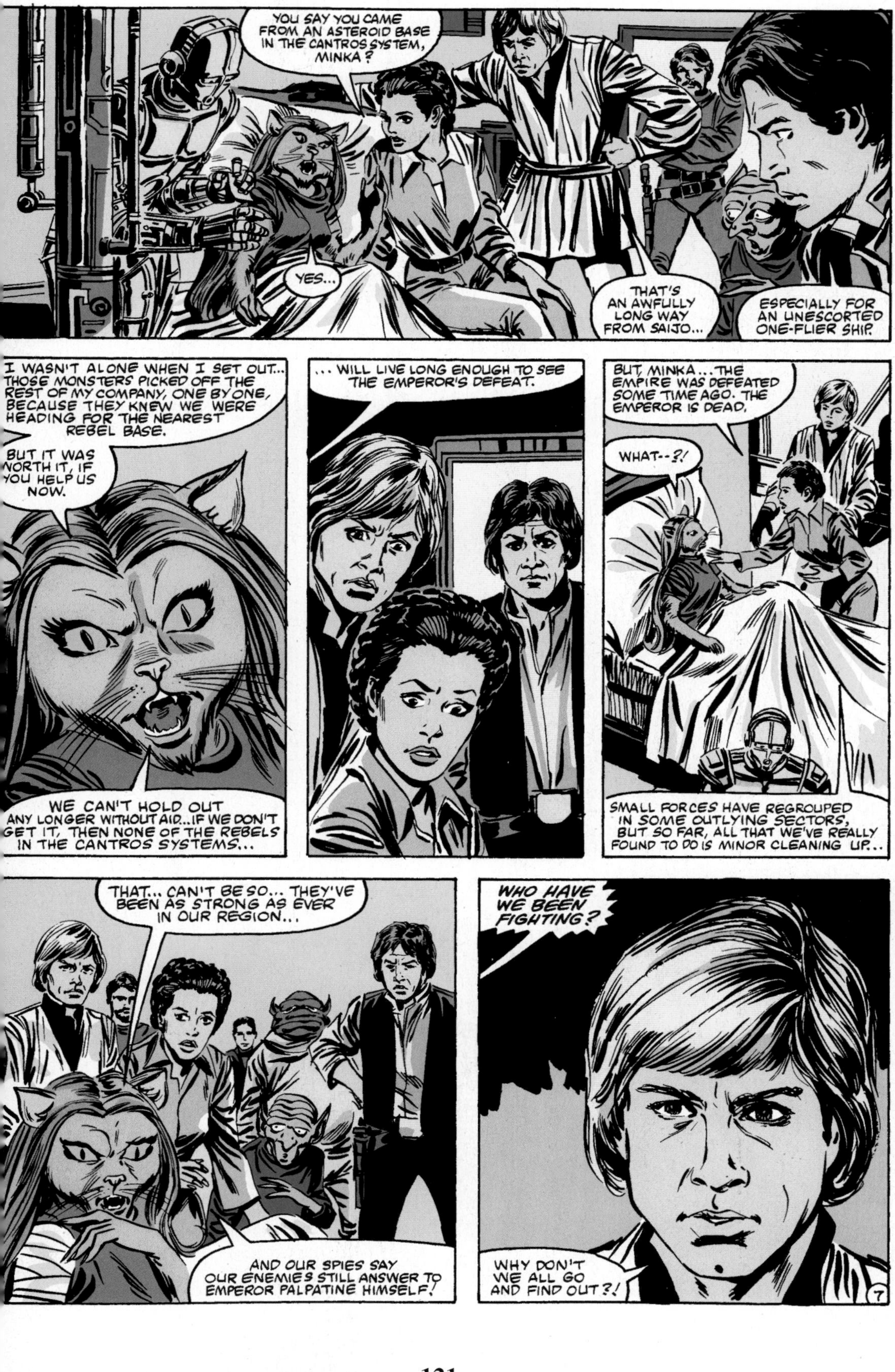
YOU SAY YOU CAME FROM AN ASTEROID BASE IN THE CANTROS SYSTEM, MINKA?
YES...
THAT'S AN AWFULLY LONG WAY FROM SAIJO...
ESPECIALLY FOR AN UNESCORTED ONE-FLIER SHIP.
I WASN'T ALONE WHEN I SET OUT... THOSE MONSTERS PICKED OFF THE REST OF MY COMPANY, ONE BY ONE, BECAUSE THEY KNEW WE WERE HEADING FOR THE NEAREST REBEL BASE.
BUT IT WAS NORTH IT, IF YOU HELP US NOW.
WE CAN'T HOLD OUT ANY LONGER WITHOUT AID...IF WE DON'T GET IT, THEN NONE OF THE REBELS IN THE CANTROS SYSTEMS...
... WILL LIVE LONG ENOUGH TO SEE THE EMPEROR'S DEFEAT.
BUT, MINKA... THE EMPIRE WAS DEFEATED SOME TIME AGO. THE EMPEROR IS DEAD.
WHAT--?!
SMALL FORCES HAVE REGROUPED IN SOME OUTLYING SECTORS, BUT SO FAR, ALL THAT WE'VE REALLY FOUND TO DO IS MINOR CLEANING UP...
THAT... CAN'T BE SO... THEY'VE BEEN AS STRONG AS EVER IN OUR REGION...
AND OUR SPIES SAY OUR ENEMIES STILL ANSWER TO EMPEROR PALPATINE HIMSELF!
WHO HAVE WE BEEN FIGHTING?
WHY DON'T WE ALL GO AND FIND OUT?!
7

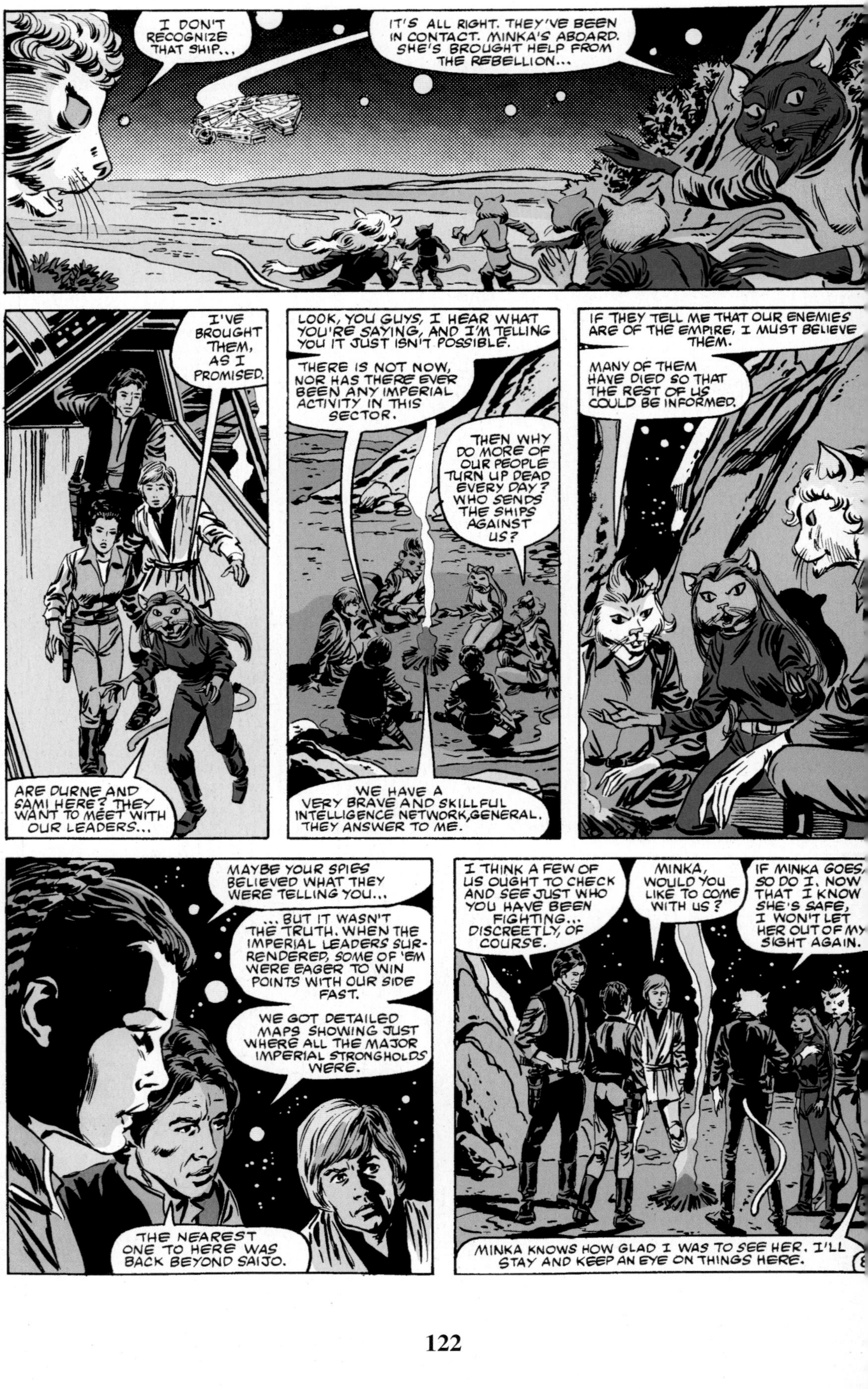
I DON'T RECOGNIZE THAT SHIP...
IT'S ALL RIGHT. THEY'VE BEEN IN CONTACT. MINKA'S ABOARD. SHE'S BROUGHT HELP FROM THE REBELLION...
I'VE BROUGHT THEM, AS I PROMISED.
ARE DURNE AND SAMI HERE? THEY WANT TO MEET WITH OUR LEADERS...
LOOK, YOU GUYS, I HEAR WHAT YOU'RE SAYING, AND I'M TELLING YOU IT JUST ISN'T POSSIBLE.
THERE IS NOT NOW, NOR HAS THERE EVER BEEN ANY IMPERIAL ACTIVITY IN THIS SECTOR.
THEN WHY DO MORE OF OUR PEOPLE TURN UP DEAD EVERY DAY? WHO SENDS THE SHIPS AGAINST US?
WE HAVE A VERY BRAVE AND SKILLFUL INTELLIGENCE NETWORK, GENERAL. THEY ANSWER TO ME.
IF THEY TELL ME THAT OUR ENEMIES ARE OF THE EMPIRE, I MUST BELIEVE THEM.
MANY OF THEM HAVE DIED SO THAT THE REST OF US COULD BE INFORMED.
MAYBE YOUR SPIES BELIEVED WHAT THEY WERE TELLING YOU...
... BUT IT WASN'T THE TRUTH. WHEN THE IMPERIAL LEADERS SURRENDERED, SOME OF 'EM WERE EAGER TO WIN POINTS WITH OUR SIDE FAST.
WE GOT DETAILED MAPS SHOWING JUST WHERE ALL THE MAJOR IMPERIAL STRONGHOLDS WERE.
THE NEAREST ONE TO HERE WAS BACK BEYOND SAIJO.
I THINK A FEW OF US OUGHT TO CHECK AND SEE JUST WHO YOU HAVE BEEN FIGHTING... DISCREETLY, OF COURSE.
MINKA, WOULD YOU LIKE TO COME WITH US?
IF MINKA GOES, SO DO I. NOW THAT I KNOW SHE'S SAFE, I WON'T LET HER OUT OF MY SIGHT AGAIN.
MINKA KNOWS HOW GLAD I WAS TO SEE HER. I'LL STAY AND KEEP AN EYE ON THINGS HERE.

THE THREE OF YOU SEEM TO KNOW SO MUCH ABOUT HOW THE FINAL BATTLES WITH THE EMPIRE WENT...

WERE YOU STATIONED VERY CLOSE TO THE HEART OF THE ACTION?

YOU COULD SAY WE *WERE* THE ACTION, SAMI.

AS A MATTER OF FACT, THE THREE OF US ARE THE ONES WHO--!

WE'RE THE ONES WHO THE LEADERS SEND OUT...

...WHEN IMPORTANT MEMBERS OF THE REBELLION ARE ELSEWHERE.

YOU KNOW SOME OF THE IMPORTANT MEMBERS OF THE REBELLION? THE HEROES? WE'VE HEARD TALES OF HOW THE EARLIER, DECISIVE BATTLES WERE WON, AND--!

SAMI, EVERYONE WHO'S WILLING TO RISK HIS LIFE FOR FREEDOM IS A HERO, NO MATTER WHO GETS TALKED ABOUT!

LUKE, WE'RE COMING IN ON THAT SO-CALLED IMPERIAL BASE NOW, AND IT LOOKS LIKE THEY WERE EXPECTING US...

BLAST!! WHOEVER THEY ARE, THEY AREN'T FRIENDLY!

HAN, PRETEND THAT THEY'VE HIT US... MAKE IT LOOK LIKE WE'RE CRASH-LANDING.

THAT SHOULDN'T BE TOO HARD, KID.

THEY *HAVE* HIT US!

9

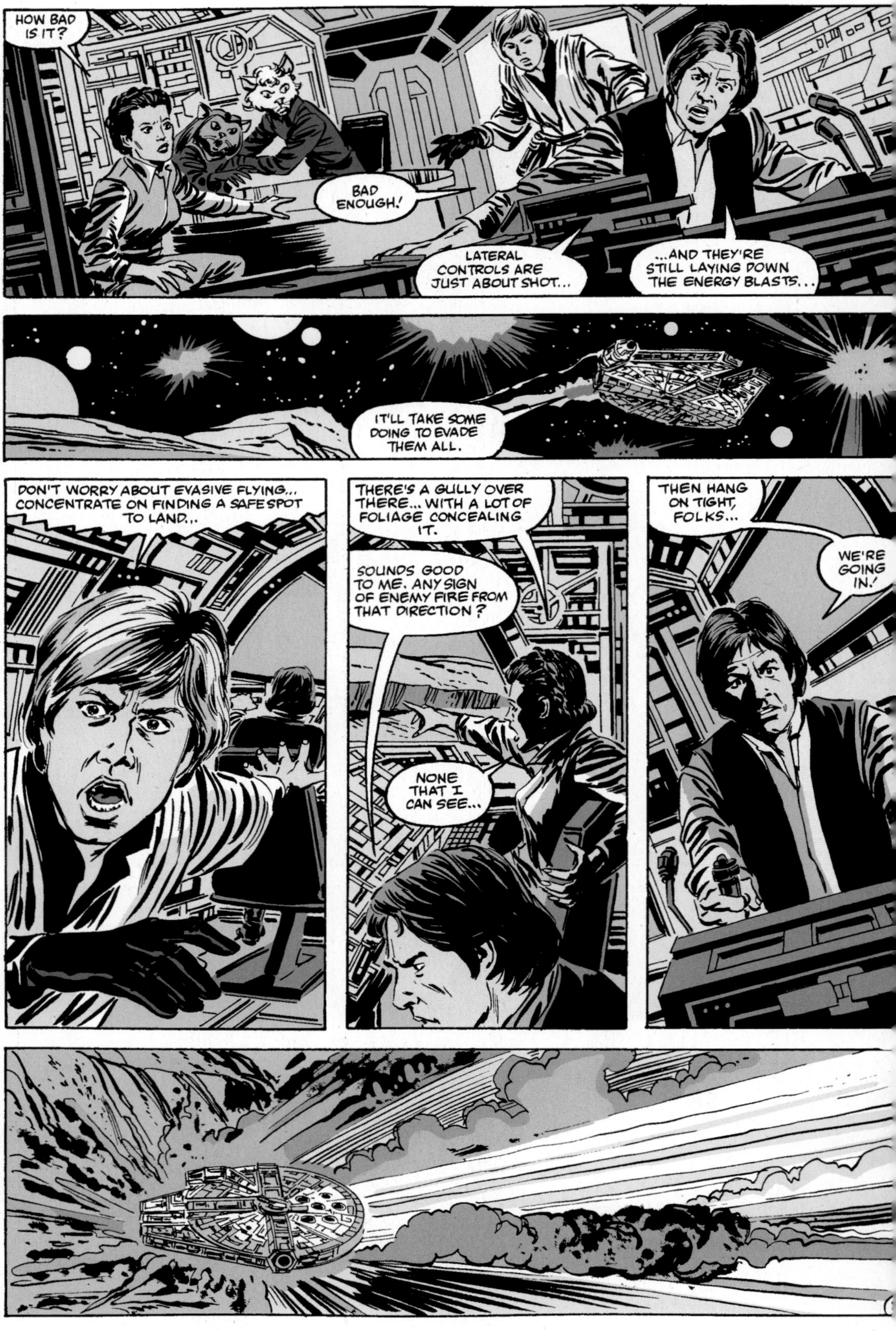
HOW BAD IS IT?
BAD ENOUGH!
LATERAL CONTROLS ARE JUST ABOUT SHOT...
...AND THEY'RE STILL LAYING DOWN THE ENERGY BLASTS...
IT'LL TAKE SOME DOING TO EVADE THEM ALL.
DON'T WORRY ABOUT EVASIVE FLYING... CONCENTRATE ON FINDING A SAFE SPOT TO LAND...
THERE'S A GULLY OVER THERE... WITH A LOT OF FOLIAGE CONCEALING IT.
SOUNDS GOOD TO ME. ANY SIGN OF ENEMY FIRE FROM THAT DIRECTION?
NONE THAT I CAN SEE...
THEN HANG ON TIGHT, FOLKS...
WE'RE GOING IN!

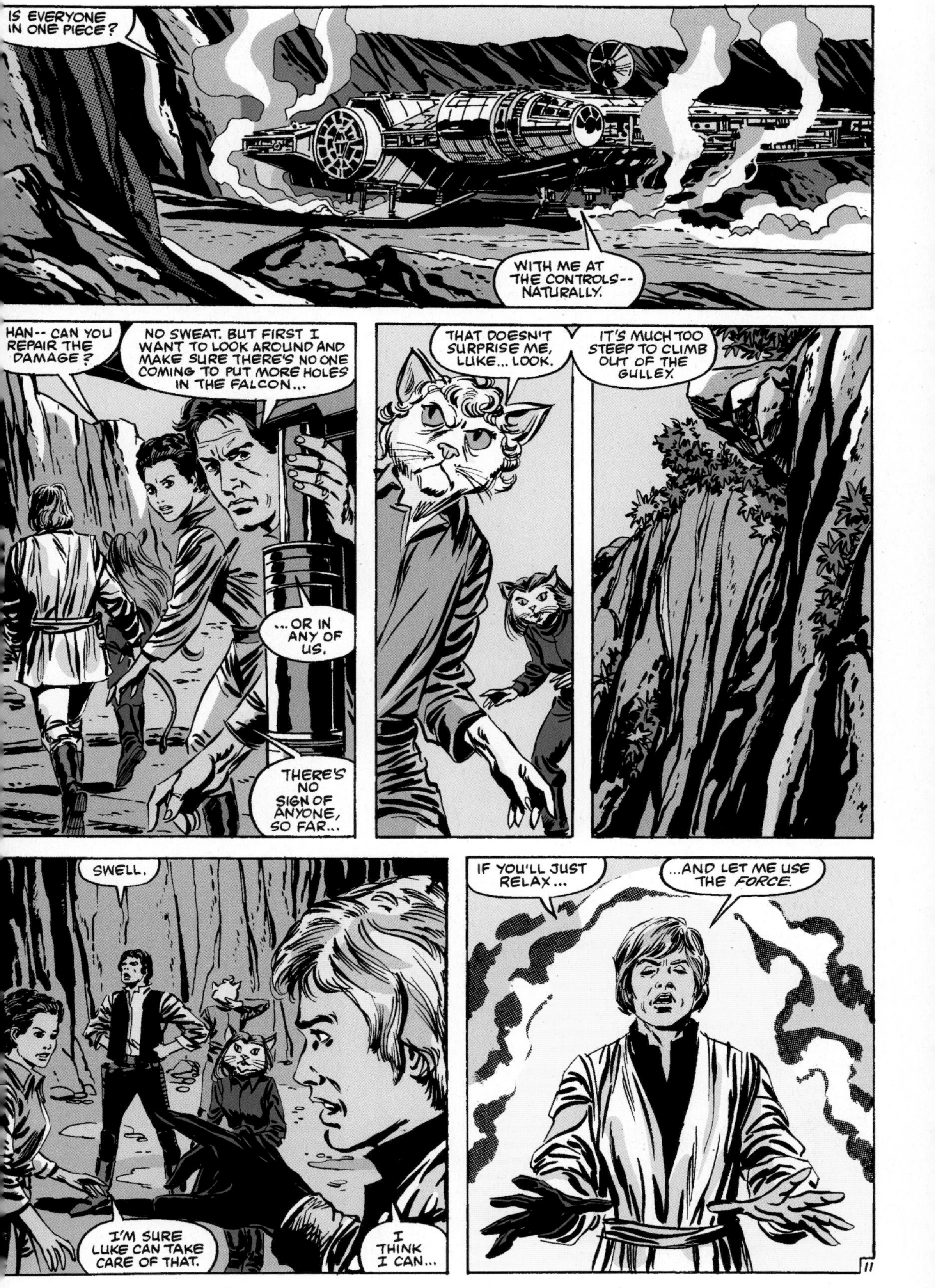

IS EVERYONE IN ONE PIECE?
WITH ME AT THE CONTROLS-- NATURALLY.
HAN-- CAN YOU REPAIR THE DAMAGE?
NO SWEAT. BUT FIRST I WANT TO LOOK AROUND AND MAKE SURE THERE'S NO ONE COMING TO PUT MORE HOLES IN THE FALCON...
...OR IN ANY OF US.
THERE'S NO SIGN OF ANYONE, SO FAR...
THAT DOESN'T SURPRISE ME, LUKE... LOOK.
IT'S MUCH TOO STEEP TO CLIMB OUT OF THE GULLEY.
SWELL.
I'M SURE LUKE CAN TAKE CARE OF THAT.
I THINK I CAN...
IF YOU'LL JUST RELAX...
...AND LET ME USE THE *FORCE*.
11

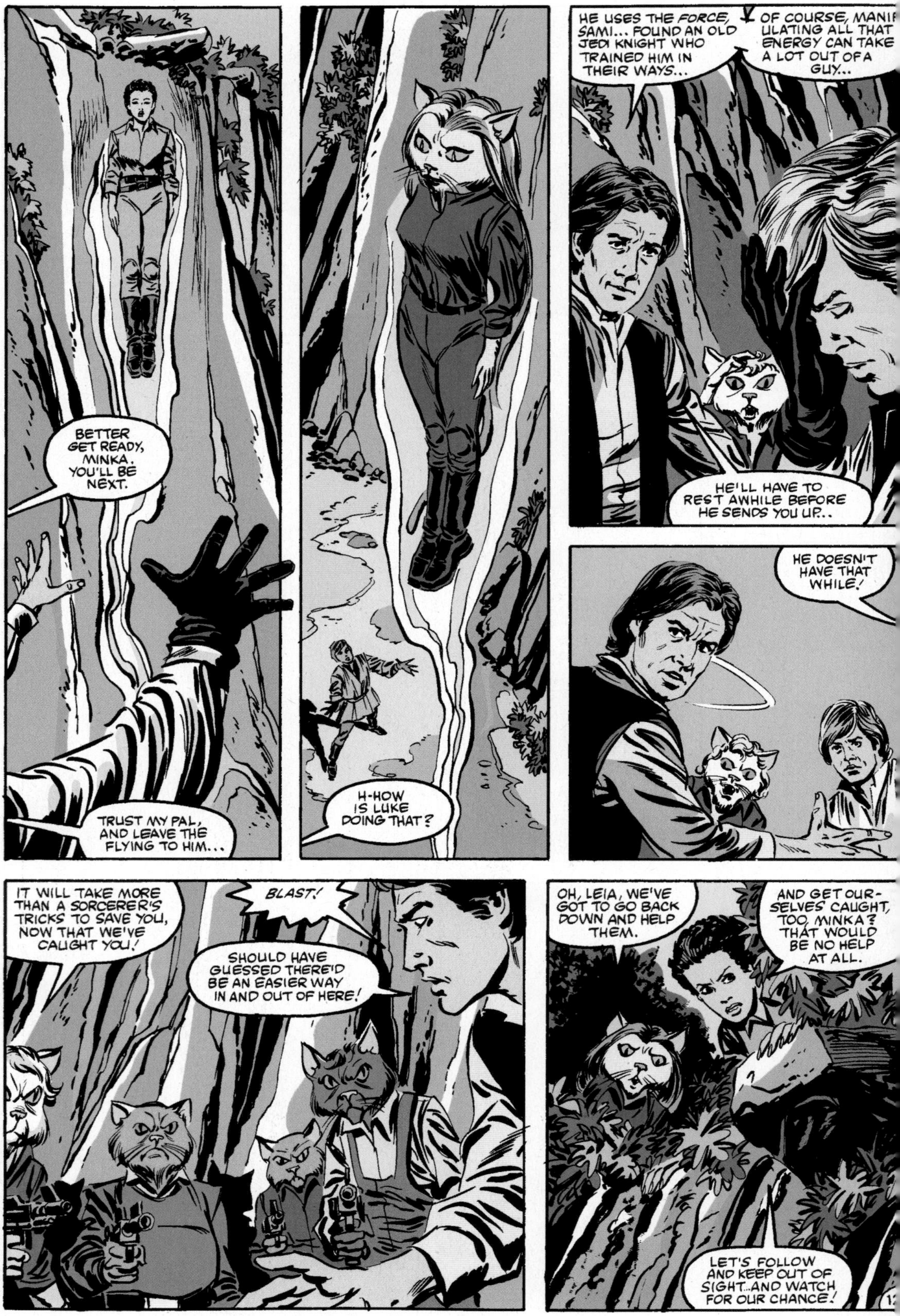
BETTER GET READY, MINKA. YOU'LL BE NEXT.
TRUST MY PAL, AND LEAVE THE FLYING TO HIM...
H-HOW IS LUKE DOING THAT?
HE USES THE FORCE, SAMI... FOUND AN OLD JEDI KNIGHT WHO TRAINED HIM IN THEIR WAYS...
OF COURSE, MANIP-ULATING ALL THAT ENERGY CAN TAKE A LOT OUT OF A GUY...
HE'LL HAVE TO REST AWHILE BEFORE HE SENDS YOU UP..
HE DOESN'T HAVE THAT WHILE!
IT WILL TAKE MORE THAN A SORCERER'S TRICKS TO SAVE YOU, NOW THAT WE'VE CAUGHT YOU!
BLAST!
SHOULD HAVE GUESSED THERE'D BE AN EASIER WAY IN AND OUT OF HERE!
OH, LEIA, WE'VE GOT TO GO BACK DOWN AND HELP THEM.
AND GET OUR-SELVES CAUGHT, TOO, MINKA? THAT WOULD BE NO HELP AT ALL.
LET'S FOLLOW AND KEEP OUT OF SIGHT...AND WATCH FOR OUR CHANCE!

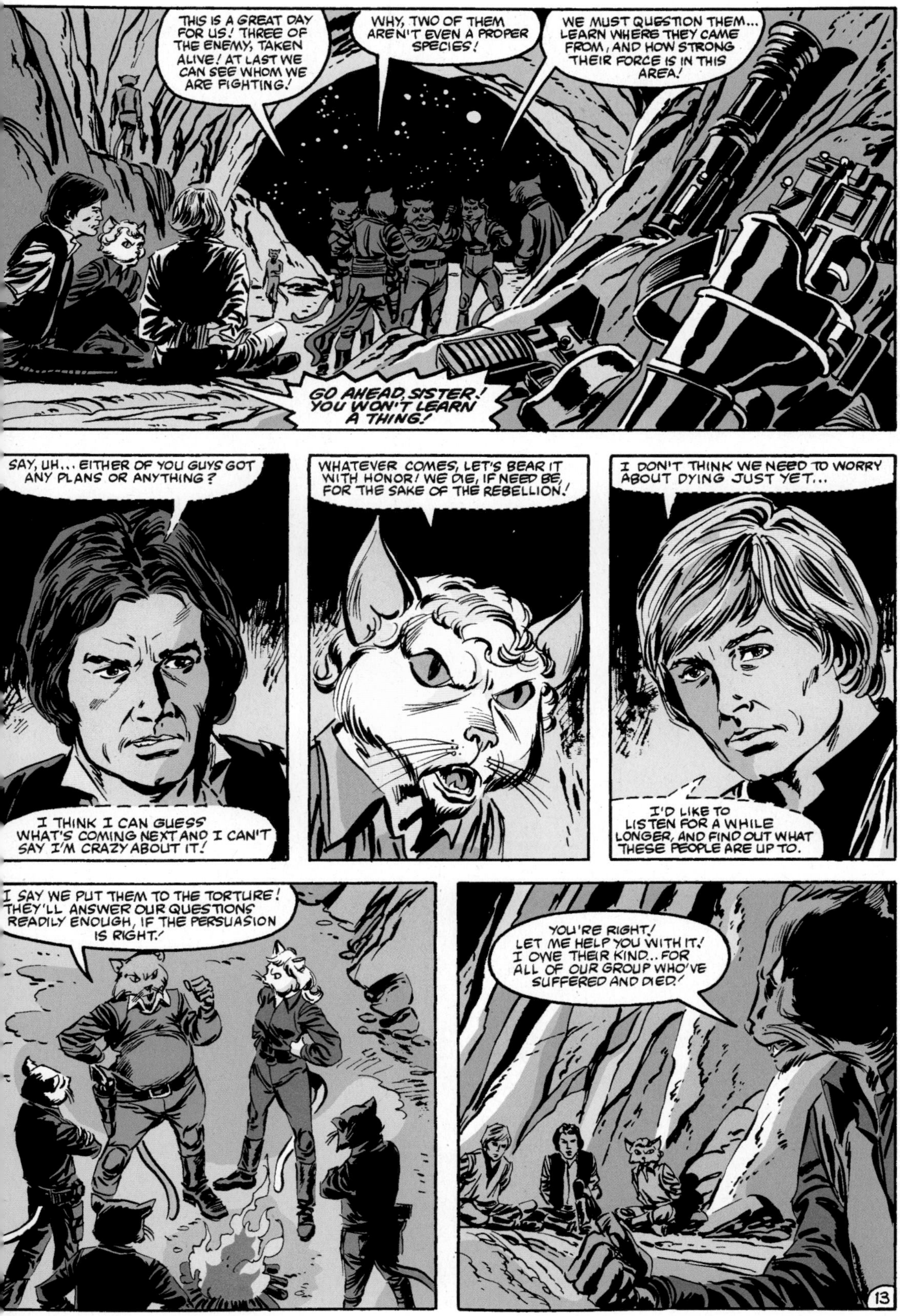
THIS IS A GREAT DAY FOR US! THREE OF THE ENEMY, TAKEN ALIVE! AT LAST WE CAN SEE WHOM WE ARE FIGHTING!
WHY, TWO OF THEM AREN'T EVEN A PROPER SPECIES!
WE MUST QUESTION THEM... LEARN WHERE THEY CAME FROM, AND HOW STRONG THEIR FORCE IS IN THIS AREA!
GO AHEAD, SISTER! YOU WON'T LEARN A THING!
SAY, UH... EITHER OF YOU GUYS GOT ANY PLANS OR ANYTHING?
I THINK I CAN GUESS WHAT'S COMING NEXT AND I CAN'T SAY I'M CRAZY ABOUT IT!
WHATEVER COMES, LET'S BEAR IT WITH HONOR! WE DIE, IF NEED BE, FOR THE SAKE OF THE REBELLION!
I DON'T THINK WE NEED TO WORRY ABOUT DYING JUST YET...
I'D LIKE TO LISTEN FOR A WHILE LONGER, AND FIND OUT WHAT THESE PEOPLE ARE UP TO.
I SAY WE PUT THEM TO THE TORTURE! THEY'LL ANSWER OUR QUESTIONS READILY ENOUGH, IF THE PERSUASION IS RIGHT!
YOU'RE RIGHT! LET ME HELP YOU WITH IT! I OWE THEIR KIND... FOR ALL OF OUR GROUP WHO'VE SUFFERED AND DIED!
13

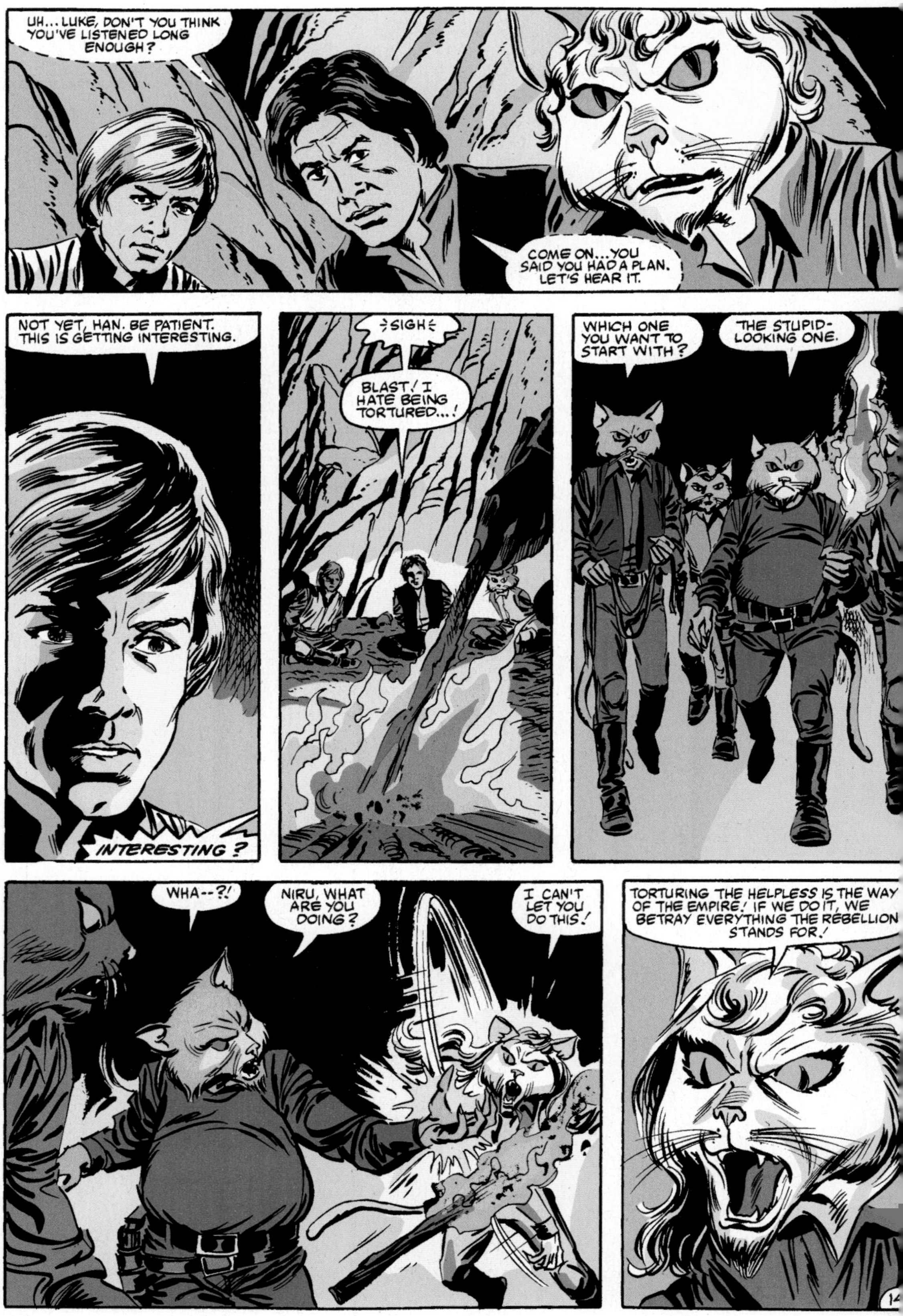
UH... LUKE, DON'T YOU THINK YOU'VE LISTENED LONG ENOUGH?
COME ON... YOU SAID YOU HAD A PLAN. LET'S HEAR IT.
NOT YET, HAN. BE PATIENT. THIS IS GETTING INTERESTING.
INTERESTING?
SIGH
BLAST! I HATE BEING TORTURED...!
WHICH ONE YOU WANT TO START WITH?
THE STUPID-LOOKING ONE.
WHA--?!
NIRU, WHAT ARE YOU DOING?
I CAN'T LET YOU DO THIS!
TORTURING THE HELPLESS IS THE WAY OF THE EMPIRE! IF WE DO IT, WE BETRAY EVERYTHING THE REBELLION STANDS FOR!

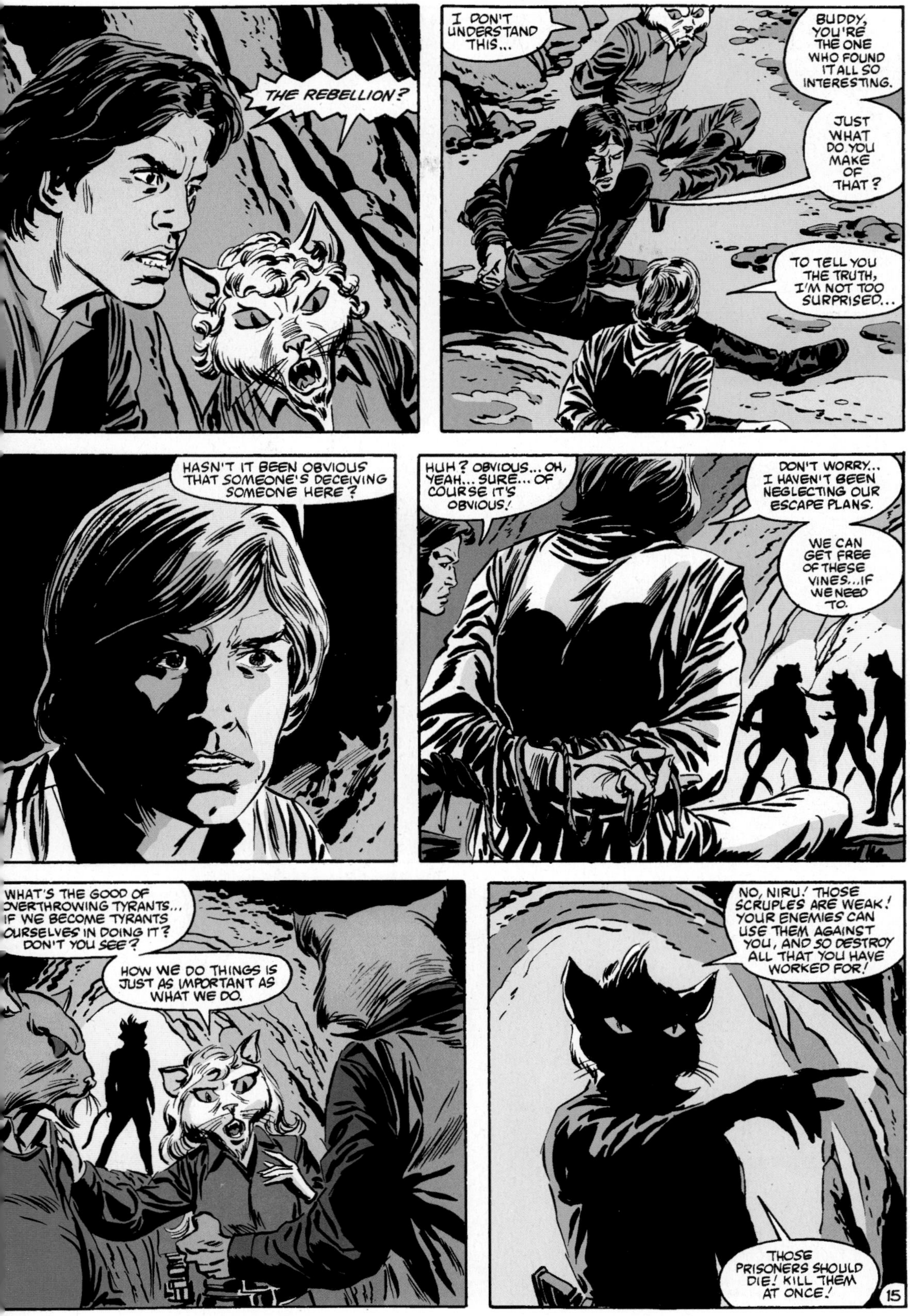
THE REBELLION?
I DON'T UNDERSTAND THIS...
BUDDY, YOU'RE THE ONE WHO FOUND IT ALL SO INTERESTING.
JUST WHAT DO YOU MAKE OF THAT?
TO TELL YOU THE TRUTH, I'M NOT TOO SURPRISED...
HASN'T IT BEEN OBVIOUS THAT SOMEONE'S DECEIVING SOMEONE HERE?
HUH? OBVIOUS... OH, YEAH... SURE... OF COURSE IT'S OBVIOUS!
DON'T WORRY... I HAVEN'T BEEN NEGLECTING OUR ESCAPE PLANS.
WE CAN GET FREE OF THESE VINES... IF WE NEED TO.
WHAT'S THE GOOD OF OVERTHROWING TYRANTS... IF WE BECOME TYRANTS OURSELVES IN DOING IT? DON'T YOU SEE?
HOW WE DO THINGS IS JUST AS IMPORTANT AS WHAT WE DO.
NO, NIRU! THOSE SCRUPLES ARE WEAK! YOUR ENEMIES CAN USE THEM AGAINST YOU, AND SO DESTROY ALL THAT YOU HAVE WORKED FOR!
THOSE PRISONERS SHOULD DIE! KILL THEM AT ONCE!
15

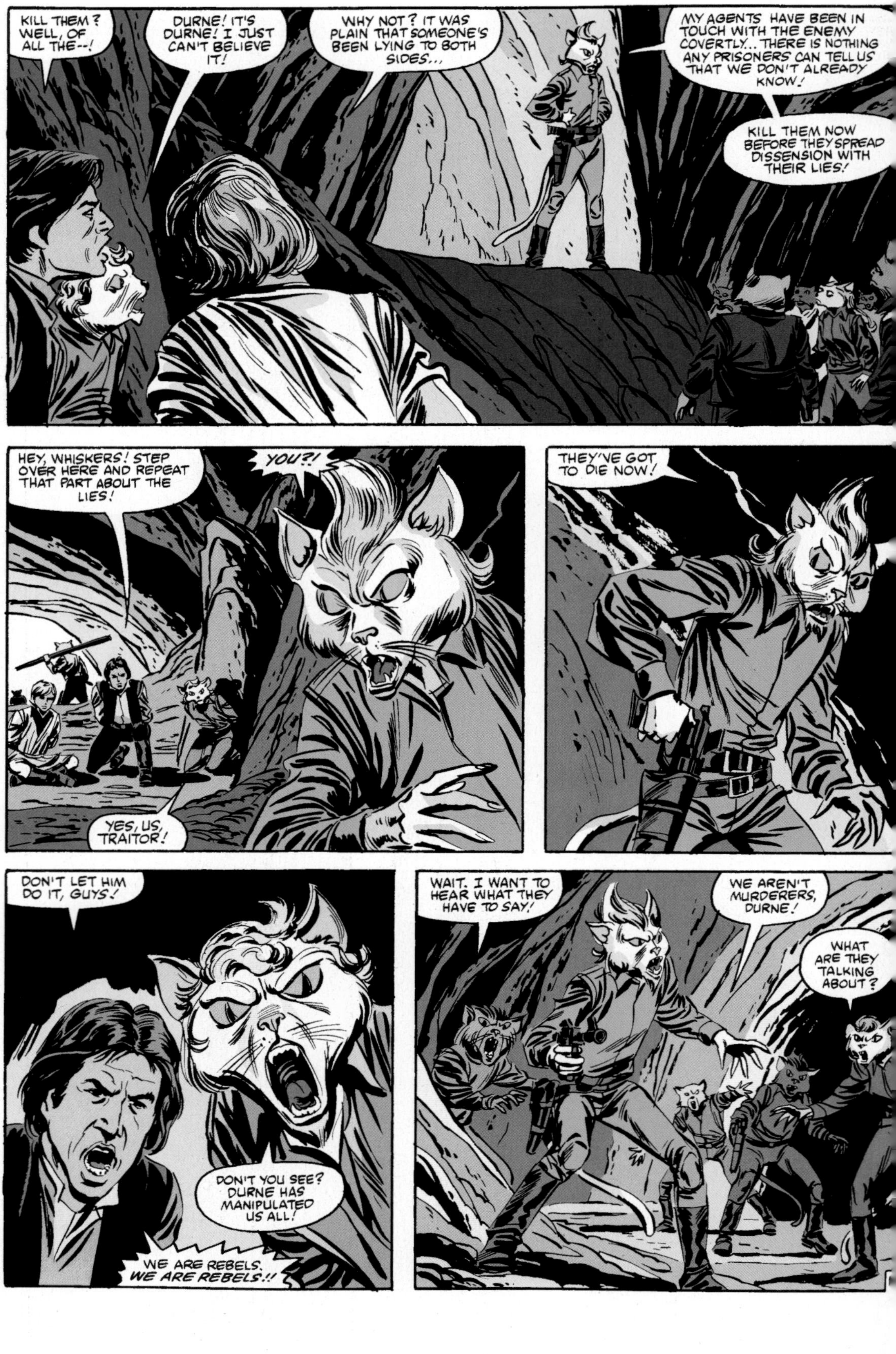
KILL THEM? WELL, OF ALL THE--!
DURNE! IT'S DURNE! I JUST CAN'T BELIEVE IT!
WHY NOT? IT WAS PLAIN THAT SOMEONE'S BEEN LYING TO BOTH SIDES...
MY AGENTS HAVE BEEN IN TOUCH WITH THE ENEMY COVERTLY... THERE IS NOTHING ANY PRISONERS CAN TELL US THAT WE DON'T ALREADY KNOW!
KILL THEM NOW BEFORE THEY SPREAD DISSENSION WITH THEIR LIES!
HEY, WHISKERS! STEP OVER HERE AND REPEAT THAT PART ABOUT THE LIES!
YOU?!
YES, US, TRAITOR!
THEY'VE GOT TO DIE NOW!
DON'T LET HIM DO IT, GUYS!
DON'T YOU SEE? DURNE HAS MANIPULATED US ALL!
WE ARE REBELS. WE ARE REBELS!!
WAIT. I WANT TO HEAR WHAT THEY HAVE TO SAY!
WE AREN'T MURDERERS, DURNE!
WHAT ARE THEY TALKING ABOUT?

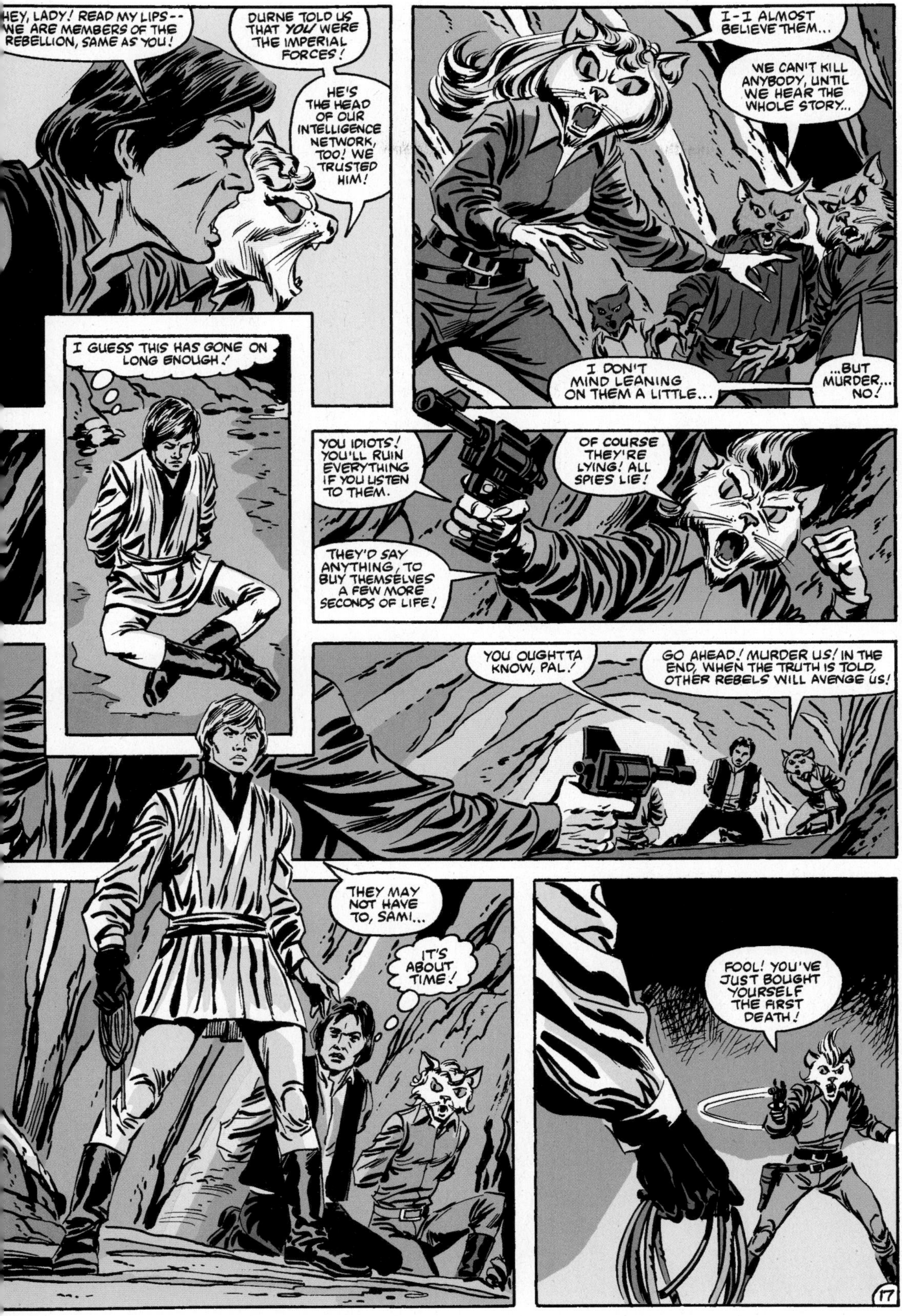
HEY, LADY! READ MY LIPS-- WE ARE MEMBERS OF THE REBELLION, SAME AS YOU!
DURNE TOLD US THAT YOU WERE THE IMPERIAL FORCES!
HE'S THE HEAD OF OUR INTELLIGENCE NETWORK, TOO! WE TRUSTED HIM!
I-I ALMOST BELIEVE THEM...
WE CAN'T KILL ANYBODY, UNTIL WE HEAR THE WHOLE STORY...
I DON'T MIND LEANING ON THEM A LITTLE...
...BUT MURDER,... NO!
I GUESS THIS HAS GONE ON LONG ENOUGH!
YOU IDIOTS! YOU'LL RUIN EVERYTHING IF YOU LISTEN TO THEM.
OF COURSE THEY'RE LYING! ALL SPIES LIE!
THEY'D SAY ANYTHING, TO BUY THEMSELVES A FEW MORE SECONDS OF LIFE!
YOU OUGHTTA KNOW, PAL!
GO AHEAD! MURDER US! IN THE END, WHEN THE TRUTH IS TOLD, OTHER REBELS WILL AVENGE US!
THEY MAY NOT HAVE TO, SAMI...
IT'S ABOUT TIME!
FOOL! YOU'VE JUST BOUGHT YOURSELF THE FIRST DEATH!
17

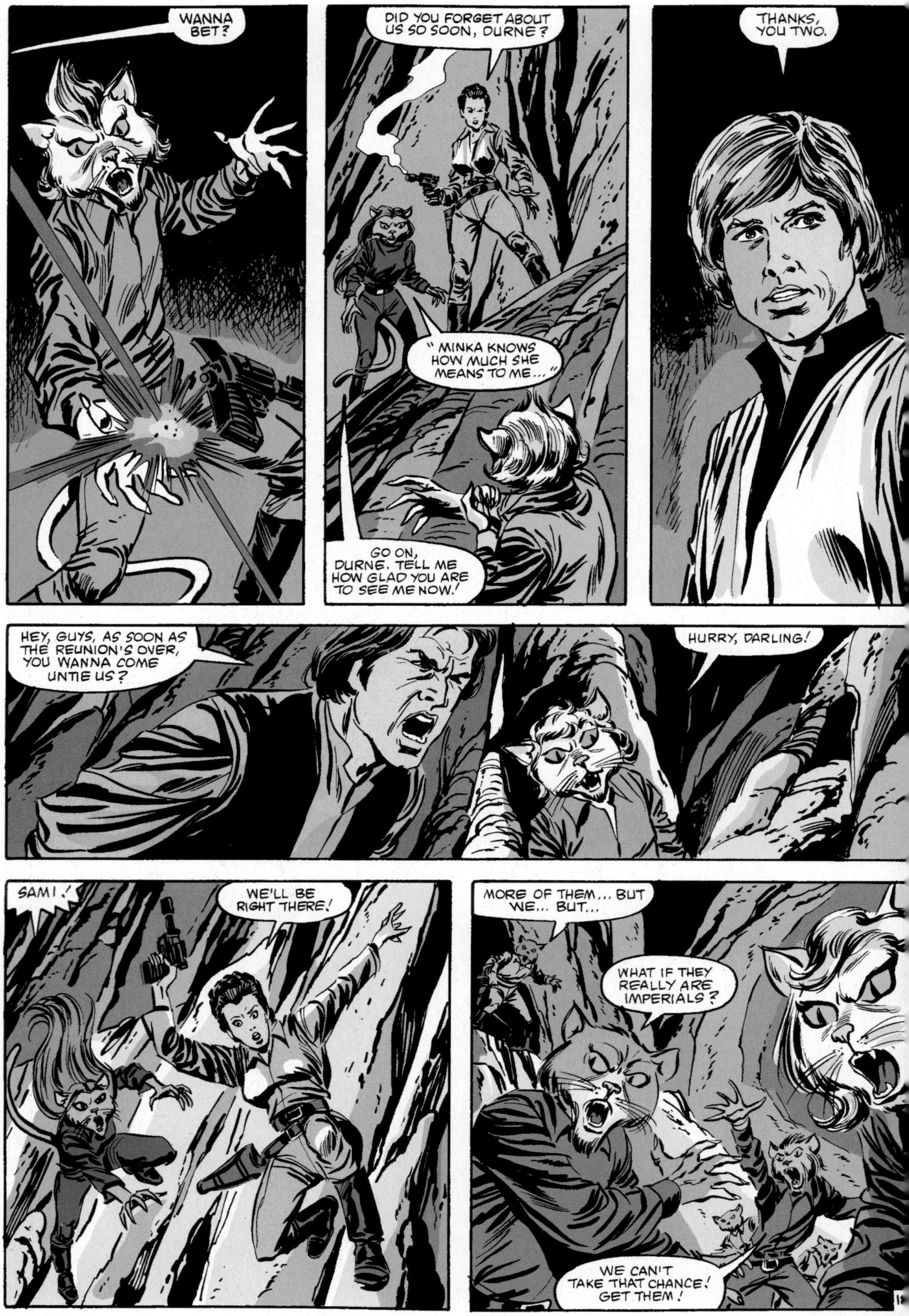
WANNA BET?
DID YOU FORGET ABOUT US SO SOON, DURNE?
"MINKA KNOWS HOW MUCH SHE MEANS TO ME..."
GO ON, DURNE. TELL ME HOW GLAD YOU ARE TO SEE ME NOW!
THANKS, YOU TWO.
HEY, GUYS, AS SOON AS THE REUNION'S OVER, YOU WANNA COME UNTIE US?
HURRY, DARLING!
SAMI!
WE'LL BE RIGHT THERE!
MORE OF THEM... BUT WE... BUT...
WHAT IF THEY REALLY ARE IMPERIALS?
WE CAN'T TAKE THAT CHANCE! GET THEM!

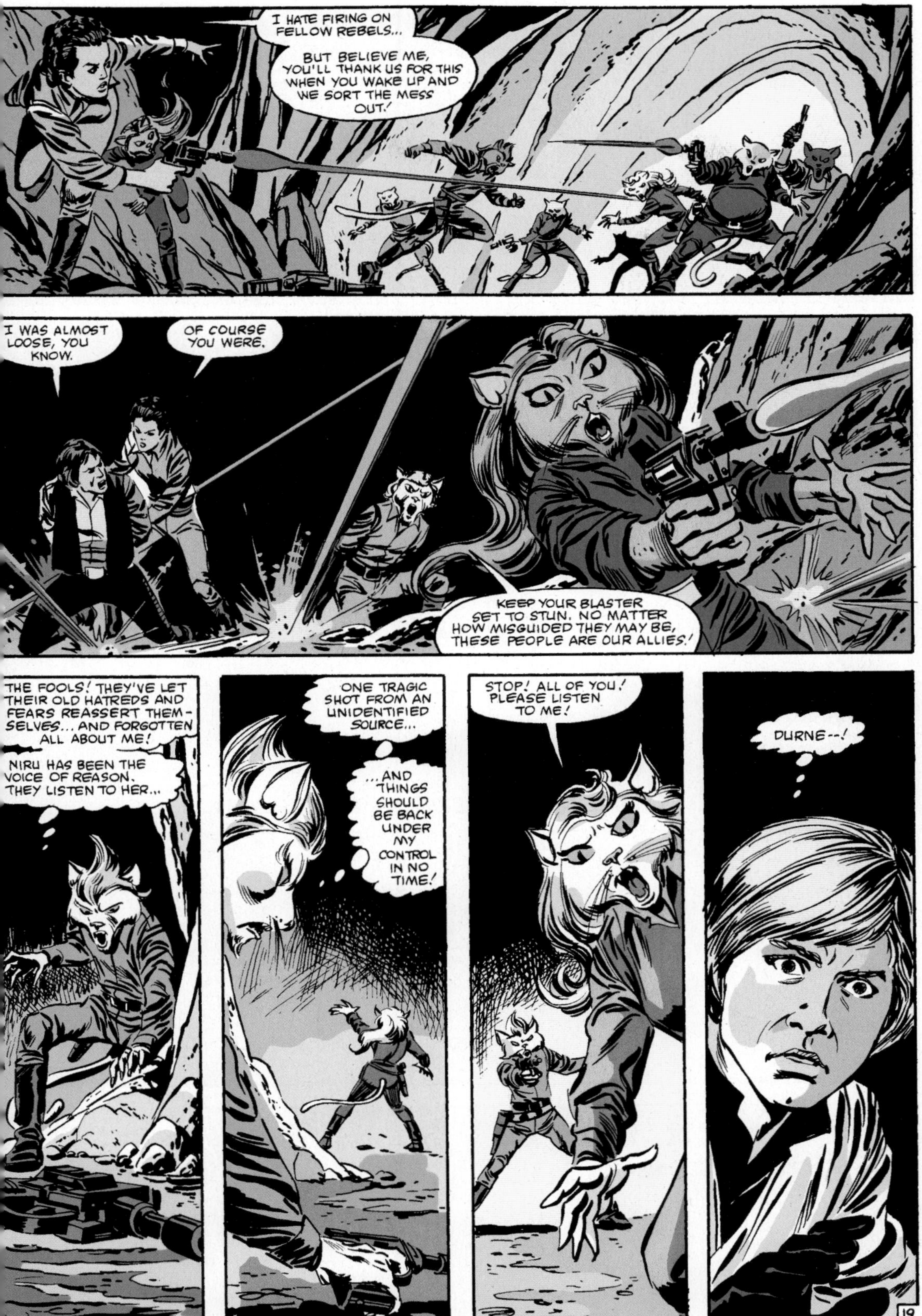
I HATE FIRING ON FELLOW REBELS...
BUT BELIEVE ME, YOU'LL THANK US FOR THIS WHEN YOU WAKE UP AND WE SORT THE MESS OUT!
I WAS ALMOST LOOSE, YOU KNOW.
OF COURSE YOU WERE.
KEEP YOUR BLASTER SET TO STUN. NO MATTER HOW MISGUIDED THEY MAY BE, THESE PEOPLE ARE OUR ALLIES!
THE FOOLS! THEY'VE LET THEIR OLD HATREDS AND FEARS REASSERT THEMSELVES... AND FORGOTTEN ALL ABOUT ME!
NIRU HAS BEEN THE VOICE OF REASON. THEY LISTEN TO HER...
ONE TRAGIC SHOT FROM AN UNIDENTIFIED SOURCE...
...AND THINGS SHOULD BE BACK UNDER MY CONTROL IN NO TIME!
STOP! ALL OF YOU! PLEASE LISTEN TO ME!
DURNE--!
19

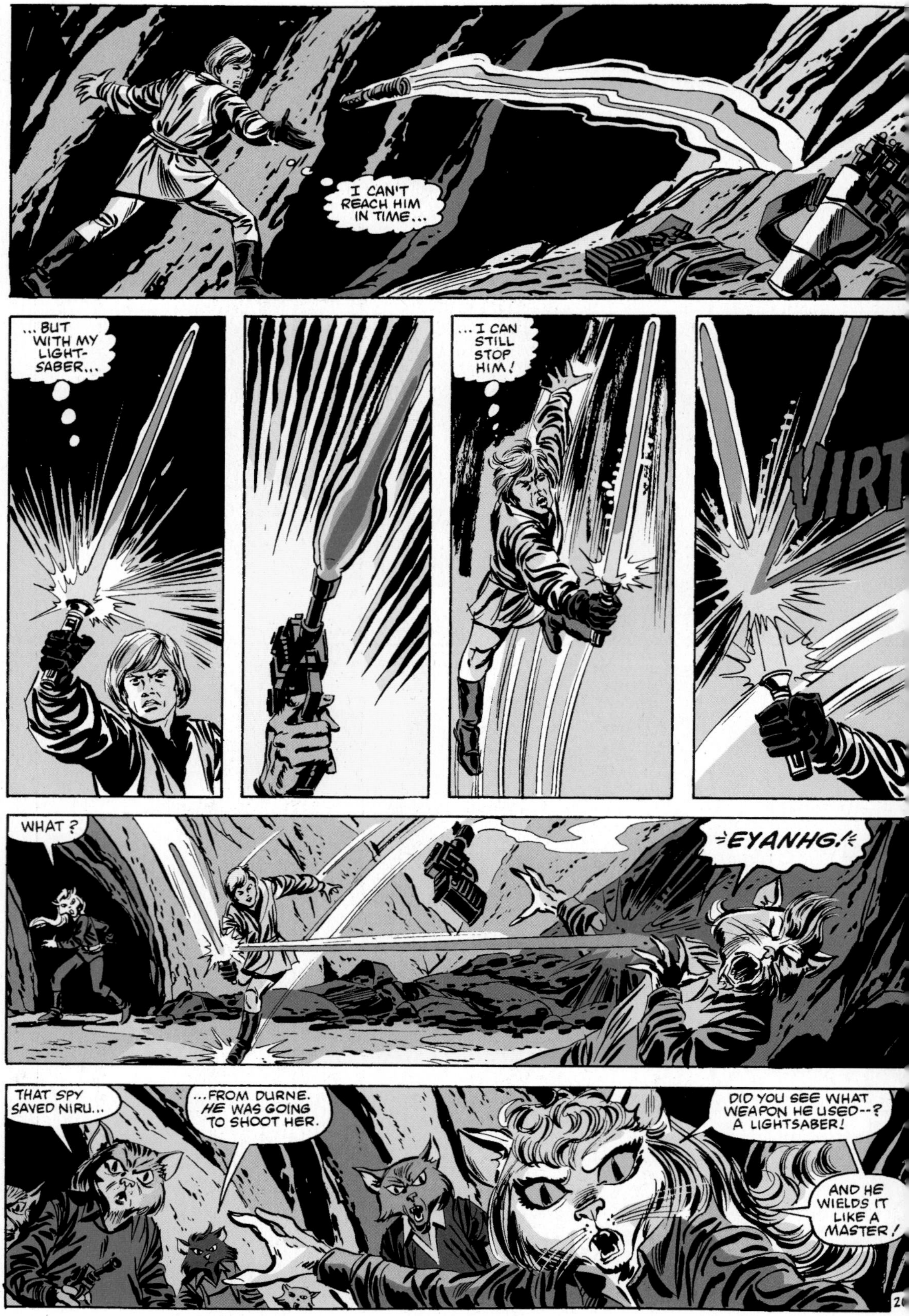
I CAN'T REACH HIM IN TIME...
...BUT WITH MY LIGHT-SABER...
...I CAN STILL STOP HIM!
VIRT
WHAT?
EYANHG!
THAT SPY SAVED NIRU...
...FROM DURNE. HE WAS GOING TO SHOOT HER.
DID YOU SEE WHAT WEAPON HE USED--? A LIGHTSABER!
AND HE WIELDS IT LIKE A MASTER!

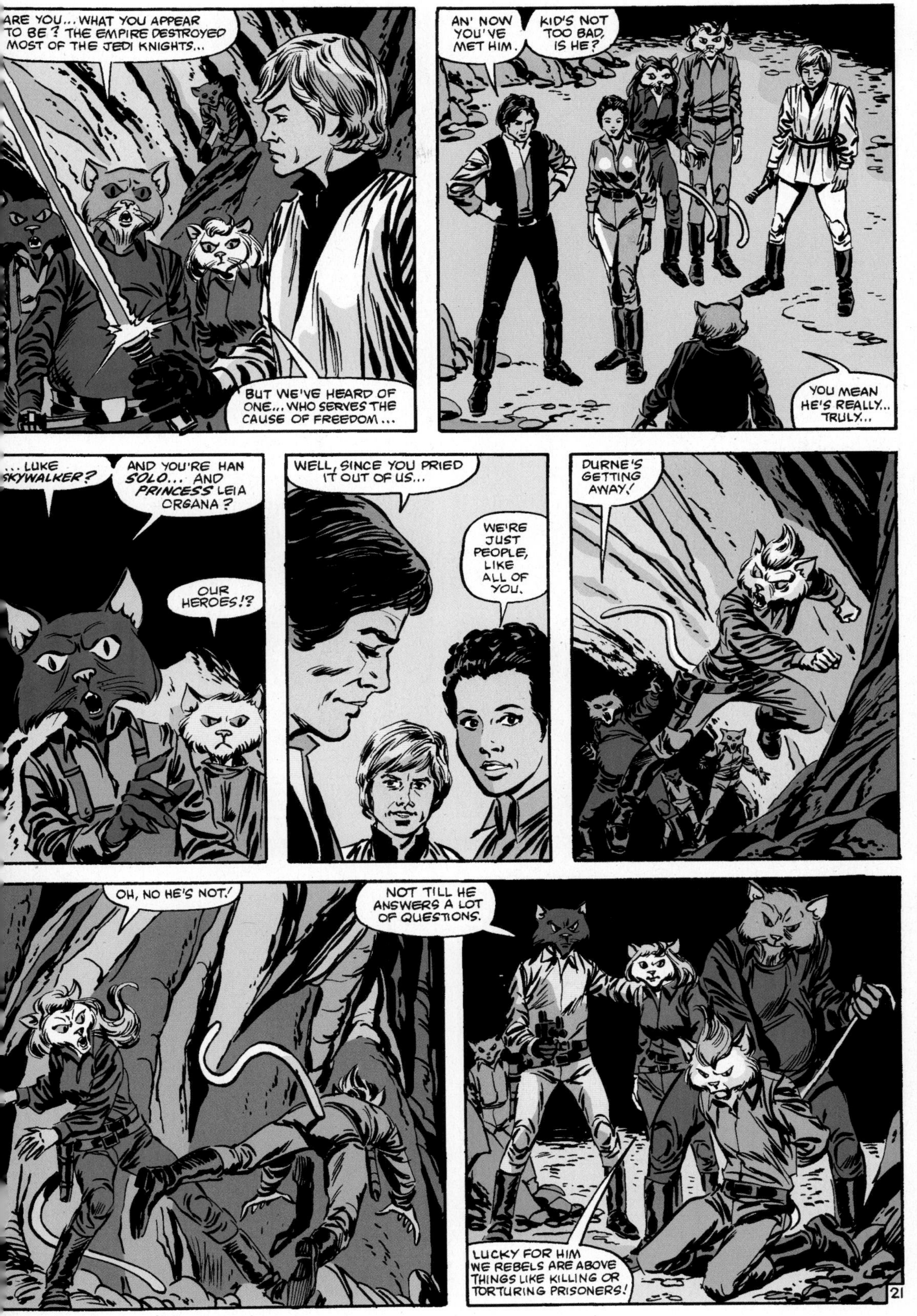
ARE YOU... WHAT YOU APPEAR TO BE? THE EMPIRE DESTROYED MOST OF THE JEDI KNIGHTS...
BUT WE'VE HEARD OF ONE... WHO SERVES THE CAUSE OF FREEDOM...
AN' NOW YOU'VE MET HIM.
KID'S NOT TOO BAD, IS HE?
YOU MEAN HE'S REALLY... TRULY...
...LUKE SKYWALKER?
AND YOU'RE HAN SOLO... AND PRINCESS LEIA ORGANA?
OUR HEROES!?
WELL, SINCE YOU PRIED IT OUT OF US...
WE'RE JUST PEOPLE, LIKE ALL OF YOU.
DURNE'S GETTING AWAY!
OH, NO HE'S NOT!
NOT TILL HE ANSWERS A LOT OF QUESTIONS.
LUCKY FOR HIM WE REBELS ARE ABOVE THINGS LIKE KILLING OR TORTURING PRISONERS!
21

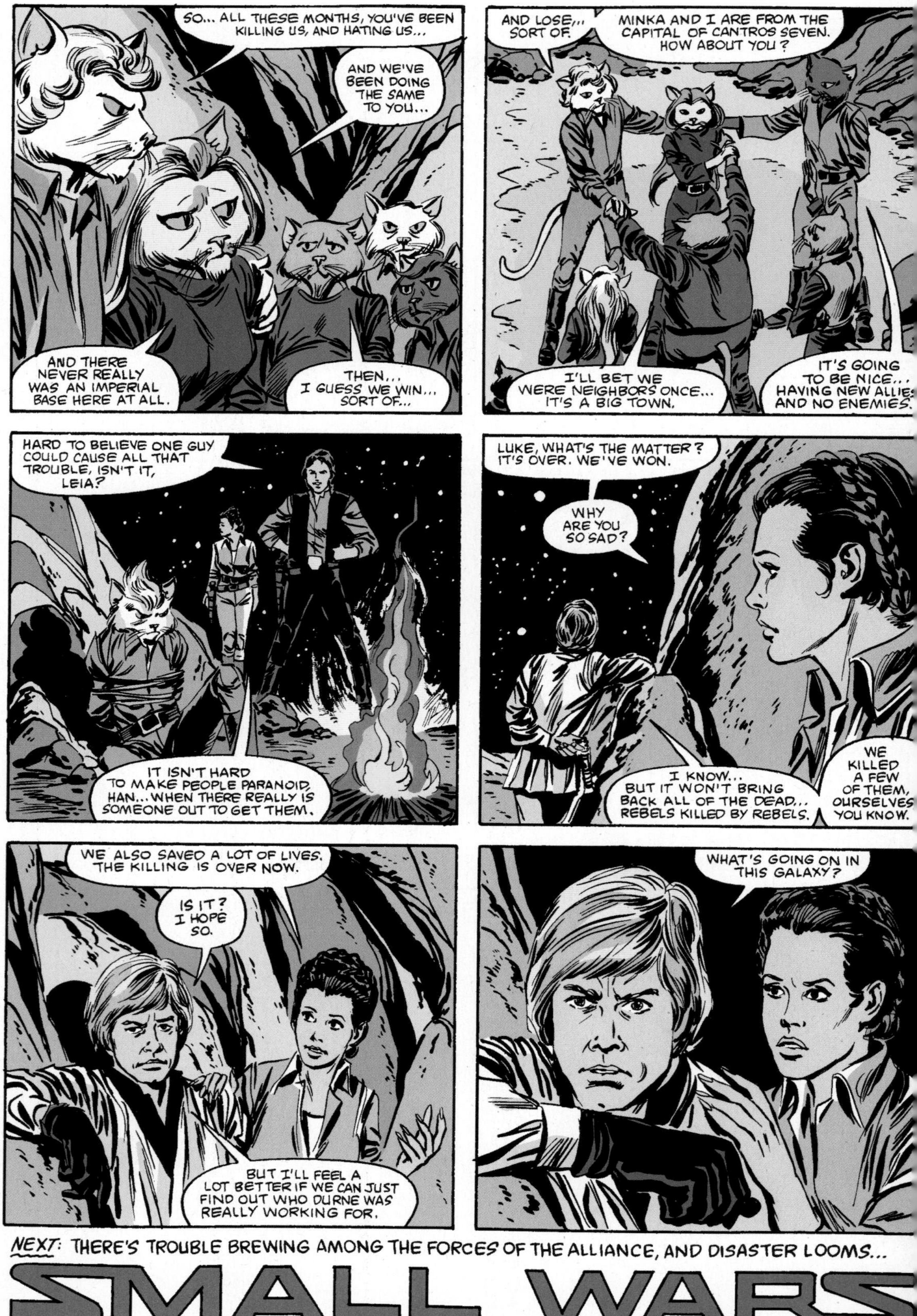
SO... ALL THESE MONTHS, YOU'VE BEEN KILLING US, AND HATING US...
AND WE'VE BEEN DOING THE SAME TO YOU...
AND THERE NEVER REALLY WAS AN IMPERIAL BASE HERE AT ALL.
THEN... I GUESS WE WIN... SORT OF...
AND LOSE,... SORT OF.
MINKA AND I ARE FROM THE CAPITAL OF CANTROS SEVEN. HOW ABOUT YOU?
I'LL BET WE WERE NEIGHBORS ONCE... IT'S A BIG TOWN.
IT'S GOING TO BE NICE... HAVING NEW ALLIES AND NO ENEMIES.
HARD TO BELIEVE ONE GUY COULD CAUSE ALL THAT TROUBLE, ISN'T IT, LEIA?
IT ISN'T HARD TO MAKE PEOPLE PARANOID, HAN... WHEN THERE REALLY IS SOMEONE OUT TO GET THEM.
LUKE, WHAT'S THE MATTER? IT'S OVER. WE'VE WON.
WHY ARE YOU SO SAD?
I KNOW... BUT IT WON'T BRING BACK ALL OF THE DEAD... REBELS KILLED BY REBELS.
WE KILLED A FEW OF THEM, OURSELVES YOU KNOW.
WE ALSO SAVED A LOT OF LIVES. THE KILLING IS OVER NOW.
IS IT? I HOPE SO.
BUT I'LL FEEL A LOT BETTER IF WE CAN JUST FIND OUT WHO DURNE WAS REALLY WORKING FOR.
WHAT'S GOING ON IN THIS GALAXY?
NEXT: THERE'S TROUBLE BREWING AMONG THE FORCES OF THE ALLIANCE, AND DISASTER LOOMS...
SMALL WARS

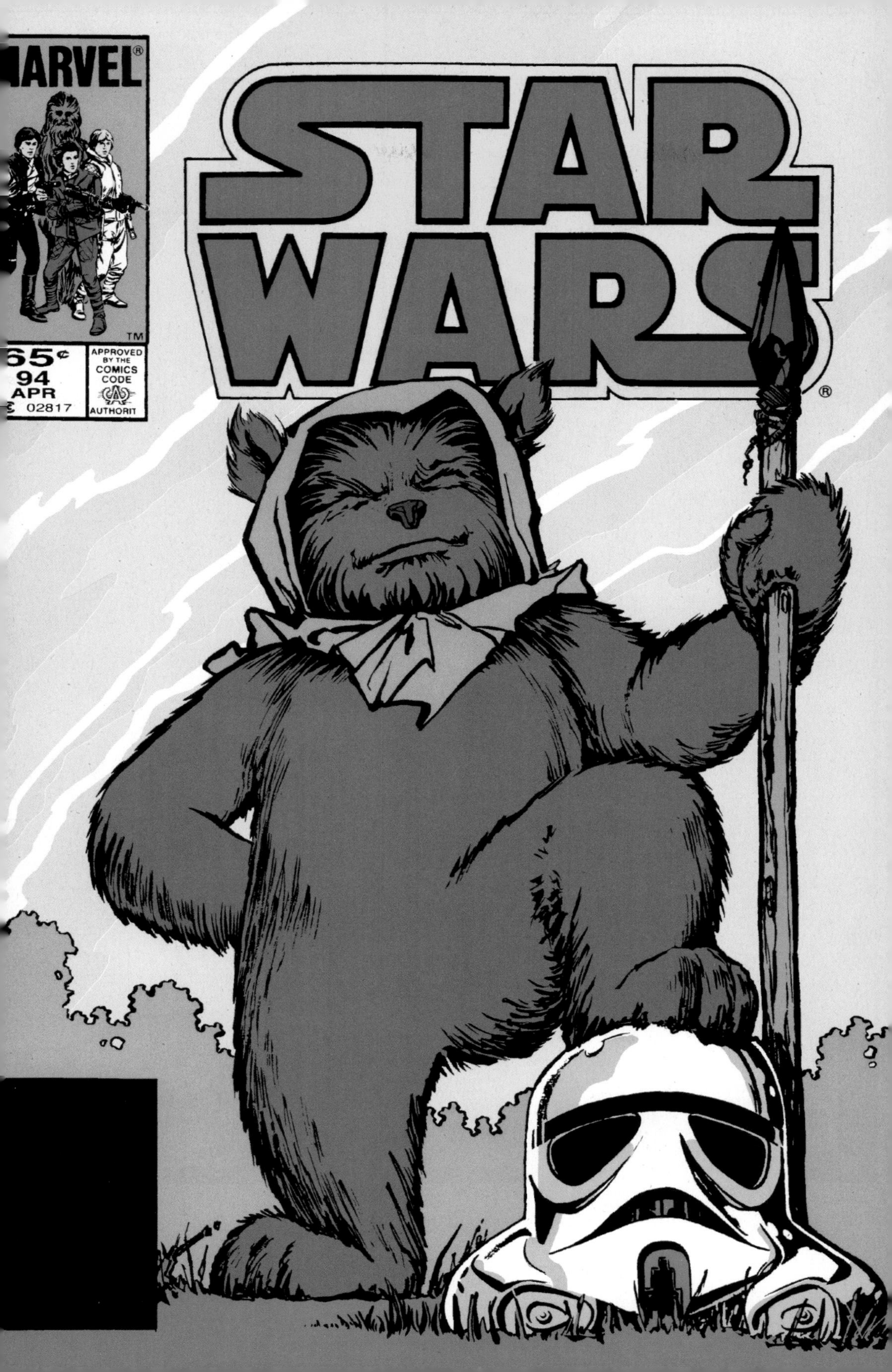
MARVEL®
STAR WARS®
65¢
94
APR
02817
APPROVED BY THE COMICS CODE AUTHORIT
TM

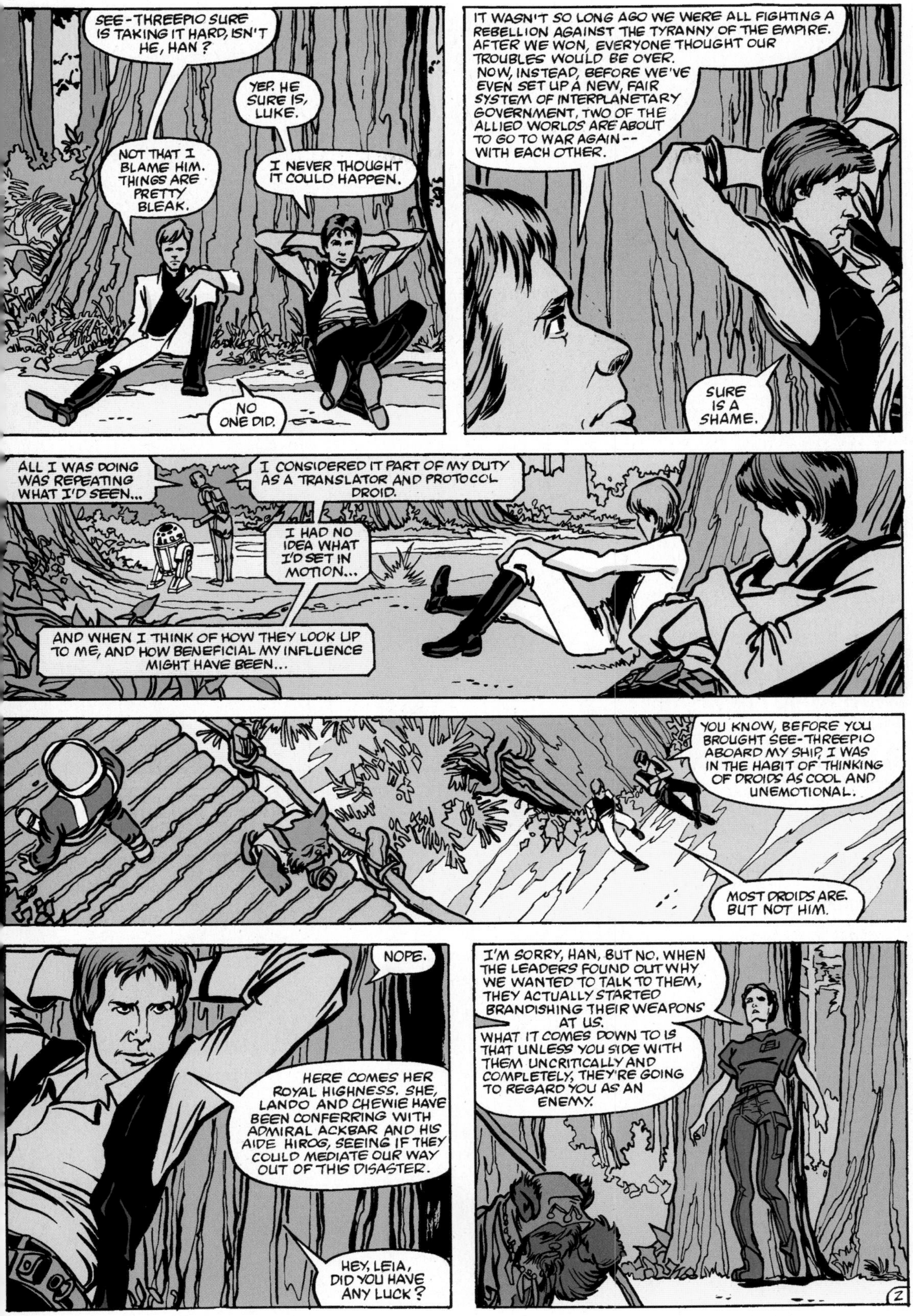
SEE-THREEPIO SURE IS TAKING IT HARD, ISN'T HE, HAN?
YEP. HE SURE IS, LUKE.
NOT THAT I BLAME HIM. THINGS ARE PRETTY BLEAK.
I NEVER THOUGHT IT COULD HAPPEN.
NO ONE DID.
IT WASN'T SO LONG AGO WE WERE ALL FIGHTING A REBELLION AGAINST THE TYRANNY OF THE EMPIRE. AFTER WE WON, EVERYONE THOUGHT OUR TROUBLES WOULD BE OVER. NOW, INSTEAD, BEFORE WE'VE EVEN SET UP A NEW, FAIR SYSTEM OF INTERPLANETARY GOVERNMENT, TWO OF THE ALLIED WORLDS ARE ABOUT TO GO TO WAR AGAIN -- WITH EACH OTHER.
SURE IS A SHAME.
ALL I WAS DOING WAS REPEATING WHAT I'D SEEN...
I CONSIDERED IT PART OF MY DUTY AS A TRANSLATOR AND PROTOCOL DROID.
I HAD NO IDEA WHAT I'D SET IN MOTION...
AND WHEN I THINK OF HOW THEY LOOK UP TO ME, AND HOW BENEFICIAL MY INFLUENCE MIGHT HAVE BEEN...
YOU KNOW, BEFORE YOU BROUGHT SEE-THREEPIO ABOARD MY SHIP, I WAS IN THE HABIT OF THINKING OF DROIDS AS COOL AND UNEMOTIONAL.
MOST DROIDS ARE. BUT NOT HIM.
NOPE.
HERE COMES HER ROYAL HIGHNESS. SHE, LANDO AND CHEWIE HAVE BEEN CONFERRING WITH ADMIRAL ACKBAR AND HIS AIDE HIROG, SEEING IF THEY COULD MEDIATE OUR WAY OUT OF THIS DISASTER.
HEY, LEIA, DID YOU HAVE ANY LUCK?
I'M SORRY, HAN, BUT NO. WHEN THE LEADERS FOUND OUT WHY WE WANTED TO TALK TO THEM, THEY ACTUALLY STARTED BRANDISHING THEIR WEAPONS AT US. WHAT IT COMES DOWN TO IS THAT UNLESS YOU SIDE WITH THEM UNCRITICALLY AND COMPLETELY, THEY'RE GOING TO REGARD YOU AS AN ENEMY.
2

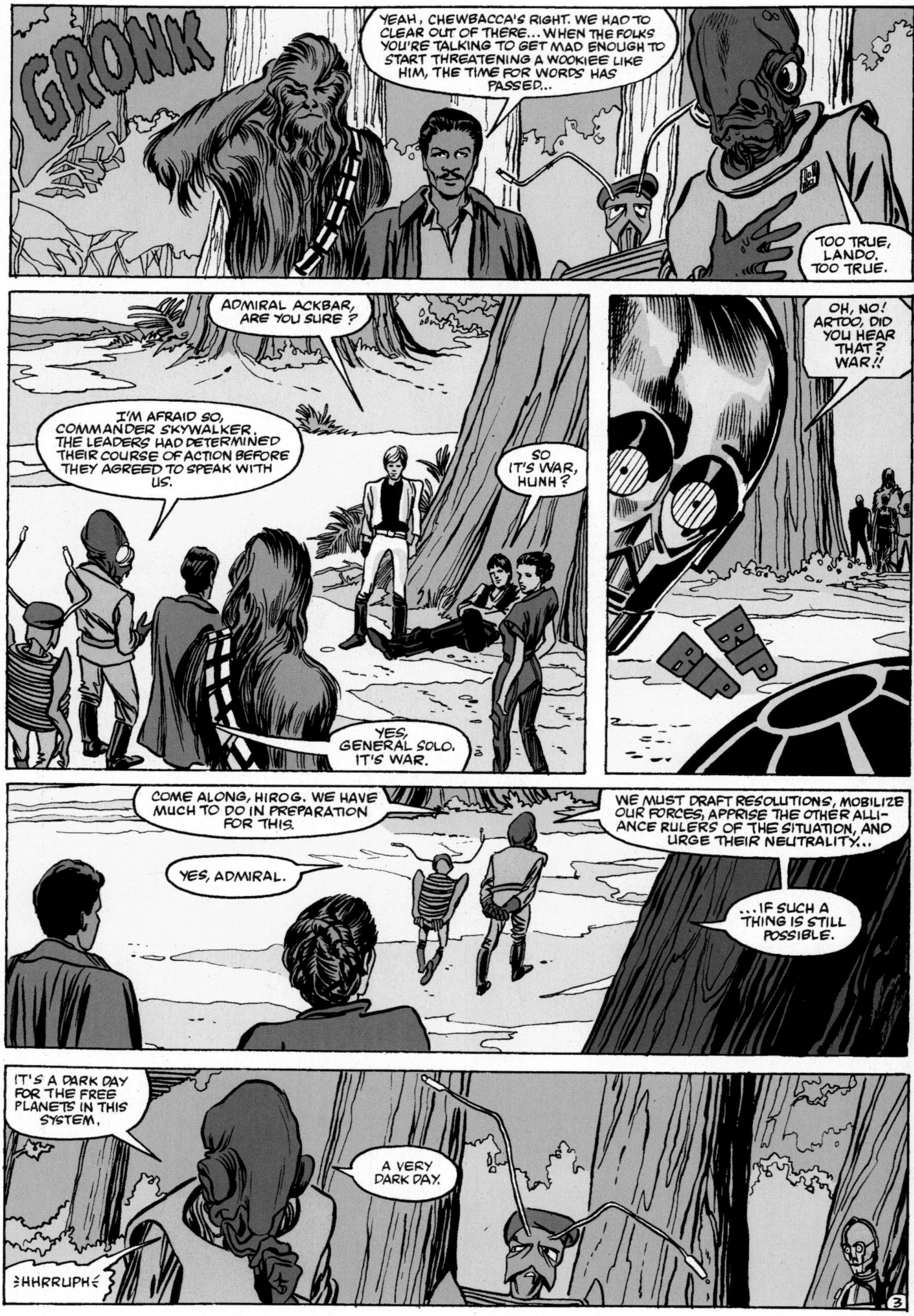
GRONK
YEAH, CHEWBACCA'S RIGHT. WE HAD TO CLEAR OUT OF THERE... WHEN THE FOLKS YOU'RE TALKING TO GET MAD ENOUGH TO START THREATENING A WOOKIEE LIKE HIM, THE TIME FOR WORDS HAS PASSED...
TOO TRUE, LANDO. TOO TRUE.
ADMIRAL ACKBAR, ARE YOU SURE?
I'M AFRAID SO, COMMANDER SKYWALKER. THE LEADERS HAD DETERMINED THEIR COURSE OF ACTION BEFORE THEY AGREED TO SPEAK WITH US.
SO IT'S WAR, HUNH?
YES, GENERAL SOLO. IT'S WAR.
OH, NO! ARTOO, DID YOU HEAR THAT? WAR!!
BIP BIP
COME ALONG, HIROG. WE HAVE MUCH TO DO IN PREPARATION FOR THIS.
YES, ADMIRAL.
WE MUST DRAFT RESOLUTIONS, MOBILIZE OUR FORCES, APPRISE THE OTHER ALLIANCE RULERS OF THE SITUATION, AND URGE THEIR NEUTRALITY...
...IF SUCH A THING IS STILL POSSIBLE.
IT'S A DARK DAY FOR THE FREE PLANETS IN THIS SYSTEM.
A VERY DARK DAY.
HHRRUPH
3

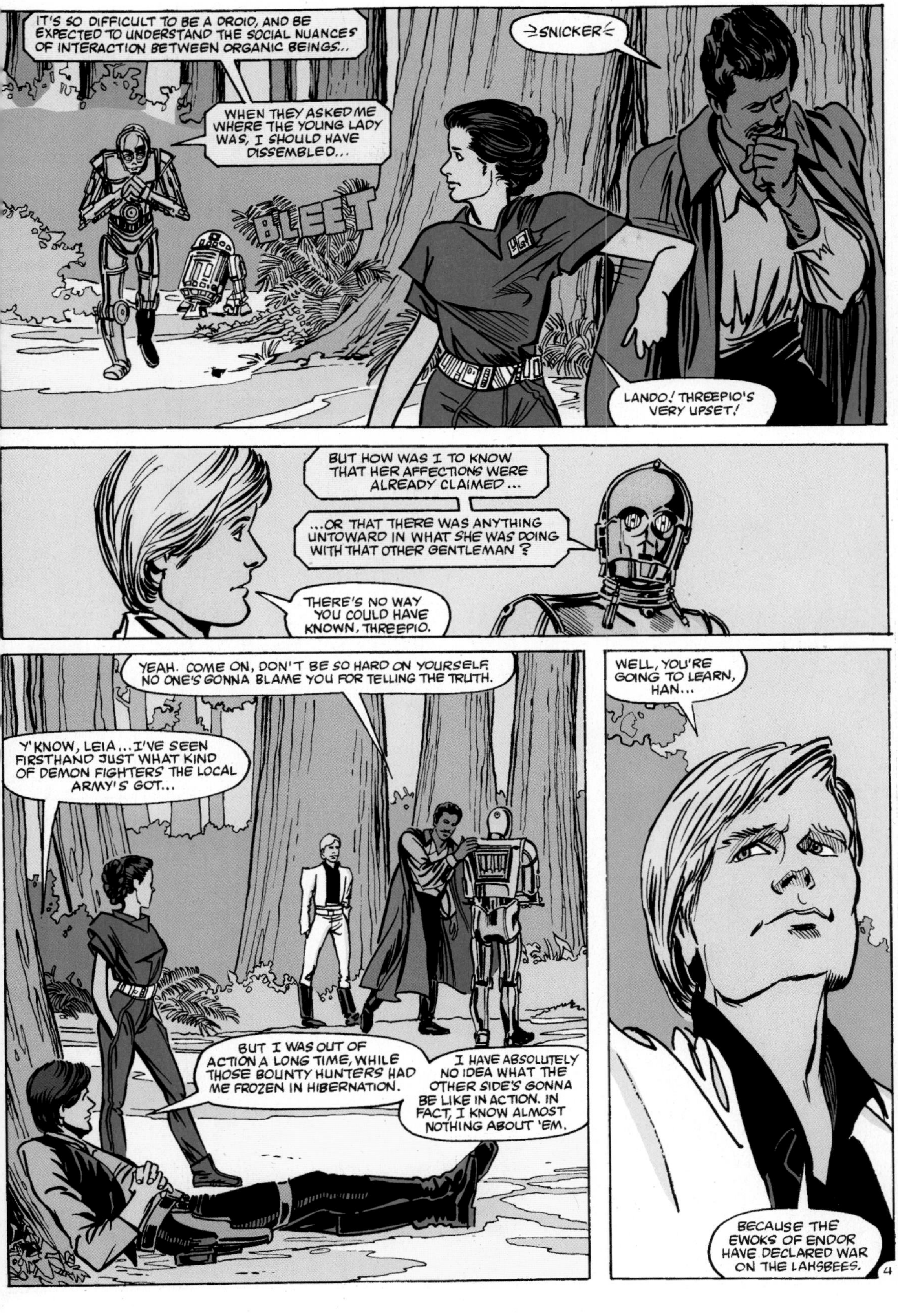

IT'S SO DIFFICULT TO BE A DROID, AND BE EXPECTED TO UNDERSTAND THE SOCIAL NUANCES OF INTERACTION BETWEEN ORGANIC BEINGS...
WHEN THEY ASKED ME WHERE THE YOUNG LADY WAS, I SHOULD HAVE DISSEMBLED...
BLEET
>SNICKER<
LANDO! THREEPIO'S VERY UPSET!
BUT HOW WAS I TO KNOW THAT HER AFFECTIONS WERE ALREADY CLAIMED...
...OR THAT THERE WAS ANYTHING UNTOWARD IN WHAT SHE WAS DOING WITH THAT OTHER GENTLEMAN?
THERE'S NO WAY YOU COULD HAVE KNOWN, THREEPIO.
YEAH. COME ON, DON'T BE SO HARD ON YOURSELF. NO ONE'S GONNA BLAME YOU FOR TELLING THE TRUTH.
Y'KNOW, LEIA... I'VE SEEN FIRSTHAND JUST WHAT KIND OF DEMON FIGHTERS THE LOCAL ARMY'S GOT...
BUT I WAS OUT OF ACTION A LONG TIME, WHILE THOSE BOUNTY HUNTERS HAD ME FROZEN IN HIBERNATION.
I HAVE ABSOLUTELY NO IDEA WHAT THE OTHER SIDE'S GONNA BE LIKE IN ACTION. IN FACT, I KNOW ALMOST NOTHING ABOUT 'EM.
WELL, YOU'RE GOING TO LEARN, HAN...
BECAUSE THE EWOKS OF ENDOR HAVE DECLARED WAR ON THE LAHSBEES.
4

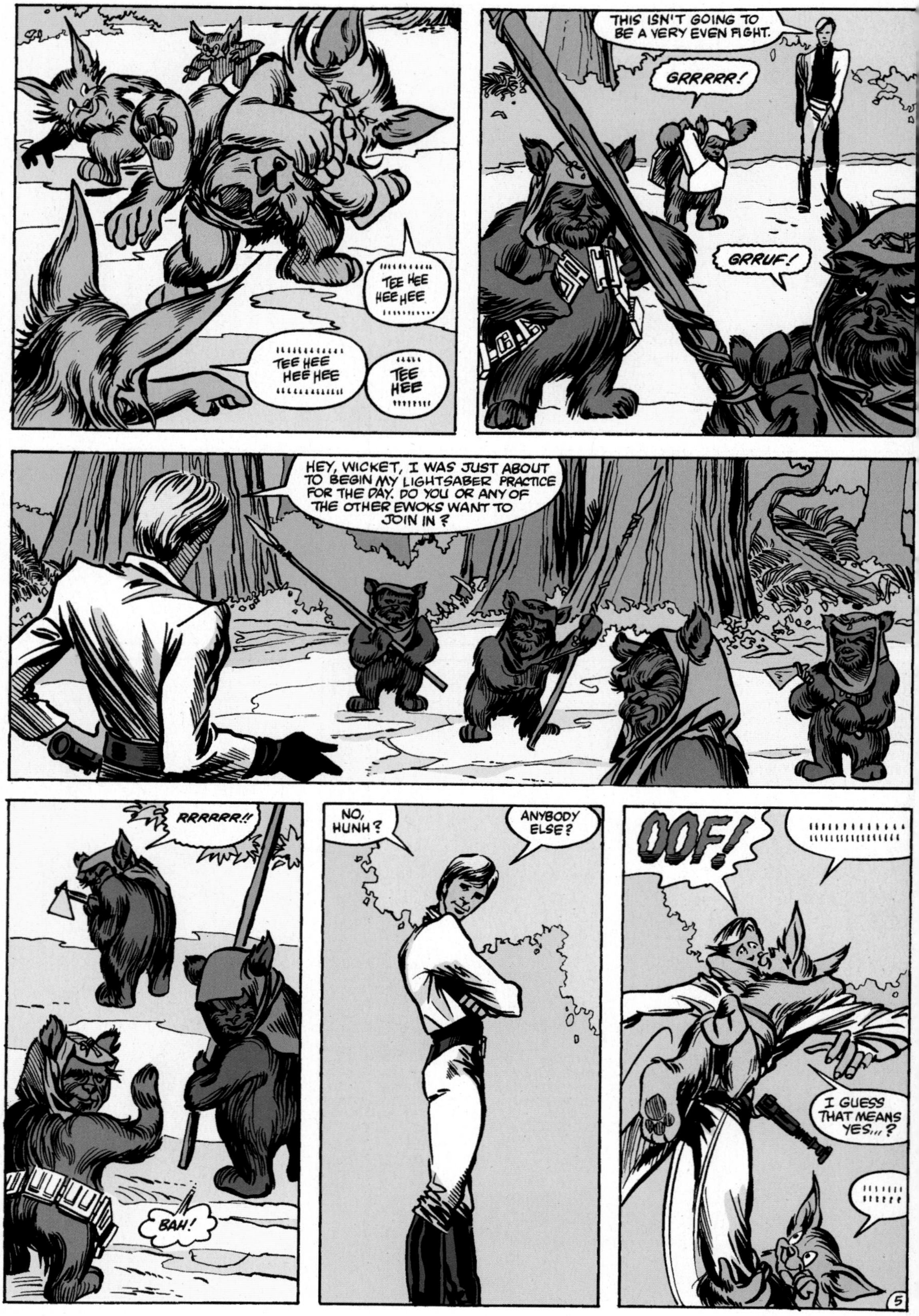
TEE HEE HEE HEE
TEE HEE HEE HEE
TEE HEE
THIS ISN'T GOING TO BE A VERY EVEN FIGHT.
GRRRRR!
GRRUF!
HEY, WICKET, I WAS JUST ABOUT TO BEGIN MY LIGHTSABER PRACTICE FOR THE DAY. DO YOU OR ANY OF THE OTHER EWOKS WANT TO JOIN IN?
RRRRRR!!
BAH!
NO, HUNH?
ANYBODY ELSE?
OOF!
I GUESS THAT MEANS YES...?
5

HIROG TO THE HIROMI MOTHER SHIP... HIROG TO THE HIROMI MOTHER SHIP... DO YOU COPY?

DO NOT, REPEAT, DO NOT BE AFRAID TO RESPOND. IT IS PERFECTLY SAFE FOR US TO CONVERSE. I HAVE USED MY POSITION AS AIDE TO ADMIRAL ACKBAR--

--TO MAKE CERTAIN THAT NO ALLIANCE PERSONNEL WILL MONITOR THIS FREQUENCY.

I AM PLEASED TO REPORT THAT ALL IS PROCEEDING ACCORDING TO PLAN. AFTER OVER TWO MILLENNIA OF WATCHING AND PLANNING, IT IS TIME FOR US -- THE HIROMI-- TO ACHIEVE OUR GLORIOUS DESTINY.

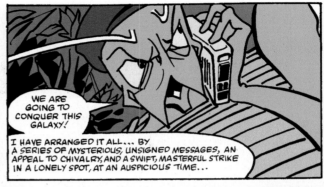

WE ARE GOING TO CONQUER THIS GALAXY!

I HAVE ARRANGED IT ALL.... BY A SERIES OF MYSTERIOUS, UNSIGNED MESSAGES, AN APPEAL TO CHIVALRY, AND A SWIFT, MASTERFUL STRIKE IN A LONELY SPOT, AT AN AUSPICIOUS TIME...

...I HAVE MADE IT APPEAR THAT ONE OF THE MOST PROMINENT OF THE DELEGATES FROM LAHSBANE HAD COMPROMISED PRINCESS KAMIDA, A LOVELY YOUNG EWOK, WHOSE TRUE SWAIN, TIPPET...

...IS A PILLAR OF BOTH HIS OWN RACE AND OF THE ALLIANCE. AND I ARRANGED FOR AN IMPARTIAL, UTTERLY TRUSTWORTHY BLABBER-MOUTH TO SEE THE MOST INCRIMINATING MOMENT OF THE WHOLE!

TIPPET IS SO JEALOUS, HE WON'T HEAR REASON, AND SO HIS ENTIRE RACE HAVE DECLARED WAR ON THE TREACHEROUS, LASCIVIOUS LAHSBEES!

THESE ARE TWO OF THE SILLIEST MOST INCONSEQUENTIAL PEOPLES I HAVE EVER ENCOUNTERED. OF COURSE, OTHER ALLIANCE RACES WILL HAVE TO TAKE SIDES!

AND AS THEIR UNITY CRUMBLES, WE CAN MOVE IN!

IT SIMPLY CAN'T FAIL!

6

AND NOW, JUST IN CASE IT SHOULD BE A HIDDEN THREAT TO US, I AM ABOUT TO OBSERVE THE ONE PHENOMENON THAT IS STILL A MYSTERY.

WE HAVE ALL HEARD LEGENDS OF THE FAMOUS JEDI KNIGHTS, AND THEIR MASTERY OF THE FORCE-- AN ENERGY FIELD THAT GIVES THEM TALENTS LIKE MIND CONTROL, TELEKINESIS AND TELEPATHY...

WELL, LUKE SKYWALKER, THE ONLY KNOWN SURVIVING JEDI, IS A COMMANDER IN THE ALLIANCE, AND I'M ABOUT TO WITNESS, FIRSTHAND, ONE OF HIS TRAINING EXERCISES!

YOU GUYS SURE YOU'VE GOT IT?

I'M GOING TO WAIT, WITH MY BACK TO YOU, AND MY EYES CLOSED. I WON'T EVEN HAVE MY LIGHTSABER ACTIVATED. YOU BE AS QUIET AS YOU CAN, AND ATTACK ME FROM AS MANY DIFFERENT DIRECTIONS AS YOU WANT.

GOOD.

OKAY. READY WHENEVER YOU ARE.

			-TEE-HEE-HEE-HEE-			
						(	(||||||||||)	)	
				//-HEE HEE-				

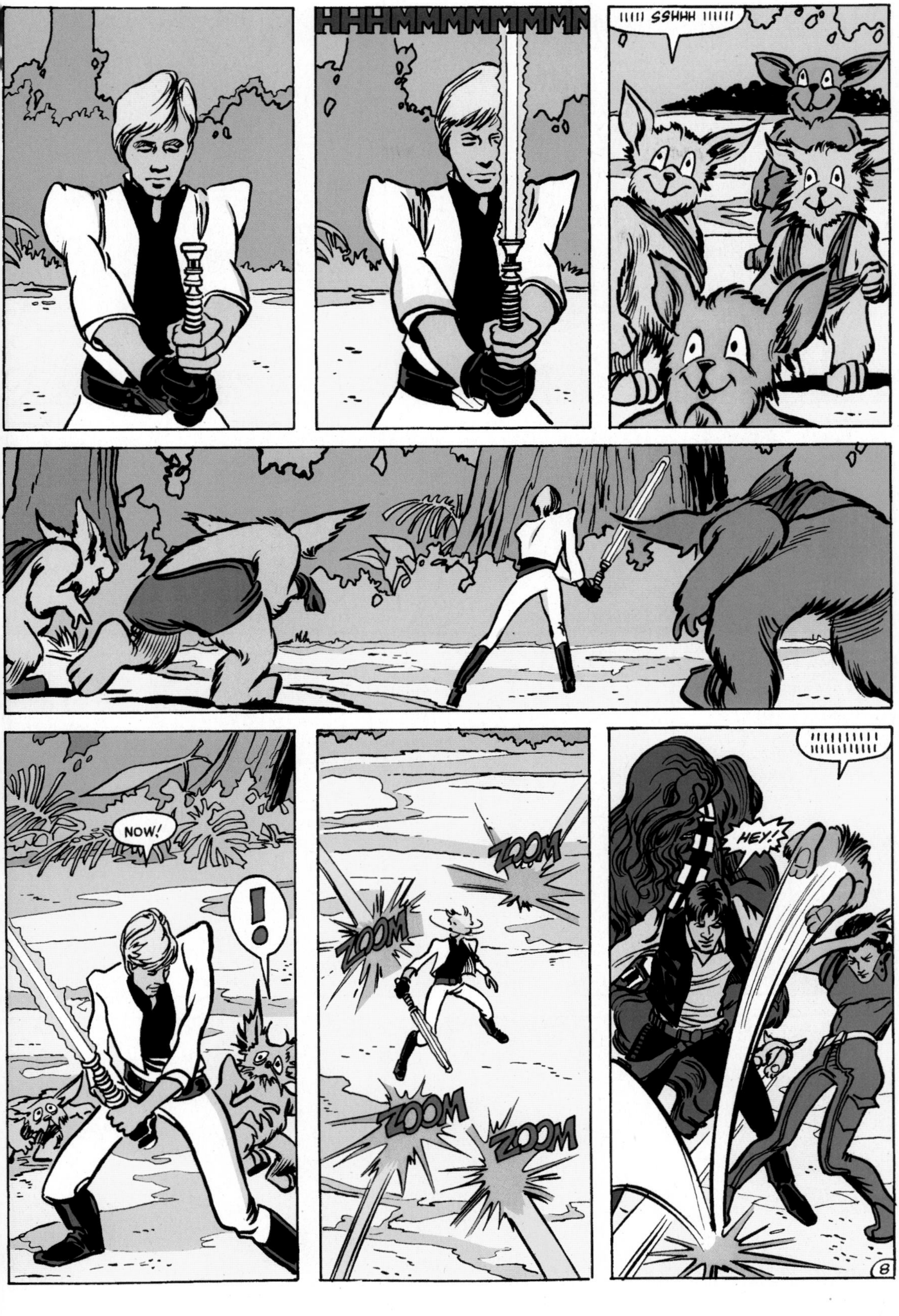
HHHHMMMMMMMMMN
!!!!! SSHHH !!!!!!
NOW!
!
ZOOM
ZOOM
ZOOM
ZOOM
!!!!!!!!!!!!
HEY!
8

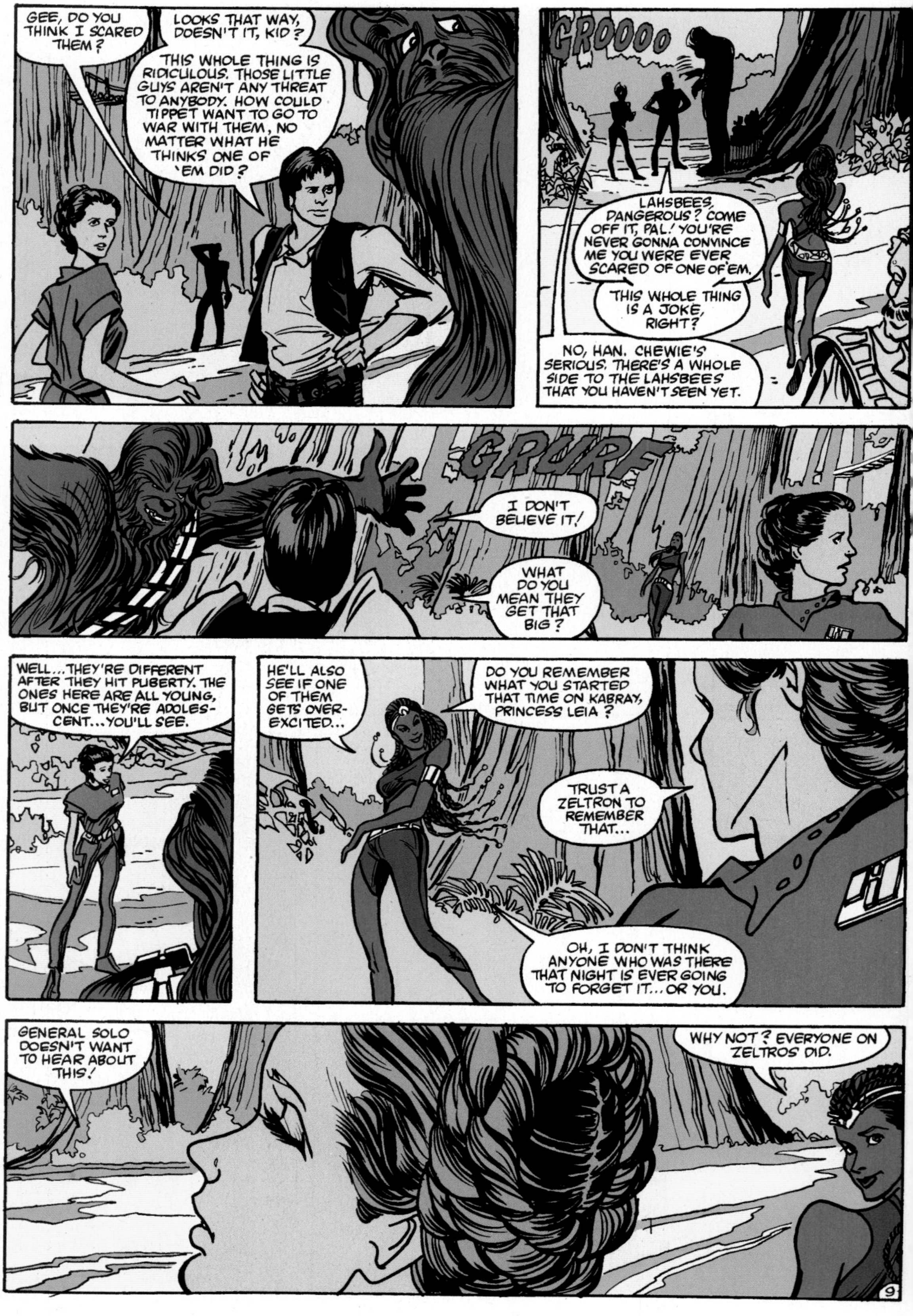
GEE, DO YOU THINK I SCARED THEM?
LOOKS THAT WAY, DOESN'T IT, KID?
THIS WHOLE THING IS RIDICULOUS. THOSE LITTLE GUYS AREN'T ANY THREAT TO ANYBODY. HOW COULD TIPPET WANT TO GO TO WAR WITH THEM, NO MATTER WHAT HE THINKS ONE OF 'EM DID?
GROOOO
LAHSBEES, DANGEROUS? COME OFF IT, PAL! YOU'RE NEVER GONNA CONVINCE ME YOU WERE EVER SCARED OF ONE OF 'EM.
THIS WHOLE THING IS A JOKE, RIGHT?
NO, HAN. CHEWIE'S SERIOUS. THERE'S A WHOLE SIDE TO THE LAHSBEES THAT YOU HAVEN'T SEEN YET.
GRURF
I DON'T BELIEVE IT!
WHAT DO YOU MEAN THEY GET THAT BIG?
WELL... THEY'RE DIFFERENT AFTER THEY HIT PUBERTY. THE ONES HERE ARE ALL YOUNG, BUT ONCE THEY'RE ADOLES-CENT... YOU'LL SEE.
HE'LL ALSO SEE IF ONE OF THEM GETS OVER-EXCITED...
DO YOU REMEMBER WHAT YOU STARTED THAT TIME ON KABRAY, PRINCESS LEIA?
TRUST A ZELTRON TO REMEMBER THAT...
OH, I DON'T THINK ANYONE WHO WAS THERE THAT NIGHT IS EVER GOING TO FORGET IT... OR YOU.
GENERAL SOLO DOESN'T WANT TO HEAR ABOUT THIS!
WHY NOT? EVERYONE ON ZELTROS DID.
9

AW, COME ON DOWN, YOU GUYS. I'M NOT GOING TO HURT YOU. I PROMISE.

I WON'T TOUCH ANY OF YOU WITH THE SABER BLADE OR HIT ANY-ONE AT ALL.

PLEASE. I REALLY NEED THE PRACTICE.

|||||| ||||||||

LUKE, WHY ARE YOU SO DETERMINED TO GO THROUGH WITH THIS?

I WAS HOPING I COULD GET BOTH SIDES TO WORK OUT WITH ME... MAYBE IF THEY ALL LET OFF A LITTLE STEAM, WE COULD GET THEM TO CALM DOWN AND TALK THINGS OVER.

BUT IT DOESN'T LOOK LIKE IT'S WORKING OUT THAT WAY.

OKAY... ONE MORE TIME.

BOFF

EEK!

|||||| ||||||

HEY! WHO'S THROWING THOSE STONES?

10

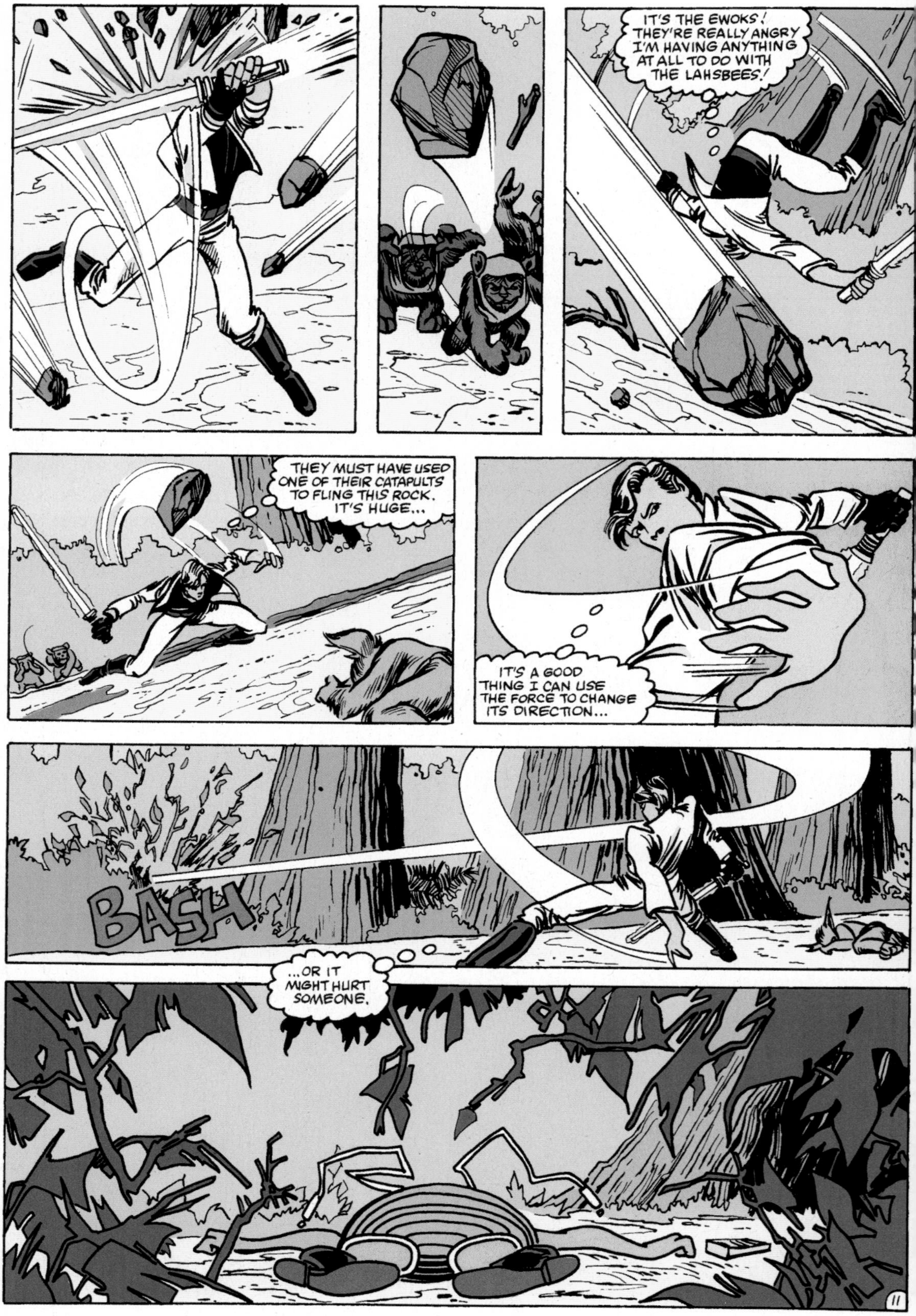
IT'S THE EWOKS! THEY'RE REALLY ANGRY I'M HAVING ANYTHING AT ALL TO DO WITH THE LAHSBEES!
THEY MUST HAVE USED ONE OF THEIR CATAPULTS TO FLING THIS ROCK. IT'S HUGE...
IT'S A GOOD THING I CAN USE THE FORCE TO CHANGE ITS DIRECTION...
BASH
...OR IT MIGHT HURT SOMEONE.
11

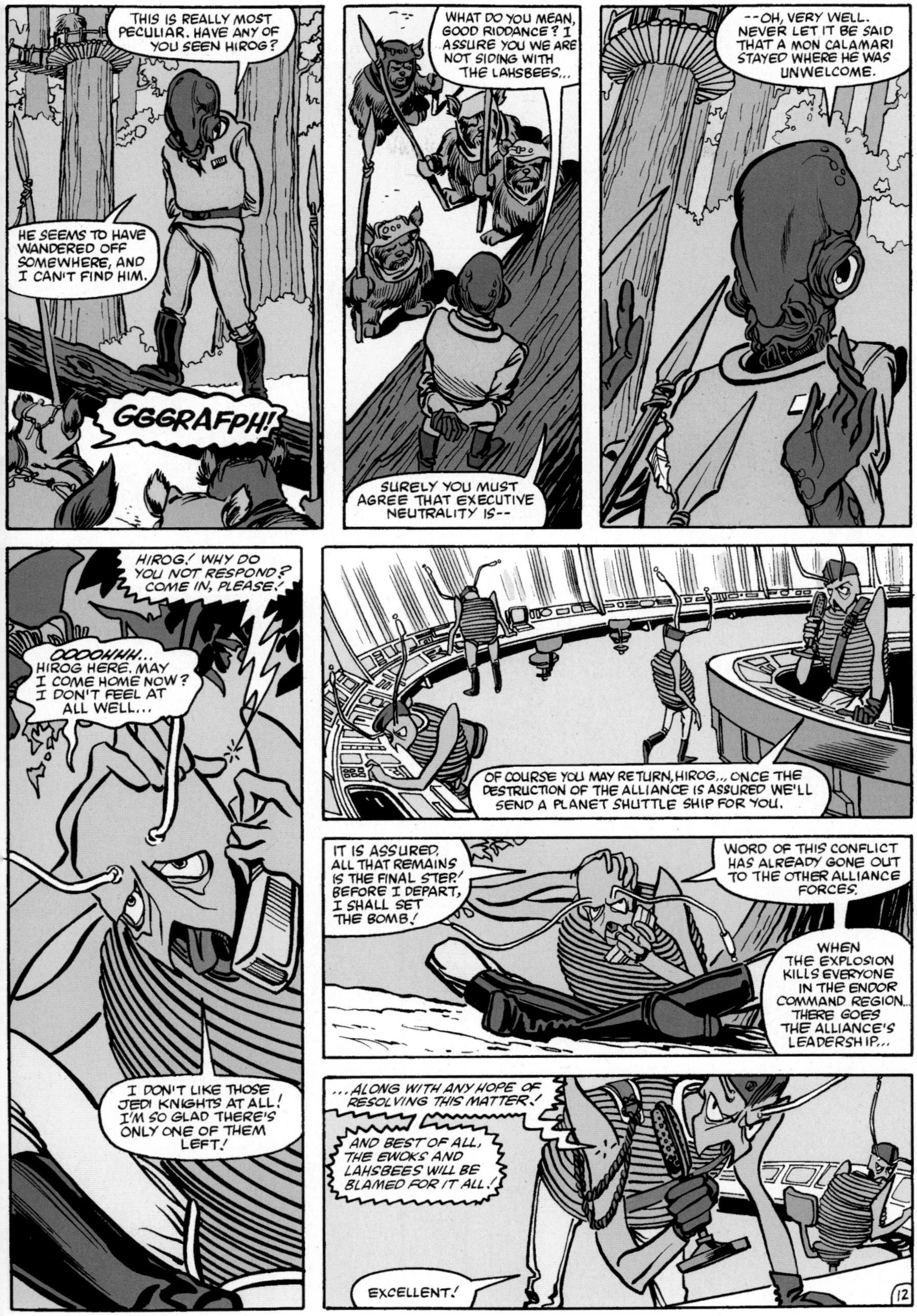
THIS IS REALLY MOST PECULIAR. HAVE ANY OF YOU SEEN HIROG?
HE SEEMS TO HAVE WANDERED OFF SOMEWHERE, AND I CAN'T FIND HIM.
GGGRAFPH!
WHAT DO YOU MEAN, GOOD RIDDANCE? I ASSURE YOU WE ARE NOT SIDING WITH THE LAHSBEES...
SURELY YOU MUST AGREE THAT EXECUTIVE NEUTRALITY IS--
--OH, VERY WELL. NEVER LET IT BE SAID THAT A MON CALAMARI STAYED WHERE HE WAS UNWELCOME.
HIROG! WHY DO YOU NOT RESPOND? COME IN, PLEASE!
OOOOHHH... HIROG HERE. MAY I COME HOME NOW? I DON'T FEEL AT ALL WELL...
I DON'T LIKE THOSE JEDI KNIGHTS AT ALL! I'M SO GLAD THERE'S ONLY ONE OF THEM LEFT!
OF COURSE YOU MAY RETURN, HIROG... ONCE THE DESTRUCTION OF THE ALLIANCE IS ASSURED WE'LL SEND A PLANET SHUTTLE SHIP FOR YOU.
IT IS ASSURED. ALL THAT REMAINS IS THE FINAL STEP! BEFORE I DEPART, I SHALL SET THE BOMB!
WORD OF THIS CONFLICT HAS ALREADY GONE OUT TO THE OTHER ALLIANCE FORCES.
WHEN THE EXPLOSION KILLS EVERYONE IN THE ENDOR COMMAND REGION... THERE GOES THE ALLIANCE'S LEADERSHIP...
...ALONG WITH ANY HOPE OF RESOLVING THIS MATTER!
AND BEST OF ALL, THE EWOKS AND LAHSBEES WILL BE BLAMED FOR IT ALL!
EXCELLENT!
12

I'M SO SURE THERE MUST BE SOMETHING I CAN DO TO ALLEVIATE THIS... IF ONLY I KNEW WHAT!

AFTER ALL, I'M THE ONLY ONE HERE WHO IS FLUENT IN THE LANGUAGES OF BOTH THE WARRING SPECIES...

BOOP

...AND THE EWOKS -- WHO ARE THE AGGRESSORS, BECAUSE OF THE PROVOCATION THEY'VE RECEIVED -- ACTUALLY REVERED ME AS A GOD AT ONE TIME.

SURELY THEY'D LISTEN, IF I COULD ONLY...

AHHOOO?

ARTOO, WHERE ARE YOU GOING?

UEET! UEETT

HEAR SOMEONE? WHO DO YOU HEAR? WHERE? NONSENSE!

HIROG TO--

EEP!

WOOO!

HIROG?!

ARTOO-DETOO! SEE-THREEPIO!

UH... LOVELY DAY WE'RE HAVING, ISN'T IT?

IS IT REALLY? WE HADN'T NOTICED!

THERE! YOU SEE HOW YOU'RE LETTING YOUR IMAGINATION GET THE BETTER OF YOU, ARTOO? IT'S ONLY HIROG!

DRAT! THIS IS GETTING COMPLICATED! I'D BETTER ACT FAST!

13

OH, YOU ARE JUST THE CUTEST LITTLE THING!

STOP WHAT YOU ARE DOING AND PUT THAT LAHSBEE DOWN!

|||||||||| |||||||||| ||||||||||||

BUT ADMIRAL ACKBAR, HE LIKES IT!

AND THAT IS PRECISELY WHY IT MUST STOP! SOME OF THOSE LAHSBEES HAVE REACHED A DANGEROUSLY ADVANCED AGE, YOU KNOW. DOESN'T THE TERM "HUHK" MEAN ANYTHING TO YOU?

SURE... I WAS ONE OF THE ZELTRONS ON KABRAY, BUT...

...OH, WELL...

||||||||| |||||||||

÷ SIGH ÷

WELL, THAT WAS A COMPLETE WASHOUT.

THE LAHSBEES DON'T WANT TO FIGHT. BUT THEY DIDN'T WANT TO FIGHT IN THE FIRST PLACE.

ALL I'VE DONE IS MAKE TIPPET AND HIS FRIENDS THINK WE'RE GANGING UP ON THEM...

THEY WON'T BELIEVE THAT PRINCESS KAMIDA AND THAT LAHSBEE WERE FRAMED SOMEHOW...

...AND THEY'RE MORE DETERMINED TO FIGHT THAN EVER.

14

NO, LUKE, MY FRIEND, ALL IS NOT LOST! WHILE YOU WERE TRYING YOUR PLAN, I FORMULATED ONE OF MY OWN!

AND IT CAN'T FAIL! IT'S BRILLIANT!

WHAT SORT OF PLAN, LANDO?

WELL, THIS WHOLE THING ISN'T REALLY GROUNDS FOR WAR, NOW IS IT? IT'S AN AFFAIR OF THE HEART.

I MANAGED TO CONVINCE BOTH SIDES TO AGREE THAT IT'S JUST A MATTER OF HONOR BETWEEN TIPPET, AND THE SENIOR LAHSBEE DELEGATE.

SO... THEY'RE GOING TO SETTLE IT BETWEEN THEMSELVES, IN SINGLE COMBAT.

MAN TO MAN, SO TO SPEAK.

RRRR...

|||||||||||||||||

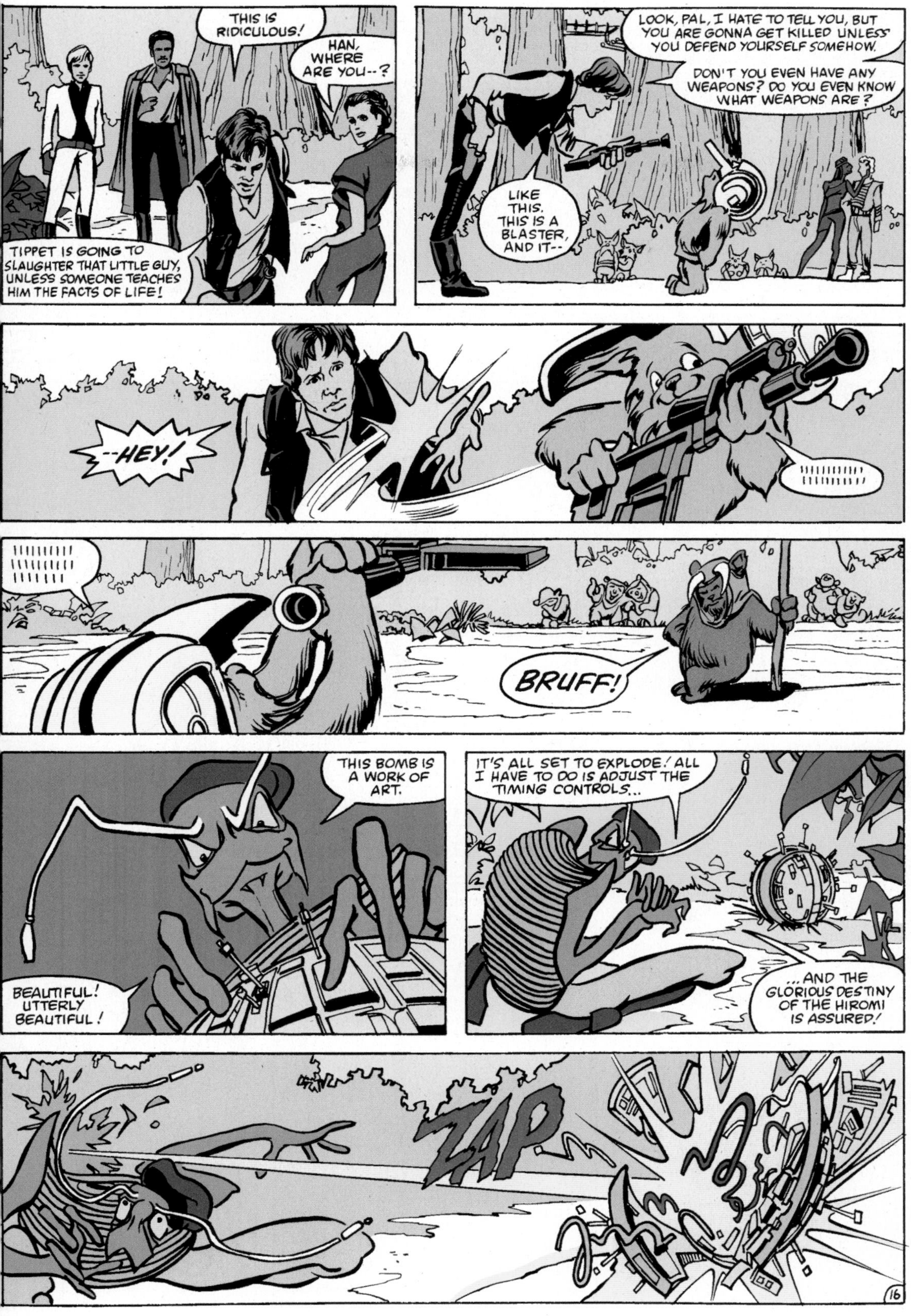
THIS IS RIDICULOUS!
HAN, WHERE ARE YOU--?
TIPPET IS GOING TO SLAUGHTER THAT LITTLE GUY, UNLESS SOMEONE TEACHES HIM THE FACTS OF LIFE!
LOOK, PAL, I HATE TO TELL YOU, BUT YOU ARE GONNA GET KILLED UNLESS YOU DEFEND YOURSELF SOMEHOW.
DON'T YOU EVEN HAVE ANY WEAPONS? DO YOU EVEN KNOW WHAT WEAPONS ARE?
LIKE THIS. THIS IS A BLASTER, AND IT--
--HEY!
BRUFF!
THIS BOMB IS A WORK OF ART.
BEAUTIFUL! UTTERLY BEAUTIFUL!
IT'S ALL SET TO EXPLODE! ALL I HAVE TO DO IS ADJUST THE TIMING CONTROLS...
...AND THE GLORIOUS DESTINY OF THE HIROMI IS ASSURED!
ZAP
16

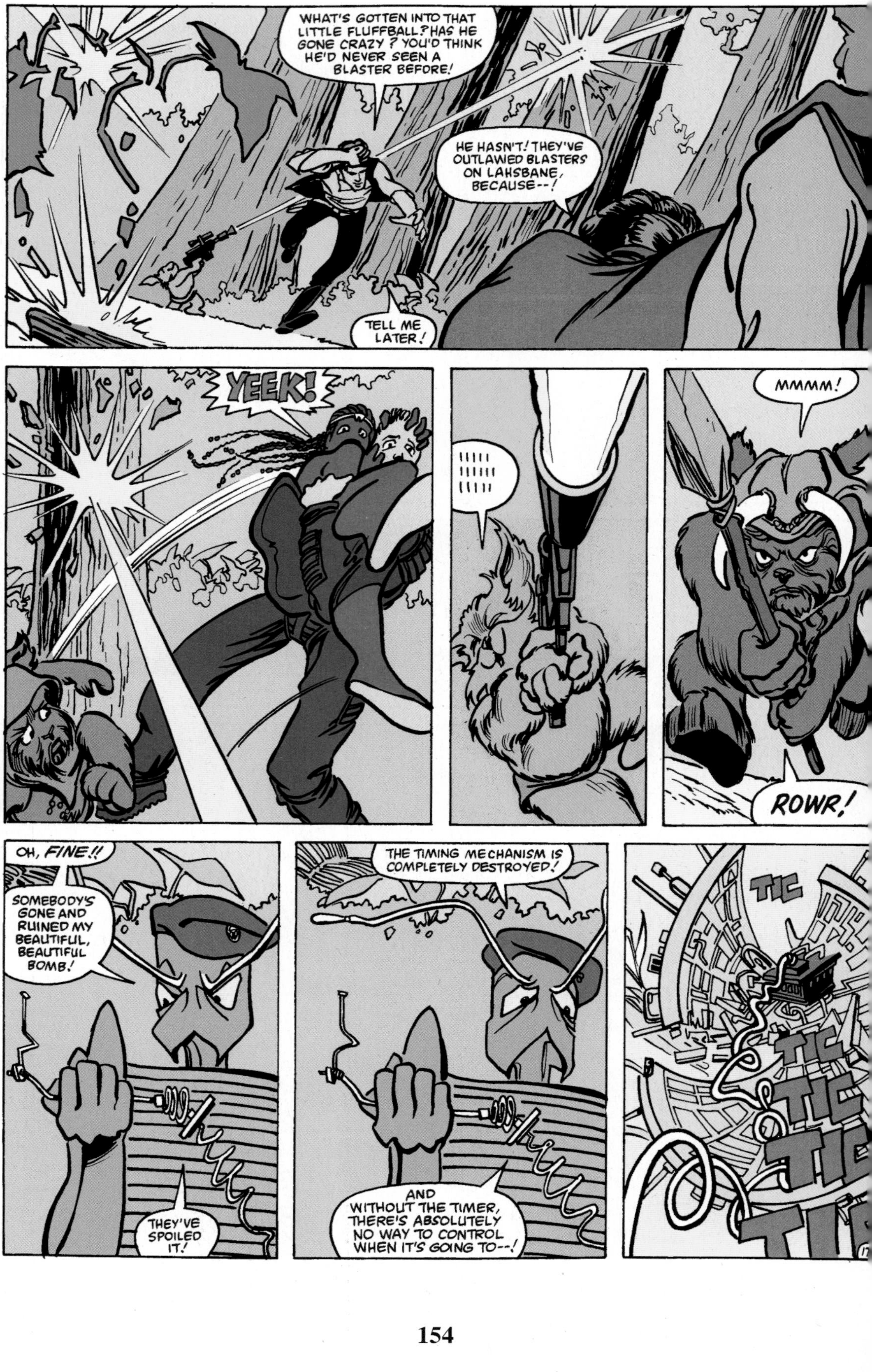
WHAT'S GOTTEN INTO THAT LITTLE FLUFFBALL? HAS HE GONE CRAZY? YOU'D THINK HE'D NEVER SEEN A BLASTER BEFORE!
HE HASN'T! THEY'VE OUTLAWED BLASTERS ON LAHSBANE, BECAUSE--!
TELL ME LATER!
YEEK!
!!!!!
!!!!!
!!!!!
MMMM!
ROWR!
OH, FINE!!
SOMEBODY'S GONE AND RUINED MY BEAUTIFUL, BEAUTIFUL BOMB!
THEY'VE SPOILED IT!
THE TIMING MECHANISM IS COMPLETELY DESTROYED!
AND WITHOUT THE TIMER, THERE'S ABSOLUTELY NO WAY TO CONTROL WHEN IT'S GOING TO--!
TIC
TIC
TIC
TIC
17

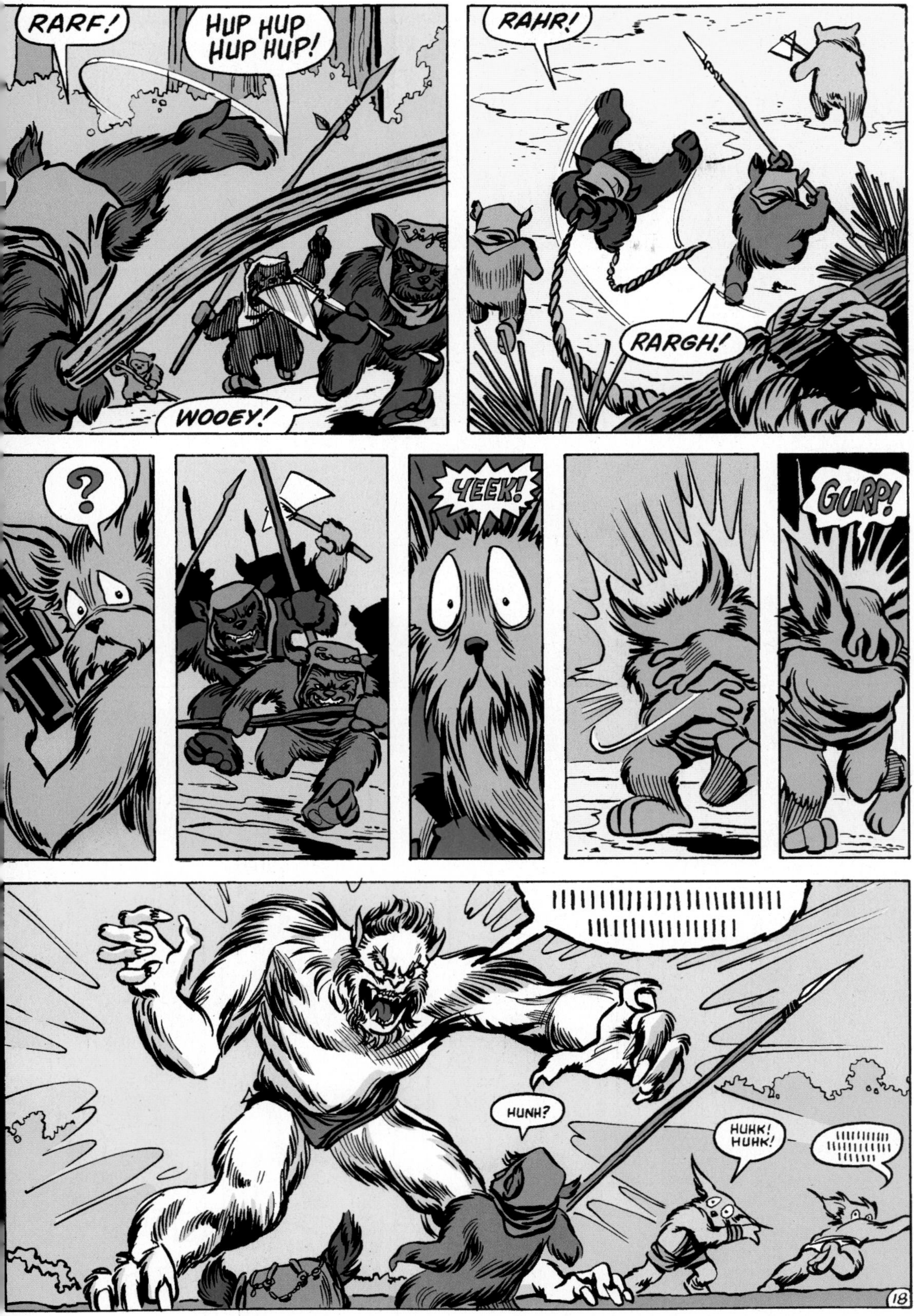
RARF!
HUP HUP HUP HUP!
WOOEY!
RAHR!
RARGH!
?
YEEK!
GURP!
HUNH?
HUHK! HUHK!
18

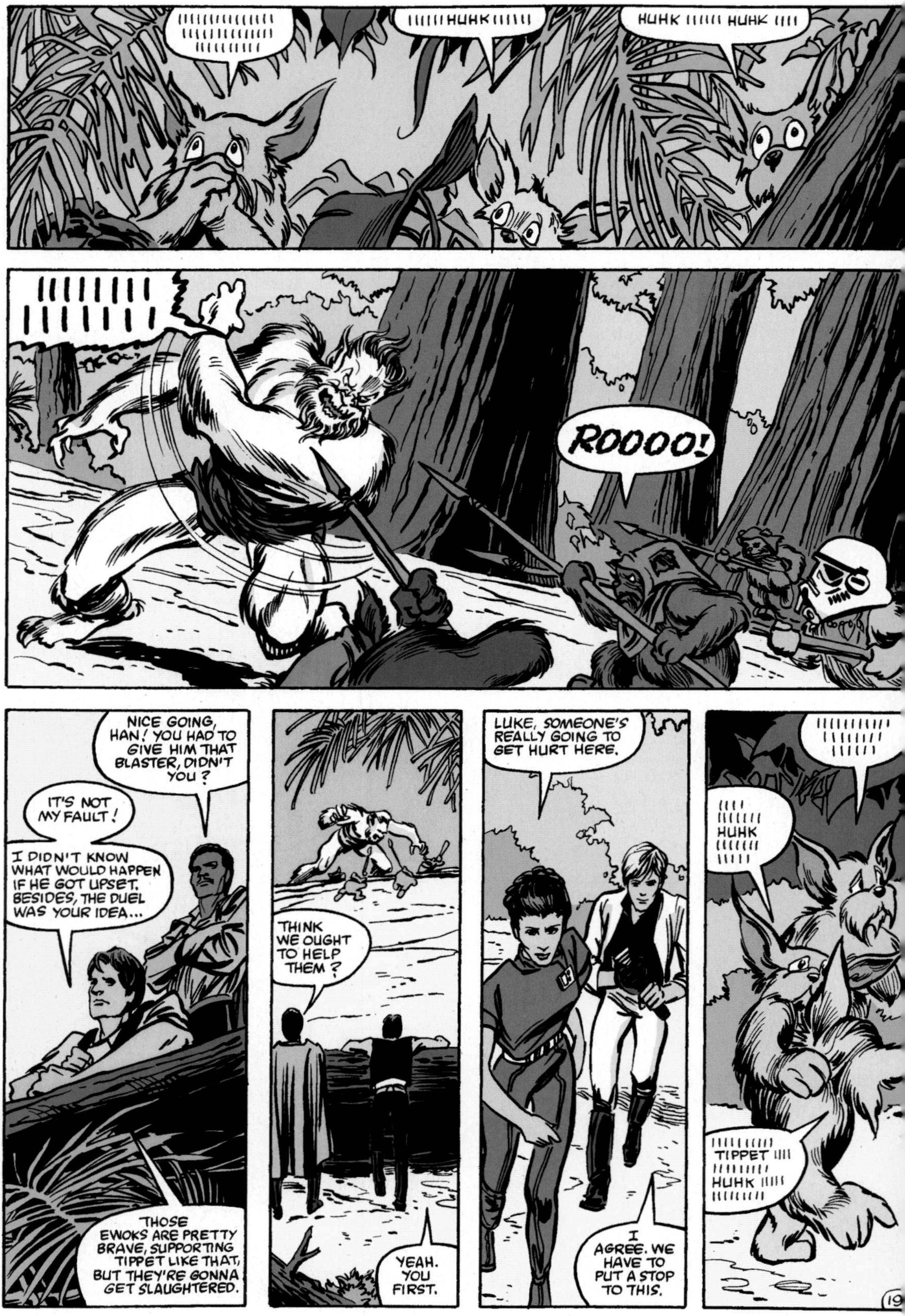
HUHK
HUHK HUHK
ROOOO!
NICE GOING, HAN! YOU HAD TO GIVE HIM THAT BLASTER, DIDN'T YOU?
IT'S NOT MY FAULT!
I DIDN'T KNOW WHAT WOULD HAPPEN IF HE GOT UPSET. BESIDES, THE DUEL WAS YOUR IDEA...
THOSE EWOKS ARE PRETTY BRAVE, SUPPORTING TIPPET LIKE THAT, BUT THEY'RE GONNA GET SLAUGHTERED.
THINK WE OUGHT TO HELP THEM?
YEAH. YOU FIRST.
LUKE, SOMEONE'S REALLY GOING TO GET HURT HERE.
I AGREE. WE HAVE TO PUT A STOP TO THIS.
HUHK
TIPPET
HUHK
19

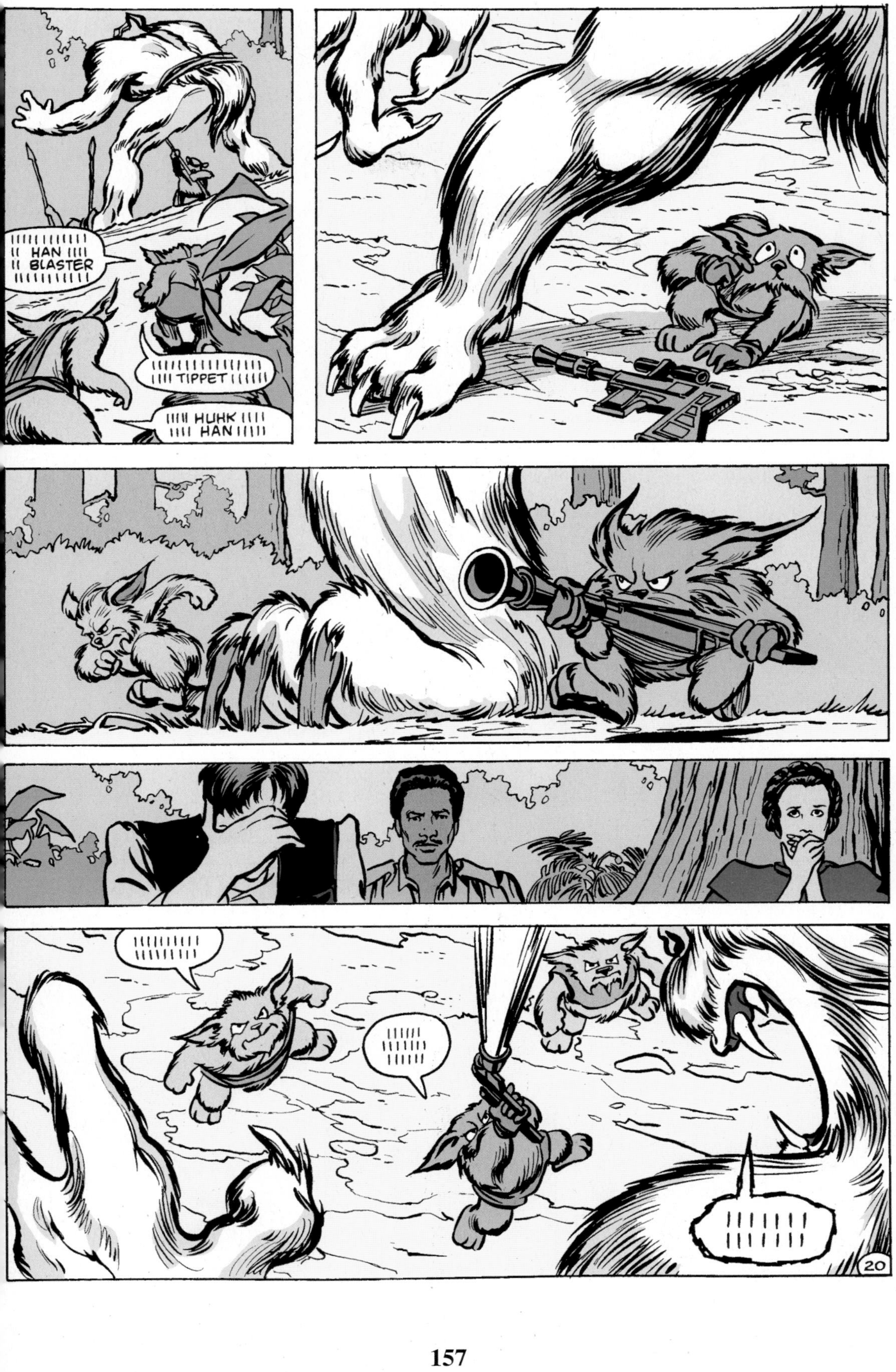
HAN BLASTER
TIPPET
HUHK HAN
20

VORP

MMRR?

|||||||||||||||||||

RUN! RUN FOR YOUR LIVES!
EVERYONE RUN! WE ARE
ALL GOING TO DIE!

MY BOMB IS GOING TO EXPLODE
AND KILL US ALL, AND I CAN'T
CONTROL IT! WE ARE ALL DOOMED!

?

?

!

HELP!
OH, HELP!
PLEASE
HELP!!!

HE-HE-HE-E-E-E-LP!!

|||||||||||
|||||||||||

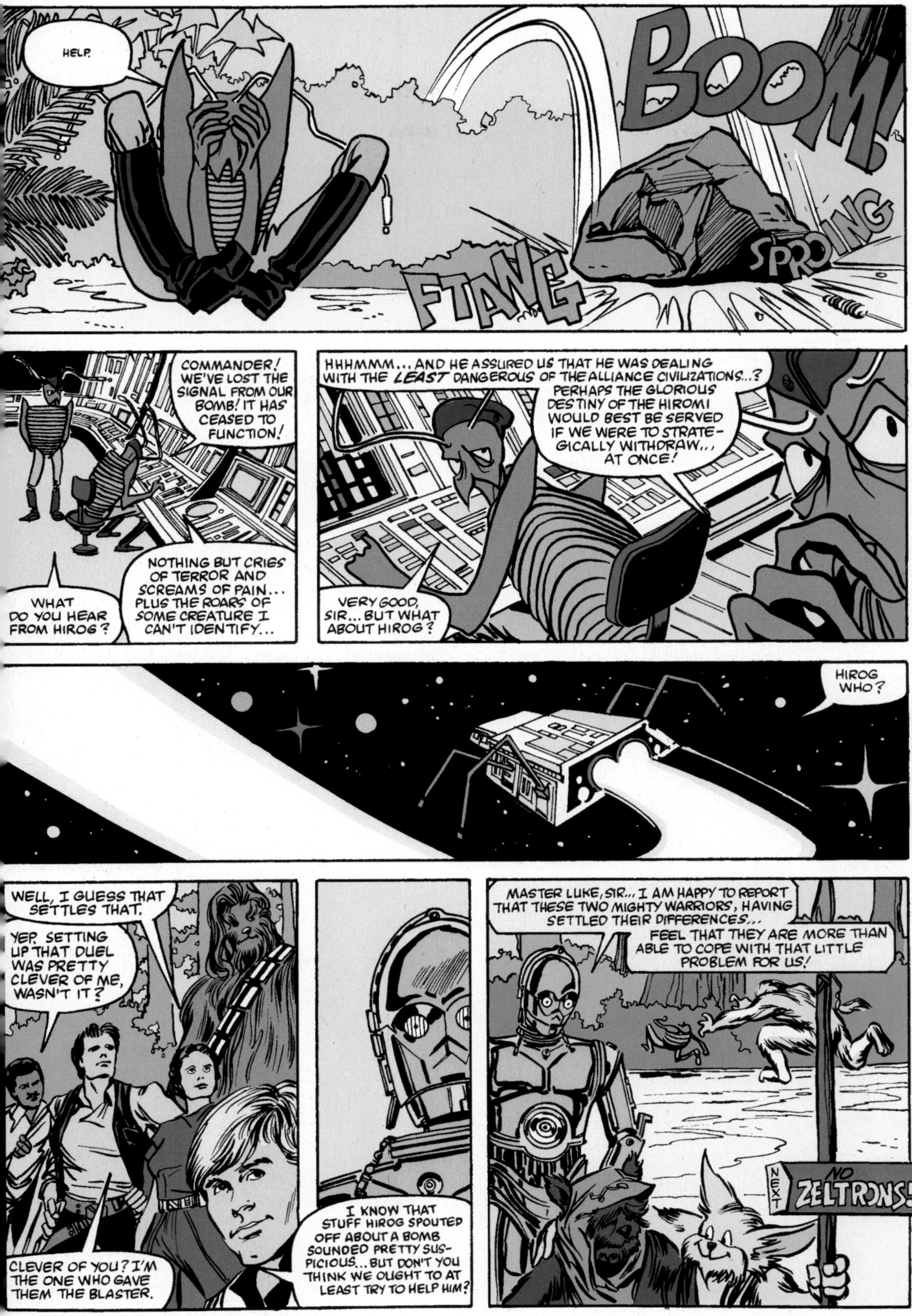

HELP.
BOOM!
SPROING
FTANG
COMMANDER! WE'VE LOST THE SIGNAL FROM OUR BOMB! IT HAS CEASED TO FUNCTION!
WHAT DO YOU HEAR FROM HIROG?
NOTHING BUT CRIES OF TERROR AND SCREAMS OF PAIN... PLUS THE ROARS OF SOME CREATURE I CAN'T IDENTIFY...
HHHMMM... AND HE ASSURED US THAT HE WAS DEALING WITH THE LEAST DANGEROUS OF THE ALLIANCE CIVILIZATIONS...?
PERHAPS THE GLORIOUS DESTINY OF THE HIROMI WOULD BEST BE SERVED IF WE WERE TO STRATEGICALLY WITHDRAW... AT ONCE!
VERY GOOD, SIR... BUT WHAT ABOUT HIROG?
HIROG WHO?
WELL, I GUESS THAT SETTLES THAT.
YEP. SETTING UP THAT DUEL WAS PRETTY CLEVER OF ME, WASN'T IT?
CLEVER OF YOU? I'M THE ONE WHO GAVE THEM THE BLASTER.
I KNOW THAT STUFF HIROG SPOUTED OFF ABOUT A BOMB SOUNDED PRETTY SUSPICIOUS... BUT DON'T YOU THINK WE OUGHT TO AT LEAST TRY TO HELP HIM?
MASTER LUKE, SIR... I AM HAPPY TO REPORT THAT THESE TWO MIGHTY WARRIORS, HAVING SETTLED THEIR DIFFERENCES...
FEEL THAT THEY ARE MORE THAN ABLE TO COPE WITH THAT LITTLE PROBLEM FOR US!
NEXT
NO ZELTRONS!

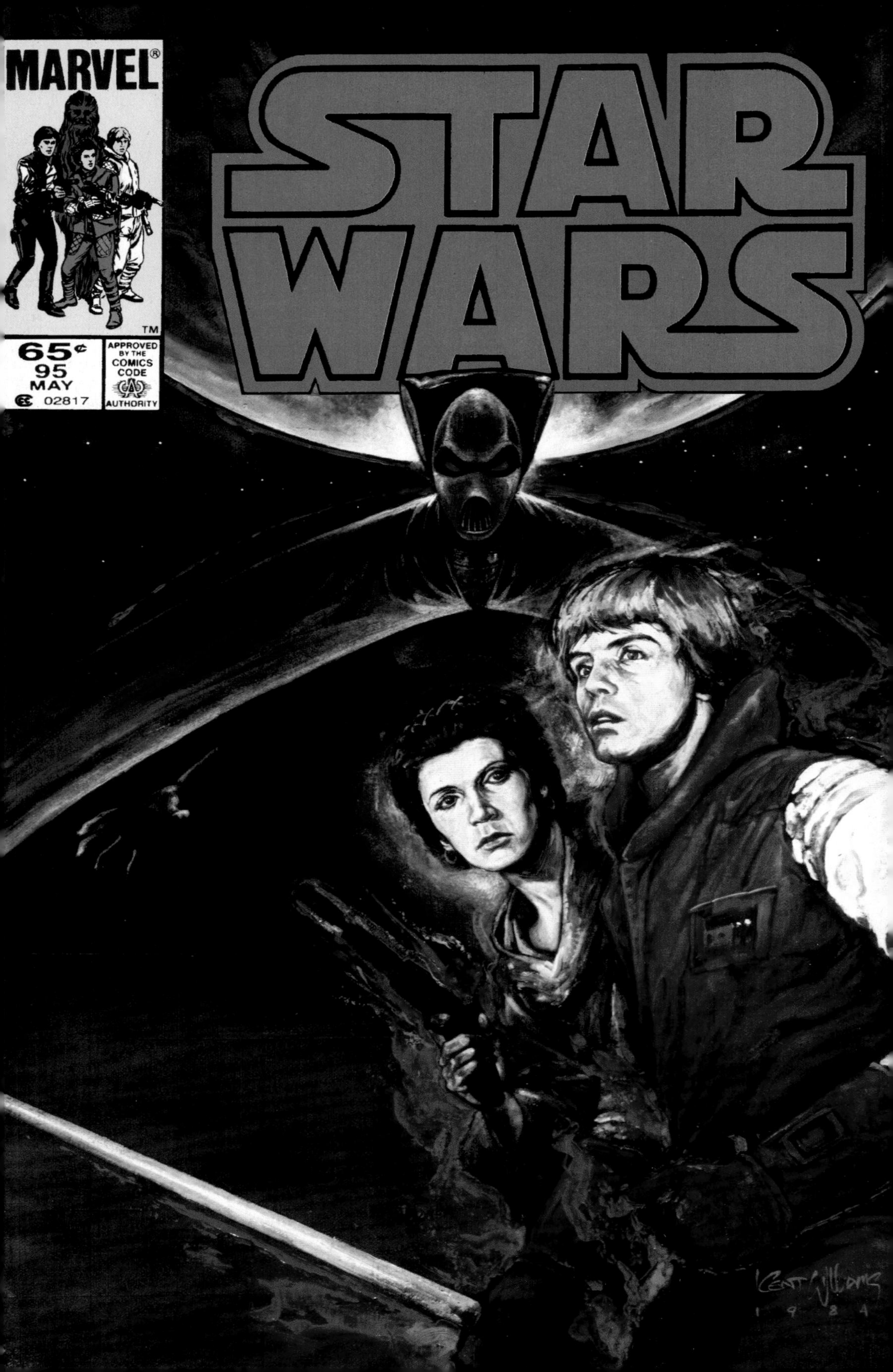
MARVEL®
STAR WARS
TM
65¢
95
MAY
02817
APPROVED BY THE COMICS CODE AUTHORITY
Kent Williams
1984

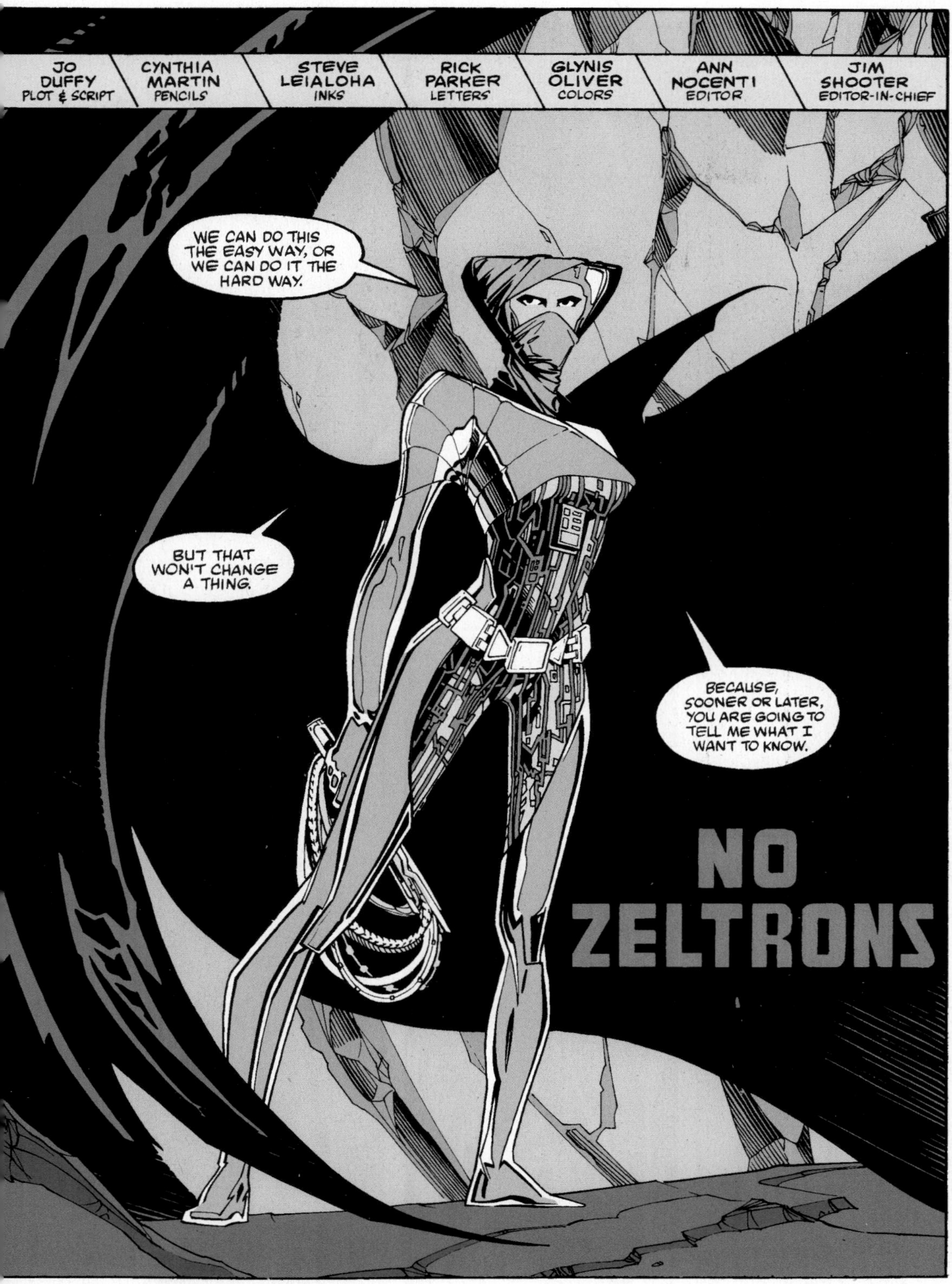

JO DUFFY PLOT & SCRIPT
CYNTHIA MARTIN PENCILS
STEVE LEIALOHA INKS
RICK PARKER LETTERS
GLYNIS OLIVER COLORS
ANN NOCENTI EDITOR
JIM SHOOTER EDITOR-IN-CHIEF
WE CAN DO THIS THE EASY WAY, OR WE CAN DO IT THE HARD WAY.
BUT THAT WON'T CHANGE A THING.
BECAUSE, SOONER OR LATER, YOU ARE GOING TO TELL ME WHAT I WANT TO KNOW.
NO ZELTRONS

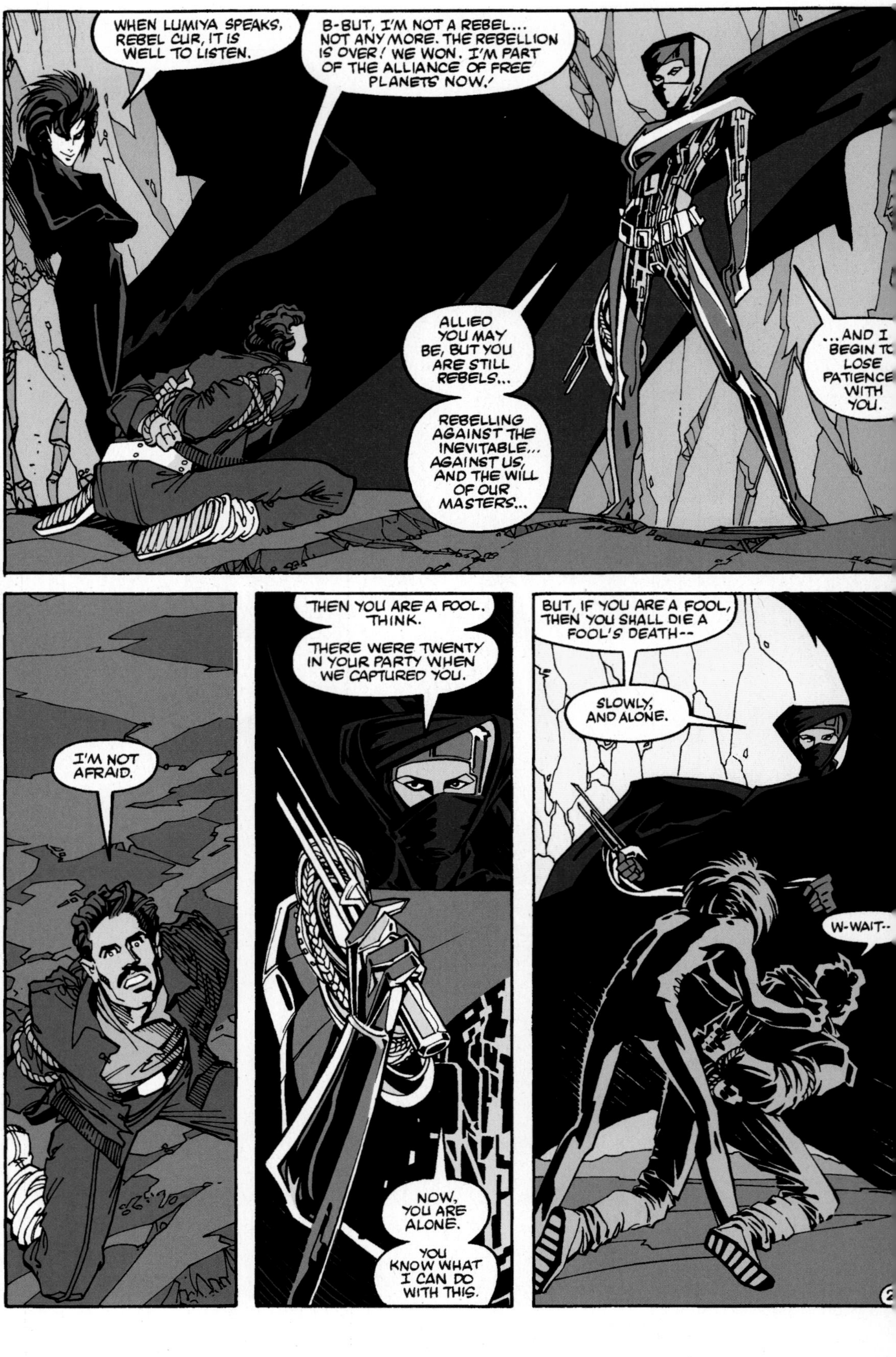
WHEN LUMIYA SPEAKS, REBEL CUR, IT IS WELL TO LISTEN.
B-BUT, I'M NOT A REBEL... NOT ANY MORE. THE REBELLION IS OVER! WE WON. I'M PART OF THE ALLIANCE OF FREE PLANETS NOW!
ALLIED YOU MAY BE, BUT YOU ARE STILL REBELS...
REBELLING AGAINST THE INEVITABLE... AGAINST US, AND THE WILL OF OUR MASTERS...
...AND I BEGIN TO LOSE PATIENCE WITH YOU.
I'M NOT AFRAID.
THEN YOU ARE A FOOL. THINK.
THERE WERE TWENTY IN YOUR PARTY WHEN WE CAPTURED YOU.
NOW, YOU ARE ALONE.
YOU KNOW WHAT I CAN DO WITH THIS.
BUT, IF YOU ARE A FOOL, THEN YOU SHALL DIE A FOOL'S DEATH--
SLOWLY, AND ALONE.
W-WAIT--

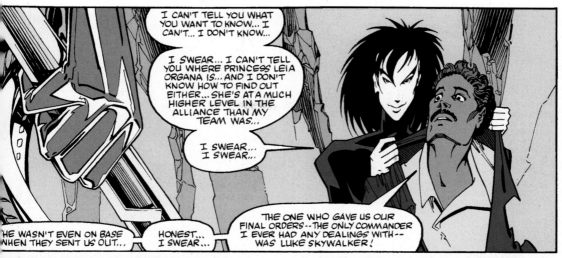

I CAN'T TELL YOU WHAT YOU WANT TO KNOW... I CAN'T... I DON'T KNOW...

I SWEAR... I CAN'T TELL YOU WHERE PRINCESS LEIA ORGANA IS... AND I DON'T KNOW HOW TO FIND OUT EITHER... SHE'S AT A MUCH HIGHER LEVEL IN THE ALLIANCE THAN MY TEAM WAS...

I SWEAR... I SWEAR...

...HE WASN'T EVEN ON BASE WHEN THEY SENT US OUT...

HONEST... I SWEAR...

THE ONE WHO GAVE US OUR FINAL ORDERS -- THE ONLY COMMANDER I EVER HAD ANY DEALINGS WITH -- WAS LUKE SKYWALKER!

SKYWALKER.

NO.

OH, NO! NOT THAT! ANYTHING BUT THAT!

TAKE IT EASY, LEIA. YOU ACT LIKE THIS IS THE END OF THE UNIVERSE, OR SOMETHING.

IT MIGHT AS WELL BE, HAN...

ADMIRAL ACKBAR... I KNOW THAT EVERYONE HAS TO MAKE SOME SAC-RIFICES FOR THE GOOD OF THE ALLIANCE ...BUT DOES IT HAVE TO BE THIS?

ISN'T THERE SOME OTHER WAY, SIR?

I'M AFRAID NOT, GENERAL SOLO.

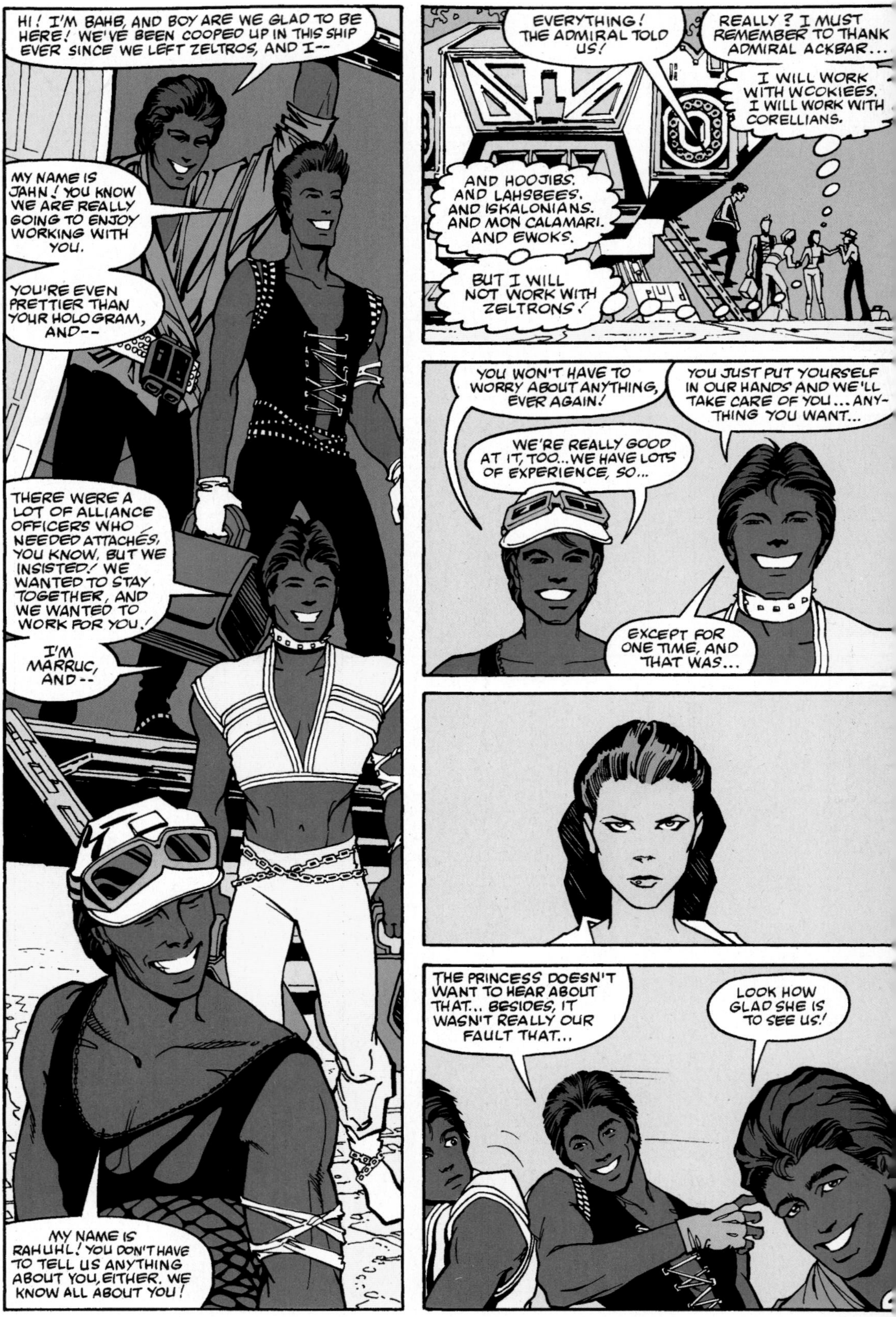
HI! I'M BAHB, AND BOY ARE WE GLAD TO BE HERE! WE'VE BEEN COOPED UP IN THIS SHIP EVER SINCE WE LEFT ZELTROS, AND I--
MY NAME IS JAHN! YOU KNOW WE ARE REALLY GOING TO ENJOY WORKING WITH YOU.
YOU'RE EVEN PRETTIER THAN YOUR HOLOGRAM, AND--
THERE WERE A LOT OF ALLIANCE OFFICERS WHO NEEDED ATTACHÉS, YOU KNOW, BUT WE INSISTED! WE WANTED TO STAY TOGETHER, AND WE WANTED TO WORK FOR YOU!
I'M MARRUC, AND--
MY NAME IS RAHUHL! YOU DON'T HAVE TO TELL US ANYTHING ABOUT YOU, EITHER. WE KNOW ALL ABOUT YOU!
EVERYTHING! THE ADMIRAL TOLD US!
REALLY? I MUST REMEMBER TO THANK ADMIRAL ACKBAR...
I WILL WORK WITH WOOKIEES. I WILL WORK WITH CORELLIANS.
AND HOOJIBS. AND LAHSBEES. AND ISKALONIANS. AND MON CALAMARI. AND EWOKS.
BUT I WILL NOT WORK WITH ZELTRONS!
YOU WON'T HAVE TO WORRY ABOUT ANYTHING, EVER AGAIN!
YOU JUST PUT YOURSELF IN OUR HANDS AND WE'LL TAKE CARE OF YOU... ANYTHING YOU WANT...
WE'RE REALLY GOOD AT IT, TOO... WE HAVE LOTS OF EXPERIENCE, SO...
EXCEPT FOR ONE TIME, AND THAT WAS...
THE PRINCESS DOESN'T WANT TO HEAR ABOUT THAT... BESIDES, IT WASN'T REALLY OUR FAULT THAT...
LOOK HOW GLAD SHE IS TO SEE US!

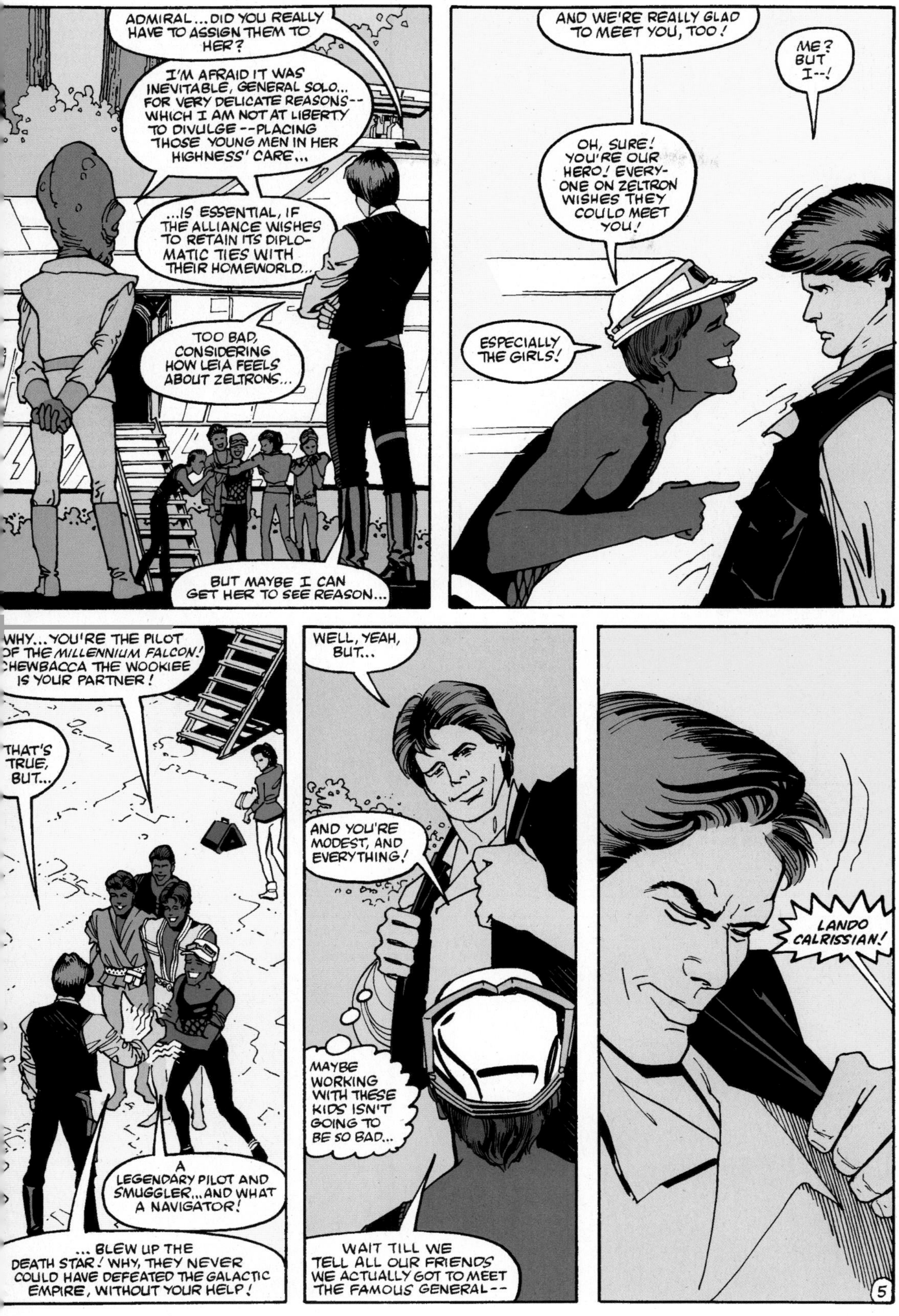
ADMIRAL... DID YOU REALLY HAVE TO ASSIGN THEM TO HER?
I'M AFRAID IT WAS INEVITABLE, GENERAL SOLO... FOR VERY DELICATE REASONS-- WHICH I AM NOT AT LIBERTY TO DIVULGE --PLACING THOSE YOUNG MEN IN HER HIGHNESS' CARE...
...IS ESSENTIAL, IF THE ALLIANCE WISHES TO RETAIN ITS DIPLOMATIC TIES WITH THEIR HOMEWORLD...
TOO BAD, CONSIDERING HOW LEIA FEELS ABOUT ZELTRONS...
BUT MAYBE I CAN GET HER TO SEE REASON...
AND WE'RE REALLY GLAD TO MEET YOU, TOO!
ME? BUT I--!
OH, SURE! YOU'RE OUR HERO! EVERYONE ON ZELTRON WISHES THEY COULD MEET YOU!
ESPECIALLY THE GIRLS!
WHY... YOU'RE THE PILOT OF THE MILLENNIUM FALCON! CHEWBACCA THE WOOKIEE IS YOUR PARTNER!
THAT'S TRUE, BUT...
A LEGENDARY PILOT AND SMUGGLER... AND WHAT A NAVIGATOR!
... BLEW UP THE DEATH STAR! WHY, THEY NEVER COULD HAVE DEFEATED THE GALACTIC EMPIRE, WITHOUT YOUR HELP!
WELL, YEAH, BUT...
AND YOU'RE MODEST, AND EVERYTHING!
MAYBE WORKING WITH THESE KIDS ISN'T GOING TO BE SO BAD...
WAIT TILL WE TELL ALL OUR FRIENDS WE ACTUALLY GOT TO MEET THE FAMOUS GENERAL--
LANDO CALRISSIAN!
5

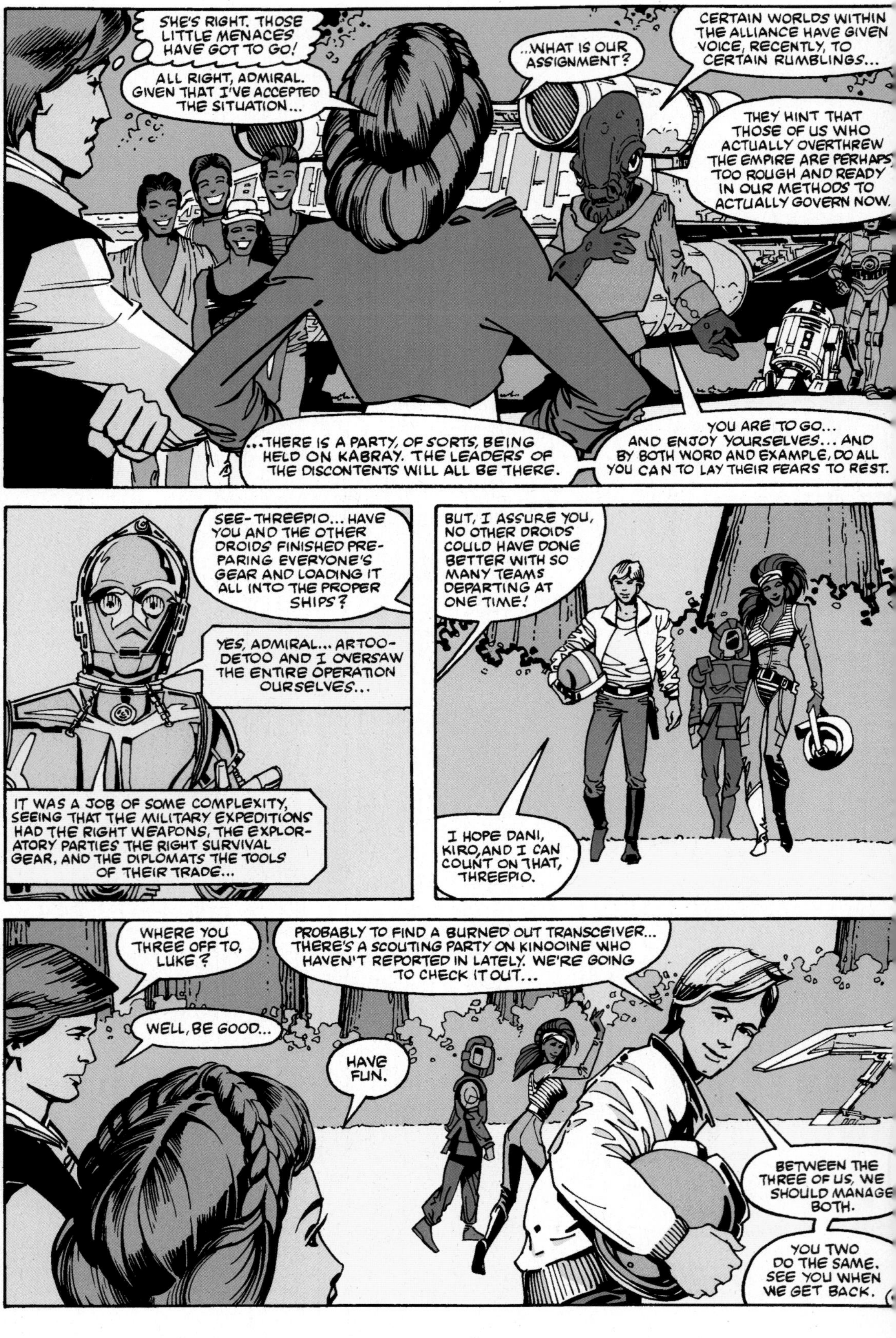
SHE'S RIGHT. THOSE LITTLE MENACES HAVE GOT TO GO!
ALL RIGHT, ADMIRAL. GIVEN THAT I'VE ACCEPTED THE SITUATION...
...WHAT IS OUR ASSIGNMENT?
CERTAIN WORLDS WITHIN THE ALLIANCE HAVE GIVEN VOICE, RECENTLY, TO CERTAIN RUMBLINGS...
THEY HINT THAT THOSE OF US WHO ACTUALLY OVERTHREW THE EMPIRE ARE PERHAPS TOO ROUGH AND READY IN OUR METHODS TO ACTUALLY GOVERN NOW.
...THERE IS A PARTY, OF SORTS, BEING HELD ON KABRAY. THE LEADERS OF THE DISCONTENTS WILL ALL BE THERE.
YOU ARE TO GO... AND ENJOY YOURSELVES... AND BY BOTH WORD AND EXAMPLE, DO ALL YOU CAN TO LAY THEIR FEARS TO REST.
SEE-THREEPIO... HAVE YOU AND THE OTHER DROIDS FINISHED PRE-PARING EVERYONE'S GEAR AND LOADING IT ALL INTO THE PROPER SHIPS?
YES, ADMIRAL... ARTOO-DETOO AND I OVERSAW THE ENTIRE OPERATION OURSELVES...
IT WAS A JOB OF SOME COMPLEXITY, SEEING THAT THE MILITARY EXPEDITIONS HAD THE RIGHT WEAPONS, THE EXPLOR-ATORY PARTIES THE RIGHT SURVIVAL GEAR, AND THE DIPLOMATS THE TOOLS OF THEIR TRADE...
BUT, I ASSURE YOU, NO OTHER DROIDS COULD HAVE DONE BETTER WITH SO MANY TEAMS DEPARTING AT ONE TIME!
I HOPE DANI, KIRO, AND I CAN COUNT ON THAT, THREEPIO.
WHERE YOU THREE OFF TO, LUKE?
PROBABLY TO FIND A BURNED OUT TRANSCEIVER... THERE'S A SCOUTING PARTY ON KINOOINE WHO HAVEN'T REPORTED IN LATELY. WE'RE GOING TO CHECK IT OUT...
WELL, BE GOOD...
HAVE FUN.
BETWEEN THE THREE OF US, WE SHOULD MANAGE BOTH.
YOU TWO DO THE SAME. SEE YOU WHEN WE GET BACK.

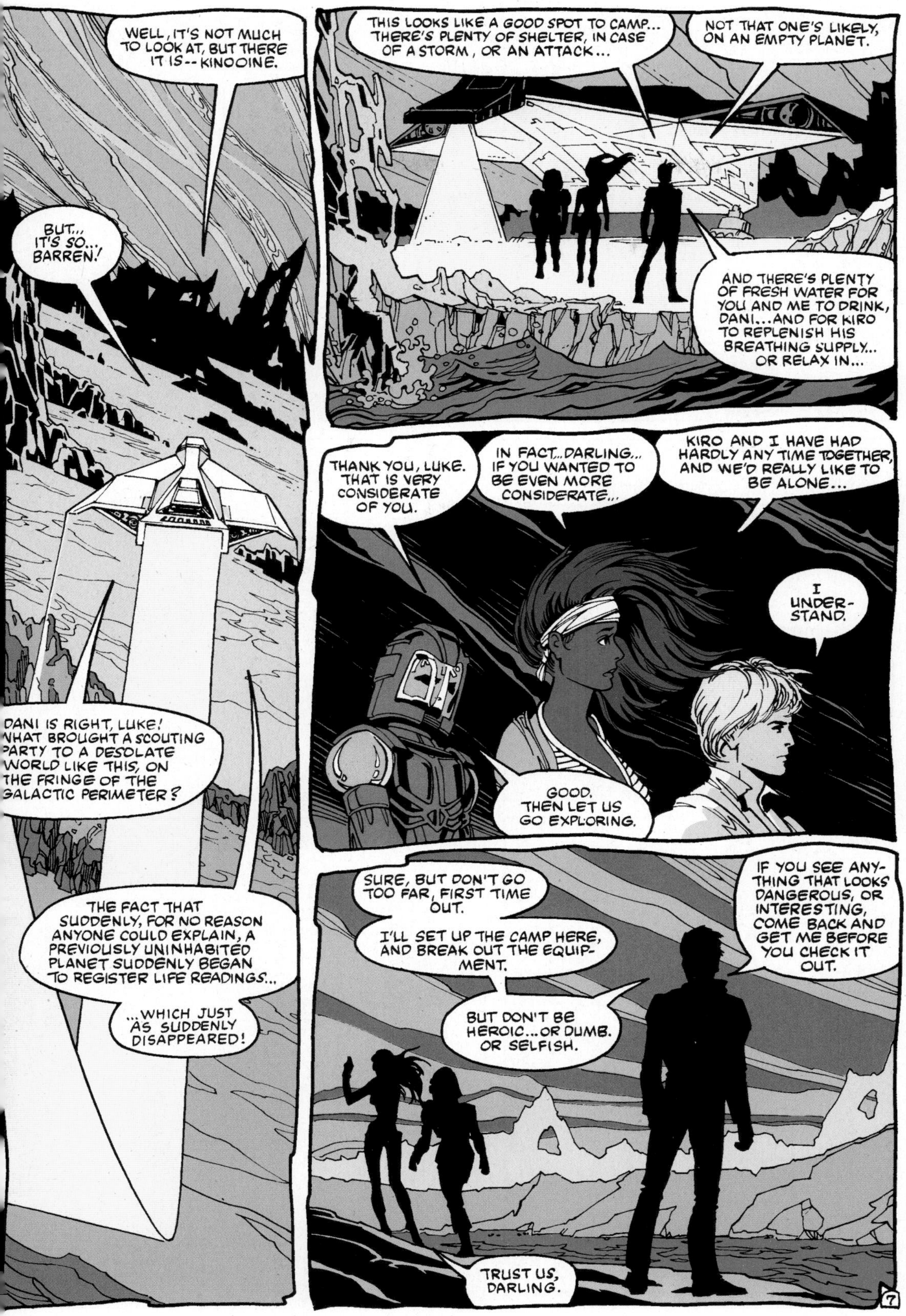
WELL, IT'S NOT MUCH TO LOOK AT, BUT THERE IT IS--KINOOINE.
BUT... IT'S SO... BARREN!
DANI IS RIGHT, LUKE! WHAT BROUGHT A SCOUTING PARTY TO A DESOLATE WORLD LIKE THIS, ON THE FRINGE OF THE GALACTIC PERIMETER?
THE FACT THAT SUDDENLY, FOR NO REASON ANYONE COULD EXPLAIN, A PREVIOUSLY UNINHABITED PLANET SUDDENLY BEGAN TO REGISTER LIFE READINGS...
...WHICH JUST AS SUDDENLY DISAPPEARED!
THIS LOOKS LIKE A GOOD SPOT TO CAMP... THERE'S PLENTY OF SHELTER, IN CASE OF A STORM, OR AN ATTACK...
NOT THAT ONE'S LIKELY, ON AN EMPTY PLANET.
AND THERE'S PLENTY OF FRESH WATER FOR YOU AND ME TO DRINK, DANI... AND FOR KIRO TO REPLENISH HIS BREATHING SUPPLY... OR RELAX IN...
THANK YOU, LUKE. THAT IS VERY CONSIDERATE OF YOU.
IN FACT... DARLING... IF YOU WANTED TO BE EVEN MORE CONSIDERATE...
KIRO AND I HAVE HAD HARDLY ANY TIME TOGETHER, AND WE'D REALLY LIKE TO BE ALONE...
I UNDER-STAND.
GOOD. THEN LET US GO EXPLORING.
SURE, BUT DON'T GO TOO FAR, FIRST TIME OUT.
I'LL SET UP THE CAMP HERE, AND BREAK OUT THE EQUIP-MENT.
IF YOU SEE ANY-THING THAT LOOKS DANGEROUS, OR INTERESTING, COME BACK AND GET ME BEFORE YOU CHECK IT OUT.
BUT DON'T BE HEROIC... OR DUMB. OR SELFISH.
TRUST US, DARLING.
7

I DON'T BELIEVE IT. I SIMPLY DON'T BELIEVE IT. AS IF THINGS WEREN'T BAD ENOUGH ALREADY!

AND DISPUTE OUR FITNESS TO ADMINISTER THE FREEDOMS WE FOUGHT FOR...

BUT NOW I'M EXPECTE[D] TO DO IT WITHOUT SO MUCH AS A DRESS TO WEAR!

NO, IT'S NOT ENOUGH THAT I HAVE TO COME BACK TO KABRAY, IN THE COMPANY OF FOUR ZELTRONS...

NOT BAD ENOUGH THAT I HAVE TO GO TO A PARTY, AND LISTEN TO A BUNCH OF PEOPLE WHO NEVER LIFTED A FINGER AGAINST THE EMPIRE YAWN AND MINCE...

I DON'T KNOW WHY YOU'RE SURPRISED. I EXPECTED SOMETHING LIKE THIS THE MINUTE I HEARD THREEPIO WAS IN CHARGE OF PACKING OUR GEAR.

I DIDN'T HEAR YOU SAY ANYTHING WHILE WE WERE STILL BACK ON ENDOR.

CHEER UP. THINK OF THE LOOK ON LUKE'S FACE, WHEN HE GOES LOOKING FOR HIS COLD WEATHER SURVIVAL SUIT... AND COMES UP WITH HALF A DOZEN PARTY DRESSES INSTEAD.

HA-HA.

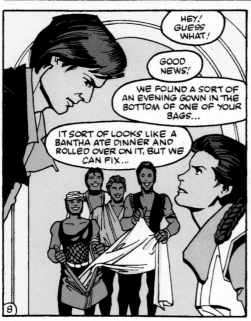

HEY! GUESS WHAT!

GOOD NEWS!

WE FOUND A SORT OF AN EVENING GOWN IN THE BOTTOM OF ONE OF YOUR BAGS...

IT SORT OF LOOKS LIKE A BANTHA ATE DINNER AND ROLLED OVER ON IT, BUT WE CAN FIX...

UM... I HAVE TO GET DRESSED. I'M SUPPOSED TO GO TO THIS PARTY TOO, YOU KNOW...

NOT THAT DRESS...I MEANT TO BURN IT, AFTER THAT BANQUET...THE AMBASSADOR UPSET HIS ENTIRE PLATE ON...I NEED A REST...

SURE, YOU JUST SLEEP, AND LEAVE EVERYTHING TO

COULD LOOK GREAT WITH A LITTLE

UNLESS THOSE ARE WINE STAINS

ALL IT NEEDS IS SOME

8

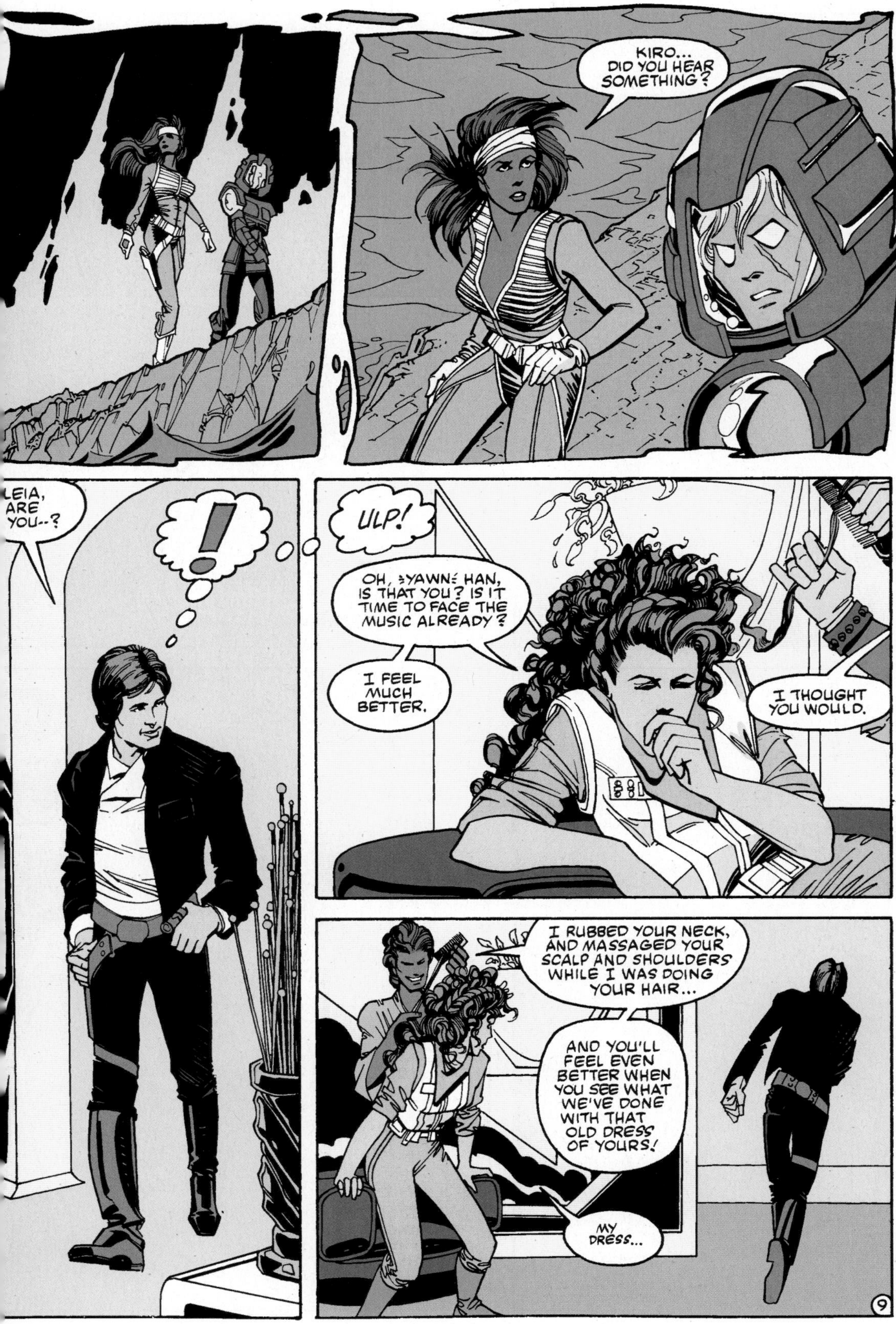
KIRO... DID YOU HEAR SOMETHING?
LEIA, ARE YOU--?
!
ULP!
OH, ≥YAWN≤ HAN, IS THAT YOU? IS IT TIME TO FACE THE MUSIC ALREADY?
I FEEL MUCH BETTER.
I THOUGHT YOU WOULD.
I RUBBED YOUR NECK, AND MASSAGED YOUR SCALP AND SHOULDERS WHILE I WAS DOING YOUR HAIR...
AND YOU'LL FEEL EVEN BETTER WHEN YOU SEE WHAT WE'VE DONE WITH THAT OLD DRESS OF YOURS!
MY DRESS...
9

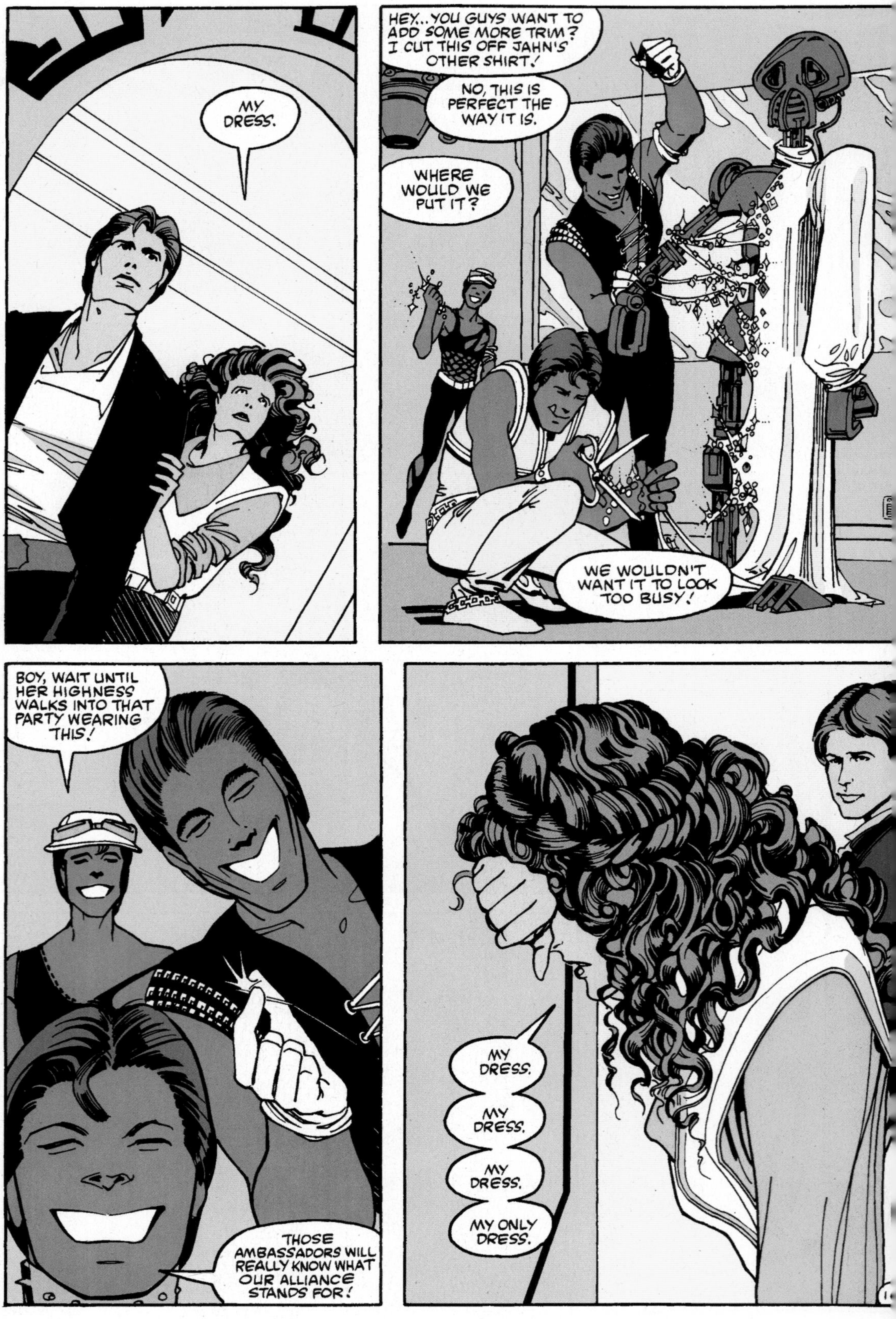
MY DRESS.
HEY... YOU GUYS WANT TO ADD SOME MORE TRIM? I CUT THIS OFF JAHN'S OTHER SHIRT!
NO, THIS IS PERFECT THE WAY IT IS.
WHERE WOULD WE PUT IT?
WE WOULDN'T WANT IT TO LOOK TOO BUSY!
BOY, WAIT UNTIL HER HIGHNESS WALKS INTO THAT PARTY WEARING THIS!
THOSE AMBASSADORS WILL REALLY KNOW WHAT OUR ALLIANCE STANDS FOR!
MY DRESS.
MY DRESS.
MY DRESS.
MY ONLY DRESS.

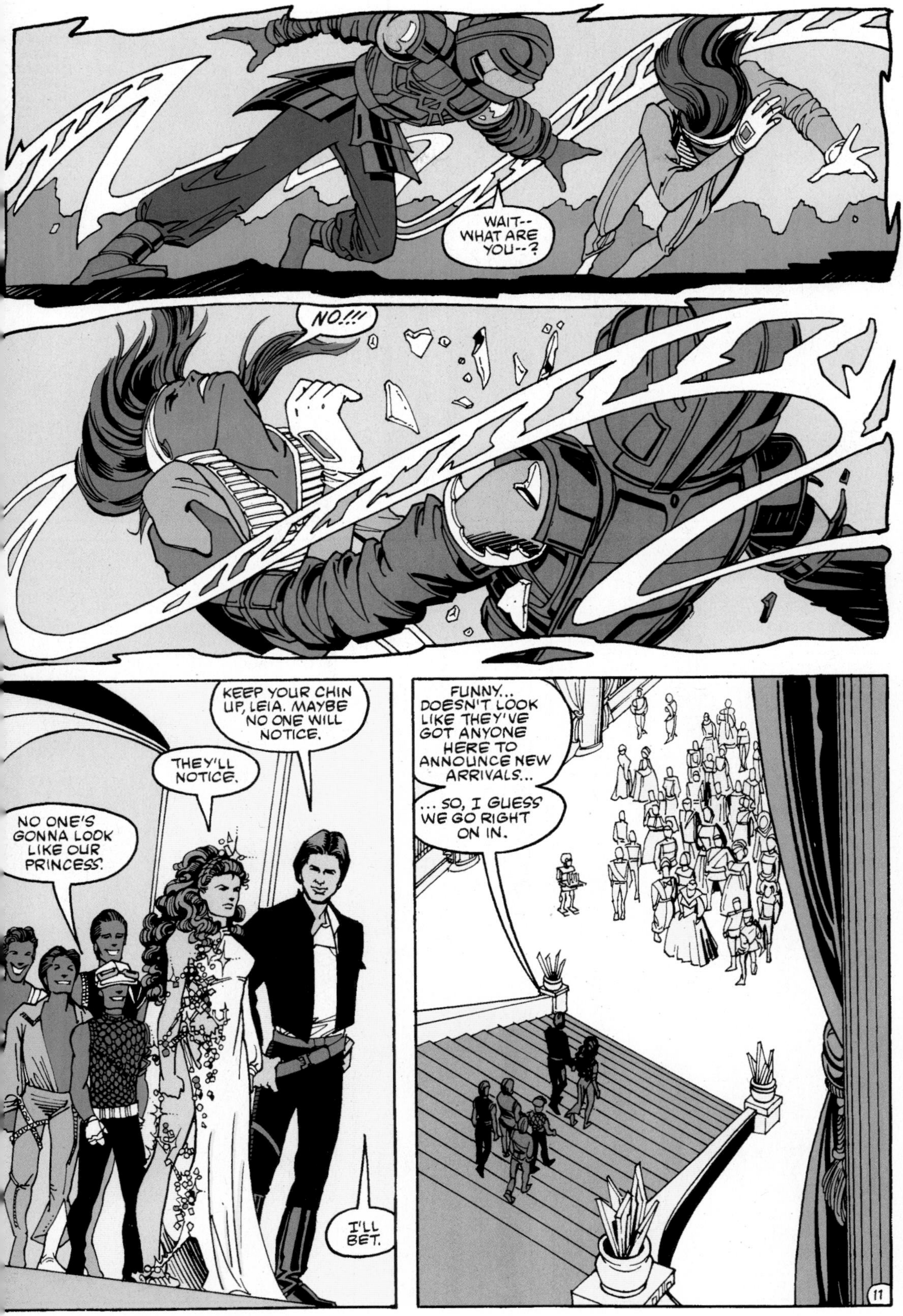
WAIT-- WHAT ARE YOU--?
NO!!!
KEEP YOUR CHIN UP, LEIA. MAYBE NO ONE WILL NOTICE.
THEY'LL NOTICE.
NO ONE'S GONNA LOOK LIKE OUR PRINCESS.
I'LL BET.
FUNNY... DOESN'T LOOK LIKE THEY'VE GOT ANYONE HERE TO ANNOUNCE NEW ARRIVALS...
...SO, I GUESS WE GO RIGHT ON IN.
11

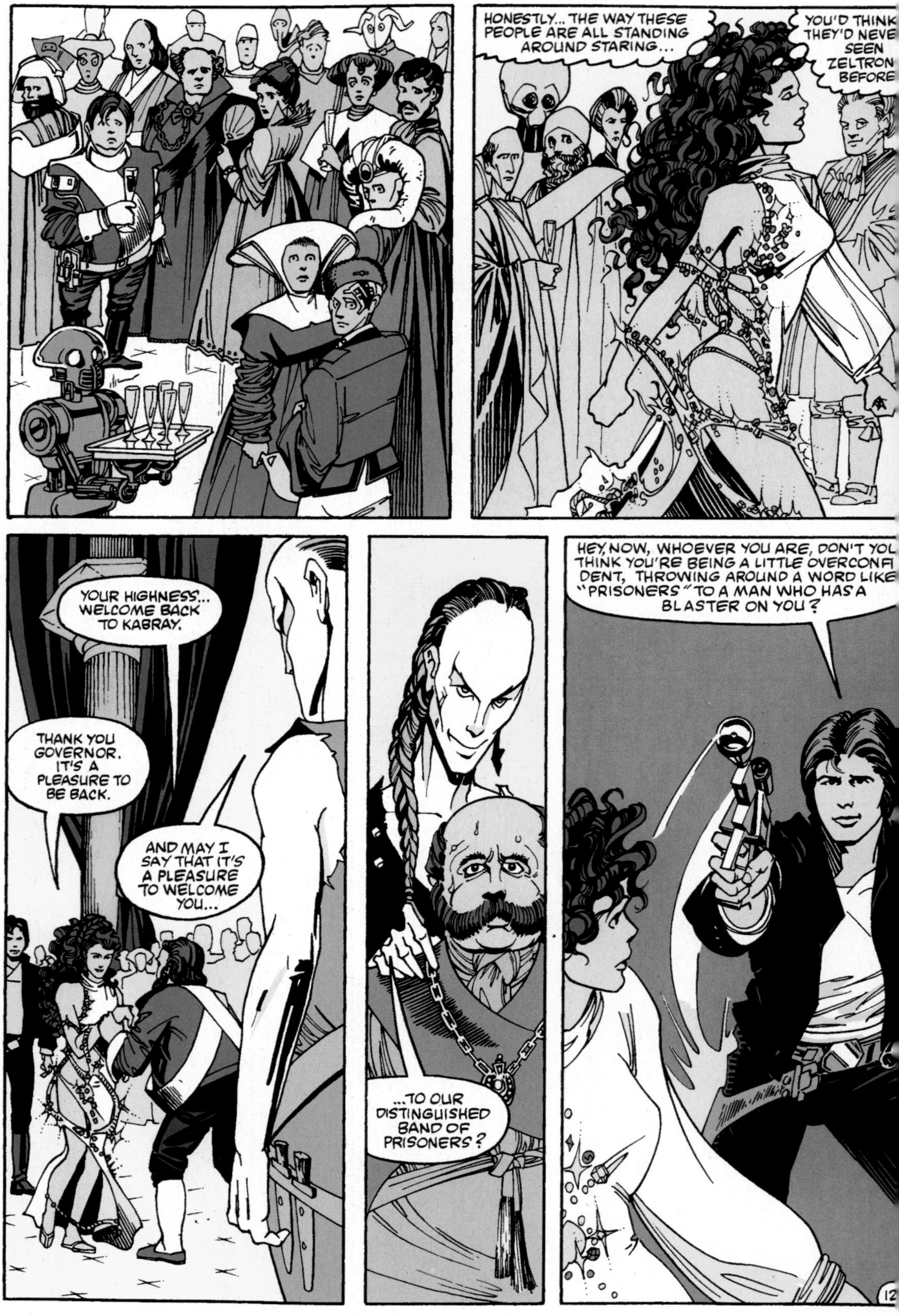
HONESTLY... THE WAY THESE PEOPLE ARE ALL STANDING AROUND STARING...
YOU'D THINK THEY'D NEVE SEEN ZELTRON BEFORE
YOUR HIGHNESS... WELCOME BACK TO KABRAY.
THANK YOU GOVERNOR. IT'S A PLEASURE TO BE BACK.
AND MAY I SAY THAT IT'S A PLEASURE TO WELCOME YOU...
...TO OUR DISTINGUISHED BAND OF PRISONERS?
HEY, NOW, WHOEVER YOU ARE, DON'T YOU THINK YOU'RE BEING A LITTLE OVERCONFI DENT, THROWING AROUND A WORD LIKE "PRISONERS" TO A MAN WHO HAS A BLASTER ON YOU?
12

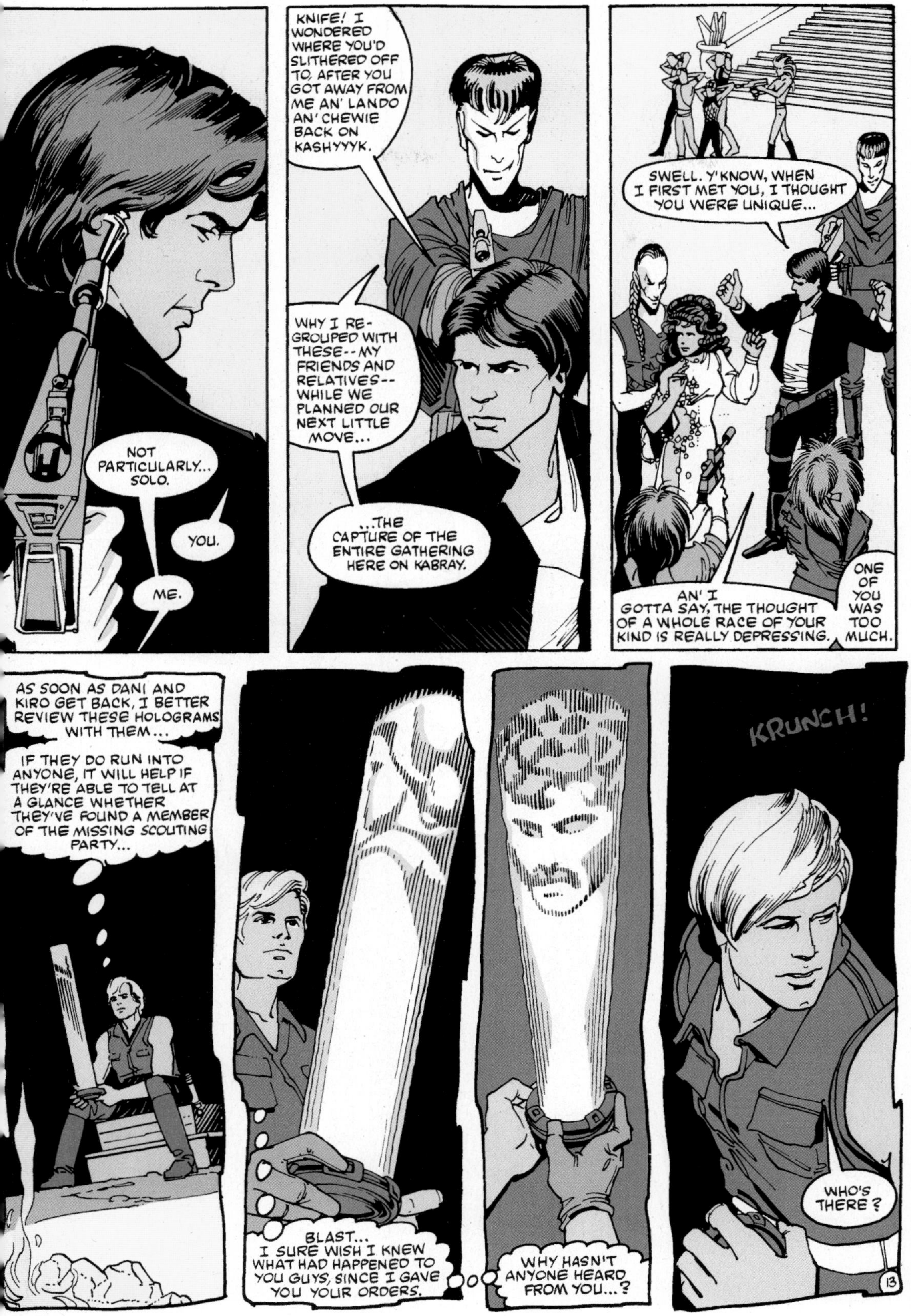
NOT PARTICULARLY... SOLO.
YOU.
ME.
KNIFE! I WONDERED WHERE YOU'D SLITHERED OFF TO, AFTER YOU GOT AWAY FROM ME AN' LANDO AN' CHEWIE BACK ON KASHYYYK.
WHY I RE-GROUPED WITH THESE--MY FRIENDS AND RELATIVES--WHILE WE PLANNED OUR NEXT LITTLE MOVE...
...THE CAPTURE OF THE ENTIRE GATHERING HERE ON KABRAY.
SWELL. Y'KNOW, WHEN I FIRST MET YOU, I THOUGHT YOU WERE UNIQUE...
AN' I GOTTA SAY, THE THOUGHT OF A WHOLE RACE OF YOUR KIND IS REALLY DEPRESSING.
ONE OF YOU WAS TOO MUCH.
AS SOON AS DANI AND KIRO GET BACK, I BETTER REVIEW THESE HOLOGRAMS WITH THEM...
IF THEY DO RUN INTO ANYONE, IT WILL HELP IF THEY'RE ABLE TO TELL AT A GLANCE WHETHER THEY'VE FOUND A MEMBER OF THE MISSING SCOUTING PARTY...
BLAST... I SURE WISH I KNEW WHAT HAD HAPPENED TO YOU GUYS, SINCE I GAVE YOU YOUR ORDERS.
WHY HASN'T ANYONE HEARD FROM YOU...?
KRUNCH!
WHO'S THERE?
13

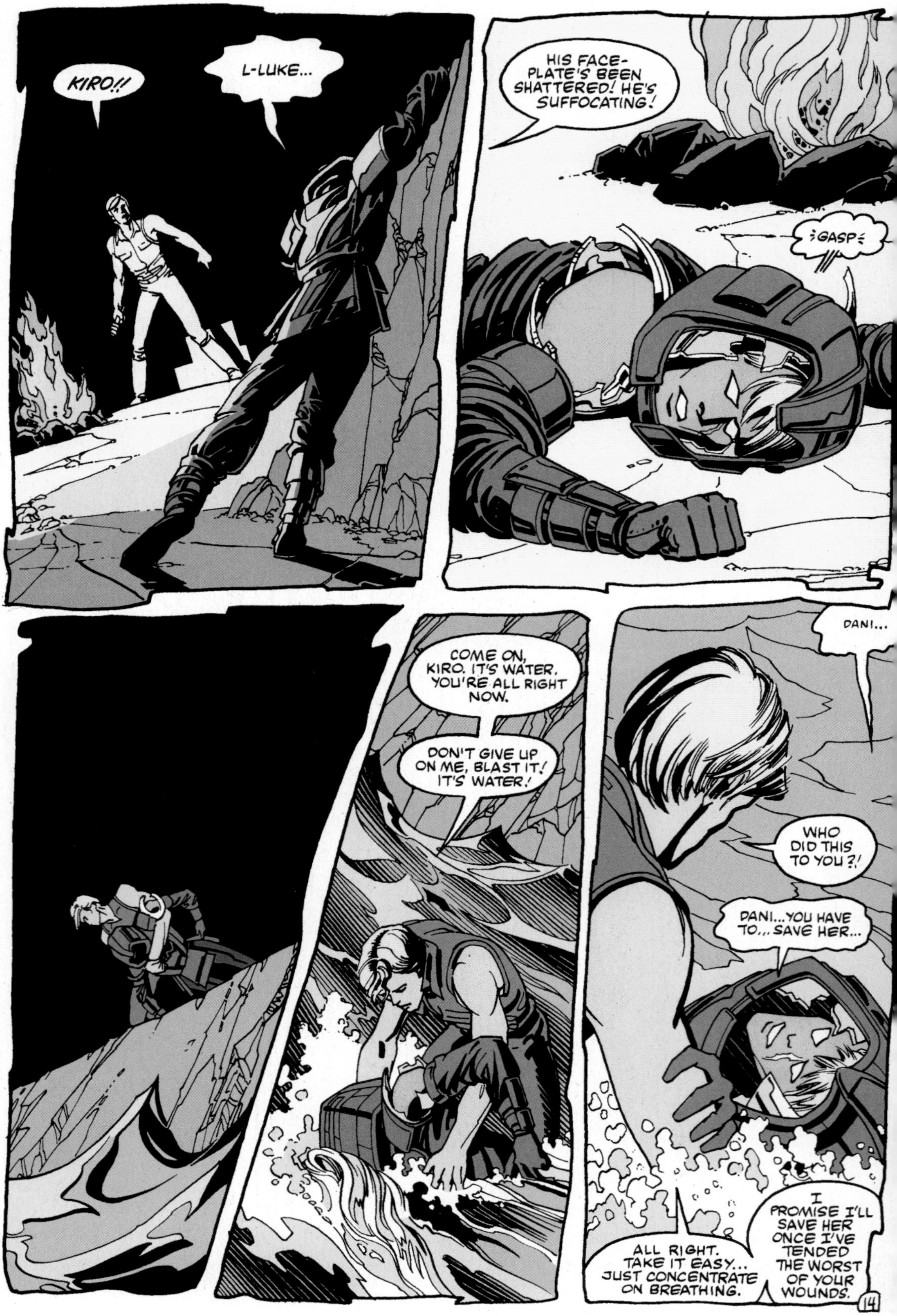
KIRO!!
L-LUKE...
HIS FACE-PLATE'S BEEN SHATTERED! HE'S SUFFOCATING!
GASP
COME ON, KIRO. IT'S WATER. YOU'RE ALL RIGHT NOW.
DON'T GIVE UP ON ME, BLAST IT! IT'S WATER!
DANI...
WHO DID THIS TO YOU?!
DANI...YOU HAVE TO... SAVE HER...
ALL RIGHT. TAKE IT EASY... JUST CONCENTRATE ON BREATHING.
I PROMISE I'LL SAVE HER ONCE I'VE TENDED THE WORST OF YOUR WOUNDS.
14

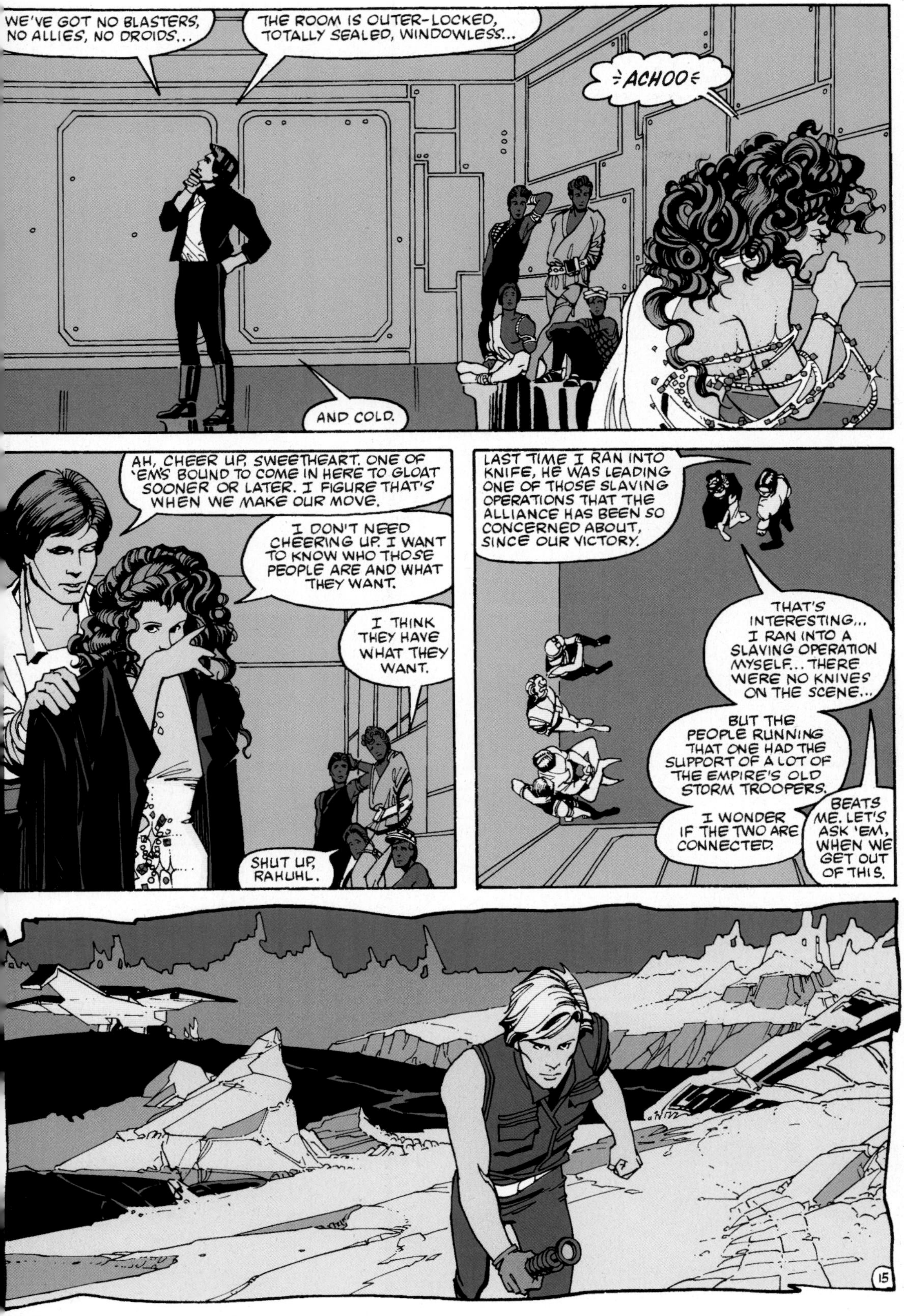
WE'VE GOT NO BLASTERS, NO ALLIES, NO DROIDS...
THE ROOM IS OUTER-LOCKED, TOTALLY SEALED, WINDOWLESS...
ACHOO
AND COLD.
AH, CHEER UP, SWEETHEART. ONE OF 'EM'S BOUND TO COME IN HERE TO GLOAT SOONER OR LATER. I FIGURE THAT'S WHEN WE MAKE OUR MOVE.
I DON'T NEED CHEERING UP. I WANT TO KNOW WHO THOSE PEOPLE ARE AND WHAT THEY WANT.
I THINK THEY HAVE WHAT THEY WANT.
SHUT UP, RAHUHL.
LAST TIME I RAN INTO KNIFE, HE WAS LEADING ONE OF THOSE SLAVING OPERATIONS THAT THE ALLIANCE HAS BEEN SO CONCERNED ABOUT, SINCE OUR VICTORY.
THAT'S INTERESTING... I RAN INTO A SLAVING OPERATION MYSELF... THERE WERE NO KNIVES ON THE SCENE...
BUT THE PEOPLE RUNNING THAT ONE HAD THE SUPPORT OF A LOT OF THE EMPIRE'S OLD STORM TROOPERS.
I WONDER IF THE TWO ARE CONNECTED.
BEATS ME. LET'S ASK 'EM, WHEN WE GET OUT OF THIS.
15

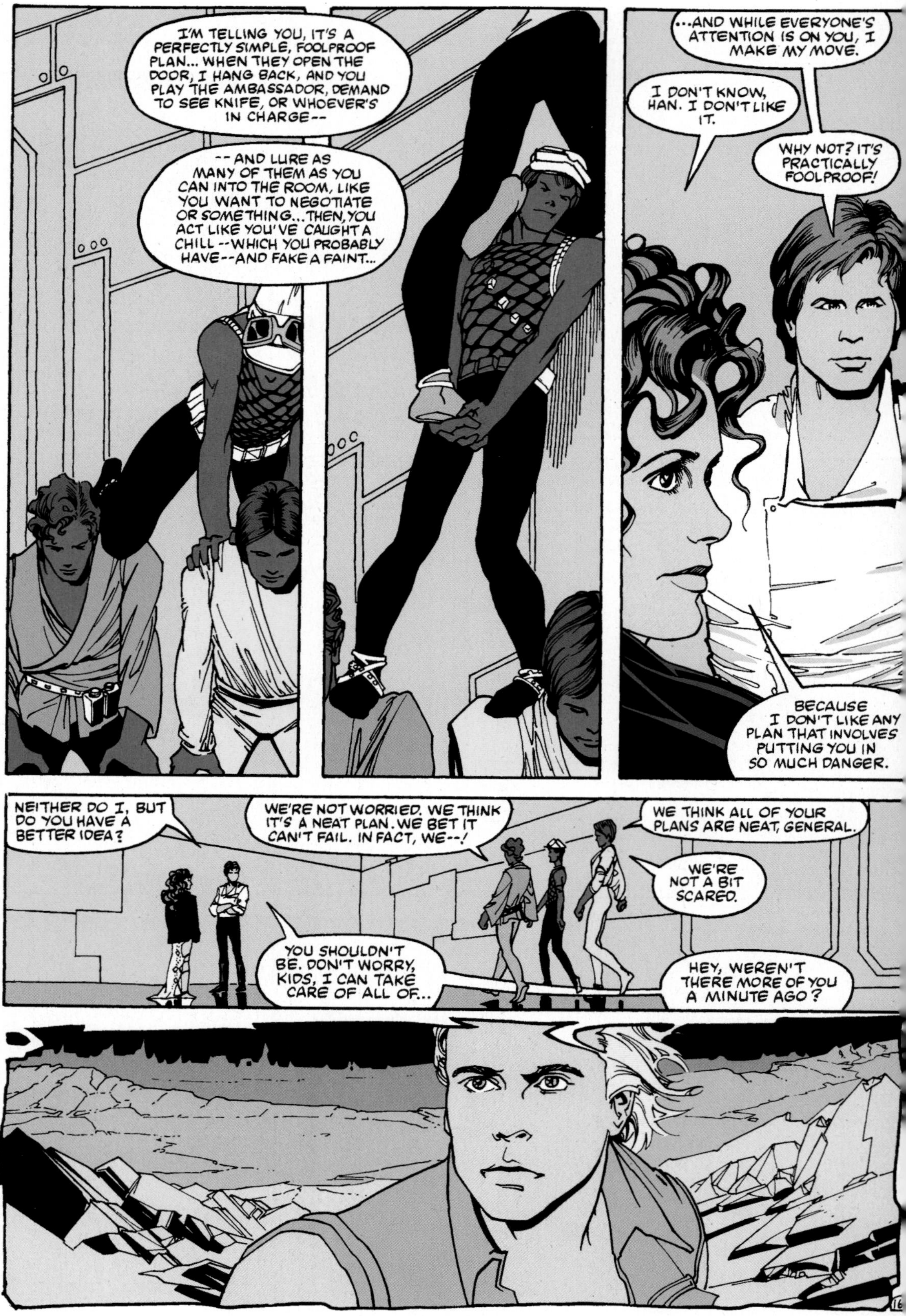
I'M TELLING YOU, IT'S A PERFECTLY SIMPLE, FOOLPROOF PLAN... WHEN THEY OPEN THE DOOR, I HANG BACK, AND YOU PLAY THE AMBASSADOR, DEMAND TO SEE KNIFE, OR WHOEVER'S IN CHARGE--
--AND LURE AS MANY OF THEM AS YOU CAN INTO THE ROOM, LIKE YOU WANT TO NEGOTIATE OR SOMETHING...THEN, YOU ACT LIKE YOU'VE CAUGHT A CHILL --WHICH YOU PROBABLY HAVE--AND FAKE A FAINT...
...AND WHILE EVERYONE'S ATTENTION IS ON YOU, I MAKE MY MOVE.
I DON'T KNOW, HAN. I DON'T LIKE IT.
WHY NOT? IT'S PRACTICALLY FOOLPROOF!
BECAUSE I DON'T LIKE ANY PLAN THAT INVOLVES PUTTING YOU IN SO MUCH DANGER.
NEITHER DO I, BUT DO YOU HAVE A BETTER IDEA?
WE'RE NOT WORRIED. WE THINK IT'S A NEAT PLAN. WE BET IT CAN'T FAIL. IN FACT, WE--!
WE THINK ALL OF YOUR PLANS ARE NEAT, GENERAL.
WE'RE NOT A BIT SCARED.
YOU SHOULDN'T BE. DON'T WORRY, KIDS, I CAN TAKE CARE OF ALL OF...
HEY, WEREN'T THERE MORE OF YOU A MINUTE AGO?

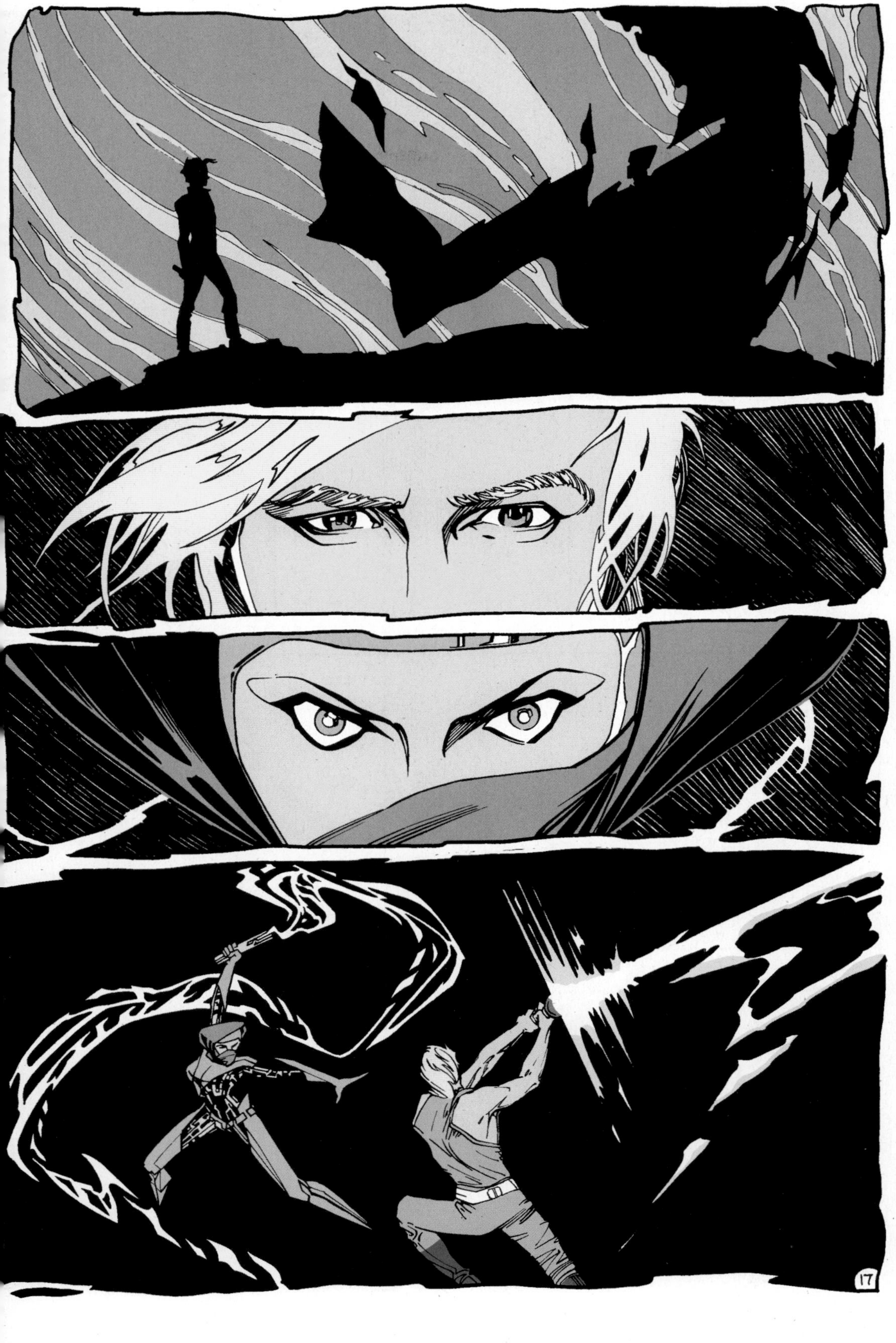
17

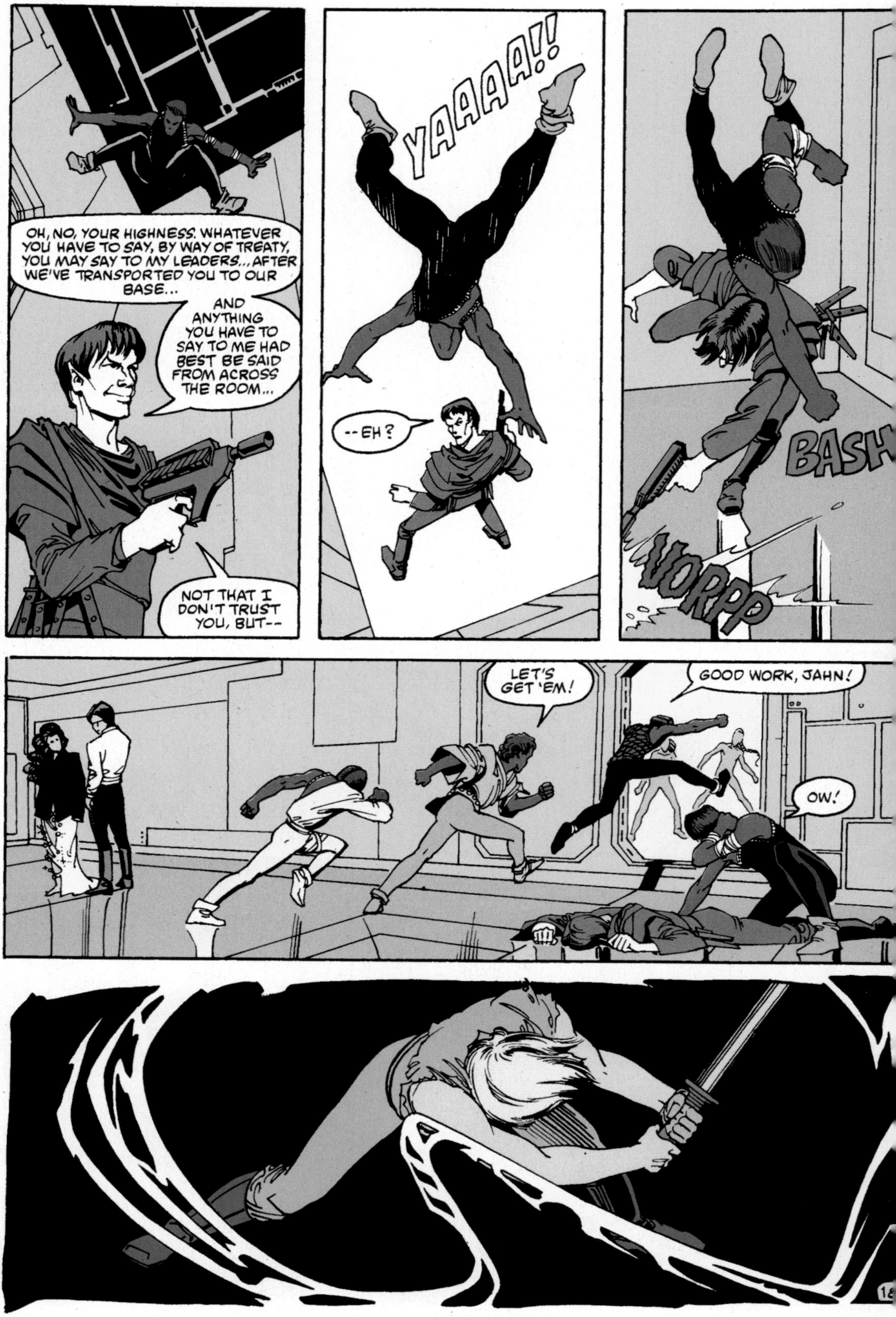

OH, NO, YOUR HIGHNESS. WHATEVER YOU HAVE TO SAY, BY WAY OF TREATY, YOU MAY SAY TO MY LEADERS... AFTER WE'VE TRANSPORTED YOU TO OUR BASE...
AND ANYTHING YOU HAVE TO SAY TO ME HAD BEST BE SAID FROM ACROSS THE ROOM...
NOT THAT I DON'T TRUST YOU, BUT--
YAAAAA!!
--EH?
BASH
VORPP
LET'S GET 'EM!
GOOD WORK, JAHN!
OW!

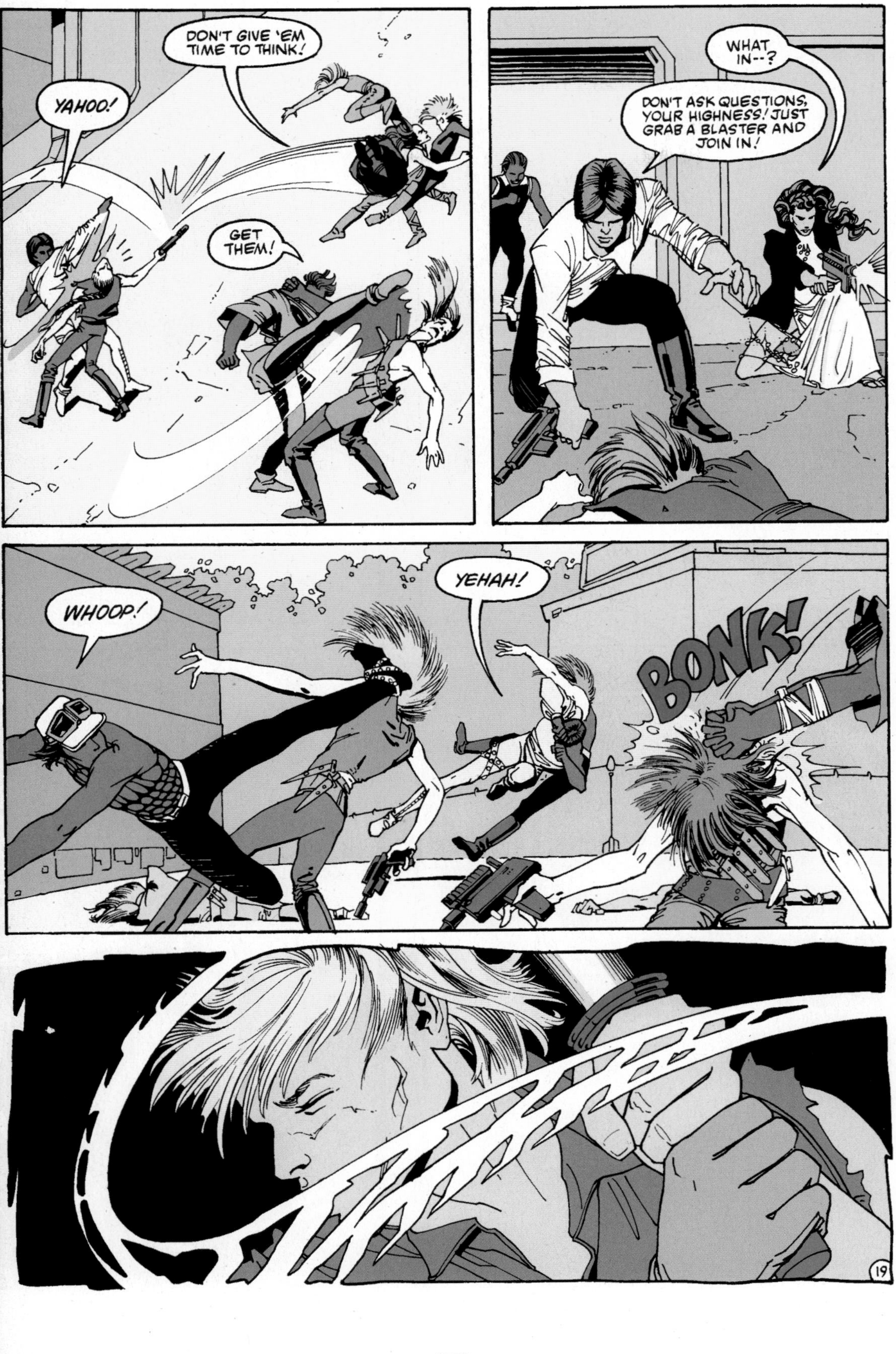
YAHOO!
DON'T GIVE 'EM TIME TO THINK!
GET THEM!
WHAT IN--?
DON'T ASK QUESTIONS, YOUR HIGHNESS! JUST GRAB A BLASTER AND JOIN IN!
WHOOP!
YEHAH!
BONK!
19

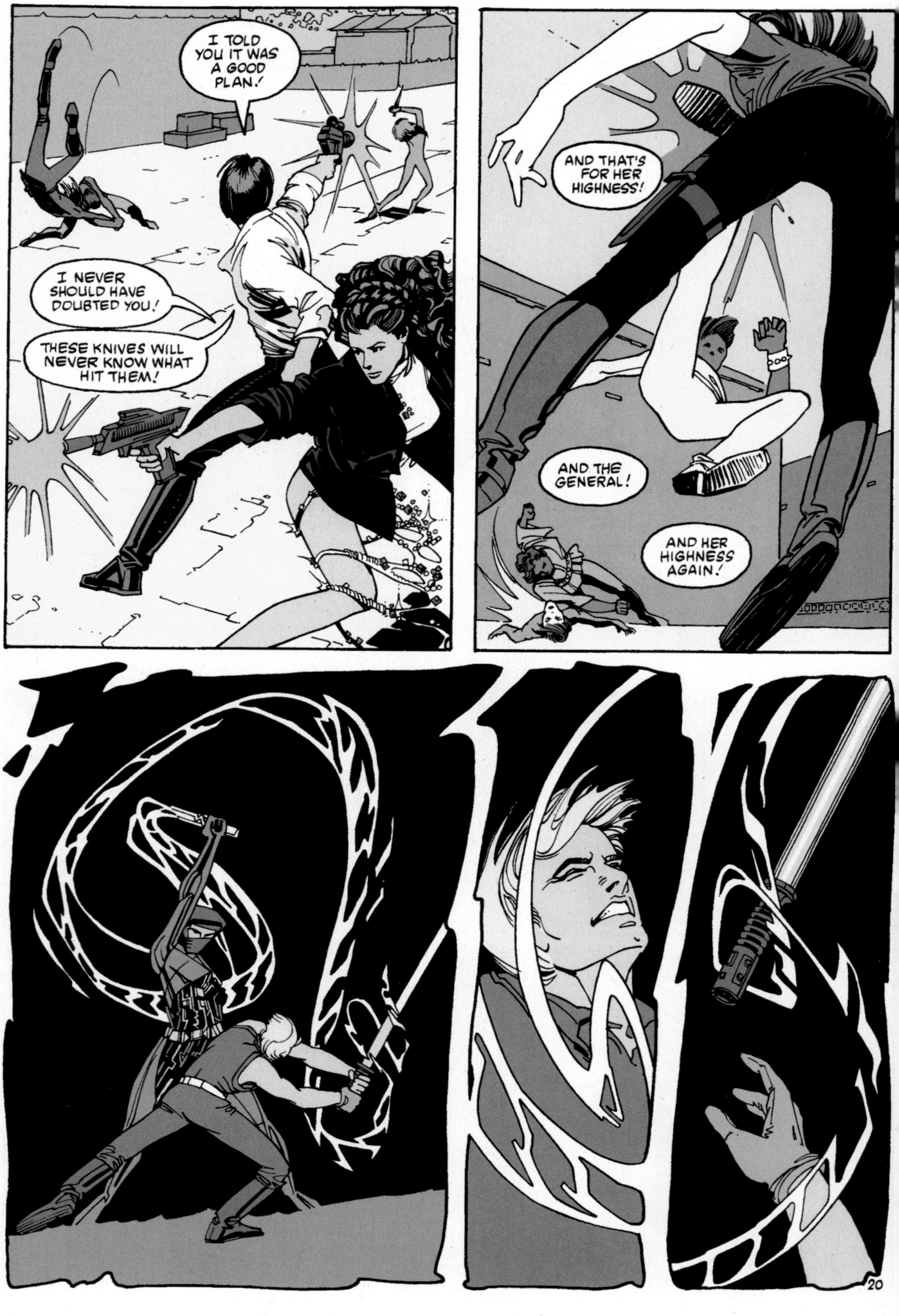
I TOLD YOU IT WAS A GOOD PLAN!
I NEVER SHOULD HAVE DOUBTED YOU!
THESE KNIVES WILL NEVER KNOW WHAT HIT THEM!
AND THAT'S FOR HER HIGHNESS!
AND THE GENERAL!
AND HER HIGHNESS AGAIN!
20

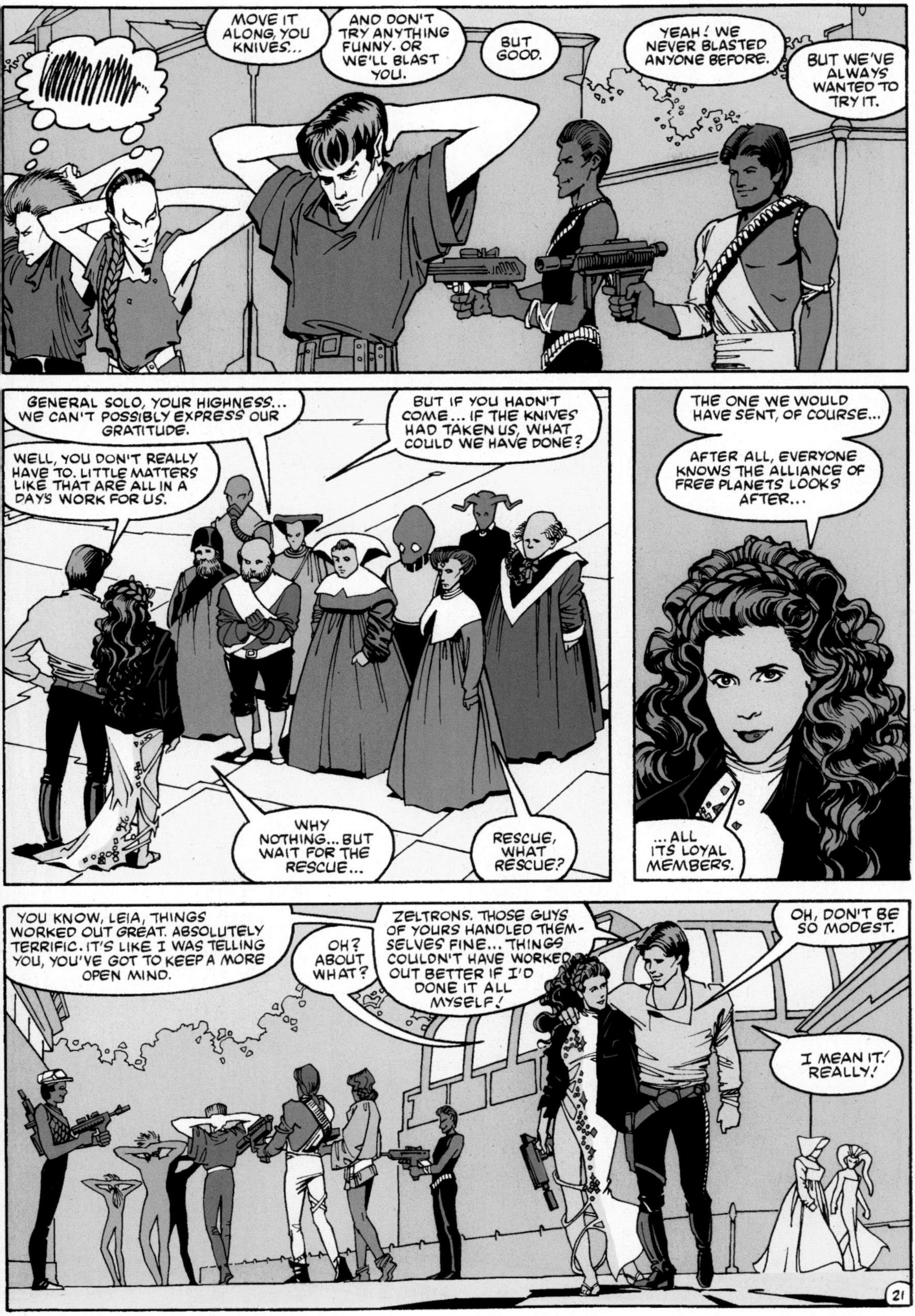
MOVE IT ALONG, YOU KNIVES...
AND DON'T TRY ANYTHING FUNNY. OR WE'LL BLAST YOU.
BUT GOOD.
YEAH! WE NEVER BLASTED ANYONE BEFORE.
BUT WE'VE ALWAYS WANTED TO TRY IT.
GENERAL SOLO, YOUR HIGHNESS... WE CAN'T POSSIBLY EXPRESS OUR GRATITUDE.
WELL, YOU DON'T REALLY HAVE TO. LITTLE MATTERS LIKE THAT ARE ALL IN A DAY'S WORK FOR US.
BUT IF YOU HADN'T COME... IF THE KNIVES HAD TAKEN US, WHAT COULD WE HAVE DONE?
WHY NOTHING... BUT WAIT FOR THE RESCUE...
RESCUE, WHAT RESCUE?
THE ONE WE WOULD HAVE SENT, OF COURSE...
AFTER ALL, EVERYONE KNOWS THE ALLIANCE OF FREE PLANETS LOOKS AFTER...
...ALL ITS LOYAL MEMBERS.
YOU KNOW, LEIA, THINGS WORKED OUT GREAT. ABSOLUTELY TERRIFIC. IT'S LIKE I WAS TELLING YOU, YOU'VE GOT TO KEEP A MORE OPEN MIND.
OH? ABOUT WHAT?
ZELTRONS. THOSE GUYS OF YOURS HANDLED THEMSELVES FINE... THINGS COULDN'T HAVE WORKED OUT BETTER IF I'D DONE IT ALL MYSELF!
OH, DON'T BE SO MODEST.
I MEAN IT! REALLY!
21

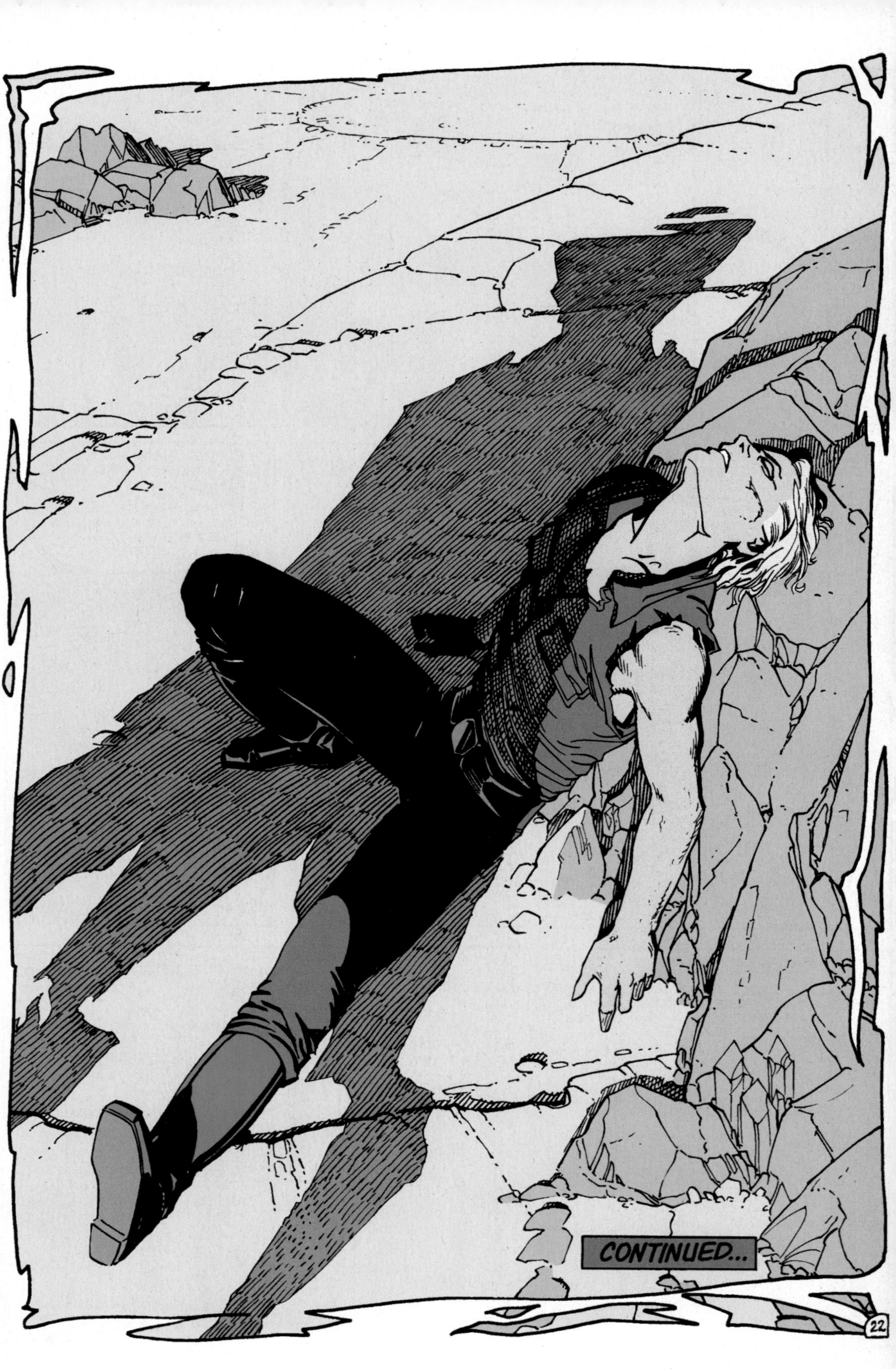
CONTINUED...
22

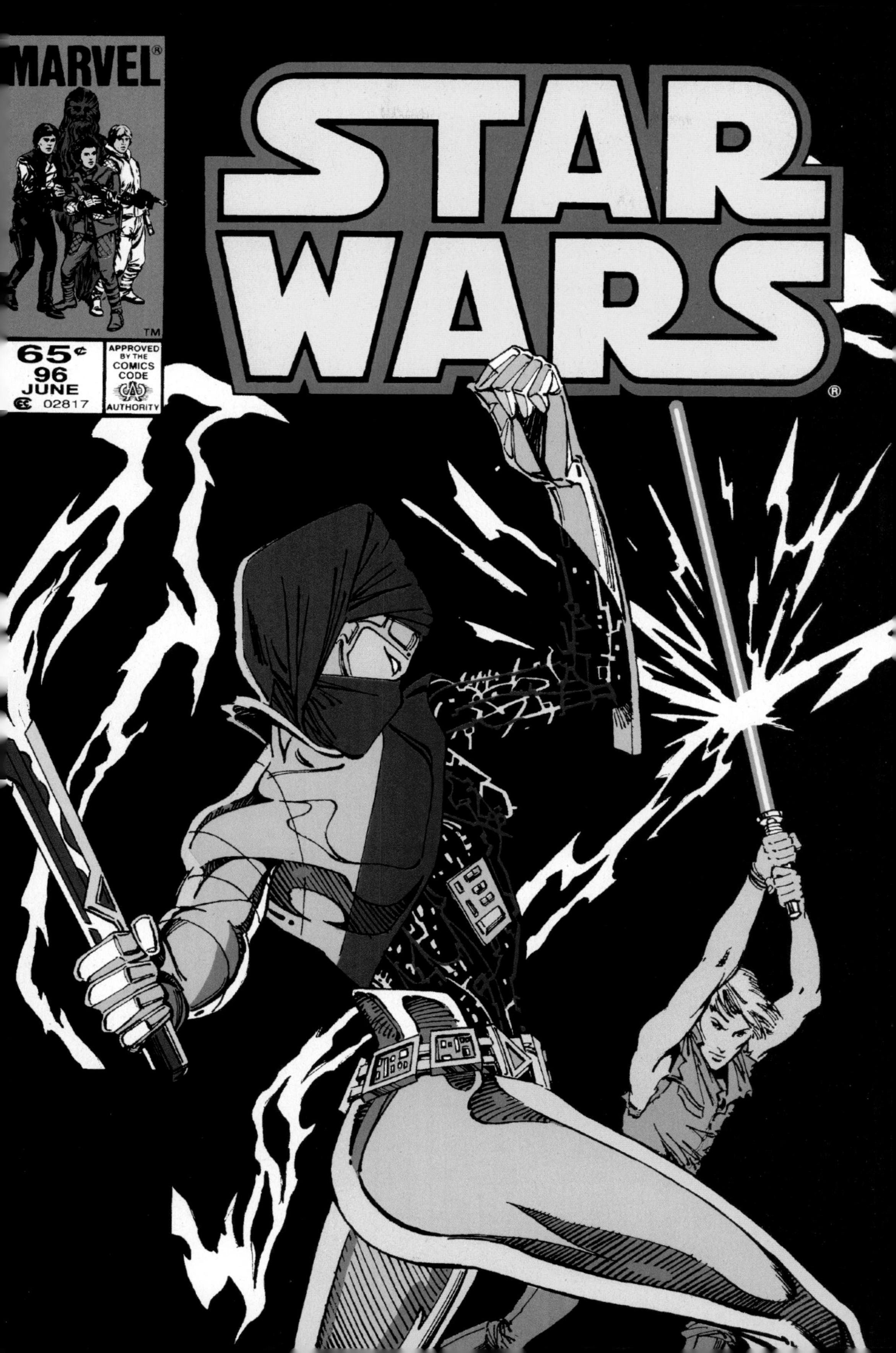
MARVEL®
STAR WARS®
TM
65¢
96
JUNE
02817
APPROVED BY THE COMICS CODE AUTHORITY

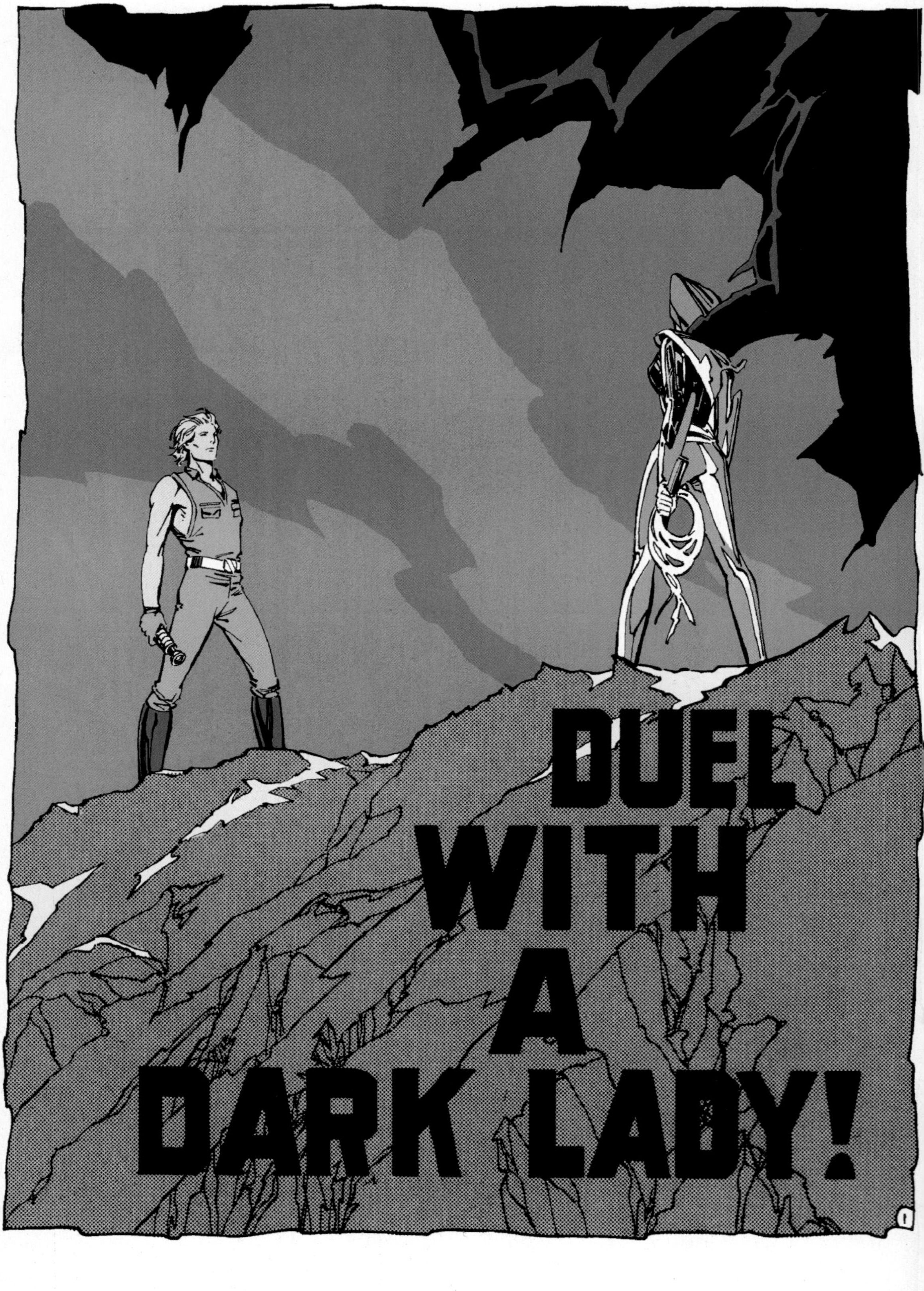
DUEL WITH A DARK LADY!

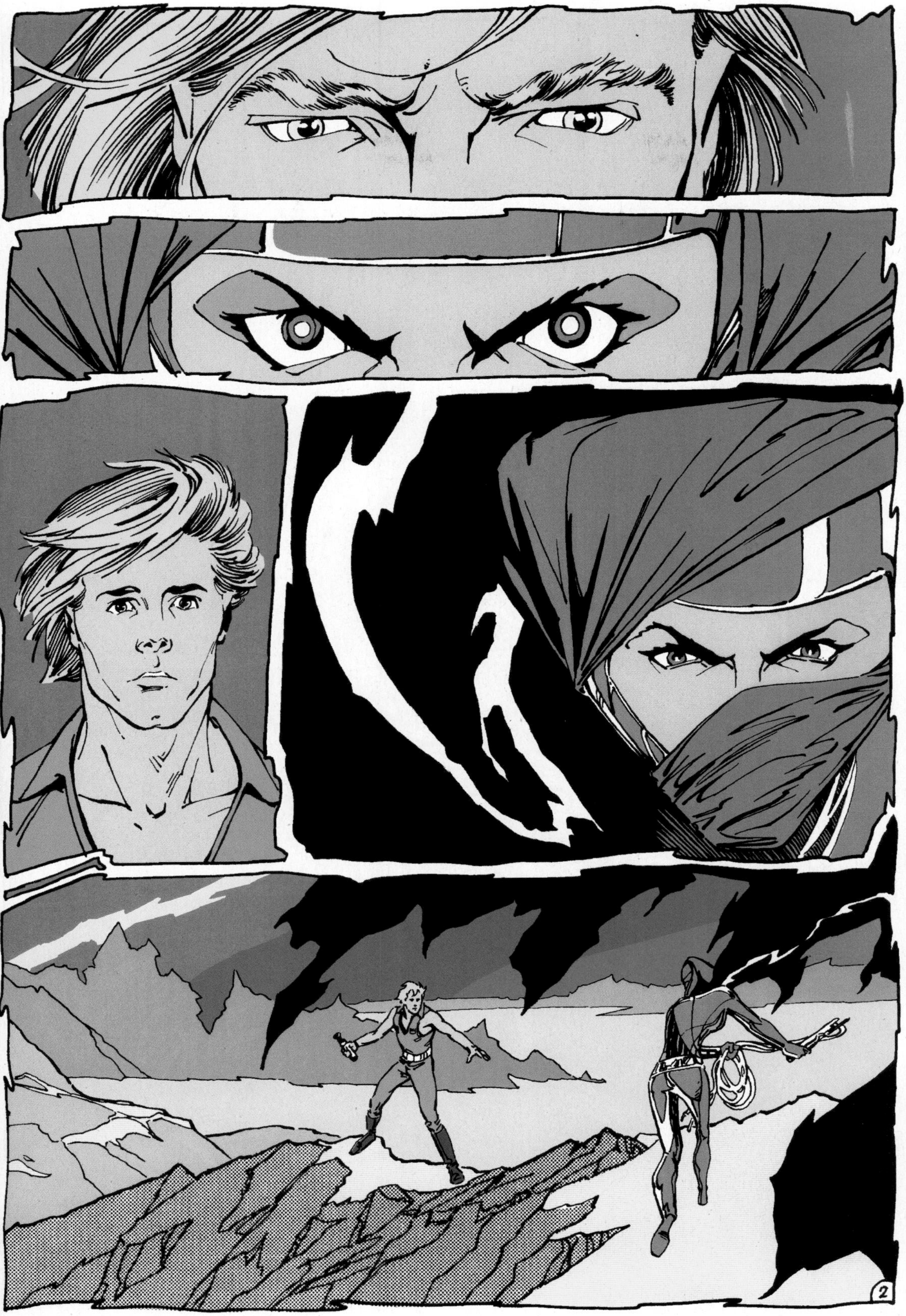
2

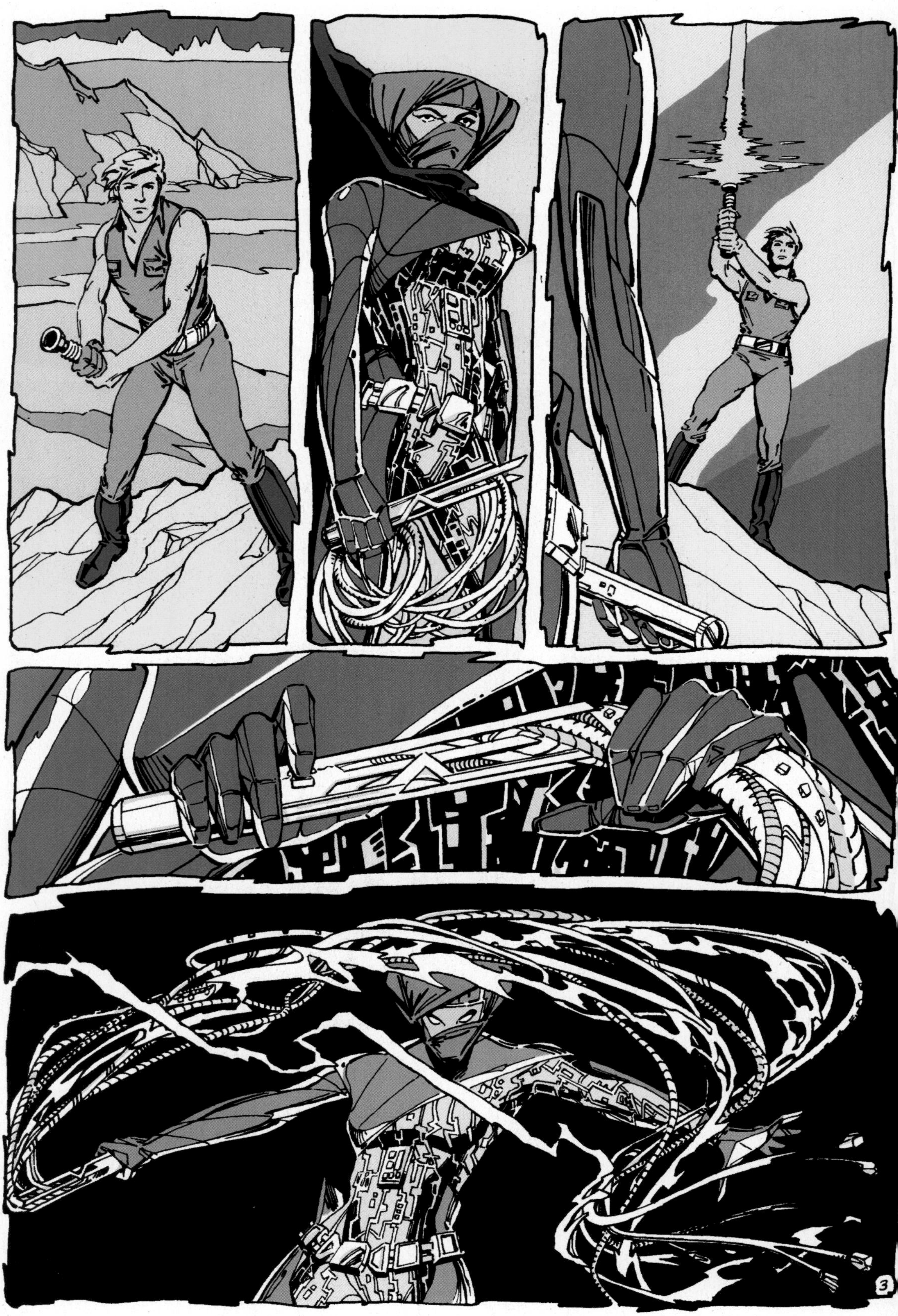

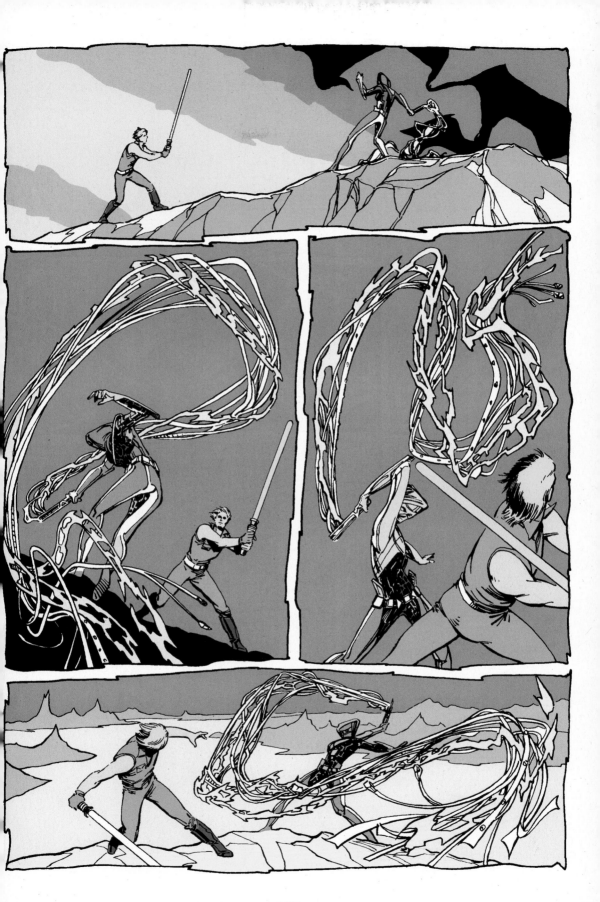

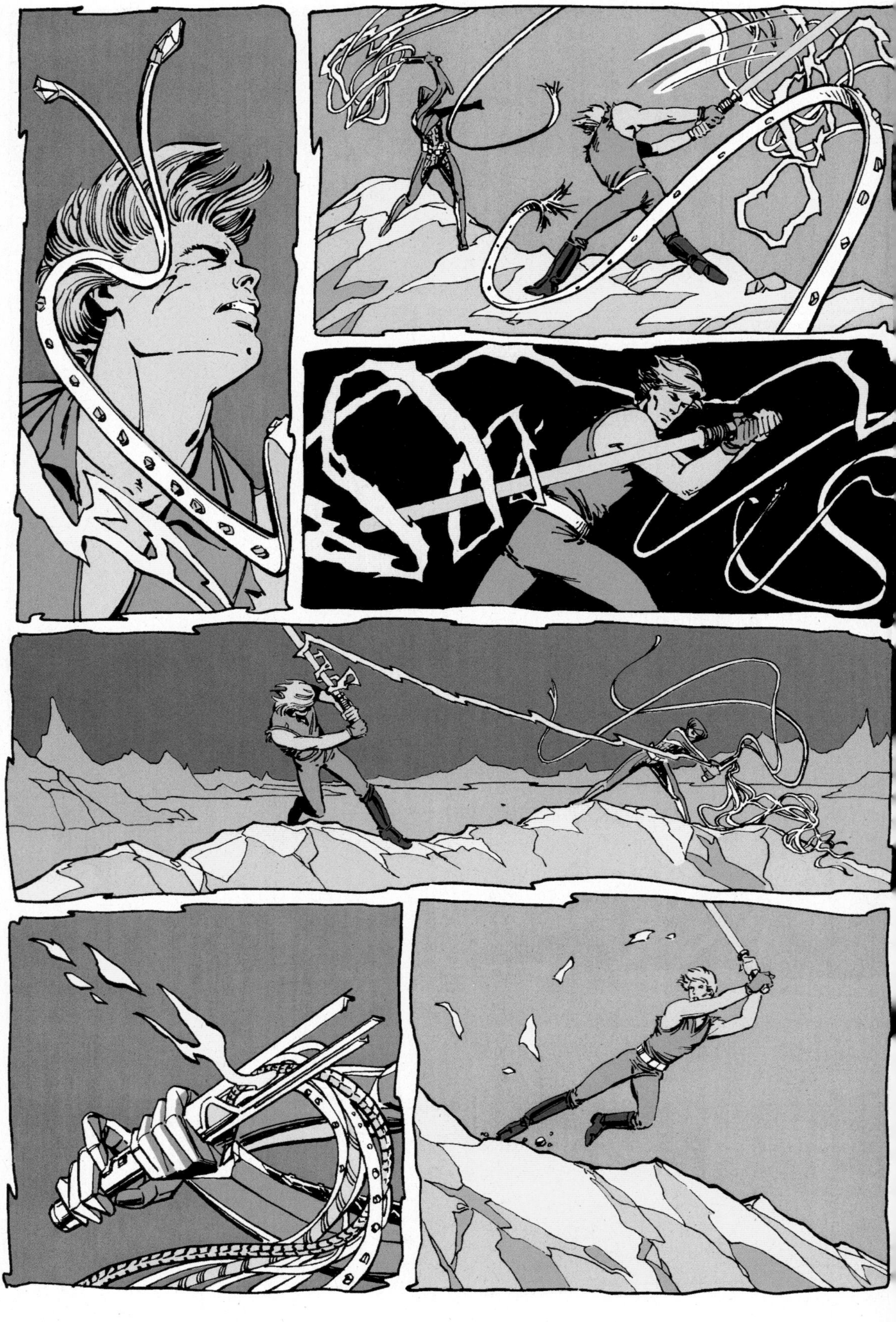

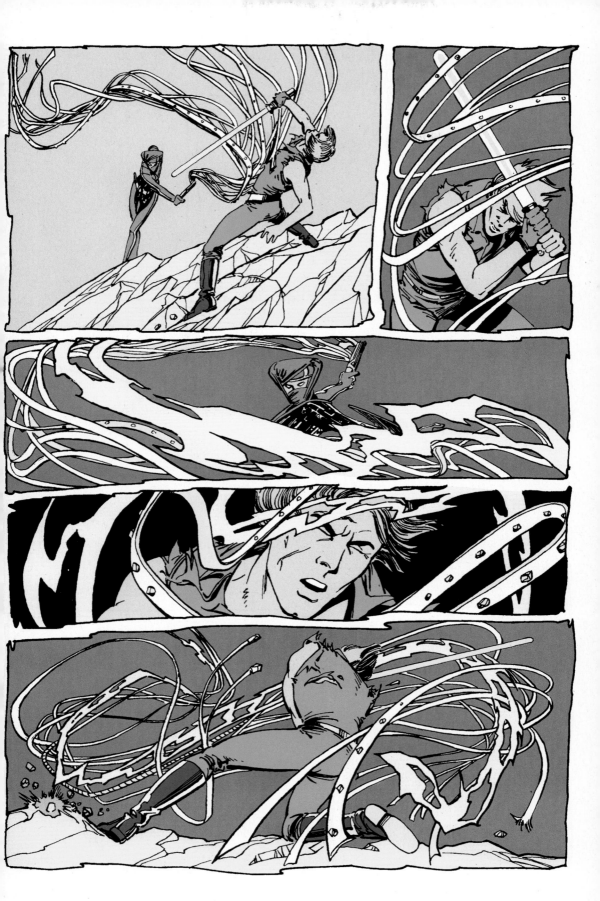

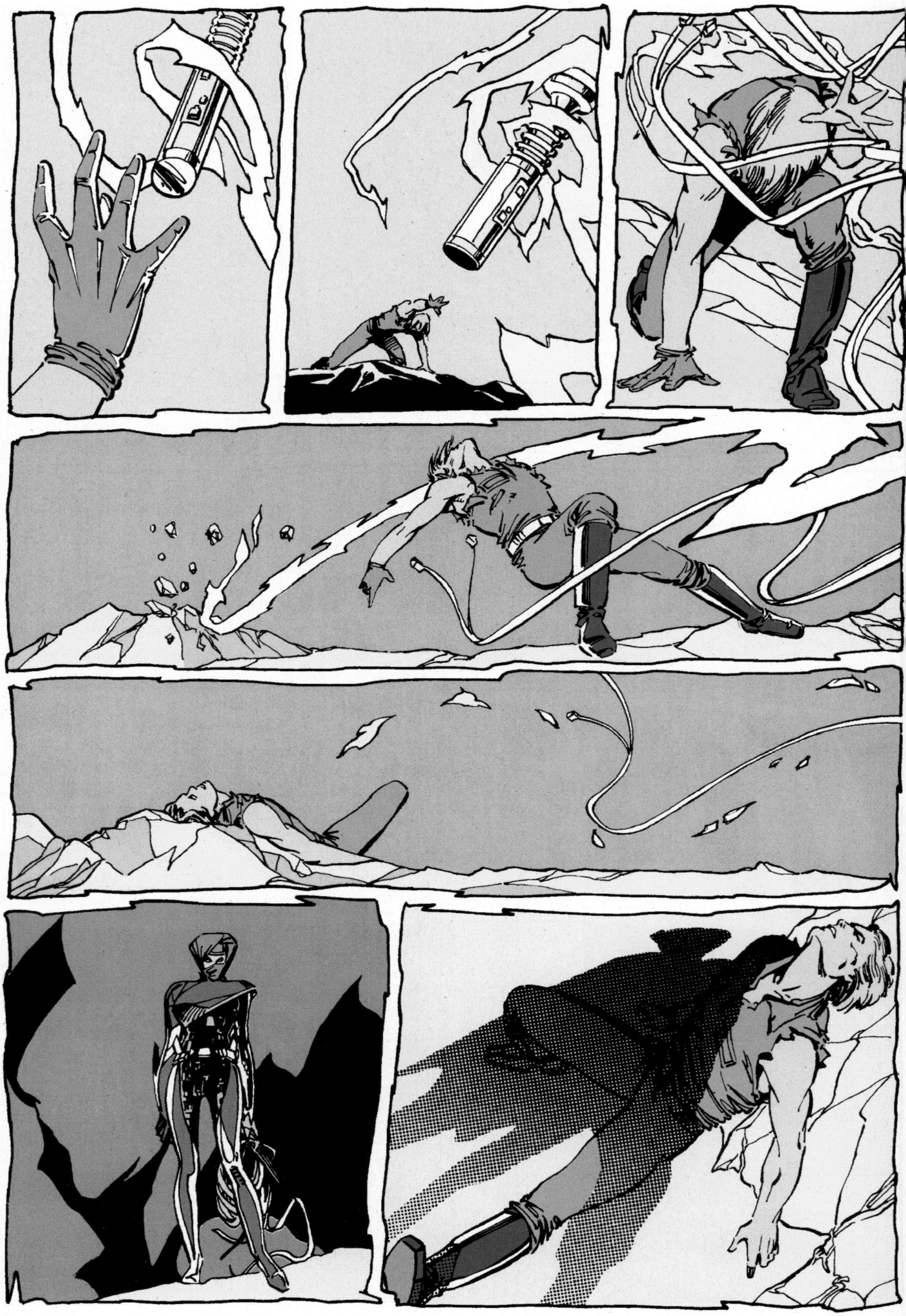

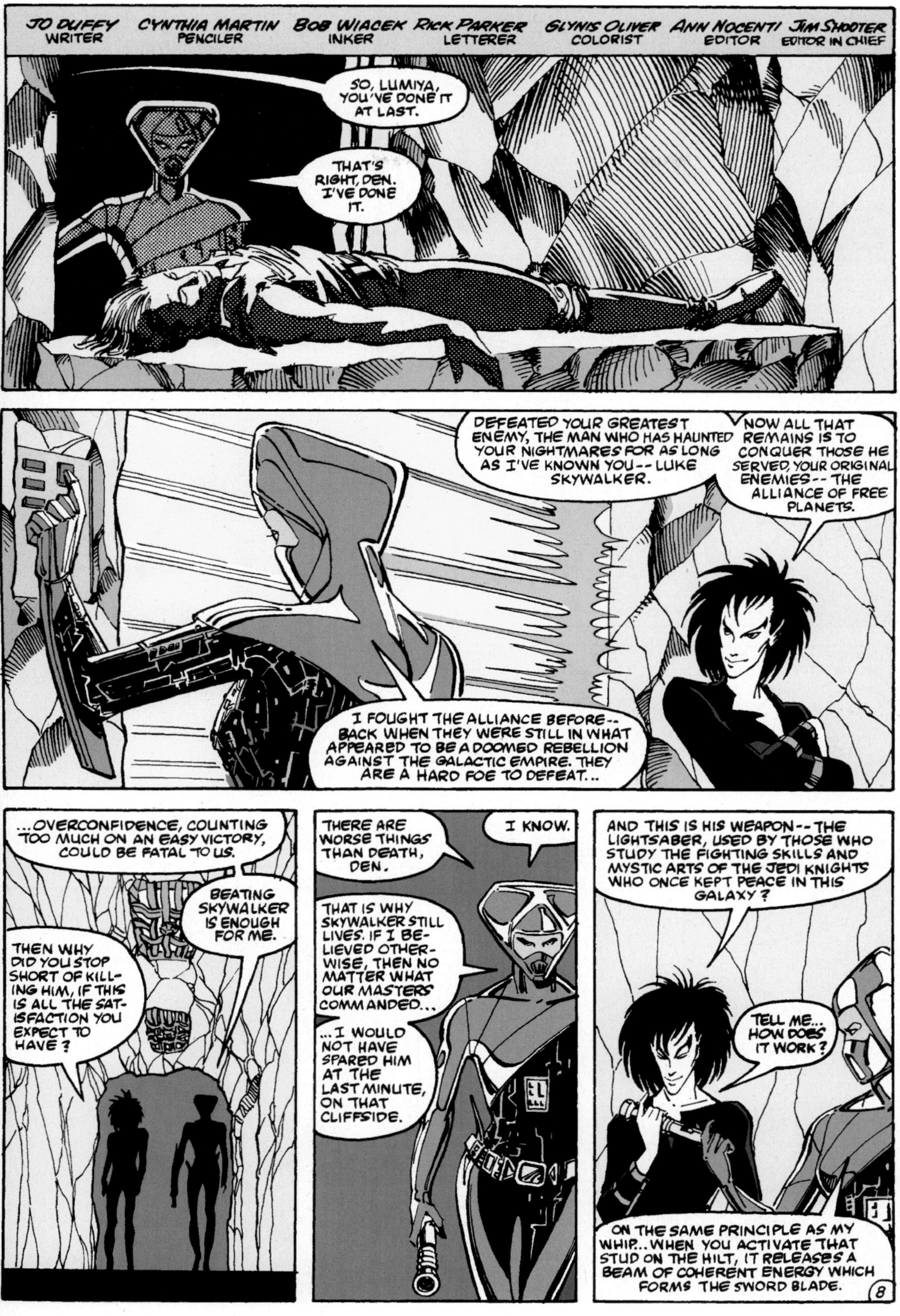
JO DUFFY WRITER
CYNTHIA MARTIN PENCILER
BOB WIACEK INKER
RICK PARKER LETTERER
GLYNIS OLIVER COLORIST
ANN NOCENTI EDITOR
JIM SHOOTER EDITOR IN CHIEF
SO, LUMIYA, YOU'VE DONE IT AT LAST.
THAT'S RIGHT, DEN. I'VE DONE IT.
DEFEATED YOUR GREATEST ENEMY, THE MAN WHO HAS HAUNTED YOUR NIGHTMARES FOR AS LONG AS I'VE KNOWN YOU-- LUKE SKYWALKER.
NOW ALL THAT REMAINS IS TO CONQUER THOSE HE SERVED, YOUR ORIGINAL ENEMIES-- THE ALLIANCE OF FREE PLANETS.
I FOUGHT THE ALLIANCE BEFORE-- BACK WHEN THEY WERE STILL IN WHAT APPEARED TO BE A DOOMED REBELLION AGAINST THE GALACTIC EMPIRE. THEY ARE A HARD FOE TO DEFEAT...
...OVERCONFIDENCE, COUNTING TOO MUCH ON AN EASY VICTORY, COULD BE FATAL TO US.
BEATING SKYWALKER IS ENOUGH FOR ME.
THEN WHY DID YOU STOP SHORT OF KILLING HIM, IF THIS IS ALL THE SATISFACTION YOU EXPECT TO HAVE?
THERE ARE WORSE THINGS THAN DEATH, DEN.
I KNOW.
THAT IS WHY SKYWALKER STILL LIVES. IF I BELIEVED OTHERWISE, THEN NO MATTER WHAT OUR MASTERS COMMANDED...
...I WOULD NOT HAVE SPARED HIM AT THE LAST MINUTE, ON THAT CLIFFSIDE.
AND THIS IS HIS WEAPON-- THE LIGHTSABER, USED BY THOSE WHO STUDY THE FIGHTING SKILLS AND MYSTIC ARTS OF THE JEDI KNIGHTS WHO ONCE KEPT PEACE IN THIS GALAXY?
TELL ME... HOW DOES IT WORK?
ON THE SAME PRINCIPLE AS MY WHIP... WHEN YOU ACTIVATE THAT STUD ON THE HILT, IT RELEASES A BEAM OF COHERENT ENERGY WHICH FORMS THE SWORD BLADE.
8

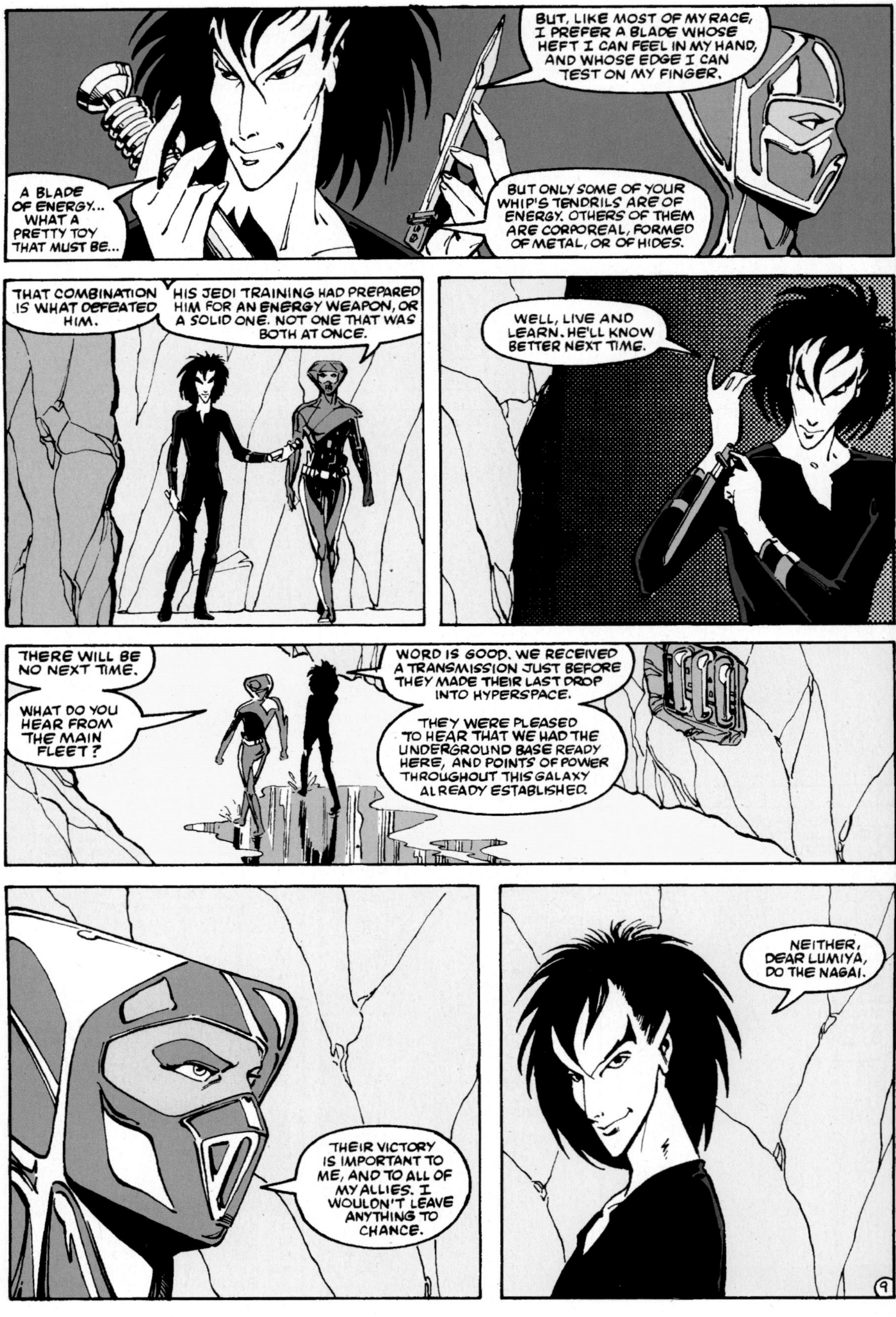
A BLADE OF ENERGY... WHAT A PRETTY TOY THAT MUST BE...
BUT, LIKE MOST OF MY RACE, I PREFER A BLADE WHOSE HEFT I CAN FEEL IN MY HAND, AND WHOSE EDGE I CAN TEST ON MY FINGER.
BUT ONLY SOME OF YOUR WHIP'S TENDRILS ARE OF ENERGY. OTHERS OF THEM ARE CORPOREAL, FORMED OF METAL, OR OF HIDES.
THAT COMBINATION IS WHAT DEFEATED HIM.
HIS JEDI TRAINING HAD PREPARED HIM FOR AN ENERGY WEAPON, OR A SOLID ONE. NOT ONE THAT WAS BOTH AT ONCE.
WELL, LIVE AND LEARN. HE'LL KNOW BETTER NEXT TIME.
THERE WILL BE NO NEXT TIME.
WHAT DO YOU HEAR FROM THE MAIN FLEET?
WORD IS GOOD. WE RECEIVED A TRANSMISSION JUST BEFORE THEY MADE THEIR LAST DROP INTO HYPERSPACE.
THEY WERE PLEASED TO HEAR THAT WE HAD THE UNDERGROUND BASE READY HERE, AND POINTS OF POWER THROUGHOUT THIS GALAXY ALREADY ESTABLISHED.
THEIR VICTORY IS IMPORTANT TO ME, AND TO ALL OF MY ALLIES. I WOULDN'T LEAVE ANYTHING TO CHANCE.
NEITHER, DEAR LUMIYA, DO THE NAGAI.
9

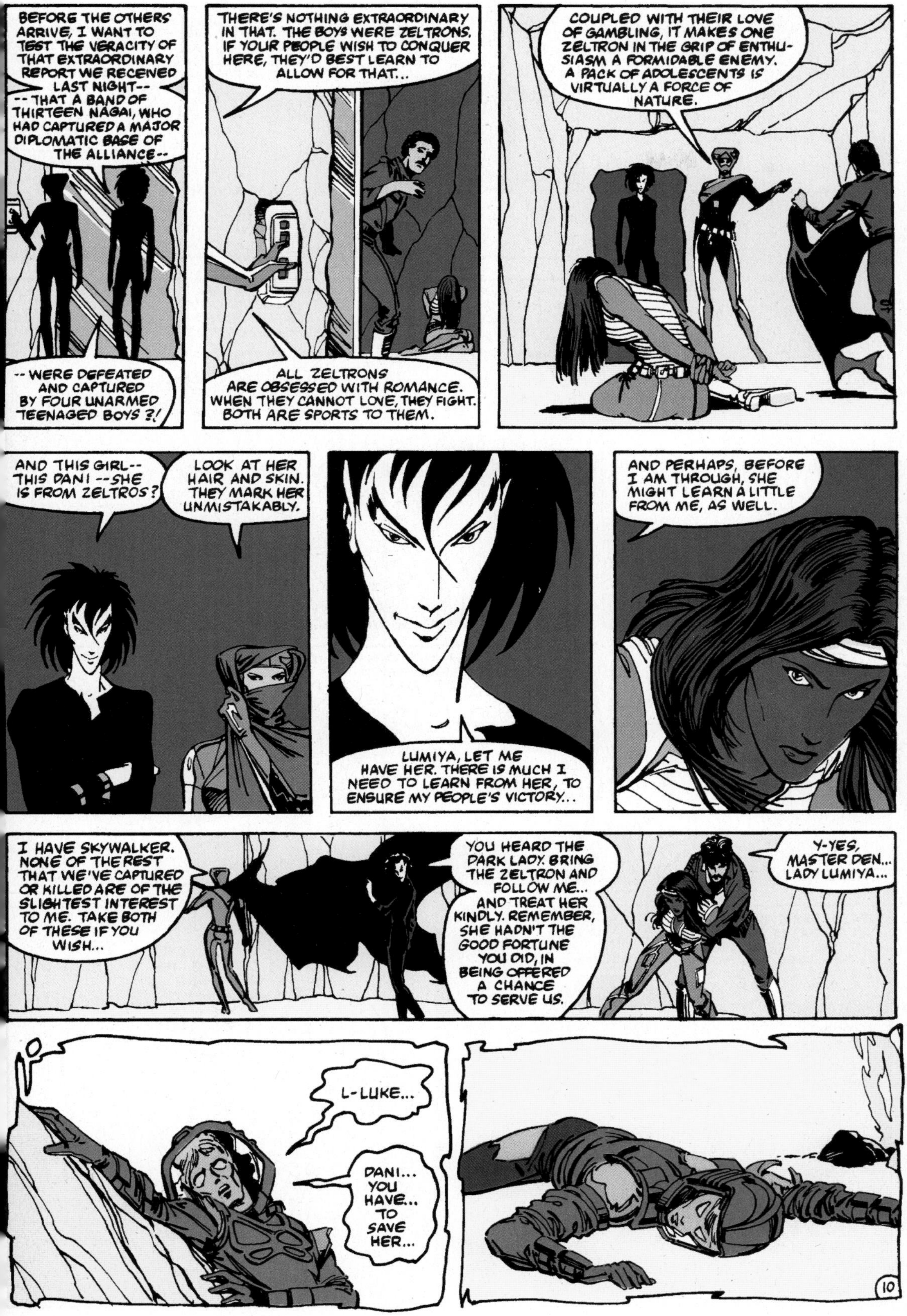
BEFORE THE OTHERS ARRIVE, I WANT TO TEST THE VERACITY OF THAT EXTRAORDINARY REPORT WE RECEIVED LAST NIGHT--
-- THAT A BAND OF THIRTEEN NAGAI, WHO HAD CAPTURED A MAJOR DIPLOMATIC BASE OF THE ALLIANCE--
-- WERE DEFEATED AND CAPTURED BY FOUR UNARMED TEENAGED BOYS ?!
THERE'S NOTHING EXTRAORDINARY IN THAT. THE BOYS WERE ZELTRONS. IF YOUR PEOPLE WISH TO CONQUER HERE, THEY'D BEST LEARN TO ALLOW FOR THAT...
ALL ZELTRONS ARE OBSESSED WITH ROMANCE. WHEN THEY CANNOT LOVE, THEY FIGHT. BOTH ARE SPORTS TO THEM.
COUPLED WITH THEIR LOVE OF GAMBLING, IT MAKES ONE ZELTRON IN THE GRIP OF ENTHUSIASM A FORMIDABLE ENEMY. A PACK OF ADOLESCENTS IS VIRTUALLY A FORCE OF NATURE.
AND THIS GIRL-- THIS DANI --SHE IS FROM ZELTROS?
LOOK AT HER HAIR AND SKIN. THEY MARK HER UNMISTAKABLY.
LUMIYA, LET ME HAVE HER. THERE IS MUCH I NEED TO LEARN FROM HER, TO ENSURE MY PEOPLE'S VICTORY...
AND PERHAPS, BEFORE I AM THROUGH, SHE MIGHT LEARN A LITTLE FROM ME, AS WELL.
I HAVE SKYWALKER. NONE OF THE REST THAT WE'VE CAPTURED OR KILLED ARE OF THE SLIGHTEST INTEREST TO ME. TAKE BOTH OF THESE IF YOU WISH...
YOU HEARD THE DARK LADY. BRING THE ZELTRON AND FOLLOW ME... AND TREAT HER KINDLY. REMEMBER, SHE HADN'T THE GOOD FORTUNE YOU DID, IN BEING OFFERED A CHANCE TO SERVE US.
Y-YES, MASTER DEN... LADY LUMIYA...
L-LUKE...
DANI... YOU HAVE... TO SAVE HER...
10

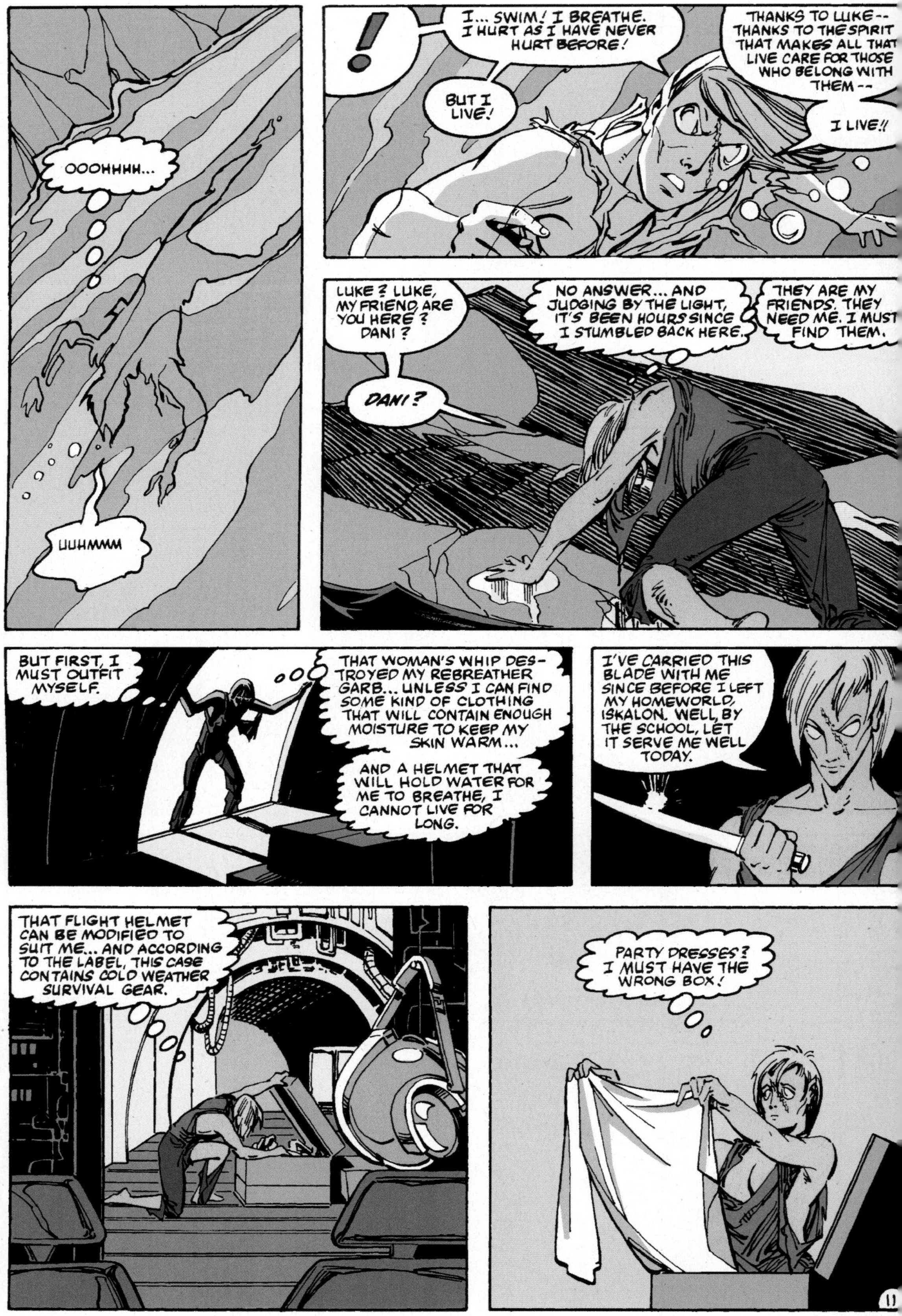
OOOHHHH...
UUHMMM
!
I... SWIM! I BREATHE. I HURT AS I HAVE NEVER HURT BEFORE!
BUT I LIVE!
THANKS TO LUKE -- THANKS TO THE SPIRIT THAT MAKES ALL THAT LIVE CARE FOR THOSE WHO BELONG WITH THEM --
I LIVE!!
LUKE? LUKE, MY FRIEND, ARE YOU HERE? DANI?
DANI?
NO ANSWER... AND JUDGING BY THE LIGHT, IT'S BEEN HOURS SINCE I STUMBLED BACK HERE.
THEY ARE MY FRIENDS. THEY NEED ME. I MUST FIND THEM.
BUT FIRST, I MUST OUTFIT MYSELF.
THAT WOMAN'S WHIP DESTROYED MY REBREATHER GARB... UNLESS I CAN FIND SOME KIND OF CLOTHING THAT WILL CONTAIN ENOUGH MOISTURE TO KEEP MY SKIN WARM...
AND A HELMET THAT WILL HOLD WATER FOR ME TO BREATHE, I CANNOT LIVE FOR LONG.
I'VE CARRIED THIS BLADE WITH ME SINCE BEFORE I LEFT MY HOMEWORLD, ISKALON. WELL, BY THE SCHOOL, LET IT SERVE ME WELL TODAY.
THAT FLIGHT HELMET CAN BE MODIFIED TO SUIT ME... AND ACCORDING TO THE LABEL, THIS CASE CONTAINS COLD WEATHER SURVIVAL GEAR.
PARTY DRESSES? I MUST HAVE THE WRONG BOX!
11

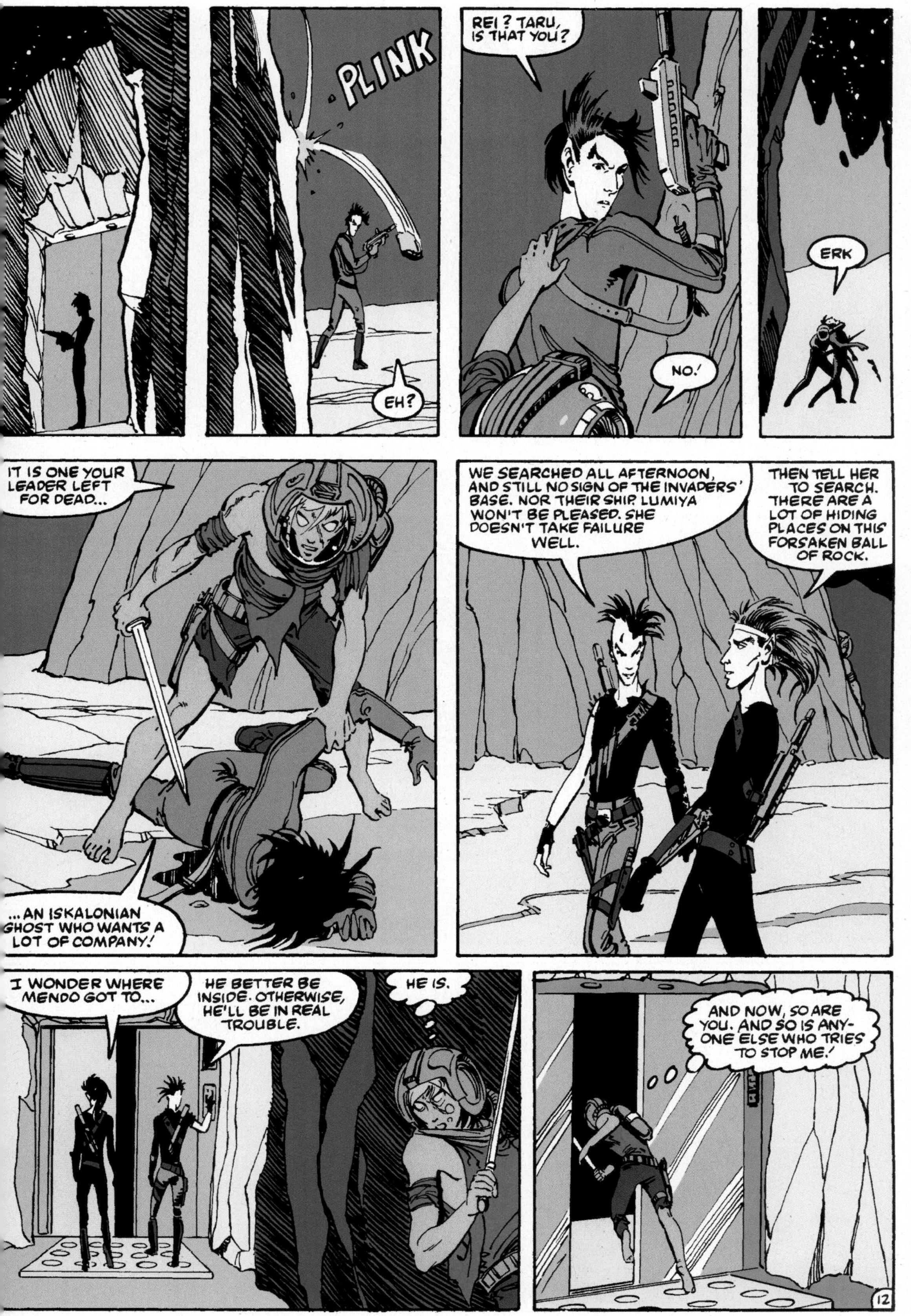
PLINK
EH?
REI? TARU, IS THAT YOU?
NO!
ERK
IT IS ONE YOUR LEADER LEFT FOR DEAD...
...AN ISKALONIAN GHOST WHO WANTS A LOT OF COMPANY!
WE SEARCHED ALL AFTERNOON, AND STILL NO SIGN OF THE INVADERS' BASE. NOR THEIR SHIP. LUMIYA WON'T BE PLEASED. SHE DOESN'T TAKE FAILURE WELL.
THEN TELL HER TO SEARCH. THERE ARE A LOT OF HIDING PLACES ON THIS FORSAKEN BALL OF ROCK.
I WONDER WHERE MENDO GOT TO...
HE BETTER BE INSIDE. OTHERWISE, HE'LL BE IN REAL TROUBLE.
HE IS.
AND NOW, SO ARE YOU. AND SO IS ANYONE ELSE WHO TRIES TO STOP ME!
12

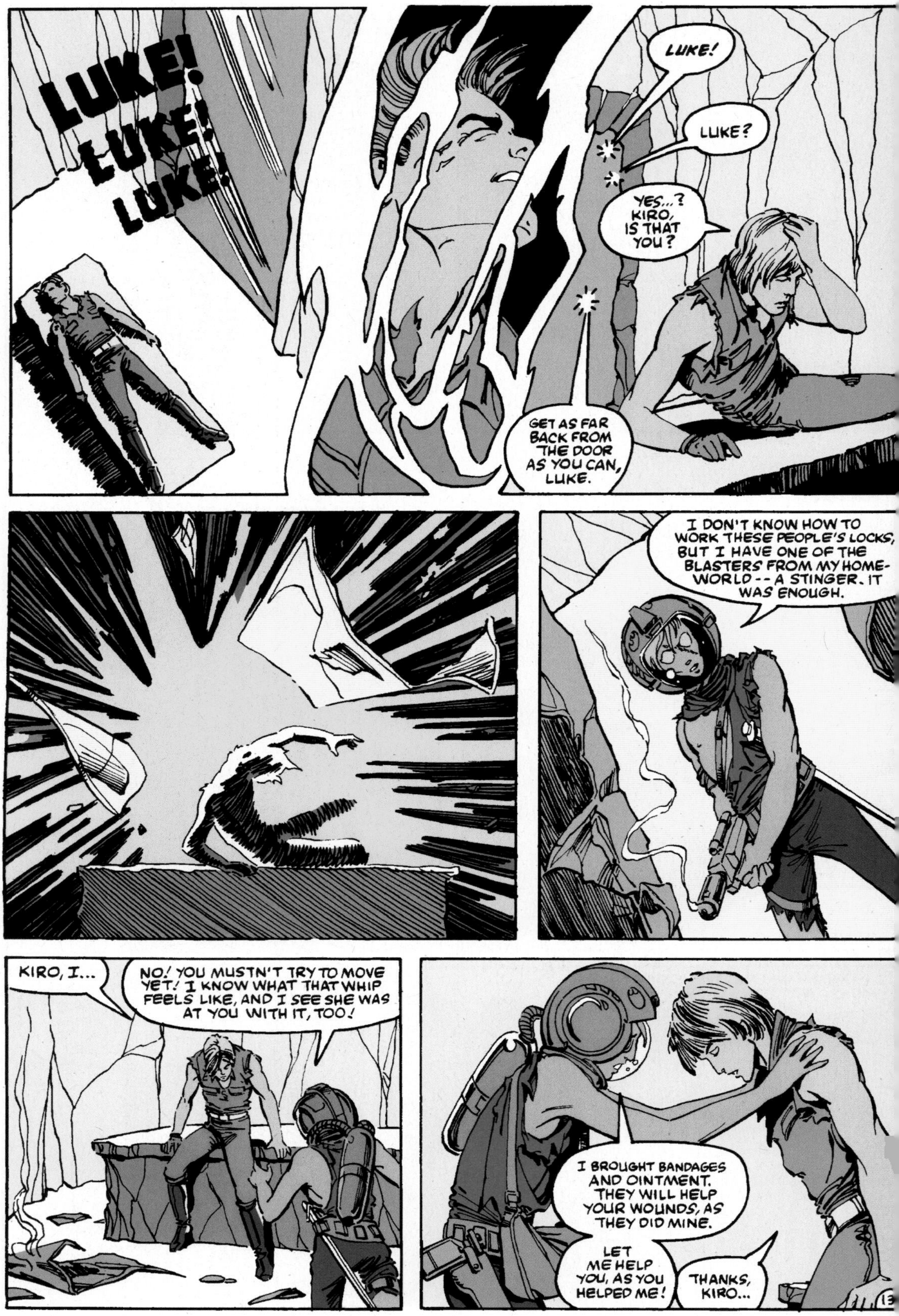
LUKE! LUKE! LUKE!
LUKE!
LUKE?
YES...? KIRO, IS THAT YOU?
GET AS FAR BACK FROM THE DOOR AS YOU CAN, LUKE.
I DON'T KNOW HOW TO WORK THESE PEOPLE'S LOCKS, BUT I HAVE ONE OF THE BLASTERS FROM MY HOME-WORLD -- A STINGER. IT WAS ENOUGH.
KIRO, I...
NO! YOU MUSTN'T TRY TO MOVE YET! I KNOW WHAT THAT WHIP FEELS LIKE, AND I SEE SHE WAS AT YOU WITH IT, TOO!
I BROUGHT BANDAGES AND OINTMENT. THEY WILL HELP YOUR WOUNDS, AS THEY DID MINE.
LET ME HELP YOU, AS YOU HELPED ME!
THANKS, KIRO...
13

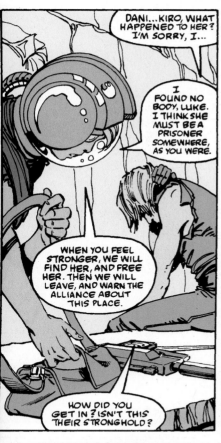

DANI...KIRO, WHAT HAPPENED TO HER? I'M SORRY, I...

I FOUND NO BODY, LUKE. I THINK SHE MUST BE A PRISONER SOMEWHERE, AS YOU WERE.

WHEN YOU FEEL STRONGER, WE WILL FIND HER, AND FREE HER. THEN WE WILL LEAVE, AND WARN THE ALLIANCE ABOUT THIS PLACE.

HOW DID YOU GET IN? ISN'T THIS THEIR STRONGHOLD?

I WAS VERY STEALTHY... AND I KILLED A FEW OF THEM...

NOT ALL, AS I WANTED TO... BUT I DIDN'T WANT TO ATTRACT ATTENTION... AND...

AND I KNEW YOU WOULD NOT LIKE IT, IF I KILLED NEEDLESSLY.

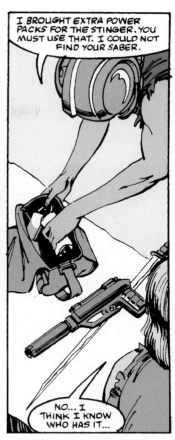

I BROUGHT EXTRA POWER PACKS FOR THE STINGER. YOU MUST USE THAT. I COULD NOT FIND YOUR SABER.

NO... I THINK I KNOW WHO HAS IT...

BUT WE CAN'T GO AFTER IT YET... NOT UNTIL WE COME UP WITH SOME SORT OF STRATEGY... OR WE'LL END UP JUST LIKE LAST TIME OR WORSE...

BUT TOGETHER WE MIGHT... ...TOGETHER.

KIRO, I THINK YOU MAY HAVE JUST SHOWN ME HOW I HAVE TO DO THIS...

I'LL NEED TO PUT SOMETHING TOGETHER. DID YOU BRING TOOLS, AS WELL AS THE EXTRA POWER PACKS?

OF COURSE.

KIRO. I... I WANT YOU TO KNOW... I STILL DON'T KNOW IF I'M GOOD ENOUGH TO BE A TEACHER. BUT IF YOU WANT...

I'LL TRAIN YOU IN THE WAYS OF THE JEDI, AS BEST I CAN. YOU DESERVE THAT.

THANK YOU, MY FRIEND.

LET US FIND DANI. THEN WE CAN PLAN FOR THE FUTURE.

14

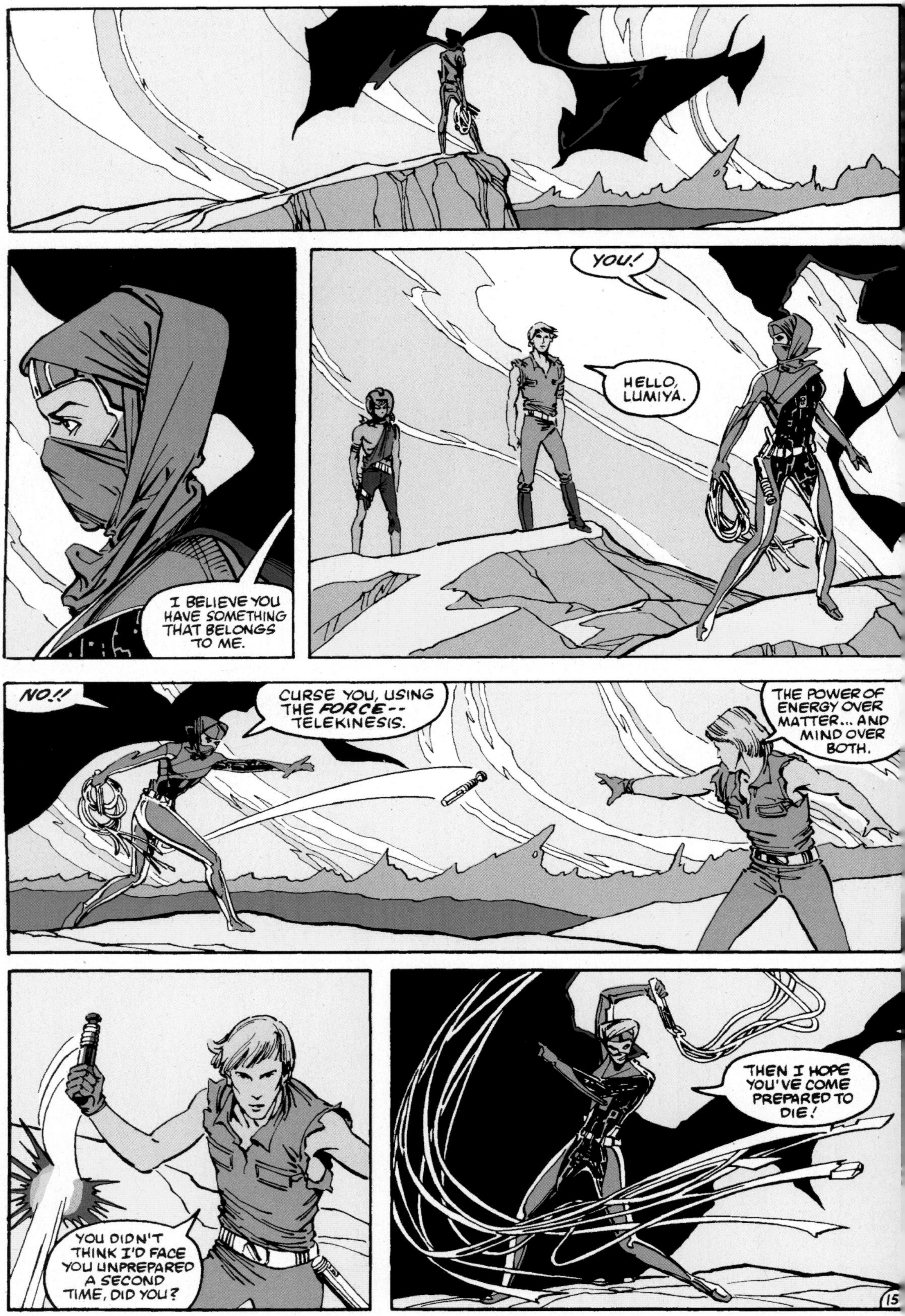

I BELIEVE YOU HAVE SOMETHING THAT BELONGS TO ME.
YOU!
HELLO, LUMIYA.
NO!!
CURSE YOU, USING THE FORCE-- TELEKINESIS.
THE POWER OF ENERGY OVER MATTER... AND MIND OVER BOTH.
YOU DIDN'T THINK I'D FACE YOU UNPREPARED A SECOND TIME, DID YOU?
THEN I HOPE YOU'VE COME PREPARED TO DIE!
15

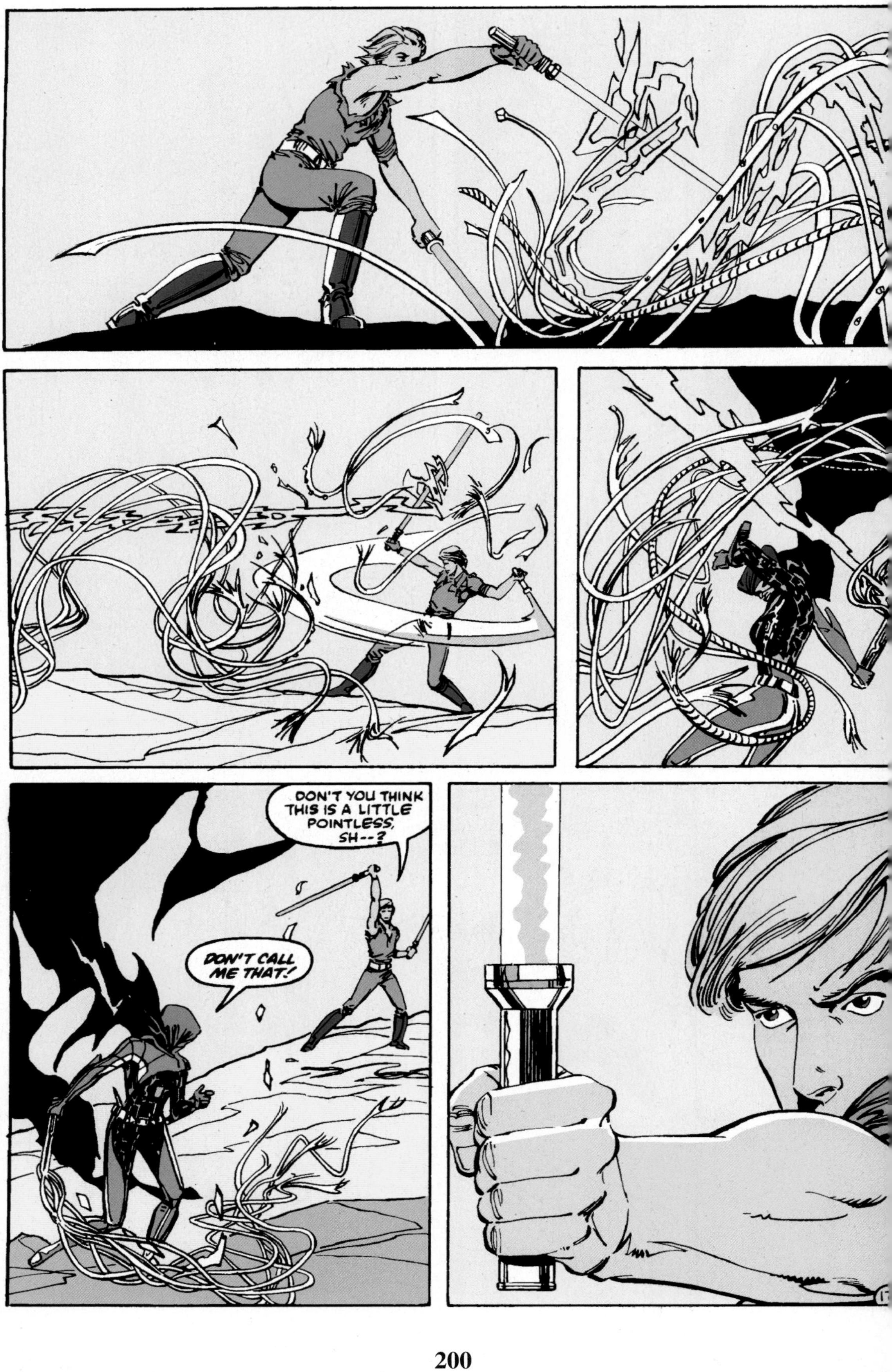
DON'T YOU THINK THIS IS A LITTLE POINTLESS, SH--?
DON'T CALL ME THAT!

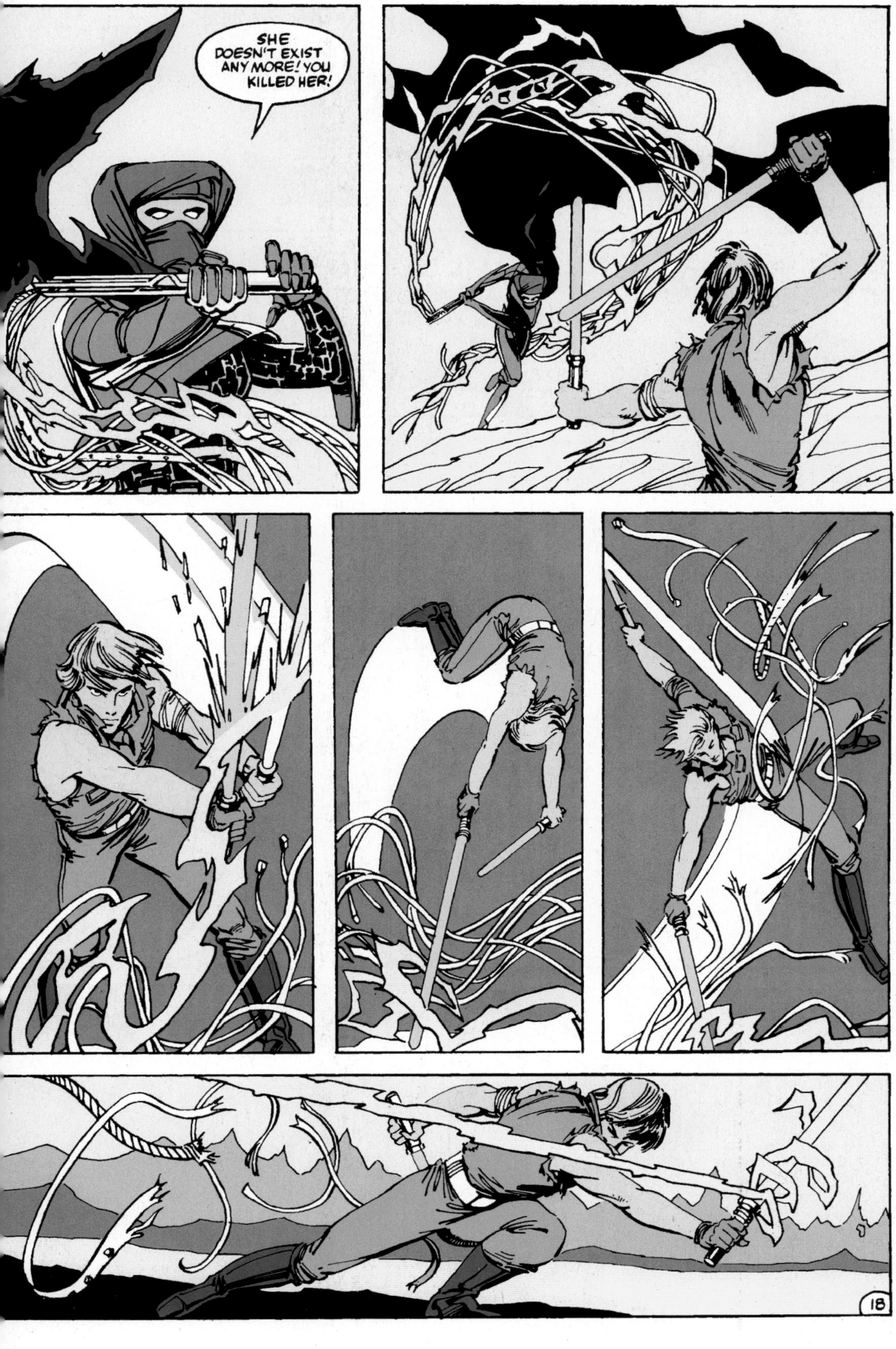
SHE DOESN'T EXIST ANY MORE! YOU KILLED HER!
18

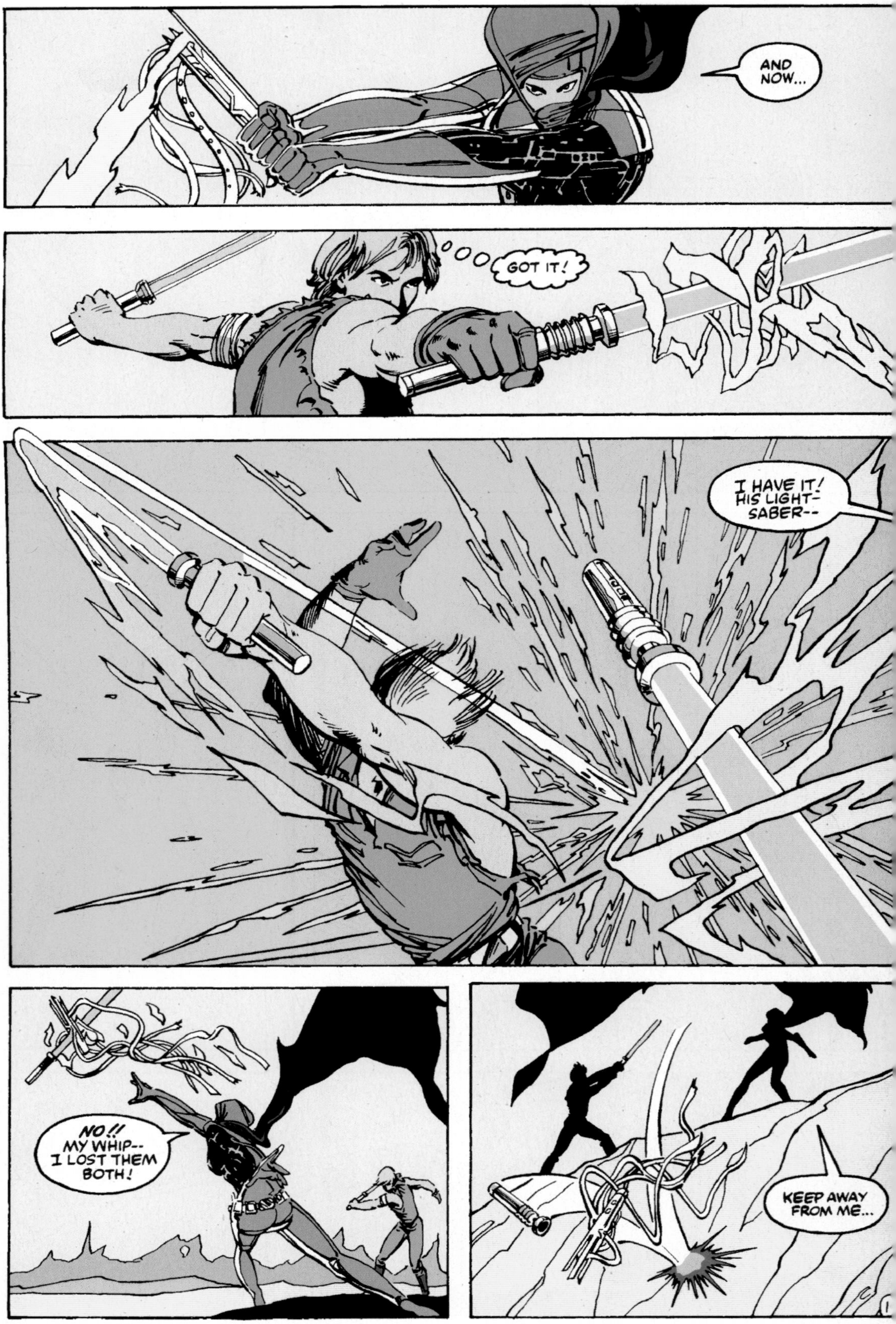
AND NOW...
GOT IT!
I HAVE IT! HIS LIGHT-SABER--
NO!! MY WHIP-- I LOST THEM BOTH!
KEEP AWAY FROM ME...

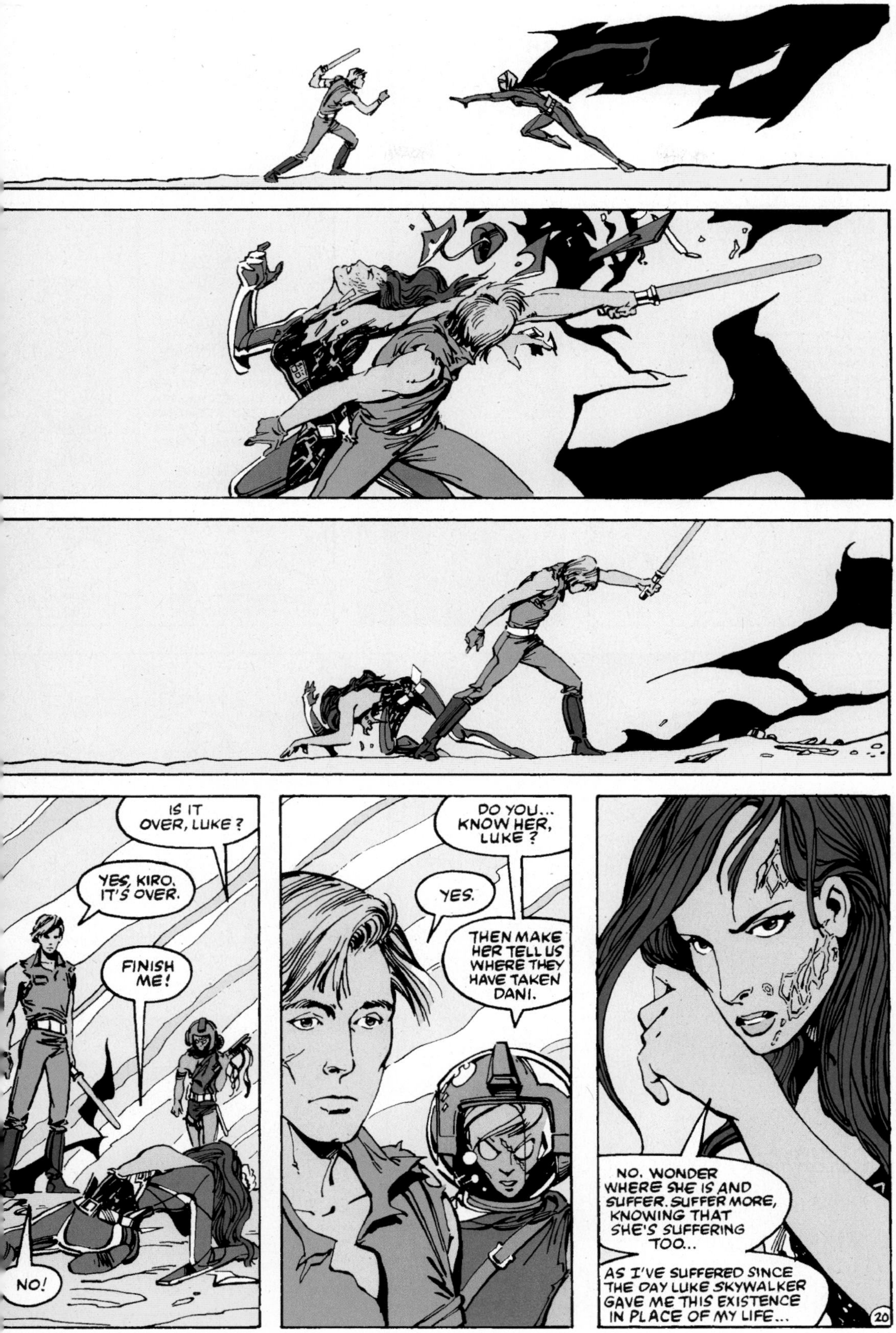
IS IT OVER, LUKE?
YES, KIRO. IT'S OVER.
FINISH ME!
NO!
DO YOU... KNOW HER, LUKE?
YES.
THEN MAKE HER TELL US WHERE THEY HAVE TAKEN DANI.
NO. WONDER WHERE SHE IS AND SUFFER. SUFFER MORE, KNOWING THAT SHE'S SUFFERING TOO...
AS I'VE SUFFERED SINCE THE DAY LUKE SKYWALKER GAVE ME THIS EXISTENCE IN PLACE OF MY LIFE...
20

As a cyborg--a mockery of life--half a woman, kept alive only by my machine parts!

I didn't know you were still alive. I didn't even know it was you I'd killed... just some imperial who was trying to kill me, and a lot of good rebels.

Luke...who is she?

I was Shira Elan Colla Brie. Now I am Lumiya. And someday, little fish man, I will spit on your grave...

As I will spit on your friend, Skywalker's, after I have seen him bereft of hope, of even the will to live...

Lumiya... the man who made you feel this way used you as a tool... but he's dead now and he wouldn't want you to go on like this...

At the end...he reconciled to the good in himself, as you can. I know it...

Believe me, as Darth Vader was my father, I...

Luke... look at the sky.

What is happening to it?

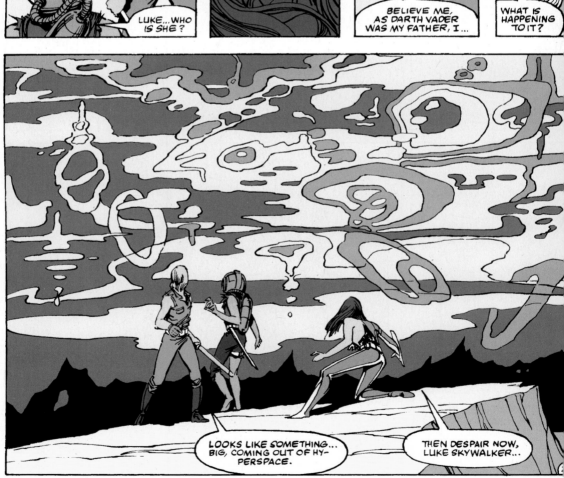

Looks like something... big, coming out of hyperspace.

Then despair now, Luke Skywalker...

204

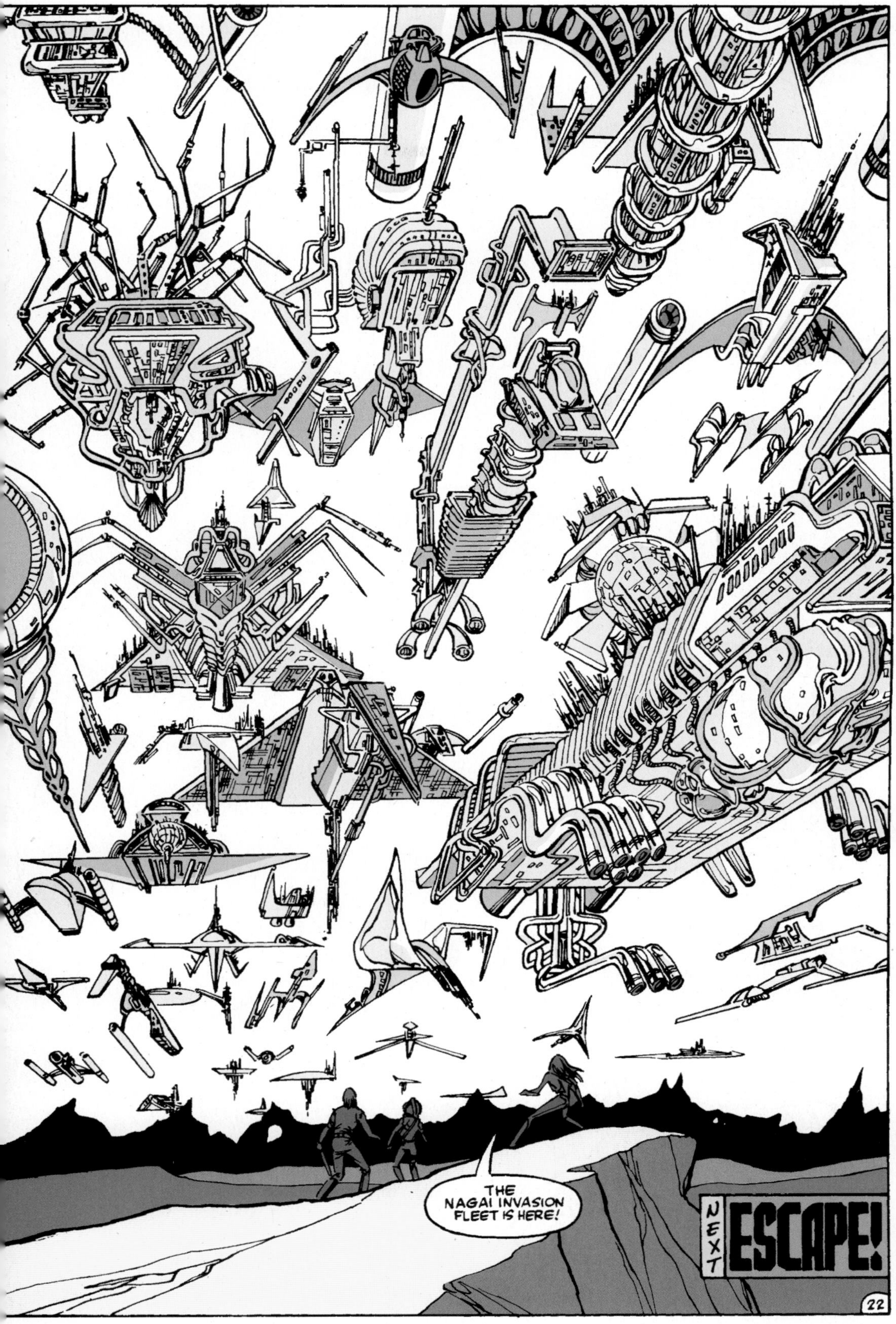
THE NAGAI INVASION FLEET IS HERE!
NEXT
ESCAPE!
22

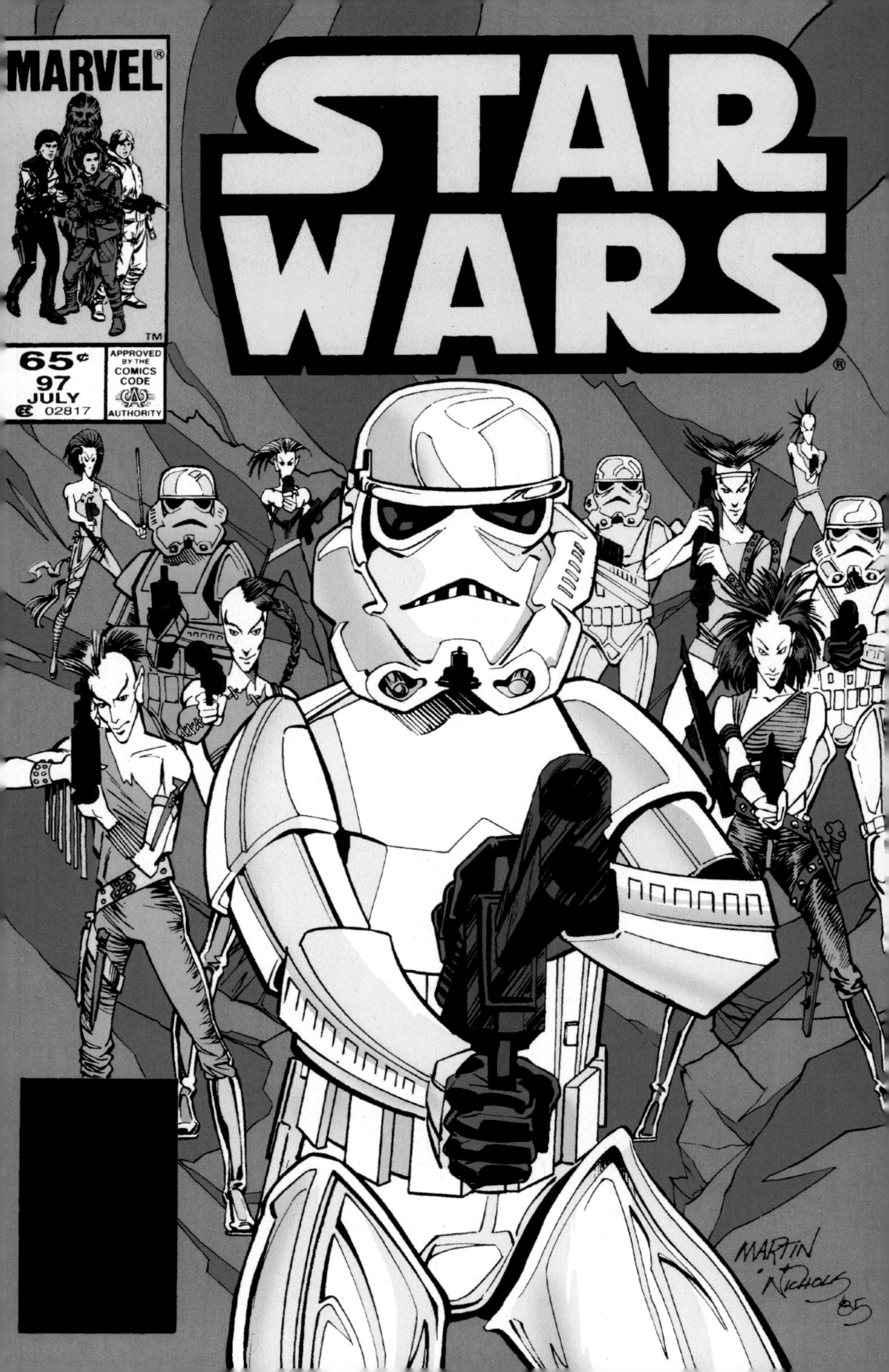
MARVEL®
STAR WARS®
TM
65¢
97
JULY
02817
APPROVED BY THE COMICS CODE AUTHORITY
MARTIN · NICHOLS '85

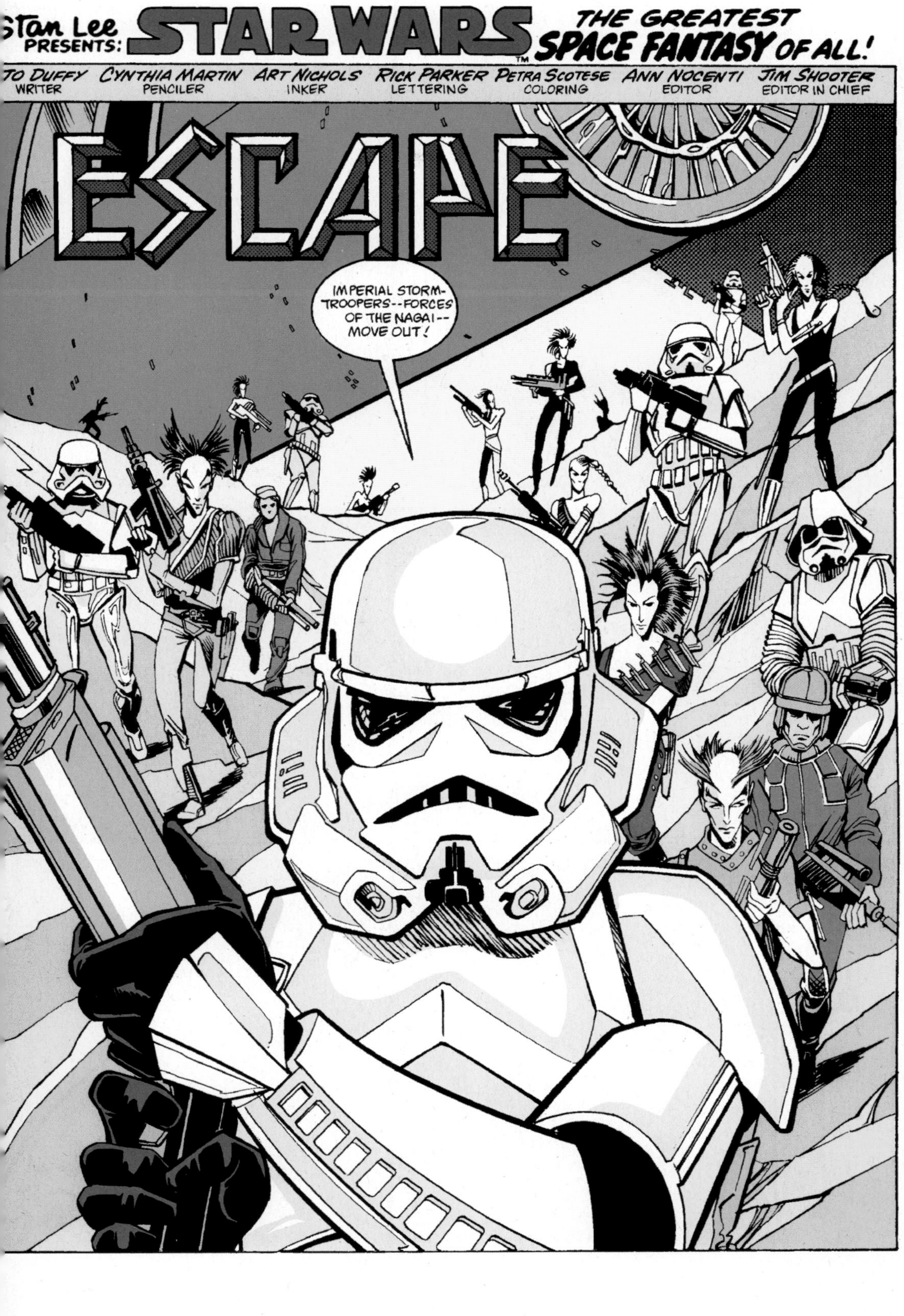
STAN LEE PRESENTS: STAR WARS THE GREATEST SPACE FANTASY OF ALL!
TO DUFFY WRITER CYNTHIA MARTIN PENCILER ART NICHOLS INKER RICK PARKER LETTERING PETRA SCOTESE COLORING ANN NOCENTI EDITOR JIM SHOOTER EDITOR IN CHIEF
ESCAPE
IMPERIAL STORM-TROOPERS--FORCES OF THE NAGAI--MOVE OUT!

208

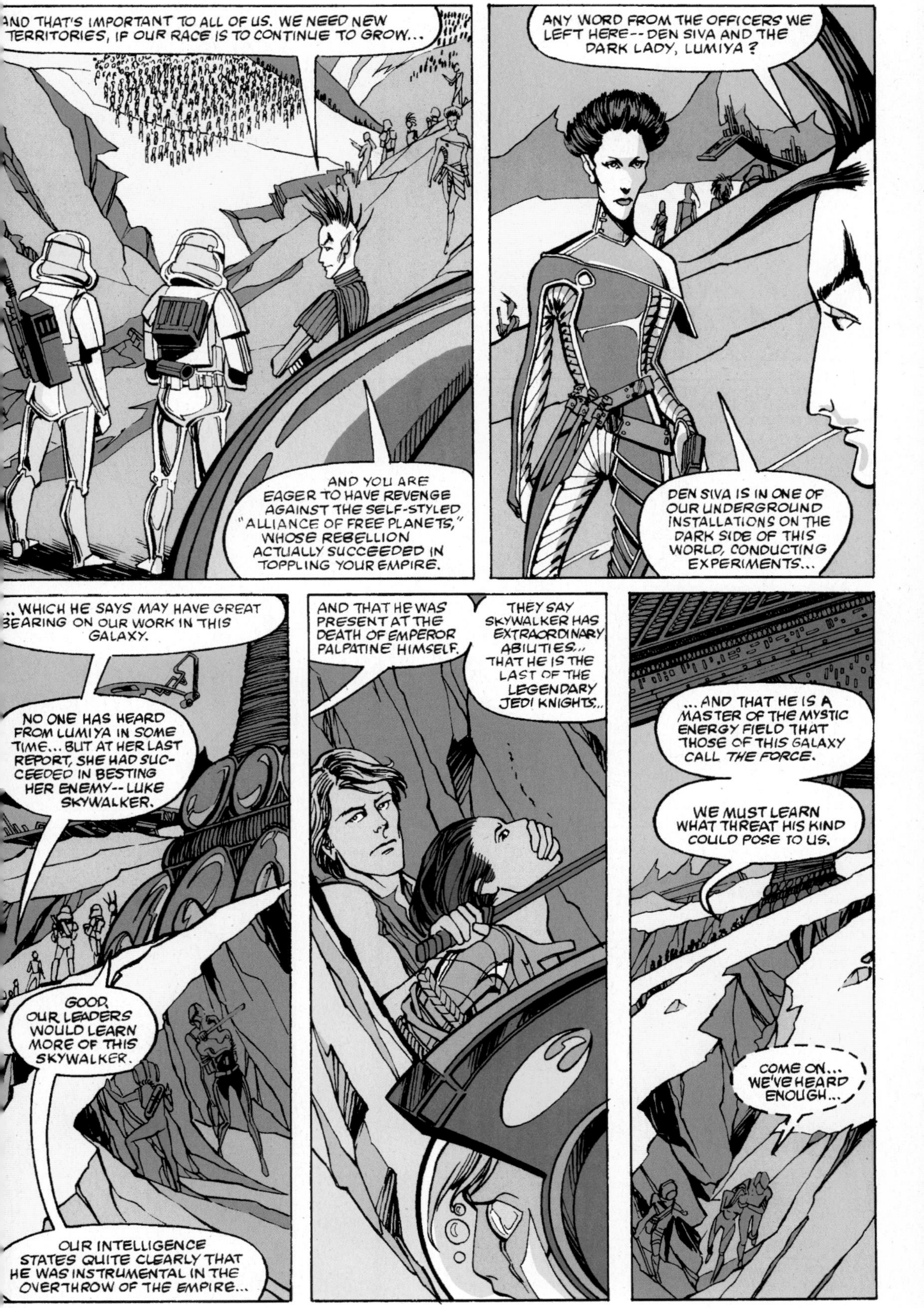
AND THAT'S IMPORTANT TO ALL OF US. WE NEED NEW TERRITORIES, IF OUR RACE IS TO CONTINUE TO GROW...
AND YOU ARE EAGER TO HAVE REVENGE AGAINST THE SELF-STYLED "ALLIANCE OF FREE PLANETS," WHOSE REBELLION ACTUALLY SUCCEEDED IN TOPPLING YOUR EMPIRE.
ANY WORD FROM THE OFFICERS WE LEFT HERE--DEN SIVA AND THE DARK LADY, LUMIYA?
DEN SIVA IS IN ONE OF OUR UNDERGROUND INSTALLATIONS ON THE DARK SIDE OF THIS WORLD, CONDUCTING EXPERIMENTS...
...WHICH HE SAYS MAY HAVE GREAT BEARING ON OUR WORK IN THIS GALAXY.
NO ONE HAS HEARD FROM LUMIYA IN SOME TIME... BUT AT HER LAST REPORT, SHE HAD SUCCEEDED IN BESTING HER ENEMY--LUKE SKYWALKER.
GOOD, OUR LEADERS WOULD LEARN MORE OF THIS SKYWALKER.
OUR INTELLIGENCE STATES QUITE CLEARLY THAT HE WAS INSTRUMENTAL IN THE OVERTHROW OF THE EMPIRE...
AND THAT HE WAS PRESENT AT THE DEATH OF EMPEROR PALPATINE HIMSELF.
THEY SAY SKYWALKER HAS EXTRAORDINARY ABILITIES... THAT HE IS THE LAST OF THE LEGENDARY JEDI KNIGHTS...
...AND THAT HE IS A MASTER OF THE MYSTIC ENERGY FIELD THAT THOSE OF THIS GALAXY CALL THE FORCE.
WE MUST LEARN WHAT THREAT HIS KIND COULD POSE TO US.
COME ON... WE'VE HEARD ENOUGH...

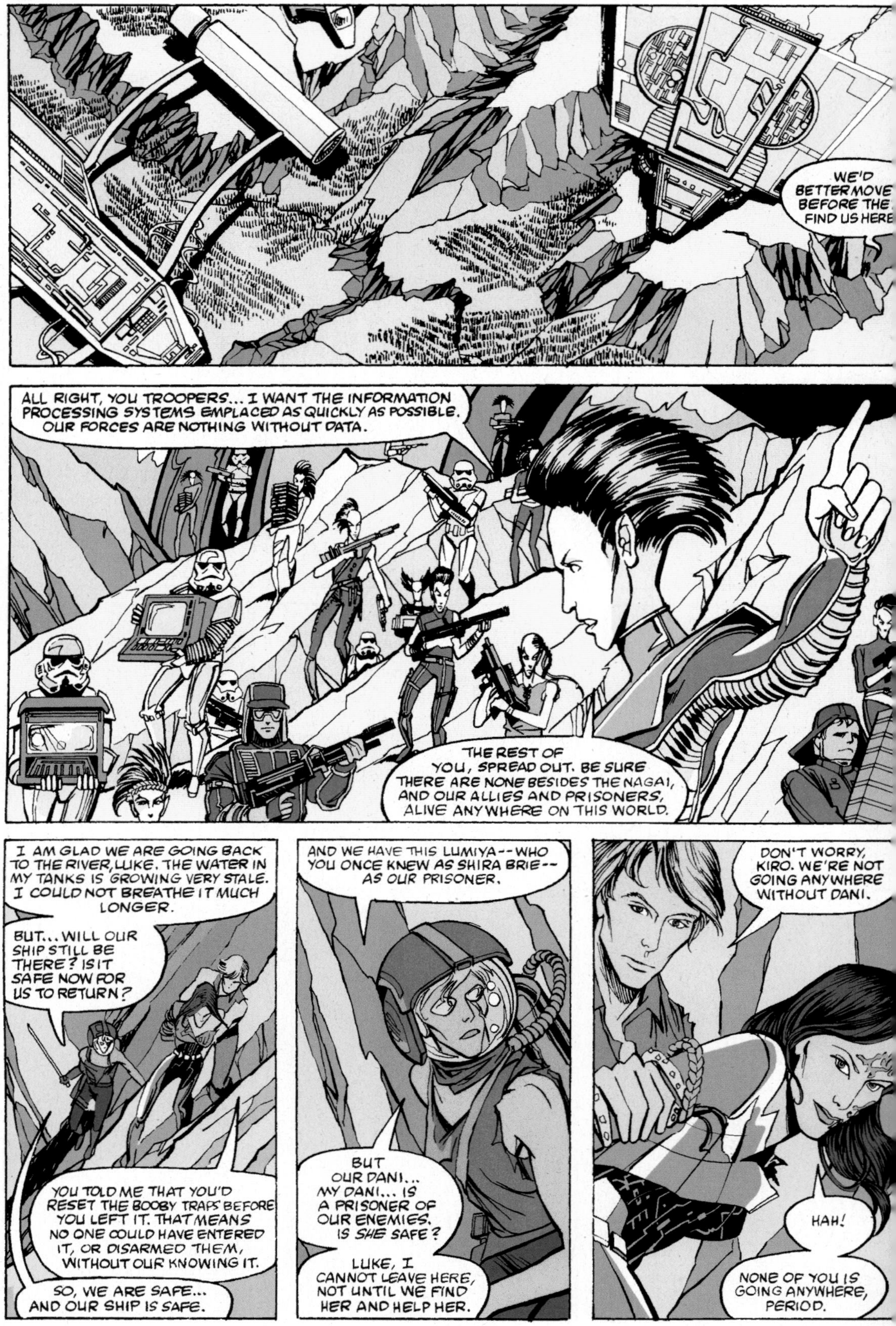
WE'D BETTER MOVE BEFORE THE FIND US HERE
ALL RIGHT, YOU TROOPERS... I WANT THE INFORMATION PROCESSING SYSTEMS EMPLACED AS QUICKLY AS POSSIBLE. OUR FORCES ARE NOTHING WITHOUT DATA.
THE REST OF YOU, SPREAD OUT. BE SURE THERE ARE NONE BESIDES THE NAGAI, AND OUR ALLIES AND PRISONERS, ALIVE ANYWHERE ON THIS WORLD.
I AM GLAD WE ARE GOING BACK TO THE RIVER, LUKE. THE WATER IN MY TANKS IS GROWING VERY STALE. I COULD NOT BREATHE IT MUCH LONGER.
BUT... WILL OUR SHIP STILL BE THERE? IS IT SAFE NOW FOR US TO RETURN?
YOU TOLD ME THAT YOU'D RESET THE BOOBY TRAPS BEFORE YOU LEFT IT. THAT MEANS NO ONE COULD HAVE ENTERED IT, OR DISARMED THEM, WITHOUT OUR KNOWING IT.
SO, WE ARE SAFE... AND OUR SHIP IS SAFE.
AND WE HAVE THIS LUMIYA--WHO YOU ONCE KNEW AS SHIRA BRIE--AS OUR PRISONER.
BUT OUR DANI... MY DANI... IS A PRISONER OF OUR ENEMIES. IS SHE SAFE?
LUKE, I CANNOT LEAVE HERE, NOT UNTIL WE FIND HER AND HELP HER.
DON'T WORRY, KIRO. WE'RE NOT GOING ANYWHERE WITHOUT DANI.
HAH!
NONE OF YOU IS GOING ANYWHERE, PERIOD.

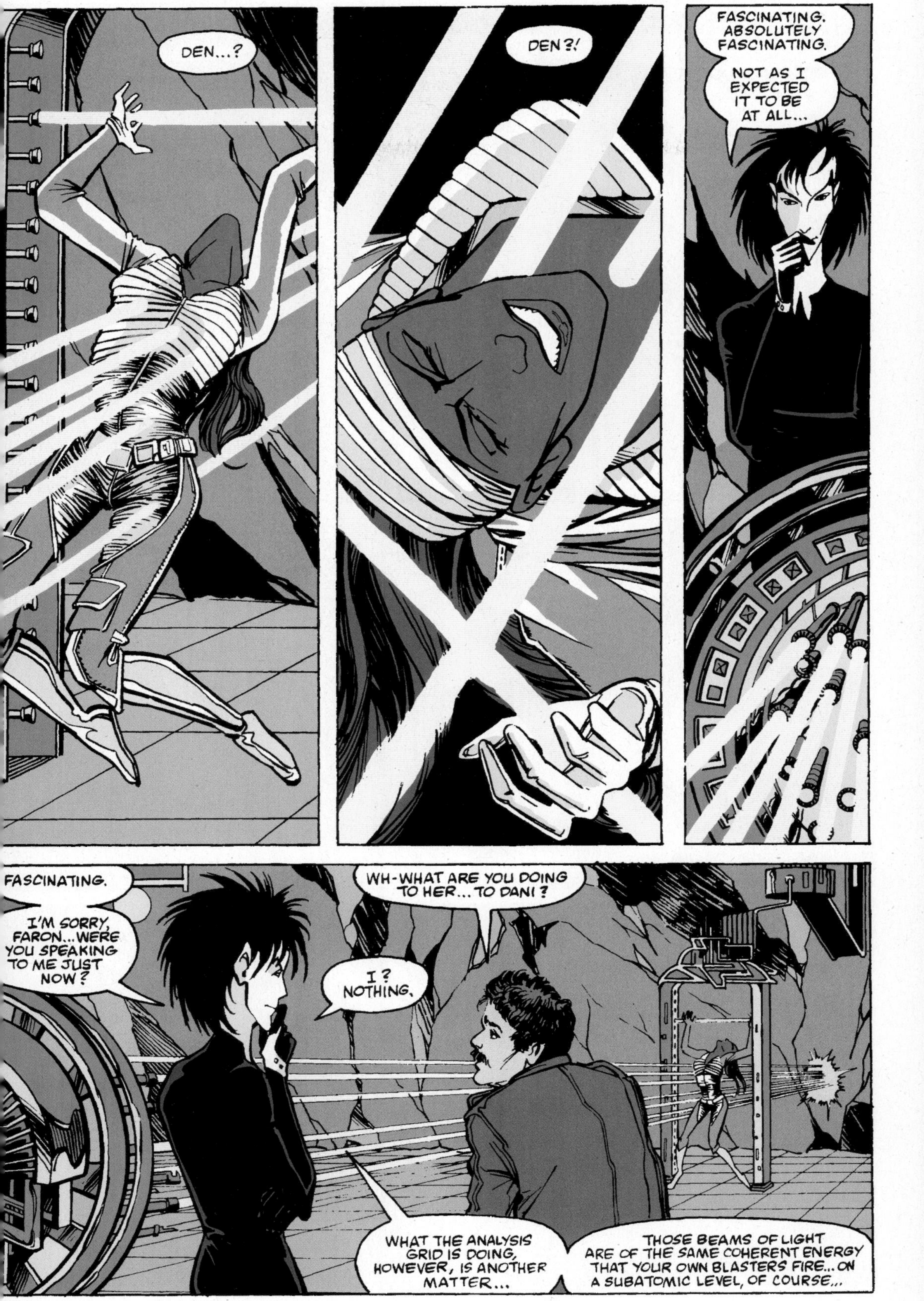
DEN...?
DEN?!
FASCINATING. ABSOLUTELY FASCINATING.
NOT AS I EXPECTED IT TO BE AT ALL...
FASCINATING.
I'M SORRY, FARON...WERE YOU SPEAKING TO ME JUST NOW?
WH-WHAT ARE YOU DOING TO HER... TO DANI?
I? NOTHING.
WHAT THE ANALYSIS GRID IS DOING, HOWEVER, IS ANOTHER MATTER...
THOSE BEAMS OF LIGHT ARE OF THE SAME COHERENT ENERGY THAT YOUR OWN BLASTERS FIRE... ON A SUBATOMIC LEVEL, OF COURSE...

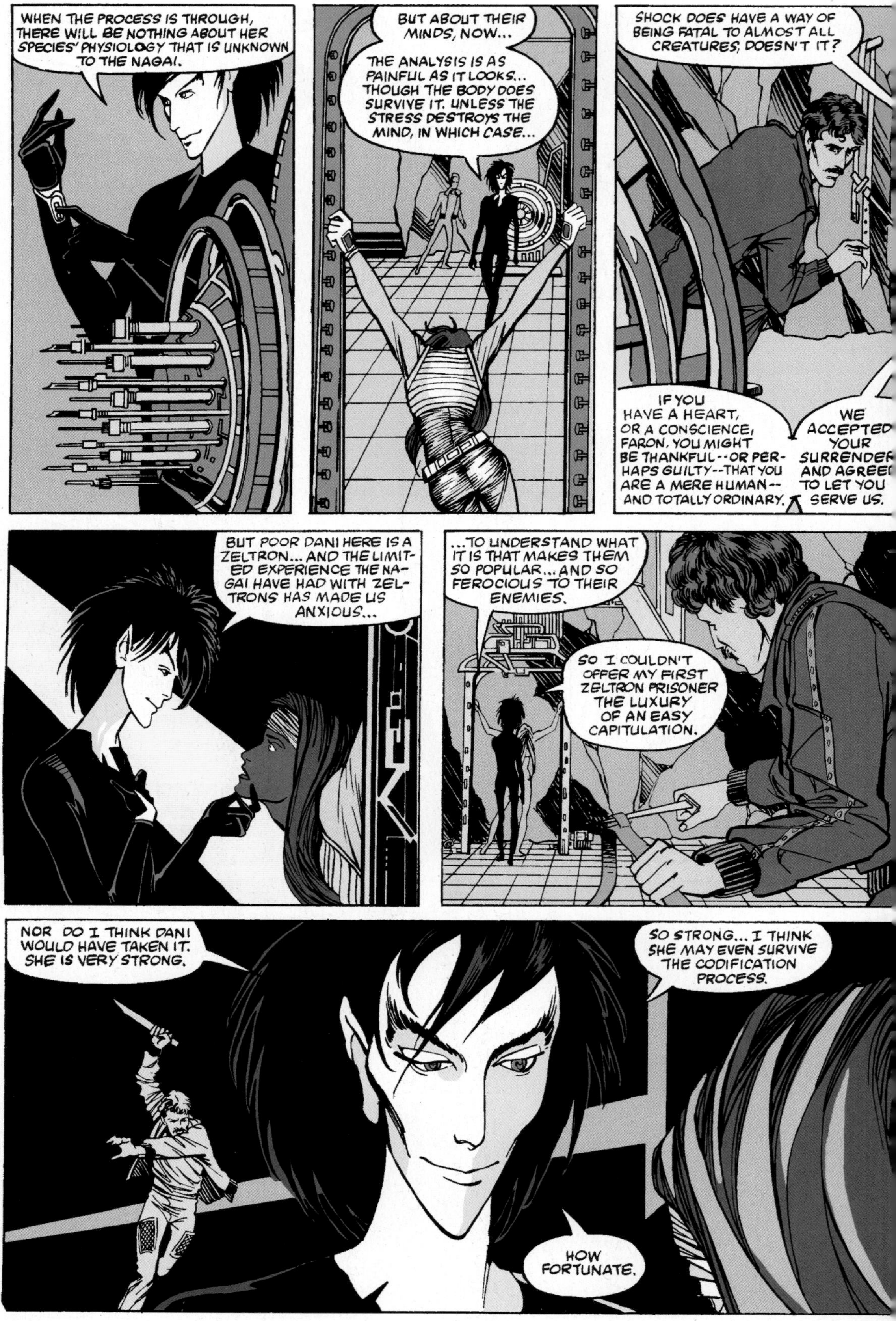
WHEN THE PROCESS IS THROUGH, THERE WILL BE NOTHING ABOUT HER SPECIES' PHYSIOLOGY THAT IS UNKNOWN TO THE NAGAI.
BUT ABOUT THEIR MINDS, NOW...
THE ANALYSIS IS AS PAINFUL AS IT LOOKS... THOUGH THE BODY DOES SURVIVE IT. UNLESS THE STRESS DESTROYS THE MIND, IN WHICH CASE...
SHOCK DOES HAVE A WAY OF BEING FATAL TO ALMOST ALL CREATURES, DOESN'T IT?
IF YOU HAVE A HEART, OR A CONSCIENCE, FARON, YOU MIGHT BE THANKFUL--OR PERHAPS GUILTY--THAT YOU ARE A MERE HUMAN--AND TOTALLY ORDINARY.
WE ACCEPTED YOUR SURRENDER AND AGREED TO LET YOU SERVE US.
BUT POOR DANI HERE IS A ZELTRON... AND THE LIMITED EXPERIENCE THE NAGAI HAVE HAD WITH ZELTRONS HAS MADE US ANXIOUS...
...TO UNDERSTAND WHAT IT IS THAT MAKES THEM SO POPULAR... AND SO FEROCIOUS TO THEIR ENEMIES.
SO I COULDN'T OFFER MY FIRST ZELTRON PRISONER THE LUXURY OF AN EASY CAPITULATION.
NOR DO I THINK DANI WOULD HAVE TAKEN IT. SHE IS VERY STRONG.
SO STRONG... I THINK SHE MAY EVEN SURVIVE THE CODIFICATION PROCESS.
HOW FORTUNATE.

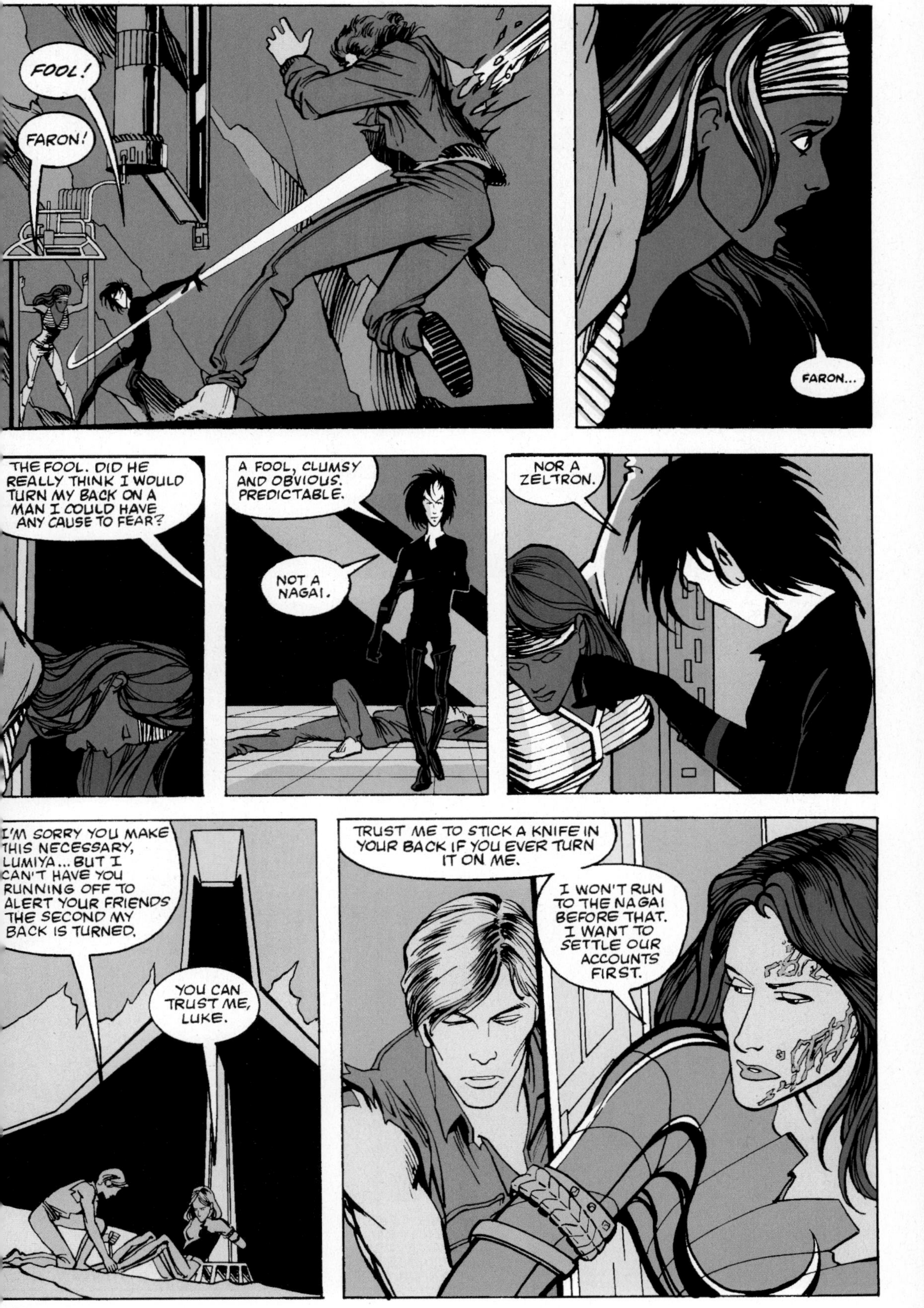
FOOL!
FARON!
FARON...
THE FOOL. DID HE REALLY THINK I WOULD TURN MY BACK ON A MAN I COULD HAVE ANY CAUSE TO FEAR?
A FOOL, CLUMSY AND OBVIOUS. PREDICTABLE.
NOT A NAGAI.
NOR A ZELTRON.
I'M SORRY YOU MAKE THIS NECESSARY, LUMIYA... BUT I CAN'T HAVE YOU RUNNING OFF TO ALERT YOUR FRIENDS THE SECOND MY BACK IS TURNED.
YOU CAN TRUST ME, LUKE.
TRUST ME TO STICK A KNIFE IN YOUR BACK IF YOU EVER TURN IT ON ME.
I WON'T RUN TO THE NAGAI BEFORE THAT. I WANT TO SETTLE OUR ACCOUNTS FIRST.

THANK YOU FOR WAITING FOR ME, LUKE... I FEEL BETTER NOW.

IT IS HARD SOMETIMES... BEING AN ISKALONIAN AMONG AIR-BREATHERS. I WISH WATER WERE HANDIER ON MOST WORLDS, SO THAT I WOULD NOT BE SUCH A BURDEN TO YOU.

YOU'RE NO BURDEN, KIRO. NOT ANY MORE THAN I WAS WHEN I VISITED YOUR PEOPLE.

IF YOU HADN'T HELPED ME OUT YESTERDAY, I'D STILL BE A PRISONER, AND WE'D ALL BE SUNK...

THANK YOU FOR FILLING MY SPARE WATER TANK.

HELP ME PUT IT ON. THEN LET US GO, AND THE NAGAI WILL BE THE ONES WHO ARE SUNK.

I'VE RESET THE DEFENSE MECHANISMS ON THE SHIP.

IF ANYONE TRIES TO ENTER IT WITHOUT DEACTIVATING THE SEQUENCE, HE'LL BE VAPORIZED.

I HOPE THE NAGAI KILL YOU.

SHORT-SIGHTED.

NO ONE KNOWS YOU'RE HERE BUT US. IF WE DIE, SO WILL YOU, OF EXPOSURE OR STARVATION.

214

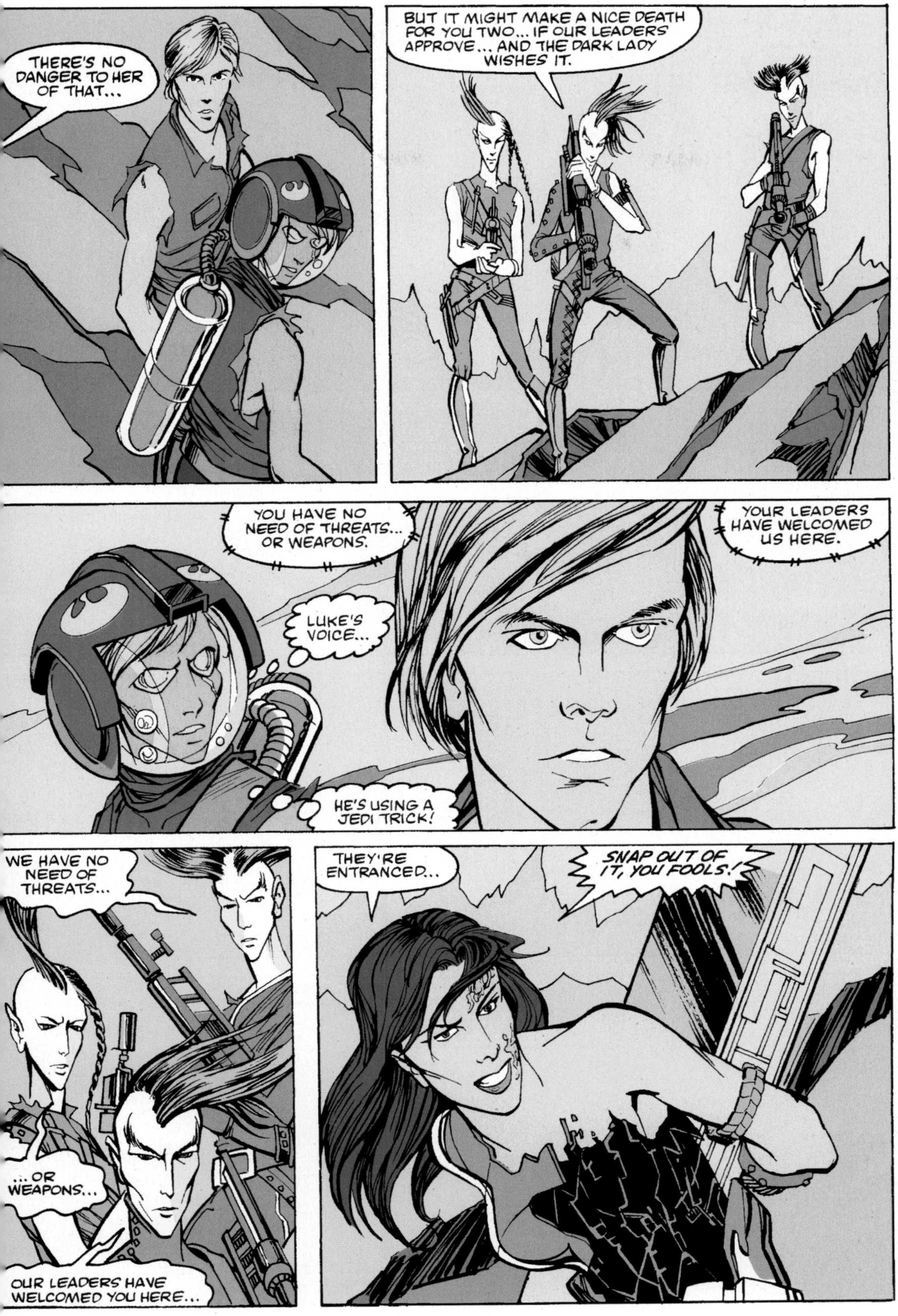
THERE'S NO DANGER TO HER OF THAT...
BUT IT MIGHT MAKE A NICE DEATH FOR YOU TWO... IF OUR LEADERS APPROVE... AND THE DARK LADY WISHES IT.
YOU HAVE NO NEED OF THREATS... OR WEAPONS.
LUKE'S VOICE...
HE'S USING A JEDI TRICK!
YOUR LEADERS HAVE WELCOMED US HERE.
WE HAVE NO NEED OF THREATS...
...OR WEAPONS...
OUR LEADERS HAVE WELCOMED YOU HERE...
THEY'RE ENTRANCED...
SNAP OUT OF IT, YOU FOOLS!

MMM...?
SHE'S RIGHT...
WE'RE...
NO!
I CAN'T LET THEM RECOVER...
UMNH!
AEGH!
HE'S...
UARRK!
I AM SORRY, LUKE... I KNOW YOU DO NOT LIKE KILLING, BUT I HAD TO.
YEAH, YOU DID. LUMIYA FORCED YOU TO. I COULDN'T HAVE RE-ASSERTED CONTROL OVER THEM, ONCE THEY KNEW WHAT I WAS DOING.
OUR DARK LADY, HERE, DOESN'T USE HER ALLIES ANY MORE KINDLY THAN SHE DID HER ENEMIES...
...BUT THAT'S WAR.

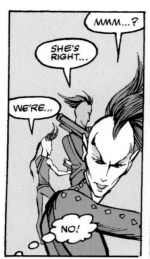

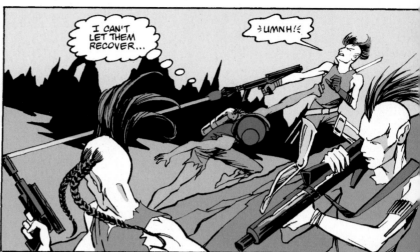

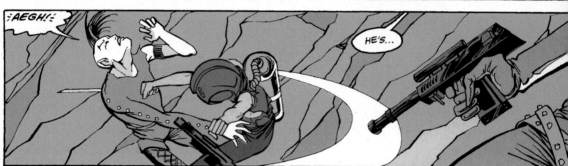

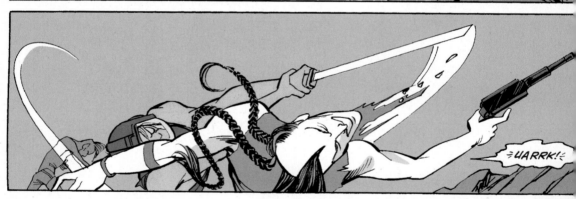

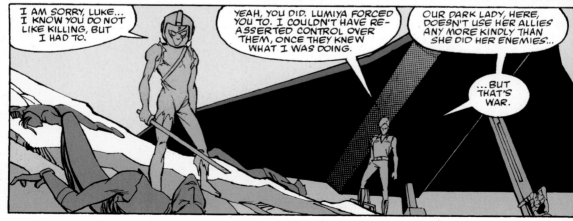

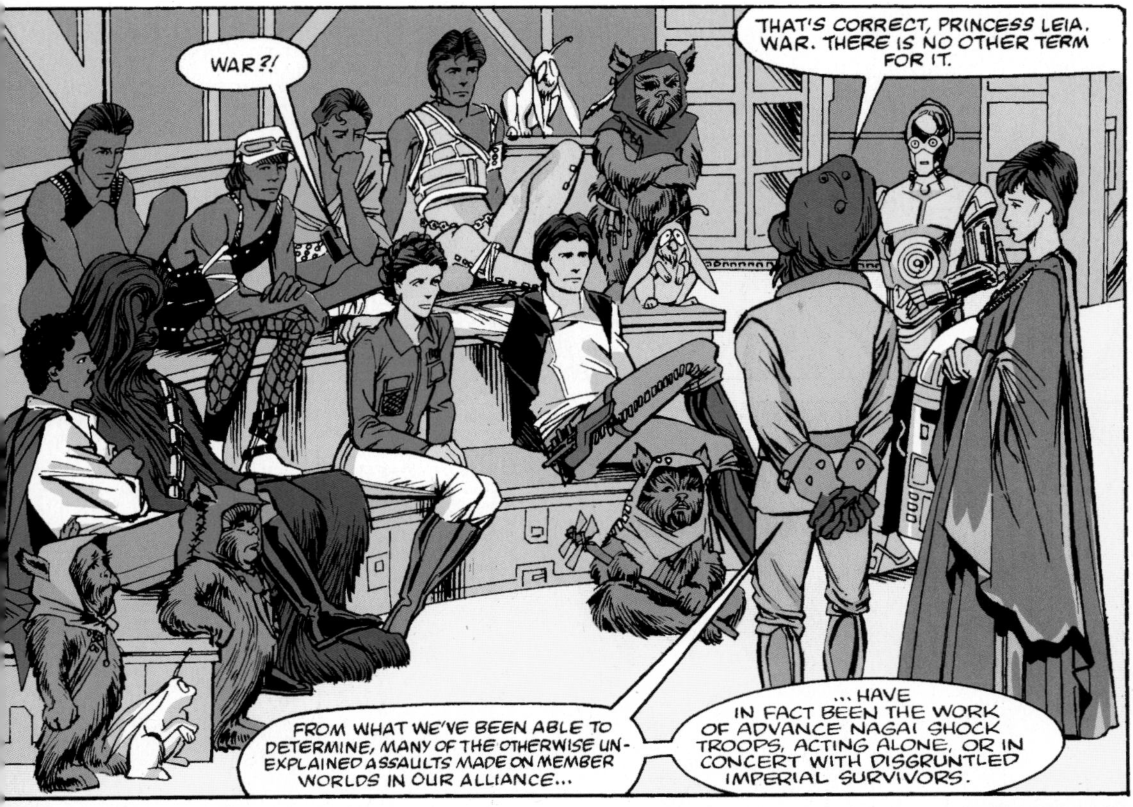
WAR?!
THAT'S CORRECT, PRINCESS LEIA. WAR. THERE IS NO OTHER TERM FOR IT.
FROM WHAT WE'VE BEEN ABLE TO DETERMINE, MANY OF THE OTHERWISE UN-EXPLAINED ASSAULTS MADE ON MEMBER WORLDS IN OUR ALLIANCE...
...HAVE IN FACT BEEN THE WORK OF ADVANCE NAGAI SHOCK TROOPS, ACTING ALONE, OR IN CONCERT WITH DISGRUNTLED IMPERIAL SURVIVORS.

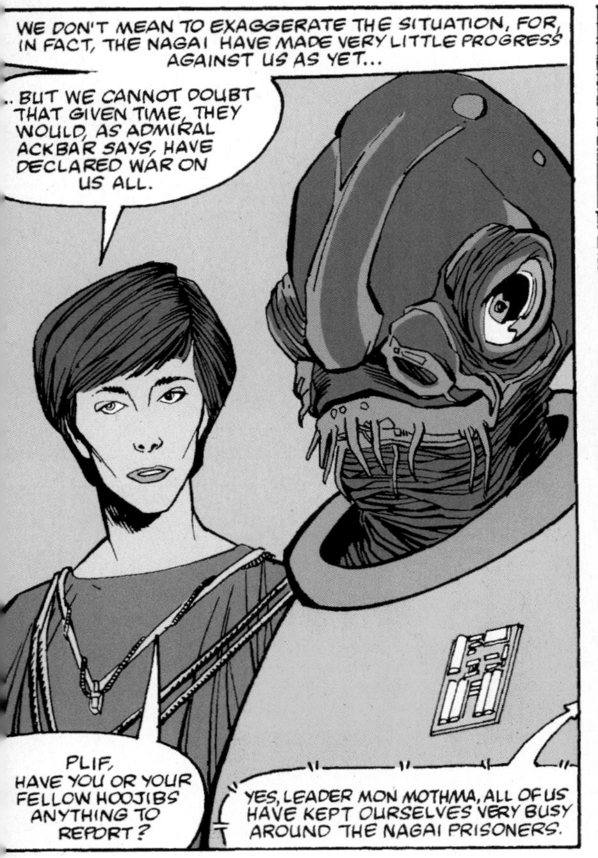
WE DON'T MEAN TO EXAGGERATE THE SITUATION, FOR, IN FACT, THE NAGAI HAVE MADE VERY LITTLE PROGRESS AGAINST US AS YET...
...BUT WE CANNOT DOUBT THAT GIVEN TIME, THEY WOULD, AS ADMIRAL ACKBAR SAYS, HAVE DECLARED WAR ON US ALL.
PLIF, HAVE YOU OR YOUR FELLOW HOOJIBS ANYTHING TO REPORT?
YES, LEADER MON MOTHMA, ALL OF US HAVE KEPT OURSELVES VERY BUSY AROUND THE NAGAI PRISONERS.

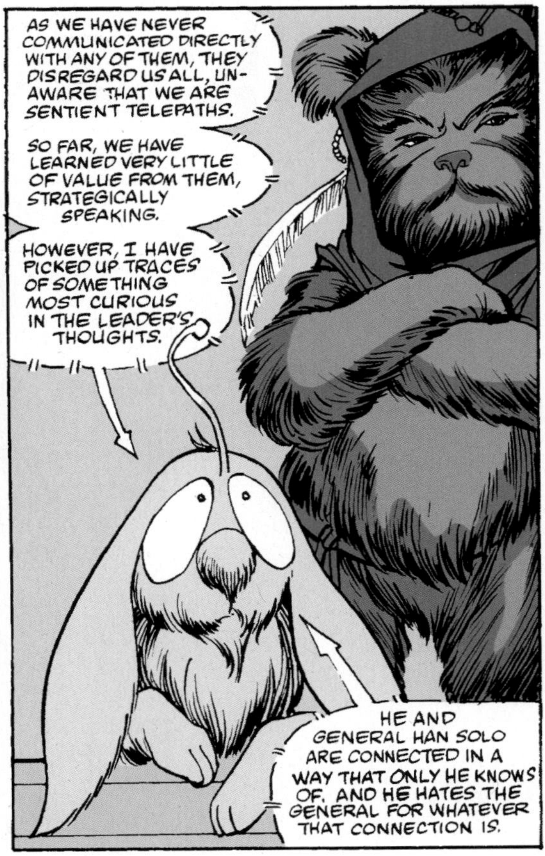
AS WE HAVE NEVER COMMUNICATED DIRECTLY WITH ANY OF THEM, THEY DISREGARD US ALL, UNAWARE THAT WE ARE SENTIENT TELEPATHS.
SO FAR, WE HAVE LEARNED VERY LITTLE OF VALUE FROM THEM, STRATEGICALLY SPEAKING.
HOWEVER, I HAVE PICKED UP TRACES OF SOMETHING MOST CURIOUS IN THE LEADER'S THOUGHTS.
HE AND GENERAL HAN SOLO ARE CONNECTED IN A WAY THAT ONLY HE KNOWS OF, AND HE HATES THE GENERAL FOR WHATEVER THAT CONNECTION IS.

I DON'T CARE IF HE'S MY LONG-LOST BROTHER!

AS LONG AS HE STAYS IN THAT CELL WHERE WE PUT HIM, KNIFE CAN HATE ME ALL HE LIKES AND KEEP HIS CONNECTIONS TO HIMSELF!

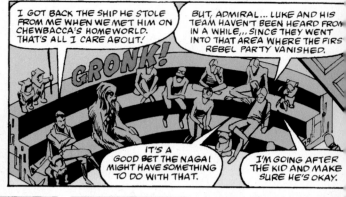

I GOT BACK THE SHIP HE STOLE FROM ME WHEN WE MET HIM ON CHEWBACCA'S HOMEWORLD. THAT'S ALL I CARE ABOUT!

BUT, ADMIRAL... LUKE AND HIS TEAM HAVEN'T BEEN HEARD FROM IN A WHILE,... SINCE THEY WENT INTO THAT AREA WHERE THE FIRST REBEL PARTY VANISHED.

GRONK!

IT'S A GOOD BET THE NAGAI MIGHT HAVE SOMETHING TO DO WITH THAT.

I'M GOING AFTER THE KID AND MAKE SURE HE'S OKAY.

NO, YOU'RE NOT.

WHAT?!

YOU CANNOT NEGLECT YOUR DUTIES FOR WHAT IS STRICTLY A PERSONAL CONCERN, GENERAL SOLO.

ADMIRAL ACKBAR, HOW CAN YOU TALK LIKE THAT? LUKE IS ONE OF THE GREATEST HEROES OF THE REBELLION!

AND SO IS HAN!

YES... AND WE APPRECIATE ALL OF OUR GOOD SOLDIERS. BUT THE REBELLION IS OVER NOW, AND WE MUST MOVE ON FROM THERE.

WE MUST SET SELFISH CONSIDERATIONS ASIDE.

HOW OUR FORCES ARE DEPLOYED--HOW OUR SOLDIERS ARE EMPLOYED --IS NOT A MATTER OF INDIVIDUAL CHOICE.

IT IS FOR OUR LEADERS TO DECIDE.

AND NONE OF YOU SITS ON THE RULING COUNCIL.

OH, REALLY?

THEN YOU CAN RUN THE NEXT WAR WITHOUT ME!

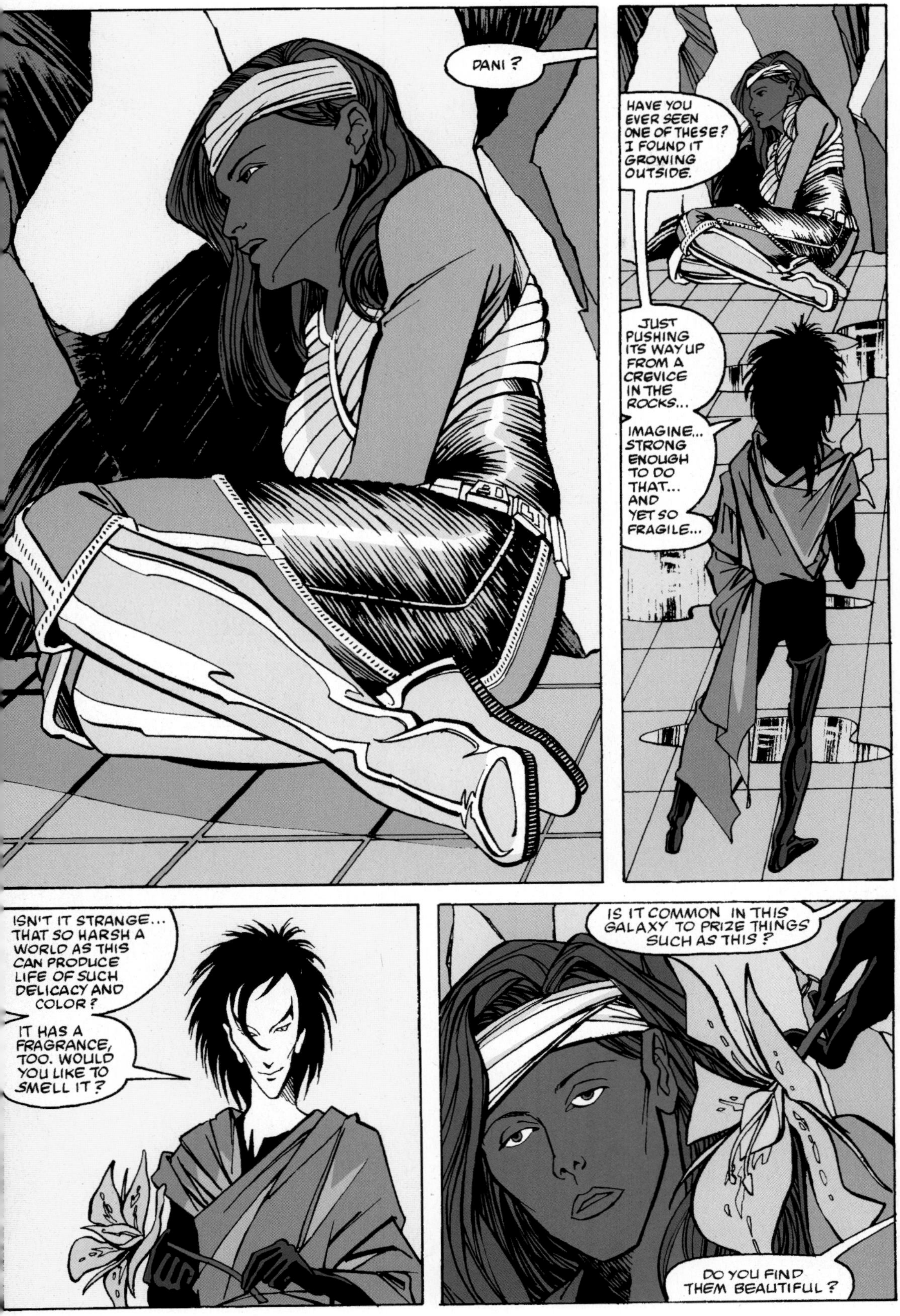
DANI?
HAVE YOU EVER SEEN ONE OF THESE? I FOUND IT GROWING OUTSIDE.
JUST PUSHING ITS WAY UP FROM A CREVICE IN THE ROCKS...
IMAGINE... STRONG ENOUGH TO DO THAT... AND YET SO FRAGILE...
ISN'T IT STRANGE... THAT SO HARSH A WORLD AS THIS CAN PRODUCE LIFE OF SUCH DELICACY AND COLOR?
IT HAS A FRAGRANCE, TOO. WOULD YOU LIKE TO SMELL IT?
IS IT COMMON IN THIS GALAXY TO PRIZE THINGS SUCH AS THIS?
DO YOU FIND THEM BEAUTIFUL?

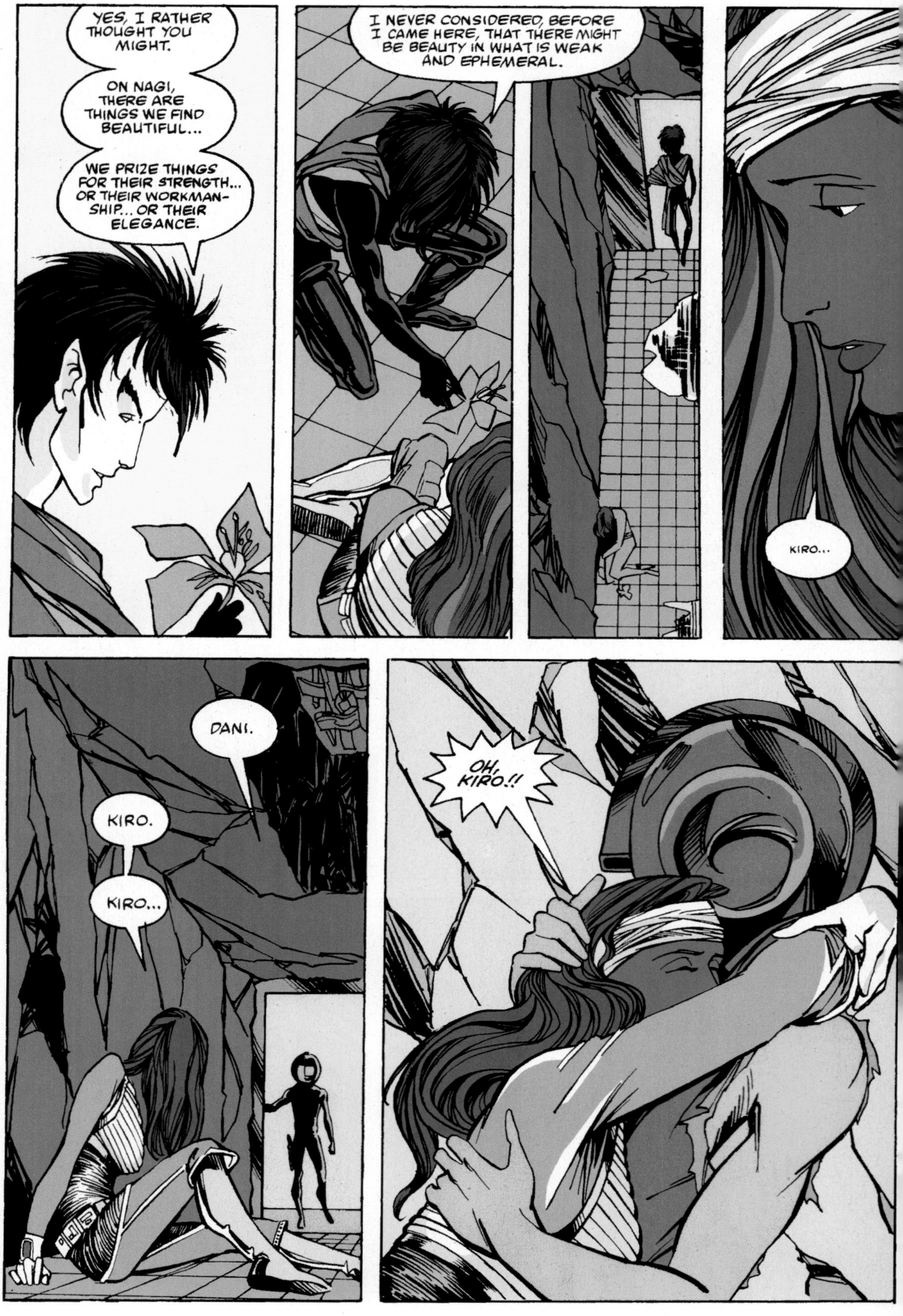
YES, I RATHER THOUGHT YOU MIGHT.
ON NAGI, THERE ARE THINGS WE FIND BEAUTIFUL...
WE PRIZE THINGS FOR THEIR STRENGTH... OR THEIR WORKMANSHIP... OR THEIR ELEGANCE.
I NEVER CONSIDERED, BEFORE I CAME HERE, THAT THERE MIGHT BE BEAUTY IN WHAT IS WEAK AND EPHEMERAL.
KIRO...
DANI.
KIRO.
KIRO...
OH, KIRO!!

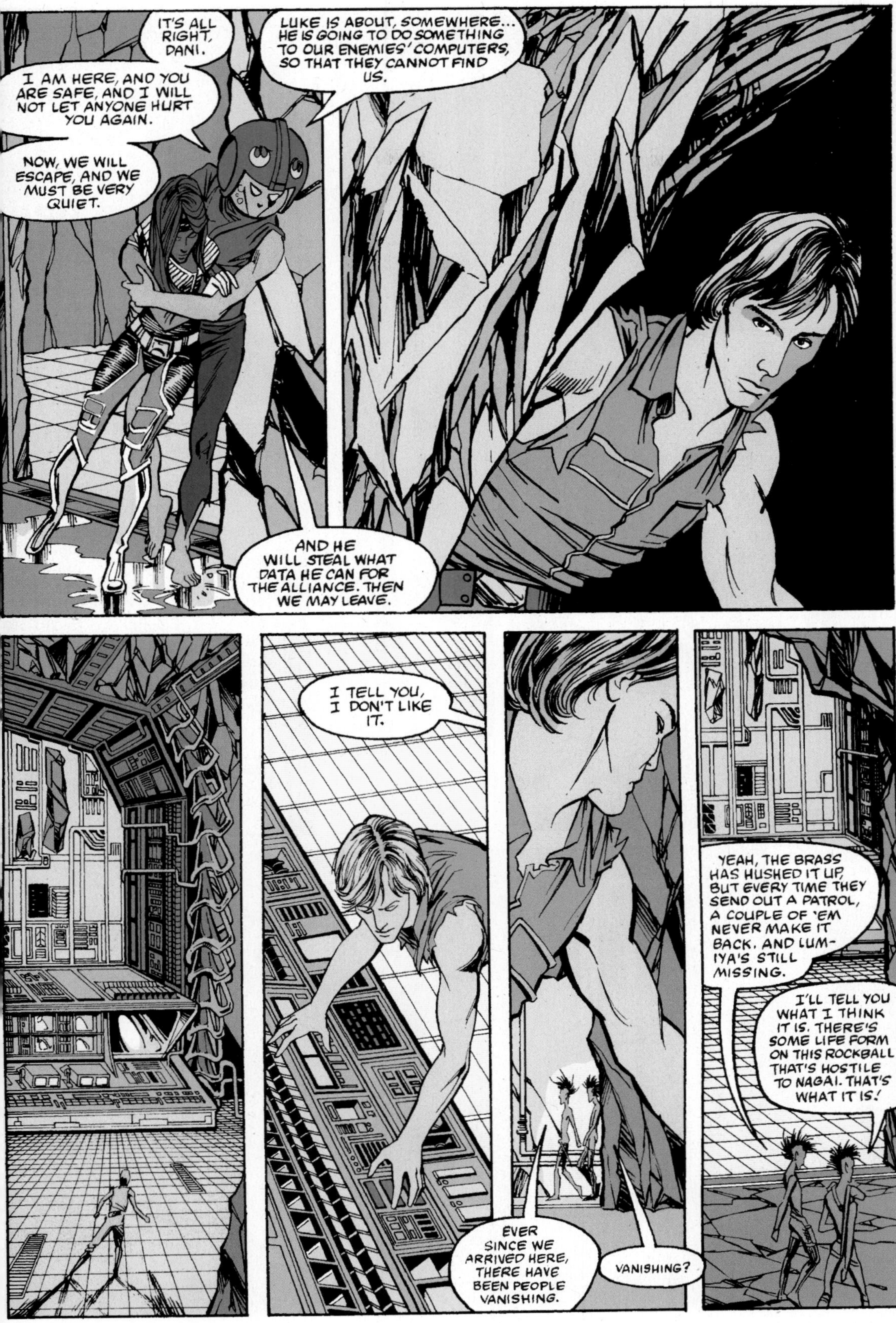
IT'S ALL RIGHT, DANI.
I AM HERE, AND YOU ARE SAFE, AND I WILL NOT LET ANYONE HURT YOU AGAIN.
NOW, WE WILL ESCAPE, AND WE MUST BE VERY QUIET.
LUKE IS ABOUT, SOMEWHERE... HE IS GOING TO DO SOMETHING TO OUR ENEMIES' COMPUTERS, SO THAT THEY CANNOT FIND US.
AND HE WILL STEAL WHAT DATA HE CAN FOR THE ALLIANCE. THEN WE MAY LEAVE.
I TELL YOU, I DON'T LIKE IT.
EVER SINCE WE ARRIVED HERE, THERE HAVE BEEN PEOPLE VANISHING.
VANISHING?
YEAH, THE BRASS HAS HUSHED IT UP, BUT EVERY TIME THEY SEND OUT A PATROL, A COUPLE OF 'EM NEVER MAKE IT BACK. AND LUMIYA'S STILL MISSING.
I'LL TELL YOU WHAT I THINK IT IS. THERE'S SOME LIFE FORM ON THIS ROCKBALL THAT'S HOSTILE TO NAGAI. THAT'S WHAT IT IS!

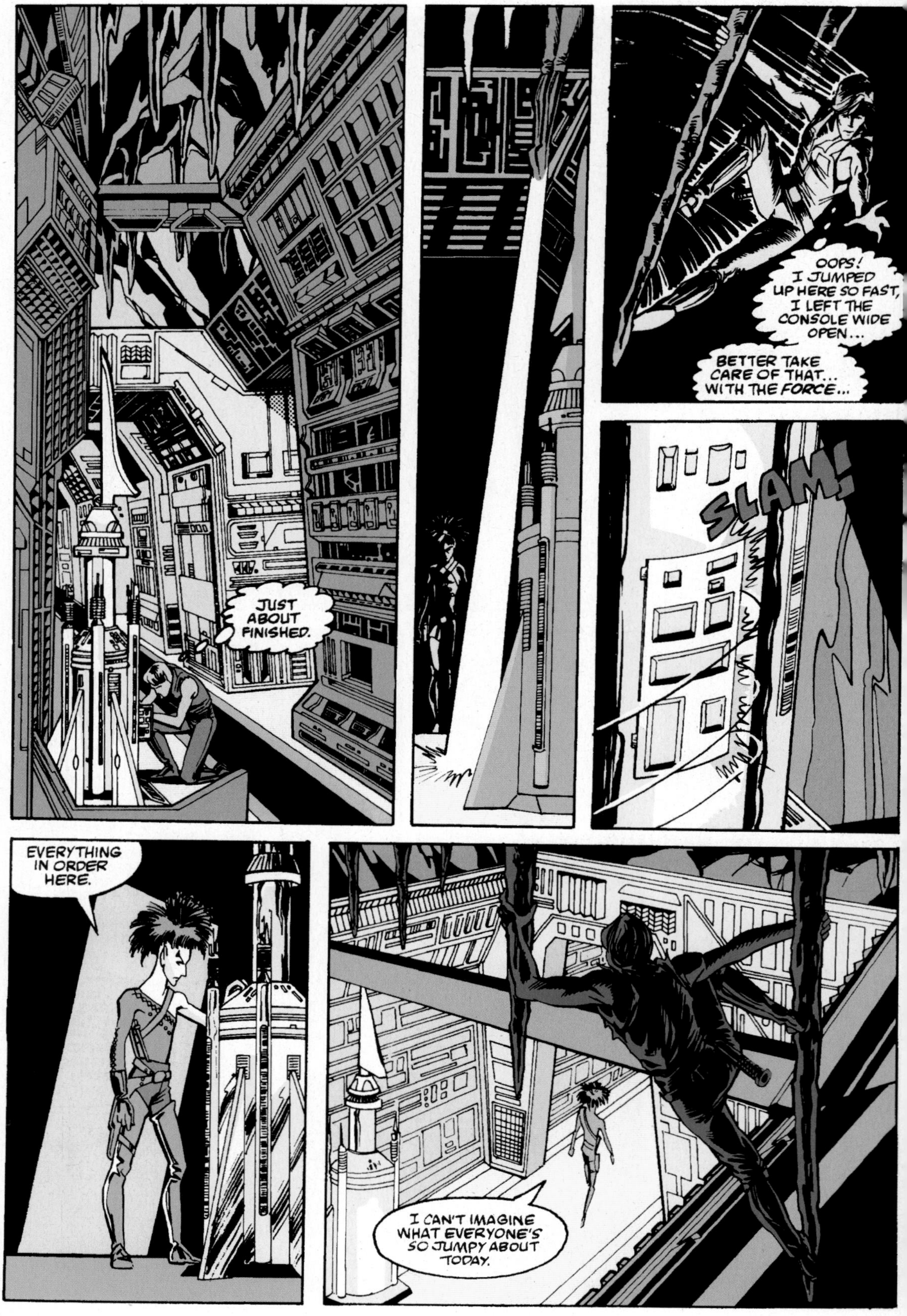
JUST ABOUT FINISHED.
OOPS! I JUMPED UP HERE SO FAST, I LEFT THE CONSOLE WIDE OPEN...
BETTER TAKE CARE OF THAT... WITH THE FORCE...
SLAM!
EVERYTHING IN ORDER HERE.
I CAN'T IMAGINE WHAT EVERYONE'S SO JUMPY ABOUT TODAY.

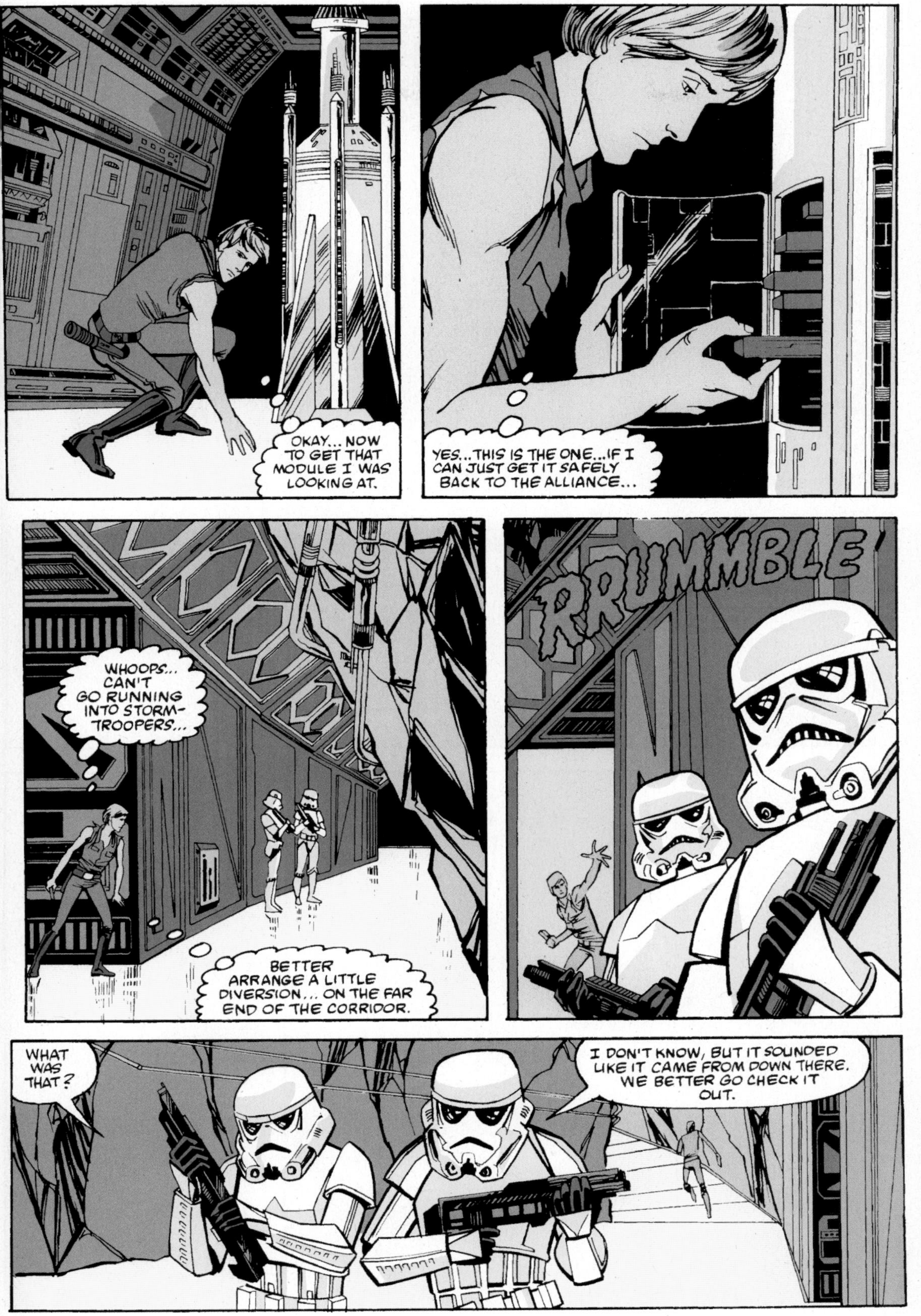

OKAY... NOW TO GET THAT MODULE I WAS LOOKING AT.
YES... THIS IS THE ONE... IF I CAN JUST GET IT SAFELY BACK TO THE ALLIANCE...
WHOOPS... CAN'T GO RUNNING INTO STORM-TROOPERS...
BETTER ARRANGE A LITTLE DIVERSION... ON THE FAR END OF THE CORRIDOR.
RRUMMBLE
WHAT WAS THAT?
I DON'T KNOW, BUT IT SOUNDED LIKE IT CAME FROM DOWN THERE. WE BETTER GO CHECK IT OUT.

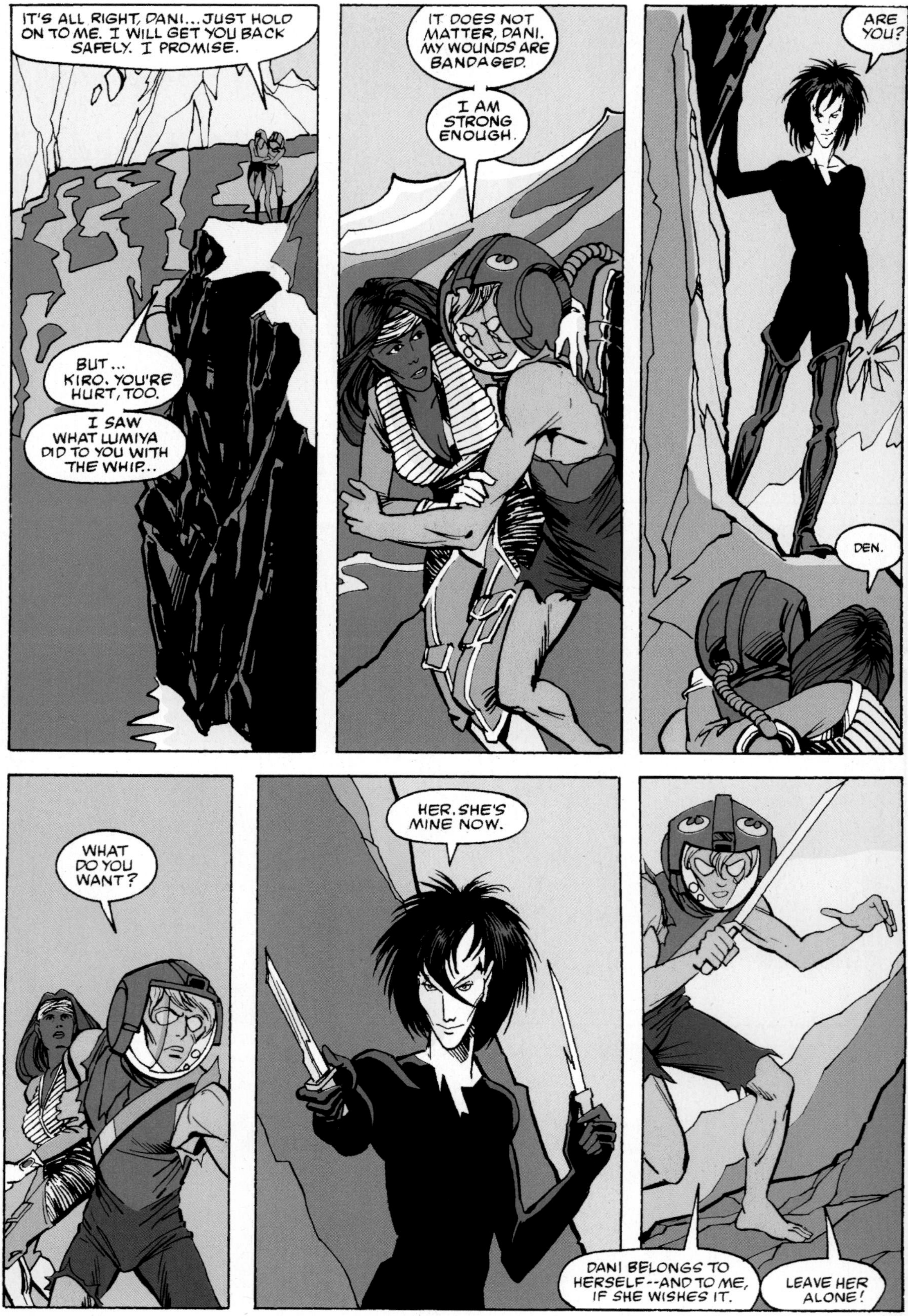
IT'S ALL RIGHT, DANI... JUST HOLD ON TO ME. I WILL GET YOU BACK SAFELY. I PROMISE.
BUT... KIRO. YOU'RE HURT, TOO.
I SAW WHAT LUMIYA DID TO YOU WITH THE WHIP...
IT DOES NOT MATTER, DANI. MY WOUNDS ARE BANDAGED.
I AM STRONG ENOUGH.
ARE YOU?
DEN.
WHAT DO YOU WANT?
HER. SHE'S MINE NOW.
DANI BELONGS TO HERSELF--AND TO ME, IF SHE WISHES IT.
LEAVE HER ALONE!

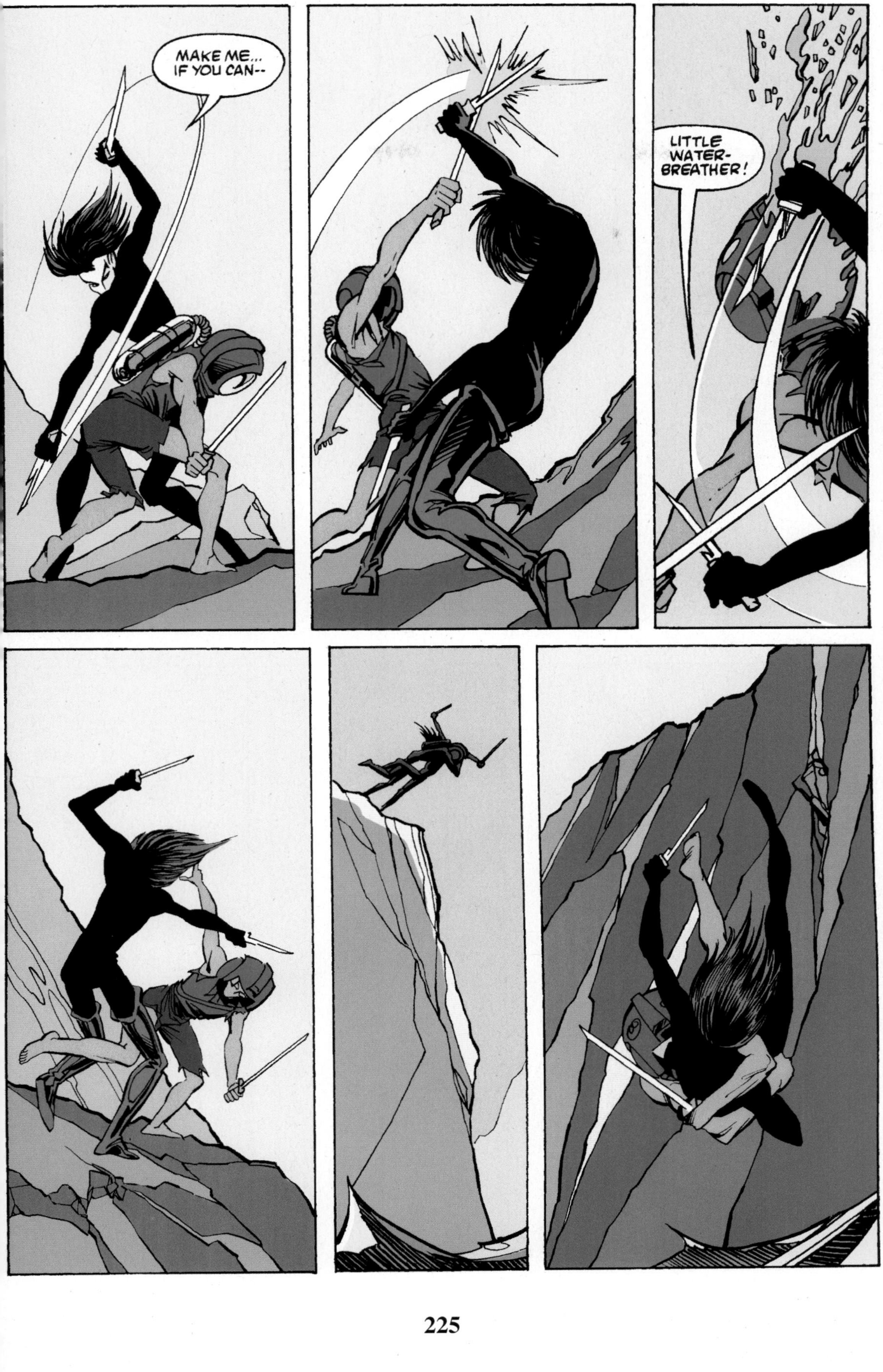
MAKE ME...
IF YOU CAN--
LITTLE WATER-BREATHER!

KIRO!

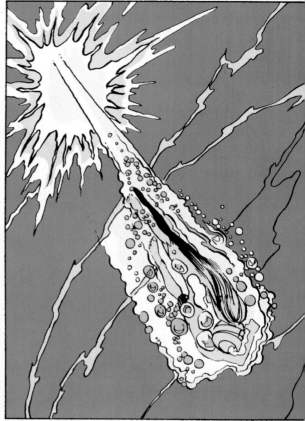

DANI? WHERE'S KIRO?

THEY'RE IN WATER... SO HE HAS THE ADVANTAGE.

PLEASE...

...LET HIM HAVE THE ADVANTAGE...

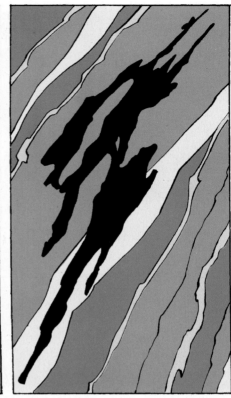

KIRO.

OH, LUKE--!

DANI, IT...

IT MIGHT NOT BE HIS BLOOD.

IT IS! YOU KNOW IT IS!

HE MAY ONLY BE WOUNDED. WE'LL LOOK. MAYBE WE CAN STILL HELP HIM...

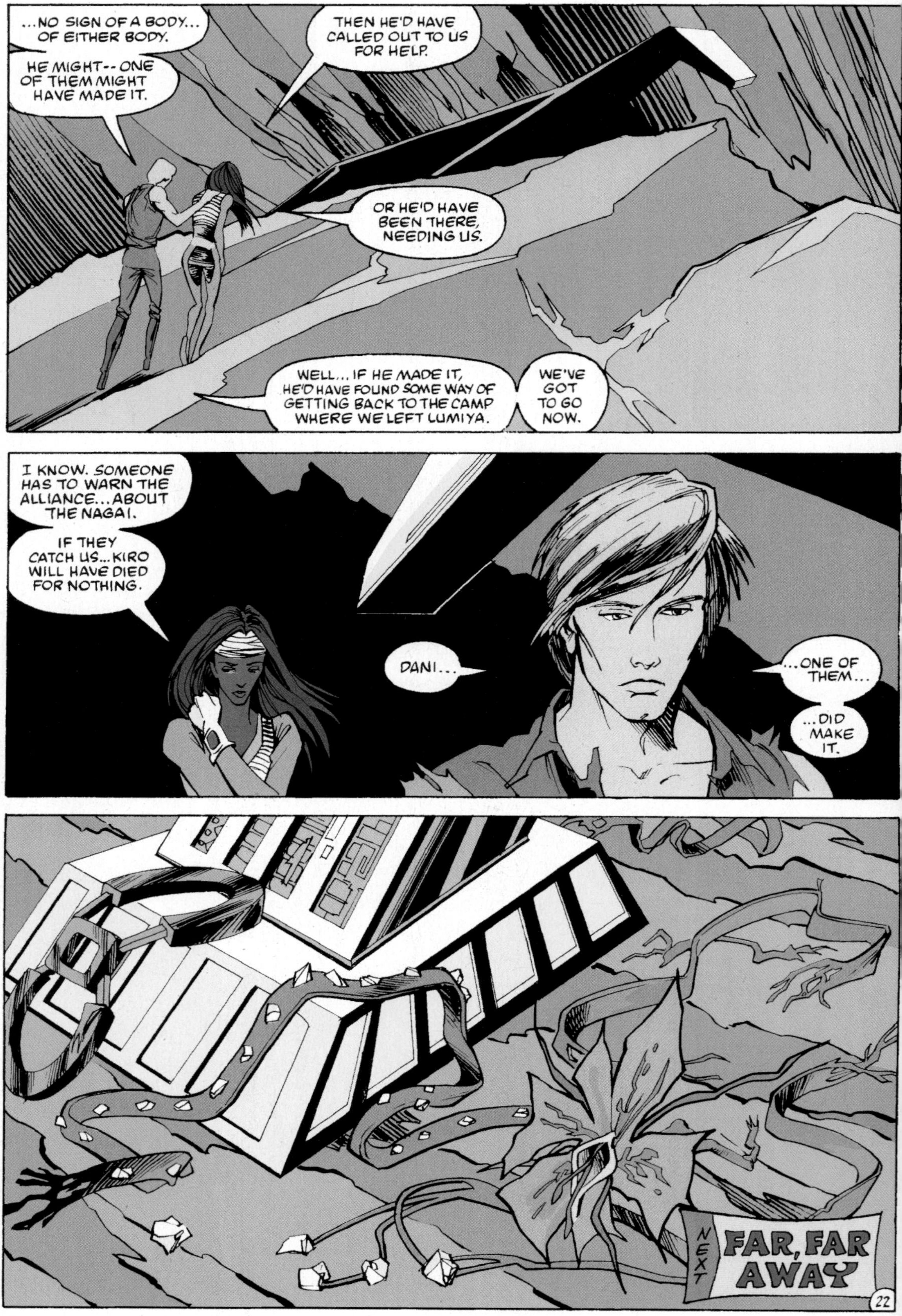
...NO SIGN OF A BODY... OF EITHER BODY.
HE MIGHT-- ONE OF THEM MIGHT HAVE MADE IT.
THEN HE'D HAVE CALLED OUT TO US FOR HELP.
OR HE'D HAVE BEEN THERE, NEEDING US.
WELL... IF HE MADE IT, HE'D HAVE FOUND SOME WAY OF GETTING BACK TO THE CAMP WHERE WE LEFT LUMIYA.
WE'VE GOT TO GO NOW.
I KNOW. SOMEONE HAS TO WARN THE ALLIANCE... ABOUT THE NAGAI.
IF THEY CATCH US... KIRO WILL HAVE DIED FOR NOTHING.
DANI...
...ONE OF THEM...
...DID MAKE IT.
NEXT
FAR, FAR AWAY
22

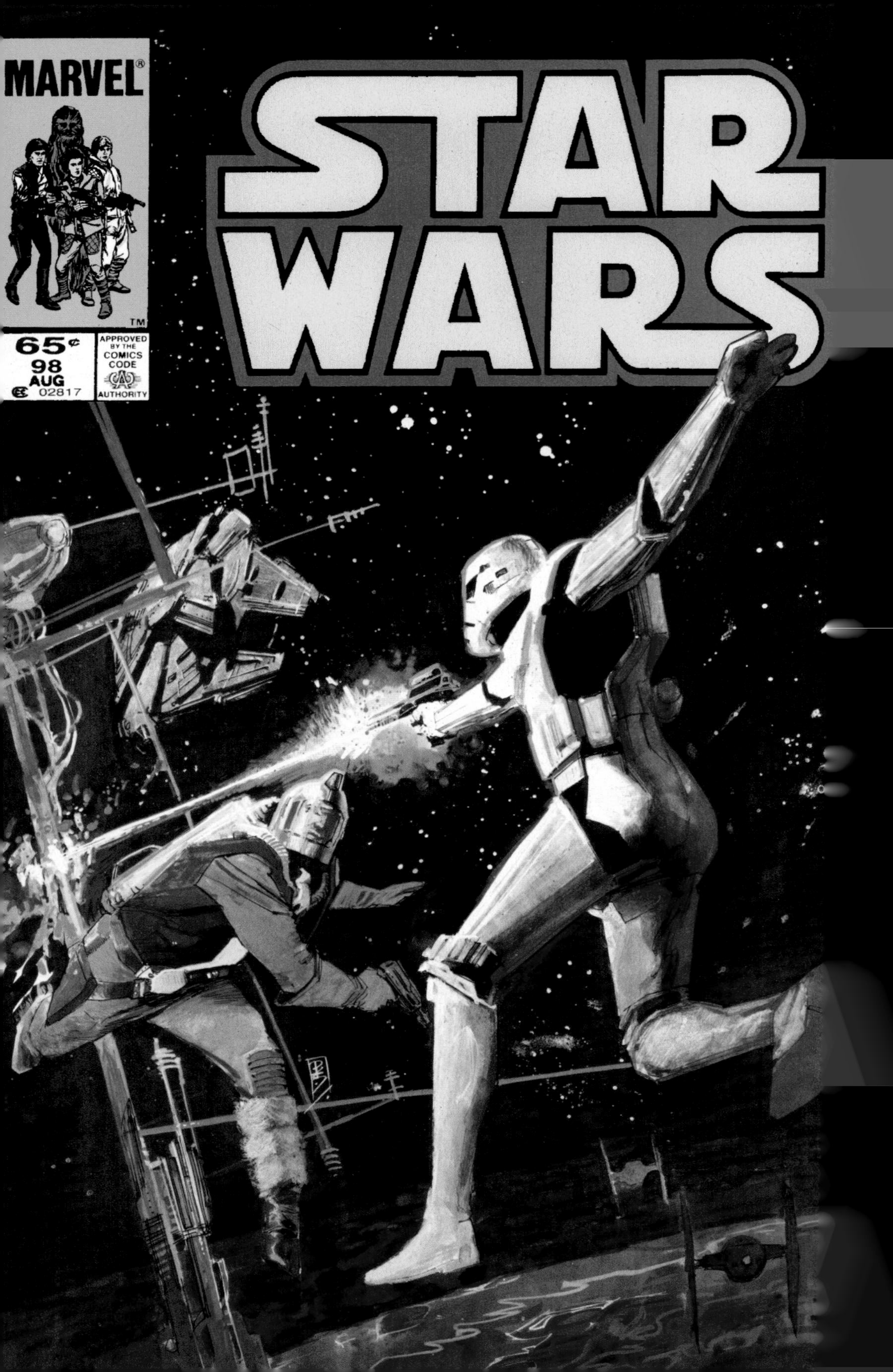

MARVEL®
STAR WARS
TM
65¢
98
AUG
02817
APPROVED BY THE COMICS CODE AUTHORITY

GENERAL SOLO! THIS REPORT NEEDS YOUR FINAL RECOMMENDATIONS! IF YOU DON'T ADD THEM SOON--

REPORT? I'VE GOT A DISASTER TO AVERT!

ARCHIE GOODWIN	AL WILLIAMSON	ED KING	GLYNIS OLIVER	ANN NOCENTI	JIM SHOOTER
WRITER	ARTIST	LETTERS	COLORIST	EDITOR	EDITOR IN CHIEF

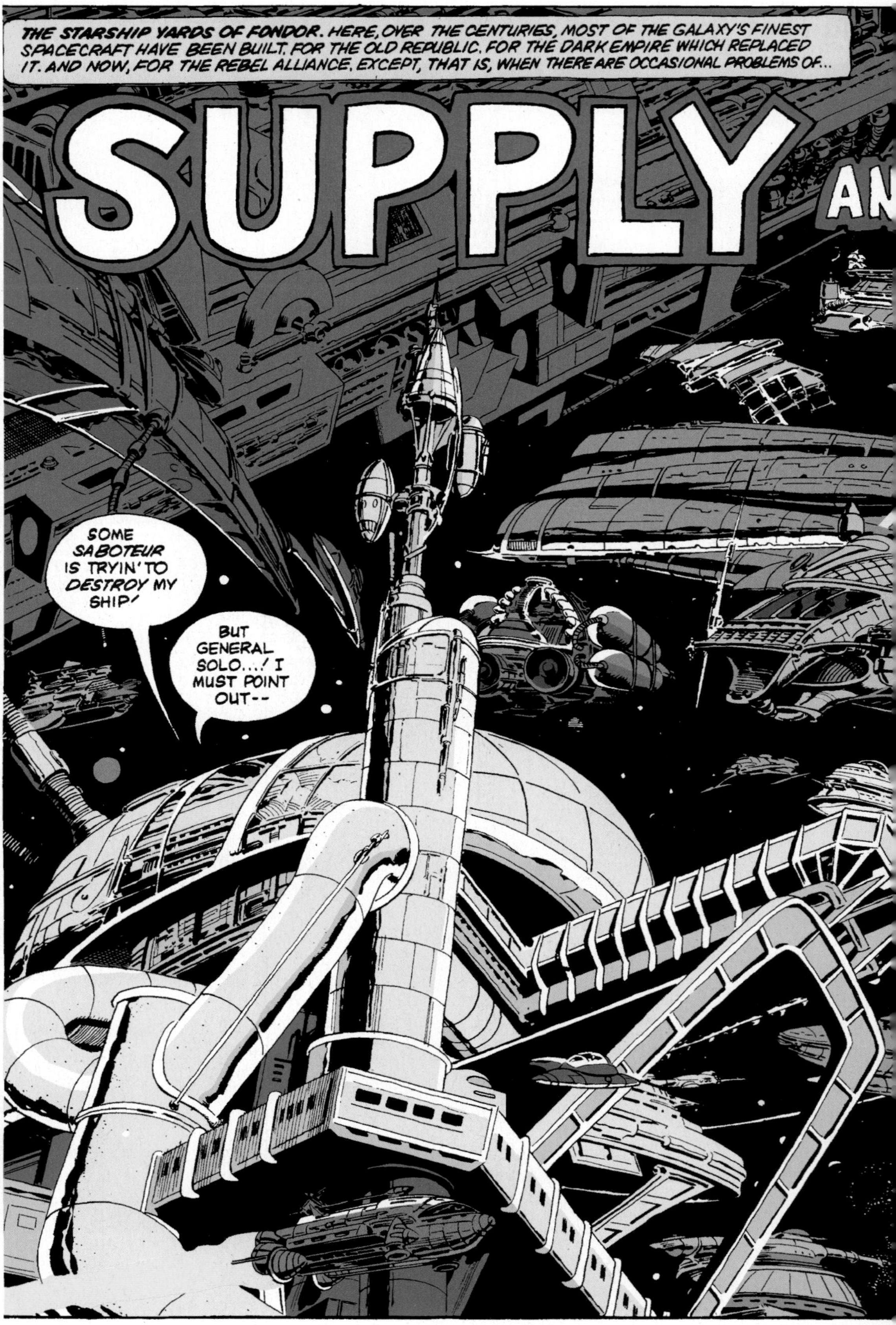
THE STARSHIP YARDS OF FONDOR. HERE, OVER THE CENTURIES, MOST OF THE GALAXY'S FINEST SPACECRAFT HAVE BEEN BUILT. FOR THE OLD REPUBLIC. FOR THE DARK EMPIRE WHICH REPLACED IT. AND NOW, FOR THE REBEL ALLIANCE. EXCEPT, THAT IS, WHEN THERE ARE OCCASIONAL PROBLEMS OF...
SUPPLY
SOME SABOTEUR IS TRYIN' TO DESTROY MY SHIP!
BUT GENERAL SOLO...! I MUST POINT OUT--

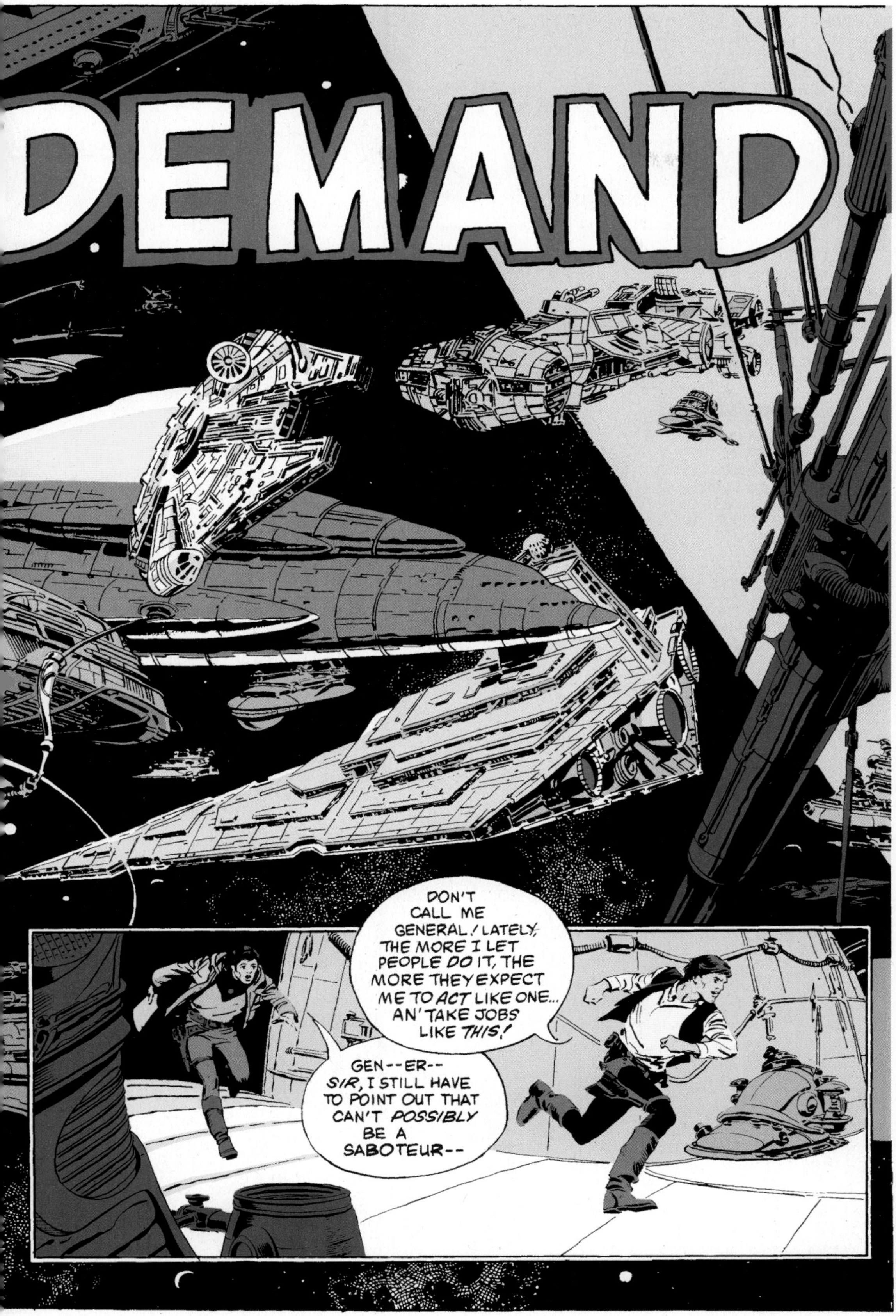
DEMAND
DON'T CALL ME GENERAL! LATELY, THE MORE I LET PEOPLE DO IT, THE MORE THEY EXPECT ME TO ACT LIKE ONE... AN' TAKE JOBS LIKE THIS!
GEN--ER--SIR, I STILL HAVE TO POINT OUT THAT CAN'T POSSIBLY BE A SABOTEUR--

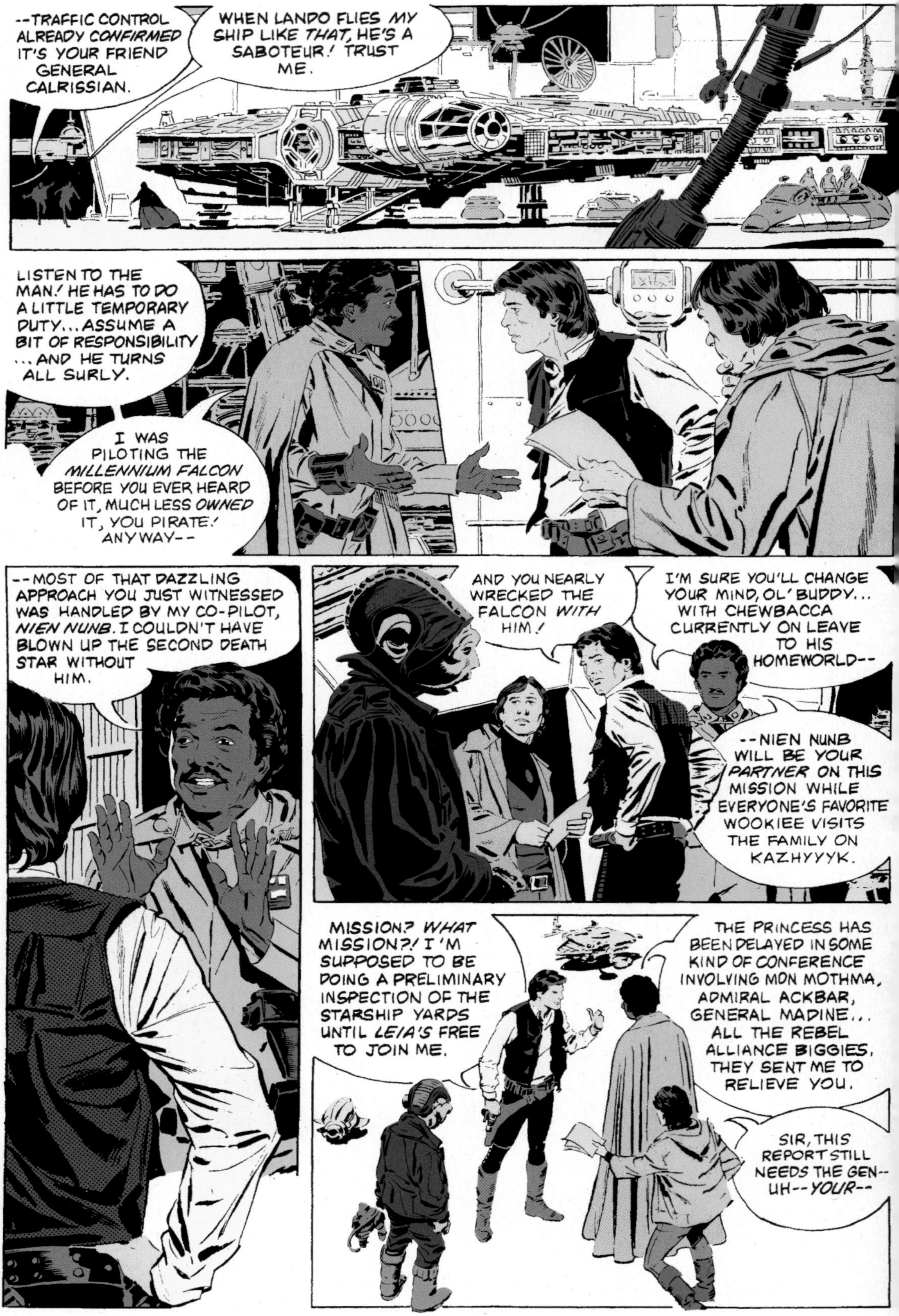
--TRAFFIC CONTROL ALREADY CONFIRMED IT'S YOUR FRIEND GENERAL CALRISSIAN.
WHEN LANDO FLIES MY SHIP LIKE THAT, HE'S A SABOTEUR! TRUST ME.
LISTEN TO THE MAN! HE HAS TO DO A LITTLE TEMPORARY DUTY... ASSUME A BIT OF RESPONSIBILITY ...AND HE TURNS ALL SURLY.
I WAS PILOTING THE MILLENNIUM FALCON BEFORE YOU EVER HEARD OF IT, MUCH LESS OWNED IT, YOU PIRATE! ANYWAY--
--MOST OF THAT DAZZLING APPROACH YOU JUST WITNESSED WAS HANDLED BY MY CO-PILOT, NIEN NUNB. I COULDN'T HAVE BLOWN UP THE SECOND DEATH STAR WITHOUT HIM.
AND YOU NEARLY WRECKED THE FALCON WITH HIM!
I'M SURE YOU'LL CHANGE YOUR MIND, OL' BUDDY... WITH CHEWBACCA CURRENTLY ON LEAVE TO HIS HOMEWORLD--
--NIEN NUNB WILL BE YOUR PARTNER ON THIS MISSION WHILE EVERYONE'S FAVORITE WOOKIEE VISITS THE FAMILY ON KAZHYYYK.
MISSION? WHAT MISSION?! I'M SUPPOSED TO BE DOING A PRELIMINARY INSPECTION OF THE STARSHIP YARDS UNTIL LEIA'S FREE TO JOIN ME.
THE PRINCESS HAS BEEN DELAYED IN SOME KIND OF CONFERENCE INVOLVING MON MOTHMA, ADMIRAL ACKBAR, GENERAL MADINE... ALL THE REBEL ALLIANCE BIGGIES. THEY SENT ME TO RELIEVE YOU.
SIR, THIS REPORT STILL NEEDS THE GEN-- UH--YOUR--

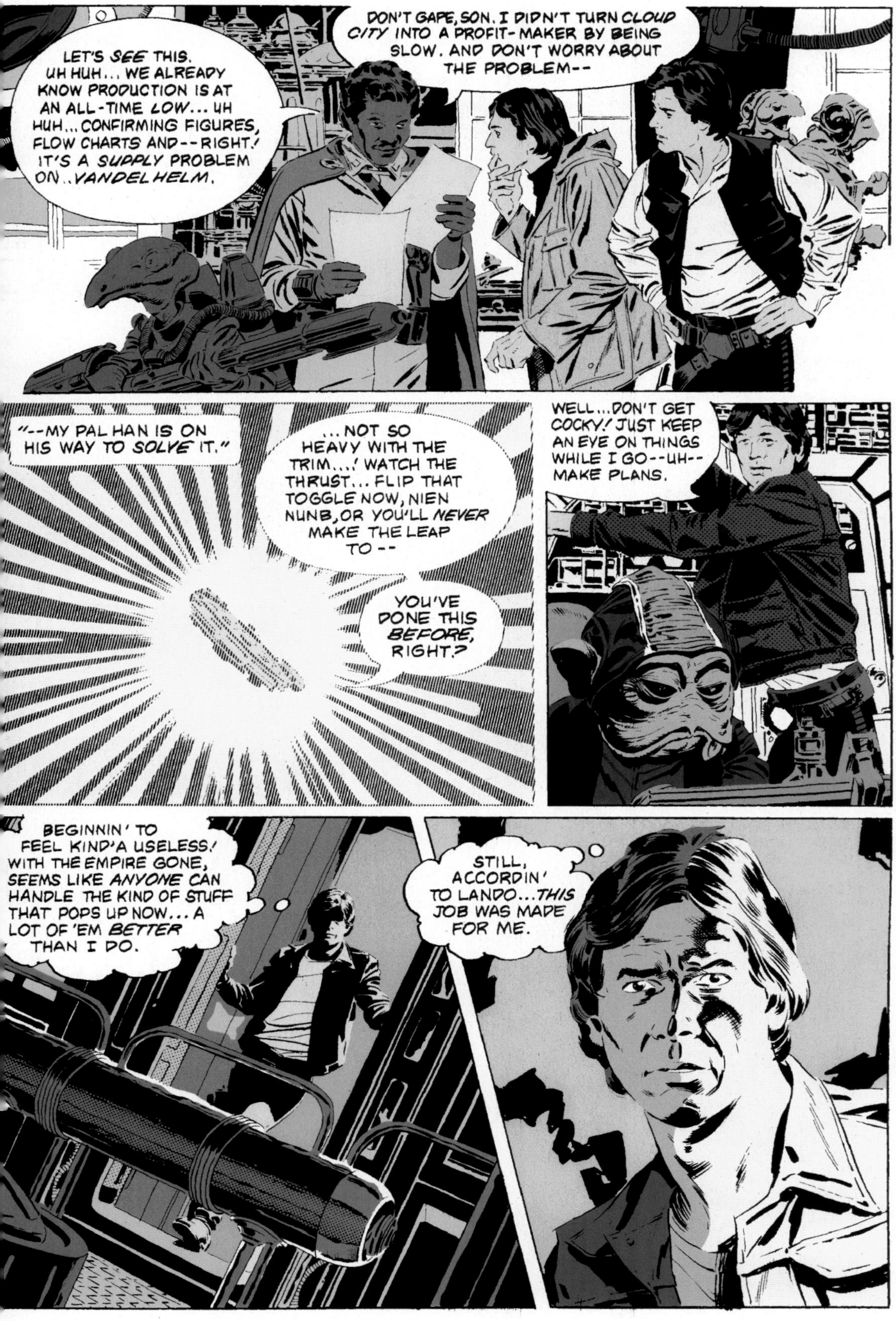
LET'S SEE THIS. UH HUH... WE ALREADY KNOW PRODUCTION IS AT AN ALL-TIME LOW... UH HUH... CONFIRMING FIGURES, FLOW CHARTS AND--RIGHT! IT'S A SUPPLY PROBLEM ON..VANDELHELM.
DON'T GAPE, SON. I DIDN'T TURN CLOUD CITY INTO A PROFIT-MAKER BY BEING SLOW. AND DON'T WORRY ABOUT THE PROBLEM--
"--MY PAL HAN IS ON HIS WAY TO SOLVE IT."
...NOT SO HEAVY WITH THE TRIM...! WATCH THE THRUST... FLIP THAT TOGGLE NOW, NIEN NUNB, OR YOU'LL NEVER MAKE THE LEAP TO--
YOU'VE DONE THIS BEFORE, RIGHT?
WELL...DON'T GET COCKY! JUST KEEP AN EYE ON THINGS WHILE I GO--UH--MAKE PLANS.
BEGINNIN' TO FEEL KIND'A USELESS! WITH THE EMPIRE GONE, SEEMS LIKE ANYONE CAN HANDLE THE KIND OF STUFF THAT POPS UP NOW... A LOT OF 'EM BETTER THAN I DO.
STILL, ACCORDIN' TO LANDO...THIS JOB WAS MADE FOR ME.

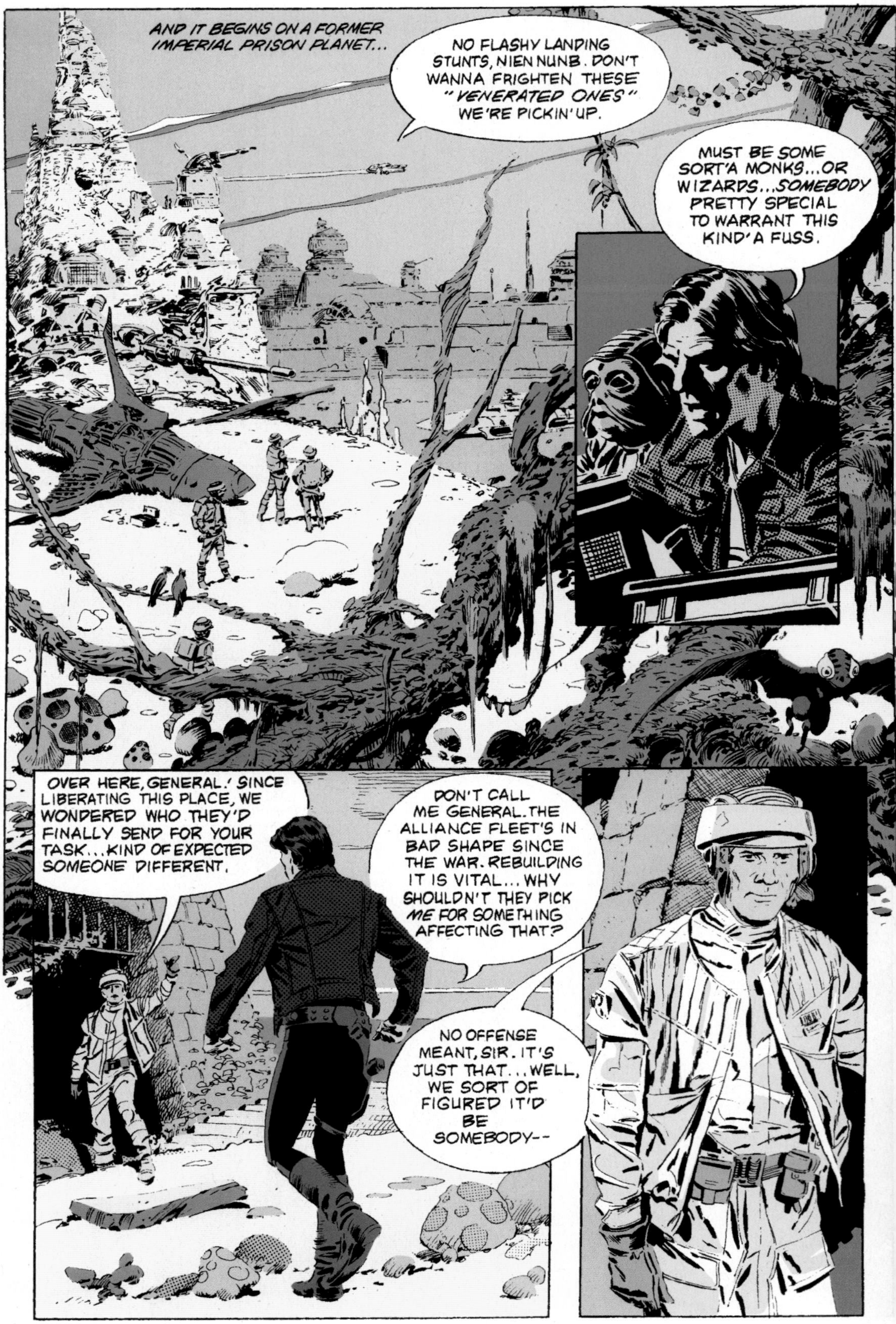
AND IT BEGINS ON A FORMER IMPERIAL PRISON PLANET...
NO FLASHY LANDING STUNTS, NIEN NUNB. DON'T WANNA FRIGHTEN THESE "VENERATED ONES" WE'RE PICKIN' UP.
MUST BE SOME SORT'A MONKS...OR WIZARDS...SOMEBODY PRETTY SPECIAL TO WARRANT THIS KIND'A FUSS.
OVER HERE, GENERAL! SINCE LIBERATING THIS PLACE, WE WONDERED WHO THEY'D FINALLY SEND FOR YOUR TASK...KIND OF EXPECTED SOMEONE DIFFERENT.
DON'T CALL ME GENERAL. THE ALLIANCE FLEET'S IN BAD SHAPE SINCE THE WAR. REBUILDING IT IS VITAL...WHY SHOULDN'T THEY PICK ME FOR SOMETHING AFFECTING THAT?
NO OFFENSE MEANT, SIR. IT'S JUST THAT...WELL, WE SORT OF FIGURED IT'D BE SOMEBODY--

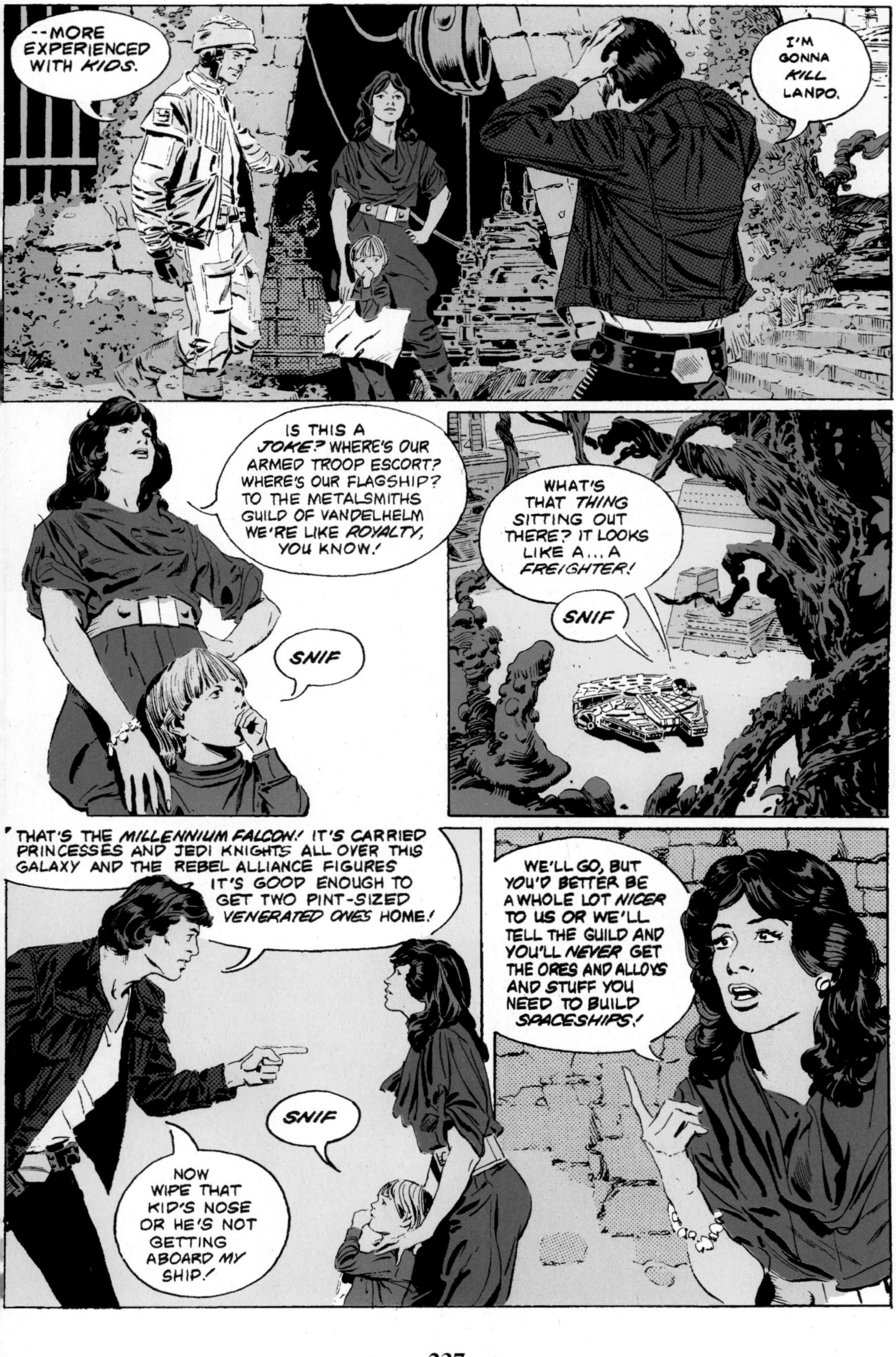
--MORE EXPERIENCED WITH KIDS.
I'M GONNA KILL LANDO.
IS THIS A JOKE? WHERE'S OUR ARMED TROOP ESCORT? WHERE'S OUR FLAGSHIP? TO THE METALSMITHS GUILD OF VANDELHELM WE'RE LIKE ROYALTY, YOU KNOW!
SNIF
WHAT'S THAT THING SITTING OUT THERE? IT LOOKS LIKE A... A FREIGHTER!
SNIF
THAT'S THE MILLENNIUM FALCON! IT'S CARRIED PRINCESSES AND JEDI KNIGHTS ALL OVER THIS GALAXY AND THE REBEL ALLIANCE FIGURES IT'S GOOD ENOUGH TO GET TWO PINT-SIZED VENERATED ONES HOME!
SNIF
NOW WIPE THAT KID'S NOSE OR HE'S NOT GETTING ABOARD MY SHIP!
WE'LL GO, BUT YOU'D BETTER BE A WHOLE LOT NICER TO US OR WE'LL TELL THE GUILD AND YOU'LL NEVER GET THE ORES AND ALLOYS AND STUFF YOU NEED TO BUILD SPACESHIPS!

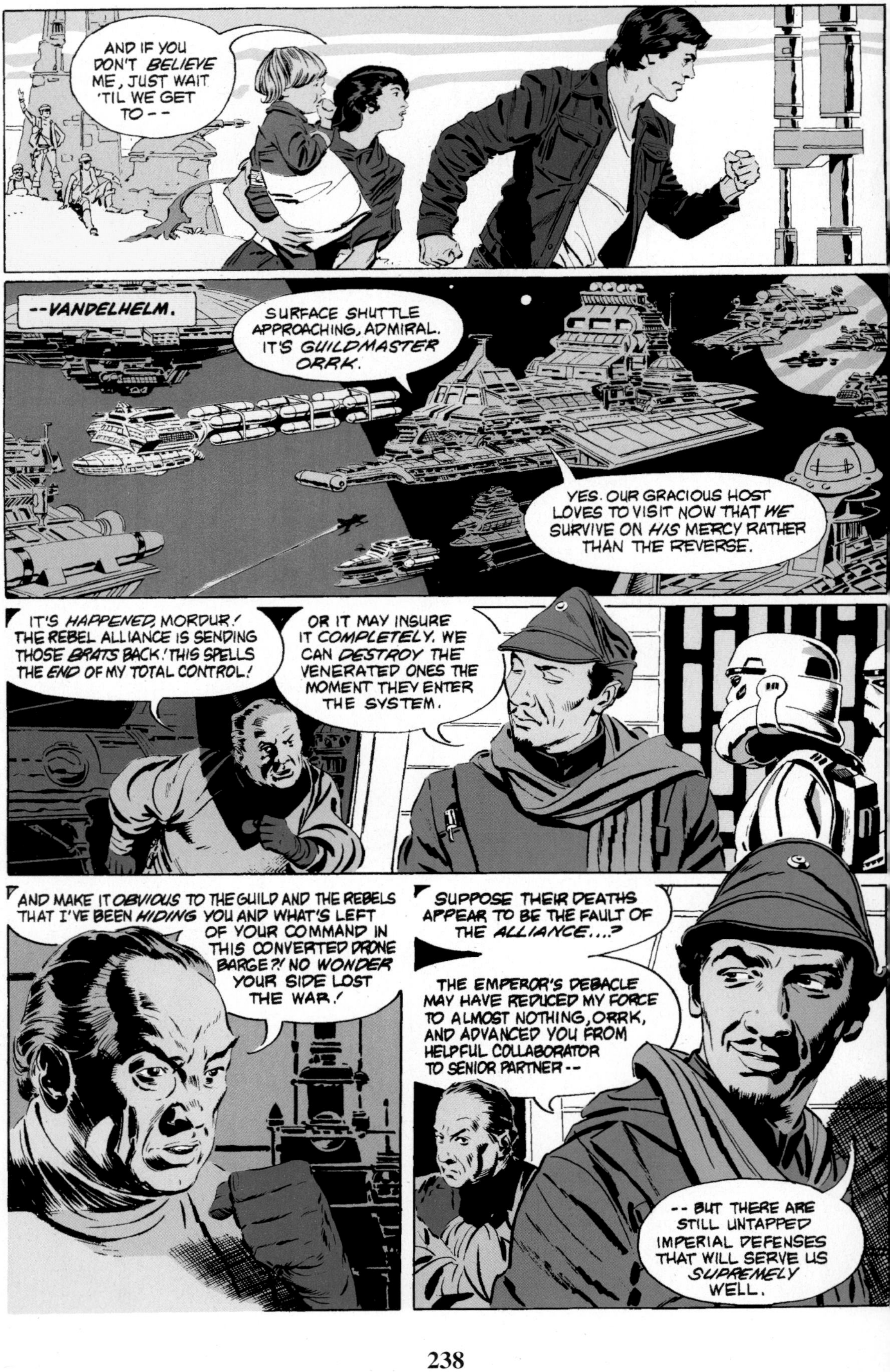
AND IF YOU DON'T BELIEVE ME, JUST WAIT 'TIL WE GET TO --
--VANDELHELM.
SURFACE SHUTTLE APPROACHING, ADMIRAL. IT'S GUILDMASTER ORRK.
YES. OUR GRACIOUS HOST LOVES TO VISIT NOW THAT WE SURVIVE ON HIS MERCY RATHER THAN THE REVERSE.
IT'S HAPPENED, MORDUR! THE REBEL ALLIANCE IS SENDING THOSE BRATS BACK! THIS SPELLS THE END OF MY TOTAL CONTROL!
OR IT MAY INSURE IT COMPLETELY. WE CAN DESTROY THE VENERATED ONES THE MOMENT THEY ENTER THE SYSTEM.
AND MAKE IT OBVIOUS TO THE GUILD AND THE REBELS THAT I'VE BEEN HIDING YOU AND WHAT'S LEFT OF YOUR COMMAND IN THIS CONVERTED DRONE BARGE?! NO WONDER YOUR SIDE LOST THE WAR!
SUPPOSE THEIR DEATHS APPEAR TO BE THE FAULT OF THE ALLIANCE....?
THE EMPEROR'S DEBACLE MAY HAVE REDUCED MY FORCE TO ALMOST NOTHING, ORRK, AND ADVANCED YOU FROM HELPFUL COLLABORATOR TO SENIOR PARTNER --
-- BUT THERE ARE STILL UNTAPPED IMPERIAL DEFENSES THAT WILL SERVE US SUPREMELY WELL.

WE'RE *TIRED* OF PLAYING HOLOGRAPHIC CHESS! IT'S LIKE EVERYTHING ELSE ON THIS SHIP... OLD AND *BORING.* TELL US ANOTHER *STORY* GENERAL SOLO...

WE *LIKED* THAT ONE ABOUT DARTH VADER COVERING YOU WITH ALL THAT FREEZING, ICKY STUFF!

SNIF

CARBONITE. AND DON'T CALL ME GENERAL. HAVE YOU WIPED THAT KID'S NOSE LATELY? WE'LL BE HITTIN' YOUR SYSTEM SOON AND I DON'T WANT--

--NIEN NUMB! WHAT ARE YOU DOING *NOW?!*

THE RESPONSE FROM THE TEMPORARY CO-PILOT IS NOT ENCOURAGING...

WE DROPPED OUT OF HYPERSPACE INTO THE MIDDLE OF AN ASTEROID SWARM?!

ASTEROIDS *DON'T EXPLODE!* LEMME AT THOSE CONTROLS!

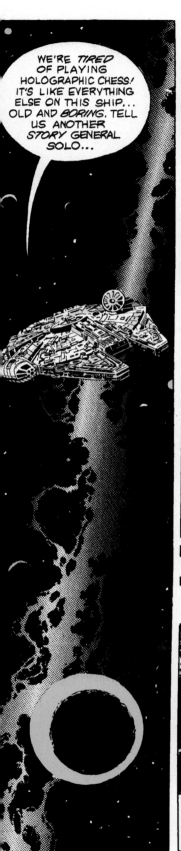

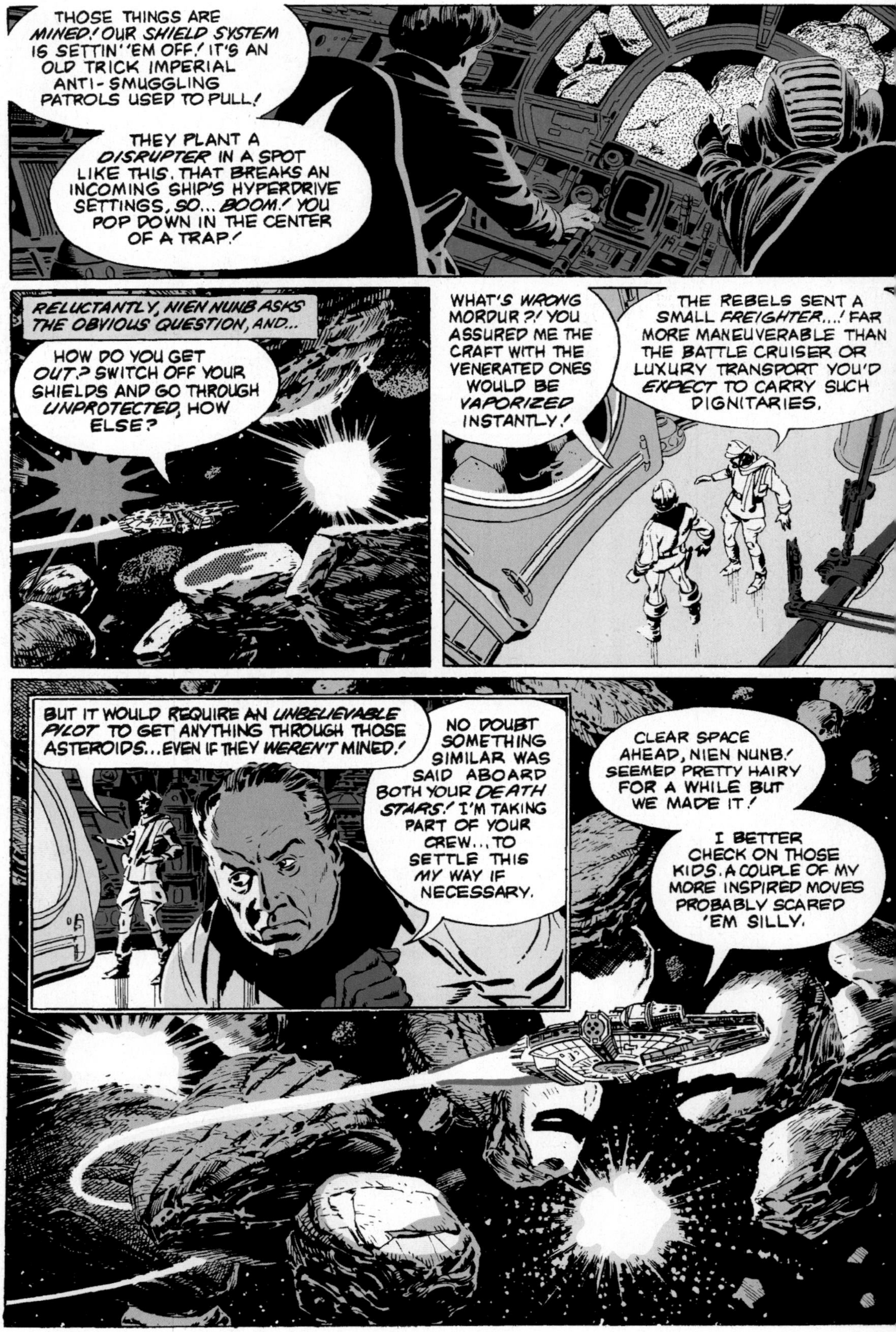
THOSE THINGS ARE MINED! OUR SHIELD SYSTEM IS SETTIN' 'EM OFF! IT'S AN OLD TRICK IMPERIAL ANTI-SMUGGLING PATROLS USED TO PULL!
THEY PLANT A DISRUPTER IN A SPOT LIKE THIS. THAT BREAKS AN INCOMING SHIP'S HYPERDRIVE SETTINGS, SO... BOOM! YOU POP DOWN IN THE CENTER OF A TRAP!
RELUCTANTLY, NIEN NUNB ASKS THE OBVIOUS QUESTION, AND...
HOW DO YOU GET OUT? SWITCH OFF YOUR SHIELDS AND GO THROUGH UNPROTECTED, HOW ELSE?
WHAT'S WRONG MORDUR ?! YOU ASSURED ME THE CRAFT WITH THE VENERATED ONES WOULD BE VAPORIZED INSTANTLY!
THE REBELS SENT A SMALL FREIGHTER...! FAR MORE MANEUVERABLE THAN THE BATTLE CRUISER OR LUXURY TRANSPORT YOU'D EXPECT TO CARRY SUCH DIGNITARIES.
BUT IT WOULD REQUIRE AN UNBELIEVABLE PILOT TO GET ANYTHING THROUGH THOSE ASTEROIDS...EVEN IF THEY WEREN'T MINED!
NO DOUBT SOMETHING SIMILAR WAS SAID ABOARD BOTH YOUR DEATH STARS! I'M TAKING PART OF YOUR CREW... TO SETTLE THIS MY WAY IF NECESSARY.
CLEAR SPACE AHEAD, NIEN NUNB! SEEMED PRETTY HAIRY FOR A WHILE BUT WE MADE IT!
I BETTER CHECK ON THOSE KIDS. A COUPLE OF MY MORE INSPIRED MOVES PROBABLY SCARED 'EM SILLY.

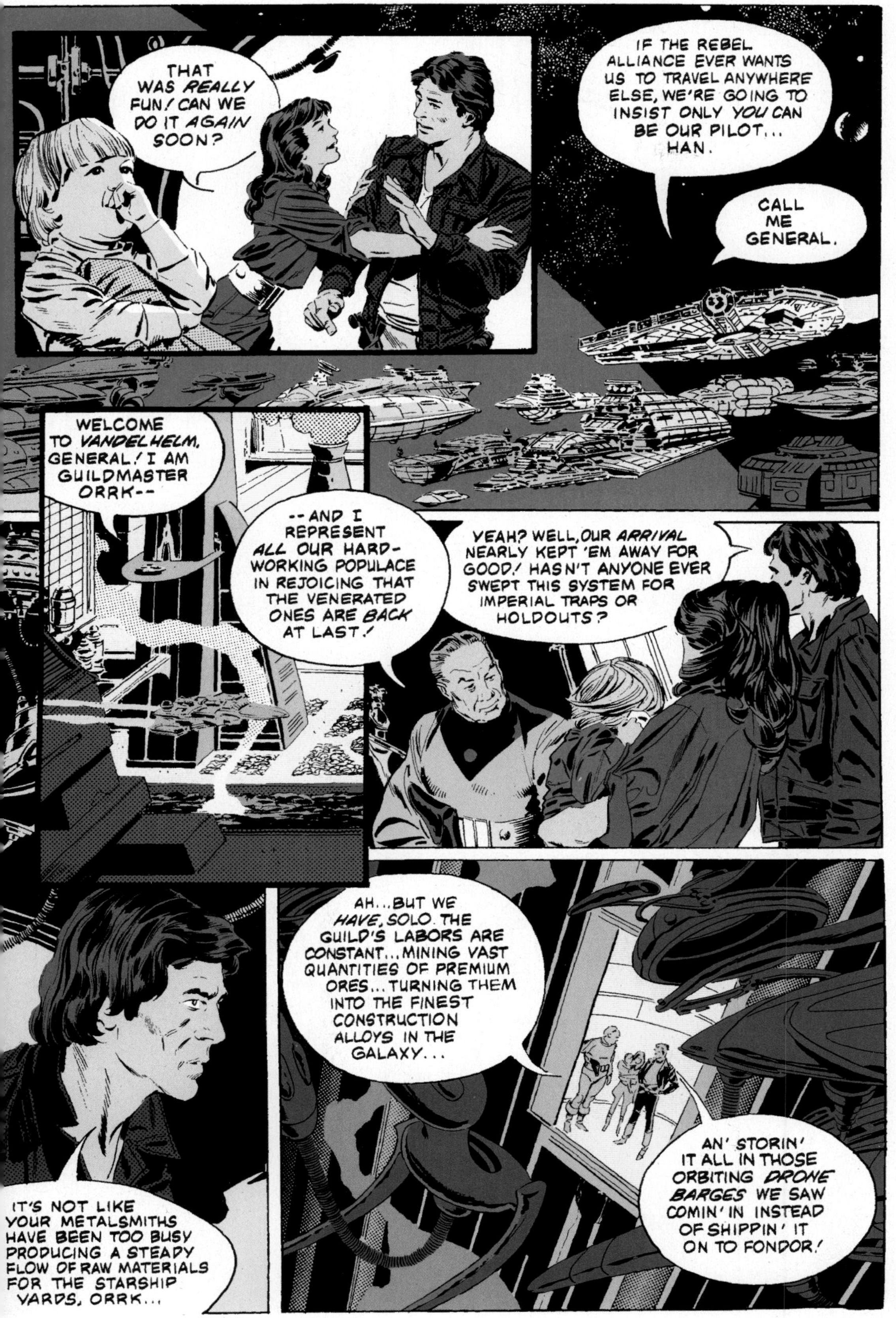
THAT WAS REALLY FUN! CAN WE DO IT AGAIN SOON?
IF THE REBEL ALLIANCE EVER WANTS US TO TRAVEL ANYWHERE ELSE, WE'RE GOING TO INSIST ONLY YOU CAN BE OUR PILOT... HAN.
CALL ME GENERAL.
WELCOME TO VANDELHELM, GENERAL! I AM GUILDMASTER ORRK--
--AND I REPRESENT ALL OUR HARD-WORKING POPULACE IN REJOICING THAT THE VENERATED ONES ARE BACK AT LAST!
YEAH? WELL, OUR ARRIVAL NEARLY KEPT 'EM AWAY FOR GOOD! HASN'T ANYONE EVER SWEPT THIS SYSTEM FOR IMPERIAL TRAPS OR HOLDOUTS?
AH...BUT WE HAVE, SOLO. THE GUILD'S LABORS ARE CONSTANT...MINING VAST QUANTITIES OF PREMIUM ORES...TURNING THEM INTO THE FINEST CONSTRUCTION ALLOYS IN THE GALAXY...
IT'S NOT LIKE YOUR METALSMITHS HAVE BEEN TOO BUSY PRODUCING A STEADY FLOW OF RAW MATERIALS FOR THE STARSHIP YARDS, ORRK...
AN' STORIN' IT ALL IN THOSE ORBITING DRONE BARGES WE SAW COMIN' IN INSTEAD OF SHIPPIN' IT ON TO FONDOR!

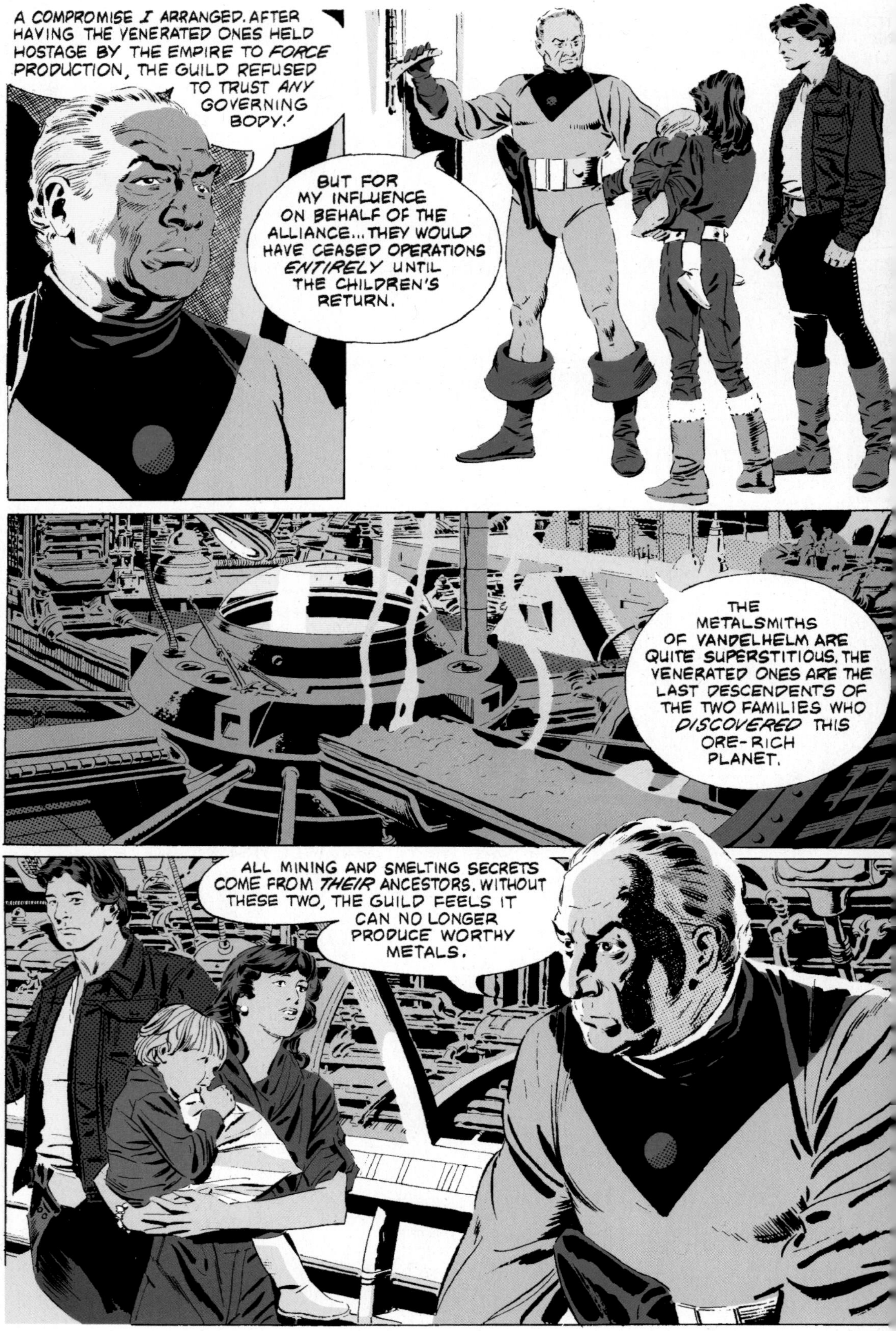
A COMPROMISE I ARRANGED. AFTER HAVING THE VENERATED ONES HELD HOSTAGE BY THE EMPIRE TO FORCE PRODUCTION, THE GUILD REFUSED TO TRUST ANY GOVERNING BODY!
BUT FOR MY INFLUENCE ON BEHALF OF THE ALLIANCE... THEY WOULD HAVE CEASED OPERATIONS ENTIRELY UNTIL THE CHILDREN'S RETURN.
THE METALSMITHS OF VANDELHELM ARE QUITE SUPERSTITIOUS. THE VENERATED ONES ARE THE LAST DESCENDENTS OF THE TWO FAMILIES WHO DISCOVERED THIS ORE-RICH PLANET.
ALL MINING AND SMELTING SECRETS COME FROM THEIR ANCESTORS. WITHOUT THESE TWO, THE GUILD FEELS IT CAN NO LONGER PRODUCE WORTHY METALS.

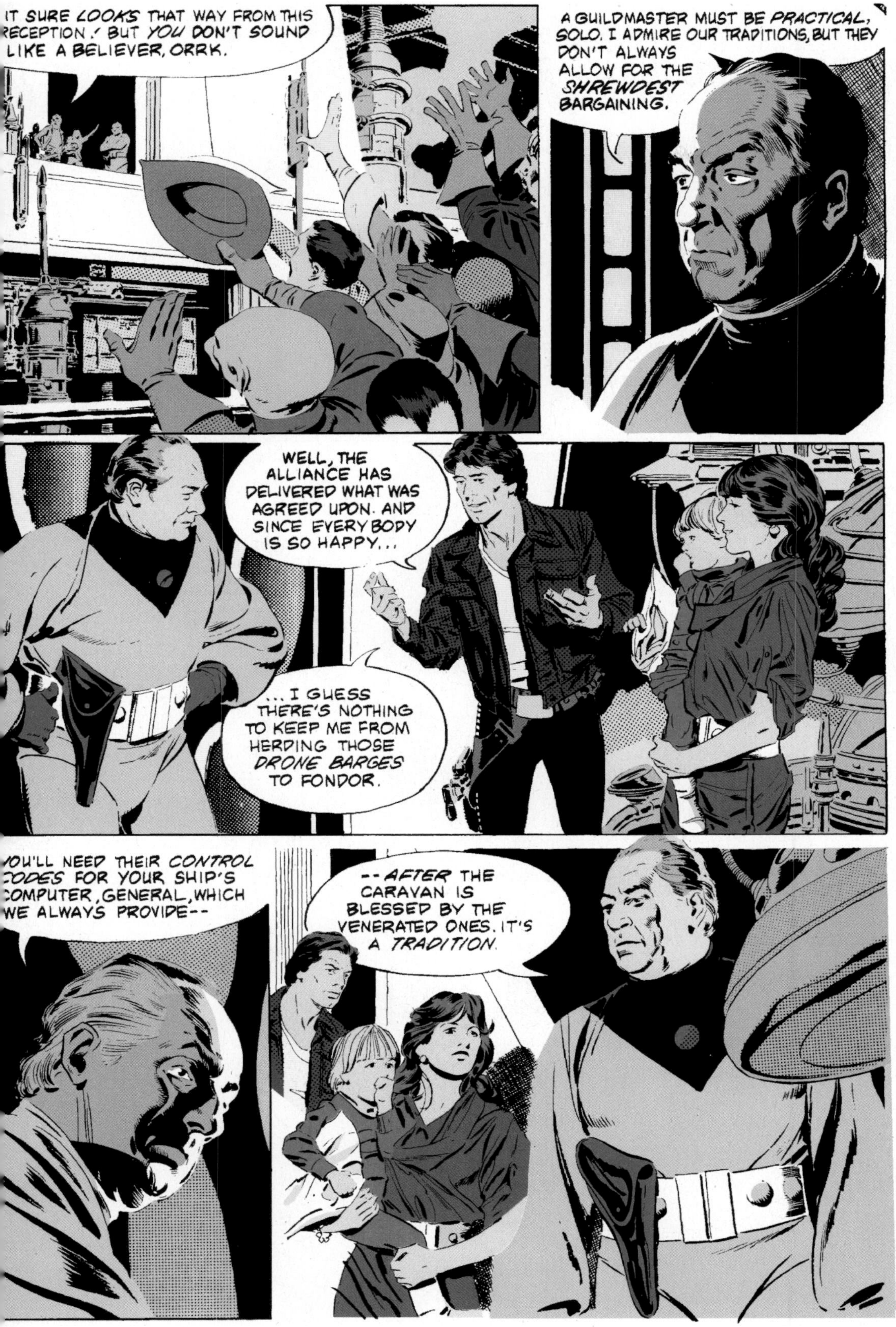
IT SURE *LOOKS* THAT WAY FROM THIS RECEPTION! BUT *YOU* DON'T SOUND LIKE A BELIEVER, ORRK.
A GUILDMASTER MUST BE *PRACTICAL*, SOLO. I ADMIRE OUR TRADITIONS, BUT THEY DON'T ALWAYS ALLOW FOR THE *SHREWDEST* BARGAINING.
WELL, THE ALLIANCE HAS DELIVERED WHAT WAS AGREED UPON. AND SINCE EVERYBODY IS SO HAPPY...
...I GUESS THERE'S NOTHING TO KEEP ME FROM HERDING THOSE *DRONE BARGES* TO FONDOR.
YOU'LL NEED THEIR *CONTROL CODES* FOR YOUR SHIP'S COMPUTER, GENERAL, WHICH WE ALWAYS PROVIDE--
--*AFTER* THE CARAVAN IS BLESSED BY THE VENERATED ONES. IT'S A *TRADITION*.

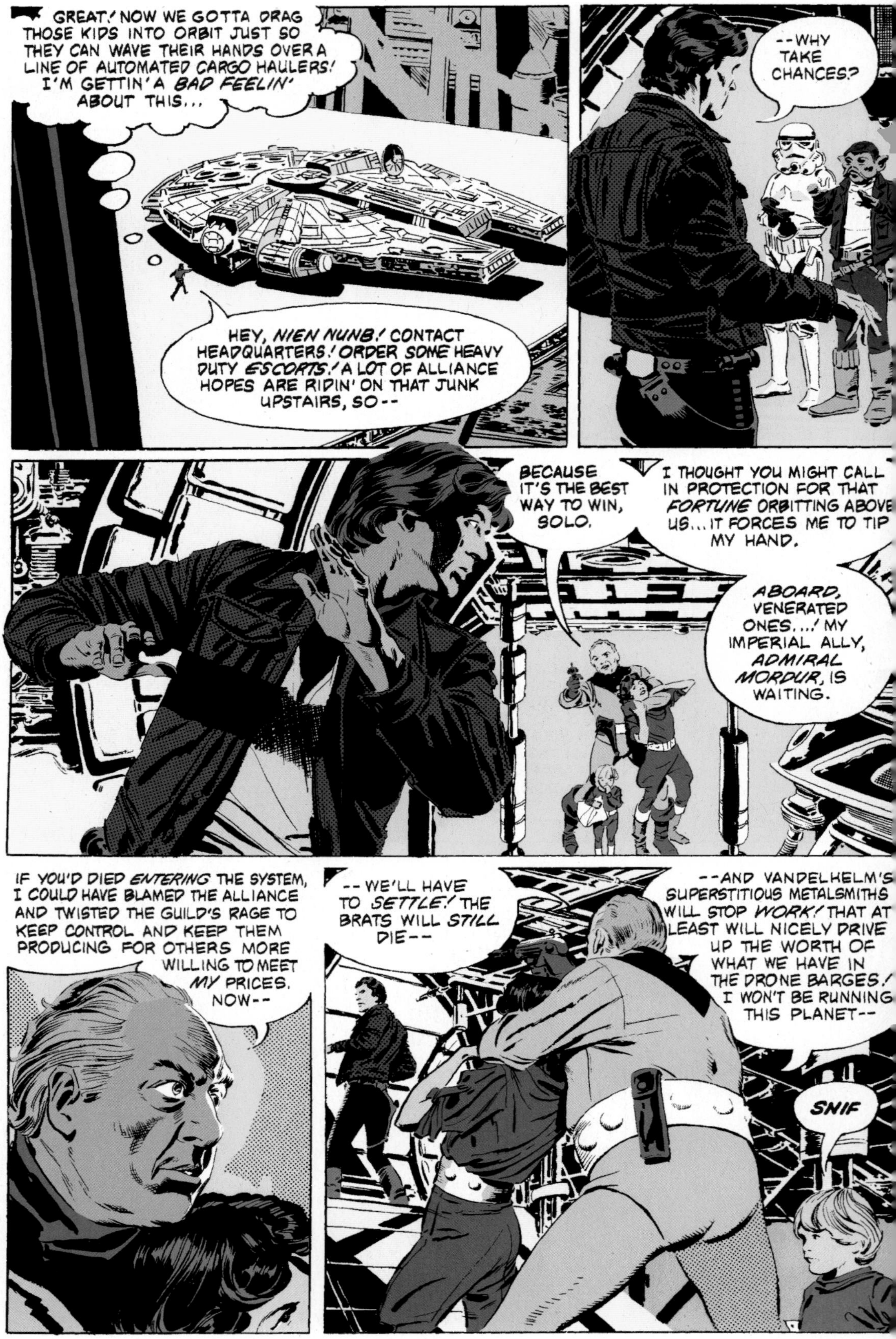
GREAT! NOW WE GOTTA DRAG THOSE KIDS INTO ORBIT JUST SO THEY CAN WAVE THEIR HANDS OVER A LINE OF AUTOMATED CARGO HAULERS! I'M GETTIN' A BAD FEELIN' ABOUT THIS...
HEY, NIEN NUNB! CONTACT HEADQUARTERS! ORDER SOME HEAVY DUTY ESCORTS! A LOT OF ALLIANCE HOPES ARE RIDIN' ON THAT JUNK UPSTAIRS, SO--
--WHY TAKE CHANCES?
BECAUSE IT'S THE BEST WAY TO WIN, SOLO.
I THOUGHT YOU MIGHT CALL IN PROTECTION FOR THAT FORTUNE ORBITTING ABOVE US... IT FORCES ME TO TIP MY HAND.
ABOARD, VENERATED ONES...! MY IMPERIAL ALLY, ADMIRAL MORDUR, IS WAITING.
IF YOU'D DIED ENTERING THE SYSTEM, I COULD HAVE BLAMED THE ALLIANCE AND TWISTED THE GUILD'S RAGE TO KEEP CONTROL AND KEEP THEM PRODUCING FOR OTHERS MORE WILLING TO MEET MY PRICES. NOW--
--WE'LL HAVE TO SETTLE! THE BRATS WILL STILL DIE--
--AND VANDELHELM'S SUPERSTITIOUS METALSMITHS WILL STOP WORK! THAT AT LEAST WILL NICELY DRIVE UP THE WORTH OF WHAT WE HAVE IN THE DRONE BARGES! I WON'T BE RUNNING THIS PLANET--
SNIF

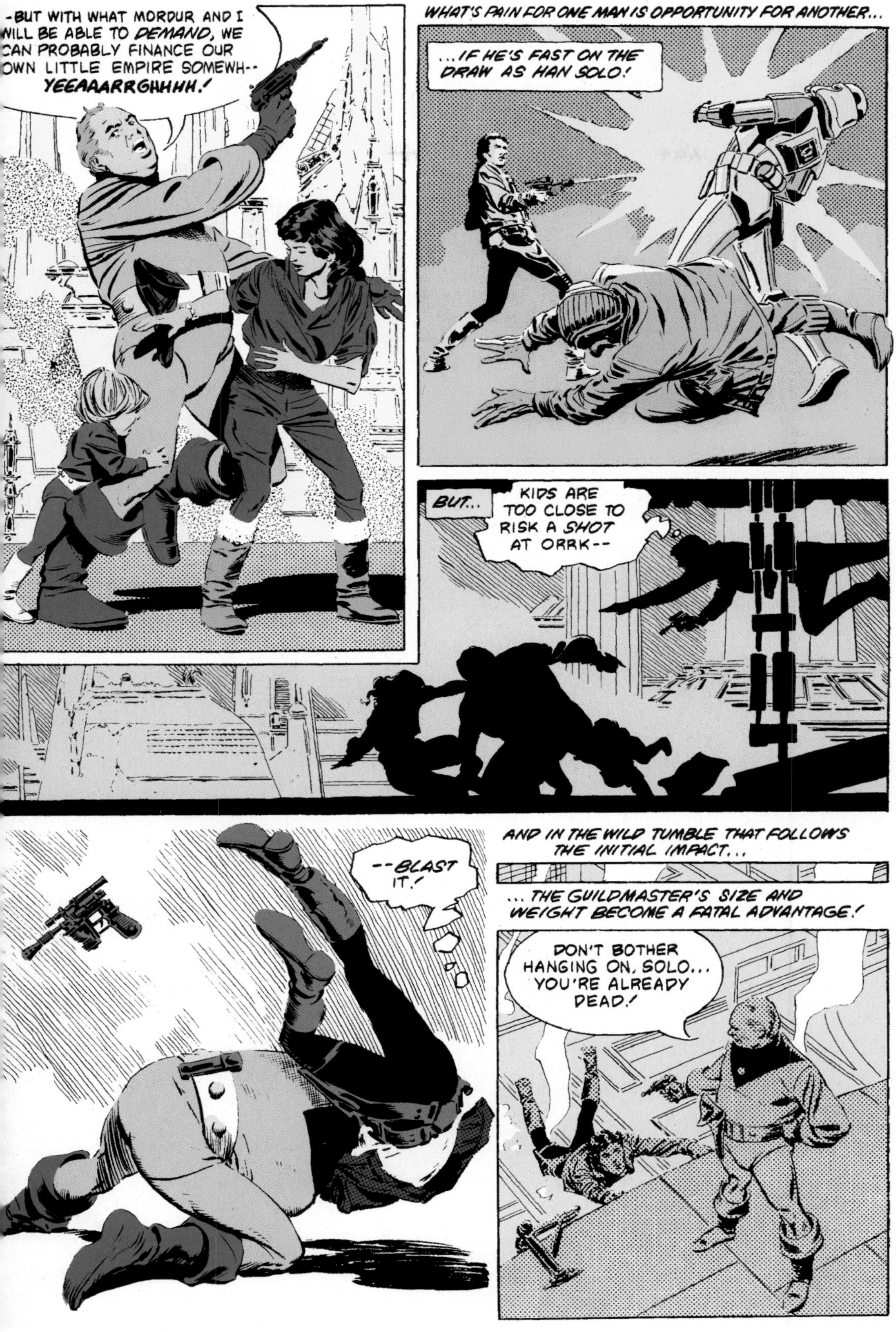
-BUT WITH WHAT MORDUR AND I WILL BE ABLE TO DEMAND, WE CAN PROBABLY FINANCE OUR OWN LITTLE EMPIRE SOMEWH-- YEEAAARRGHHHH!
WHAT'S PAIN FOR ONE MAN IS OPPORTUNITY FOR ANOTHER...
...IF HE'S FAST ON THE DRAW AS HAN SOLO!
BUT...
KIDS ARE TOO CLOSE TO RISK A SHOT AT ORRK--
--BLAST IT!
AND IN THE WILD TUMBLE THAT FOLLOWS THE INITIAL IMPACT...
...THE GUILDMASTER'S SIZE AND WEIGHT BECOME A FATAL ADVANTAGE!
DON'T BOTHER HANGING ON, SOLO... YOU'RE ALREADY DEAD!

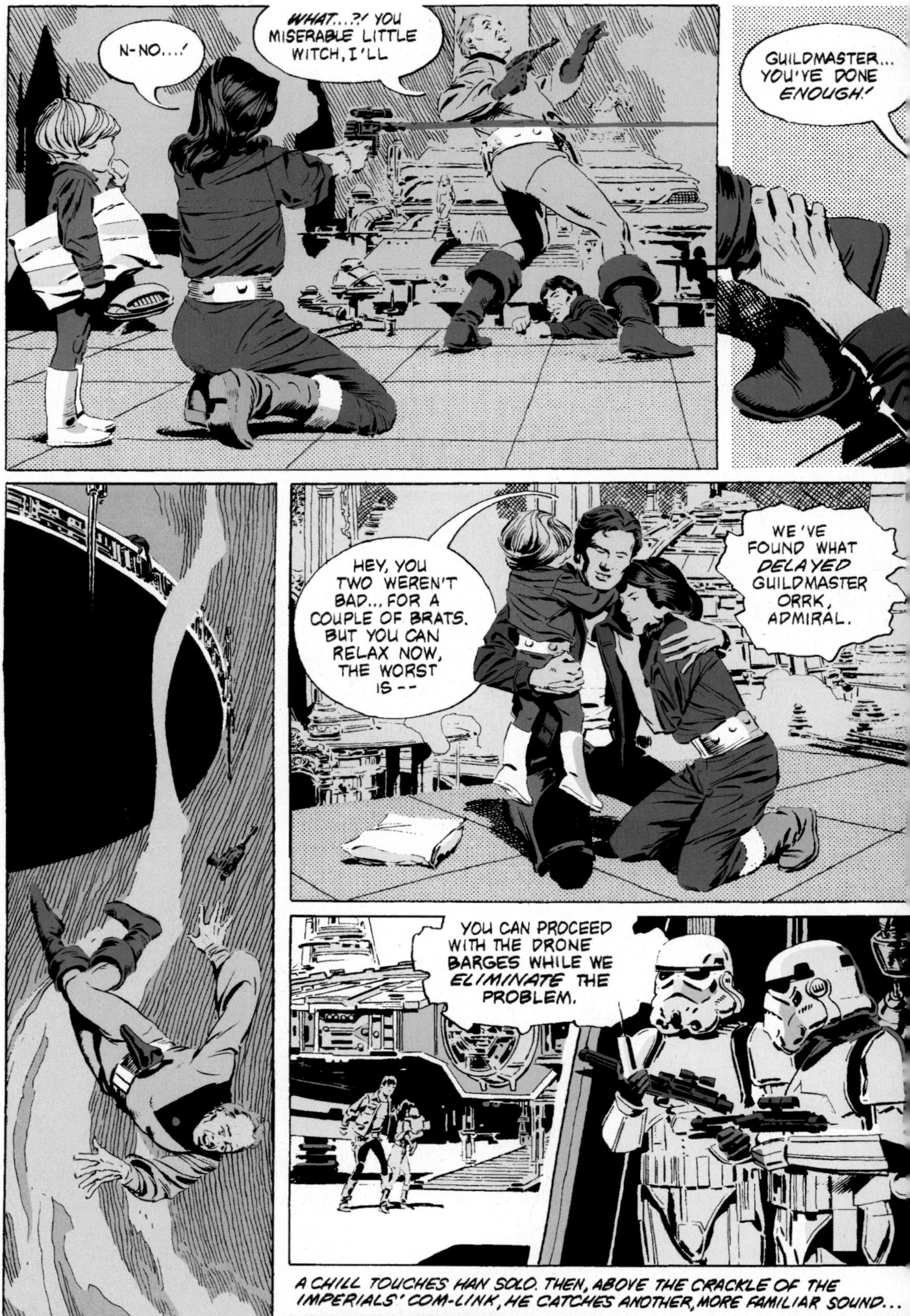
N-NO...!
WHAT...?! YOU MISERABLE LITTLE WITCH, I'LL
GUILDMASTER... YOU'VE DONE ENOUGH!
HEY, YOU TWO WEREN'T BAD... FOR A COUPLE OF BRATS. BUT YOU CAN RELAX NOW, THE WORST IS --
WE'VE FOUND WHAT DELAYED GUILDMASTER ORRK, ADMIRAL.
YOU CAN PROCEED WITH THE DRONE BARGES WHILE WE ELIMINATE THE PROBLEM.
A CHILL TOUCHES HAN SOLO. THEN, ABOVE THE CRACKLE OF THE IMPERIALS' COM-LINK, HE CATCHES ANOTHER, MORE FAMILIAR SOUND...

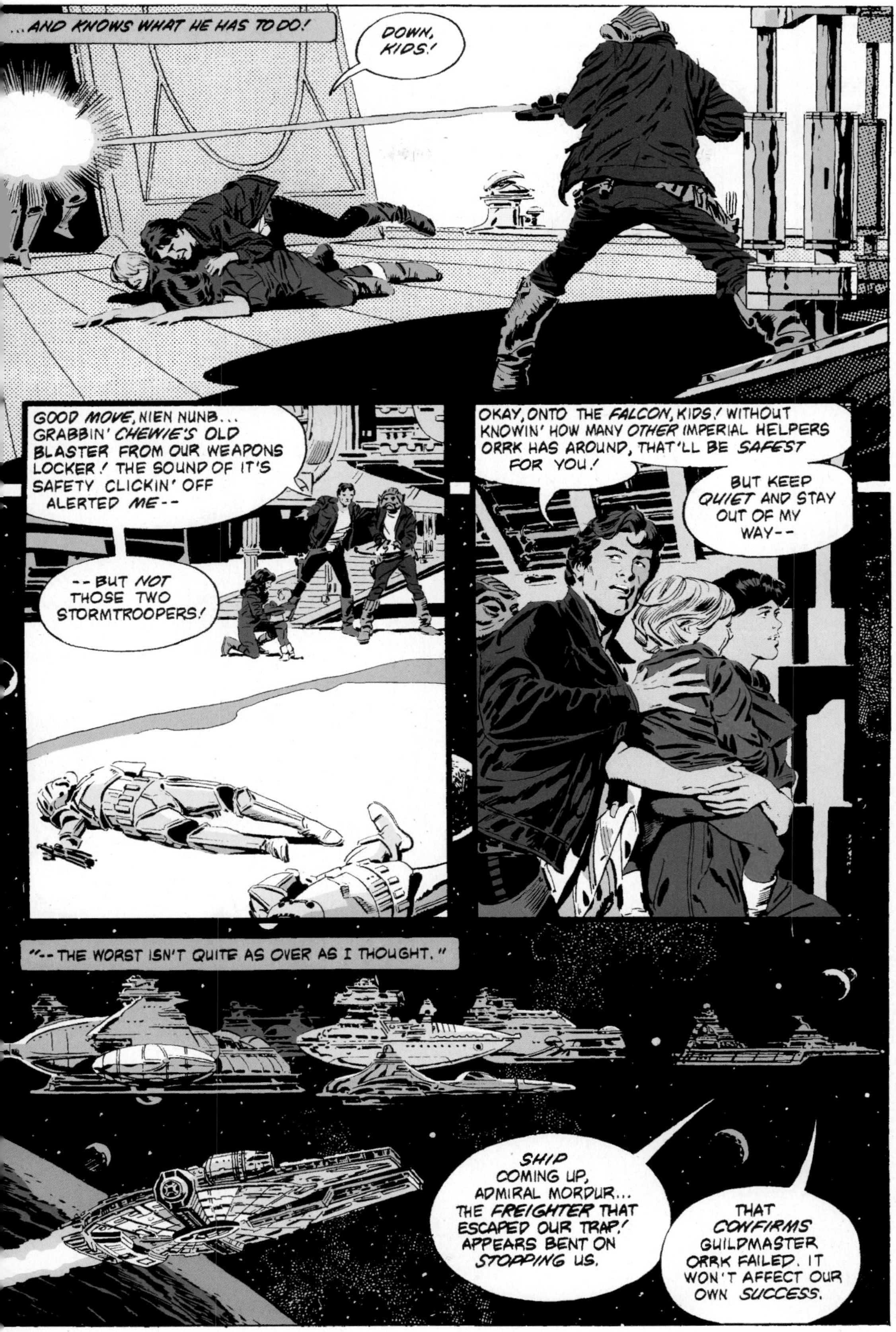
...AND KNOWS WHAT HE HAS TO DO!
DOWN, KIDS!
GOOD MOVE, NIEN NUNB... GRABBIN' CHEWIE'S OLD BLASTER FROM OUR WEAPONS LOCKER! THE SOUND OF IT'S SAFETY CLICKIN' OFF ALERTED ME--
--BUT NOT THOSE TWO STORMTROOPERS!
OKAY, ONTO THE FALCON, KIDS! WITHOUT KNOWIN' HOW MANY OTHER IMPERIAL HELPERS ORRK HAS AROUND, THAT'LL BE SAFEST FOR YOU!
BUT KEEP QUIET AND STAY OUT OF MY WAY--
"--THE WORST ISN'T QUITE AS OVER AS I THOUGHT."
SHIP COMING UP, ADMIRAL MORDUR... THE FREIGHTER THAT ESCAPED OUR TRAP! APPEARS BENT ON STOPPING US.
THAT CONFIRMS GUILDMASTER ORRK FAILED. IT WON'T AFFECT OUR OWN SUCCESS.

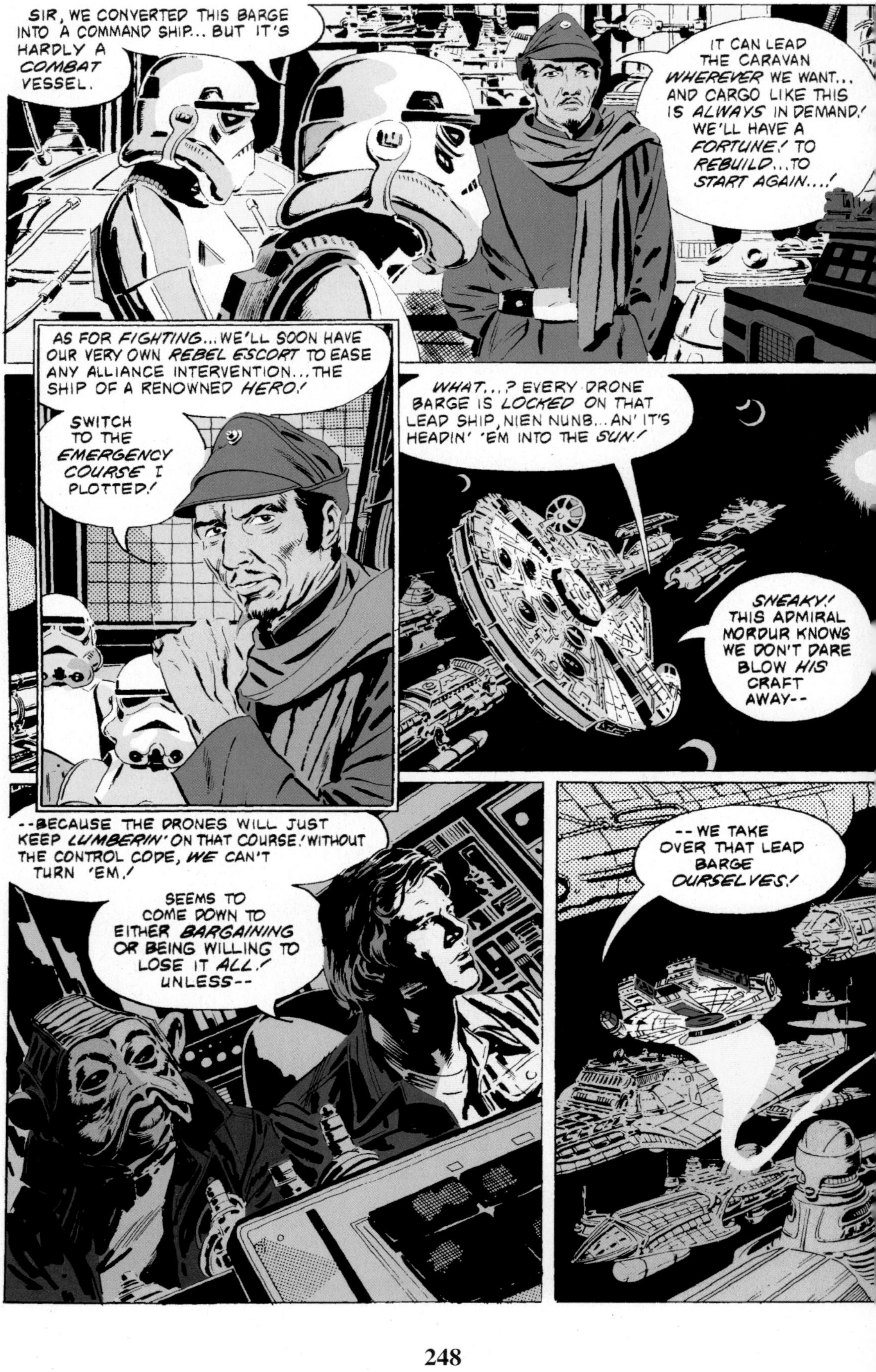
SIR, WE CONVERTED THIS BARGE INTO A COMMAND SHIP... BUT IT'S HARDLY A COMBAT VESSEL.
IT CAN LEAD THE CARAVAN WHEREVER WE WANT... AND CARGO LIKE THIS IS ALWAYS IN DEMAND! WE'LL HAVE A FORTUNE! TO REBUILD...TO START AGAIN...!
AS FOR FIGHTING... WE'LL SOON HAVE OUR VERY OWN REBEL ESCORT TO EASE ANY ALLIANCE INTERVENTION...THE SHIP OF A RENOWNED HERO!
SWITCH TO THE EMERGENCY COURSE I PLOTTED!
WHAT...? EVERY DRONE BARGE IS LOCKED ON THAT LEAD SHIP, NIEN NUNB...AN' IT'S HEADIN' 'EM INTO THE SUN!
SNEAKY! THIS ADMIRAL MORDUR KNOWS WE DON'T DARE BLOW HIS CRAFT AWAY--
--BECAUSE THE DRONES WILL JUST KEEP LUMBERIN' ON THAT COURSE! WITHOUT THE CONTROL CODE, WE CAN'T TURN 'EM!
SEEMS TO COME DOWN TO EITHER BARGAINING OR BEING WILLING TO LOSE IT ALL! UNLESS--
--WE TAKE OVER THAT LEAD BARGE OURSELVES!

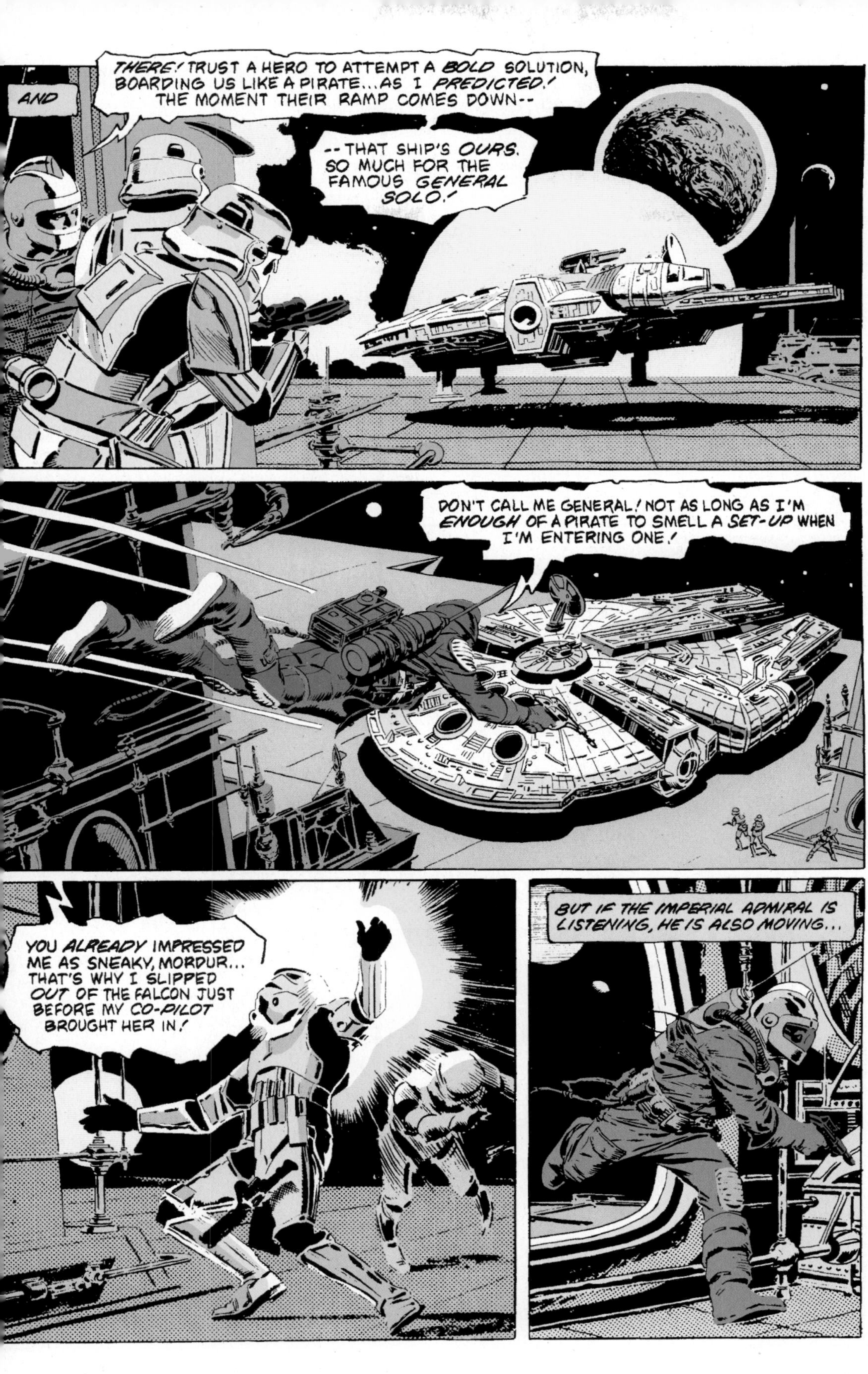
AND
THERE! TRUST A HERO TO ATTEMPT A BOLD SOLUTION, BOARDING US LIKE A PIRATE...AS I PREDICTED! THE MOMENT THEIR RAMP COMES DOWN--
--THAT SHIP'S OURS. SO MUCH FOR THE FAMOUS GENERAL SOLO!
DON'T CALL ME GENERAL! NOT AS LONG AS I'M ENOUGH OF A PIRATE TO SMELL A SET-UP WHEN I'M ENTERING ONE!
YOU ALREADY IMPRESSED ME AS SNEAKY, MORDUR... THAT'S WHY I SLIPPED OUT OF THE FALCON JUST BEFORE MY CO-PILOT BROUGHT HER IN!
BUT IF THE IMPERIAL ADMIRAL IS LISTENING, HE IS ALSO MOVING...

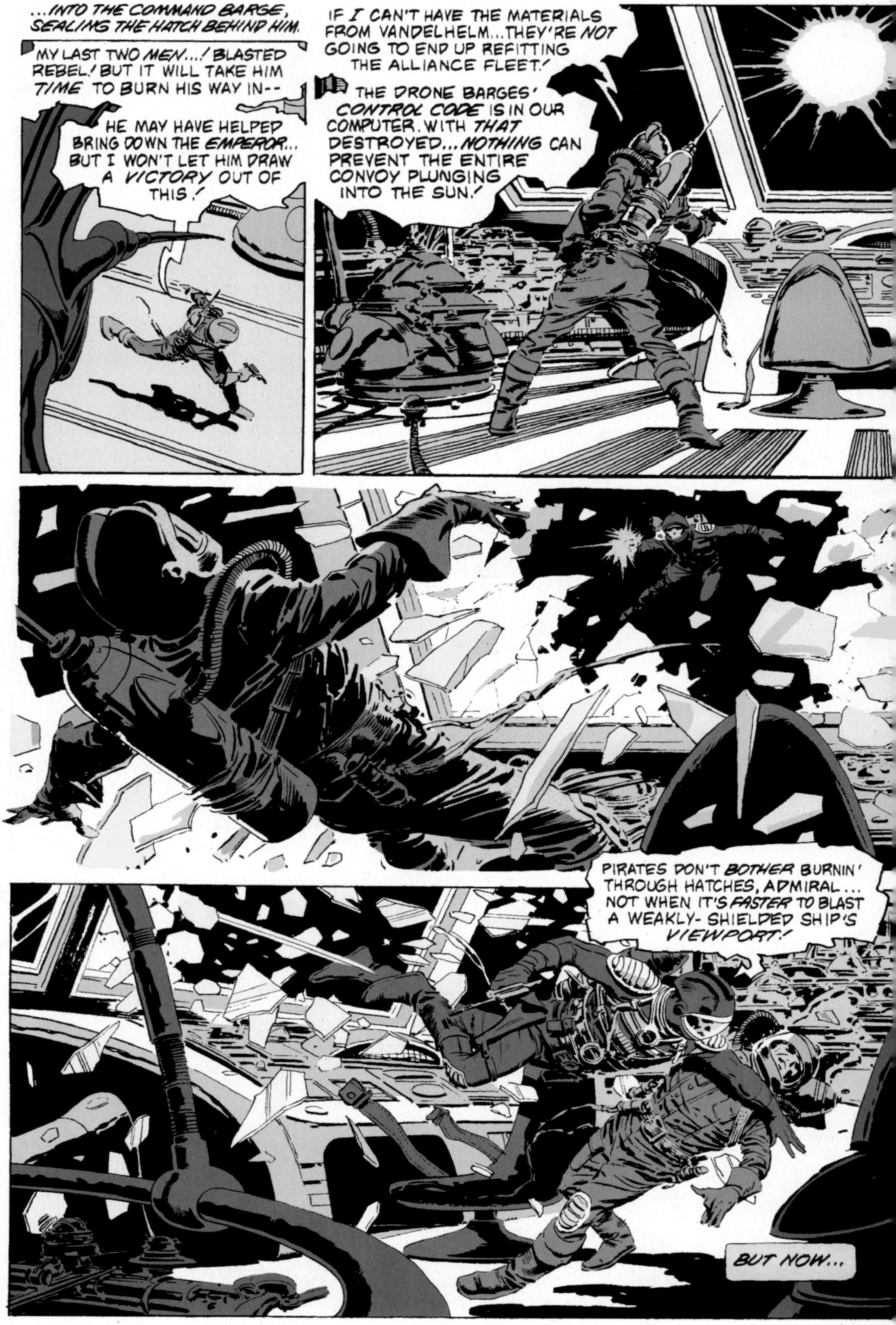
...INTO THE COMMAND BARGE, SEALING THE HATCH BEHIND HIM.
MY LAST TWO MEN...! BLASTED REBEL! BUT IT WILL TAKE HIM TIME TO BURN HIS WAY IN--
HE MAY HAVE HELPED BRING DOWN THE EMPEROR... BUT I WON'T LET HIM DRAW A VICTORY OUT OF THIS!
IF I CAN'T HAVE THE MATERIALS FROM VANDELHELM...THEY'RE NOT GOING TO END UP REFITTING THE ALLIANCE FLEET!
THE DRONE BARGES' CONTROL CODE IS IN OUR COMPUTER. WITH THAT DESTROYED...NOTHING CAN PREVENT THE ENTIRE CONVOY PLUNGING INTO THE SUN!
PIRATES DON'T BOTHER BURNIN' THROUGH HATCHES, ADMIRAL... NOT WHEN IT'S FASTER TO BLAST A WEAKLY-SHIELDED SHIP'S VIEWPORT!
BUT NOW...

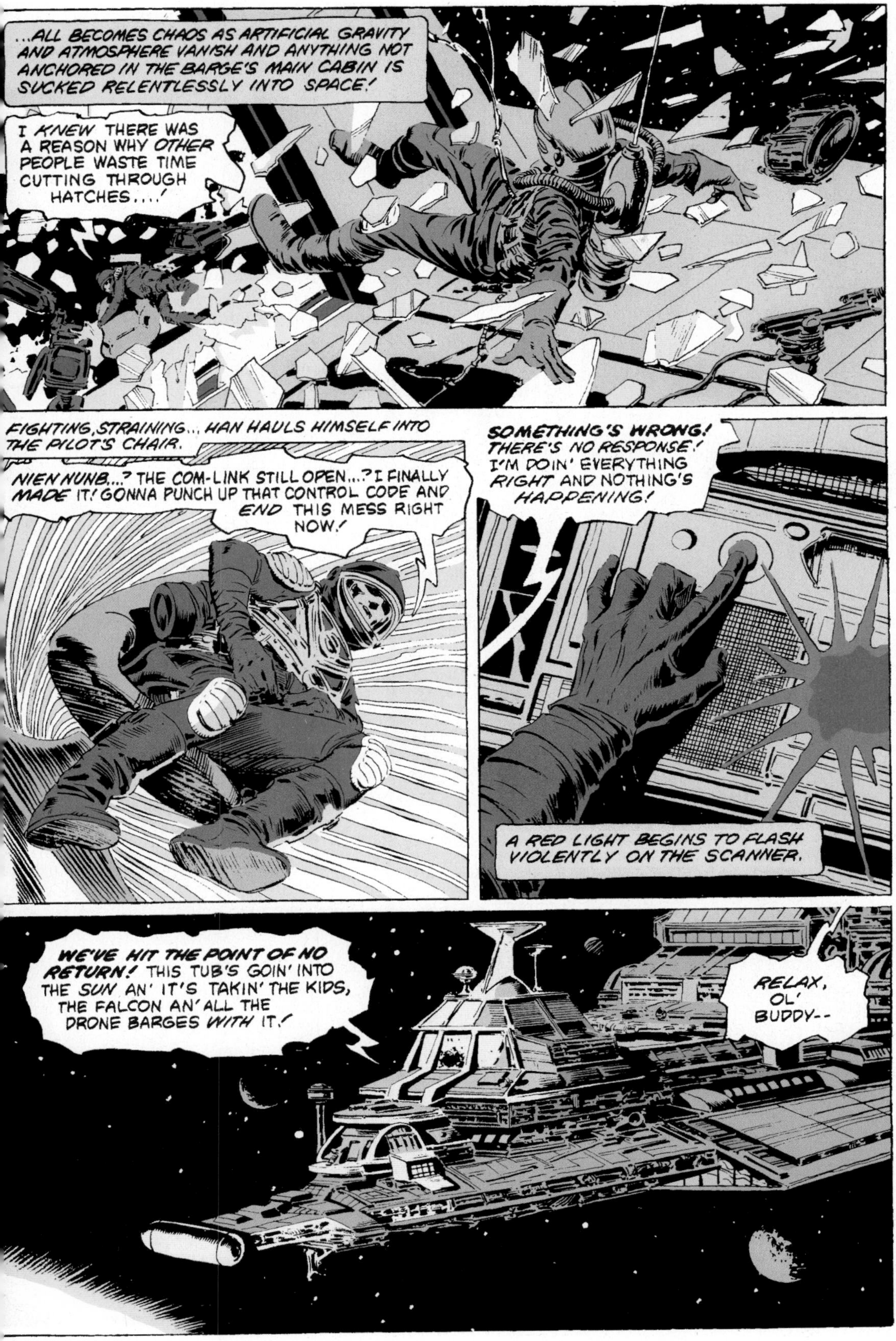

...ALL BECOMES CHAOS AS ARTIFICIAL GRAVITY AND ATMOSPHERE VANISH AND ANYTHING NOT ANCHORED IN THE BARGE'S MAIN CABIN IS SUCKED RELENTLESSLY INTO SPACE!
I KNEW THERE WAS A REASON WHY OTHER PEOPLE WASTE TIME CUTTING THROUGH HATCHES....!
FIGHTING, STRAINING... HAN HAULS HIMSELF INTO THE PILOT'S CHAIR.
NIEN NUNB...? THE COM-LINK STILL OPEN...? I FINALLY MADE IT! GONNA PUNCH UP THAT CONTROL CODE AND END THIS MESS RIGHT NOW!
SOMETHING'S WRONG! THERE'S NO RESPONSE! I'M DOIN' EVERYTHING RIGHT AND NOTHING'S HAPPENING!
A RED LIGHT BEGINS TO FLASH VIOLENTLY ON THE SCANNER.
WE'VE HIT THE POINT OF NO RETURN! THIS TUB'S GOIN' INTO THE SUN AN' IT'S TAKIN' THE KIDS, THE FALCON AN' ALL THE DRONE BARGES WITH IT!
RELAX, OL' BUDDY--

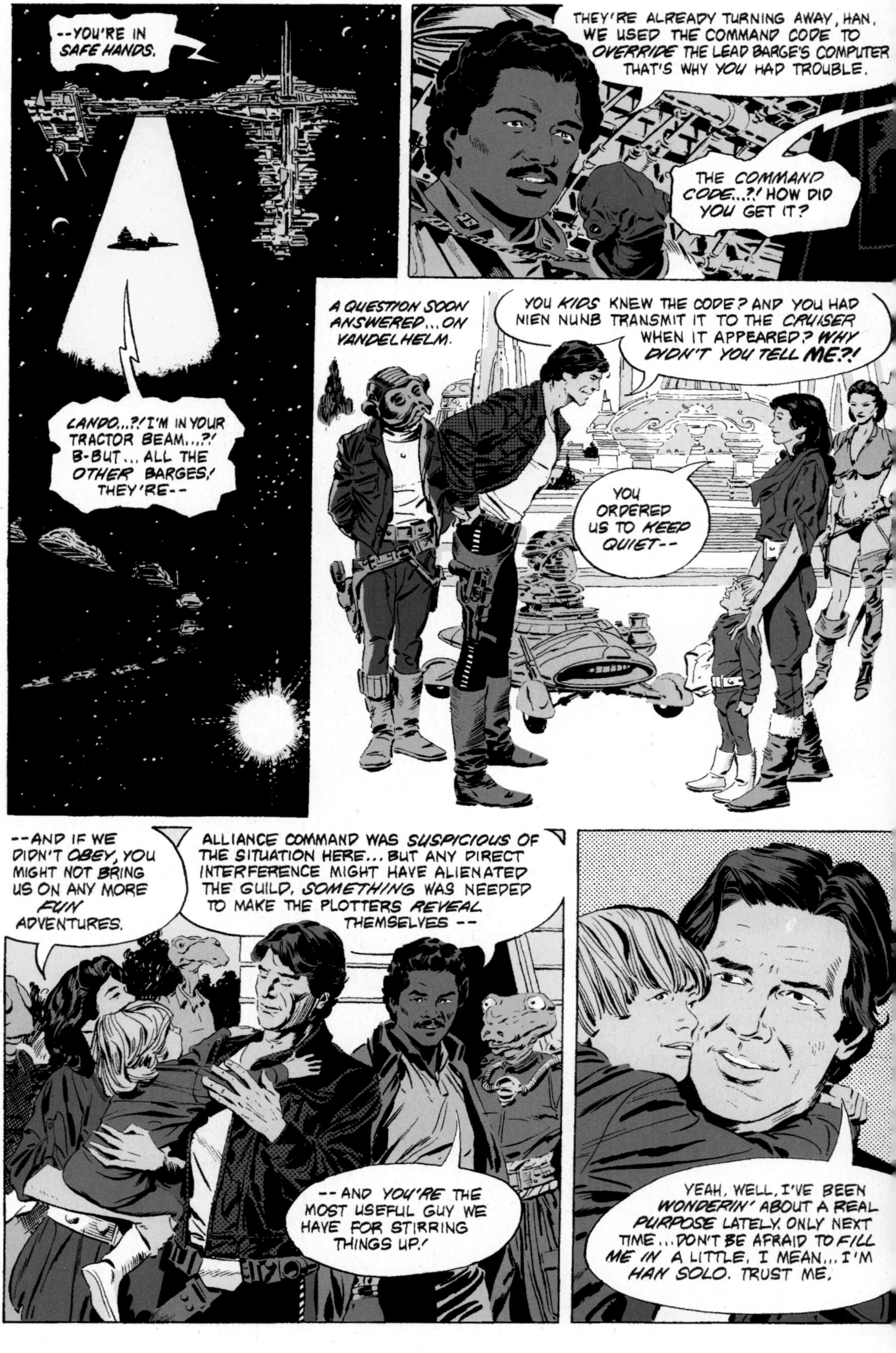
--YOU'RE IN SAFE HANDS.
THEY'RE ALREADY TURNING AWAY, HAN. WE USED THE COMMAND CODE TO OVERRIDE THE LEAD BARGE'S COMPUTER. THAT'S WHY YOU HAD TROUBLE.
THE COMMAND CODE...?! HOW DID YOU GET IT?
LANDO...?! I'M IN YOUR TRACTOR BEAM...?! B-BUT... ALL THE OTHER BARGES! THEY'RE--
A QUESTION SOON ANSWERED... ON VANDELHELM.
YOU KIDS KNEW THE CODE? AND YOU HAD NIEN NUNB TRANSMIT IT TO THE CRUISER WHEN IT APPEARED? WHY DIDN'T YOU TELL ME?!
YOU ORDERED US TO KEEP QUIET--
--AND IF WE DIDN'T OBEY, YOU MIGHT NOT BRING US ON ANY MORE FUN ADVENTURES.
ALLIANCE COMMAND WAS SUSPICIOUS OF THE SITUATION HERE... BUT ANY DIRECT INTERFERENCE MIGHT HAVE ALIENATED THE GUILD. SOMETHING WAS NEEDED TO MAKE THE PLOTTERS REVEAL THEMSELVES --
-- AND YOU'RE THE MOST USEFUL GUY WE HAVE FOR STIRRING THINGS UP!
YEAH, WELL, I'VE BEEN WONDERIN' ABOUT A REAL PURPOSE LATELY. ONLY NEXT TIME... DON'T BE AFRAID TO FILL ME IN A LITTLE. I MEAN... I'M HAN SOLO. TRUST ME.

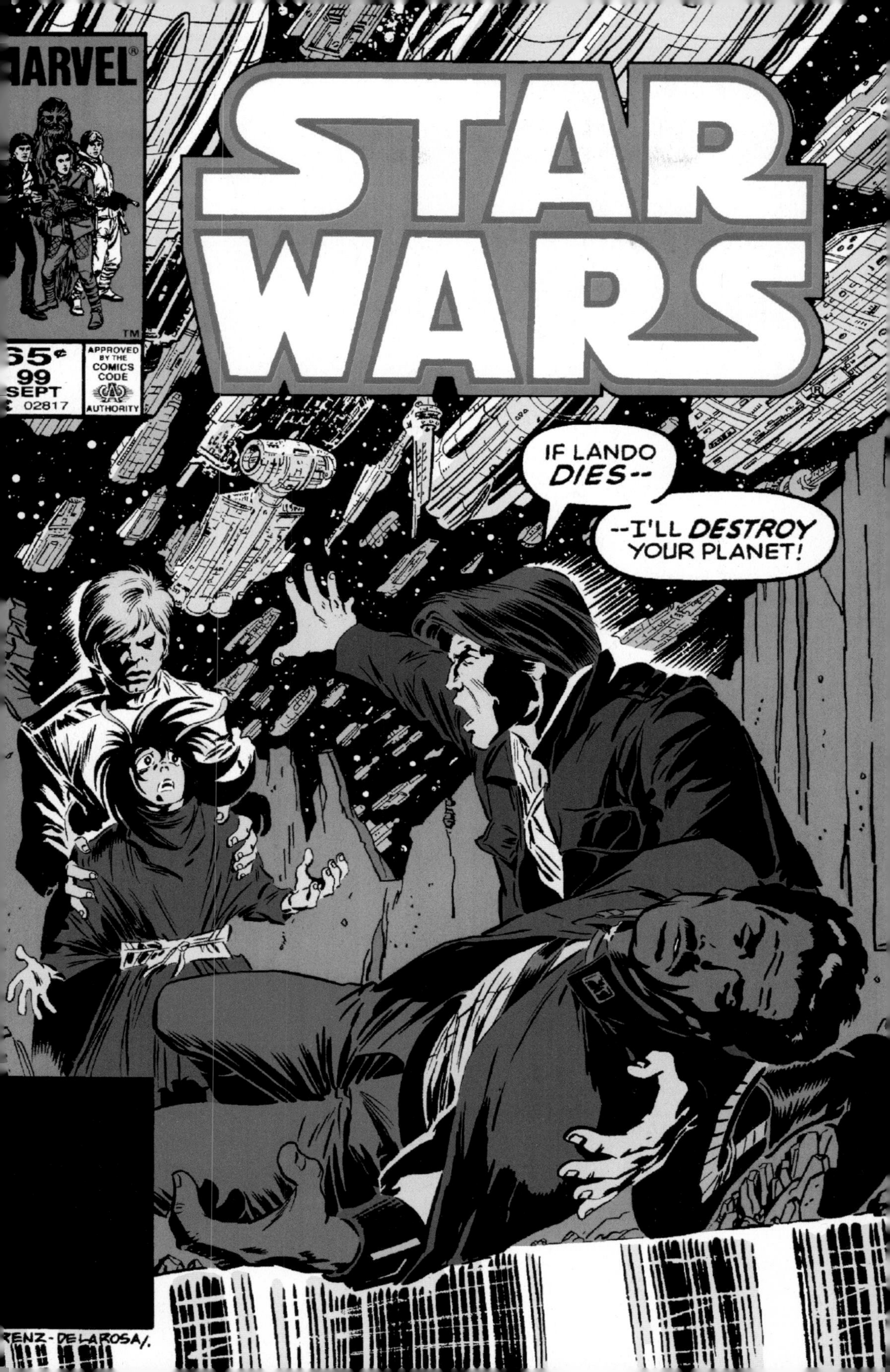
MARVEL
STAR WARS
65¢
99
SEPT
02817
APPROVED BY THE COMICS CODE AUTHORITY
IF LANDO DIES--
--I'LL DESTROY YOUR PLANET!
RENZ-DELAROSA/.

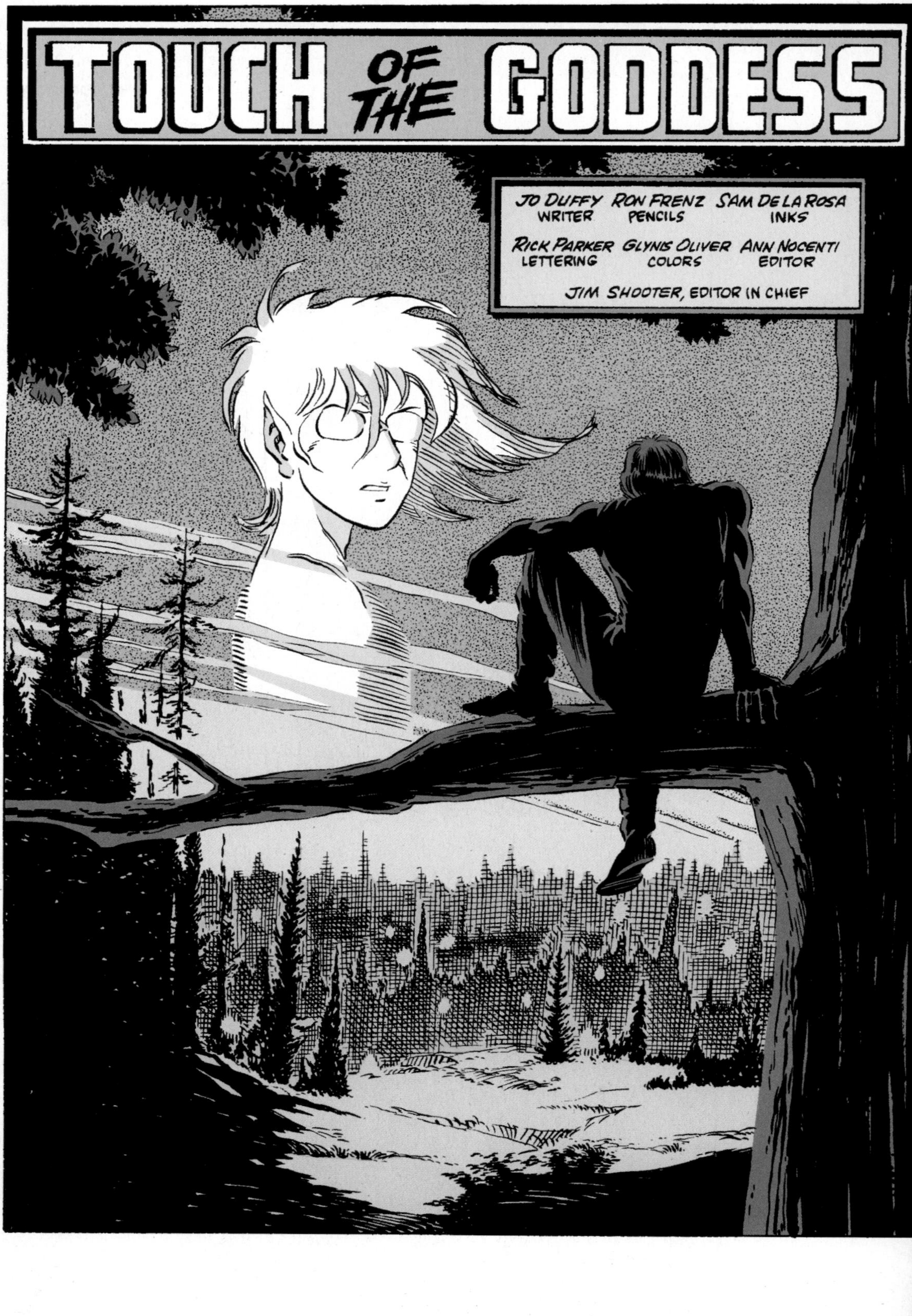
TOUCH OF THE GODDESS
JO DUFFY WRITER
RON FRENZ PENCILS
SAM DE LA ROSA INKS
RICK PARKER LETTERING
GLYNIS OLIVER COLORS
ANN NOCENTI EDITOR
JIM SHOOTER, EDITOR IN CHIEF

LUKE... WHAT ARE YOU THINKING ABOUT?

ABOUT LIFE...AND FRIENDSHIP.

ABOUT KIRO.

ARE YOU BLAMING YOURSELF... FOR HIS DEATH?

WHY NOT? LANDO, I AM RESPONSIBLE.

IT'S NOT LIKE YOU'RE THE ONE WHO KILLED HIM.

NO. BUT HE LEFT HIS HOME, AND HIS PEOPLE, AND DIED IN THE WATERS OF AN ASTEROID LIGHT YEARS FROM WHERE HE BELONGED...

BECAUSE OF ME.

A LOT OF PEOPLE HAVE DIED SINCE THE REBELLION BEGAN.

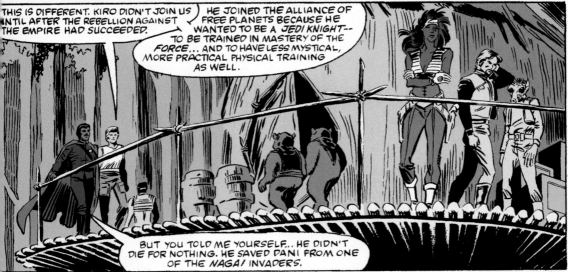

THIS IS DIFFERENT. KIRO DIDN'T JOIN US UNTIL AFTER THE REBELLION AGAINST THE EMPIRE HAD SUCCEEDED.

HE JOINED THE ALLIANCE OF FREE PLANETS BECAUSE HE WANTED TO BE A JEDI KNIGHT-- TO BE TRAINED IN MASTERY OF THE FORCE... AND TO HAVE LESS MYSTICAL, MORE PRACTICAL PHYSICAL TRAINING AS WELL.

BUT YOU TOLD ME YOURSELF... HE DIDN'T DIE FOR NOTHING. HE SAVED DANI FROM ONE OF THE NAGAI INVADERS.

YEAH... AND JUST LOOK AT DANI NOW...

SHE LOVED HIM, LANDO... REALLY LOVED HIM. AND NOW SHE'S HURTING SO MUCH, NOT EVEN HER CLOSEST FRIENDS CAN REACH HER.

CAN YOU BELIEVE IT? A ZELTRON WHO CAN'T BE TOUCHED.

SHE'S NOT THE ONLY UNHAPPY ZELTRON WE HAVE AROUND THE ALLIANCE THESE DAYS.

PRINCESS LEIA'S ATTACHES ARE GLUMMER THAN I EVER THOUGHT THEY COULD BE.

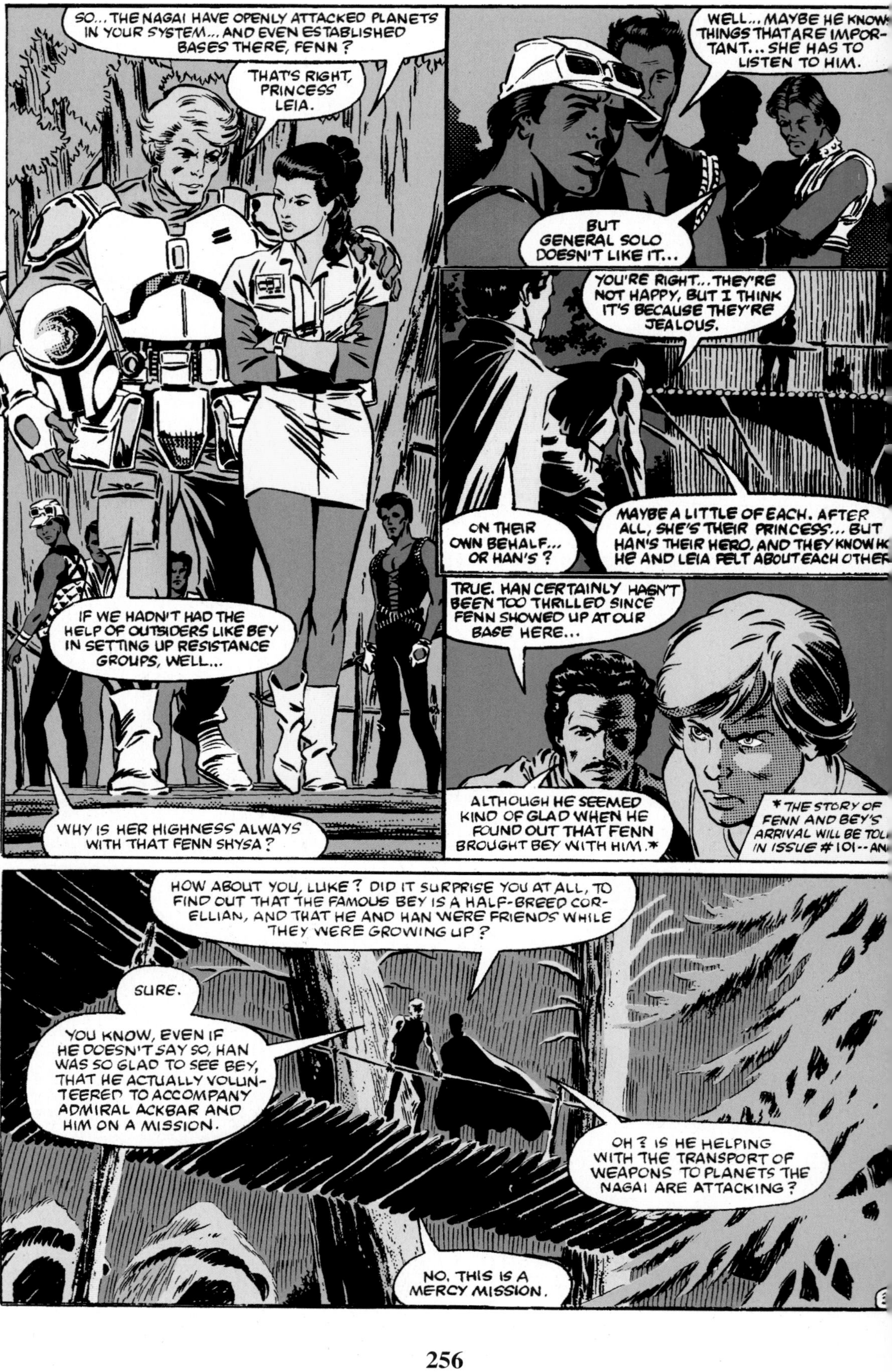
SO... THE NAGAI HAVE OPENLY ATTACKED PLANETS IN YOUR SYSTEM... AND EVEN ESTABLISHED BASES THERE, FENN ?
THAT'S RIGHT, PRINCESS LEIA.
IF WE HADN'T HAD THE HELP OF OUTSIDERS LIKE BEY IN SETTING UP RESISTANCE GROUPS, WELL...
WHY IS HER HIGHNESS ALWAYS WITH THAT FENN SHYSA ?
WELL... MAYBE HE KNOWS THINGS THAT ARE IMPORTANT... SHE HAS TO LISTEN TO HIM.
BUT GENERAL SOLO DOESN'T LIKE IT...
YOU'RE RIGHT... THEY'RE NOT HAPPY, BUT I THINK IT'S BECAUSE THEY'RE JEALOUS.
ON THEIR OWN BEHALF... OR HAN'S ?
MAYBE A LITTLE OF EACH. AFTER ALL, SHE'S THEIR PRINCESS... BUT HAN'S THEIR HERO, AND THEY KNOW H HE AND LEIA FELT ABOUT EACH OTHE
TRUE. HAN CERTAINLY HASN'T BEEN TOO THRILLED SINCE FENN SHOWED UP AT OUR BASE HERE...
ALTHOUGH HE SEEMED KIND OF GLAD WHEN HE FOUND OUT THAT FENN BROUGHT BEY WITH HIM.*
* THE STORY OF FENN AND BEY'S ARRIVAL WILL BE TOL IN ISSUE #101--AN
HOW ABOUT YOU, LUKE ? DID IT SURPRISE YOU AT ALL, TO FIND OUT THAT THE FAMOUS BEY IS A HALF-BREED CORELLIAN, AND THAT HE AND HAN WERE FRIENDS WHILE THEY WERE GROWING UP ?
SURE.
YOU KNOW, EVEN IF HE DOESN'T SAY SO, HAN WAS SO GLAD TO SEE BEY, THAT HE ACTUALLY VOLUNTEERED TO ACCOMPANY ADMIRAL ACKBAR AND HIM ON A MISSION.
OH ? IS HE HELPING WITH THE TRANSPORT OF WEAPONS TO PLANETS THE NAGAI ARE ATTACKING ?
NO, THIS IS A MERCY MISSION.

SO, GENERAL SOLO... HAVE YOU AND BEY BOTH TAKEN THE PROTECTIVE PRECONTAINMENT RADIATION BATHS?

YOU BET, ADMIRAL. BEFORE WE LEFT THE ALLIANCE FLEET.

MY PEOPLE WOULD NOT HAVE GIVEN THE *MILLENNIUM FALCON* PERMISSION TO LAND, HAD WE NOT BEEN ASSURED THAT ITS PILOT AND PASSENGER WERE SHIELDED, ADMIRAL.

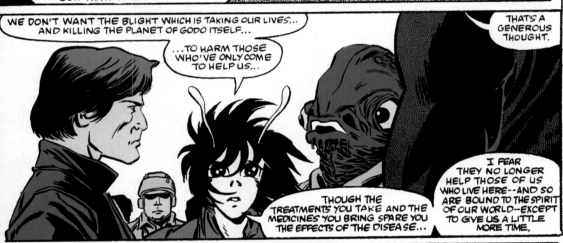

WE DON'T WANT THE BLIGHT WHICH IS TAKING OUR LIVES... AND KILLING THE PLANET OF GODO ITSELF...

...TO HARM THOSE WHO'VE ONLY COME TO HELP US...

THAT'S A GENEROUS THOUGHT.

THOUGH THE TREATMENTS YOU TAKE AND THE MEDICINES YOU BRING SPARE YOU THE EFFECTS OF THE DISEASE...

I FEAR THEY NO LONGER HELP THOSE OF US WHO LIVE HERE--AND SO ARE BOUND TO THE SPIRIT OF OUR WORLD--EXCEPT TO GIVE US A LITTLE MORE TIME.

IT'S INCREDIBLE. YOU CAN SEE... GODO ONCE HOUSED A GREAT CIVILIZATION...

BUT NOW... IT'S LIKE THE PLANET ITSELF ISN'T FIT TO SUPPORT LIFE.

IT'S MORE THAN THAT, HAN... IT SEEMS TO BE POISONING ALL THE LIFE THAT WALKS UPON IT.

ADMIRAL... CAN WE WALK AROUND HERE... CHECK THINGS OUT... TALK TO SOME PEOPLE?

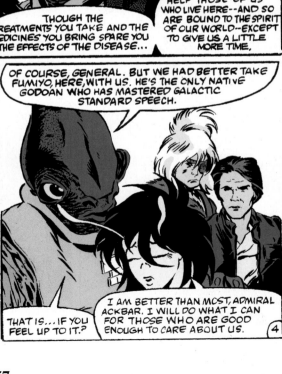

OF COURSE, GENERAL. BUT WE HAD BETTER TAKE FUMIYO, HERE, WITH US. HE'S THE ONLY NATIVE GODOAN WHO HAS MASTERED GALACTIC STANDARD SPEECH.

THAT IS... IF YOU FEEL UP TO IT?

I AM BETTER THAN MOST, ADMIRAL ACKBAR. I WILL DO WHAT I CAN FOR THOSE WHO ARE GOOD ENOUGH TO CARE ABOUT US.

4

257

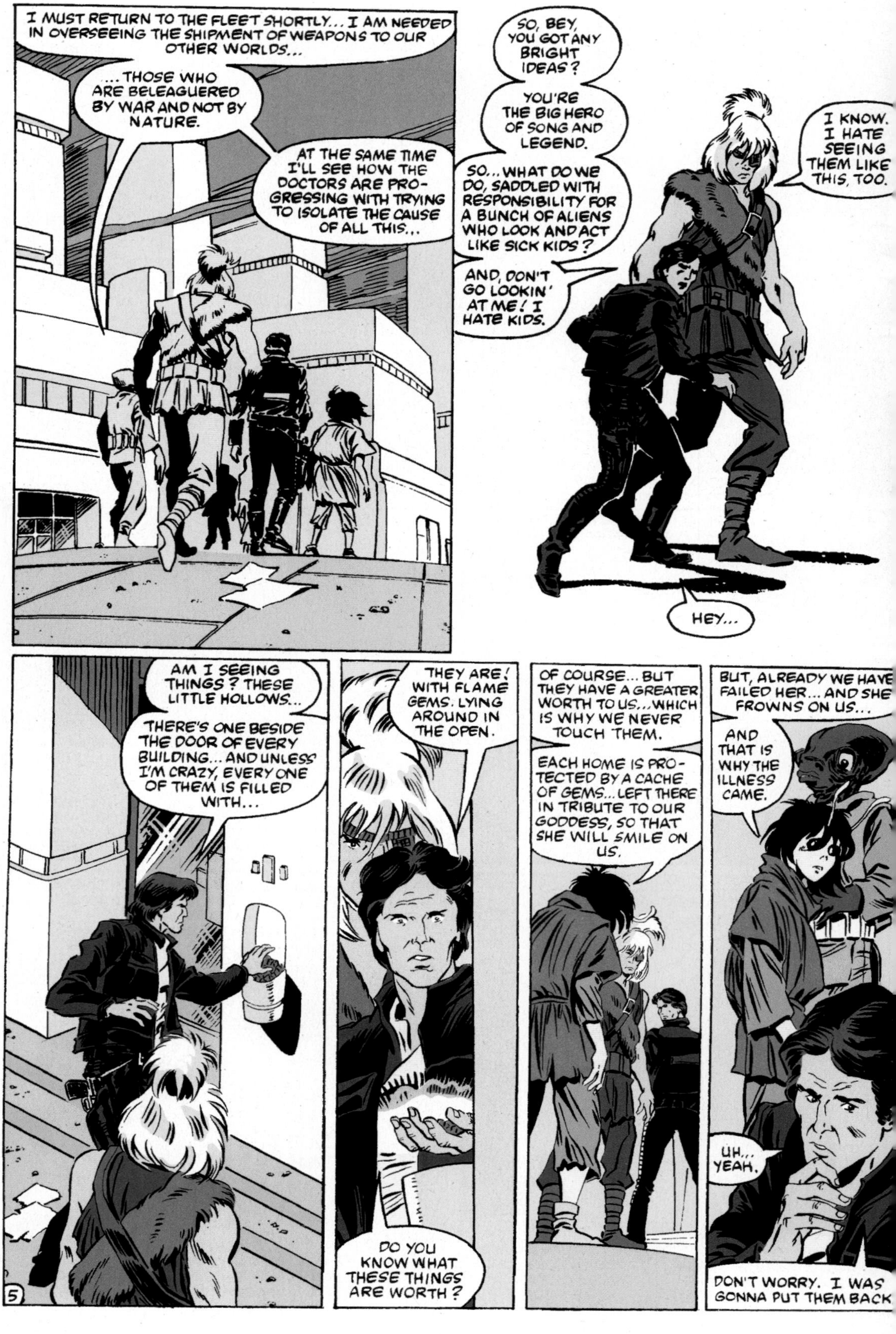
I MUST RETURN TO THE FLEET SHORTLY... I AM NEEDED IN OVERSEEING THE SHIPMENT OF WEAPONS TO OUR OTHER WORLDS...
...THOSE WHO ARE BELEAGUERED BY WAR AND NOT BY NATURE.
AT THE SAME TIME I'LL SEE HOW THE DOCTORS ARE PRO-GRESSING WITH TRYING TO ISOLATE THE CAUSE OF ALL THIS...
SO, BEY, YOU GOT ANY BRIGHT IDEAS?
YOU'RE THE BIG HERO OF SONG AND LEGEND.
SO... WHAT DO WE DO, SADDLED WITH RESPONSIBILITY FOR A BUNCH OF ALIENS WHO LOOK AND ACT LIKE SICK KIDS?
AND, DON'T GO LOOKIN' AT ME! I HATE KIDS.
I KNOW. I HATE SEEING THEM LIKE THIS, TOO.
HEY...
AM I SEEING THINGS? THESE LITTLE HOLLOWS...
THERE'S ONE BESIDE THE DOOR OF EVERY BUILDING... AND UNLESS I'M CRAZY, EVERY ONE OF THEM IS FILLED WITH...
THEY ARE! WITH FLAME GEMS. LYING AROUND IN THE OPEN.
DO YOU KNOW WHAT THESE THINGS ARE WORTH?
OF COURSE... BUT THEY HAVE A GREATER WORTH TO US... WHICH IS WHY WE NEVER TOUCH THEM.
EACH HOME IS PRO-TECTED BY A CACHE OF GEMS... LEFT THERE IN TRIBUTE TO OUR GODDESS, SO THAT SHE WILL SMILE ON US.
BUT, ALREADY WE HAVE FAILED HER... AND SHE FROWNS ON US...
AND THAT IS WHY THE ILLNESS CAME.
UH... YEAH.
DON'T WORRY. I WAS GONNA PUT THEM BACK
5

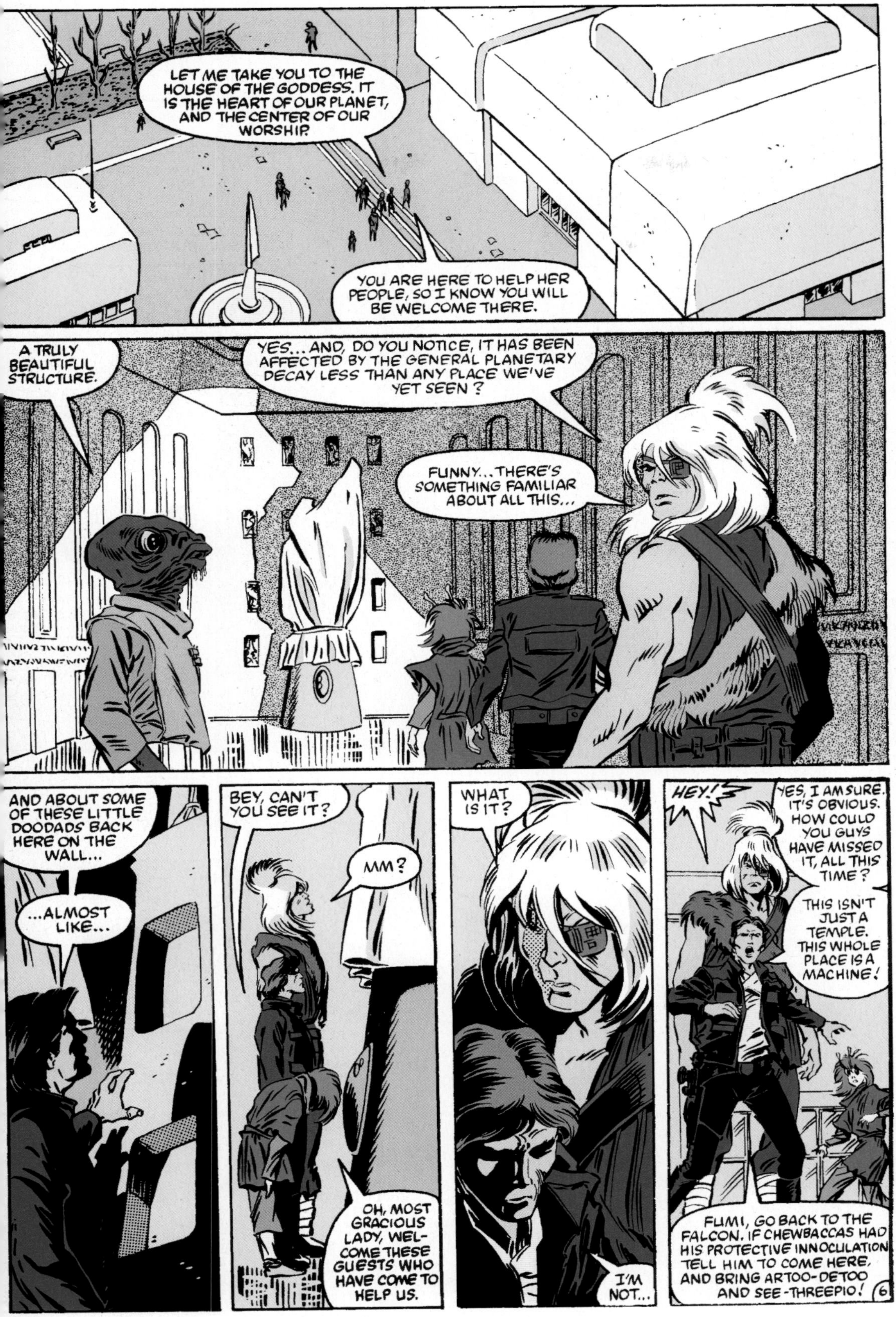
LET ME TAKE YOU TO THE HOUSE OF THE GODDESS. IT IS THE HEART OF OUR PLANET, AND THE CENTER OF OUR WORSHIP.
YOU ARE HERE TO HELP HER PEOPLE, SO I KNOW YOU WILL BE WELCOME THERE.
A TRULY BEAUTIFUL STRUCTURE.
YES... AND, DO YOU NOTICE, IT HAS BEEN AFFECTED BY THE GENERAL PLANETARY DECAY LESS THAN ANY PLACE WE'VE YET SEEN?
FUNNY... THERE'S SOMETHING FAMILIAR ABOUT ALL THIS...
AND ABOUT SOME OF THESE LITTLE DOODADS BACK HERE ON THE WALL...
...ALMOST LIKE...
BEY, CAN'T YOU SEE IT?
MM?
OH, MOST GRACIOUS LADY, WEL-COME THESE GUESTS WHO HAVE COME TO HELP US.
WHAT IS IT?
I'M NOT...
HEY!
YES, I AM SURE. IT'S OBVIOUS. HOW COULD YOU GUYS HAVE MISSED IT, ALL THIS TIME?
THIS ISN'T JUST A TEMPLE. THIS WHOLE PLACE IS A MACHINE!
FLIMI, GO BACK TO THE FALCON. IF CHEWBACCAS HAD HIS PROTECTIVE INNOCULATION TELL HIM TO COME HERE, AND BRING ARTOO-DETOO AND SEE-THREEPIO!
6

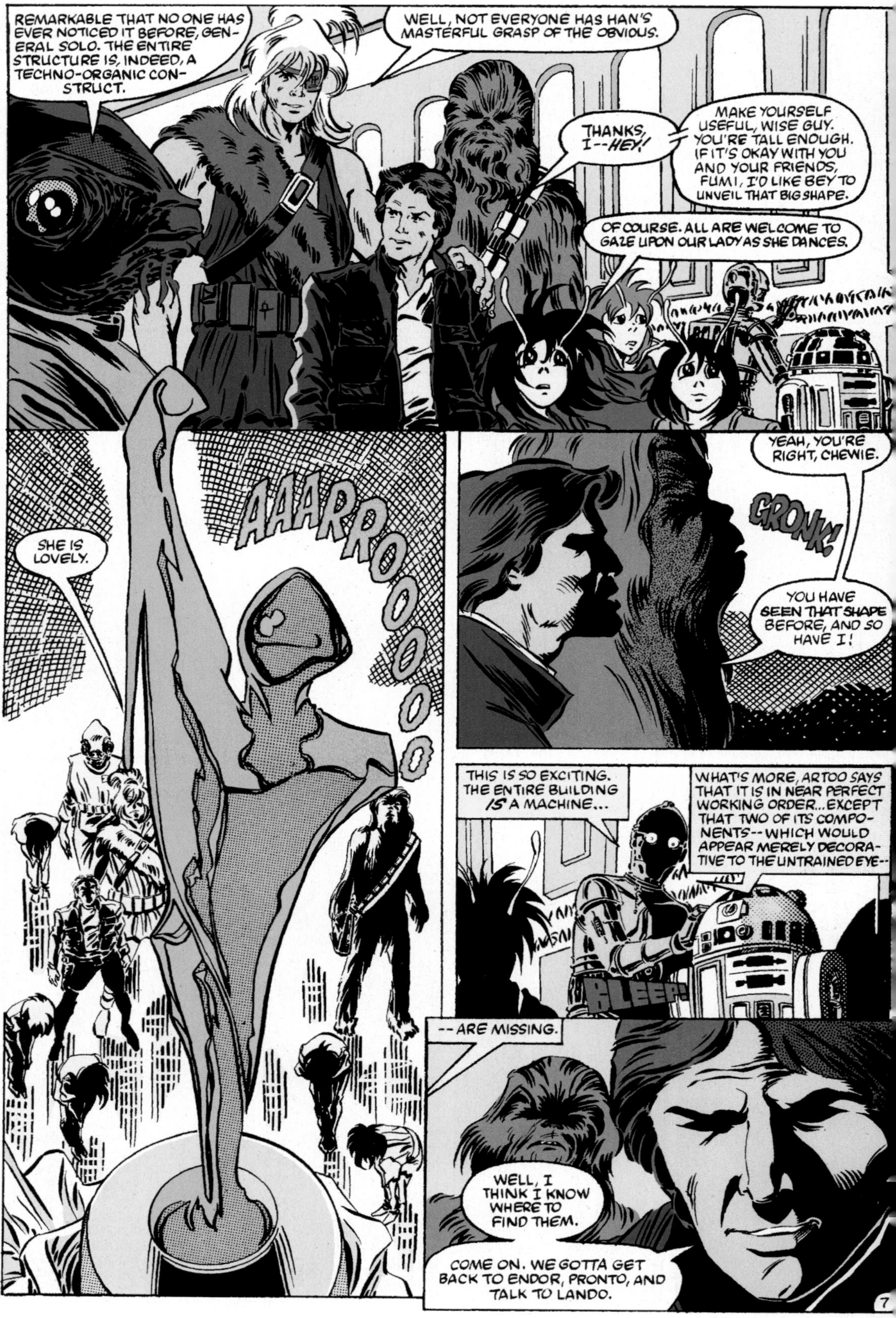
REMARKABLE THAT NO ONE HAS EVER NOTICED IT BEFORE, GENERAL SOLO. THE ENTIRE STRUCTURE IS, INDEED, A TECHNO-ORGANIC CONSTRUCT.
WELL, NOT EVERYONE HAS HAN'S MASTERFUL GRASP OF THE OBVIOUS.
THANKS, I--HEY!
MAKE YOURSELF USEFUL, WISE GUY. YOU'RE TALL ENOUGH. IF IT'S OKAY WITH YOU AND YOUR FRIENDS, FUMI, I'D LIKE BEY TO UNVEIL THAT BIG SHAPE.
OF COURSE. ALL ARE WELCOME TO GAZE UPON OUR LADY AS SHE DANCES.
AAARROOOOOOO
SHE IS LOVELY.
YEAH, YOU'RE RIGHT, CHEWIE.
GRONK!
YOU HAVE SEEN THAT SHAPE BEFORE, AND SO HAVE I!
THIS IS SO EXCITING. THE ENTIRE BUILDING IS A MACHINE...
WHAT'S MORE, ARTOO SAYS THAT IT IS IN NEAR PERFECT WORKING ORDER...EXCEPT THAT TWO OF ITS' COMPONENTS--WHICH WOULD APPEAR MERELY DECORATIVE TO THE UNTRAINED EYE--
BLEEP!
--ARE MISSING.
WELL, I THINK I KNOW WHERE TO FIND THEM.
COME ON. WE GOTTA GET BACK TO ENDOR, PRONTO, AND TALK TO LANDO.
7

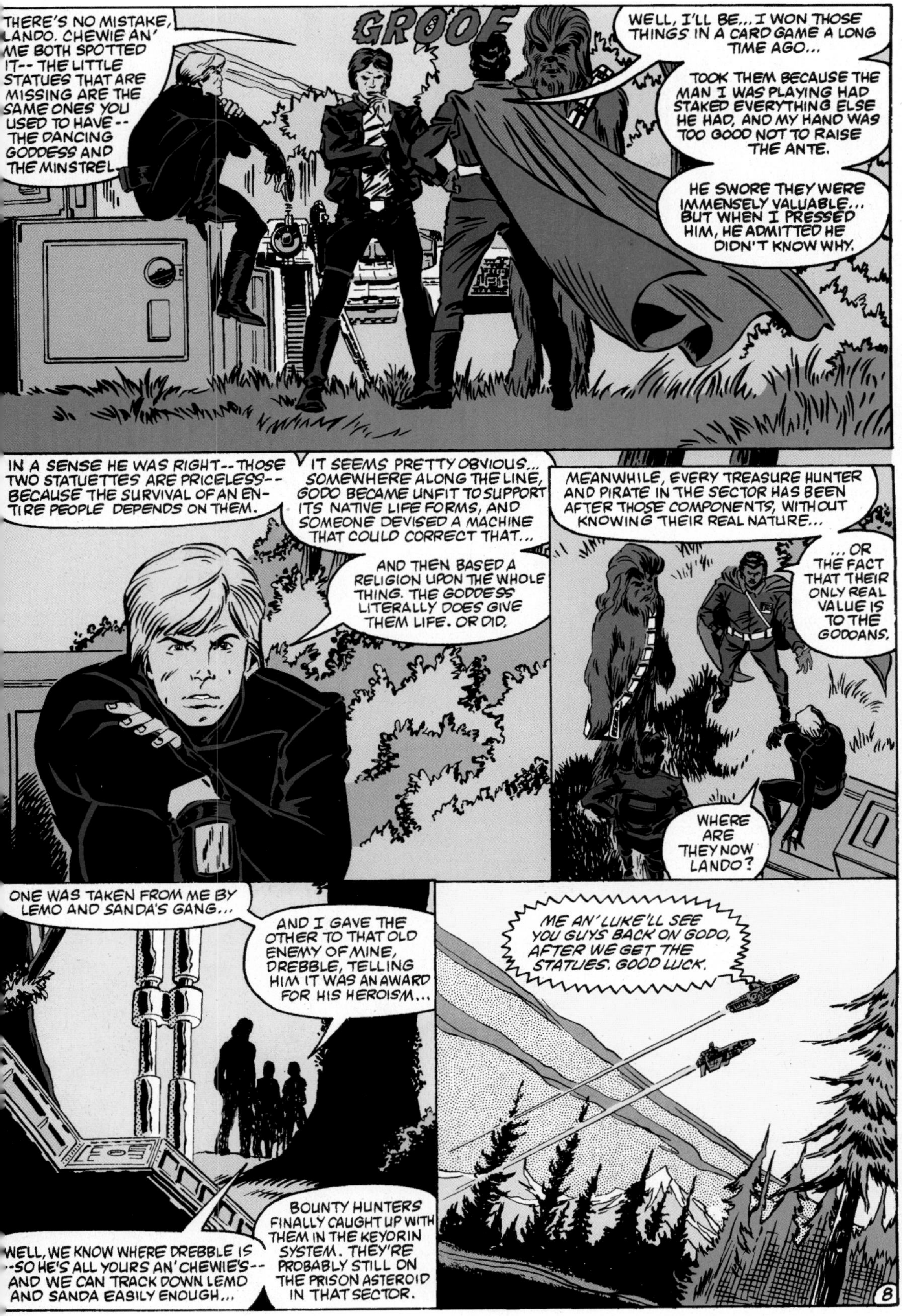
THERE'S NO MISTAKE, LANDO. CHEWIE AN' ME BOTH SPOTTED IT-- THE LITTLE STATUES THAT ARE MISSING ARE THE SAME ONES YOU USED TO HAVE-- THE DANCING GODDESS AND THE MINSTREL.
GROOF
WELL, I'LL BE... I WON THOSE THINGS IN A CARD GAME A LONG TIME AGO...
TOOK THEM BECAUSE THE MAN I WAS PLAYING HAD STAKED EVERYTHING ELSE HE HAD, AND MY HAND WAS TOO GOOD NOT TO RAISE THE ANTE.
HE SWORE THEY WERE IMMENSELY VALUABLE... BUT WHEN I PRESSED HIM, HE ADMITTED HE DIDN'T KNOW WHY.
IN A SENSE HE WAS RIGHT--THOSE TWO STATUETTES ARE PRICELESS-- BECAUSE THE SURVIVAL OF AN ENTIRE PEOPLE DEPENDS ON THEM.
IT SEEMS PRETTY OBVIOUS... SOMEWHERE ALONG THE LINE, GODO BECAME UNFIT TO SUPPORT ITS NATIVE LIFE FORMS, AND SOMEONE DEVISED A MACHINE THAT COULD CORRECT THAT...
AND THEN BASED A RELIGION UPON THE WHOLE THING. THE GODDESS LITERALLY DOES GIVE THEM LIFE. OR DID.
MEANWHILE, EVERY TREASURE HUNTER AND PIRATE IN THE SECTOR HAS BEEN AFTER THOSE COMPONENTS, WITHOUT KNOWING THEIR REAL NATURE...
...OR THE FACT THAT THEIR ONLY REAL VALUE IS TO THE GODOANS.
WHERE ARE THEY NOW LANDO?
ONE WAS TAKEN FROM ME BY LEMO AND SANDA'S GANG...
AND I GAVE THE OTHER TO THAT OLD ENEMY OF MINE, DREBBLE, TELLING HIM IT WAS AN AWARD FOR HIS HEROISM...
BOUNTY HUNTERS FINALLY CAUGHT UP WITH THEM IN THE KEYORIN SYSTEM. THEY'RE PROBABLY STILL ON THE PRISON ASTEROID IN THAT SECTOR.
WELL, WE KNOW WHERE DREBBLE IS --SO HE'S ALL YOURS AN' CHEWIE'S-- AND WE CAN TRACK DOWN LEMO AND SANDA EASILY ENOUGH...
ME AN' LUKE'LL SEE YOU GUYS BACK ON GODO, AFTER WE GET THE STATUES. GOOD LUCK.
8

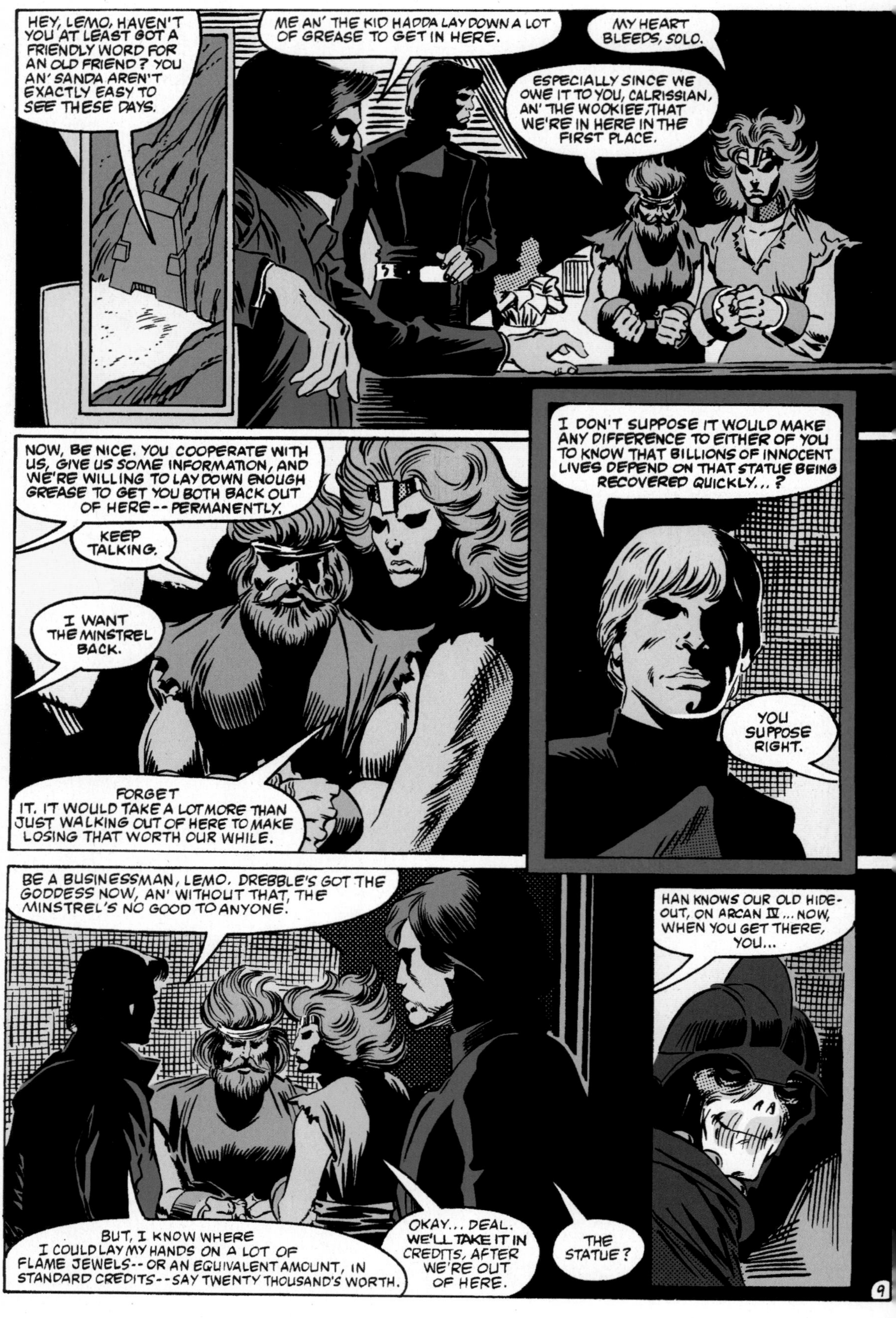
HEY, LEMO, HAVEN'T YOU AT LEAST GOT A FRIENDLY WORD FOR AN OLD FRIEND? YOU AN' SANDA AREN'T EXACTLY EASY TO SEE THESE DAYS.
ME AN' THE KID HADDA LAY DOWN A LOT OF GREASE TO GET IN HERE.
MY HEART BLEEDS, SOLO.
ESPECIALLY SINCE WE OWE IT TO YOU, CALRISSIAN, AN' THE WOOKIEE, THAT WE'RE IN HERE IN THE FIRST PLACE.
NOW, BE NICE. YOU COOPERATE WITH US, GIVE US SOME INFORMATION, AND WE'RE WILLING TO LAY DOWN ENOUGH GREASE TO GET YOU BOTH BACK OUT OF HERE--PERMANENTLY.
KEEP TALKING.
I WANT THE MINSTREL BACK.
FORGET IT. IT WOULD TAKE A LOT MORE THAN JUST WALKING OUT OF HERE TO MAKE LOSING THAT WORTH OUR WHILE.
I DON'T SUPPOSE IT WOULD MAKE ANY DIFFERENCE TO EITHER OF YOU TO KNOW THAT BILLIONS OF INNOCENT LIVES DEPEND ON THAT STATUE BEING RECOVERED QUICKLY...?
YOU SUPPOSE RIGHT.
BE A BUSINESSMAN, LEMO. DREBBLE'S GOT THE GODDESS NOW, AN' WITHOUT THAT, THE MINSTREL'S NO GOOD TO ANYONE.
BUT, I KNOW WHERE I COULD LAY MY HANDS ON A LOT OF FLAME JEWELS--OR AN EQUIVALENT AMOUNT, IN STANDARD CREDITS--SAY TWENTY THOUSAND'S WORTH.
OKAY... DEAL. WE'LL TAKE IT IN CREDITS, AFTER WE'RE OUT OF HERE.
THE STATUE?
HAN KNOWS OUR OLD HIDE-OUT, ON ARCAN IV... NOW, WHEN YOU GET THERE, YOU...
9

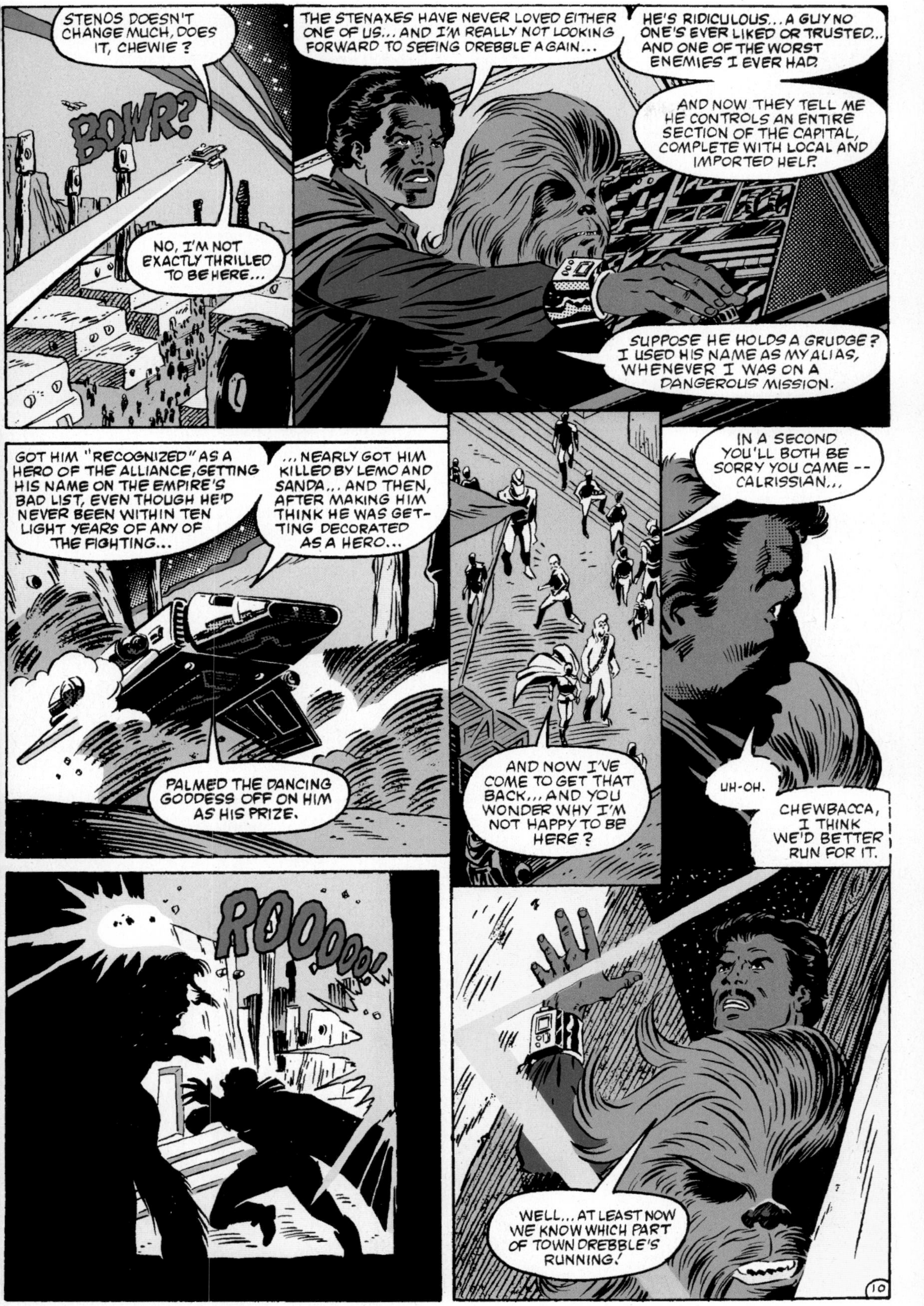
STENOS DOESN'T CHANGE MUCH, DOES IT, CHEWIE?
BOWR?
NO, I'M NOT EXACTLY THRILLED TO BE HERE...
THE STENAXES HAVE NEVER LOVED EITHER ONE OF US... AND I'M REALLY NOT LOOKING FORWARD TO SEEING DREBBLE AGAIN...
HE'S RIDICULOUS... A GUY NO ONE'S EVER LIKED OR TRUSTED... AND ONE OF THE WORST ENEMIES I EVER HAD.
AND NOW THEY TELL ME HE CONTROLS AN ENTIRE SECTION OF THE CAPITAL, COMPLETE WITH LOCAL AND IMPORTED HELP.
SUPPOSE HE HOLDS A GRUDGE? I USED HIS NAME AS MY ALIAS, WHENEVER I WAS ON A DANGEROUS MISSION.
GOT HIM "RECOGNIZED" AS A HERO OF THE ALLIANCE, GETTING HIS NAME ON THE EMPIRE'S BAD LIST, EVEN THOUGH HE'D NEVER BEEN WITHIN TEN LIGHT YEARS OF ANY OF THE FIGHTING...
...NEARLY GOT HIM KILLED BY LEMO AND SANDA... AND THEN, AFTER MAKING HIM THINK HE WAS GETTING DECORATED AS A HERO...
PALMED THE DANCING GODDESS OFF ON HIM AS HIS PRIZE.
AND NOW I'VE COME TO GET THAT BACK... AND YOU WONDER WHY I'M NOT HAPPY TO BE HERE?
IN A SECOND YOU'LL BOTH BE SORRY YOU CAME -- CALRISSIAN...
UH-OH.
CHEWBACCA, I THINK WE'D BETTER RUN FOR IT.
ROOOOOO!
WELL... AT LEAST NOW WE KNOW WHICH PART OF TOWN DREBBLE'S RUNNING!
10

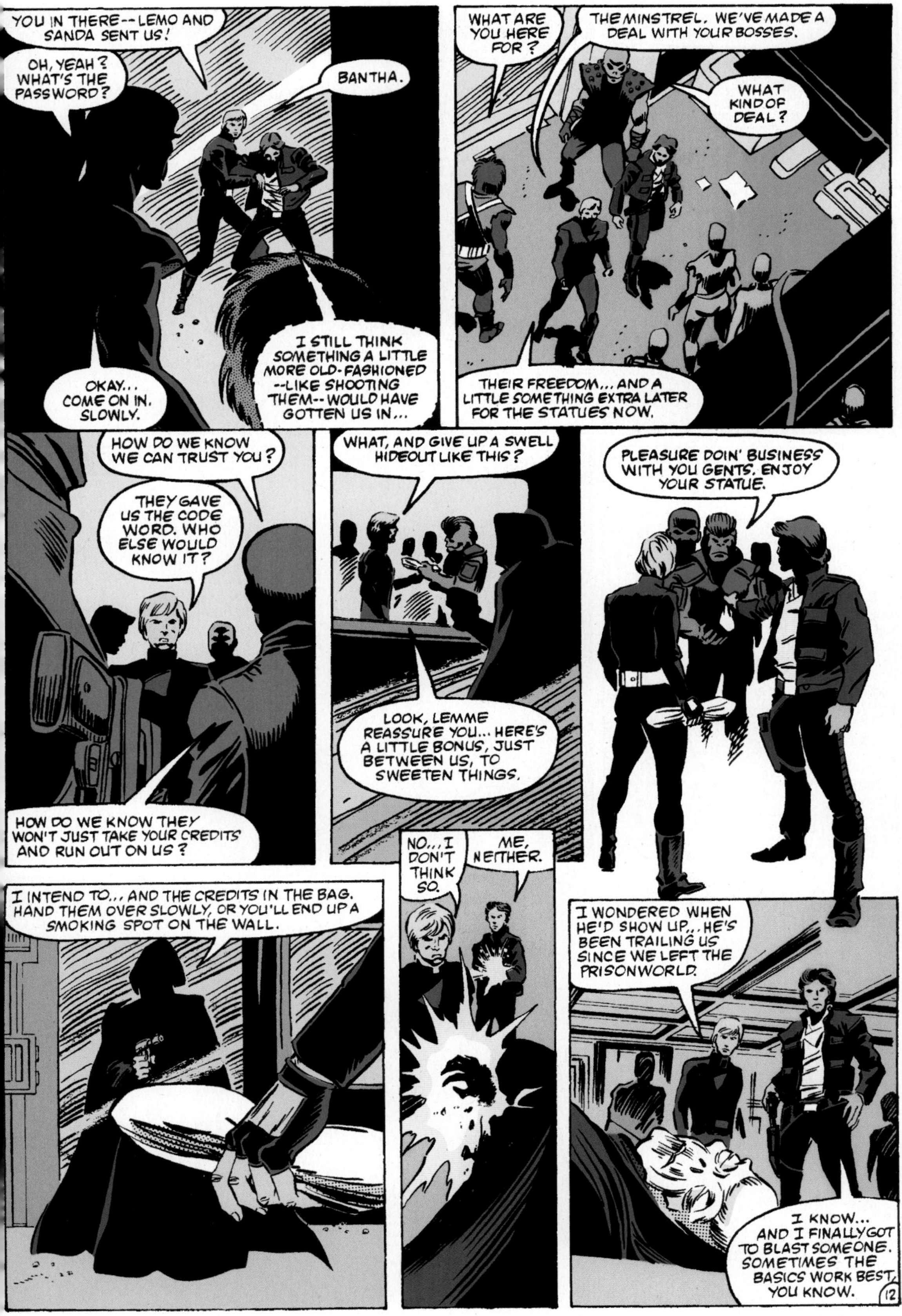
YOU IN THERE--LEMO AND SANDA SENT US!
OH, YEAH? WHAT'S THE PASSWORD?
BANTHA.
OKAY... COME ON IN. SLOWLY.
I STILL THINK SOMETHING A LITTLE MORE OLD-FASHIONED --LIKE SHOOTING THEM--WOULD HAVE GOTTEN US IN...
WHAT ARE YOU HERE FOR?
THE MINSTREL. WE'VE MADE A DEAL WITH YOUR BOSSES.
WHAT KIND OF DEAL?
THEIR FREEDOM... AND A LITTLE SOMETHING EXTRA LATER FOR THE STATUES NOW.
HOW DO WE KNOW WE CAN TRUST YOU?
THEY GAVE US THE CODE WORD. WHO ELSE WOULD KNOW IT?
HOW DO WE KNOW THEY WON'T JUST TAKE YOUR CREDITS AND RUN OUT ON US?
WHAT, AND GIVE UP A SWELL HIDEOUT LIKE THIS?
LOOK, LEMME REASSURE YOU... HERE'S A LITTLE BONUS, JUST BETWEEN US, TO SWEETEN THINGS.
PLEASURE DOIN' BUSINESS WITH YOU GENTS. ENJOY YOUR STATUE.
I INTEND TO... AND THE CREDITS IN THE BAG. HAND THEM OVER SLOWLY, OR YOU'LL END UP A SMOKING SPOT ON THE WALL.
NO... I DON'T THINK SO.
ME, NEITHER.
I WONDERED WHEN HE'D SHOW UP... HE'S BEEN TRAILING US SINCE WE LEFT THE PRISONWORLD.
I KNOW... AND I FINALLY GOT TO BLAST SOMEONE. SOMETIMES THE BASICS WORK BEST, YOU KNOW.
12

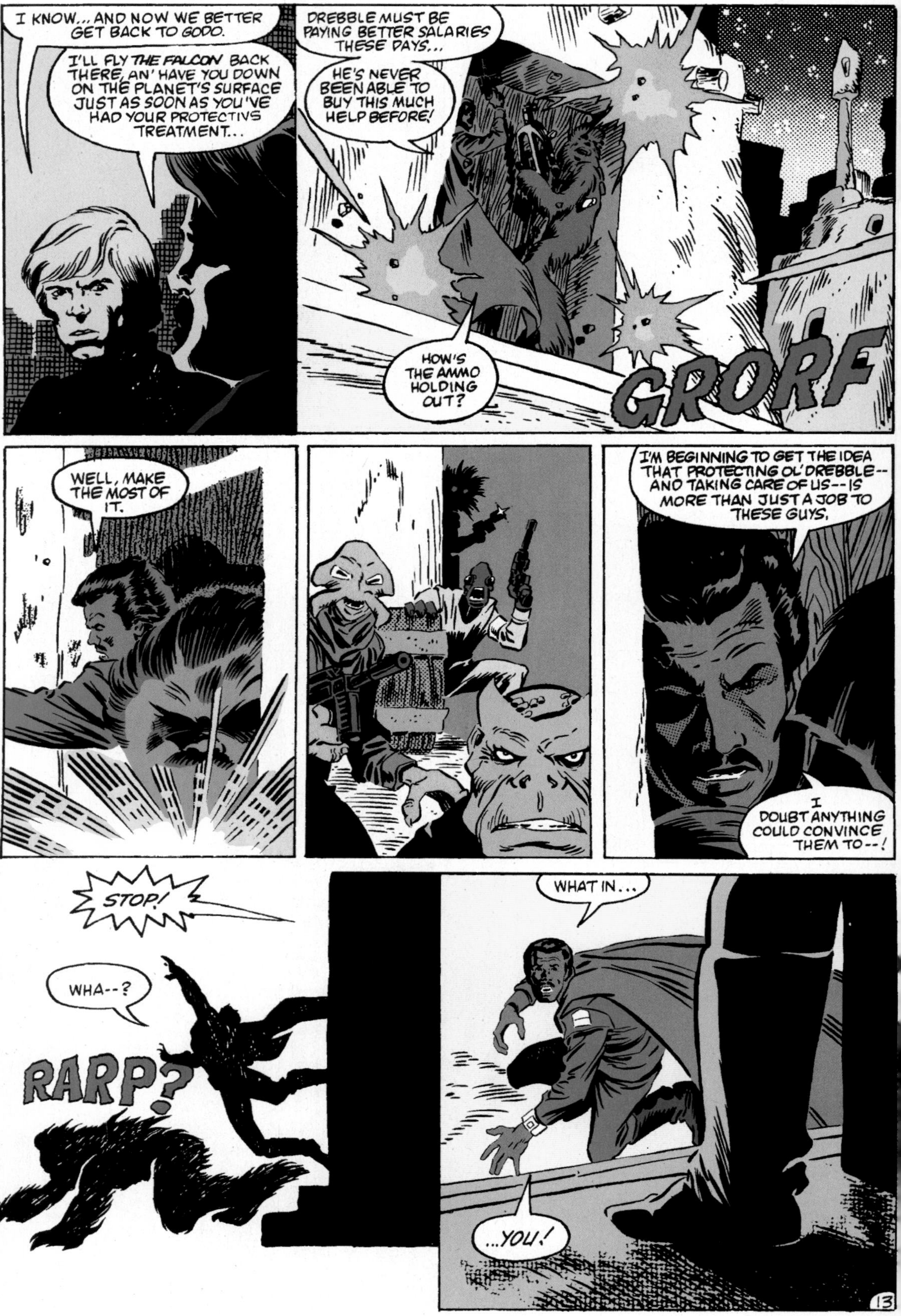
I KNOW... AND NOW WE BETTER GET BACK TO GODO.
I'LL FLY THE FALCON BACK THERE, AN' HAVE YOU DOWN ON THE PLANET'S SURFACE JUST AS SOON AS YOU'VE HAD YOUR PROTECTIVS TREATMENT...
DREBBLE MUST BE PAYING BETTER SALARIES THESE DAYS...
HE'S NEVER BEEN ABLE TO BUY THIS MUCH HELP BEFORE!
HOW'S THE AMMO HOLDING OUT?
GRORF
WELL, MAKE THE MOST OF IT.
I'M BEGINNING TO GET THE IDEA THAT PROTECTING OL' DREBBLE-- AND TAKING CARE OF US-- IS MORE THAN JUST A JOB TO THESE GUYS.
I DOUBT ANYTHING COULD CONVINCE THEM TO--!
STOP!
WHA--?
RARP?
WHAT IN...
...YOU!
13

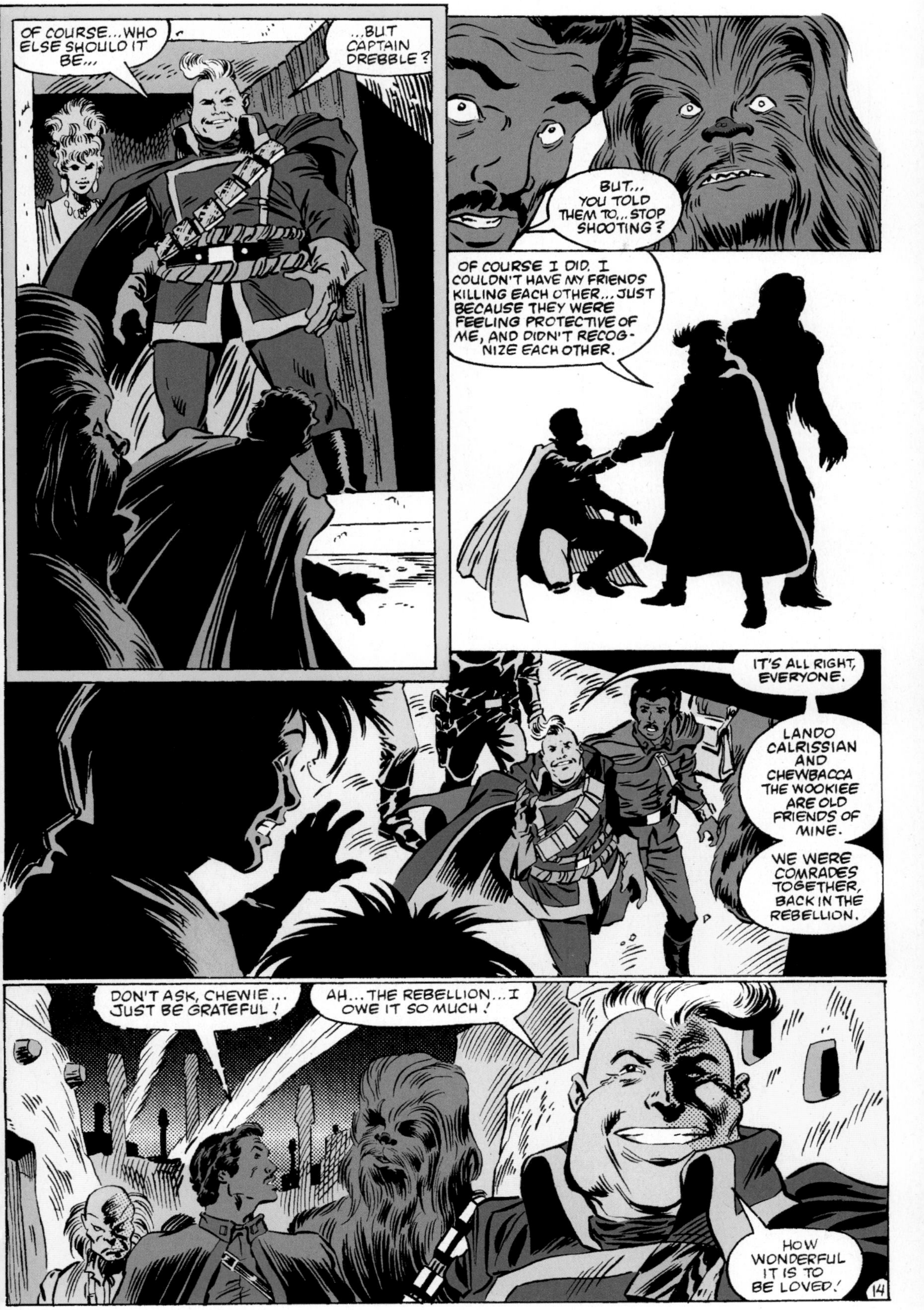
OF COURSE...WHO ELSE SHOULD IT BE...
...BUT CAPTAIN DREBBLE?
BUT... YOU TOLD THEM TO... STOP SHOOTING?
OF COURSE I DID. I COULDN'T HAVE MY FRIENDS KILLING EACH OTHER... JUST BECAUSE THEY WERE FEELING PROTECTIVE OF ME, AND DIDN'T RECOGNIZE EACH OTHER.
IT'S ALL RIGHT, EVERYONE.
LANDO CALRISSIAN AND CHEWBACCA THE WOOKIEE ARE OLD FRIENDS OF MINE.
WE WERE COMRADES TOGETHER, BACK IN THE REBELLION.
DON'T ASK, CHEWIE... JUST BE GRATEFUL!
AH... THE REBELLION... I OWE IT SO MUCH!
HOW WONDERFUL IT IS TO BE LOVED!
14

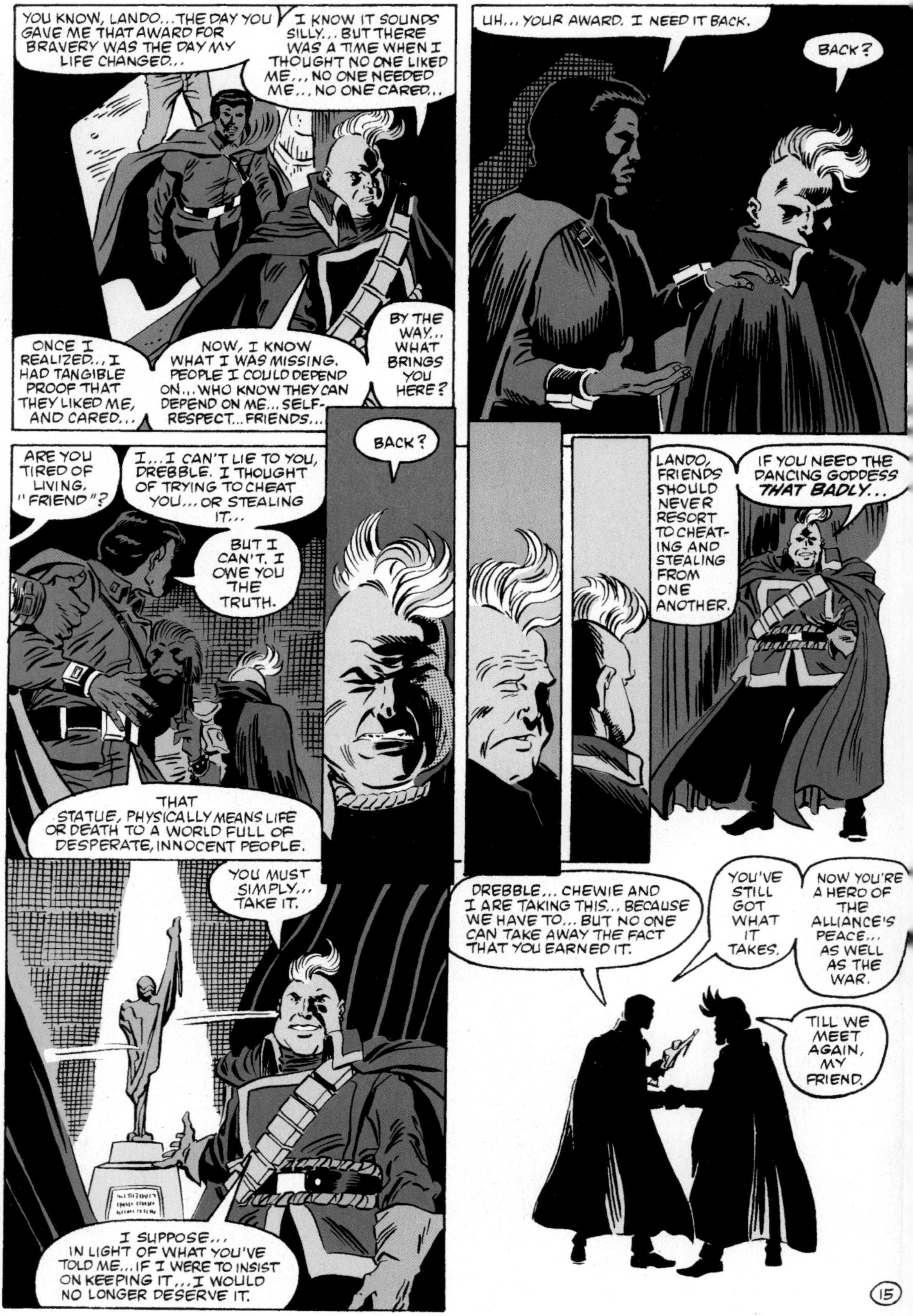
YOU KNOW, LANDO... THE DAY YOU GAVE ME THAT AWARD FOR BRAVERY WAS THE DAY MY LIFE CHANGED...
I KNOW IT SOUNDS SILLY... BUT THERE WAS A TIME WHEN I THOUGHT NO ONE LIKED ME... NO ONE NEEDED ME... NO ONE CARED...
ONCE I REALIZED... I HAD TANGIBLE PROOF THAT THEY LIKED ME, AND CARED...
NOW, I KNOW WHAT I WAS MISSING. PEOPLE I COULD DEPEND ON... WHO KNOW THEY CAN DEPEND ON ME... SELF-RESPECT... FRIENDS...
BY THE WAY... WHAT BRINGS YOU HERE?
UH... YOUR AWARD. I NEED IT BACK.
BACK?
ARE YOU TIRED OF LIVING, "FRIEND"?
I... I CAN'T LIE TO YOU, DREBBLE. I THOUGHT OF TRYING TO CHEAT YOU... OR STEALING IT...
BUT I CAN'T. I OWE YOU THE TRUTH.
THAT STATUE, PHYSICALLY MEANS LIFE OR DEATH TO A WORLD FULL OF DESPERATE, INNOCENT PEOPLE.
BACK?
LANDO, FRIENDS SHOULD NEVER RESORT TO CHEATING AND STEALING FROM ONE ANOTHER.
IF YOU NEED THE DANCING GODDESS *THAT BADLY...*
YOU MUST SIMPLY... TAKE IT.
I SUPPOSE... IN LIGHT OF WHAT YOU'VE TOLD ME... IF I WERE TO INSIST ON KEEPING IT... I WOULD NO LONGER DESERVE IT.
DREBBLE... CHEWIE AND I ARE TAKING THIS... BECAUSE WE HAVE TO... BUT NO ONE CAN TAKE AWAY THE FACT THAT YOU EARNED IT.
YOU'VE STILL GOT WHAT IT TAKES.
NOW YOU'RE A HERO OF THE ALLIANCE'S PEACE... AS WELL AS THE WAR.
TILL WE MEET AGAIN, MY FRIEND.
15

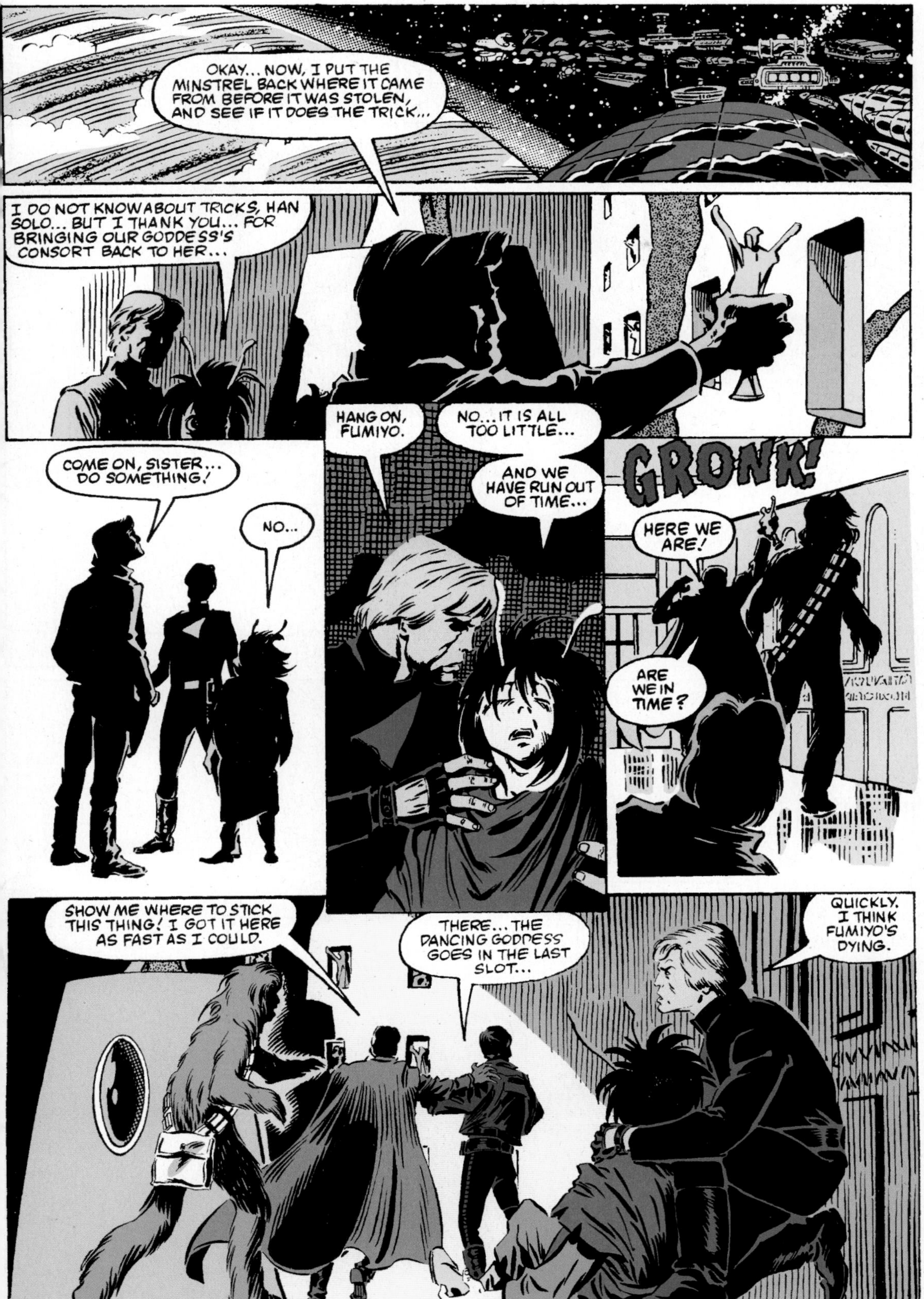
OKAY... NOW, I PUT THE MINSTREL BACK WHERE IT CAME FROM BEFORE IT WAS STOLEN, AND SEE IF IT DOES THE TRICK...
I DO NOT KNOW ABOUT TRICKS, HAN SOLO... BUT I THANK YOU... FOR BRINGING OUR GODDESS'S CONSORT BACK TO HER...
COME ON, SISTER... DO SOMETHING!
NO...
HANG ON, FUMIYO.
NO... IT IS ALL TOO LITTLE...
AND WE HAVE RUN OUT OF TIME...
GRONK!
HERE WE ARE!
ARE WE IN TIME?
SHOW ME WHERE TO STICK THIS THING! I GOT IT HERE AS FAST AS I COULD.
THERE... THE DANCING GODDESS GOES IN THE LAST SLOT...
QUICKLY. I THINK FUMIYO'S DYING.
16

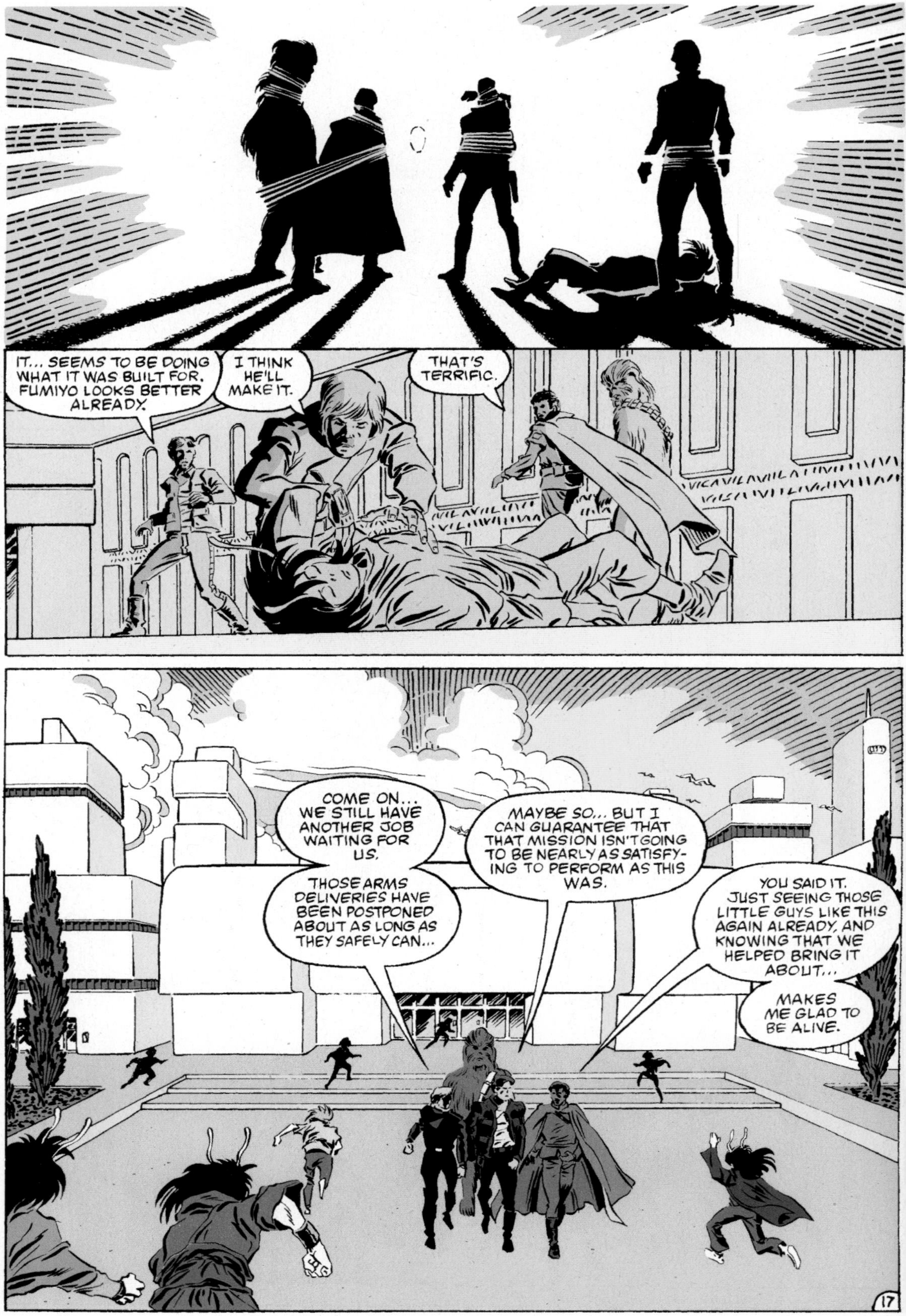
IT... SEEMS TO BE DOING WHAT IT WAS BUILT FOR. FUMIYO LOOKS BETTER ALREADY.
I THINK HE'LL MAKE IT.
THAT'S TERRIFIC.
COME ON... WE STILL HAVE ANOTHER JOB WAITING FOR US.
THOSE ARMS DELIVERIES HAVE BEEN POSTPONED ABOUT AS LONG AS THEY SAFELY CAN...
MAYBE SO... BUT I CAN GUARANTEE THAT THAT MISSION ISN'T GOING TO BE NEARLY AS SATISFY-ING TO PERFORM AS THIS WAS.
YOU SAID IT. JUST SEEING THOSE LITTLE GUYS LIKE THIS AGAIN ALREADY, AND KNOWING THAT WE HELPED BRING IT ABOUT...
MAKES ME GLAD TO BE ALIVE.
17

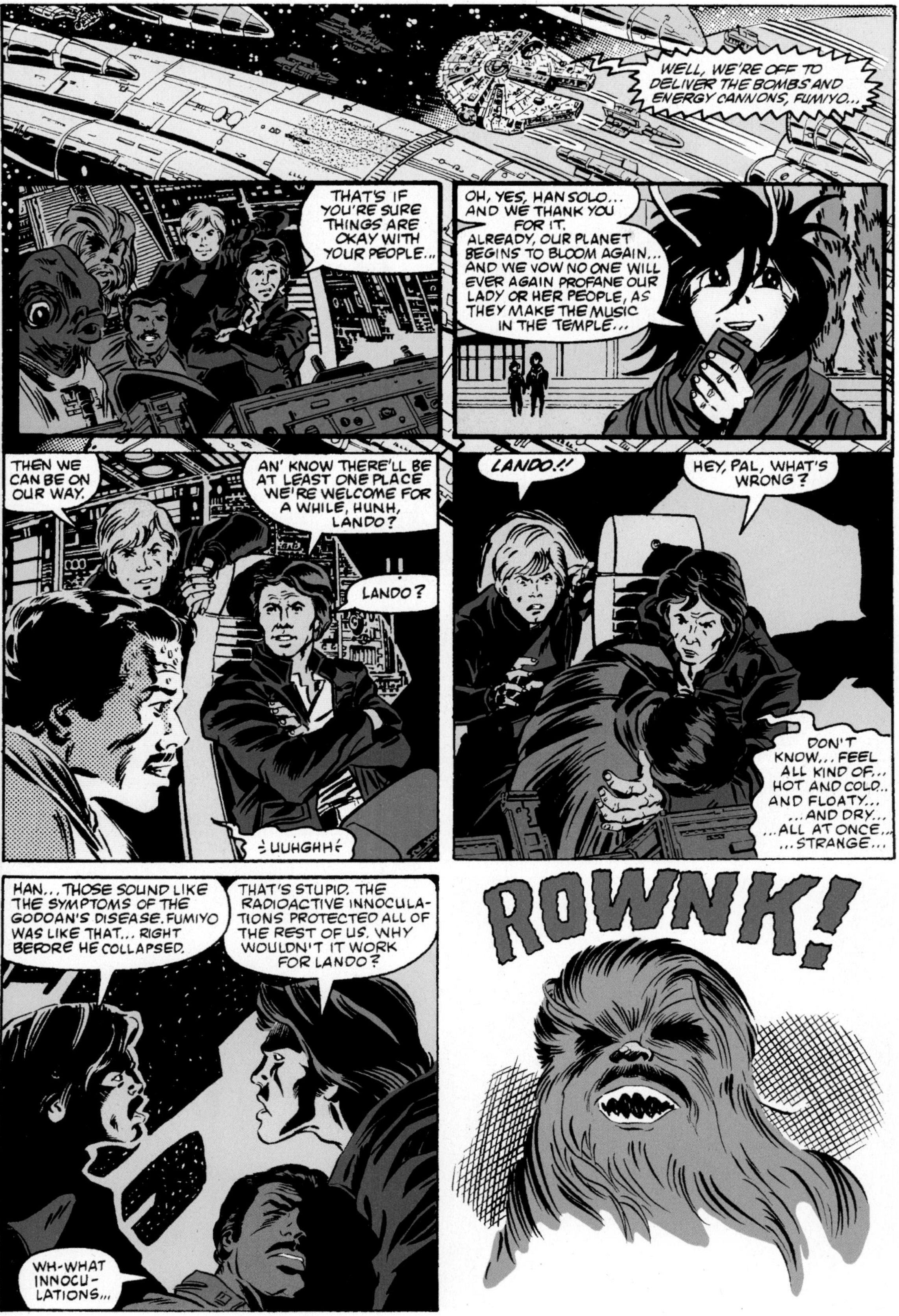
WELL, WE'RE OFF TO DELIVER THE BOMBS AND ENERGY CANNONS, FUMIYO...
THAT'S IF YOU'RE SURE THINGS ARE OKAY WITH YOUR PEOPLE...
OH, YES, HAN SOLO... AND WE THANK YOU FOR IT.
ALREADY, OUR PLANET BEGINS TO BLOOM AGAIN... AND WE VOW NO ONE WILL EVER AGAIN PROFANE OUR LADY OR HER PEOPLE, AS THEY MAKE THE MUSIC IN THE TEMPLE...
THEN WE CAN BE ON OUR WAY.
AN' KNOW THERE'LL BE AT LEAST ONE PLACE WE'RE WELCOME FOR A WHILE, HUNH, LANDO?
LANDO?
UUHGHH
LANDO.!!
HEY, PAL, WHAT'S WRONG?
DON'T KNOW... FEEL ALL KIND OF... HOT AND COLD... AND FLOATY... ...AND DRY... ...ALL AT ONCE... ...STRANGE...
HAN... THOSE SOUND LIKE THE SYMPTOMS OF THE GODOAN'S DISEASE. FUMIYO WAS LIKE THAT... RIGHT BEFORE HE COLLAPSED.
THAT'S STUPID. THE RADIOACTIVE INNOCULATIONS PROTECTED ALL OF THE REST OF US. WHY WOULDN'T IT WORK FOR LANDO?
WH-WHAT INNOCULATIONS...
ROWNK!

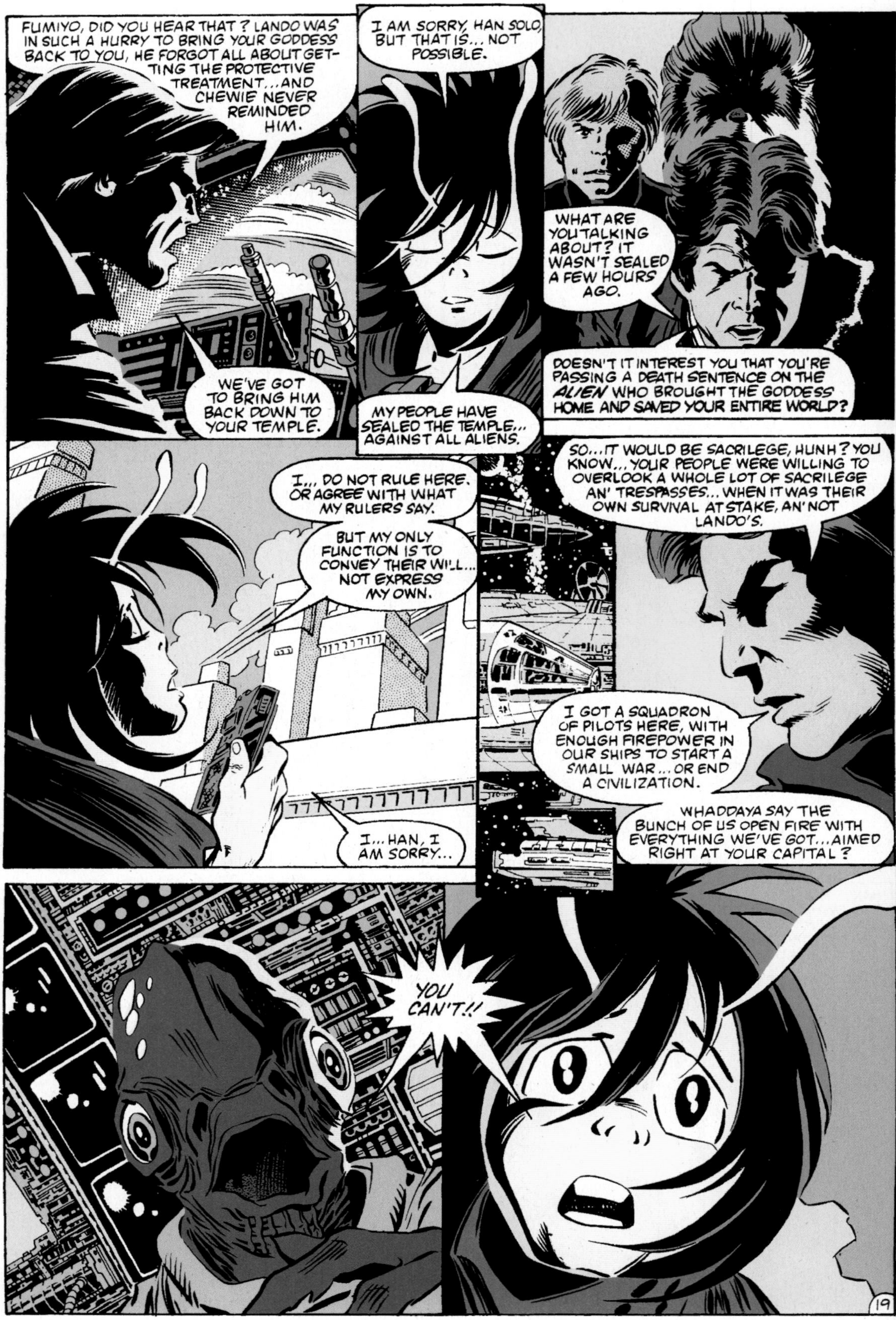
FUMIYO, DID YOU HEAR THAT? LANDO WAS IN SUCH A HURRY TO BRING YOUR GODDESS BACK TO YOU, HE FORGOT ALL ABOUT GETTING THE PROTECTIVE TREATMENT... AND CHEWIE NEVER REMINDED HIM.
WE'VE GOT TO BRING HIM BACK DOWN TO YOUR TEMPLE.
I AM SORRY, HAN SOLO, BUT THAT IS... NOT POSSIBLE.
MY PEOPLE HAVE SEALED THE TEMPLE... AGAINST ALL ALIENS.
WHAT ARE YOU TALKING ABOUT? IT WASN'T SEALED A FEW HOURS AGO.
DOESN'T IT INTEREST YOU THAT YOU'RE PASSING A DEATH SENTENCE ON THE ALIEN WHO BROUGHT THE GODDESS HOME AND SAVED YOUR ENTIRE WORLD?
I... DO NOT RULE HERE. OR AGREE WITH WHAT MY RULERS SAY.
BUT MY ONLY FUNCTION IS TO CONVEY THEIR WILL... NOT EXPRESS MY OWN.
I... HAN, I AM SORRY...
SO... IT WOULD BE SACRILEGE, HUNH? YOU KNOW... YOUR PEOPLE WERE WILLING TO OVERLOOK A WHOLE LOT OF SACRILEGE AN' TRESPASSES... WHEN IT WAS THEIR OWN SURVIVAL AT STAKE, AN' NOT LANDO'S.
I GOT A SQUADRON OF PILOTS HERE, WITH ENOUGH FIREPOWER IN OUR SHIPS TO START A SMALL WAR... OR END A CIVILIZATION.
WHADDAYA SAY THE BUNCH OF US OPEN FIRE WITH EVERYTHING WE'VE GOT... AIMED RIGHT AT YOUR CAPITAL?
YOU CAN'T!!
19

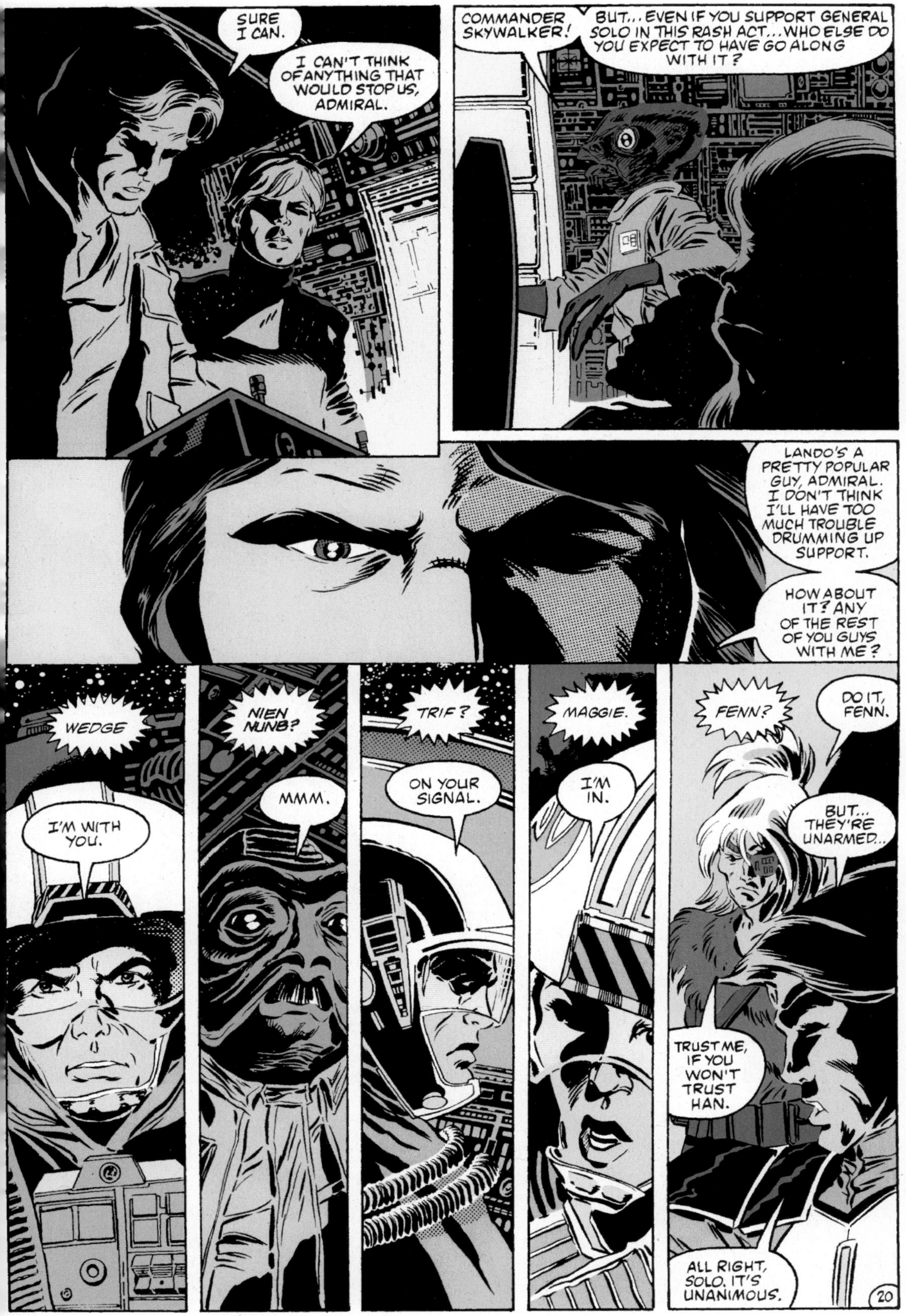
SURE I CAN.
I CAN'T THINK OF ANYTHING THAT WOULD STOP US, ADMIRAL.
COMMANDER SKYWALKER!
BUT... EVEN IF YOU SUPPORT GENERAL SOLO IN THIS RASH ACT... WHO ELSE DO YOU EXPECT TO HAVE GO ALONG WITH IT?
LANDO'S A PRETTY POPULAR GUY, ADMIRAL. I DON'T THINK I'LL HAVE TOO MUCH TROUBLE DRUMMING UP SUPPORT.
HOW ABOUT IT? ANY OF THE REST OF YOU GUYS WITH ME?
WEDGE
I'M WITH YOU.
NIEN NUNB?
MMM.
TRIF?
ON YOUR SIGNAL.
MAGGIE.
I'M IN.
FENN?
DO IT, FENN.
BUT... THEY'RE UNARMED...
TRUST ME, IF YOU WON'T TRUST HAN.
ALL RIGHT, SOLO. IT'S UNANIMOUS.
20

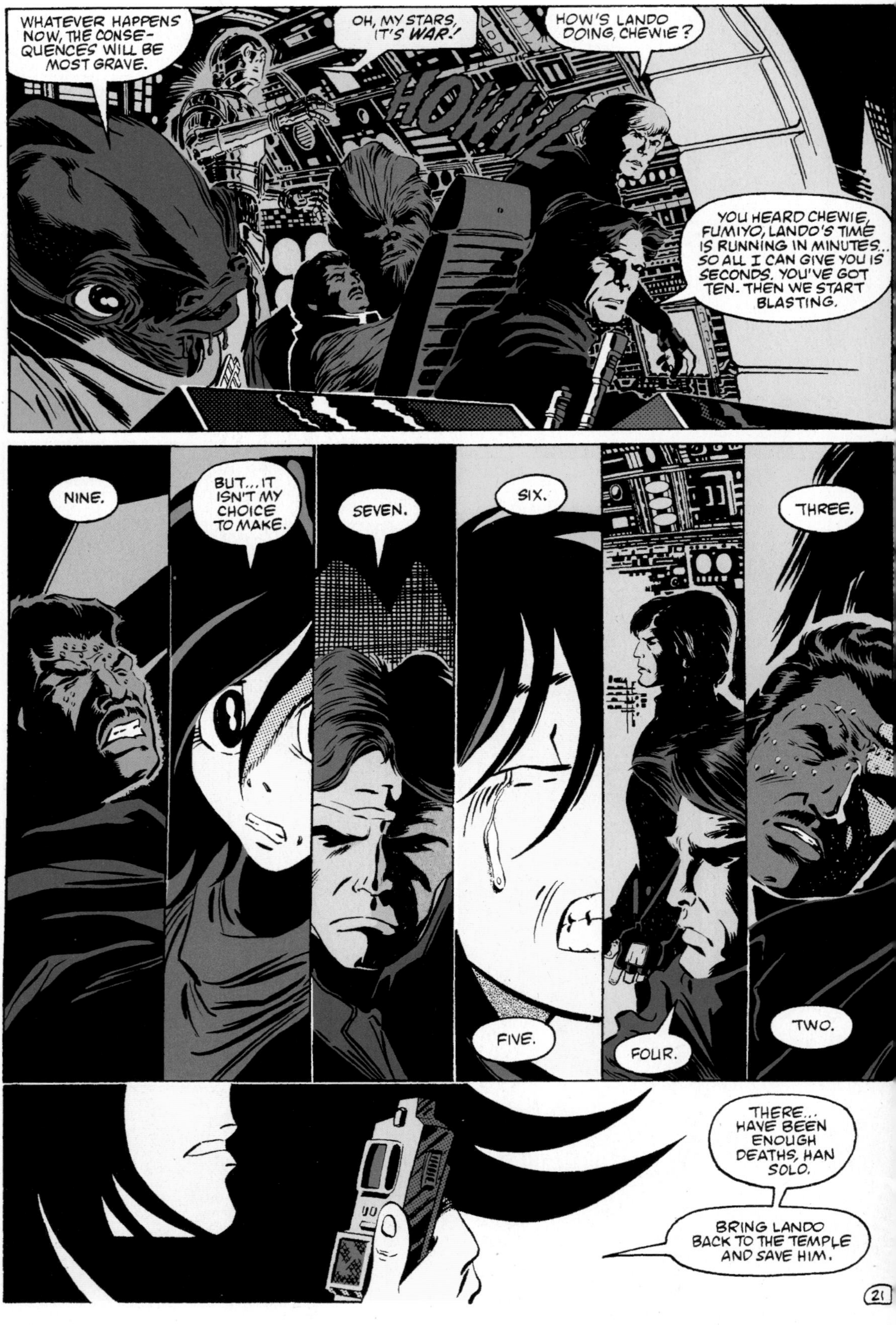
WHATEVER HAPPENS NOW, THE CONSE-QUENCES WILL BE MOST GRAVE.
OH, MY STARS, IT'S WAR!
HOWWL
HOW'S LANDO DOING, CHEWIE?
YOU HEARD CHEWIE, FUMIYO, LANDO'S TIME IS RUNNING IN MINUTES... SO ALL I CAN GIVE YOU IS SECONDS. YOU'VE GOT TEN. THEN WE START BLASTING.
NINE.
BUT... IT ISN'T MY CHOICE TO MAKE.
SEVEN.
SIX.
FIVE.
FOUR.
THREE.
TWO.
THERE... HAVE BEEN ENOUGH DEATHS, HAN SOLO.
BRING LANDO BACK TO THE TEMPLE AND SAVE HIM.
21

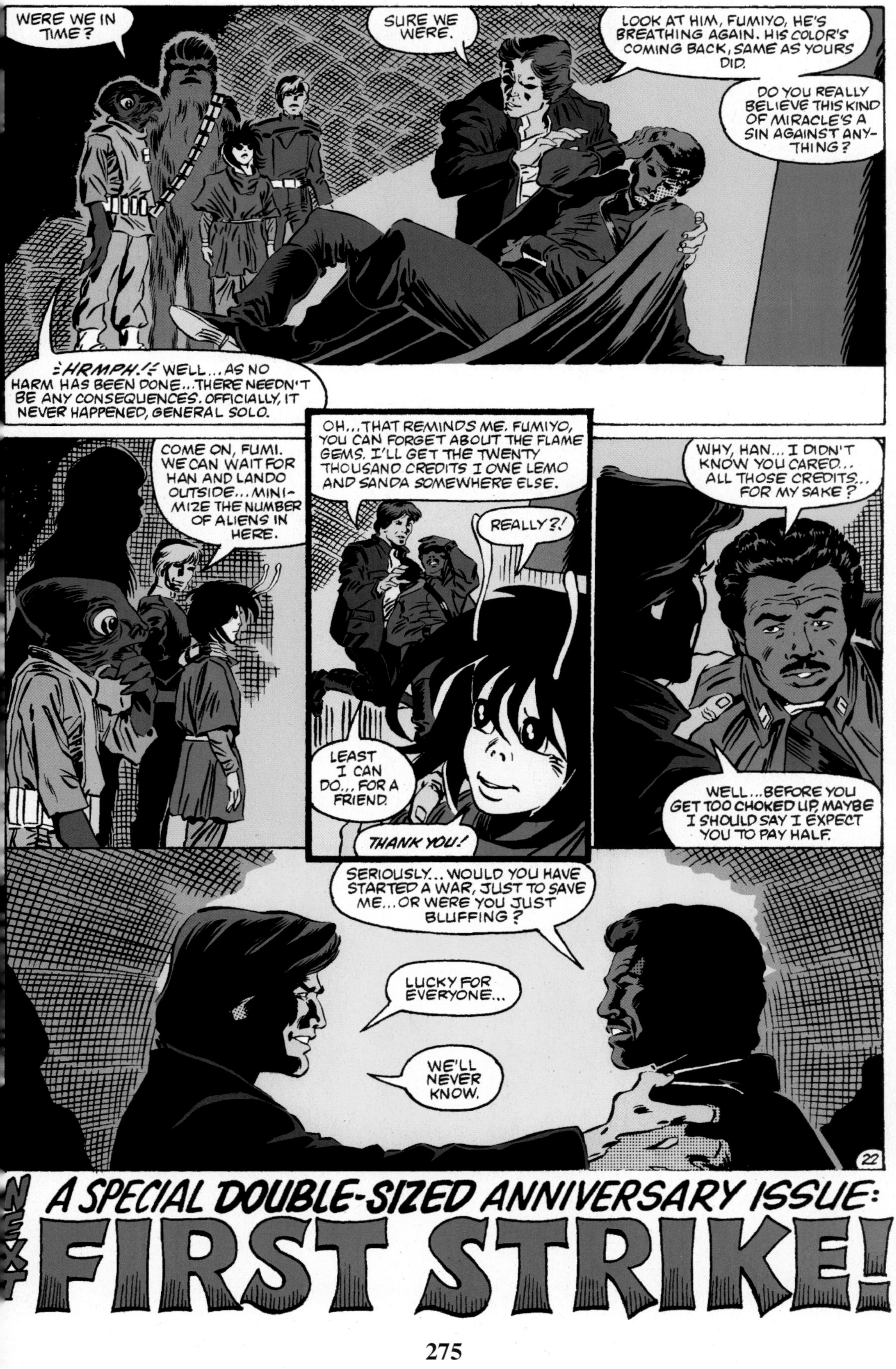
WERE WE IN TIME?
SURE WE WERE.
LOOK AT HIM, FUMIYO, HE'S BREATHING AGAIN. HIS COLOR'S COMING BACK, SAME AS YOURS DID.
DO YOU REALLY BELIEVE THIS KIND OF MIRACLE'S A SIN AGAINST ANYTHING?
:HRMPH!: WELL... AS NO HARM HAS BEEN DONE... THERE NEEDN'T BE ANY CONSEQUENCES. OFFICIALLY, IT NEVER HAPPENED, GENERAL SOLO.
COME ON, FUMI. WE CAN WAIT FOR HAN AND LANDO OUTSIDE... MINIMIZE THE NUMBER OF ALIENS IN HERE.
OH... THAT REMINDS ME. FUMIYO, YOU CAN FORGET ABOUT THE FLAME GEMS. I'LL GET THE TWENTY THOUSAND CREDITS I OWE LEMO AND SANDA SOMEWHERE ELSE.
REALLY?!
LEAST I CAN DO... FOR A FRIEND.
THANK YOU!
WHY, HAN... I DIDN'T KNOW YOU CARED... ALL THOSE CREDITS... FOR MY SAKE?
WELL... BEFORE YOU GET TOO CHOKED UP, MAYBE I SHOULD SAY I EXPECT YOU TO PAY HALF.
SERIOUSLY... WOULD YOU HAVE STARTED A WAR, JUST TO SAVE ME... OR WERE YOU JUST BLUFFING?
LUCKY FOR EVERYONE...
WE'LL NEVER KNOW.
22
NEXT
A SPECIAL DOUBLE-SIZED ANNIVERSARY ISSUE:
FIRST STRIKE!

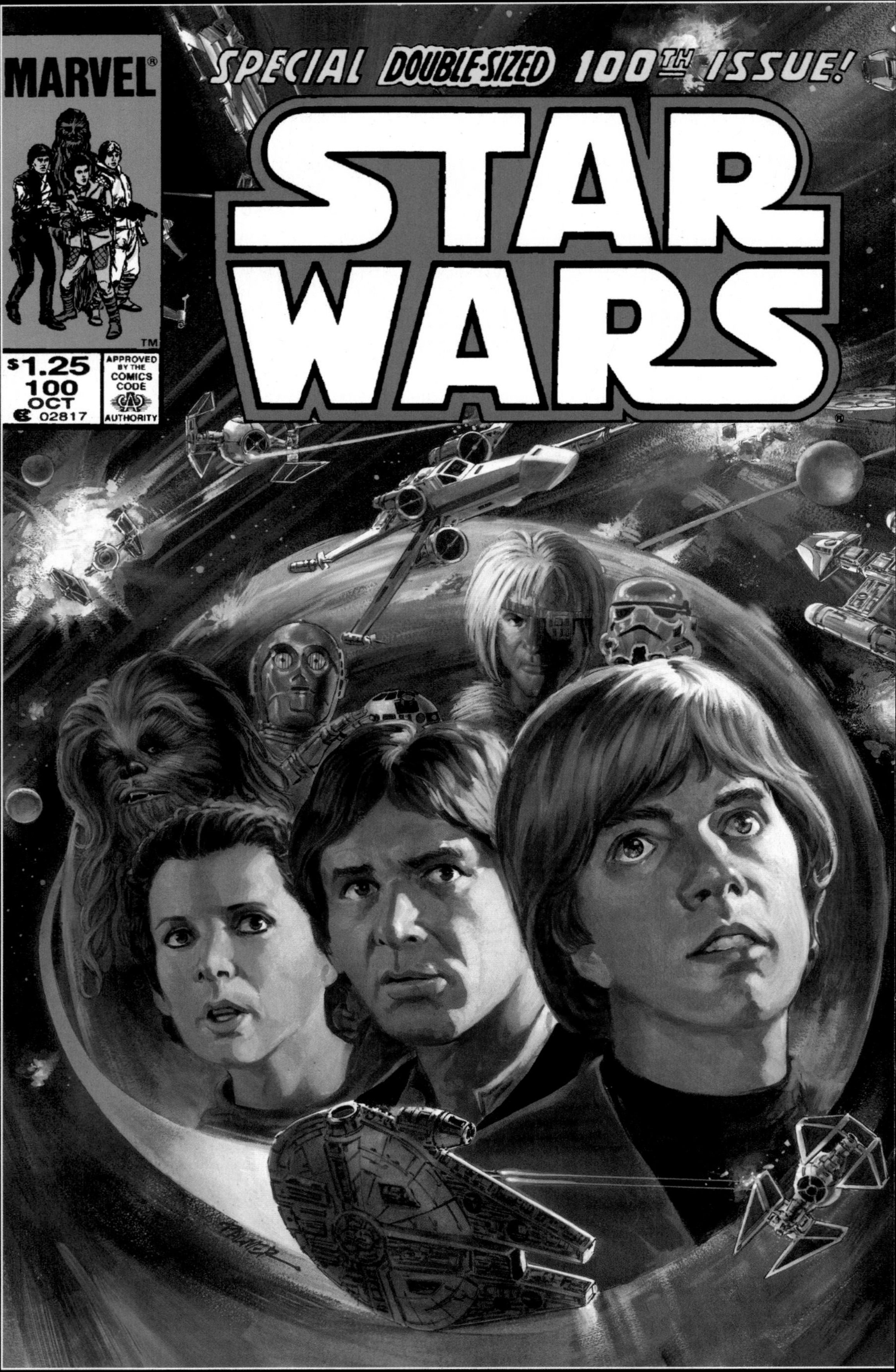
MARVEL®
SPECIAL DOUBLE-SIZED 100TH ISSUE!
STAR WARS
TM
$1.25
100
OCT
02817
APPROVED BY THE COMICS CODE AUTHORITY

FIRST STRIKE

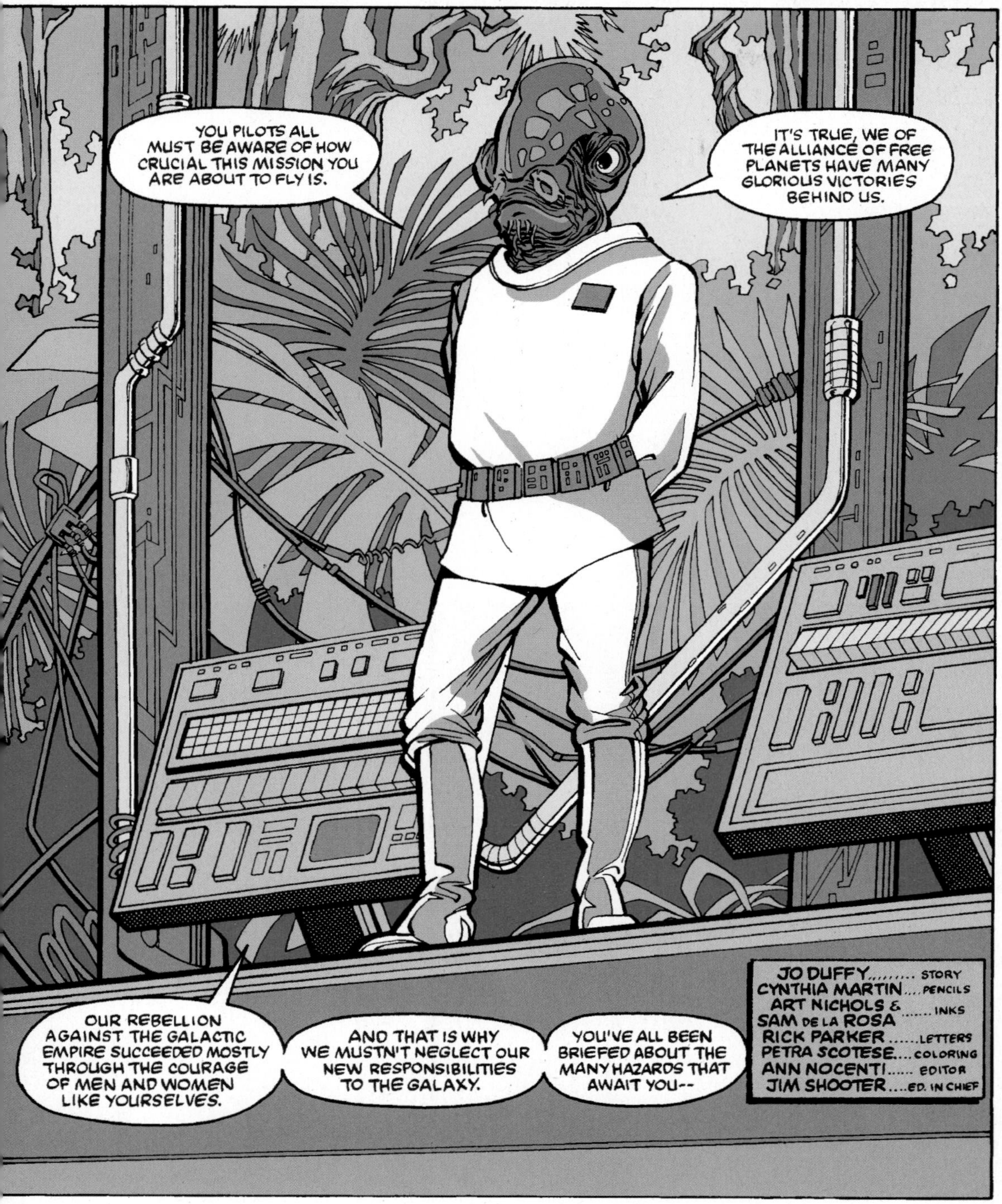
YOU PILOTS ALL MUST BE AWARE OF HOW CRUCIAL THIS MISSION YOU ARE ABOUT TO FLY IS.
IT'S TRUE, WE OF THE ALLIANCE OF FREE PLANETS HAVE MANY GLORIOUS VICTORIES BEHIND US.
OUR REBELLION AGAINST THE GALACTIC EMPIRE SUCCEEDED MOSTLY THROUGH THE COURAGE OF MEN AND WOMEN LIKE YOURSELVES.
AND THAT IS WHY WE MUSTN'T NEGLECT OUR NEW RESPONSIBILITIES TO THE GALAXY.
YOU'VE ALL BEEN BRIEFED ABOUT THE MANY HAZARDS THAT AWAIT YOU--
JO DUFFY........ STORY
CYNTHIA MARTIN.... PENCILS
ART NICHOLS & SAM DE LA ROSA....... INKS
RICK PARKER....... LETTERS
PETRA SCOTESE..... COLORING
ANN NOCENTI...... EDITOR
JIM SHOOTER.... ED. IN CHIEF

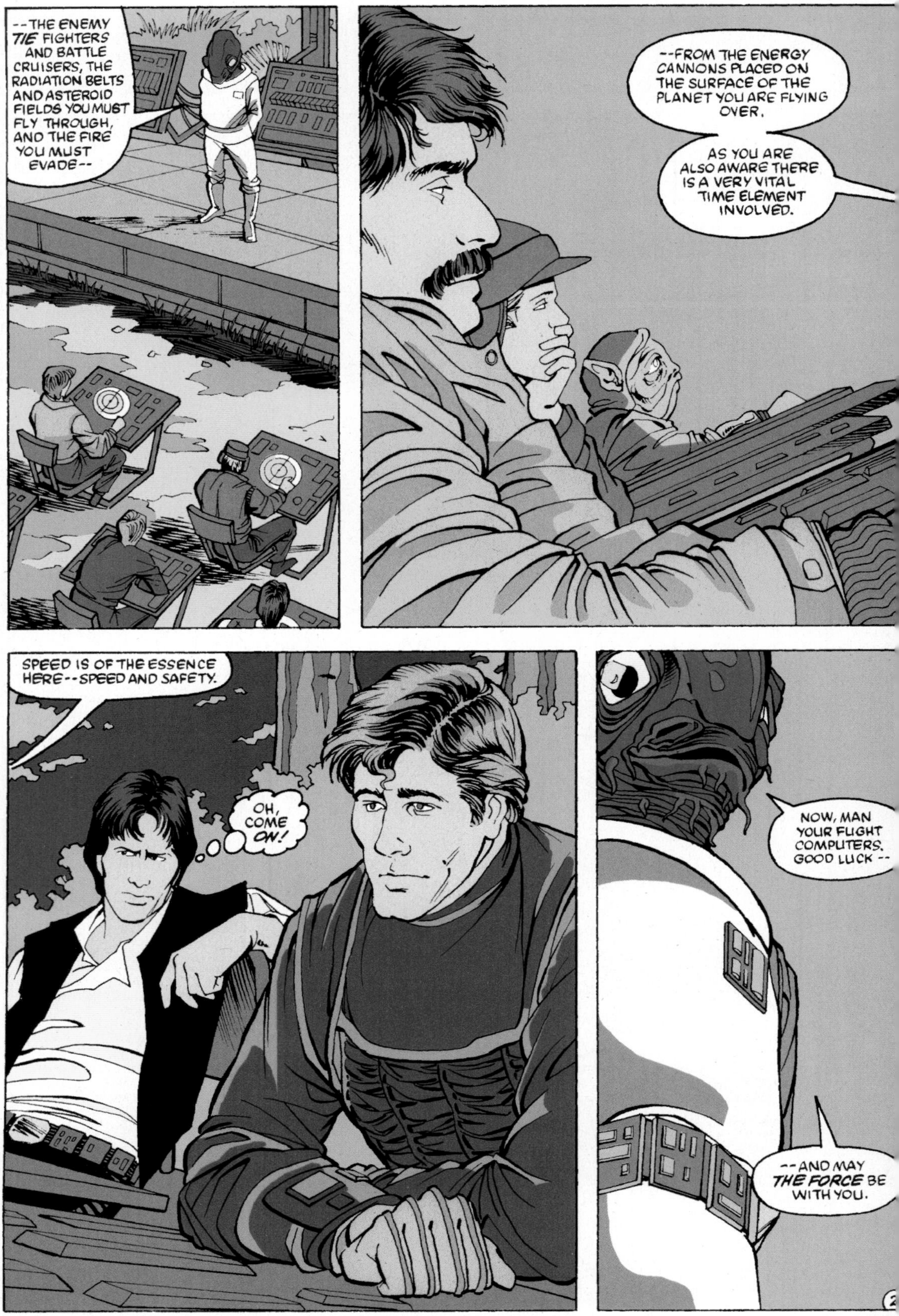
--THE ENEMY TIE FIGHTERS AND BATTLE CRUISERS, THE RADIATION BELTS AND ASTEROID FIELDS YOU MUST FLY THROUGH, AND THE FIRE YOU MUST EVADE--
--FROM THE ENERGY CANNONS PLACED ON THE SURFACE OF THE PLANET YOU ARE FLYING OVER.
AS YOU ARE ALSO AWARE THERE IS A VERY VITAL TIME ELEMENT INVOLVED.
SPEED IS OF THE ESSENCE HERE--SPEED AND SAFETY.
OH, COME ON!
NOW, MAN YOUR FLIGHT COMPUTERS. GOOD LUCK--
--AND MAY THE FORCE BE WITH YOU.

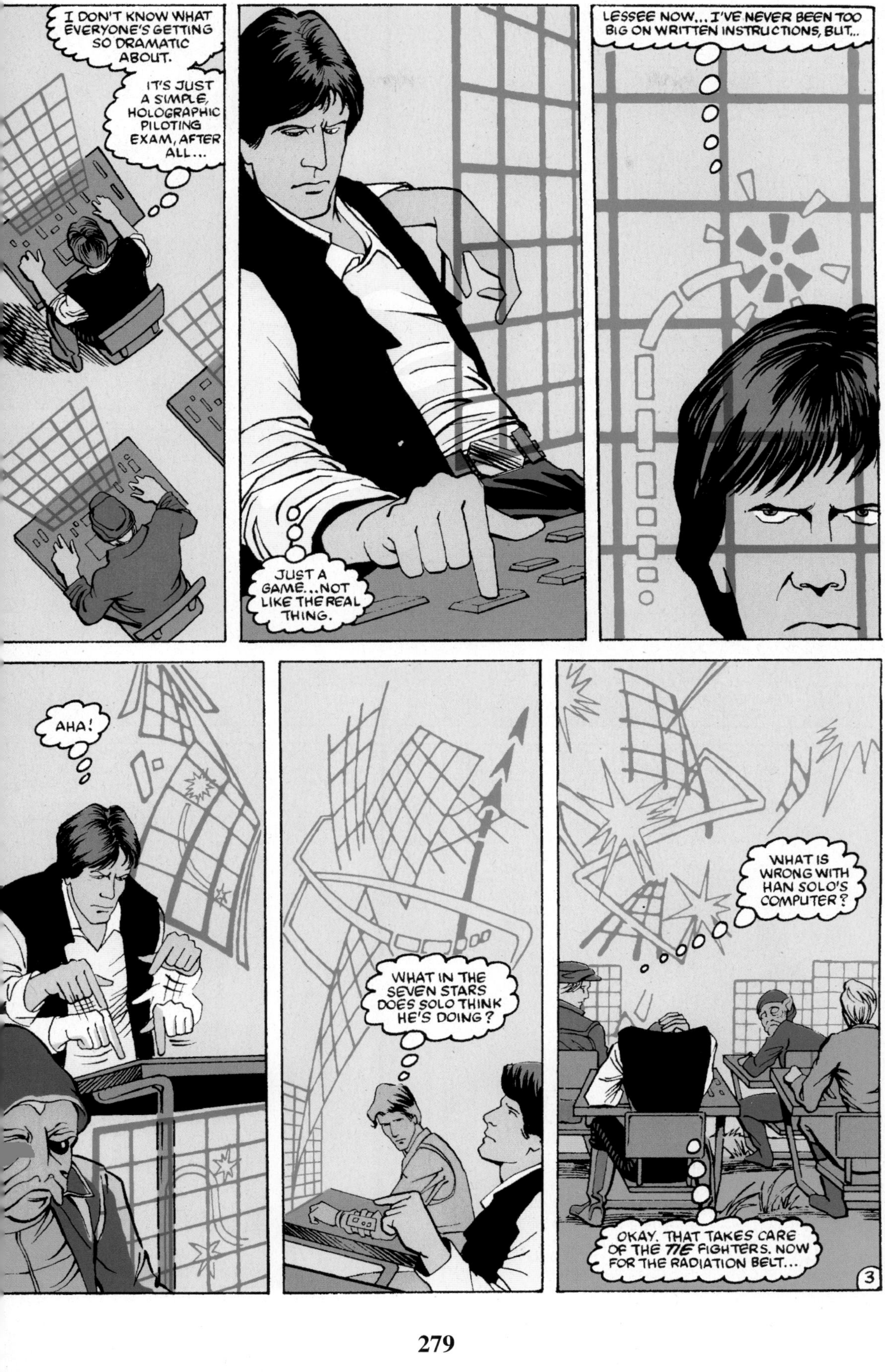
I DON'T KNOW WHAT EVERYONE'S GETTING SO DRAMATIC ABOUT.
IT'S JUST A SIMPLE, HOLOGRAPHIC PILOTING EXAM, AFTER ALL...
JUST A GAME...NOT LIKE THE REAL THING.
LESSEE NOW... I'VE NEVER BEEN TOO BIG ON WRITTEN INSTRUCTIONS, BUT...
AHA!
WHAT IN THE SEVEN STARS DOES SOLO THINK HE'S DOING?
WHAT IS WRONG WITH HAN SOLO'S COMPUTER?
OKAY. THAT TAKES CARE OF THE TIE FIGHTERS. NOW FOR THE RADIATION BELT...
3

LUKE, LANDO, I CAN TELL YOU ONE THING. IF ANYONE BESIDES ADMIRAL ACKBAR HAD ORDERED ME TO TAKE THAT TEST, I WOULDN'T HAVE STOOD FOR IT.

WHY NOT? YOU PASSED, DIDN'T YOU?

'COURSE I DID, BUT... THERE'S A BIG DIFFERENCE BETWEEN BEING ABLE TO HANDLE A DANGEROUS SET-UP AND BEING ABLE TO TELL A COMPUTER HOW TO DO IT, IN TERMS IT CAN UNDERSTAND.

HERE COMES HER ROYAL HIGHNESS. MAYBE SHE CAN EXPLAIN WHAT THE TESTING WAS ALL ABOUT IN THE FIRST PLACE...

LEIA?

LEIA, I--!

AH, PRINCESS LEIA. YOU LOOK AS LOVELY AS EVER TODAY.

FENN SHYSA-- AGAIN!

THANK YOU, FENN...

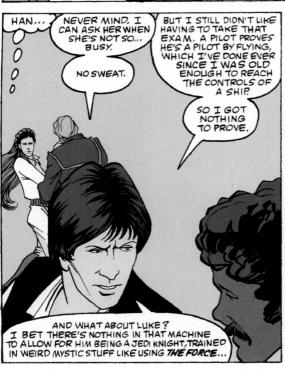

HAN...

NEVER MIND. I CAN ASK HER WHEN SHE'S NOT SO... BUSY.

NO SWEAT.

BUT I STILL DIDN'T LIKE HAVING TO TAKE THAT EXAM. A PILOT PROVES HE'S A PILOT BY FLYING, WHICH I'VE DONE EVER SINCE I WAS OLD ENOUGH TO REACH THE CONTROLS OF A SHIP.

SO I GOT NOTHING TO PROVE.

AND WHAT ABOUT LUKE? I BET THERE'S NOTHING IN THAT MACHINE TO ALLOW FOR HIM BEING A JEDI KNIGHT, TRAINED IN WEIRD MYSTIC STUFF LIKE USING *THE FORCE*...

HE DOESN'T EVEN USE A TARGETING COMPUTER WHEN HE FLIES.

SO, WHO CAME UP WITH THE DUMB IDEA OF TESTING US?

UH, HAN..., I DIDN'T SEE YOUR FRIEND, BEY, SIGNED UP FOR ANY OF THE TESTING SESSIONS.

HE'S NOT.

SPEAKING OF BEY, ISN'T THAT HIM OVER THERE, TALKING TO FENN AND LEIA?

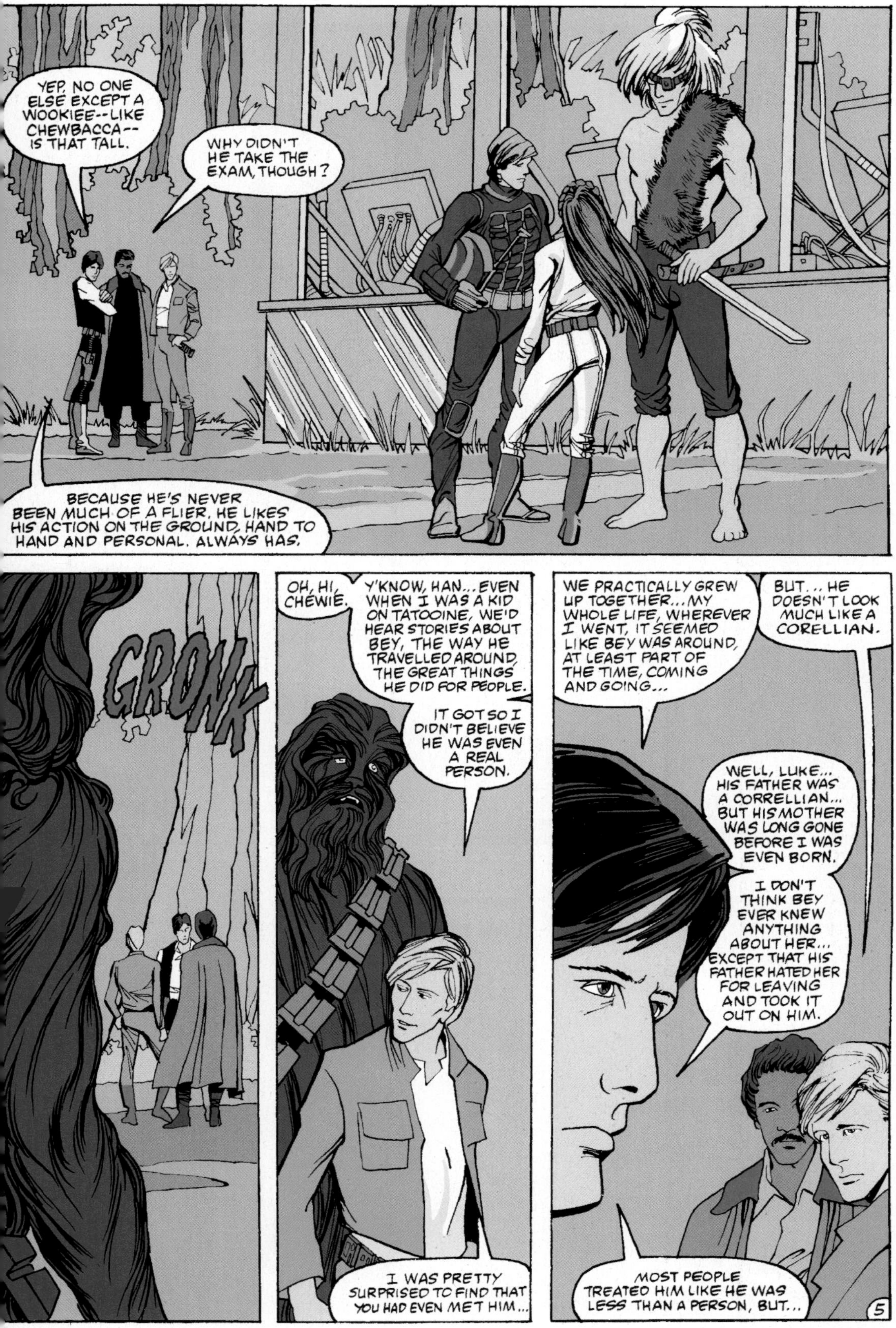
YEP, NO ONE ELSE EXCEPT A WOOKIEE--LIKE CHEWBACCA--IS THAT TALL.
WHY DIDN'T HE TAKE THE EXAM, THOUGH?
BECAUSE HE'S NEVER BEEN MUCH OF A FLIER. HE LIKES HIS ACTION ON THE GROUND, HAND TO HAND AND PERSONAL. ALWAYS HAS.
GRONK
OH, HI, CHEWIE.
Y'KNOW, HAN... EVEN WHEN I WAS A KID ON TATOOINE, WE'D HEAR STORIES ABOUT BEY, THE WAY HE TRAVELLED AROUND, THE GREAT THINGS HE DID FOR PEOPLE.
IT GOT SO I DIDN'T BELIEVE HE WAS EVEN A REAL PERSON.
I WAS PRETTY SURPRISED TO FIND THAT YOU HAD EVEN MET HIM...
WE PRACTICALLY GREW UP TOGETHER... MY WHOLE LIFE, WHEREVER I WENT, IT SEEMED LIKE BEY WAS AROUND, AT LEAST PART OF THE TIME, COMING AND GOING...
BUT... HE DOESN'T LOOK MUCH LIKE A CORELLIAN.
WELL, LUKE... HIS FATHER WAS A CORRELLIAN... BUT HIS MOTHER WAS LONG GONE BEFORE I WAS EVEN BORN.
I DON'T THINK BEY EVER KNEW ANYTHING ABOUT HER... EXCEPT THAT HIS FATHER HATED HER FOR LEAVING AND TOOK IT OUT ON HIM.
MOST PEOPLE TREATED HIM LIKE HE WAS LESS THAN A PERSON, BUT...
5

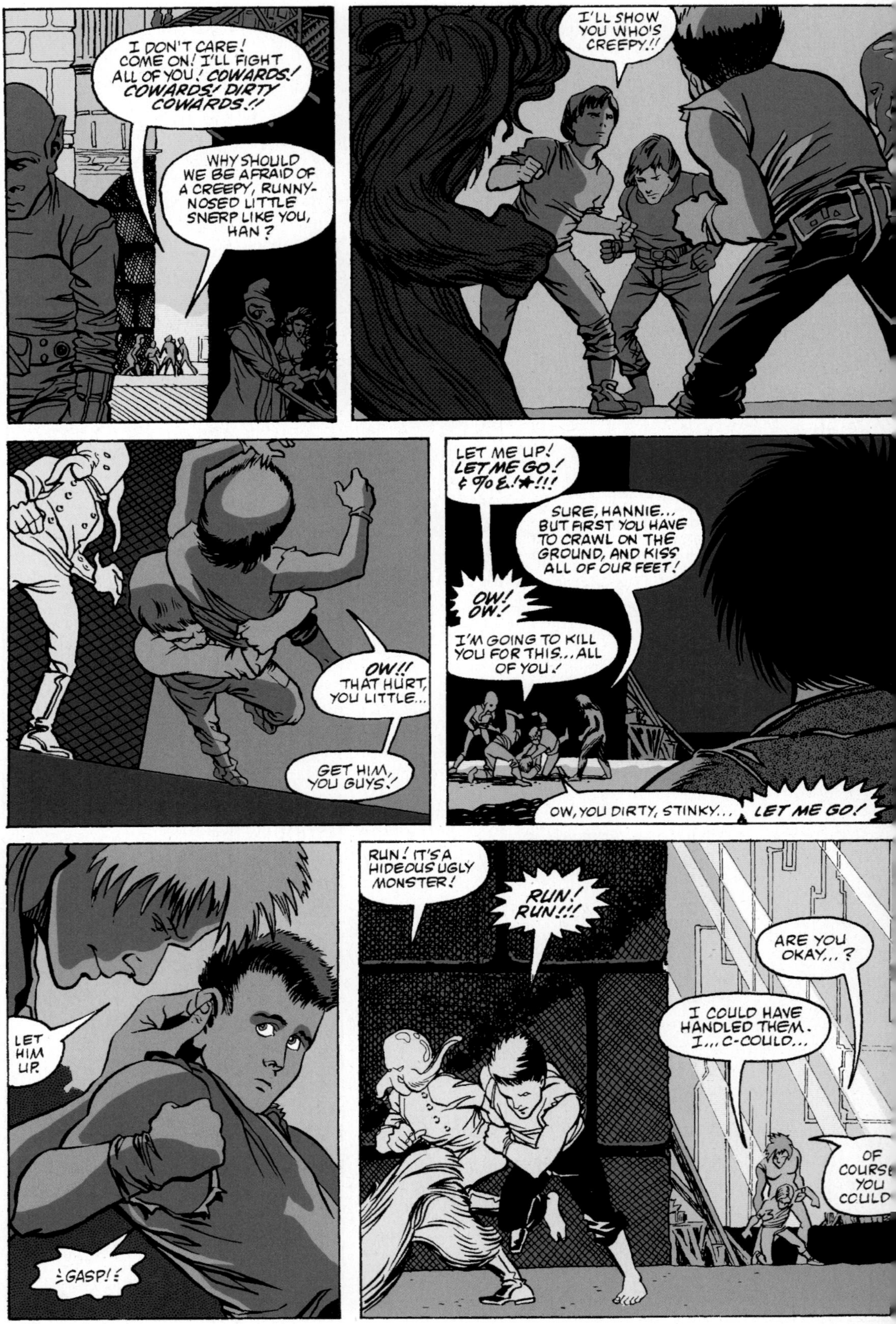
I DON'T CARE! COME ON! I'LL FIGHT ALL OF YOU! COWARDS! COWARDS! DIRTY COWARDS!!
WHY SHOULD WE BE AFRAID OF A CREEPY, RUNNY-NOSED LITTLE SNERP LIKE YOU, HAN?
I'LL SHOW YOU WHO'S CREEPY!!
OW!! THAT HURT, YOU LITTLE...
GET HIM, YOU GUYS!
LET ME UP! LET ME GO! ¢%©£!★!!!
SURE, HANNIE... BUT FIRST YOU HAVE TO CRAWL ON THE GROUND, AND KISS ALL OF OUR FEET!
OW! OW!
I'M GOING TO KILL YOU FOR THIS... ALL OF YOU!
OW, YOU DIRTY, STINKY...
LET ME GO!
LET HIM UP.
GASP!
RUN! IT'S A HIDEOUS UGLY MONSTER!
RUN! RUN!!!
ARE YOU OKAY...?
I COULD HAVE HANDLED THEM. I... C-COULD...
OF COURSE YOU COULD

...UT WHY DO I HAVE TO LEARN HIS STUFF, BEY?

YOU DON'T HAVE TO, HAN.

BUT I WAS CONCERNED ABOUT MY LITTLE BUDDY...

...OING ROUGH S LIFE...

BEING KNOWN AS A MAN WHO'LL NEVER BE ANY BIGGER THAN THE SIZE OF THE BLASTER HE'S CARRYING.

WHAT?!?

=OOF=

=ACK=

FIGHT WITH YOUR HEAD, HAN...

USE YOUR ENERGY... NOT YOUR ANGER...

WHOOP!

THE BLOODSTRIPE, HUNH? YOU WON THE BLOODSTRIPE? THAT MEANS MORE THAN A MILLION MEDALS! YOU MUST BE PROUD.

MM...

SOMEDAY, I'M GONNA WEAR THE BLOODSTRIPE, TOO. YOU'LL SEE!

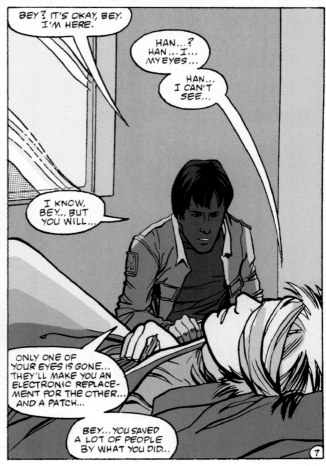
BEY? IT'S OKAY, BEY. I'M HERE.

HAN...? HAN... I... MY EYES...

HAN... I CAN'T SEE...

I KNOW, BEY... BUT YOU WILL...

ONLY ONE OF YOUR EYES IS GONE... THEY'LL MAKE YOU AN ELECTRONIC REPLACEMENT FOR THE OTHER... AND A PATCH...

BEY... YOU SAVED A LOT OF PEOPLE BY WHAT YOU DID...

7

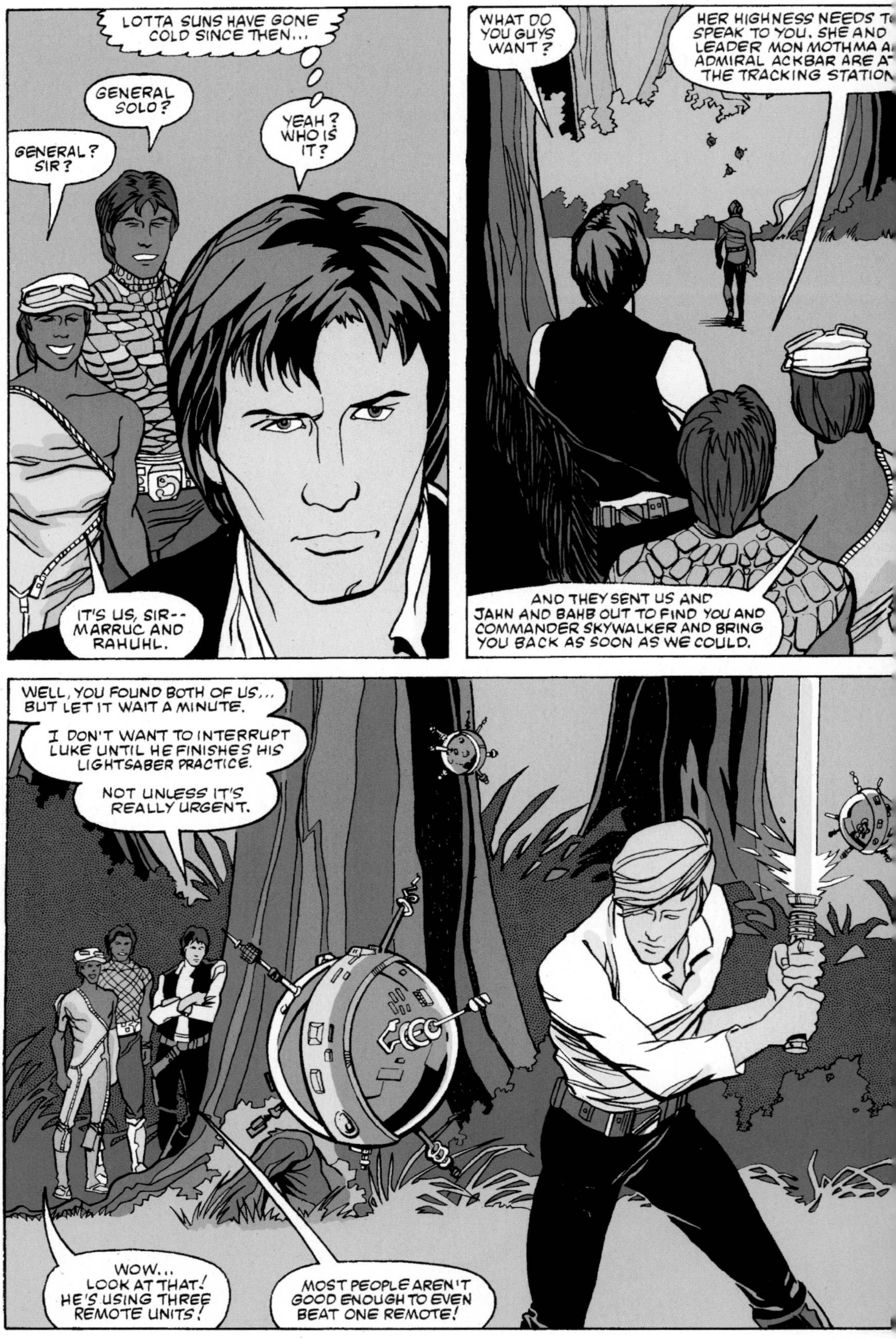
LOTTA SUNS HAVE GONE COLD SINCE THEN...
GENERAL? SIR?
GENERAL SOLO?
YEAH? WHO IS IT?
IT'S US, SIR-- MARRUC AND RAHUHL.
WHAT DO YOU GUYS WANT?
HER HIGHNESS NEEDS TO SPEAK TO YOU. SHE AND LEADER MON MOTHMA AND ADMIRAL ACKBAR ARE AT THE TRACKING STATION
AND THEY SENT US AND JAHN AND BAHB OUT TO FIND YOU AND COMMANDER SKYWALKER AND BRING YOU BACK AS SOON AS WE COULD.
WELL, YOU FOUND BOTH OF US... BUT LET IT WAIT A MINUTE.
I DON'T WANT TO INTERRUPT LUKE UNTIL HE FINISHES HIS LIGHTSABER PRACTICE.
NOT UNLESS IT'S REALLY URGENT.
WOW... LOOK AT THAT! HE'S USING THREE REMOTE UNITS!
MOST PEOPLE AREN'T GOOD ENOUGH TO EVEN BEAT ONE REMOTE!

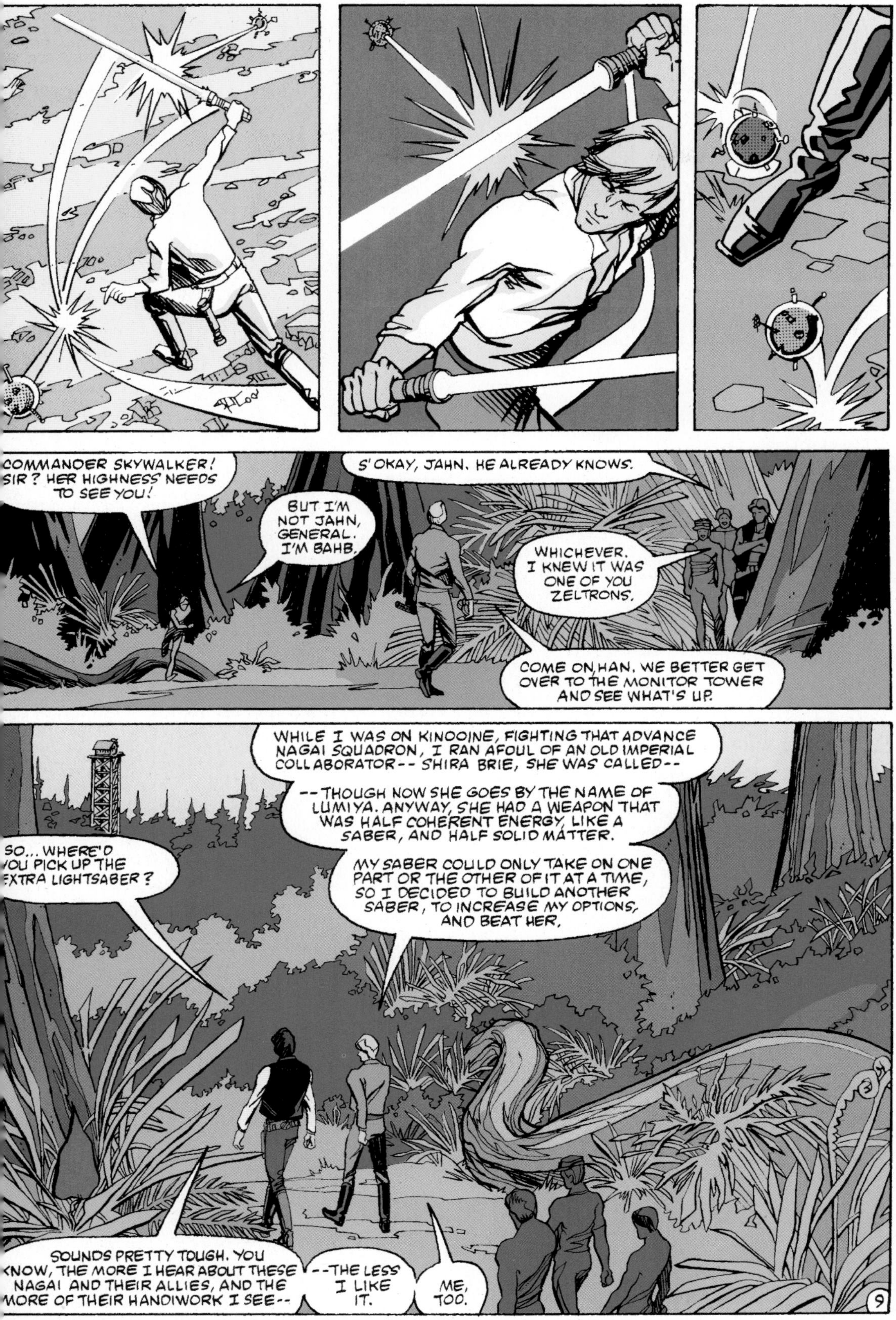
COMMANDER SKYWALKER! SIR? HER HIGHNESS NEEDS TO SEE YOU!
S'OKAY, JAHN. HE ALREADY KNOWS.
BUT I'M NOT JAHN, GENERAL. I'M BAHB.
WHICHEVER. I KNEW IT WAS ONE OF YOU ZELTRONS.
COME ON, HAN. WE BETTER GET OVER TO THE MONITOR TOWER AND SEE WHAT'S UP.
SO... WHERE'D YOU PICK UP THE EXTRA LIGHTSABER?
WHILE I WAS ON KINOOINE, FIGHTING THAT ADVANCE NAGAI SQUADRON, I RAN AFOUL OF AN OLD IMPERIAL COLLABORATOR-- SHIRA BRIE, SHE WAS CALLED--
--THOUGH NOW SHE GOES BY THE NAME OF LUMIYA. ANYWAY, SHE HAD A WEAPON THAT WAS HALF COHERENT ENERGY, LIKE A SABER, AND HALF SOLID MATTER.
MY SABER COULD ONLY TAKE ON ONE PART OR THE OTHER OF IT AT A TIME, SO I DECIDED TO BUILD ANOTHER SABER, TO INCREASE MY OPTIONS, AND BEAT HER.
SOUNDS PRETTY TOUGH. YOU KNOW, THE MORE I HEAR ABOUT THESE NAGAI AND THEIR ALLIES, AND THE MORE OF THEIR HANDIWORK I SEE--
--THE LESS I LIKE IT.
ME, TOO.
9

SO... WHAT'S UP?

JUST A SHORT WHILE AGO, HER HIGHNESS, WORKING IN CONJUNCTION WITH HER ZELTRON ATTACHÉS, AND THE DROIDS WHO MAN THIS STATION, DETECTED SOMETHING WHICH CAUSES US ALL GRAVE CONCERN.

LEIA, IF YOU'D TELL THE GENERAL, AND THE REST OF THE PILOTS...

A LARGE NUMBER OF SMALL CRAFT, FLYING SWIFTLY AND IN FORMATION, HAVE BEEN DETECTED, BEARING FOR THIS MOON.

WE'VE HAD NO COMMUNICATIONS FROM ANY OTHER WORLDS IN THE ALLIANCE, AND SINCE WE'VE HAD OUR TEMPORARY HEADQUARTERS HERE FOR SOME TIME...

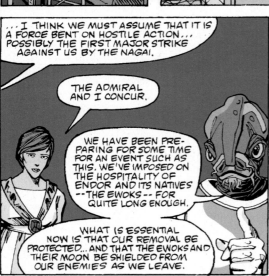

... I THINK WE MUST ASSUME THAT IT IS A FORCE BENT ON HOSTILE ACTION... POSSIBLY THE FIRST MAJOR STRIKE AGAINST US BY THE NAGAI.

THE ADMIRAL AND I CONCUR.

WE HAVE BEEN PREPARING FOR SOME TIME FOR AN EVENT SUCH AS THIS. WE'VE IMPOSED ON THE HOSPITALITY OF ENDOR AND ITS NATIVES --THE EWOKS-- FOR QUITE LONG ENOUGH.

WHAT IS ESSENTIAL NOW IS THAT OUR REMOVAL BE PROTECTED... AND THAT THE EWOKS AND THEIR MOON BE SHIELDED FROM OUR ENEMIES AS WE LEAVE.

NO SWEAT. YOU GOT ALL YOUR BEST PILOTS RIGHT HERE, AND WE ALL KNOW WHAT SQUADRONS WE FLY WITH. IF OUR SHIPS ARE READY, WE CAN JUST--!

YOUR SHIPS ARE READY... AND WE'D LIKE ALL OF YOU, EXCEPT COMMANDER SKYWALKER AND GENERAL SOLO, TO MAN THEM, AT ONCE, WHILE WE COMMENCE THE EVACUATION.

GENERAL CALRISSIAN WILL COMMAND THE DEFENSES, AND HER HIGHNESS, PRINCESS LEIA ORGANA, WILL CONTINUE TO RUN THIS MONITORING STATION UNTIL EVERYONE ELSE HAS LEFT.

GREAT! MEANWHILE, WHAT DO YOU WANT ME AN' LUKE TO DO? WHY AREN'T WE FLYING?

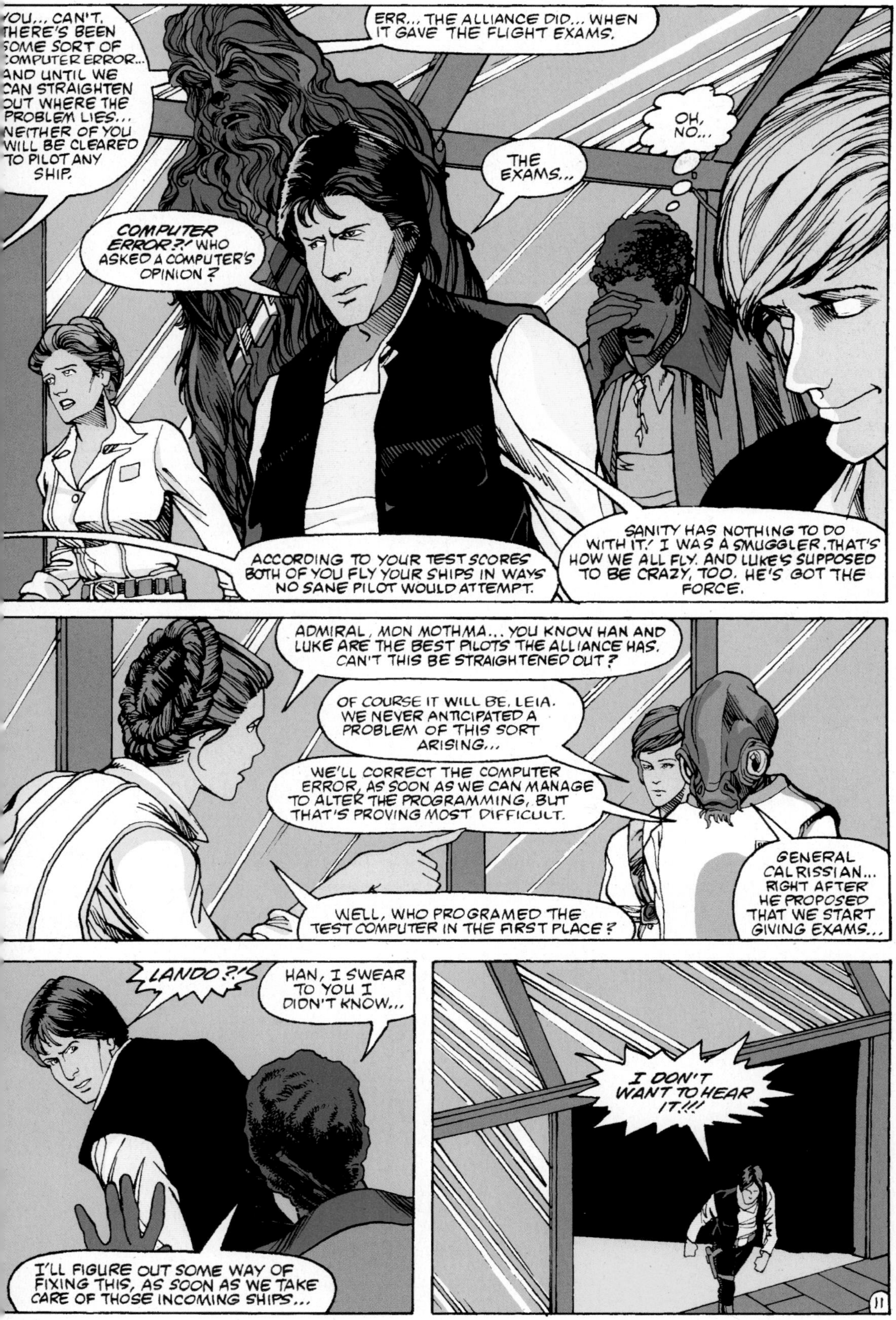
YOU... CAN'T. THERE'S BEEN SOME SORT OF COMPUTER ERROR... AND UNTIL WE CAN STRAIGHTEN OUT WHERE THE PROBLEM LIES... NEITHER OF YOU WILL BE CLEARED TO PILOT ANY SHIP.
COMPUTER ERROR?! WHO ASKED A COMPUTER'S OPINION?
ERR... THE ALLIANCE DID... WHEN IT GAVE THE FLIGHT EXAMS.
THE EXAMS...
OH, NO...
ACCORDING TO YOUR TEST SCORES BOTH OF YOU FLY YOUR SHIPS IN WAYS NO SANE PILOT WOULD ATTEMPT.
SANITY HAS NOTHING TO DO WITH IT! I WAS A SMUGGLER. THAT'S HOW WE ALL FLY. AND LUKE'S SUPPOSED TO BE CRAZY, TOO. HE'S GOT THE FORCE.
ADMIRAL, MON MOTHMA... YOU KNOW HAN AND LUKE ARE THE BEST PILOTS THE ALLIANCE HAS. CAN'T THIS BE STRAIGHTENED OUT?
OF COURSE IT WILL BE, LEIA. WE NEVER ANTICIPATED A PROBLEM OF THIS SORT ARISING...
WE'LL CORRECT THE COMPUTER ERROR, AS SOON AS WE CAN MANAGE TO ALTER THE PROGRAMMING, BUT THAT'S PROVING MOST DIFFICULT.
WELL, WHO PROGRAMED THE TEST COMPUTER IN THE FIRST PLACE?
GENERAL CALRISSIAN... RIGHT AFTER HE PROPOSED THAT WE START GIVING EXAMS...
LANDO?!
HAN, I SWEAR TO YOU I DIDN'T KNOW...
I'LL FIGURE OUT SOME WAY OF FIXING THIS, AS SOON AS WE TAKE CARE OF THOSE INCOMING SHIPS...
I DON'T WANT TO HEAR IT!!!
11

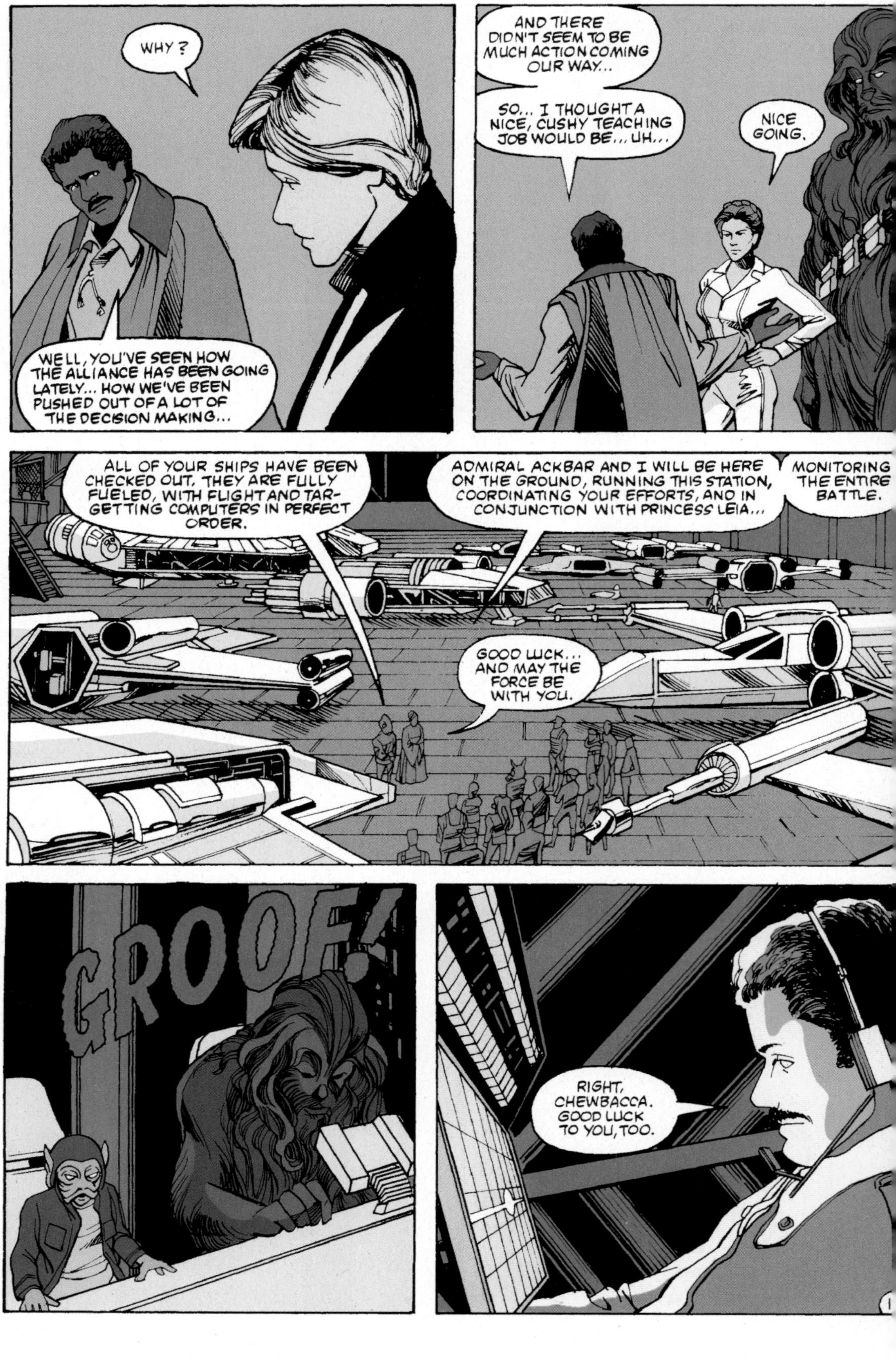
WHY?
WELL, YOU'VE SEEN HOW THE ALLIANCE HAS BEEN GOING LATELY... HOW WE'VE BEEN PUSHED OUT OF A LOT OF THE DECISION MAKING...
AND THERE DIDN'T SEEM TO BE MUCH ACTION COMING OUR WAY...
SO... I THOUGHT A NICE, CUSHY TEACHING JOB WOULD BE... UH...
NICE GOING.
ALL OF YOUR SHIPS HAVE BEEN CHECKED OUT. THEY ARE FULLY FUELED, WITH FLIGHT AND TARGETTING COMPUTERS IN PERFECT ORDER.
ADMIRAL ACKBAR AND I WILL BE HERE ON THE GROUND, RUNNING THIS STATION, COORDINATING YOUR EFFORTS, AND IN CONJUNCTION WITH PRINCESS LEIA...
MONITORING THE ENTIRE BATTLE.
GOOD LUCK... AND MAY THE FORCE BE WITH YOU.
GROOF!
RIGHT, CHEWBACCA. GOOD LUCK TO YOU, TOO.

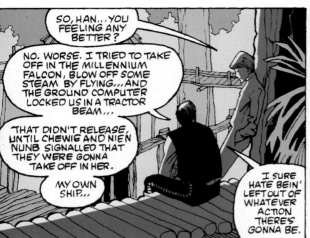

SO, HAN... YOU FEELING ANY BETTER?

NO. WORSE. I TRIED TO TAKE OFF IN THE MILLENNIUM FALCON, BLOW OFF SOME STEAM BY FLYING,...AND THE GROUND COMPUTER LOCKED US IN A TRACTOR BEAM...

THAT DIDN'T RELEASE, UNTIL CHEWIE AND NIEN NUNB SIGNALLED THAT THEY WERE GONNA TAKE OFF IN HER.

MY OWN SHIP...

I SURE HATE BEIN' LEFT OUT OF WHATEVER ACTION THERE'S GONNA BE.

WELL, WE MAY NOT HAVE TO MISS IT ENTIRELY.

TIPPET WAS TELLING ME HE AND SOME OF THE OTHER EWOKS SPOTTED SOMETHING STRANGE EARLIER TODAY, BUT THEY COULDN'T REALLY DESCRIBE IT.

WANT TO GRAB A COUPLE OF SPEEDER BIKES AND CHECK IT OUT?

SURE.

THERE'S TIPPET NOW.

LET'S LEAVE THE BIKES OVER HERE, SO WE CAN SNEAK UP ON WHATEVER'S GOT THE LITTLE FUZZBALLS SO NERVOUS...

RIGHT...

WELL, I'LL...

⑬

289

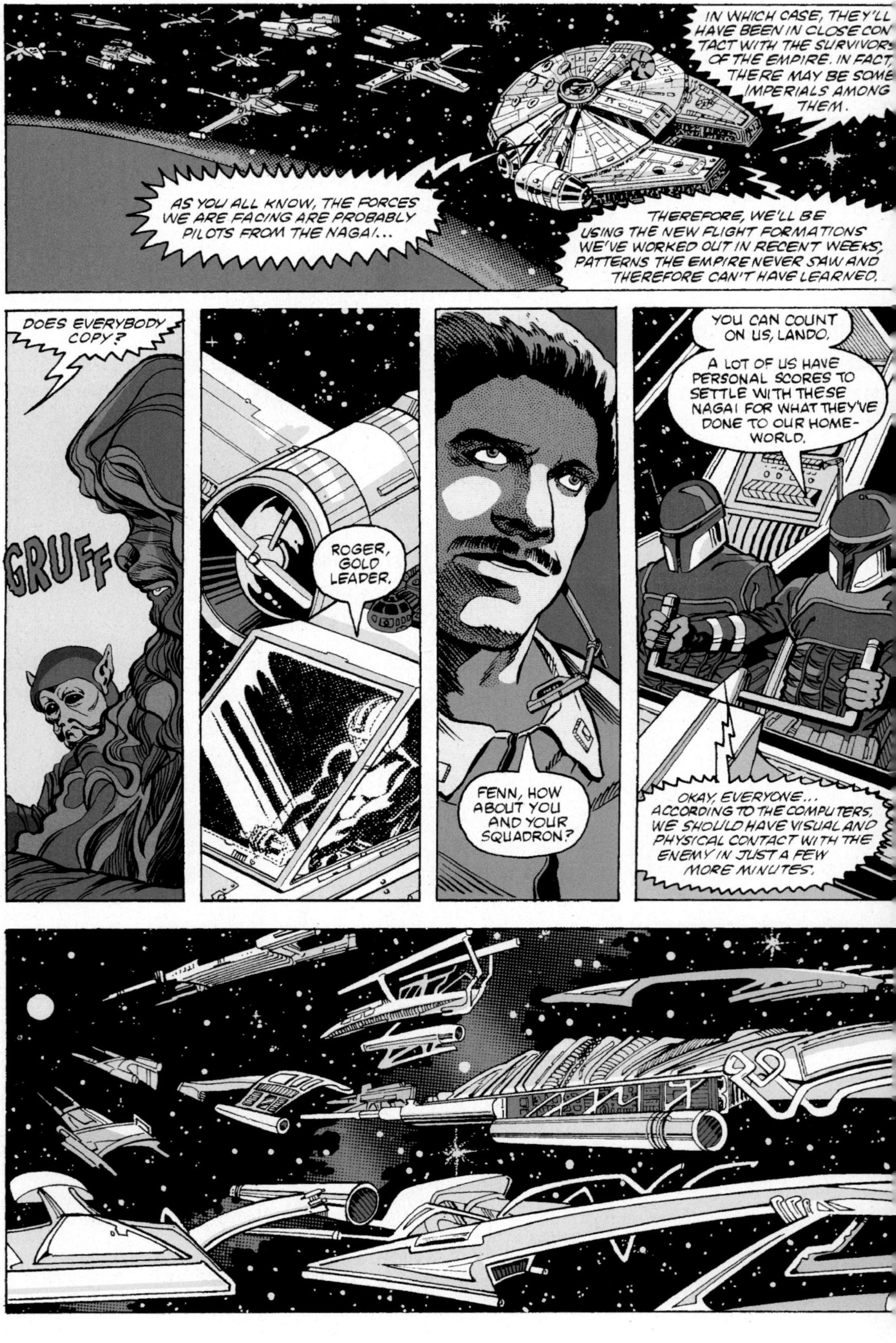

AS YOU ALL KNOW, THE FORCES WE ARE FACING ARE PROBABLY PILOTS FROM THE NAGAI...
IN WHICH CASE, THEY'LL HAVE BEEN IN CLOSE CONTACT WITH THE SURVIVORS OF THE EMPIRE. IN FACT, THERE MAY BE SOME IMPERIALS AMONG THEM.
THEREFORE, WE'LL BE USING THE NEW FLIGHT FORMATIONS WE'VE WORKED OUT IN RECENT WEEKS, PATTERNS THE EMPIRE NEVER SAW AND THEREFORE CAN'T HAVE LEARNED.
DOES EVERYBODY COPY?
GRUFF
ROGER, GOLD LEADER.
FENN, HOW ABOUT YOU AND YOUR SQUADRON?
YOU CAN COUNT ON US, LANDO.
A LOT OF US HAVE PERSONAL SCORES TO SETTLE WITH THESE NAGAI FOR WHAT THEY'VE DONE TO OUR HOME-WORLD.
OKAY, EVERYONE... ACCORDING TO THE COMPUTERS, WE SHOULD HAVE VISUAL AND PHYSICAL CONTACT WITH THE ENEMY IN JUST A FEW MORE MINUTES.

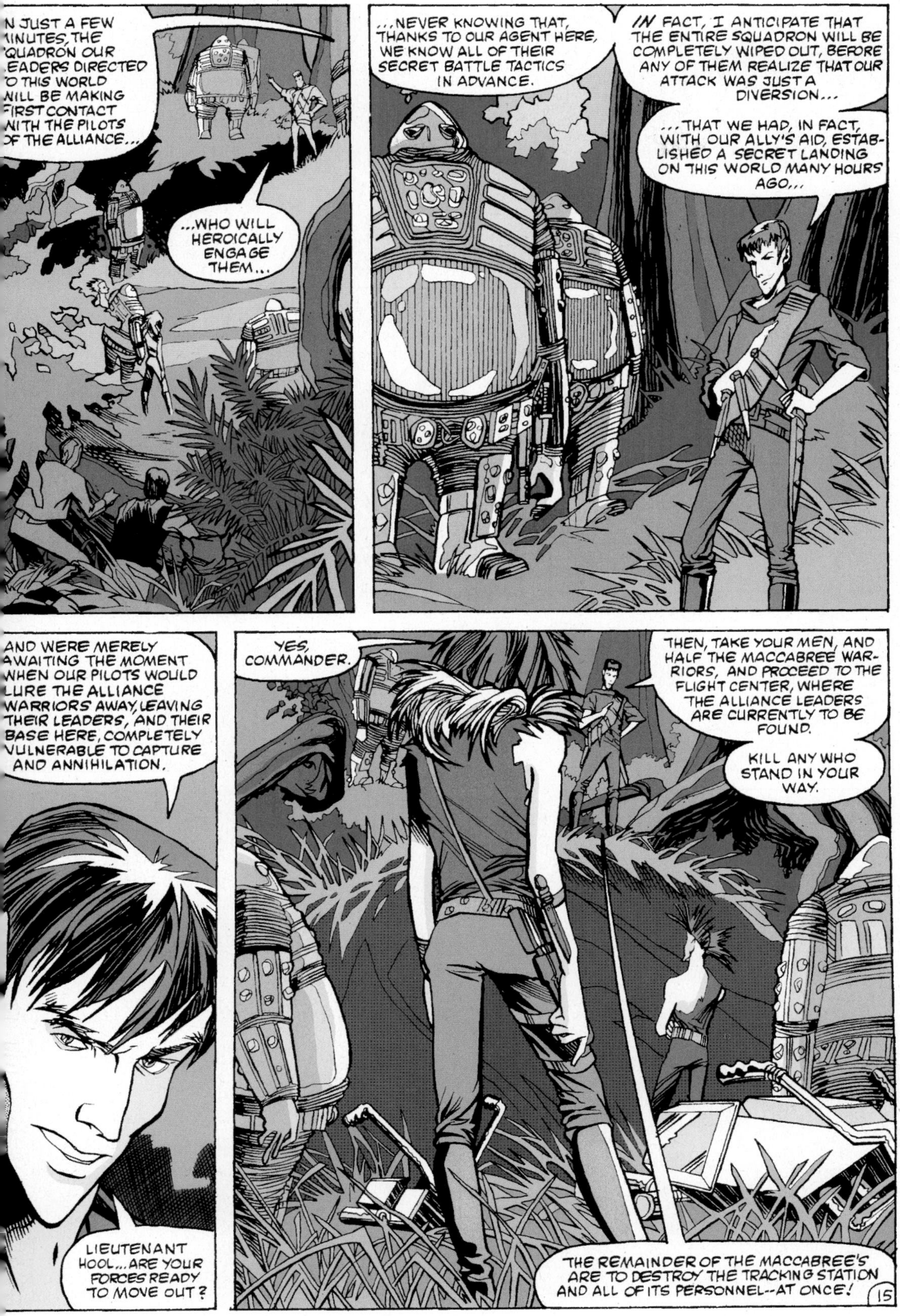
N JUST A FEW MINUTES, THE SQUADRON OUR LEADERS DIRECTED TO THIS WORLD WILL BE MAKING FIRST CONTACT WITH THE PILOTS OF THE ALLIANCE...
...WHO WILL HEROICALLY ENGAGE THEM...
...NEVER KNOWING THAT, THANKS TO OUR AGENT HERE, WE KNOW ALL OF THEIR SECRET BATTLE TACTICS IN ADVANCE.
IN FACT, I ANTICIPATE THAT THE ENTIRE SQUADRON WILL BE COMPLETELY WIPED OUT, BEFORE ANY OF THEM REALIZE THAT OUR ATTACK WAS JUST A DIVERSION...
...THAT WE HAD, IN FACT, WITH OUR ALLY'S AID, ESTABLISHED A SECRET LANDING ON THIS WORLD MANY HOURS AGO,...
AND WERE MERELY AWAITING THE MOMENT WHEN OUR PILOTS WOULD LURE THE ALLIANCE WARRIORS AWAY, LEAVING THEIR LEADERS, AND THEIR BASE HERE, COMPLETELY VULNERABLE TO CAPTURE AND ANNIHILATION.
LIEUTENANT HOOL...ARE YOUR FORCES READY TO MOVE OUT?
YES, COMMANDER.
THEN, TAKE YOUR MEN, AND HALF THE MACCABREE WARRIORS, AND PROCEED TO THE FLIGHT CENTER, WHERE THE ALLIANCE LEADERS ARE CURRENTLY TO BE FOUND.
KILL ANY WHO STAND IN YOUR WAY.
THE REMAINDER OF THE MACCABREE'S ARE TO DESTROY THE TRACKING STATION AND ALL OF ITS PERSONNEL--AT ONCE!
15

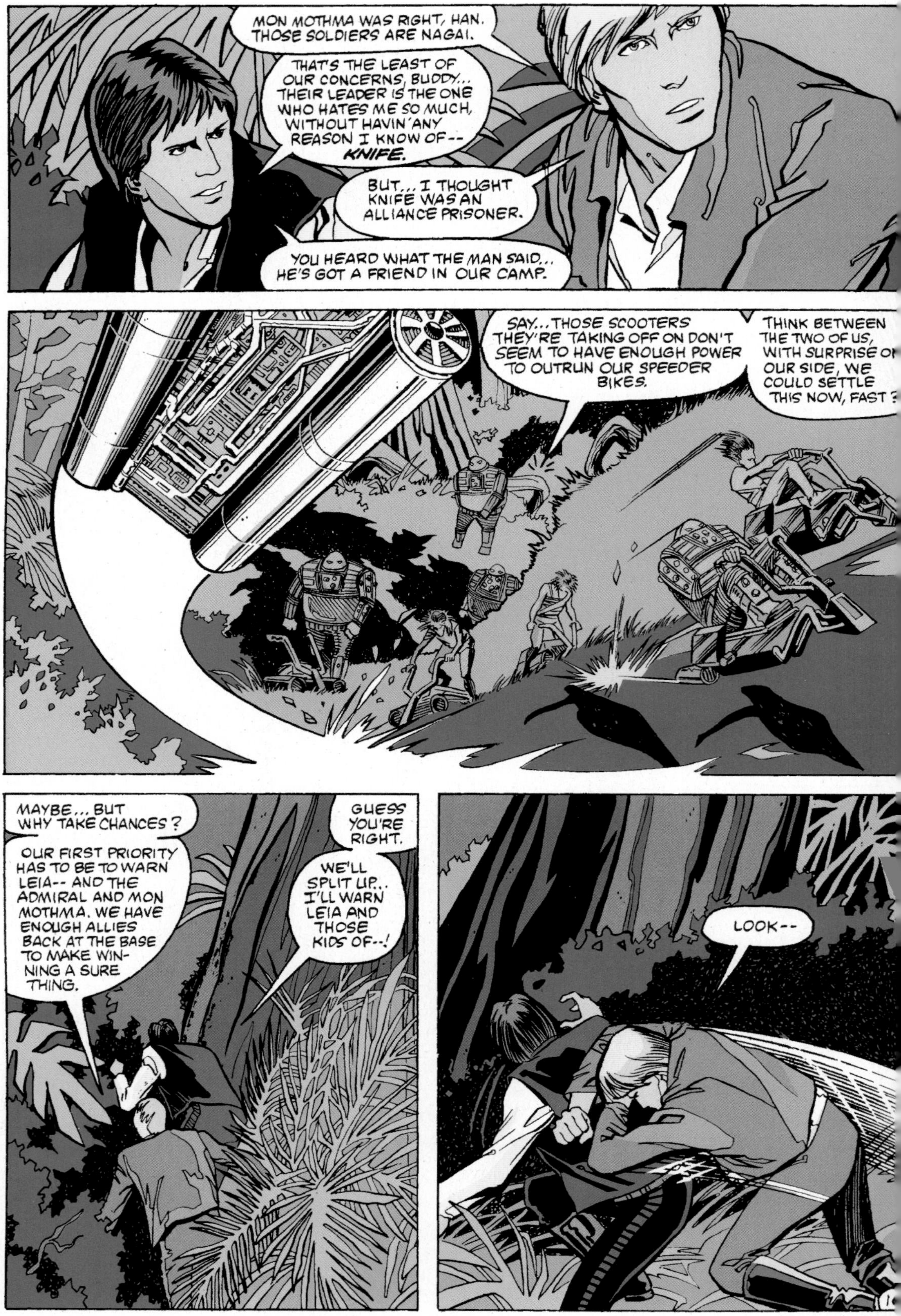
MON MOTHMA WAS RIGHT, HAN. THOSE SOLDIERS ARE NAGAI.
THAT'S THE LEAST OF OUR CONCERNS, BUDDY... THEIR LEADER IS THE ONE WHO HATES ME SO MUCH, WITHOUT HAVIN' ANY REASON I KNOW OF-- KNIFE.
BUT... I THOUGHT KNIFE WAS AN ALLIANCE PRISONER.
YOU HEARD WHAT THE MAN SAID... HE'S GOT A FRIEND IN OUR CAMP.
SAY... THOSE SCOOTERS THEY'RE TAKING OFF ON DON'T SEEM TO HAVE ENOUGH POWER TO OUTRUN OUR SPEEDER BIKES.
THINK BETWEEN THE TWO OF US, WITH SURPRISE ON OUR SIDE, WE COULD SETTLE THIS NOW, FAST?
MAYBE... BUT WHY TAKE CHANCES?
OUR FIRST PRIORITY HAS TO BE TO WARN LEIA-- AND THE ADMIRAL AND MON MOTHMA. WE HAVE ENOUGH ALLIES BACK AT THE BASE TO MAKE WINNING A SURE THING.
GUESS YOU'RE RIGHT.
WE'LL SPLIT UP.. I'LL WARN LEIA AND THOSE KIDS OF--!
LOOK--

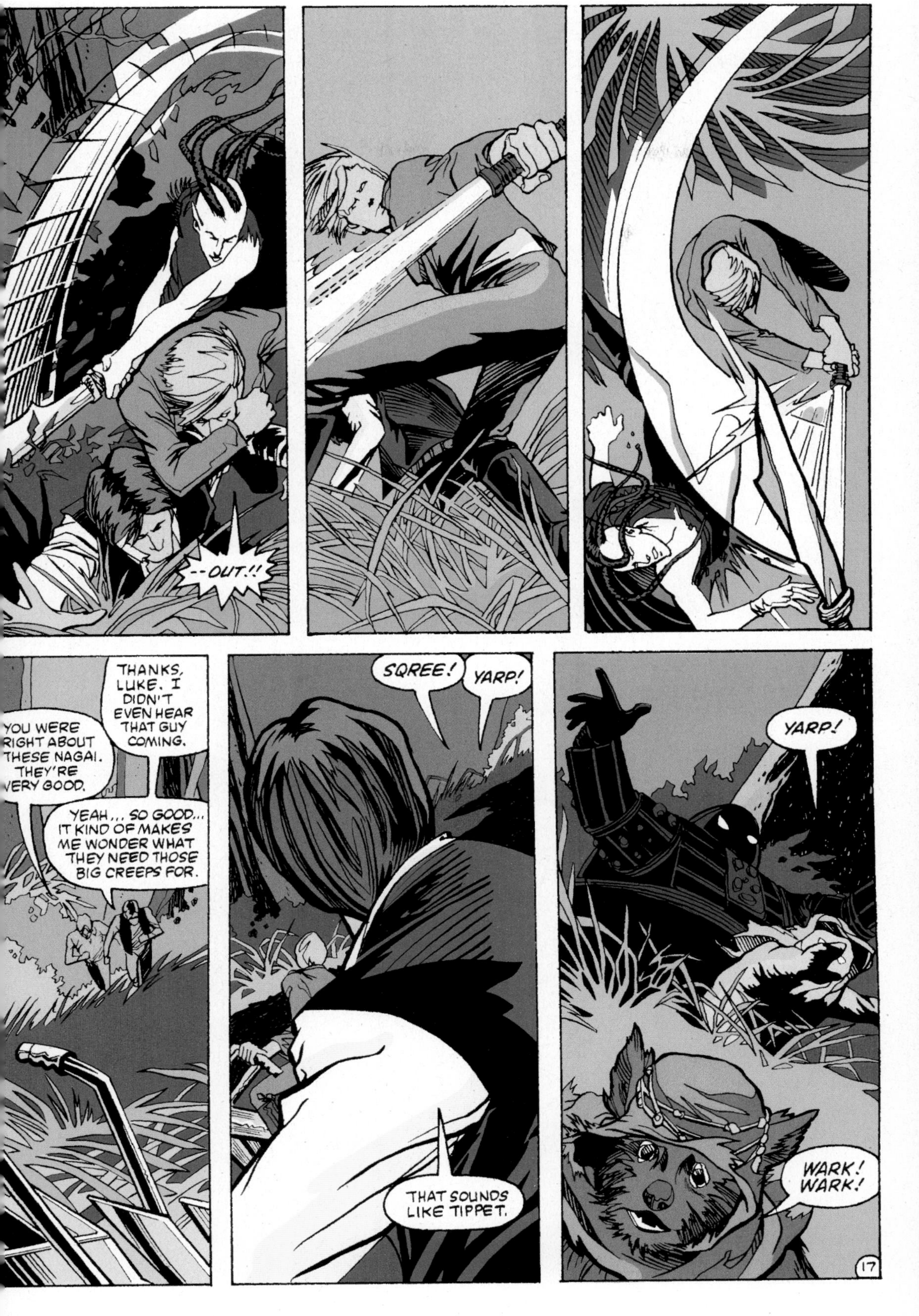
--OUT.!!
THANKS, LUKE. I DIDN'T EVEN HEAR THAT GUY COMING.
YOU WERE RIGHT ABOUT THESE NAGAI. THEY'RE VERY GOOD.
YEAH... SO GOOD... IT KIND OF MAKES ME WONDER WHAT THEY NEED THOSE BIG CREEPS FOR.
SQREE!
YARP!
THAT SOUNDS LIKE TIPPET.
YARP!
WARK! WARK!
17

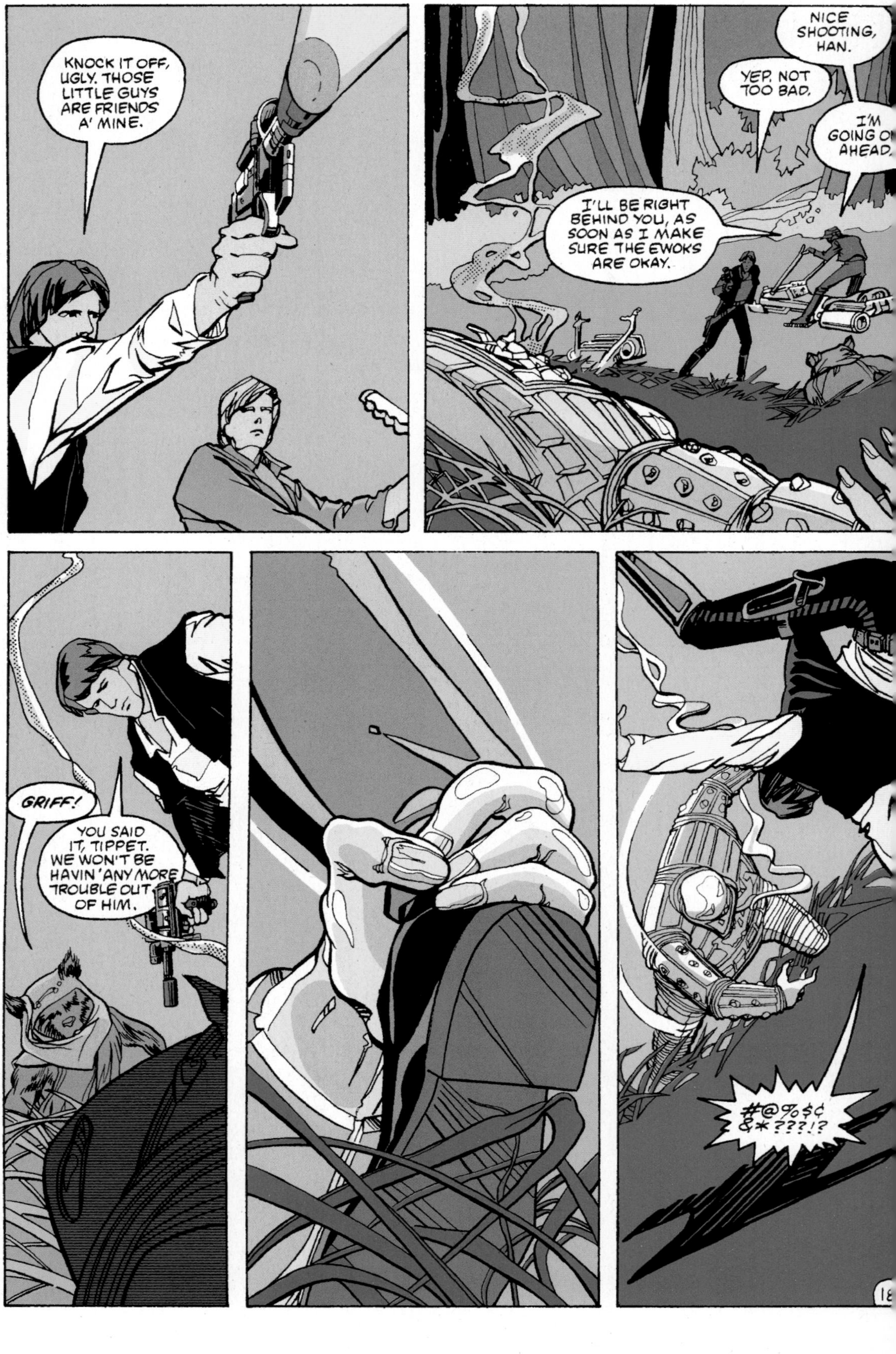
KNOCK IT OFF, UGLY. THOSE LITTLE GUYS ARE FRIENDS A' MINE.
NICE SHOOTING, HAN.
YEP. NOT TOO BAD.
I'M GOING ON AHEAD.
I'LL BE RIGHT BEHIND YOU, AS SOON AS I MAKE SURE THE EWOKS ARE OKAY.
GRIFF!
YOU SAID IT, TIPPET. WE WON'T BE HAVIN' ANY MORE TROUBLE OUT OF HIM.
#@%$¢ &*???!?
18

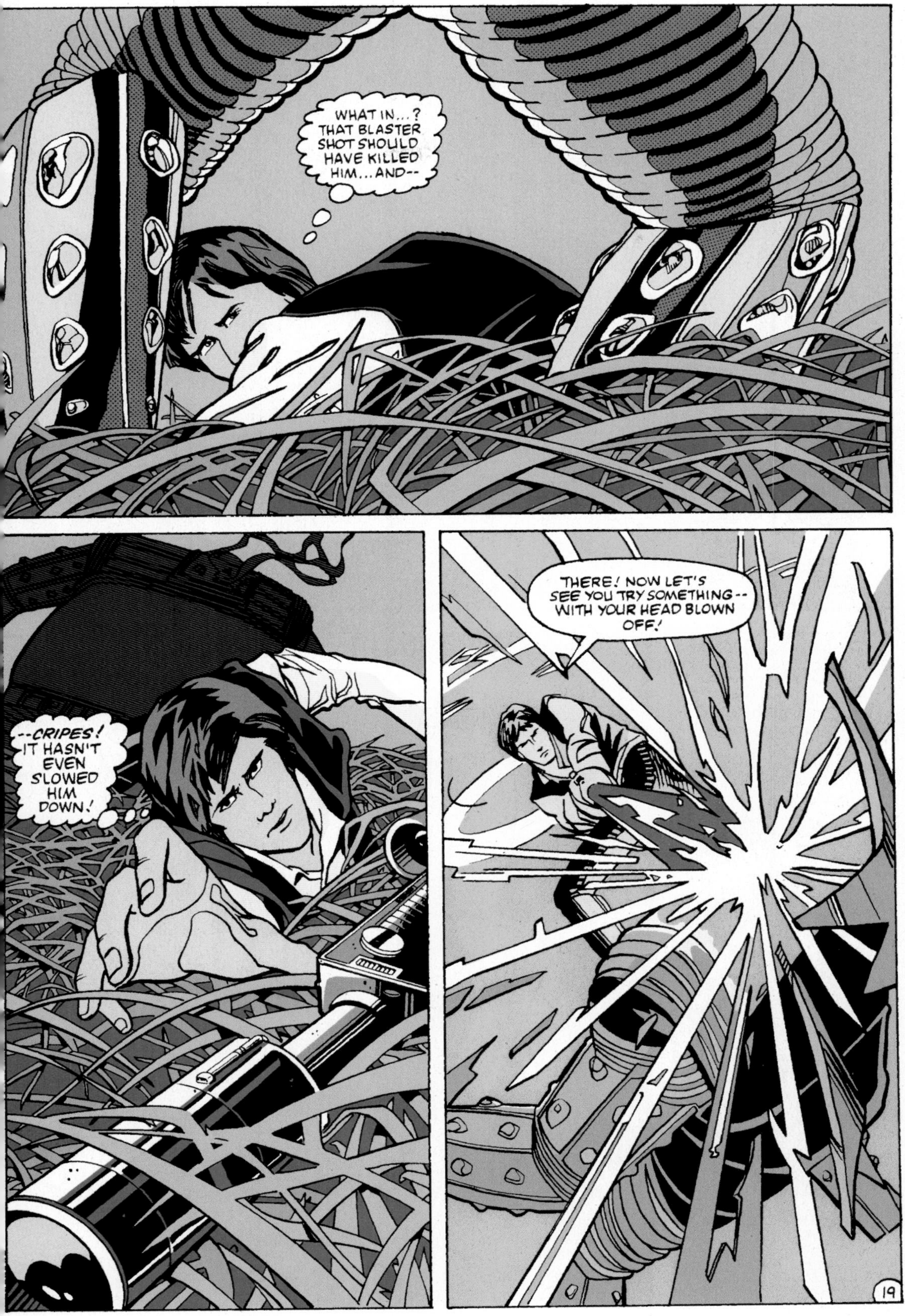
WHAT IN...? THAT BLASTER SHOT SHOULD HAVE KILLED HIM...AND--
--CRIPES! IT HASN'T EVEN SLOWED HIM DOWN!
THERE! NOW LET'S SEE YOU TRY SOMETHING-- WITH YOUR HEAD BLOWN OFF!
19

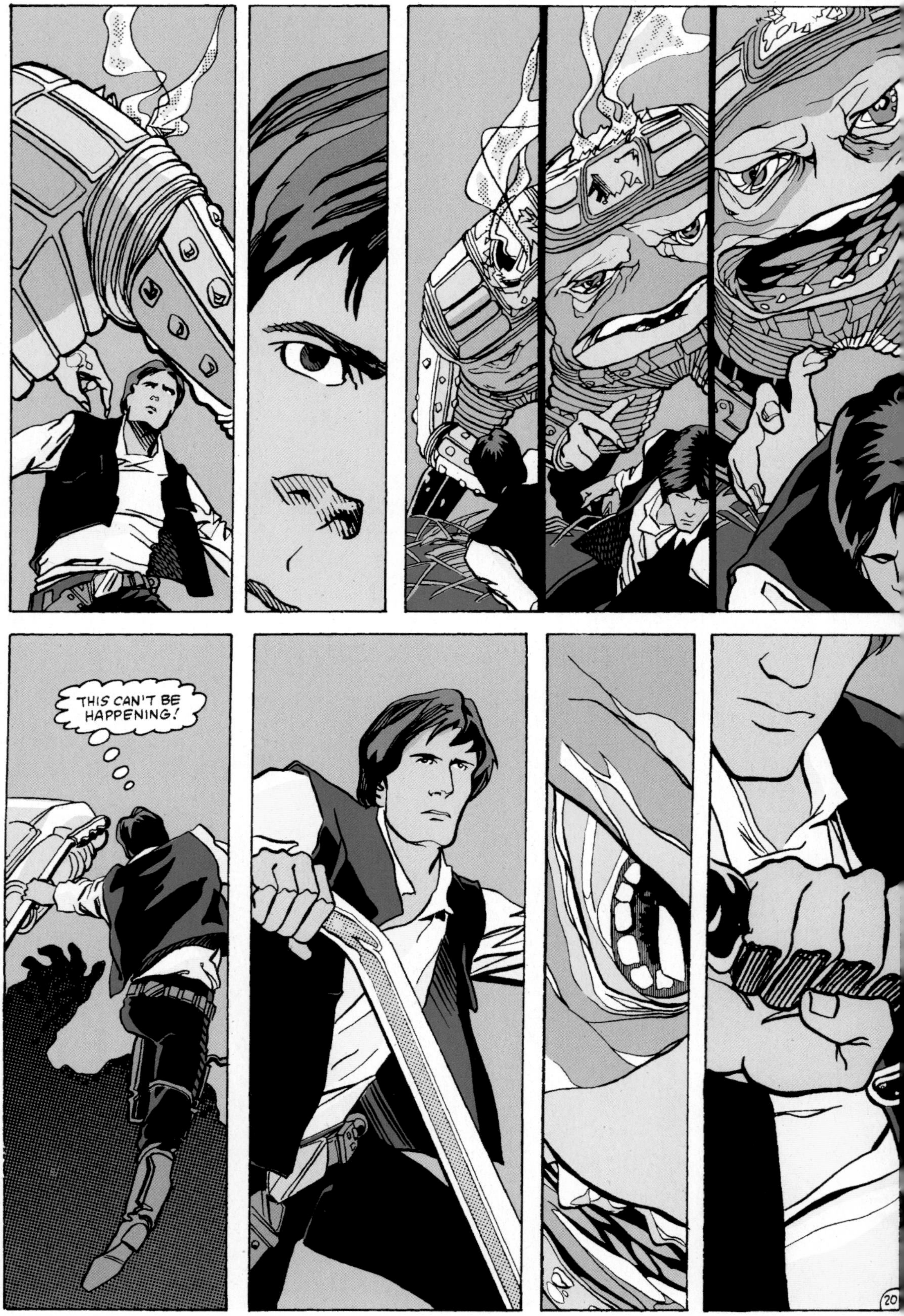
THIS CAN'T BE HAPPENING!
20

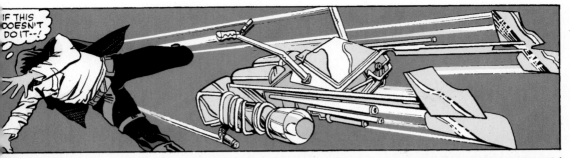

IF THIS DOESN'T DO IT--!

≡HUHF≡

≡HFH≡

≡HFH≡

WELL, THERE GOES MY SPEEDER BIKE...

I'VE GOT TO...

AN'... LUKE DOESN'T KNOW WHAT HE'S UP AGAINST.

OH, NO.

LEIA.

21

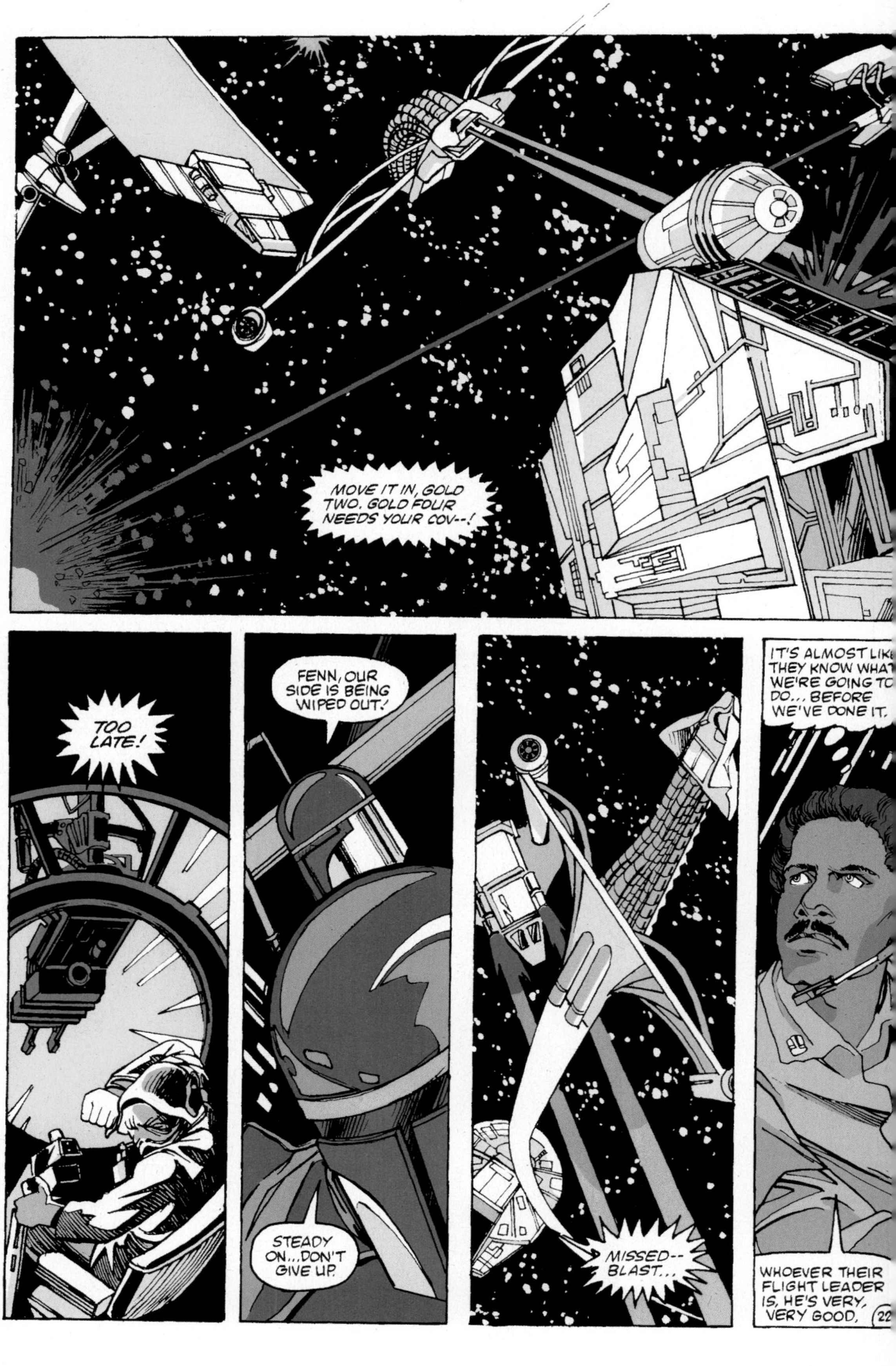
MOVE IT IN, GOLD TWO. GOLD FOUR NEEDS YOUR COV--!
TOO LATE!
FENN, OUR SIDE IS BEING WIPED OUT!
STEADY ON... DON'T GIVE UP.
MISSED-- BLAST...
IT'S ALMOST LIKE THEY KNOW WHAT WE'RE GOING TO DO... BEFORE WE'VE DONE IT.
WHOEVER THEIR FLIGHT LEADER IS, HE'S VERY, VERY GOOD.
22

...HE'S VERY VERY GOOD.

AH, REVENGE IS SWEET! I WONDER HOW MANY OF THOSE FOOLS WILL DIE BEFORE THEY REALIZE THE TRUTH--THAT THEY WERE BETRAYED BEFORE WE EVER ARRIVED HERE.

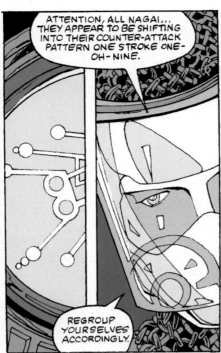

ATTENTION, ALL NAGAI... THEY APPEAR TO BE SHIFTING INTO THEIR COUNTER-ATTACK PATTERN ONE STROKE ONE-OH-NINE.

REGROUP YOURSELVES ACCORDINGLY.

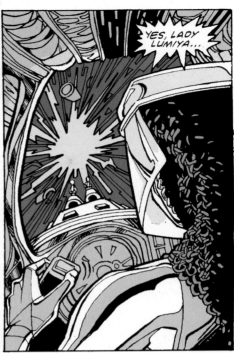

YES, LADY LUMIYA...

BLEEP BRVEET?

OF COURSE I CAN SEE HOW BADLY THE BATTLE IS GOING FOR OUR SQUA-DRON, ARTOO-DETOO... BUT DON'T GO ANNOUNCING IT FOR EVERYONE TO HEAR.

IT WOULD BE VERY BAD FOR MORALE IF WE WERE TO AN-NOUNCE THAT WE'RE DOOMED.

GRAVE AS MATTERS ARE, SEE-THREEPIO, I DON'T THINK WE'VE COME TO AS BAD A PASS AS THAT, YET.

NONETHELESS, ADMIRAL, THE OUT-LOOK IS NOT GOOD.

OUR EVACUATION...?

WOULD BE SUICIDE, WITH AN ENEMY AS FORMIDABLE AND WELL PREPARED AS THAT SQUADRON, WAITING ABOVE US.

23

299

OUR PILOTS ARE GONNA WIN THIS FIGHT, AREN'T THEY YOUR HIGHNESS?

I DON'T KNOW, JAHN... I HOPE SO, BUT...

THEY HAVE TO WIN. THEY'RE THE BEST THERE IS.

I WISH WE WERE PILOTS, TOO, THEN WE'D BE UP THERE, AND--

AND YOU MIGHT BE GETTING KILLED RIGHT NOW, I'M GLAD YOU'RE HERE WITH ME.

KILLED? BUT...

ALL ALLIANCE CHANNELS ARE SUPPOSED TO BE ENCODED AND SCRAMBLED... BUT THE WAY THE NAGAI ARE MANEUVERING...

... RIGHT ON OUR PILOTS ALMOST BEFORE THEY MOVE, I'D ALMOST SWEAR THAT SOMEHOW, OUR COMMUNICATIONS ARE BEING MONITORED.

BUT, THAT'S CRAZY!

WHERE WOULD THEY GET OUR FREQUENCIES?

IT'S PRETTY DARK OUT NOW... I'M GONNA LET IN A LITTLE FRESH AI--

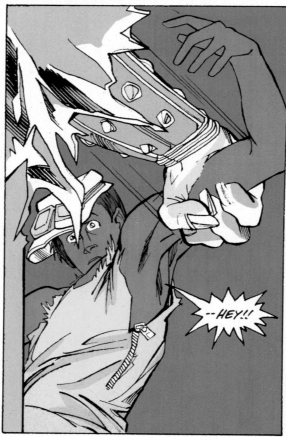

--HEY!!

RAHUHL!!

HELP-- HURRY.

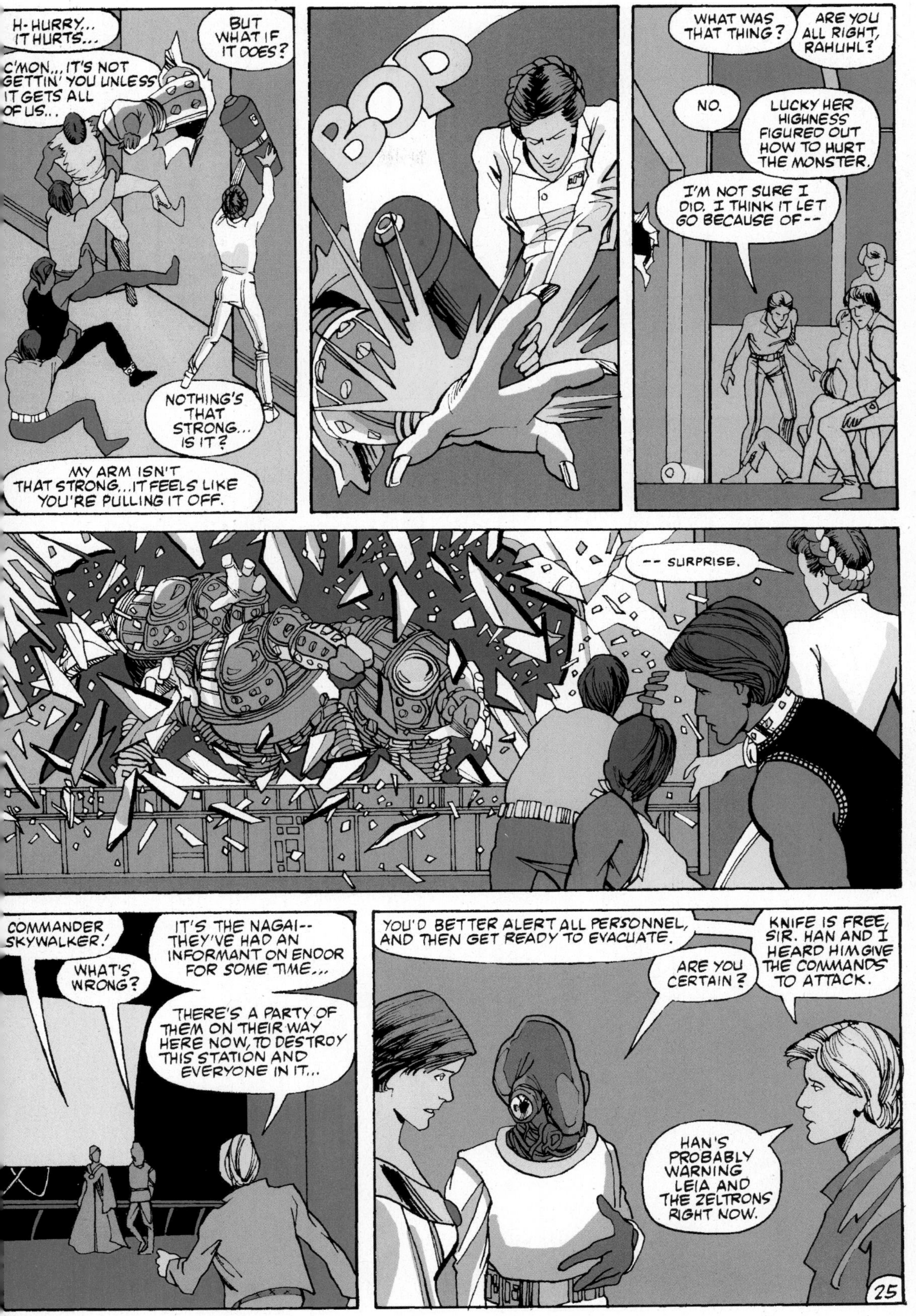
H-HURRY... IT HURTS...
BUT WHAT IF IT DOES?
C'MON... IT'S NOT GETTIN' YOU UNLESS IT GETS ALL OF US...
NOTHING'S THAT STRONG... IS IT?
MY ARM ISN'T THAT STRONG... IT FEELS LIKE YOU'RE PULLING IT OFF.
BOP
WHAT WAS THAT THING?
ARE YOU ALL RIGHT, RAHUHL?
NO.
LUCKY HER HIGHNESS FIGURED OUT HOW TO HURT THE MONSTER.
I'M NOT SURE I DID. I THINK IT LET GO BECAUSE OF --
-- SURPRISE.
COMMANDER SKYWALKER!
WHAT'S WRONG?
IT'S THE NAGAI-- THEY'VE HAD AN INFORMANT ON ENDOR FOR SOME TIME...
THERE'S A PARTY OF THEM ON THEIR WAY HERE NOW, TO DESTROY THIS STATION AND EVERYONE IN IT...
KNIFE IS FREE, SIR. HAN AND I HEARD HIM GIVE THE COMMANDS TO ATTACK.
ARE YOU CERTAIN?
YOU'D BETTER ALERT ALL PERSONNEL, AND THEN GET READY TO EVACUATE.
HAN'S PROBABLY WARNING LEIA AND THE ZELTRONS RIGHT NOW.
25

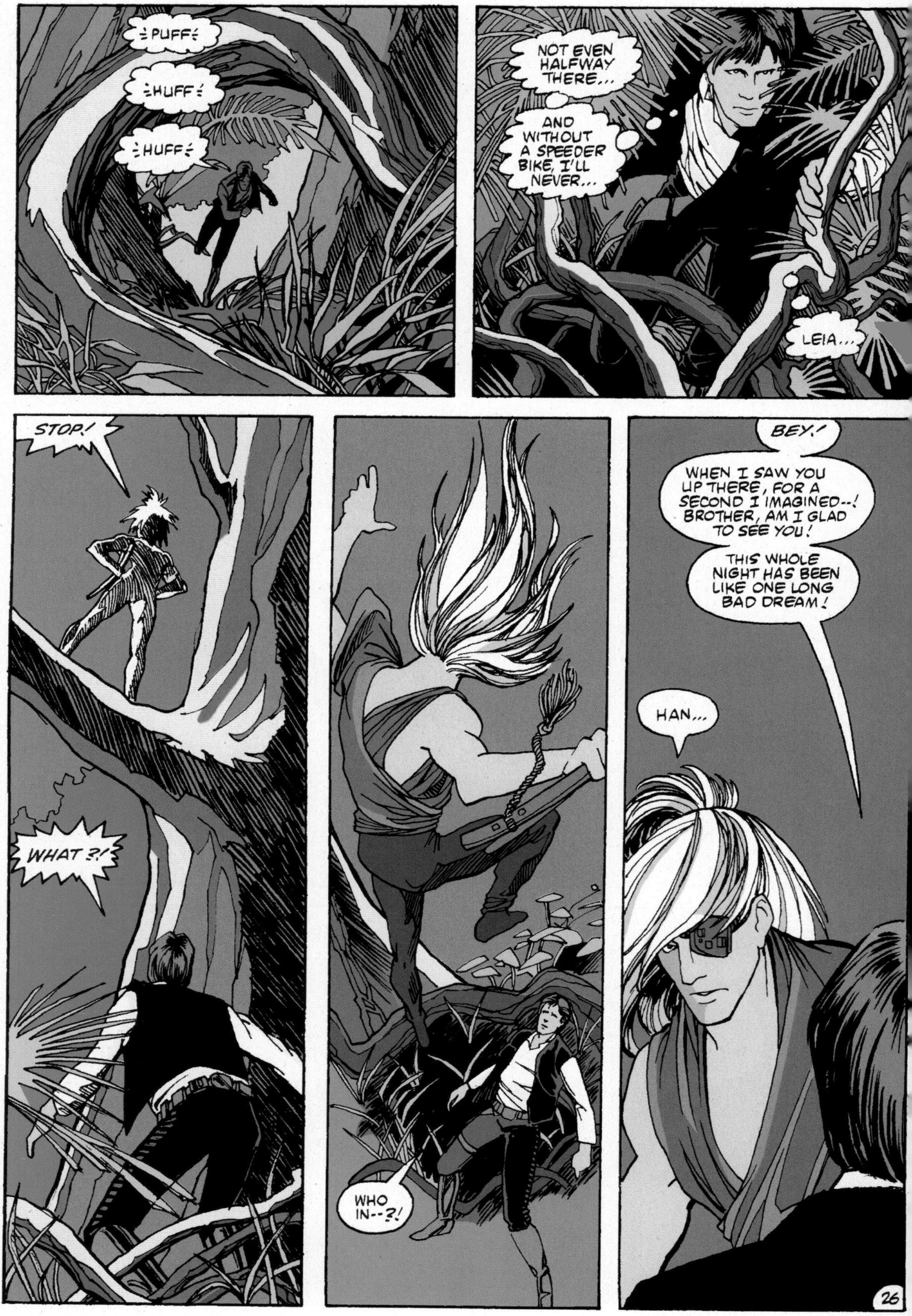
PUFF
HUFF
HUFF
NOT EVEN HALFWAY THERE...
AND WITHOUT A SPEEDER BIKE, I'LL NEVER...
LEIA...
STOP!
WHAT?!
WHO IN--?!
BEY!
WHEN I SAW YOU UP THERE, FOR A SECOND I IMAGINED--! BROTHER, AM I GLAD TO SEE YOU!
THIS WHOLE NIGHT HAS BEEN LIKE ONE LONG BAD DREAM!
HAN...
26

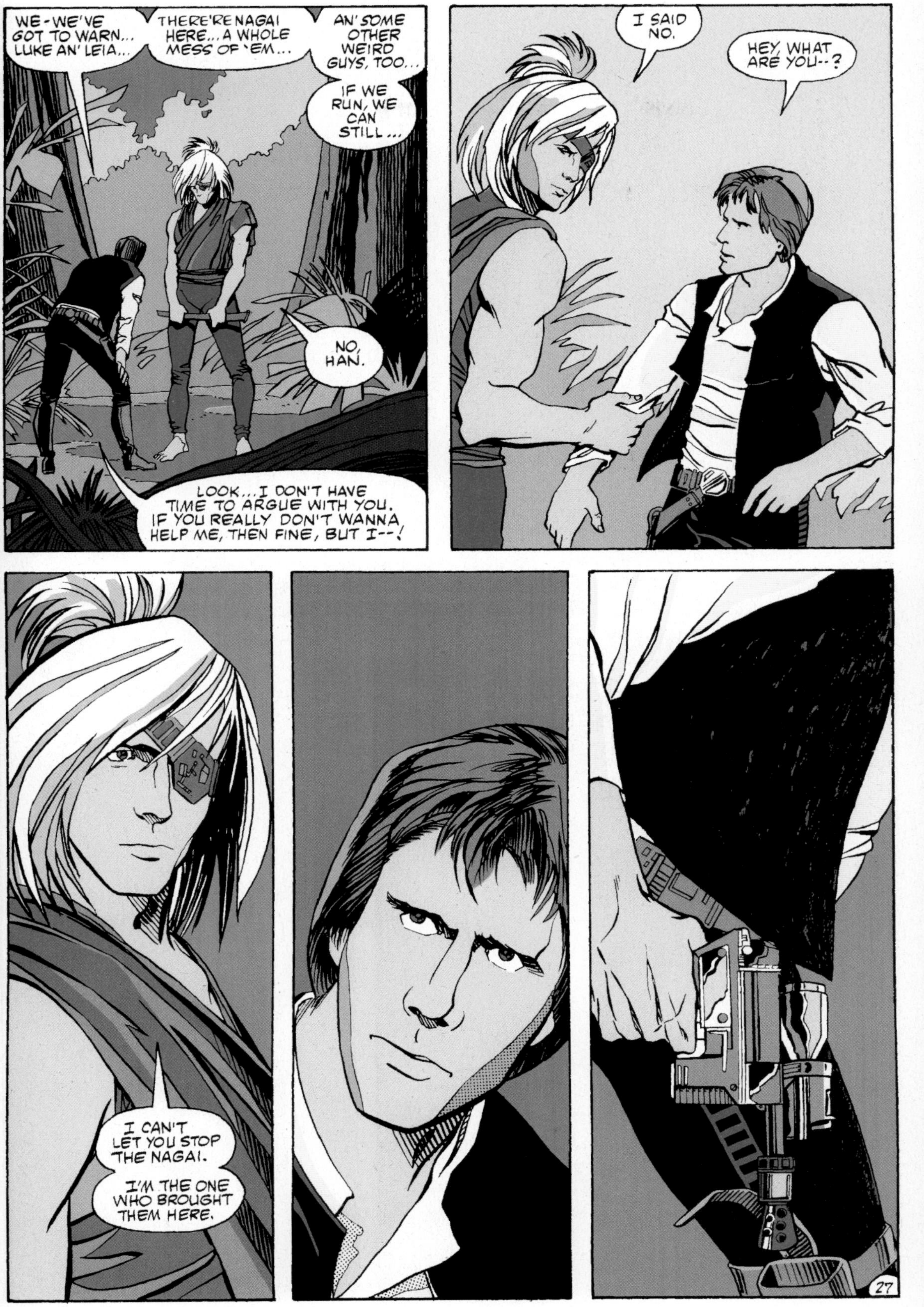
WE-WE'VE GOT TO WARN... LUKE AN' LEIA...
THERE'RE NAGAI HERE... A WHOLE MESS OF 'EM...
AN' SOME OTHER WEIRD GUYS, TOO...
IF WE RUN, WE CAN STILL...
NO, HAN.
LOOK... I DON'T HAVE TIME TO ARGUE WITH YOU. IF YOU REALLY DON'T WANNA HELP ME, THEN FINE, BUT I--!
I SAID NO.
HEY, WHAT ARE YOU--?
I CAN'T LET YOU STOP THE NAGAI.
I'M THE ONE WHO BROUGHT THEM HERE.
27

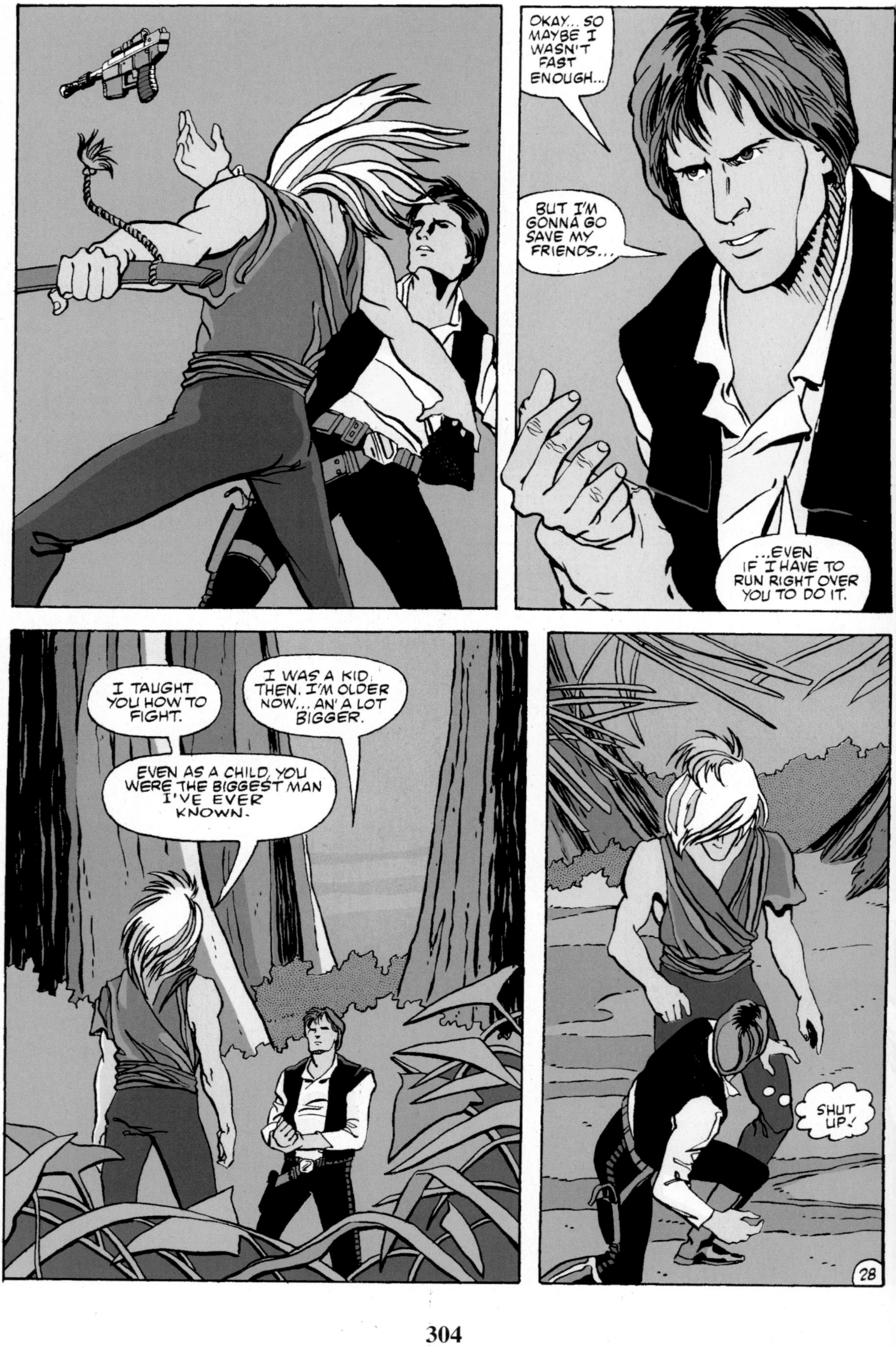
OKAY... SO MAYBE I WASN'T FAST ENOUGH...
BUT I'M GONNA GO SAVE MY FRIENDS...
...EVEN IF I HAVE TO RUN RIGHT OVER YOU TO DO IT.
I TAUGHT YOU HOW TO FIGHT.
I WAS A KID THEN. I'M OLDER NOW... AN' A LOT BIGGER.
EVEN AS A CHILD, YOU WERE THE BIGGEST MAN I'VE EVER KNOWN.
SHUT UP!
28

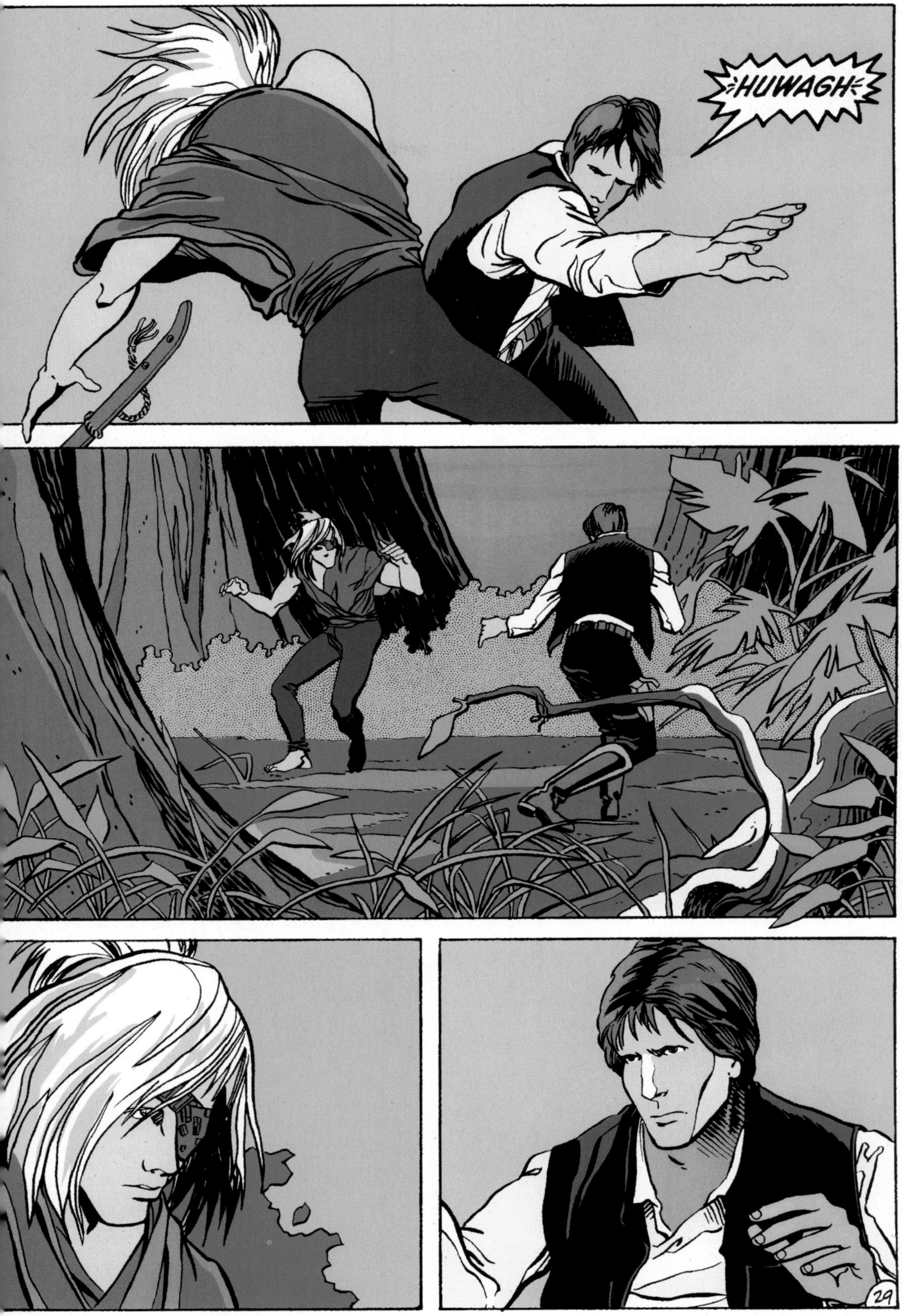
HUWAGH
29

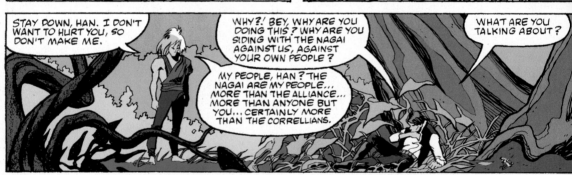

STAY DOWN, HAN. I DON'T WANT TO HURT YOU, SO DON'T MAKE ME.

WHY?! BEY, WHY ARE YOU DOING THIS? WHY ARE YOU SIDING WITH THE NAGAI AGAINST US, AGAINST YOUR OWN PEOPLE?

WHAT ARE YOU TALKING ABOUT?

MY PEOPLE, HAN? THE NAGAI ARE MY PEOPLE... MORE THAN THE ALLIANCE... MORE THAN ANYONE BUT YOU... CERTAINLY MORE THAN THE CORRELLIANS.

ALL THOSE TRIPS I TOOK, RAMBLING AROUND FROM PLANET TO PLANET, LEARNING WHAT I COULD, MAKING FRIENDS WHERE I COULD...

THE DAY FINALLY CAME WHEN GOOD LUCK AND BAD INSTRUMENTS FORCED ME TO WHERE NONE OF US HAD EVER BEEN -- BEYOND THE GALACTIC PERIMETER.

AND, OUT THERE, I LEARNED SOMETHING... MY MOTHER WAS AN ADVANCE SCOUT FOR THE NAGAI FLEET, WHO WANDERED INTO CORRELLI, AND SAW A GALAXY THAT MIGHT SOME-DAY BE FIT FOR TAKE-OVER...

AND SO, AFTER SHE'D LEARNED ALL SHE COULD, SHE WENT HOME, AND TOLD HER PEOPLE TO WAIT... WAIT UNTIL THE REBELLION HAD DONE THE WORK FOR THEM, AND THEY COULD COME HERE AND PICK UP THE PIECES OF WHICHEVER SIDE SURVIVED.

30

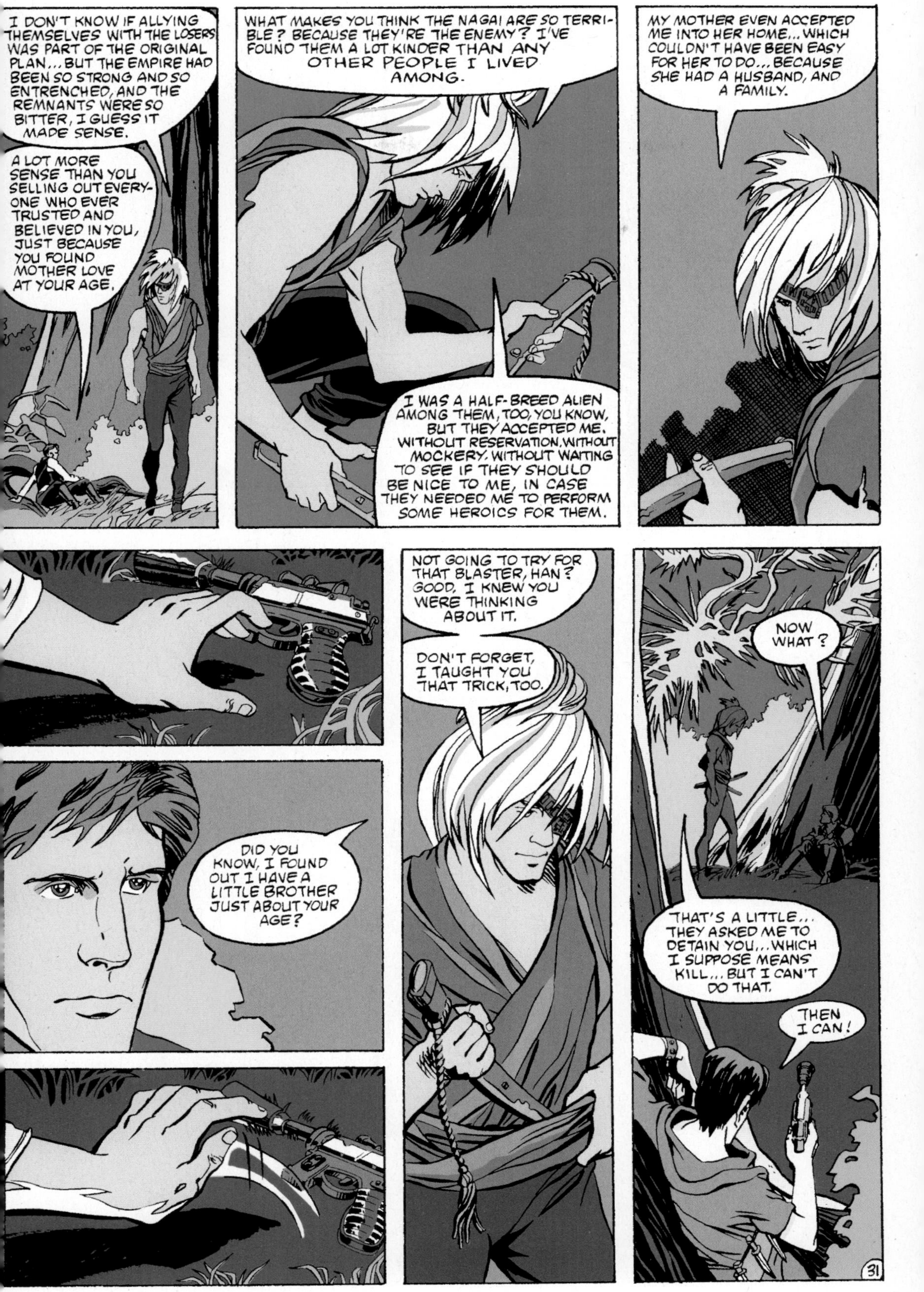
I DON'T KNOW IF ALLYING THEMSELVES WITH THE LOSERS WAS PART OF THE ORIGINAL PLAN... BUT THE EMPIRE HAD BEEN SO STRONG AND SO ENTRENCHED, AND THE REMNANTS WERE SO BITTER, I GUESS IT MADE SENSE.
A LOT MORE SENSE THAN YOU SELLING OUT EVERYONE WHO EVER TRUSTED AND BELIEVED IN YOU, JUST BECAUSE YOU FOUND MOTHER LOVE AT YOUR AGE.
WHAT MAKES YOU THINK THE NAGAI ARE SO TERRIBLE? BECAUSE THEY'RE THE ENEMY? I'VE FOUND THEM A LOT KINDER THAN ANY OTHER PEOPLE I LIVED AMONG.
I WAS A HALF-BREED ALIEN AMONG THEM, TOO, YOU KNOW, BUT THEY ACCEPTED ME. WITHOUT RESERVATION, WITHOUT MOCKERY. WITHOUT WAITING TO SEE IF THEY SHOULD BE NICE TO ME, IN CASE THEY NEEDED ME TO PERFORM SOME HEROICS FOR THEM.
MY MOTHER EVEN ACCEPTED ME INTO HER HOME... WHICH COULDN'T HAVE BEEN EASY FOR HER TO DO... BECAUSE SHE HAD A HUSBAND, AND A FAMILY.
DID YOU KNOW, I FOUND OUT I HAVE A LITTLE BROTHER JUST ABOUT YOUR AGE?
NOT GOING TO TRY FOR THAT BLASTER, HAN? GOOD, I KNEW YOU WERE THINKING ABOUT IT.
DON'T FORGET, I TAUGHT YOU THAT TRICK, TOO.
NOW WHAT?
THAT'S A LITTLE... THEY ASKED ME TO DETAIN YOU... WHICH I SUPPOSE MEANS KILL... BUT I CAN'T DO THAT.
THEN I CAN!
31

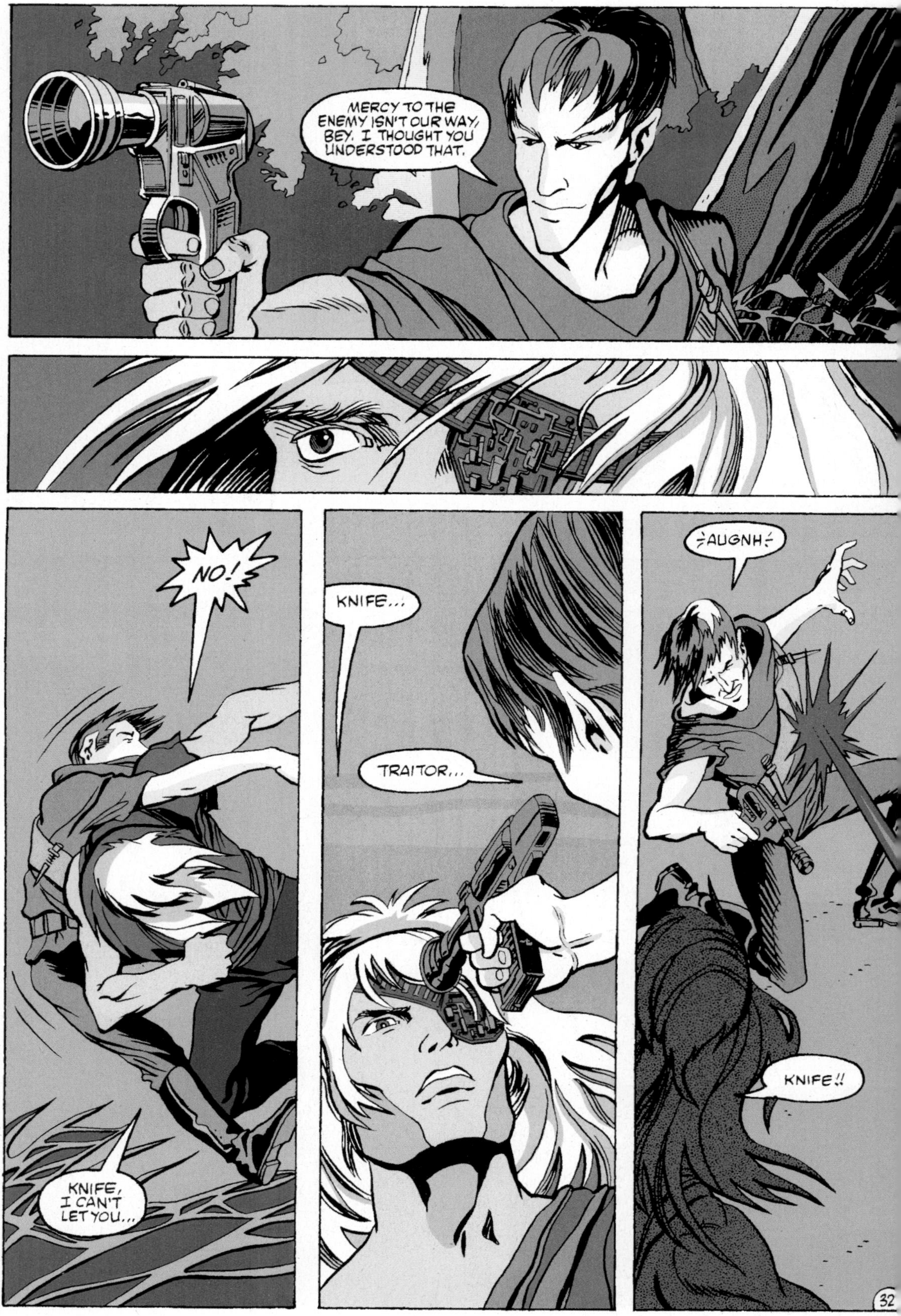
MERCY TO THE ENEMY ISN'T OUR WAY, BEY. I THOUGHT YOU UNDERSTOOD THAT.
NO!
KNIFE, I CAN'T LET YOU...
KNIFE...
TRAITOR...
AUGNH
KNIFE!!
32

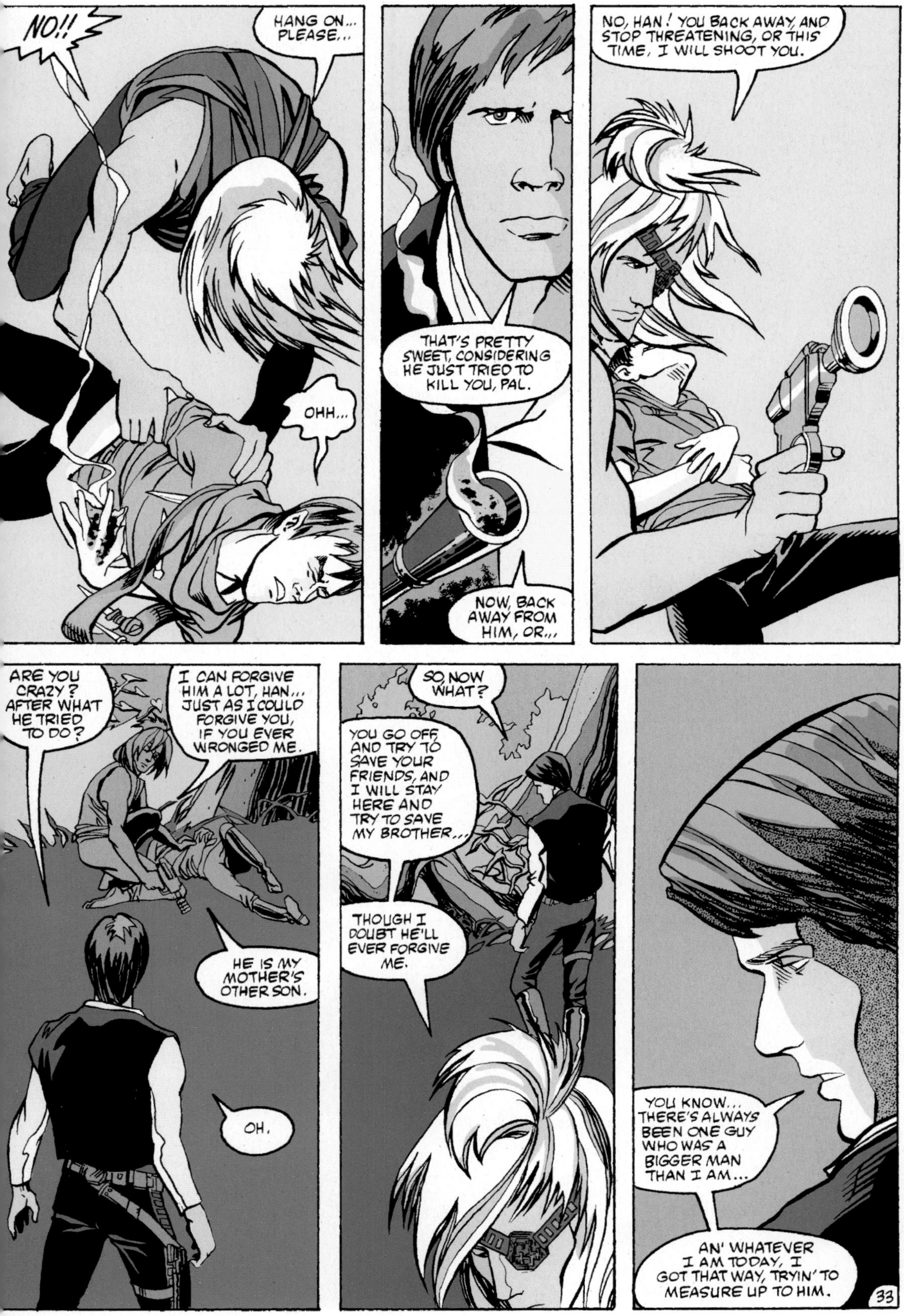

NO!!
HANG ON... PLEASE...
OHH...
THAT'S PRETTY SWEET, CONSIDERING HE JUST TRIED TO KILL YOU, PAL.
NOW, BACK AWAY FROM HIM, OR...
NO, HAN! YOU BACK AWAY, AND STOP THREATENING, OR THIS TIME, I WILL SHOOT YOU.
ARE YOU CRAZY? AFTER WHAT HE TRIED TO DO?
I CAN FORGIVE HIM A LOT, HAN... JUST AS I COULD FORGIVE YOU, IF YOU EVER WRONGED ME.
HE IS MY MOTHER'S OTHER SON.
OH.
SO, NOW WHAT?
YOU GO OFF AND TRY TO SAVE YOUR FRIENDS, AND I WILL STAY HERE AND TRY TO SAVE MY BROTHER...
THOUGH I DOUBT HE'LL EVER FORGIVE ME.
YOU KNOW... THERE'S ALWAYS BEEN ONE GUY WHO WAS A BIGGER MAN THAN I AM...
AN' WHATEVER I AM TODAY, I GOT THAT WAY, TRYIN' TO MEASURE UP TO HIM.
33

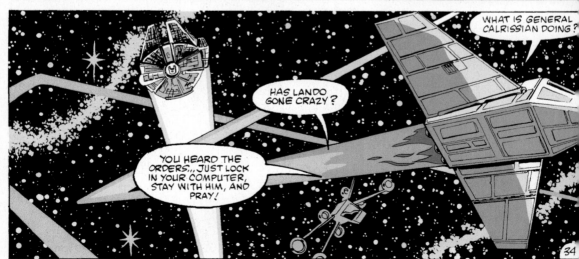

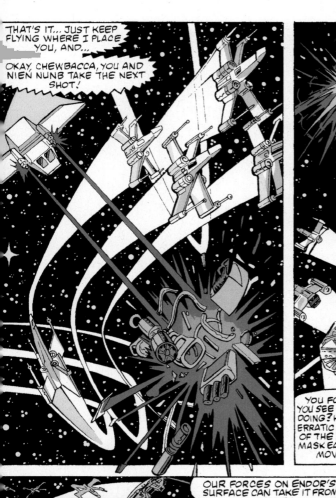

THAT'S IT... JUST KEEP FLYING WHERE I PLACE YOU, AND...

OKAY, CHEWBACCA, YOU AND NIEN NUNB TAKE THE NEXT SHOT!

YOU FOOLS! CAN'T YOU SEE WHAT HE'S DOING? HE'S USING THE ERRATIC FLIGHT PATHS OF THE SHIPS TO MASK EACH OTHER'S MOVEMENTS...

AND PICKING YOU ALL OFF AT WILL!

THIS WASN'T IN THE PLANS, ANYWHERE. SOUND RETREAT!

OUR FORCES ON ENDOR'S SURFACE CAN TAKE IT FROM HERE!

CALRISSIAN... I'VE NEVER SEEN FLYING LIKE THAT IN MY LIFE! ARE YOU A PILOT-- OR A MAGICIAN?

HOW DID YOU THINK OF SUCH A CRAZY STUNT?

I DIDN'T.

I JUST USED ONE OF HAN'S TRICKS.

35

311

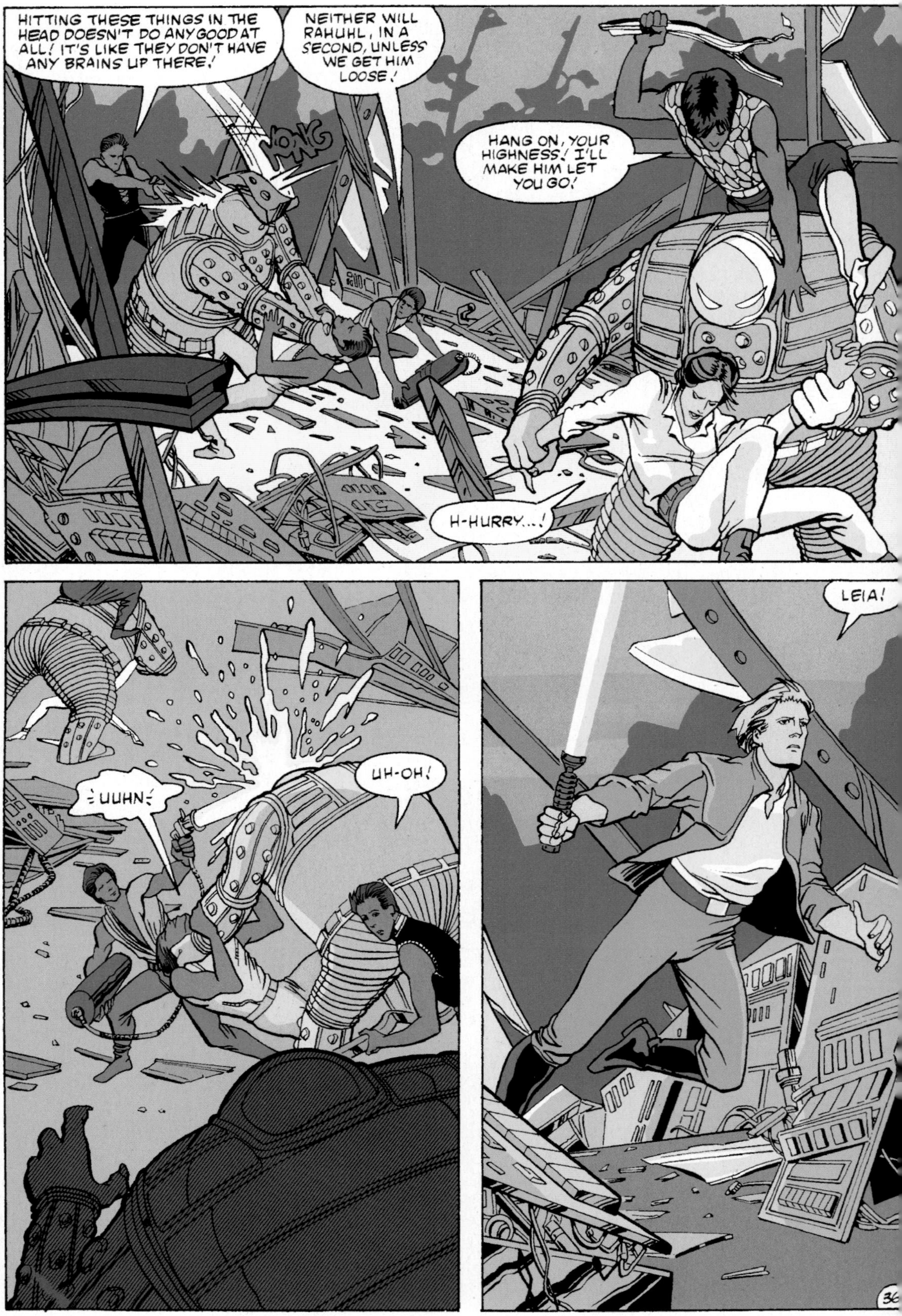
HITTING THESE THINGS IN THE HEAD DOESN'T DO ANY GOOD AT ALL! IT'S LIKE THEY DON'T HAVE ANY BRAINS UP THERE!
NEITHER WILL RAHUHL, IN A SECOND, UNLESS WE GET HIM LOOSE!
WONG
HANG ON, YOUR HIGHNESS! I'LL MAKE HIM LET YOU GO!
H-HURRY...!
UUHN
UH-OH!
LEIA!
36

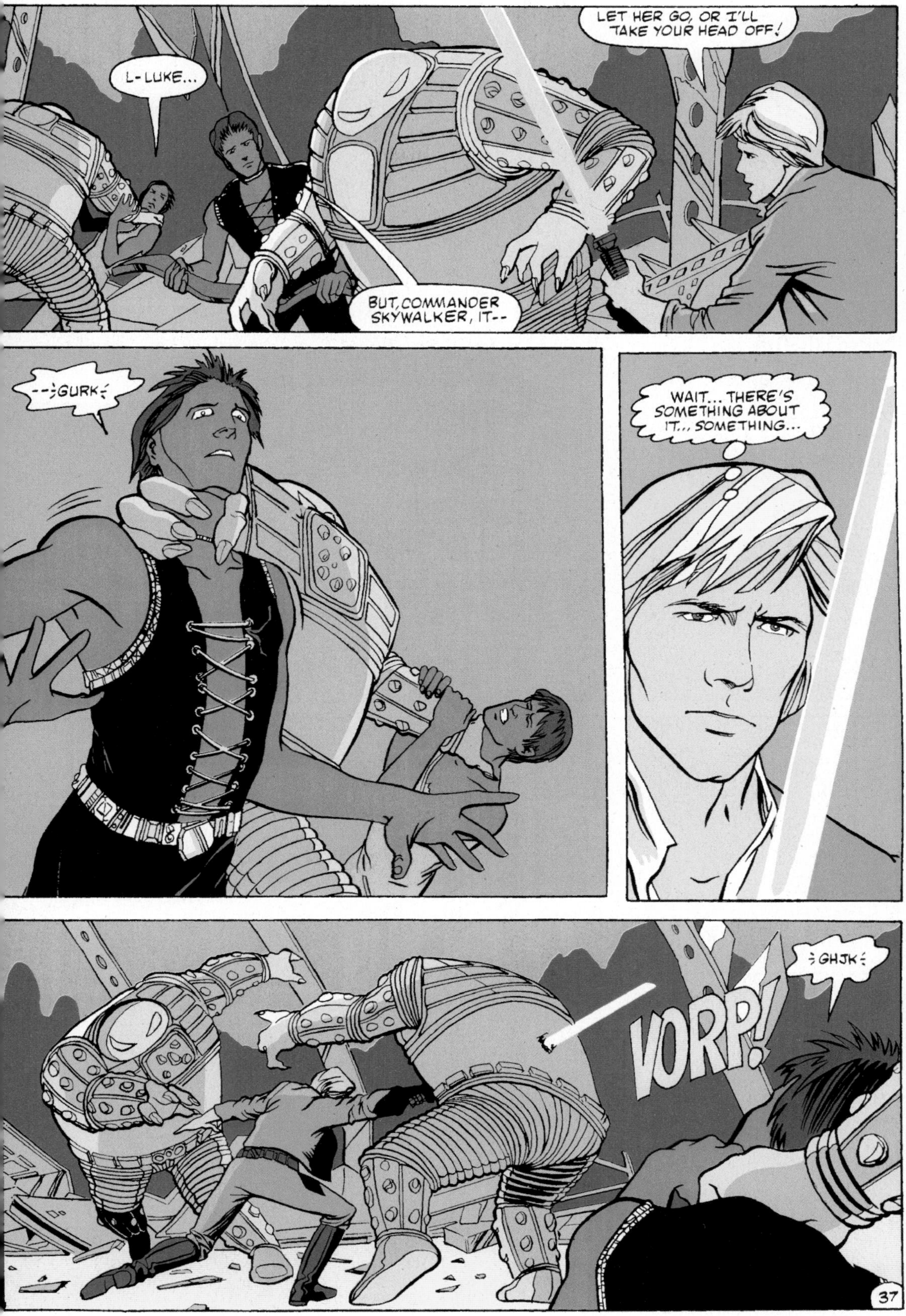
L-LUKE...
LET HER GO, OR I'LL TAKE YOUR HEAD OFF!
BUT, COMMANDER SKYWALKER, IT--
--GURK--
WAIT... THERE'S SOMETHING ABOUT IT... SOMETHING...
GHJK
VORP!
37

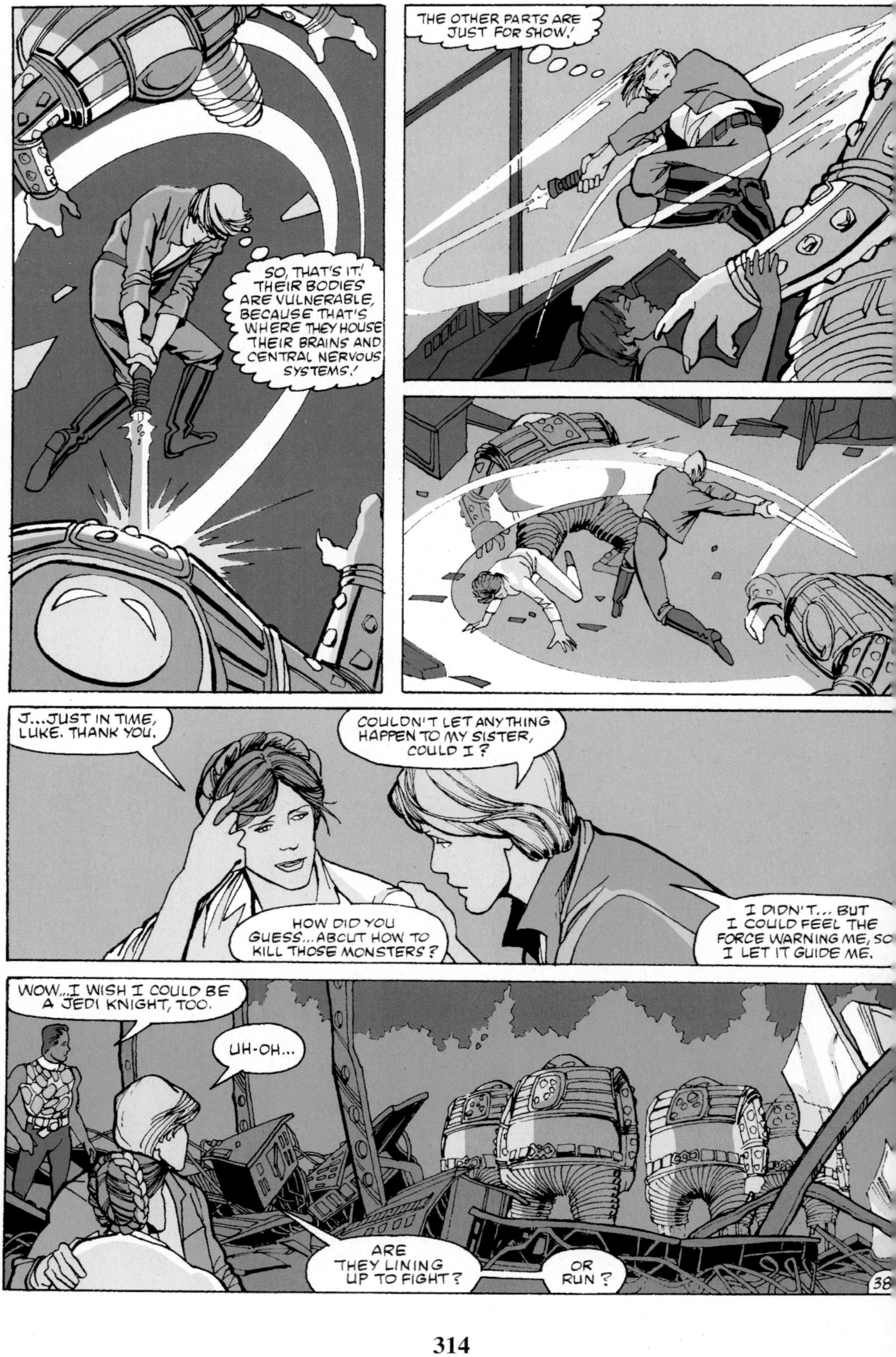
SO, THAT'S IT! THEIR BODIES ARE VULNERABLE, BECAUSE THAT'S WHERE THEY HOUSE THEIR BRAINS AND CENTRAL NERVOUS SYSTEMS!
THE OTHER PARTS ARE JUST FOR SHOW!
J...JUST IN TIME, LUKE. THANK YOU.
COULDN'T LET ANYTHING HAPPEN TO MY SISTER, COULD I?
HOW DID YOU GUESS... ABOUT HOW TO KILL THOSE MONSTERS?
I DIDN'T... BUT I COULD FEEL THE FORCE WARNING ME, SO I LET IT GUIDE ME.
WOW...I WISH I COULD BE A JEDI KNIGHT, TOO.
UH-OH...
ARE THEY LINING UP TO FIGHT?
OR RUN?
38

LOOKIT WHAT THEY'RE DOING! THEIR ARMS AND LEGS ARE--!

I DON'T THINK THOSE WERE "THEIR" ARMS AND LEGS, MARRUC...

THEY MUST HAVE GOTTEN THEM ON LOAN FROM THE NAGAI.

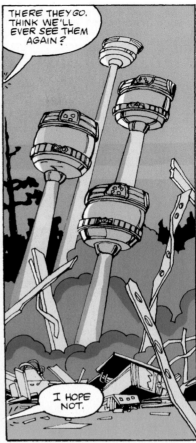

THERE THEY GO. THINK WE'LL EVER SEE THEM AGAIN?

I HOPE NOT.

⸰PUFF⸰

⸰HFH⸰

⸰HFPH⸰

⸰HFPH⸰

LEIA...

THE ELEVATOR... WAS OUT...HADDA...

HAN!

WHEN I SAW THE BUILDING WRECKED, I THOUGHT...

I THOUGHT THEY'D...

THOUGHT YOU WERE...

OH, HAN...

39

315

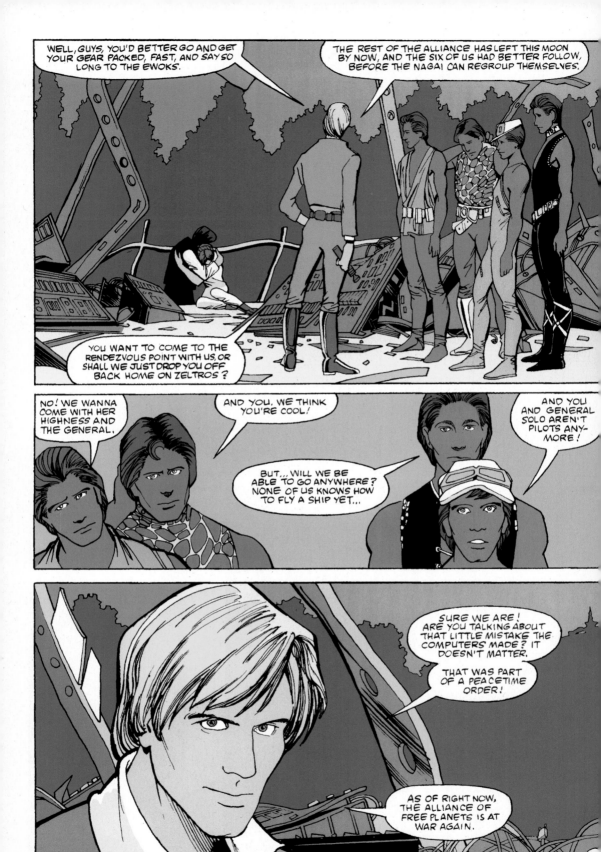

WELL, GUYS, YOU'D BETTER GO AND GET YOUR GEAR PACKED, FAST, AND SAY SO LONG TO THE EWOKS.

THE REST OF THE ALLIANCE HAS LEFT THIS MOON BY NOW, AND THE SIX OF US HAD BETTER FOLLOW, BEFORE THE NAGAI CAN REGROUP THEMSELVES.

YOU WANT TO COME TO THE RENDEZVOUS POINT WITH US, OR SHALL WE JUST DROP YOU OFF BACK HOME ON ZELTROS?

NO! WE WANNA COME WITH HER HIGHNESS AND THE GENERAL,

AND YOU, WE THINK YOU'RE COOL!

BUT... WILL WE BE ABLE TO GO ANYWHERE? NONE OF US KNOWS HOW TO FLY A SHIP YET...

AND YOU AND GENERAL SOLO AREN'T PILOTS ANY-MORE!

SURE WE ARE! ARE YOU TALKING ABOUT THAT LITTLE MISTAKE THE COMPUTERS MADE? IT DOESN'T MATTER.

THAT WAS PART OF A PEACETIME ORDER!

AS OF RIGHT NOW, THE ALLIANCE OF FREE PLANETS IS AT WAR AGAIN.

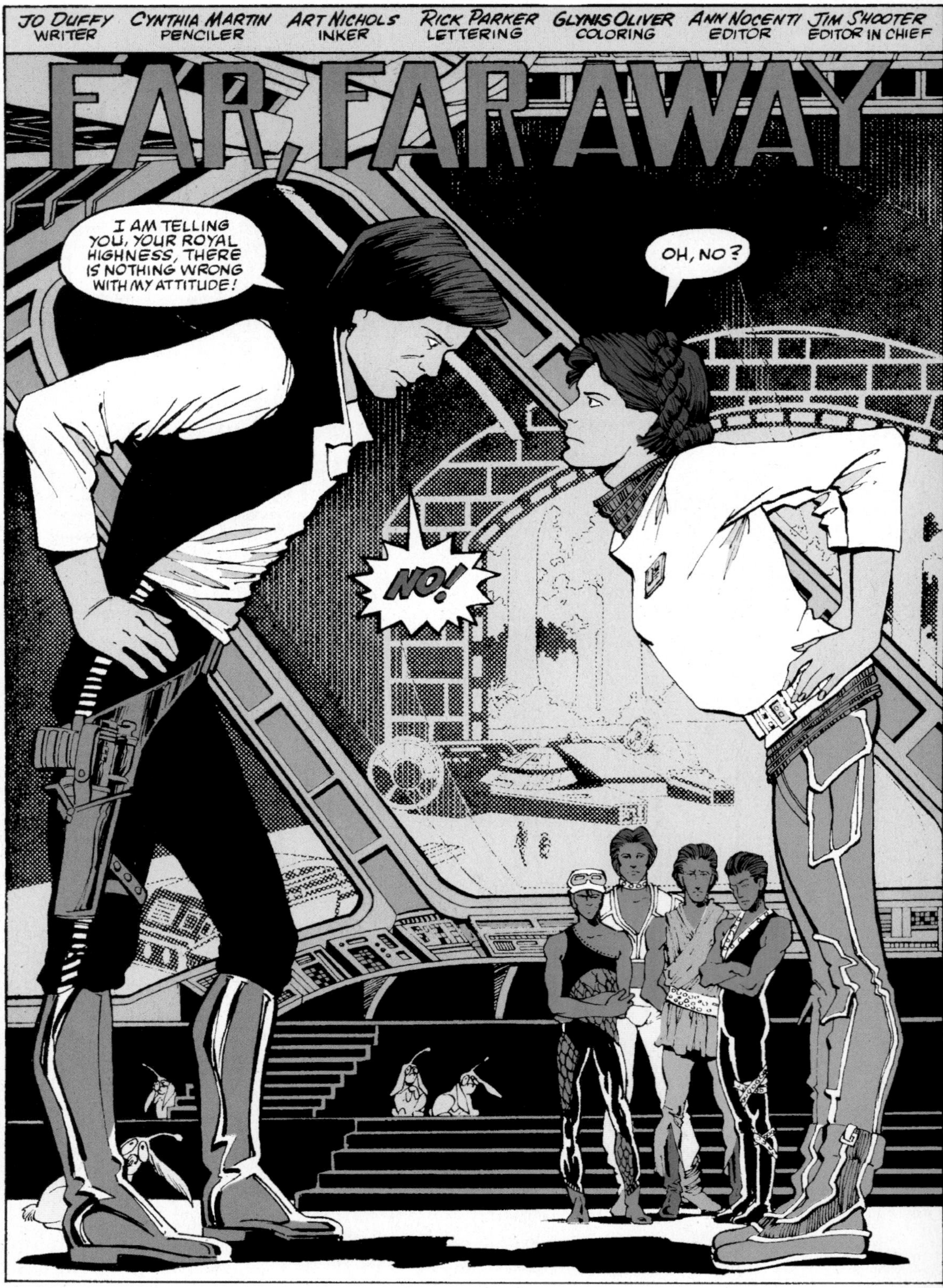
JO DUFFY WRITER
CYNTHIA MARTIN PENCILER
ART NICHOLS INKER
RICK PARKER LETTERING
GLYNIS OLIVER COLORING
ANN NOCENTI EDITOR
JIM SHOOTER EDITOR IN CHIEF
FAR, FAR AWAY
I AM TELLING YOU, YOUR ROYAL HIGHNESS, THERE IS NOTHING WRONG WITH MY ATTITUDE!
OH, NO?
NO!

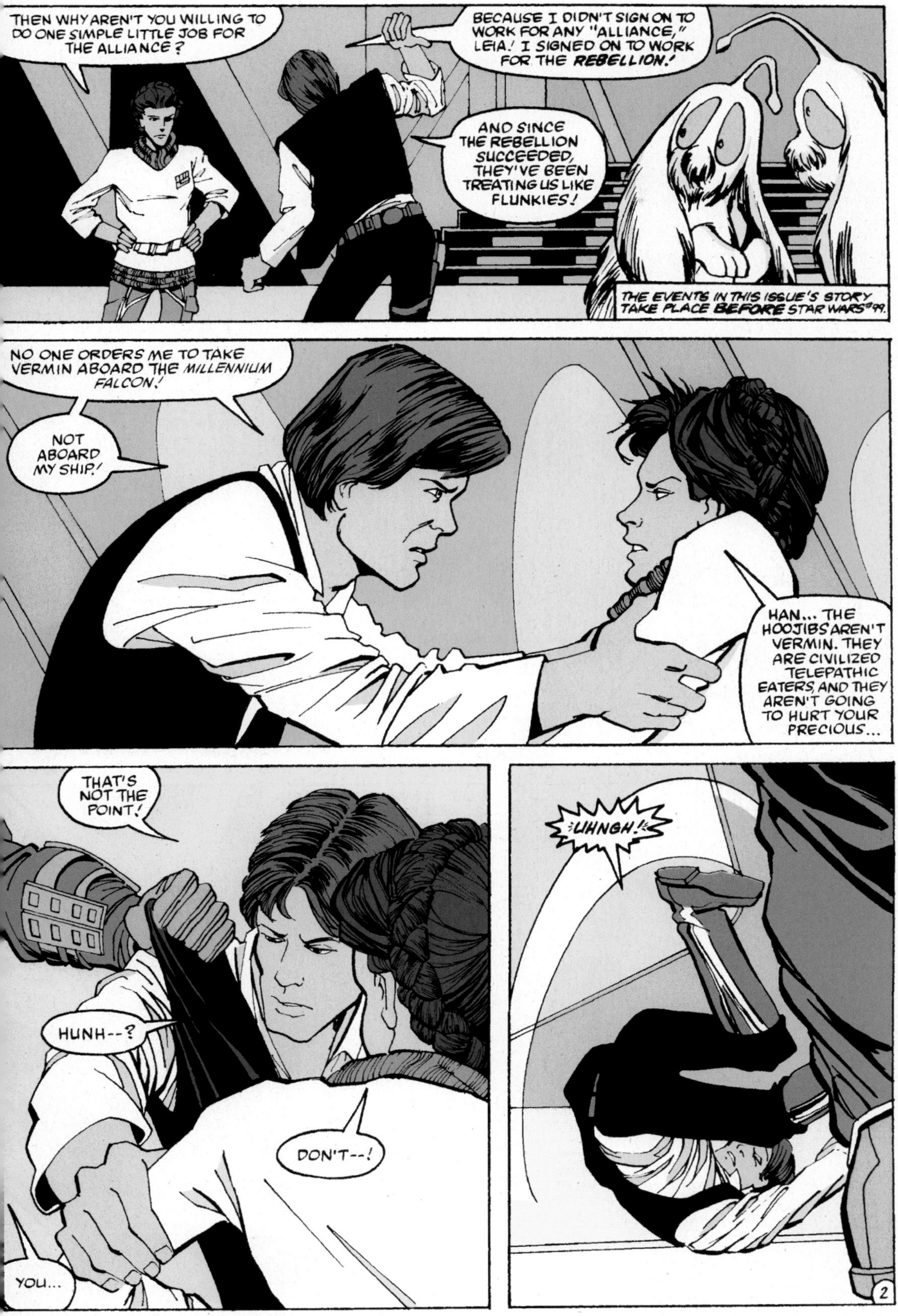
THEN WHY AREN'T YOU WILLING TO DO ONE SIMPLE LITTLE JOB FOR THE ALLIANCE?
BECAUSE I DIDN'T SIGN ON TO WORK FOR ANY "ALLIANCE," LEIA! I SIGNED ON TO WORK FOR THE REBELLION!
AND SINCE THE REBELLION SUCCEEDED, THEY'VE BEEN TREATING US LIKE FLUNKIES!
THE EVENTS IN THIS ISSUE'S STORY TAKE PLACE BEFORE STAR WARS #99.
NO ONE ORDERS ME TO TAKE VERMIN ABOARD THE MILLENNIUM FALCON!
NOT ABOARD MY SHIP!
HAN... THE HOOJIBS AREN'T VERMIN. THEY ARE CIVILIZED TELEPATHIC EATERS, AND THEY AREN'T GOING TO HURT YOUR PRECIOUS...
THAT'S NOT THE POINT!
HUNH--?
DON'T--!
YOU...
UHNGH!
2

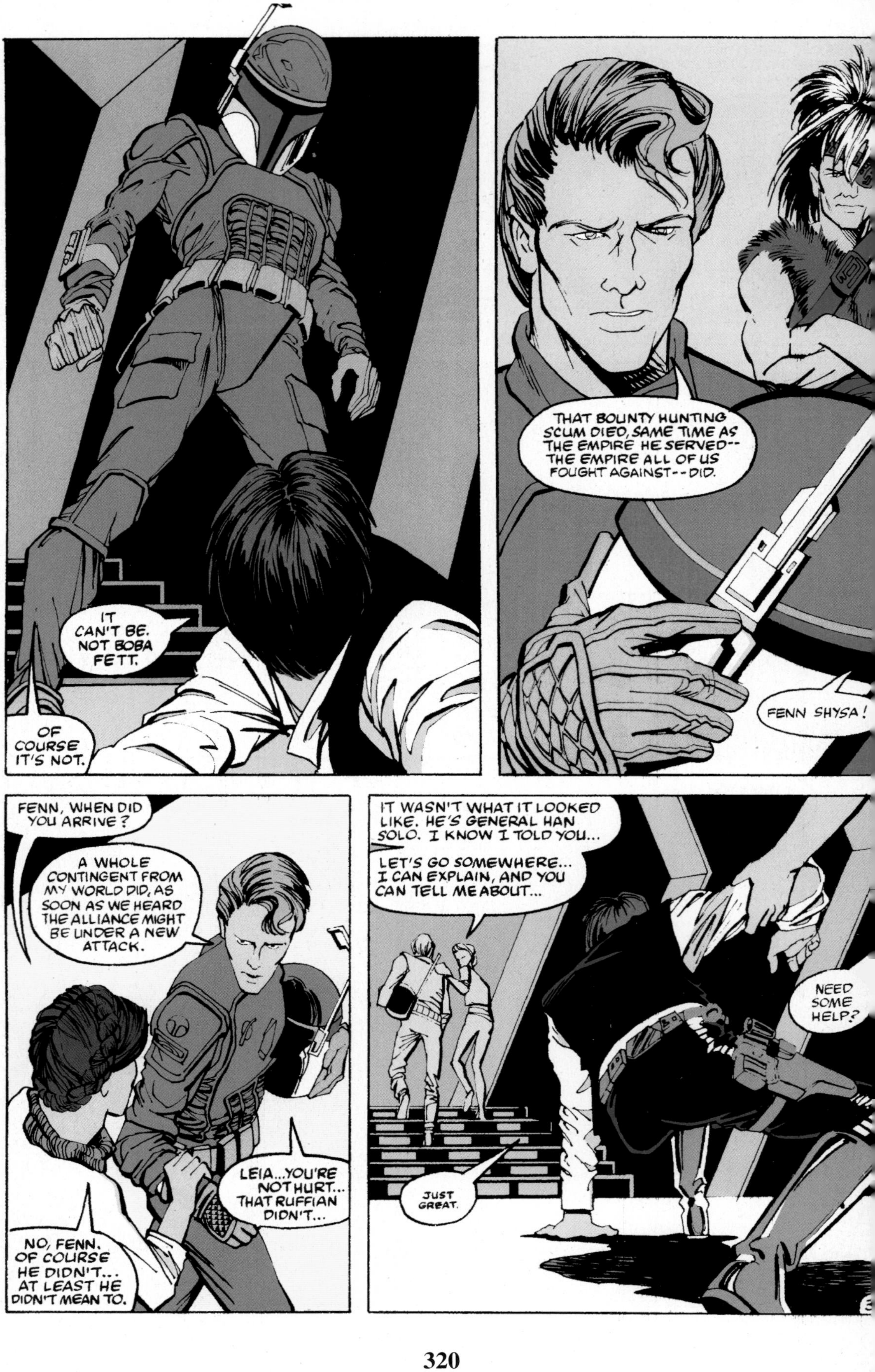
IT CAN'T BE. NOT BOBA FETT.
OF COURSE IT'S NOT.
THAT BOUNTY HUNTING SCUM DIED, SAME TIME AS THE EMPIRE HE SERVED-- THE EMPIRE ALL OF US FOUGHT AGAINST--DID.
FENN SHYSA!
FENN, WHEN DID YOU ARRIVE?
A WHOLE CONTINGENT FROM MY WORLD DID, AS SOON AS WE HEARD THE ALLIANCE MIGHT BE UNDER A NEW ATTACK.
LEIA...YOU'RE NOT HURT... THAT RUFFIAN DIDN'T...
NO, FENN. OF COURSE HE DIDN'T... AT LEAST HE DIDN'T MEAN TO.
IT WASN'T WHAT IT LOOKED LIKE. HE'S GENERAL HAN SOLO. I KNOW I TOLD YOU...
LET'S GO SOMEWHERE... I CAN EXPLAIN, AND YOU CAN TELL ME ABOUT...
NEED SOME HELP?
JUST GREAT.

BEY??!? WHEN DID YOU COME IN? WHERE DID YOU COME FROM?

I'VE BEEN HERE AND THERE. I WAS ON FENN'S HOMEWORLD, WHEN THE CALL FROM YOUR ADMIRAL ACKBAR CAME IN.

IT SOUNDED LIKE IT MIGHT BE AMUSING, SO I CAME WITH HIM.

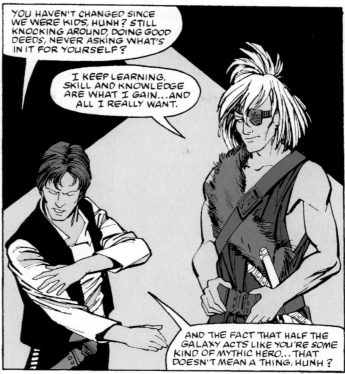

YOU HAVEN'T CHANGED SINCE WE WERE KIDS, HUNH? STILL KNOCKING AROUND, DOING GOOD DEEDS, NEVER ASKING WHAT'S IN IT FOR YOURSELF?

I KEEP LEARNING. SKILL AND KNOWLEDGE ARE WHAT I GAIN...AND ALL I REALLY WANT.

AND THE FACT THAT HALF THE GALAXY ACTS LIKE YOU'RE SOME KIND OF MYTHIC HERO...THAT DOESN'T MEAN A THING, HUNH?

AND YOU... ARE YOU STILL IN IT FOR THE MONEY... OR HAVE YOU FINALLY FOUND ANYTHING ELSE THAT MEANS MORE TO YOU?

I DON'T KNOW WHAT YOU'RE TALKING ABOUT. THE MONEY'S GOOD.

THAT GIRL... THE PRINCESS? SHE'S RESPECTED THROUGHOUT THE ALLIANCE...SHE MEANS SOMETHING TO YOU?

IS IT MUTUAL?

NONE OF YOUR BUSINESS.

YOU'RE STILL YOUR USUAL SELF, HAN. HAVEN'T YOU LEARNED YET?

IF YOU CARE FOR SOMEONE, TREAT HER WELL. TELL HER THAT YOU CARE.

I DON'T HAVE TO TELL LEIA! SHE KNOWS HOW I FEEL!

MMM?

THAT'S ENOUGH!

4

HAN, WE'VE BEEN THROUGH ALL THAT... THESE BALLS OF COHERENT ENERGY HAVE BEEN APPEARING THROUGHOUT THIS SECTOR OF SPACE...

I STILL THINK THIS IS RIDICULOUS. WHAT DO YOU NEED ME AND MY SHIP FOR?

...THROWING OFF NAVIGATION, AND SPONTANEOUSLY RELOCATING ENTIRE SHIPS...

WE NEED PLIF AND HIS FELLOW HOOJIBS -- AND A COUPLE OF DROIDS, LIKE ARTOO-DETOO, OR SEE-THREEPIO -- TO RECORD AND ANALYZE THE PHENOMENON.

THIS IS THE LARGEST ONE TO SHOW UP SO FAR, AND YOUR SHIP IS THE ONLY ONE WITH THE MANEUVERABILITY TO...

HAN...

I DON'T UNDERSTAND. WHERE DID THE MILLEN-NIUM FALCON AND ALL OF THAT ENERGY GO?

DIDN'T YOU HEAR? SHE SAID IT HAD BEEN MOVING SHIPS, THAT ENERGY, WITHOUT EXPLANATION...

HAN..

WHAT'S HAPPENING?

I DON'T KNOW... JUST HANG ON, AND LET ME NAVIGATE THROUGH IT.

BLEEP!

I AGREE WITH ARTOO, GENERAL SOLO! I WANT TO KNOW WHERE WE ARE!

BEATS ME, THREEPIO!

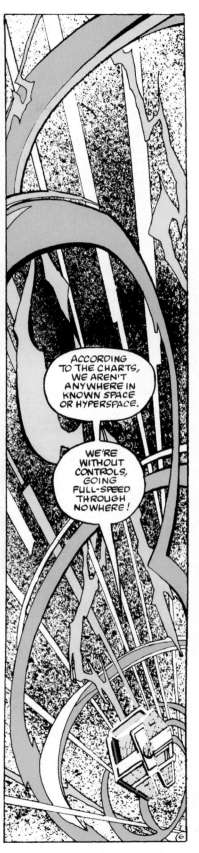

ACCORDING TO THE CHARTS, WE AREN'T ANYWHERE IN KNOWN SPACE OR HYPERSPACE.

WE'RE WITHOUT CONTROLS, GOING FULL-SPEED THROUGH NOWHERE!

6

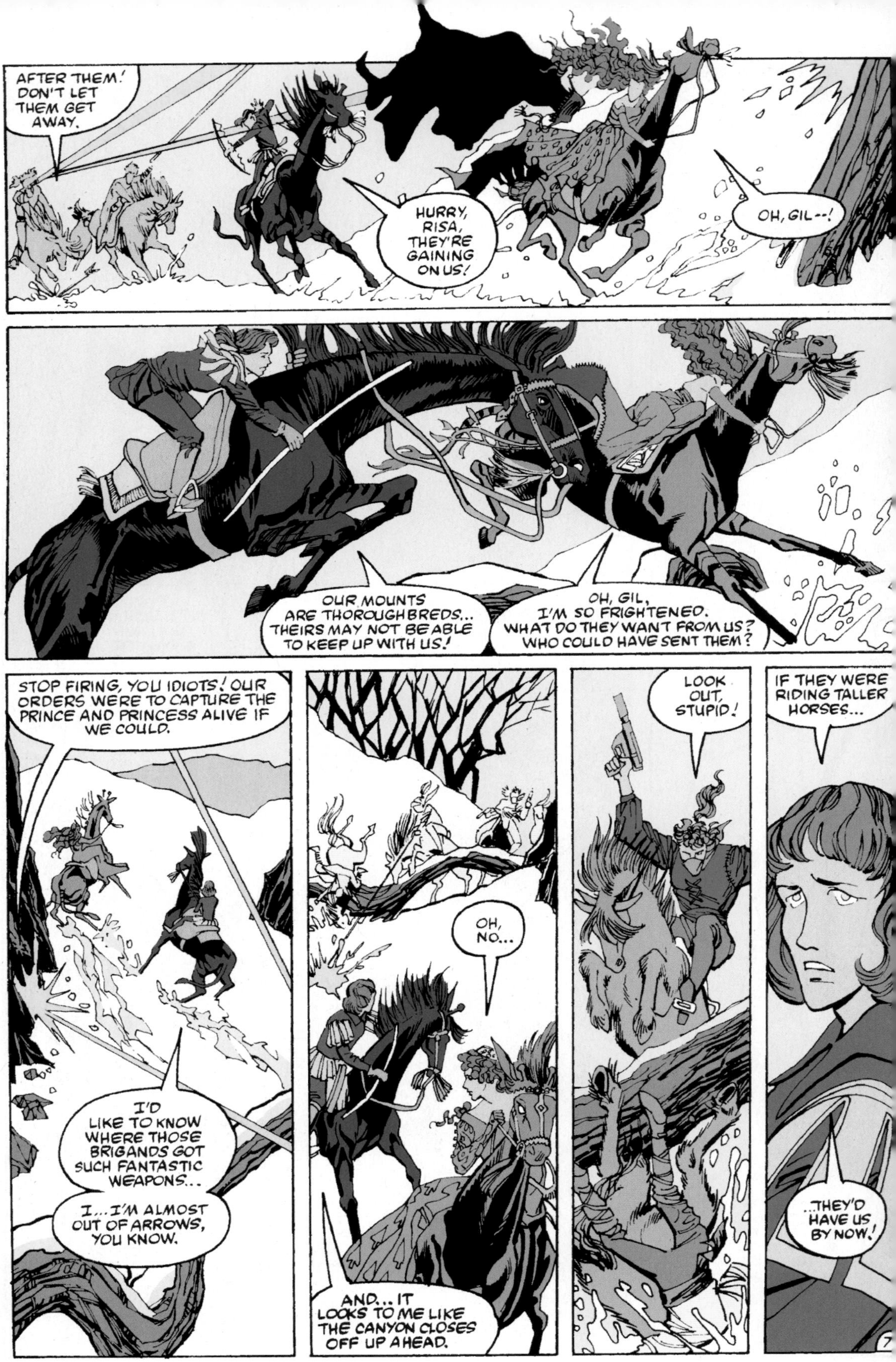
AFTER THEM! DON'T LET THEM GET AWAY.
HURRY, RISA, THEY'RE GAINING ON US!
OH, GIL--!
OUR MOUNTS ARE THOROUGHBREDS... THEIRS MAY NOT BE ABLE TO KEEP UP WITH US!
OH, GIL, I'M SO FRIGHTENED. WHAT DO THEY WANT FROM US? WHO COULD HAVE SENT THEM?
STOP FIRING, YOU IDIOTS! OUR ORDERS WERE TO CAPTURE THE PRINCE AND PRINCESS ALIVE IF WE COULD.
I'D LIKE TO KNOW WHERE THOSE BRIGANDS GOT SUCH FANTASTIC WEAPONS...
I... I'M ALMOST OUT OF ARROWS, YOU KNOW.
OH, NO...
AND... IT LOOKS TO ME LIKE THE CANYON CLOSES OFF UP AHEAD.
LOOK OUT, STUPID!
IF THEY WERE RIDING TALLER HORSES...
...THEY'D HAVE US BY NOW!
7

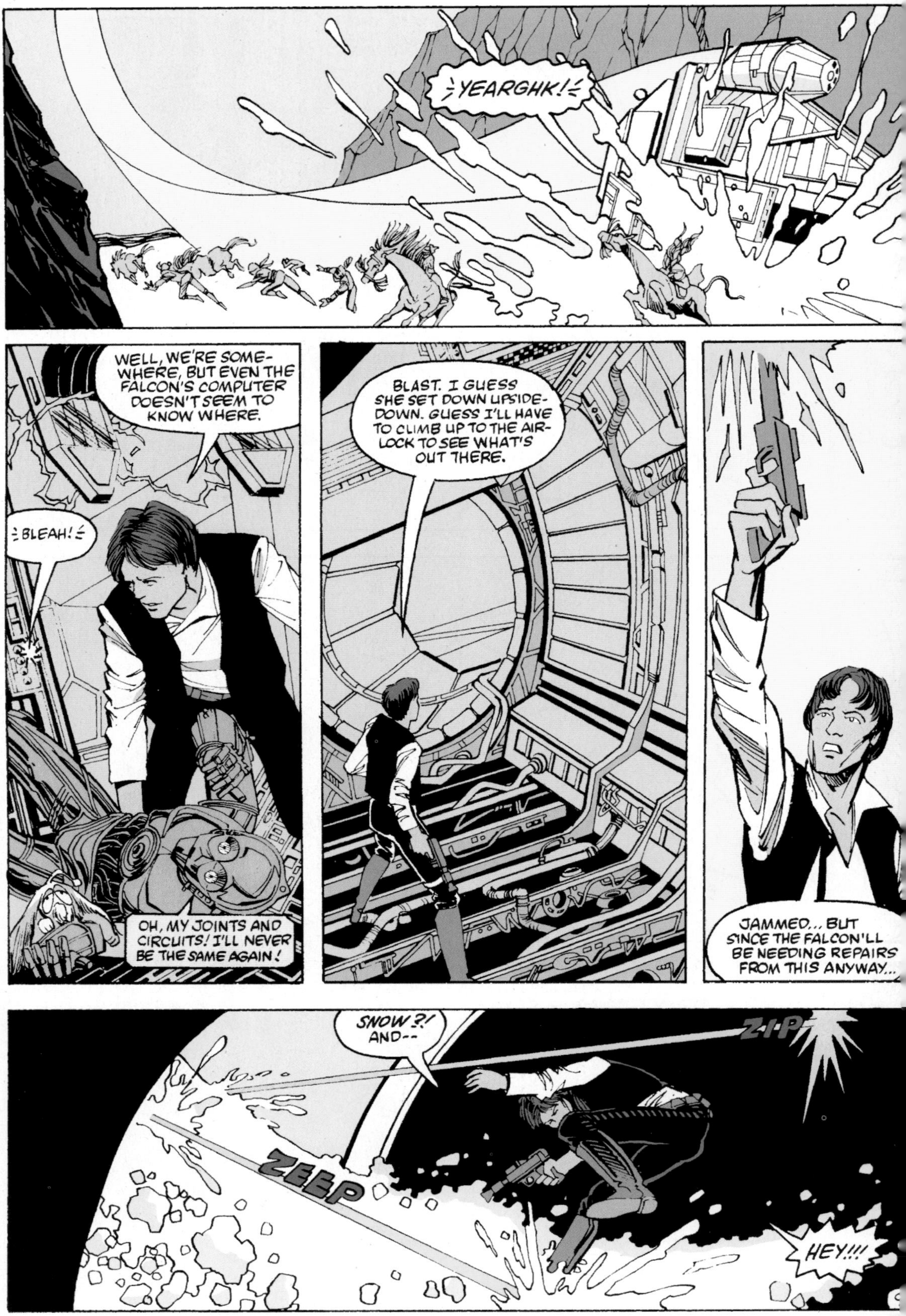
YEARGHK!
WELL, WE'RE SOMEWHERE, BUT EVEN THE FALCON'S COMPUTER DOESN'T SEEM TO KNOW WHERE.
BLEAH!
OH, MY JOINTS AND CIRCUITS! I'LL NEVER BE THE SAME AGAIN!
BLAST. I GUESS SHE SET DOWN UPSIDE-DOWN. GUESS I'LL HAVE TO CLIMB UP TO THE AIRLOCK TO SEE WHAT'S OUT THERE.
JAMMED... BUT SINCE THE FALCON'LL BE NEEDING REPAIRS FROM THIS ANYWAY...
SNOW?! AND--
ZIP
ZEEP
HEY!!!

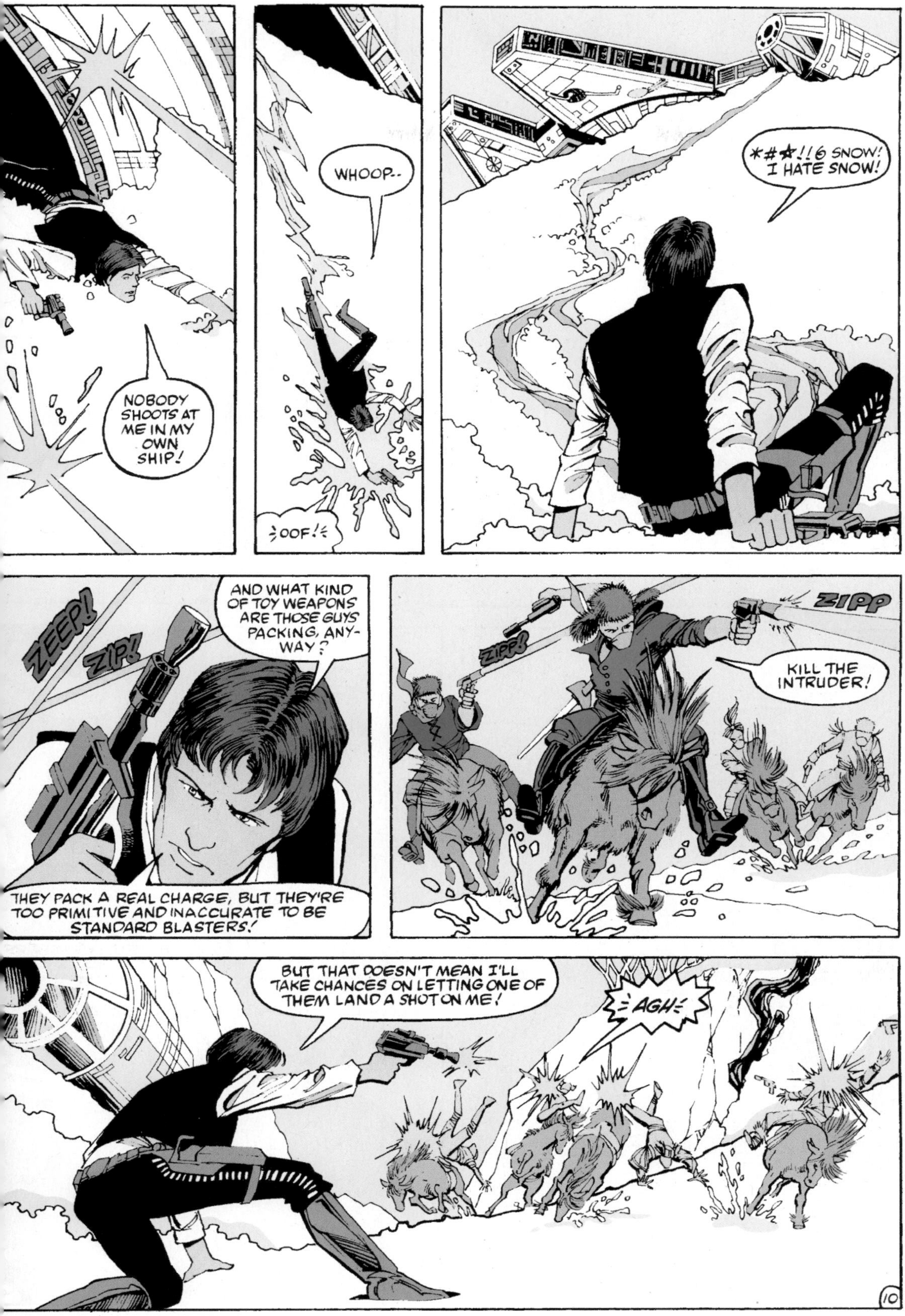
NOBODY SHOOTS AT ME IN MY OWN SHIP!
WHOOP--
OOF!
*#☆!!6 SNOW! I HATE SNOW!
ZEEP!
ZIP!
AND WHAT KIND OF TOY WEAPONS ARE THOSE GUYS PACKING, ANYWAY?
THEY PACK A REAL CHARGE, BUT THEY'RE TOO PRIMITIVE AND INACCURATE TO BE STANDARD BLASTERS!
ZIPP
ZIPP
KILL THE INTRUDER!
BUT THAT DOESN'T MEAN I'LL TAKE CHANCES ON LETTING ONE OF THEM LAND A SHOT ON ME!
AGH
10

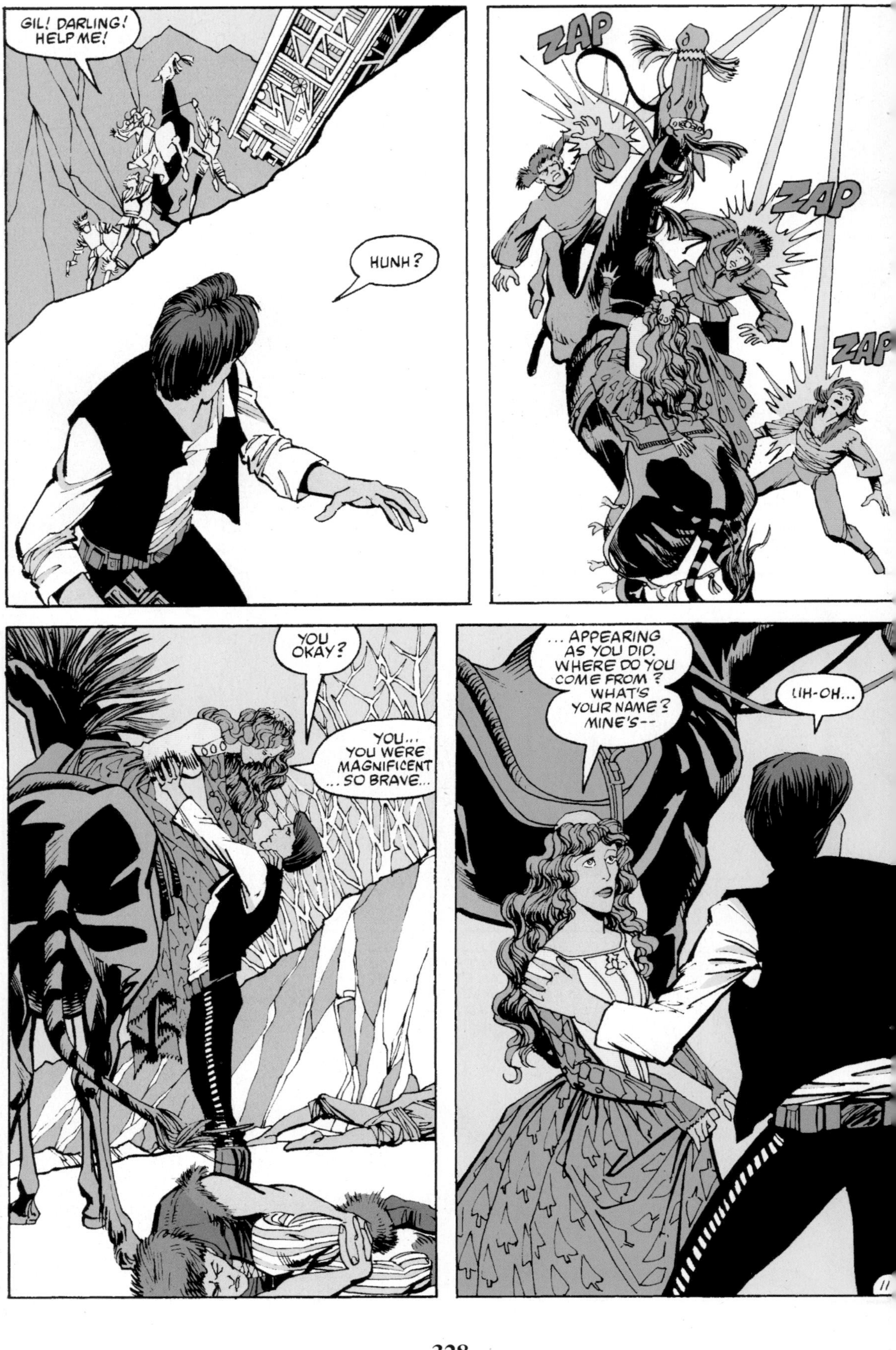
GIL! DARLING! HELP ME!
HUNH?
ZAP
ZAP
ZAP
YOU OKAY?
YOU... YOU WERE MAGNIFICENT ...SO BRAVE...
...APPEARING AS YOU DID. WHERE DO YOU COME FROM? WHAT'S YOUR NAME? MINE'S--
UH-OH...
11

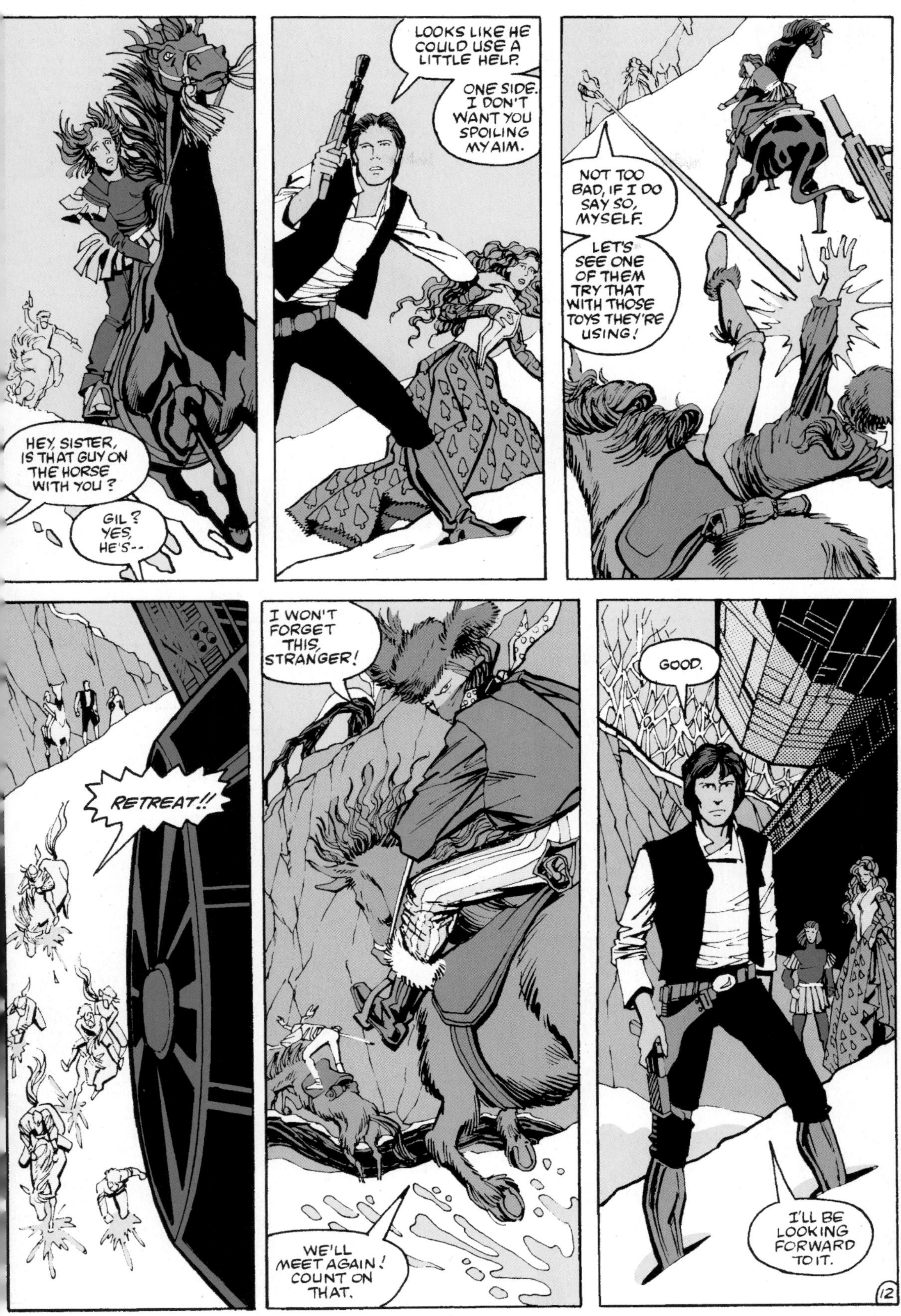
HEY, SISTER, IS THAT GUY ON THE HORSE WITH YOU?
GIL? YES, HE'S--
LOOKS LIKE HE COULD USE A LITTLE HELP.
ONE SIDE. I DON'T WANT YOU SPOILING MY AIM.
NOT TOO BAD, IF I DO SAY SO, MYSELF.
LET'S SEE ONE OF THEM TRY THAT WITH THOSE TOYS THEY'RE USING!
RETREAT!!
I WON'T FORGET THIS, STRANGER!
WE'LL MEET AGAIN! COUNT ON THAT.
GOOD.
I'LL BE LOOKING FORWARD TO IT.
12

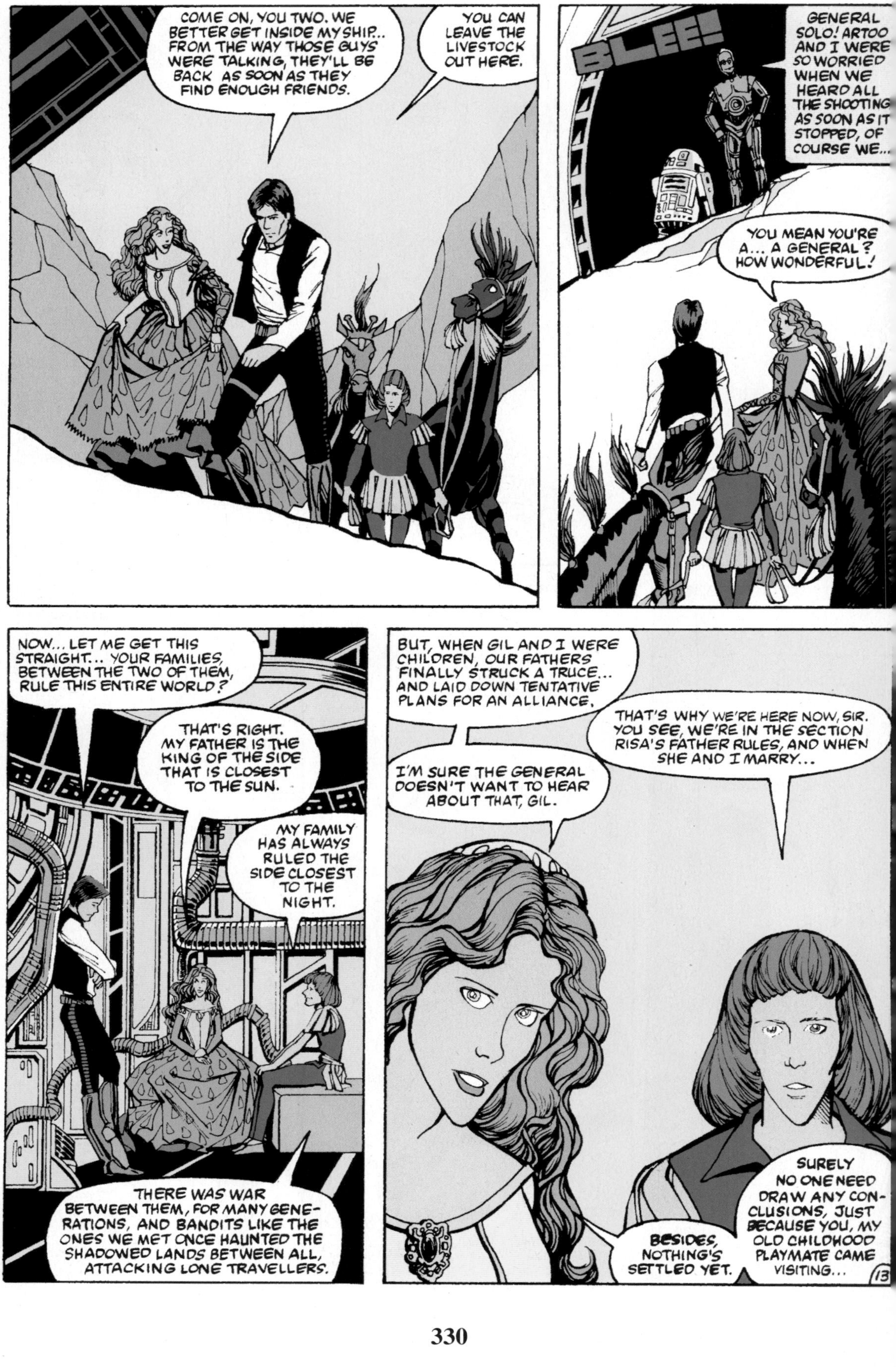

COME ON, YOU TWO. WE BETTER GET INSIDE MY SHIP... FROM THE WAY THOSE GUYS WERE TALKING, THEY'LL BE BACK AS SOON AS THEY FIND ENOUGH FRIENDS.
YOU CAN LEAVE THE LIVESTOCK OUT HERE.
BLEE!
GENERAL SOLO! ARTOO AND I WERE SO WORRIED WHEN WE HEARD ALL THE SHOOTING AS SOON AS IT STOPPED, OF COURSE WE...
YOU MEAN YOU'RE A... A GENERAL? HOW WONDERFUL!
NOW... LET ME GET THIS STRAIGHT... YOUR FAMILIES, BETWEEN THE TWO OF THEM, RULE THIS ENTIRE WORLD?
THAT'S RIGHT. MY FATHER IS THE KING OF THE SIDE THAT IS CLOSEST TO THE SUN.
MY FAMILY HAS ALWAYS RULED THE SIDE CLOSEST TO THE NIGHT.
THERE WAS WAR BETWEEN THEM, FOR MANY GENERATIONS, AND BANDITS LIKE THE ONES WE MET ONCE HAUNTED THE SHADOWED LANDS BETWEEN ALL, ATTACKING LONE TRAVELLERS.
BUT, WHEN GIL AND I WERE CHILDREN, OUR FATHERS FINALLY STRUCK A TRUCE... AND LAID DOWN TENTATIVE PLANS FOR AN ALLIANCE.
THAT'S WHY WE'RE HERE NOW, SIR. YOU SEE, WE'RE IN THE SECTION RISA'S FATHER RULES, AND WHEN SHE AND I MARRY...
I'M SURE THE GENERAL DOESN'T WANT TO HEAR ABOUT THAT, GIL.
BESIDES, NOTHING'S SETTLED YET.
SURELY NO ONE NEED DRAW ANY CONCLUSIONS, JUST BECAUSE YOU, MY OLD CHILDHOOD PLAYMATE CAME VISITING...
13

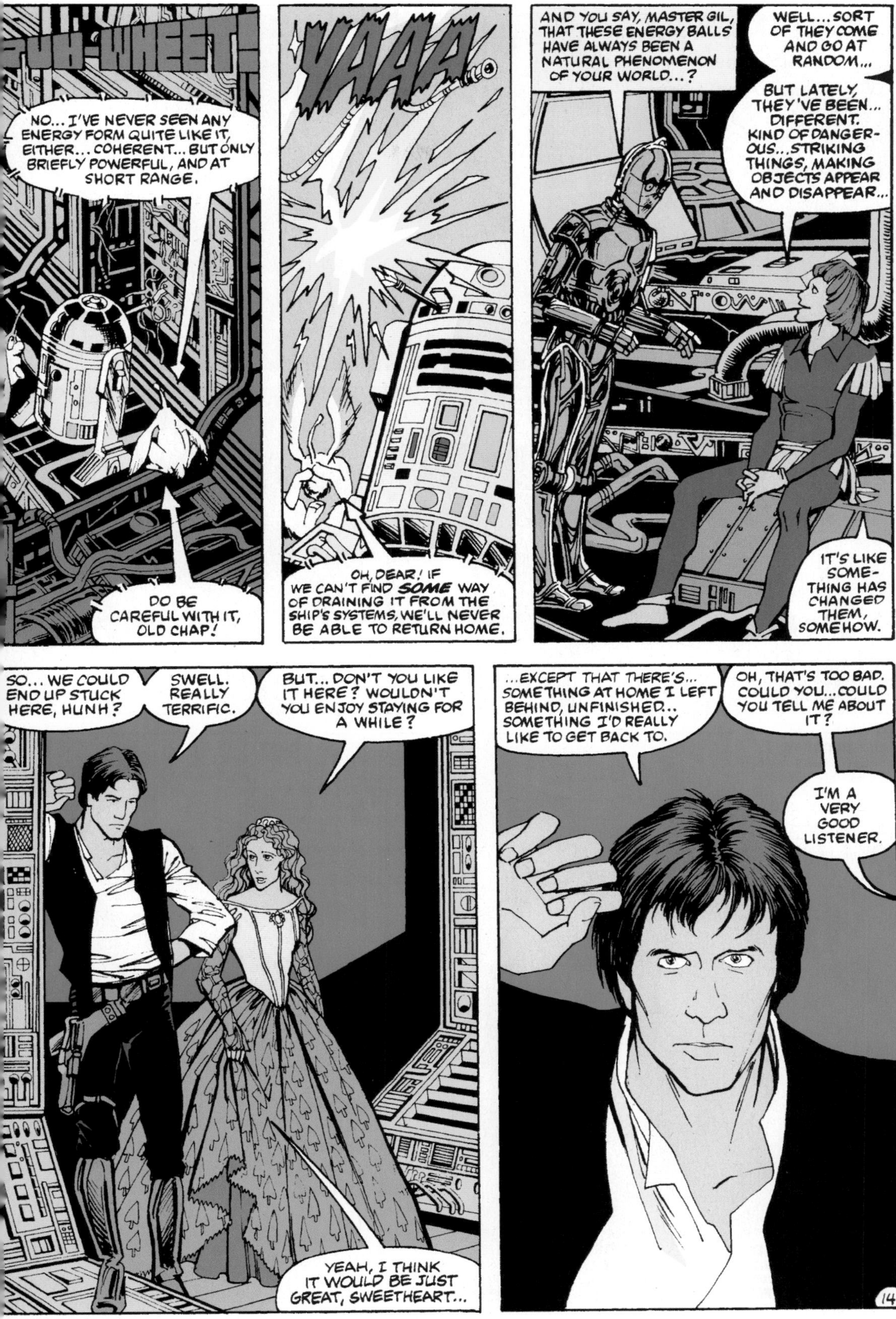
FWEE-WHEET!
NO... I'VE NEVER SEEN ANY ENERGY FORM QUITE LIKE IT, EITHER... COHERENT... BUT ONLY BRIEFLY POWERFUL, AND AT SHORT RANGE.
DO BE CAREFUL WITH IT, OLD CHAP!
YAAA
OH, DEAR! IF WE CAN'T FIND SOME WAY OF DRAINING IT FROM THE SHIP'S SYSTEMS, WE'LL NEVER BE ABLE TO RETURN HOME.
AND YOU SAY, MASTER GIL, THAT THESE ENERGY BALLS HAVE ALWAYS BEEN A NATURAL PHENOMENON OF YOUR WORLD...?
WELL... SORT OF. THEY COME AND GO AT RANDOM...
BUT LATELY, THEY'VE BEEN... DIFFERENT. KIND OF DANGEROUS... STRIKING THINGS, MAKING OBJECTS APPEAR AND DISAPPEAR...
IT'S LIKE SOMETHING HAS CHANGED THEM, SOMEHOW.
SO... WE COULD END UP STUCK HERE, HUNH?
SWELL. REALLY TERRIFIC.
BUT... DON'T YOU LIKE IT HERE? WOULDN'T YOU ENJOY STAYING FOR A WHILE?
YEAH, I THINK IT WOULD BE JUST GREAT, SWEETHEART...
...EXCEPT THAT THERE'S... SOMETHING AT HOME I LEFT BEHIND, UNFINISHED... SOMETHING I'D REALLY LIKE TO GET BACK TO.
OH, THAT'S TOO BAD. COULD YOU... COULD YOU TELL ME ABOUT IT?
I'M A VERY GOOD LISTENER.
14

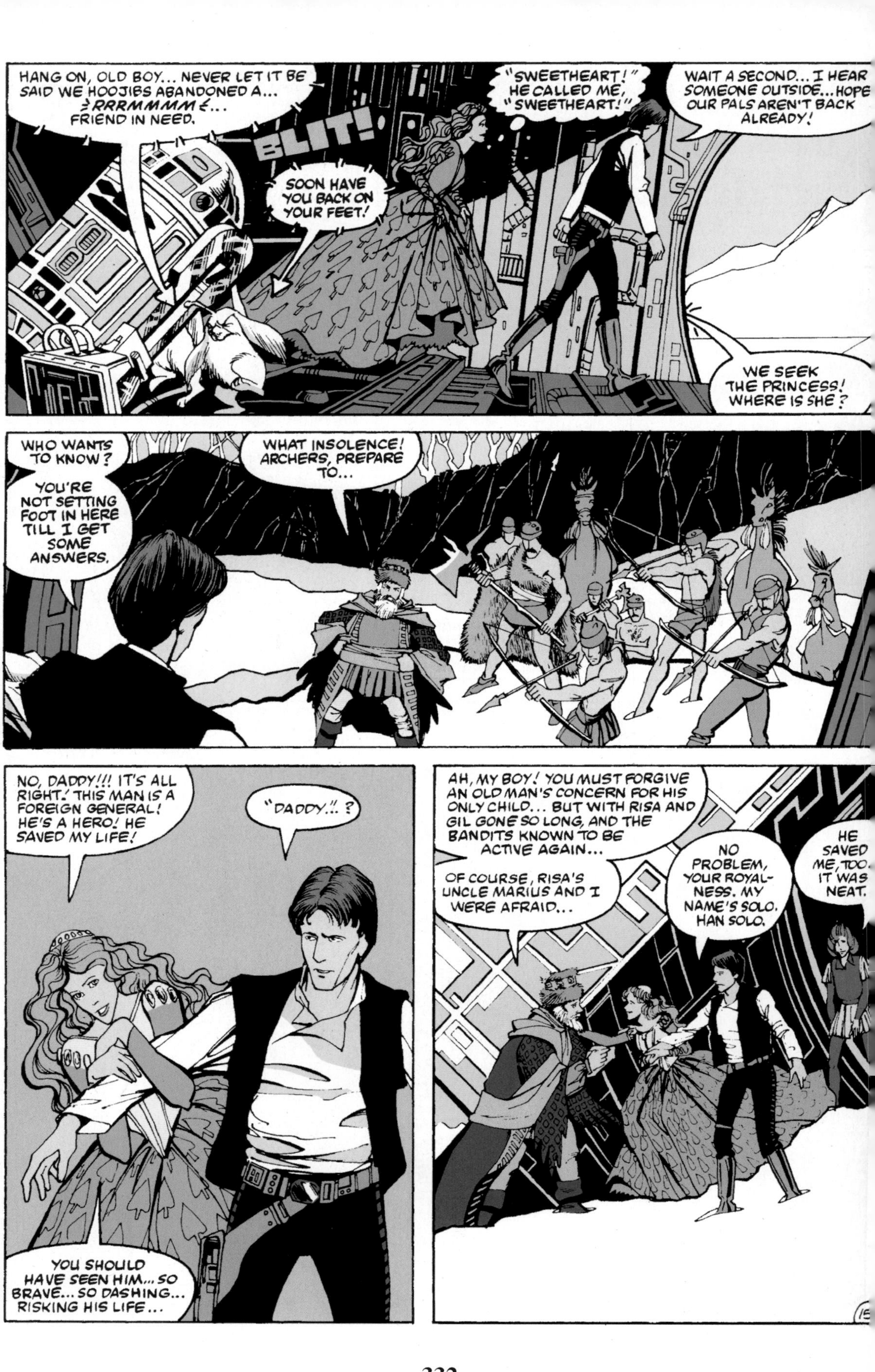
HANG ON, OLD BOY... NEVER LET IT BE SAID WE HOOJIBS ABANDONED A... ≷RRRMMMM≶... FRIEND IN NEED.
BLIT!
SOON HAVE YOU BACK ON YOUR FEET!
"SWEETHEART!" HE CALLED ME, "SWEETHEART!"
WAIT A SECOND... I HEAR SOMEONE OUTSIDE... HOPE OUR PALS AREN'T BACK ALREADY!
WE SEEK THE PRINCESS! WHERE IS SHE?
WHO WANTS TO KNOW?
YOU'RE NOT SETTING FOOT IN HERE TILL I GET SOME ANSWERS.
WHAT INSOLENCE! ARCHERS, PREPARE TO...
NO, DADDY!!! IT'S ALL RIGHT! THIS MAN IS A FOREIGN GENERAL! HE'S A HERO! HE SAVED MY LIFE!
"DADDY"!.. ?
YOU SHOULD HAVE SEEN HIM... SO BRAVE... SO DASHING... RISKING HIS LIFE...
AH, MY BOY! YOU MUST FORGIVE AN OLD MAN'S CONCERN FOR HIS ONLY CHILD... BUT WITH RISA AND GIL GONE SO LONG, AND THE BANDITS KNOWN TO BE ACTIVE AGAIN...
OF COURSE, RISA'S UNCLE MARIUS AND I WERE AFRAID...
NO PROBLEM, YOUR ROYAL-NESS. MY NAME'S SOLO. HAN SOLO.
HE SAVED ME, TOO. IT WAS NEAT.
15

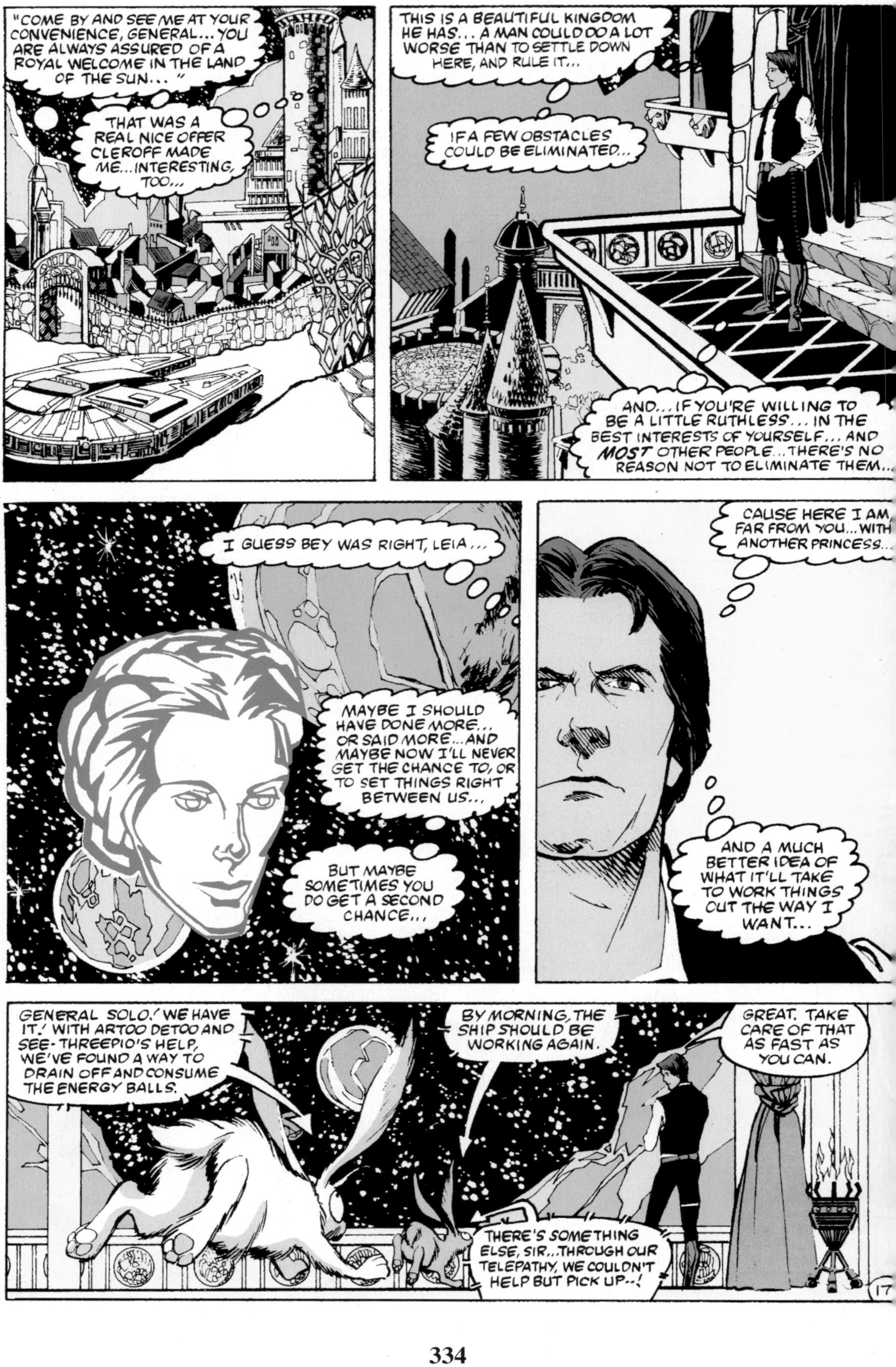
"COME BY AND SEE ME AT YOUR CONVENIENCE, GENERAL... YOU ARE ALWAYS ASSURED OF A ROYAL WELCOME IN THE LAND OF THE SUN..."
THAT WAS A REAL NICE OFFER CLEROFF MADE ME... INTERESTING, TOO...
THIS IS A BEAUTIFUL KINGDOM HE HAS... A MAN COULD DO A LOT WORSE THAN TO SETTLE DOWN HERE, AND RULE IT...
IF A FEW OBSTACLES COULD BE ELIMINATED...
AND... IF YOU'RE WILLING TO BE A LITTLE RUTHLESS... IN THE BEST INTERESTS OF YOURSELF... AND MOST OTHER PEOPLE... THERE'S NO REASON NOT TO ELIMINATE THEM...
I GUESS BEY WAS RIGHT, LEIA...
MAYBE I SHOULD HAVE DONE MORE... OR SAID MORE... AND MAYBE NOW I'LL NEVER GET THE CHANCE TO, OR TO SET THINGS RIGHT BETWEEN US...
BUT MAYBE SOMETIMES YOU DO GET A SECOND CHANCE...
CAUSE HERE I AM FAR FROM YOU... WITH ANOTHER PRINCESS...
AND A MUCH BETTER IDEA OF WHAT IT'LL TAKE TO WORK THINGS OUT THE WAY I WANT...
GENERAL SOLO! WE HAVE IT! WITH ARTOO DETOO AND SEE-THREEPIO'S HELP, WE'VE FOUND A WAY TO DRAIN OFF AND CONSUME THE ENERGY BALLS.
BY MORNING, THE SHIP SHOULD BE WORKING AGAIN.
GREAT. TAKE CARE OF THAT AS FAST AS YOU CAN.
THERE'S SOMETHING ELSE, SIR... THROUGH OUR TELEPATHY, WE COULDN'T HELP BUT PICK UP--!
17

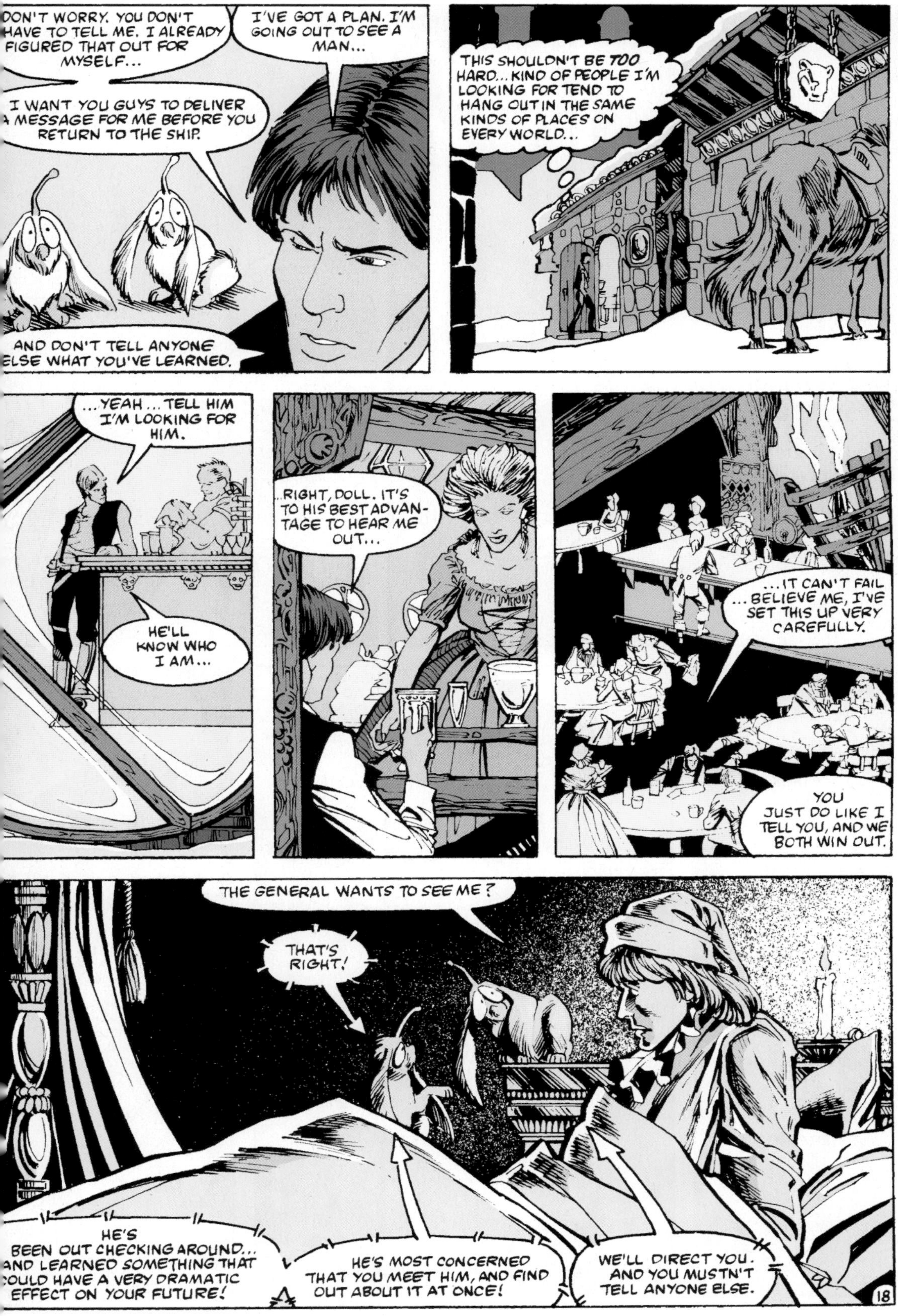
DON'T WORRY. YOU DON'T HAVE TO TELL ME. I ALREADY FIGURED THAT OUT FOR MYSELF...
I'VE GOT A PLAN. I'M GOING OUT TO SEE A MAN...
I WANT YOU GUYS TO DELIVER A MESSAGE FOR ME BEFORE YOU RETURN TO THE SHIP.
AND DON'T TELL ANYONE ELSE WHAT YOU'VE LEARNED.
THIS SHOULDN'T BE TOO HARD... KIND OF PEOPLE I'M LOOKING FOR TEND TO HANG OUT IN THE SAME KINDS OF PLACES ON EVERY WORLD...
...YEAH ... TELL HIM I'M LOOKING FOR HIM.
HE'LL KNOW WHO I AM...
...RIGHT, DOLL. IT'S TO HIS BEST ADVANTAGE TO HEAR ME OUT...
...IT CAN'T FAIL ... BELIEVE ME, I'VE SET THIS UP VERY CAREFULLY.
YOU JUST DO LIKE I TELL YOU, AND WE BOTH WIN OUT.
THE GENERAL WANTS TO SEE ME?
THAT'S RIGHT!
HE'S BEEN OUT CHECKING AROUND... AND LEARNED SOMETHING THAT COULD HAVE A VERY DRAMATIC EFFECT ON YOUR FUTURE!
HE'S MOST CONCERNED THAT YOU MEET HIM, AND FIND OUT ABOUT IT AT ONCE!
WE'LL DIRECT YOU. AND YOU MUSTN'T TELL ANYONE ELSE.
18

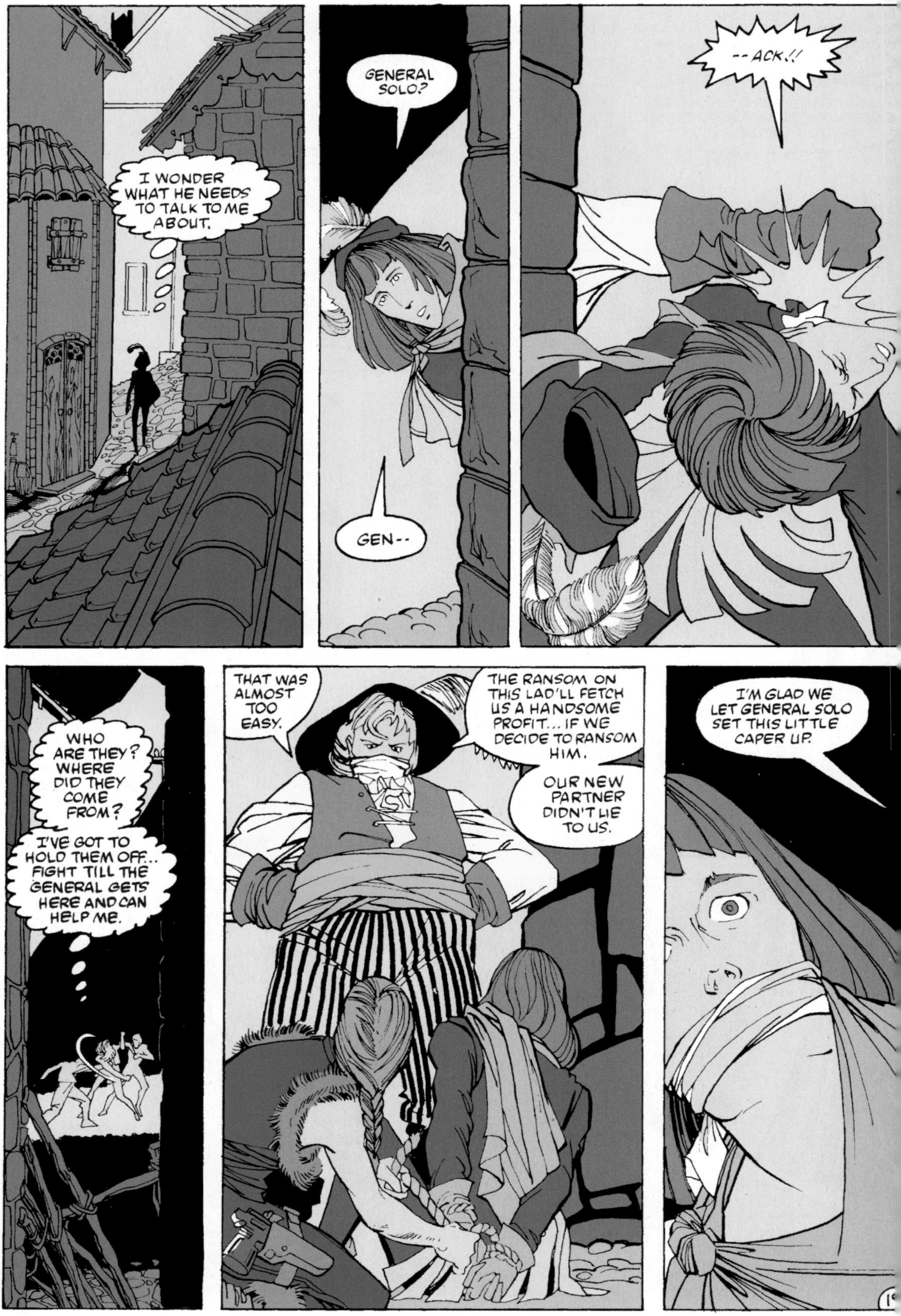
I WONDER WHAT HE NEEDS TO TALK TO ME ABOUT.
GENERAL SOLO?
GEN--
--ACK!!
WHO ARE THEY? WHERE DID THEY COME FROM?
I'VE GOT TO HOLD THEM OFF... FIGHT TILL THE GENERAL GETS HERE AND CAN HELP ME.
THAT WAS ALMOST TOO EASY.
THE RANSOM ON THIS LAD'LL FETCH US A HANDSOME PROFIT... IF WE DECIDE TO RANSOM HIM.
OUR NEW PARTNER DIDN'T LIE TO US.
I'M GLAD WE LET GENERAL SOLO SET THIS LITTLE CAPER UP.

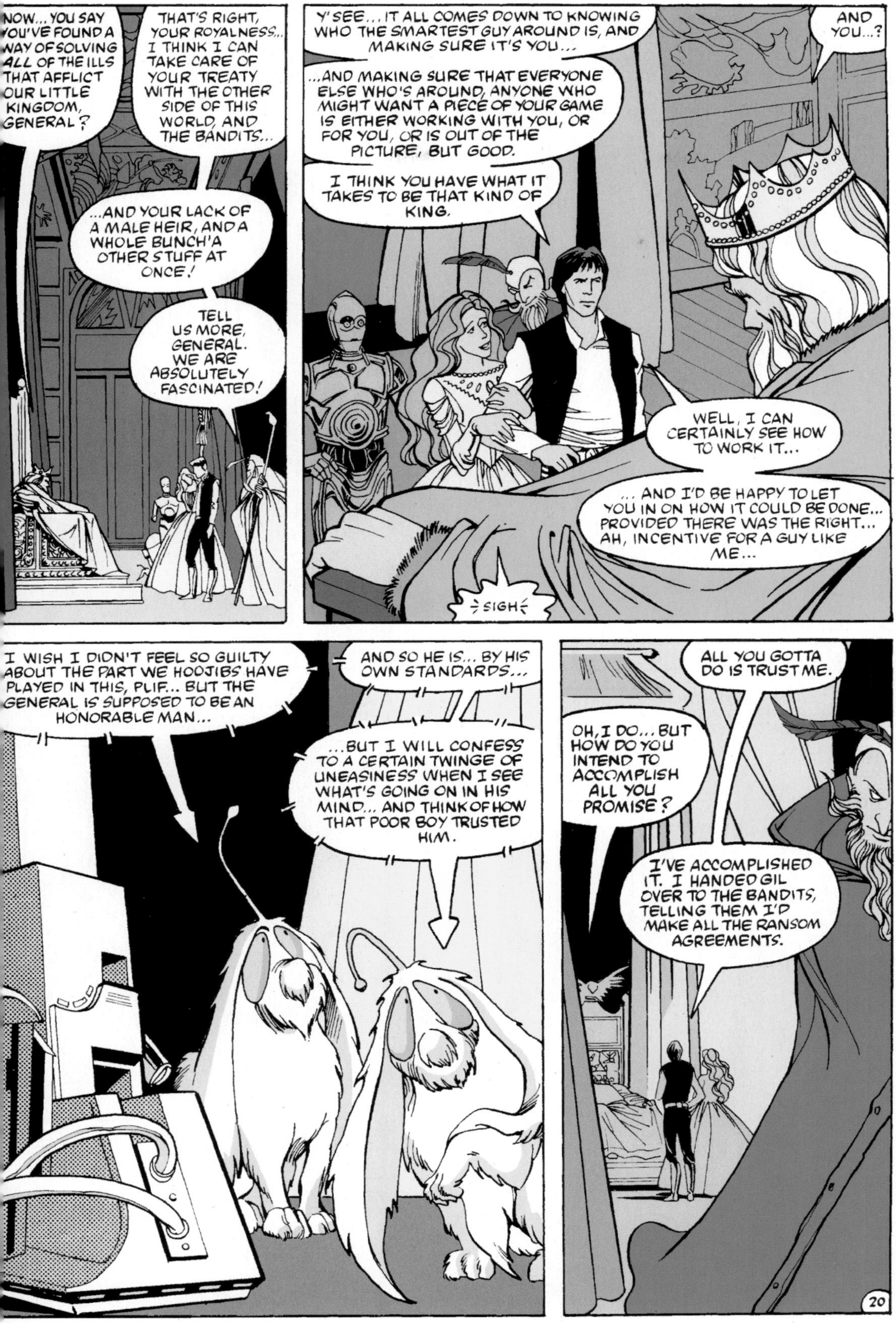
NOW... YOU SAY YOU'VE FOUND A WAY OF SOLVING ALL OF THE ILLS THAT AFFLICT OUR LITTLE KINGDOM, GENERAL?
THAT'S RIGHT, YOUR ROYALNESS... I THINK I CAN TAKE CARE OF YOUR TREATY WITH THE OTHER SIDE OF THIS WORLD, AND THE BANDITS...
...AND YOUR LACK OF A MALE HEIR, AND A WHOLE BUNCH'A OTHER STUFF AT ONCE!
TELL US MORE, GENERAL. WE ARE ABSOLUTELY FASCINATED!
Y'SEE... IT ALL COMES DOWN TO KNOWING WHO THE SMARTEST GUY AROUND IS, AND MAKING SURE IT'S YOU...
...AND MAKING SURE THAT EVERYONE ELSE WHO'S AROUND, ANYONE WHO MIGHT WANT A PIECE OF YOUR GAME IS EITHER WORKING WITH YOU, OR FOR YOU, OR IS OUT OF THE PICTURE, BUT GOOD.
I THINK YOU HAVE WHAT IT TAKES TO BE THAT KIND OF KING.
AND YOU...?
WELL, I CAN CERTAINLY SEE HOW TO WORK IT...
... AND I'D BE HAPPY TO LET YOU IN ON HOW IT COULD BE DONE... PROVIDED THERE WAS THE RIGHT... AH, INCENTIVE FOR A GUY LIKE ME...
SIGH
I WISH I DIDN'T FEEL SO GUILTY ABOUT THE PART WE HOOJIBS HAVE PLAYED IN THIS, PLIF... BUT THE GENERAL IS SUPPOSED TO BE AN HONORABLE MAN...
AND SO HE IS... BY HIS OWN STANDARDS...
...BUT I WILL CONFESS TO A CERTAIN TWINGE OF UNEASINESS WHEN I SEE WHAT'S GOING ON IN HIS MIND... AND THINK OF HOW THAT POOR BOY TRUSTED HIM.
ALL YOU GOTTA DO IS TRUST ME.
OH, I DO... BUT HOW DO YOU INTEND TO ACCOMPLISH ALL YOU PROMISE?
I'VE ACCOMPLISHED IT. I HANDED GIL OVER TO THE BANDITS, TELLING THEM I'D MAKE ALL THE RANSOM AGREEMENTS.
20

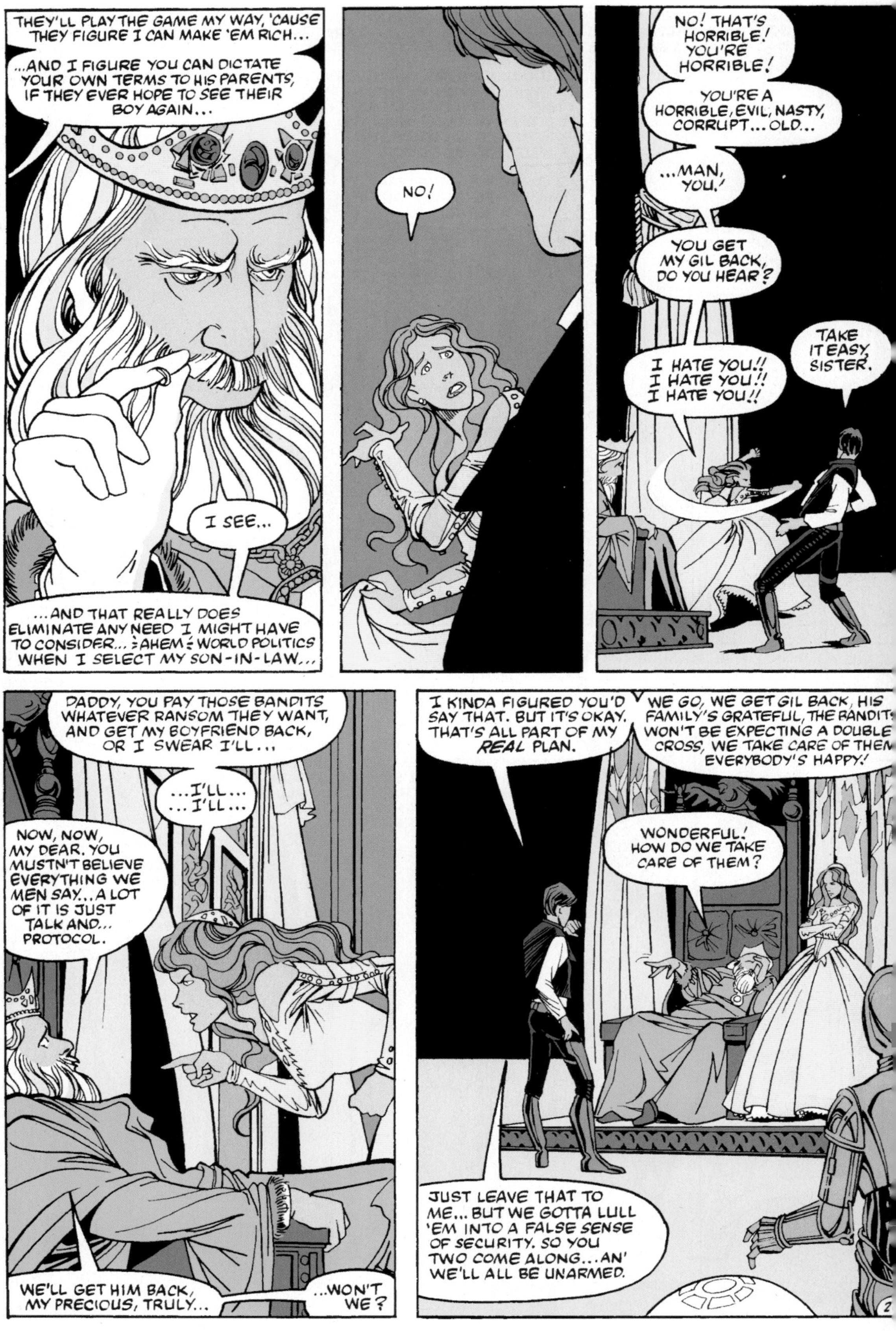
THEY'LL PLAY THE GAME MY WAY, 'CAUSE THEY FIGURE I CAN MAKE 'EM RICH...
...AND I FIGURE YOU CAN DICTATE YOUR OWN TERMS TO HIS PARENTS, IF THEY EVER HOPE TO SEE THEIR BOY AGAIN...
I SEE...
...AND THAT REALLY DOES ELIMINATE ANY NEED I MIGHT HAVE TO CONSIDER... AHEM WORLD POLITICS WHEN I SELECT MY SON-IN-LAW...
NO!
NO! THAT'S HORRIBLE! YOU'RE HORRIBLE!
YOU'RE A HORRIBLE, EVIL, NASTY, CORRUPT... OLD...
...MAN, YOU!
YOU GET MY GIL BACK, DO YOU HEAR?
I HATE YOU!! I HATE YOU!! I HATE YOU!!
TAKE IT EASY, SISTER.
DADDY, YOU PAY THOSE BANDITS WHATEVER RANSOM THEY WANT, AND GET MY BOYFRIEND BACK, OR I SWEAR I'LL...
...I'LL... ...I'LL...
NOW, NOW, MY DEAR. YOU MUSTN'T BELIEVE EVERYTHING WE MEN SAY... A LOT OF IT IS JUST TALK AND... PROTOCOL.
WE'LL GET HIM BACK, MY PRECIOUS, TRULY...
...WON'T WE?
I KINDA FIGURED YOU'D SAY THAT. BUT IT'S OKAY. THAT'S ALL PART OF MY REAL PLAN.
WE GO, WE GET GIL BACK, HIS FAMILY'S GRATEFUL, THE BANDITS WON'T BE EXPECTING A DOUBLE CROSS, WE TAKE CARE OF THEM EVERYBODY'S HAPPY!
WONDERFUL! HOW DO WE TAKE CARE OF THEM?
JUST LEAVE THAT TO ME... BUT WE GOTTA LULL 'EM INTO A FALSE SENSE OF SECURITY. SO YOU TWO COME ALONG... AN' WE'LL ALL BE UNARMED.
2

HOWEVER, I REALLY DON'T SEE THAT A GLIB ALIEN HAS MUCH USE TO US AT ALL, AS A HOSTAGE OR ANYTHING ELSE.

WELL! GOOD OLD UNCLE MARIUS. I WAS WONDERING WHEN YOU'D GET AROUND TO SHOWING UP.

OH, COME NOW! YOU CAN'T HAVE KNOWN THAT I WAS THE GENIUS BEHIND THESE BANDITS AND THEIR NEW WEAPONS. CONFESS. I SURPRISED YOU!

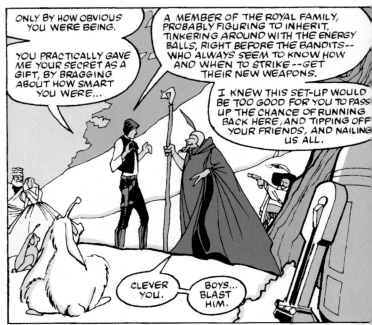

ONLY BY HOW OBVIOUS YOU WERE BEING.

YOU PRACTICALLY GAVE ME YOUR SECRET AS A GIFT, BY BRAGGING ABOUT HOW SMART YOU WERE...

A MEMBER OF THE ROYAL FAMILY, PROBABLY FIGURING TO INHERIT, TINKERING AROUND WITH THE ENERGY BALLS, RIGHT BEFORE THE BANDITS-- WHO ALWAYS SEEM TO KNOW HOW AND WHEN TO STRIKE--GET THEIR NEW WEAPONS.

I KNEW THIS SET-UP WOULD BE TOO GOOD FOR YOU TO PASS UP THE CHANCE OF RUNNING BACK HERE, AND TIPPING OFF YOUR FRIENDS, AND NAILING US ALL.

CLEVER YOU.

BOYS... BLAST HIM.

ARTOO, BLAST HIM.

I SAID I WOULDN'T CARRY A WEAPON. I DIDN'T SAY ANYTHING ABOUT NOT GIVING ONE TO A DROID.

OH... AN' ANOTHER THING, GUYS...

...AFTER YOU TOLD ME WHERE YOUR HIDEOUT WAS, I SENT A COUPLE OF HOOJIBS ALONG. THEY DRAINED ALL THE POWER OUT OF YOUR LITTLE POPGUNS...

AND I LEFT A MESSAGE WITH THE ROYAL GUARD. I FIGURE THEY SHOULD BE ALONG TO MOP YOU UP ANY TIME NOW.

CLICK

CLICK

ARTOO'LL COVER YOU UNTIL THEN.

SO LONG, FOLKS. PLEASURE DOIN' BUSINESS WITH YOU.

A REMARKABLE MAN...DASHING AND AUDACIOUS.

TOO BAD HE COULDN'T STAY FOR THE WEDDING.

I HOPE HE NEVER COMES BACK.

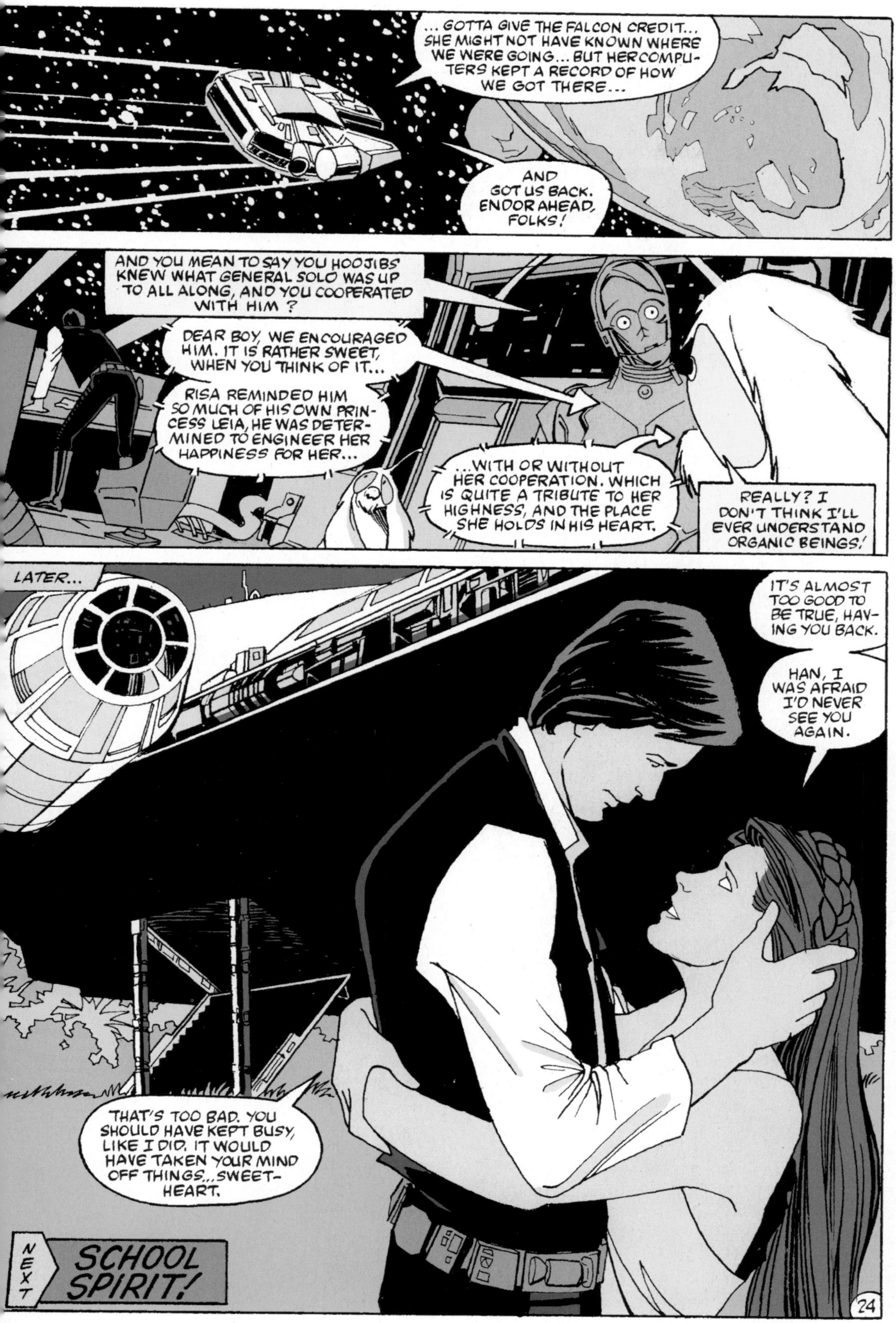

...GOTTA GIVE THE FALCON CREDIT... SHE MIGHT NOT HAVE KNOWN WHERE WE WERE GOING... BUT HER COMPUTERS KEPT A RECORD OF HOW WE GOT THERE...
AND GOT US BACK. ENDOR AHEAD, FOLKS!
AND YOU MEAN TO SAY YOU HOOJIBS KNEW WHAT GENERAL SOLO WAS UP TO ALL ALONG, AND YOU COOPERATED WITH HIM?
DEAR BOY, WE ENCOURAGED HIM. IT IS RATHER SWEET, WHEN YOU THINK OF IT...
RISA REMINDED HIM SO MUCH OF HIS OWN PRINCESS LEIA, HE WAS DETERMINED TO ENGINEER HER HAPPINESS FOR HER...
...WITH OR WITHOUT HER COOPERATION. WHICH IS QUITE A TRIBUTE TO HER HIGHNESS, AND THE PLACE SHE HOLDS IN HIS HEART.
REALLY? I DON'T THINK I'LL EVER UNDERSTAND ORGANIC BEINGS!
LATER...
IT'S ALMOST TOO GOOD TO BE TRUE, HAVING YOU BACK.
HAN, I WAS AFRAID I'D NEVER SEE YOU AGAIN.
THAT'S TOO BAD. YOU SHOULD HAVE KEPT BUSY, LIKE I DID. IT WOULD HAVE TAKEN YOUR MIND OFF THINGS... SWEETHEART.
NEXT
SCHOOL SPIRIT!
24

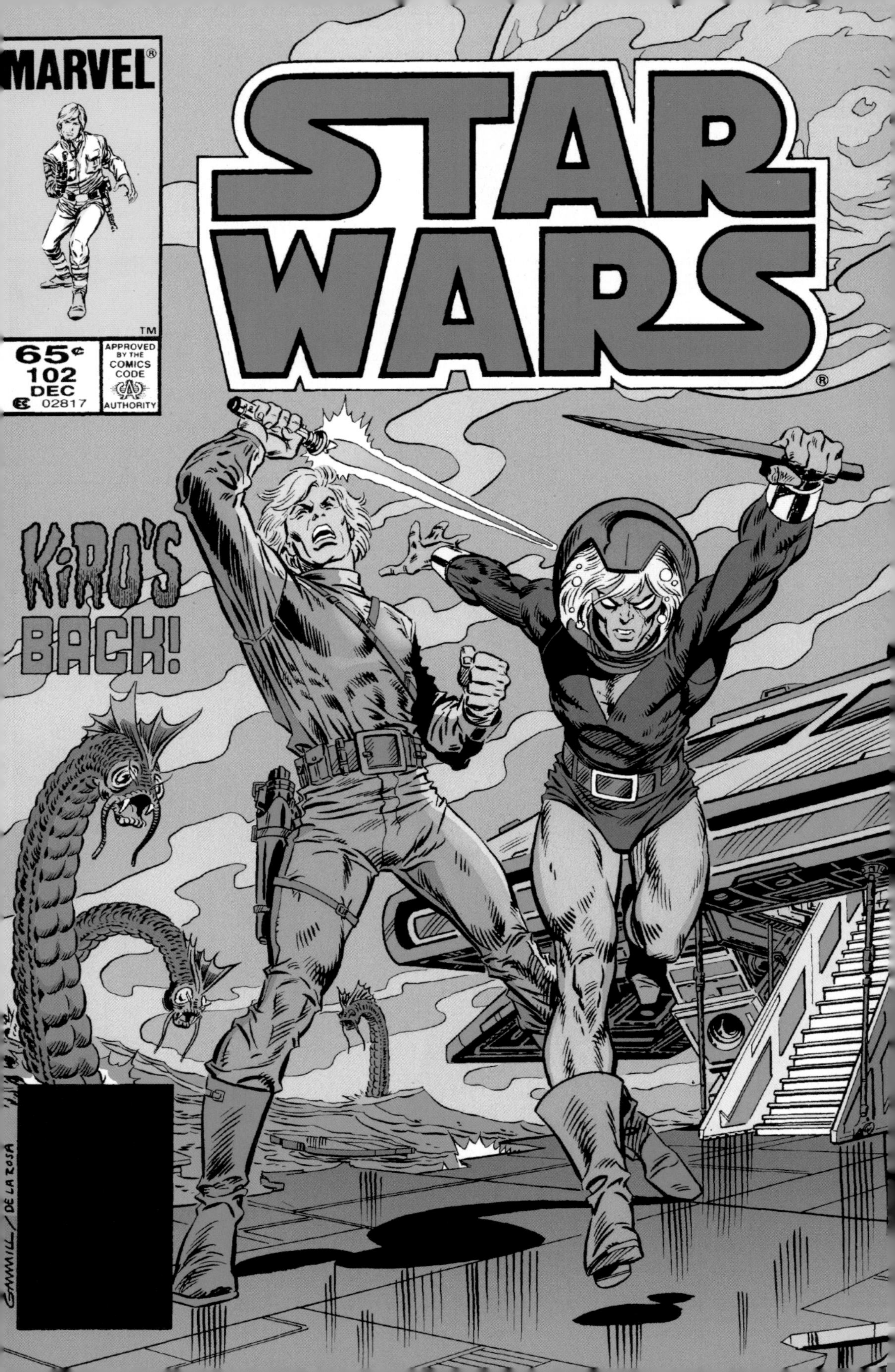
MARVEL®
STAR WARS®
TM
65¢
102
DEC
02817
APPROVED BY THE COMICS CODE AUTHORITY
KIRO'S BACK!
GAMMILL / DE LA ROSA

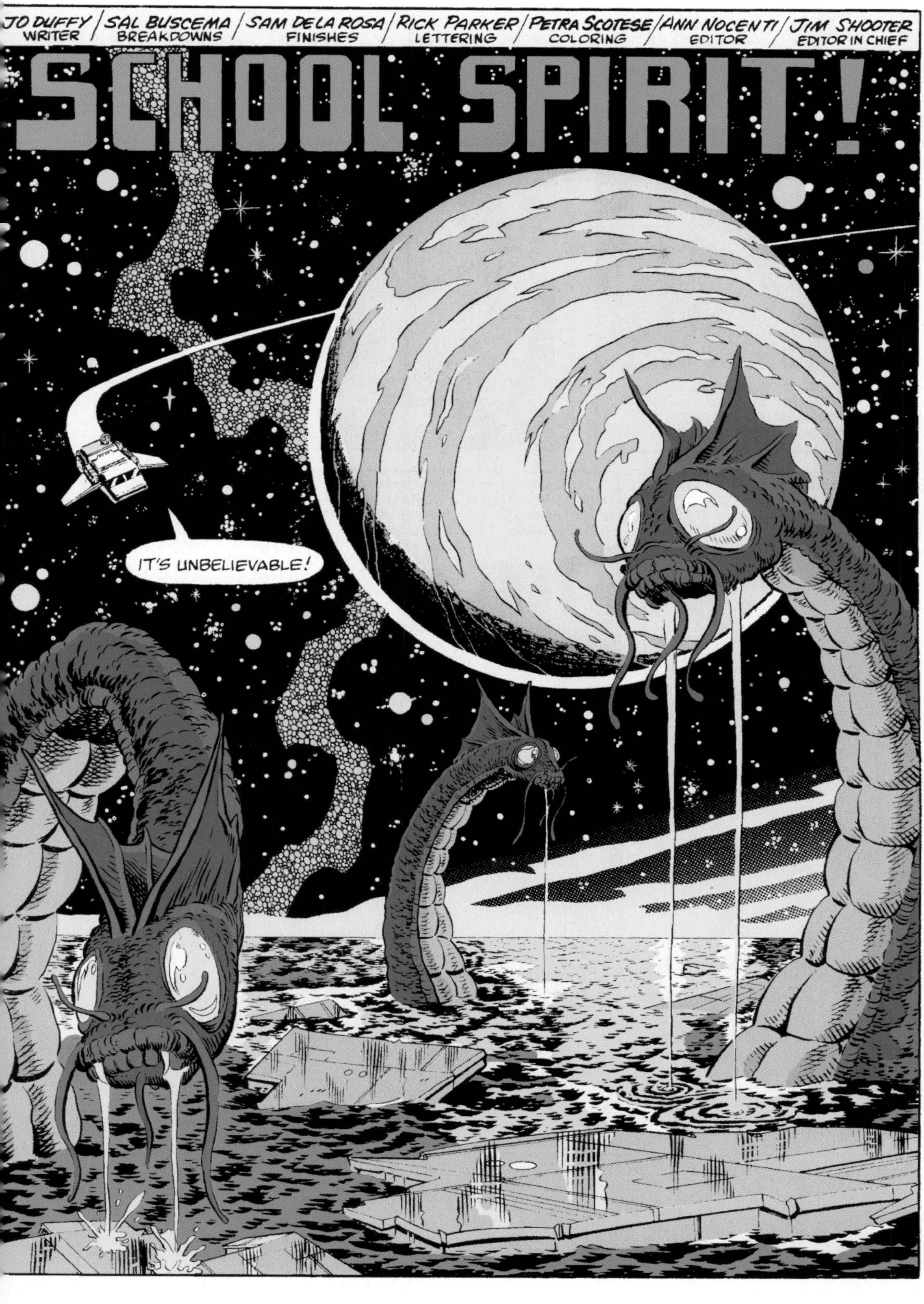
JO DUFFY WRITER / SAL BUSCEMA BREAKDOWNS / SAM DE LA ROSA FINISHES / RICK PARKER LETTERING / PETRA SCOTESE COLORING / ANN NOCENTI EDITOR / JIM SHOOTER EDITOR IN CHIEF
SCHOOL SPIRIT!
IT'S UNBELIEVABLE!

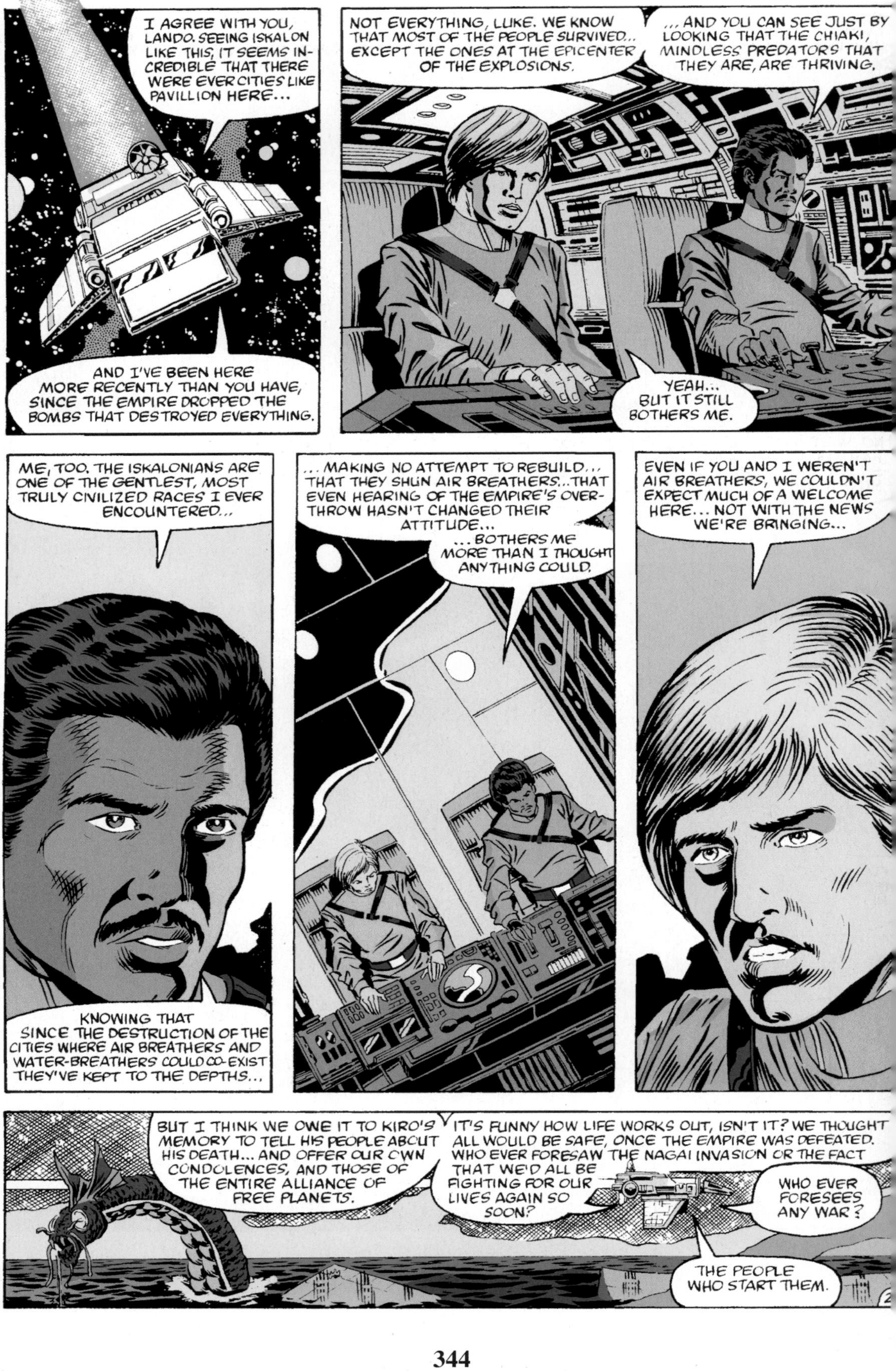
I AGREE WITH YOU, LANDO. SEEING ISKALON LIKE THIS, IT SEEMS INCREDIBLE THAT THERE WERE EVER CITIES LIKE PAVILLION HERE...
AND I'VE BEEN HERE MORE RECENTLY THAN YOU HAVE, SINCE THE EMPIRE DROPPED THE BOMBS THAT DESTROYED EVERYTHING.
NOT EVERYTHING, LUKE. WE KNOW THAT MOST OF THE PEOPLE SURVIVED... EXCEPT THE ONES AT THE EPICENTER OF THE EXPLOSIONS.
...AND YOU CAN SEE JUST BY LOOKING THAT THE CHIAKI, MINDLESS PREDATORS THAT THEY ARE, ARE THRIVING.
YEAH... BUT IT STILL BOTHERS ME.
ME, TOO. THE ISKALONIANS ARE ONE OF THE GENTLEST, MOST TRULY CIVILIZED RACES I EVER ENCOUNTERED...
KNOWING THAT SINCE THE DESTRUCTION OF THE CITIES WHERE AIR BREATHERS AND WATER-BREATHERS COULD CO-EXIST THEY'VE KEPT TO THE DEPTHS...
...MAKING NO ATTEMPT TO REBUILD... THAT THEY SHUN AIR BREATHERS... THAT EVEN HEARING OF THE EMPIRE'S OVERTHROW HASN'T CHANGED THEIR ATTITUDE...
...BOTHERS ME MORE THAN I THOUGHT ANYTHING COULD.
EVEN IF YOU AND I WEREN'T AIR BREATHERS, WE COULDN'T EXPECT MUCH OF A WELCOME HERE... NOT WITH THE NEWS WE'RE BRINGING...
BUT I THINK WE OWE IT TO KIRO'S MEMORY TO TELL HIS PEOPLE ABOUT HIS DEATH... AND OFFER OUR OWN CONDOLENCES, AND THOSE OF THE ENTIRE ALLIANCE OF FREE PLANETS.
IT'S FUNNY HOW LIFE WORKS OUT, ISN'T IT? WE THOUGHT ALL WOULD BE SAFE, ONCE THE EMPIRE WAS DEFEATED. WHO EVER FORESAW THE NAGAI INVASION OR THE FACT THAT WE'D ALL BE FIGHTING FOR OUR LIVES AGAIN SO SOON?
WHO EVER FORESEES ANY WAR?
THE PEOPLE WHO START THEM.

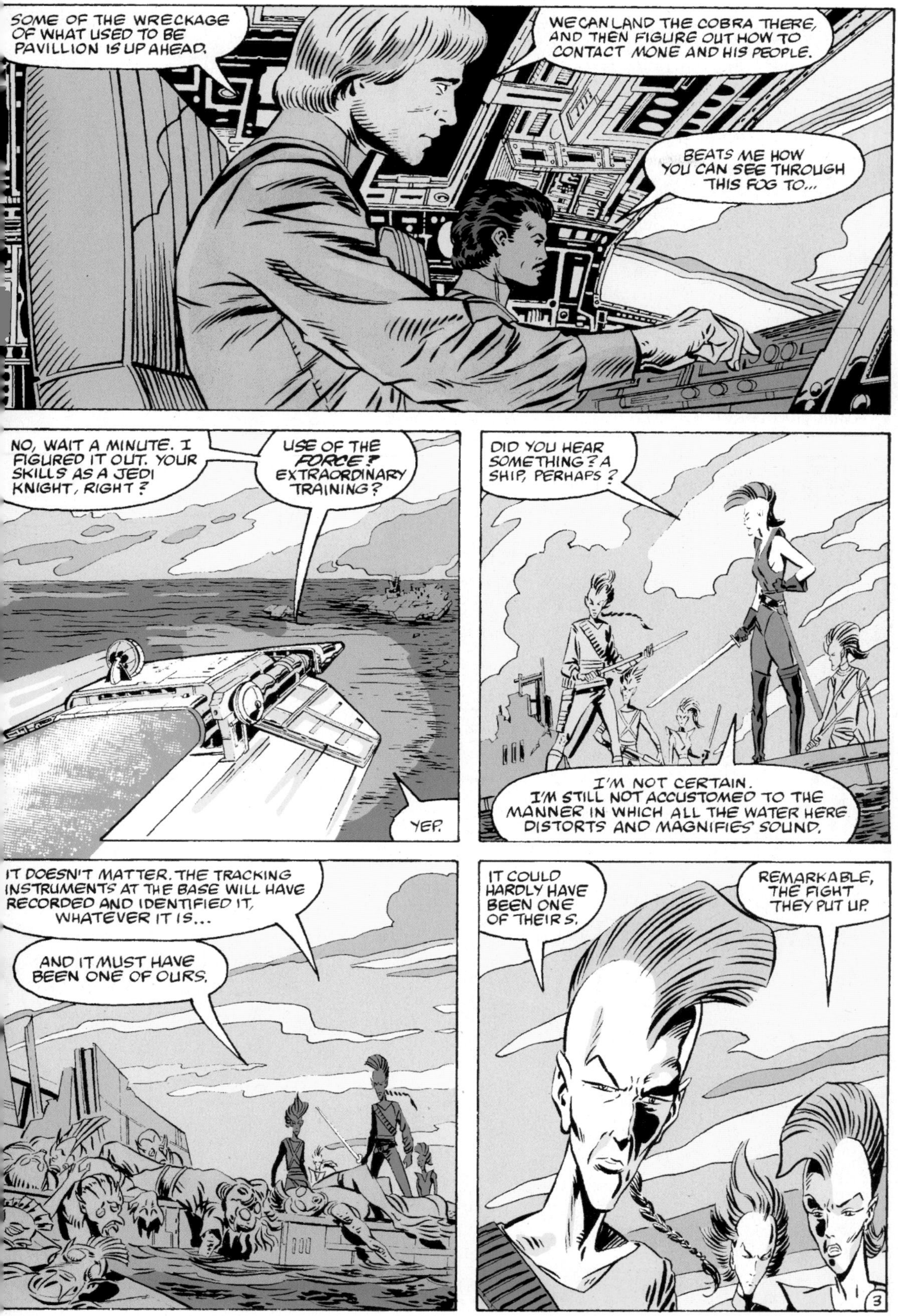
SOME OF THE WRECKAGE OF WHAT USED TO BE PAVILLION IS UP AHEAD.
WE CAN LAND THE COBRA THERE, AND THEN FIGURE OUT HOW TO CONTACT MONE AND HIS PEOPLE.
BEATS ME HOW YOU CAN SEE THROUGH THIS FOG TO...
NO, WAIT A MINUTE. I FIGURED IT OUT. YOUR SKILLS AS A JEDI KNIGHT, RIGHT?
USE OF THE FORCE? EXTRAORDINARY TRAINING?
YEP.
DID YOU HEAR SOMETHING? A SHIP, PERHAPS?
I'M NOT CERTAIN. I'M STILL NOT ACCUSTOMED TO THE MANNER IN WHICH ALL THE WATER HERE DISTORTS AND MAGNIFIES SOUND.
IT DOESN'T MATTER. THE TRACKING INSTRUMENTS AT THE BASE WILL HAVE RECORDED AND IDENTIFIED IT, WHATEVER IT IS...
AND IT MUST HAVE BEEN ONE OF OURS.
IT COULD HARDLY HAVE BEEN ONE OF THEIRS.
REMARKABLE, THE FIGHT THEY PUT UP.
3

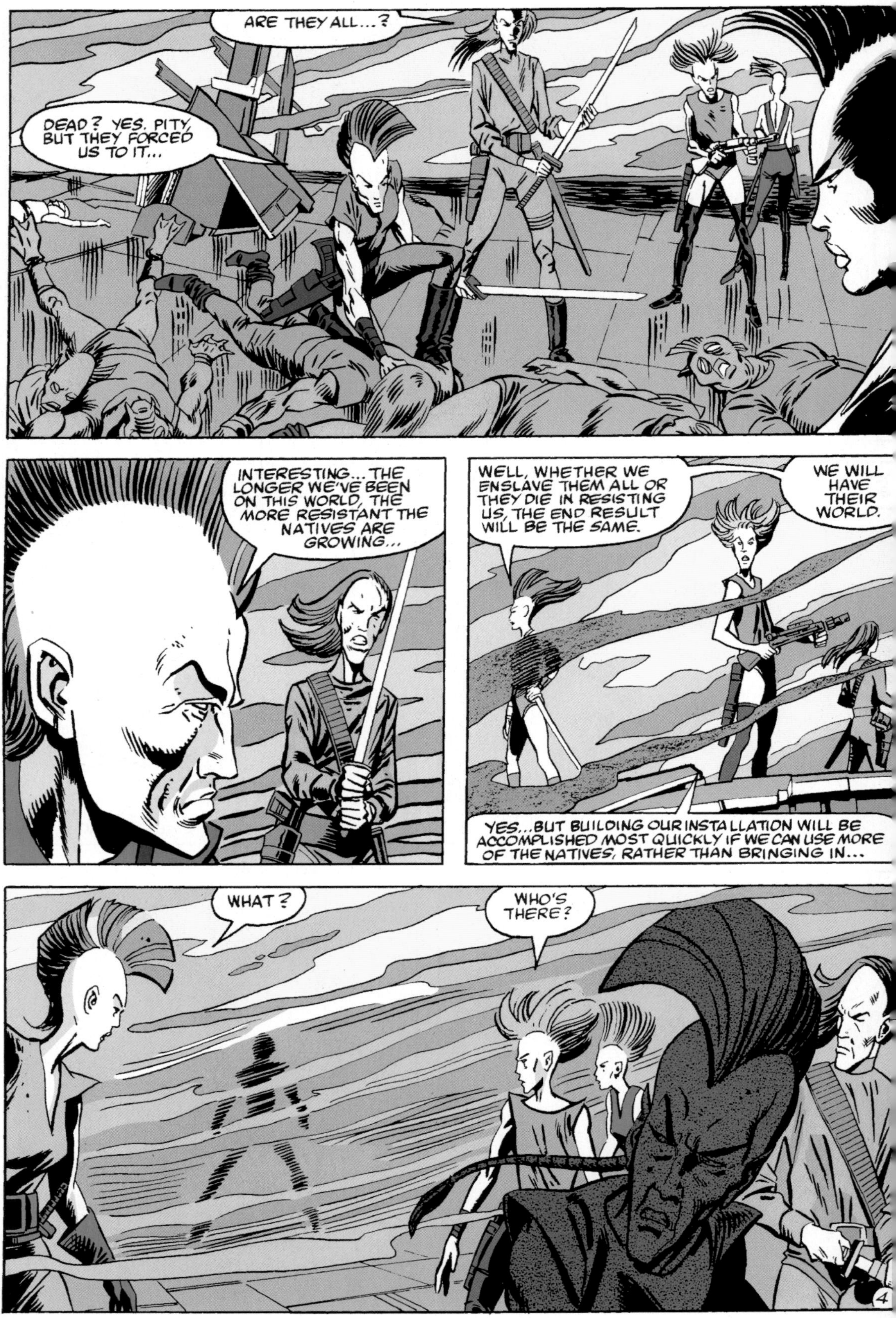
ARE THEY ALL...?
DEAD? YES. PITY, BUT THEY FORCED US TO IT...
INTERESTING... THE LONGER WE'VE BEEN ON THIS WORLD, THE MORE RESISTANT THE NATIVES ARE GROWING...
WELL, WHETHER WE ENSLAVE THEM ALL OR THEY DIE IN RESISTING US, THE END RESULT WILL BE THE SAME.
WE WILL HAVE THEIR WORLD.
YES...BUT BUILDING OUR INSTALLATION WILL BE ACCOMPLISHED MOST QUICKLY IF WE CAN USE MORE OF THE NATIVES, RATHER THAN BRINGING IN...
WHAT?
WHO'S THERE?
4

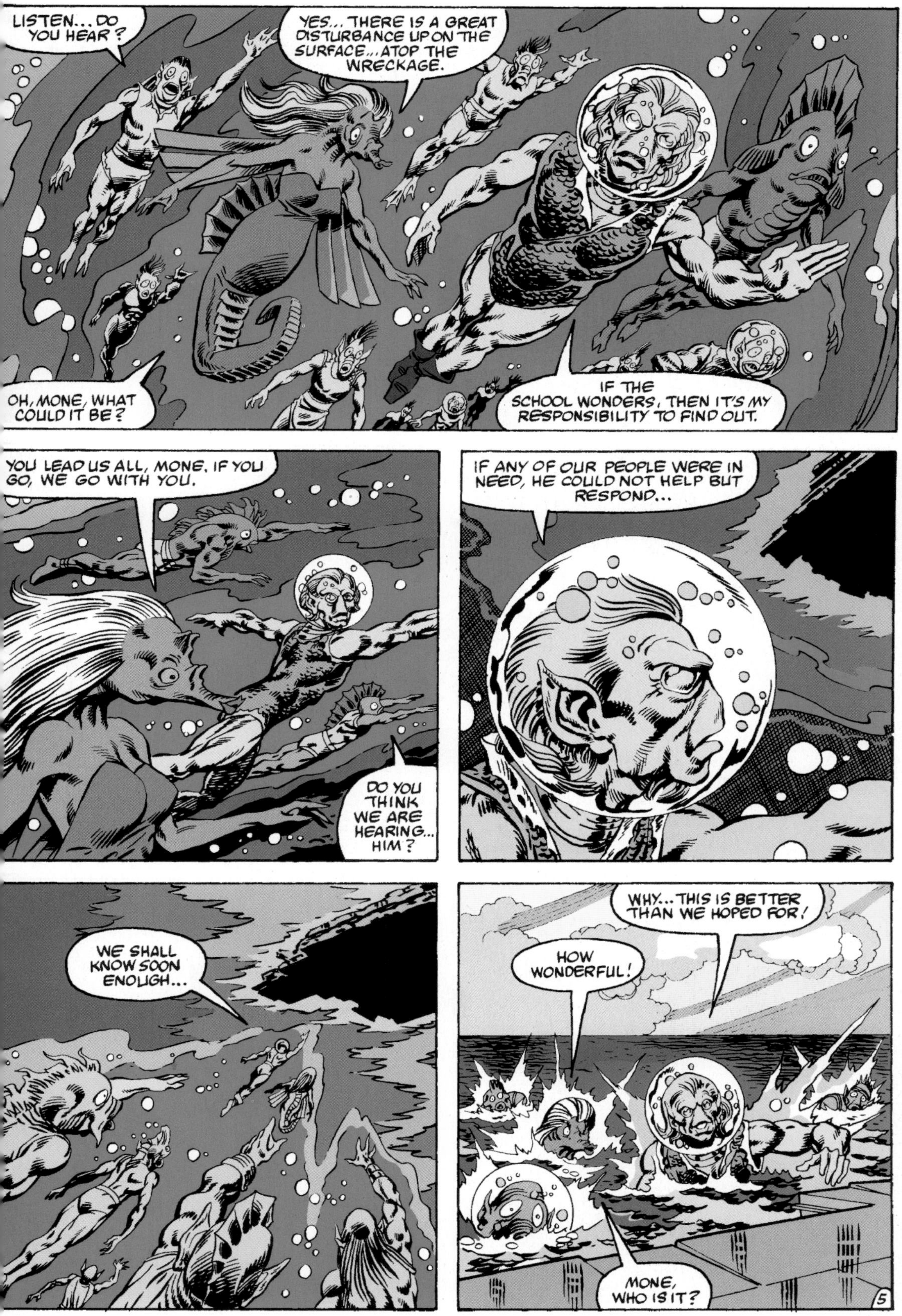
LISTEN... DO YOU HEAR?
YES... THERE IS A GREAT DISTURBANCE UPON THE SURFACE... ATOP THE WRECKAGE.
OH, MONE, WHAT COULD IT BE?
IF THE SCHOOL WONDERS, THEN IT'S MY RESPONSIBILITY TO FIND OUT.
YOU LEAD US ALL, MONE. IF YOU GO, WE GO WITH YOU.
DO YOU THINK WE ARE HEARING... HIM?
IF ANY OF OUR PEOPLE WERE IN NEED, HE COULD NOT HELP BUT RESPOND...
WE SHALL KNOW SOON ENOUGH...
WHY... THIS IS BETTER THAN WE HOPED FOR!
HOW WONDERFUL!
MONE, WHO IS IT?
5

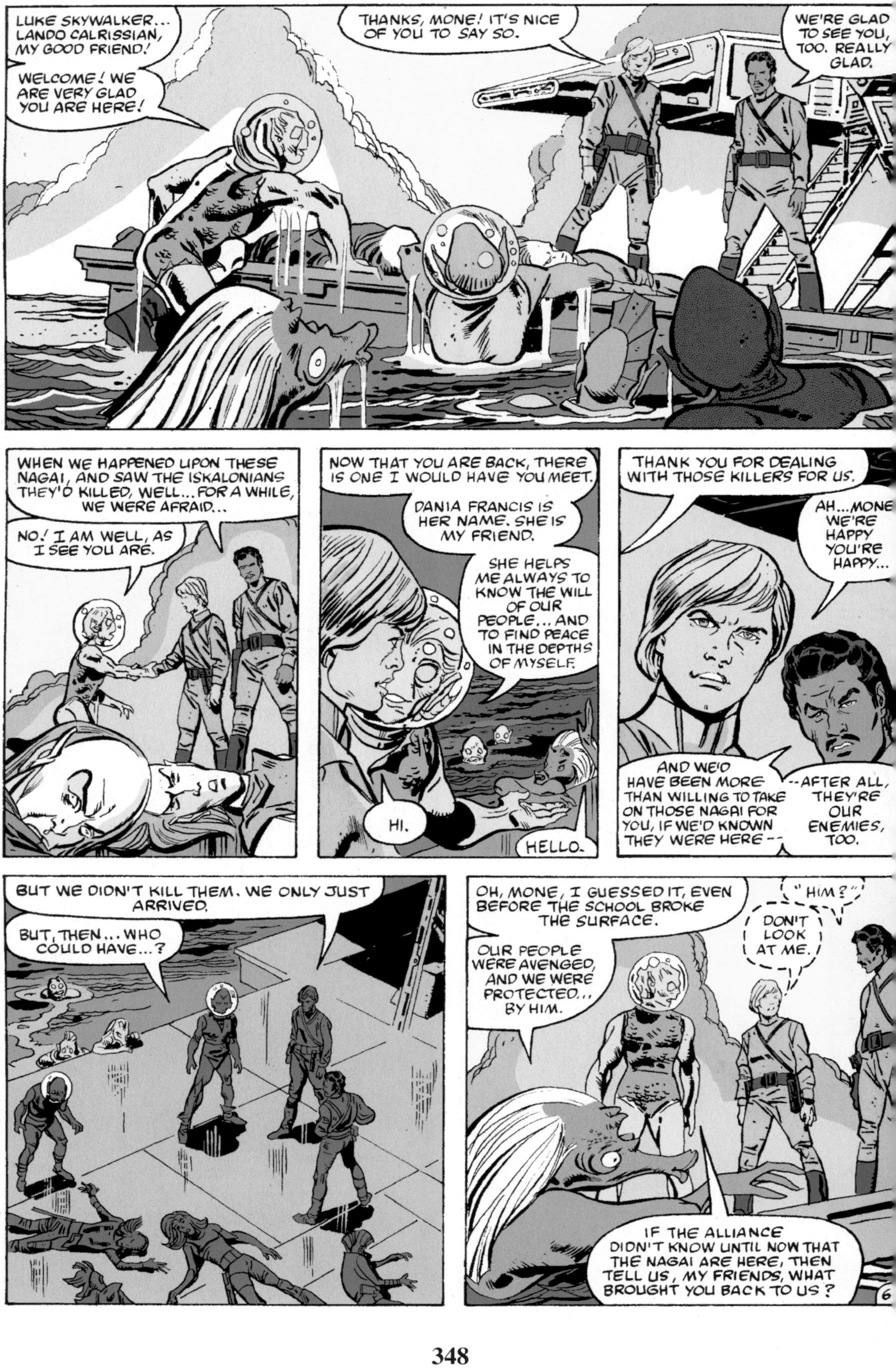

LUKE SKYWALKER... LANDO CALRISSIAN, MY GOOD FRIEND!
WELCOME! WE ARE VERY GLAD YOU ARE HERE!
THANKS, MONE! IT'S NICE OF YOU TO SAY SO.
WE'RE GLAD TO SEE YOU, TOO. REALLY GLAD.
WHEN WE HAPPENED UPON THESE NAGAI, AND SAW THE ISKALONIANS THEY'D KILLED, WELL... FOR A WHILE, WE WERE AFRAID...
NO! I AM WELL, AS I SEE YOU ARE.
NOW THAT YOU ARE BACK, THERE IS ONE I WOULD HAVE YOU MEET.
DANIA FRANCIS IS HER NAME. SHE IS MY FRIEND.
SHE HELPS ME ALWAYS TO KNOW THE WILL OF OUR PEOPLE... AND TO FIND PEACE IN THE DEPTHS OF MYSELF.
HI.
HELLO.
THANK YOU FOR DEALING WITH THOSE KILLERS FOR US.
AH... MONE WE'RE HAPPY YOU'RE HAPPY...
AND WE'D HAVE BEEN MORE THAN WILLING TO TAKE ON THOSE NAGAI FOR YOU, IF WE'D KNOWN THEY WERE HERE--
--AFTER ALL, THEY'RE OUR ENEMIES, TOO.
BUT WE DIDN'T KILL THEM. WE ONLY JUST ARRIVED.
BUT, THEN... WHO COULD HAVE...?
OH, MONE, I GUESSED IT, EVEN BEFORE THE SCHOOL BROKE THE SURFACE.
OUR PEOPLE WERE AVENGED, AND WE WERE PROTECTED... BY HIM.
"HIM?"
DON'T LOOK AT ME.
IF THE ALLIANCE DIDN'T KNOW UNTIL NOW THAT THE NAGAI ARE HERE, THEN TELL US, MY FRIENDS, WHAT BROUGHT YOU BACK TO US?
6

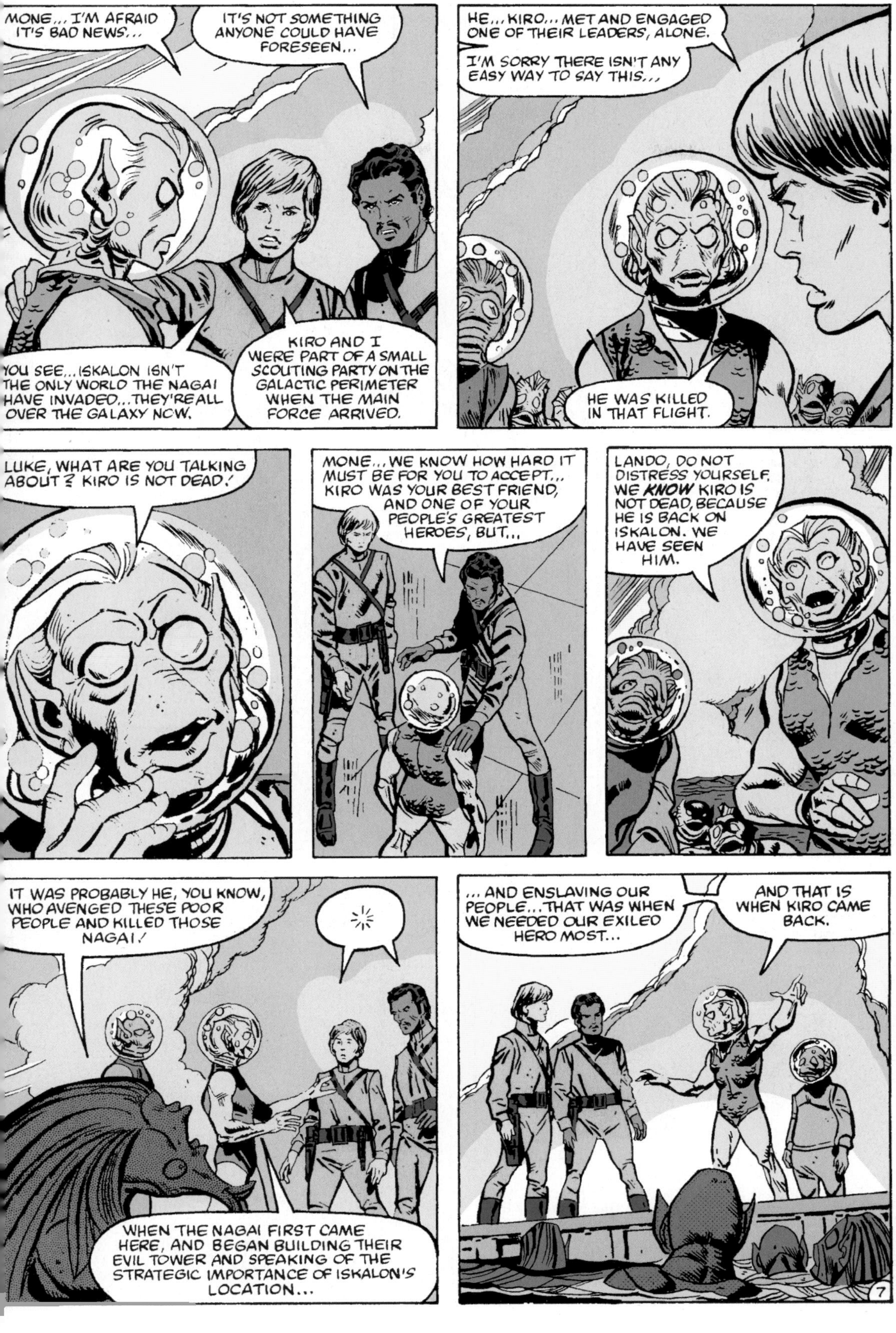
MONE... I'M AFRAID IT'S BAD NEWS...
IT'S NOT SOMETHING ANYONE COULD HAVE FORESEEN...
YOU SEE... ISKALON ISN'T THE ONLY WORLD THE NAGAI HAVE INVADED... THEY'RE ALL OVER THE GALAXY NOW.
KIRO AND I WERE PART OF A SMALL SCOUTING PARTY ON THE GALACTIC PERIMETER WHEN THE MAIN FORCE ARRIVED.
HE... KIRO... MET AND ENGAGED ONE OF THEIR LEADERS, ALONE.
I'M SORRY THERE ISN'T ANY EASY WAY TO SAY THIS...
HE WAS KILLED IN THAT FLIGHT.
LUKE, WHAT ARE YOU TALKING ABOUT? KIRO IS NOT DEAD!
MONE... WE KNOW HOW HARD IT MUST BE FOR YOU TO ACCEPT... KIRO WAS YOUR BEST FRIEND, AND ONE OF YOUR PEOPLE'S GREATEST HEROES, BUT...
LANDO, DO NOT DISTRESS YOURSELF. WE KNOW KIRO IS NOT DEAD, BECAUSE HE IS BACK ON ISKALON. WE HAVE SEEN HIM.
IT WAS PROBABLY HE, YOU KNOW, WHO AVENGED THESE POOR PEOPLE AND KILLED THOSE NAGAI!
WHEN THE NAGAI FIRST CAME HERE, AND BEGAN BUILDING THEIR EVIL TOWER AND SPEAKING OF THE STRATEGIC IMPORTANCE OF ISKALON'S LOCATION...
... AND ENSLAVING OUR PEOPLE... THAT WAS WHEN WE NEEDED OUR EXILED HERO MOST...
AND THAT IS WHEN KIRO CAME BACK.
7

IT WAS A TWO-PASSENGER CRAFT, NOT ANY KNOWN CLASS OF MILITARY CRAFT, SO IT MAY BE PRIVATELY OWNED.

ANY WORD AS YET ON THAT SHIP THAT CAME IN?

DEFINITELY NOT ONE OF OURS, SIR.

THEY MADE NO ATTEMPT TO IDENTIFY THEMSELVES, AND OBTAINED NO CLEARANCES WHATSOEVER.

TAKE A PARTY OF HUNTERS, AND SOME OF THE STORM TROOPERS AND CHECK OUT THEIR LANDING SITE.

BRING SOME OF THE NEW WEAPONS. THEY'VE PROVEN PARTICULARLY EFFICACIOUS AGAINST THE SLAVES WE TESTED THEM ON.

IT'S TIME WE CHECKED OUT HOW THEY PERFORM IN THE FIELD.

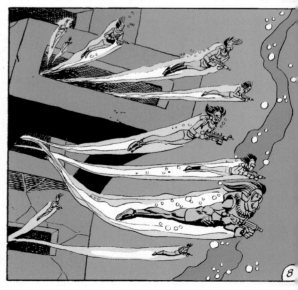

8

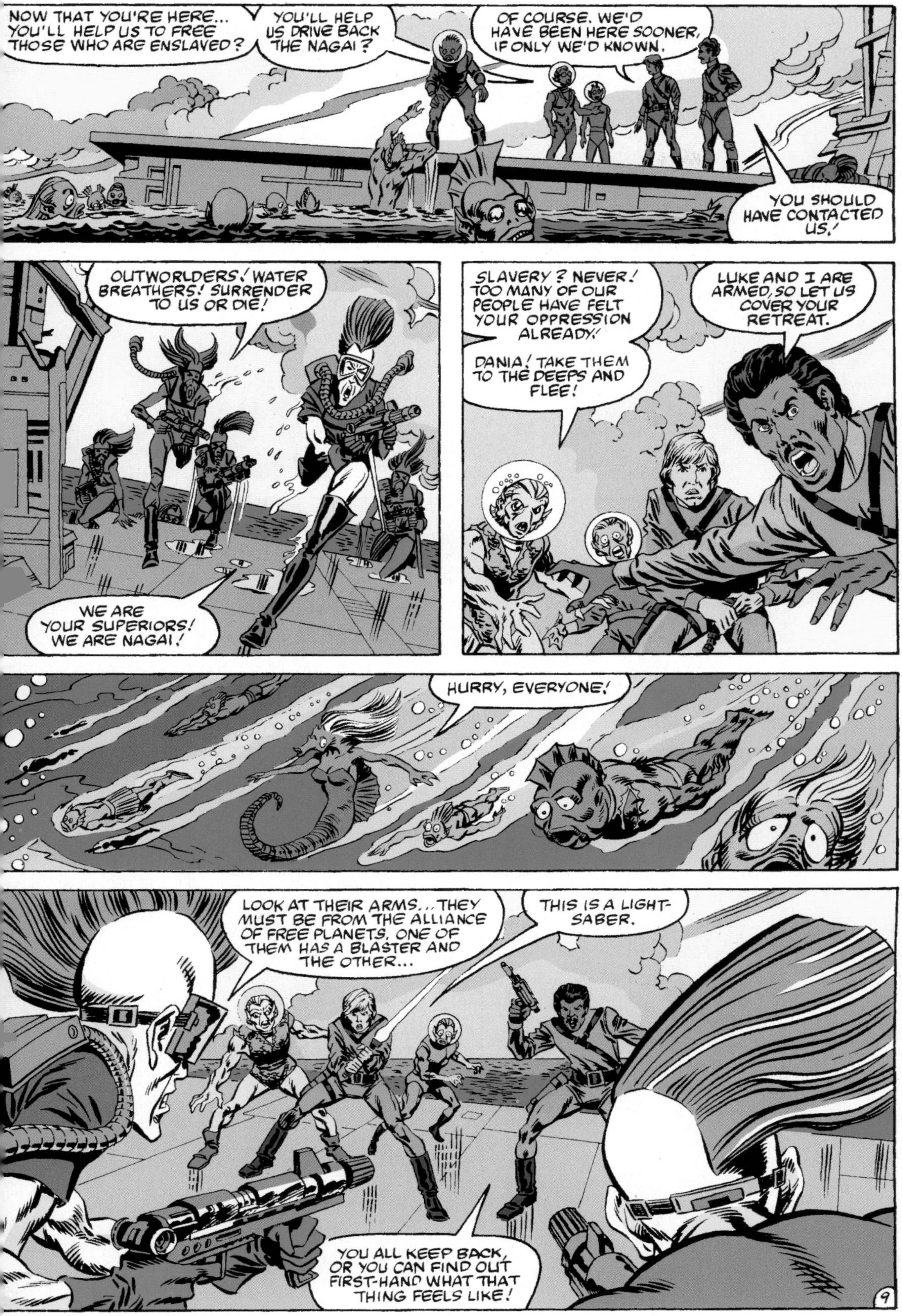
NOW THAT YOU'RE HERE... YOU'LL HELP US TO FREE THOSE WHO ARE ENSLAVED?
YOU'LL HELP US DRIVE BACK THE NAGAI?
OF COURSE. WE'D HAVE BEEN HERE SOONER, IF ONLY WE'D KNOWN.
YOU SHOULD HAVE CONTACTED US!
OUTWORLDERS! WATER BREATHERS! SURRENDER TO US OR DIE!
WE ARE YOUR SUPERIORS! WE ARE NAGAI!
SLAVERY? NEVER! TOO MANY OF OUR PEOPLE HAVE FELT YOUR OPPRESSION ALREADY!
DANIA! TAKE THEM TO THE DEEPS AND FLEE!
LUKE AND I ARE ARMED, SO LET US COVER YOUR RETREAT.
HURRY, EVERYONE!
LOOK AT THEIR ARMS... THEY MUST BE FROM THE ALLIANCE OF FREE PLANETS. ONE OF THEM HAS A BLASTER AND THE OTHER...
THIS IS A LIGHT-SABER.
YOU ALL KEEP BACK, OR YOU CAN FIND OUT FIRST-HAND WHAT THAT THING FEELS LIKE!
9

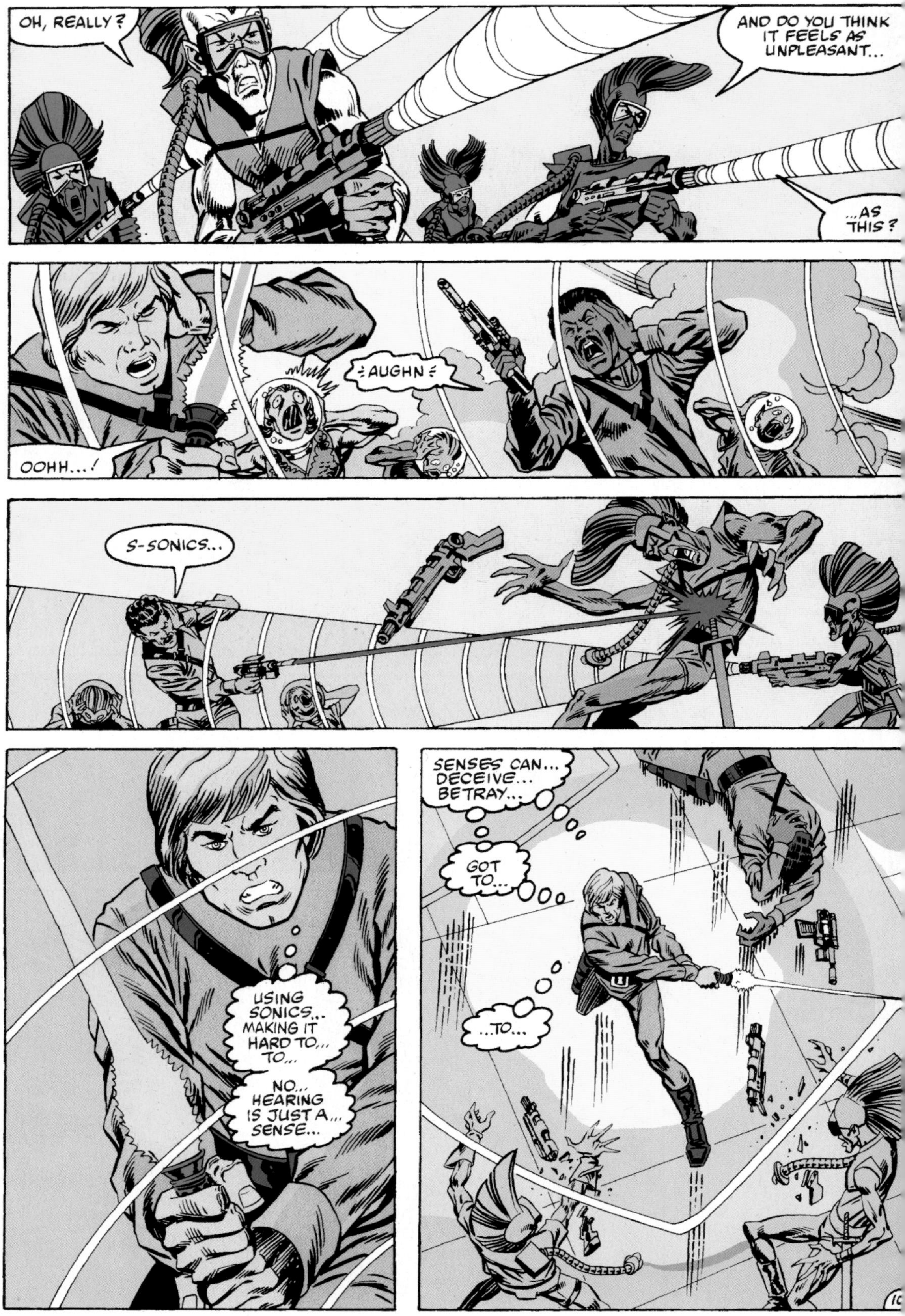
OH, REALLY?
AND DO YOU THINK IT FEELS AS UNPLEASANT...
...AS THIS?
AUGHN
OOHH...!
S-SONICS...
USING SONICS... MAKING IT HARD TO... TO...
NO... HEARING IS JUST A... SENSE...
SENSES CAN... DECEIVE... BETRAY...
GOT TO...
...TO...

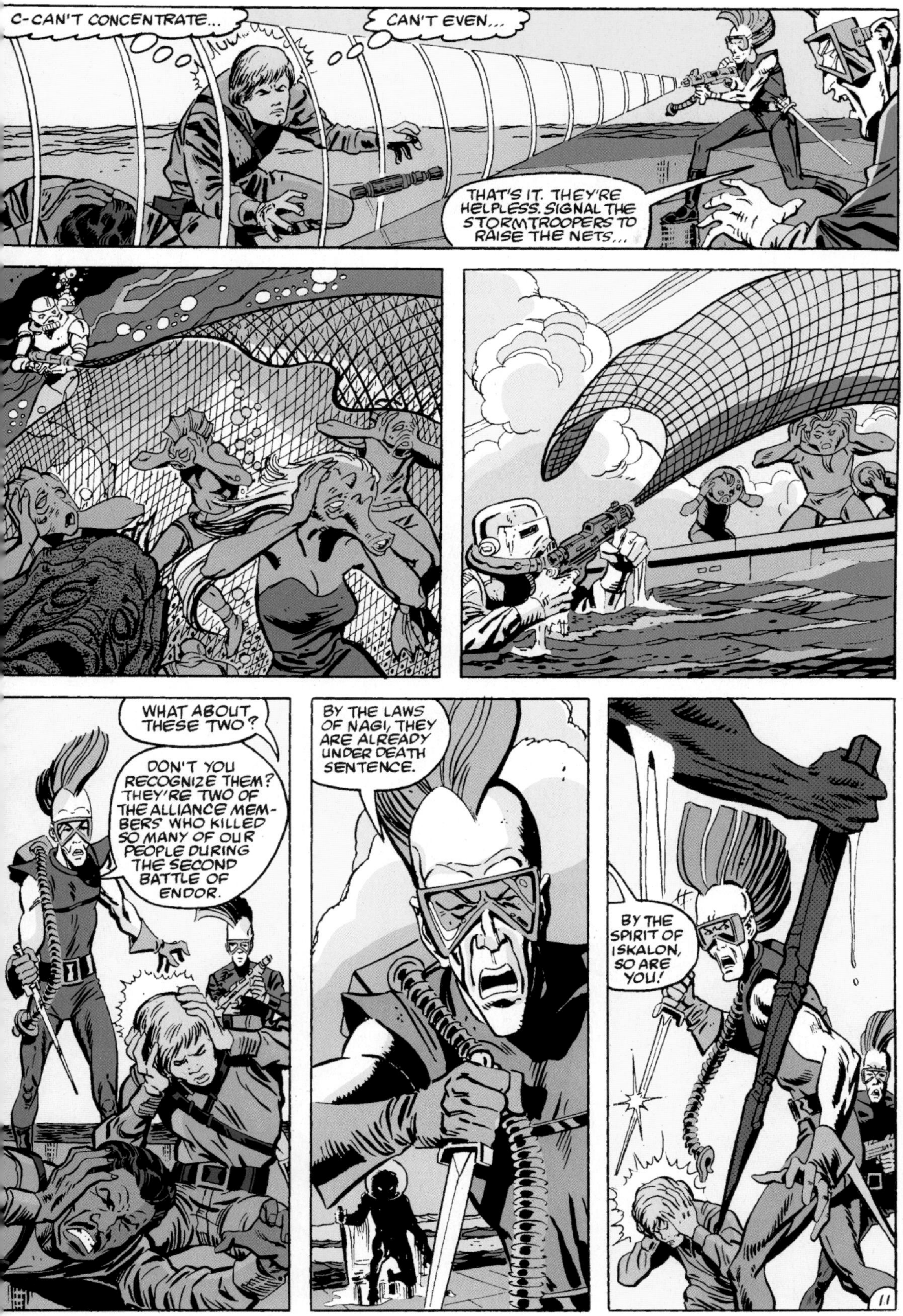
C-CAN'T CONCENTRATE...
CAN'T EVEN...
THAT'S IT. THEY'RE HELPLESS. SIGNAL THE STORMTROOPERS TO RAISE THE NETS...
WHAT ABOUT THESE TWO?
DON'T YOU RECOGNIZE THEM? THEY'RE TWO OF THE ALLIANCE MEMBERS WHO KILLED SO MANY OF OUR PEOPLE DURING THE SECOND BATTLE OF ENDOR.
BY THE LAWS OF NAGI, THEY ARE ALREADY UNDER DEATH SENTENCE.
BY THE SPIRIT OF ISKALON, SO ARE YOU!
11

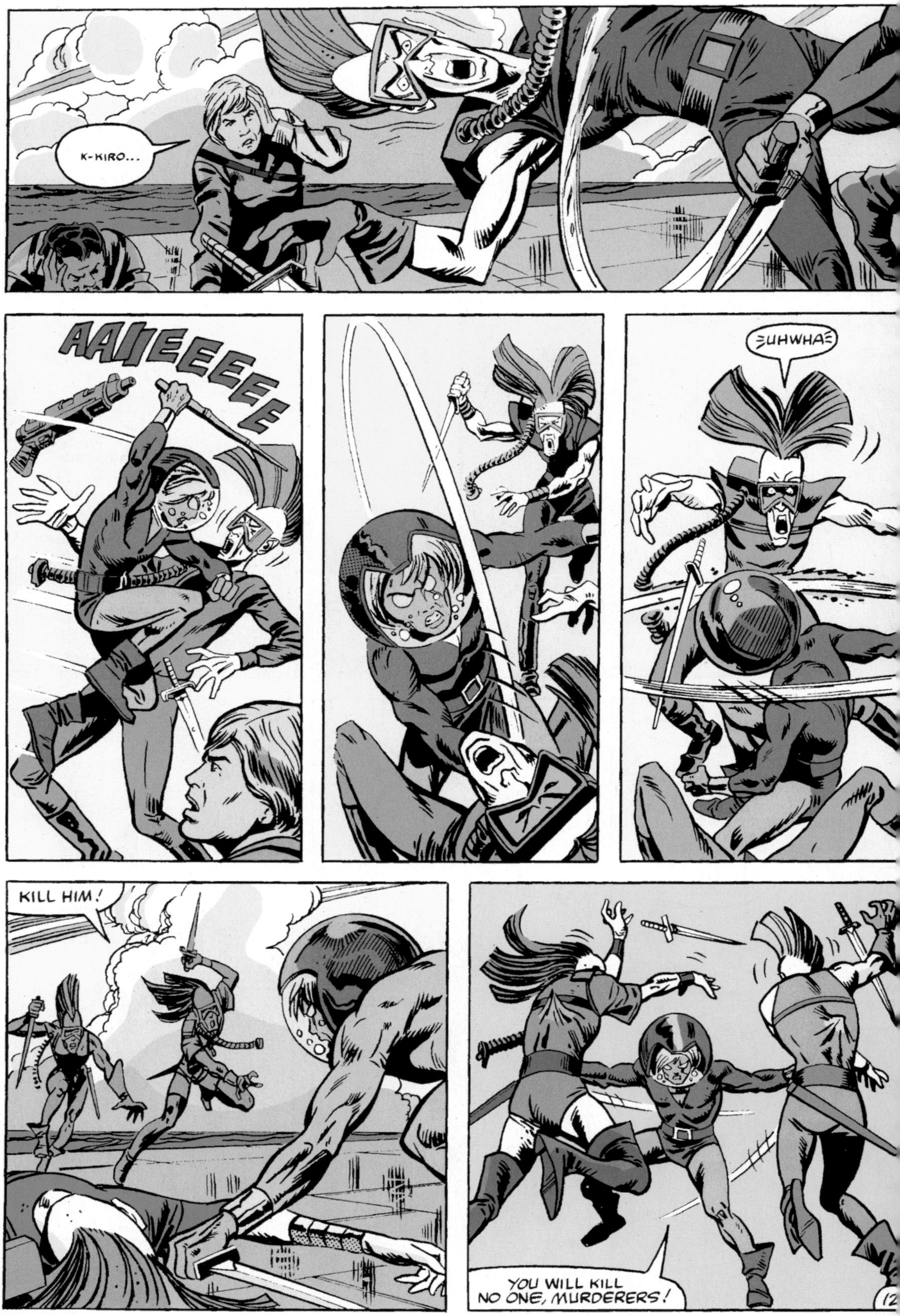
K-KIRO...
AAIIEEEEE
UHWHA
KILL HIM!
YOU WILL KILL NO ONE, MURDERERS!
12

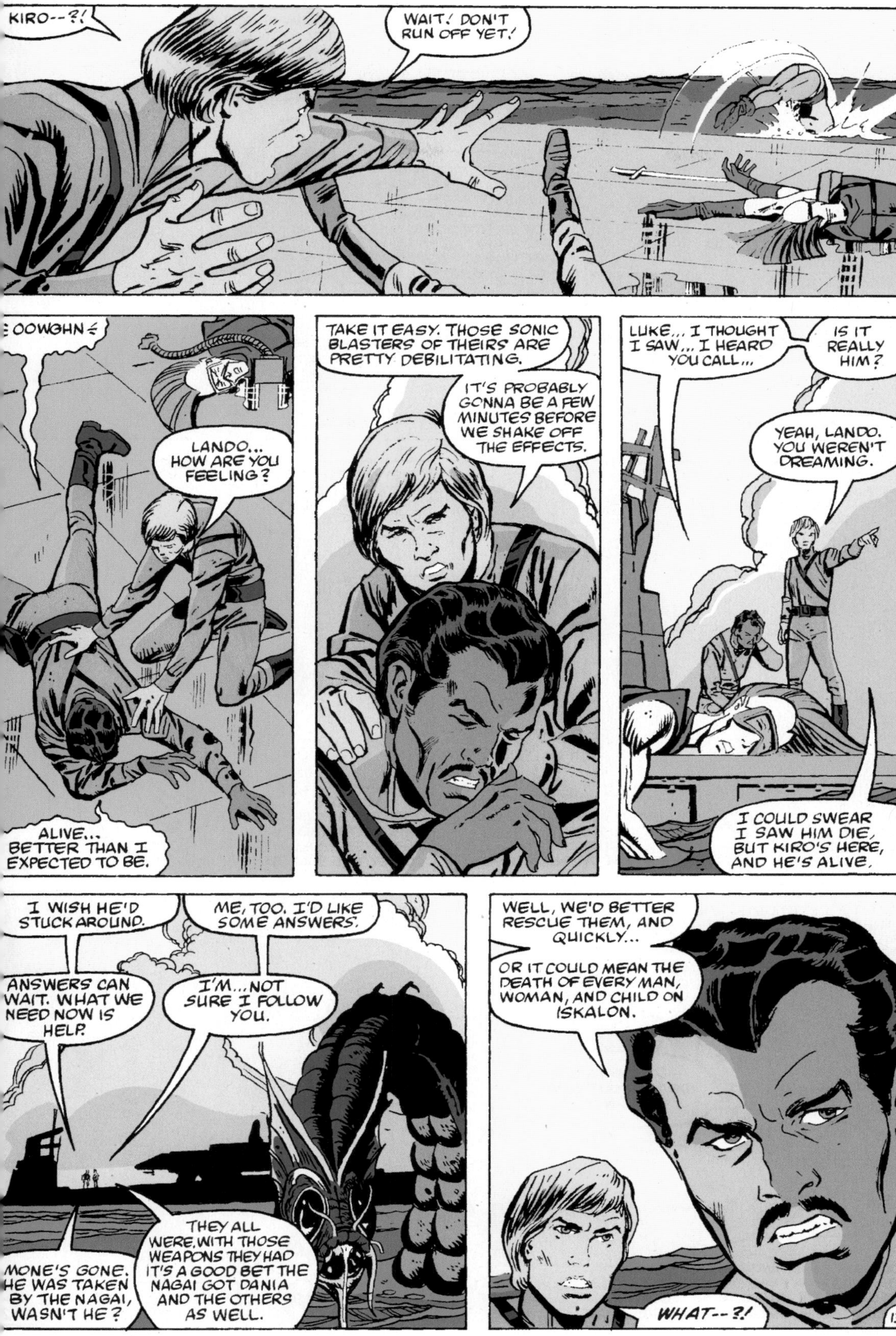
KIRO--?!
WAIT! DON'T RUN OFF YET!
OOWGHN
LANDO... HOW ARE YOU FEELING?
ALIVE... BETTER THAN I EXPECTED TO BE.
TAKE IT EASY. THOSE SONIC BLASTERS OF THEIRS ARE PRETTY DEBILITATING.
IT'S PROBABLY GONNA BE A FEW MINUTES BEFORE WE SHAKE OFF THE EFFECTS.
LUKE... I THOUGHT I SAW... I HEARD YOU CALL...
IS IT REALLY HIM?
YEAH, LANDO. YOU WEREN'T DREAMING.
I COULD SWEAR I SAW HIM DIE, BUT KIRO'S HERE, AND HE'S ALIVE.
I WISH HE'D STUCK AROUND.
ME, TOO. I'D LIKE SOME ANSWERS.
ANSWERS CAN WAIT. WHAT WE NEED NOW IS HELP.
I'M... NOT SURE I FOLLOW YOU.
MONE'S GONE. HE WAS TAKEN BY THE NAGAI, WASN'T HE?
THEY ALL WERE. WITH THOSE WEAPONS THEY HAD IT'S A GOOD BET THE NAGAI GOT DANIA AND THE OTHERS AS WELL.
WELL, WE'D BETTER RESCUE THEM, AND QUICKLY...
OR IT COULD MEAN THE DEATH OF EVERY MAN, WOMAN, AND CHILD ON ISKALON.
WHAT--?!
13

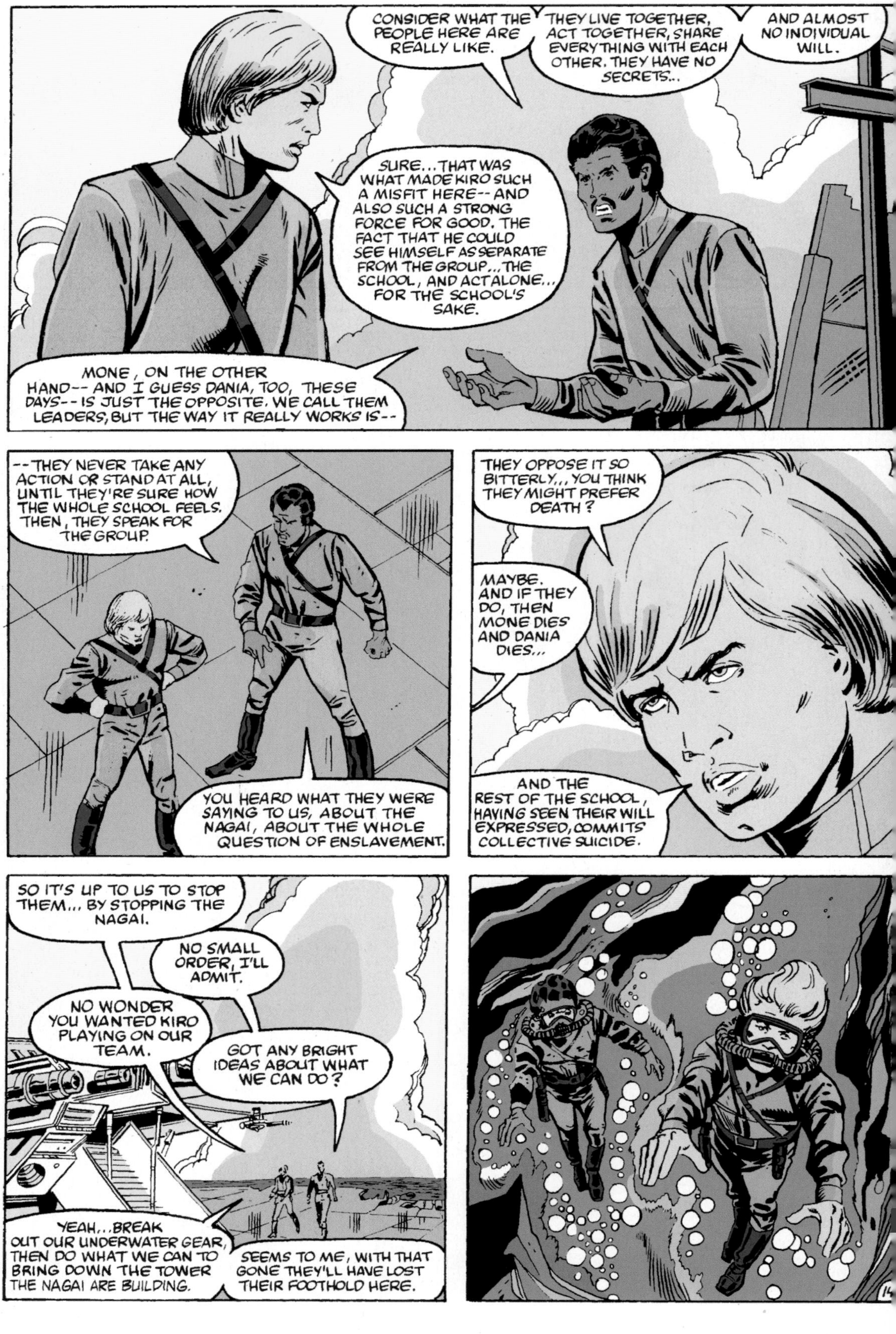
CONSIDER WHAT THE PEOPLE HERE ARE REALLY LIKE.
THEY LIVE TOGETHER, ACT TOGETHER, SHARE EVERYTHING WITH EACH OTHER. THEY HAVE NO SECRETS...
AND ALMOST NO INDIVIDUAL WILL.
SURE...THAT WAS WHAT MADE KIRO SUCH A MISFIT HERE-- AND ALSO SUCH A STRONG FORCE FOR GOOD. THE FACT THAT HE COULD SEE HIMSELF AS SEPARATE FROM THE GROUP... THE SCHOOL, AND ACT ALONE... FOR THE SCHOOL'S SAKE.
MONE, ON THE OTHER HAND-- AND I GUESS DANIA, TOO, THESE DAYS-- IS JUST THE OPPOSITE. WE CALL THEM LEADERS, BUT THE WAY IT REALLY WORKS IS--
--THEY NEVER TAKE ANY ACTION OR STAND AT ALL, UNTIL THEY'RE SURE HOW THE WHOLE SCHOOL FEELS. THEN, THEY SPEAK FOR THE GROUP.
YOU HEARD WHAT THEY WERE SAYING TO US, ABOUT THE NAGAI, ABOUT THE WHOLE QUESTION OF ENSLAVEMENT.
THEY OPPOSE IT SO BITTERLY... YOU THINK THEY MIGHT PREFER DEATH?
MAYBE. AND IF THEY DO, THEN MONE DIES AND DANIA DIES...
AND THE REST OF THE SCHOOL, HAVING SEEN THEIR WILL EXPRESSED, COMMITS COLLECTIVE SUICIDE.
SO IT'S UP TO US TO STOP THEM... BY STOPPING THE NAGAI.
NO SMALL ORDER, I'LL ADMIT.
NO WONDER YOU WANTED KIRO PLAYING ON OUR TEAM.
GOT ANY BRIGHT IDEAS ABOUT WHAT WE CAN DO?
YEAH... BREAK OUT OUR UNDERWATER GEAR, THEN DO WHAT WE CAN TO BRING DOWN THE TOWER THE NAGAI ARE BUILDING.
SEEMS TO ME, WITH THAT GONE THEY'LL HAVE LOST THEIR FOOTHOLD HERE.
14

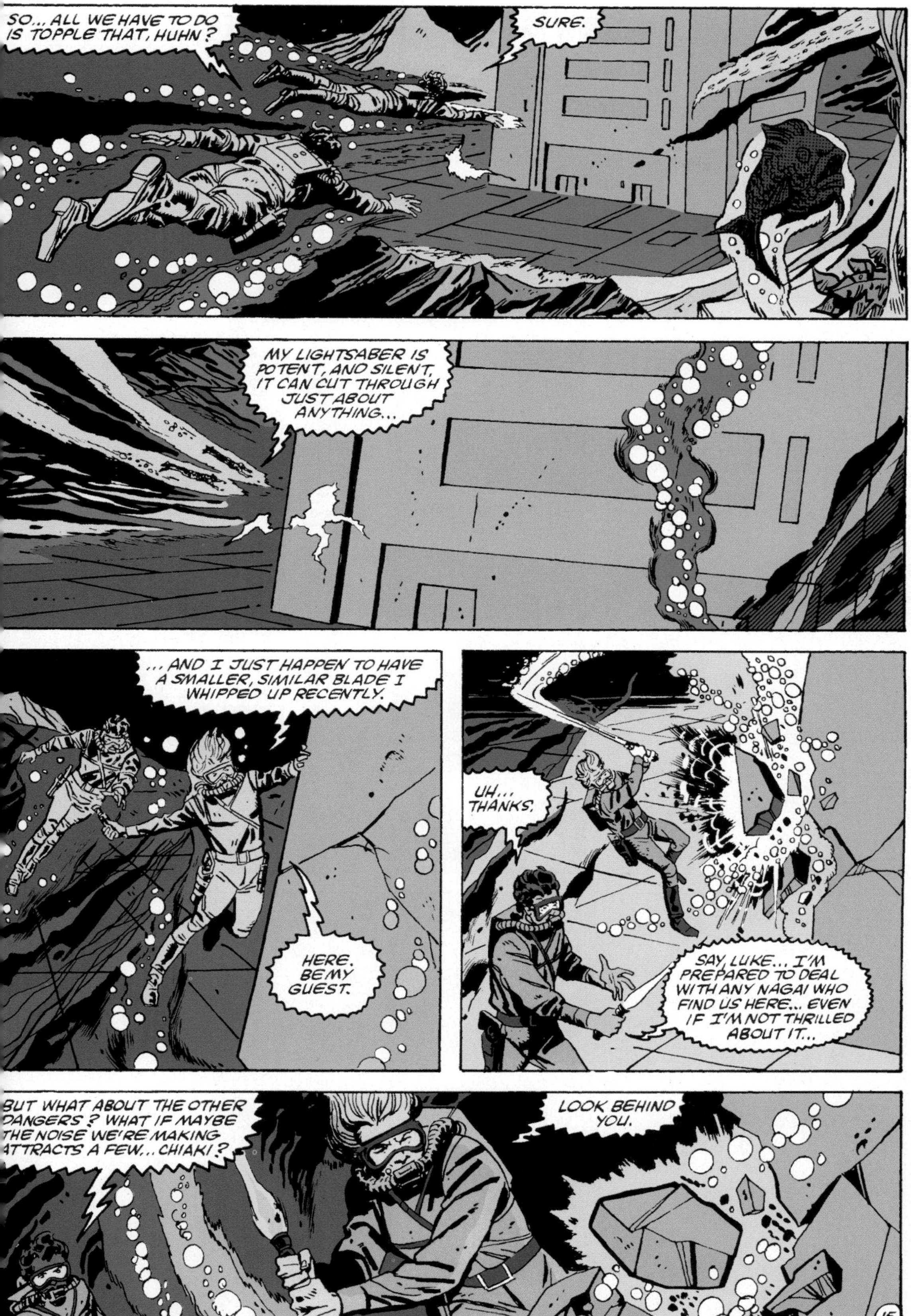
SO... ALL WE HAVE TO DO IS TOPPLE THAT, HUHN?
SURE.
MY LIGHTSABER IS POTENT, AND SILENT. IT CAN CUT THROUGH JUST ABOUT ANYTHING...
...AND I JUST HAPPEN TO HAVE A SMALLER, SIMILAR BLADE I WHIPPED UP RECENTLY.
HERE. BE MY GUEST.
UH... THANKS.
SAY, LUKE... I'M PREPARED TO DEAL WITH ANY NAGAI WHO FIND US HERE... EVEN IF I'M NOT THRILLED ABOUT IT...
BUT WHAT ABOUT THE OTHER DANGERS? WHAT IF MAYBE THE NOISE WE'RE MAKING ATTRACTS A FEW... CHIAKI?
LOOK BEHIND YOU.
15

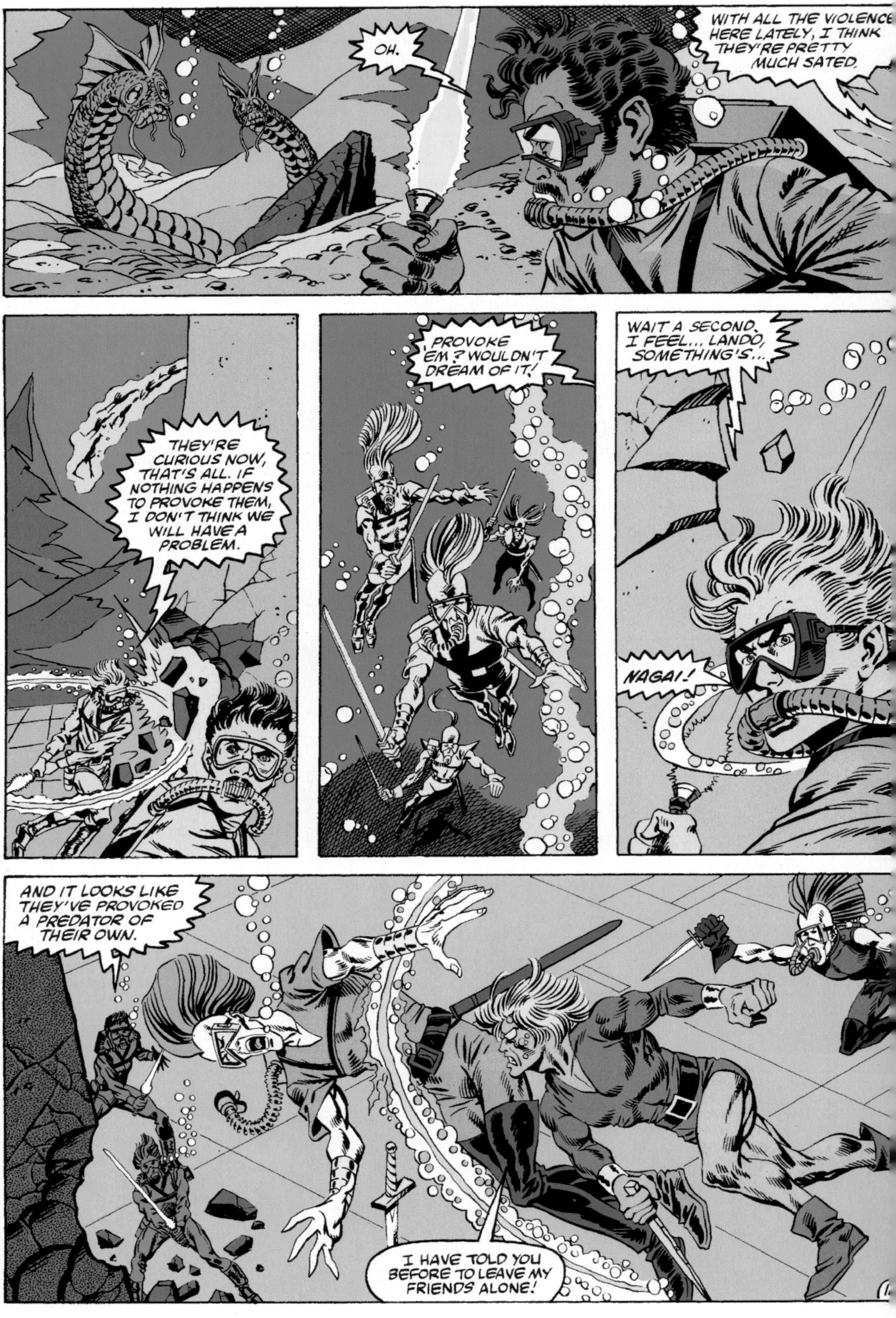
OH.
WITH ALL THE VIOLENCE HERE LATELY, I THINK THEY'RE PRETTY MUCH SATED.
THEY'RE CURIOUS NOW, THAT'S ALL. IF NOTHING HAPPENS TO PROVOKE THEM, I DON'T THINK WE WILL HAVE A PROBLEM.
PROVOKE 'EM ? WOULDN'T DREAM OF IT!
WAIT A SECOND. I FEEL... LANDO, SOMETHING'S...
NAGAI!
AND IT LOOKS LIKE THEY'VE PROVOKED A PREDATOR OF THEIR OWN.
I HAVE TOLD YOU BEFORE TO LEAVE MY FRIENDS ALONE!

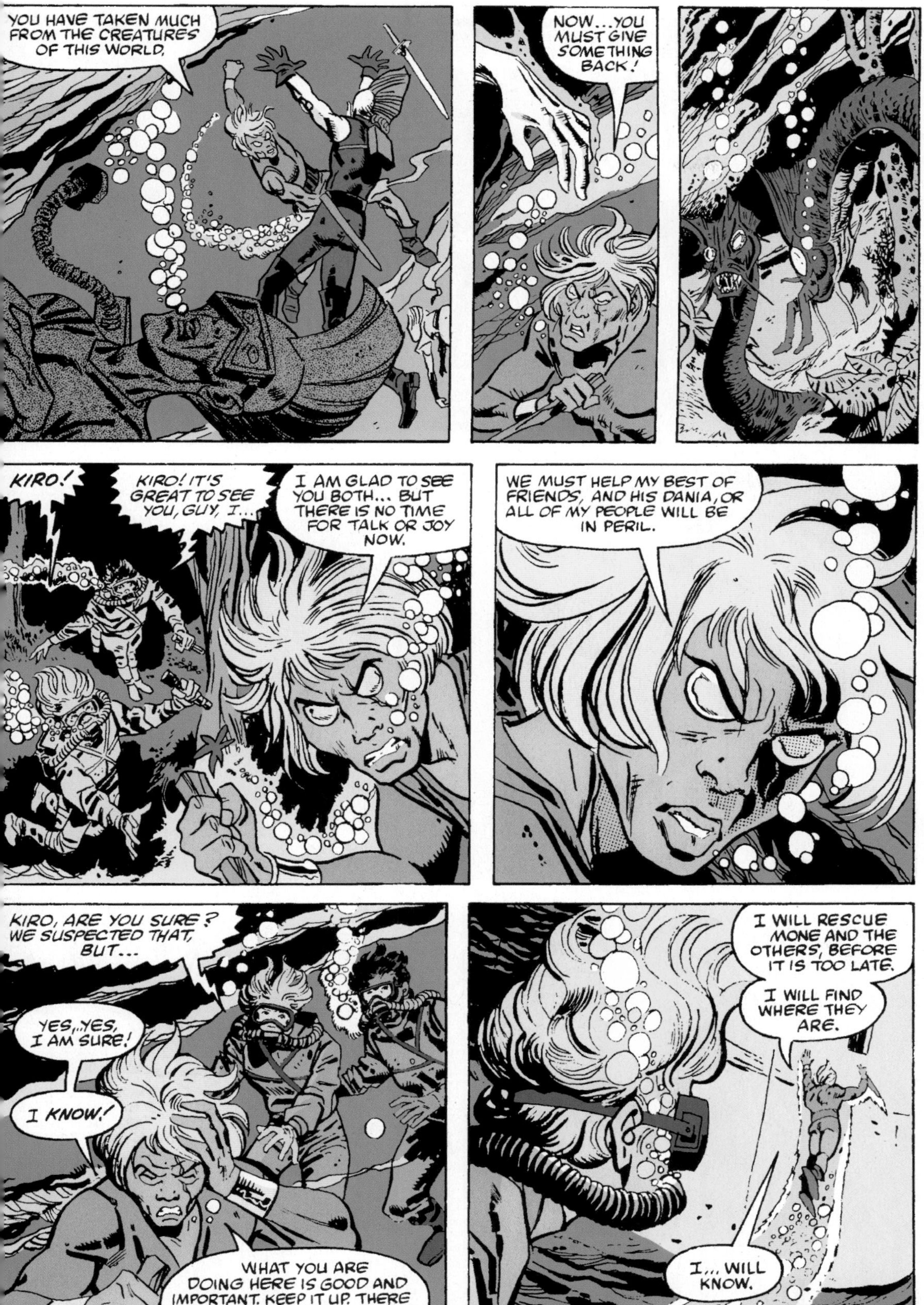
YOU HAVE TAKEN MUCH FROM THE CREATURES OF THIS WORLD,
NOW... YOU MUST GIVE SOMETHING BACK!
KIRO!
KIRO! IT'S GREAT TO SEE YOU, GUY, I...
I AM GLAD TO SEE YOU BOTH... BUT THERE IS NO TIME FOR TALK OR JOY NOW.
WE MUST HELP MY BEST OF FRIENDS, AND HIS DANIA, OR ALL OF MY PEOPLE WILL BE IN PERIL.
KIRO, ARE YOU SURE? WE SUSPECTED THAT, BUT...
YES,..YES, I AM SURE!
I KNOW!
WHAT YOU ARE DOING HERE IS GOOD AND IMPORTANT. KEEP IT UP. THERE SHOULD BE NO MORE GUARDS UNTIL THE LATE CYCLE.
I WILL RESCUE MONE AND THE OTHERS, BEFORE IT IS TOO LATE.
I WILL FIND WHERE THEY ARE.
I... WILL KNOW.
17

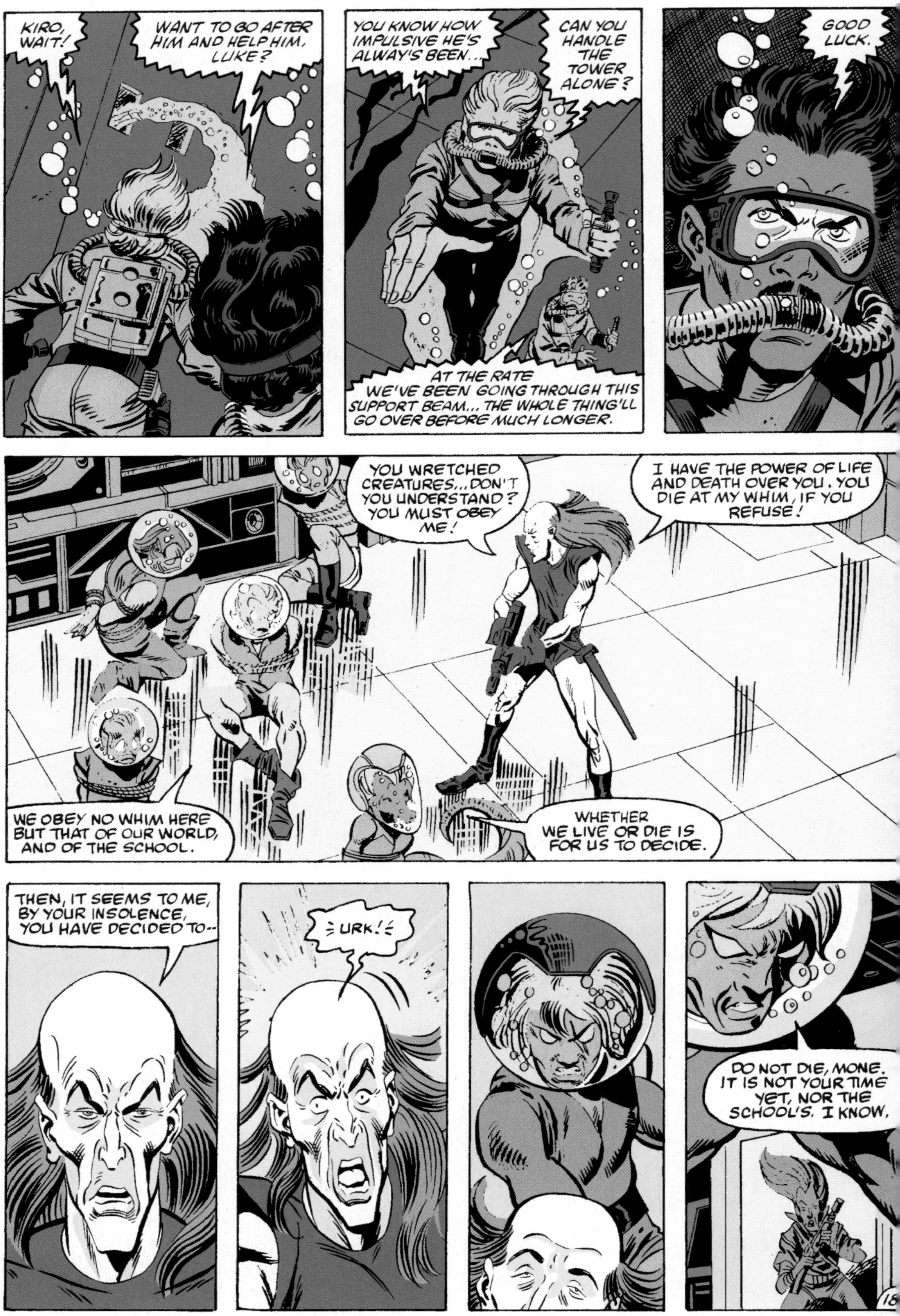
KIRO, WAIT!
WANT TO GO AFTER HIM AND HELP HIM, LUKE?
YOU KNOW HOW IMPULSIVE HE'S ALWAYS BEEN...
CAN YOU HANDLE THE TOWER ALONE?
AT THE RATE WE'VE BEEN GOING THROUGH THIS SUPPORT BEAM... THE WHOLE THING'LL GO OVER BEFORE MUCH LONGER.
GOOD LUCK.
YOU WRETCHED CREATURES... DON'T YOU UNDERSTAND? YOU MUST OBEY ME!
I HAVE THE POWER OF LIFE AND DEATH OVER YOU. YOU DIE AT MY WHIM, IF YOU REFUSE!
WE OBEY NO WHIM HERE BUT THAT OF OUR WORLD, AND OF THE SCHOOL.
WHETHER WE LIVE OR DIE IS FOR US TO DECIDE.
THEN, IT SEEMS TO ME, BY YOUR INSOLENCE, YOU HAVE DECIDED TO--
URK!
DO NOT DIE, MONE. IT IS NOT YOUR TIME YET, NOR THE SCHOOL'S. I KNOW.
18

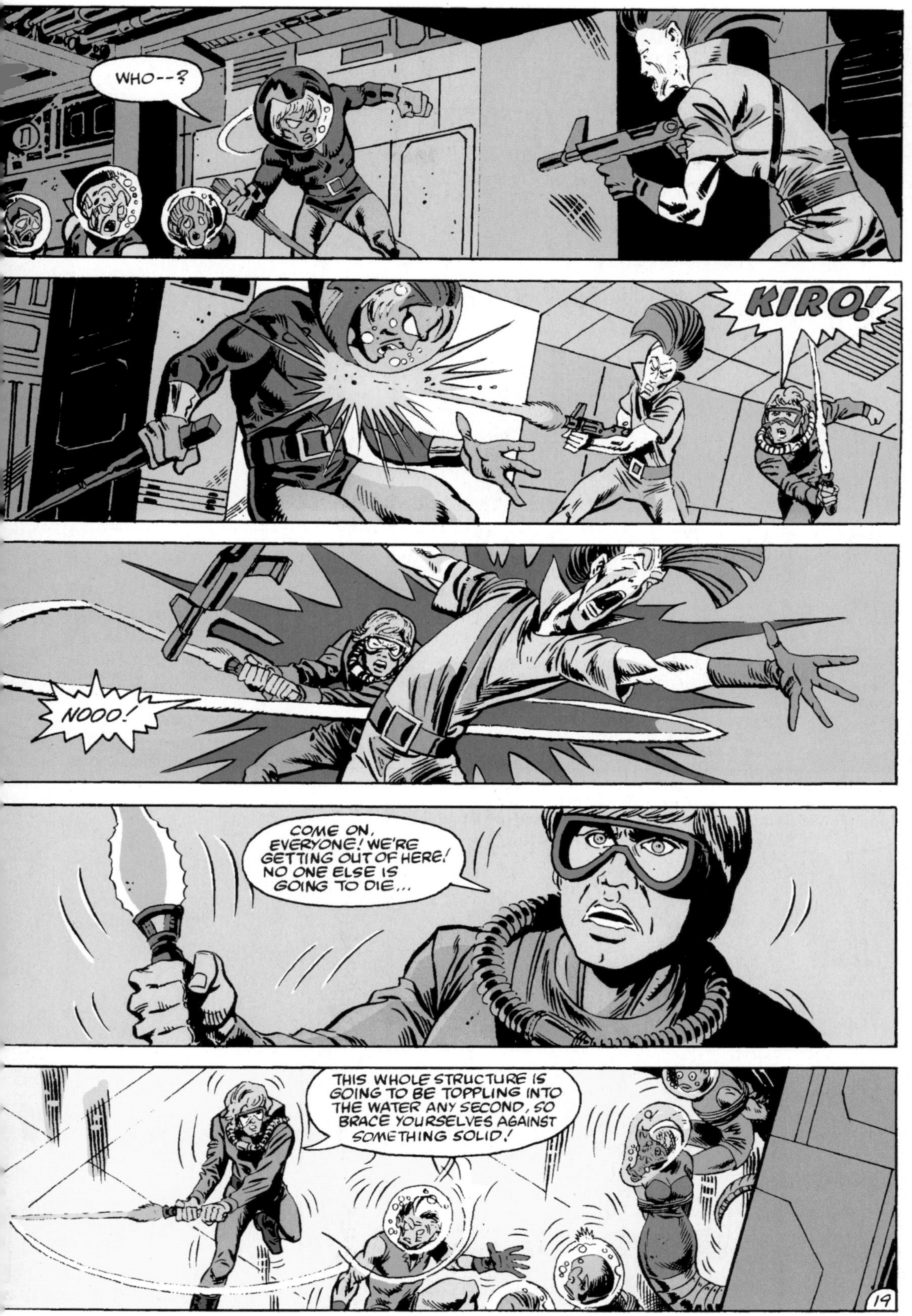

WHO--?
KIRO!
NOOO!
COME ON, EVERYONE! WE'RE GETTING OUT OF HERE! NO ONE ELSE IS GOING TO DIE...
THIS WHOLE STRUCTURE IS GOING TO BE TOPPLING INTO THE WATER ANY SECOND, SO BRACE YOURSELVES AGAINST SOMETHING SOLID!
19

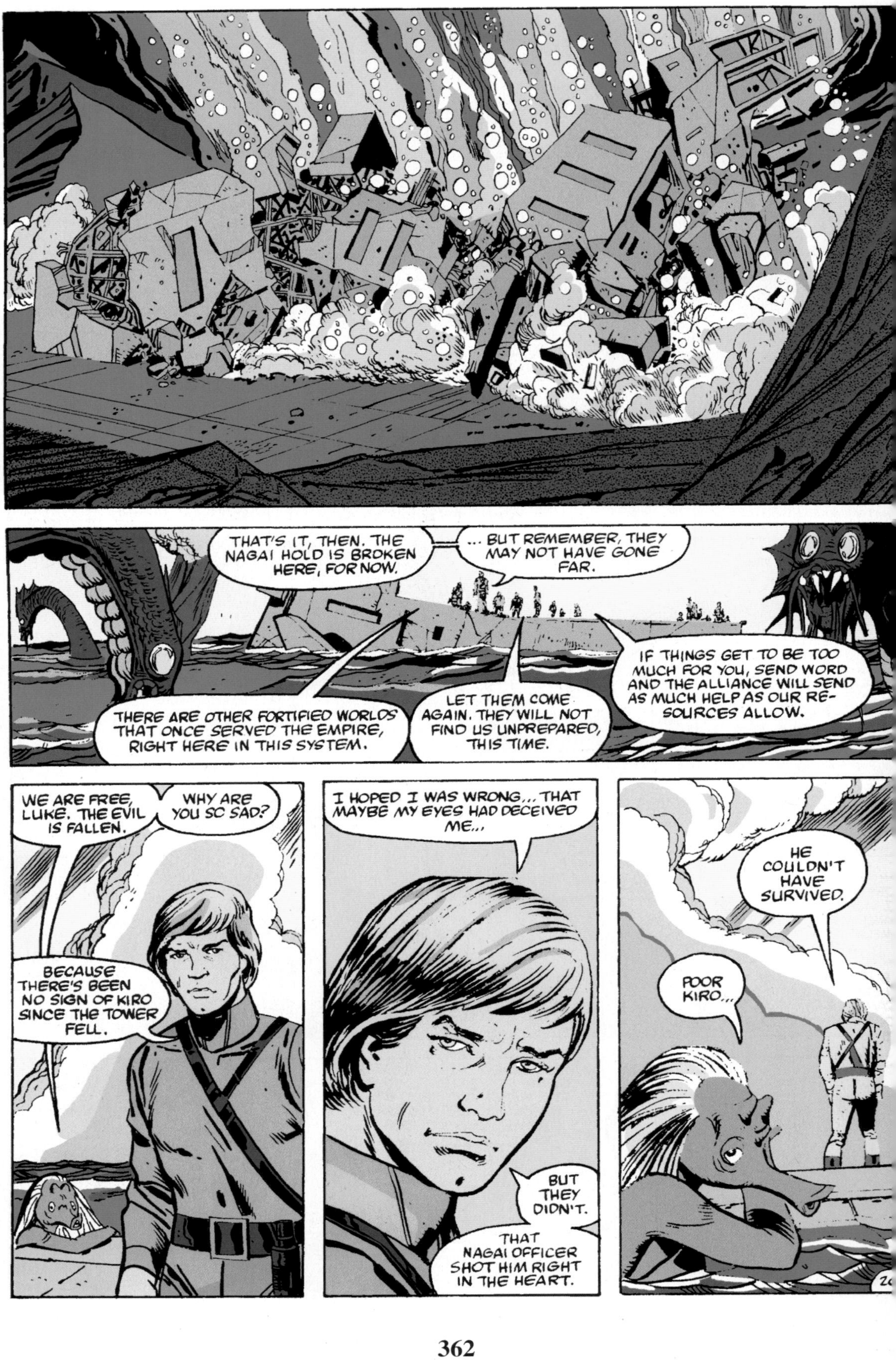
THAT'S IT, THEN. THE NAGAI HOLD IS BROKEN HERE, FOR NOW.
... BUT REMEMBER, THEY MAY NOT HAVE GONE FAR.
THERE ARE OTHER FORTIFIED WORLDS THAT ONCE SERVED THE EMPIRE, RIGHT HERE IN THIS SYSTEM.
LET THEM COME AGAIN. THEY WILL NOT FIND US UNPREPARED, THIS TIME.
IF THINGS GET TO BE TOO MUCH FOR YOU, SEND WORD AND THE ALLIANCE WILL SEND AS MUCH HELP AS OUR RE-SOURCES ALLOW.
WE ARE FREE, LUKE. THE EVIL IS FALLEN.
WHY ARE YOU SO SAD?
BECAUSE THERE'S BEEN NO SIGN OF KIRO SINCE THE TOWER FELL.
I HOPED I WAS WRONG... THAT MAYBE MY EYES HAD DECEIVED ME...
BUT THEY DIDN'T.
THAT NAGAI OFFICER SHOT HIM RIGHT IN THE HEART.
HE COULDN'T HAVE SURVIVED.
POOR KIRO...

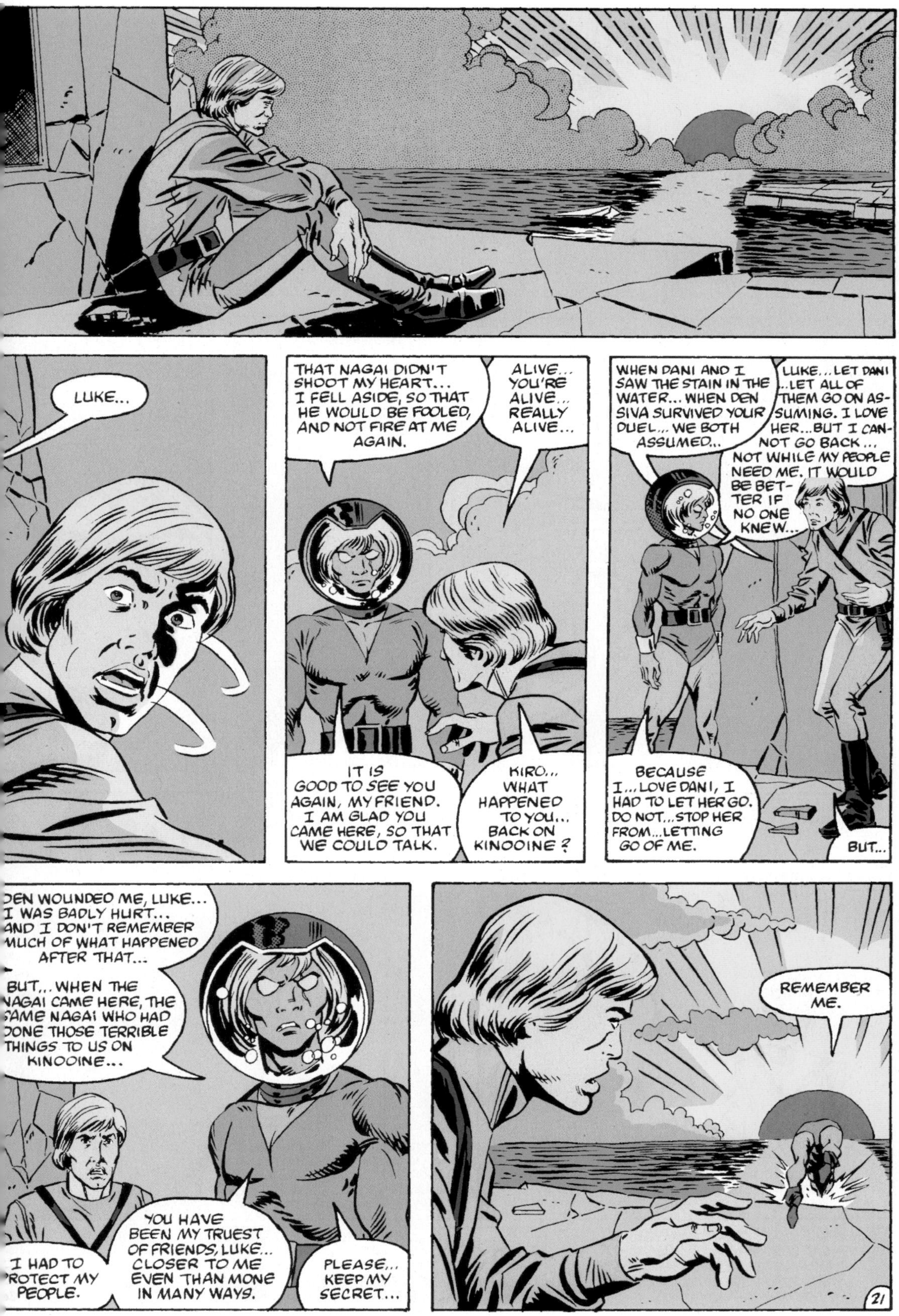
LUKE...
THAT NAGAI DIDN'T SHOOT MY HEART... I FELL ASIDE, SO THAT HE WOULD BE FOOLED, AND NOT FIRE AT ME AGAIN.
ALIVE... YOU'RE ALIVE... REALLY ALIVE...
IT IS GOOD TO SEE YOU AGAIN, MY FRIEND. I AM GLAD YOU CAME HERE, SO THAT WE COULD TALK.
KIRO... WHAT HAPPENED TO YOU... BACK ON KINOOINE?
WHEN DANI AND I SAW THE STAIN IN THE WATER... WHEN DEN SIVA SURVIVED YOUR DUEL... WE BOTH ASSUMED...
LUKE... LET DANI ...LET ALL OF THEM GO ON ASSUMING. I LOVE HER... BUT I CANNOT GO BACK... NOT WHILE MY PEOPLE NEED ME. IT WOULD BE BETTER IF NO ONE KNEW...
BECAUSE I... LOVE DANI, I HAD TO LET HER GO. DO NOT... STOP HER FROM... LETTING GO OF ME.
BUT...
DEN WOUNDED ME, LUKE... I WAS BADLY HURT... AND I DON'T REMEMBER MUCH OF WHAT HAPPENED AFTER THAT...
BUT... WHEN THE NAGAI CAME HERE, THE SAME NAGAI WHO HAD DONE THOSE TERRIBLE THINGS TO US ON KINOOINE...
I HAD TO PROTECT MY PEOPLE.
YOU HAVE BEEN MY TRUEST OF FRIENDS, LUKE... CLOSER TO ME EVEN THAN MONE IN MANY WAYS.
PLEASE... KEEP MY SECRET...
REMEMBER ME.
21

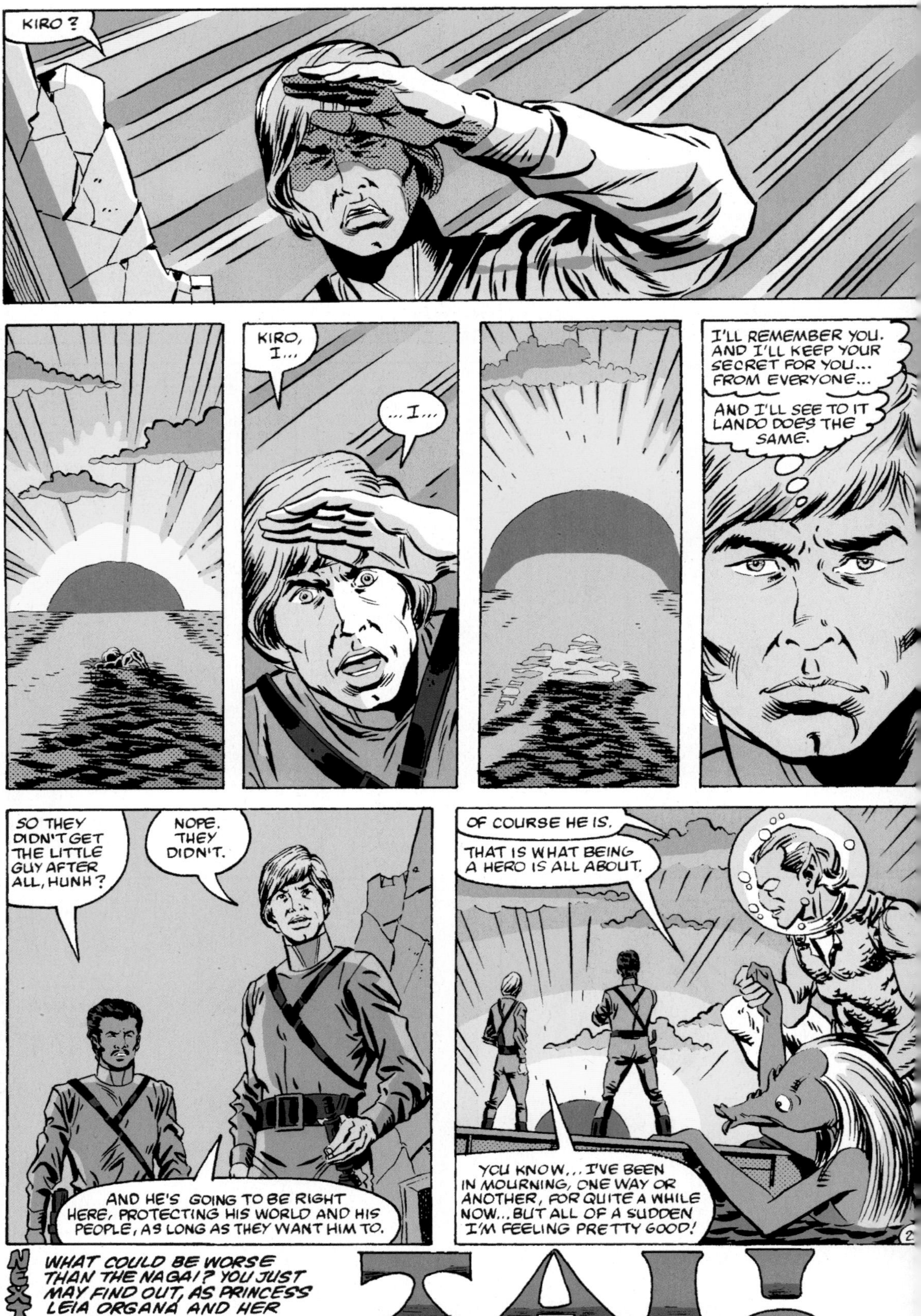
KIRO?
KIRO, I...
...I...
I'LL REMEMBER YOU. AND I'LL KEEP YOUR SECRET FOR YOU... FROM EVERYONE...
AND I'LL SEE TO IT LANDO DOES THE SAME.
SO THEY DIDN'T GET THE LITTLE GUY AFTER ALL, HUNH?
NOPE. THEY DIDN'T.
AND HE'S GOING TO BE RIGHT HERE, PROTECTING HIS WORLD AND HIS PEOPLE, AS LONG AS THEY WANT HIM TO.
OF COURSE HE IS.
THAT IS WHAT BEING A HERO IS ALL ABOUT.
YOU KNOW... I'VE BEEN IN MOURNING, ONE WAY OR ANOTHER, FOR QUITE A WHILE NOW... BUT ALL OF A SUDDEN I'M FEELING PRETTY GOOD!
NEXT
WHAT COULD BE WORSE THAN THE NAGAI? YOU JUST MAY FIND OUT, AS PRINCESS LEIA ORGANA AND HER ENTOURAGE MEET:
TAI!

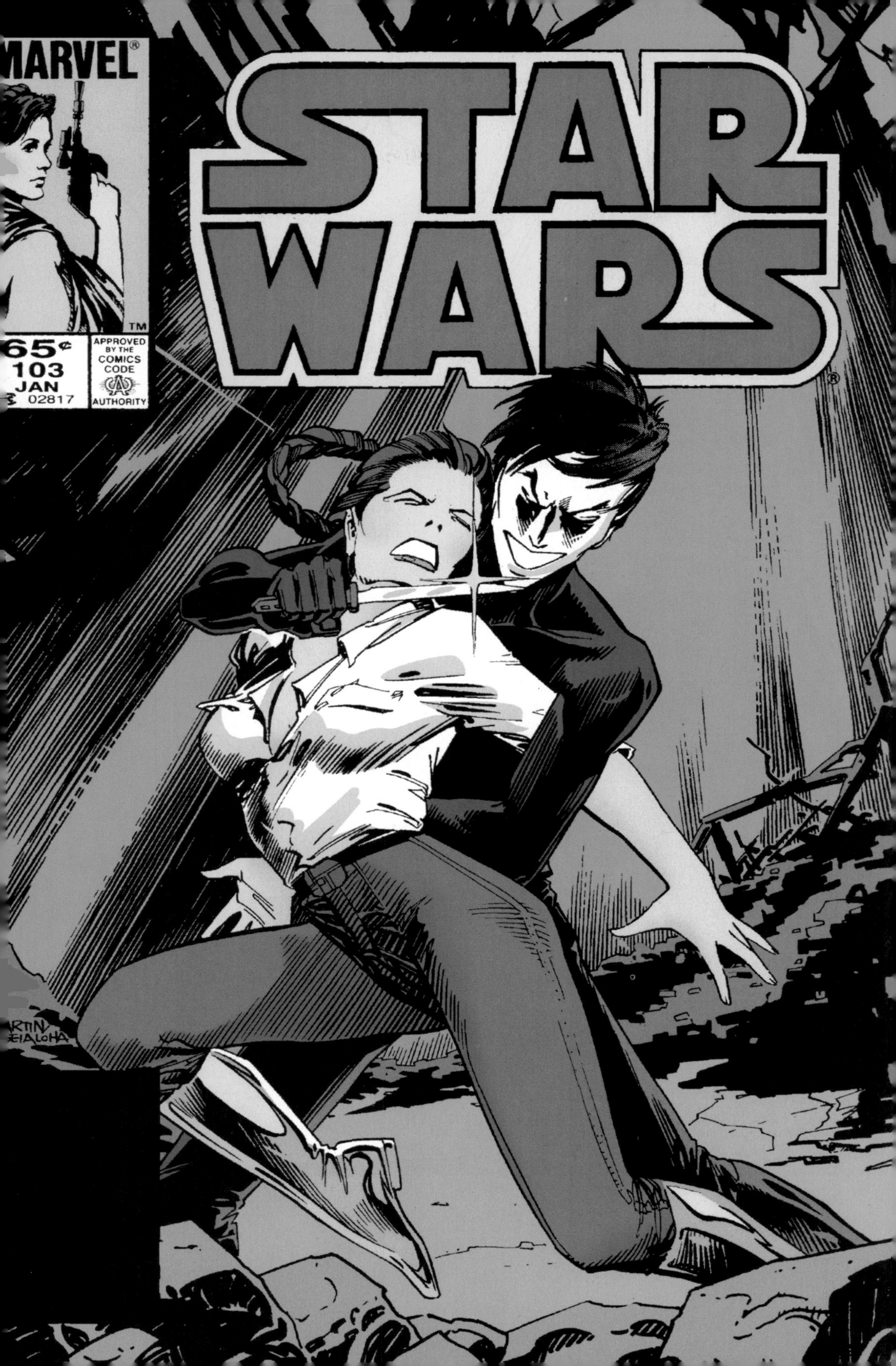
MARVEL®
STAR WARS®
TM
65¢
103
JAN
02817
APPROVED BY THE COMICS CODE AUTHORITY

JO DUFFY WRITER CYNTHIA MARTIN PENCILER ART NICHOLS INKER RICK PARKER LETTERING M. WRIGHTSON COLORING ANN NOCENTI EDITOR JIM SHOOTER EDITOR IN CHIEF

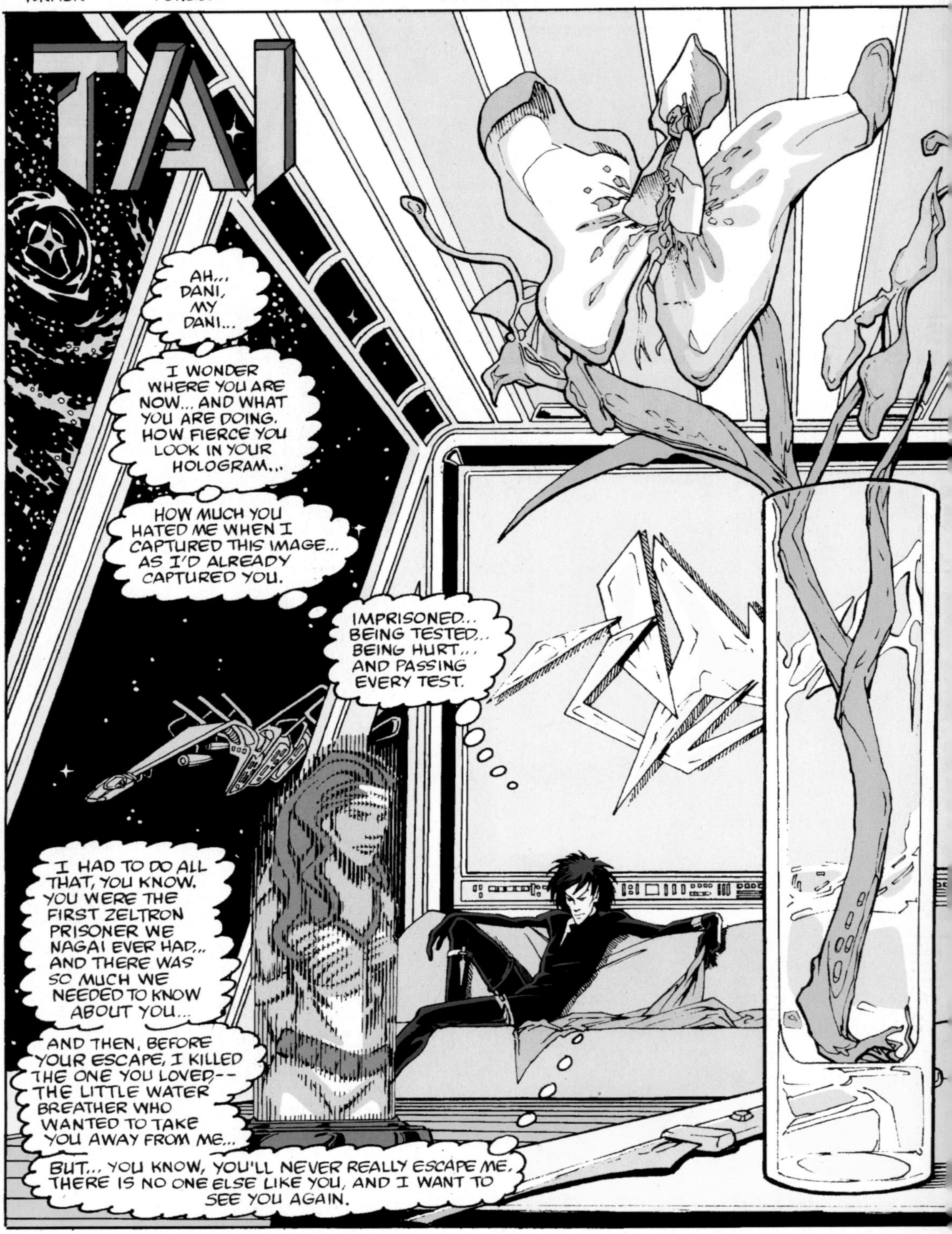

TAI
AH... DANI, MY DANI...
I WONDER WHERE YOU ARE NOW... AND WHAT YOU ARE DOING. HOW FIERCE YOU LOOK IN YOUR HOLOGRAM...
HOW MUCH YOU HATED ME WHEN I CAPTURED THIS IMAGE... AS I'D ALREADY CAPTURED YOU.
IMPRISONED... BEING TESTED... BEING HURT... AND PASSING EVERY TEST.
I HAD TO DO ALL THAT, YOU KNOW. YOU WERE THE FIRST ZELTRON PRISONER WE NAGAI EVER HAD... AND THERE WAS SO MUCH WE NEEDED TO KNOW ABOUT YOU...
AND THEN, BEFORE YOUR ESCAPE, I KILLED THE ONE YOU LOVED-- THE LITTLE WATER BREATHER WHO WANTED TO TAKE YOU AWAY FROM ME...
BUT... YOU KNOW, YOU'LL NEVER REALLY ESCAPE ME. THERE IS NO ONE ELSE LIKE YOU, AND I WANT TO SEE YOU AGAIN.

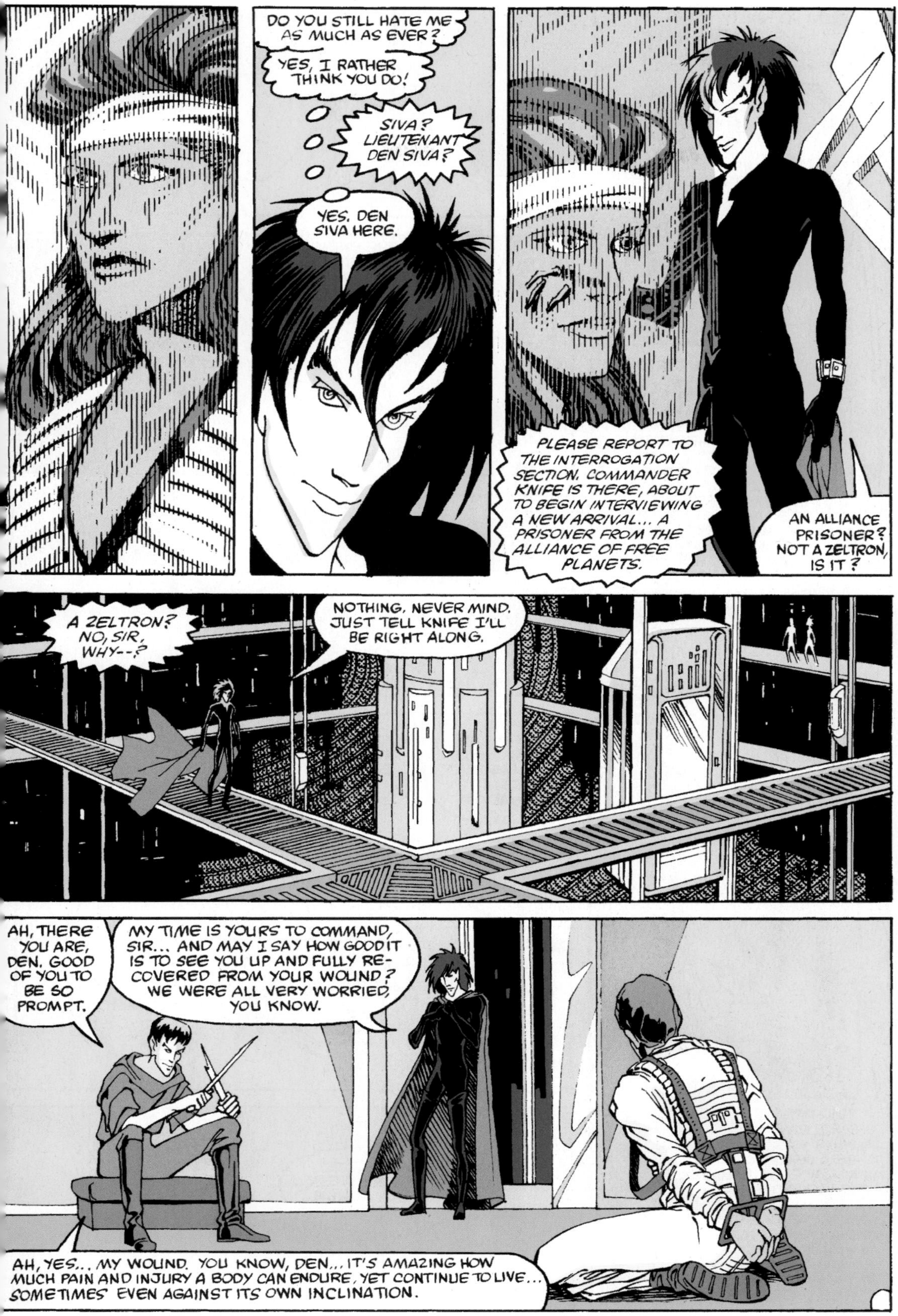
DO YOU STILL HATE ME AS MUCH AS EVER?
YES, I RATHER THINK YOU DO!
SIVA? LIEUTENANT DEN SIVA?
YES. DEN SIVA HERE.
PLEASE REPORT TO THE INTERROGATION SECTION. COMMANDER KNIFE IS THERE, ABOUT TO BEGIN INTERVIEWING A NEW ARRIVAL... A PRISONER FROM THE ALLIANCE OF FREE PLANETS.
AN ALLIANCE PRISONER? NOT A ZELTRON, IS IT?
A ZELTRON? NO, SIR, WHY--?
NOTHING. NEVER MIND. JUST TELL KNIFE I'LL BE RIGHT ALONG.
AH, THERE YOU ARE, DEN. GOOD OF YOU TO BE SO PROMPT.
MY TIME IS YOURS TO COMMAND, SIR... AND MAY I SAY HOW GOOD IT IS TO SEE YOU UP AND FULLY RE-COVERED FROM YOUR WOUND? WE WERE ALL VERY WORRIED, YOU KNOW.
AH, YES... MY WOUND. YOU KNOW, DEN... IT'S AMAZING HOW MUCH PAIN AND INJURY A BODY CAN ENDURE, YET CONTINUE TO LIVE... SOMETIMES EVEN AGAINST ITS OWN INCLINATION.

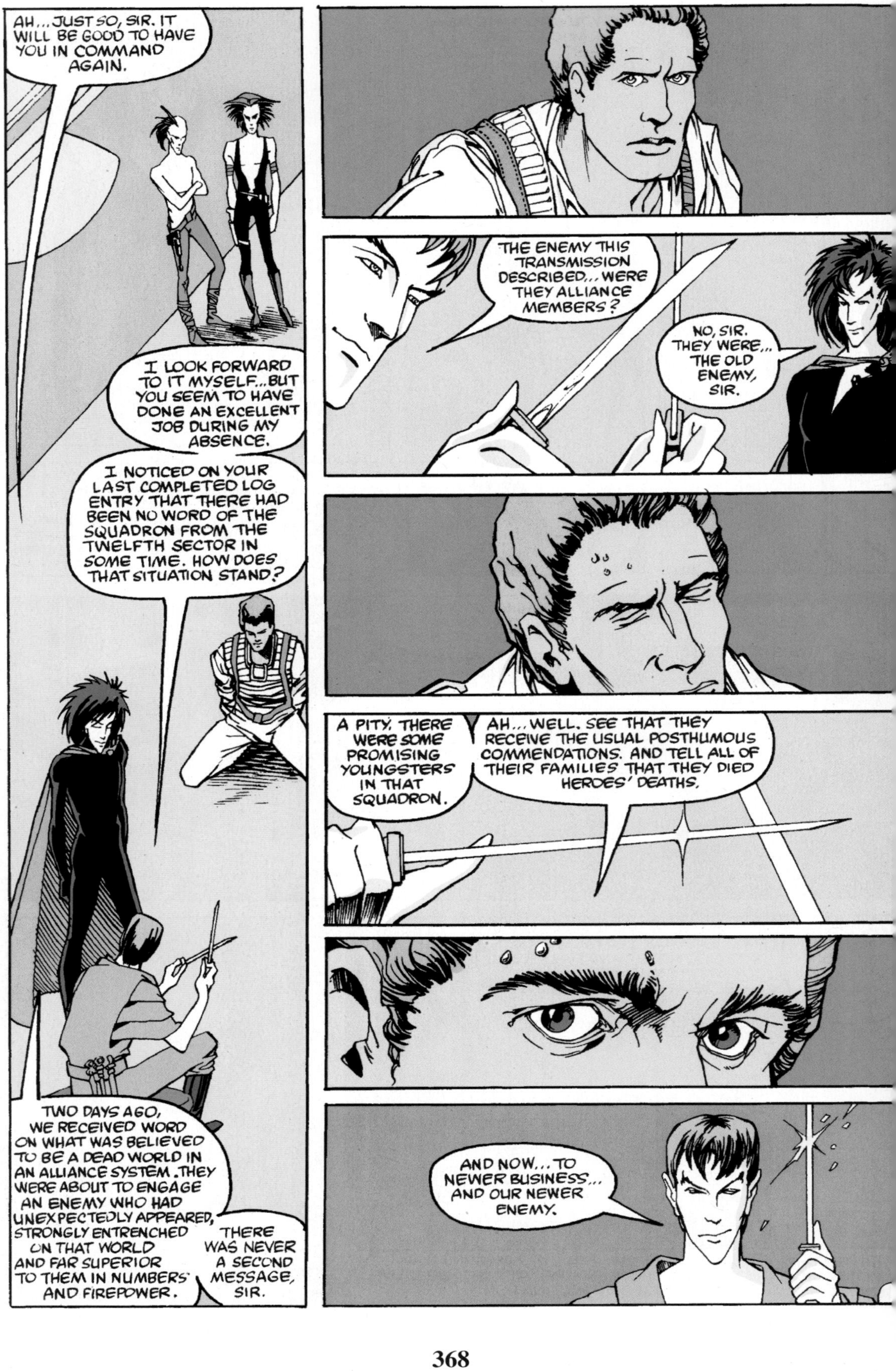
AH... JUST SO, SIR. IT WILL BE GOOD TO HAVE YOU IN COMMAND AGAIN.
I LOOK FORWARD TO IT MYSELF... BUT YOU SEEM TO HAVE DONE AN EXCELLENT JOB DURING MY ABSENCE.
I NOTICED ON YOUR LAST COMPLETED LOG ENTRY THAT THERE HAD BEEN NO WORD OF THE SQUADRON FROM THE TWELFTH SECTOR IN SOME TIME. HOW DOES THAT SITUATION STAND?
TWO DAYS AGO, WE RECEIVED WORD ON WHAT WAS BELIEVED TO BE A DEAD WORLD IN AN ALLIANCE SYSTEM. THEY WERE ABOUT TO ENGAGE AN ENEMY WHO HAD UNEXPECTEDLY APPEARED, STRONGLY ENTRENCHED ON THAT WORLD AND FAR SUPERIOR TO THEM IN NUMBERS AND FIREPOWER.
THERE WAS NEVER A SECOND MESSAGE, SIR.
THE ENEMY THIS TRANSMISSION DESCRIBED... WERE THEY ALLIANCE MEMBERS?
NO, SIR. THEY WERE... THE OLD ENEMY, SIR.
A PITY. THERE WERE SOME PROMISING YOUNGSTERS IN THAT SQUADRON.
AH... WELL. SEE THAT THEY RECEIVE THE USUAL POSTHUMOUS COMMENDATIONS. AND TELL ALL OF THEIR FAMILIES THAT THEY DIED HEROES' DEATHS.
AND NOW... TO NEWER BUSINESS... AND OUR NEWER ENEMY.

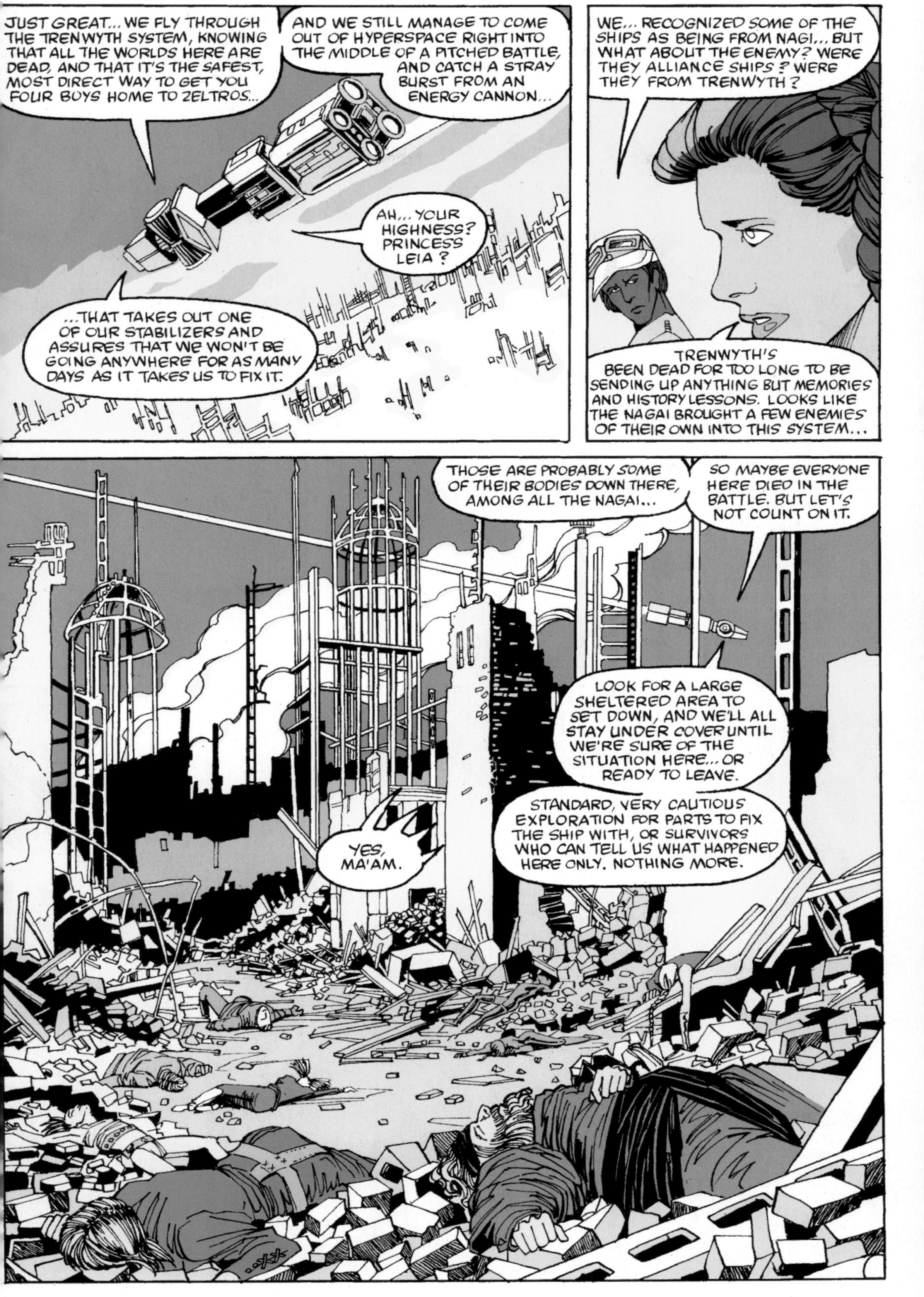

JUST GREAT... WE FLY THROUGH THE TRENWYTH SYSTEM, KNOWING THAT ALL THE WORLDS HERE ARE DEAD, AND THAT IT'S THE SAFEST, MOST DIRECT WAY TO GET YOU FOUR BOYS HOME TO ZELTROS...
AND WE STILL MANAGE TO COME OUT OF HYPERSPACE RIGHT INTO THE MIDDLE OF A PITCHED BATTLE, AND CATCH A STRAY BURST FROM AN ENERGY CANNON...
...THAT TAKES OUT ONE OF OUR STABILIZERS AND ASSURES THAT WE WON'T BE GOING ANYWHERE FOR AS MANY DAYS AS IT TAKES US TO FIX IT.
AH... YOUR HIGHNESS? PRINCESS LEIA?
WE... RECOGNIZED SOME OF THE SHIPS AS BEING FROM NAGI... BUT WHAT ABOUT THE ENEMY? WERE THEY ALLIANCE SHIPS? WERE THEY FROM TRENWYTH?
TRENWYTH'S BEEN DEAD FOR TOO LONG TO BE SENDING UP ANYTHING BUT MEMORIES AND HISTORY LESSONS. LOOKS LIKE THE NAGAI BROUGHT A FEW ENEMIES OF THEIR OWN INTO THIS SYSTEM...
THOSE ARE PROBABLY SOME OF THEIR BODIES DOWN THERE, AMONG ALL THE NAGAI...
SO MAYBE EVERYONE HERE DIED IN THE BATTLE. BUT LET'S NOT COUNT ON IT.
LOOK FOR A LARGE SHELTERED AREA TO SET DOWN, AND WE'LL ALL STAY UNDER COVER UNTIL WE'RE SURE OF THE SITUATION HERE... OR READY TO LEAVE.
STANDARD, VERY CAUTIOUS EXPLORATION FOR PARTS TO FIX THE SHIP WITH, OR SURVIVORS WHO CAN TELL US WHAT HAPPENED HERE ONLY. NOTHING MORE.
YES, MA'AM.

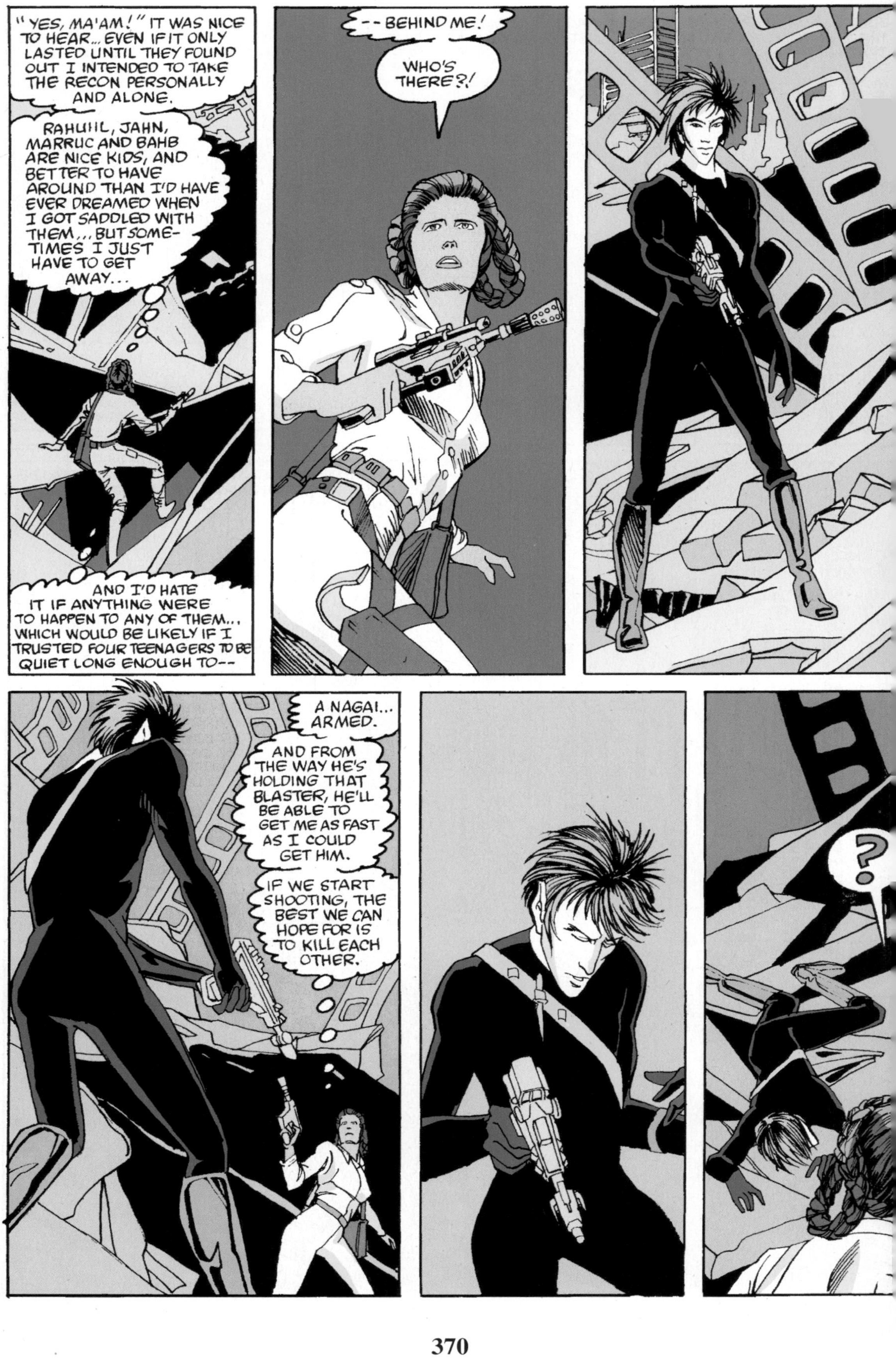
"YES, MA'AM!" IT WAS NICE TO HEAR... EVEN IF IT ONLY LASTED UNTIL THEY FOUND OUT I INTENDED TO TAKE THE RECON PERSONALLY AND ALONE.
RAHUHL, JAHN, MARRUC AND BAHB ARE NICE KIDS, AND BETTER TO HAVE AROUND THAN I'D HAVE EVER DREAMED WHEN I GOT SADDLED WITH THEM... BUT SOMETIMES I JUST HAVE TO GET AWAY...
AND I'D HATE IT IF ANYTHING WERE TO HAPPEN TO ANY OF THEM... WHICH WOULD BE LIKELY IF I TRUSTED FOUR TEENAGERS TO BE QUIET LONG ENOUGH TO--
--BEHIND ME!
WHO'S THERE?!
A NAGAI... ARMED.
AND FROM THE WAY HE'S HOLDING THAT BLASTER, HE'LL BE ABLE TO GET ME AS FAST AS I COULD GET HIM.
IF WE START SHOOTING, THE BEST WE CAN HOPE FOR IS TO KILL EACH OTHER.
?

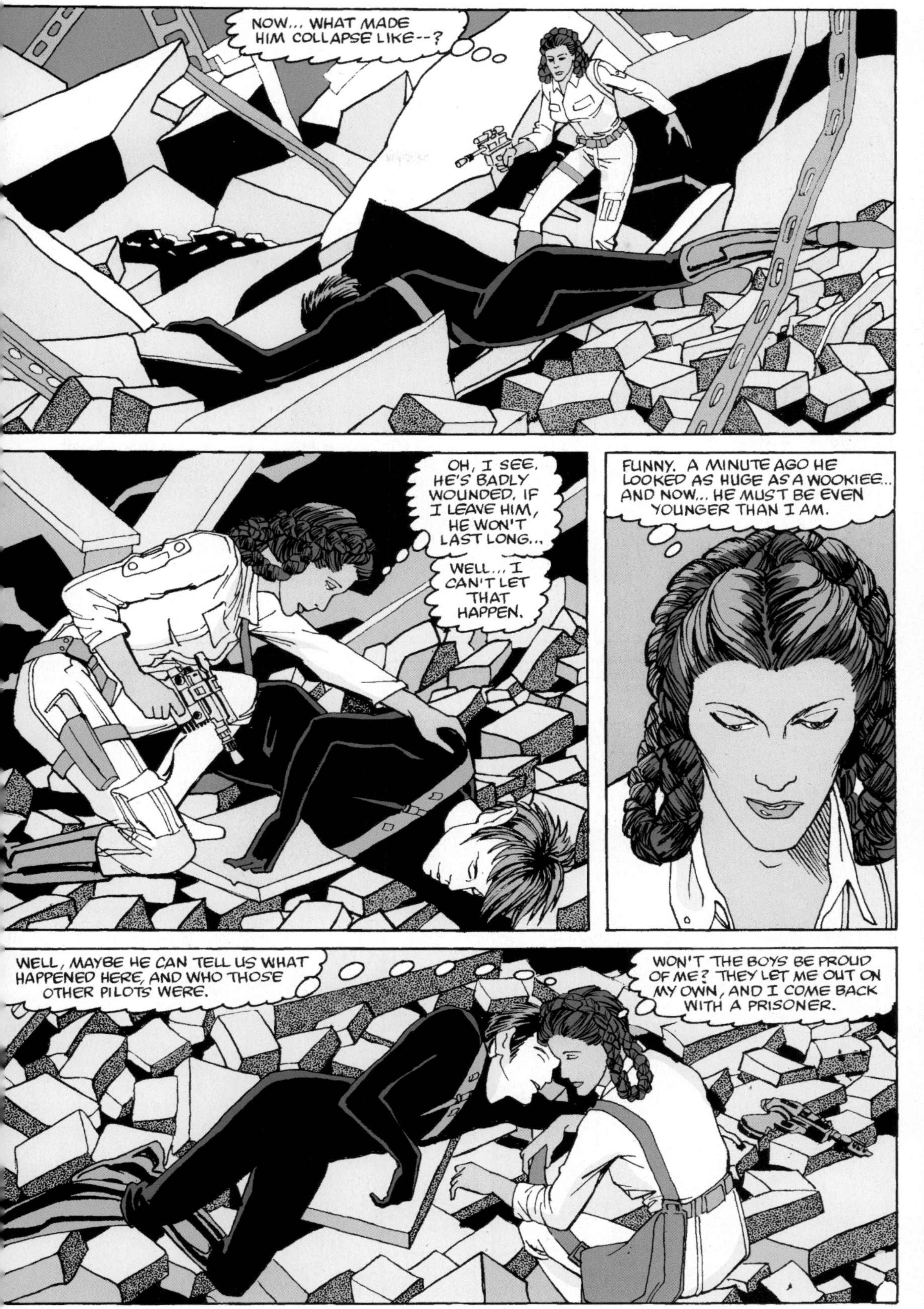
NOW... WHAT MADE HIM COLLAPSE LIKE--?
OH, I SEE. HE'S BADLY WOUNDED. IF I LEAVE HIM, HE WON'T LAST LONG...
WELL... I CAN'T LET THAT HAPPEN.
FUNNY. A MINUTE AGO HE LOOKED AS HUGE AS A WOOKIEE... AND NOW... HE MUST BE EVEN YOUNGER THAN I AM.
WELL, MAYBE HE CAN TELL US WHAT HAPPENED HERE, AND WHO THOSE OTHER PILOTS WERE.
WON'T THE BOYS BE PROUD OF ME? THEY LET ME OUT ON MY OWN, AND I COME BACK WITH A PRISONER.

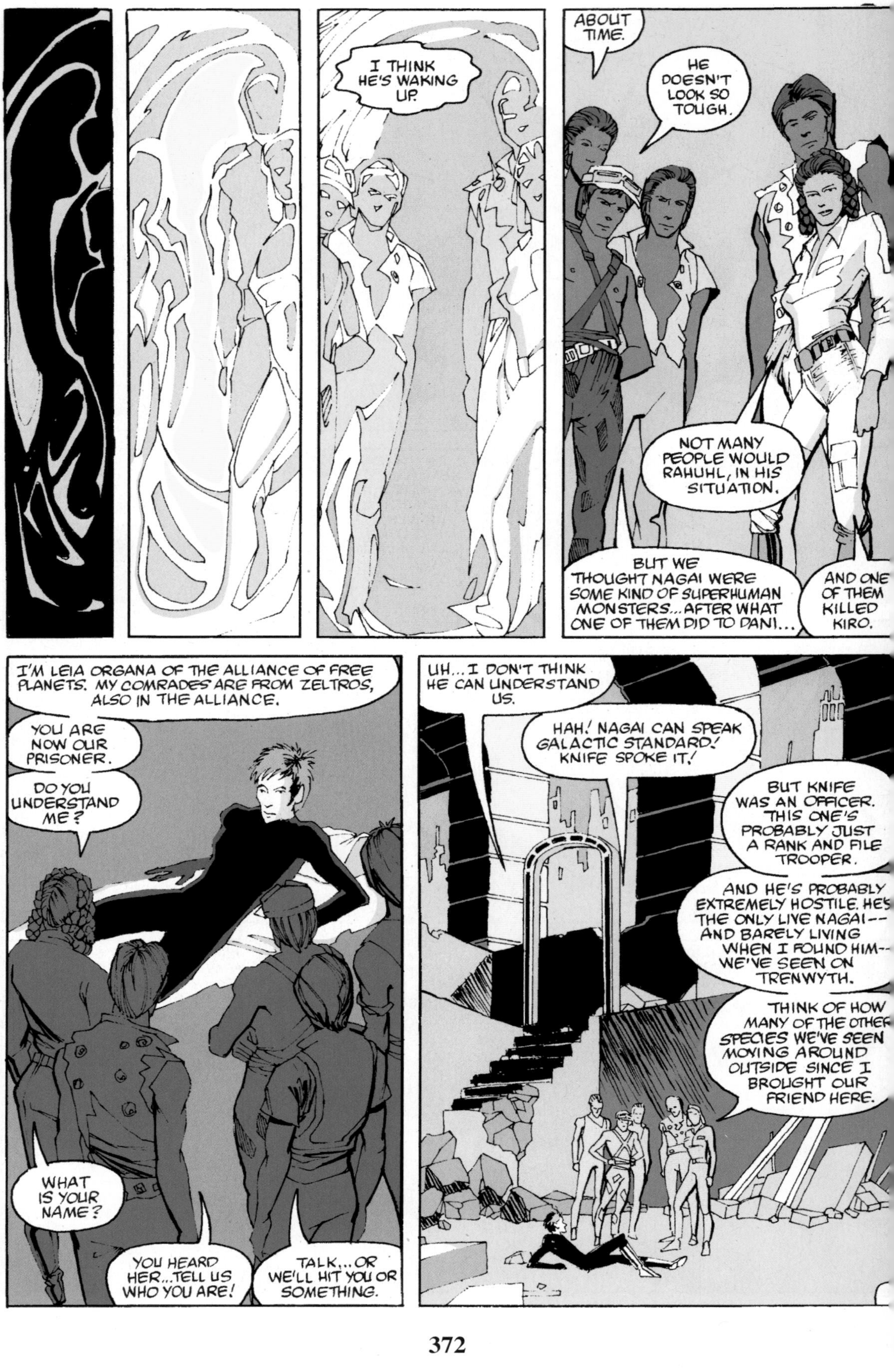
I THINK HE'S WAKING UP.
ABOUT TIME.
HE DOESN'T LOOK SO TOUGH.
NOT MANY PEOPLE WOULD RAHUHL, IN HIS SITUATION.
BUT WE THOUGHT NAGAI WERE SOME KIND OF SUPERHUMAN MONSTERS... AFTER WHAT ONE OF THEM DID TO DANI...
AND ONE OF THEM KILLED KIRO.
I'M LEIA ORGANA OF THE ALLIANCE OF FREE PLANETS. MY COMRADES ARE FROM ZELTROS, ALSO IN THE ALLIANCE.
YOU ARE NOW OUR PRISONER.
DO YOU UNDERSTAND ME?
WHAT IS YOUR NAME?
YOU HEARD HER...TELL US WHO YOU ARE!
TALK,...OR WE'LL HIT YOU OR SOMETHING.
UH...I DON'T THINK HE CAN UNDERSTAND US.
HAH! NAGAI CAN SPEAK GALACTIC STANDARD! KNIFE SPOKE IT!
BUT KNIFE WAS AN OFFICER. THIS ONE'S PROBABLY JUST A RANK AND FILE TROOPER.
AND HE'S PROBABLY EXTREMELY HOSTILE. HE'S THE ONLY LIVE NAGAI--- AND BARELY LIVING WHEN I FOUND HIM-- WE'VE SEEN ON TRENWYTH.
THINK OF HOW MANY OF THE OTHER SPECIES WE'VE SEEN MOVING AROUND OUTSIDE SINCE I BROUGHT OUR FRIEND HERE.

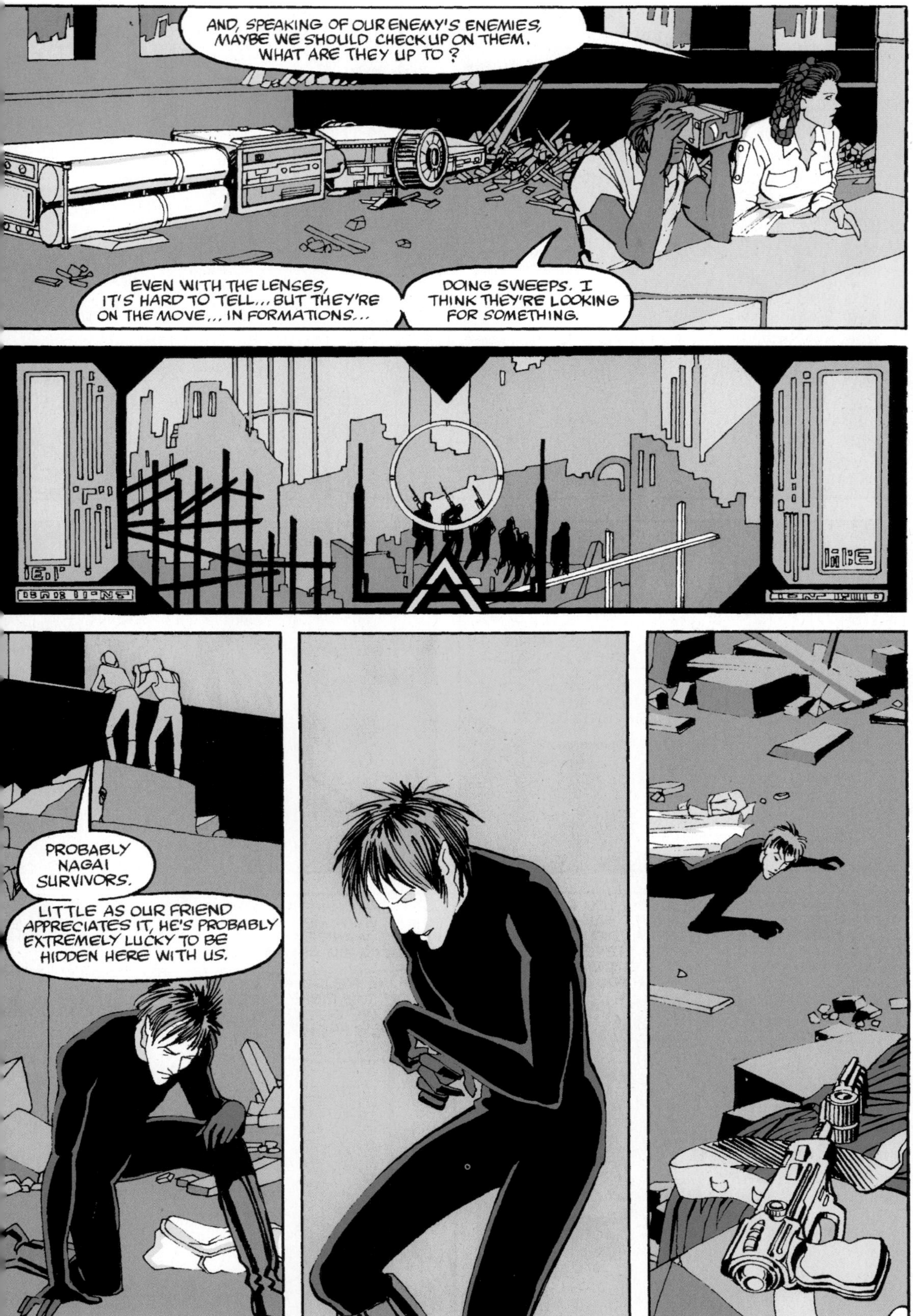
AND, SPEAKING OF OUR ENEMY'S ENEMIES, MAYBE WE SHOULD CHECK UP ON THEM. WHAT ARE THEY UP TO ?
EVEN WITH THE LENSES, IT'S HARD TO TELL... BUT THEY'RE ON THE MOVE... IN FORMATIONS...
DOING SWEEPS. I THINK THEY'RE LOOKING FOR SOMETHING.
PROBABLY NAGAI SURVIVORS.
LITTLE AS OUR FRIEND APPRECIATES IT, HE'S PROBABLY EXTREMELY LUCKY TO BE HIDDEN HERE WITH US.

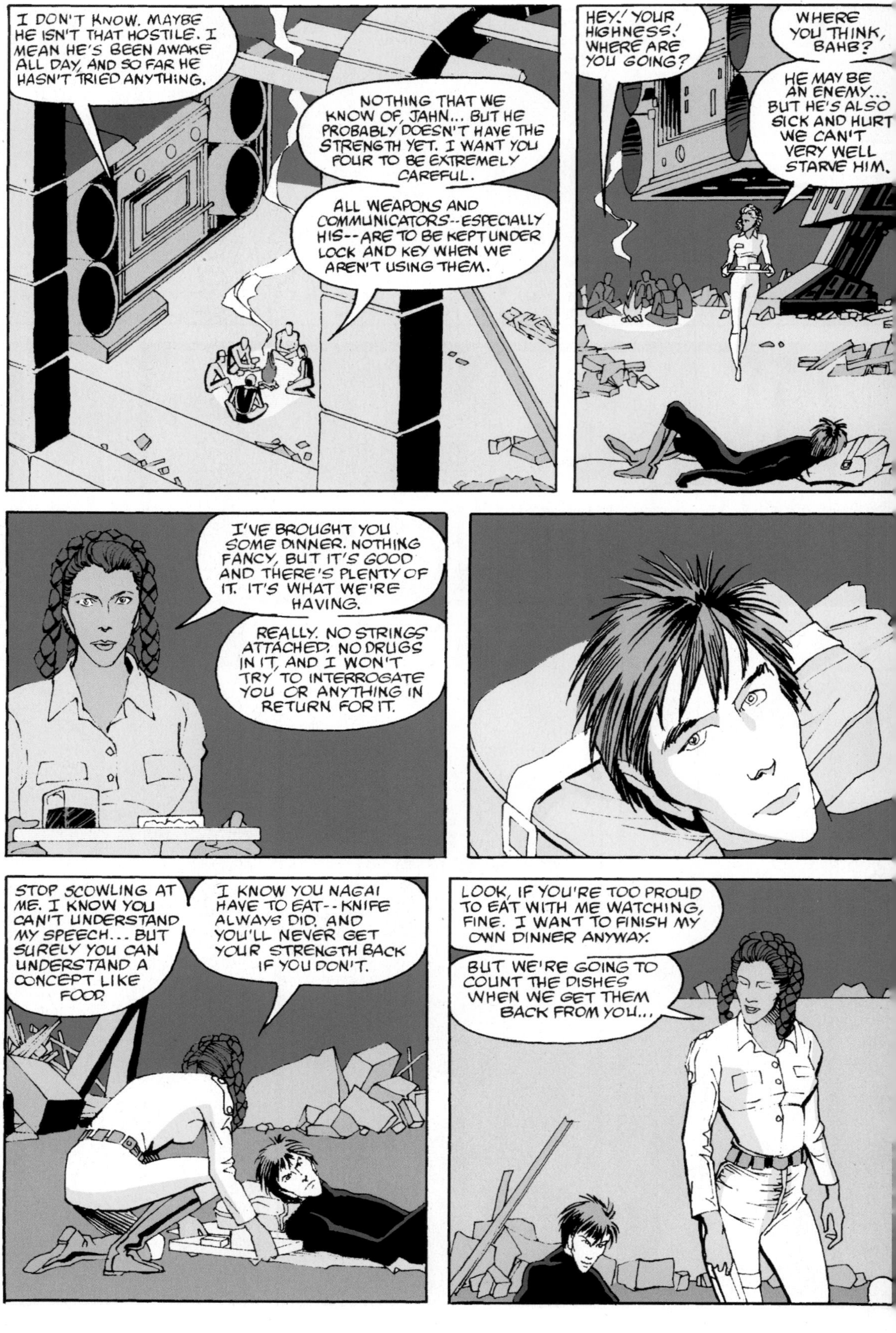
I DON'T KNOW. MAYBE HE ISN'T THAT HOSTILE. I MEAN HE'S BEEN AWAKE ALL DAY, AND SO FAR HE HASN'T TRIED ANYTHING.
NOTHING THAT WE KNOW OF, JAHN... BUT HE PROBABLY DOESN'T HAVE THE STRENGTH YET. I WANT YOU FOUR TO BE EXTREMELY CAREFUL.
ALL WEAPONS AND COMMUNICATORS--ESPECIALLY HIS--ARE TO BE KEPT UNDER LOCK AND KEY WHEN WE AREN'T USING THEM.
HEY! YOUR HIGHNESS! WHERE ARE YOU GOING?
WHERE YOU THINK, BAHB?
HE MAY BE AN ENEMY... BUT HE'S ALSO SICK AND HURT. WE CAN'T VERY WELL STARVE HIM.
I'VE BROUGHT YOU SOME DINNER. NOTHING FANCY, BUT IT'S GOOD AND THERE'S PLENTY OF IT. IT'S WHAT WE'RE HAVING.
REALLY. NO STRINGS ATTACHED. NO DRUGS IN IT, AND I WON'T TRY TO INTERROGATE YOU OR ANYTHING IN RETURN FOR IT.
STOP SCOWLING AT ME. I KNOW YOU CAN'T UNDERSTAND MY SPEECH... BUT SURELY YOU CAN UNDERSTAND A CONCEPT LIKE FOOD.
I KNOW YOU NAGAI HAVE TO EAT--KNIFE ALWAYS DID. AND YOU'LL NEVER GET YOUR STRENGTH BACK IF YOU DON'T.
LOOK, IF YOU'RE TOO PROUD TO EAT WITH ME WATCHING, FINE. I WANT TO FINISH MY OWN DINNER ANYWAY.
BUT WE'RE GOING TO COUNT THE DISHES WHEN WE GET THEM BACK FROM YOU...

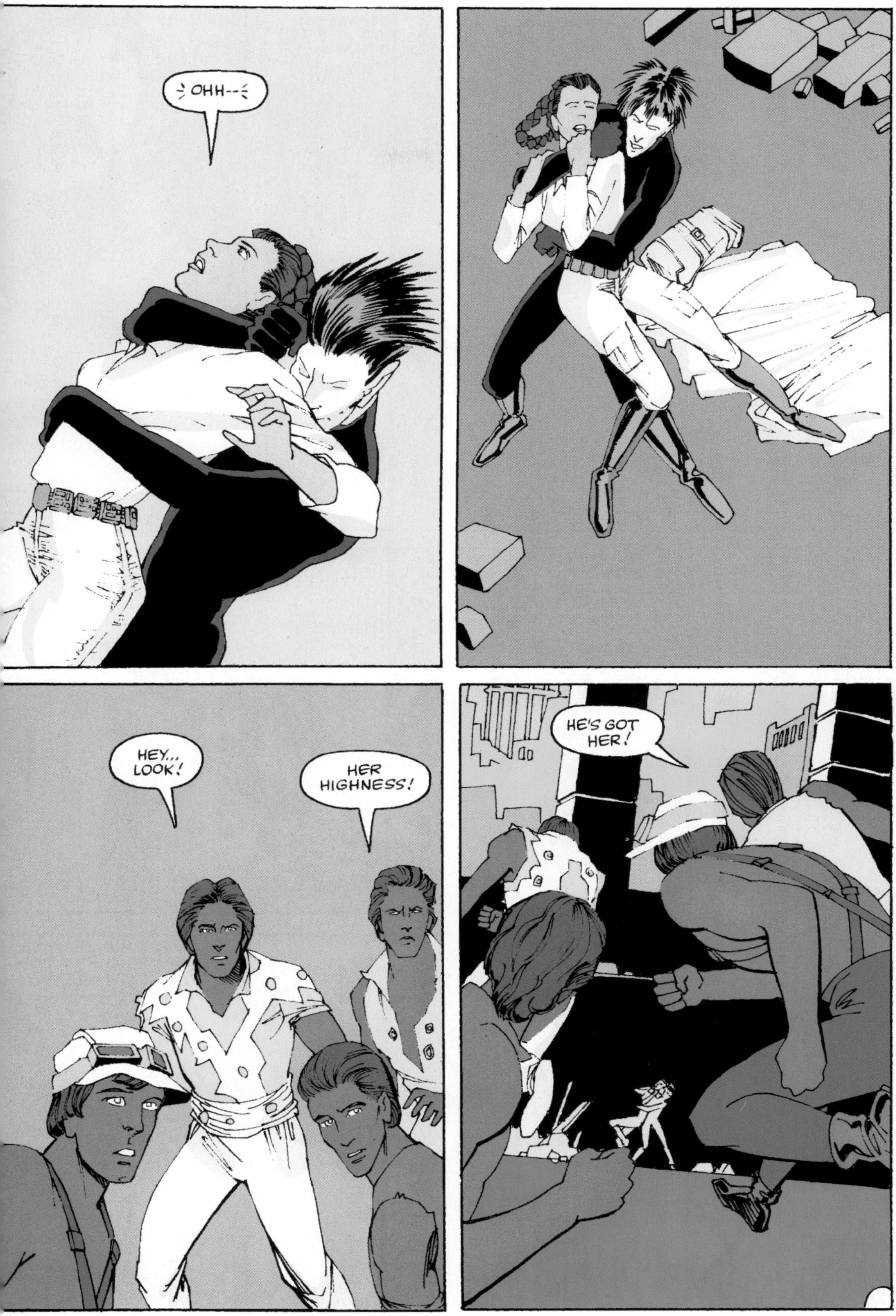
OHH--
HEY... LOOK!
HER HIGHNESS!
HE'S GOT HER!

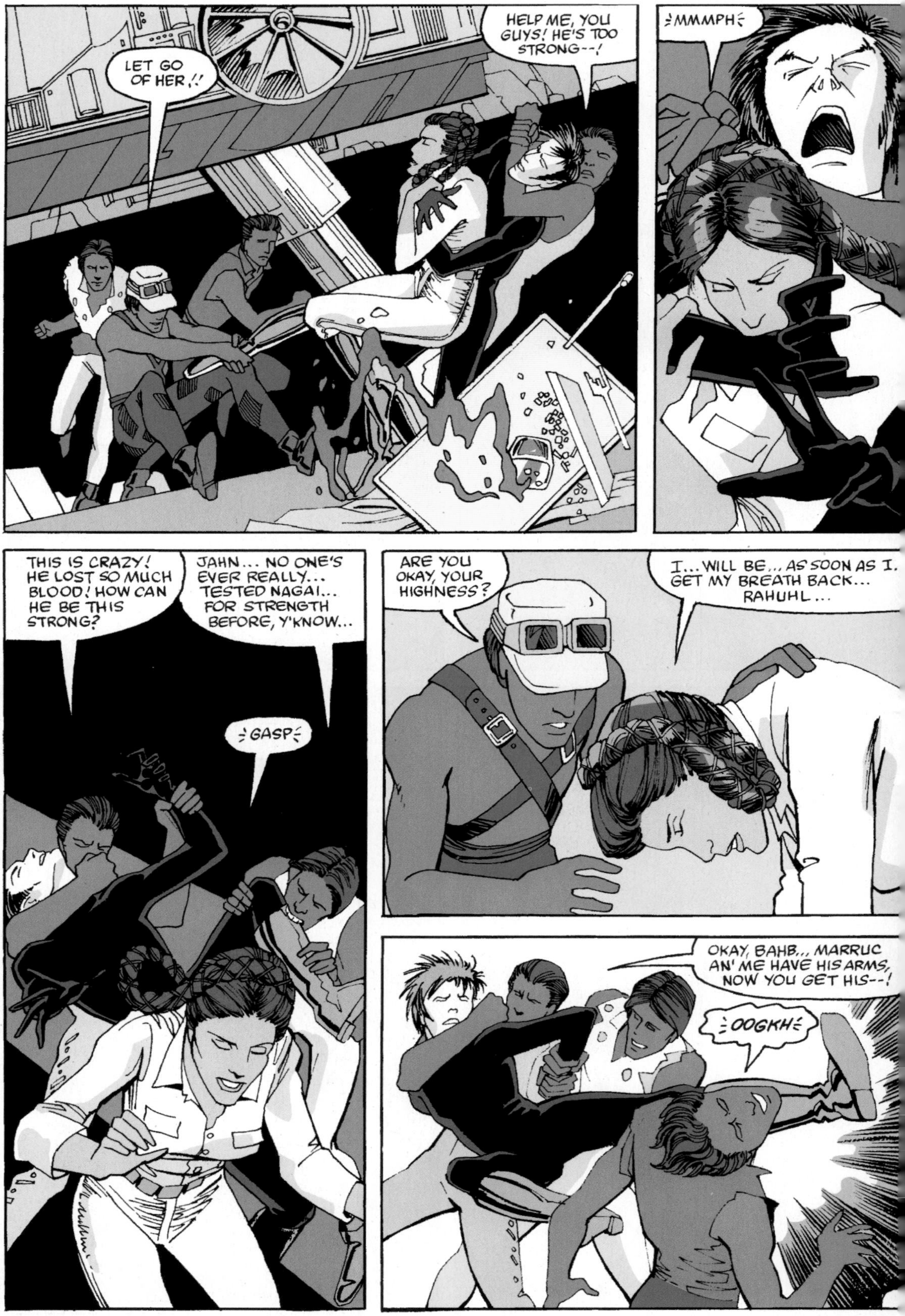
LET GO OF HER!!
HELP ME, YOU GUYS! HE'S TOO STRONG--!
MMMPH
THIS IS CRAZY! HE LOST SO MUCH BLOOD! HOW CAN HE BE THIS STRONG?
JAHN... NO ONE'S EVER REALLY... TESTED NAGAI... FOR STRENGTH BEFORE, Y'KNOW...
GASP
ARE YOU OKAY, YOUR HIGHNESS?
I... WILL BE... AS SOON AS I GET MY BREATH BACK... RAHUHL...
OKAY, BAHB... MARRUC AN' ME HAVE HIS ARMS, NOW YOU GET HIS--!
OOGKH

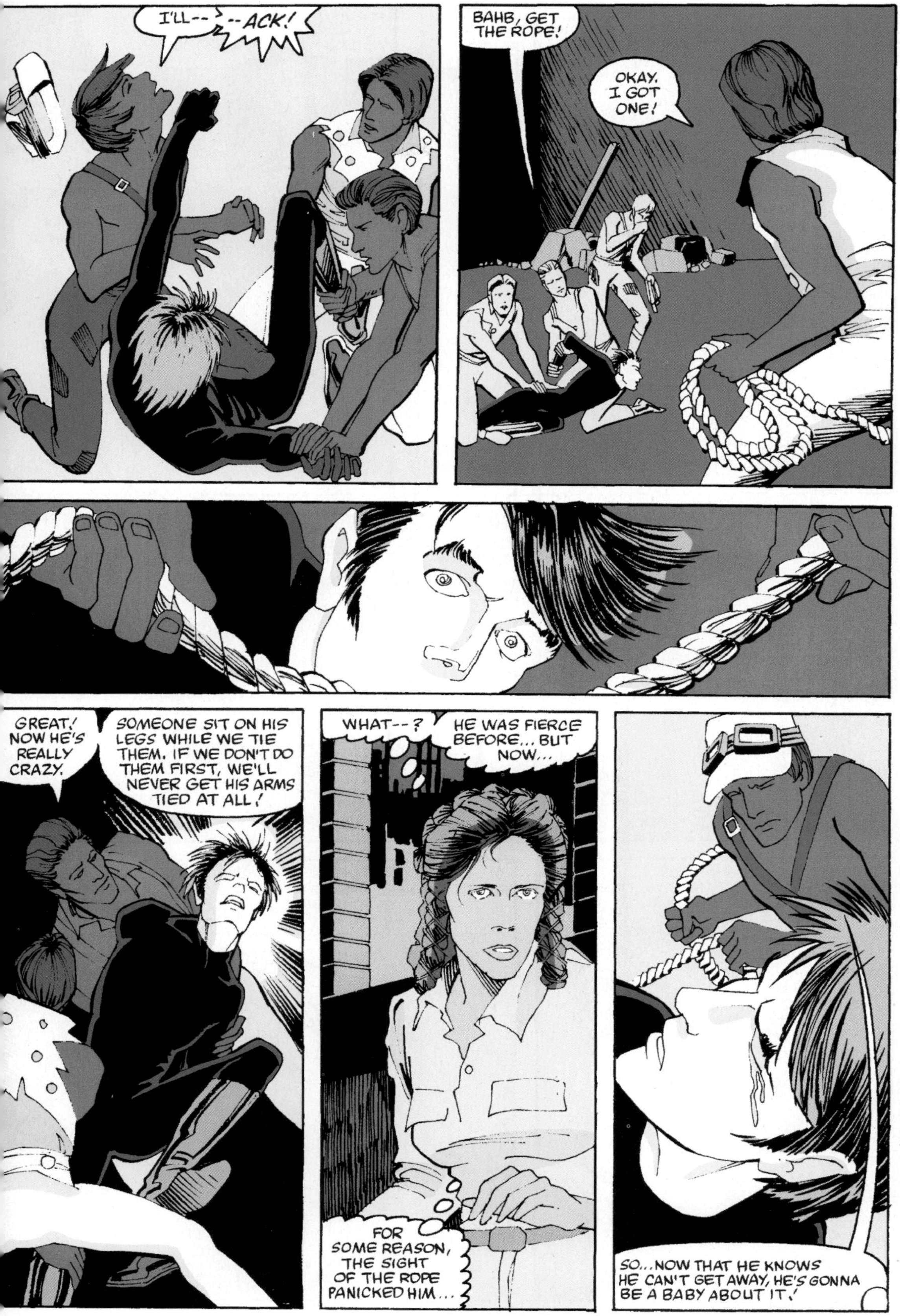
I'LL--
--ACK!
BAHB, GET THE ROPE!
OKAY. I GOT ONE!
GREAT! NOW HE'S REALLY CRAZY.
SOMEONE SIT ON HIS LEGS WHILE WE TIE THEM. IF WE DON'T DO THEM FIRST, WE'LL NEVER GET HIS ARMS TIED AT ALL!
WHAT--?
HE WAS FIERCE BEFORE... BUT NOW...
FOR SOME REASON, THE SIGHT OF THE ROPE PANICKED HIM...
SO...NOW THAT HE KNOWS HE CAN'T GET AWAY, HE'S GONNA BE A BABY ABOUT IT!

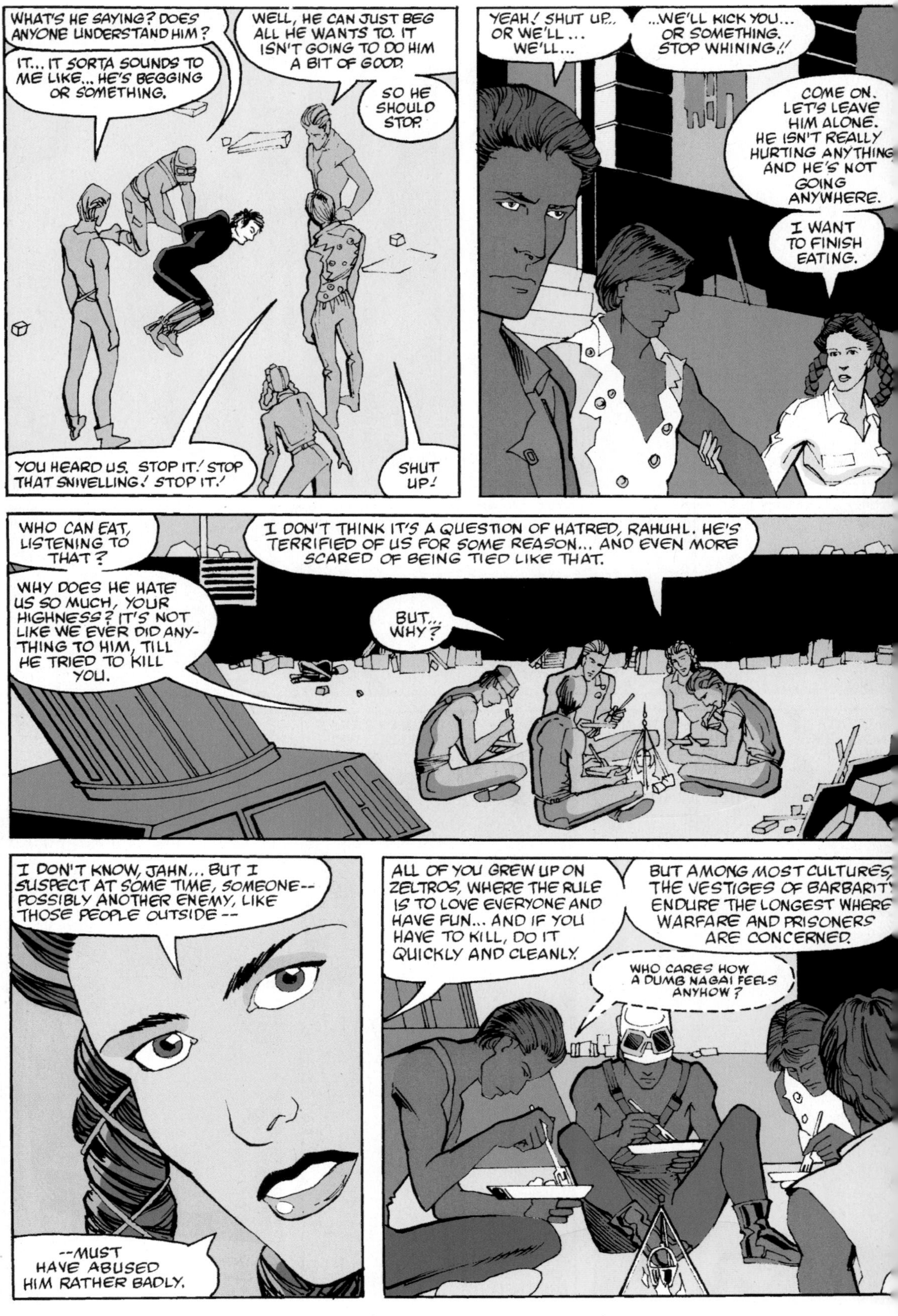
WHAT'S HE SAYING? DOES ANYONE UNDERSTAND HIM?
IT... IT SORTA SOUNDS TO ME LIKE... HE'S BEGGING OR SOMETHING.
WELL, HE CAN JUST BEG ALL HE WANTS TO. IT ISN'T GOING TO DO HIM A BIT OF GOOD.
SO HE SHOULD STOP.
YOU HEARD US. STOP IT! STOP THAT SNIVELLING! STOP IT!
SHUT UP!
YEAH! SHUT UP... OR WE'LL... WE'LL...
...WE'LL KICK YOU... OR SOMETHING. STOP WHINING!!
COME ON. LET'S LEAVE HIM ALONE. HE ISN'T REALLY HURTING ANYTHING AND HE'S NOT GOING ANYWHERE.
I WANT TO FINISH EATING.
WHO CAN EAT, LISTENING TO THAT?
WHY DOES HE HATE US SO MUCH, YOUR HIGHNESS? IT'S NOT LIKE WE EVER DID ANY-THING TO HIM, TILL HE TRIED TO KILL YOU.
I DON'T THINK IT'S A QUESTION OF HATRED, RAHUHL. HE'S TERRIFIED OF US FOR SOME REASON... AND EVEN MORE SCARED OF BEING TIED LIKE THAT.
BUT... WHY?
I DON'T KNOW, JAHN... BUT I SUSPECT AT SOME TIME, SOMEONE-- POSSIBLY ANOTHER ENEMY, LIKE THOSE PEOPLE OUTSIDE --
--MUST HAVE ABUSED HIM RATHER BADLY.
ALL OF YOU GREW UP ON ZELTROS, WHERE THE RULE IS TO LOVE EVERYONE AND HAVE FUN... AND IF YOU HAVE TO KILL, DO IT QUICKLY AND CLEANLY.
BUT AMONG MOST CULTURES, THE VESTIGES OF BARBARITY ENDURE THE LONGEST WHERE WARFARE AND PRISONERS ARE CONCERNED.
WHO CARES HOW A DUMB NAGAI FEELS ANYHOW?

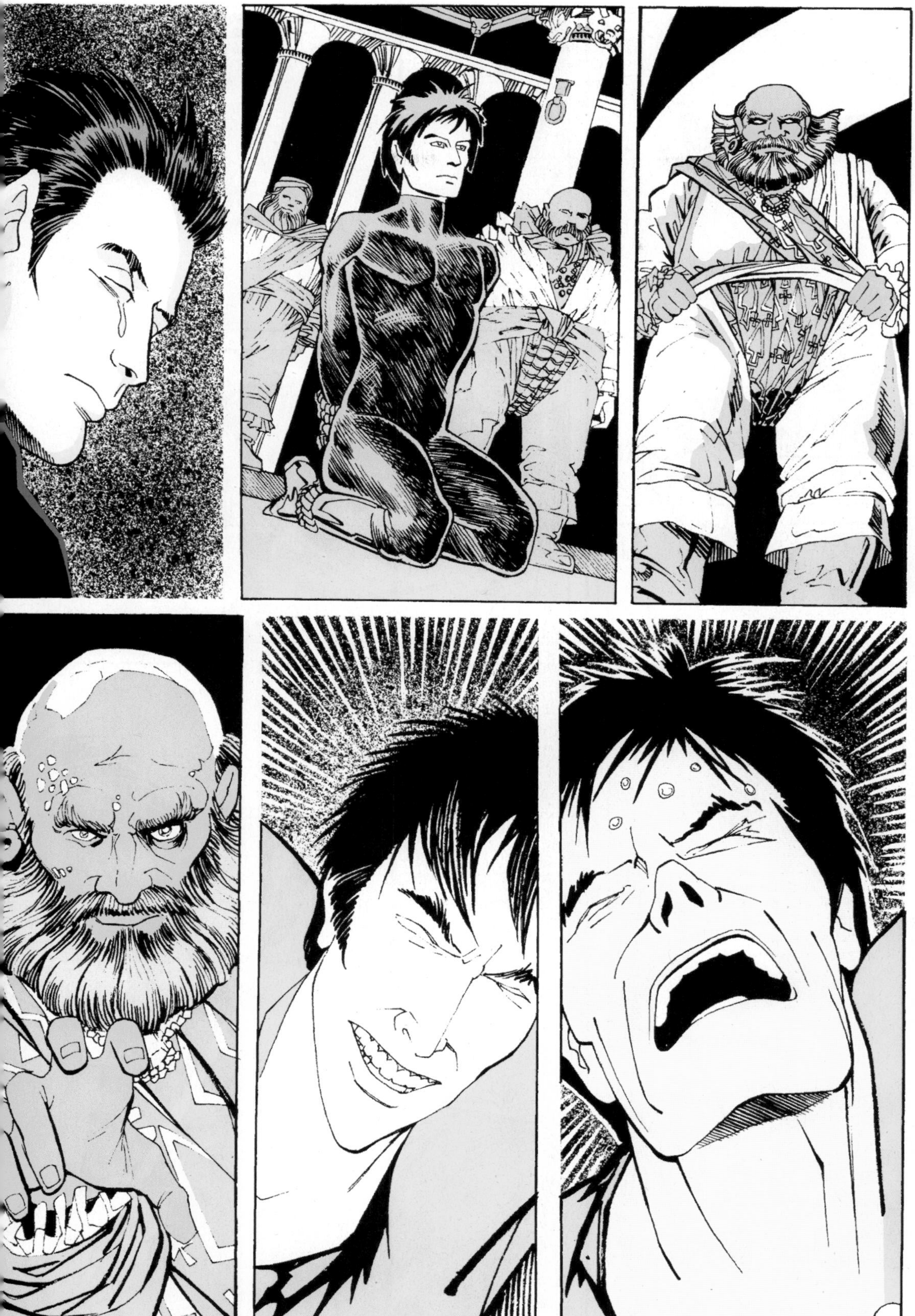

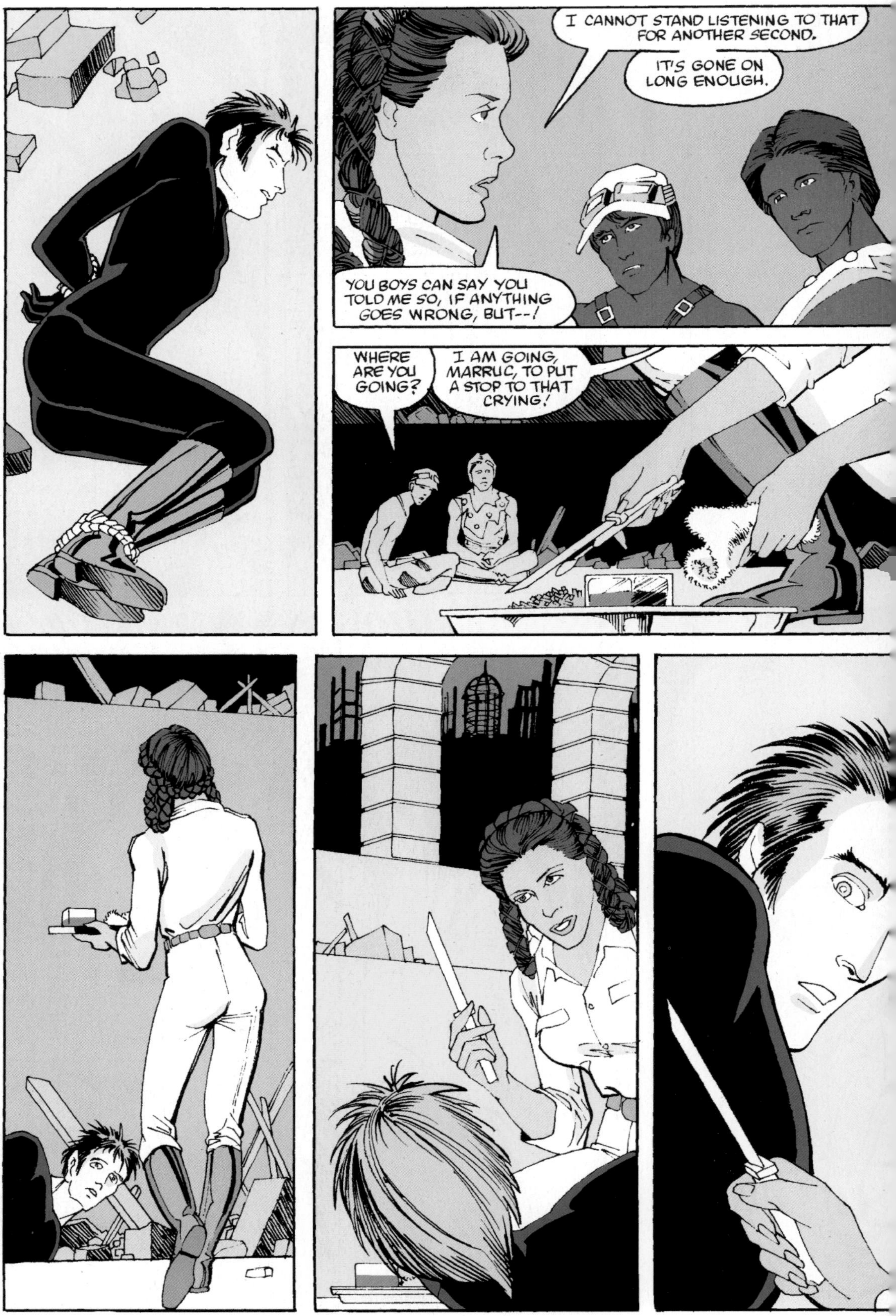
I CANNOT STAND LISTENING TO THAT FOR ANOTHER SECOND.
IT'S GONE ON LONG ENOUGH.
YOU BOYS CAN SAY YOU TOLD ME SO, IF ANYTHING GOES WRONG, BUT--!
WHERE ARE YOU GOING?
I AM GOING, MARRUC, TO PUT A STOP TO THAT CRYING!

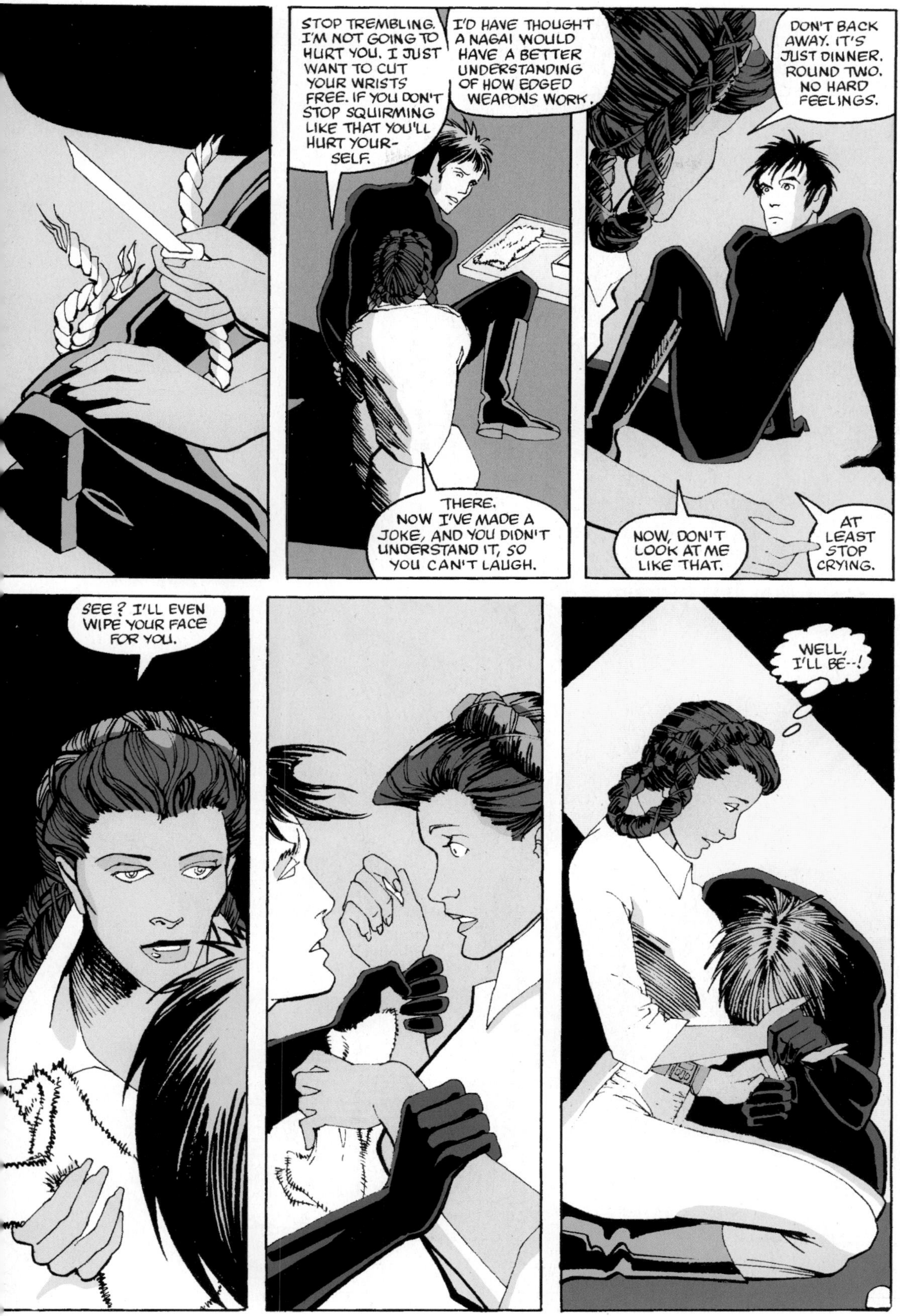
STOP TREMBLING. I'M NOT GOING TO HURT YOU. I JUST WANT TO CUT YOUR WRISTS FREE. IF YOU DON'T STOP SQUIRMING LIKE THAT YOU'LL HURT YOURSELF.
I'D HAVE THOUGHT A NAGAI WOULD HAVE A BETTER UNDERSTANDING OF HOW EDGED WEAPONS WORK.
THERE. NOW I'VE MADE A JOKE, AND YOU DIDN'T UNDERSTAND IT, SO YOU CAN'T LAUGH.
DON'T BACK AWAY. IT'S JUST DINNER. ROUND TWO. NO HARD FEELINGS.
NOW, DON'T LOOK AT ME LIKE THAT.
AT LEAST STOP CRYING.
SEE? I'LL EVEN WIPE YOUR FACE FOR YOU.
WELL, I'LL BE--!

... HEALING WELL. I DON'T THINK IT WILL CAUSE YOU ANY TROUBLE, ONCE YOU'RE BACK ON YOUR FEET.

... FINALLY FOUND THE SECOND FLAW IN THE DAMAGED COMPONENT? THEN WE CAN BE OUT OF HERE IN THE NEXT DAY OR TWO!

THAT IS A CAUSE FOR CELEBRATION...

FUNNY... OUR PRISONER HASN'T TRIED ANYTHING RECENTLY. I THINK HE REALLY TRUSTS US, BUT...

YOU'VE NOTICED IT, HAVEN'T YOU, YOUR HIGHNESS? HE'S ALWAYS LOOKING AT YOU!

I BET HE HAS A CRUSH ON YOU.

BIG DEAL. YOU HAVE A CRUSH ON HER YOURSELF!

NO DOUBT ABOUT IT, YOUR HIGHNESS. IT LOOKS LIKE THEY'RE FINALLY MOVING OUT.

WONDERFUL, THEN WE'LL BE ABLE TO LEAVE WHEN OUR SHIP'S READY WITHOUT RISKING A CONFRONTATION.

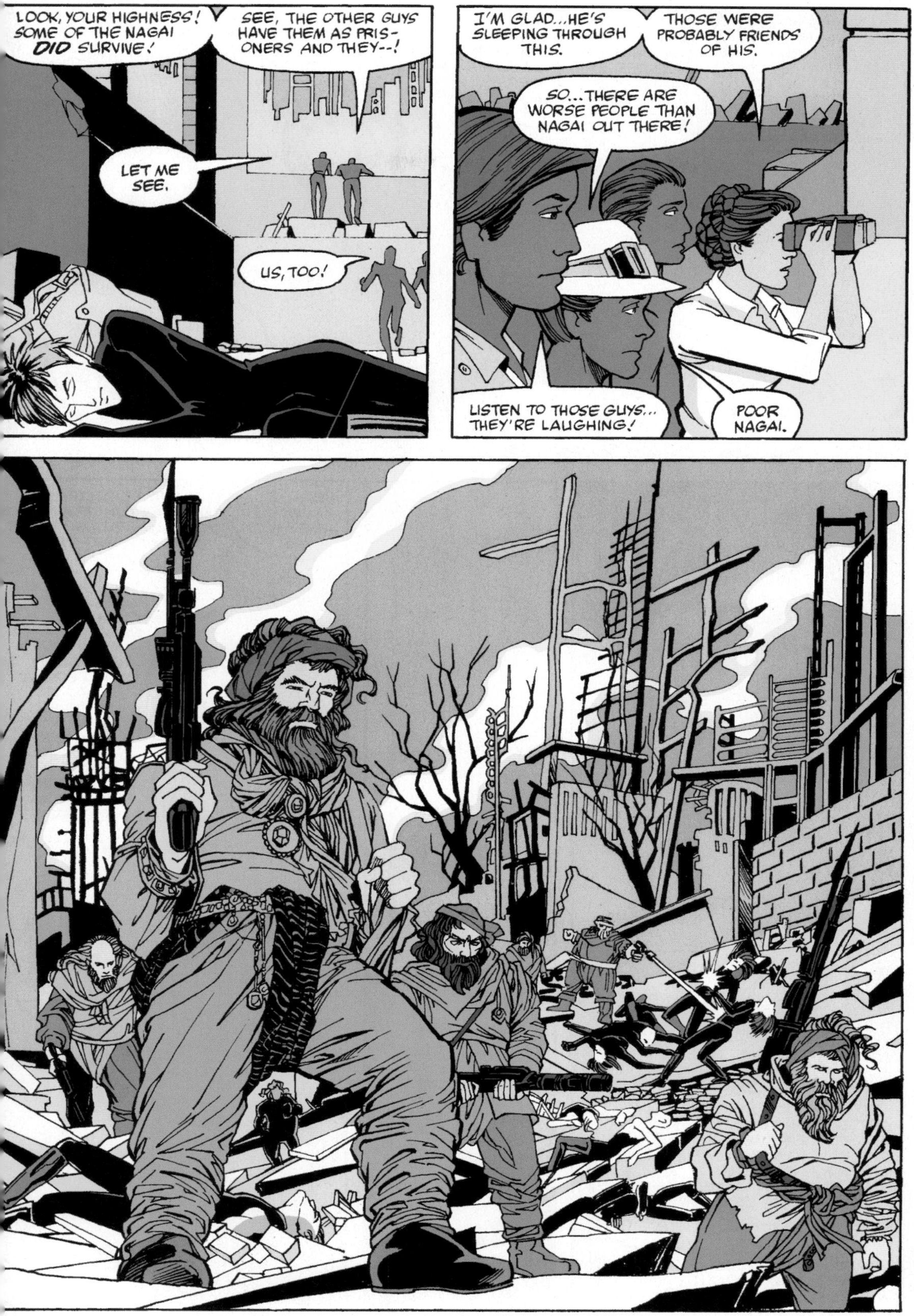
LOOK, YOUR HIGHNESS! SOME OF THE NAGAI DID SURVIVE!
SEE, THE OTHER GUYS HAVE THEM AS PRIS-ONERS AND THEY--!
LET ME SEE.
US, TOO!
I'M GLAD...HE'S SLEEPING THROUGH THIS.
THOSE WERE PROBABLY FRIENDS OF HIS.
SO...THERE ARE WORSE PEOPLE THAN NAGAI OUT THERE!
LISTEN TO THOSE GUYS... THEY'RE LAUGHING!
POOR NAGAI.

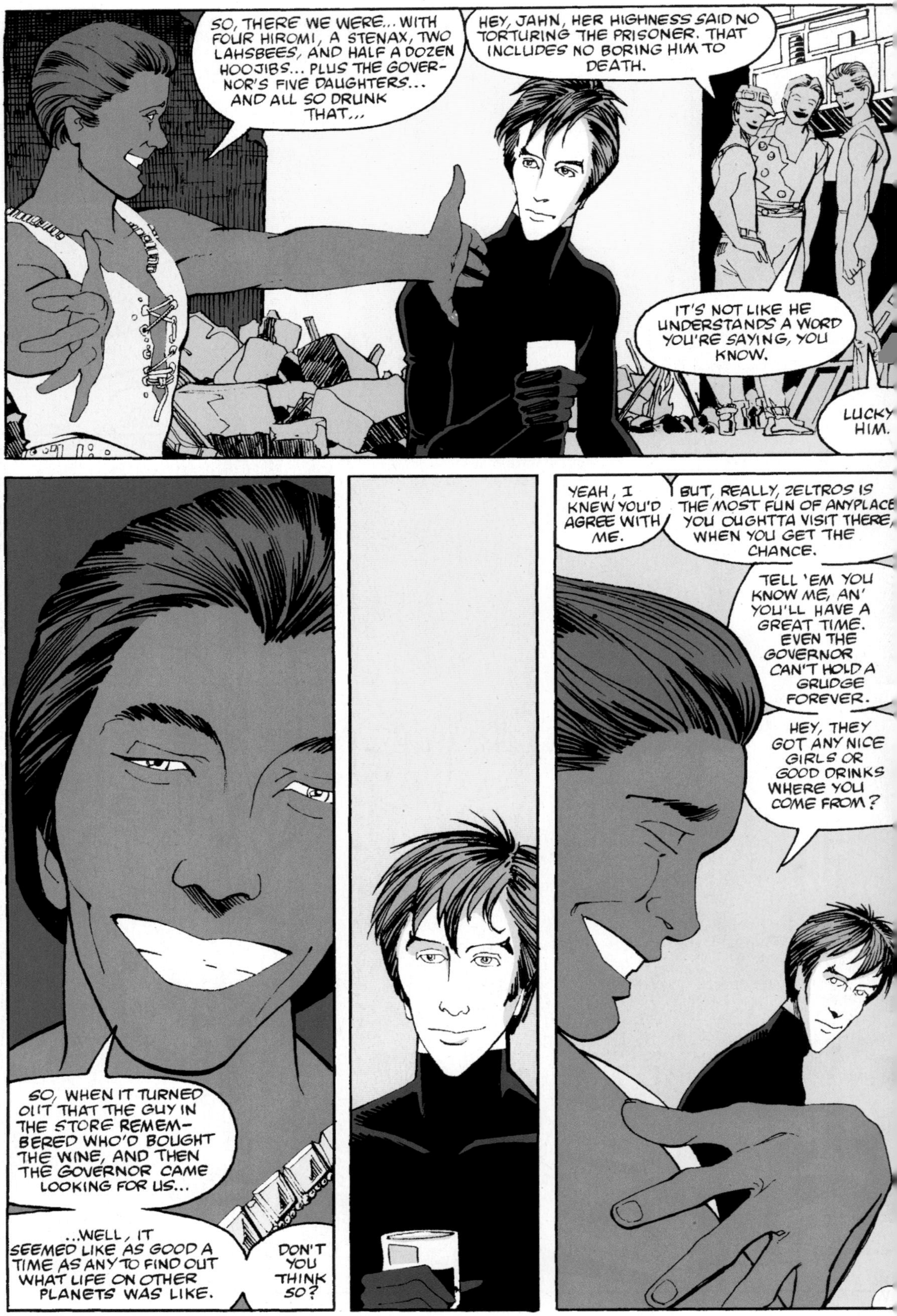
SO, THERE WE WERE... WITH FOUR HIROMI, A STENAX, TWO LAHSBEES, AND HALF A DOZEN HOOJIBS... PLUS THE GOVERNOR'S FIVE DAUGHTERS... AND ALL SO DRUNK THAT...
HEY, JAHN, HER HIGHNESS SAID NO TORTURING THE PRISONER. THAT INCLUDES NO BORING HIM TO DEATH.
IT'S NOT LIKE HE UNDERSTANDS A WORD YOU'RE SAYING, YOU KNOW.
LUCKY HIM.
SO, WHEN IT TURNED OUT THAT THE GUY IN THE STORE REMEMBERED WHO'D BOUGHT THE WINE, AND THEN THE GOVERNOR CAME LOOKING FOR US...
...WELL, IT SEEMED LIKE AS GOOD A TIME AS ANY TO FIND OUT WHAT LIFE ON OTHER PLANETS WAS LIKE.
DON'T YOU THINK SO?
YEAH, I KNEW YOU'D AGREE WITH ME.
BUT, REALLY, ZELTROS IS THE MOST FUN OF ANYPLACE YOU OUGHTTA VISIT THERE, WHEN YOU GET THE CHANCE.
TELL 'EM YOU KNOW ME, AN' YOU'LL HAVE A GREAT TIME. EVEN THE GOVERNOR CAN'T HOLD A GRUDGE FOREVER.
HEY, THEY GOT ANY NICE GIRLS OR GOOD DRINKS WHERE YOU COME FROM?

... CHECKS OUT JUST FINE. AND SINCE THOSE OTHER PEOPLE REALLY DO SEEM TO HAVE LEFT TRENWYTH, WE CAN BE ON OUR WAY JUST AS SOON AS YOU FOUR GET THE GEAR PACKED.

RIGHT.

WHICH LEAVES ME JUST ONE MORE LITTLE THING TO TAKE CARE OF.

LOOK... WE'RE GOING NOW. CAN YOU UNDERSTAND ME?

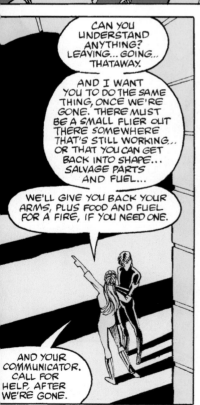

CAN YOU UNDERSTAND ANYTHING? LEAVING... GOING... THATAWAY.

AND I WANT YOU TO DO THE SAME THING, ONCE WE'RE GONE. THERE MUST BE A SMALL FLIER OUT THERE SOMEWHERE THAT'S STILL WORKING... OR THAT YOU CAN GET BACK INTO SHAPE... SALVAGE PARTS AND FUEL...

WE'LL GIVE YOU BACK YOUR ARMS, PLUS FOOD AND FUEL FOR A FIRE, IF YOU NEED ONE.

AND YOUR COMMUNICATOR. CALL FOR HELP, AFTER WE'RE GONE.

LISTEN... I'M AN ALLIANCE OFFICER. WE SHOULD TAKE YOU BACK WITH US, AS A PRISONER... BUT AFTER ALL WE'VE BEEN THROUGH, I JUST CAN'T!

AREN'T YOU GETTING ANY OF THIS? SHOO! SCRAM! GO!

WHAT ARE YOU WAITING FOR?

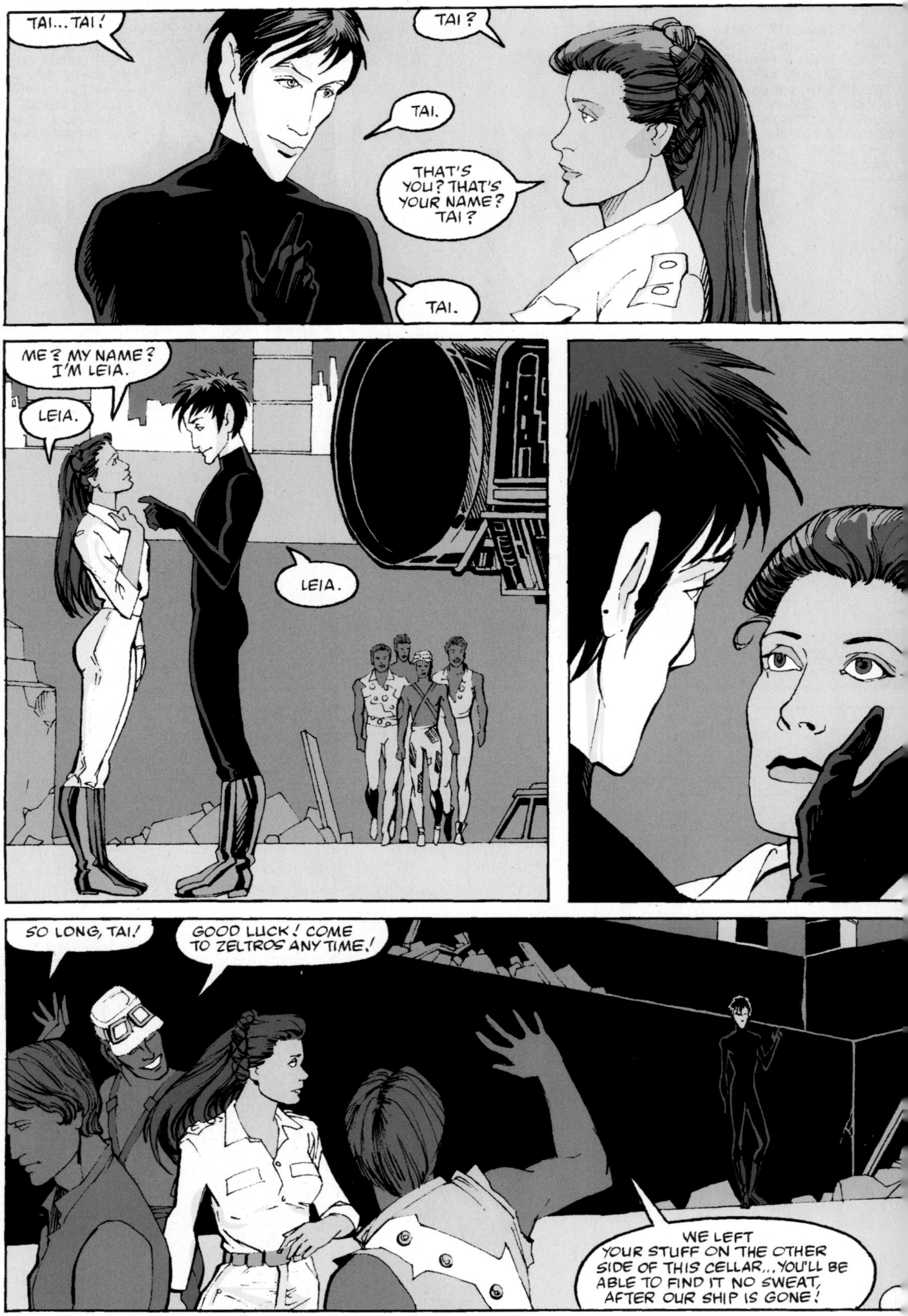
TAI... TAI!
TAI?
TAI.
THAT'S YOU? THAT'S YOUR NAME? TAI?
TAI.
ME? MY NAME? I'M LEIA.
LEIA.
LEIA.
SO LONG, TAI!
GOOD LUCK! COME TO ZELTROS ANY TIME!
WE LEFT YOUR STUFF ON THE OTHER SIDE OF THIS CELLAR... YOU'LL BE ABLE TO FIND IT NO SWEAT, AFTER OUR SHIP IS GONE!

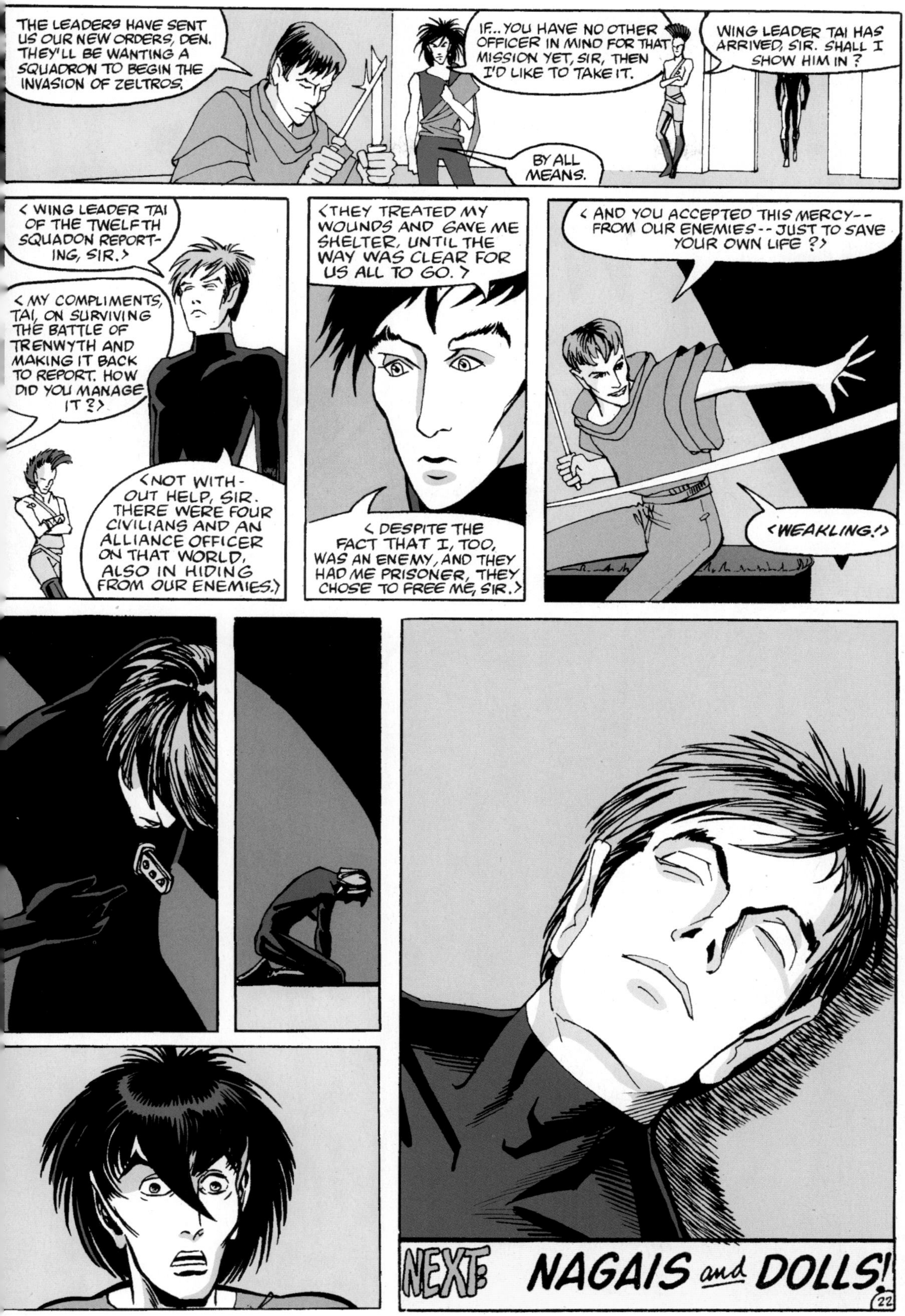

THE LEADERS HAVE SENT US OUR NEW ORDERS, DEN. THEY'LL BE WANTING A SQUADRON TO BEGIN THE INVASION OF ZELTROS.
IF... YOU HAVE NO OTHER OFFICER IN MIND FOR THAT MISSION YET, SIR, THEN I'D LIKE TO TAKE IT.
BY ALL MEANS.
WING LEADER TAI HAS ARRIVED, SIR. SHALL I SHOW HIM IN?
< WING LEADER TAI OF THE TWELFTH SQUADON REPORTING, SIR. >
< MY COMPLIMENTS, TAI, ON SURVIVING THE BATTLE OF TRENWYTH AND MAKING IT BACK TO REPORT. HOW DID YOU MANAGE IT? >
<NOT WITHOUT HELP, SIR. THERE WERE FOUR CIVILIANS AND AN ALLIANCE OFFICER ON THAT WORLD, ALSO IN HIDING FROM OUR ENEMIES.>
<THEY TREATED MY WOUNDS AND GAVE ME SHELTER, UNTIL THE WAY WAS CLEAR FOR US ALL TO GO.>
< DESPITE THE FACT THAT I, TOO, WAS AN ENEMY, AND THEY HAD ME PRISONER, THEY CHOSE TO FREE ME, SIR.>
< AND YOU ACCEPTED THIS MERCY-- FROM OUR ENEMIES-- JUST TO SAVE YOUR OWN LIFE?>
<WEAKLING!>
NEXT: NAGAIS and DOLLS!
22

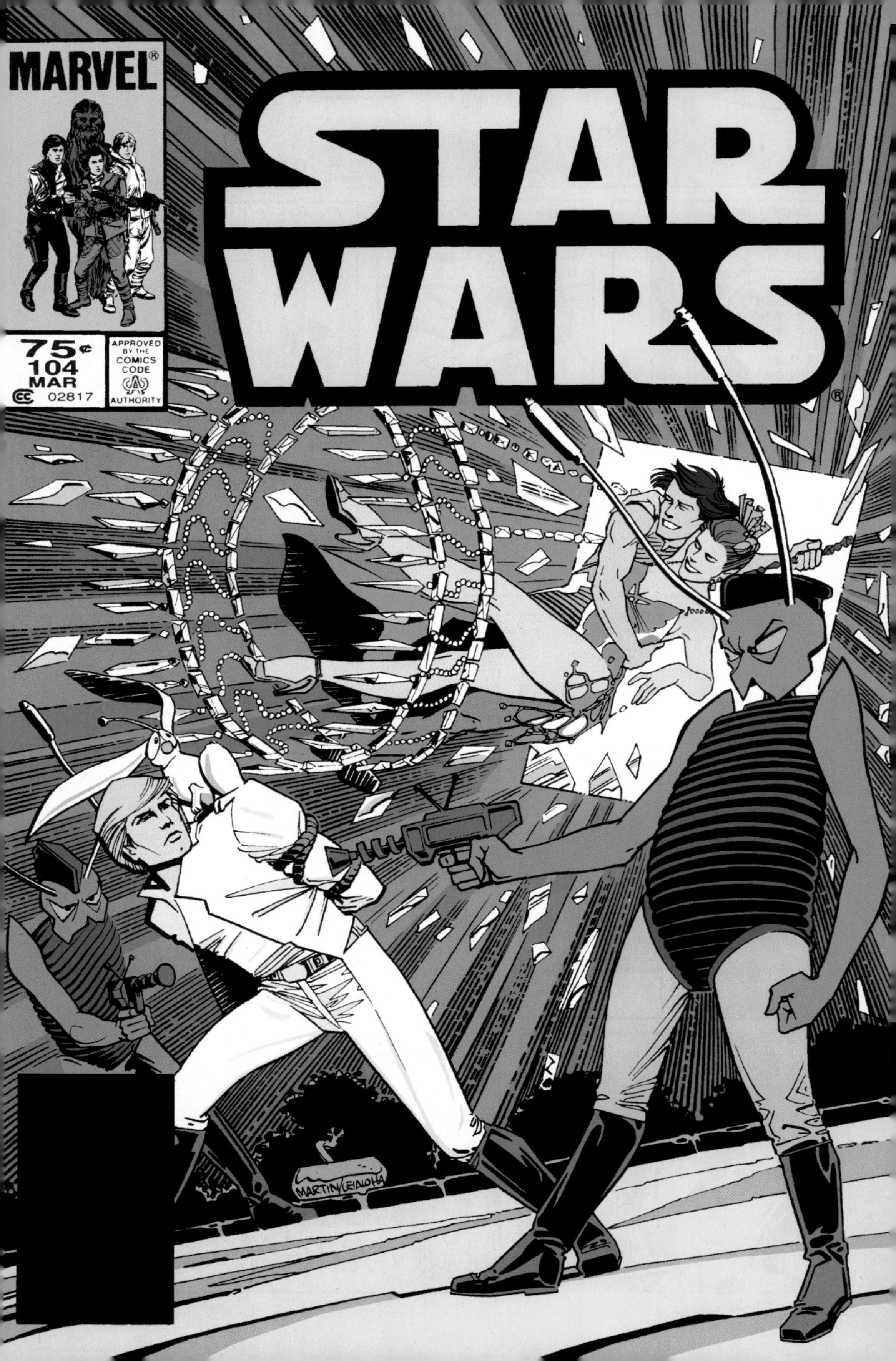
MARVEL®
STAR WARS®
75¢
104
MAR
02817
APPROVED BY THE COMICS CODE AUTHORITY
MARTIN/LEIALOHA

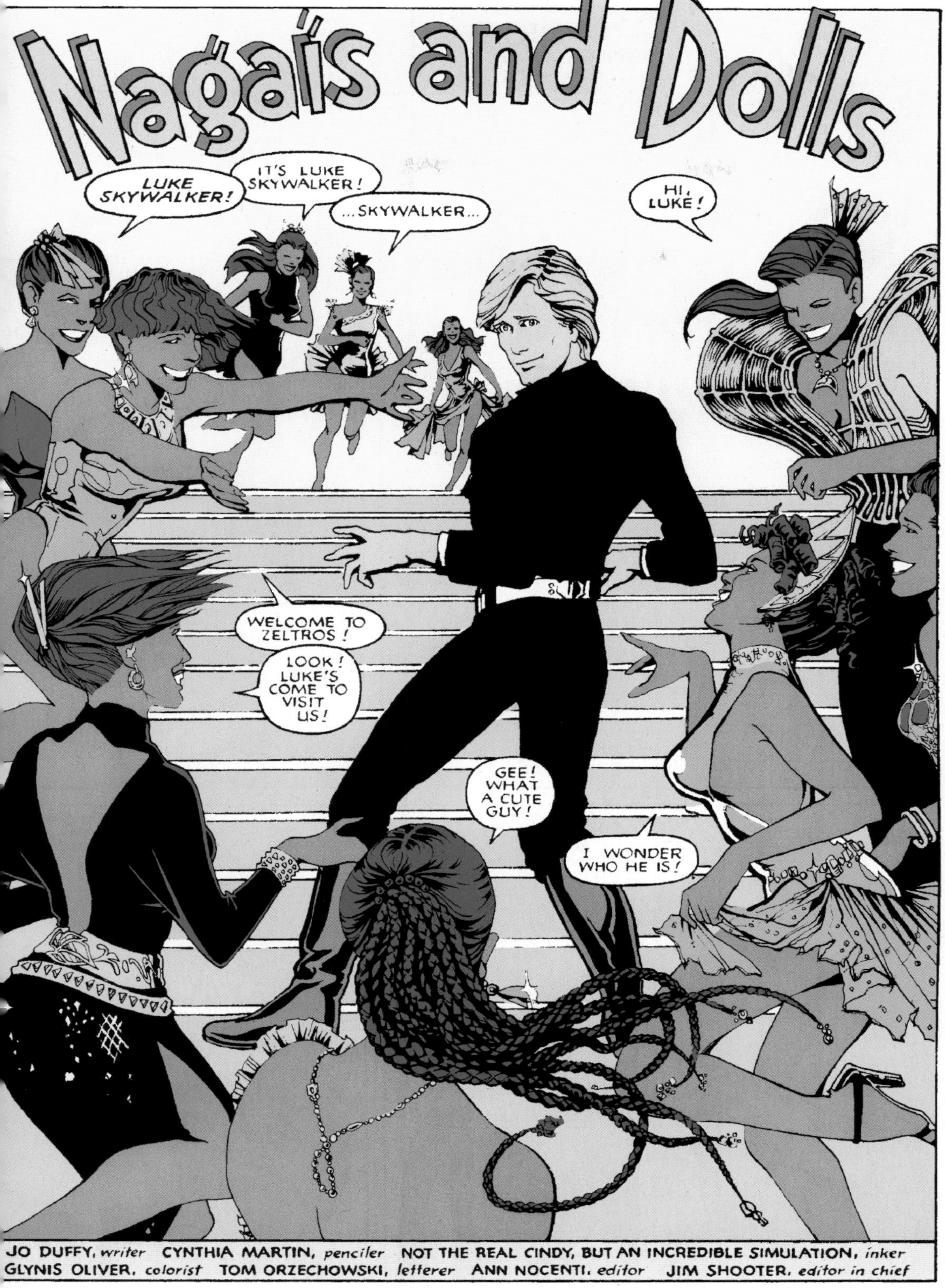
Nagaís and Dolls
LUKE SKYWALKER!
IT'S LUKE SKYWALKER!
...SKYWALKER...
HI, LUKE!
WELCOME TO ZELTROS!
LOOK! LUKE'S COME TO VISIT US!
GEE! WHAT A CUTE GUY!
I WONDER WHO HE IS!
JO DUFFY, writer CYNTHIA MARTIN, penciler NOT THE REAL CINDY, BUT AN INCREDIBLE SIMULATION, inker
GLYNIS OLIVER, colorist TOM ORZECHOWSKI, letterer ANN NOCENTI, editor JIM SHOOTER, editor in chief

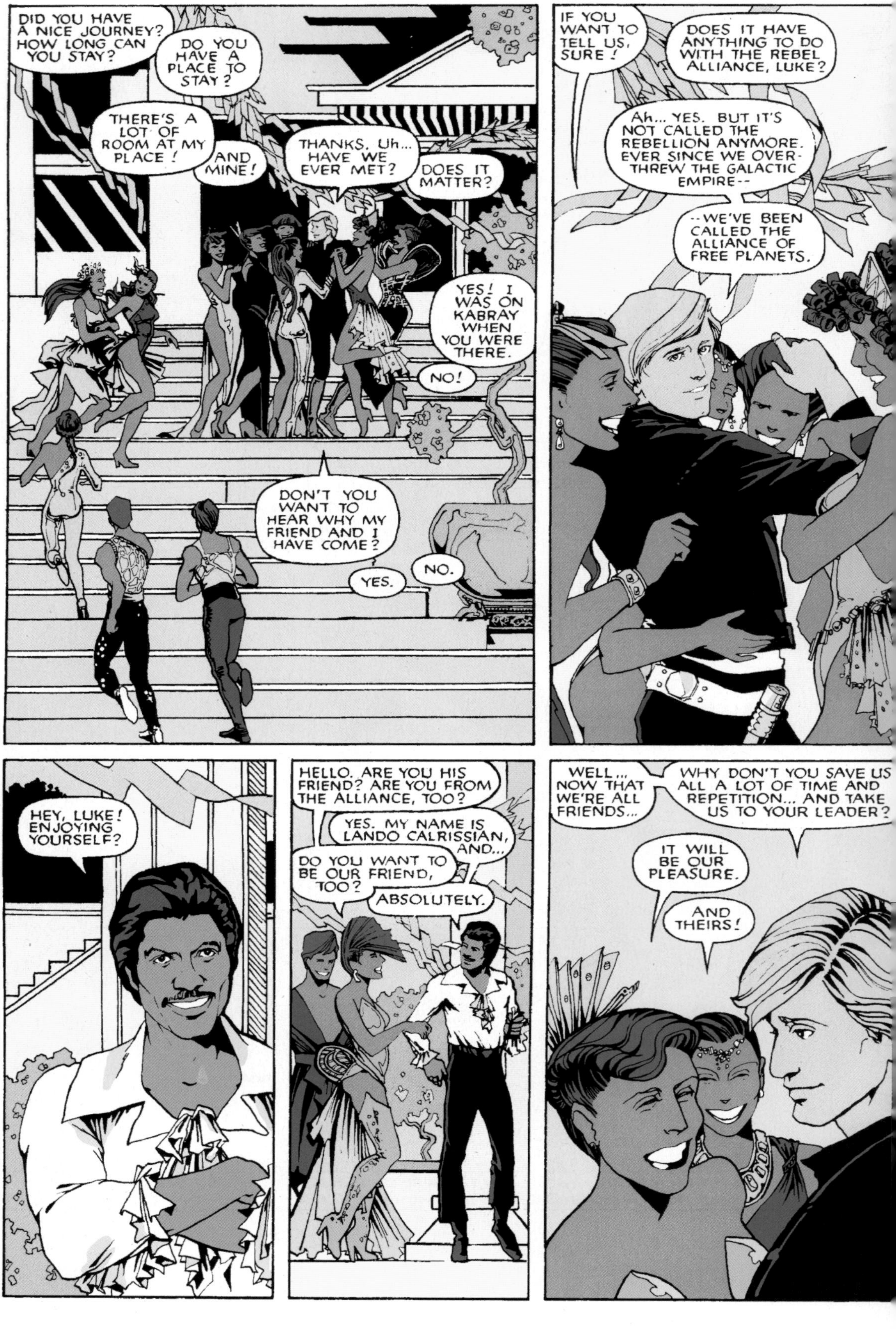
DID YOU HAVE A NICE JOURNEY? HOW LONG CAN YOU STAY?
DO YOU HAVE A PLACE TO STAY?
THERE'S A LOT OF ROOM AT MY PLACE!
AND MINE!
THANKS. Uh... HAVE WE EVER MET?
DOES IT MATTER?
YES! I WAS ON KABRAY WHEN YOU WERE THERE.
NO!
DON'T YOU WANT TO HEAR WHY MY FRIEND AND I HAVE COME?
YES.
NO.
IF YOU WANT TO TELL US, SURE!
DOES IT HAVE ANYTHING TO DO WITH THE REBEL ALLIANCE, LUKE?
Ah... YES. BUT IT'S NOT CALLED THE REBELLION ANYMORE. EVER SINCE WE OVERTHREW THE GALACTIC EMPIRE--
--WE'VE BEEN CALLED THE ALLIANCE OF FREE PLANETS.
HEY, LUKE! ENJOYING YOURSELF?
HELLO. ARE YOU HIS FRIEND? ARE YOU FROM THE ALLIANCE, TOO?
YES. MY NAME IS LANDO CALRISSIAN, AND...
DO YOU WANT TO BE OUR FRIEND, TOO?
ABSOLUTELY.
WELL... NOW THAT WE'RE ALL FRIENDS...
WHY DON'T YOU SAVE US ALL A LOT OF TIME AND REPETITION... AND TAKE US TO YOUR LEADER?
IT WILL BE OUR PLEASURE.
AND THEIRS!

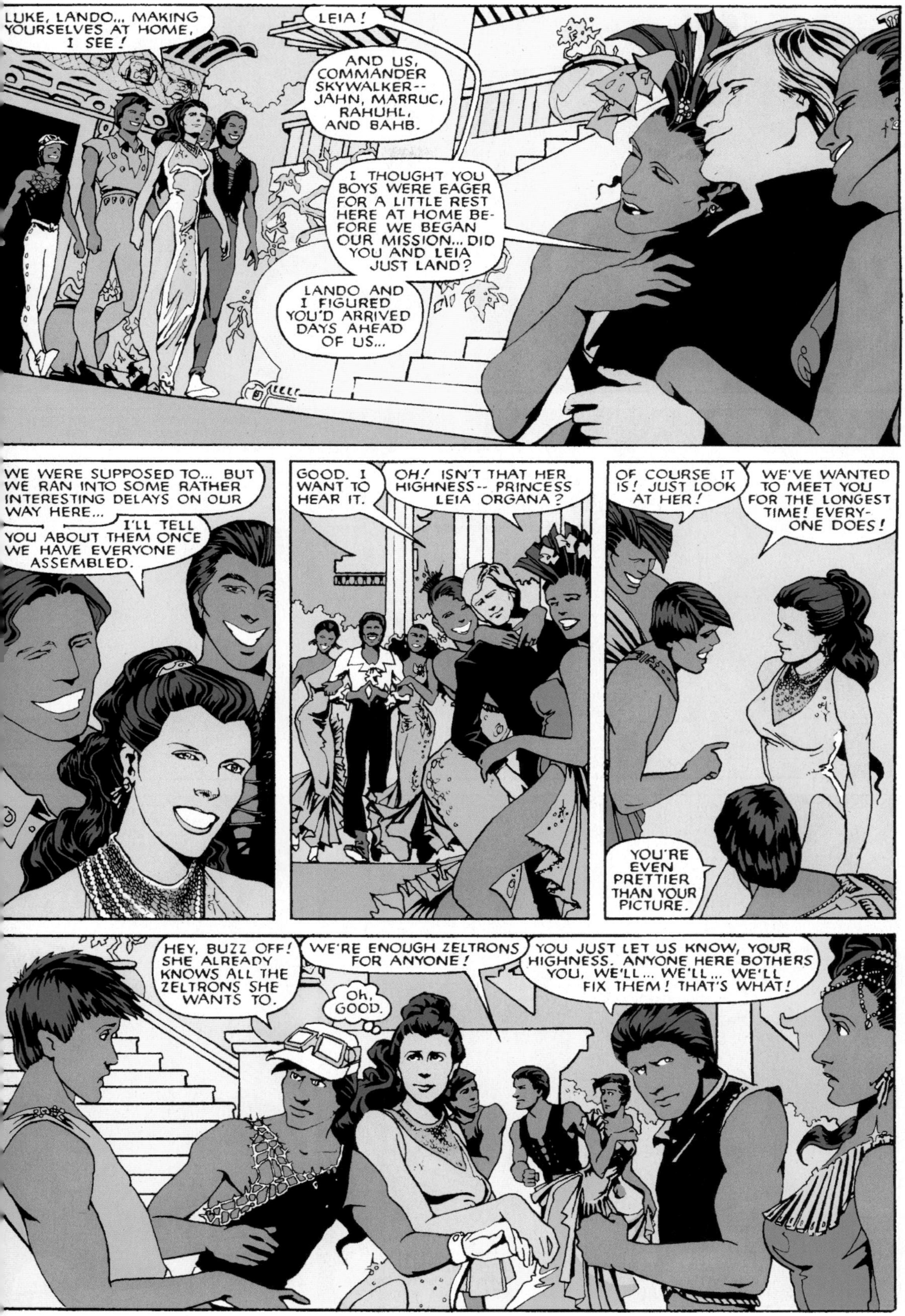

LUKE, LANDO... MAKING YOURSELVES AT HOME, I SEE!
LEIA!
AND US, COMMANDER SKYWALKER-- JAHN, MARRUC, RAHUHL, AND BAHB.
I THOUGHT YOU BOYS WERE EAGER FOR A LITTLE REST HERE AT HOME BEFORE WE BEGAN OUR MISSION... DID YOU AND LEIA JUST LAND?
LANDO AND I FIGURED YOU'D ARRIVED DAYS AHEAD OF US...
WE WERE SUPPOSED TO... BUT WE RAN INTO SOME RATHER INTERESTING DELAYS ON OUR WAY HERE...
I'LL TELL YOU ABOUT THEM ONCE WE HAVE EVERYONE ASSEMBLED.
GOOD. I WANT TO HEAR IT.
OH! ISN'T THAT HER HIGHNESS-- PRINCESS LEIA ORGANA?
OF COURSE IT IS! JUST LOOK AT HER!
WE'VE WANTED TO MEET YOU FOR THE LONGEST TIME! EVERYONE DOES!
YOU'RE EVEN PRETTIER THAN YOUR PICTURE.
HEY, BUZZ OFF! SHE ALREADY KNOWS ALL THE ZELTRONS SHE WANTS TO.
WE'RE ENOUGH ZELTRONS FOR ANYONE!
Oh, GOOD.
YOU JUST LET US KNOW, YOUR HIGHNESS. ANYONE HERE BOTHERS YOU, WE'LL... WE'LL... WE'LL FIX THEM! THAT'S WHAT!

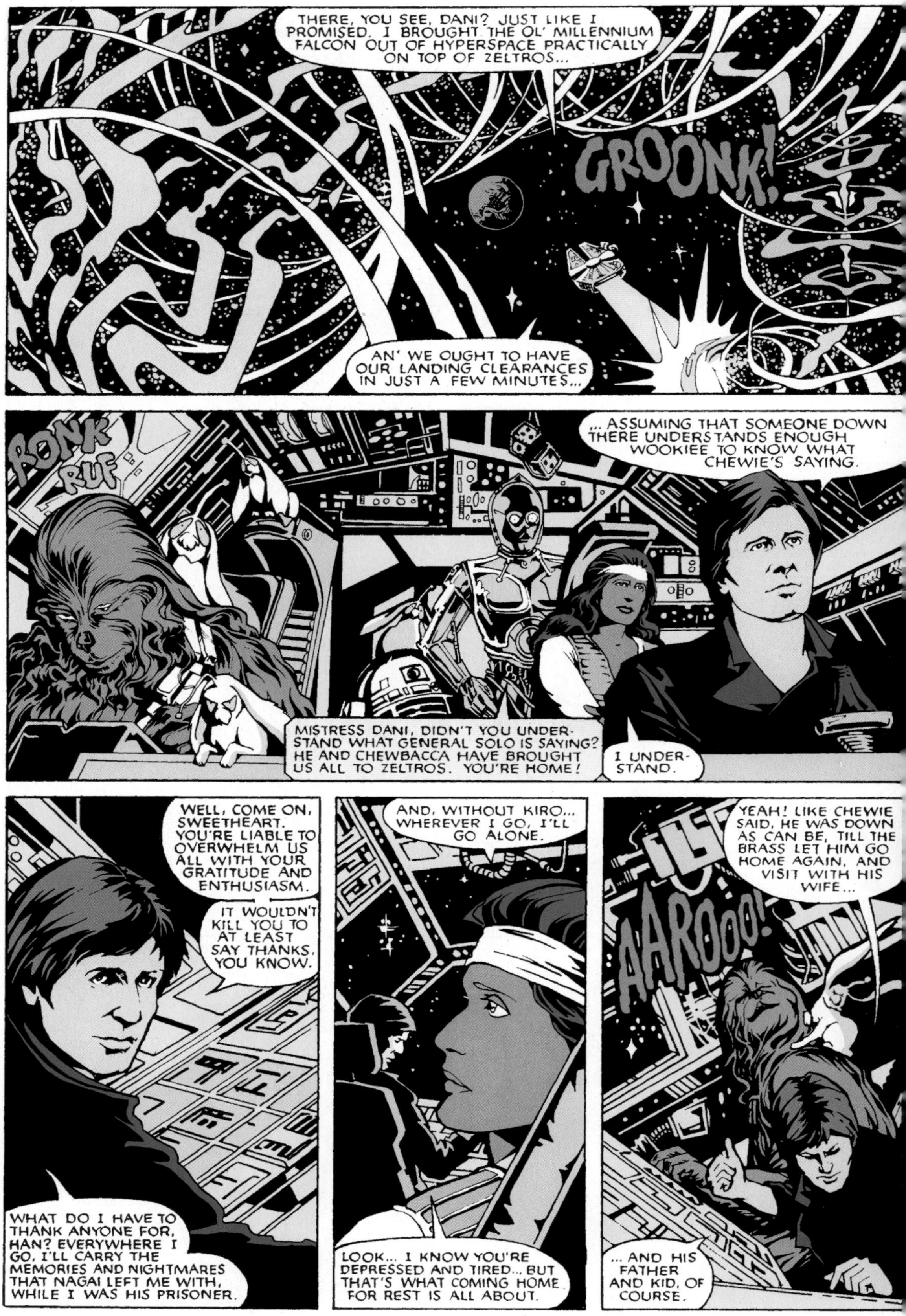
THERE, YOU SEE, DANI? JUST LIKE I PROMISED. I BROUGHT THE OL' MILLENNIUM FALCON OUT OF HYPERSPACE PRACTICALLY ON TOP OF ZELTROS...
GROONK!
AN' WE OUGHT TO HAVE OUR LANDING CLEARANCES IN JUST A FEW MINUTES...
RONK RUF
...ASSUMING THAT SOMEONE DOWN THERE UNDERSTANDS ENOUGH WOOKIEE TO KNOW WHAT CHEWIE'S SAYING.
MISTRESS DANI, DIDN'T YOU UNDERSTAND WHAT GENERAL SOLO IS SAYING? HE AND CHEWBACCA HAVE BROUGHT US ALL TO ZELTROS. YOU'RE HOME!
I UNDERSTAND.
WELL, COME ON, SWEETHEART. YOU'RE LIABLE TO OVERWHELM US ALL WITH YOUR GRATITUDE AND ENTHUSIASM.
IT WOULDN'T KILL YOU TO AT LEAST SAY THANKS, YOU KNOW.
WHAT DO I HAVE TO THANK ANYONE FOR, HAN? EVERYWHERE I GO, I'LL CARRY THE MEMORIES AND NIGHTMARES THAT NAGAI LEFT ME WITH, WHILE I WAS HIS PRISONER.
AND, WITHOUT KIRO... WHEREVER I GO, I'LL GO ALONE.
LOOK... I KNOW YOU'RE DEPRESSED AND TIRED... BUT THAT'S WHAT COMING HOME FOR REST IS ALL ABOUT.
YEAH! LIKE CHEWIE SAID, HE WAS DOWN AS CAN BE, TILL THE BRASS LET HIM GO HOME AGAIN, AND VISIT WITH HIS WIFE...
AAROOO!
...AND HIS FATHER AND KID, OF COURSE.

INDEED, MISTRESS DANI... ARTOO-DETOO AND I ARE MERELY DROIDS, AND NOT ORGANIC BEINGS. BUT I'M CERTAIN IF WE HAD HOMES, VISITING THEM WOULD BRIGHTEN OUR FEELINGS... IF WE HAD FEELINGS.

AND WE HOOJIBS ARE ALWAYS PLEASED TO RETURN TO OUR WORLD, ARBRA.

BUT KIRO WAS... HE... I WOULD HAVE STAYED WITH HIM FOREVER.

AND THAT NAGAI-- THAT DEN SIVA-- TOOK HIM AWAY FROM ME.

IT'S DIFFERENT FOR YOU. PRINCESS LEIA IS STILL ALIVE.

BUT THE NAGAI ROBBED ME OF SOMEONE I LOVE!

WHAT MAKES YOU THINK I'M DIFFERENT?

THIS IS WAR, SISTER. EVERYONE'S LOST PEOPLE THAT THEY CARE ABOUT.

THEN YOU SHOULD UNDER-STAND HOW I FEEL. I'M NOT HOME FOR MYSELF. I'M HERE FOR KIRO...

... AND FOR ALL THE KIROS AND DANIS AND HANS WHO HAVEN'T SUFFERED YET IN THIS WAR.

I WANT TO DO EVERY-THING IN MY POWER TO CONVINCE MY PEOPLE'S RULERS THAT WE SHOULD ENTER THIS WAR, WHOLEHEARTEDLY...

... AND HELP THE ALLIANCE OF FREE PLANETS TO EXTERMINATE THE NAGAI!

PLIF... SINCE HER EXPERIENCE WITH THIS DEN SIVA... DANI HAS CHANGED SO. ALL HER PEACE AND JOY ARE GONE.

YES... AND BEING TELEPATHIC, WE ARE MORE AWARE OF HER PAIN AND ANGER THAN THE REST OF HER FRIENDS. POOR DANI.

HELLO! WELCOME, WHOEVER YOU ARE!

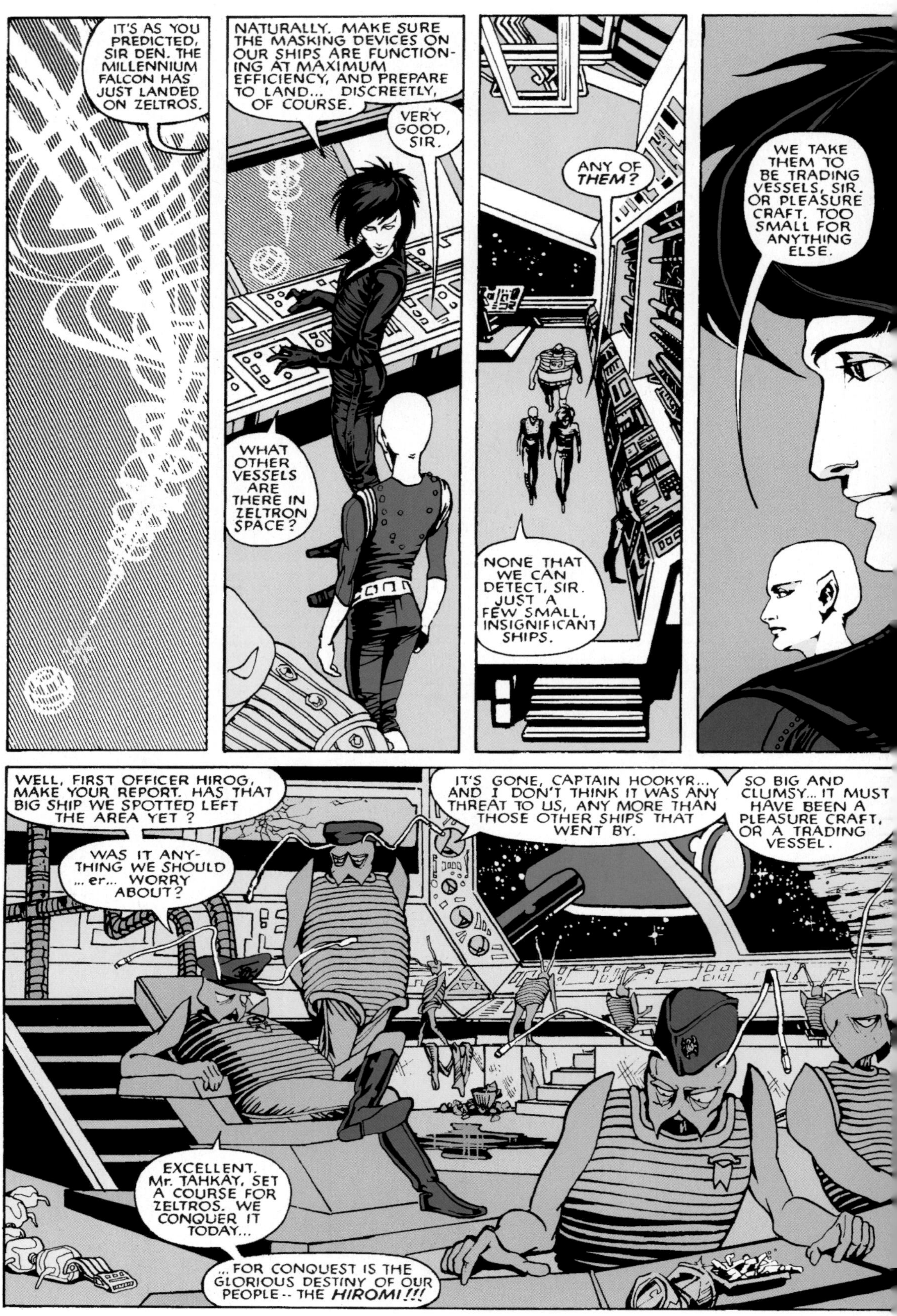
IT'S AS YOU PREDICTED, SIR DEN. THE MILLENNIUM FALCON HAS JUST LANDED ON ZELTROS.
NATURALLY. MAKE SURE THE MASKING DEVICES ON OUR SHIPS ARE FUNCTIONING AT MAXIMUM EFFICIENCY, AND PREPARE TO LAND... DISCREETLY, OF COURSE.
VERY GOOD, SIR.
WHAT OTHER VESSELS ARE THERE IN ZELTRON SPACE?
ANY OF *THEM?*
NONE THAT WE CAN DETECT, SIR. JUST A FEW SMALL, INSIGNIFICANT SHIPS.
WE TAKE THEM TO BE TRADING VESSELS, SIR. OR PLEASURE CRAFT. TOO SMALL FOR ANYTHING ELSE.
WELL, FIRST OFFICER HIROG, MAKE YOUR REPORT. HAS THAT BIG SHIP WE SPOTTED LEFT THE AREA YET ?
WAS IT ANYTHING WE *SHOULD* ...er... WORRY ABOUT?
IT'S GONE, CAPTAIN HOOKYR... AND I DON'T THINK IT WAS ANY THREAT TO US, ANY MORE THAN THOSE OTHER SHIPS THAT WENT BY.
SO BIG AND CLUMSY... IT MUST HAVE BEEN A PLEASURE CRAFT, OR A TRADING VESSEL.
EXCELLENT. Mr. TAHKAY, SET A COURSE FOR ZELTROS. WE CONQUER IT TODAY...
...FOR CONQUEST IS THE GLORIOUS DESTINY OF OUR PEOPLE -- THE *HIROMI!!!*

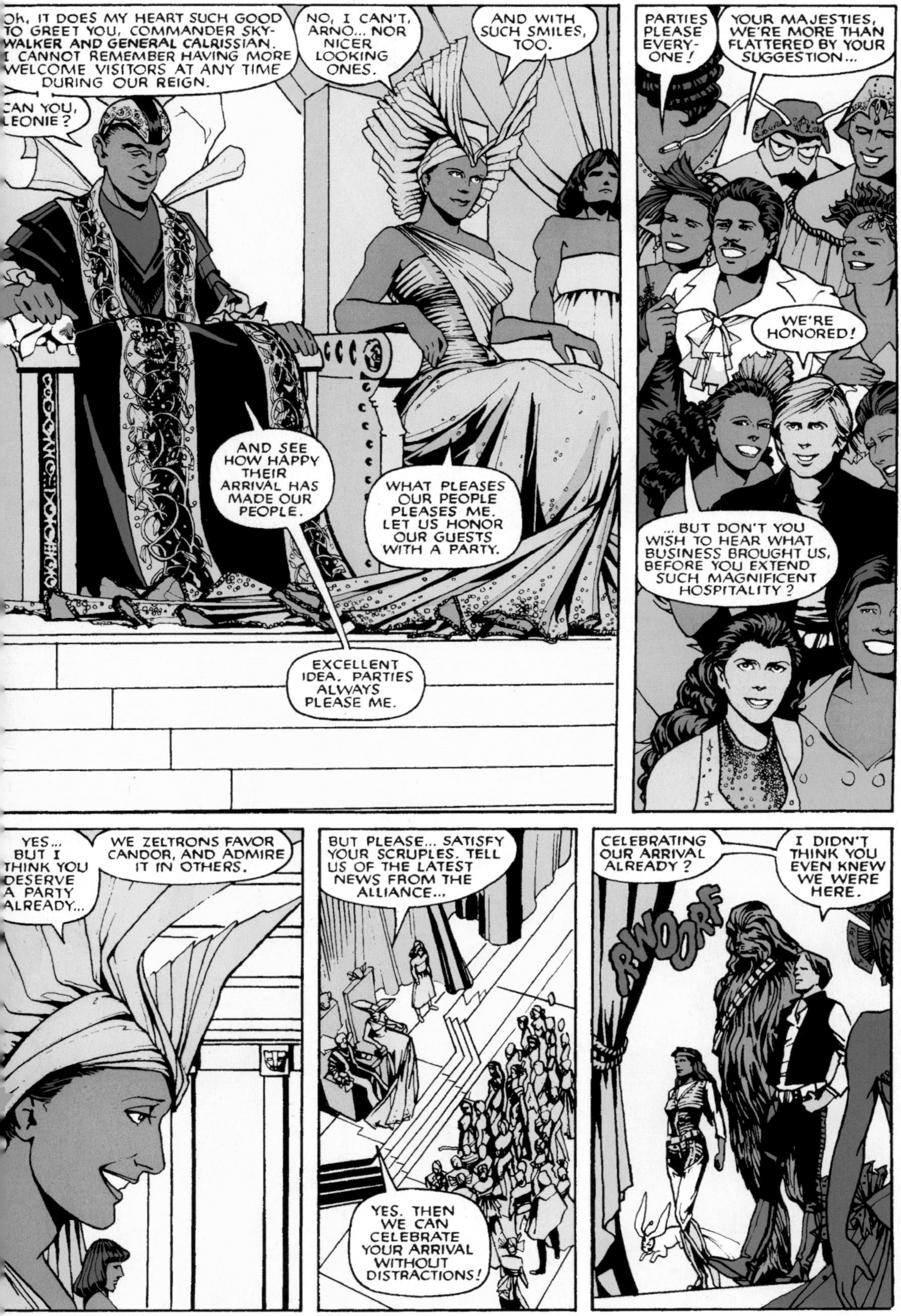
Oh, IT DOES MY HEART SUCH GOOD TO GREET YOU, COMMANDER SKY-WALKER AND GENERAL CALRISSIAN. I CANNOT REMEMBER HAVING MORE WELCOME VISITORS AT ANY TIME DURING OUR REIGN.
CAN YOU, LEONIE?
NO, I CAN'T, ARNO... NOR NICER LOOKING ONES.
AND WITH SUCH SMILES, TOO.
AND SEE HOW HAPPY THEIR ARRIVAL HAS MADE OUR PEOPLE.
WHAT PLEASES OUR PEOPLE PLEASES ME. LET US HONOR OUR GUESTS WITH A PARTY.
EXCELLENT IDEA. PARTIES ALWAYS PLEASE ME.
PARTIES PLEASE EVERY-ONE!
YOUR MAJESTIES, WE'RE MORE THAN FLATTERED BY YOUR SUGGESTION...
WE'RE HONORED!
...BUT DON'T YOU WISH TO HEAR WHAT BUSINESS BROUGHT US, BEFORE YOU EXTEND SUCH MAGNIFICENT HOSPITALITY?
YES... BUT I THINK YOU DESERVE A PARTY ALREADY...
WE ZELTRONS FAVOR CANDOR, AND ADMIRE IT IN OTHERS.
BUT PLEASE... SATISFY YOUR SCRUPLES. TELL US OF THE LATEST NEWS FROM THE ALLIANCE...
YES. THEN WE CAN CELEBRATE YOUR ARRIVAL WITHOUT DISTRACTIONS!
CELEBRATING OUR ARRIVAL ALREADY?
I DIDN'T THINK YOU EVEN KNEW WE WERE HERE.
RWOORF

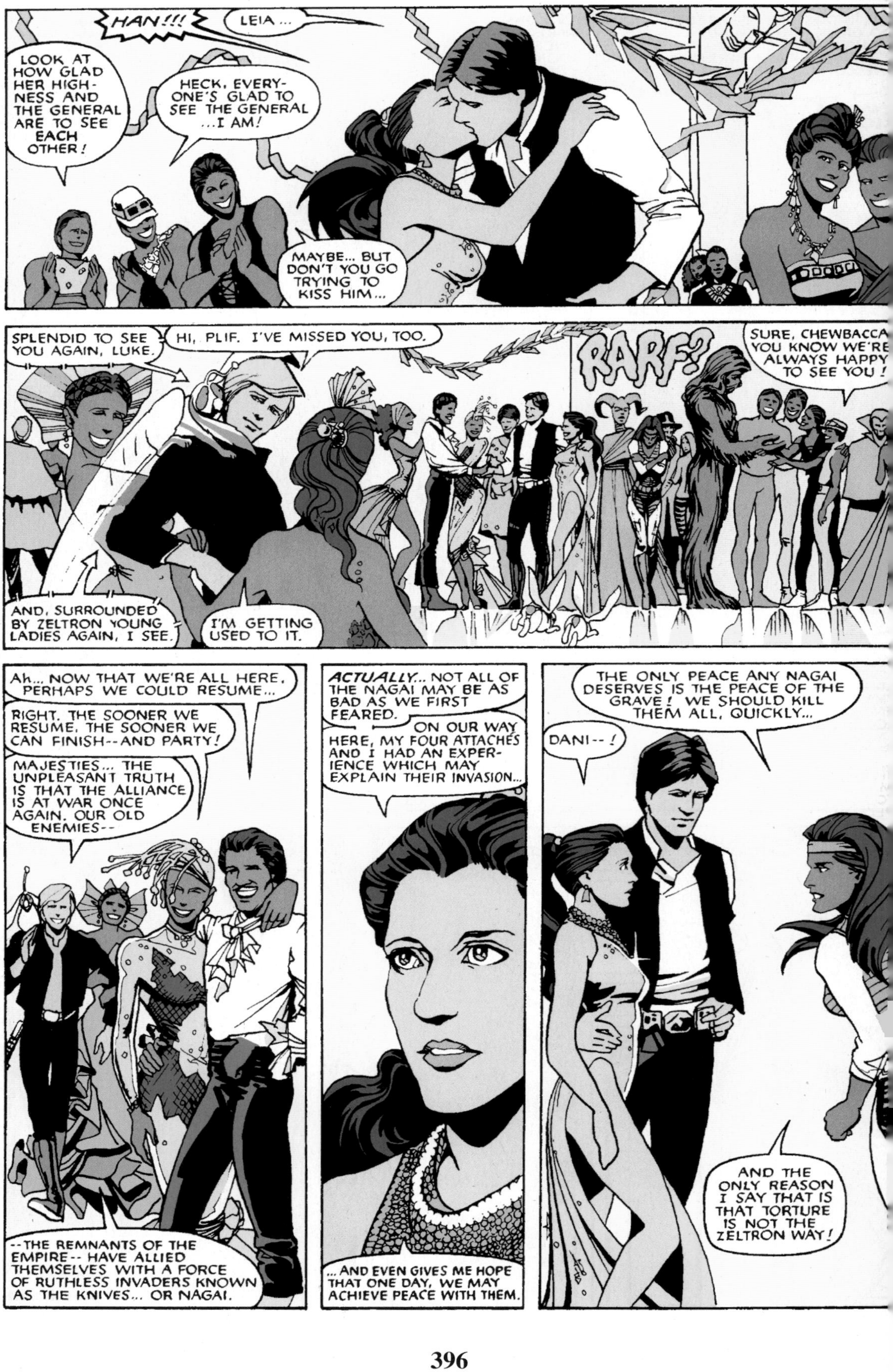
HAN!!!
LEIA...
LOOK AT HOW GLAD HER HIGHNESS AND THE GENERAL ARE TO SEE EACH OTHER!
HECK, EVERYONE'S GLAD TO SEE THE GENERAL ...I AM!
MAYBE... BUT DON'T YOU GO TRYING TO KISS HIM...
SPLENDID TO SEE YOU AGAIN, LUKE.
HI, PLIF. I'VE MISSED YOU, TOO.
AND, SURROUNDED BY ZELTRON YOUNG LADIES AGAIN, I SEE.
I'M GETTING USED TO IT.
RARF?
SURE, CHEWBACCA YOU KNOW WE'RE ALWAYS HAPPY TO SEE YOU!
Ah... NOW THAT WE'RE ALL HERE, PERHAPS WE COULD RESUME...
RIGHT. THE SOONER WE RESUME, THE SOONER WE CAN FINISH--AND PARTY!
MAJESTIES... THE UNPLEASANT TRUTH IS THAT THE ALLIANCE IS AT WAR ONCE AGAIN. OUR OLD ENEMIES--
--THE REMNANTS OF THE EMPIRE-- HAVE ALLIED THEMSELVES WITH A FORCE OF RUTHLESS INVADERS KNOWN AS THE KNIVES... OR NAGAI.
ACTUALLY... NOT ALL OF THE NAGAI MAY BE AS BAD AS WE FIRST FEARED.
ON OUR WAY HERE, MY FOUR ATTACHES AND I HAD AN EXPERIENCE WHICH MAY EXPLAIN THEIR INVASION...
...AND EVEN GIVES ME HOPE THAT ONE DAY, WE MAY ACHIEVE PEACE WITH THEM.
THE ONLY PEACE ANY NAGAI DESERVES IS THE PEACE OF THE GRAVE! WE SHOULD KILL THEM ALL, QUICKLY...
DANI--!
AND THE ONLY REASON I SAY THAT IS THAT TORTURE IS NOT THE ZELTRON WAY!

ANNOUNCING THE ROYAL GOVERNOR OF THE NORTHERN PROVINCE--

--HIS EXCELLENCY *VERTAG!*

GOVERNOR... VERTAG...?

THE ONE WHOSE FIVE DAUGHTERS WE...

RIGHT BEFORE WE LEFT HOME?

WHAT DO YOU THINK, JAHN...

I THINK... I HOPE HER HIGHNESS UNDERSTANDS...

THAT I SUDDENLY REMEMBERED AN URGENT APPOINTMENT...

YEAH... LIKE, IN THE *SOUTHERN* PROVINCE.

'SCUSE US... 'BYE... ONE SIDE, PLEASE...

ANI... BELIEVE ME, I KNOW WHAT IT'S LIKE TO SUFFER AT THE HANDS OF AN ENEMY, AND TO LOSE SOMEONE YOU LOVE...

...BUT WE'RE THINKING AND MAKING DECISIONS FOR ALL THE FREE PEOPLE IN THE GALAXY NOW.

THINK OF HOW MANY OF THEM WILL SUFFER IF THERE'S AN ALL-OUT WAR... A WAR THAT MIGHT BE AVERTED.

DON'T TALK DOWN TO ME, LEIA!

THOSE FREE PEOPLE WON'T STAY FREE FOR VERY LONG UNLESS ALL THE NAGAI ARE DEAD.

THIS IS A LITTLE... AWKWARD... OUR LEADERS SENT US HERE TO ASK FOR YOUR SUPPORT IN THE COMING WAR... BUT IF WAR *CAN* BE AVOIDED...

DEPENDS ON WHAT IT IS LEIA'S FOUND OUT...

BUT, FROM WHAT I'VE *SEEN* SO FAR, IT'S SAFER HAVING DINNER WITH A SARLACC THAN IT IS TRUSTING A NAGAI.

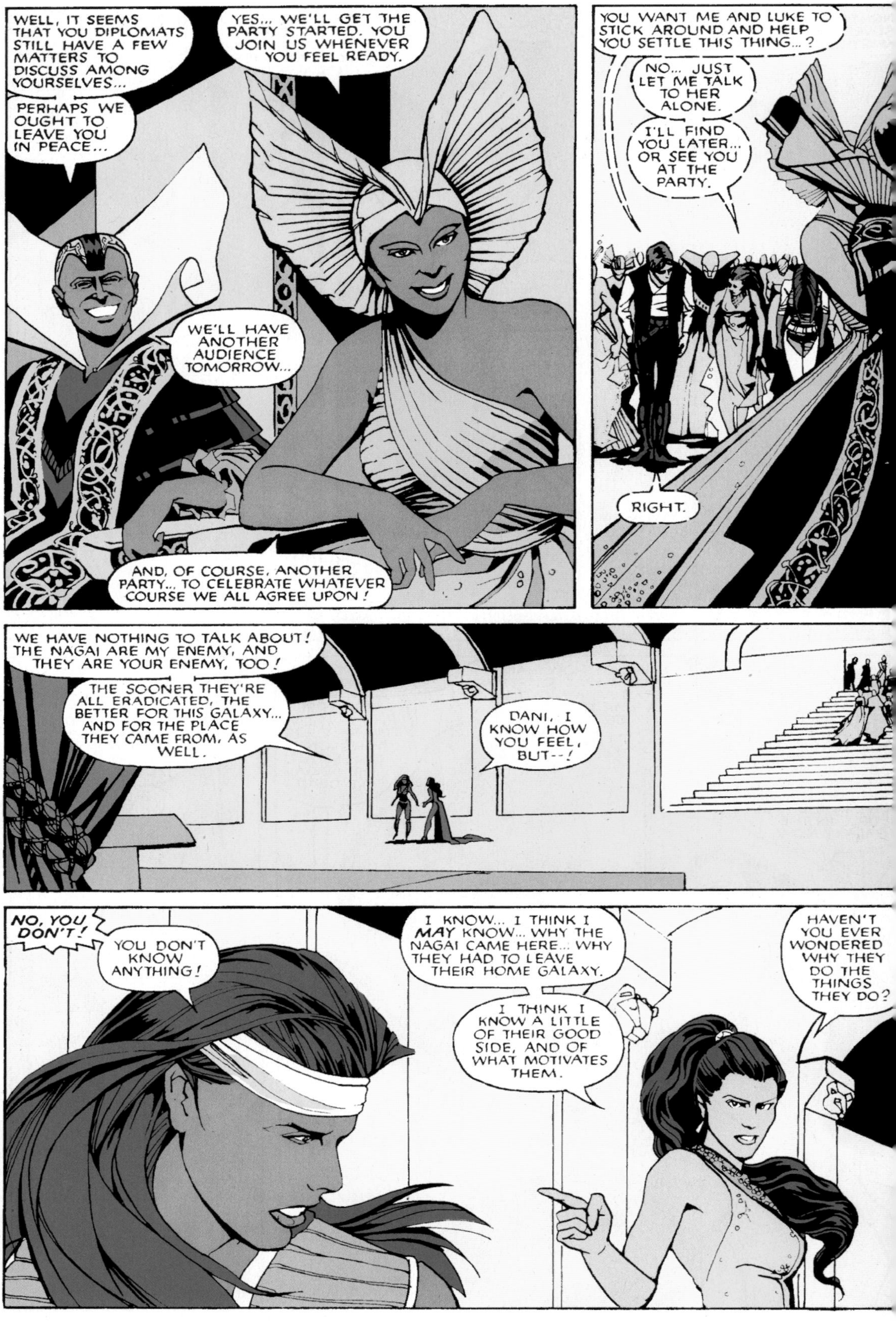

WELL, IT SEEMS THAT YOU DIPLOMATS STILL HAVE A FEW MATTERS TO DISCUSS AMONG YOURSELVES...
PERHAPS WE OUGHT TO LEAVE YOU IN PEACE...
YES... WE'LL GET THE PARTY STARTED. YOU JOIN US WHENEVER YOU FEEL READY.
WE'LL HAVE ANOTHER AUDIENCE TOMORROW...
AND, OF COURSE, ANOTHER PARTY... TO CELEBRATE WHATEVER COURSE WE ALL AGREE UPON!
YOU WANT ME AND LUKE TO STICK AROUND AND HELP YOU SETTLE THIS THING...?
NO... JUST LET ME TALK TO HER ALONE.
I'LL FIND YOU LATER... OR SEE YOU AT THE PARTY.
RIGHT.
WE HAVE NOTHING TO TALK ABOUT! THE NAGAI ARE MY ENEMY, AND THEY ARE YOUR ENEMY, TOO!
THE SOONER THEY'RE ALL ERADICATED, THE BETTER FOR THIS GALAXY... AND FOR THE PLACE THEY CAME FROM, AS WELL.
DANI, I KNOW HOW YOU FEEL, BUT--!
NO, YOU DON'T!
YOU DON'T KNOW ANYTHING!
I KNOW... I THINK I *MAY* KNOW... WHY THE NAGAI CAME HERE... WHY THEY HAD TO LEAVE THEIR HOME GALAXY.
I THINK I KNOW A LITTLE OF THEIR GOOD SIDE, AND OF WHAT MOTIVATES THEM.
HAVEN'T YOU EVER WONDERED WHY THEY DO THE THINGS THEY DO?

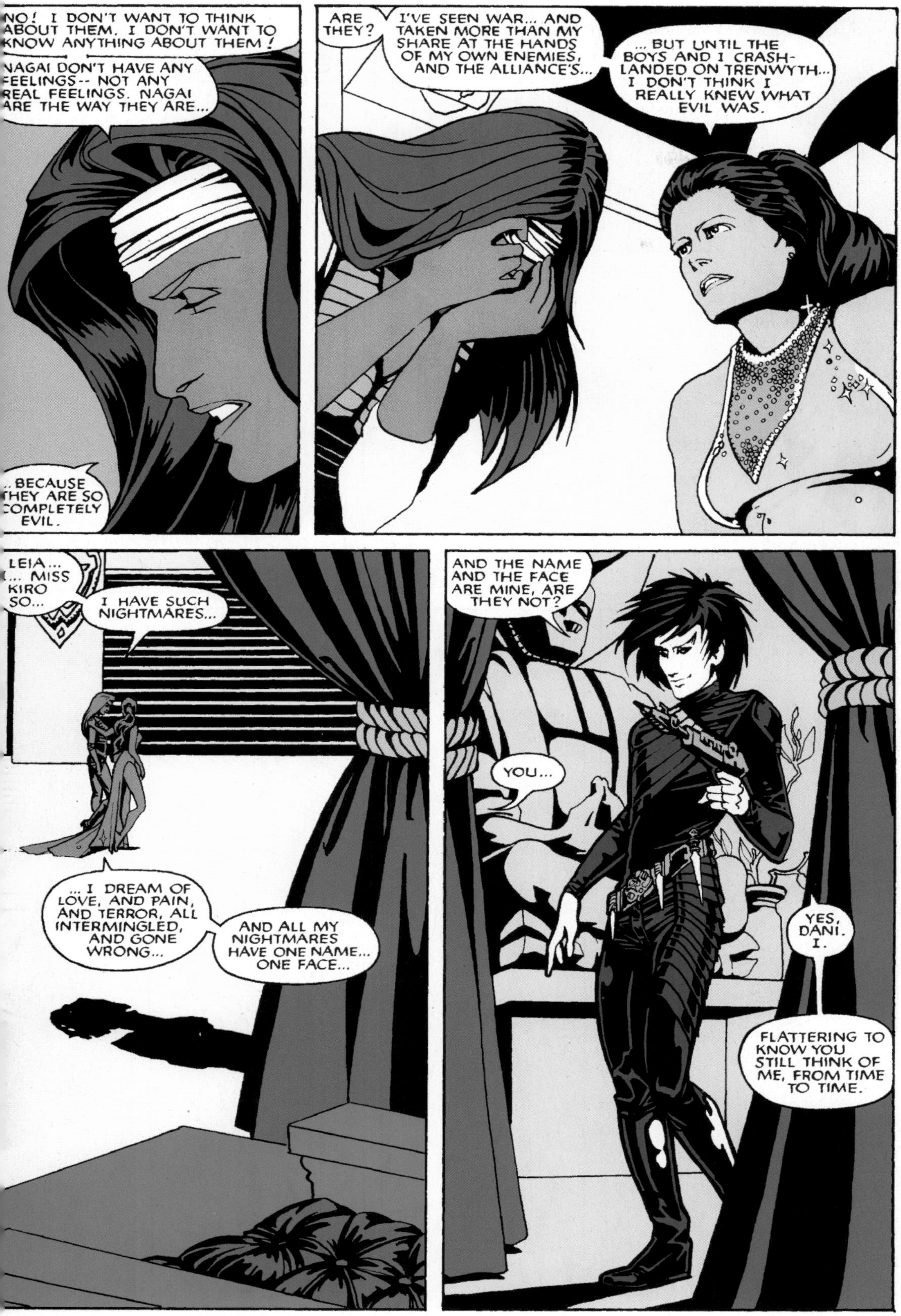

NO! I DON'T WANT TO THINK ABOUT THEM. I DON'T WANT TO KNOW ANYTHING ABOUT THEM!
NAGAI DON'T HAVE ANY FEELINGS-- NOT ANY REAL FEELINGS. NAGAI ARE THE WAY THEY ARE...
..BECAUSE THEY ARE SO COMPLETELY EVIL.
ARE THEY?
I'VE SEEN WAR... AND TAKEN MORE THAN MY SHARE AT THE HANDS OF MY OWN ENEMIES, AND THE ALLIANCE'S...
...BUT UNTIL THE BOYS AND I CRASH-LANDED ON TRENWYTH... I DON'T THINK I REALLY KNEW WHAT EVIL WAS.
LEIA... ...MISS KIRO SO...
I HAVE SUCH NIGHTMARES...
...I DREAM OF LOVE, AND PAIN, AND TERROR, ALL INTERMINGLED, AND GONE WRONG...
AND ALL MY NIGHTMARES HAVE ONE NAME... ONE FACE...
AND THE NAME AND THE FACE ARE MINE, ARE THEY NOT?
YOU...
YES, DANI. I.
FLATTERING TO KNOW YOU STILL THINK OF ME, FROM TIME TO TIME.

LEIA... LET ME TAKE CARE OF HIM!

RUN! GET HELP! WARN THE OTHERS!

DANI, I...

YES, PRINCESS, DO.

WE WANT TO BE ALONE TOGETHER. WE HAVE SO MUCH TO CATCH UP ON.

SHE'S...

...RIGHT.

OH, FOR SHAME! AND HERE I THOUGHT YOU MIGHT HAVE MISSED ME, JUST A LITTLE.

I'M SORRY, MY DEAR, BUT I CAN'T LET YOU GO...

AND EVEN IF MY PEOPLE ALLOWED THAT...

I... I WILL NEVER ALLOW YOU TO ESCAPE ME AGAIN!

SWAK

NOW, DEN?

NOW.

NO!

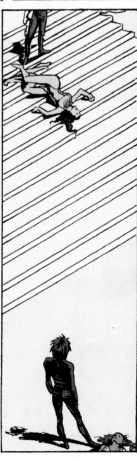

400

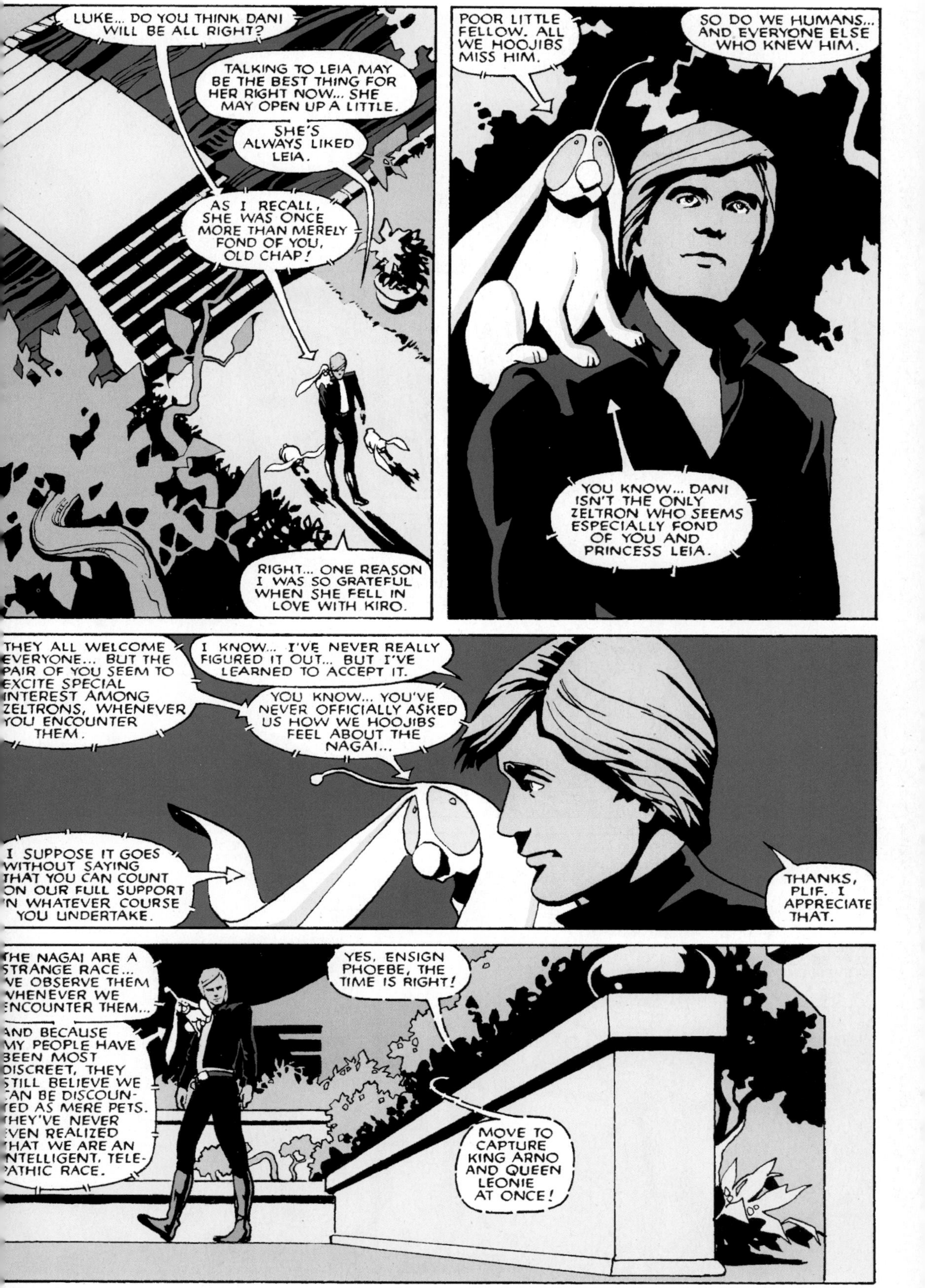

LUKE... DO YOU THINK DANI WILL BE ALL RIGHT?
TALKING TO LEIA MAY BE THE BEST THING FOR HER RIGHT NOW... SHE MAY OPEN UP A LITTLE.
SHE'S ALWAYS LIKED LEIA.
AS I RECALL, SHE WAS ONCE MORE THAN MERELY FOND OF YOU, OLD CHAP!
RIGHT... ONE REASON I WAS SO GRATEFUL WHEN SHE FELL IN LOVE WITH KIRO.
POOR LITTLE FELLOW. ALL WE HOOJIBS MISS HIM.
SO DO WE HUMANS... AND EVERYONE ELSE WHO KNEW HIM.
YOU KNOW... DANI ISN'T THE ONLY ZELTRON WHO SEEMS ESPECIALLY FOND OF YOU AND PRINCESS LEIA.
THEY ALL WELCOME EVERYONE... BUT THE PAIR OF YOU SEEM TO EXCITE SPECIAL INTEREST AMONG ZELTRONS, WHENEVER YOU ENCOUNTER THEM.
I KNOW... I'VE NEVER REALLY FIGURED IT OUT... BUT I'VE LEARNED TO ACCEPT IT.
YOU KNOW... YOU'VE NEVER OFFICIALLY ASKED US HOW WE HOOJIBS FEEL ABOUT THE NAGAI...
I SUPPOSE IT GOES WITHOUT SAYING THAT YOU CAN COUNT ON OUR FULL SUPPORT IN WHATEVER COURSE YOU UNDERTAKE.
THANKS, PLIF. I APPRECIATE THAT.
THE NAGAI ARE A STRANGE RACE... WE OBSERVE THEM WHENEVER WE ENCOUNTER THEM...
AND BECAUSE MY PEOPLE HAVE BEEN MOST DISCREET, THEY STILL BELIEVE WE CAN BE DISCOUNTED AS MERE PETS. THEY'VE NEVER EVEN REALIZED THAT WE ARE AN INTELLIGENT, TELEPATHIC RACE.
YES, ENSIGN PHOEBE, THE TIME IS RIGHT!
MOVE TO CAPTURE KING ARNO AND QUEEN LEONIE AT ONCE!

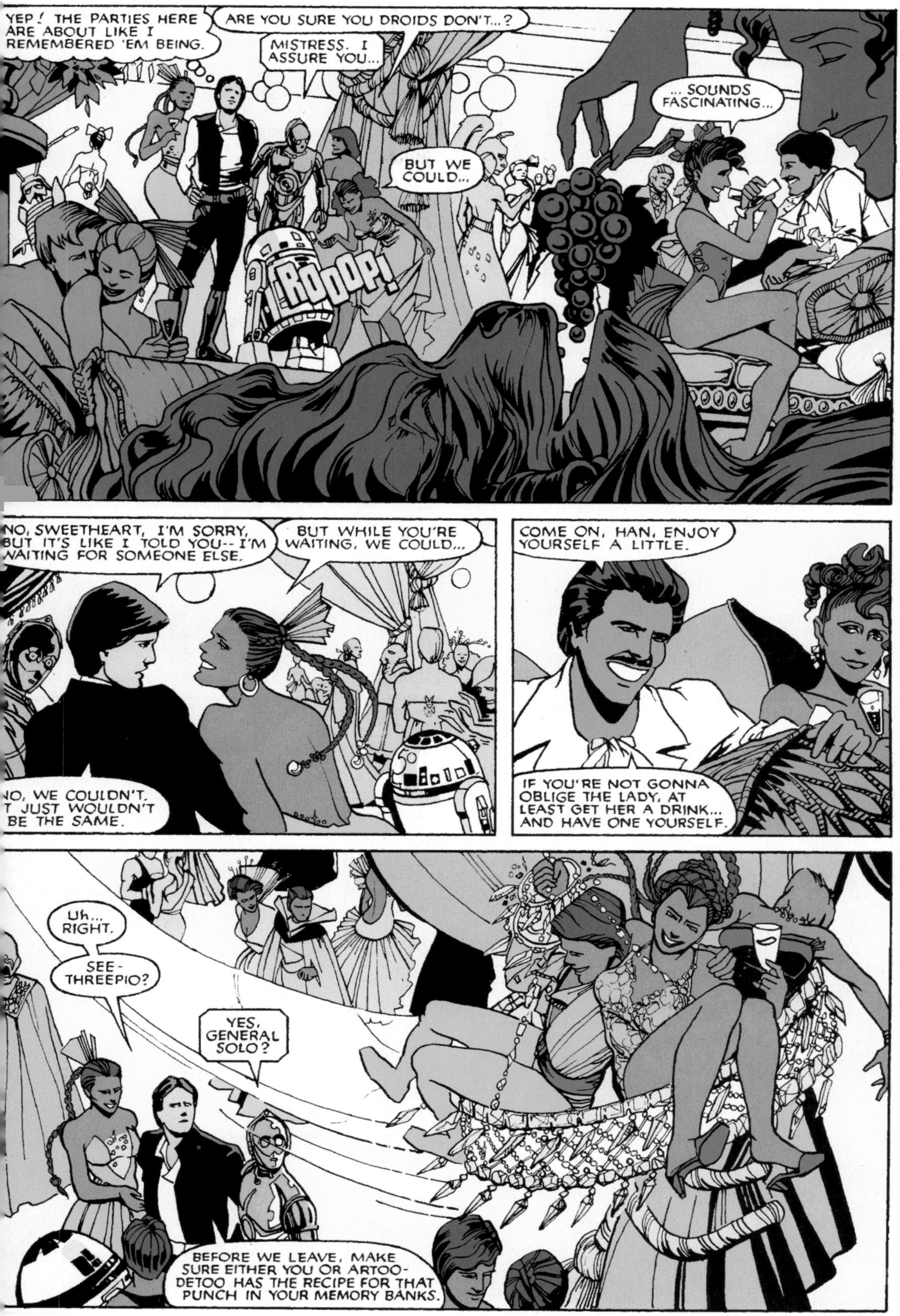
YEP! THE PARTIES HERE ARE ABOUT LIKE I REMEMBERED 'EM BEING.
ARE YOU SURE YOU DROIDS DON'T...?
MISTRESS. I ASSURE YOU...
BUT WE COULD...
... SOUNDS FASCINATING...
ROOOP!
NO, SWEETHEART, I'M SORRY, BUT IT'S LIKE I TOLD YOU-- I'M WAITING FOR SOMEONE ELSE.
BUT WHILE YOU'RE WAITING, WE COULD...
NO, WE COULDN'T. IT JUST WOULDN'T BE THE SAME.
COME ON, HAN, ENJOY YOURSELF A LITTLE.
IF YOU'RE NOT GONNA OBLIGE THE LADY, AT LEAST GET HER A DRINK... AND HAVE ONE YOURSELF.
Uh... RIGHT.
SEE-THREEPIO?
YES, GENERAL SOLO?
BEFORE WE LEAVE, MAKE SURE EITHER YOU OR ARTOO-DETOO HAS THE RECIPE FOR THAT PUNCH IN YOUR MEMORY BANKS.

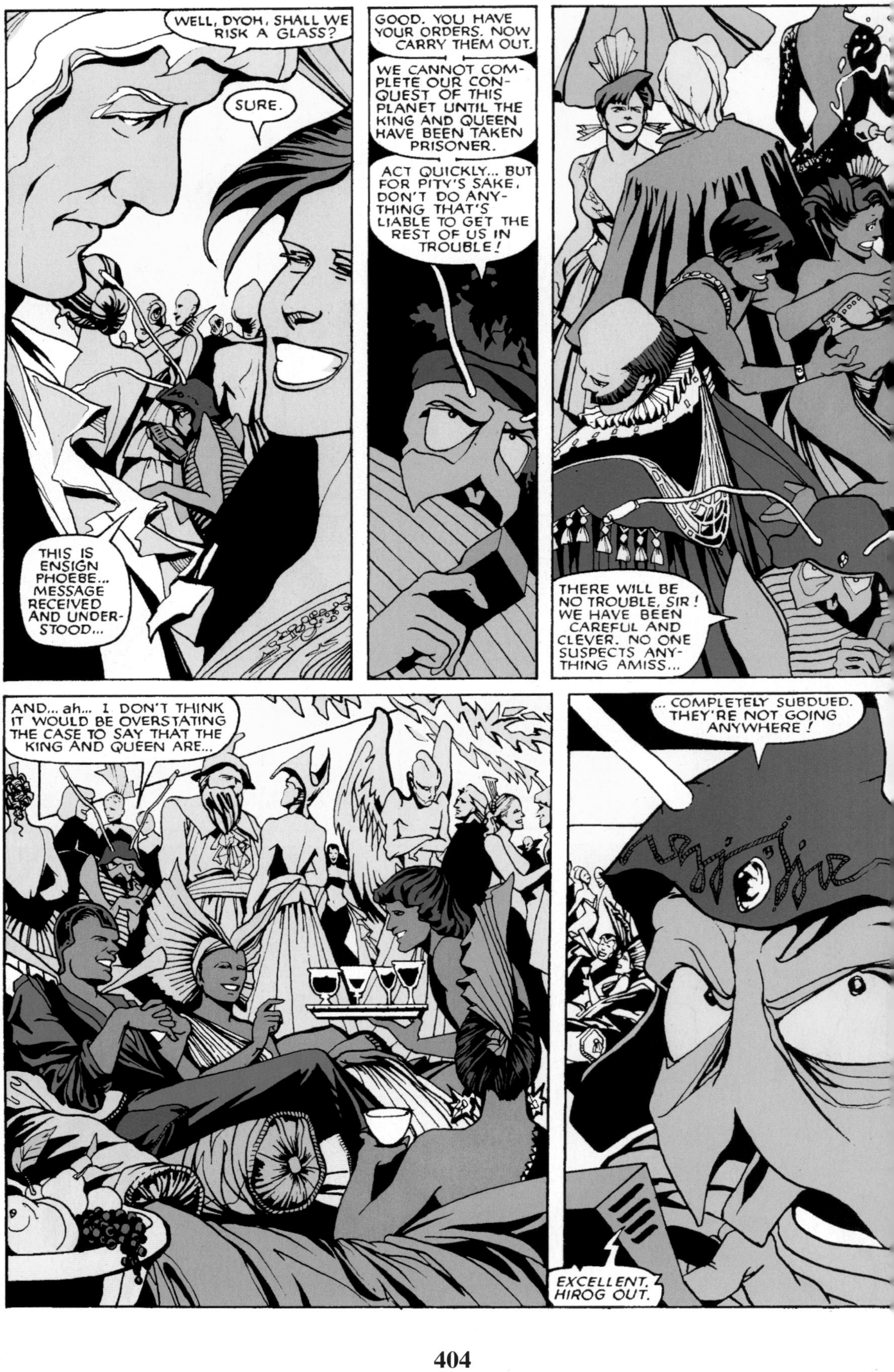
WELL, DYOH, SHALL WE RISK A GLASS?
SURE.
THIS IS ENSIGN PHOEBE... MESSAGE RECEIVED AND UNDERSTOOD...
GOOD. YOU HAVE YOUR ORDERS. NOW CARRY THEM OUT.
WE CANNOT COMPLETE OUR CONQUEST OF THIS PLANET UNTIL THE KING AND QUEEN HAVE BEEN TAKEN PRISONER.
ACT QUICKLY... BUT FOR PITY'S SAKE, DON'T DO ANYTHING THAT'S LIABLE TO GET THE REST OF US IN TROUBLE!
THERE WILL BE NO TROUBLE, SIR! WE HAVE BEEN CAREFUL AND CLEVER. NO ONE SUSPECTS ANYTHING AMISS...
AND... ah... I DON'T THINK IT WOULD BE OVERSTATING THE CASE TO SAY THAT THE KING AND QUEEN ARE...
...COMPLETELY SUBDUED. THEY'RE NOT GOING ANYWHERE!
EXCELLENT. HIROG OUT.

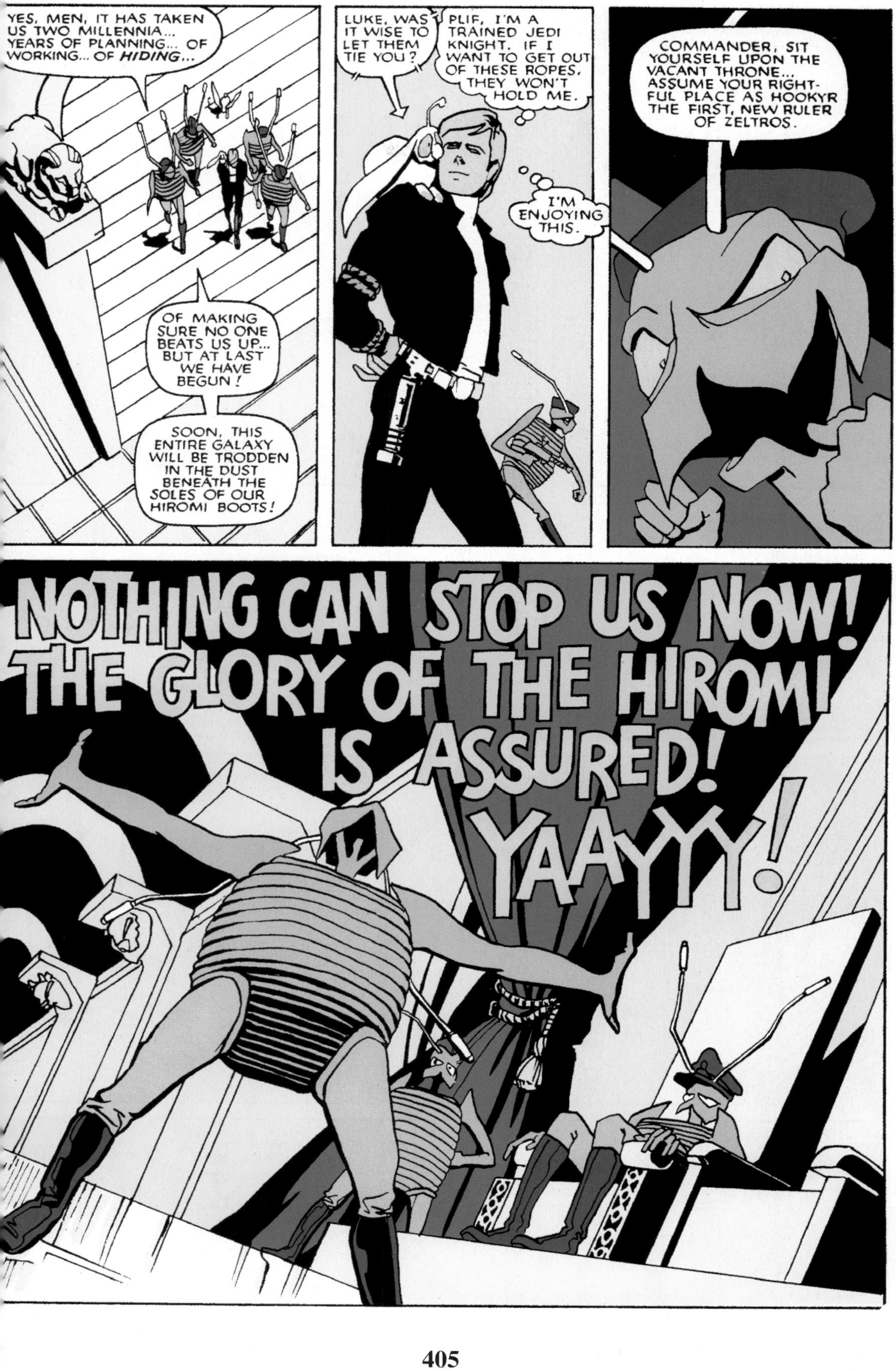
YES, MEN, IT HAS TAKEN US TWO MILLENNIA... YEARS OF PLANNING... OF WORKING... OF HIDING...
OF MAKING SURE NO ONE BEATS US UP... BUT AT LAST WE HAVE BEGUN!
SOON, THIS ENTIRE GALAXY WILL BE TRODDEN IN THE DUST BENEATH THE SOLES OF OUR HIROMI BOOTS!
LUKE, WAS IT WISE TO LET THEM TIE YOU?
PLIF, I'M A TRAINED JEDI KNIGHT. IF I WANT TO GET OUT OF THESE ROPES, THEY WON'T HOLD ME.
I'M ENJOYING THIS.
COMMANDER, SIT YOURSELF UPON THE VACANT THRONE... ASSUME YOUR RIGHTFUL PLACE AS HOOKYR THE FIRST, NEW RULER OF ZELTROS.
NOTHING CAN STOP US NOW! THE GLORY OF THE HIROMI IS ASSURED!
YAAYYY!

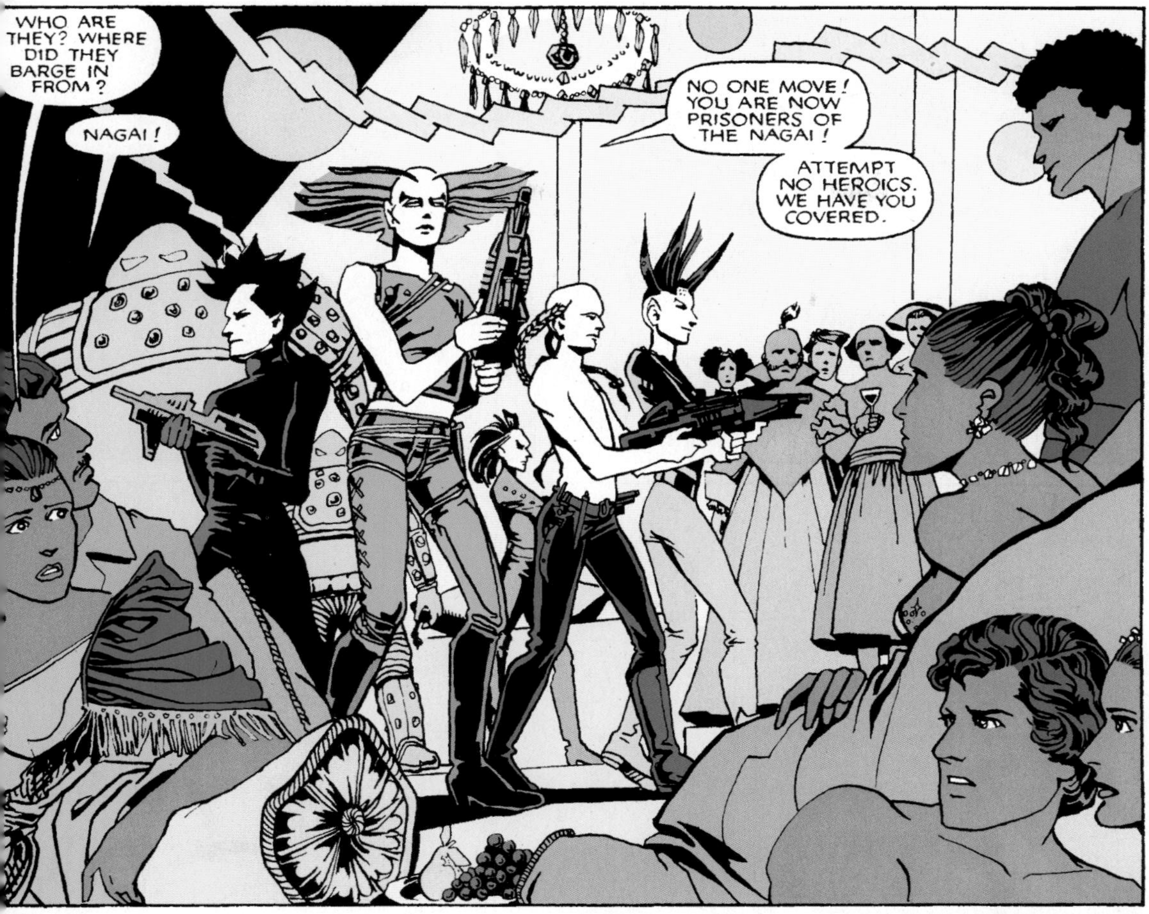
WHO ARE THEY? WHERE DID THEY BARGE IN FROM?
NAGAI!
NO ONE MOVE! YOU ARE NOW PRISONERS OF THE NAGAI!
ATTEMPT NO HEROICS. WE HAVE YOU COVERED.

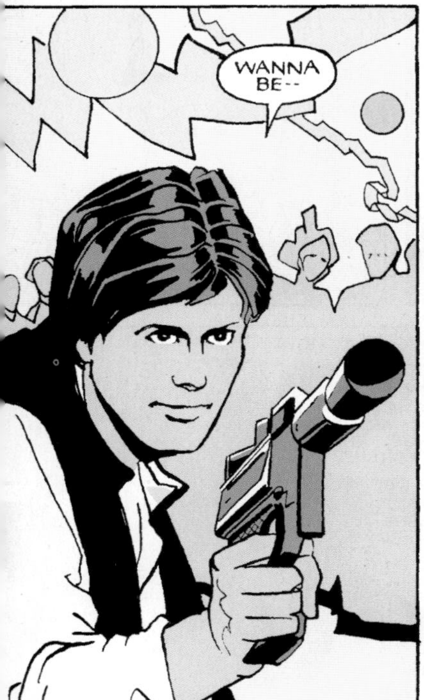
WANNA BE--

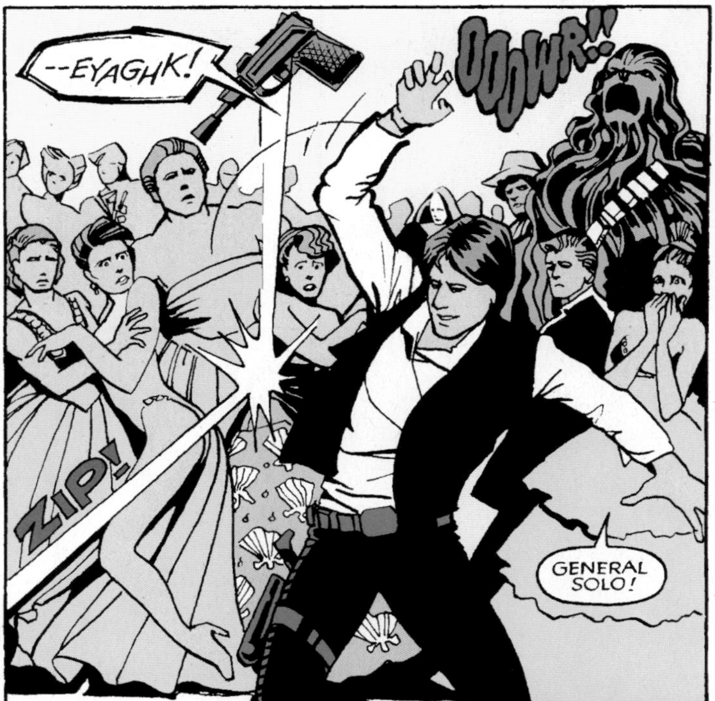
--EYAGHK!
OOOWR!!
ZIP!
GENERAL SOLO!

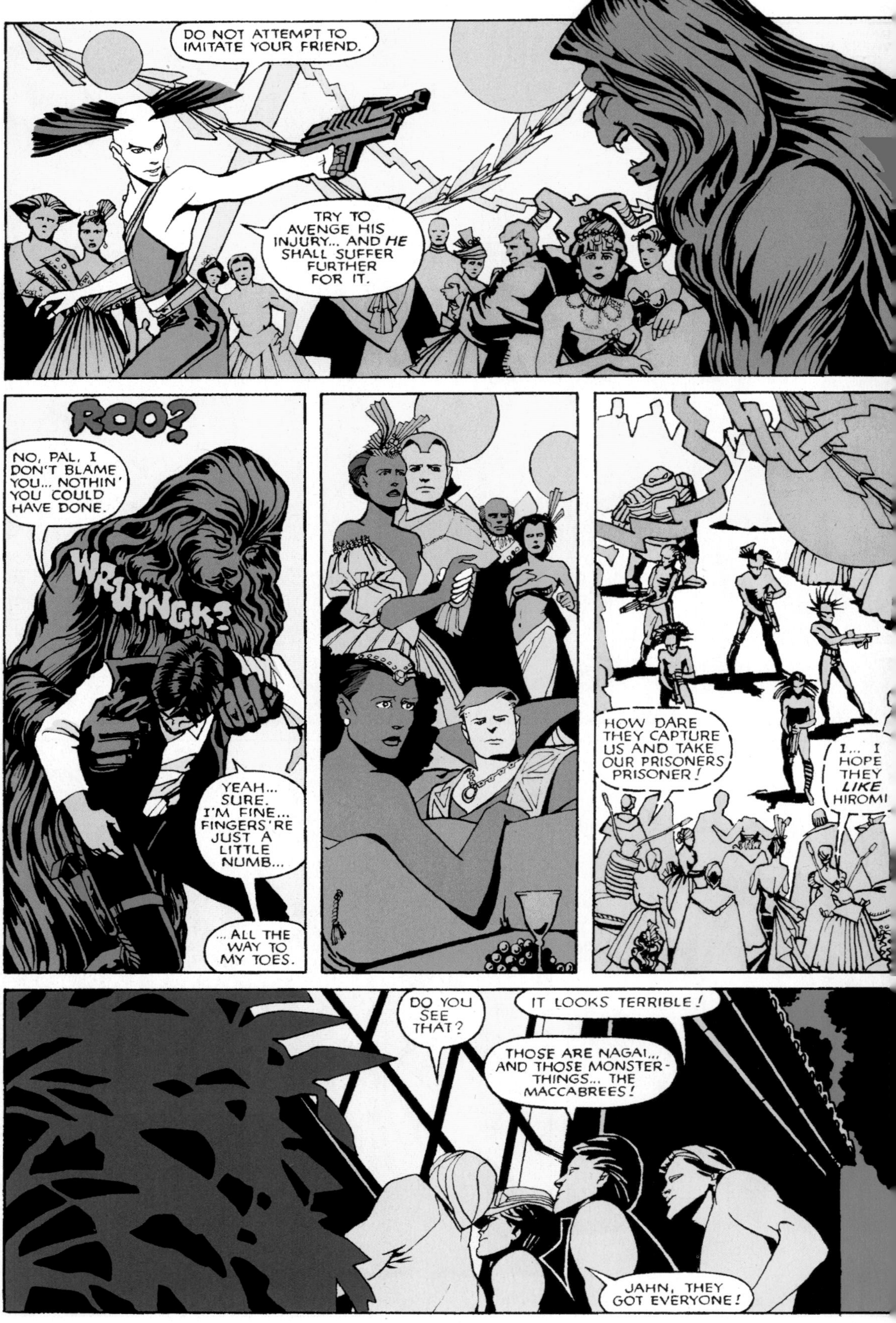
DO NOT ATTEMPT TO IMITATE YOUR FRIEND.
TRY TO AVENGE HIS INJURY... AND HE SHALL SUFFER FURTHER FOR IT.
ROO?
NO, PAL, I DON'T BLAME YOU... NOTHIN' YOU COULD HAVE DONE.
WRUYNGK?
YEAH... SURE. I'M FINE... FINGERS'RE JUST A LITTLE NUMB...
...ALL THE WAY TO MY TOES.
HOW DARE THEY CAPTURE US AND TAKE OUR PRISONERS PRISONER!
I... I HOPE THEY LIKE HIROMI
DO YOU SEE THAT?
IT LOOKS TERRIBLE!
THOSE ARE NAGAI... AND THOSE MONSTER-THINGS... THE MACCABREES!
JAHN, THEY GOT EVERYONE!

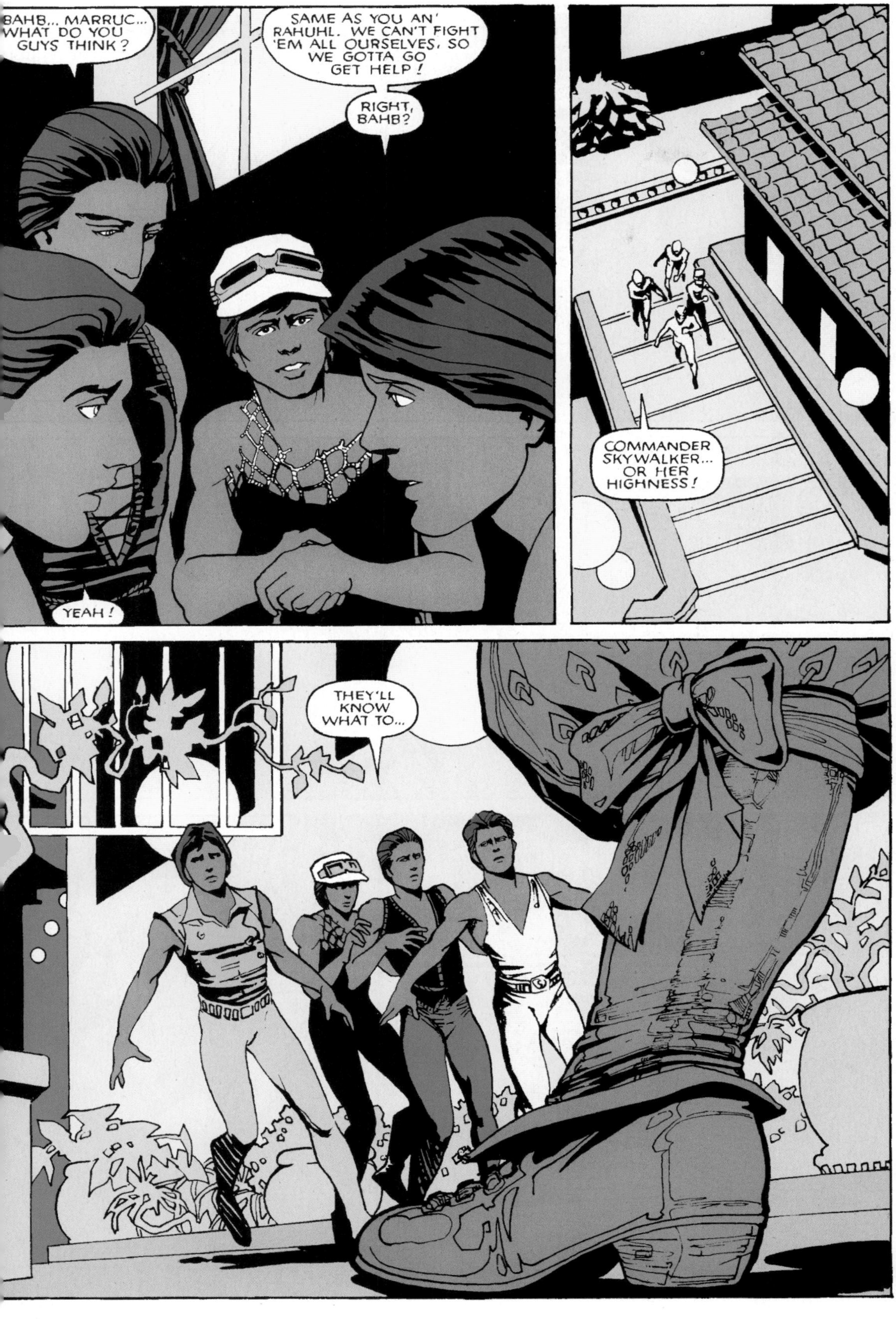
BAHB... MARRUC... WHAT DO YOU GUYS THINK?
SAME AS YOU AN' RAHUHL. WE CAN'T FIGHT 'EM ALL OURSELVES, SO WE GOTTA GO GET HELP!
RIGHT, BAHB?
YEAH!
COMMANDER SKYWALKER... OR HER HIGHNESS!
THEY'LL KNOW WHAT TO...

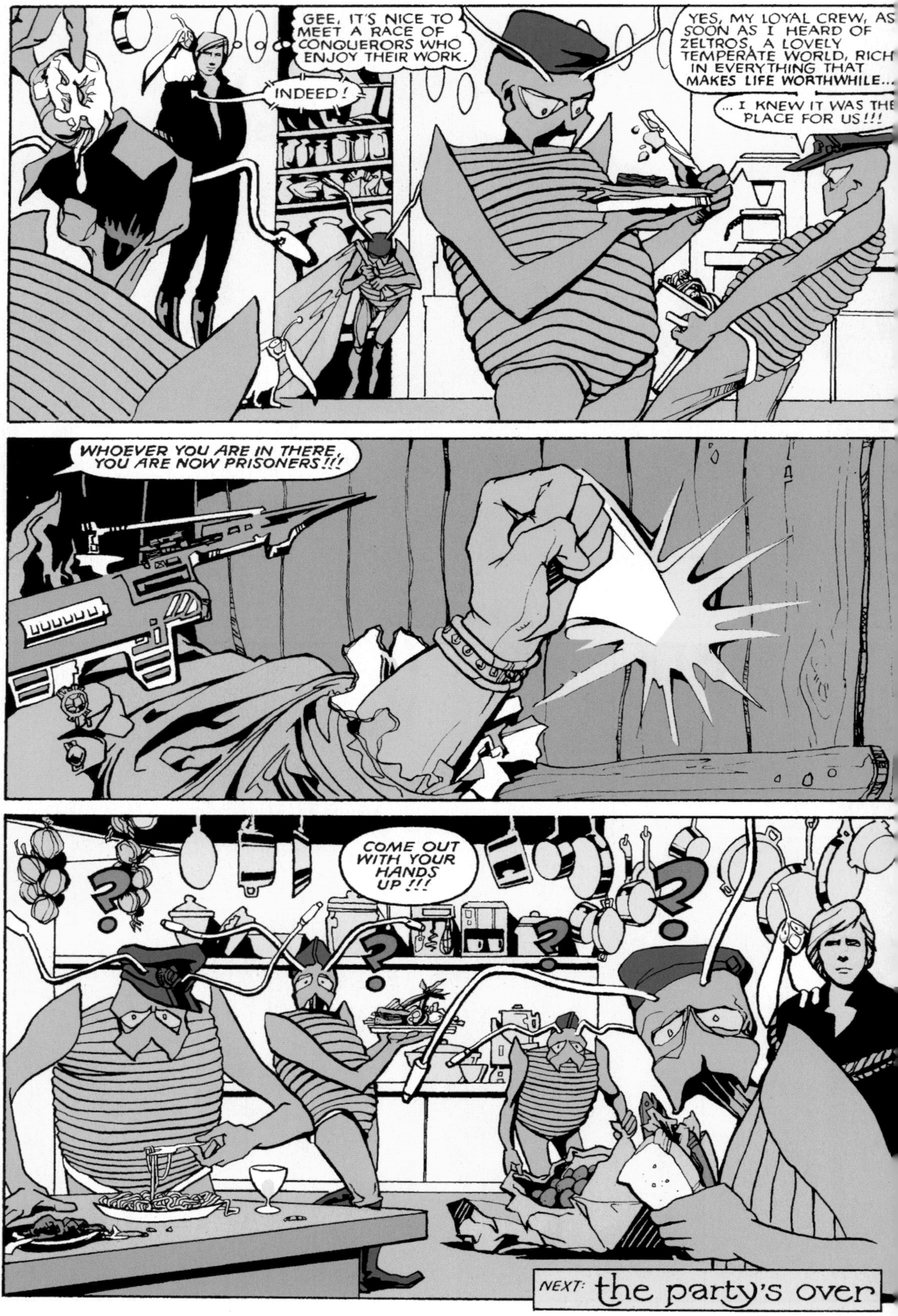
GEE, IT'S NICE TO MEET A RACE OF CONQUERORS WHO ENJOY THEIR WORK.
INDEED!
YES, MY LOYAL CREW, AS SOON AS I HEARD OF ZELTROS, A LOVELY TEMPERATE WORLD, RICH IN EVERYTHING THAT MAKES LIFE WORTHWHILE...
... I KNEW IT WAS THE PLACE FOR US!!!
WHOEVER YOU ARE IN THERE, YOU ARE NOW PRISONERS!!!
COME OUT WITH YOUR HANDS UP!!!
NEXT: the party's over

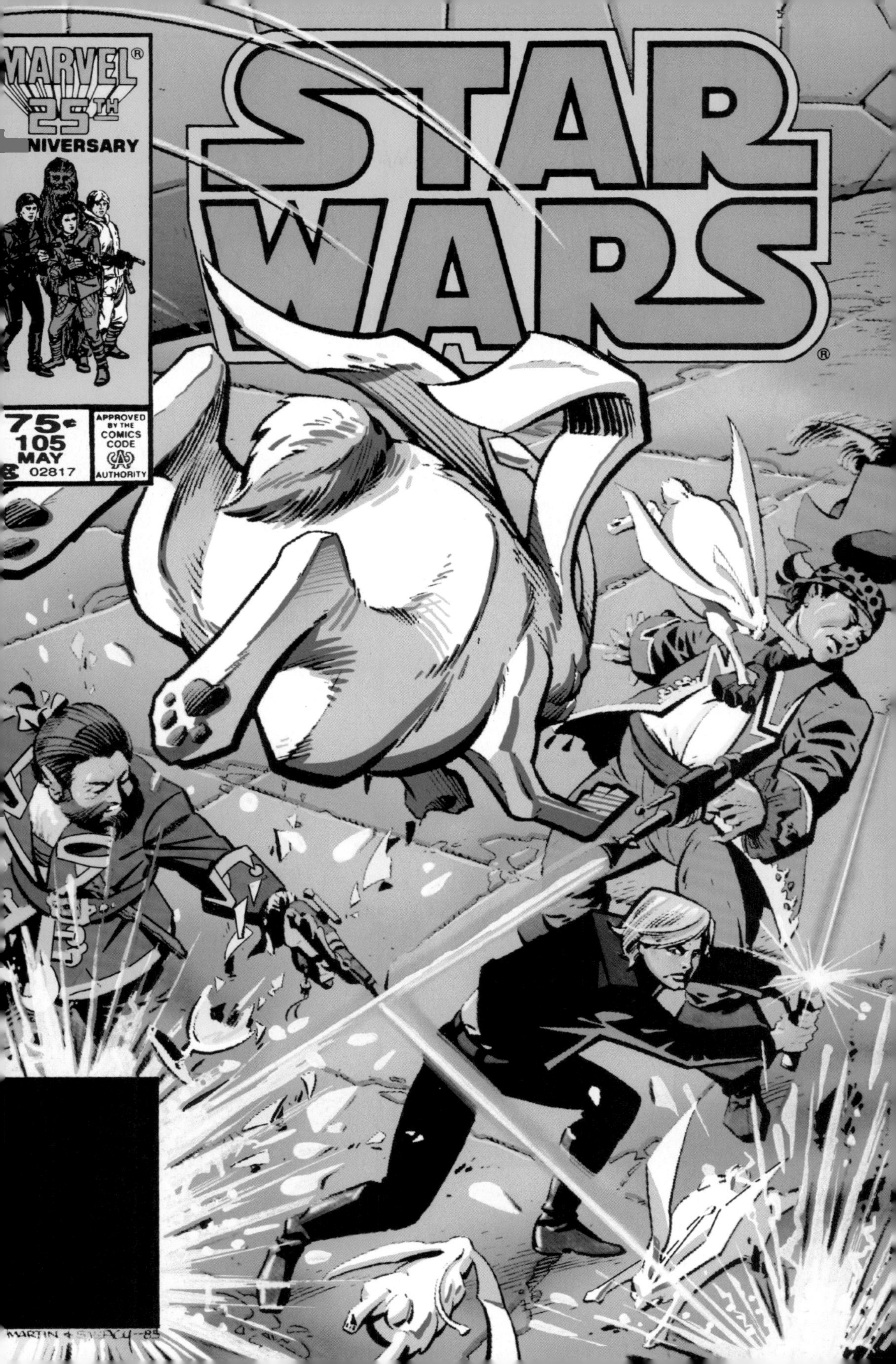
MARVEL 25TH ANNIVERSARY
75¢
105
MAY
02817
APPROVED BY THE COMICS CODE AUTHORITY
STAR WARS

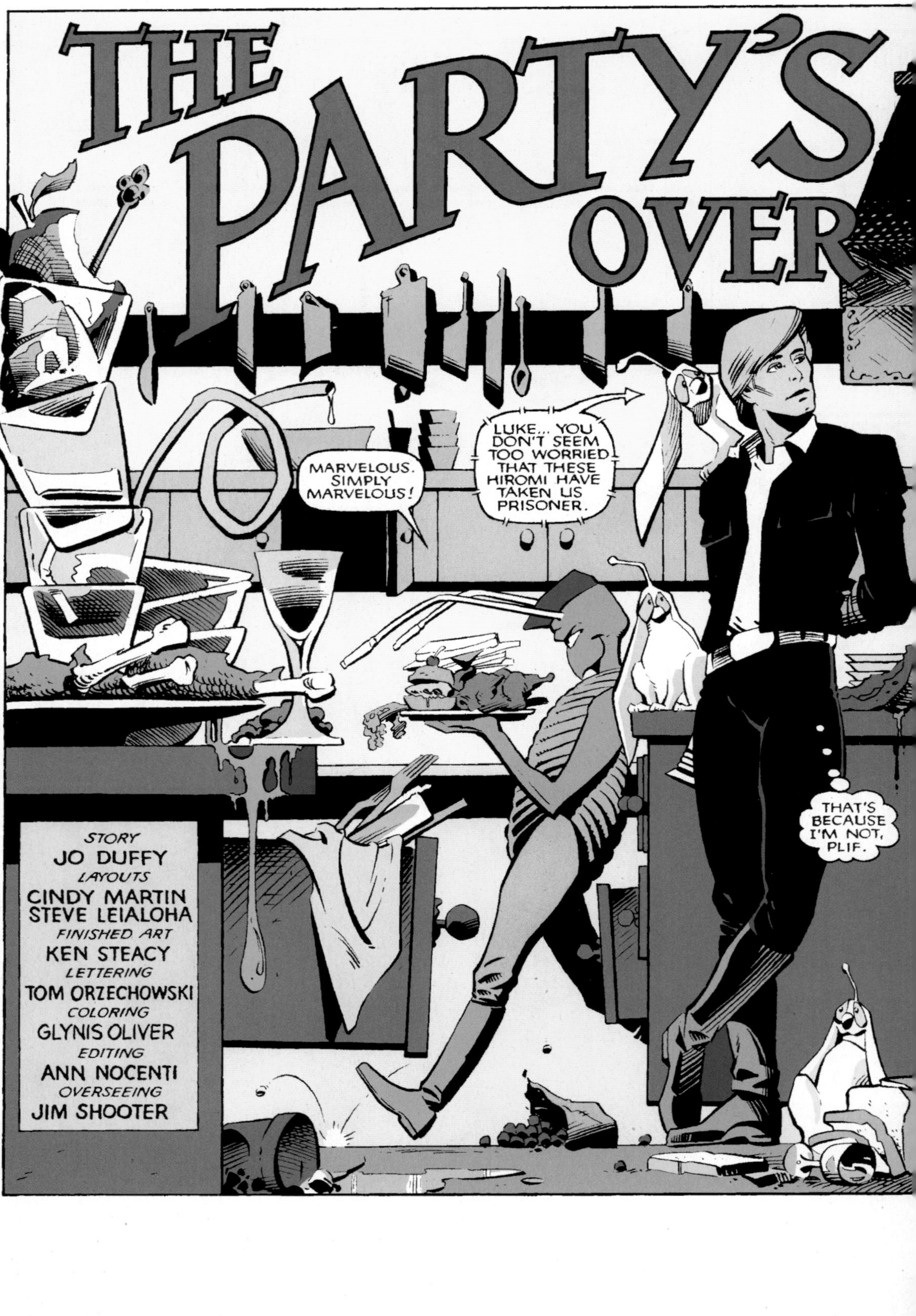
THE PARTY'S OVER
MARVELOUS. SIMPLY MARVELOUS!
LUKE... YOU DON'T SEEM TOO WORRIED THAT THESE HIROMI HAVE TAKEN US PRISONER.
THAT'S BECAUSE I'M NOT, PLIF.
STORY
JO DUFFY
LAYOUTS
CINDY MARTIN
STEVE LEIALOHA
FINISHED ART
KEN STEACY
LETTERING
TOM ORZECHOWSKI
COLORING
GLYNIS OLIVER
EDITING
ANN NOCENTI
OVERSEEING
JIM SHOOTER

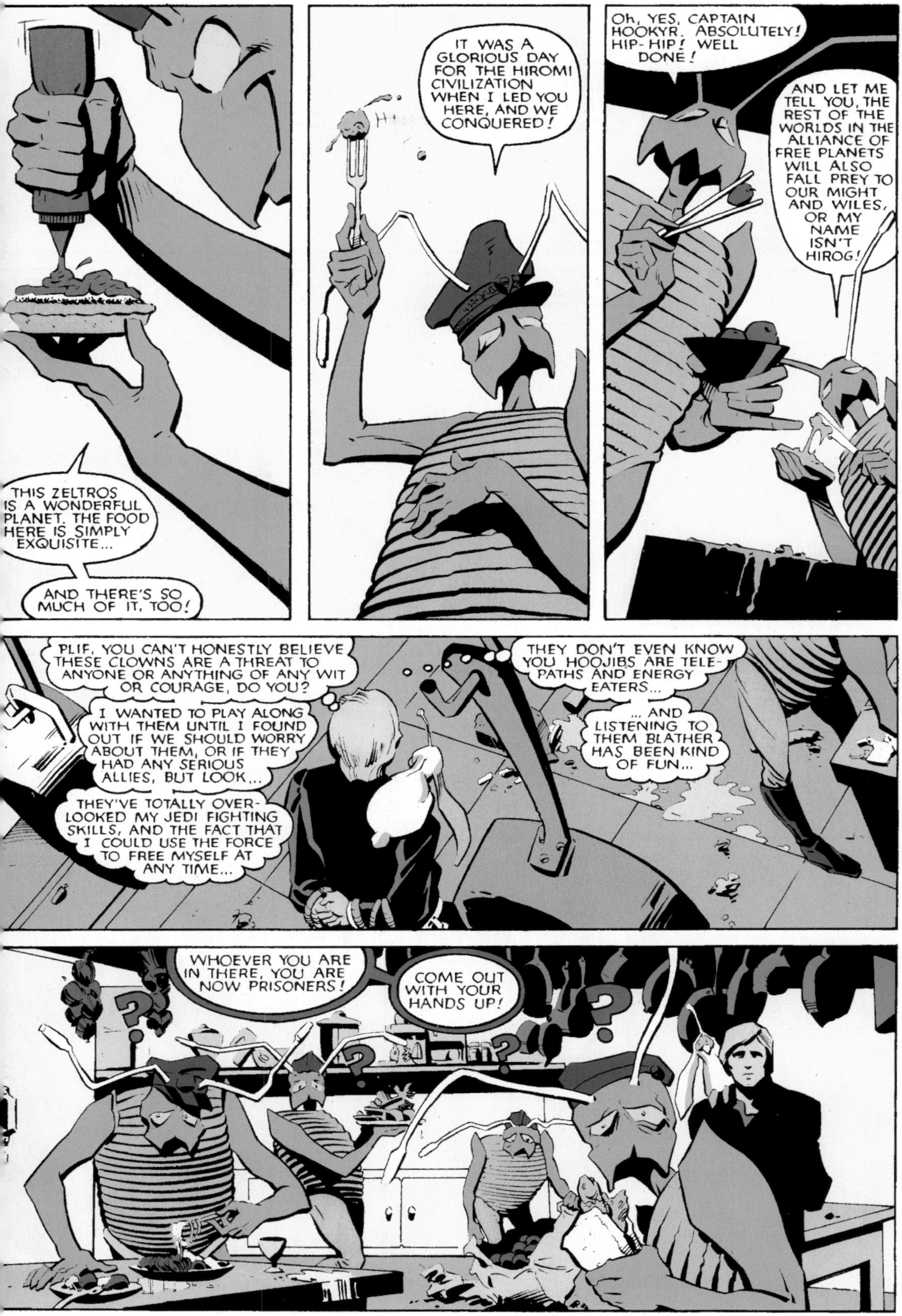
THIS ZELTROS IS A WONDERFUL PLANET. THE FOOD HERE IS SIMPLY EXQUISITE...
AND THERE'S SO MUCH OF IT, TOO!
IT WAS A GLORIOUS DAY FOR THE HIROMI CIVILIZATION WHEN I LED YOU HERE, AND WE CONQUERED!
Oh, YES, CAPTAIN HOOKYR. ABSOLUTELY! HIP-HIP! WELL DONE!
AND LET ME TELL YOU, THE REST OF THE WORLDS IN THE ALLIANCE OF FREE PLANETS WILL ALSO FALL PREY TO OUR MIGHT AND WILES, OR MY NAME ISN'T HIROG!
PLIF, YOU CAN'T HONESTLY BELIEVE THESE CLOWNS ARE A THREAT TO ANYONE OR ANYTHING OF ANY WIT OR COURAGE, DO YOU?
I WANTED TO PLAY ALONG WITH THEM UNTIL I FOUND OUT IF WE SHOULD WORRY ABOUT THEM, OR IF THEY HAD ANY SERIOUS ALLIES, BUT LOOK...
THEY'VE TOTALLY OVER-LOOKED MY JEDI FIGHTING SKILLS, AND THE FACT THAT I COULD USE THE FORCE TO FREE MYSELF AT ANY TIME...
THEY DON'T EVEN KNOW YOU HOOJIBS ARE TELE-PATHS AND ENERGY EATERS...
... AND LISTENING TO THEM BLATHER HAS BEEN KIND OF FUN...
WHOEVER YOU ARE IN THERE, YOU ARE NOW PRISONERS!
COME OUT WITH YOUR HANDS UP!

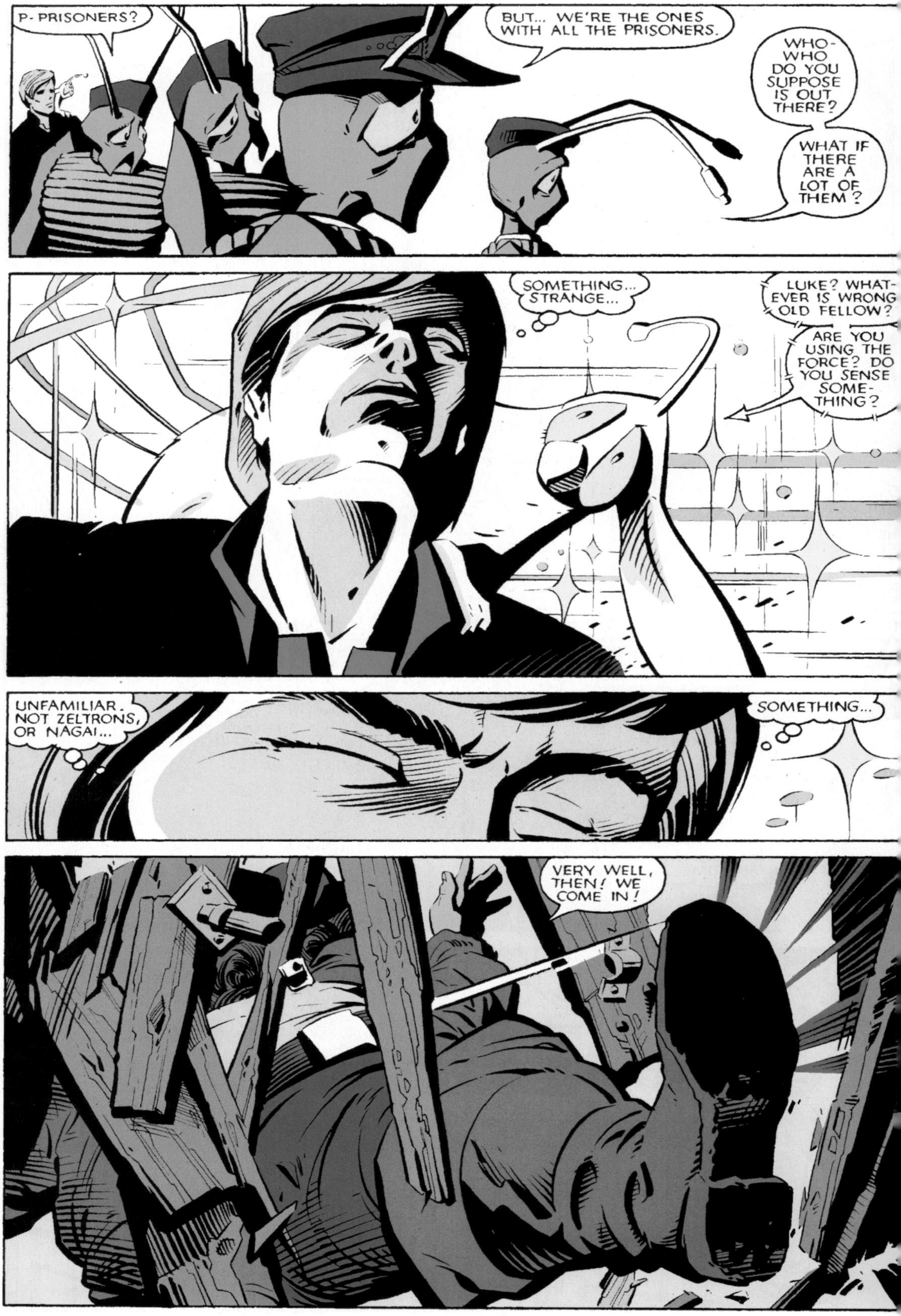
P-PRISONERS?
BUT... WE'RE THE ONES WITH ALL THE PRISONERS.
WHO-WHO DO YOU SUPPOSE IS OUT THERE?
WHAT IF THERE ARE A LOT OF THEM?
SOMETHING... STRANGE...
LUKE? WHAT-EVER IS WRONG OLD FELLOW?
ARE YOU USING THE FORCE? DO YOU SENSE SOME-THING?
UNFAMILIAR. NOT ZELTRONS, OR NAGAI...
SOMETHING...
VERY WELL, THEN! WE COME IN!

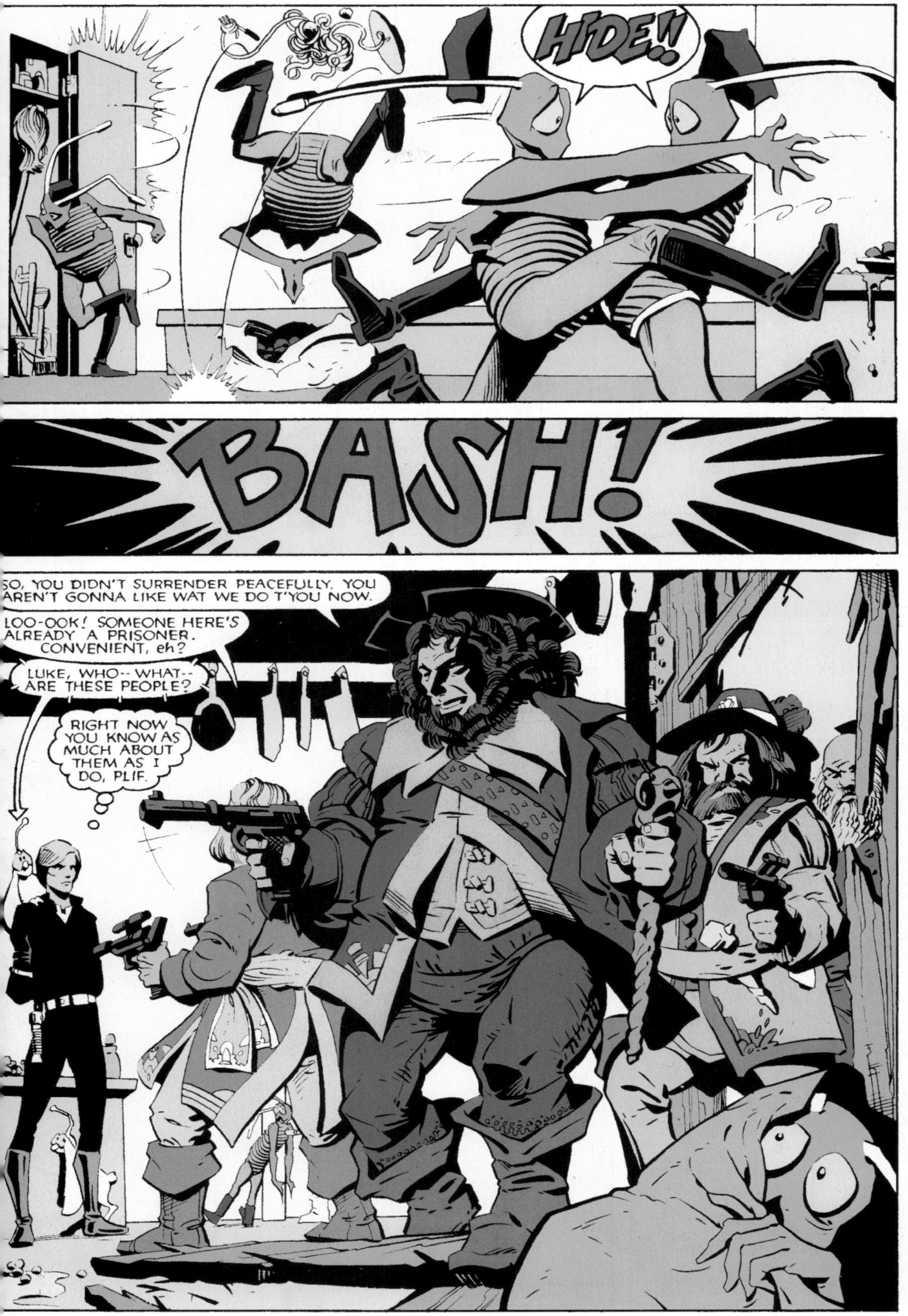

HI'DE!!
BASH!
SO, YOU DIDN'T SURRENDER PEACEFULLY. YOU AREN'T GONNA LIKE WAT WE DO T'YOU NOW.
LOO-OOK! SOMEONE HERE'S ALREADY A PRISONER. CONVENIENT, eh?
LUKE, WHO-- WHAT-- ARE THESE PEOPLE?
RIGHT NOW YOU KNOW AS MUCH ABOUT THEM AS I DO, PLIF.

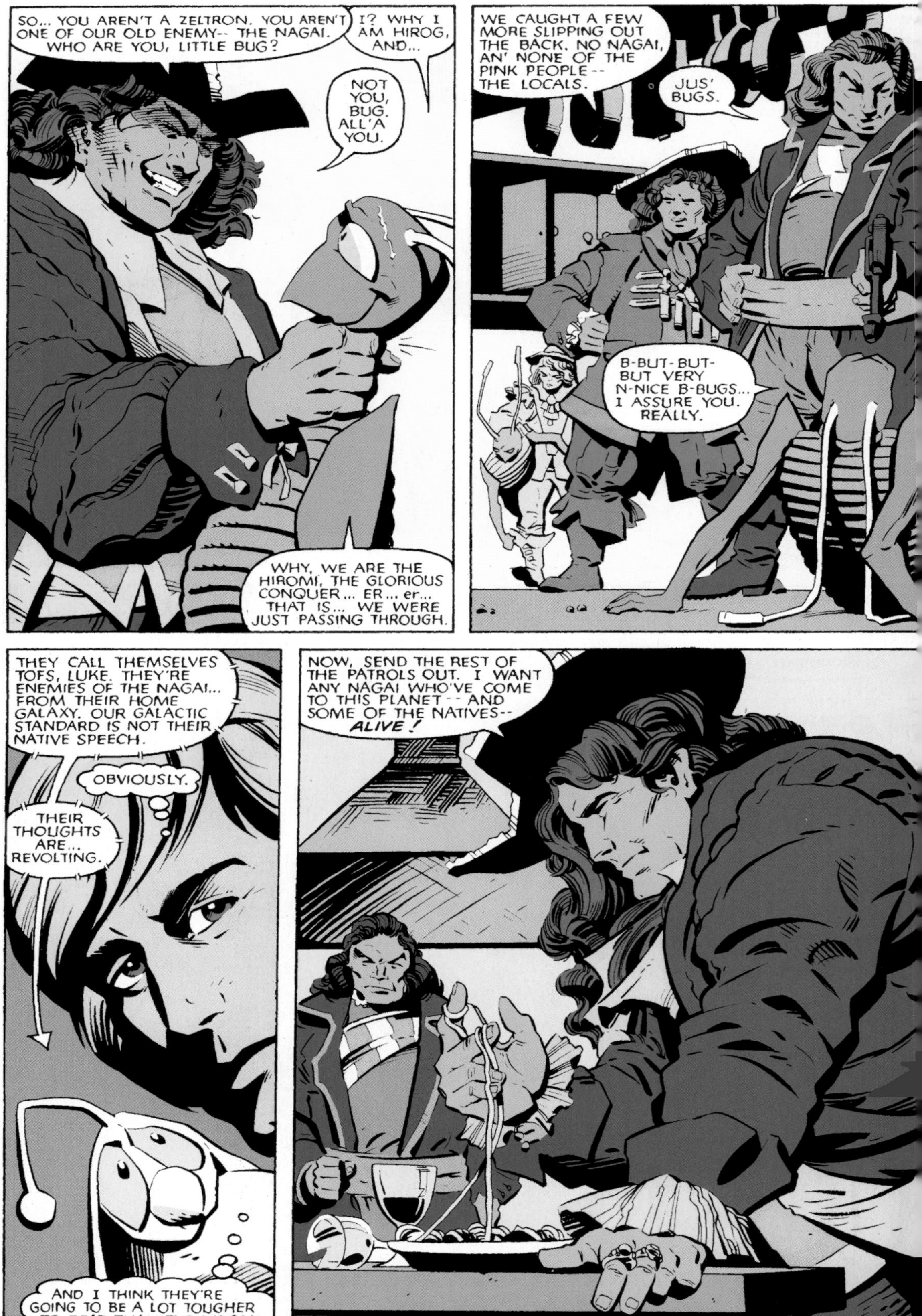
SO... YOU AREN'T A ZELTRON. YOU AREN'T ONE OF OUR OLD ENEMY-- THE NAGAI. WHO ARE YOU, LITTLE BUG?
I? WHY I AM HIROG, AND...
NOT YOU, BUG. ALL'A YOU.
WHY, WE ARE THE HIROMI, THE GLORIOUS CONQUER... ER... er... THAT IS... WE WERE JUST PASSING THROUGH.
WE CAUGHT A FEW MORE SLIPPING OUT THE BACK. NO NAGAI, AN' NONE OF THE PINK PEOPLE-- THE LOCALS.
JUS' BUGS.
B-BUT-BUT-BUT VERY N-NICE B-BUGS... I ASSURE YOU. REALLY.
THEY CALL THEMSELVES TOFS, LUKE. THEY'RE ENEMIES OF THE NAGAI... FROM THEIR HOME GALAXY. OUR GALACTIC STANDARD IS NOT THEIR NATIVE SPEECH.
OBVIOUSLY.
THEIR THOUGHTS ARE... REVOLTING.
AND I THINK THEY'RE GOING TO BE A LOT TOUGHER TO BEAT THAN THE HIROMI.
NOW, SEND THE REST OF THE PATROLS OUT. I WANT ANY NAGAI WHO'VE COME TO THIS PLANET-- AND SOME OF THE NATIVES-- ALIVE!

WH-WHO ARE THESE PEOPLE? WHY ARE THEY HERE?

THEY'RE CALLED THE NAGAI, SWEETHEART... AN' THE BIG CYBORGS ARE THEIR HEAVYWEIGHTS-- THE MACCABREE.

AN' YOU CAN BET THEY AREN'T HERE TO JOIN THE PARTY.

YOU SOUND PRETTY DISGUSTED, HAN.

HROWL!

YEAH, LANDO, LIKE CHEWIE SAID, THE SITUATION IS DISGUSTING.

WE COME HERE TO ZELTROS TO CONVINCE THEM TO JOIN THE ALLIANCE OF FREE PLANETS' DEFENSE AGAINST THE NAGAI...

YEAH... AND THE KING AND QUEEN GAVE US SUCH A BIG WELCOME... THAT A NAGAI INVASION RIGHT HERE CATCHES US FLAT-FOOTED.

HOW'S YOUR WOUNDED WRIST?

I'LL LIVE. IF I CAN GET MY HAND AROUND A BLASTER, I THINK I CAN FIRE IT.

BUT YOU WON'T GET YOUR HAND AROUND A BLASTER, ALIEN. WE NAGAI KNOW YOUR REPUTATION.

WE HAVE ALREADY DISPATCHED ANOTHER SQUADRON TO ROUND UP ANY OTHER OF YOUR ALLIES WHO MAY BE ON THIS PLANET...

IN FACT, IT'S TIME TO COMMUNICATE...

DEN SIVA? LIEUTENANT SIVA, ACKNOWLEDGE, PLEASE.

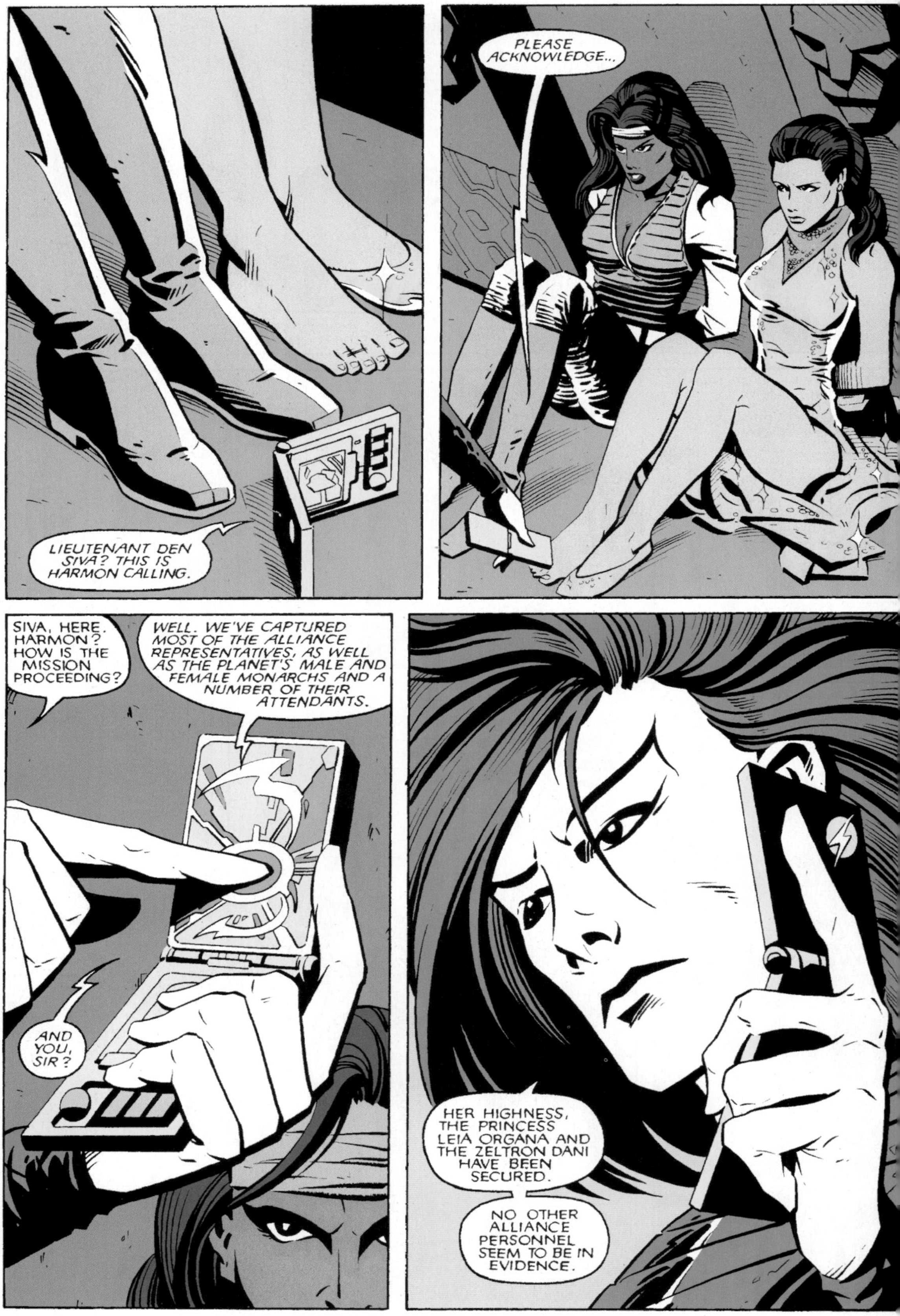
LIEUTENANT DEN SIVA? THIS IS HARMON CALLING.
PLEASE ACKNOWLEDGE...
SIVA, HERE. HARMON? HOW IS THE MISSION PROCEEDING?
WELL. WE'VE CAPTURED MOST OF THE ALLIANCE REPRESENTATIVES, AS WELL AS THE PLANET'S MALE AND FEMALE MONARCHS AND A NUMBER OF THEIR ATTENDANTS.
AND YOU, SIR?
HER HIGHNESS, THE PRINCESS LEIA ORGANA AND THE ZELTRON DANI HAVE BEEN SECURED.
NO OTHER ALLIANCE PERSONNEL SEEM TO BE IN EVIDENCE.

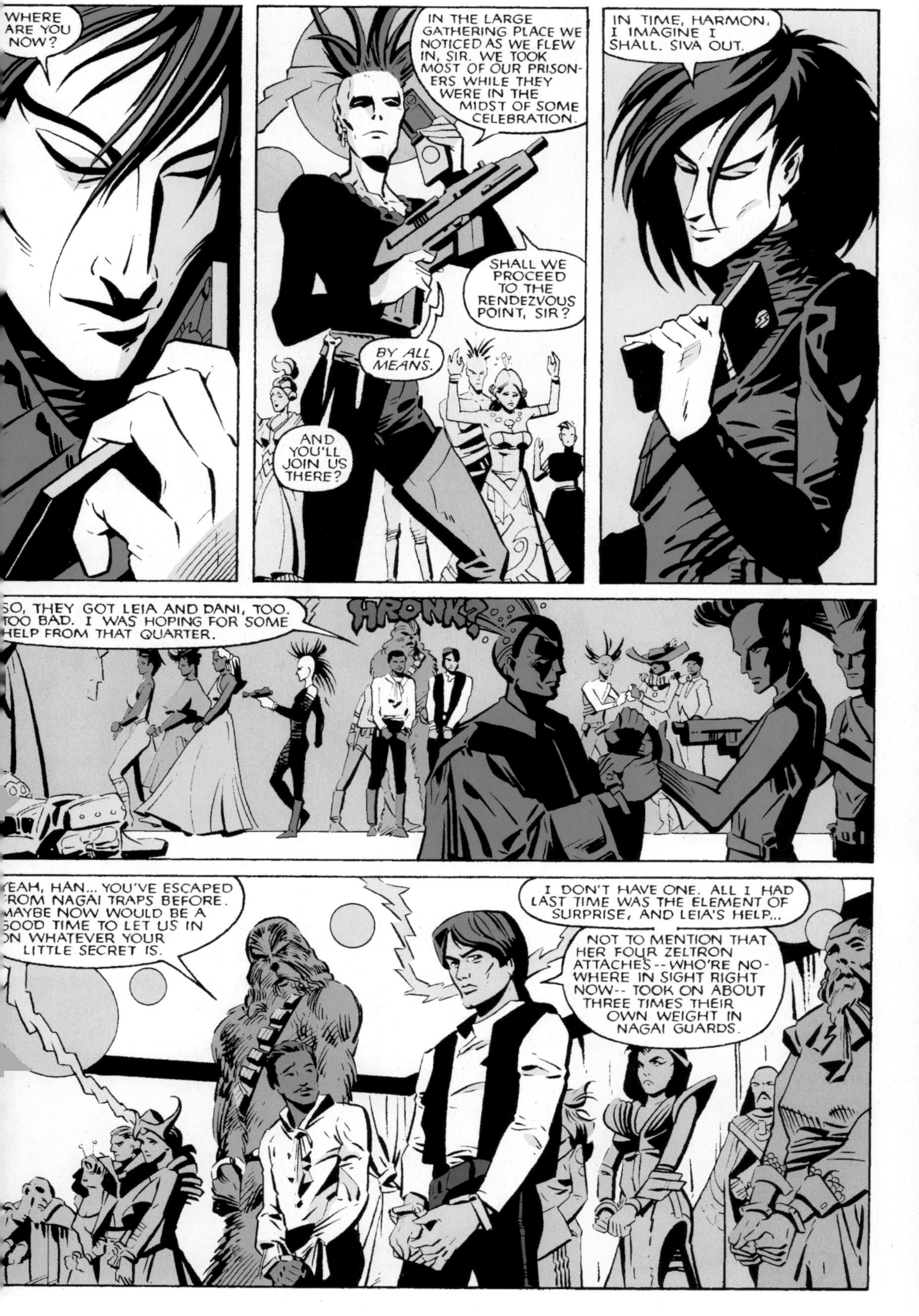
WHERE ARE YOU NOW?
IN THE LARGE GATHERING PLACE WE NOTICED AS WE FLEW IN, SIR. WE TOOK MOST OF OUR PRISONERS WHILE THEY WERE IN THE MIDST OF SOME CELEBRATION.
SHALL WE PROCEED TO THE RENDEZVOUS POINT, SIR?
BY ALL MEANS.
AND YOU'LL JOIN US THERE?
IN TIME, HARMON, I IMAGINE I SHALL. SIVA OUT.
SO, THEY GOT LEIA AND DANI, TOO. TOO BAD. I WAS HOPING FOR SOME HELP FROM THAT QUARTER.
HRONK?
YEAH, HAN... YOU'VE ESCAPED FROM NAGAI TRAPS BEFORE. MAYBE NOW WOULD BE A GOOD TIME TO LET US IN ON WHATEVER YOUR LITTLE SECRET IS.
I DON'T HAVE ONE. ALL I HAD LAST TIME WAS THE ELEMENT OF SURPRISE, AND LEIA'S HELP...
NOT TO MENTION THAT HER FOUR ZELTRON ATTACHÉS--WHO'RE NO-WHERE IN SIGHT RIGHT NOW-- TOOK ON ABOUT THREE TIMES THEIR OWN WEIGHT IN NAGAI GUARDS.

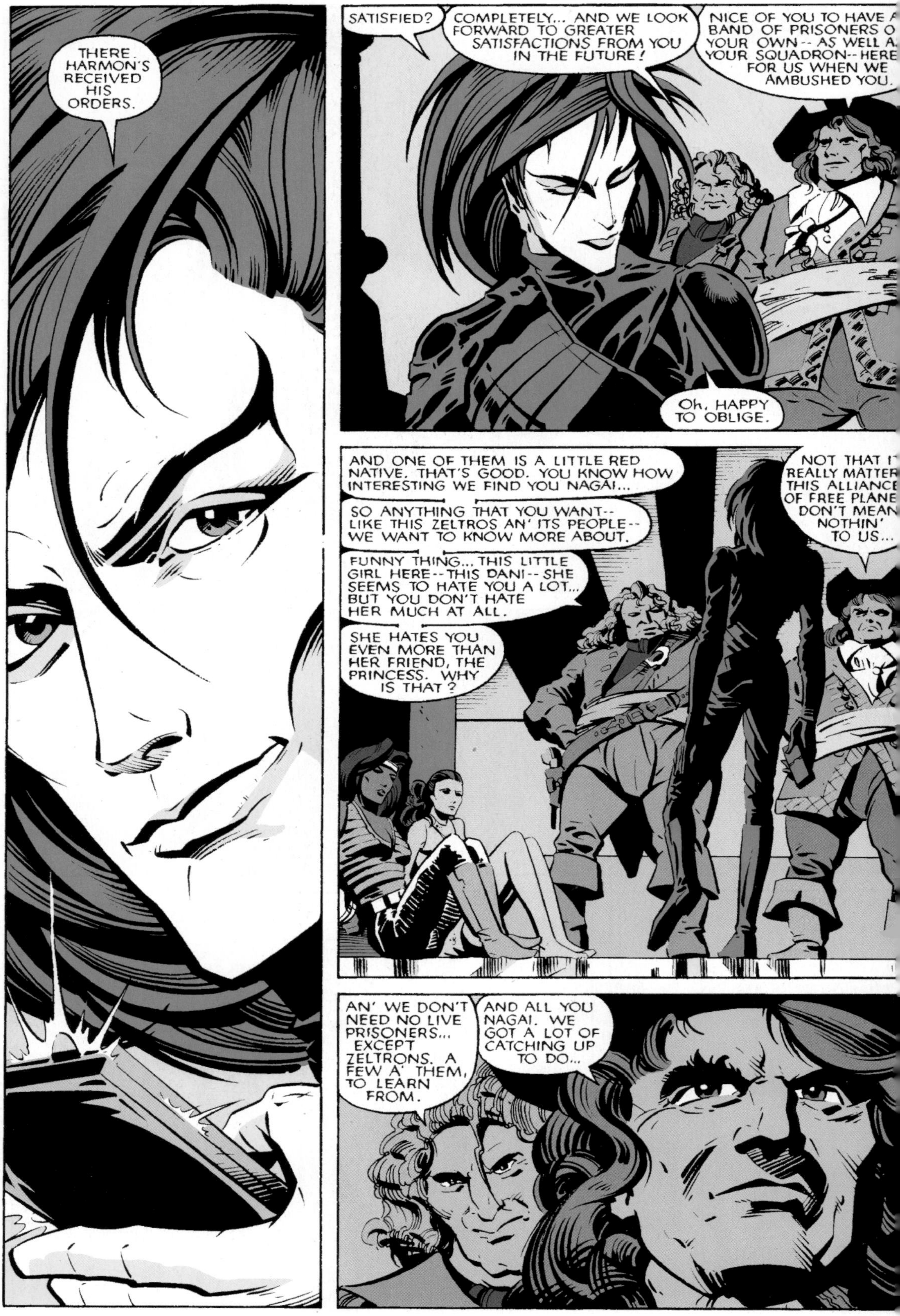
THERE. HARMON'S RECEIVED HIS ORDERS.
SATISFIED?
COMPLETELY... AND WE LOOK FORWARD TO GREATER SATISFACTIONS FROM YOU IN THE FUTURE!
NICE OF YOU TO HAVE A BAND OF PRISONERS O YOUR OWN-- AS WELL A YOUR SQUADRON-- HERE FOR US WHEN WE AMBUSHED YOU.
Oh, HAPPY TO OBLIGE.
AND ONE OF THEM IS A LITTLE RED NATIVE. THAT'S GOOD. YOU KNOW HOW INTERESTING WE FIND YOU NAGAI...
NOT THAT I REALLY MATTER THIS ALLIANC OF FREE PLANE DON'T MEAN NOTHIN' TO US...
SO ANYTHING THAT YOU WANT-- LIKE THIS ZELTROS AN' ITS PEOPLE-- WE WANT TO KNOW MORE ABOUT.
FUNNY THING... THIS LITTLE GIRL HERE--THIS DANI--SHE SEEMS TO HATE YOU A LOT... BUT YOU DON'T HATE HER MUCH AT ALL.
SHE HATES YOU EVEN MORE THAN HER FRIEND, THE PRINCESS. WHY IS THAT?
AN' WE DON'T NEED NO LIVE PRISONERS... EXCEPT ZELTRONS. A FEW A' THEM, TO LEARN FROM.
AND ALL YOU NAGAI. WE GOT A LOT OF CATCHING UP TO DO...

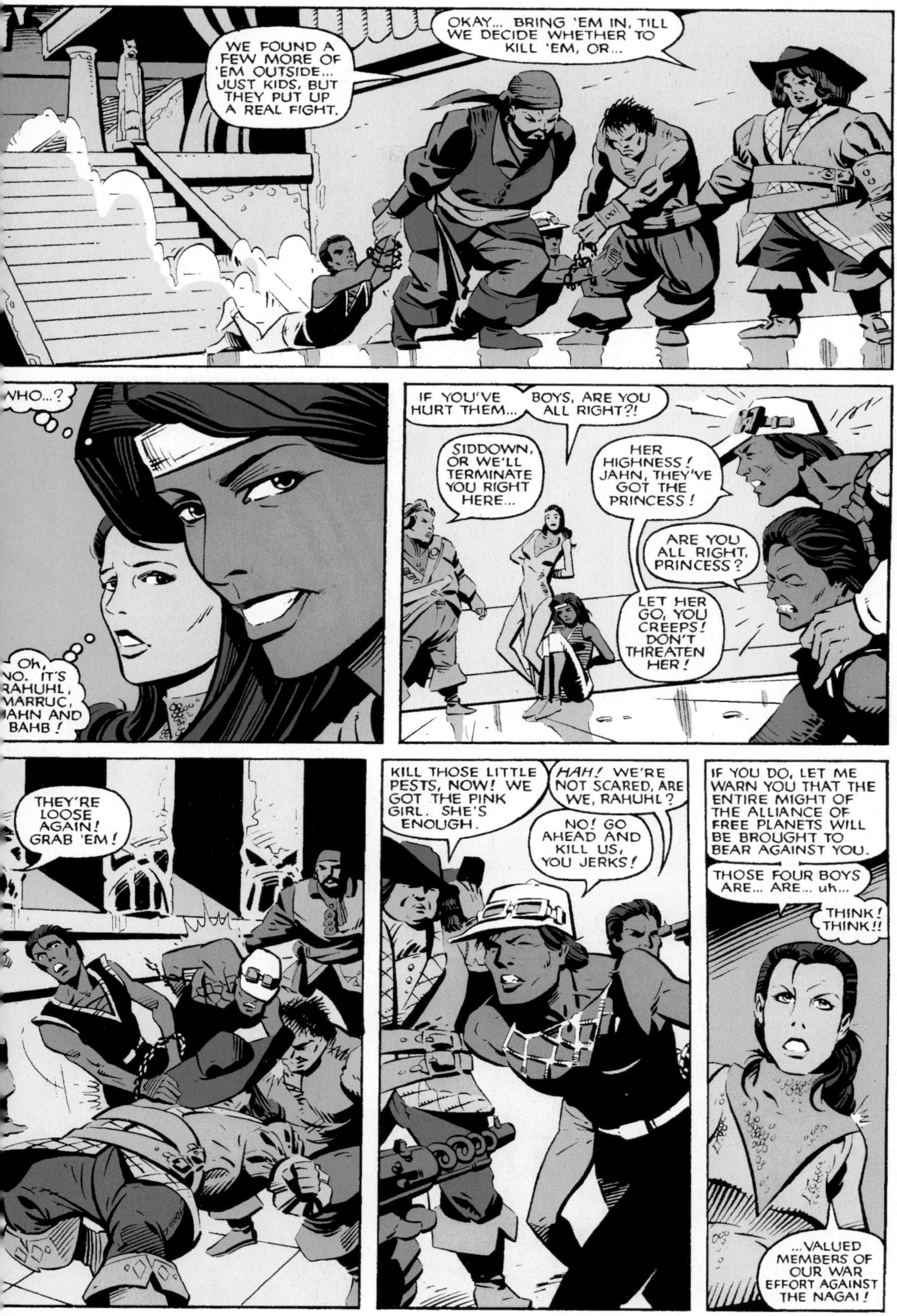
WE FOUND A FEW MORE OF 'EM OUTSIDE... JUST KIDS, BUT THEY PUT UP A REAL FIGHT.
OKAY... BRING 'EM IN, TILL WE DECIDE WHETHER TO KILL 'EM, OR...
WHO...?
Oh, NO. IT'S RAHUHL, MARRUC, JAHN AND BAHB!
IF YOU'VE HURT THEM...
BOYS, ARE YOU ALL RIGHT?!
SIDDOWN, OR WE'LL TERMINATE YOU RIGHT HERE...
HER HIGHNESS! JAHN, THEY'VE GOT THE PRINCESS!
ARE YOU ALL RIGHT, PRINCESS?
LET HER GO, YOU CREEPS! DON'T THREATEN HER!
THEY'RE LOOSE AGAIN! GRAB 'EM!
KILL THOSE LITTLE PESTS, NOW! WE GOT THE PINK GIRL. SHE'S ENOUGH.
HAH! WE'RE NOT SCARED, ARE WE, RAHUHL?
NO! GO AHEAD AND KILL US, YOU JERKS!
IF YOU DO, LET ME WARN YOU THAT THE ENTIRE MIGHT OF THE ALLIANCE OF FREE PLANETS WILL BE BROUGHT TO BEAR AGAINST YOU.
THOSE FOUR BOYS ARE... ARE... uh...
THINK! THINK!!
...VALUED MEMBERS OF OUR WAR EFFORT AGAINST THE NAGAI!

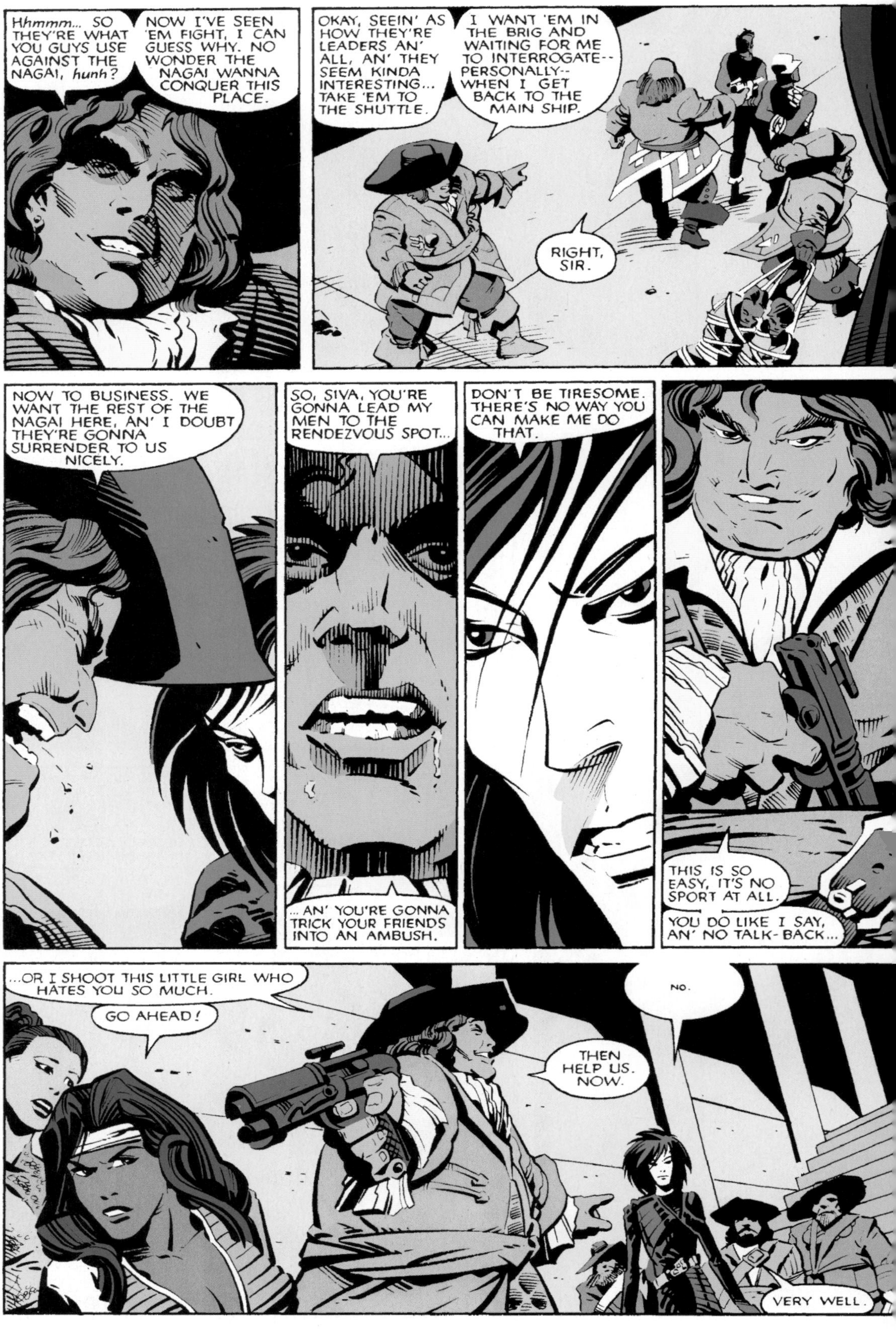
Hhmmm... SO THEY'RE WHAT YOU GUYS USE AGAINST THE NAGAI, hunh?
NOW I'VE SEEN 'EM FIGHT, I CAN GUESS WHY. NO WONDER THE NAGAI WANNA CONQUER THIS PLACE.
OKAY, SEEIN' AS HOW THEY'RE LEADERS AN' ALL, AN' THEY SEEM KINDA INTERESTING... TAKE 'EM TO THE SHUTTLE.
I WANT 'EM IN THE BRIG AND WAITING FOR ME TO INTERROGATE-- PERSONALLY-- WHEN I GET BACK TO THE MAIN SHIP.
RIGHT, SIR.
NOW TO BUSINESS. WE WANT THE REST OF THE NAGAI HERE, AN' I DOUBT THEY'RE GONNA SURRENDER TO US NICELY.
SO, SIVA, YOU'RE GONNA LEAD MY MEN TO THE RENDEZVOUS SPOT...
...AN' YOU'RE GONNA TRICK YOUR FRIENDS INTO AN AMBUSH.
DON'T BE TIRESOME. THERE'S NO WAY YOU CAN MAKE ME DO THAT.
THIS IS SO EASY, IT'S NO SPORT AT ALL.
YOU DO LIKE I SAY, AN' NO TALK-BACK...
...OR I SHOOT THIS LITTLE GIRL WHO HATES YOU SO MUCH.
GO AHEAD!
NO.
THEN HELP US. NOW.
VERY WELL.

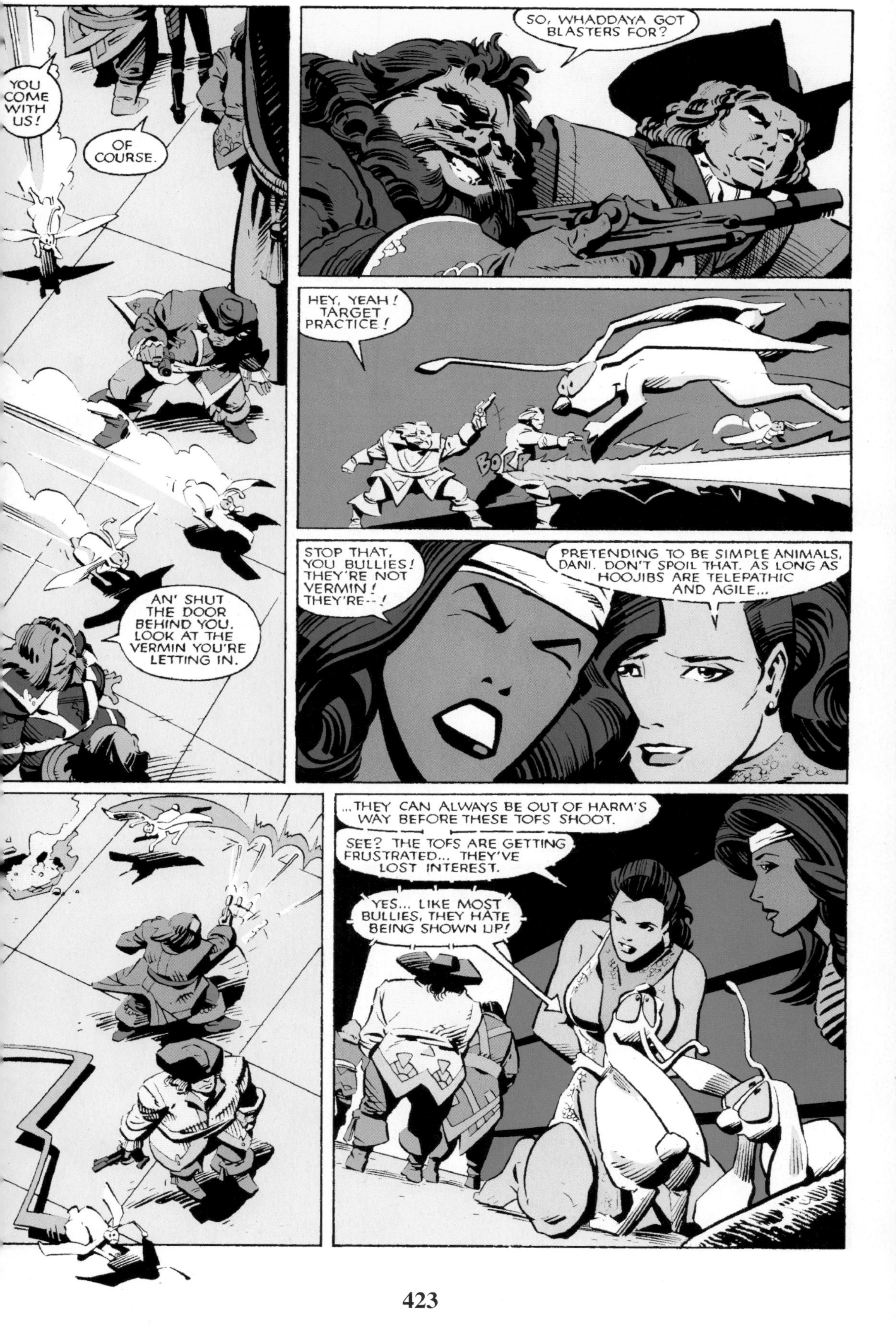
YOU COME WITH US!
OF COURSE.
SO, WHADDAYA GOT BLASTERS FOR?
HEY, YEAH! TARGET PRACTICE!
BORP
AN' SHUT THE DOOR BEHIND YOU. LOOK AT THE VERMIN YOU'RE LETTING IN.
STOP THAT, YOU BULLIES! THEY'RE NOT VERMIN! THEY'RE--!
PRETENDING TO BE SIMPLE ANIMALS, DANI. DON'T SPOIL THAT. AS LONG AS HOOJIBS ARE TELEPATHIC AND AGILE...
...THEY CAN ALWAYS BE OUT OF HARM'S WAY BEFORE THESE TOFS SHOOT.
SEE? THE TOFS ARE GETTING FRUSTRATED... THEY'VE LOST INTEREST.
YES... LIKE MOST BULLIES, THEY HATE BEING SHOWN UP!

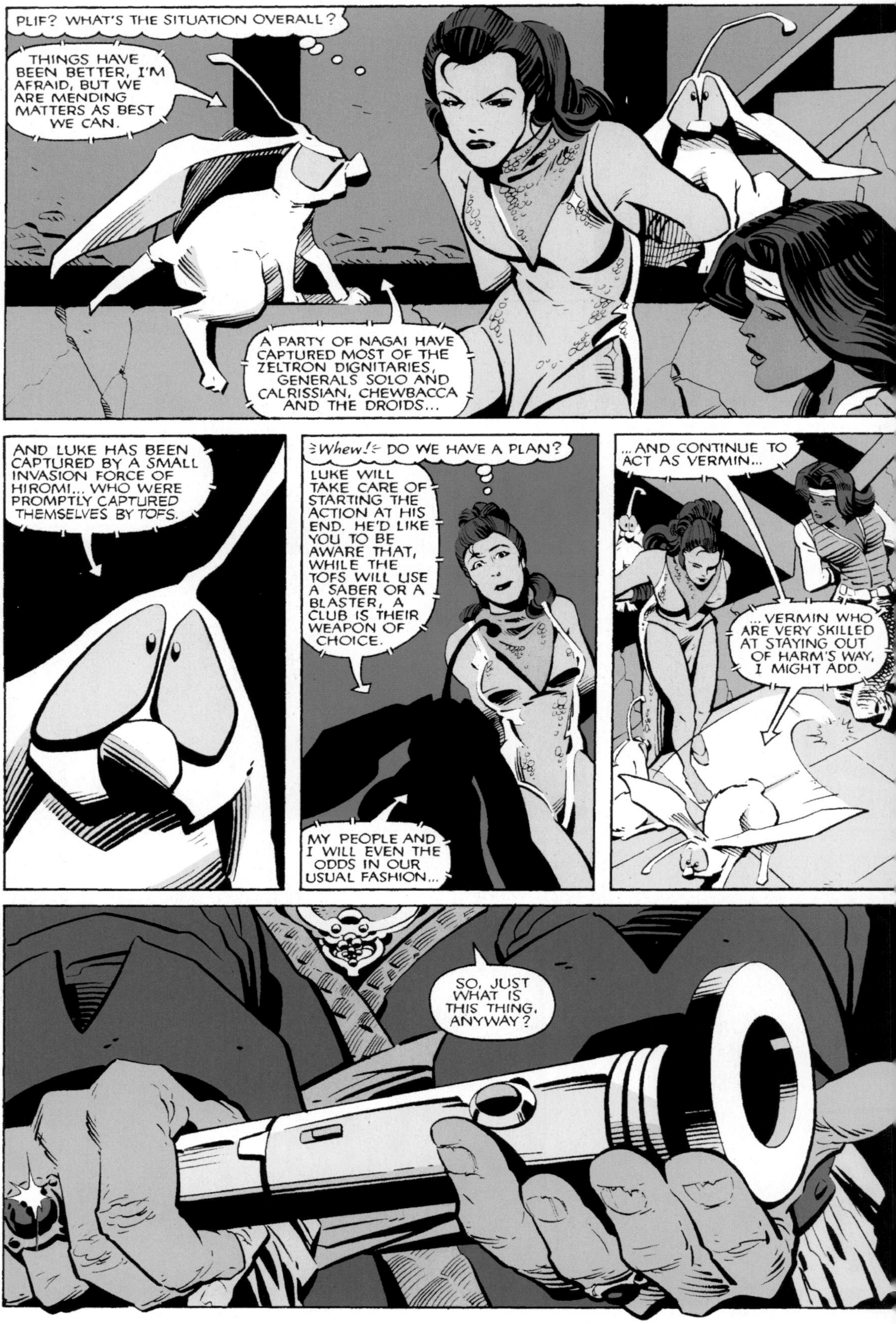
PLIF? WHAT'S THE SITUATION OVERALL?
THINGS HAVE BEEN BETTER, I'M AFRAID, BUT WE ARE MENDING MATTERS AS BEST WE CAN.
A PARTY OF NAGAI HAVE CAPTURED MOST OF THE ZELTRON DIGNITARIES, GENERALS SOLO AND CALRISSIAN, CHEWBACCA AND THE DROIDS...
AND LUKE HAS BEEN CAPTURED BY A SMALL INVASION FORCE OF HIROMI... WHO WERE PROMPTLY CAPTURED THEMSELVES BY TOFS.
Whew! DO WE HAVE A PLAN?
LUKE WILL TAKE CARE OF STARTING THE ACTION AT HIS END. HE'D LIKE YOU TO BE AWARE THAT, WHILE THE TOFS WILL USE A SABER OR A BLASTER, A CLUB IS THEIR WEAPON OF CHOICE.
MY PEOPLE AND I WILL EVEN THE ODDS IN OUR USUAL FASHION...
...AND CONTINUE TO ACT AS VERMIN...
...VERMIN WHO ARE VERY SKILLED AT STAYING OUT OF HARM'S WAY, I MIGHT ADD.
SO, JUST WHAT IS THIS THING, ANYWAY?

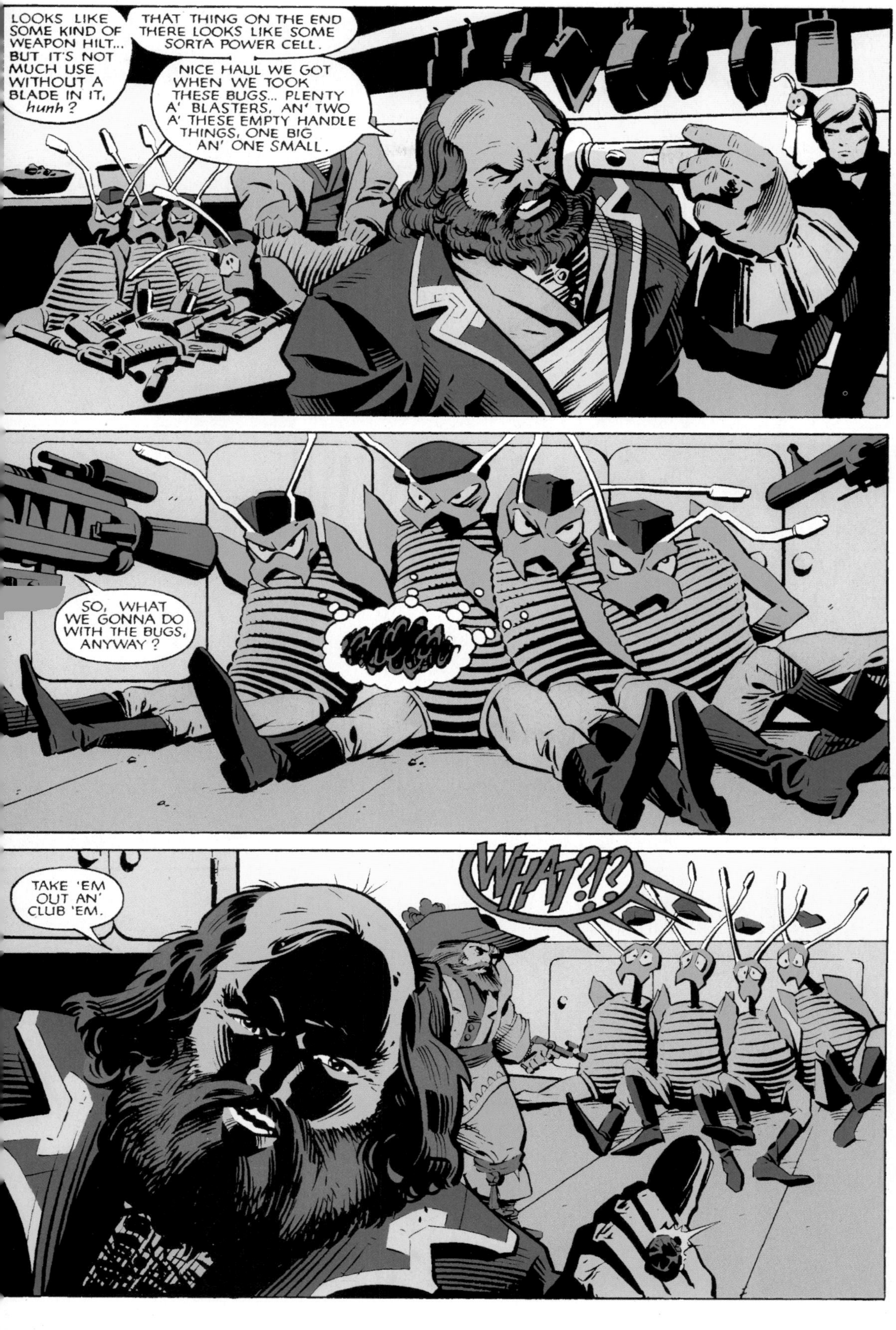
LOOKS LIKE SOME KIND OF WEAPON HILT... BUT IT'S NOT MUCH USE WITHOUT A BLADE IN IT, *hunh*?
THAT THING ON THE END THERE LOOKS LIKE SOME SORTA POWER CELL.
NICE HAUL WE GOT WHEN WE TOOK THESE BUGS... PLENTY A' BLASTERS, AN' TWO A' THESE EMPTY HANDLE THINGS, ONE BIG AN' ONE SMALL.
SO, WHAT WE GONNA DO WITH THE BUGS, ANYWAY?
TAKE 'EM OUT AN' CLUB 'EM.
WHAT?!?

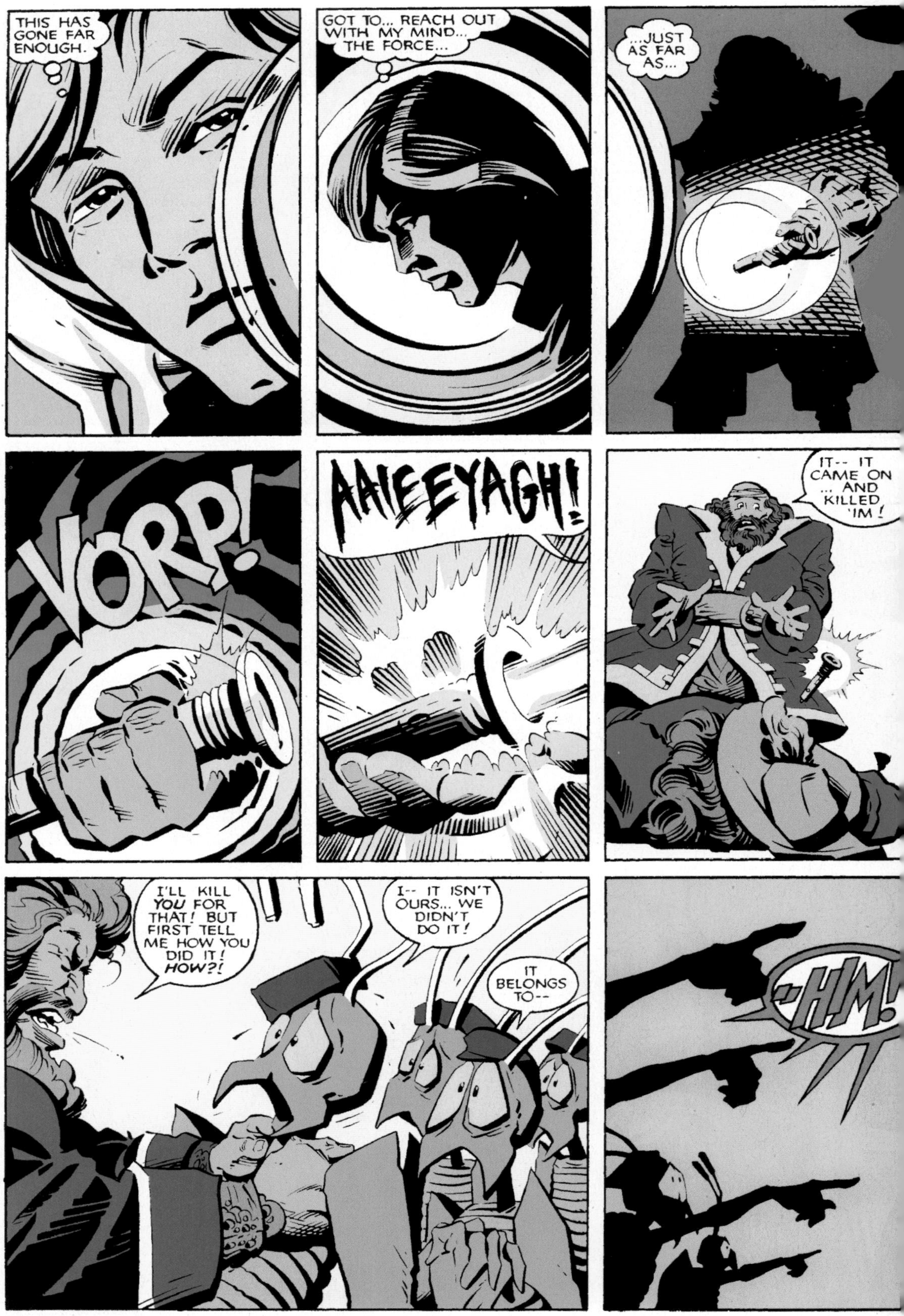
THIS HAS GONE FAR ENOUGH.
GOT TO... REACH OUT WITH MY MIND... THE FORCE...
...JUST AS FAR AS...
VORP!
AAIEEYAGH!
IT-- IT CAME ON ... AND KILLED 'IM!
I'LL KILL YOU FOR THAT! BUT FIRST TELL ME HOW YOU DID IT! HOW?!
I-- IT ISN'T OURS... WE DIDN'T DO IT!
IT BELONGS TO--
-HIM!

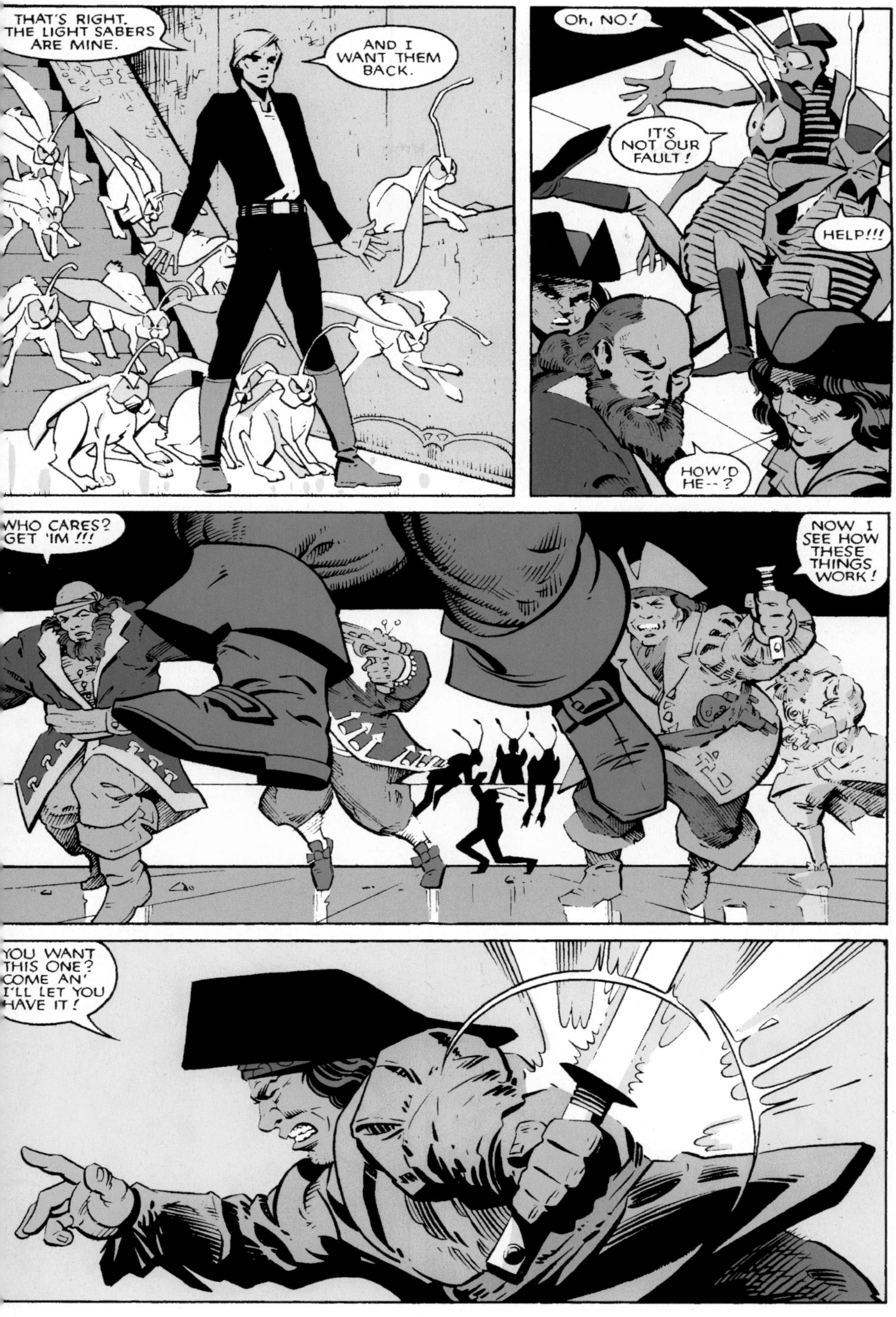
THAT'S RIGHT. THE LIGHT SABERS ARE MINE.
AND I WANT THEM BACK.
Oh, NO!
IT'S NOT OUR FAULT!
HELP!!!
HOW'D HE--?
WHO CARES? GET 'IM!!!
NOW I SEE HOW THESE THINGS WORK!
YOU WANT THIS ONE? COME AN' I'LL LET YOU HAVE IT!

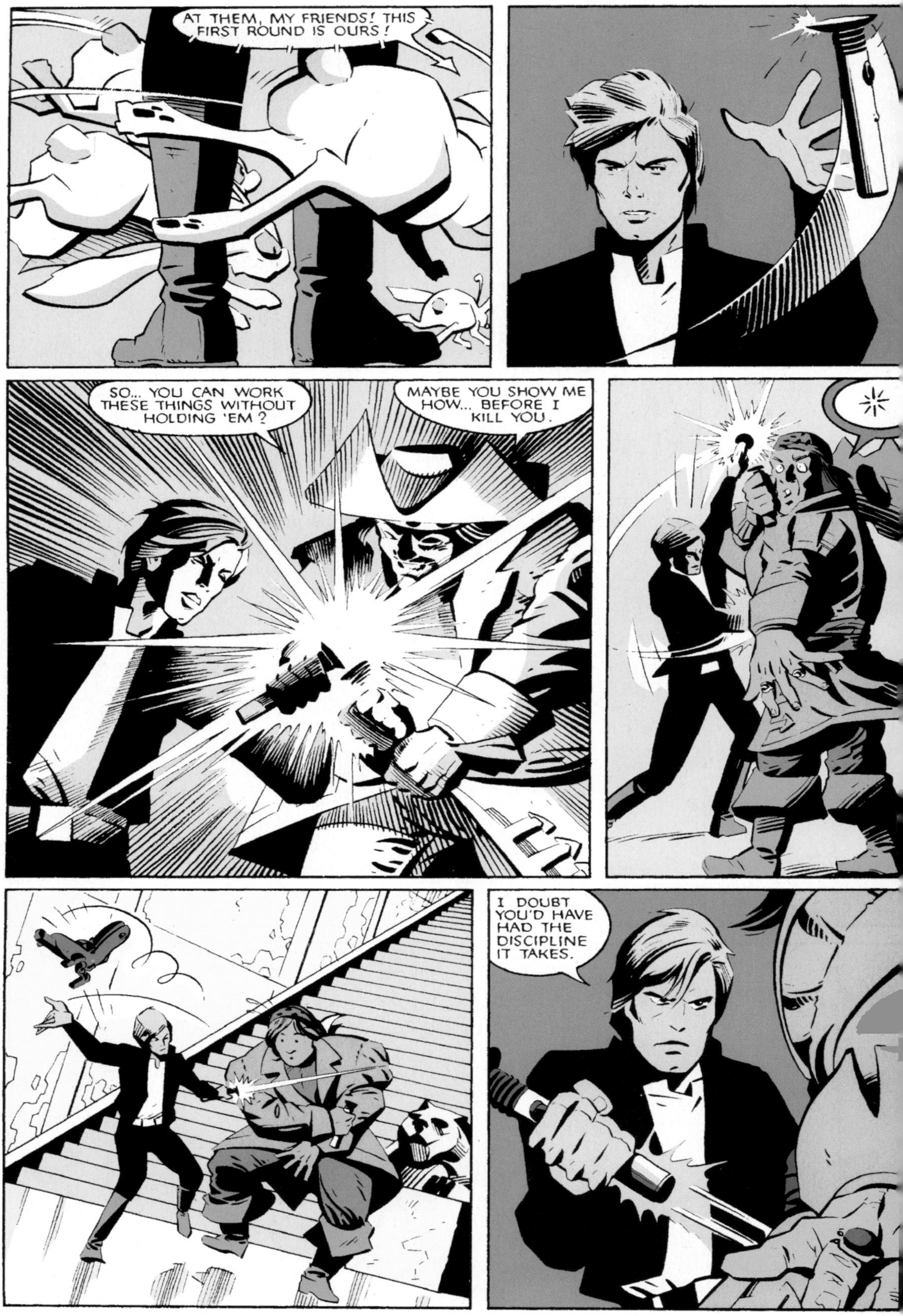
AT THEM, MY FRIENDS! THIS FIRST ROUND IS OURS!
SO... YOU CAN WORK THESE THINGS WITHOUT HOLDING 'EM?
MAYBE YOU SHOW ME HOW... BEFORE I KILL YOU.
I DOUBT YOU'D HAVE HAD THE DISCIPLINE IT TAKES.

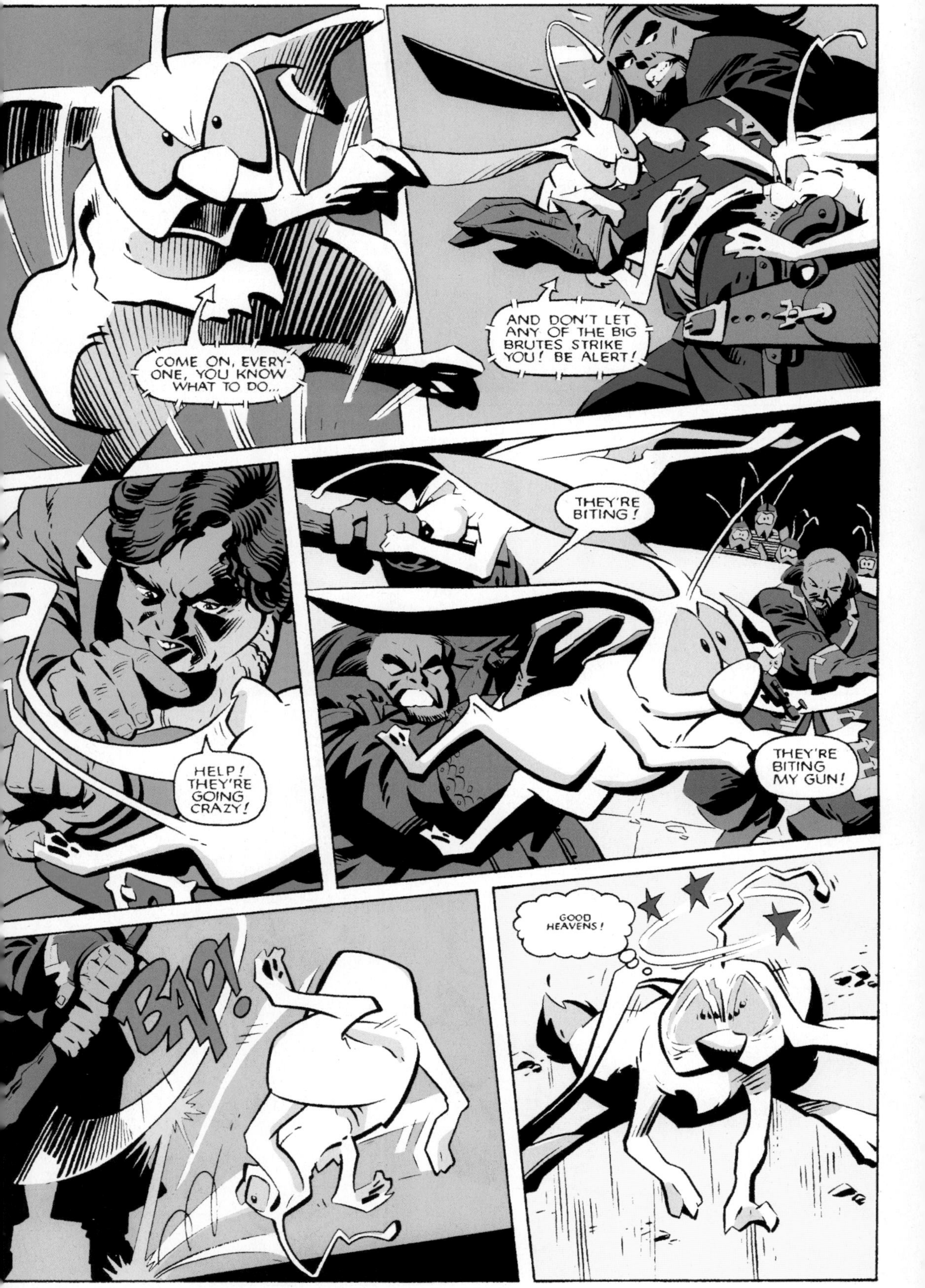
COME ON, EVERY-ONE, YOU KNOW WHAT TO DO...
AND DON'T LET ANY OF THE BIG BRUTES STRIKE YOU! BE ALERT!
HELP! THEY'RE GOING CRAZY!
THEY'RE BITING!
THEY'RE BITING MY GUN!
BAP!
GOOD HEAVENS!

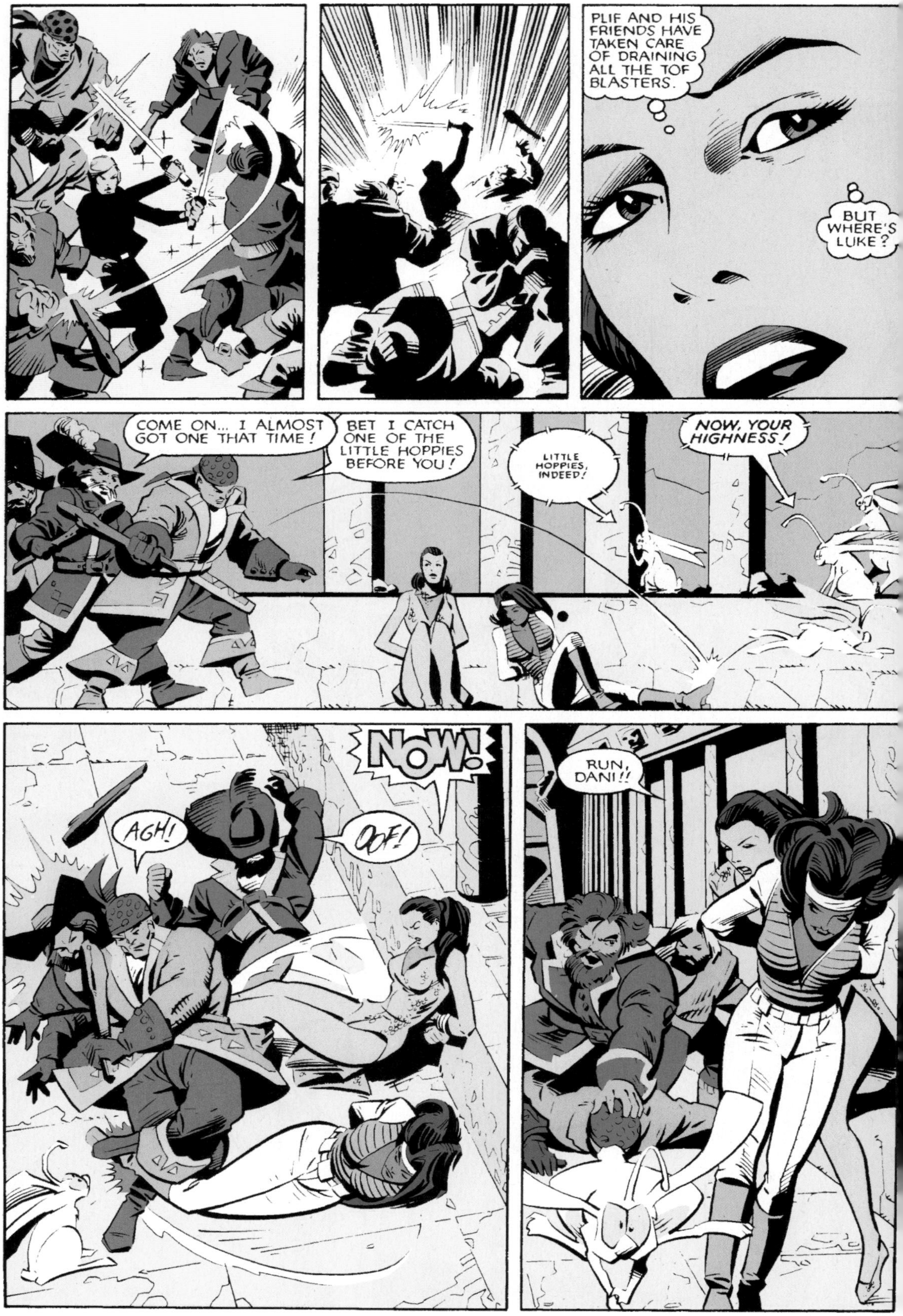

PLIF AND HIS FRIENDS HAVE TAKEN CARE OF DRAINING ALL THE TOF BLASTERS.
BUT WHERE'S LUKE?
COME ON... I ALMOST GOT ONE THAT TIME!
BET I CATCH ONE OF THE LITTLE HOPPIES BEFORE YOU!
LITTLE HOPPIES, INDEED!
NOW, YOUR HIGHNESS!
NOW!
AGH!
OOF!
RUN, DANI!!

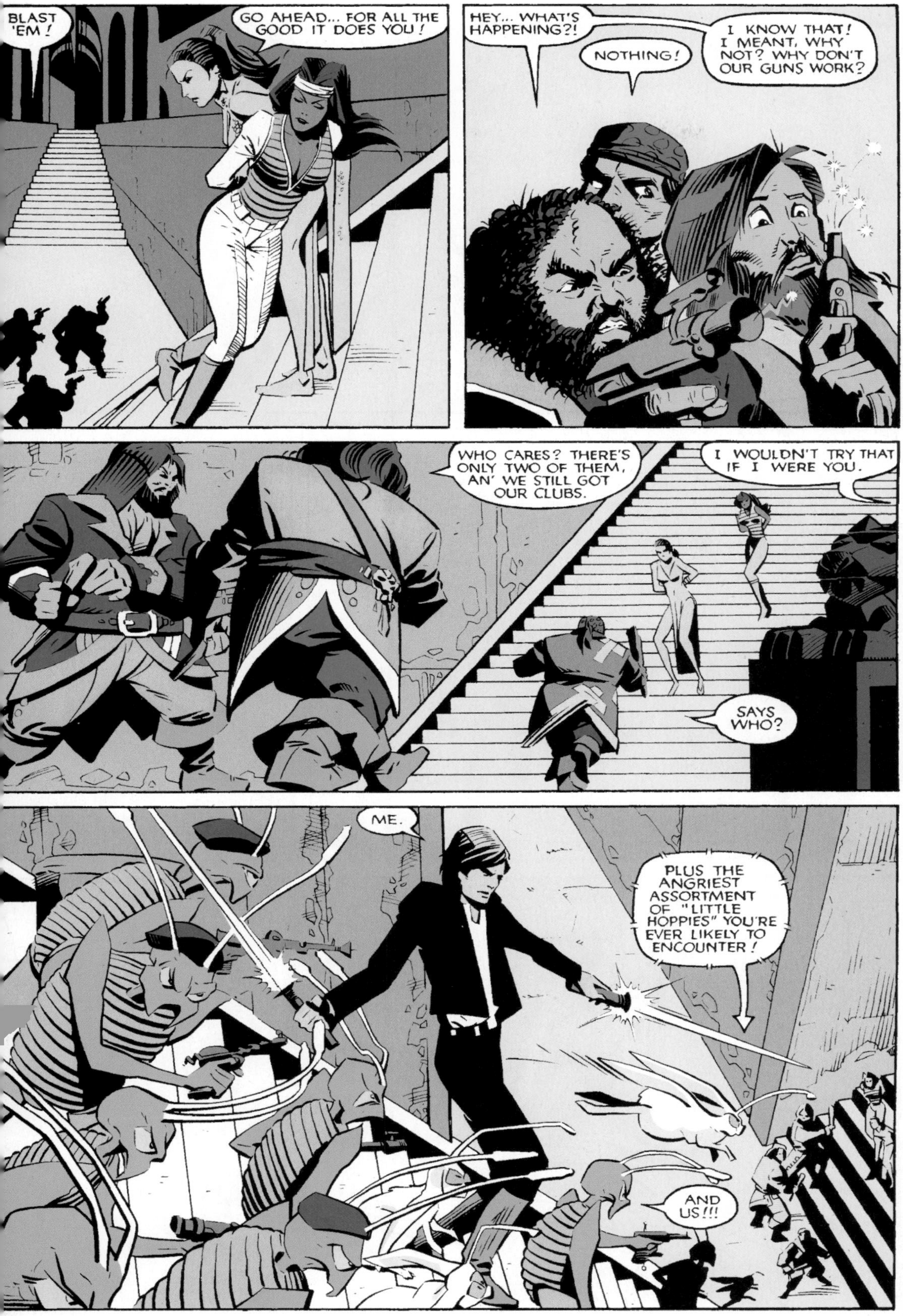
BLAST 'EM!
GO AHEAD... FOR ALL THE GOOD IT DOES YOU!
HEY... WHAT'S HAPPENING?!
NOTHING!
I KNOW THAT! I MEANT, WHY NOT? WHY DON'T OUR GUNS WORK?
WHO CARES? THERE'S ONLY TWO OF THEM, AN' WE STILL GOT OUR CLUBS.
I WOULDN'T TRY THAT IF I WERE YOU.
SAYS WHO?
ME.
PLUS THE ANGRIEST ASSORTMENT OF "LITTLE HOPPIES" YOU'RE EVER LIKELY TO ENCOUNTER!
AND US!!!

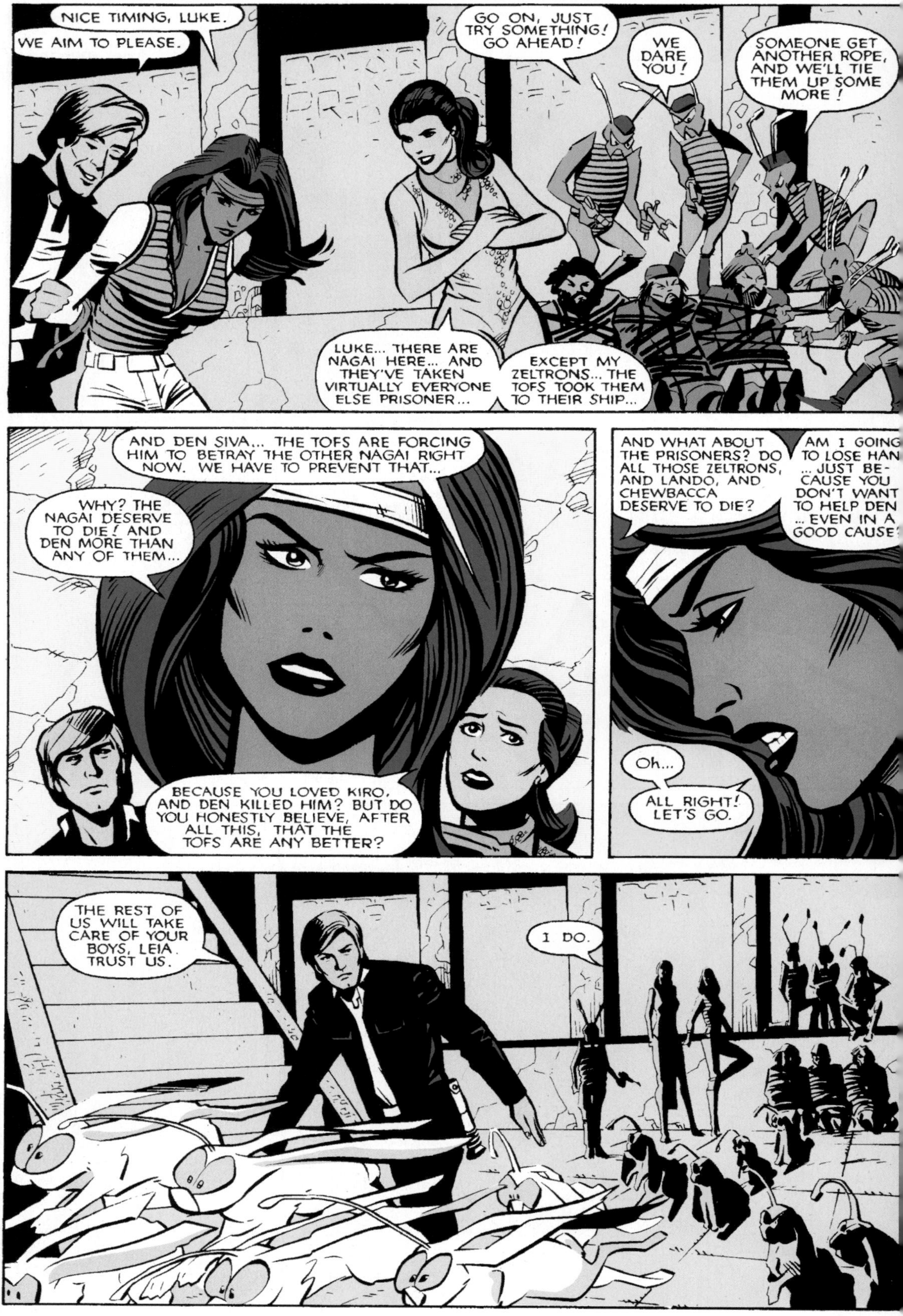
NICE TIMING, LUKE.
WE AIM TO PLEASE.
GO ON, JUST TRY SOMETHING! GO AHEAD!
WE DARE YOU!
SOMEONE GET ANOTHER ROPE, AND WE'LL TIE THEM UP SOME MORE!
LUKE... THERE ARE NAGAI HERE... AND THEY'VE TAKEN VIRTUALLY EVERYONE ELSE PRISONER...
EXCEPT MY ZELTRONS... THE TOFS TOOK THEM TO THEIR SHIP...
AND DEN SIVA... THE TOFS ARE FORCING HIM TO BETRAY THE OTHER NAGAI RIGHT NOW. WE HAVE TO PREVENT THAT...
WHY? THE NAGAI DESERVE TO DIE! AND DEN MORE THAN ANY OF THEM...
BECAUSE YOU LOVED KIRO, AND DEN KILLED HIM? BUT DO YOU HONESTLY BELIEVE, AFTER ALL THIS, THAT THE TOFS ARE ANY BETTER?
AND WHAT ABOUT THE PRISONERS? DO ALL THOSE ZELTRONS, AND LANDO, AND CHEWBACCA DESERVE TO DIE?
AM I GOING TO LOSE HAN ... JUST BECAUSE YOU DON'T WANT TO HELP DEN ... EVEN IN A GOOD CAUSE?
Oh...
ALL RIGHT! LET'S GO.
THE REST OF US WILL TAKE CARE OF YOUR BOYS, LEIA. TRUST US.
I DO.

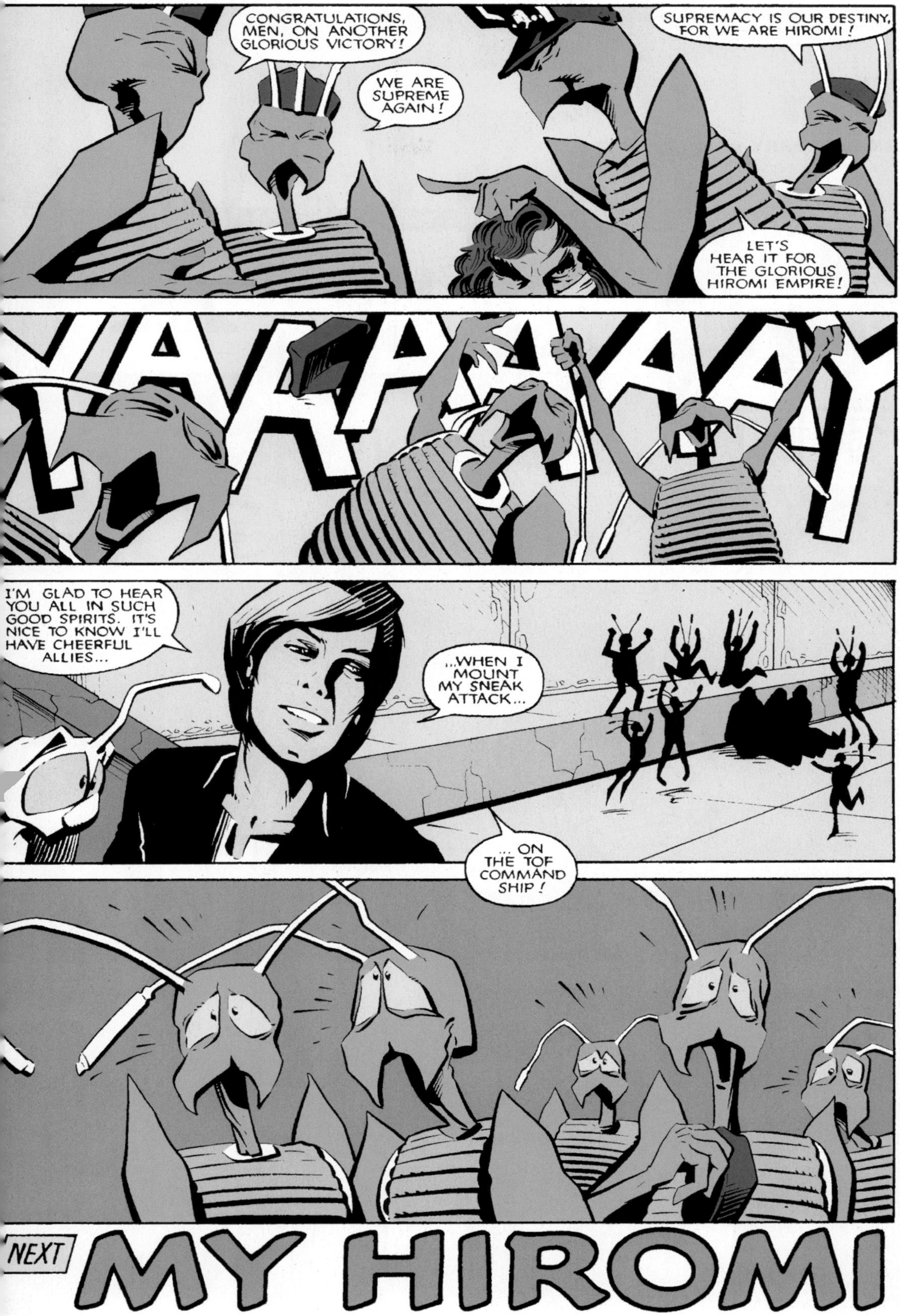
CONGRATULATIONS, MEN, ON ANOTHER GLORIOUS VICTORY!
WE ARE SUPREME AGAIN!
SUPREMACY IS OUR DESTINY, FOR WE ARE HIROMI!
LET'S HEAR IT FOR THE GLORIOUS HIROMI EMPIRE!
YAAAAAY
I'M GLAD TO HEAR YOU ALL IN SUCH GOOD SPIRITS. IT'S NICE TO KNOW I'LL HAVE CHEERFUL ALLIES...
...WHEN I MOUNT MY SNEAK ATTACK...
... ON THE TOF COMMAND SHIP!
NEXT
MY HIROMI

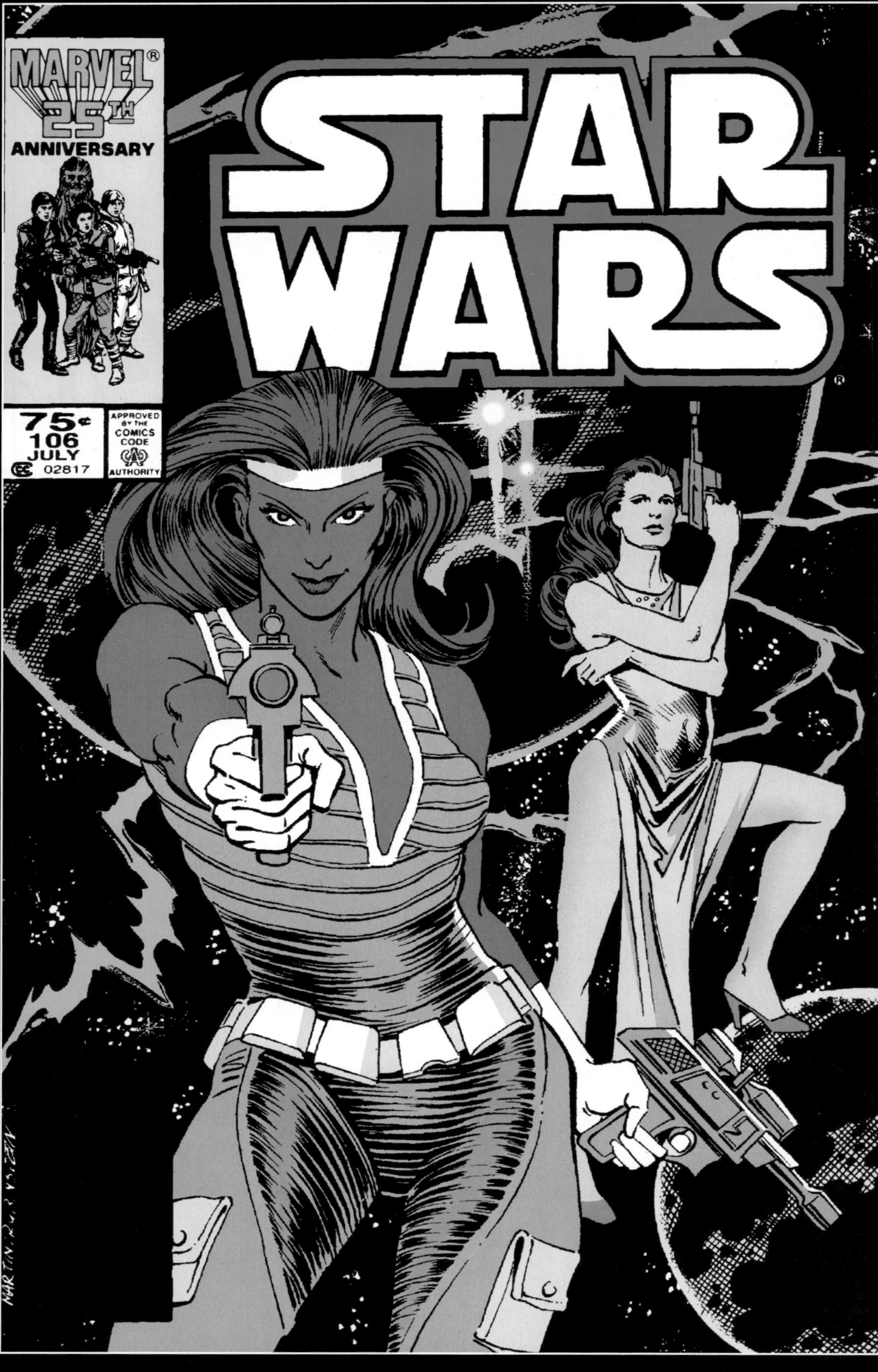
MARVEL®
25TH
ANNIVERSARY
STAR WARS®
75¢
106
JULY
02817
APPROVED BY THE COMICS CODE AUTHORITY
MARTINEZ

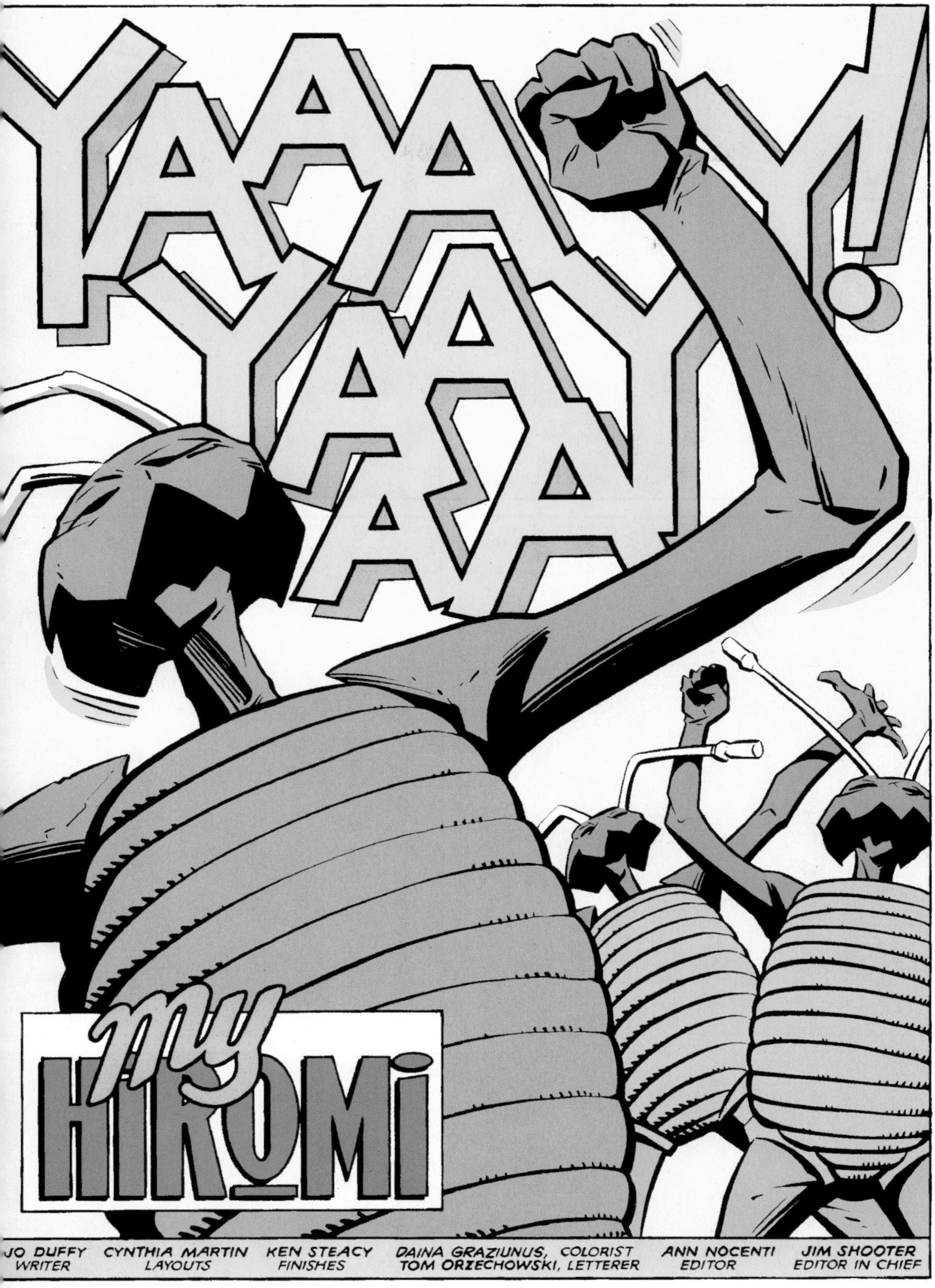
YAAAAY! YAAAAY
My HIROMI
JO DUFFY WRITER
CYNTHIA MARTIN LAYOUTS
KEN STEACY FINISHES
DAINA GRAZIUNUS, COLORIST
TOM ORZECHOWSKI, LETTERER
ANN NOCENTI EDITOR
JIM SHOOTER EDITOR IN CHIEF

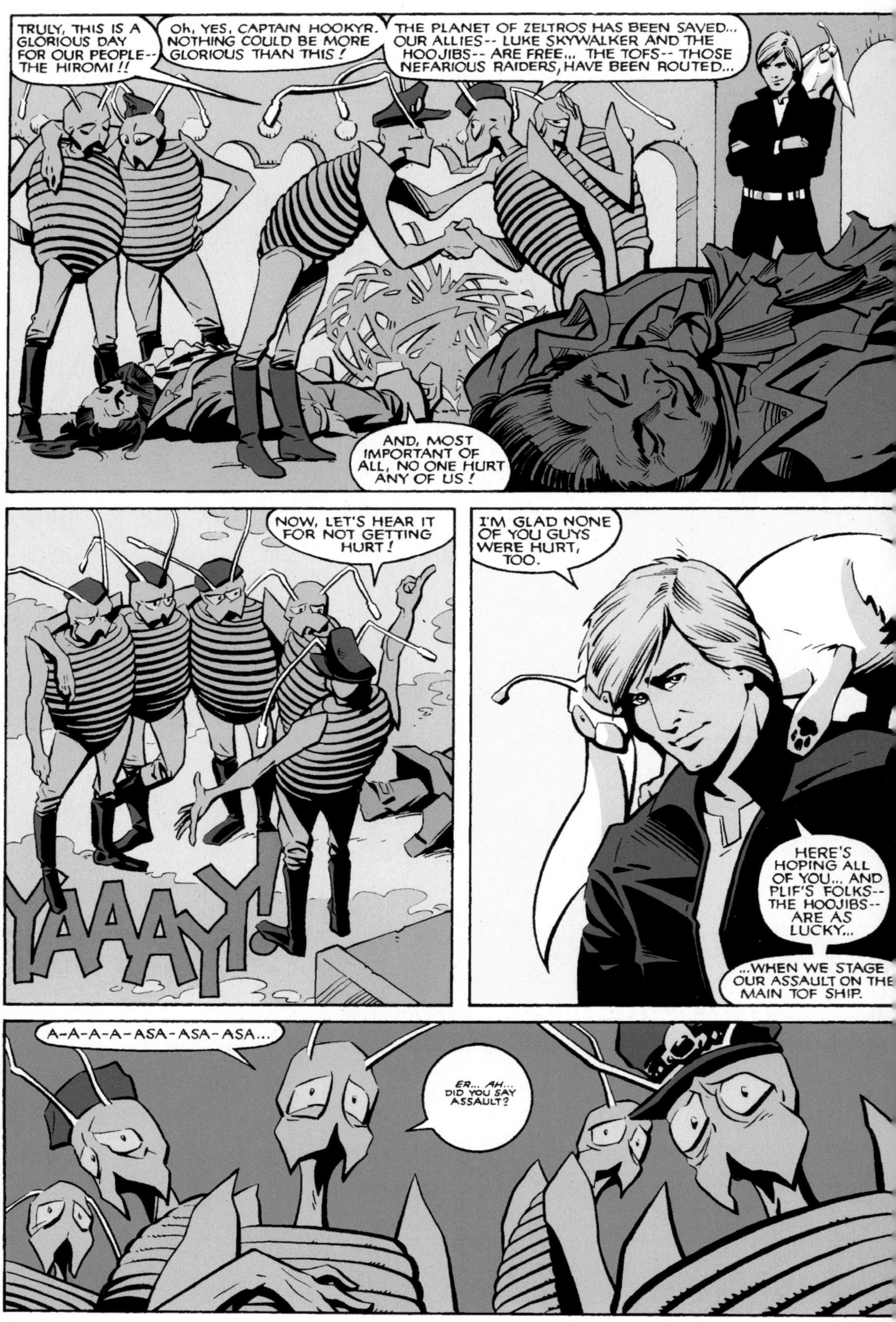

TRULY, THIS IS A GLORIOUS DAY FOR OUR PEOPLE-- THE HIROMI!!
Oh, YES, CAPTAIN HOOKYR. NOTHING COULD BE MORE GLORIOUS THAN THIS!
THE PLANET OF ZELTROS HAS BEEN SAVED... OUR ALLIES-- LUKE SKYWALKER AND THE HOOJIBS-- ARE FREE... THE TOFS-- THOSE NEFARIOUS RAIDERS, HAVE BEEN ROUTED...
AND, MOST IMPORTANT OF ALL, NO ONE HURT ANY OF US!
NOW, LET'S HEAR IT FOR NOT GETTING HURT!
YAAAY!
I'M GLAD NONE OF YOU GUYS WERE HURT, TOO.
HERE'S HOPING ALL OF YOU... AND PLIF'S FOLKS-- THE HOOJIBS-- ARE AS LUCKY...
...WHEN WE STAGE OUR ASSAULT ON THE MAIN TOF SHIP.
A-A-A-A-ASA-ASA-ASA...
ER... AH... DID YOU SAY ASSAULT?

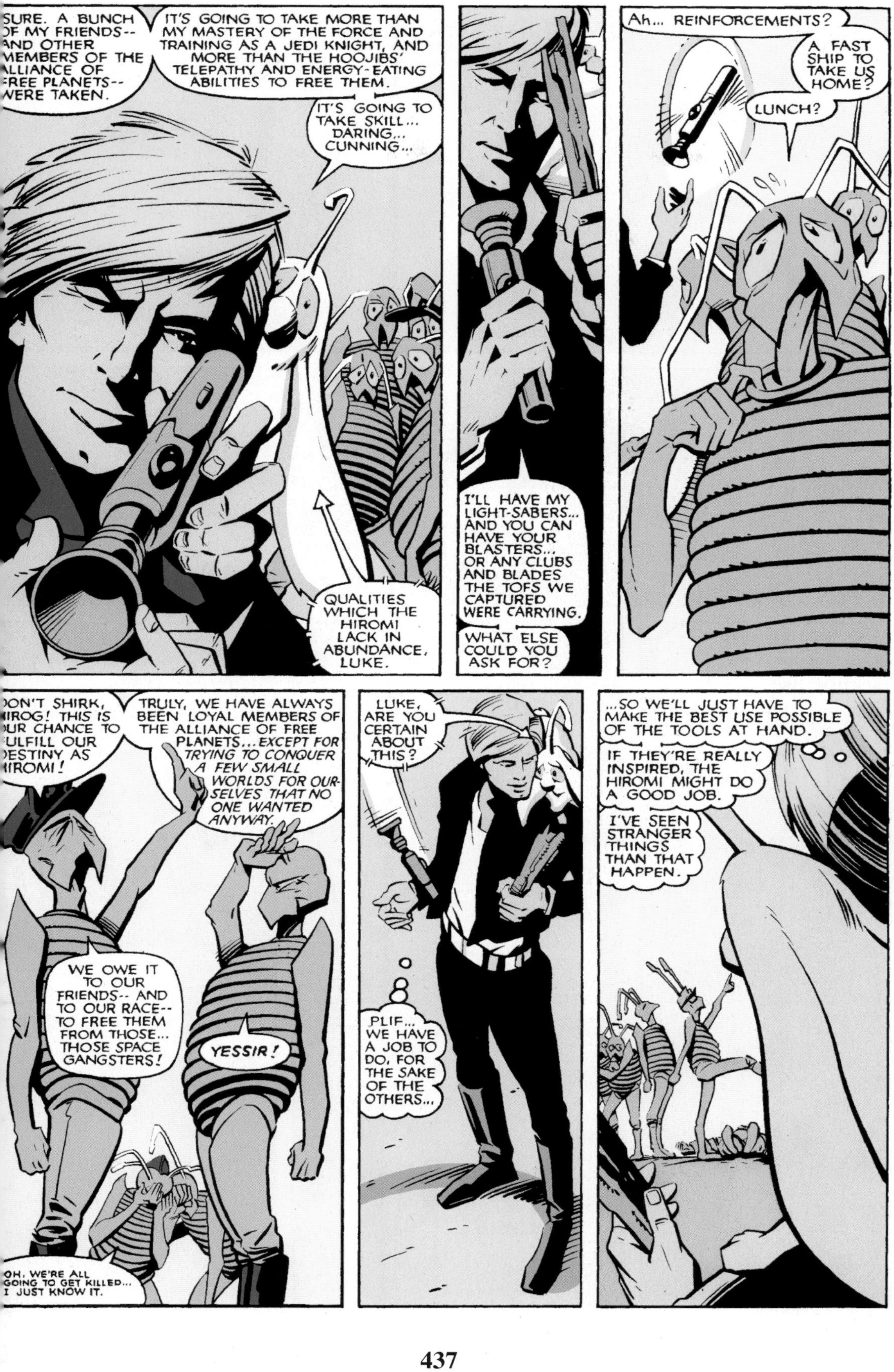
SURE. A BUNCH OF MY FRIENDS-- AND OTHER MEMBERS OF THE ALLIANCE OF FREE PLANETS-- WERE TAKEN.
IT'S GOING TO TAKE MORE THAN MY MASTERY OF THE FORCE AND TRAINING AS A JEDI KNIGHT, AND MORE THAN THE HOOJIBS' TELEPATHY AND ENERGY-EATING ABILITIES TO FREE THEM.
IT'S GOING TO TAKE SKILL... DARING... CUNNING...
QUALITIES WHICH THE HIROMI LACK IN ABUNDANCE, LUKE.
I'LL HAVE MY LIGHT-SABERS... AND YOU CAN HAVE YOUR BLASTERS... OR ANY CLUBS AND BLADES THE TOFS WE CAPTURED WERE CARRYING.
WHAT ELSE COULD YOU ASK FOR?
Ah... REINFORCEMENTS?
A FAST SHIP TO TAKE US HOME?
LUNCH?
DON'T SHIRK, HIROG! THIS IS OUR CHANCE TO FULFILL OUR DESTINY AS HIROMI!
TRULY, WE HAVE ALWAYS BEEN LOYAL MEMBERS OF THE ALLIANCE OF FREE PLANETS... EXCEPT FOR TRYING TO CONQUER A FEW SMALL WORLDS FOR OURSELVES THAT NO ONE WANTED ANYWAY.
WE OWE IT TO OUR FRIENDS-- AND TO OUR RACE-- TO FREE THEM FROM THOSE... THOSE SPACE GANGSTERS!
YESSIR!
OH, WE'RE ALL GOING TO GET KILLED... I JUST KNOW IT.
LUKE, ARE YOU CERTAIN ABOUT THIS?
PLIF... WE HAVE A JOB TO DO, FOR THE SAKE OF THE OTHERS...
...SO WE'LL JUST HAVE TO MAKE THE BEST USE POSSIBLE OF THE TOOLS AT HAND.
IF THEY'RE REALLY INSPIRED, THE HIROMI MIGHT DO A GOOD JOB.
I'VE SEEN STRANGER THINGS THAN THAT HAPPEN.

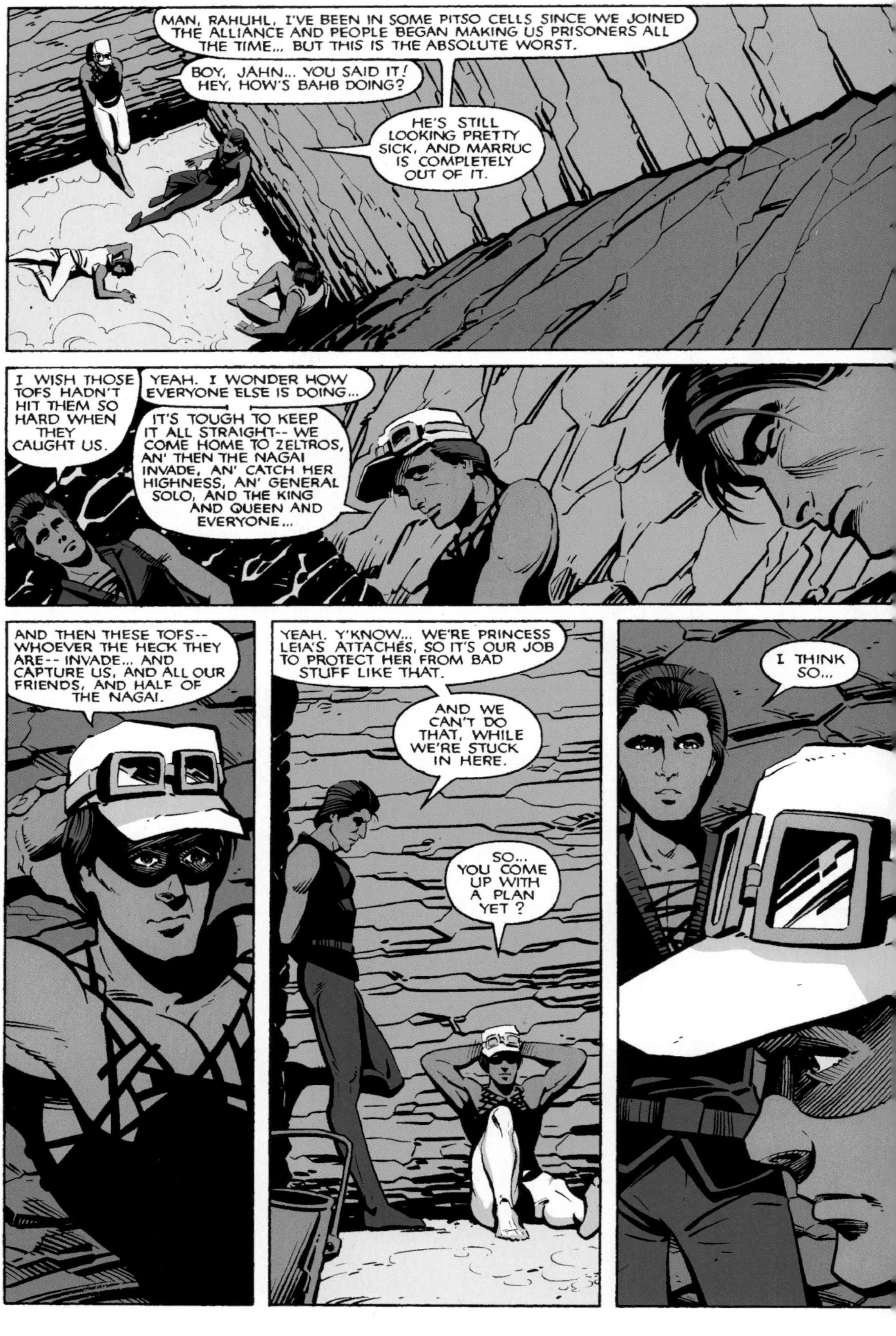
MAN, RAHUHL, I'VE BEEN IN SOME PITSO CELLS SINCE WE JOINED THE ALLIANCE AND PEOPLE BEGAN MAKING US PRISONERS ALL THE TIME... BUT THIS IS THE ABSOLUTE WORST.
BOY, JAHN... YOU SAID IT! HEY, HOW'S BAHB DOING?
HE'S STILL LOOKING PRETTY SICK, AND MARRUC IS COMPLETELY OUT OF IT.
I WISH THOSE TOFS HADN'T HIT THEM SO HARD WHEN THEY CAUGHT US.
YEAH. I WONDER HOW EVERYONE ELSE IS DOING...
IT'S TOUGH TO KEEP IT ALL STRAIGHT-- WE COME HOME TO ZELTROS, AN' THEN THE NAGAI INVADE, AN' CATCH HER HIGHNESS, AN' GENERAL SOLO, AND THE KING AND QUEEN AND EVERYONE...
AND THEN THESE TOFS-- WHOEVER THE HECK THEY ARE-- INVADE... AND CAPTURE US, AND ALL OUR FRIENDS, AND HALF OF THE NAGAI.
YEAH. Y'KNOW... WE'RE PRINCESS LEIA'S ATTACHÉS, SO IT'S OUR JOB TO PROTECT HER FROM BAD STUFF LIKE THAT.
AND WE CAN'T DO THAT, WHILE WE'RE STUCK IN HERE.
SO... YOU COME UP WITH A PLAN YET?
I THINK SO...

NOW LISTEN, YOU GUYS...

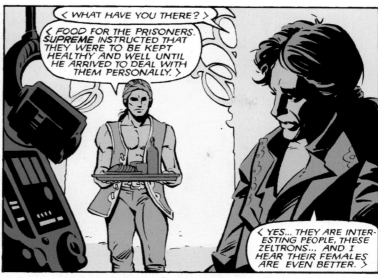

< WHAT HAVE YOU THERE? >

< FOOD FOR THE PRISONERS. SUPREME INSTRUCTED THAT THEY WERE TO BE KEPT HEALTHY AND WELL UNTIL HE ARRIVED TO DEAL WITH THEM PERSONALLY. >

< YES... THEY ARE INTERESTING PEOPLE, THESE ZELTRONS... AND I HEAR THEIR FEMALES ARE EVEN BETTER. >

< TRULY, IT IS WELL THAT WE CAME TO THIS GALAXY IN PURSUIT OF OUR OLD ENEMY-- THE NAGAI. >

< THAT FOOD YOU ARE TAKING IS FOR THE PRISONERS. >

< INDEED. >

< IF THEY ARE DISPLEASED... TELL THEM TO ADDRESS THEIR COMPLAINTS TO ME...! >

NOW--

OOWWW!

439

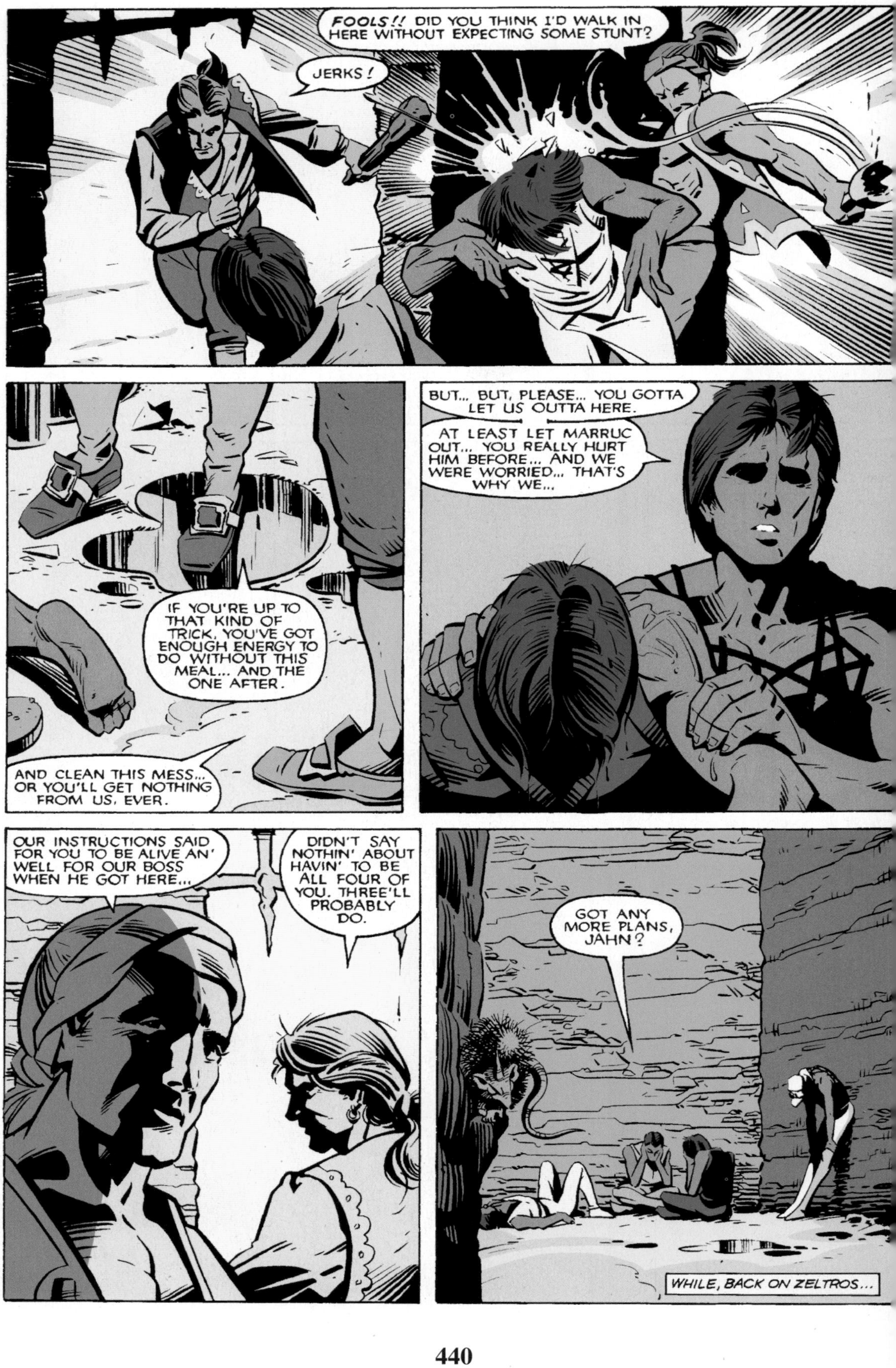
FOOLS!! DID YOU THINK I'D WALK IN HERE WITHOUT EXPECTING SOME STUNT?
JERKS!
IF YOU'RE UP TO THAT KIND OF TRICK, YOU'VE GOT ENOUGH ENERGY TO DO WITHOUT THIS MEAL... AND THE ONE AFTER.
AND CLEAN THIS MESS... OR YOU'LL GET NOTHING FROM US, EVER.
BUT... BUT, PLEASE... YOU GOTTA LET US OUTTA HERE.
AT LEAST LET MARRUC OUT... YOU REALLY HURT HIM BEFORE... AND WE WERE WORRIED... THAT'S WHY WE...
OUR INSTRUCTIONS SAID FOR YOU TO BE ALIVE AN' WELL FOR OUR BOSS WHEN HE GOT HERE...
DIDN'T SAY NOTHIN' ABOUT HAVIN' TO BE ALL FOUR OF YOU. THREE'LL PROBABLY DO.
WHILE, BACK ON ZELTROS...
GOT ANY MORE PLANS, JAHN?

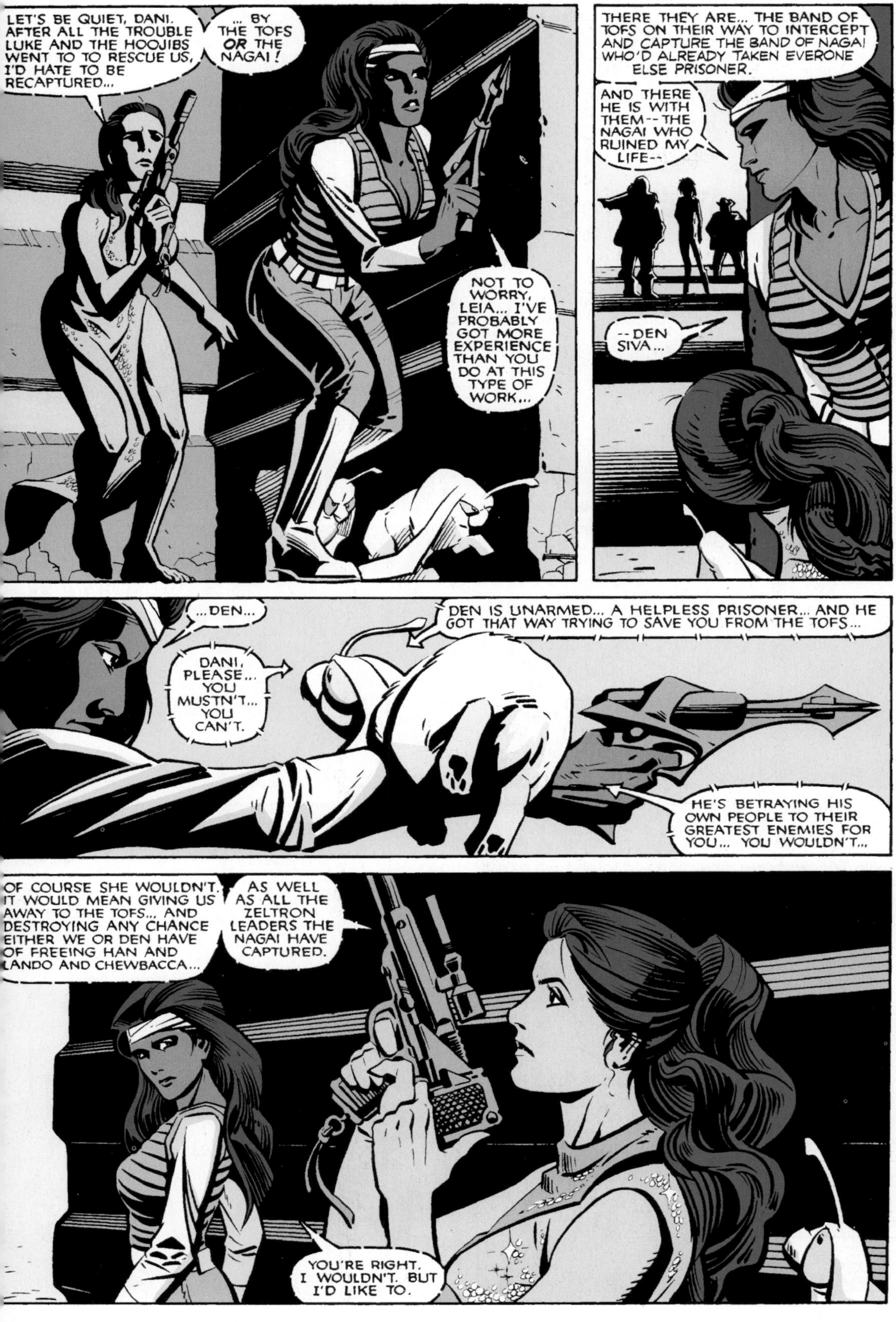
LET'S BE QUIET, DANI. AFTER ALL THE TROUBLE LUKE AND THE HOOJIBS WENT TO TO RESCUE US, I'D HATE TO BE RECAPTURED...
... BY THE TOFS OR THE NAGAI!
NOT TO WORRY, LEIA... I'VE PROBABLY GOT MORE EXPERIENCE THAN YOU DO AT THIS TYPE OF WORK...
THERE THEY ARE... THE BAND OF TOFS ON THEIR WAY TO INTERCEPT AND CAPTURE THE BAND OF NAGAI WHO'D ALREADY TAKEN EVERONE ELSE PRISONER.
AND THERE HE IS WITH THEM--THE NAGAI WHO RUINED MY LIFE--
--DEN SIVA...
...DEN...
DEN IS UNARMED... A HELPLESS PRISONER... AND HE GOT THAT WAY TRYING TO SAVE YOU FROM THE TOFS...
DANI, PLEASE... YOU MUSTN'T... YOU CAN'T.
HE'S BETRAYING HIS OWN PEOPLE TO THEIR GREATEST ENEMIES FOR YOU... YOU WOULDN'T...
OF COURSE SHE WOULDN'T. IT WOULD MEAN GIVING US AWAY TO THE TOFS... AND DESTROYING ANY CHANCE EITHER WE OR DEN HAVE OF FREEING HAN AND LANDO AND CHEWBACCA...
AS WELL AS ALL THE ZELTRON LEADERS THE NAGAI HAVE CAPTURED.
YOU'RE RIGHT. I WOULDN'T. BUT I'D LIKE TO.

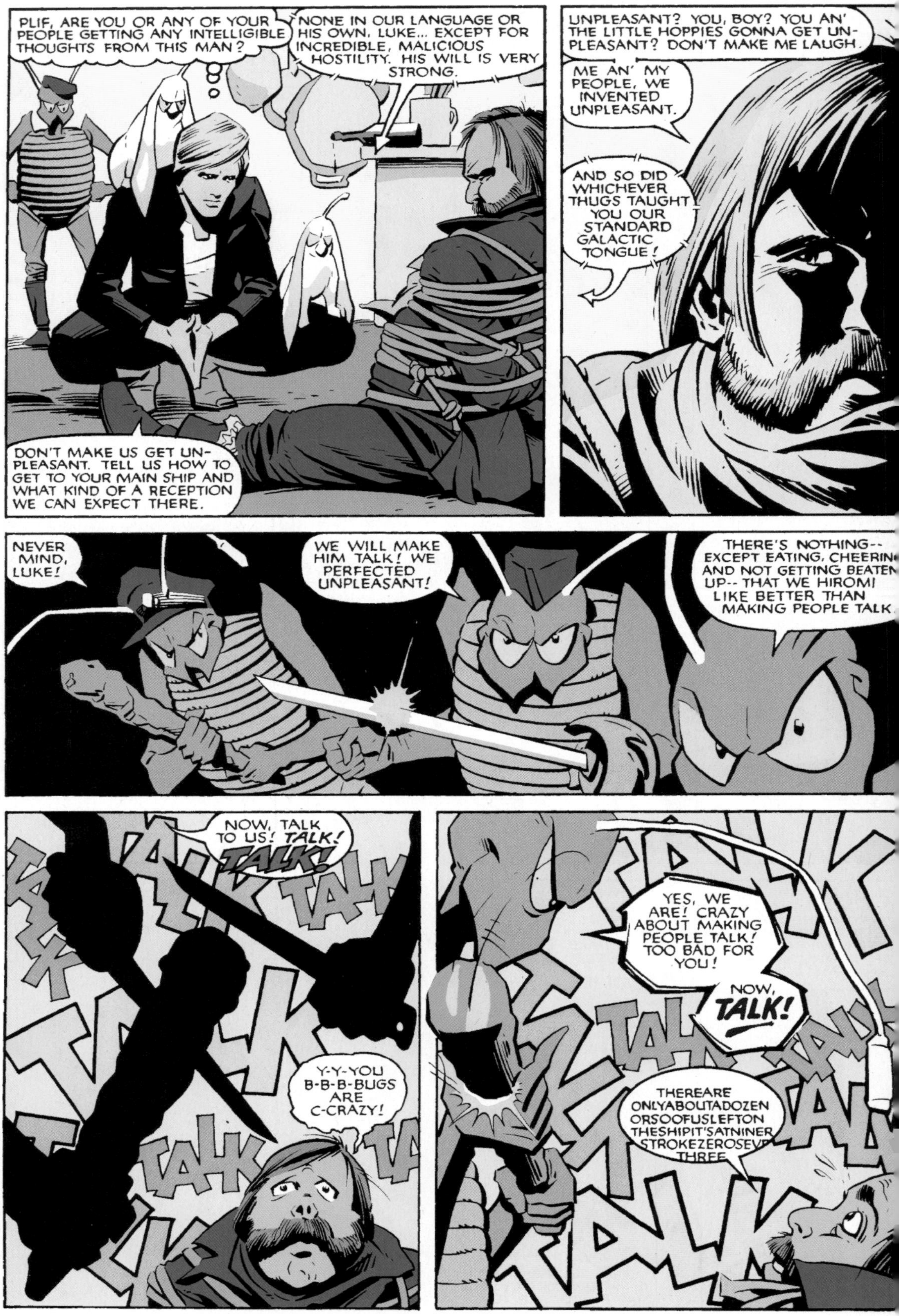
PLIF, ARE YOU OR ANY OF YOUR PEOPLE GETTING ANY INTELLIGIBLE THOUGHTS FROM THIS MAN?
NONE IN OUR LANGUAGE OR HIS OWN, LUKE... EXCEPT FOR INCREDIBLE, MALICIOUS HOSTILITY. HIS WILL IS VERY STRONG.
DON'T MAKE US GET UNPLEASANT. TELL US HOW TO GET TO YOUR MAIN SHIP AND WHAT KIND OF A RECEPTION WE CAN EXPECT THERE.
UNPLEASANT? YOU, BOY? YOU AN' THE LITTLE HOPPIES GONNA GET UNPLEASANT? DON'T MAKE ME LAUGH.
ME AN' MY PEOPLE, WE INVENTED UNPLEASANT.
AND SO DID WHICHEVER THUGS TAUGHT YOU OUR STANDARD GALACTIC TONGUE!
NEVER MIND, LUKE!
WE WILL MAKE HIM TALK! WE PERFECTED UNPLEASANT!
THERE'S NOTHING-- EXCEPT EATING, CHEERIN AND NOT GETTING BEATEN UP-- THAT WE HIROMI LIKE BETTER THAN MAKING PEOPLE TALK.
NOW, TALK TO US! TALK! TALK!
TALK TALK TALK TALK TALK TALK
Y-Y-YOU B-B-B-BUGS ARE C-CRAZY!
YES, WE ARE! CRAZY ABOUT MAKING PEOPLE TALK! TOO BAD FOR YOU!
NOW, TALK!
TALK TALK TALK TALK
THEREARE ONLYABOUTADOZEN ORSOOFUSLEFTON THESHIPIT'SATNINER STROKEZEROSEV THREE

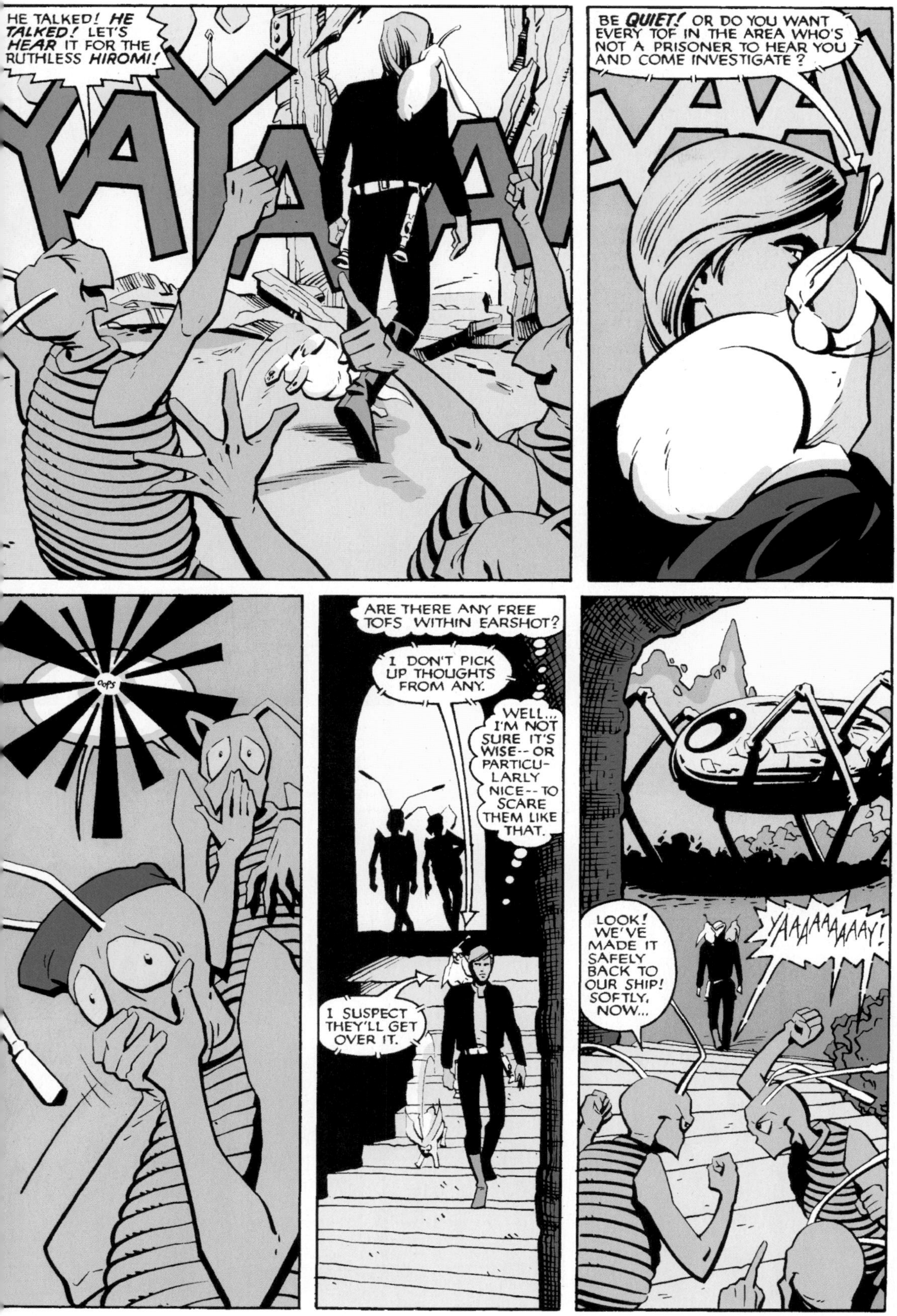

HE TALKED! HE TALKED! LET'S HEAR IT FOR THE RUTHLESS HIROMI!
YAYAYAA
BE QUIET! OR DO YOU WANT EVERY TOF IN THE AREA WHO'S NOT A PRISONER TO HEAR YOU AND COME INVESTIGATE?
OOPS
ARE THERE ANY FREE TOFS WITHIN EARSHOT?
I DON'T PICK UP THOUGHTS FROM ANY.
WELL... I'M NOT SURE IT'S WISE--OR PARTICULARLY NICE--TO SCARE THEM LIKE THAT.
I SUSPECT THEY'LL GET OVER IT.
LOOK! WE'VE MADE IT SAFELY BACK TO OUR SHIP! SOFTLY, NOW...
YAAAAAAAAY!

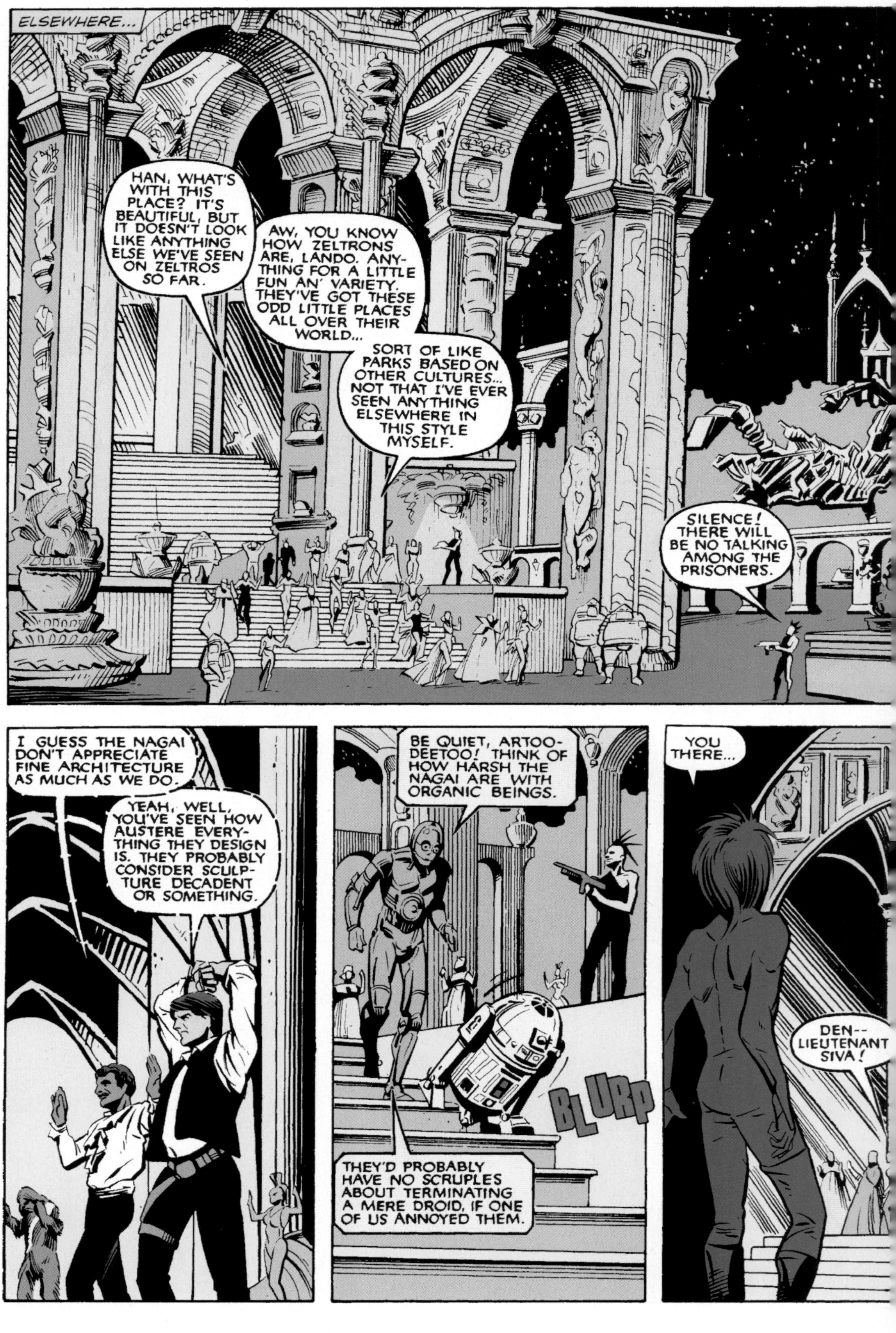
ELSEWHERE...
HAN, WHAT'S WITH THIS PLACE? IT'S BEAUTIFUL, BUT IT DOESN'T LOOK LIKE ANYTHING ELSE WE'VE SEEN ON ZELTROS SO FAR.
AW, YOU KNOW HOW ZELTRONS ARE, LANDO. ANYTHING FOR A LITTLE FUN AN' VARIETY. THEY'VE GOT THESE ODD LITTLE PLACES ALL OVER THEIR WORLD...
SORT OF LIKE PARKS BASED ON OTHER CULTURES... NOT THAT I'VE EVER SEEN ANYTHING ELSEWHERE IN THIS STYLE MYSELF.
SILENCE! THERE WILL BE NO TALKING AMONG THE PRISONERS.
I GUESS THE NAGAI DON'T APPRECIATE FINE ARCHITECTURE AS MUCH AS WE DO.
YEAH, WELL, YOU'VE SEEN HOW AUSTERE EVERYTHING THEY DESIGN IS. THEY PROBABLY CONSIDER SCULPTURE DECADENT OR SOMETHING.
BE QUIET, ARTOO-DEETOO! THINK OF HOW HARSH THE NAGAI ARE WITH ORGANIC BEINGS.
BLURP
THEY'D PROBABLY HAVE NO SCRUPLES ABOUT TERMINATING A MERE DROID, IF ONE OF US ANNOYED THEM.
YOU THERE...
DEN-- LIEUTENANT SIVA!

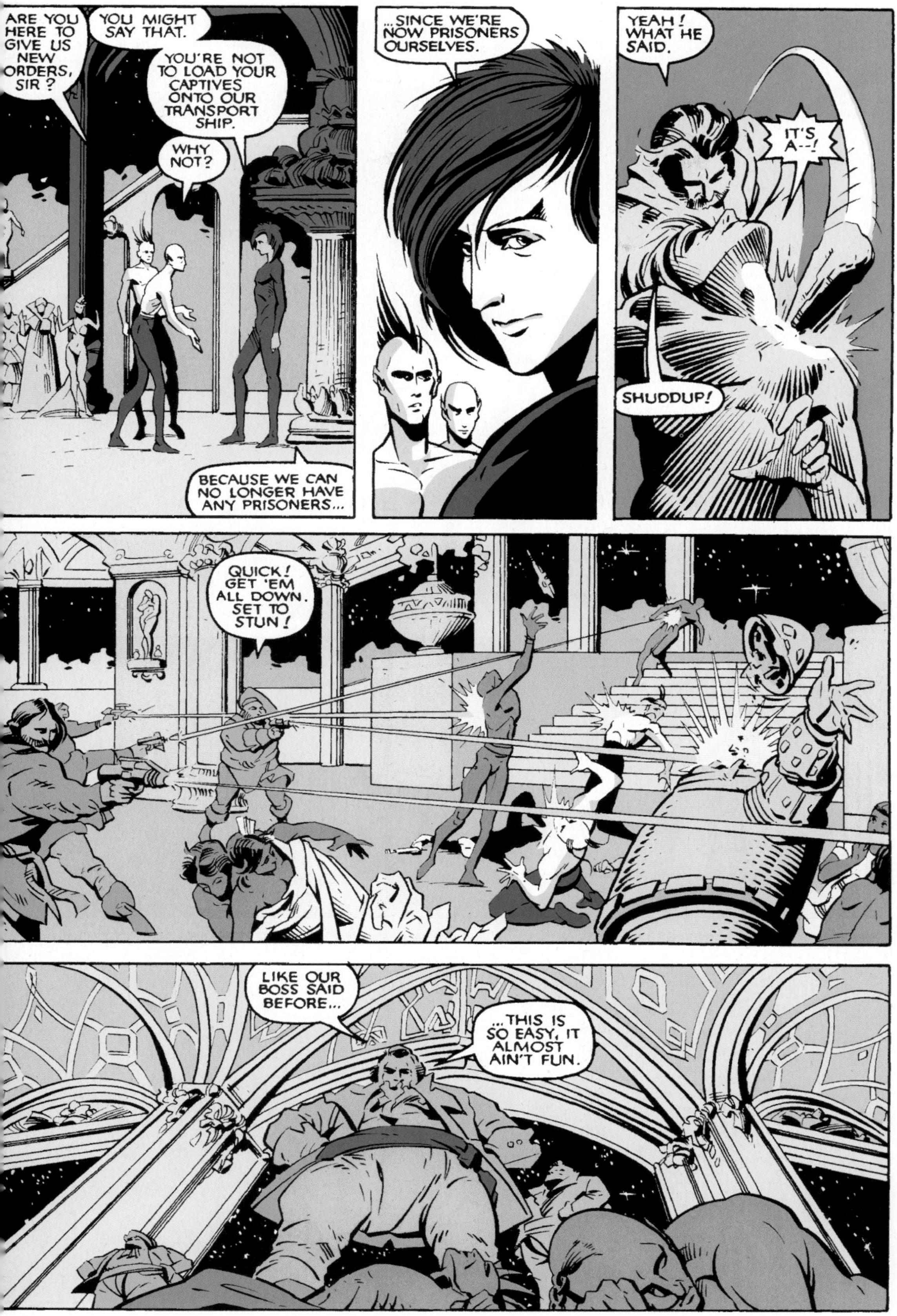
ARE YOU HERE TO GIVE US NEW ORDERS, SIR?
YOU MIGHT SAY THAT.
YOU'RE NOT TO LOAD YOUR CAPTIVES ONTO OUR TRANSPORT SHIP.
WHY NOT?
BECAUSE WE CAN NO LONGER HAVE ANY PRISONERS...
...SINCE WE'RE NOW PRISONERS OURSELVES.
YEAH! WHAT HE SAID.
IT'S A--!
SHUDDUP!
QUICK! GET 'EM ALL DOWN. SET TO STUN!
LIKE OUR BOSS SAID BEFORE...
...THIS IS SO EASY, IT ALMOST AIN'T FUN.

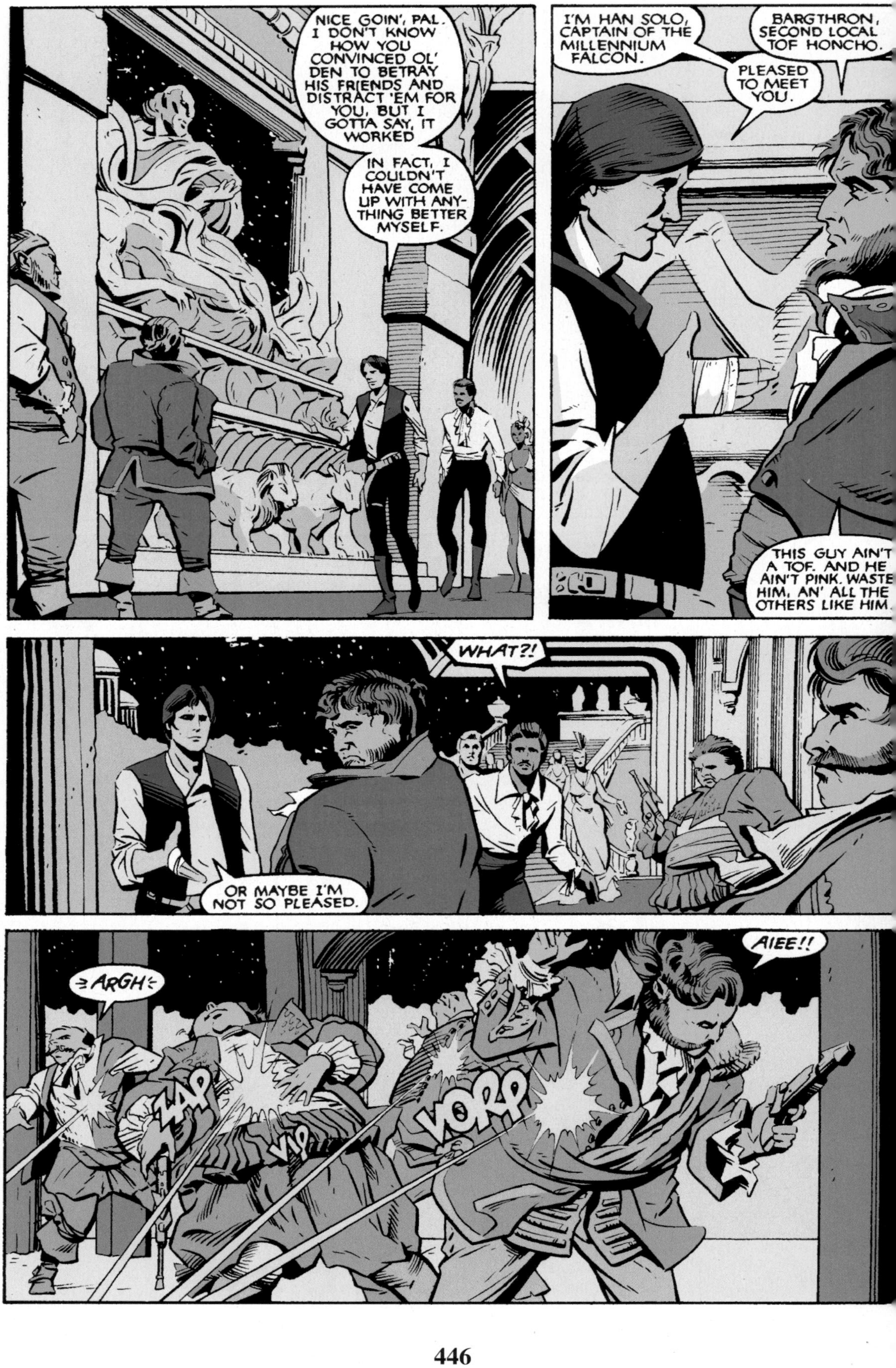
NICE GOIN', PAL. I DON'T KNOW HOW YOU CONVINCED OL' DEN TO BETRAY HIS FRIENDS AND DISTRACT 'EM FOR YOU, BUT I GOTTA SAY, IT WORKED
IN FACT, I COULDN'T HAVE COME UP WITH ANYTHING BETTER MYSELF.
I'M HAN SOLO, CAPTAIN OF THE MILLENNIUM FALCON.
BARGTHRON, SECOND LOCAL TOF HONCHO.
PLEASED TO MEET YOU.
THIS GUY AIN'T A TOF. AND HE AIN'T PINK. WASTE HIM, AN' ALL THE OTHERS LIKE HIM.
WHAT?!
OR MAYBE I'M NOT SO PLEASED.
AIEE!!
ARGH
ZAP
VORP

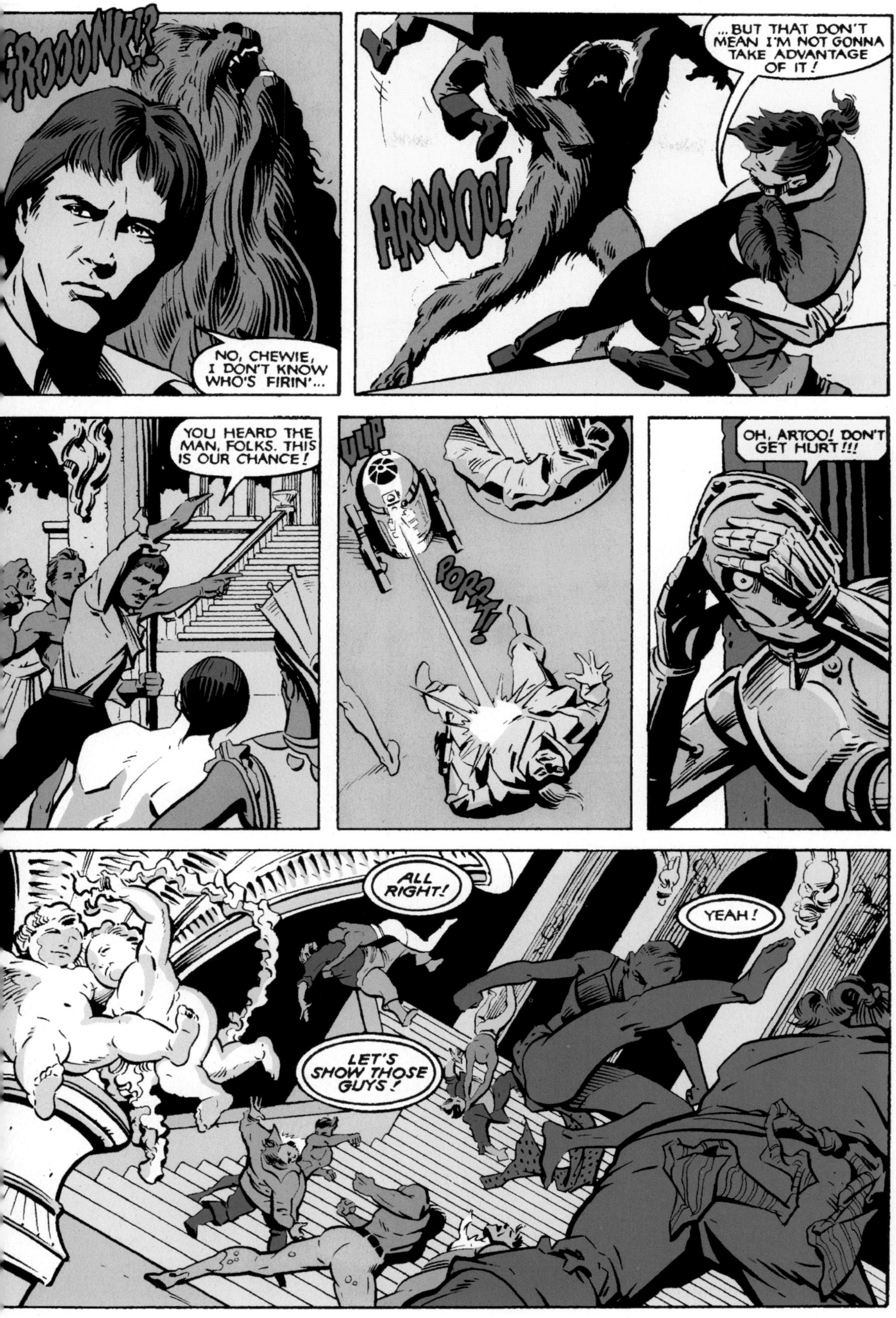
GROOONK!?
NO, CHEWIE, I DON'T KNOW WHO'S FIRIN'...
...BUT THAT DON'T MEAN I'M NOT GONNA TAKE ADVANTAGE OF IT!
AROOOO!
YOU HEARD THE MAN, FOLKS. THIS IS OUR CHANCE!
ULP
PORRT!
OH, ARTOO! DON'T GET HURT!!!
ALL RIGHT!
YEAH!
LET'S SHOW THOSE GUYS!

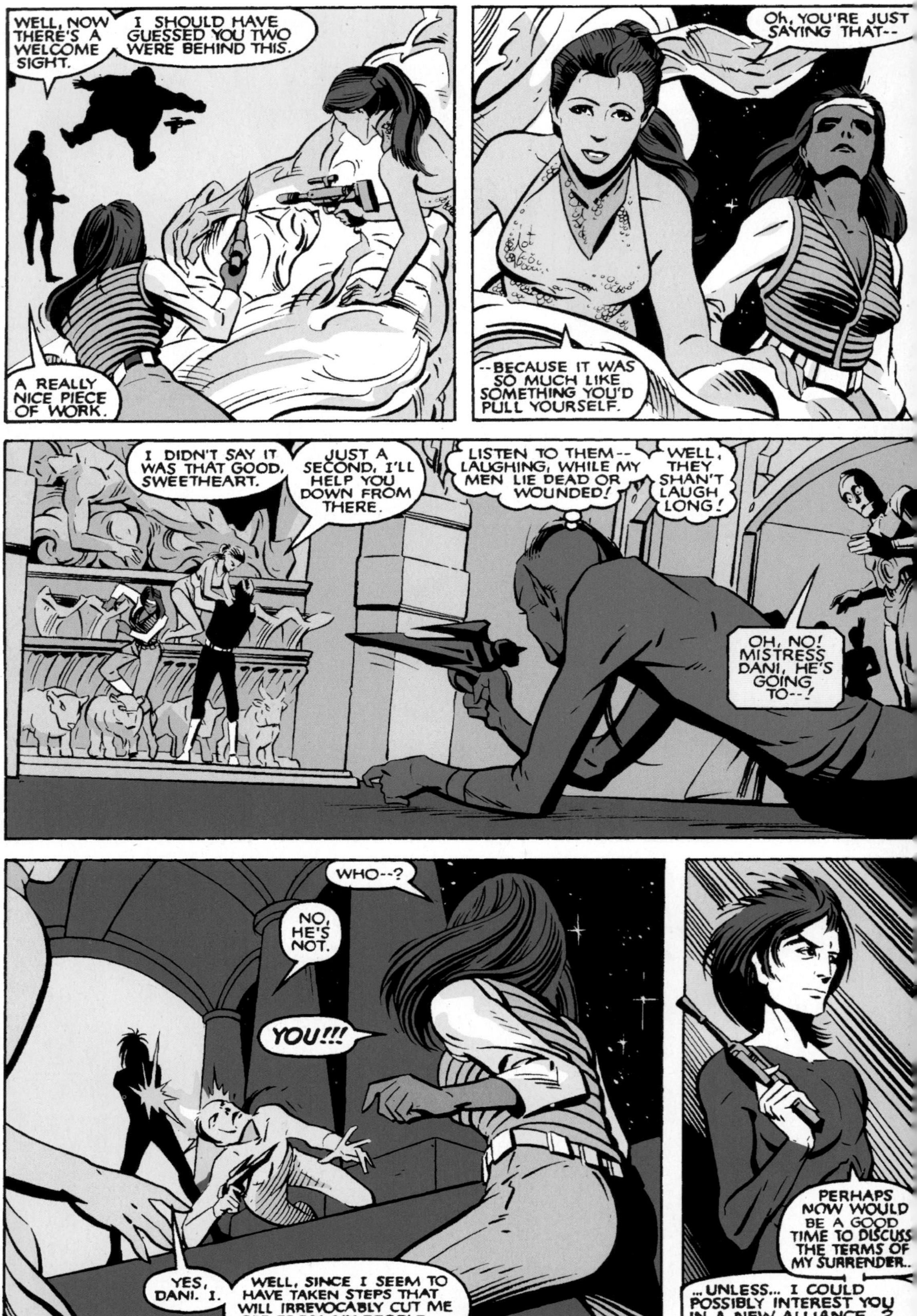
WELL, NOW THERE'S A WELCOME SIGHT.
I SHOULD HAVE GUESSED YOU TWO WERE BEHIND THIS.
A REALLY NICE PIECE OF WORK.
Oh, YOU'RE JUST SAYING THAT--
--BECAUSE IT WAS SO MUCH LIKE SOMETHING YOU'D PULL YOURSELF.
I DIDN'T SAY IT WAS THAT GOOD, SWEETHEART.
JUST A SECOND, I'LL HELP YOU DOWN FROM THERE.
LISTEN TO THEM-- LAUGHING, WHILE MY MEN LIE DEAD OR WOUNDED!
WELL, THEY SHAN'T LAUGH LONG!
OH, NO! MISTRESS DANI, HE'S GOING TO--!
WHO--?
NO, HE'S NOT.
YOU!!!
YES, DANI. I.
WELL, SINCE I SEEM TO HAVE TAKEN STEPS THAT WILL IRREVOCABLY CUT ME OFF FROM MY PEOPLE--
PERHAPS NOW WOULD BE A GOOD TIME TO DISCUSS THE TERMS OF MY SURRENDER..
...UNLESS... I COULD POSSIBLY INTEREST YOU IN A NEW ALLIANCE...?

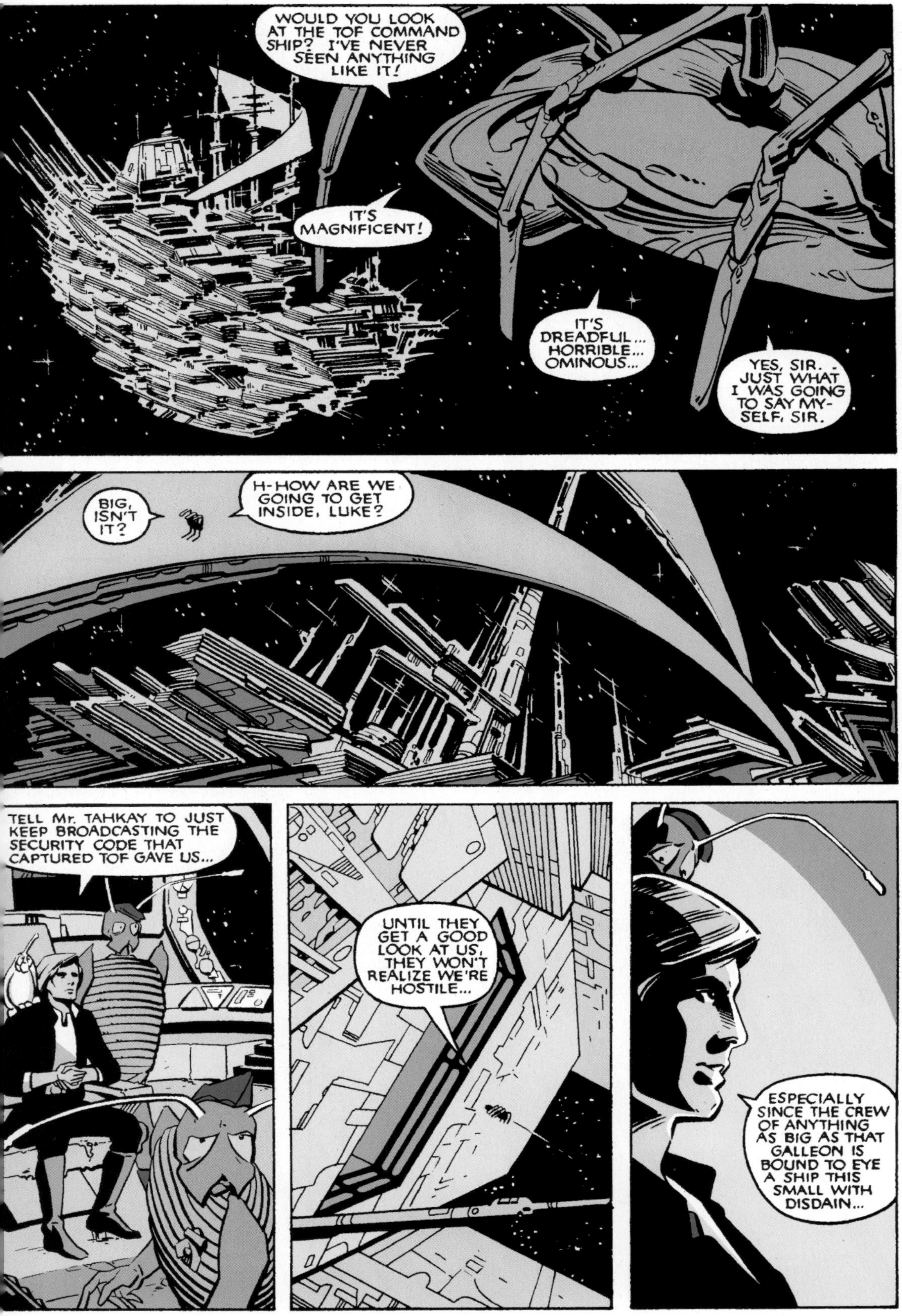
WOULD YOU LOOK AT THE TOF COMMAND SHIP? I'VE NEVER SEEN ANYTHING LIKE IT!
IT'S MAGNIFICENT!
IT'S DREADFUL... HORRIBLE... OMINOUS...
YES, SIR. JUST WHAT I WAS GOING TO SAY MY-SELF, SIR.
BIG, ISN'T IT?
H-HOW ARE WE GOING TO GET INSIDE, LUKE?
TELL Mr. TAHKAY TO JUST KEEP BROADCASTING THE SECURITY CODE THAT CAPTURED TOF GAVE US...
UNTIL THEY GET A GOOD LOOK AT US, THEY WON'T REALIZE WE'RE HOSTILE...
ESPECIALLY SINCE THE CREW OF ANYTHING AS BIG AS THAT GALLEON IS BOUND TO EYE A SHIP THIS SMALL WITH DISDAIN...

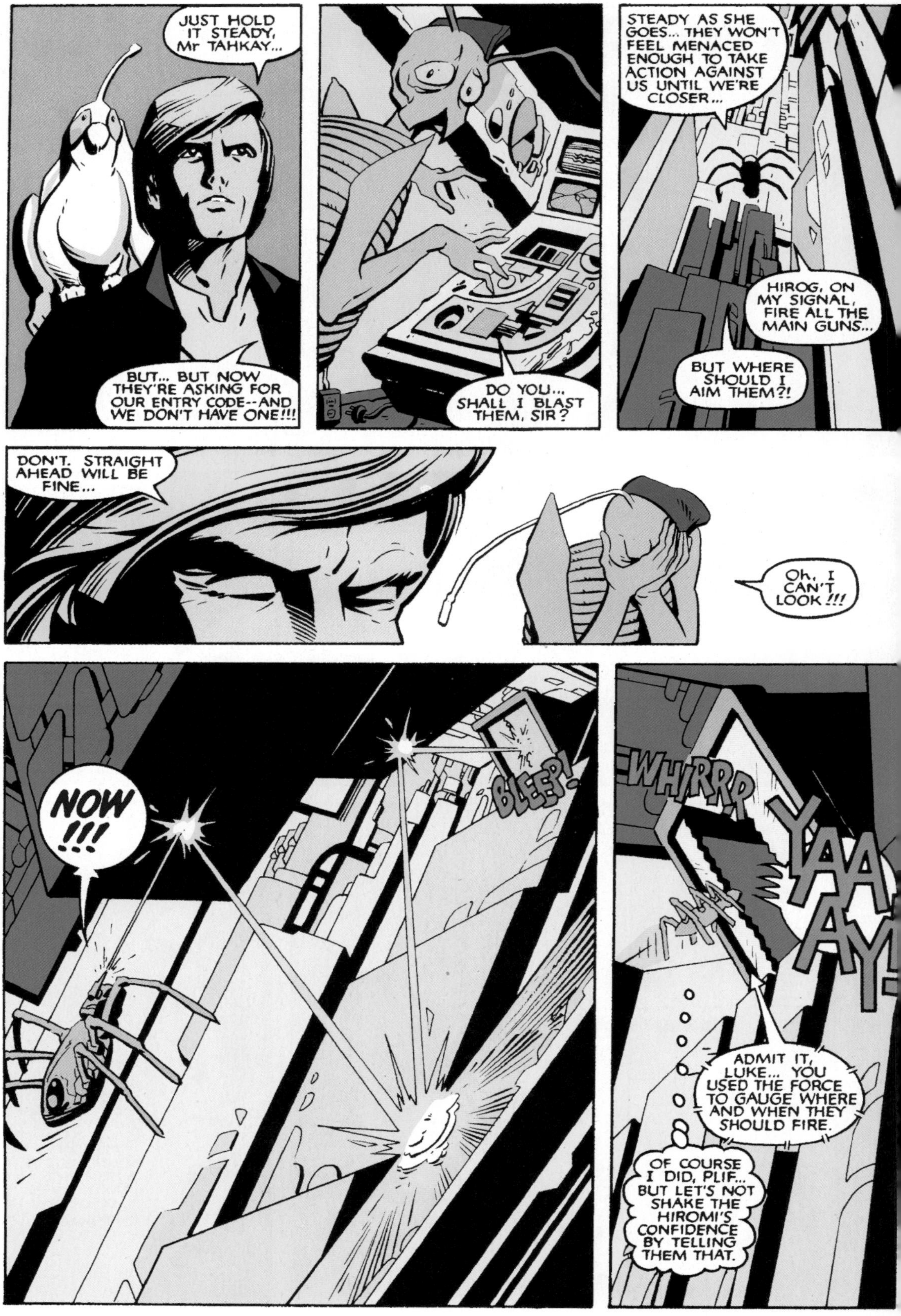
JUST HOLD IT STEADY, Mr TAHKAY...
BUT... BUT NOW THEY'RE ASKING FOR OUR ENTRY CODE--AND WE DON'T HAVE ONE!!!
DO YOU... SHALL I BLAST THEM, SIR?
STEADY AS SHE GOES... THEY WON'T FEEL MENACED ENOUGH TO TAKE ACTION AGAINST US UNTIL WE'RE CLOSER...
HIROG, ON MY SIGNAL, FIRE ALL THE MAIN GUNS...
BUT WHERE SHOULD I AIM THEM?!
DON'T. STRAIGHT AHEAD WILL BE FINE...
Oh, I CAN'T LOOK!!!
NOW!!!
BLEEP!
WHIRRRR
YAAAY!
ADMIT IT, LUKE... YOU USED THE FORCE TO GAUGE WHERE AND WHEN THEY SHOULD FIRE.
OF COURSE I DID, PLIF... BUT LET'S NOT SHAKE THE HIROMI'S CONFIDENCE BY TELLING THEM THAT.

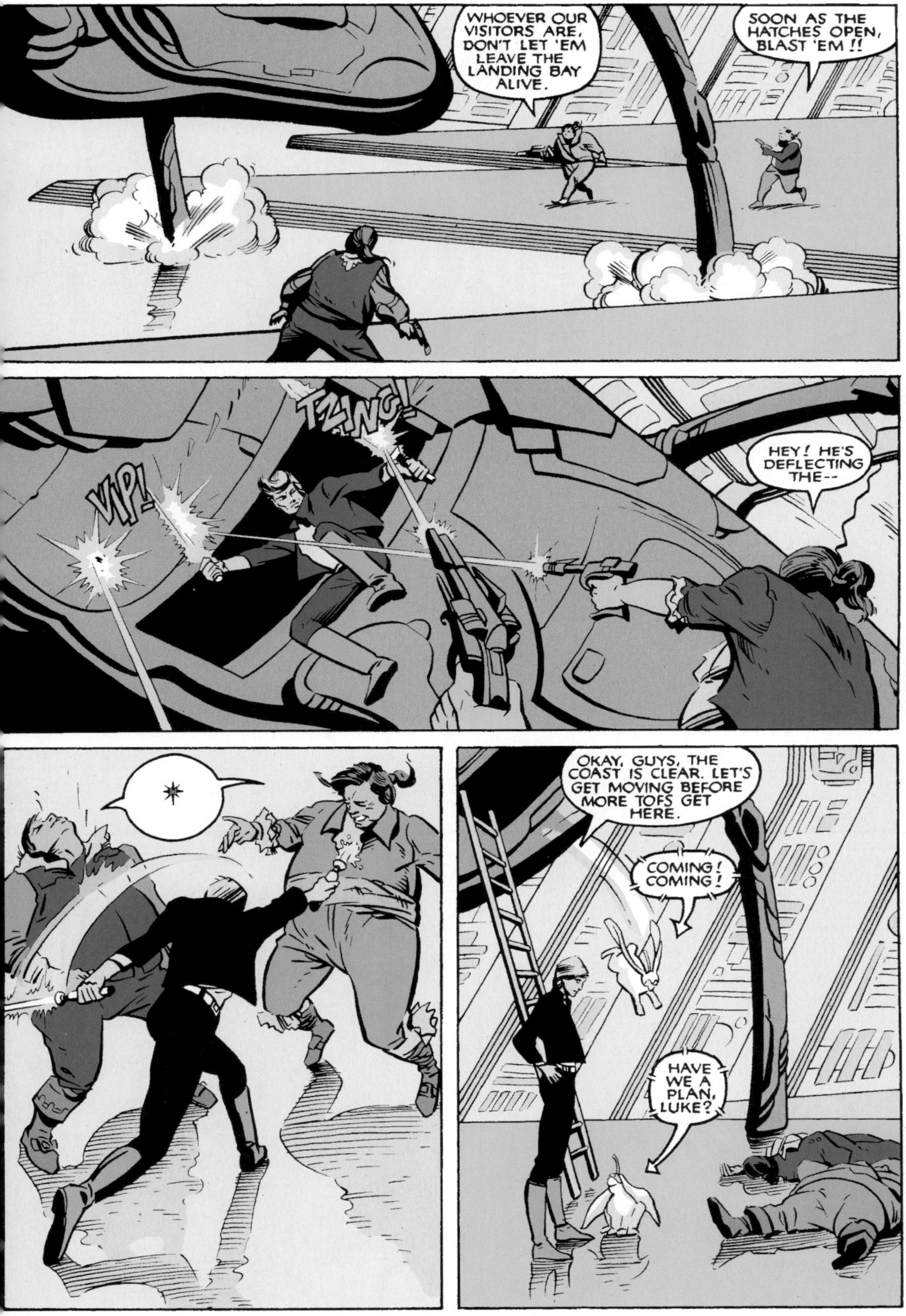
WHOEVER OUR VISITORS ARE, DON'T LET 'EM LEAVE THE LANDING BAY ALIVE.
SOON AS THE HATCHES OPEN, BLAST 'EM !!
TZING!
VIP!
HEY! HE'S DEFLECTING THE--
OKAY, GUYS, THE COAST IS CLEAR. LET'S GET MOVING BEFORE MORE TOFS GET HERE.
COMING! COMING!
HAVE WE A PLAN, LUKE?

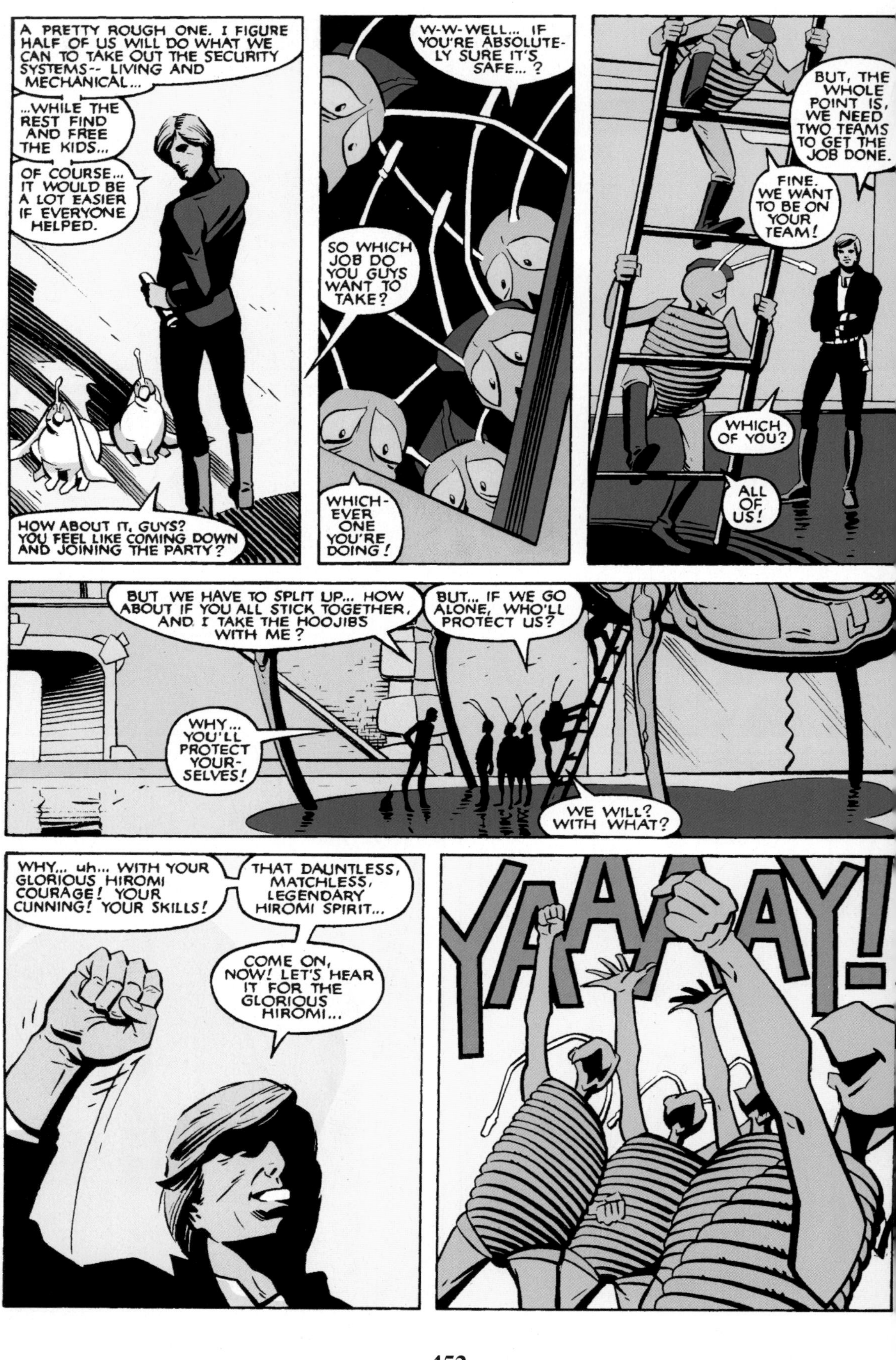

A PRETTY ROUGH ONE. I FIGURE HALF OF US WILL DO WHAT WE CAN TO TAKE OUT THE SECURITY SYSTEMS-- LIVING AND MECHANICAL...
...WHILE THE REST FIND AND FREE THE KIDS...
OF COURSE... IT WOULD BE A LOT EASIER IF EVERYONE HELPED.
HOW ABOUT IT, GUYS? YOU FEEL LIKE COMING DOWN AND JOINING THE PARTY?
W-W-WELL... IF YOU'RE ABSOLUTELY SURE IT'S SAFE...?
SO WHICH JOB DO YOU GUYS WANT TO TAKE?
WHICHEVER ONE YOU'RE DOING!
BUT, THE WHOLE POINT IS, WE NEED TWO TEAMS TO GET THE JOB DONE.
FINE. WE WANT TO BE ON YOUR TEAM!
WHICH OF YOU?
ALL OF US!
BUT WE HAVE TO SPLIT UP... HOW ABOUT IF YOU ALL STICK TOGETHER, AND I TAKE THE HOOJIBS WITH ME?
BUT... IF WE GO ALONE, WHO'LL PROTECT US?
WHY... YOU'LL PROTECT YOURSELVES!
WE WILL? WITH WHAT?
WHY... uh... WITH YOUR GLORIOUS HIROMI COURAGE! YOUR CUNNING! YOUR SKILLS!
THAT DAUNTLESS, MATCHLESS, LEGENDARY HIROMI SPIRIT...
COME ON, NOW! LET'S HEAR IT FOR THE GLORIOUS HIROMI...
YAAAAY!

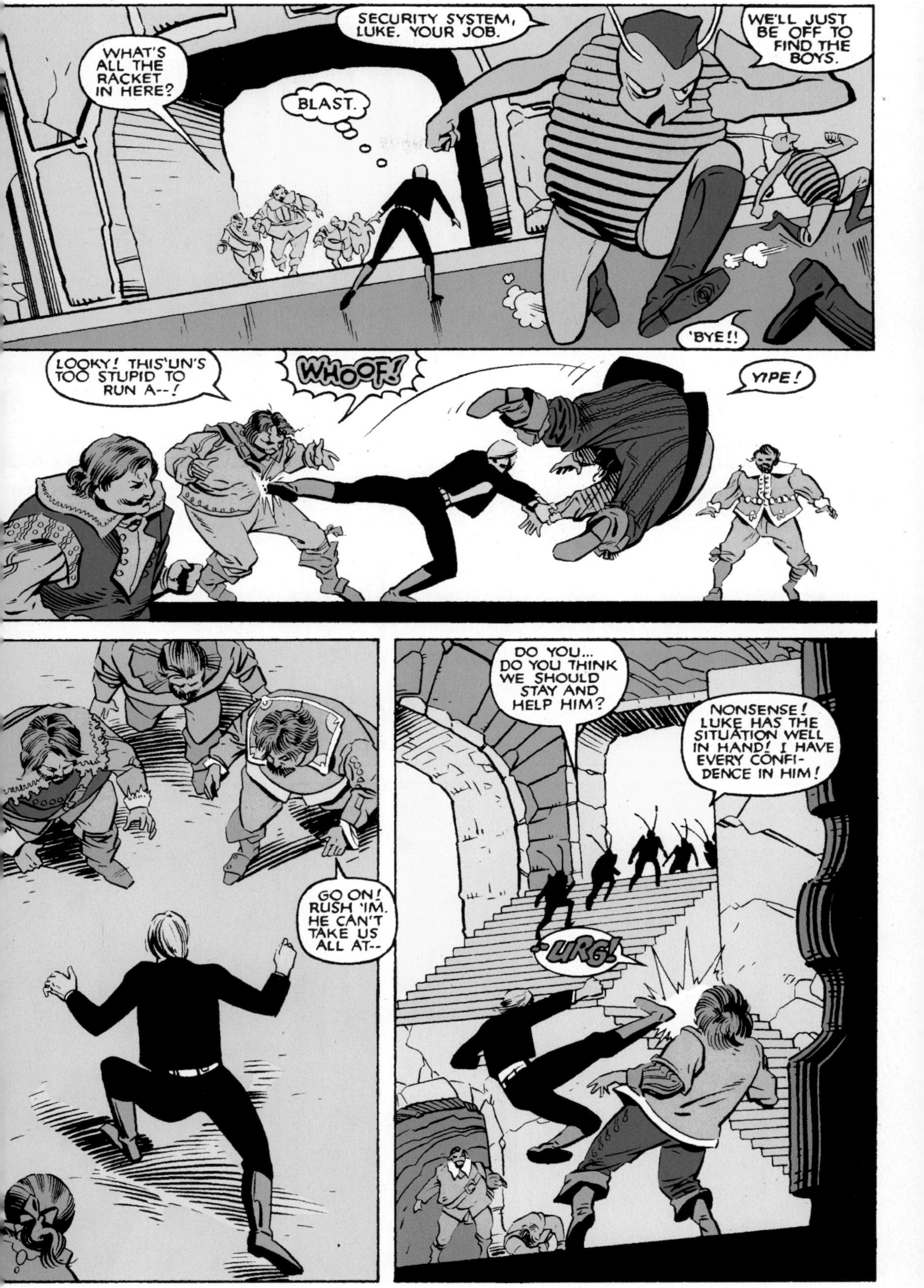
WHAT'S ALL THE RACKET IN HERE?
SECURITY SYSTEM, LUKE. YOUR JOB.
BLAST.
WE'LL JUST BE OFF TO FIND THE BOYS.
'BYE!!
LOOKY! THIS'UN'S TOO STUPID TO RUN A--!
WHOOF!
YIPE!
GO ON! RUSH 'IM. HE CAN'T TAKE US ALL AT--
DO YOU... DO YOU THINK WE SHOULD STAY AND HELP HIM?
NONSENSE! LUKE HAS THE SITUATION WELL IN HAND! I HAVE EVERY CONFI-DENCE IN HIM!
URG!

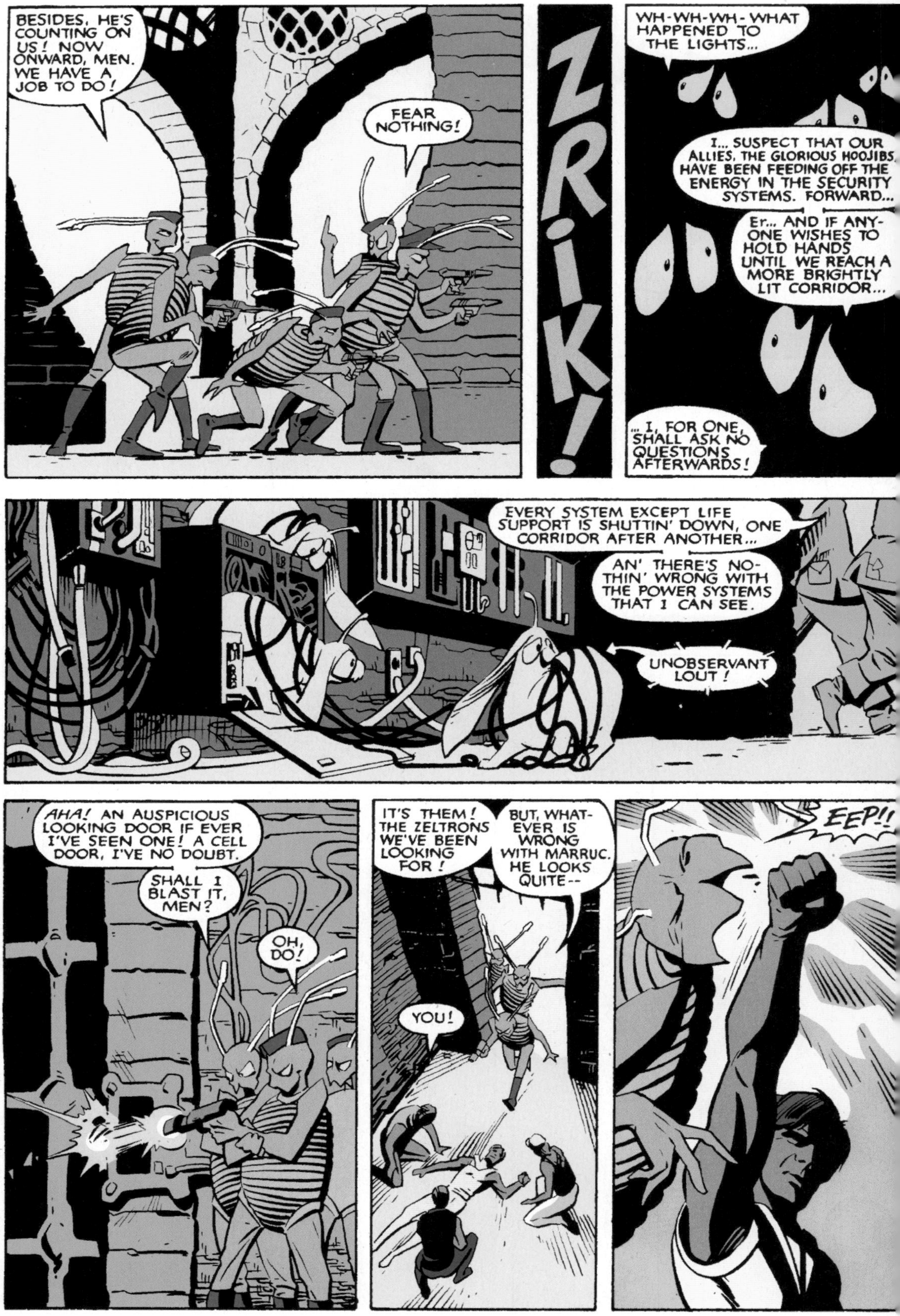

BESIDES, HE'S COUNTING ON US! NOW ONWARD, MEN. WE HAVE A JOB TO DO!
FEAR NOTHING!
ZRiK!
WH-WH-WH-WHAT HAPPENED TO THE LIGHTS...
I... SUSPECT THAT OUR ALLIES, THE GLORIOUS HOOJIBS, HAVE BEEN FEEDING OFF THE ENERGY IN THE SECURITY SYSTEMS. FORWARD...
Er... AND IF ANY-ONE WISHES TO HOLD HANDS UNTIL WE REACH A MORE BRIGHTLY LIT CORRIDOR...
...I, FOR ONE, SHALL ASK NO QUESTIONS AFTERWARDS!
EVERY SYSTEM EXCEPT LIFE SUPPORT IS SHUTTIN' DOWN, ONE CORRIDOR AFTER ANOTHER...
AN' THERE'S NO-THIN' WRONG WITH THE POWER SYSTEMS THAT I CAN SEE.
UNOBSERVANT LOUT!
AHA! AN AUSPICIOUS LOOKING DOOR IF EVER I'VE SEEN ONE! A CELL DOOR, I'VE NO DOUBT.
SHALL I BLAST IT, MEN?
OH, DO!
IT'S THEM! THE ZELTRONS WE'VE BEEN LOOKING FOR!
BUT, WHAT-EVER IS WRONG WITH MARRUC. HE LOOKS QUITE--
YOU!
EEP!!

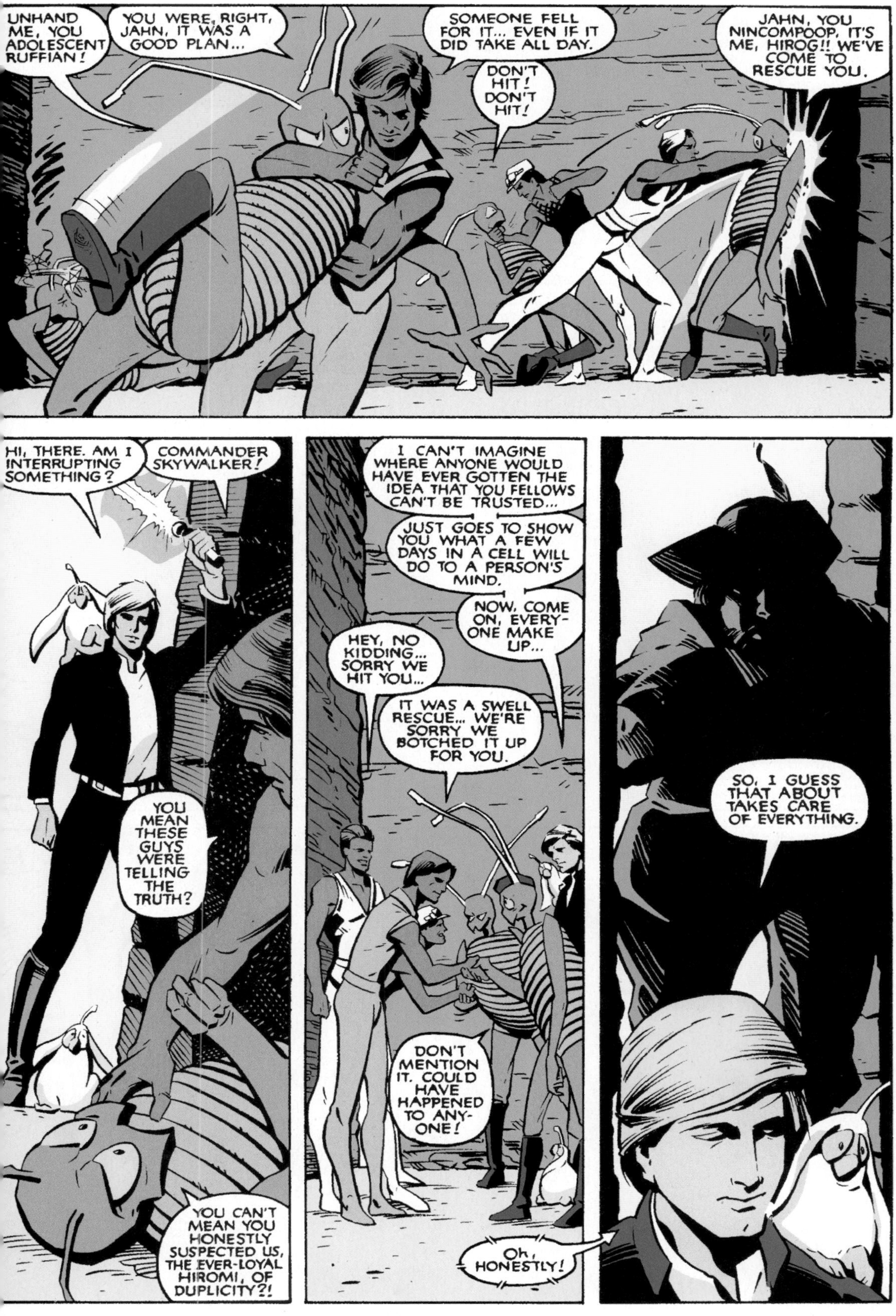
UNHAND ME, YOU ADOLESCENT RUFFIAN!
YOU WERE RIGHT, JAHN, IT WAS A GOOD PLAN...
SOMEONE FELL FOR IT... EVEN IF IT DID TAKE ALL DAY.
DON'T HIT! DON'T HIT!
JAHN, YOU NINCOMPOOP, IT'S ME, HIROG!! WE'VE COME TO RESCUE YOU.
HI, THERE. AM I INTERRUPTING SOMETHING?
COMMANDER SKYWALKER!
YOU MEAN THESE GUYS WERE TELLING THE TRUTH?
YOU CAN'T MEAN YOU HONESTLY SUSPECTED US, THE EVER-LOYAL HIROMI, OF DUPLICITY?!
I CAN'T IMAGINE WHERE ANYONE WOULD HAVE EVER GOTTEN THE IDEA THAT YOU FELLOWS CAN'T BE TRUSTED...
JUST GOES TO SHOW YOU WHAT A FEW DAYS IN A CELL WILL DO TO A PERSON'S MIND.
NOW, COME ON, EVERY-ONE MAKE UP...
HEY, NO KIDDING... SORRY WE HIT YOU...
IT WAS A SWELL RESCUE... WE'RE SORRY WE BOTCHED IT UP FOR YOU.
DON'T MENTION IT. COULD HAVE HAPPENED TO ANY-ONE!
Oh, HONESTLY!
SO, I GUESS THAT ABOUT TAKES CARE OF EVERYTHING.

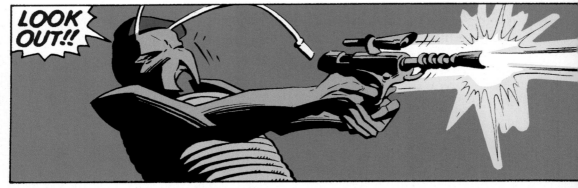

LOOK OUT!!

NICE SHOOTING, HIROG. LUCKY FOR ME YOU SPOTTED THAT TOF...

NOW WE BETTER CLEAR OUT OF HERE. TOUGH AS WE ALL ARE, I DON'T KNOW IF FIFTEEN OR SO OF US ARE ENOUGH TO TAKE ON THIS WHOLE GALLEON...

...SO I PLANTED SOME EXPLOSIVES IN A FEW OF THEIR MAIN SYSTEMS.

WE'D BETTER BE AWAY BEFORE THEY BLOW...

BE RIGHT WITH YOU, LUKE...

A TOF! WE ACTUALLY BEAT A TOF...

IN A FAIR FIGHT!

BY OUR-SELVES...

IMAGINE!!

SO, LET'S HEAR IT--

YAAAYAYY!

NEXT: OLD FRIENDS AND NEW UNITE FOR THE *FINAL CHAPTER* IN MARVEL'S CONTINUING ADVENTURES OF LUKE SKYWALKER--

ALL TOGETHER NOW!

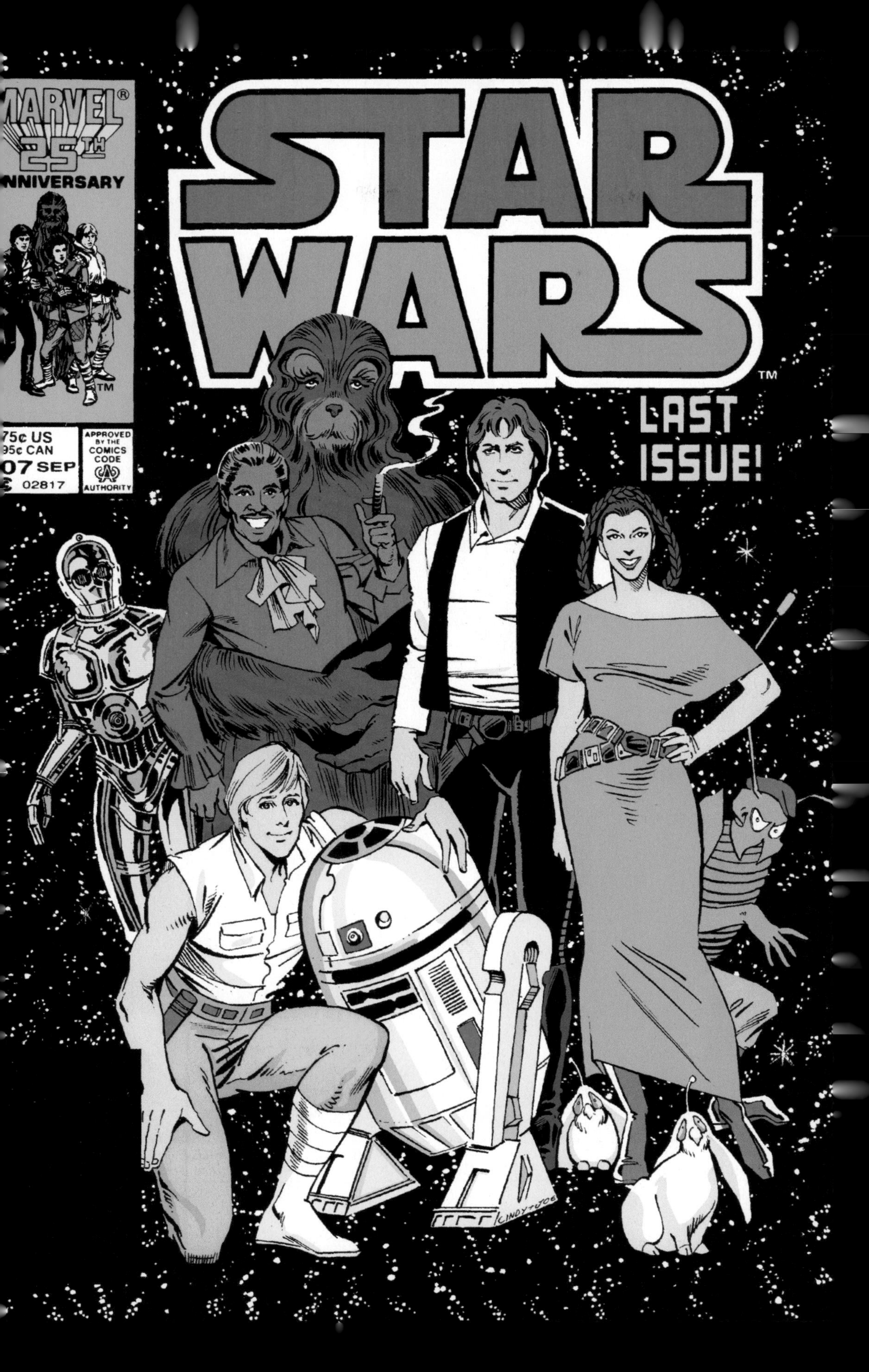
MARVEL®
25TH
ANNIVERSARY
STAR WARS™
LAST ISSUE!
75¢ US
95¢ CAN
107 SEP
02817
APPROVED BY THE COMICS CODE AUTHORITY
CINDY+JOE

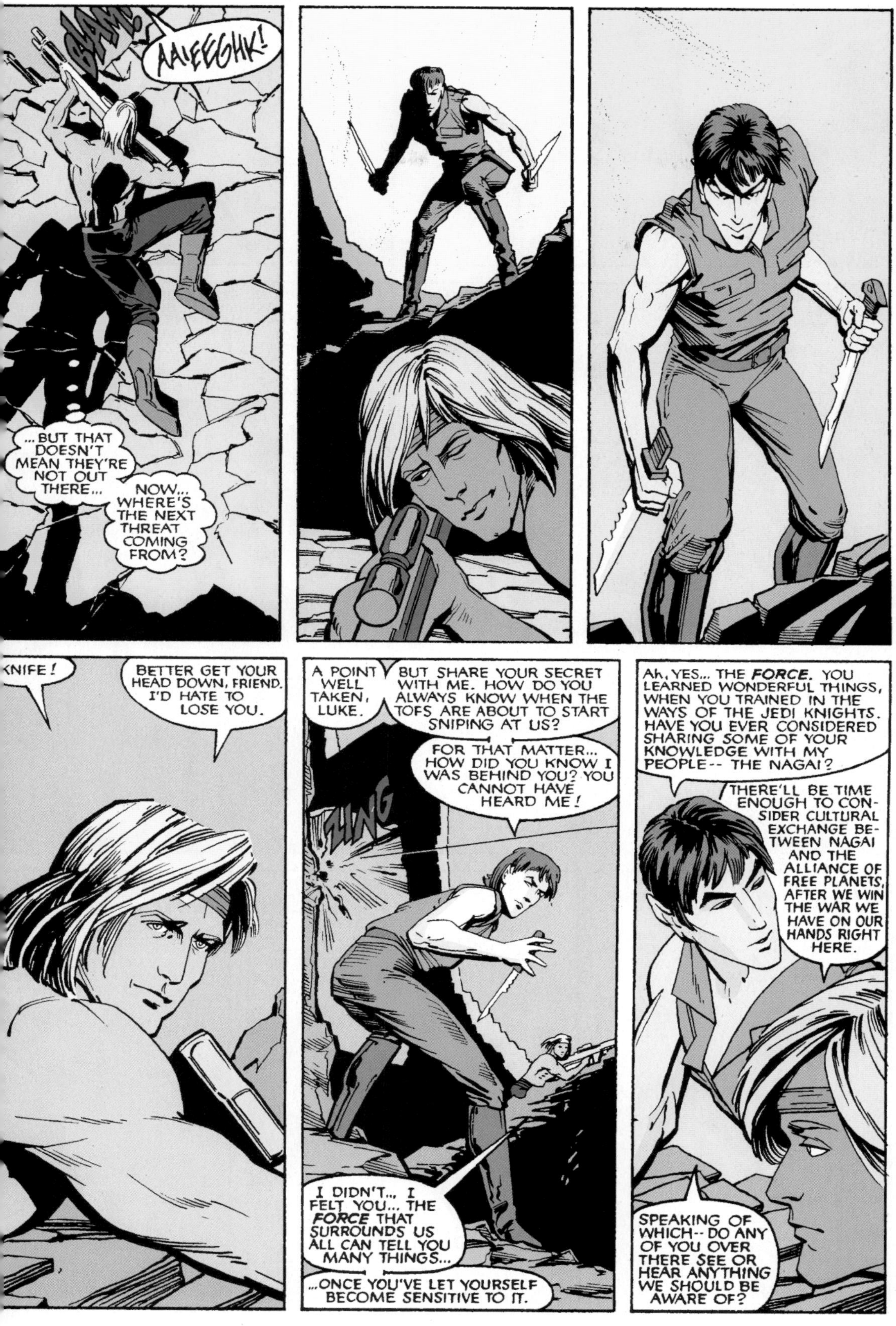
BLAM!
AAIEEGHK!
...BUT THAT DOESN'T MEAN THEY'RE NOT OUT THERE...
NOW... WHERE'S THE NEXT THREAT COMING FROM?
KNIFE!
BETTER GET YOUR HEAD DOWN, FRIEND. I'D HATE TO LOSE YOU.
A POINT WELL TAKEN, LUKE.
BUT SHARE YOUR SECRET WITH ME. HOW DO YOU ALWAYS KNOW WHEN THE TOFS ARE ABOUT TO START SNIPING AT US?
FOR THAT MATTER... HOW DID YOU KNOW I WAS BEHIND YOU? YOU CANNOT HAVE HEARD ME!
ZING
I DIDN'T... I FELT YOU... THE FORCE THAT SURROUNDS US ALL CAN TELL YOU MANY THINGS...
...ONCE YOU'VE LET YOURSELF BECOME SENSITIVE TO IT.
AH, YES... THE FORCE. YOU LEARNED WONDERFUL THINGS, WHEN YOU TRAINED IN THE WAYS OF THE JEDI KNIGHTS. HAVE YOU EVER CONSIDERED SHARING SOME OF YOUR KNOWLEDGE WITH MY PEOPLE-- THE NAGAI?
THERE'LL BE TIME ENOUGH TO CONSIDER CULTURAL EXCHANGE BETWEEN NAGAI AND THE ALLIANCE OF FREE PLANETS, AFTER WE WIN THE WAR WE HAVE ON OUR HANDS RIGHT HERE.
SPEAKING OF WHICH-- DO ANY OF YOU OVER THERE SEE OR HEAR ANYTHING WE SHOULD BE AWARE OF?

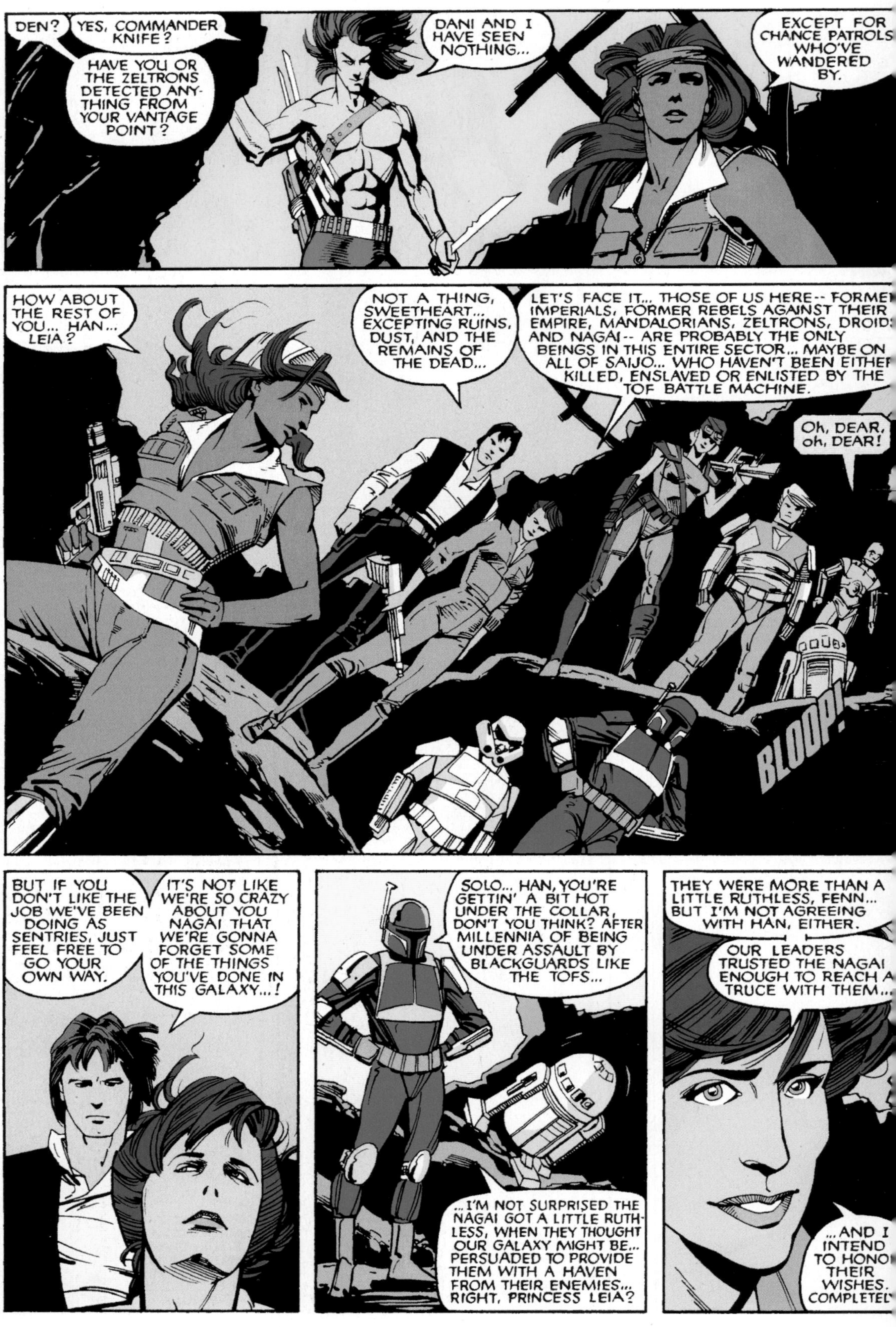
DEN?
YES, COMMANDER KNIFE?
HAVE YOU OR THE ZELTRONS DETECTED ANYTHING FROM YOUR VANTAGE POINT?
DANI AND I HAVE SEEN NOTHING...
EXCEPT FOR CHANCE PATROLS WHO'VE WANDERED BY.
HOW ABOUT THE REST OF YOU... HAN... LEIA?
NOT A THING, SWEETHEART... EXCEPTING RUINS, DUST, AND THE REMAINS OF THE DEAD...
LET'S FACE IT... THOSE OF US HERE-- FORMER IMPERIALS, FORMER REBELS AGAINST THEIR EMPIRE, MANDALORIANS, ZELTRONS, DROIDS AND NAGAI-- ARE PROBABLY THE ONLY BEINGS IN THIS ENTIRE SECTOR... MAYBE ON ALL OF SAIJO... WHO HAVEN'T BEEN EITHER KILLED, ENSLAVED OR ENLISTED BY THE TOF BATTLE MACHINE.
Oh, DEAR, oh, DEAR!
BLOOP!
BUT IF YOU DON'T LIKE THE JOB WE'VE BEEN DOING AS SENTRIES, JUST FEEL FREE TO GO YOUR OWN WAY.
IT'S NOT LIKE WE'RE SO CRAZY ABOUT YOU NAGAI THAT WE'RE GONNA FORGET SOME OF THE THINGS YOU'VE DONE IN THIS GALAXY...!
SOLO... HAN, YOU'RE GETTIN' A BIT HOT UNDER THE COLLAR, DON'T YOU THINK? AFTER MILLENNIA OF BEING UNDER ASSAULT BY BLACKGUARDS LIKE THE TOFS...
...I'M NOT SURPRISED THE NAGAI GOT A LITTLE RUTHLESS, WHEN THEY THOUGHT OUR GALAXY MIGHT BE... PERSUADED TO PROVIDE THEM WITH A HAVEN FROM THEIR ENEMIES... RIGHT, PRINCESS LEIA?
THEY WERE MORE THAN A LITTLE RUTHLESS, FENN... BUT I'M NOT AGREEING WITH HAN, EITHER.
OUR LEADERS TRUSTED THE NAGAI ENOUGH TO REACH A TRUCE WITH THEM...
...AND I INTEND TO HONO THEIR WISHES. COMPLETEL

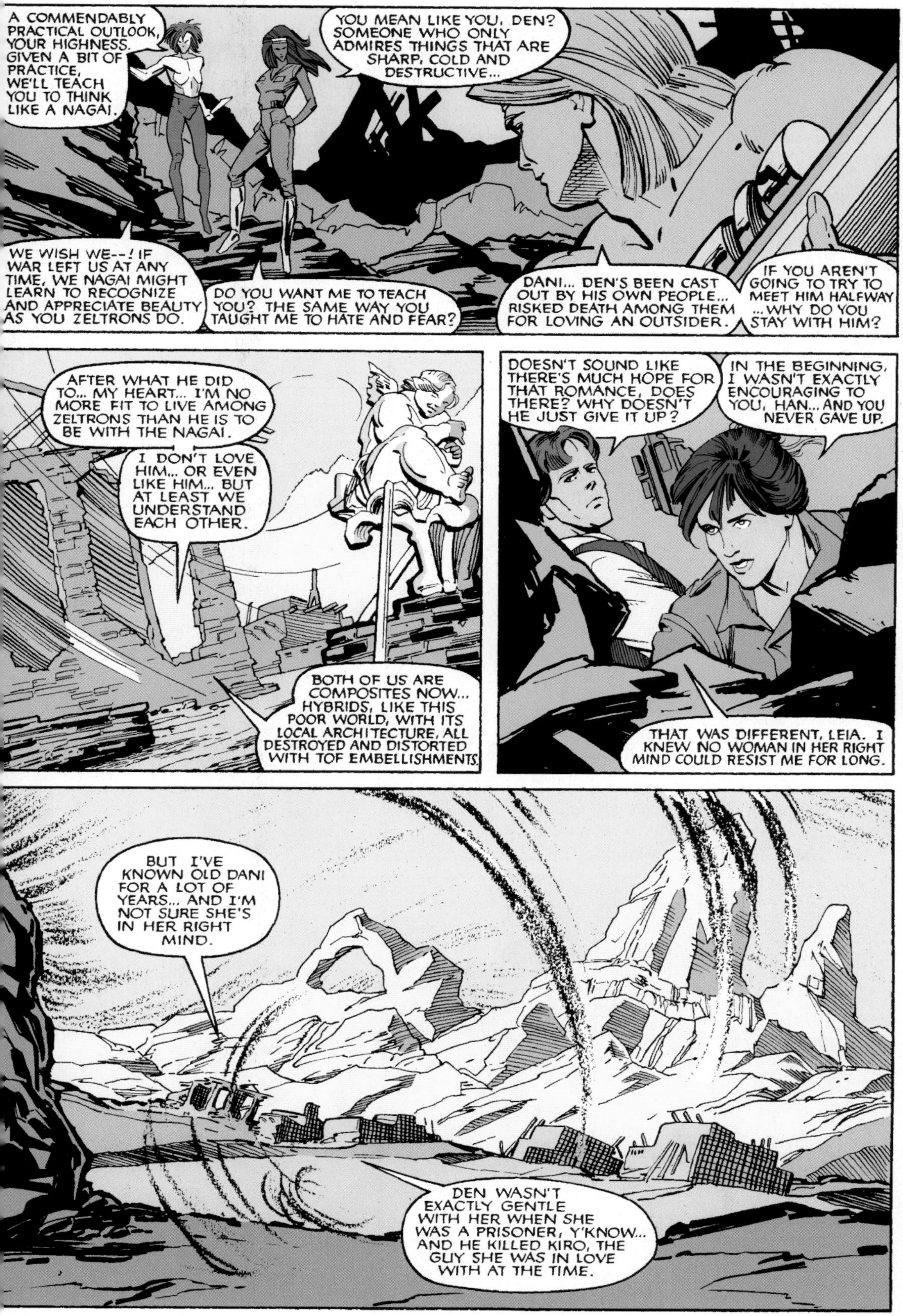
A COMMENDABLY PRACTICAL OUTLOOK, YOUR HIGHNESS. GIVEN A BIT OF PRACTICE, WE'LL TEACH YOU TO THINK LIKE A NAGAI.
YOU MEAN LIKE YOU, DEN? SOMEONE WHO ONLY ADMIRES THINGS THAT ARE SHARP, COLD AND DESTRUCTIVE...
WE WISH WE--! IF WAR LEFT US AT ANY TIME, WE NAGAI MIGHT LEARN TO RECOGNIZE AND APPRECIATE BEAUTY AS YOU ZELTRONS DO.
DO YOU WANT ME TO TEACH YOU? THE SAME WAY YOU TAUGHT ME TO HATE AND FEAR?
DANI... DEN'S BEEN CAST OUT BY HIS OWN PEOPLE... RISKED DEATH AMONG THEM FOR LOVING AN OUTSIDER.
IF YOU AREN'T GOING TO TRY TO MEET HIM HALFWAY ...WHY DO YOU STAY WITH HIM?
AFTER WHAT HE DID TO... MY HEART... I'M NO MORE FIT TO LIVE AMONG ZELTRONS THAN HE IS TO BE WITH THE NAGAI.
I DON'T LOVE HIM... OR EVEN LIKE HIM... BUT AT LEAST WE UNDERSTAND EACH OTHER.
BOTH OF US ARE COMPOSITES NOW... HYBRIDS, LIKE THIS POOR WORLD, WITH ITS LOCAL ARCHITECTURE, ALL DESTROYED AND DISTORTED WITH TOF EMBELLISHMENTS.
DOESN'T SOUND LIKE THERE'S MUCH HOPE FOR THAT ROMANCE, DOES THERE? WHY DOESN'T HE JUST GIVE IT UP?
IN THE BEGINNING, I WASN'T EXACTLY ENCOURAGING TO YOU, HAN... AND YOU NEVER GAVE UP.
THAT WAS DIFFERENT, LEIA. I KNEW NO WOMAN IN HER RIGHT MIND COULD RESIST ME FOR LONG.
BUT I'VE KNOWN OLD DANI FOR A LOT OF YEARS... AND I'M NOT SURE SHE'S IN HER RIGHT MIND.
DEN WASN'T EXACTLY GENTLE WITH HER WHEN SHE WAS A PRISONER, Y'KNOW... AND HE KILLED KIRO, THE GUY SHE WAS IN LOVE WITH AT THE TIME.

TEMPERS ARE FRAYING AND I'M NOT SURPRISED, CONSIDERING WHAT'S AT STAKE HERE, AND HOW SMALL OUR CHANCES OF SUCCEEDING--

--AT THIS MISSION ADMIRAL ACKBAR AND MON MOTHMA ASSIGNED US.

WE MUST PUT ASIDE OUR PERSONAL FEELINGS AND GRUDGES... IT IS OUR ONLY HOPE.

NOW, I KNOW MOST OF YOU ARE FAMILIAR WITH THE PLANET SAIJO, ONE OF THE WORLDS ON THE RIM OF THE GALAXY. ONE OF THE EARLIEST BATTLES BETWEEN OUR PEOPLE AND YOU NAGAI WAS FOUGHT THERE...

...JUST AS IT HAD PREVIOUSLY BEEN THE SITE OF SOME OF THE BLOODIEST AND BITTEREST DISPUTES BETWEEN US, WHEN SOME OF THOSE HERE STILL SUPPORTED THE GALACTIC EMPEROR, AND THE REST WERE IN REBELLION AGAINST HIM.

THE WORLD ITSELF IS SPARSELY POPULATED, AND ITS INHABITANTS HAVE RAISED ONLY THE MOST PRIMITIVE OF STRUCTURES...

... BUT IT HAS EVER THRIVED AS A SPACEPORT AND A TRADING POST AMONG THE OUTER WORLDS.

SINCE WE LEARNED OF THE NAGAI INCURSIONS THERE, LONG BEFORE WE ACCEPTED THEM INTO OUR ALLIANCE, WE HAVE HAD OUR FINEST INTELLIGENCE AGENTS IN THE OUTER WORLDS KEEPING TRACK OF ALL THE COMINGS AND GOINGS ON SAIJO...

AND WE NOW KNOW, WITH ABSOLUTE CERTAINTY, THAT NEITHER THE NATIVES NOR THE NAGAI ARE IN POWER THERE.

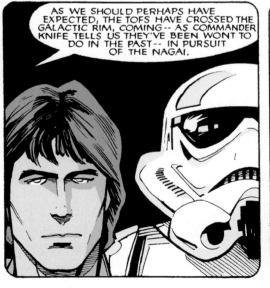

AS WE SHOULD PERHAPS HAVE EXPECTED, THE TOFS HAVE CROSSED THE GALACTIC RIM, COMING -- AS COMMANDER KNIFE TELLS US THEY'VE BEEN WONT TO DO IN THE PAST-- IN PURSUIT OF THE NAGAI.

AND THE SUPREME COMMANDER OF ALL THEIR FORCES ON THIS EXPEDITION HAS MADE SAIJO HIS PERSONAL BASE -- THE BASE OF OPERATIONS OF THE CROWN PRINCE OF TOF, HEIR TO THE THRONE OF THEIR ENTIRE CIVILIZATION.

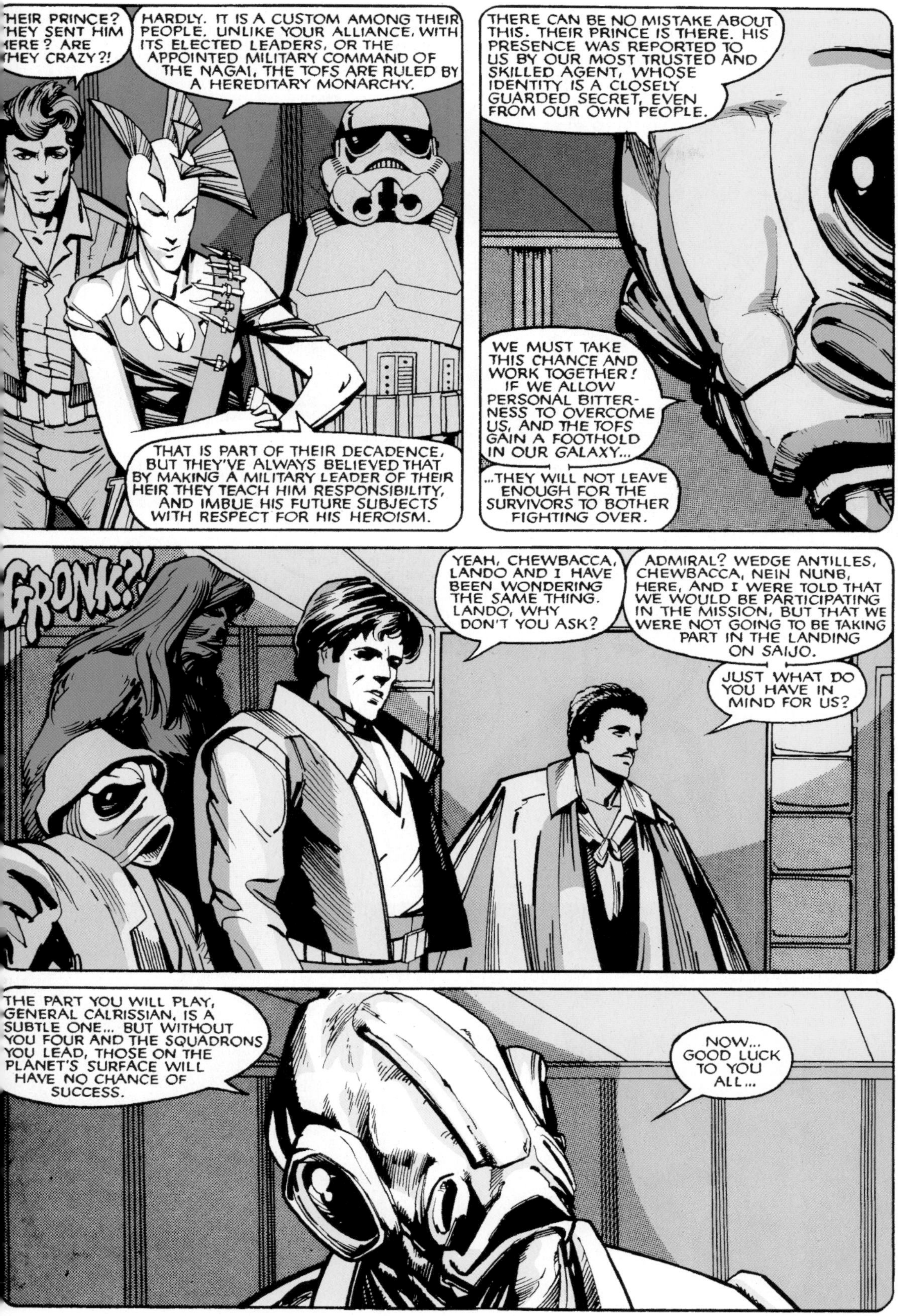
THEIR PRINCE? THEY SENT HIM HERE? ARE THEY CRAZY?!
HARDLY. IT IS A CUSTOM AMONG THEIR PEOPLE. UNLIKE YOUR ALLIANCE, WITH ITS ELECTED LEADERS, OR THE APPOINTED MILITARY COMMAND OF THE NAGAI, THE TOFS ARE RULED BY A HEREDITARY MONARCHY.
THAT IS PART OF THEIR DECADENCE, BUT THEY'VE ALWAYS BELIEVED THAT BY MAKING A MILITARY LEADER OF THEIR HEIR THEY TEACH HIM RESPONSIBILITY, AND IMBUE HIS FUTURE SUBJECTS WITH RESPECT FOR HIS HEROISM.
THERE CAN BE NO MISTAKE ABOUT THIS. THEIR PRINCE IS THERE. HIS PRESENCE WAS REPORTED TO US BY OUR MOST TRUSTED AND SKILLED AGENT, WHOSE IDENTITY IS A CLOSELY GUARDED SECRET, EVEN FROM OUR OWN PEOPLE.
WE MUST TAKE THIS CHANCE AND WORK TOGETHER! IF WE ALLOW PERSONAL BITTERNESS TO OVERCOME US, AND THE TOFS GAIN A FOOTHOLD IN OUR GALAXY...
...THEY WILL NOT LEAVE ENOUGH FOR THE SURVIVORS TO BOTHER FIGHTING OVER.
GRONK?!
YEAH, CHEWBACCA, LANDO AND I HAVE BEEN WONDERING THE SAME THING. LANDO, WHY DON'T YOU ASK?
ADMIRAL? WEDGE ANTILLES, CHEWBACCA, NEIN NUNB, HERE, AND I WERE TOLD THAT WE WOULD BE PARTICIPATING IN THE MISSION, BUT THAT WE WERE NOT GOING TO BE TAKING PART IN THE LANDING ON SAIJO.
JUST WHAT DO YOU HAVE IN MIND FOR US?
THE PART YOU WILL PLAY, GENERAL CALRISSIAN, IS A SUBTLE ONE... BUT WITHOUT YOU FOUR AND THE SQUADRONS YOU LEAD, THOSE ON THE PLANET'S SURFACE WILL HAVE NO CHANCE OF SUCCESS.
NOW... GOOD LUCK TO YOU ALL...

"...AND MAY THE FORCE BE WITH YOU." NOT A BAD SEND-OFF, WHEN YOU THINK OF IT. WITH WHAT'S COMING UP, THE MORE THAT'S POSITIVE WE HAVE WITH US, THE BETTER.

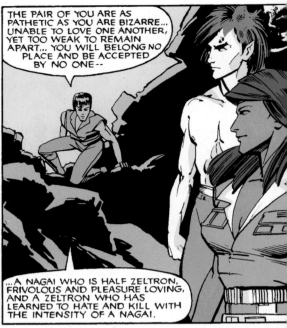

THE PAIR OF YOU ARE AS PATHETIC AS YOU ARE BIZARRE... UNABLE TO LOVE ONE ANOTHER, YET TOO WEAK TO REMAIN APART... YOU WILL BELONG NO PLACE AND BE ACCEPTED BY NO ONE--

...A NAGAI WHO IS HALF ZELTRON, FRIVOLOUS AND PLEASURE LOVING, AND A ZELTRON WHO HAS LEARNED TO HATE AND KILL WITH THE INTENSITY OF A NAGAI.

FUNNY, I THOUGHT YOU NAGAI LIKED HYBRIDS... OR WAS THAT JUST WHAT YOU TOLD BEY WHEN HE WANDERED INTO YOUR SECTOR OF SPACE, SO THAT YOU COULD GAIN HIS CONFIDENCE AND CONVINCE HIM TO BETRAY THE REST OF US?

BEY WAS HALF CORELLIAN, LIKE YOU, SOLO... BUT HE WAS ALSO HALF NAGAI... HALF MY BROTHER. FOR THAT I WELCOMED HIM.

AND HE WAS WEAK! FOR YOUR SAKE, HE ALSO BETRAYED US NAGAI.

IN FUTURE, WHEN I DEAL WITH THOSE WHO ARE NOT TRUE NAGAI, I SHALL REMEMBER THAT!

THIS IS THE MERRI-WEATHER... BULK CRUISER MERRIWEATHER, REQUESTING LANDING CLEARANCE, THAT WE MAY CONDUCT NORMAL TRADE. WE BRING SUPPLIES FROM TOF CENTRAL.

SAIJO? HAVE WE PERMISSION TO LAND?

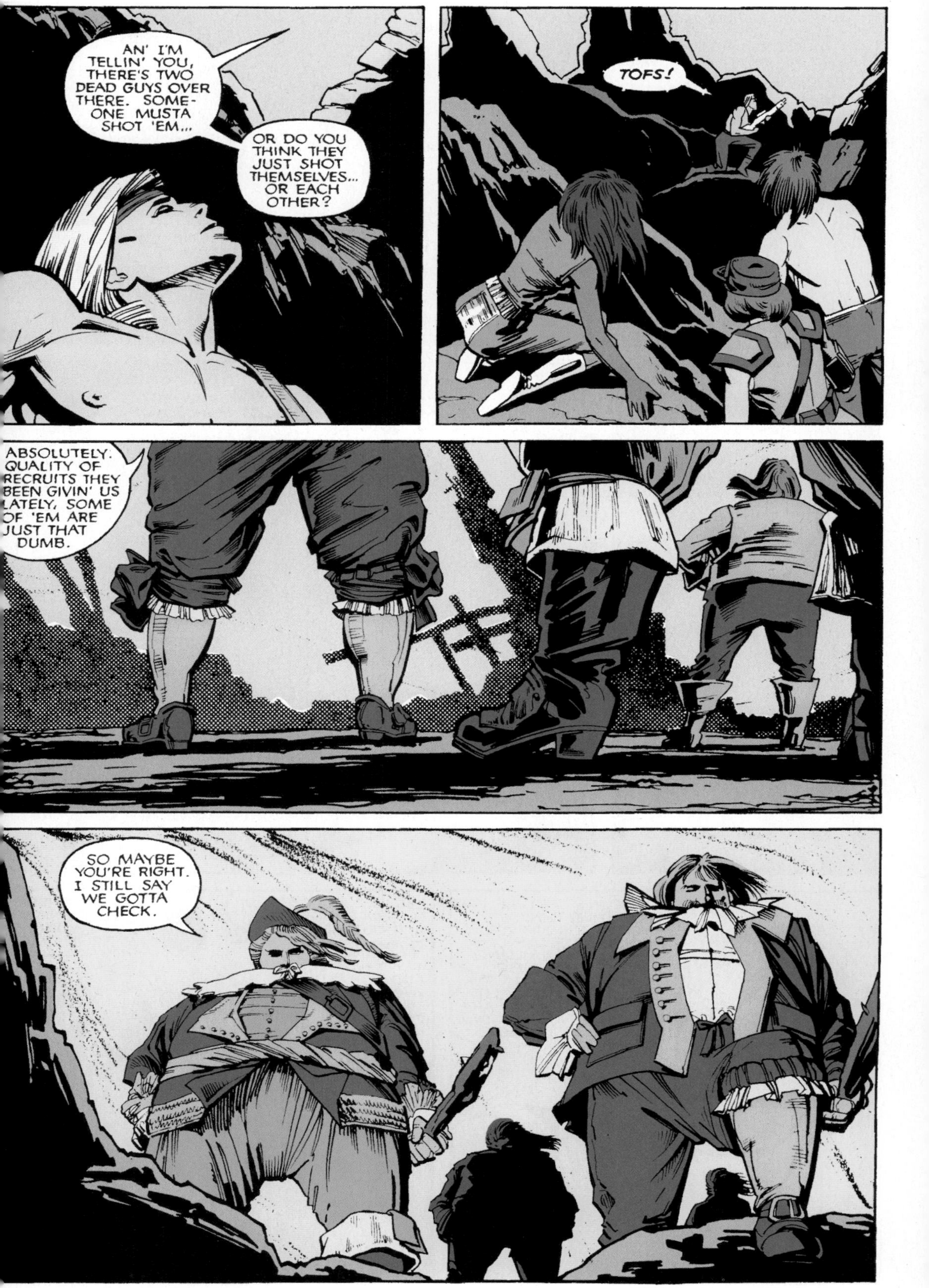
AN' I'M TELLIN' YOU, THERE'S TWO DEAD GUYS OVER THERE. SOME-ONE MUSTA SHOT 'EM...
OR DO YOU THINK THEY JUST SHOT THEMSELVES... OR EACH OTHER?
TOFS!
ABSOLUTELY. QUALITY OF RECRUITS THEY BEEN GIVIN' US LATELY, SOME OF 'EM ARE JUST THAT DUMB.
SO MAYBE YOU'RE RIGHT. I STILL SAY WE GOTTA CHECK.

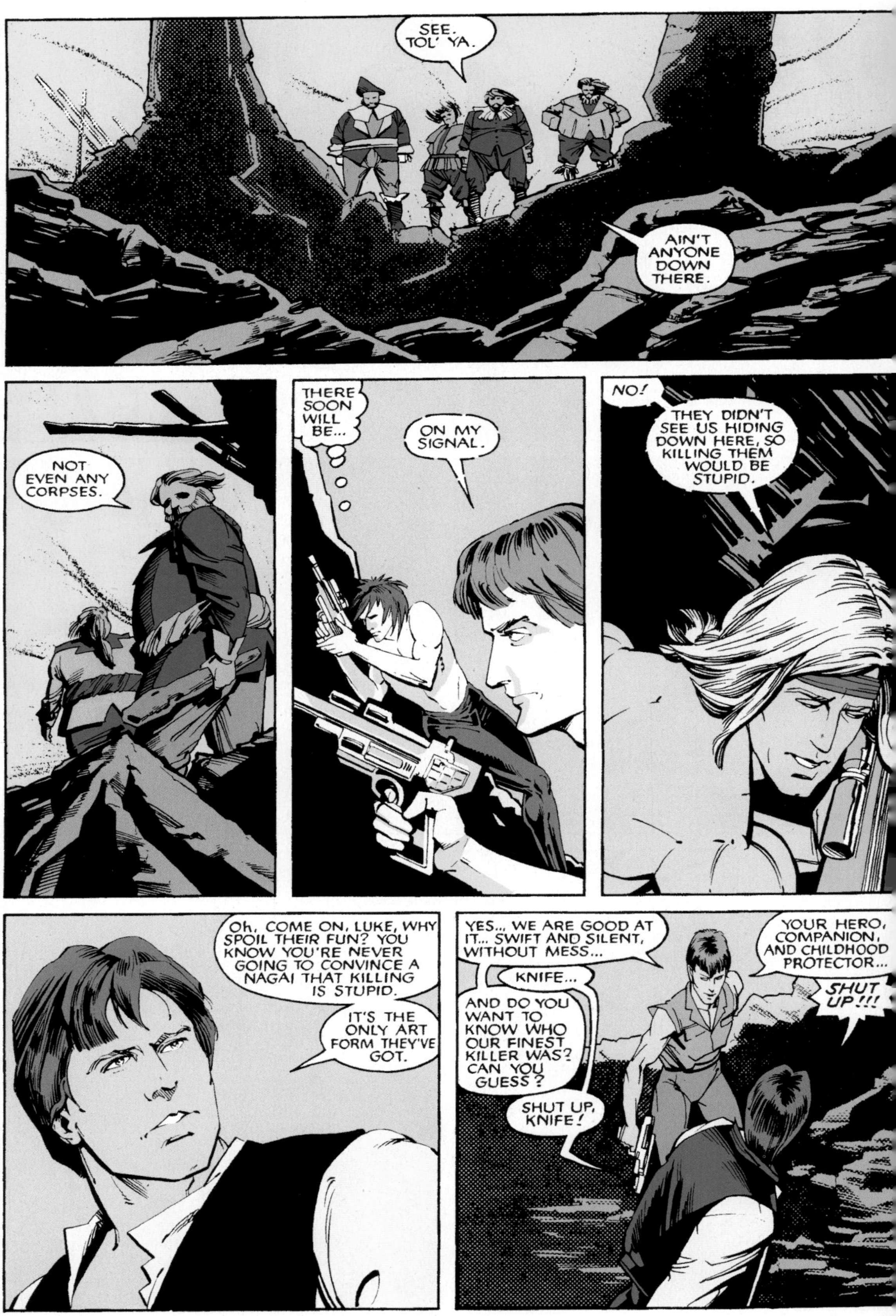
SEE. TOL' YA.
AIN'T ANYONE DOWN THERE.
NOT EVEN ANY CORPSES.
THERE SOON WILL BE...
ON MY SIGNAL.
NO!
THEY DIDN'T SEE US HIDING DOWN HERE, SO KILLING THEM WOULD BE STUPID.
Oh, COME ON, LUKE, WHY SPOIL THEIR FUN? YOU KNOW YOU'RE NEVER GOING TO CONVINCE A NAGAI THAT KILLING IS STUPID.
IT'S THE ONLY ART FORM THEY'VE GOT.
YES... WE ARE GOOD AT IT... SWIFT AND SILENT, WITHOUT MESS...
KNIFE...
AND DO YOU WANT TO KNOW WHO OUR FINEST KILLER WAS? CAN YOU GUESS?
SHUT UP, KNIFE!
YOUR HERO, COMPANION, AND CHILDHOOD PROTECTOR...
SHUT UP!!!

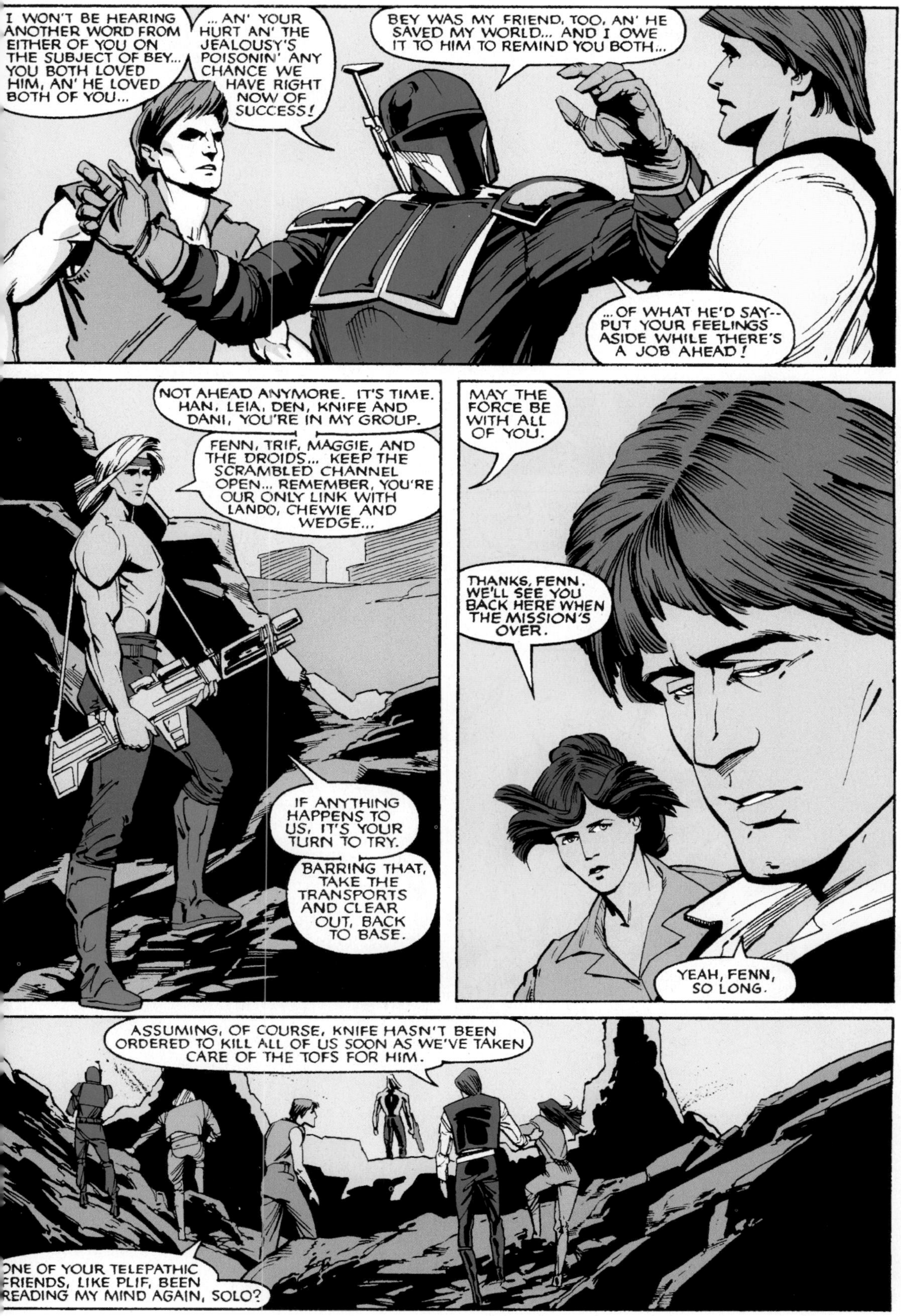
I WON'T BE HEARING ANOTHER WORD FROM EITHER OF YOU ON THE SUBJECT OF BEY... YOU BOTH LOVED HIM, AN' HE LOVED BOTH OF YOU...
... AN' YOUR HURT AN' THE JEALOUSY'S POISONIN' ANY CHANCE WE HAVE RIGHT NOW OF SUCCESS!
BEY WAS MY FRIEND, TOO, AN' HE SAVED MY WORLD... AND I OWE IT TO HIM TO REMIND YOU BOTH...
...OF WHAT HE'D SAY-- PUT YOUR FEELINGS ASIDE WHILE THERE'S A JOB AHEAD!
NOT AHEAD ANYMORE. IT'S TIME. HAN, LEIA, DEN, KNIFE AND DANI, YOU'RE IN MY GROUP.
FENN, TRIF, MAGGIE, AND THE DROIDS... KEEP THE SCRAMBLED CHANNEL OPEN... REMEMBER, YOU'RE OUR ONLY LINK WITH LANDO, CHEWIE AND WEDGE...
IF ANYTHING HAPPENS TO US, IT'S YOUR TURN TO TRY.
BARRING THAT, TAKE THE TRANSPORTS AND CLEAR OUT, BACK TO BASE.
MAY THE FORCE BE WITH ALL OF YOU.
THANKS, FENN. WE'LL SEE YOU BACK HERE WHEN THE MISSION'S OVER.
YEAH, FENN, SO LONG.
ASSUMING, OF COURSE, KNIFE HASN'T BEEN ORDERED TO KILL ALL OF US SOON AS WE'VE TAKEN CARE OF THE TOFS FOR HIM.
ONE OF YOUR TELEPATHIC FRIENDS, LIKE PLIF, BEEN READING MY MIND AGAIN, SOLO?

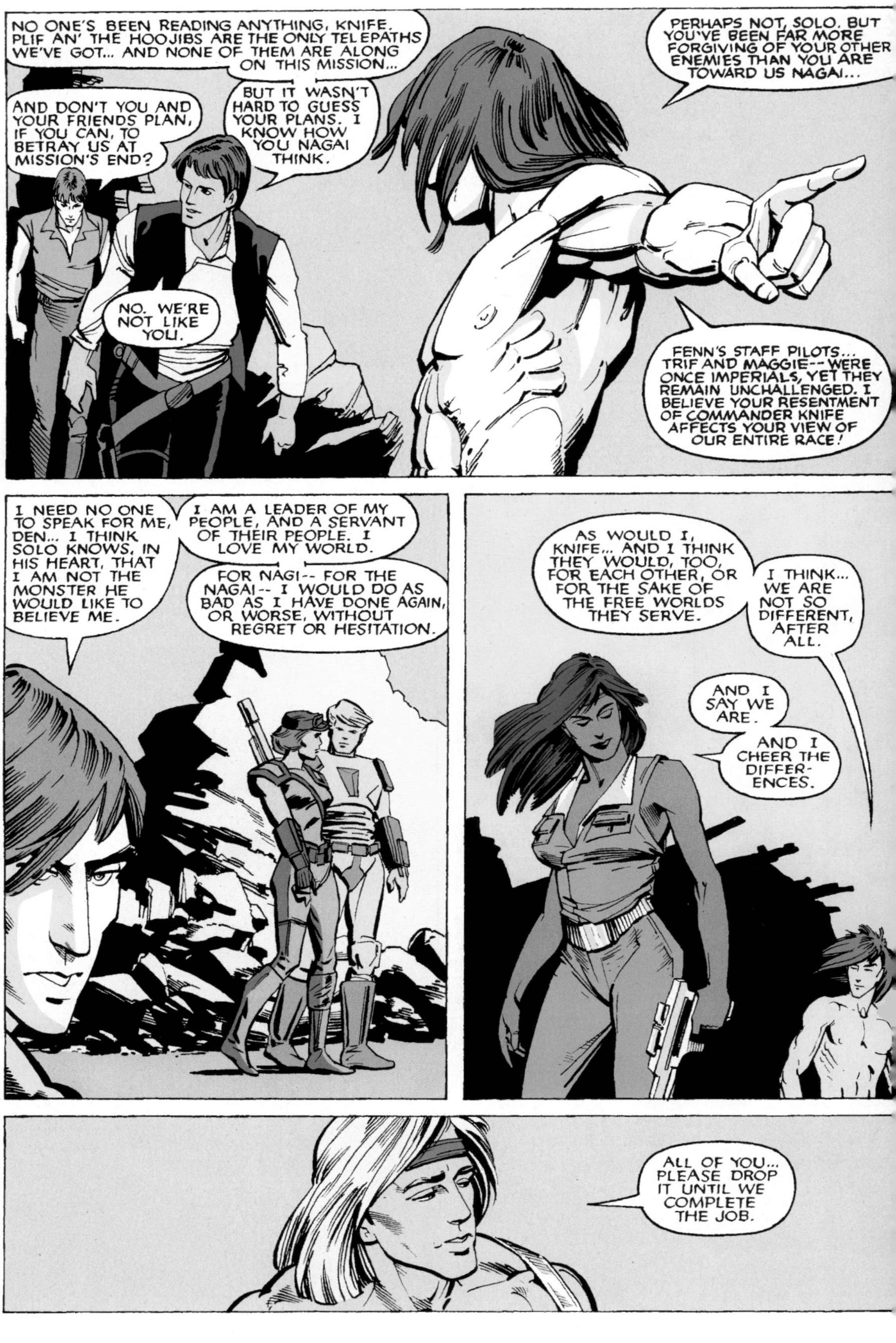
NO ONE'S BEEN READING ANYTHING, KNIFE. PLIF AN' THE HOOJIBS ARE THE ONLY TELEPATHS WE'VE GOT... AND NONE OF THEM ARE ALONG ON THIS MISSION...
AND DON'T YOU AND YOUR FRIENDS PLAN, IF YOU CAN, TO BETRAY US AT MISSION'S END?
BUT IT WASN'T HARD TO GUESS YOUR PLANS. I KNOW HOW YOU NAGAI THINK.
NO. WE'RE NOT LIKE YOU.
PERHAPS NOT, SOLO. BUT YOU'VE BEEN FAR MORE FORGIVING OF YOUR OTHER ENEMIES THAN YOU ARE TOWARD US NAGAI...
FENN'S STAFF PILOTS... TRIF AND MAGGIE-- WERE ONCE IMPERIALS, YET THEY REMAIN UNCHALLENGED. I BELIEVE YOUR RESENTMENT OF COMMANDER KNIFE AFFECTS YOUR VIEW OF OUR ENTIRE RACE!
I NEED NO ONE TO SPEAK FOR ME, DEN... I THINK SOLO KNOWS, IN HIS HEART, THAT I AM NOT THE MONSTER HE WOULD LIKE TO BELIEVE ME.
I AM A LEADER OF MY PEOPLE, AND A SERVANT OF THEIR PEOPLE. I LOVE MY WORLD.
FOR NAGI-- FOR THE NAGAI-- I WOULD DO AS BAD AS I HAVE DONE AGAIN, OR WORSE, WITHOUT REGRET OR HESITATION.
AS WOULD I, KNIFE... AND I THINK THEY WOULD, TOO, FOR EACH OTHER, OR FOR THE SAKE OF THE FREE WORLDS THEY SERVE.
I THINK... WE ARE NOT SO DIFFERENT, AFTER ALL.
AND I SAY WE ARE.
AND I CHEER THE DIFFERENCES.
ALL OF YOU... PLEASE DROP IT UNTIL WE COMPLETE THE JOB.

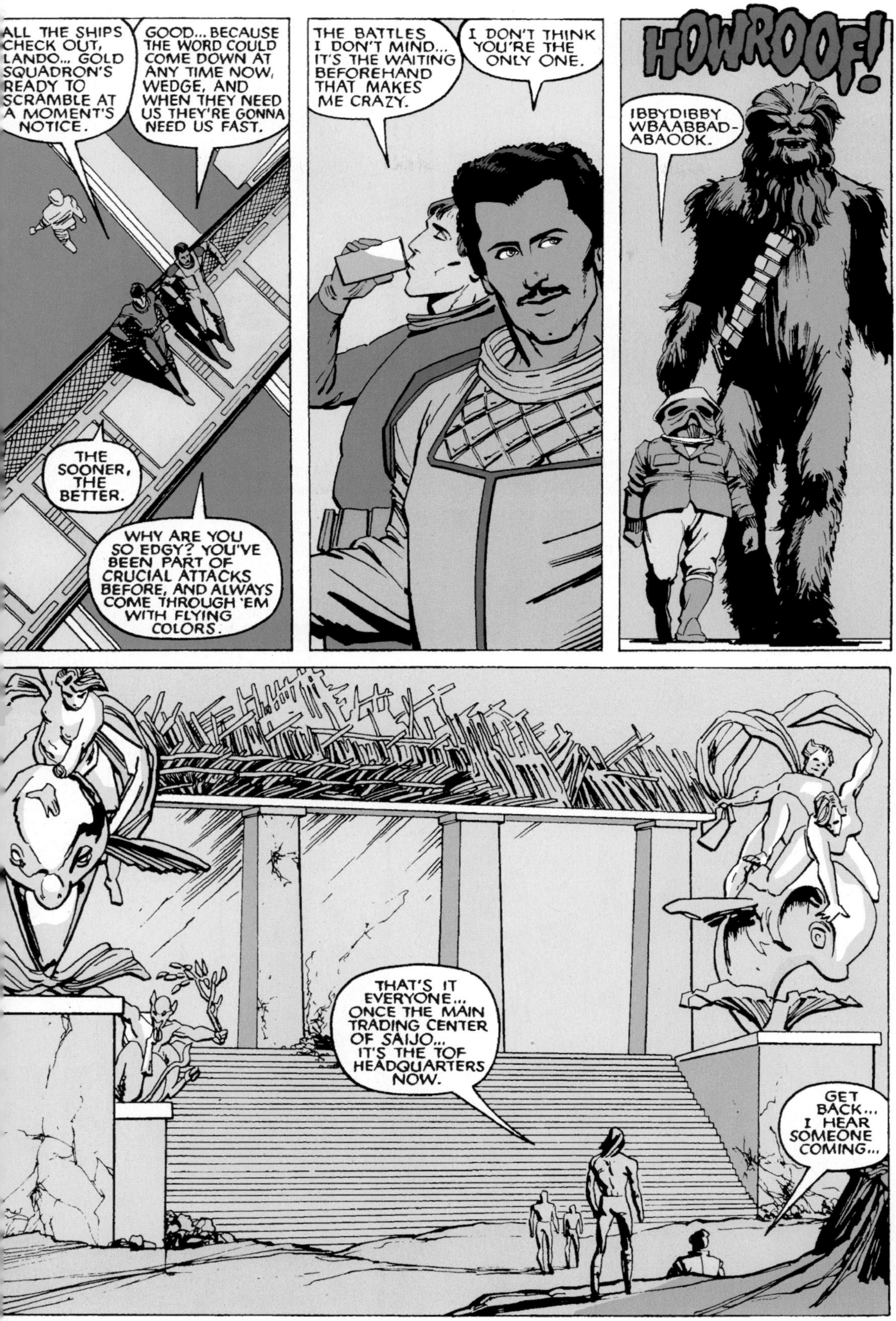

ALL THE SHIPS CHECK OUT, LANDO... GOLD SQUADRON'S READY TO SCRAMBLE AT A MOMENT'S NOTICE.
GOOD... BECAUSE THE WORD COULD COME DOWN AT ANY TIME NOW, WEDGE, AND WHEN THEY NEED US THEY'RE GONNA NEED US FAST.
THE SOONER, THE BETTER.
WHY ARE YOU SO EDGY? YOU'VE BEEN PART OF CRUCIAL ATTACKS BEFORE, AND ALWAYS COME THROUGH 'EM WITH FLYING COLORS.
THE BATTLES I DON'T MIND... IT'S THE WAITING BEFOREHAND THAT MAKES ME CRAZY.
I DON'T THINK YOU'RE THE ONLY ONE.
HOWROOF!
IBBYDIBBY WBAABBAD-ABAOOK.
THAT'S IT EVERYONE... ONCE THE MAIN TRADING CENTER OF SAIJO... IT'S THE TOF HEADQUARTERS NOW.
GET BACK... I HEAR SOMEONE COMING...

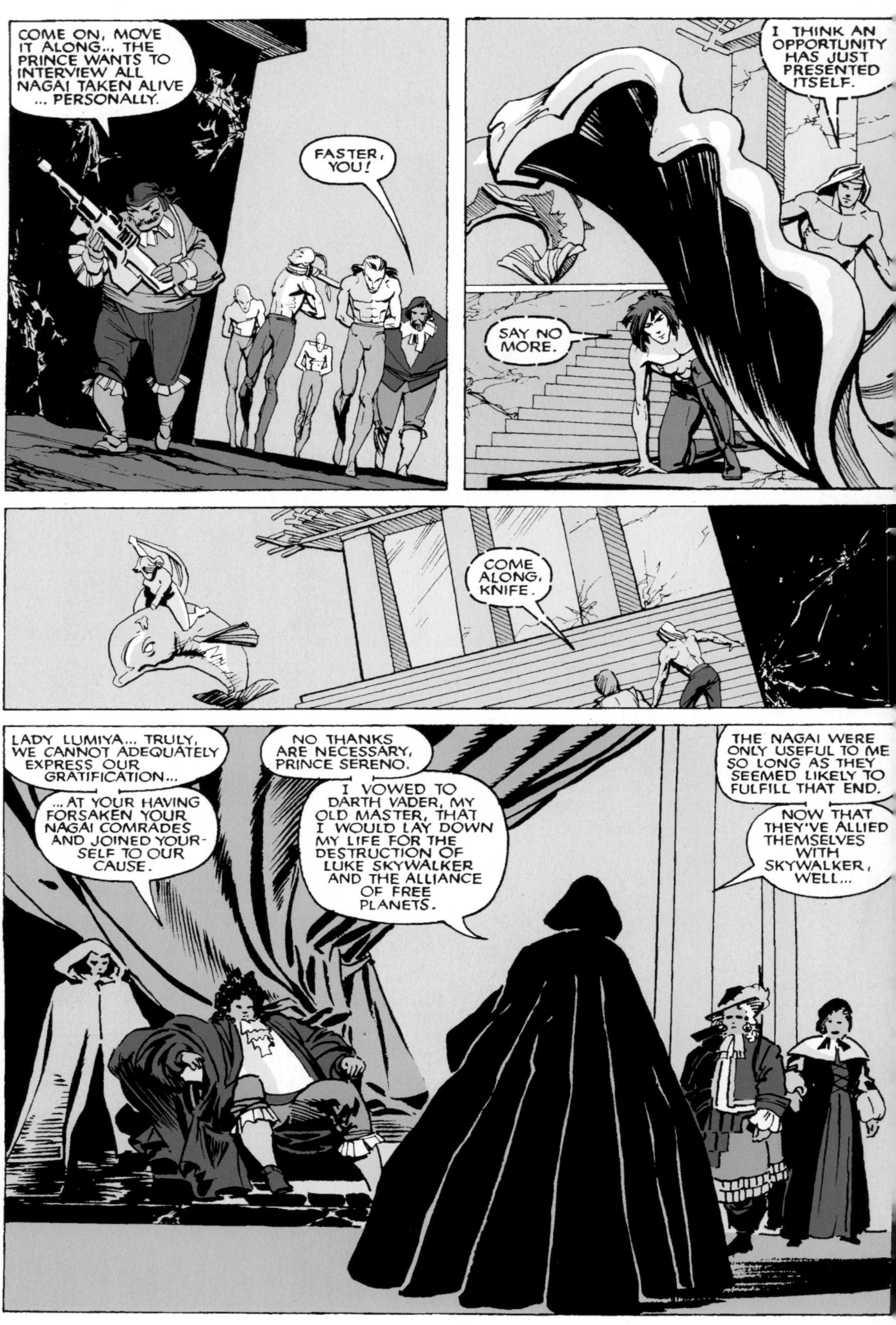
COME ON, MOVE IT ALONG... THE PRINCE WANTS TO INTERVIEW ALL NAGAI TAKEN ALIVE ... PERSONALLY.
FASTER, YOU!
I THINK AN OPPORTUNITY HAS JUST PRESENTED ITSELF.
SAY NO MORE.
COME ALONG, KNIFE.
LADY LUMIYA... TRULY, WE CANNOT ADEQUATELY EXPRESS OUR GRATIFICATION...
...AT YOUR HAVING FORSAKEN YOUR NAGAI COMRADES AND JOINED YOURSELF TO OUR CAUSE.
NO THANKS ARE NECESSARY, PRINCE SERENO.
I VOWED TO DARTH VADER, MY OLD MASTER, THAT I WOULD LAY DOWN MY LIFE FOR THE DESTRUCTION OF LUKE SKYWALKER AND THE ALLIANCE OF FREE PLANETS.
THE NAGAI WERE ONLY USEFUL TO ME SO LONG AS THEY SEEMED LIKELY TO FULFILL THAT END.
NOW THAT THEY'VE ALLIED THEMSELVES WITH SKYWALKER, WELL...

REPORTING, SIRE!

I... I... BRING THE NAGAI CAPTIVES, AS ORDERED!

Oh, YES... THEY'RE LOVELY, AREN'T THEY? AND DO THEY HATE US? AND FEAR US?

WE'LL HAVE SOME NICE DIVERSIONS... LATER.

SOONER AND MORE DIVERTING THAN YOU THINK!

S-SIRE... FORGIVE ME... I... THEY ARE REALLY--

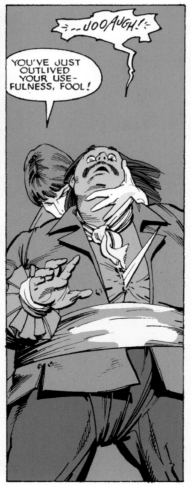

--UOOAUGH!

YOU'VE JUST OUTLIVED YOUR USE-FULNESS, FOOL!

WHAT IS THE MEANING OF--?

PRINCE SERENO! YOU ARE NOW A PRISONER OF WAR!

SURRENDER AND TELL YOUR SUBJECTS TO DO LIKEWISE--

--IN THE NAME OF NAGI--

--AND THE ALLIANCE OF FREE PLANETS!!

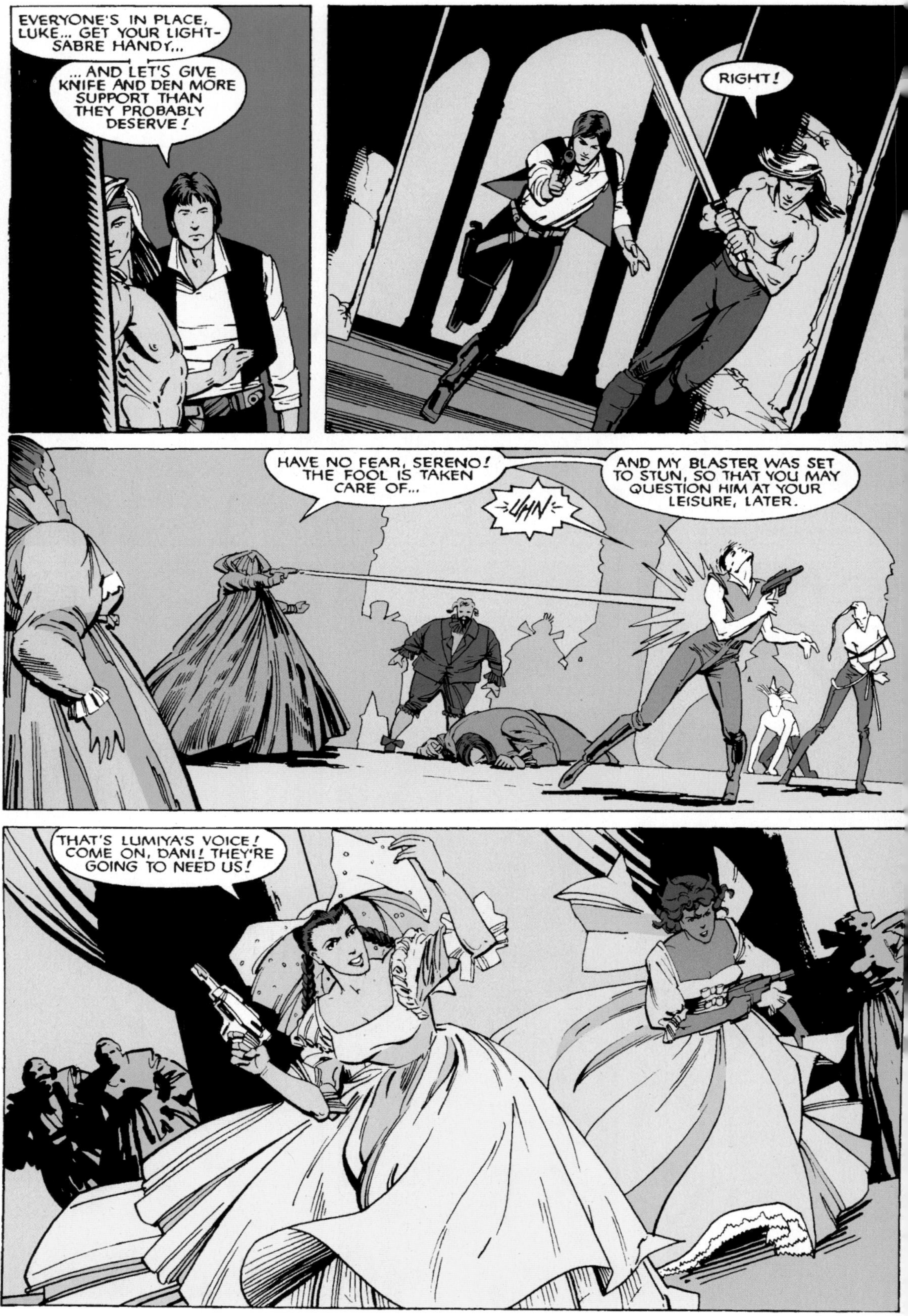
EVERYONE'S IN PLACE, LUKE... GET YOUR LIGHT-SABRE HANDY...
...AND LET'S GIVE KNIFE AND DEN MORE SUPPORT THAN THEY PROBABLY DESERVE!
RIGHT!
HAVE NO FEAR, SERENO! THE FOOL IS TAKEN CARE OF...
UHN
AND MY BLASTER WAS SET TO STUN, SO THAT YOU MAY QUESTION HIM AT YOUR LEISURE, LATER.
THAT'S LUMIYA'S VOICE! COME ON, DANI! THEY'RE GOING TO NEED US!

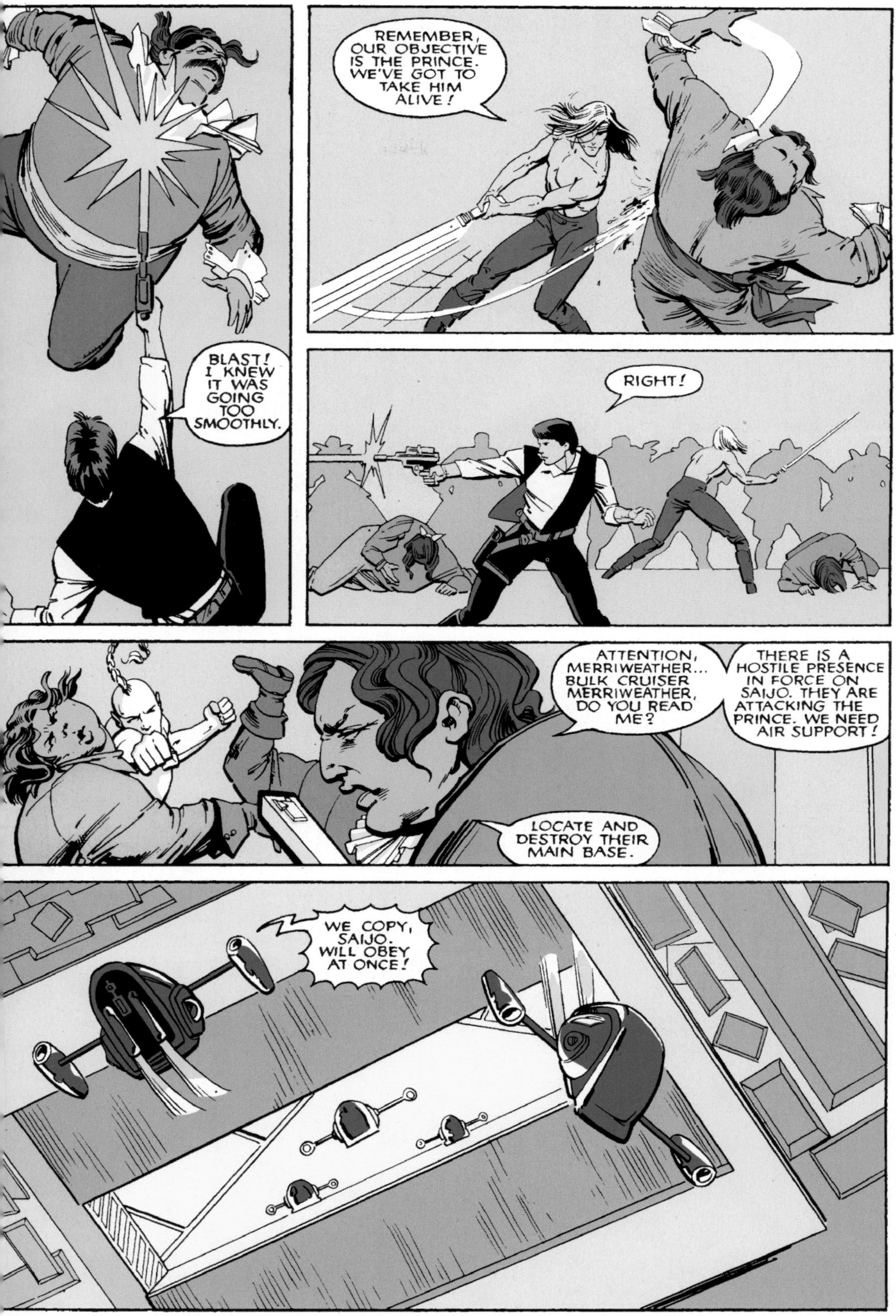
REMEMBER, OUR OBJECTIVE IS THE PRINCE. WE'VE GOT TO TAKE HIM ALIVE!
BLAST! I KNEW IT WAS GOING TOO SMOOTHLY.
RIGHT!
ATTENTION, MERRIWEATHER... BULK CRUISER MERRIWEATHER, DO YOU READ ME?
THERE IS A HOSTILE PRESENCE IN FORCE ON SAIJO. THEY ARE ATTACKING THE PRINCE. WE NEED AIR SUPPORT!
LOCATE AND DESTROY THEIR MAIN BASE.
WE COPY, SAIJO. WILL OBEY AT ONCE!

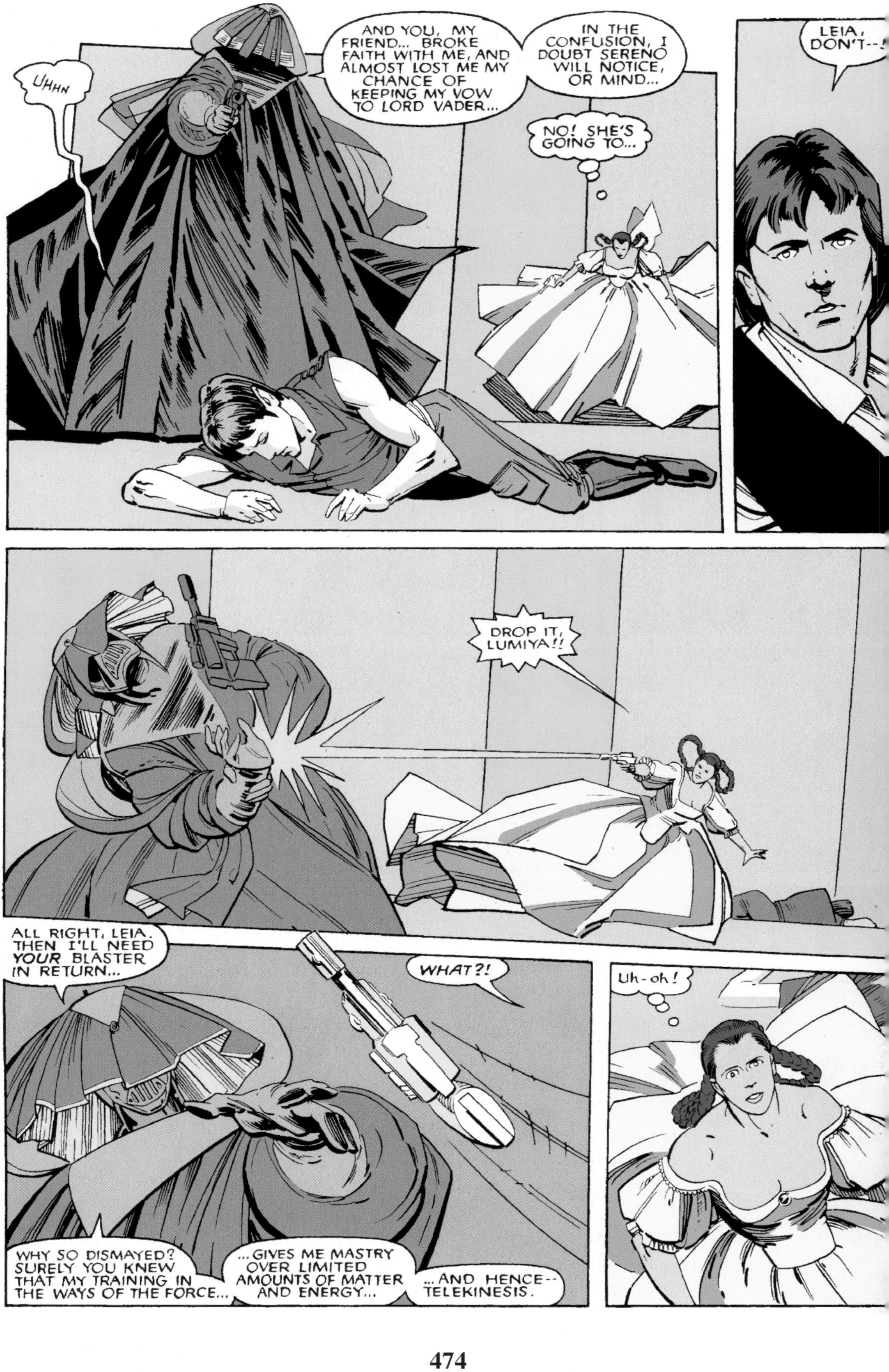
UHHN
AND YOU, MY FRIEND... BROKE FAITH WITH ME, AND ALMOST LOST ME MY CHANCE OF KEEPING MY VOW TO LORD VADER...
IN THE CONFUSION, I DOUBT SERENO WILL NOTICE, OR MIND...
NO! SHE'S GOING TO...
LEIA, DON'T--!
DROP IT, LUMIYA!!
ALL RIGHT, LEIA. THEN I'LL NEED YOUR BLASTER IN RETURN...
WHAT?!
Uh-oh!
WHY SO DISMAYED? SURELY YOU KNEW THAT MY TRAINING IN THE WAYS OF THE FORCE...
...GIVES ME MASTRY OVER LIMITED AMOUNTS OF MATTER AND ENERGY...
...AND HENCE-- TELEKINESIS.

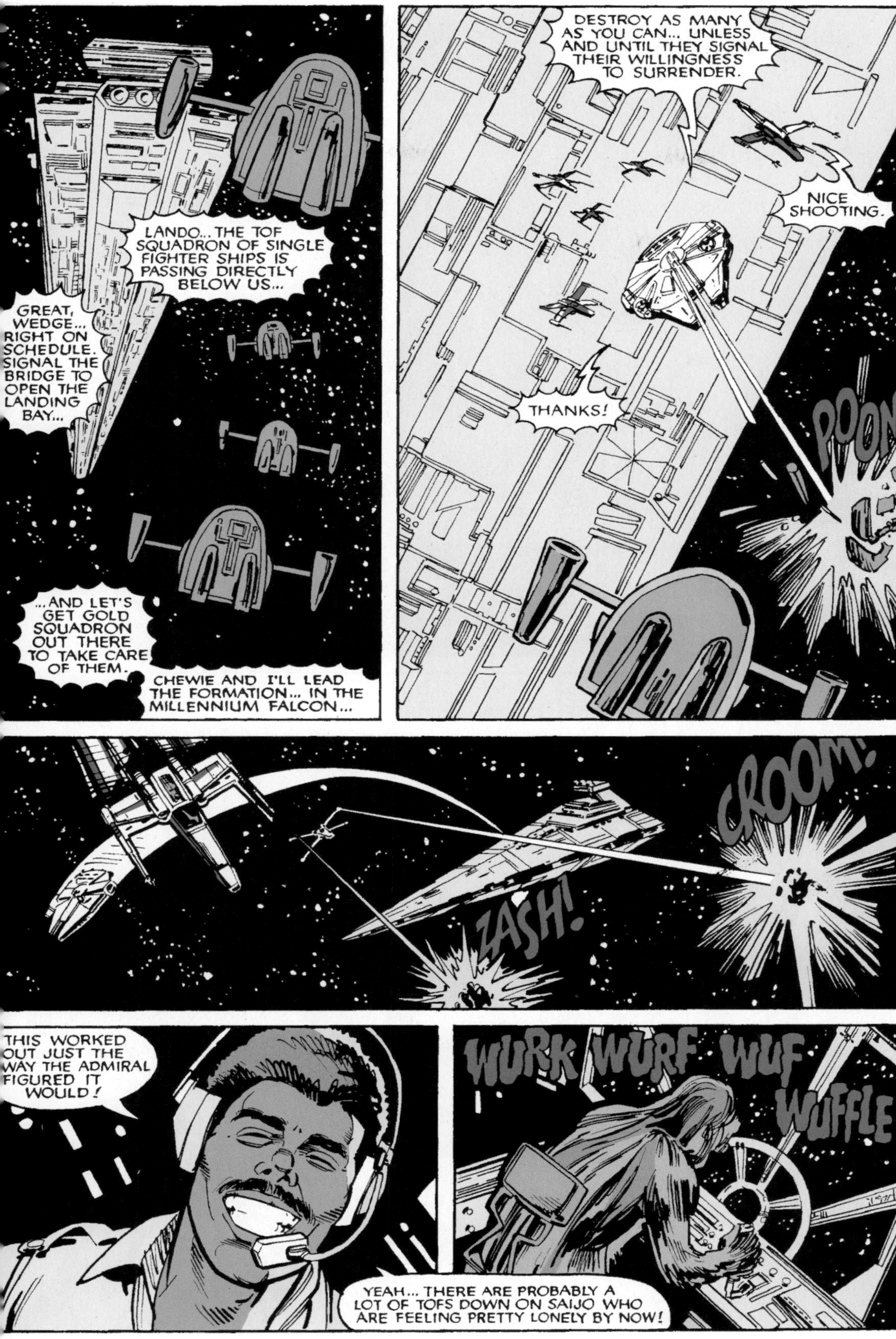

LANDO... THE TOF SQUADRON OF SINGLE FIGHTER SHIPS IS PASSING DIRECTLY BELOW US...
GREAT, WEDGE... RIGHT ON SCHEDULE. SIGNAL THE BRIDGE TO OPEN THE LANDING BAY...
...AND LET'S GET GOLD SQUADRON OUT THERE TO TAKE CARE OF THEM.
CHEWIE AND I'LL LEAD THE FORMATION... IN THE MILLENNIUM FALCON...
DESTROY AS MANY AS YOU CAN... UNLESS AND UNTIL THEY SIGNAL THEIR WILLINGNESS TO SURRENDER.
NICE SHOOTING.
THANKS!
POOM!
CROOM!
ZASH!
THIS WORKED OUT JUST THE WAY THE ADMIRAL FIGURED IT WOULD!
WURK WURF WUF WUFFLE
YEAH... THERE ARE PROBABLY A LOT OF TOFS DOWN ON SAIJO WHO ARE FEELING PRETTY LONELY BY NOW!

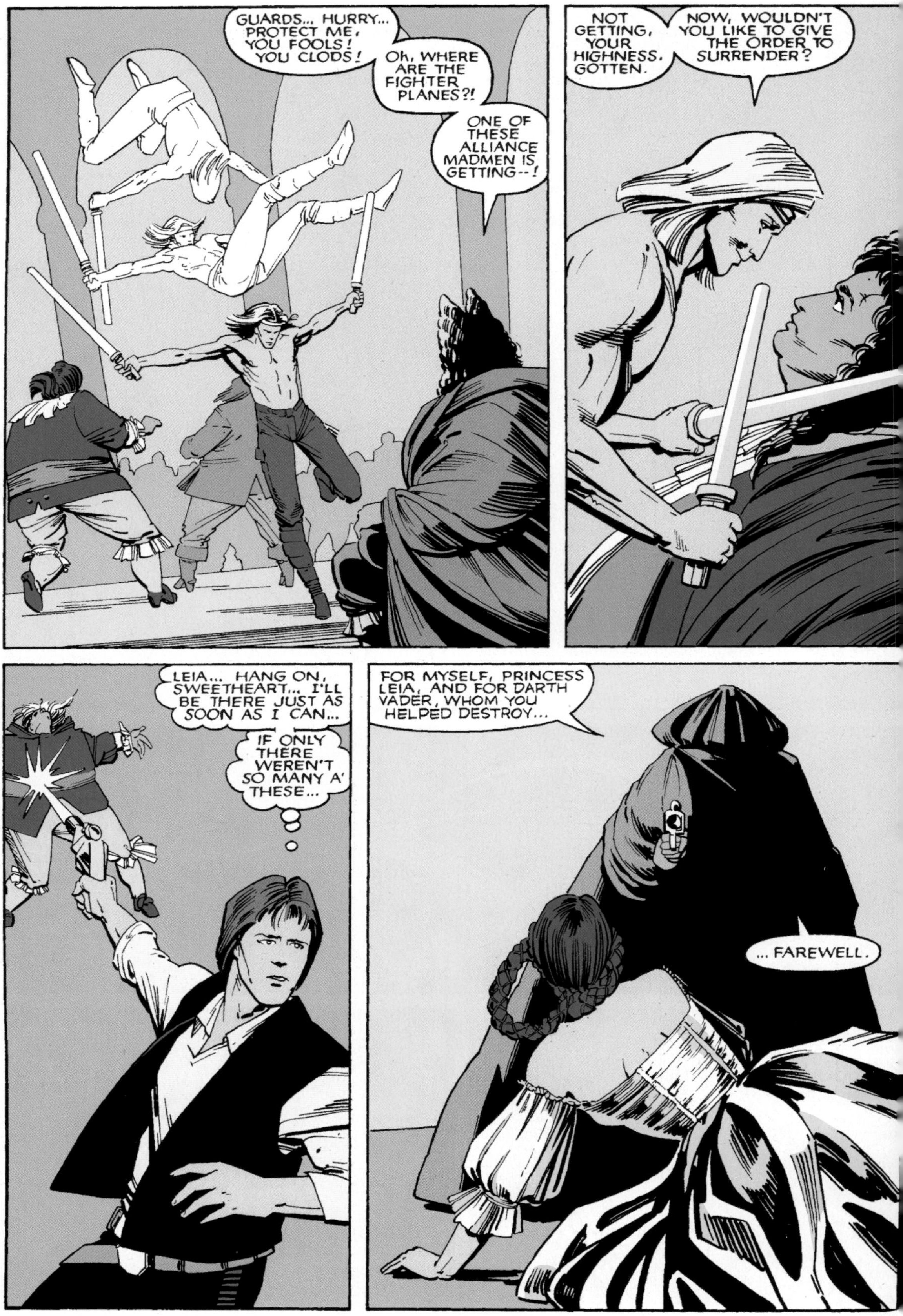
GUARDS... HURRY... PROTECT ME, YOU FOOLS! YOU CLODS!
Oh, WHERE ARE THE FIGHTER PLANES?!
ONE OF THESE ALLIANCE MADMEN IS GETTING--!
NOT GETTING, YOUR HIGHNESS. GOTTEN.
NOW, WOULDN'T YOU LIKE TO GIVE THE ORDER TO SURRENDER?
LEIA... HANG ON, SWEETHEART... I'LL BE THERE JUST AS SOON AS I CAN...
IF ONLY THERE WEREN'T SO MANY A' THESE...
FOR MYSELF, PRINCESS LEIA, AND FOR DARTH VADER, WHOM YOU HELPED DESTROY...
... FAREWELL.

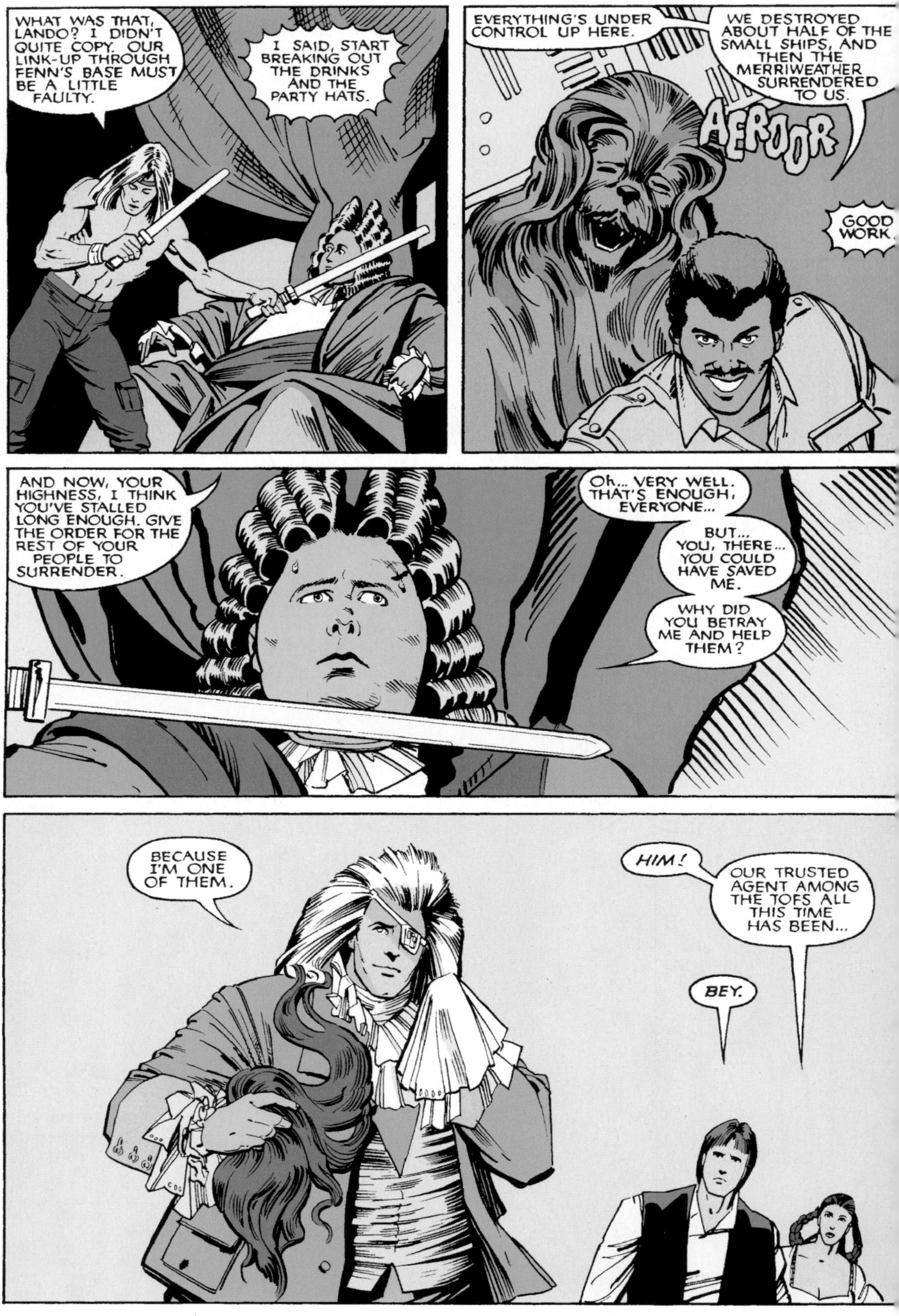
WHAT WAS THAT, LANDO? I DIDN'T QUITE COPY. OUR LINK-UP THROUGH FENN'S BASE MUST BE A LITTLE FAULTY.
I SAID, START BREAKING OUT THE DRINKS AND THE PARTY HATS.
EVERYTHING'S UNDER CONTROL UP HERE.
WE DESTROYED ABOUT HALF OF THE SMALL SHIPS, AND THEN THE MERRIWEATHER SURRENDERED TO US.
AEROOR
GOOD WORK.
AND NOW, YOUR HIGHNESS, I THINK YOU'VE STALLED LONG ENOUGH. GIVE THE ORDER FOR THE REST OF YOUR PEOPLE TO SURRENDER.
Oh... VERY WELL. THAT'S ENOUGH, EVERYONE...
BUT... YOU, THERE... YOU COULD HAVE SAVED ME.
WHY DID YOU BETRAY ME AND HELP THEM?
BECAUSE I'M ONE OF THEM.
HIM!
OUR TRUSTED AGENT AMONG THE TOFS ALL THIS TIME HAS BEEN...
BEY.

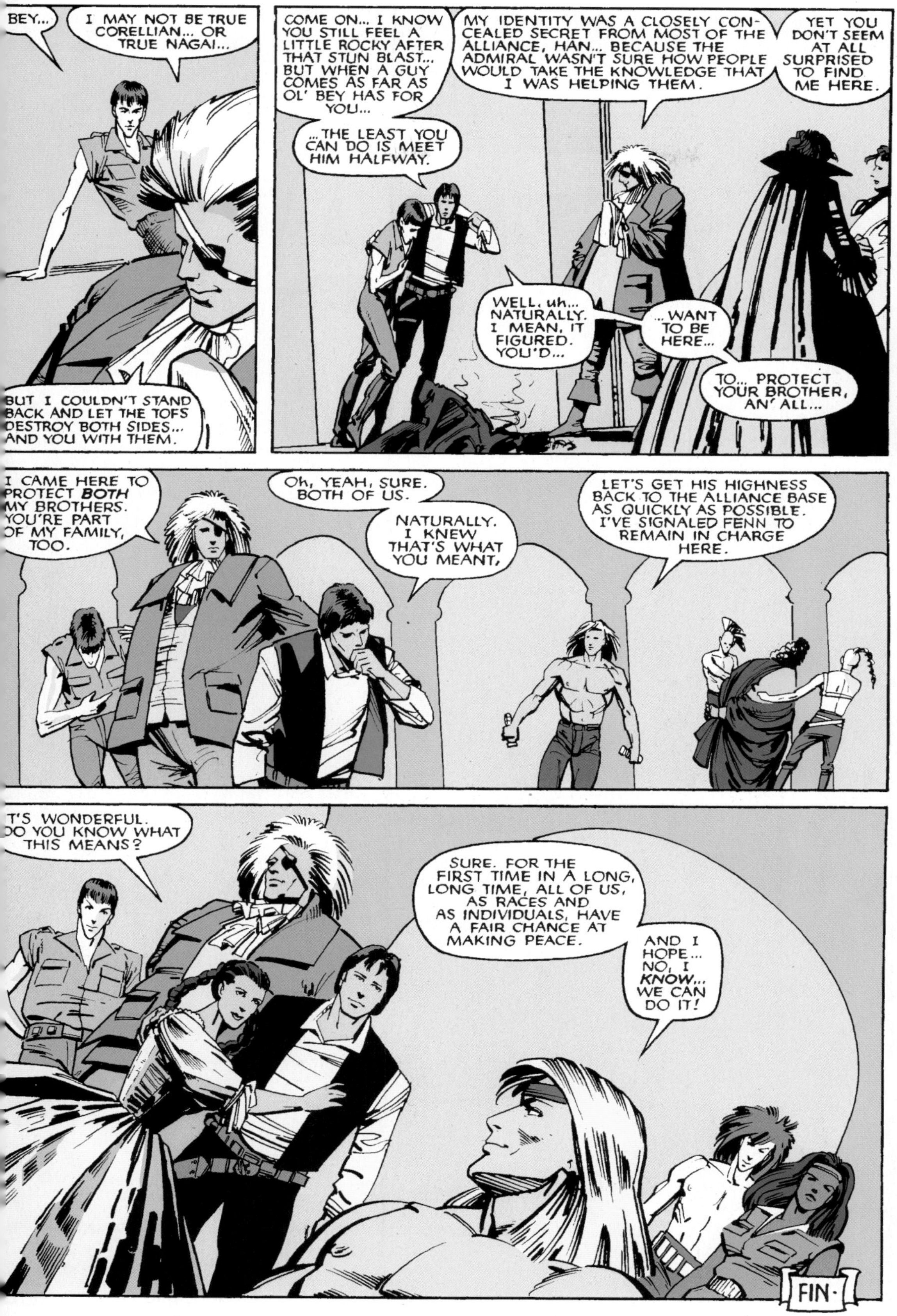
BEY...
I MAY NOT BE TRUE CORELLIAN... OR TRUE NAGAI...
BUT I COULDN'T STAND BACK AND LET THE TOFS DESTROY BOTH SIDES... AND YOU WITH THEM.
COME ON... I KNOW YOU STILL FEEL A LITTLE ROCKY AFTER THAT STUN BLAST... BUT WHEN A GUY COMES AS FAR AS OL' BEY HAS FOR YOU...
...THE LEAST YOU CAN DO IS MEET HIM HALFWAY.
MY IDENTITY WAS A CLOSELY CONCEALED SECRET FROM MOST OF THE ALLIANCE, HAN... BECAUSE THE ADMIRAL WASN'T SURE HOW PEOPLE WOULD TAKE THE KNOWLEDGE THAT I WAS HELPING THEM.
YET YOU DON'T SEEM AT ALL SURPRISED TO FIND ME HERE.
WELL, uh... NATURALLY. I MEAN, IT FIGURED. YOU'D...
...WANT TO BE HERE...
TO... PROTECT YOUR BROTHER, AN' ALL...
I CAME HERE TO PROTECT BOTH MY BROTHERS. YOU'RE PART OF MY FAMILY, TOO.
Oh, YEAH, SURE. BOTH OF US.
NATURALLY. I KNEW THAT'S WHAT YOU MEANT.
LET'S GET HIS HIGHNESS BACK TO THE ALLIANCE BASE AS QUICKLY AS POSSIBLE. I'VE SIGNALED FENN TO REMAIN IN CHARGE HERE.
IT'S WONDERFUL. DO YOU KNOW WHAT THIS MEANS?
SURE. FOR THE FIRST TIME IN A LONG, LONG TIME, ALL OF US, AS RACES AND AS INDIVIDUALS, HAVE A FAIR CHANCE AT MAKING PEACE.
AND I HOPE... NO, I KNOW... WE CAN DO IT!
FIN·

MARVEL'S ORIGINAL *STAR WARS* SERIES ENDED IN 1986 WITH #107. OVER THIRTY YEARS LATER, AS PART OF THE 80TH ANNIVERSARY CELEBRATION IN 2019, MARVEL PUBLISHED *STAR WARS #108* — A NOSTALGIC ONE-SHOT TH REVISITED THE TIMEFRAME AND CHARACTERS OF THE ORIGINAL SERIES.

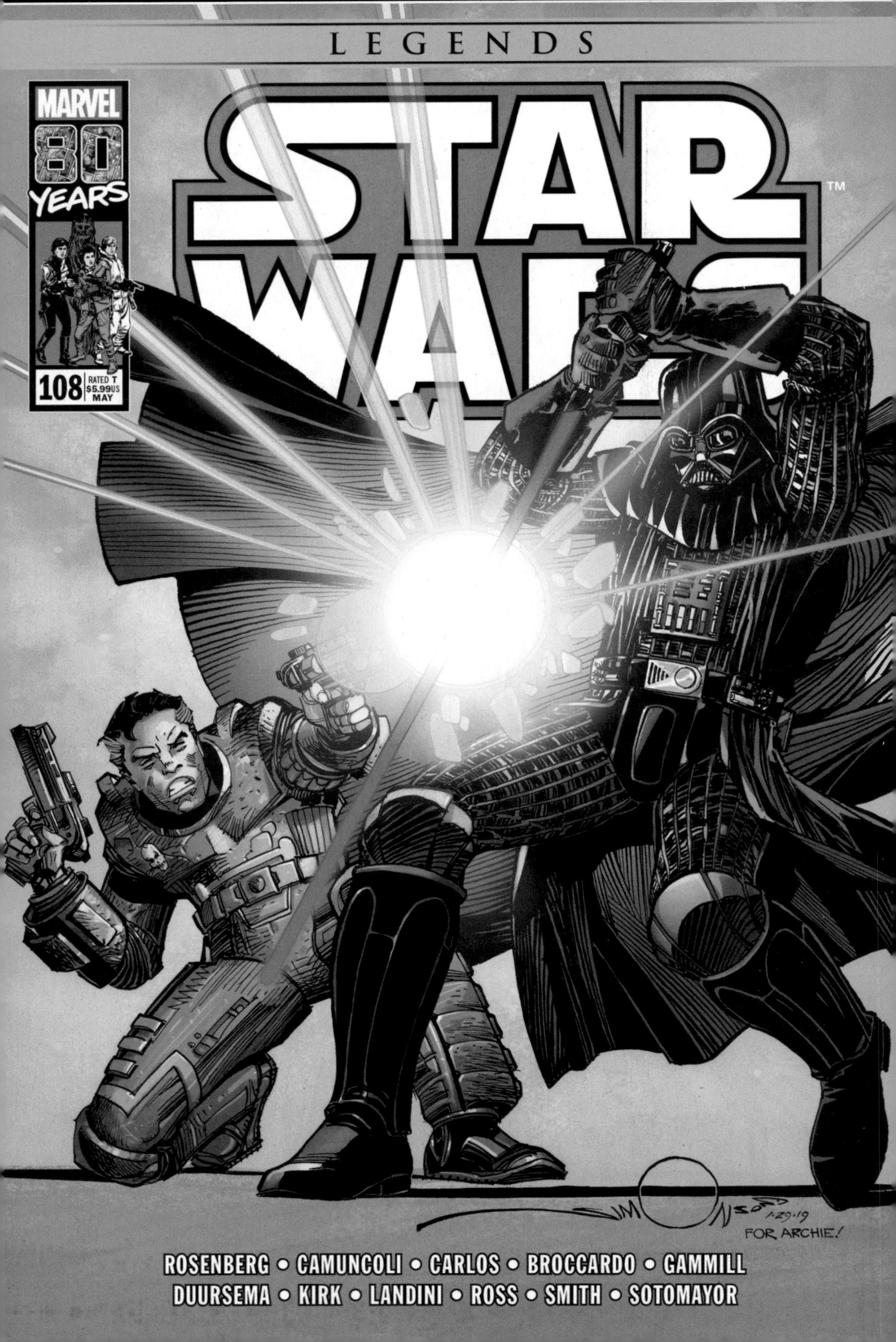

LEGENDS
MARVEL
80 YEARS
108
RATED T
$5.99US
MAY
STAR WARS
TM
SIMONSON 1.29.19
FOR ARCHIE!
ROSENBERG • CAMUNCOLI • CARLOS • BROCCARDO • GAMMILL
DUURSEMA • KIRK • LANDINI • ROSS • SMITH • SOTOMAYOR

Long ago in a galaxy far, far away...

The cosmic civil war is over! The Empire has fallen. The tyrannical Dark Lords of the Sith who ruled the galaxy, Emperor Palpatine and Darth Vader, are destroyed, and the heroic Rebel Alliance has restored freedom to the star systems with the formation of the New Republic.

But a long-forgotten threat, one more terrible than even the Sith, is still out there in the wilds of deep space, and its return could annihilate all life in the galaxy! Once again, only the freedom fighters Princess Leia Organa, Luke Skywalker and Han Solo can hope to stand against the forces of evil. This is their story!

STAR WARS

"FOREVER CRIMSON"

MATTHEW ROSENBERG
writer

CHAPTER 1: GIUSEPPE CAMUNCOLI & CAM SMITH; ANDREA BROCCARDO

CHAPTER 2: KERRY GAMMILL & ZE CARLOS

CHAPTER 3: ANDREA BROCCARDO

CHAPTER 4: JAN DUURSEMA

CHAPTER 5: ANDREA BROCCARDO

CHAPTER 6: STEFANO LANDINI

CHAPTER 7: LUKE ROSS

CHAPTER 8: LEONARD KIRK

CHRIS SOTOMAYOR   **VC's CLAYTON COWLES**
color artist   *letterer*

WALTER SIMONSON & ANTONIO FABELA   **JOHN TYLER CHRISTOPHER; MICHAEL GOLDEN**
cover artists   *variant cover artists*

CARMINE INFANTINO, DAN GREEN & DEAN WHITE
remastered variant

CARLOS LAO   **TOM GRONEMAN**   **MARK PANICCIA**
graphic designer   *assistant editor*   *editor*

C.B. CEBULSKI   **JOE QUESADA**   **DAN BUCKLEY**
editor in chief   *chief creative officer*   *president*

dedicated to **ARCHIE GOODWIN**

——————————— **FOR LUCASFILM** ———————————

ROBERT SIMPSON *senior editor* • **MICHAEL SIGLAIN** *creative director*
JAMES WAUGH, LELAND CHEE & MATT MARTIN *Lucasfilm story group*
very special thanks to **PABLO HIDALGO**

CHAPTER I

THE LEGEND OF VALANCE THE HUNTER!

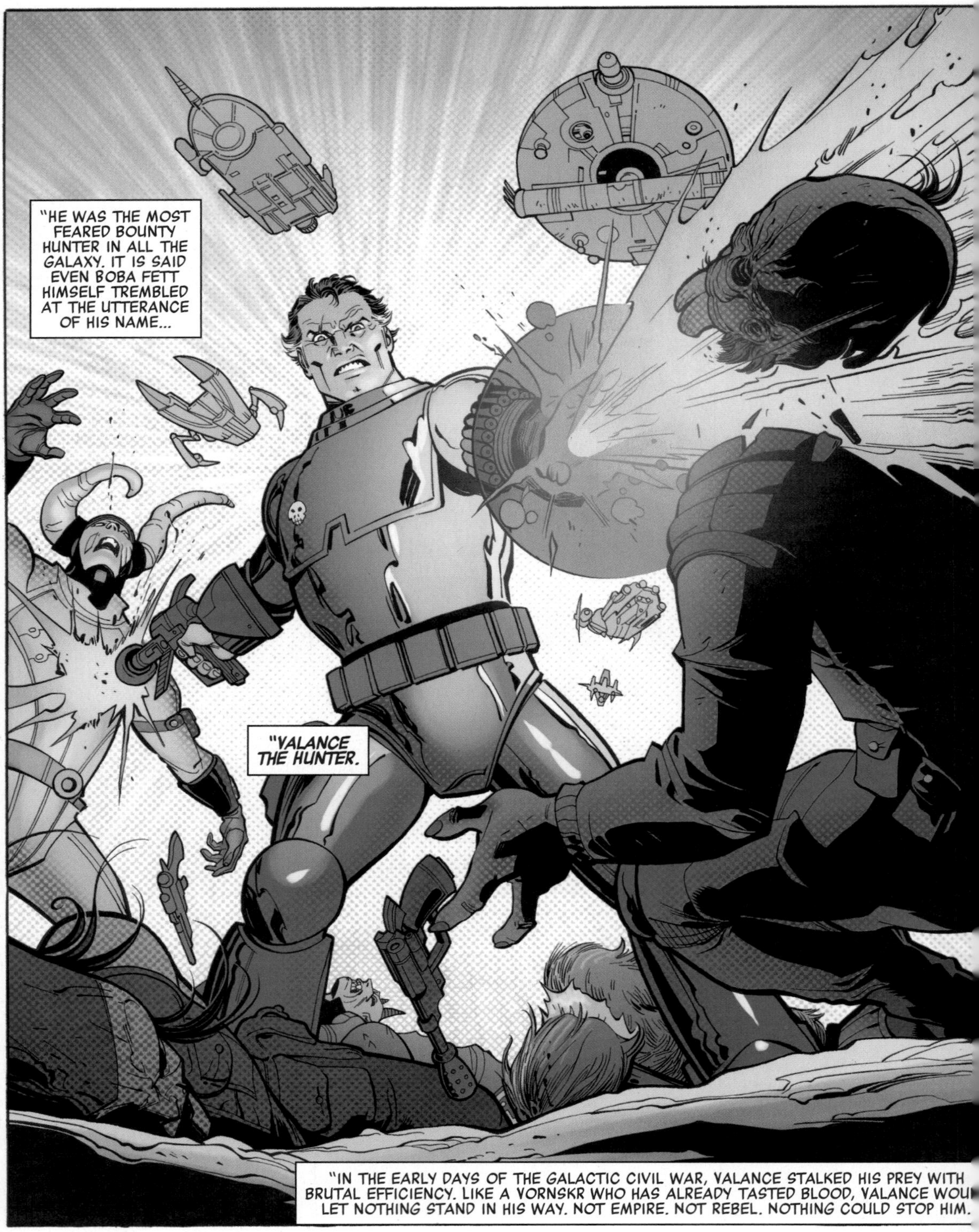
"HE WAS THE MOST FEARED BOUNTY HUNTER IN ALL THE GALAXY. IT IS SAID EVEN BOBA FETT HIMSELF TREMBLED AT THE UTTERANCE OF HIS NAME...
"VALANCE THE HUNTER.
"IN THE EARLY DAYS OF THE GALACTIC CIVIL WAR, VALANCE STALKED HIS PREY WITH BRUTAL EFFICIENCY. LIKE A VORNSKR WHO HAS ALREADY TASTED BLOOD, VALANCE WOU LET NOTHING STAND IN HIS WAY. NOT EMPIRE. NOT REBEL. NOTHING COULD STOP HIM.

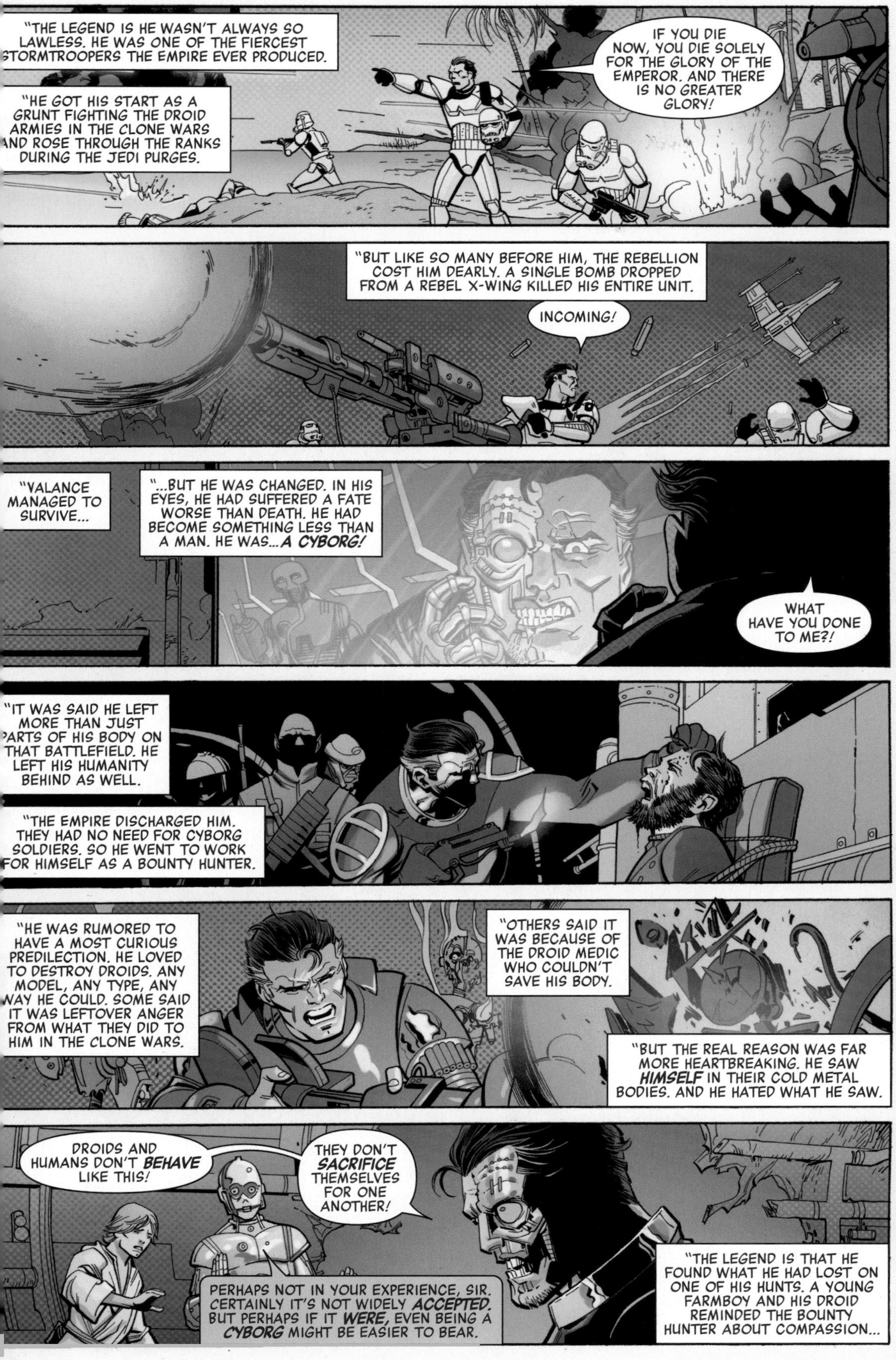
"THE LEGEND IS HE WASN'T ALWAYS SO LAWLESS. HE WAS ONE OF THE FIERCEST STORMTROOPERS THE EMPIRE EVER PRODUCED.
"HE GOT HIS START AS A GRUNT FIGHTING THE DROID ARMIES IN THE CLONE WARS AND ROSE THROUGH THE RANKS DURING THE JEDI PURGES.
IF YOU DIE NOW, YOU DIE SOLELY FOR THE GLORY OF THE EMPEROR. AND THERE IS NO GREATER GLORY!
"BUT LIKE SO MANY BEFORE HIM, THE REBELLION COST HIM DEARLY. A SINGLE BOMB DROPPED FROM A REBEL X-WING KILLED HIS ENTIRE UNIT.
INCOMING!
"VALANCE MANAGED TO SURVIVE...
"...BUT HE WAS CHANGED. IN HIS EYES, HE HAD SUFFERED A FATE WORSE THAN DEATH. HE HAD BECOME SOMETHING LESS THAN A MAN. HE WAS... ***A CYBORG!***
WHAT HAVE YOU DONE TO ME?!
"IT WAS SAID HE LEFT MORE THAN JUST PARTS OF HIS BODY ON THAT BATTLEFIELD. HE LEFT HIS HUMANITY BEHIND AS WELL.
"THE EMPIRE DISCHARGED HIM. THEY HAD NO NEED FOR CYBORG SOLDIERS. SO HE WENT TO WORK FOR HIMSELF AS A BOUNTY HUNTER.
"HE WAS RUMORED TO HAVE A MOST CURIOUS PREDILECTION. HE LOVED TO DESTROY DROIDS. ANY MODEL, ANY TYPE, ANY WAY HE COULD. SOME SAID IT WAS LEFTOVER ANGER FROM WHAT THEY DID TO HIM IN THE CLONE WARS.
"OTHERS SAID IT WAS BECAUSE OF THE DROID MEDIC WHO COULDN'T SAVE HIS BODY.
"BUT THE REAL REASON WAS FAR MORE HEARTBREAKING. HE SAW ***HIMSELF*** IN THEIR COLD METAL BODIES. AND HE HATED WHAT HE SAW.
DROIDS AND HUMANS DON'T ***BEHAVE*** LIKE THIS!
THEY DON'T ***SACRIFICE*** THEMSELVES FOR ONE ANOTHER!
PERHAPS NOT IN YOUR EXPERIENCE, SIR. CERTAINLY IT'S NOT WIDELY ***ACCEPTED.*** BUT PERHAPS IF IT ***WERE,*** EVEN BEING A ***CYBORG*** MIGHT BE EASIER TO BEAR.
"THE LEGEND IS THAT HE FOUND WHAT HE HAD LOST ON ONE OF HIS HUNTS. A YOUNG FARMBOY AND HIS DROID REMINDED THE BOUNTY HUNTER ABOUT COMPASSION...

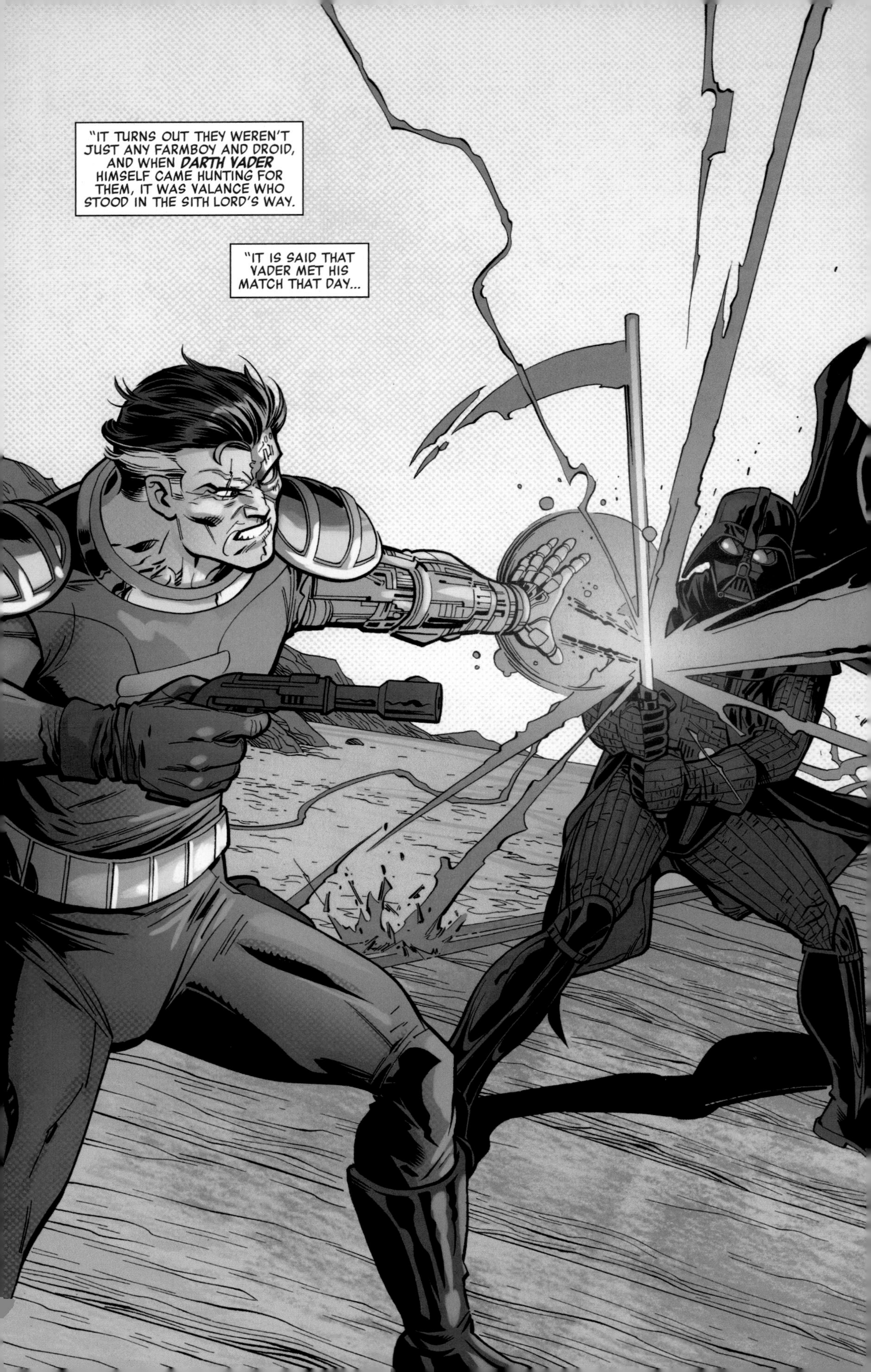
"IT TURNS OUT THEY WEREN'T JUST ANY FARMBOY AND DROID, AND WHEN DARTH VADER HIMSELF CAME HUNTING FOR THEM, IT WAS VALANCE WHO STOOD IN THE SITH LORD'S WAY.
"IT IS SAID THAT VADER MET HIS MATCH THAT DAY...

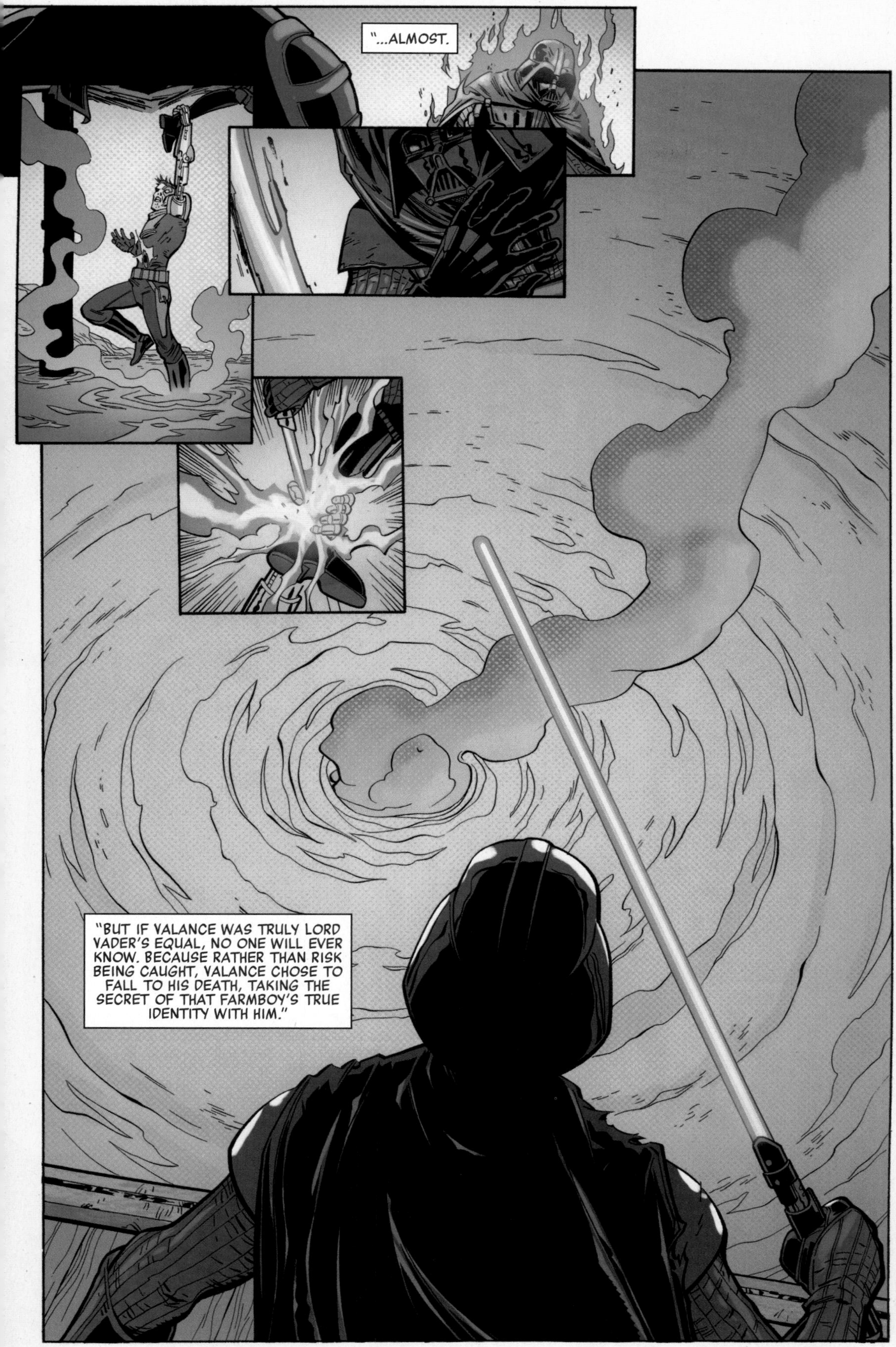
"...ALMOST.
"BUT IF VALANCE WAS TRULY LORD VADER'S EQUAL, NO ONE WILL EVER KNOW. BECAUSE RATHER THAN RISK BEING CAUGHT, VALANCE CHOSE TO FALL TO HIS DEATH, TAKING THE SECRET OF THAT FARMBOY'S TRUE IDENTITY WITH HIM."

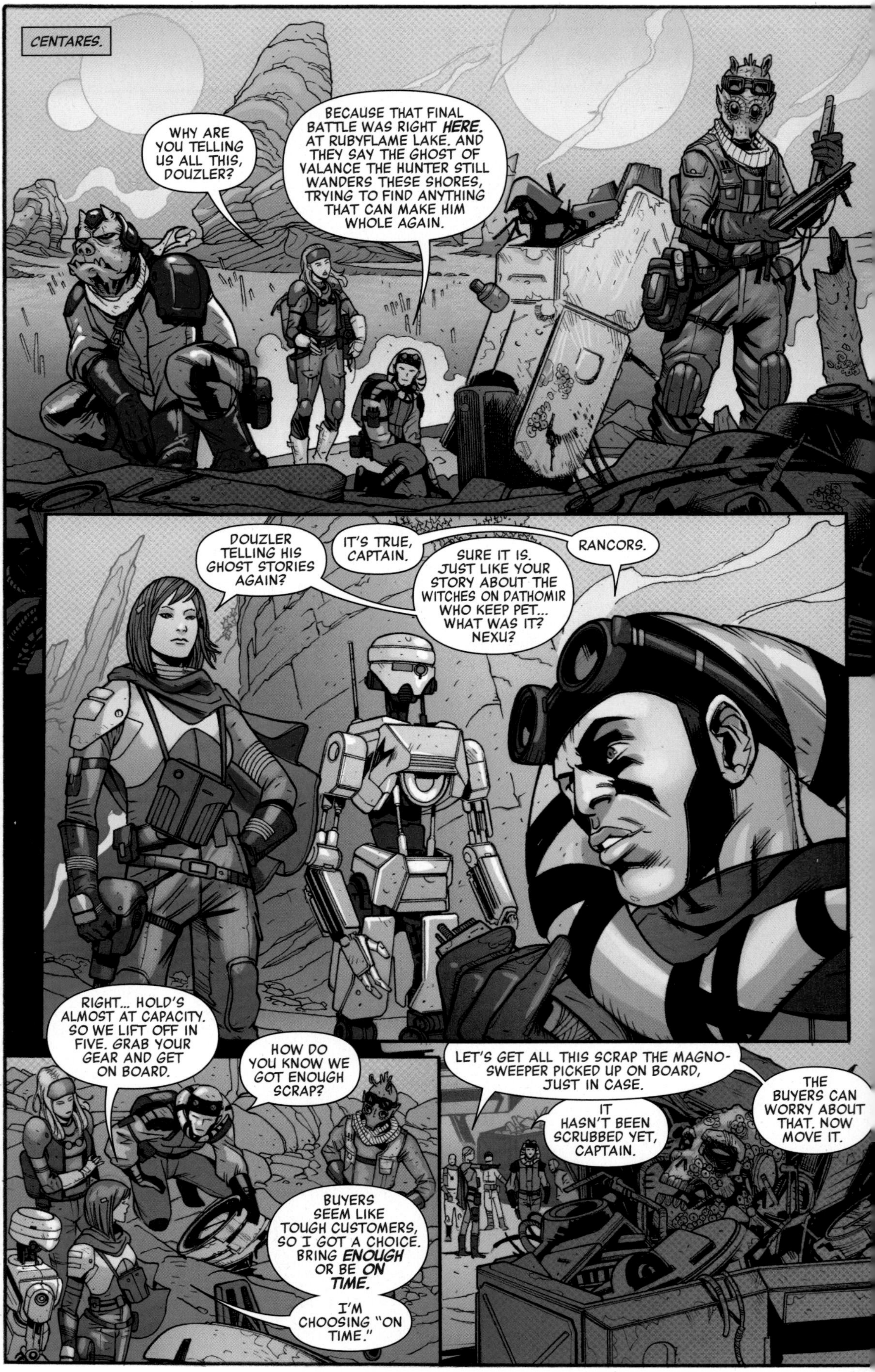
CENTARES.
WHY ARE YOU TELLING US ALL THIS, DOUZLER?
BECAUSE THAT FINAL BATTLE WAS RIGHT HERE. AT RUBYFLAME LAKE. AND THEY SAY THE GHOST OF VALANCE THE HUNTER STILL WANDERS THESE SHORES, TRYING TO FIND ANYTHING THAT CAN MAKE HIM WHOLE AGAIN.
DOUZLER TELLING HIS GHOST STORIES AGAIN?
IT'S TRUE, CAPTAIN.
SURE IT IS. JUST LIKE YOUR STORY ABOUT THE WITCHES ON DATHOMIR WHO KEEP PET... WHAT WAS IT? NEXU?
RANCORS.
RIGHT... HOLD'S ALMOST AT CAPACITY. SO WE LIFT OFF IN FIVE. GRAB YOUR GEAR AND GET ON BOARD.
HOW DO YOU KNOW WE GOT ENOUGH SCRAP?
BUYERS SEEM LIKE TOUGH CUSTOMERS, SO I GOT A CHOICE. BRING ENOUGH OR BE ON TIME.
I'M CHOOSING "ON TIME."
LET'S GET ALL THIS SCRAP THE MAGNO-SWEEPER PICKED UP ON BOARD, JUST IN CASE.
IT HASN'T BEEN SCRUBBED YET, CAPTAIN.
THE BUYERS CAN WORRY ABOUT THAT. NOW MOVE IT.

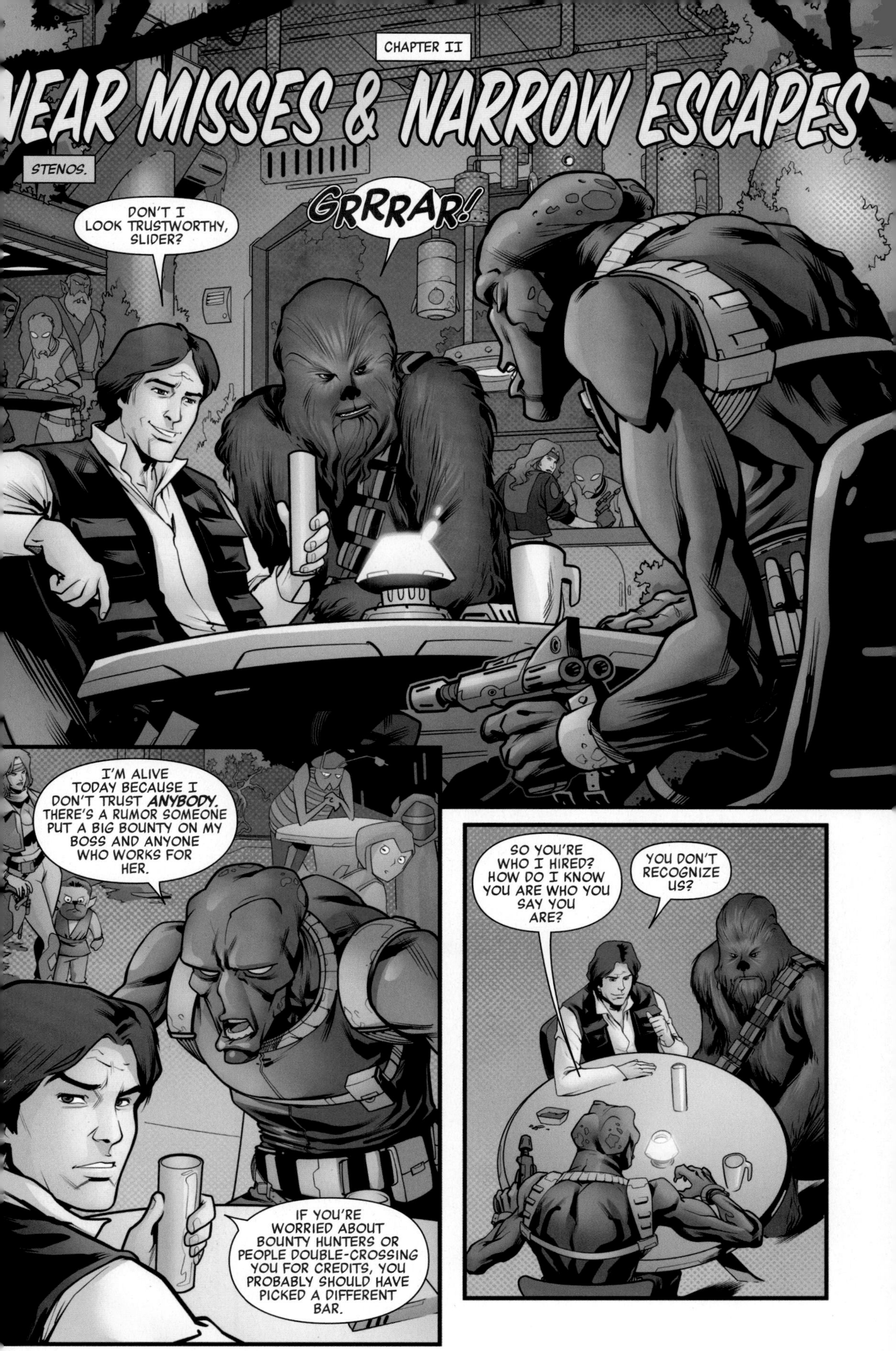
CHAPTER II
NEAR MISSES & NARROW ESCAPES
STENOS.
DON'T I LOOK TRUSTWORTHY, SLIDER?
GRRRAR!
I'M ALIVE TODAY BECAUSE I DON'T TRUST ANYBODY. THERE'S A RUMOR SOMEONE PUT A BIG BOUNTY ON MY BOSS AND ANYONE WHO WORKS FOR HER.
IF YOU'RE WORRIED ABOUT BOUNTY HUNTERS OR PEOPLE DOUBLE-CROSSING YOU FOR CREDITS, YOU PROBABLY SHOULD HAVE PICKED A DIFFERENT BAR.
SO YOU'RE WHO I HIRED? HOW DO I KNOW YOU ARE WHO YOU SAY YOU ARE?
YOU DON'T RECOGNIZE US?

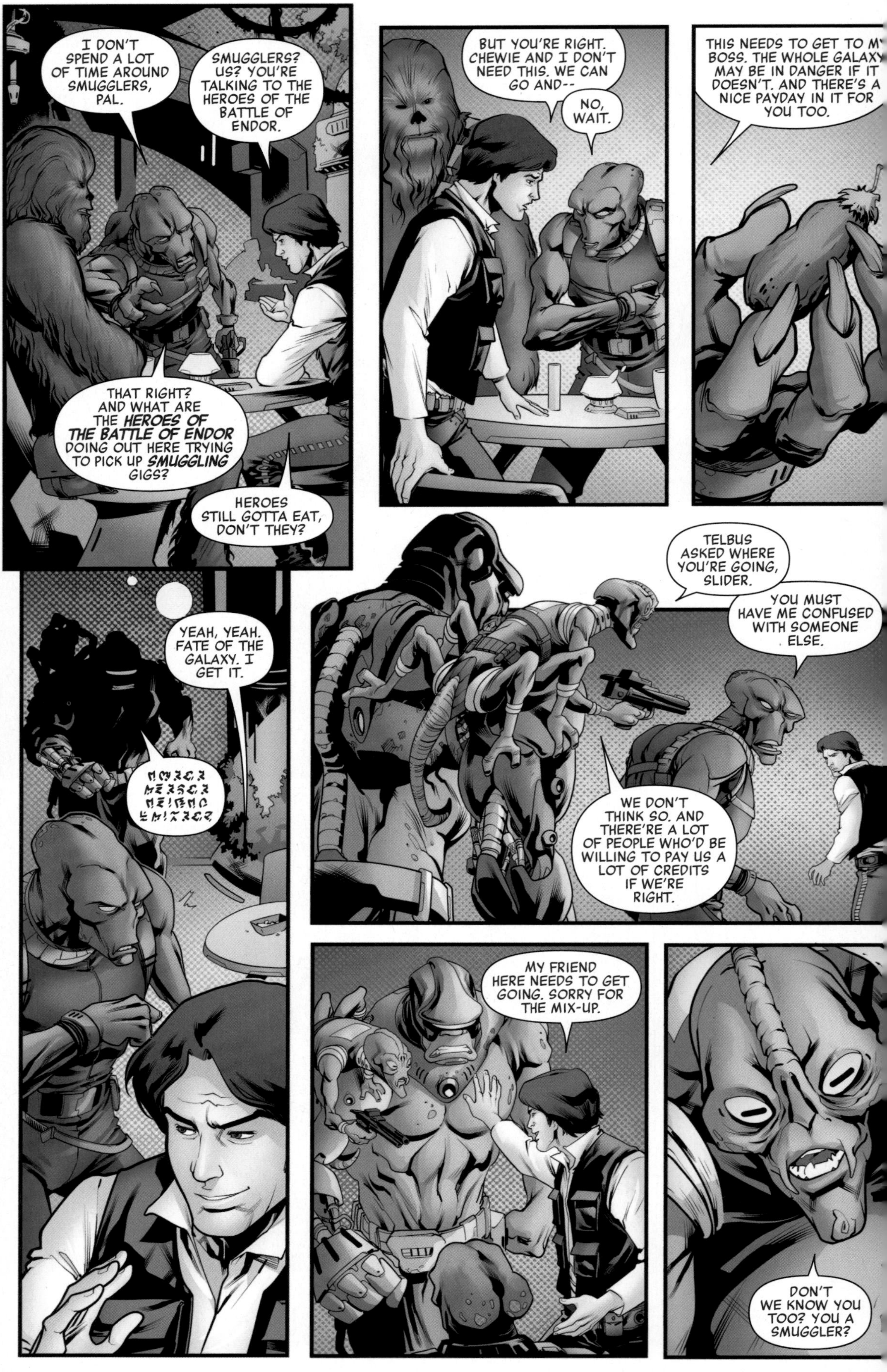
I DON'T SPEND A LOT OF TIME AROUND SMUGGLERS, PAL.
SMUGGLERS? US? YOU'RE TALKING TO THE HEROES OF THE BATTLE OF ENDOR.
THAT RIGHT? AND WHAT ARE THE HEROES OF THE BATTLE OF ENDOR DOING OUT HERE TRYING TO PICK UP SMUGGLING GIGS?
HEROES STILL GOTTA EAT, DON'T THEY?
BUT YOU'RE RIGHT. CHEWIE AND I DON'T NEED THIS. WE CAN GO AND--
NO, WAIT.
THIS NEEDS TO GET TO MY BOSS. THE WHOLE GALAXY MAY BE IN DANGER IF IT DOESN'T. AND THERE'S A NICE PAYDAY IN IT FOR YOU TOO.
YEAH, YEAH. FATE OF THE GALAXY. I GET IT.
TELBUS ASKED WHERE YOU'RE GOING, SLIDER.
YOU MUST HAVE ME CONFUSED WITH SOMEONE ELSE.
WE DON'T THINK SO. AND THERE'RE A LOT OF PEOPLE WHO'D BE WILLING TO PAY US A LOT OF CREDITS IF WE'RE RIGHT.
MY FRIEND HERE NEEDS TO GET GOING. SORRY FOR THE MIX-UP.
DON'T WE KNOW YOU TOO? YOU A SMUGGLER?

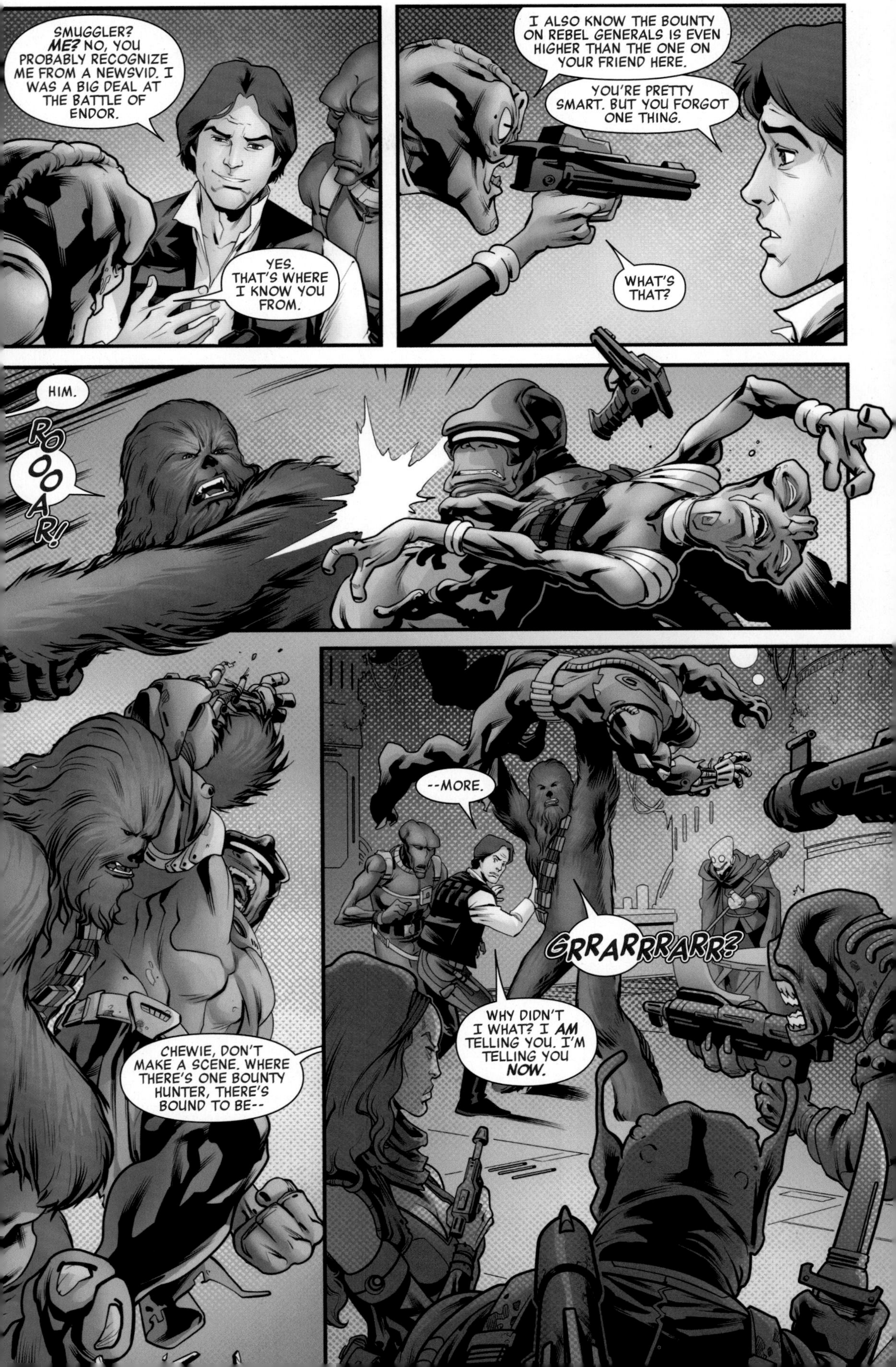
SMUGGLER? ME? NO, YOU PROBABLY RECOGNIZE ME FROM A NEWSVID. I WAS A BIG DEAL AT THE BATTLE OF ENDOR.
YES. THAT'S WHERE I KNOW YOU FROM.
I ALSO KNOW THE BOUNTY ON REBEL GENERALS IS EVEN HIGHER THAN THE ONE ON YOUR FRIEND HERE.
YOU'RE PRETTY SMART. BUT YOU FORGOT ONE THING.
WHAT'S THAT?
HIM.
ROOOOAR!
CHEWIE, DON'T MAKE A SCENE. WHERE THERE'S ONE BOUNTY HUNTER, THERE'S BOUND TO BE--
--MORE.
GRRARRRARR?
WHY DIDN'T I WHAT? I AM TELLING YOU. I'M TELLING YOU NOW.

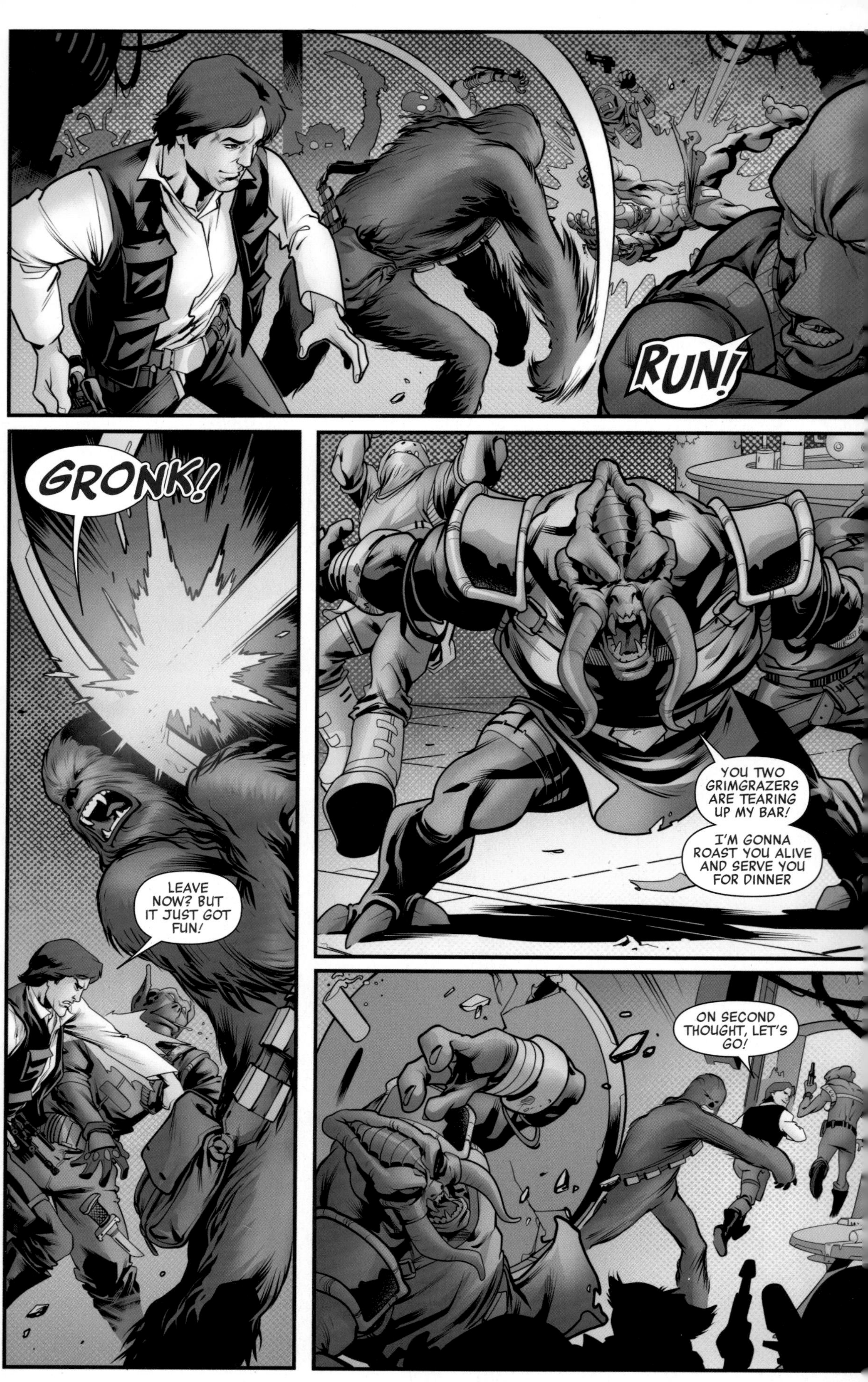
RUN!
GRONK!
LEAVE NOW? BUT IT JUST GOT FUN!
YOU TWO GRIMGRAZERS ARE TEARING UP MY BAR!
I'M GONNA ROAST YOU ALIVE AND SERVE YOU FOR DINNER
ON SECOND THOUGHT, LET'S GO!

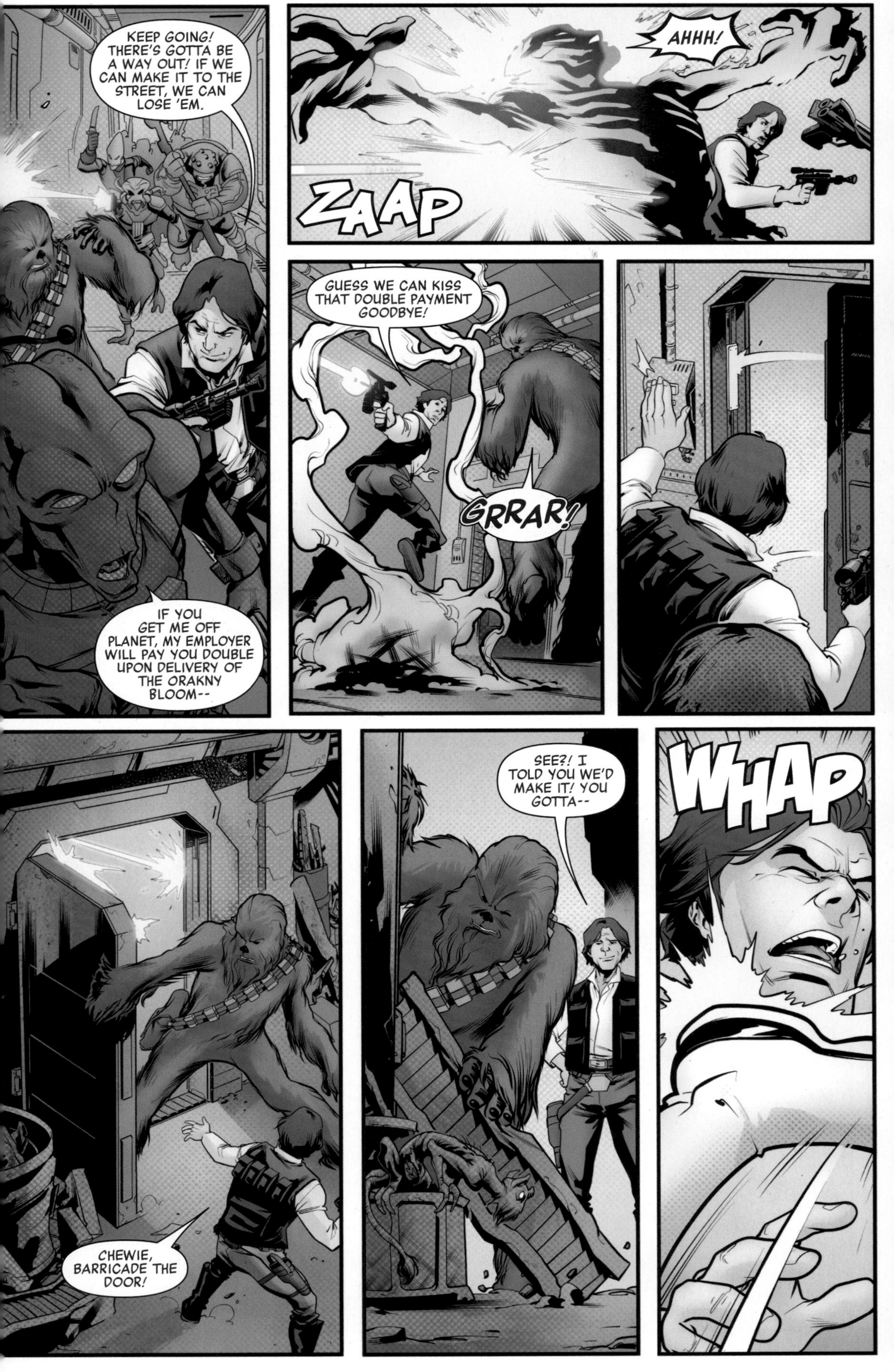
KEEP GOING! THERE'S GOTTA BE A WAY OUT! IF WE CAN MAKE IT TO THE STREET, WE CAN LOSE 'EM.
IF YOU GET ME OFF PLANET, MY EMPLOYER WILL PAY YOU DOUBLE UPON DELIVERY OF THE ORAKNY BLOOM--
AHHH!
ZAAP
GUESS WE CAN KISS THAT DOUBLE PAYMENT GOODBYE!
GRRAR!
CHEWIE, BARRICADE THE DOOR!
SEE?! I TOLD YOU WE'D MAKE IT! YOU GOTTA--
WHAP

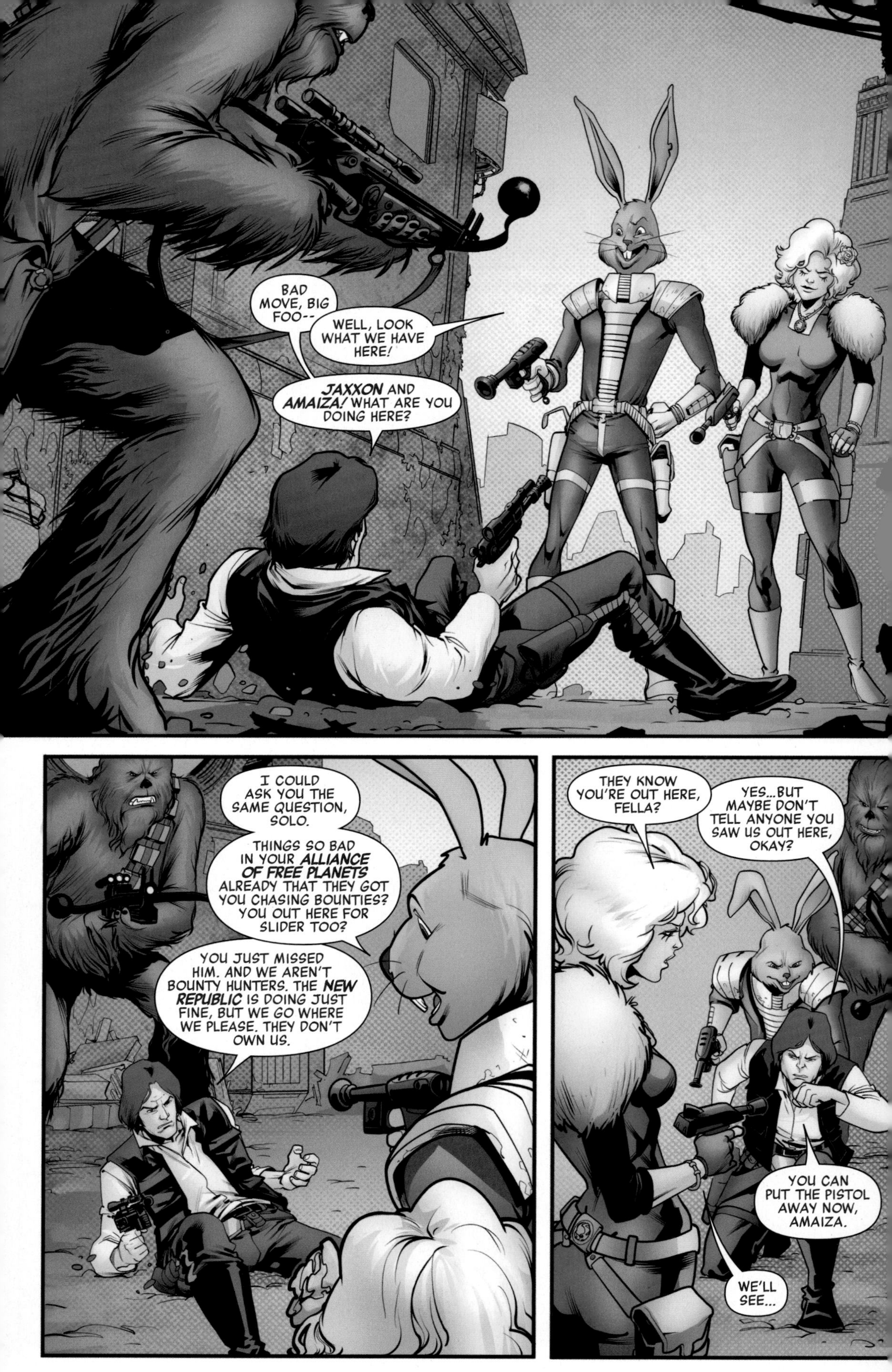
BAD MOVE, BIG FOO--
WELL, LOOK WHAT WE HAVE HERE!
JAXXON AND AMAIZA! WHAT ARE YOU DOING HERE?
I COULD ASK YOU THE SAME QUESTION, SOLO.
THINGS SO BAD IN YOUR ALLIANCE OF FREE PLANETS ALREADY THAT THEY GOT YOU CHASING BOUNTIES? YOU OUT HERE FOR SLIDER TOO?
YOU JUST MISSED HIM. AND WE AREN'T BOUNTY HUNTERS. THE NEW REPUBLIC IS DOING JUST FINE, BUT WE GO WHERE WE PLEASE. THEY DON'T OWN US.
THEY KNOW YOU'RE OUT HERE, FELLA?
YES...BUT MAYBE DON'T TELL ANYONE YOU SAW US OUT HERE, OKAY?
YOU CAN PUT THE PISTOL AWAY NOW, AMAIZA.
WE'LL SEE...

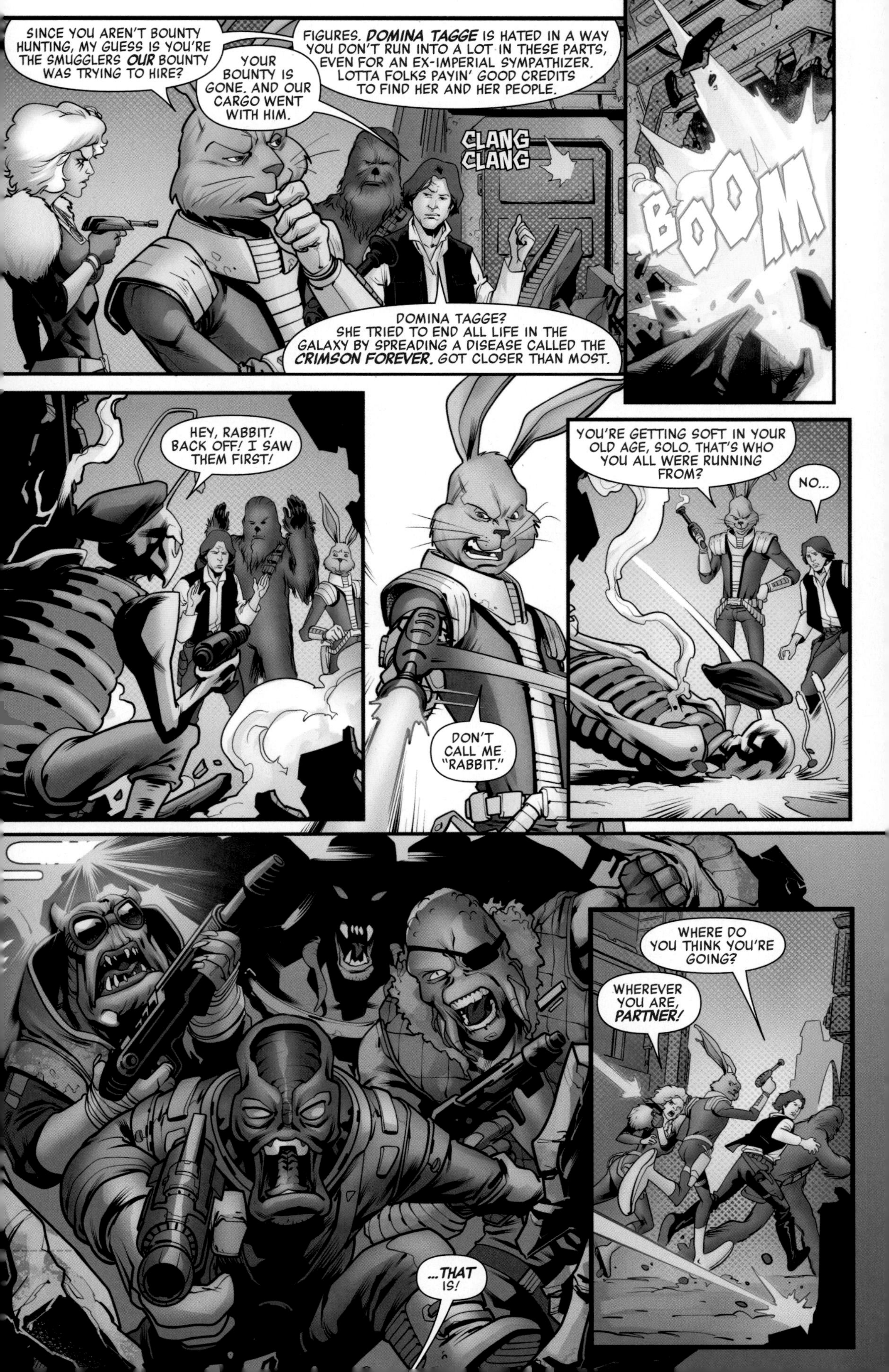
SINCE YOU AREN'T BOUNTY HUNTING, MY GUESS IS YOU'RE THE SMUGGLERS OUR BOUNTY WAS TRYING TO HIRE?
YOUR BOUNTY IS GONE. AND OUR CARGO WENT WITH HIM.
FIGURES. DOMINA TAGGE IS HATED IN A WAY YOU DON'T RUN INTO A LOT IN THESE PARTS, EVEN FOR AN EX-IMPERIAL SYMPATHIZER. LOTTA FOLKS PAYIN' GOOD CREDITS TO FIND HER AND HER PEOPLE.
CLANG CLANG
DOMINA TAGGE? SHE TRIED TO END ALL LIFE IN THE GALAXY BY SPREADING A DISEASE CALLED THE CRIMSON FOREVER. GOT CLOSER THAN MOST.
BOOM
HEY, RABBIT! BACK OFF! I SAW THEM FIRST!
DON'T CALL ME "RABBIT."
YOU'RE GETTING SOFT IN YOUR OLD AGE, SOLO. THAT'S WHO YOU ALL WERE RUNNING FROM?
NO...
...THAT IS!
WHERE DO YOU THINK YOU'RE GOING?
WHEREVER YOU ARE, PARTNER!

CHAPTER III

A SCAVENGER'S MISTAKE

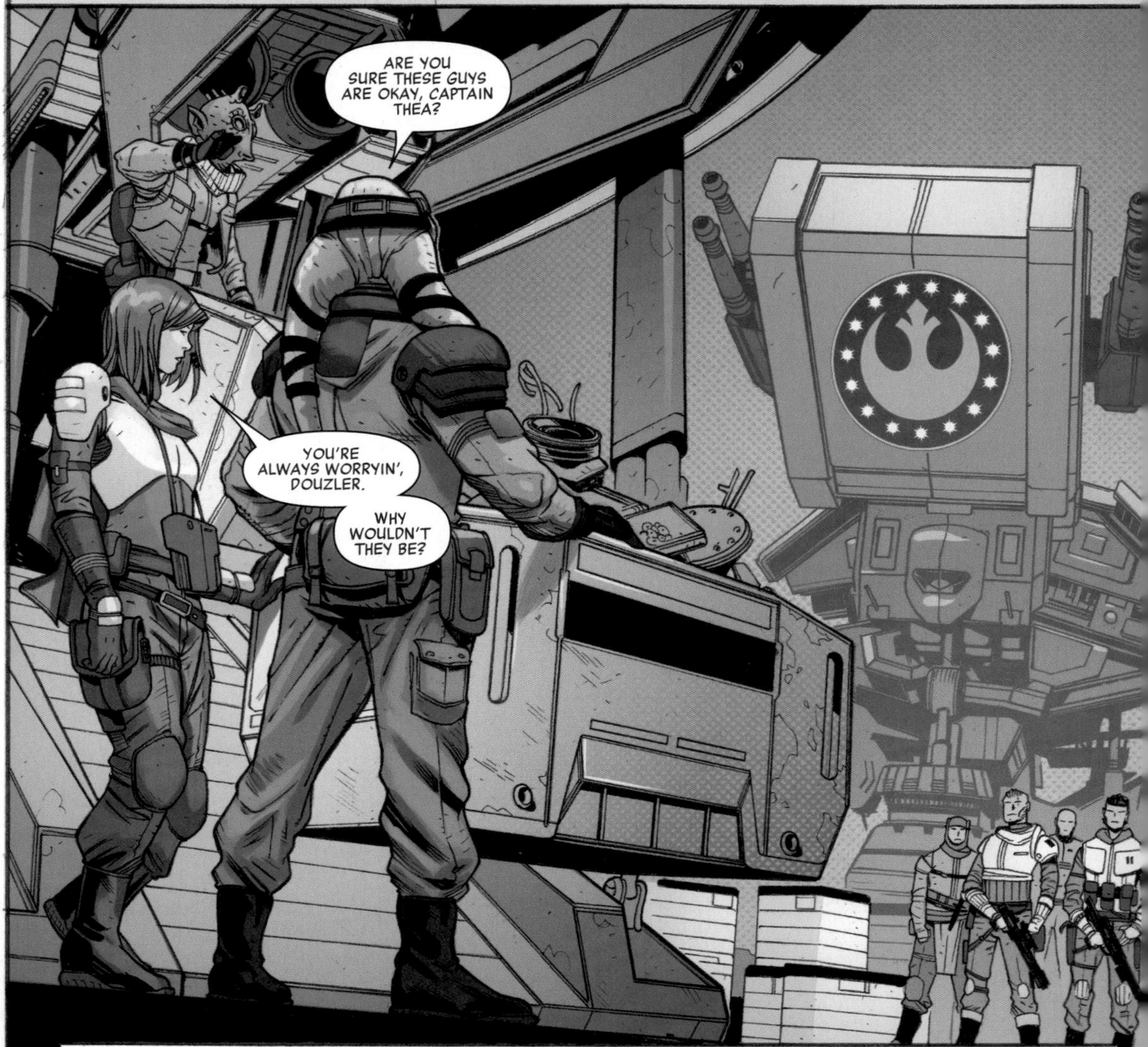
ARE YOU SURE THESE GUYS ARE OKAY, CAPTAIN THEA?
YOU'RE ALWAYS WORRYIN', DOUZLER.
WHY WOULDN'T THEY BE?

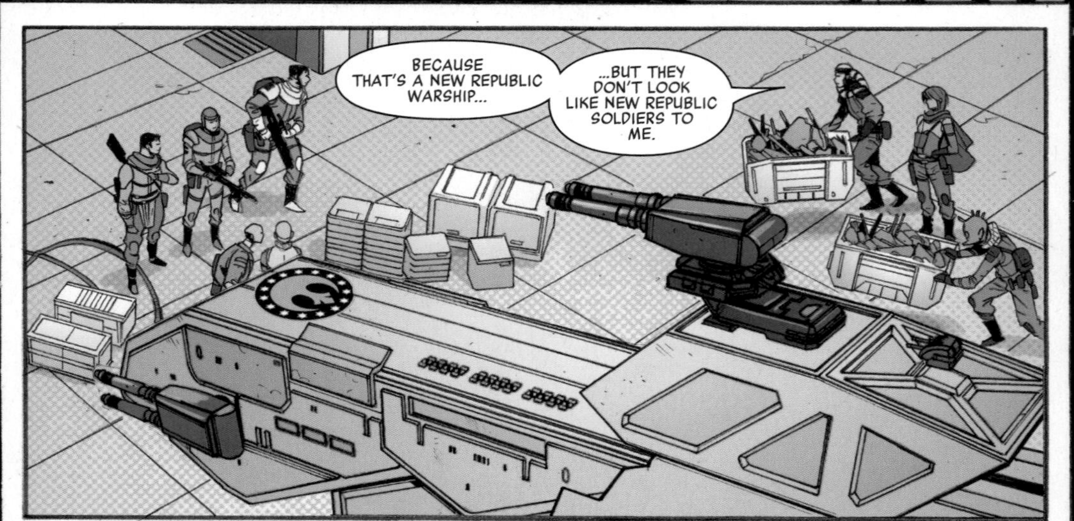
BECAUSE THAT'S A NEW REPUBLIC WARSHIP...
...BUT THEY DON'T LOOK LIKE NEW REPUBLIC SOLDIERS TO ME.

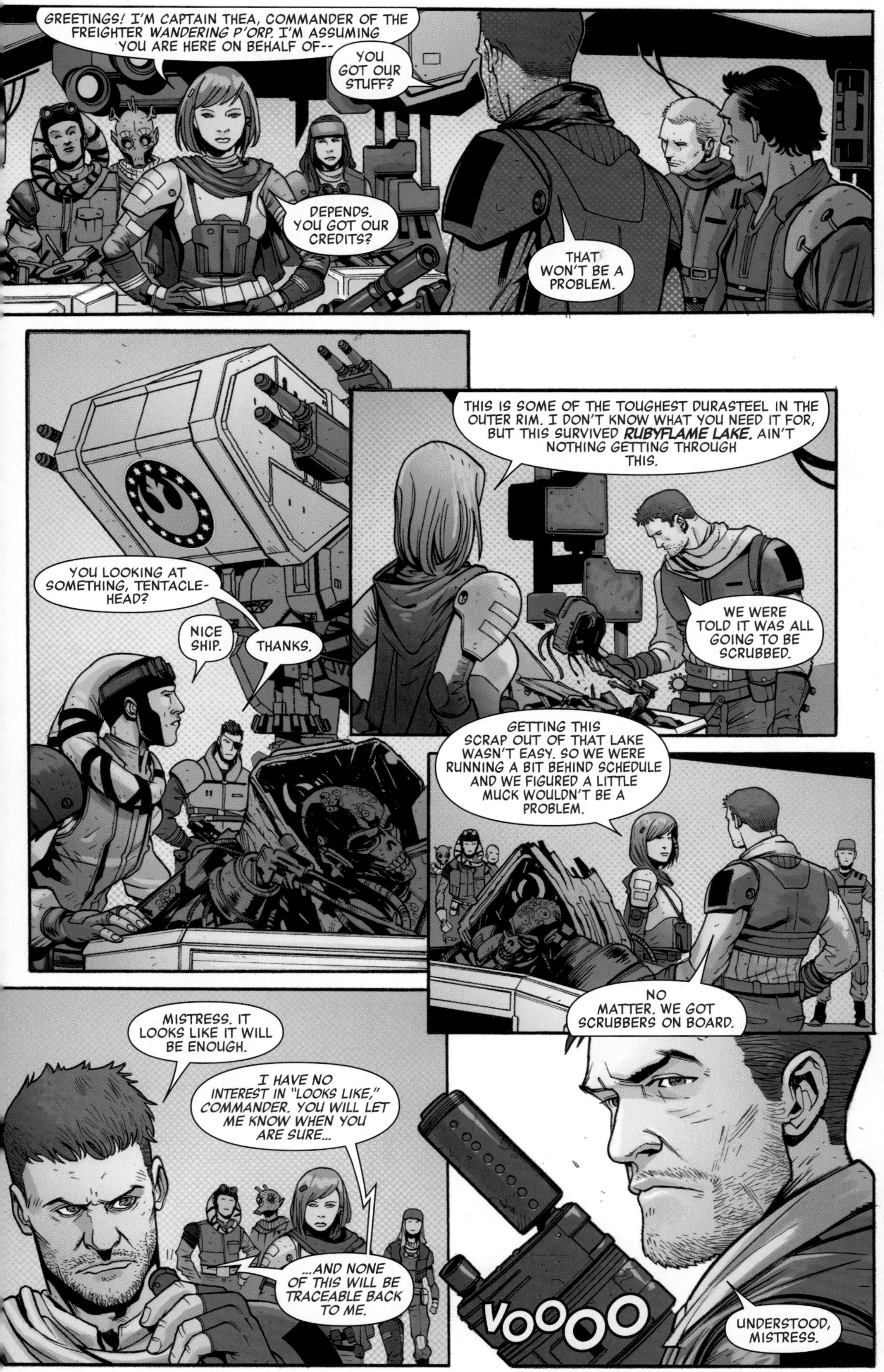
GREETINGS! I'M CAPTAIN THEA, COMMANDER OF THE FREIGHTER *WANDERING P'ORP.* I'M ASSUMING YOU ARE HERE ON BEHALF OF--
YOU GOT OUR STUFF?
DEPENDS. YOU GOT OUR CREDITS?
THAT WON'T BE A PROBLEM.
THIS IS SOME OF THE TOUGHEST DURASTEEL IN THE OUTER RIM. I DON'T KNOW WHAT YOU NEED IT FOR, BUT THIS SURVIVED **RUBYFLAME LAKE.** AIN'T NOTHING GETTING THROUGH THIS.
WE WERE TOLD IT WAS ALL GOING TO BE SCRUBBED.
YOU LOOKING AT SOMETHING, TENTACLE-HEAD?
NICE SHIP.
THANKS.
GETTING THIS SCRAP OUT OF THAT LAKE WASN'T EASY. SO WE WERE RUNNING A BIT BEHIND SCHEDULE AND WE FIGURED A LITTLE MUCK WOULDN'T BE A PROBLEM.
NO MATTER. WE GOT SCRUBBERS ON BOARD.
MISTRESS. IT LOOKS LIKE IT WILL BE ENOUGH.
I HAVE NO INTEREST IN "LOOKS LIKE," COMMANDER. YOU WILL LET ME KNOW WHEN YOU ARE SURE...
...AND NONE OF THIS WILL BE TRACEABLE BACK TO ME.
VOOOOO
UNDERSTOOD, MISTRESS.

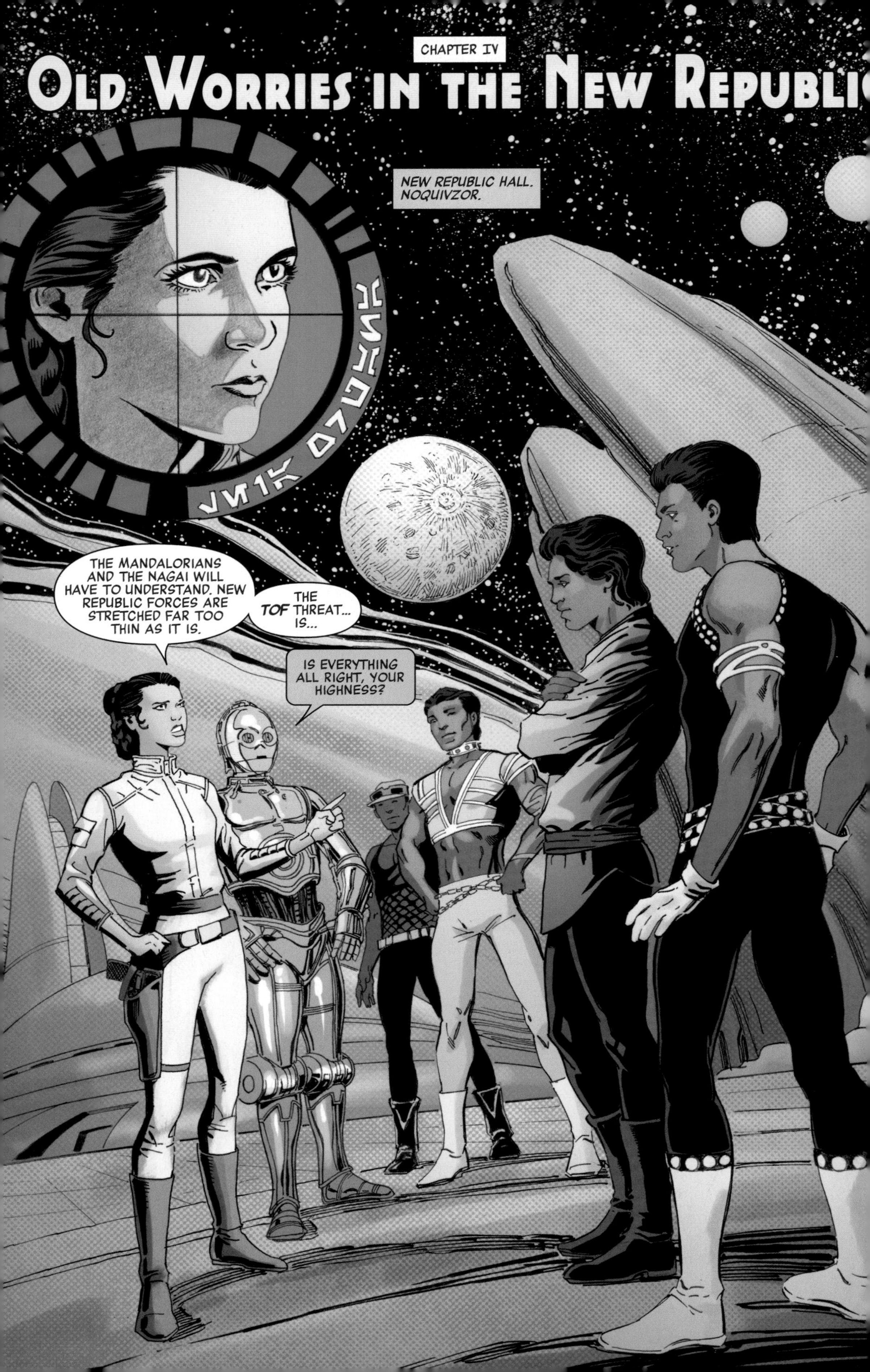
CHAPTER IV
OLD WORRIES IN THE NEW REPUBLIC
NEW REPUBLIC HALL. NOQUIVZOR.
THE MANDALORIANS AND THE NAGAI WILL HAVE TO UNDERSTAND. NEW REPUBLIC FORCES ARE STRETCHED FAR TOO THIN AS IT IS.
THE TOF THREAT... IS...
IS EVERYTHING ALL RIGHT, YOUR HIGHNESS?

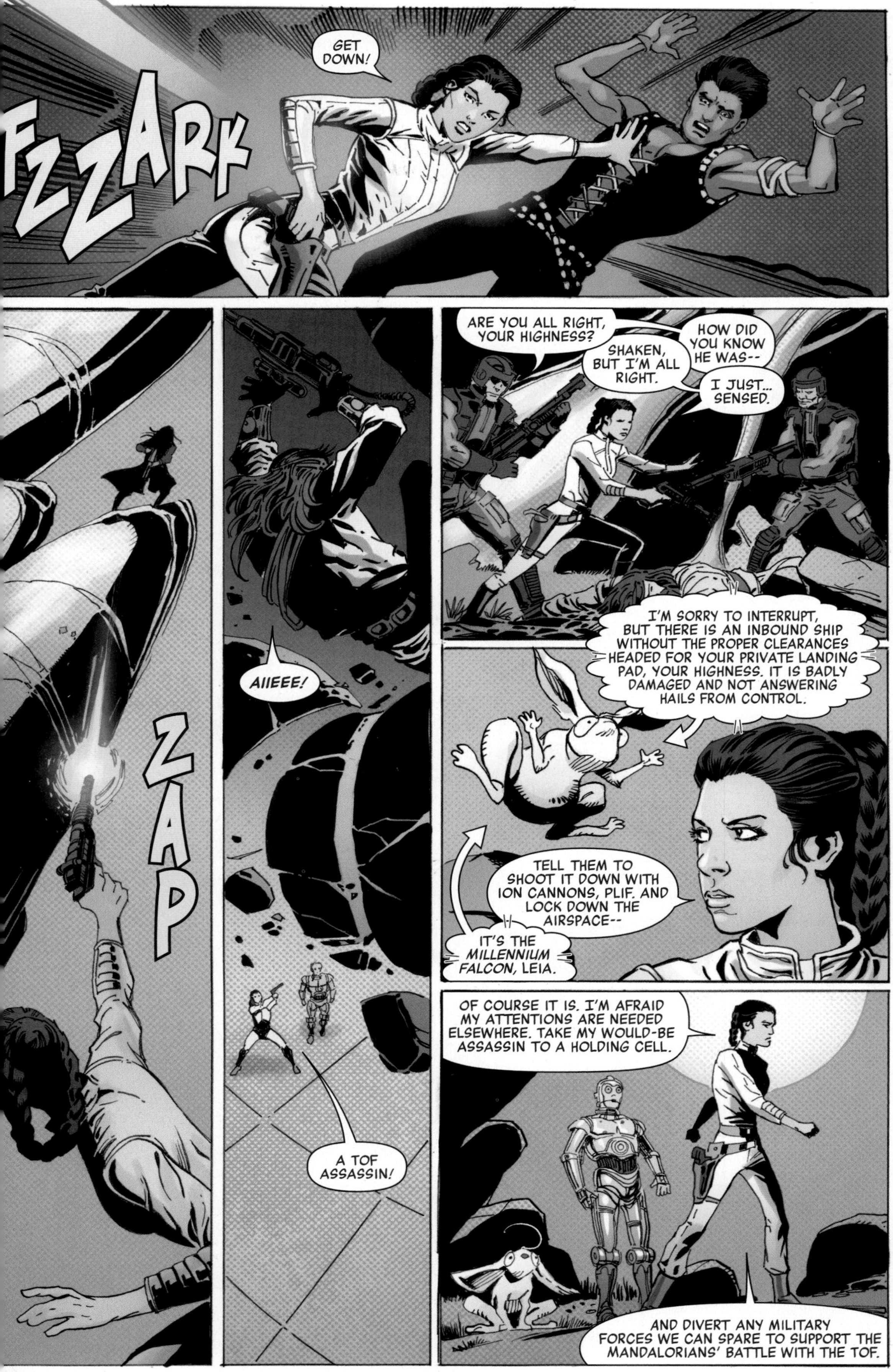
GET DOWN!
FZZARK
ZAP
AIIEEE!
A TOF ASSASSIN!
ARE YOU ALL RIGHT, YOUR HIGHNESS?
SHAKEN, BUT I'M ALL RIGHT.
HOW DID YOU KNOW HE WAS--
I JUST... SENSED.
I'M SORRY TO INTERRUPT, BUT THERE IS AN INBOUND SHIP WITHOUT THE PROPER CLEARANCES HEADED FOR YOUR PRIVATE LANDING PAD, YOUR HIGHNESS. IT IS BADLY DAMAGED AND NOT ANSWERING HAILS FROM CONTROL.
TELL THEM TO SHOOT IT DOWN WITH ION CANNONS, PLIF. AND LOCK DOWN THE AIRSPACE--
IT'S THE *MILLENNIUM FALCON*, LEIA.
OF COURSE IT IS. I'M AFRAID MY ATTENTIONS ARE NEEDED ELSEWHERE. TAKE MY WOULD-BE ASSASSIN TO A HOLDING CELL.
AND DIVERT ANY MILITARY FORCES WE CAN SPARE TO SUPPORT THE MANDALORIANS' BATTLE WITH THE TOF.

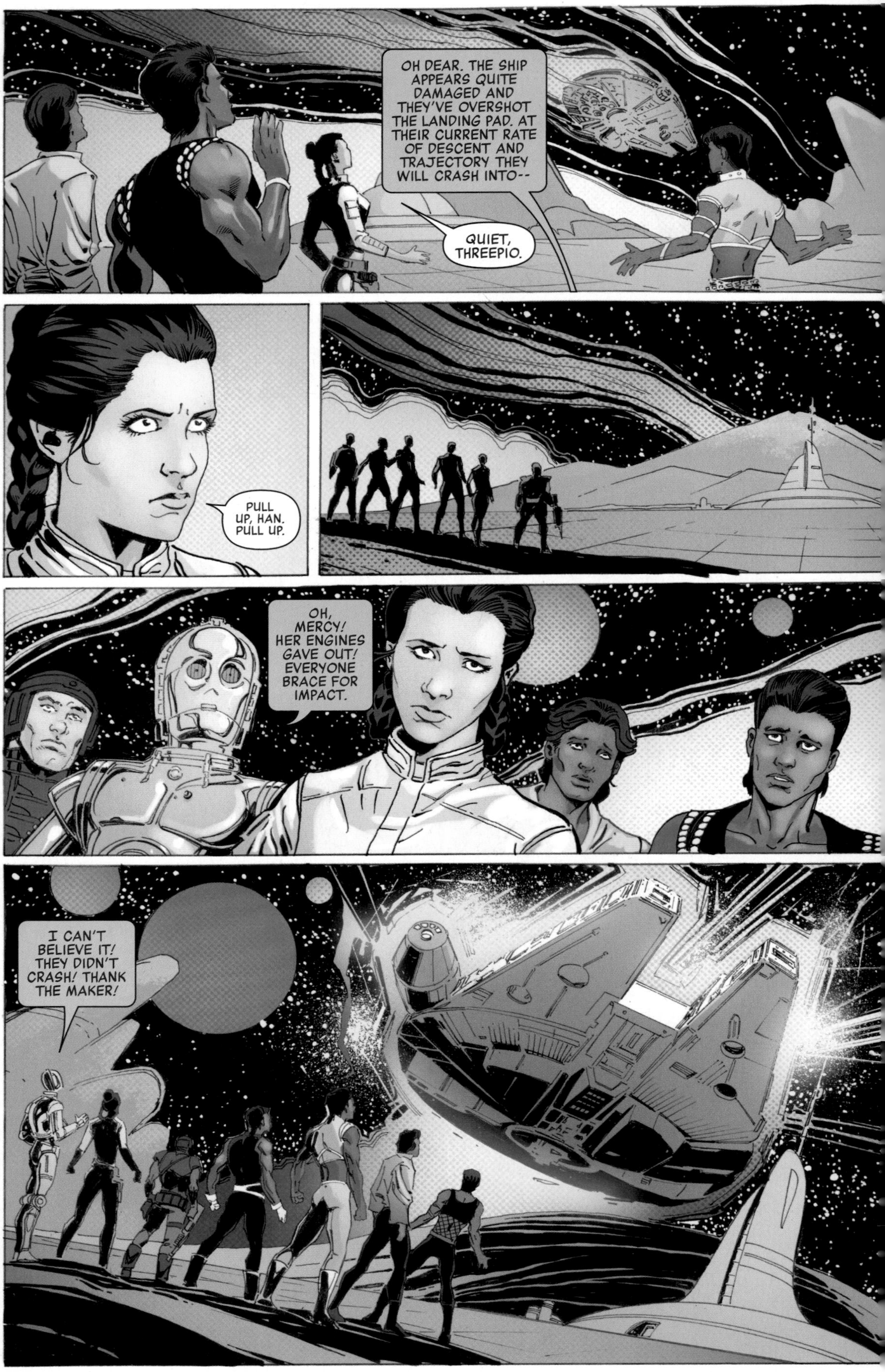
OH DEAR. THE SHIP APPEARS QUITE DAMAGED AND THEY'VE OVERSHOT THE LANDING PAD. AT THEIR CURRENT RATE OF DESCENT AND TRAJECTORY THEY WILL CRASH INTO--
QUIET, THREEPIO.
PULL UP, HAN. PULL UP.
OH, MERCY! HER ENGINES GAVE OUT! EVERYONE BRACE FOR IMPACT.
I CAN'T BELIEVE IT! THEY DIDN'T CRASH! THANK THE MAKER!

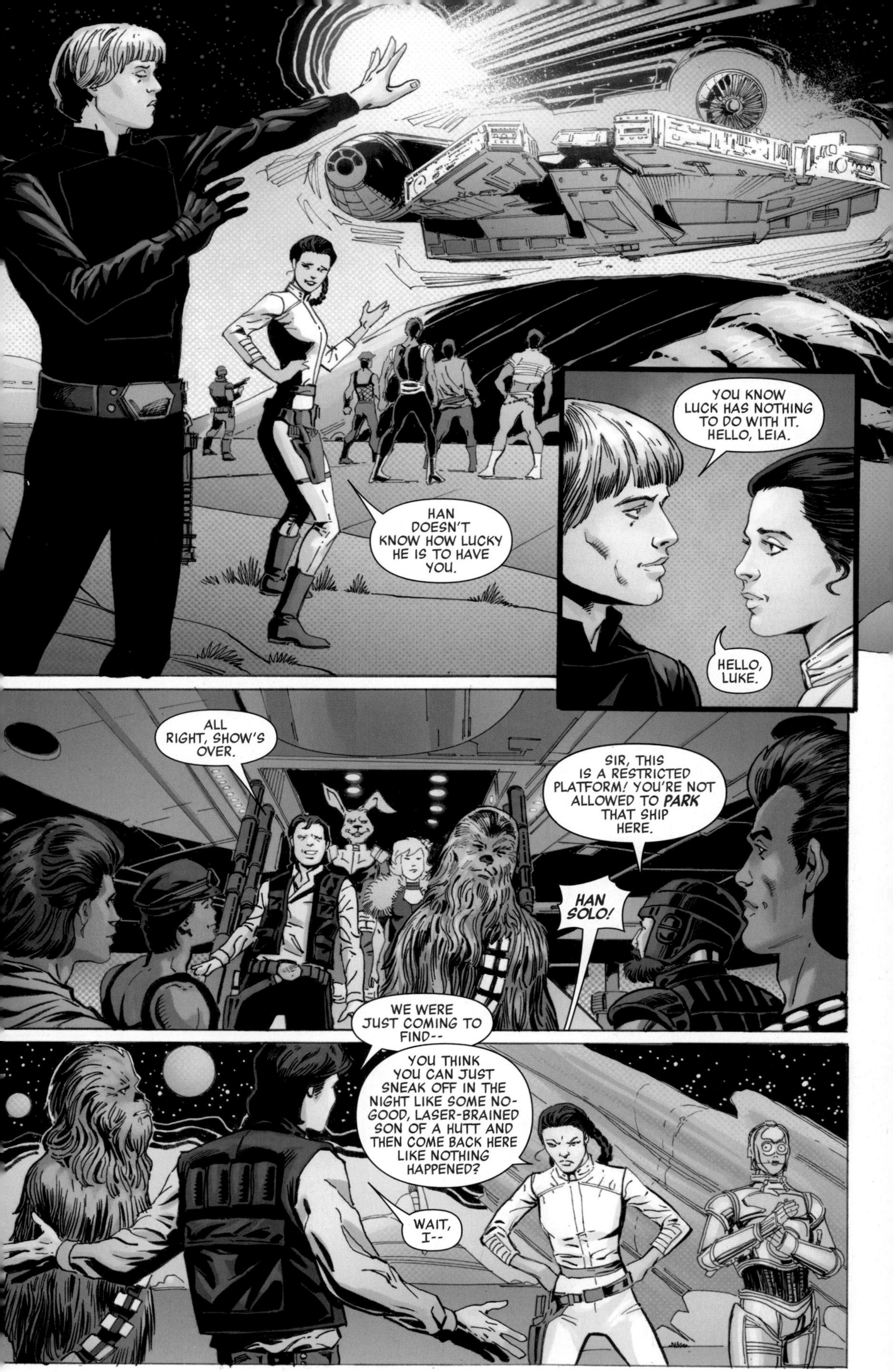
HAN DOESN'T KNOW HOW LUCKY HE IS TO HAVE YOU.
YOU KNOW LUCK HAS NOTHING TO DO WITH IT. HELLO, LEIA.
HELLO, LUKE.
ALL RIGHT, SHOW'S OVER.
SIR, THIS IS A RESTRICTED PLATFORM! YOU'RE NOT ALLOWED TO PARK THAT SHIP HERE.
HAN SOLO!
WE WERE JUST COMING TO FIND--
YOU THINK YOU CAN JUST SNEAK OFF IN THE NIGHT LIKE SOME NO-GOOD, LASER-BRAINED SON OF A HUTT AND THEN COME BACK HERE LIKE NOTHING HAPPENED?
WAIT, I--

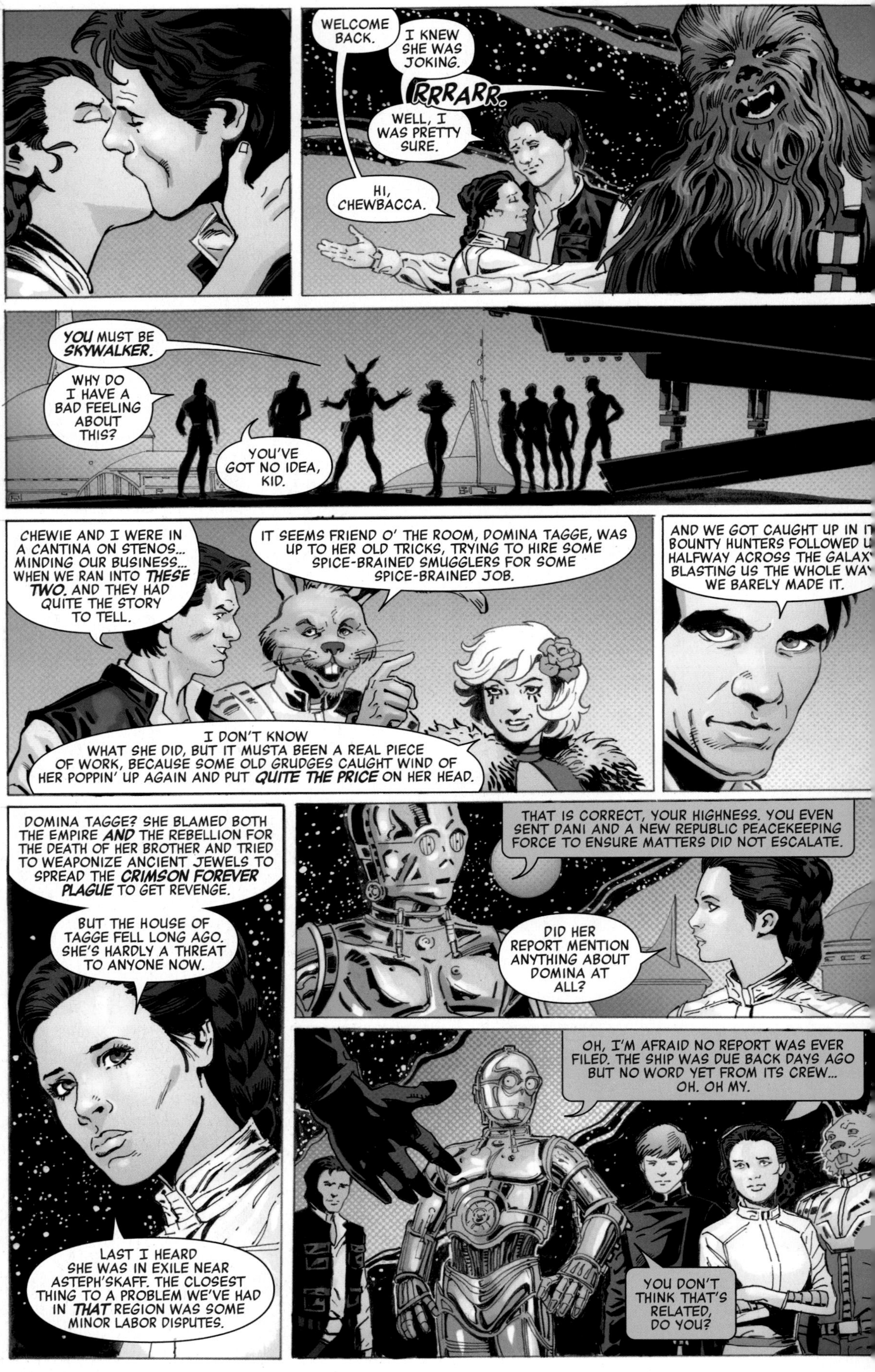
WELCOME BACK.
I KNEW SHE WAS JOKING.
RRRARR.
WELL, I WAS PRETTY SURE.
HI, CHEWBACCA.
YOU MUST BE SKYWALKER.
WHY DO I HAVE A BAD FEELING ABOUT THIS?
YOU'VE GOT NO IDEA, KID.
CHEWIE AND I WERE IN A CANTINA ON STENOS... MINDING OUR BUSINESS... WHEN WE RAN INTO THESE TWO. AND THEY HAD QUITE THE STORY TO TELL.
IT SEEMS FRIEND O' THE ROOM, DOMINA TAGGE, WAS UP TO HER OLD TRICKS, TRYING TO HIRE SOME SPICE-BRAINED SMUGGLERS FOR SOME SPICE-BRAINED JOB.
I DON'T KNOW WHAT SHE DID, BUT IT MUSTA BEEN A REAL PIECE OF WORK, BECAUSE SOME OLD GRUDGES CAUGHT WIND OF HER POPPIN' UP AGAIN AND PUT QUITE THE PRICE ON HER HEAD.
DOMINA TAGGE? SHE BLAMED BOTH THE EMPIRE AND THE REBELLION FOR THE DEATH OF HER BROTHER AND TRIED TO WEAPONIZE ANCIENT JEWELS TO SPREAD THE CRIMSON FOREVER PLAGUE TO GET REVENGE.
BUT THE HOUSE OF TAGGE FELL LONG AGO. SHE'S HARDLY A THREAT TO ANYONE NOW.
LAST I HEARD SHE WAS IN EXILE NEAR ASTEPH'SKAFF. THE CLOSEST THING TO A PROBLEM WE'VE HAD IN THAT REGION WAS SOME MINOR LABOR DISPUTES.
THAT IS CORRECT, YOUR HIGHNESS. YOU EVEN SENT DANI AND A NEW REPUBLIC PEACEKEEPING FORCE TO ENSURE MATTERS DID NOT ESCALATE.
DID HER REPORT MENTION ANYTHING ABOUT DOMINA AT ALL?
OH, I'M AFRAID NO REPORT WAS EVER FILED. THE SHIP WAS DUE BACK DAYS AGO BUT NO WORD YET FROM ITS CREW... OH. OH MY.
YOU DON'T THINK THAT'S RELATED, DO YOU?

CHAPTER V

FOR FEAR OF WHAT MIGHT WAKE

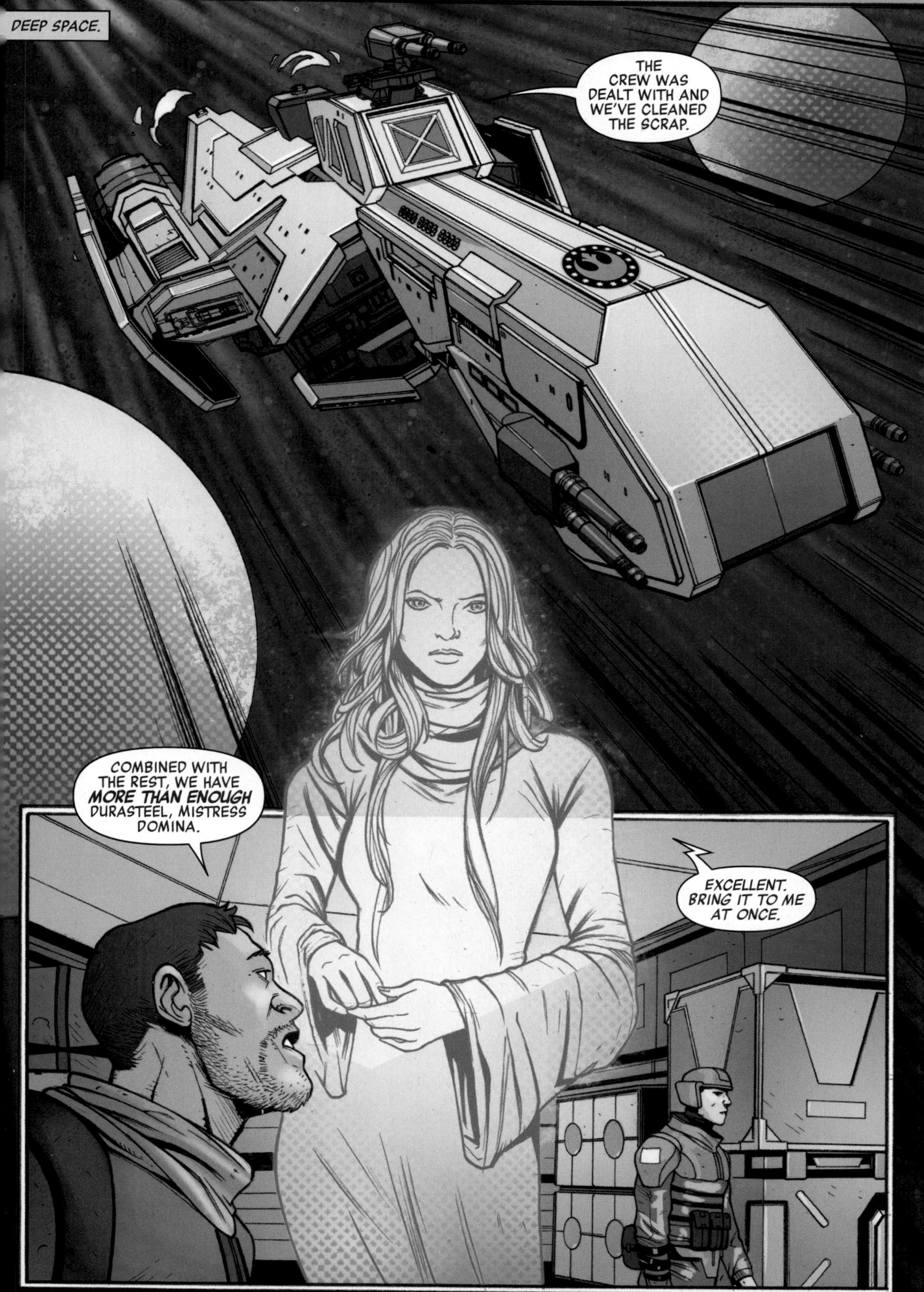
DEEP SPACE.
THE CREW WAS DEALT WITH AND WE'VE CLEANED THE SCRAP.
COMBINED WITH THE REST, WE HAVE MORE THAN ENOUGH DURASTEEL, MISTRESS DOMINA.
EXCELLENT. BRING IT TO ME AT ONCE.

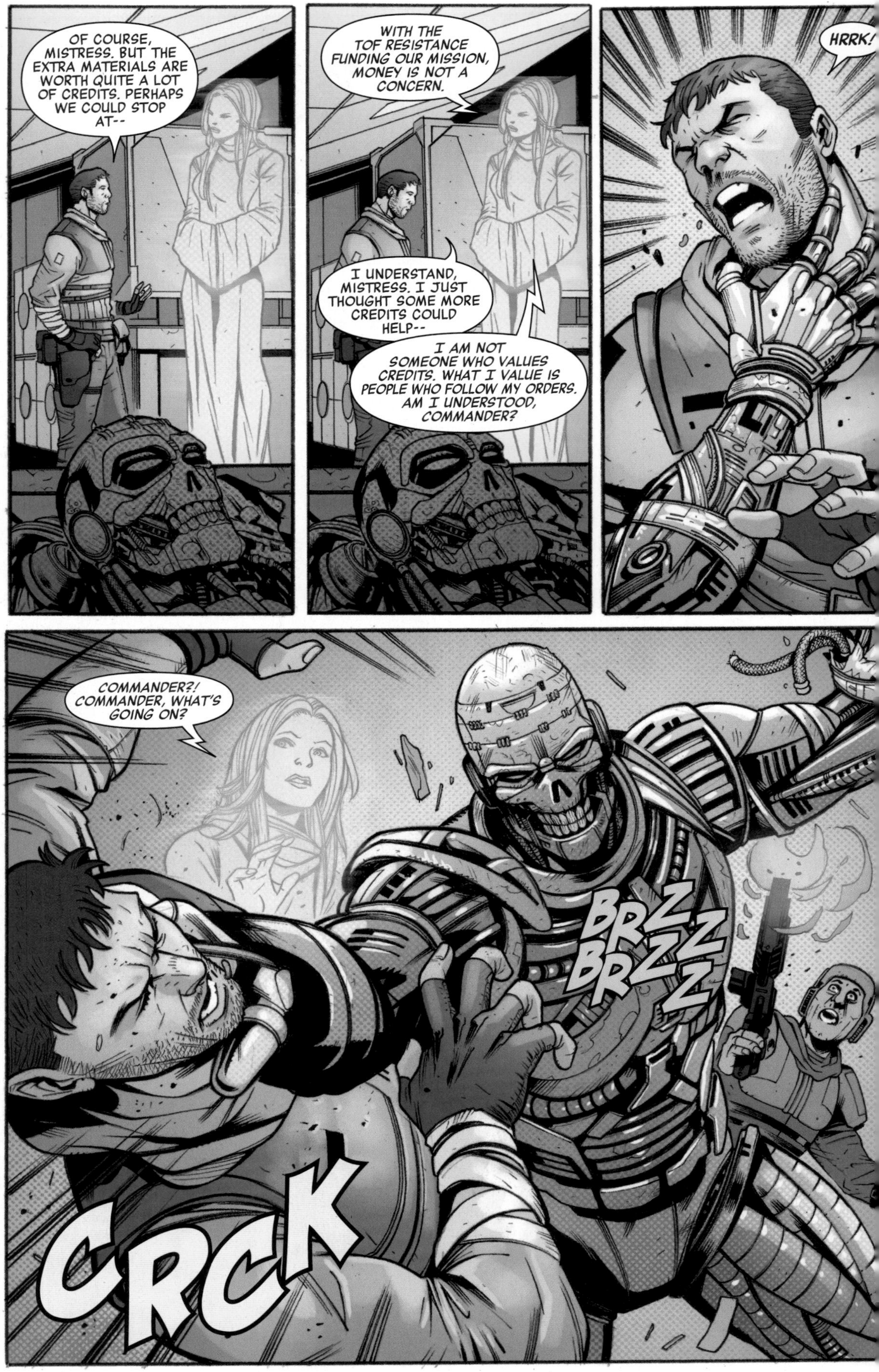
OF COURSE, MISTRESS. BUT THE EXTRA MATERIALS ARE WORTH QUITE A LOT OF CREDITS. PERHAPS WE COULD STOP AT--
WITH THE TOF RESISTANCE FUNDING OUR MISSION, MONEY IS NOT A CONCERN.
I UNDERSTAND, MISTRESS. I JUST THOUGHT SOME MORE CREDITS COULD HELP--
I AM NOT SOMEONE WHO VALUES CREDITS. WHAT I VALUE IS PEOPLE WHO FOLLOW MY ORDERS. AM I UNDERSTOOD, COMMANDER?
HRRK!
COMMANDER?! COMMANDER, WHAT'S GOING ON?
BRZZZ BRZZZ
CRCK

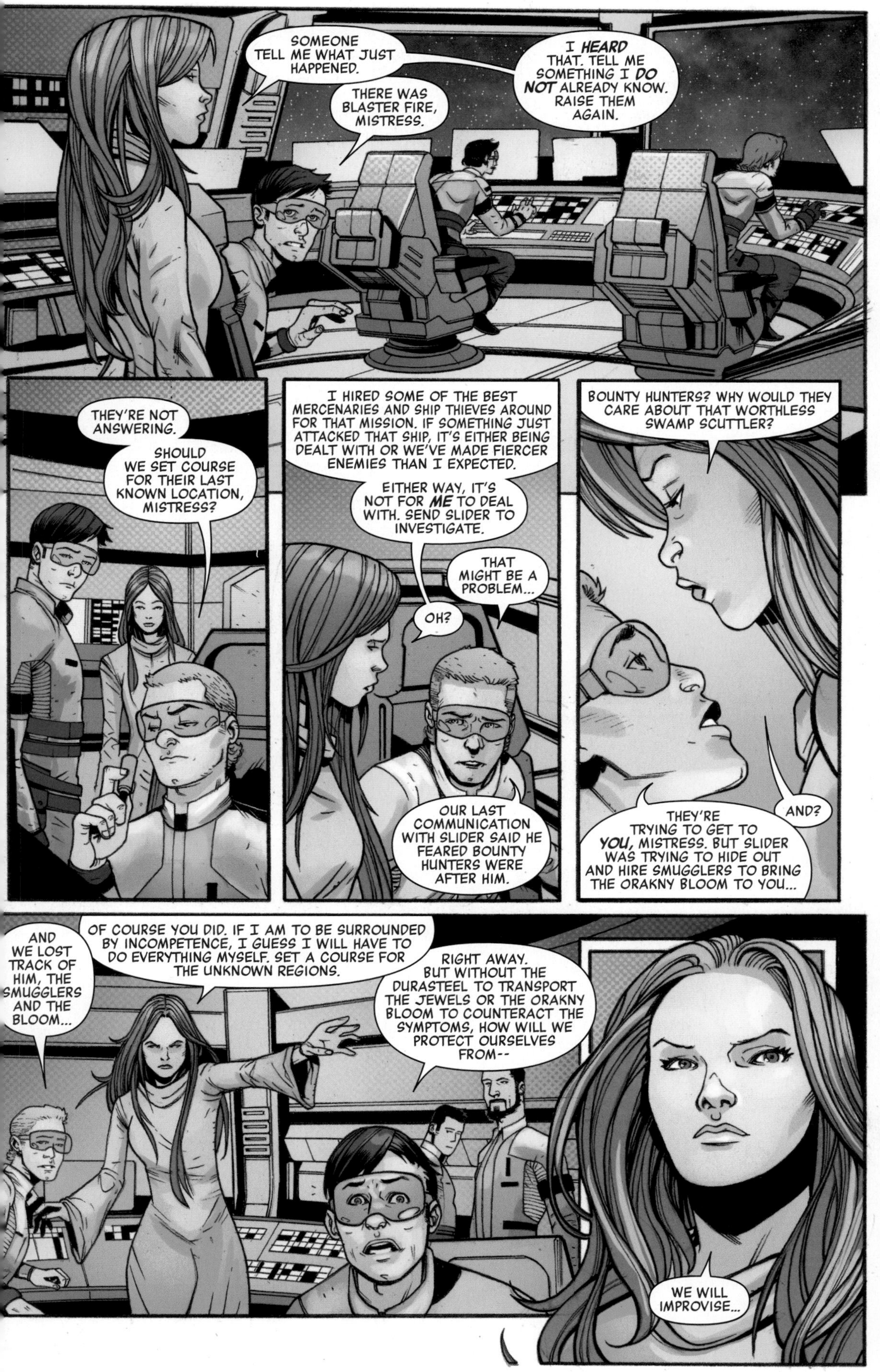
SOMEONE TELL ME WHAT JUST HAPPENED.
THERE WAS BLASTER FIRE, MISTRESS.
I **HEARD** THAT. TELL ME SOMETHING I **DO NOT** ALREADY KNOW. RAISE THEM AGAIN.
THEY'RE NOT ANSWERING.
SHOULD WE SET COURSE FOR THEIR LAST KNOWN LOCATION, MISTRESS?
I HIRED SOME OF THE BEST MERCENARIES AND SHIP THIEVES AROUND FOR THAT MISSION. IF SOMETHING JUST ATTACKED THAT SHIP, IT'S EITHER BEING DEALT WITH OR WE'VE MADE FIERCER ENEMIES THAN I EXPECTED.
EITHER WAY, IT'S NOT FOR **ME** TO DEAL WITH. SEND SLIDER TO INVESTIGATE.
THAT MIGHT BE A PROBLEM...
OH?
OUR LAST COMMUNICATION WITH SLIDER SAID HE FEARED BOUNTY HUNTERS WERE AFTER HIM.
BOUNTY HUNTERS? WHY WOULD THEY CARE ABOUT THAT WORTHLESS SWAMP SCUTTLER?
AND?
THEY'RE TRYING TO GET TO **YOU,** MISTRESS. BUT SLIDER WAS TRYING TO HIDE OUT AND HIRE SMUGGLERS TO BRING THE ORAKNY BLOOM TO YOU...
AND WE LOST TRACK OF HIM, THE SMUGGLERS AND THE BLOOM...
OF COURSE YOU DID. IF I AM TO BE SURROUNDED BY INCOMPETENCE, I GUESS I WILL HAVE TO DO EVERYTHING MYSELF. SET A COURSE FOR THE UNKNOWN REGIONS.
RIGHT AWAY. BUT WITHOUT THE DURASTEEL TO TRANSPORT THE JEWELS OR THE ORAKNY BLOOM TO COUNTERACT THE SYMPTOMS, HOW WILL WE PROTECT OURSELVES FROM--
WE WILL IMPROVISE...

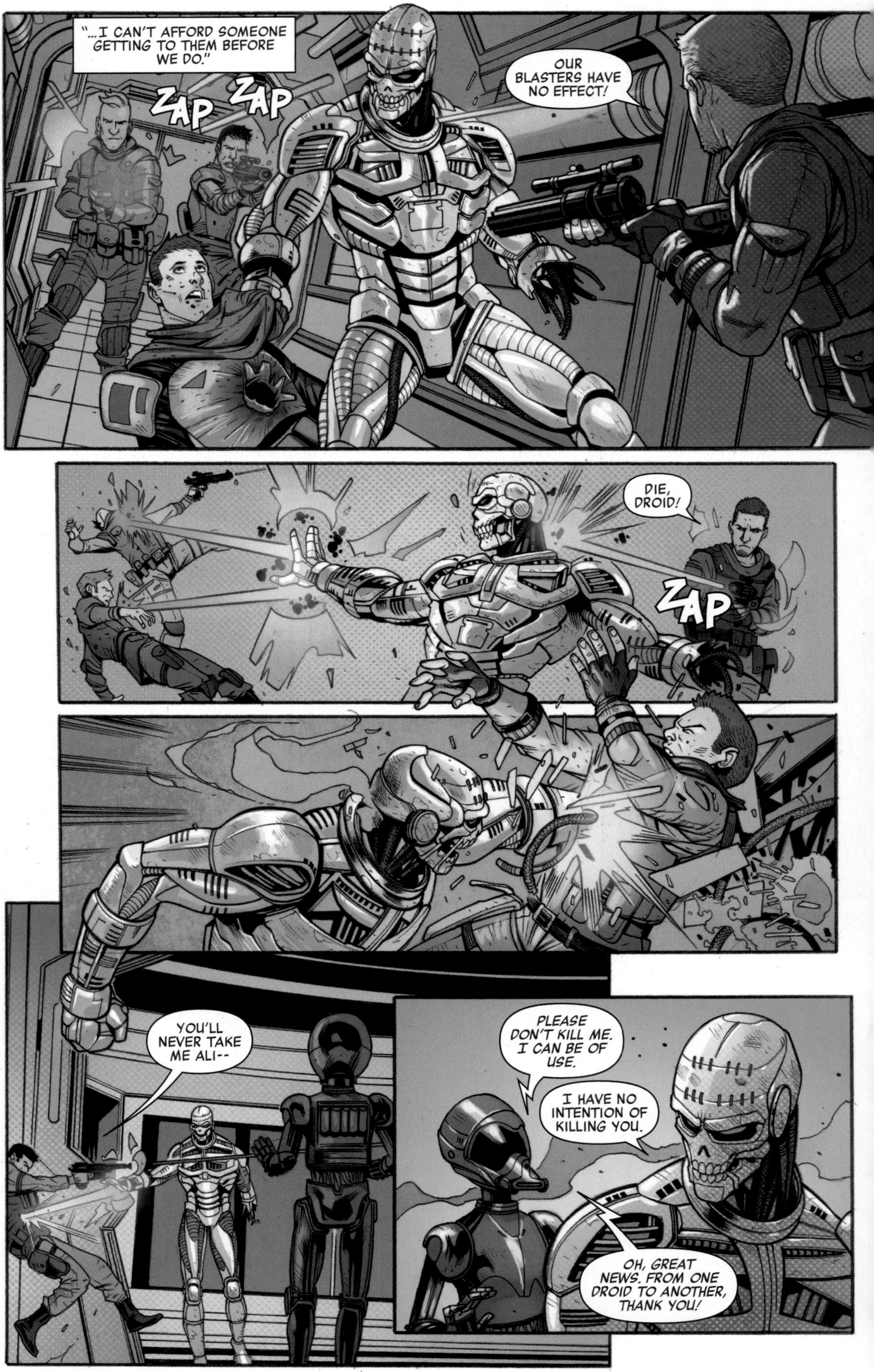
"...I CAN'T AFFORD SOMEONE GETTING TO THEM BEFORE WE DO."
ZAP ZAP
OUR BLASTERS HAVE NO EFFECT!
DIE, DROID!
ZAP
YOU'LL NEVER TAKE ME ALI--
PLEASE DON'T KILL ME. I CAN BE OF USE.
I HAVE NO INTENTION OF KILLING YOU.
OH, GREAT NEWS. FROM ONE DROID TO ANOTHER, THANK YOU!

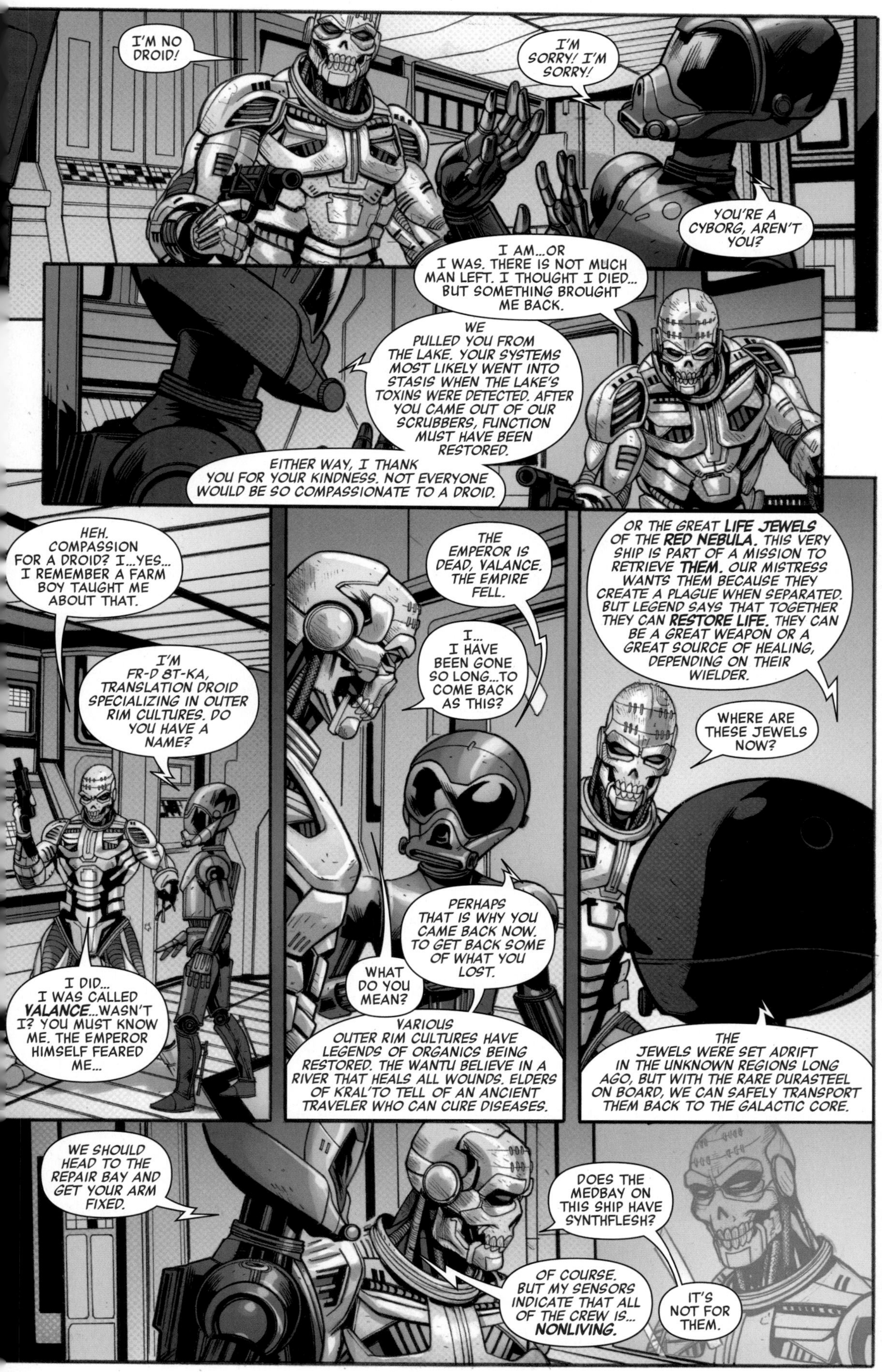

I'M NO DROID!
I'M SORRY! I'M SORRY!
YOU'RE A CYBORG, AREN'T YOU?
I AM...OR I WAS. THERE IS NOT MUCH MAN LEFT. I THOUGHT I DIED... BUT SOMETHING BROUGHT ME BACK.
WE PULLED YOU FROM THE LAKE. YOUR SYSTEMS MOST LIKELY WENT INTO STASIS WHEN THE LAKE'S TOXINS WERE DETECTED. AFTER YOU CAME OUT OF OUR SCRUBBERS, FUNCTION MUST HAVE BEEN RESTORED.
EITHER WAY, I THANK YOU FOR YOUR KINDNESS. NOT EVERYONE WOULD BE SO COMPASSIONATE TO A DROID.
HEH. COMPASSION FOR A DROID? I...YES... I REMEMBER A FARM BOY TAUGHT ME ABOUT THAT.
I'M FR-D 8T-KA, TRANSLATION DROID SPECIALIZING IN OUTER RIM CULTURES. DO YOU HAVE A NAME?
I DID... I WAS CALLED VALANCE...WASN'T I? YOU MUST KNOW ME. THE EMPEROR HIMSELF FEARED ME...
THE EMPEROR IS DEAD, VALANCE. THE EMPIRE FELL.
I... I HAVE BEEN GONE SO LONG...TO COME BACK AS THIS?
PERHAPS THAT IS WHY YOU CAME BACK NOW. TO GET BACK SOME OF WHAT YOU LOST.
WHAT DO YOU MEAN?
VARIOUS OUTER RIM CULTURES HAVE LEGENDS OF ORGANICS BEING RESTORED. THE WANTU BELIEVE IN A RIVER THAT HEALS ALL WOUNDS. ELDERS OF KRAL'TO TELL OF AN ANCIENT TRAVELER WHO CAN CURE DISEASES.
OR THE GREAT LIFE JEWELS OF THE RED NEBULA. THIS VERY SHIP IS PART OF A MISSION TO RETRIEVE THEM. OUR MISTRESS WANTS THEM BECAUSE THEY CREATE A PLAGUE WHEN SEPARATED. BUT LEGEND SAYS THAT TOGETHER THEY CAN RESTORE LIFE. THEY CAN BE A GREAT WEAPON OR A GREAT SOURCE OF HEALING, DEPENDING ON THEIR WIELDER.
WHERE ARE THESE JEWELS NOW?
THE JEWELS WERE SET ADRIFT IN THE UNKNOWN REGIONS LONG AGO, BUT WITH THE RARE DURASTEEL ON BOARD, WE CAN SAFELY TRANSPORT THEM BACK TO THE GALACTIC CORE.
WE SHOULD HEAD TO THE REPAIR BAY AND GET YOUR ARM FIXED.
DOES THE MEDBAY ON THIS SHIP HAVE SYNTHFLESH?
OF COURSE. BUT MY SENSORS INDICATE THAT ALL OF THE CREW IS... NONLIVING.
IT'S NOT FOR THEM.

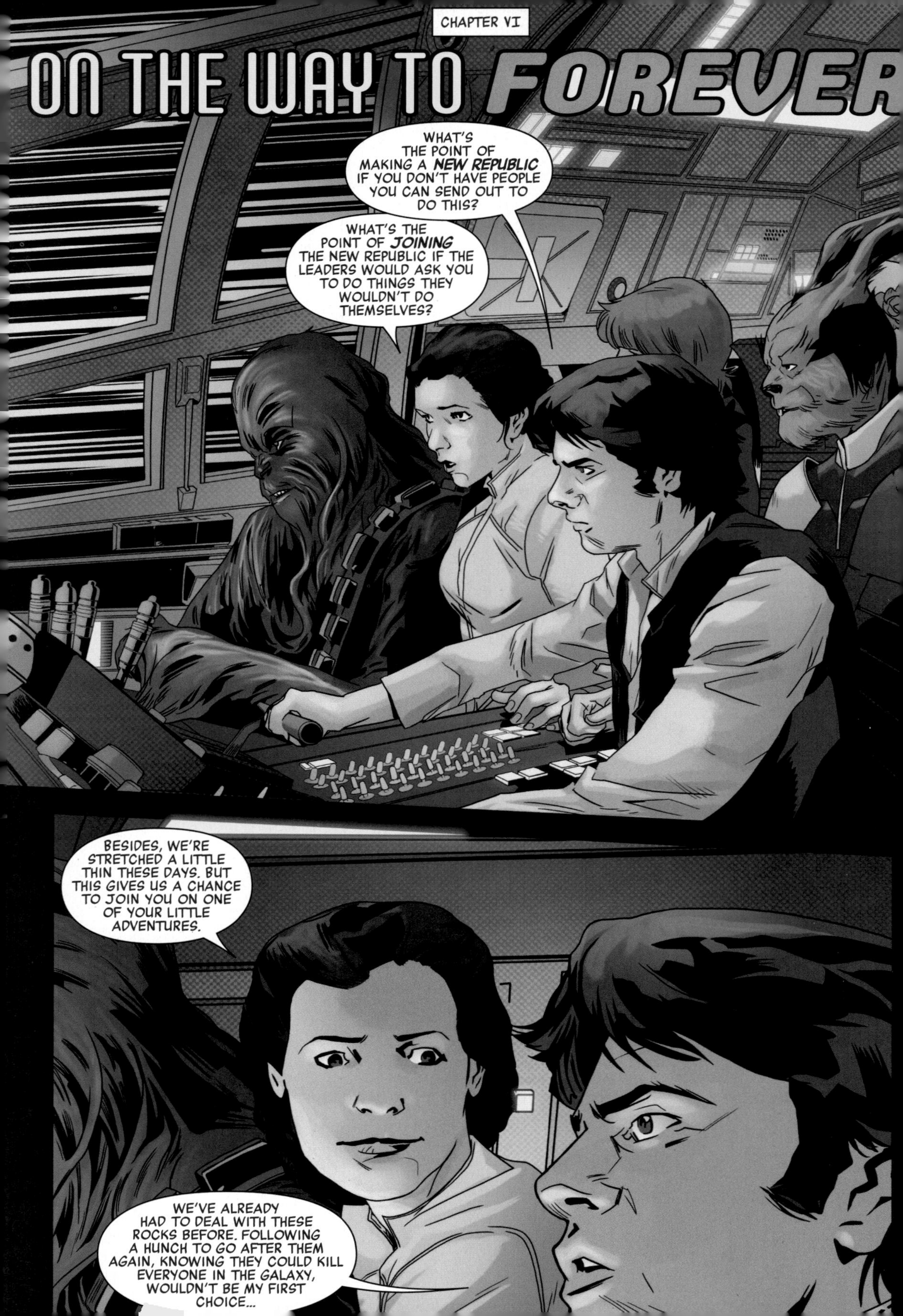

CHAPTER VI
ON THE WAY TO FOREVER
WHAT'S THE POINT OF MAKING A NEW REPUBLIC IF YOU DON'T HAVE PEOPLE YOU CAN SEND OUT TO DO THIS?
WHAT'S THE POINT OF JOINING THE NEW REPUBLIC IF THE LEADERS WOULD ASK YOU TO DO THINGS THEY WOULDN'T DO THEMSELVES?
BESIDES, WE'RE STRETCHED A LITTLE THIN THESE DAYS. BUT THIS GIVES US A CHANCE TO JOIN YOU ON ONE OF YOUR LITTLE ADVENTURES.
WE'VE ALREADY HAD TO DEAL WITH THESE ROCKS BEFORE. FOLLOWING A HUNCH TO GO AFTER THEM AGAIN, KNOWING THEY COULD KILL EVERYONE IN THE GALAXY, WOULDN'T BE MY FIRST CHOICE...

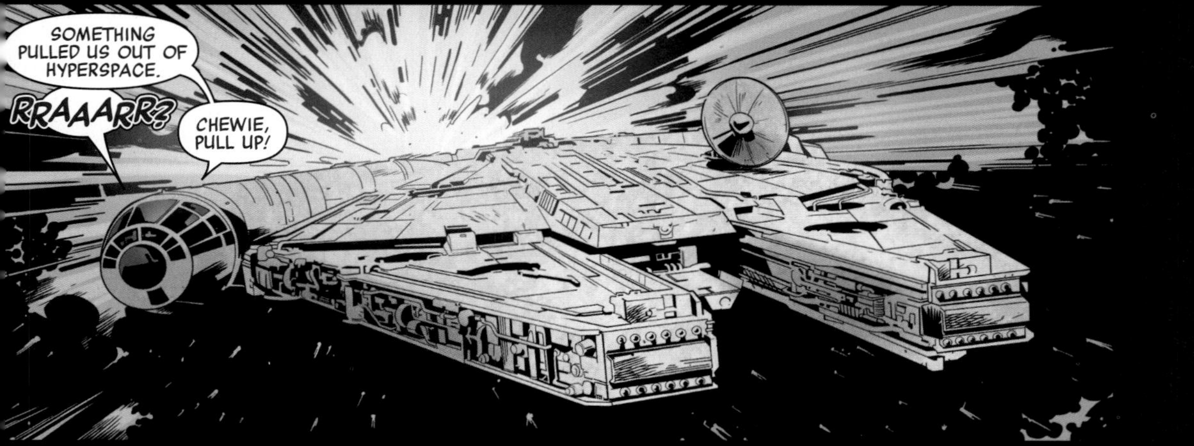
SOMETHING PULLED US OUT OF HYPERSPACE.
RRAAARR?
CHEWIE, PULL UP!

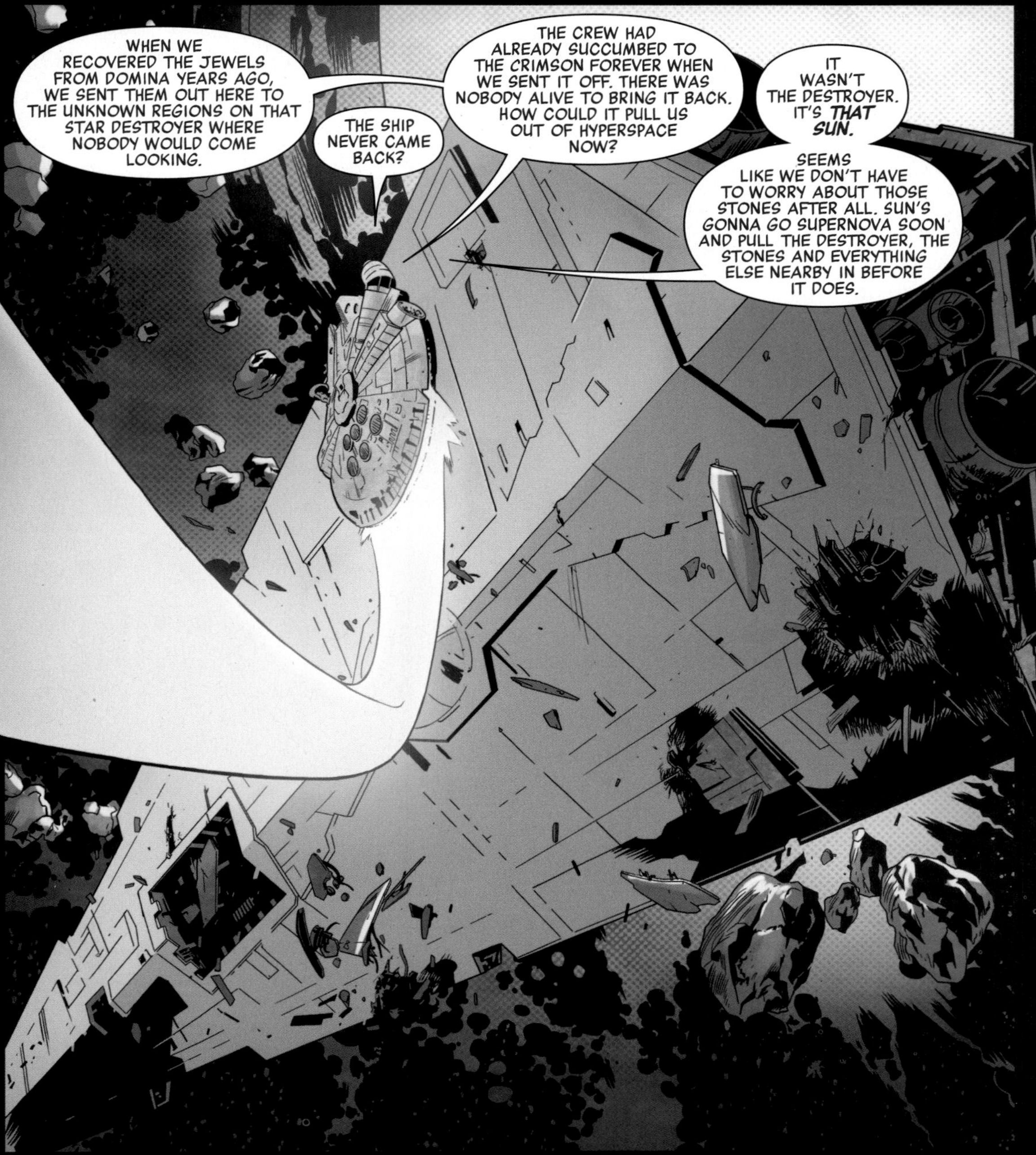
WHEN WE RECOVERED THE JEWELS FROM DOMINA YEARS AGO, WE SENT THEM OUT HERE TO THE UNKNOWN REGIONS ON THAT STAR DESTROYER WHERE NOBODY WOULD COME LOOKING.
THE SHIP NEVER CAME BACK?
THE CREW HAD ALREADY SUCCUMBED TO THE CRIMSON FOREVER WHEN WE SENT IT OFF. THERE WAS NOBODY ALIVE TO BRING IT BACK. HOW COULD IT PULL US OUT OF HYPERSPACE NOW?
IT WASN'T THE DESTROYER. IT'S ***THAT SUN.***
SEEMS LIKE WE DON'T HAVE TO WORRY ABOUT THOSE STONES AFTER ALL. SUN'S GONNA GO SUPERNOVA SOON AND PULL THE DESTROYER, THE STONES AND EVERYTHING ELSE NEARBY IN BEFORE IT DOES.

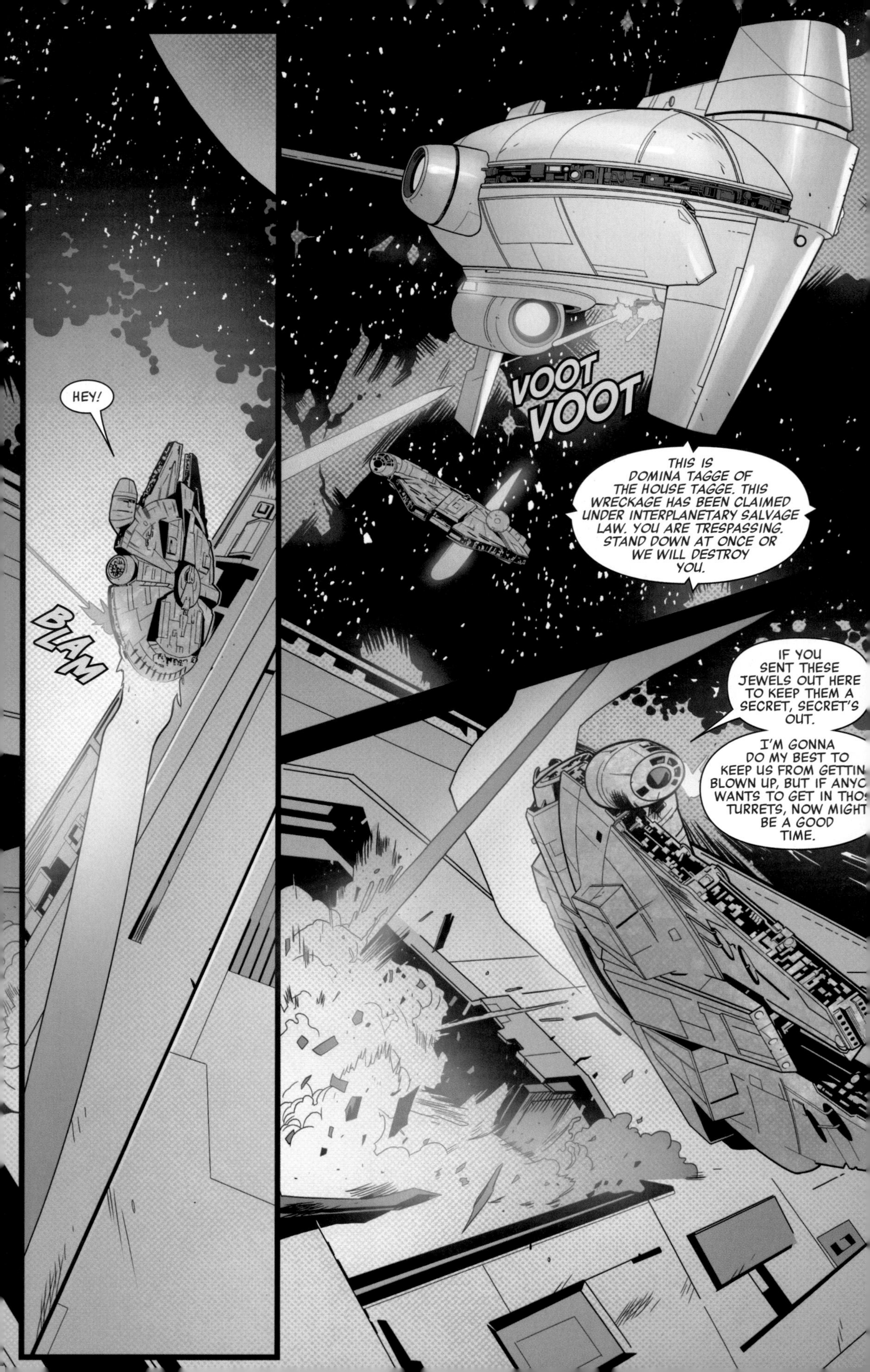
HEY!
BLAM
VOOT VOOT
THIS IS DOMINA TAGGE OF THE HOUSE TAGGE. THIS WRECKAGE HAS BEEN CLAIMED UNDER INTERPLANETARY SALVAGE LAW. YOU ARE TRESPASSING. STAND DOWN AT ONCE OR WE WILL DESTROY YOU.
IF YOU SENT THESE JEWELS OUT HERE TO KEEP THEM A SECRET, SECRET'S OUT.
I'M GONNA DO MY BEST TO KEEP US FROM GETTIN BLOWN UP, BUT IF ANYO WANTS TO GET IN THOS TURRETS, NOW MIGHT BE A GOOD TIME.

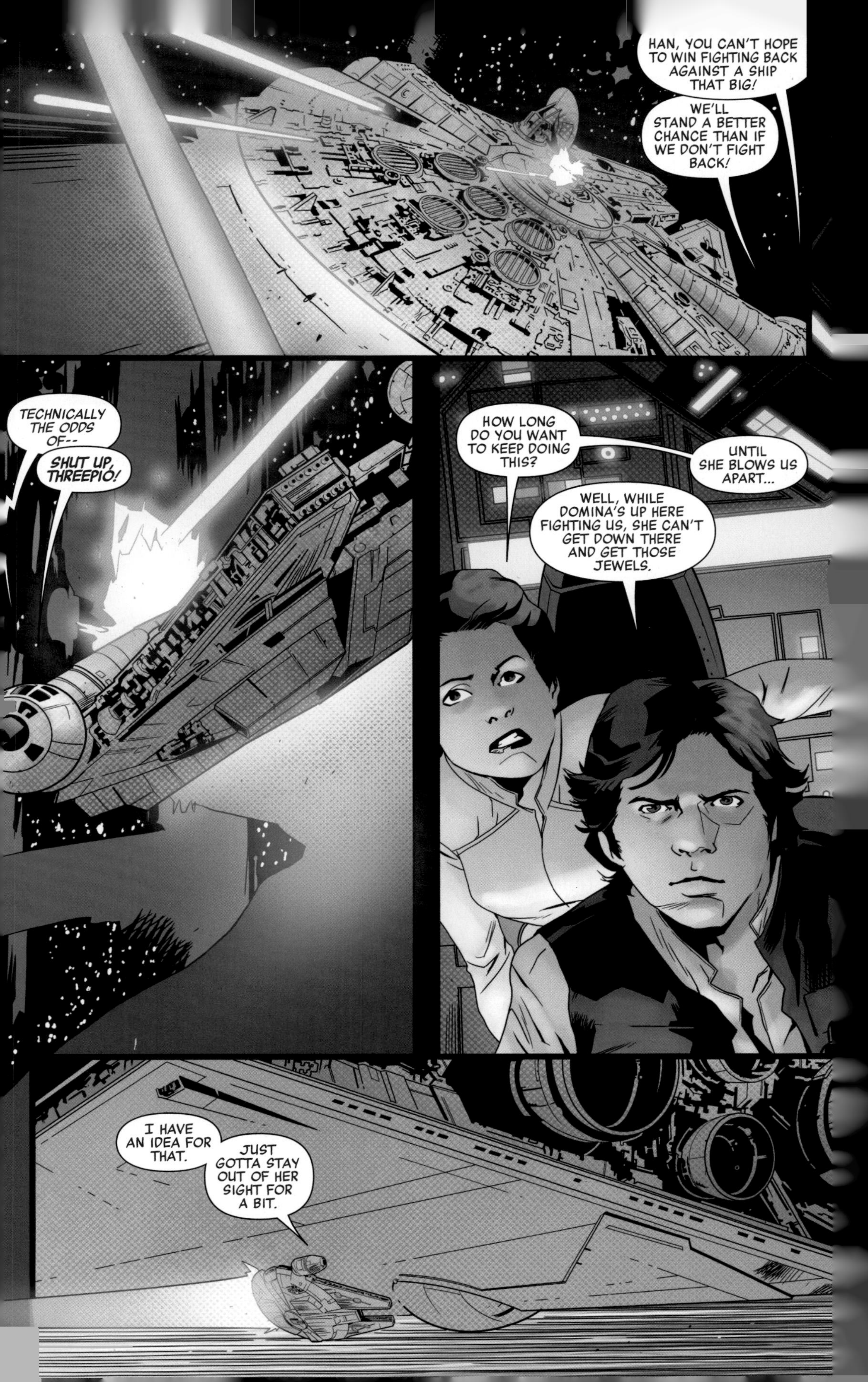
HAN, YOU CAN'T HOPE TO WIN FIGHTING BACK AGAINST A SHIP THAT BIG!
WE'LL STAND A BETTER CHANCE THAN IF WE DON'T FIGHT BACK!
TECHNICALLY THE ODDS OF--
SHUT UP, THREEPIO!
HOW LONG DO YOU WANT TO KEEP DOING THIS?
UNTIL SHE BLOWS US APART...
WELL, WHILE DOMINA'S UP HERE FIGHTING US, SHE CAN'T GET DOWN THERE AND GET THOSE JEWELS.
I HAVE AN IDEA FOR THAT.
JUST GOTTA STAY OUT OF HER SIGHT FOR A BIT.

CHAPTER VII

SNATCHED AWAY FROM THE SUN

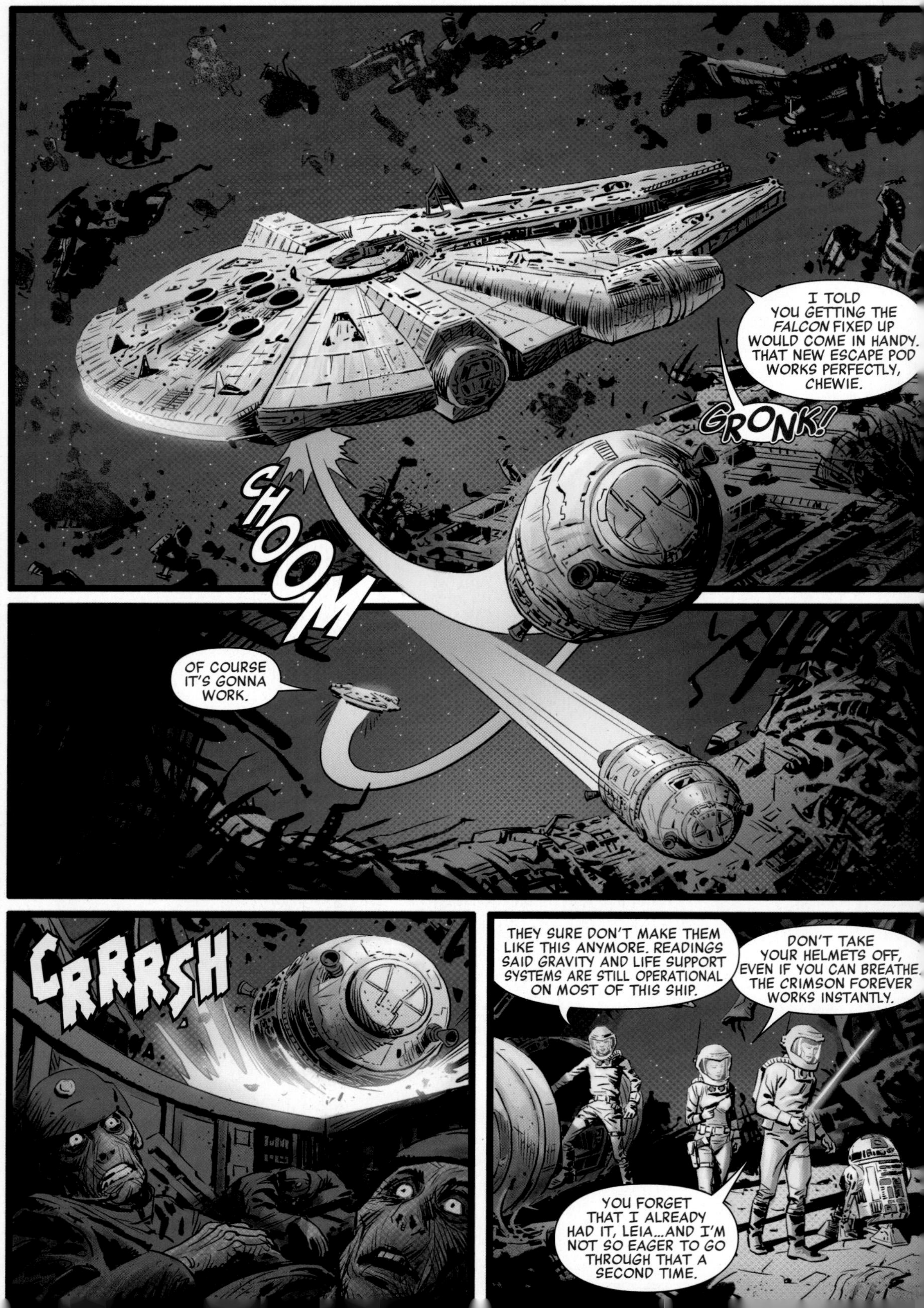
I TOLD YOU GETTING THE FALCON FIXED UP WOULD COME IN HANDY. THAT NEW ESCAPE POD WORKS PERFECTLY, CHEWIE.
GRONK!
CHOOM
OF COURSE IT'S GONNA WORK.
CRRRSH
THEY SURE DON'T MAKE THEM LIKE THIS ANYMORE. READINGS SAID GRAVITY AND LIFE SUPPORT SYSTEMS ARE STILL OPERATIONAL ON MOST OF THIS SHIP.
DON'T TAKE YOUR HELMETS OFF, EVEN IF YOU CAN BREATHE. THE CRIMSON FOREVER WORKS INSTANTLY.
YOU FORGET THAT I ALREADY HAD IT, LEIA...AND I'M NOT SO EAGER TO GO THROUGH THAT A SECOND TIME.

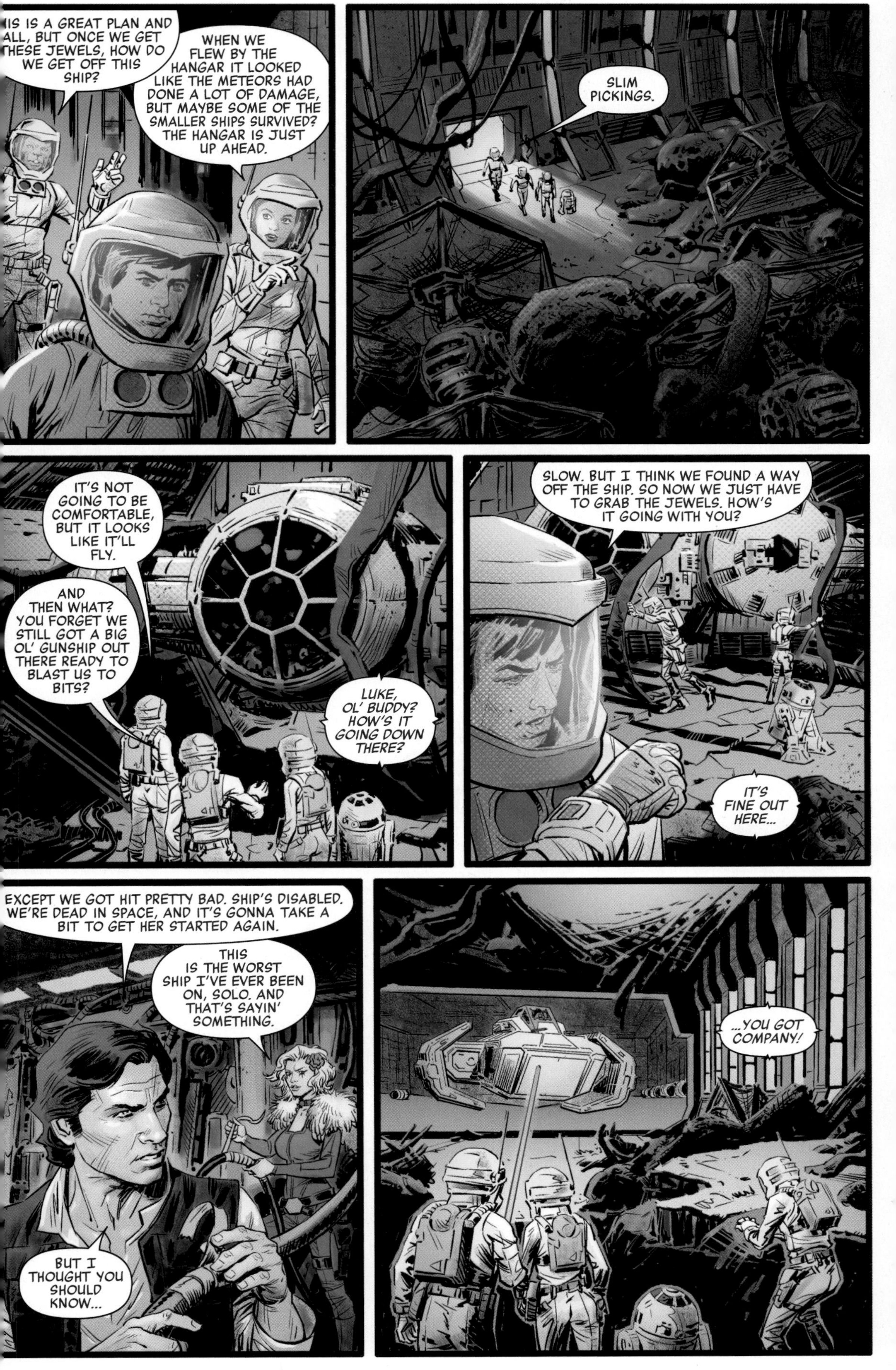

IS IS A GREAT PLAN AND ALL, BUT ONCE WE GET THESE JEWELS, HOW DO WE GET OFF THIS SHIP?
WHEN WE FLEW BY THE HANGAR IT LOOKED LIKE THE METEORS HAD DONE A LOT OF DAMAGE, BUT MAYBE SOME OF THE SMALLER SHIPS SURVIVED? THE HANGAR IS JUST UP AHEAD.
SLIM PICKINGS.
IT'S NOT GOING TO BE COMFORTABLE, BUT IT LOOKS LIKE IT'LL FLY.
AND THEN WHAT? YOU FORGET WE STILL GOT A BIG OL' GUNSHIP OUT THERE READY TO BLAST US TO BITS?
LUKE, OL' BUDDY? HOW'S IT GOING DOWN THERE?
SLOW. BUT I THINK WE FOUND A WAY OFF THE SHIP. SO NOW WE JUST HAVE TO GRAB THE JEWELS. HOW'S IT GOING WITH YOU?
IT'S FINE OUT HERE...
EXCEPT WE GOT HIT PRETTY BAD. SHIP'S DISABLED. WE'RE DEAD IN SPACE, AND IT'S GONNA TAKE A BIT TO GET HER STARTED AGAIN.
THIS IS THE WORST SHIP I'VE EVER BEEN ON, SOLO. AND THAT'S SAYIN' SOMETHING.
BUT I THOUGHT YOU SHOULD KNOW...
...YOU GOT COMPANY!

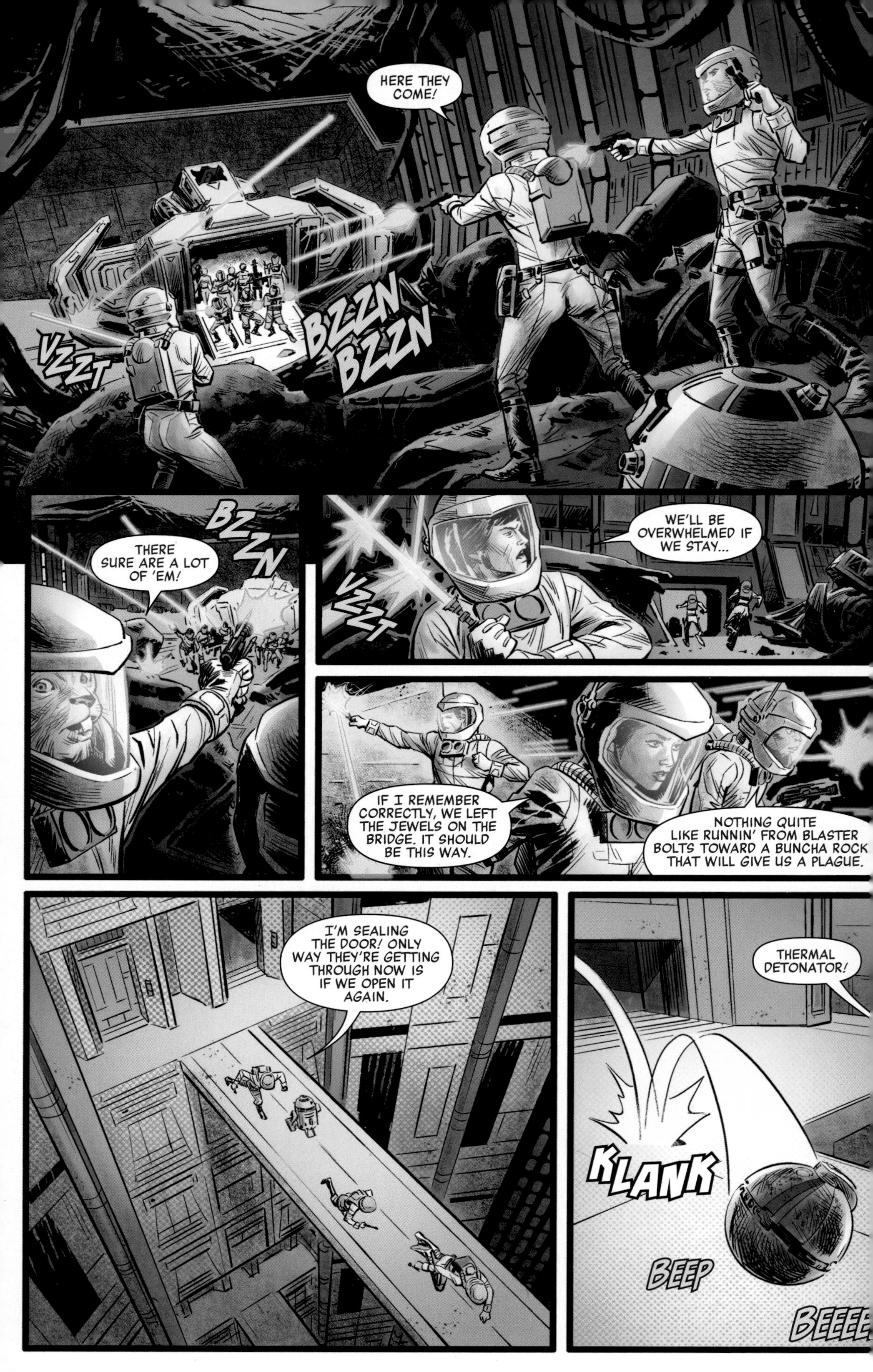
HERE THEY COME!
VZZT
BZZN BZZN
THERE SURE ARE A LOT OF 'EM!
BZZN
WE'LL BE OVERWHELMED IF WE STAY...
VZZT
IF I REMEMBER CORRECTLY, WE LEFT THE JEWELS ON THE BRIDGE. IT SHOULD BE THIS WAY.
NOTHING QUITE LIKE RUNNIN' FROM BLASTER BOLTS TOWARD A BUNCHA ROCK THAT WILL GIVE US A PLAGUE.
I'M SEALING THE DOOR! ONLY WAY THEY'RE GETTING THROUGH NOW IS IF WE OPEN IT AGAIN.
THERMAL DETONATOR!
KLANK
BEEP
BEEEE

KABOOM

WELL, GETTING BACK JUST GOT A LITTLE HARDER.

BWEE-BWOOO

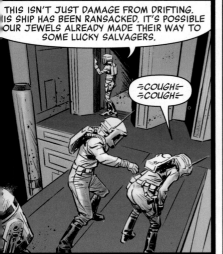

THIS ISN'T JUST DAMAGE FROM DRIFTING. IS SHIP HAS BEEN RANSACKED. IT'S POSSIBLE OUR JEWELS ALREADY MADE THEIR WAY TO SOME LUCKY SALVAGERS.

=COUGH= =COUGH=

YOU OKAY?

SOMETHING'S WRONG.

THE BLAST TORE A HOLE IN YOUR SUIT. I CAN PATCH IT.

THE CRIMSON FOREVER IS WORKING MUCH FASTER THAN IT DID BEFORE. THERE'S A LOT WE STILL DON'T KNOW ABOUT IT.

DON'T WORRY. WHEN WE FIND THE JEWELS, WE WILL PUT THEM TOGETHER AND REVERSE YOUR SYMPTOMS--

HELLO, GORGEOUS. NOW WHERE'S YOUR FRIEND?

GUESS YOU'RE THE LUCKY SALVAGER.

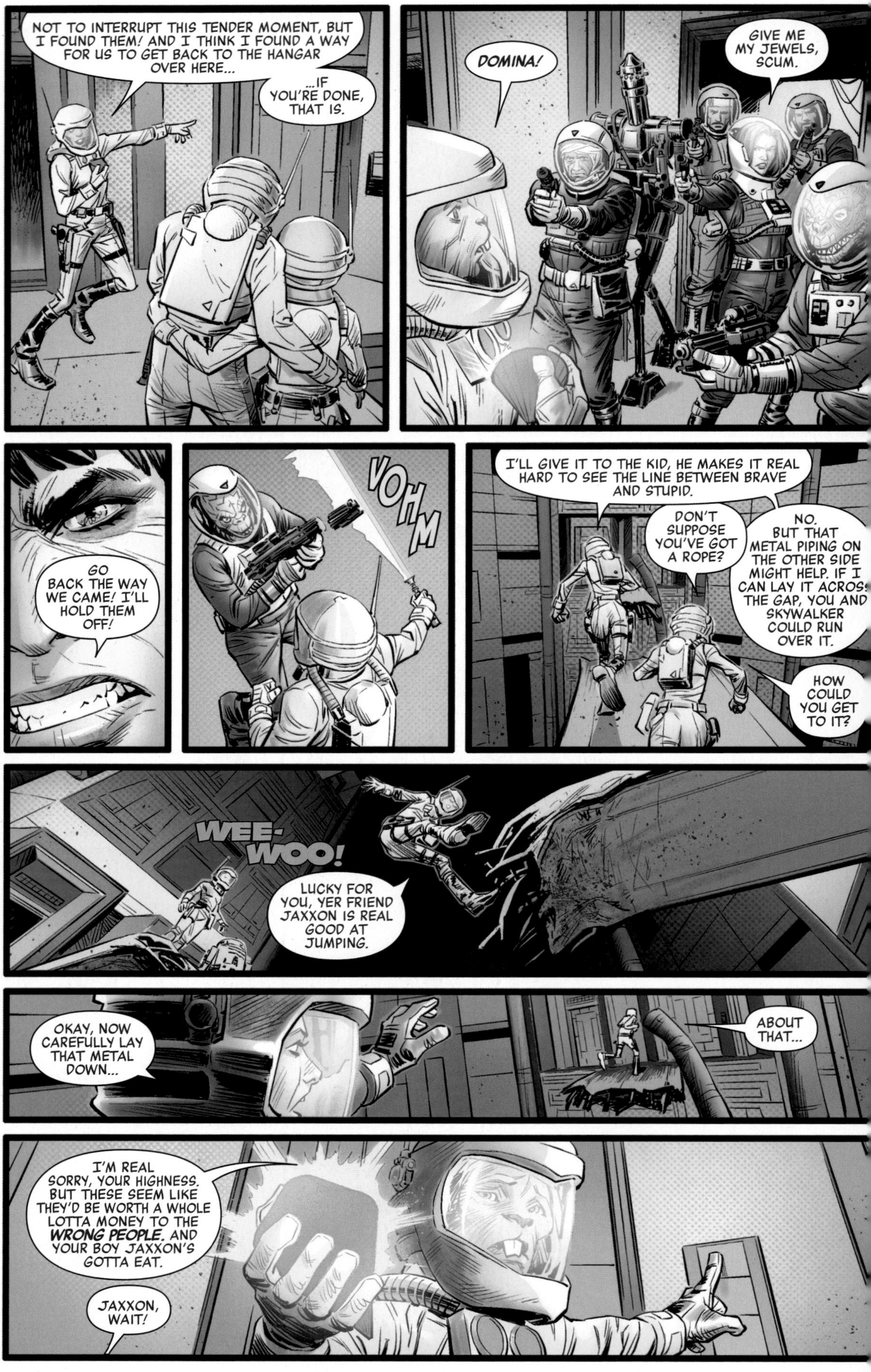
NOT TO INTERRUPT THIS TENDER MOMENT, BUT I FOUND THEM! AND I THINK I FOUND A WAY FOR US TO GET BACK TO THE HANGAR OVER HERE...
...IF YOU'RE DONE, THAT IS.
DOMINA!
GIVE ME MY JEWELS, SCUM.
GO BACK THE WAY WE CAME! I'LL HOLD THEM OFF!
VOHM
I'LL GIVE IT TO THE KID, HE MAKES IT REAL HARD TO SEE THE LINE BETWEEN BRAVE AND STUPID.
DON'T SUPPOSE YOU'VE GOT A ROPE?
NO. BUT THAT METAL PIPING ON THE OTHER SIDE MIGHT HELP. IF I CAN LAY IT ACROSS THE GAP, YOU AND SKYWALKER COULD RUN OVER IT.
HOW COULD YOU GET TO IT?
WEE-WOO!
LUCKY FOR YOU, YER FRIEND JAXXON IS REAL GOOD AT JUMPING.
OKAY, NOW CAREFULLY LAY THAT METAL DOWN...
ABOUT THAT...
I'M REAL SORRY, YOUR HIGHNESS. BUT THESE SEEM LIKE THEY'D BE WORTH A WHOLE LOTTA MONEY TO THE WRONG PEOPLE. AND YOUR BOY JAXXON'S GOTTA EAT.
JAXXON, WAIT!

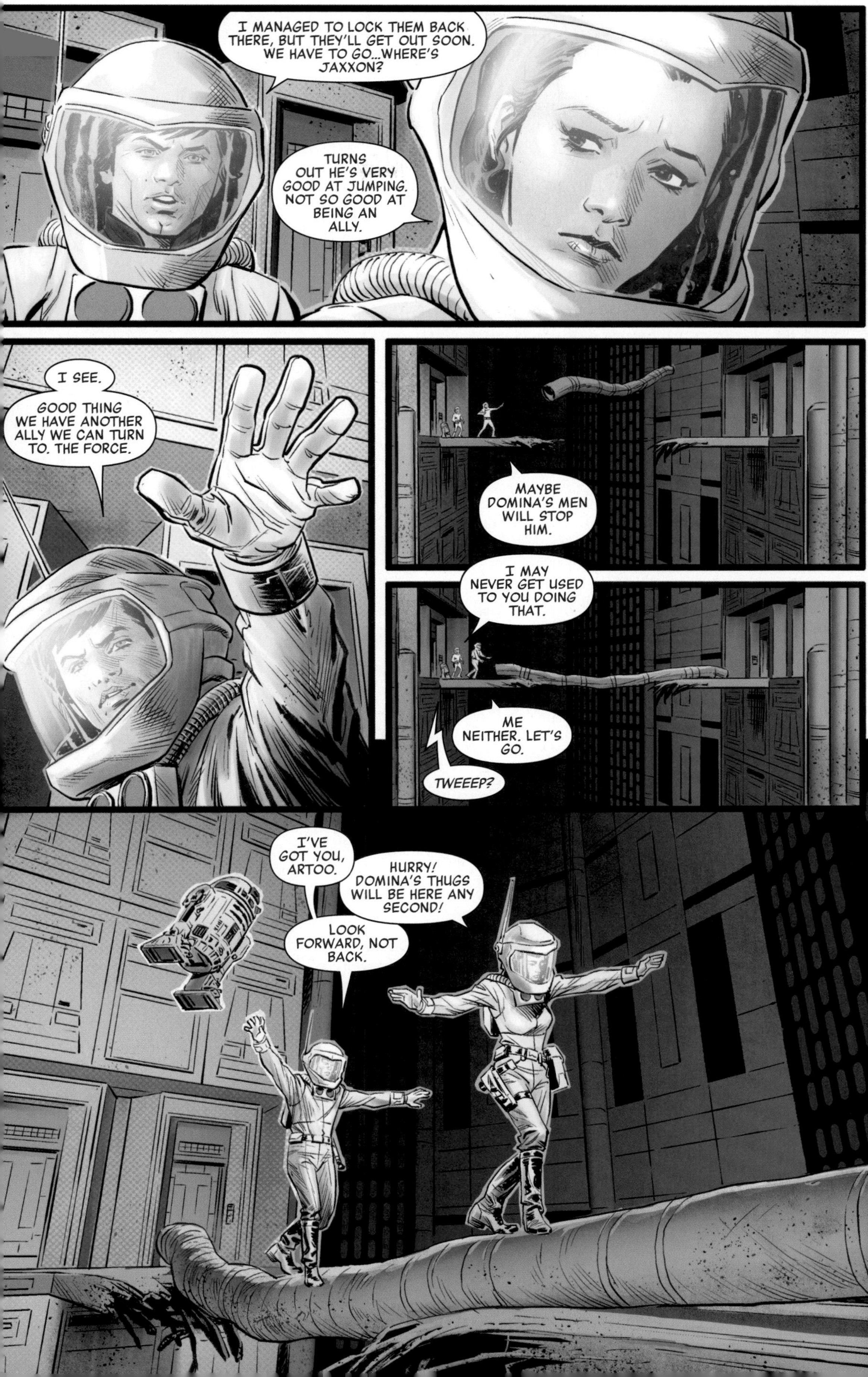
I MANAGED TO LOCK THEM BACK THERE, BUT THEY'LL GET OUT SOON. WE HAVE TO GO...WHERE'S JAXXON?
TURNS OUT HE'S VERY GOOD AT JUMPING. NOT SO GOOD AT BEING AN ALLY.
I SEE.
GOOD THING WE HAVE ANOTHER ALLY WE CAN TURN TO. THE FORCE.
MAYBE DOMINA'S MEN WILL STOP HIM.
I MAY NEVER GET USED TO YOU DOING THAT.
ME NEITHER. LET'S GO.
TWEEEP?
I'VE GOT YOU, ARTOO.
HURRY! DOMINA'S THUGS WILL BE HERE ANY SECOND!
LOOK FORWARD, NOT BACK.

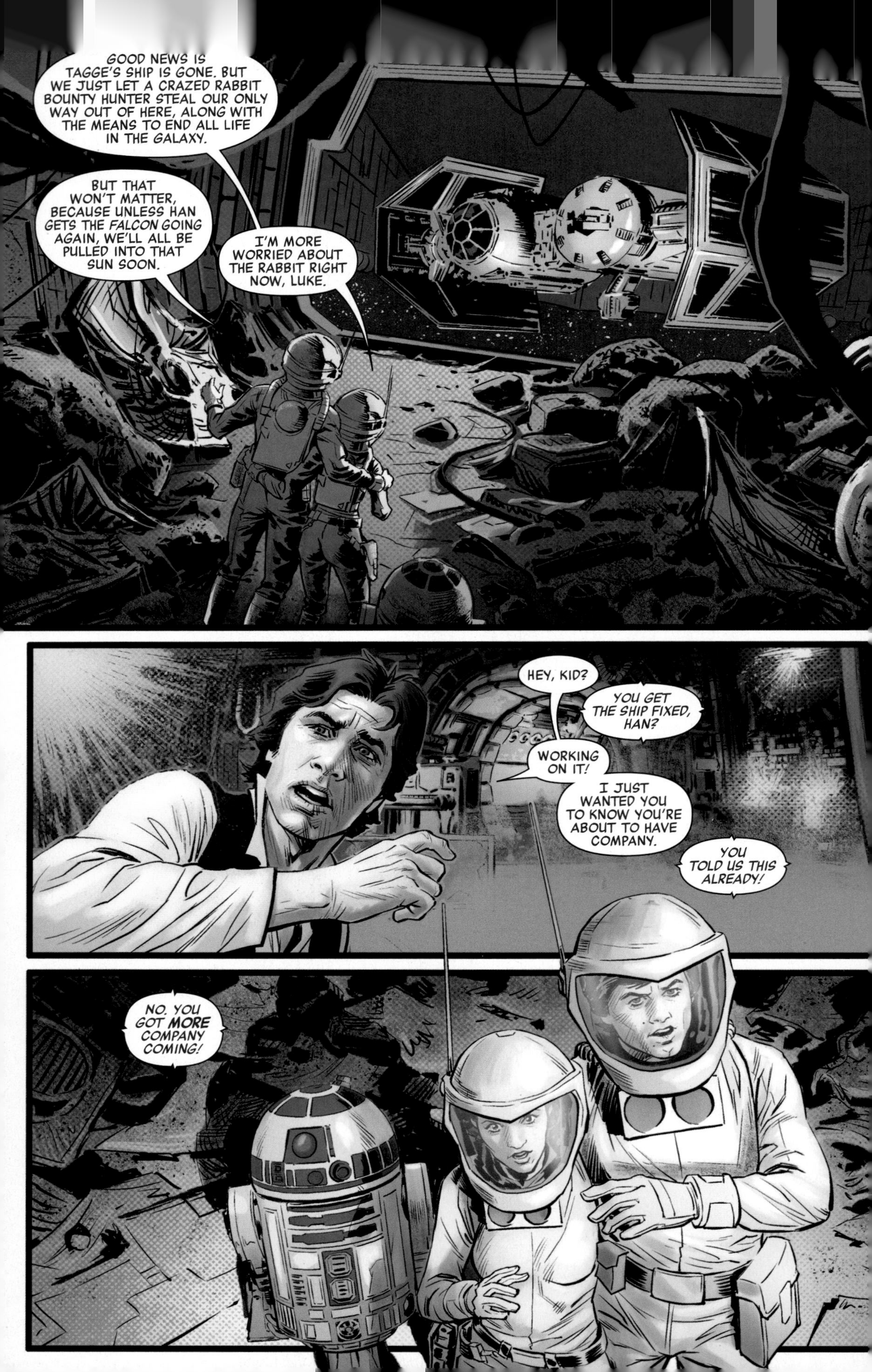
GOOD NEWS IS TAGGE'S SHIP IS GONE. BUT WE JUST LET A CRAZED RABBIT BOUNTY HUNTER STEAL OUR ONLY WAY OUT OF HERE, ALONG WITH THE MEANS TO END ALL LIFE IN THE GALAXY.
BUT THAT WON'T MATTER, BECAUSE UNLESS HAN GETS THE *FALCON* GOING AGAIN, WE'LL ALL BE PULLED INTO THAT SUN SOON.
I'M MORE WORRIED ABOUT THE RABBIT RIGHT NOW, LUKE.
HEY, KID?
YOU GET THE SHIP FIXED, HAN?
WORKING ON IT!
I JUST WANTED YOU TO KNOW YOU'RE ABOUT TO HAVE COMPANY.
YOU TOLD US THIS ALREADY!
NO. YOU GOT **MORE** COMPANY COMING!

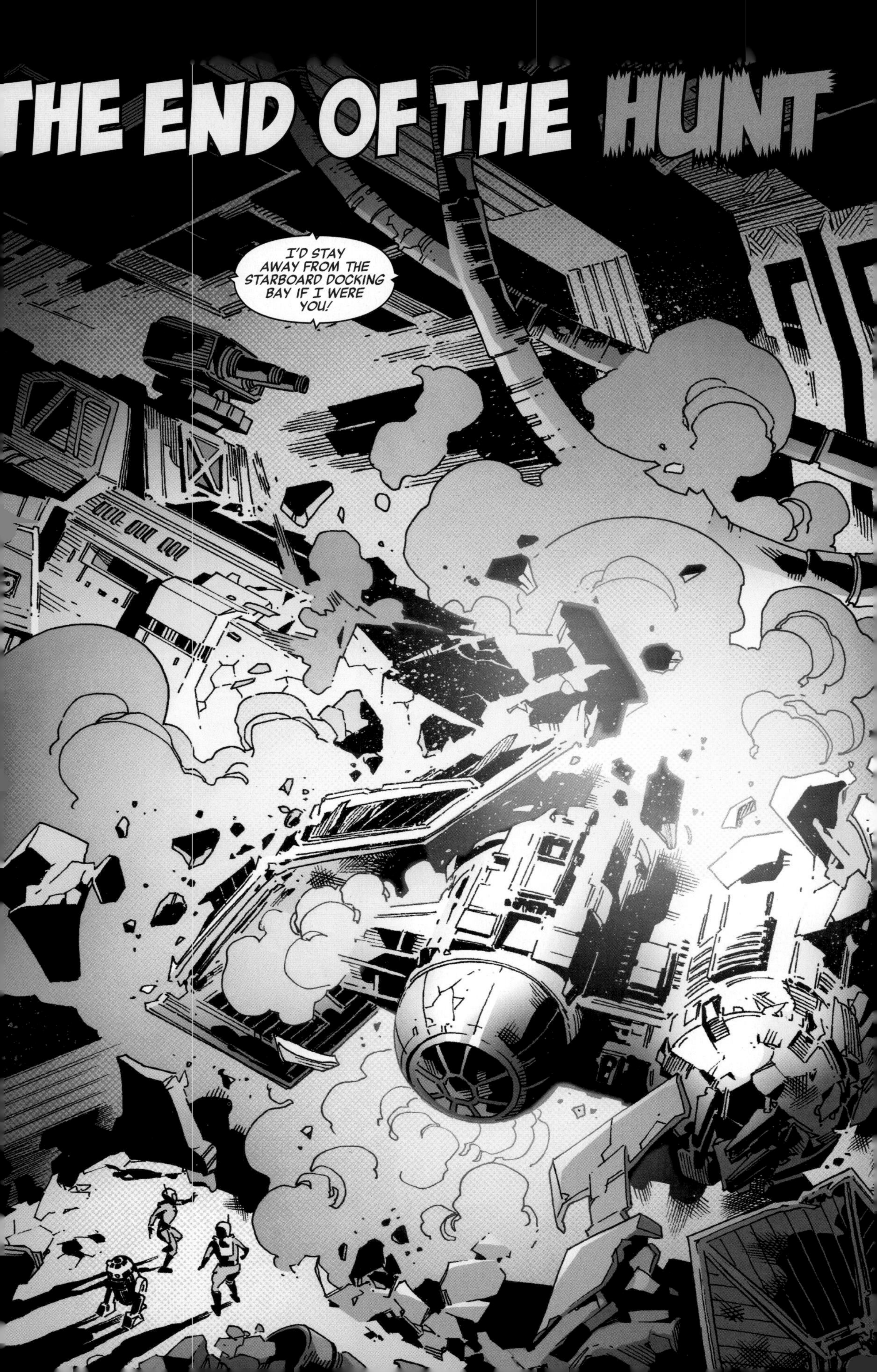
THE END OF THE HUNT
I'D STAY AWAY FROM THE STARBOARD DOCKING BAY IF I WERE YOU!

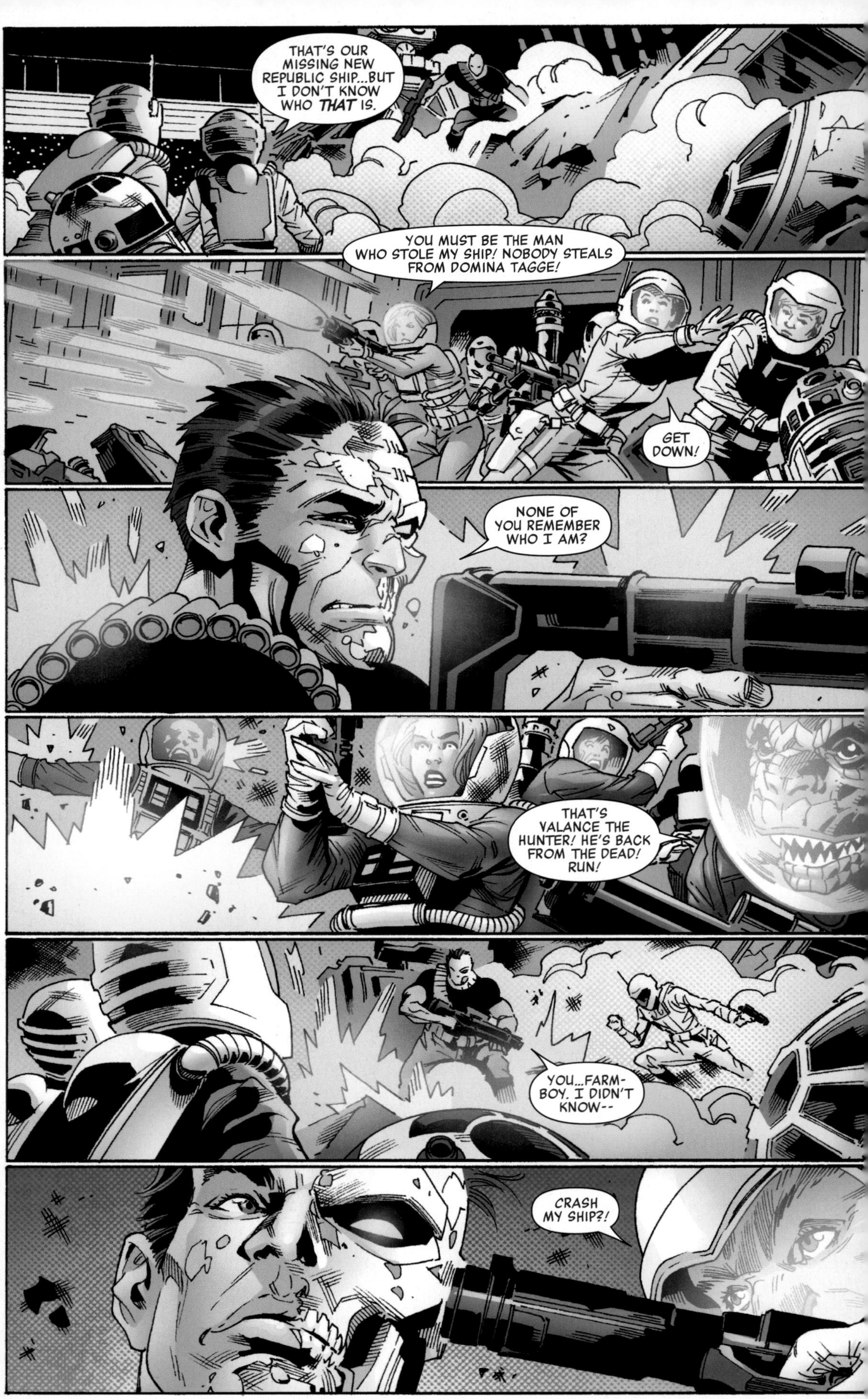
THAT'S OUR MISSING NEW REPUBLIC SHIP...BUT I DON'T KNOW WHO *THAT* IS.
YOU MUST BE THE MAN WHO STOLE MY SHIP! NOBODY STEALS FROM DOMINA TAGGE!
GET DOWN!
NONE OF YOU REMEMBER WHO I AM?
THAT'S VALANCE THE HUNTER! HE'S BACK FROM THE DEAD! RUN!
YOU...FARM-BOY. I DIDN'T KNOW--
CRASH MY SHIP?!

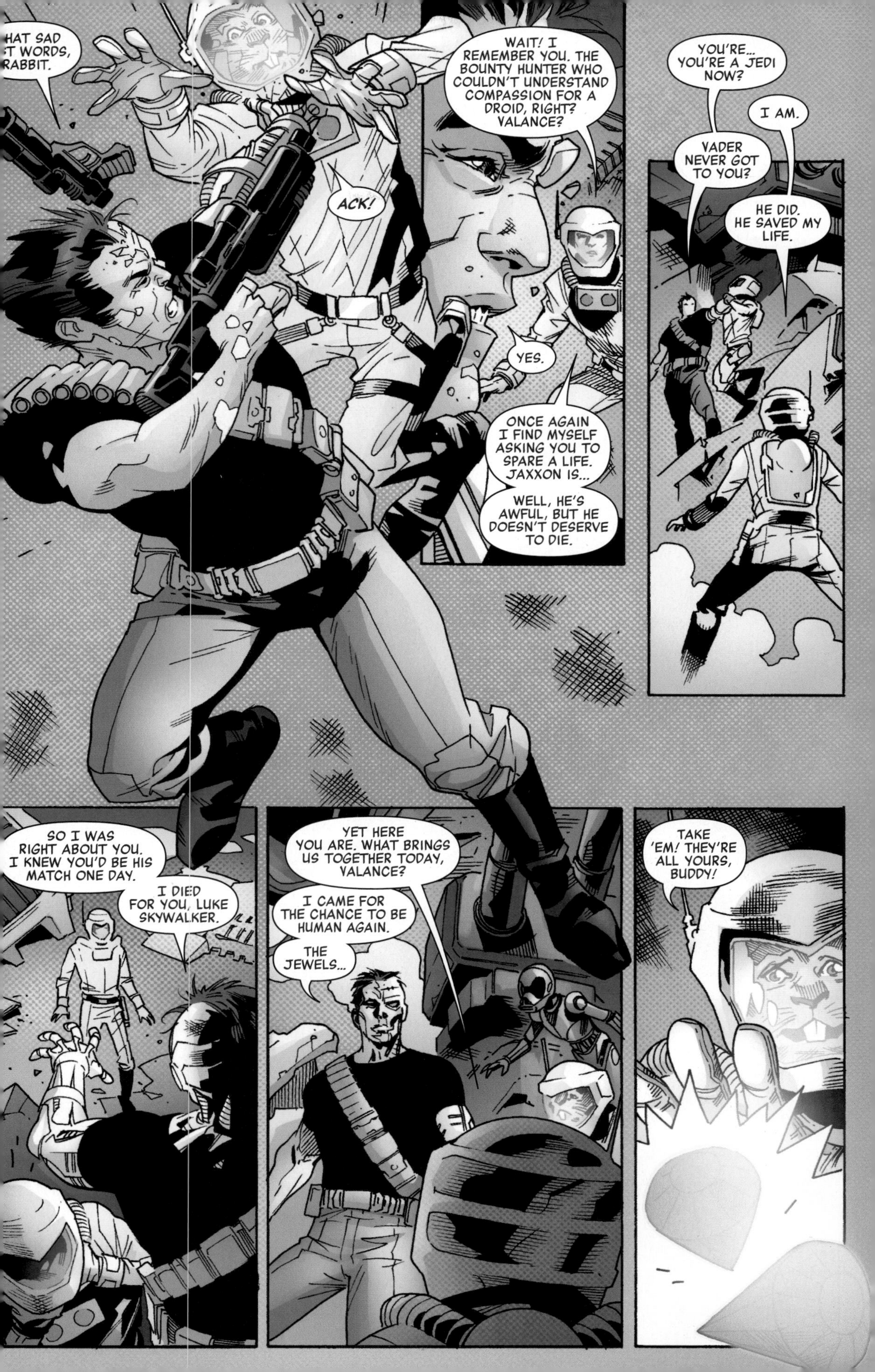
HAT SAD
T WORDS,
RABBIT.
ACK!
WAIT! I REMEMBER YOU. THE BOUNTY HUNTER WHO COULDN'T UNDERSTAND COMPASSION FOR A DROID, RIGHT? VALANCE?
YES.
ONCE AGAIN I FIND MYSELF ASKING YOU TO SPARE A LIFE. JAXXON IS...
WELL, HE'S AWFUL, BUT HE DOESN'T DESERVE TO DIE.
YOU'RE... YOU'RE A JEDI NOW?
I AM.
VADER NEVER GOT TO YOU?
HE DID. HE SAVED MY LIFE.
SO I WAS RIGHT ABOUT YOU. I KNEW YOU'D BE HIS MATCH ONE DAY.
I DIED FOR YOU, LUKE SKYWALKER.
YET HERE YOU ARE. WHAT BRINGS US TOGETHER TODAY, VALANCE?
I CAME FOR THE CHANCE TO BE HUMAN AGAIN.
THE JEWELS...
TAKE 'EM! THEY'RE ALL YOURS, BUDDY!

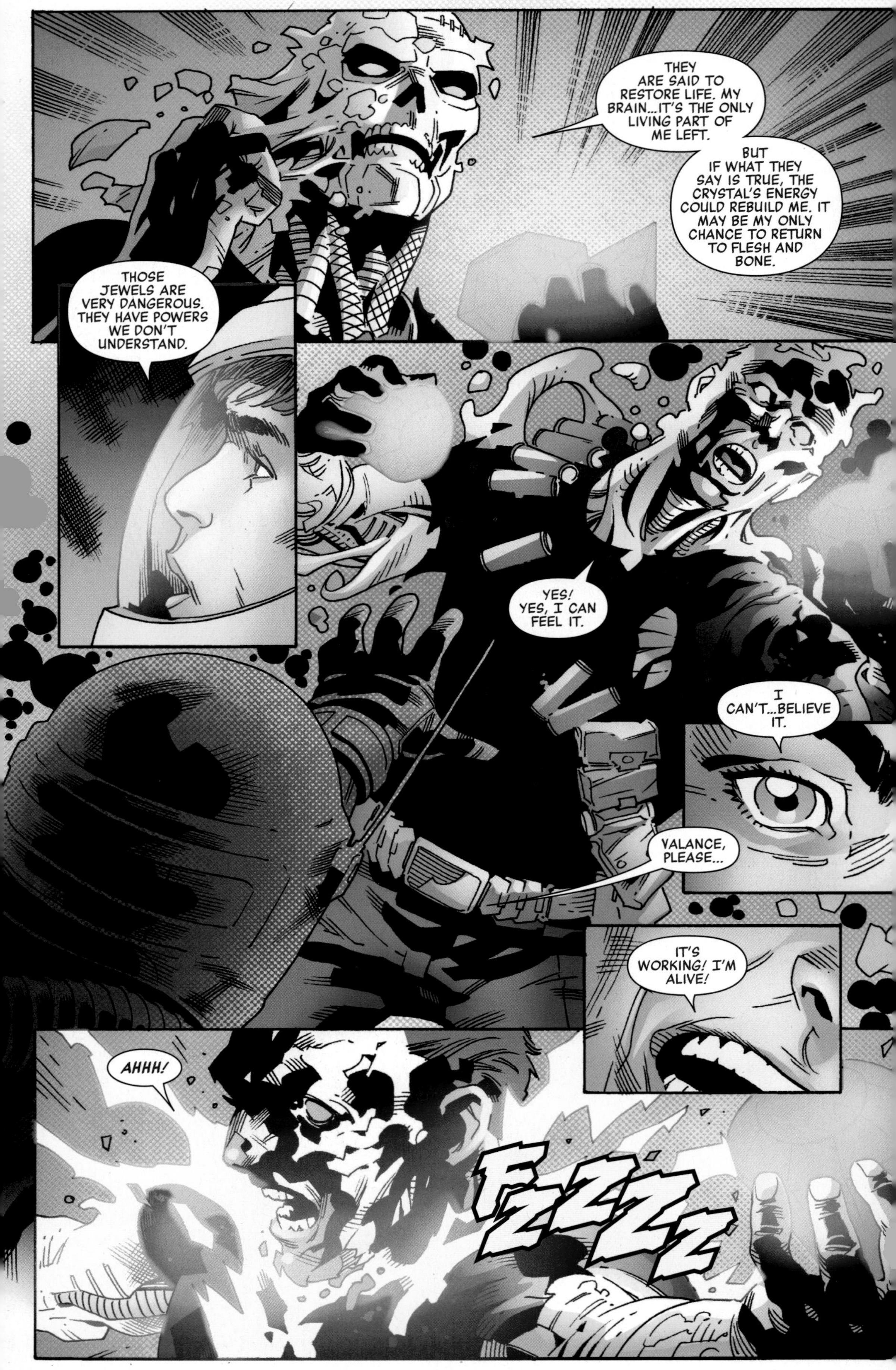
THEY ARE SAID TO RESTORE LIFE. MY BRAIN...IT'S THE ONLY LIVING PART OF ME LEFT.
BUT IF WHAT THEY SAY IS TRUE, THE CRYSTAL'S ENERGY COULD REBUILD ME. IT MAY BE MY ONLY CHANCE TO RETURN TO FLESH AND BONE.
THOSE JEWELS ARE VERY DANGEROUS. THEY HAVE POWERS WE DON'T UNDERSTAND.
YES! YES, I CAN FEEL IT.
I CAN'T...BELIEVE IT.
VALANCE, PLEASE...
IT'S WORKING! I'M ALIVE!
AHHH!
FZZZZ

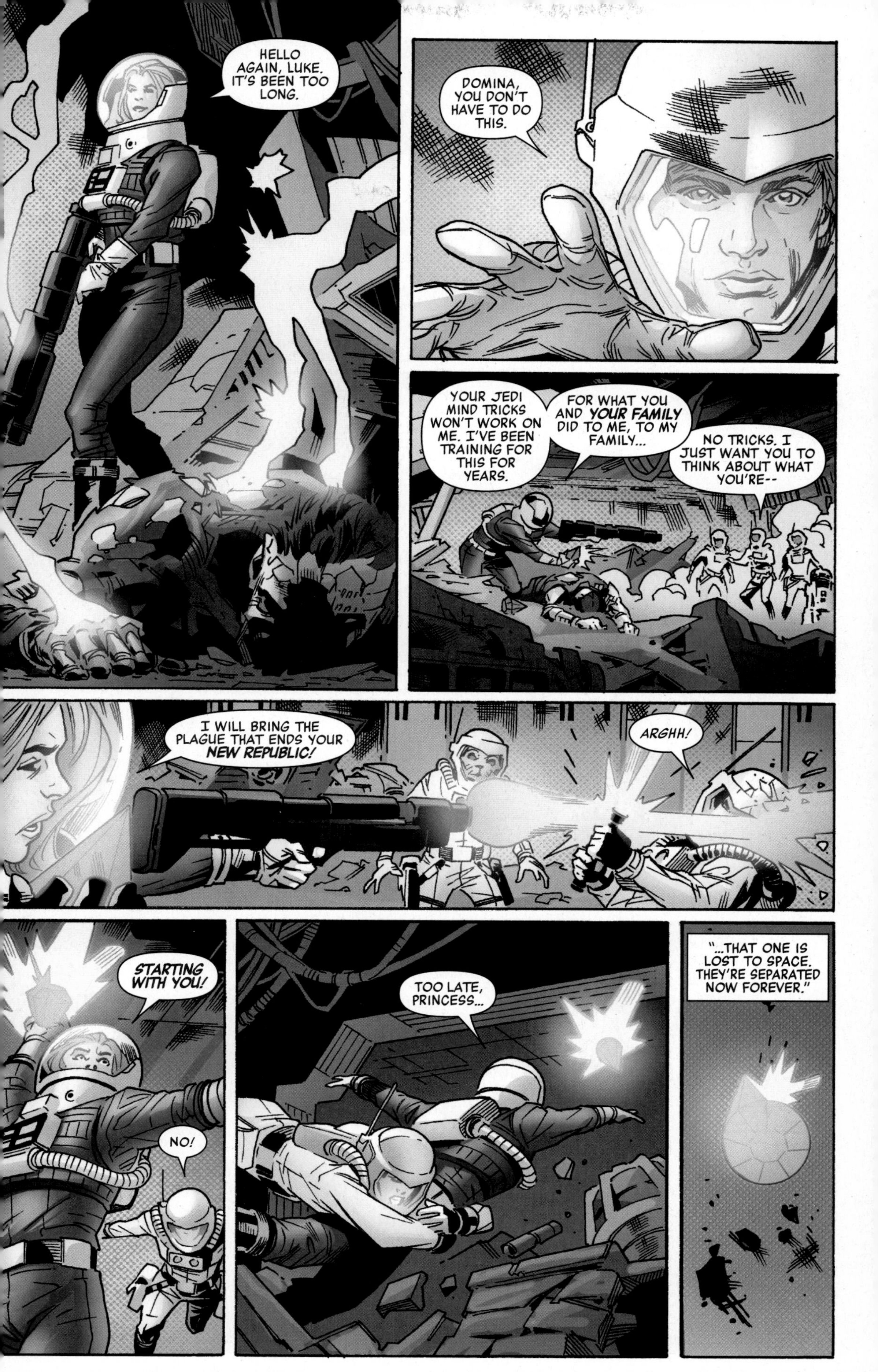
HELLO AGAIN, LUKE. IT'S BEEN TOO LONG.
DOMINA, YOU DON'T HAVE TO DO THIS.
YOUR JEDI MIND TRICKS WON'T WORK ON ME. I'VE BEEN TRAINING FOR THIS FOR YEARS.
FOR WHAT YOU AND YOUR FAMILY DID TO ME, TO MY FAMILY...
NO TRICKS. I JUST WANT YOU TO THINK ABOUT WHAT YOU'RE--
I WILL BRING THE PLAGUE THAT ENDS YOUR NEW REPUBLIC!
ARGHH!
STARTING WITH YOU!
NO!
TOO LATE, PRINCESS...
"...THAT ONE IS LOST TO SPACE. THEY'RE SEPARATED NOW FOREVER."

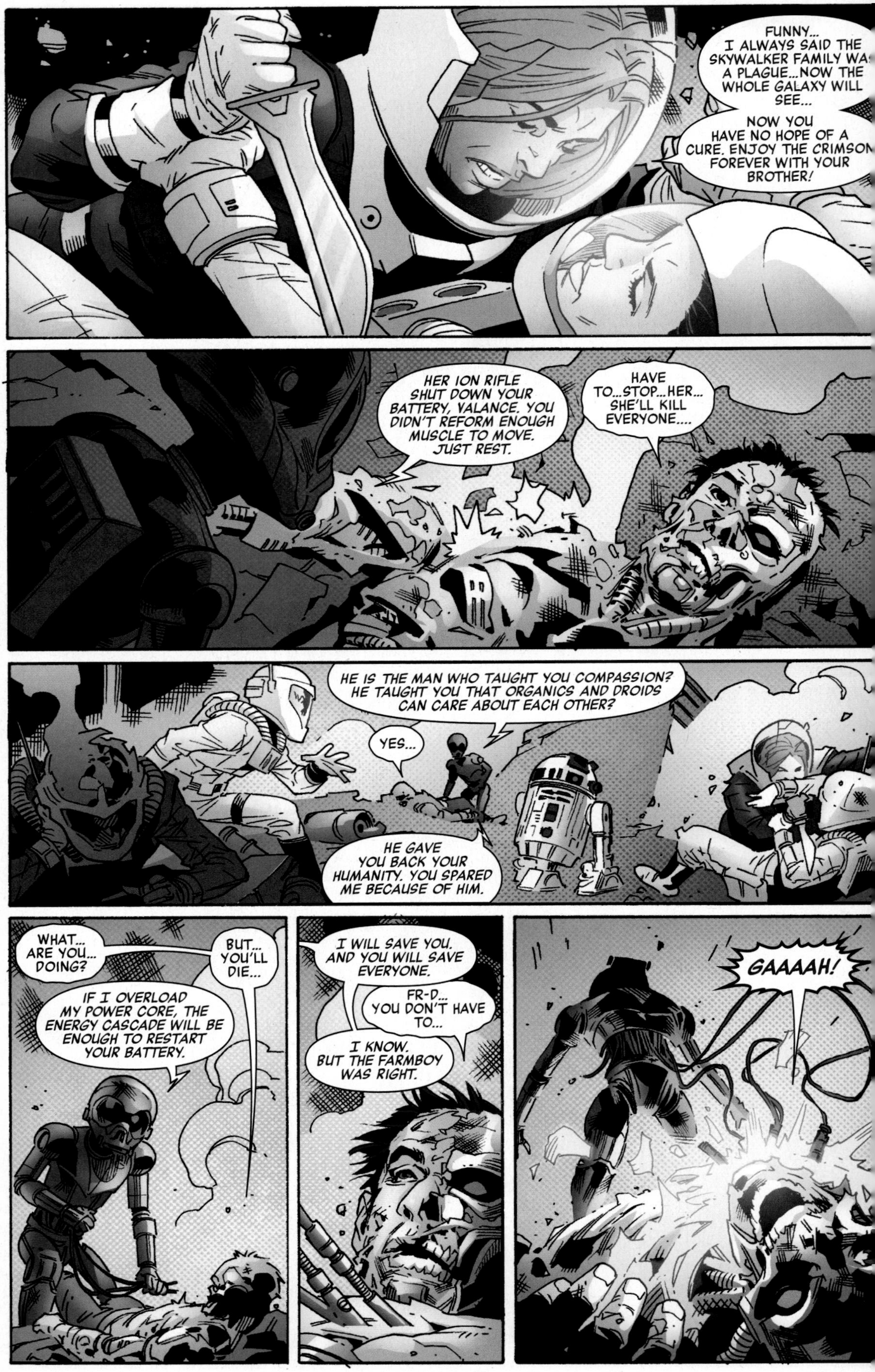
FUNNY... I ALWAYS SAID THE SKYWALKER FAMILY WAS A PLAGUE...NOW THE WHOLE GALAXY WILL SEE...
NOW YOU HAVE NO HOPE OF A CURE. ENJOY THE CRIMSON FOREVER WITH YOUR BROTHER!
HER ION RIFLE SHUT DOWN YOUR BATTERY, VALANCE. YOU DIDN'T REFORM ENOUGH MUSCLE TO MOVE. JUST REST.
HAVE TO...STOP...HER... SHE'LL KILL EVERYONE....
HE IS THE MAN WHO TAUGHT YOU COMPASSION? HE TAUGHT YOU THAT ORGANICS AND DROIDS CAN CARE ABOUT EACH OTHER?
YES...
HE GAVE YOU BACK YOUR HUMANITY. YOU SPARED ME BECAUSE OF HIM.
WHAT... ARE YOU... DOING?
IF I OVERLOAD MY POWER CORE, THE ENERGY CASCADE WILL BE ENOUGH TO RESTART YOUR BATTERY.
BUT... YOU'LL DIE...
I WILL SAVE YOU. AND YOU WILL SAVE EVERYONE.
FR-D... YOU DON'T HAVE TO...
I KNOW. BUT THE FARMBOY WAS RIGHT.
GAAAAH!

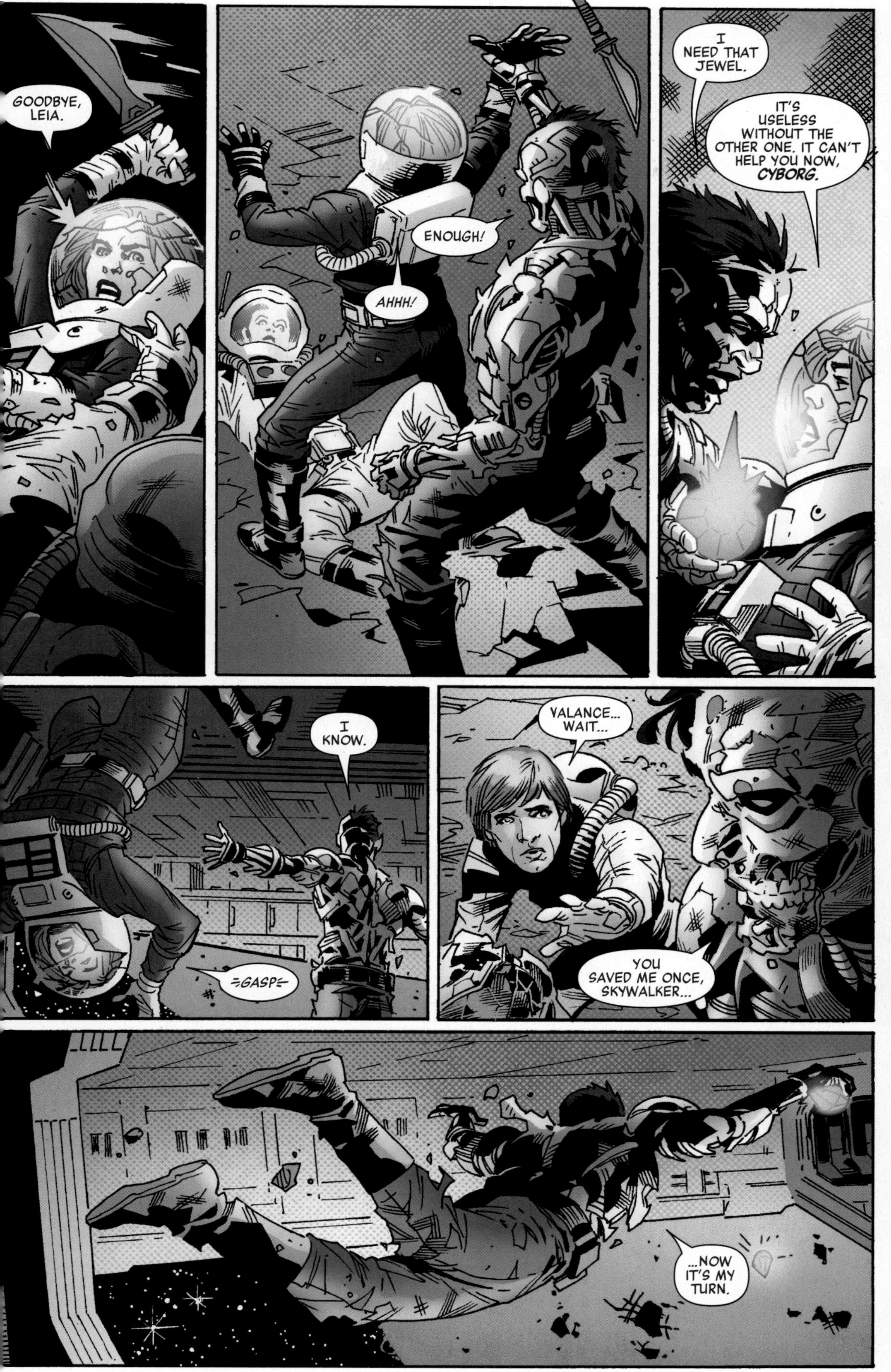
GOODBYE, LEIA.
ENOUGH!
AHHH!
I NEED THAT JEWEL.
IT'S USELESS WITHOUT THE OTHER ONE. IT CAN'T HELP YOU NOW, CYBORG.
I KNOW.
=GASP=
VALANCE... WAIT...
YOU SAVED ME ONCE, SKYWALKER...
...NOW IT'S MY TURN.

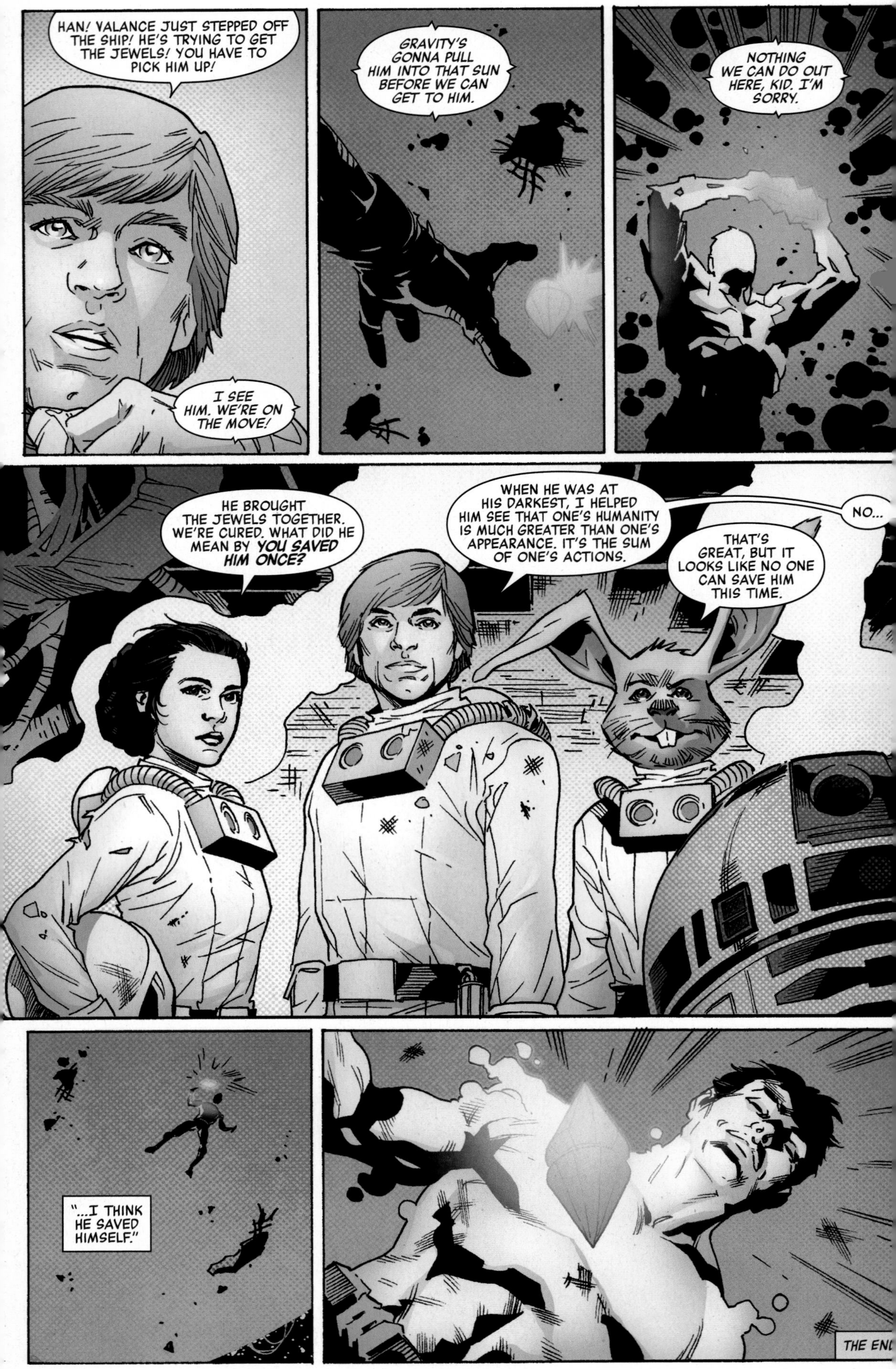
HAN! VALANCE JUST STEPPED OFF THE SHIP! HE'S TRYING TO GET THE JEWELS! YOU HAVE TO PICK HIM UP!
I SEE HIM. WE'RE ON THE MOVE!
GRAVITY'S GONNA PULL HIM INTO THAT SUN BEFORE WE CAN GET TO HIM.
NOTHING WE CAN DO OUT HERE, KID. I'M SORRY.
HE BROUGHT THE JEWELS TOGETHER. WE'RE CURED. WHAT DID HE MEAN BY YOU SAVED HIM ONCE?
WHEN HE WAS AT HIS DARKEST, I HELPED HIM SEE THAT ONE'S HUMANITY IS MUCH GREATER THAN ONE'S APPEARANCE. IT'S THE SUM OF ONE'S ACTIONS.
THAT'S GREAT, BUT IT LOOKS LIKE NO ONE CAN SAVE HIM THIS TIME.
NO...
"...I THINK HE SAVED HIMSELF."
THE END

CELEBRATING MARVEL'S FIRST STAR WARS COMICS

MARVEL'S STAR WARS series in the late '70s and early '80s was an important part of many fans' comic reading experience. It was the only way we could quench the thirst we had for more adventures featuring George Lucas' incredible creations. We did, after all, have to wait the near eternity of three years between movies.

Unbeknownst to us, the creators on the comic faced a very difficult challenge. With the understandable secrecy that comes with protecting a huge blockbuster's plots, twists and cliffhangers, the writers and artists had what seemed to many an impossible task: tell interesting and compelling stories while protecting the details of the movies.

In order to do that, new characters had to be introduced along with stories that worked around the established continuity. Out of necessity, a whole different continuity was created. One I thought we'd never be able to revisit.

Thanks to the good people at Lucasfilm, we were given the opportunity to take an unprecedented trip down memory lane in celebration of Marvel's 0th anniversary and the special relationship Marvel has had with the epic space fantasy that started over four decades ago.

One of my favorite of the new characters was Valance the Hunter. A deadly cyborg bounty hunter, he debuted after the introduction of such other colorful comics-only characters as Jaxxon and Amaiza Foxtrain. While a version of Valance was introduced into current cannon via the HAN SOLO: IMPERIAL CADET miniseries, how fun would it be to bring him, Jaxxon, Amaiza and even the devious Domina Tagge back for one special story, taking place in that now-classic non-canon universe?

40¢ 27 SEPT 02817
MARVEL COMICS GROUP
ADVENTURES BEYOND THE GREATEST SPACE-FANTASY FILM OF ALL!
STAR WARS
LUKE AND THREEPIO STALKED BY THE SINISTER CYBORG!
RETURN OF THE HUNTER!

40¢ 29 NOV 02817
MARVEL COMICS GROUP
ADVENTURES BEYOND THE GREATEST SPACE-FANTASY FILM OF ALL!
STAR WARS
DARK ENCOUNTER!

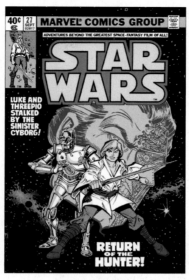

I called Walter Simonson to discuss those early days and, since he was the co-creator of Valance, see if he had any interest in doing a cover or interior work, and he mentioned that he once wanted to do a sequel to "The Crimson Forever," the story for the oversized 50th issue written by legendary Archie Goodwin and illustrated by Al Williamson, Simonson and Tom Palmer. Writer Matt Rosenberg—whom I'd professed my love for those early Star Wars comics to on many an occasion—Tom Groneman and myself enthusiastically listened and began connecting dots. A few days and a couple of omnibuses later, Matt presented a pitch for the special issue you hold in your hands now.

While this is meant to celebrate some of those unique and original characters Marvel created decades ago, we also want to thank all the wonderful, talented and amazing creators who contributed to the series' 107-issue run. We wouldn't have such a rich tapestry to celebrate if it weren't for all their hard work.

Mark Paniccia
Senior Editor
MARVEL COMICS

THE STARS OF MARVEL'S ORIGINAL STAR WARS

by Jess Harrold

STAR WARS
30¢ 1 JULY 02817
MARVEL COMICS GROUP
THE GREATEST SPACE-FANTASY FILM OF ALL!
STAR WARS
FABULOUS FIRST ISSUE!
ENTER LUKE SKYWALKER! WILL HE SAVE THE GALAXY— OR DESTROY IT?
MARVEL'S EPIC OFFICIAL ADAPTATION OF —A FILM BY GEORGE LUCAS—

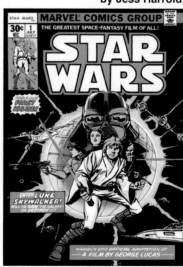

For 107 issues across nine years — not forgetting three Annuals and the four-issue Return of the Jedi — Marvel's original Star Wars series adapted and expanded George Lucas' epic saga. It did so throughout with a stellar cast of creators to rival anything a Hollywood space opera could bring to the silver screen. And every writer, artist and editor shared one thing in common: a huge passion for Star Wars.

Right from the start, Roy Thomas — after sharing dinner with Lucas himself — persuaded Stan Lee and Marvel to take a chance on the then-unknown sci-fi property, while Howard Chaykin was the illustrator handpicked by the filmmakers to tell the story of the first film in comic book form. They were followed on the book by a veritable "who's who" of the industry — too many to list here, but including such luminaries as Archie Goodwin, Carmine Infantino, Walter Simonson, Louise Simonson, Al Williamson, David Michelinie, Ann Nocenti, Chris Claremont and Tom Palmer. And writing almost every issue from #70 to the book's end was a writer whose love of the source material knew no bounds: Jo Duffy.

60¢
70
APR
MARVEL COMICS GROUP
STAR WARS
FEATURING HAN SOLO IN "THE STENAX SHUFFLE!"

"It was huge!" Duffy says. "I loved the movies. I adored and admired the wonderful work done by my predecessors on the Marvel title. Like me, every one of those people was a fan of the material and brought a wholehearted approach to it." Duffy says Goodwin wrote wonderful tales: "I still tear up when I remember [Goodwin's] story about Jolli the bandit (Star Wars #15)." Referring to Michelinie, Duffy adds, "You don't get Plif the Hoojib out of somebody who does not madly love Star Wars."

And she is full of praise for her major artistic collaborators, Ron Frenz, Tom Palmer and Cynthia Martin. "Ron was perhaps the only person on the planet who loved Star Wars as much, if not more, than I did," Duffy says. "He was so enthusiastic — at the time he bore a more-than-slight resemblance to Mark Hamill. Everybody gave him a hard time at every signing, because he was this fresh-faced, floppy-haired blond kid, looking like he's not just illustrating the adventures of Luke, he's probably going out with a lightsaber and fighting the Empire after the office is closed for the day!

"Working with Ron was just unbelievable fun. Artistically he's very generous, and he's got a tremendous sense of humor. When we did that story where Leia and Dani the Zeltron are bickering and having adventures and they're trying to stop a balloon and end up being whisked off a cliff by that balloon [Star Wars #73], I couldn't have done that with anybody but Ron.

"And Tom Palmer made everybody involved look even better than they already were. Tom is the Jedi master of bringing out the best in every artist he collaborates with."

Of Martin, with whom Duffy brought the book to an end, she says: "Cyndi's artwork is remarkable, she's very talented. She basically got that job because she came up to me at a convention with unbelievable samples, including some Star Wars pieces. Her work was unlike anything anybody else was doing at the time. Like Ron, she had an absolute love of Star Wars."

Duffy commenced her run prior to the events of Return of the Jedi and continued it for three years beyond the film's release. Hard as it is to imagine now, for a time that made her pretty much the only person on the planet writing new Star Wars stories. That came with certain restrictions, but necessity proved the mother of invention. "I was not allowed to advance the mythos beyond Return of the Jedi," she says. "But, with those characters, and with that world, even not being able to deal with the big narrative, there was so much to do."

This included introducing notable new characters, such as the Corellian smuggler Rik Duel and his gang, including Dani the Zeltron, as well as the invading army of the Nagai.

"I was having a whale of a time," she says. "It was like, if I can't deal with the Empire, and Darth Vader is dead, then okay, new people are going to invade! I was having a wonderful time, and the book sold right up to the end. I could have gone on with that story for years. It was not to be, but we had a hell of a fun time planning it!"

Though Duffy was disappointed that she could not continue her story past Star Wars #107, she is delighted that the series still resonates with fans several decades on — and that #108 is seeing print at last. "I am ecstatic that anybody wants to do it," she says, "and I am absolutely cheering for the great result I know Marvel is going to have with it."

MARVEL
25
ANNIVERSARY
STAR WARS
LAST ISSUE!
75¢ US
107 SEP

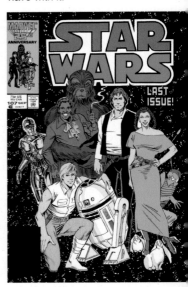

David Michelinie, writer: "I can't compare my love of Star Wars with Jo's because I don't know the depth of her passion. But, as for me, if I'd had twins I would have named them 'Luke' and 'Leia' — which might have been a little embarrassing if they were both boys! On Star Wars, I did my best to emulate the tone and feel of the first two movies. And since those movies offered action, drama and fun, it seemed a good idea to do the same with my stories. I really liked the "Shira's Story" arc (Star Wars #60-63), which put Luke on the outs with the rebellion. "Shadeshine!" (Star Wars Annual #2) also stands out for me, since it was the only chance I had to write Han Solo. He was busy being trapped in carbonite at the time, and I had to sneak in a flashback story in order to use the character!"

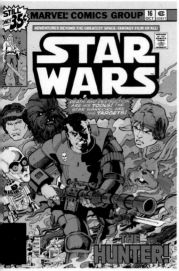

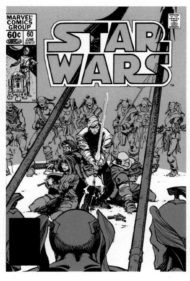

STILL ONLY 35¢
MARVEL COMICS GROUP
16 OCT
ADVENTURES BEYOND THE GREATEST SPACE-FANTASY FILM OF ALL!
STAR WARS
DEATH AND DESTRUCTION ARE HIS TOOLS! THE STAR WARRIORS ARE HIS TARGETS!
THE HUNTER!

.ouise Simonson, editor: "One of he things we all found most amusing vas that when you proposed a story ınd sent the plot in to Lucas for ıpproval, if they said, 'oh, you can't do hat,' we'd say, okay, that's happening ı the next movie! Obviously, Han /as in carbonite, and we couldn't ıave Luke and Leia romantically ıvolved, or Luke facing off against /ader in real life — so we put in a :ouple of Vader holograms every now ınd then, or symbolically on a cover!"

Valter Simonson, penciler: "I'm ɫelighted that our run is remembered :indly today, so long after we did it. Ve went back to Cloud City, I got ɔ draw Lobot. It was fun. Billy Dee Villiams (Lando) was not that hard to ɫraw, I don't know why. Some people ıre very difficult to draw — Luke was ı little tricky. He had a very handsome ace, but not a lot of lines — he was ı young guy. But Billy Dee Williams, I ɲnjoyed drawing him.

Ve had a conference call about Star Wars #108. I couldn't draw it, I ıad too much other stuff to do — I vould have loved to, because it was ı sequel to Archie Goodwin's story from Star Wars #50]. It may be that he idea of doing a sequel to 'The Crimson Forever' was my original dea — I'm a big Archie Goodwin an, and of course he was a good riend, so I thought of that story. And Star Wars #108 includes Valance the Hunter, whom Archie invented and I ɫrew back in #16 — a bounty hunter ı the Star Wars universe before he second film came out, so we kinda liked that. I haven't drawn him commercially since 1978, but it was fun to go back and draw him again [on the cover to Star Wars #108]. I thought it would be cool to have him fighting Darth Vader. I always enjoyed drawing Vader — and I didn't get to do it a lot in the comic. I put a 'For Archie' at the bottom of the cover, and Marvel was cool letting me do that."

MARVEL COMICS GROUP
60¢ 60 JUNE
STAR WARS

Ron Frenz, penciler: "I had followed the book and was a big fan of the movies, so it was a great pleasure to land the assignment. Jo was my first experience with a regular creative partner, talking on the phone, becoming friends, trading ideas, becoming involved in storytelling. She taught me a lot about collaboration, leaving your ego at the door, and was an incredibly talented technical writer. She really knows the craft. My greatest memory of working with her was that her stories were fun. We did some wonderfully dark, dramatic stories, like "Ellie" (Star Wars #80), but she was also very much of a mind to keep the fun of the Star Wars movies in her stories. I like the splash page of Star Wars #81 — it's just Han Solo with his hands on his chest, going 'It's me!', because Jo loved that line in Return, 'Hey, it's me.' I was invited along with Jo and Archie to go to the Denver premiere of Return of the Jedi. It was my first time on a plane. I rented a tux, and Archie was in a tux, and Jo looked gorgeous in a gown — and the gentleman that hosted us went in jeans and sandals!"

Tom Palmer, inker: "Star Wars #81 has a special cover with a backstory. We were not allowed to use Han Solo in any issues while he was frozen since Empire Strikes Back, and his release in Return of the Jedi opened the door to welcoming his return with a cover. Jo Duffy approached me to do a painting with Han and I jumped at it. I did some sketches and settled on a montage with other Star Wars icons. Lucasfilm supplied photos of the movie and in my batch there was a large head of Han Solo, as you see it on the cover, with his blaster up by his face, gazing to the right. That was the door to the bunker. I had my cover — and it is my favorite!"

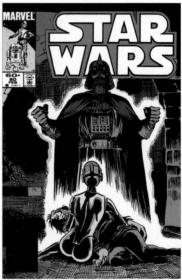

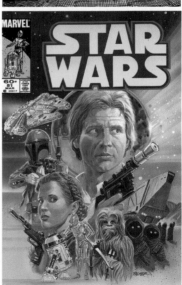

MARVEL
STAR WARS
60¢ 80

MARVEL
STAR WARS
60¢ 81 MAR

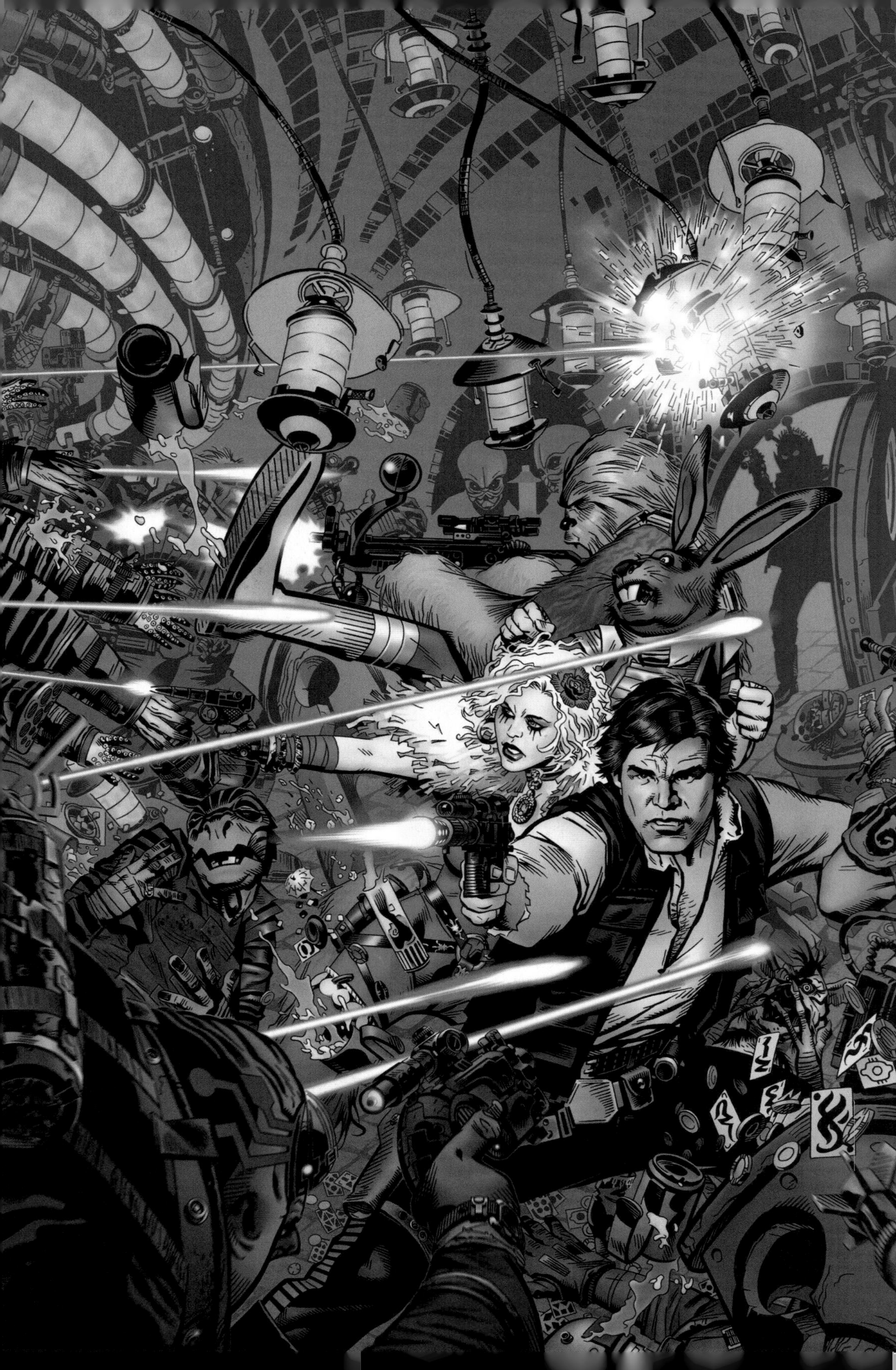

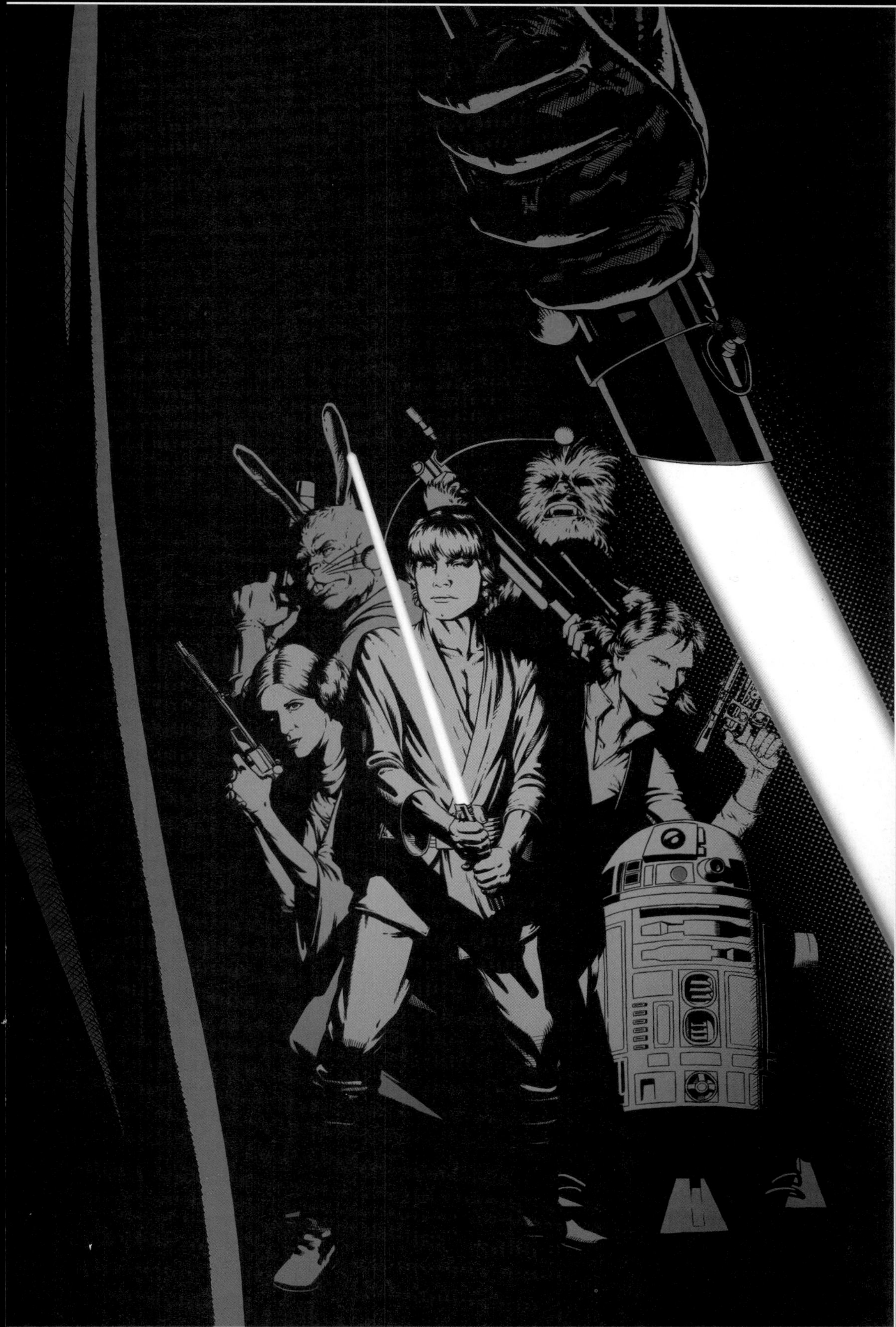

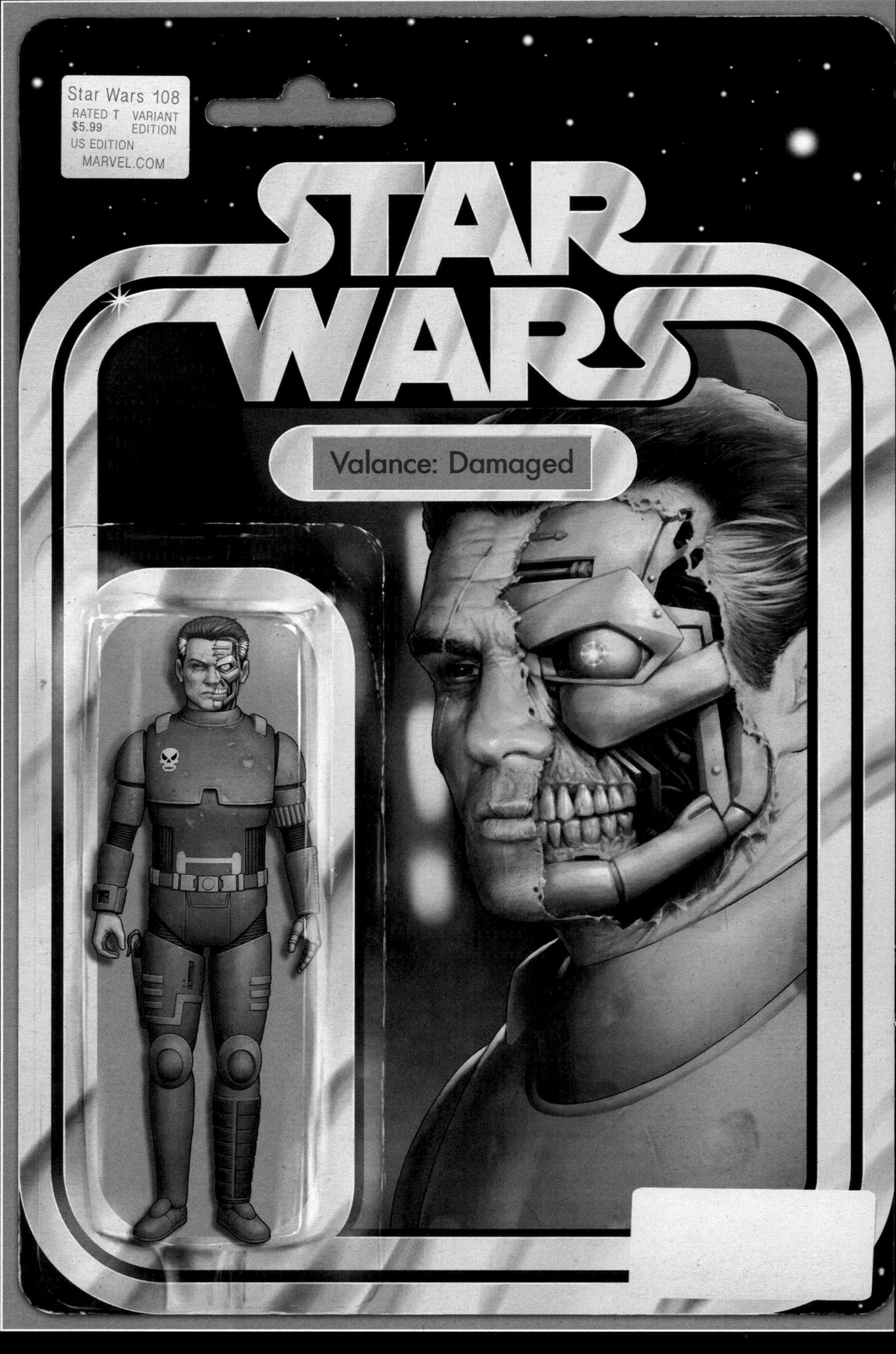
Star Wars 108
RATED T VARIANT
$5.99 EDITION
US EDITION
MARVEL.COM
STAR WARS
Valance: Damaged

STAR WARS #108 **ACTION FIGURE VARIANT BY JOHN TYLER CHRISTOPHER**

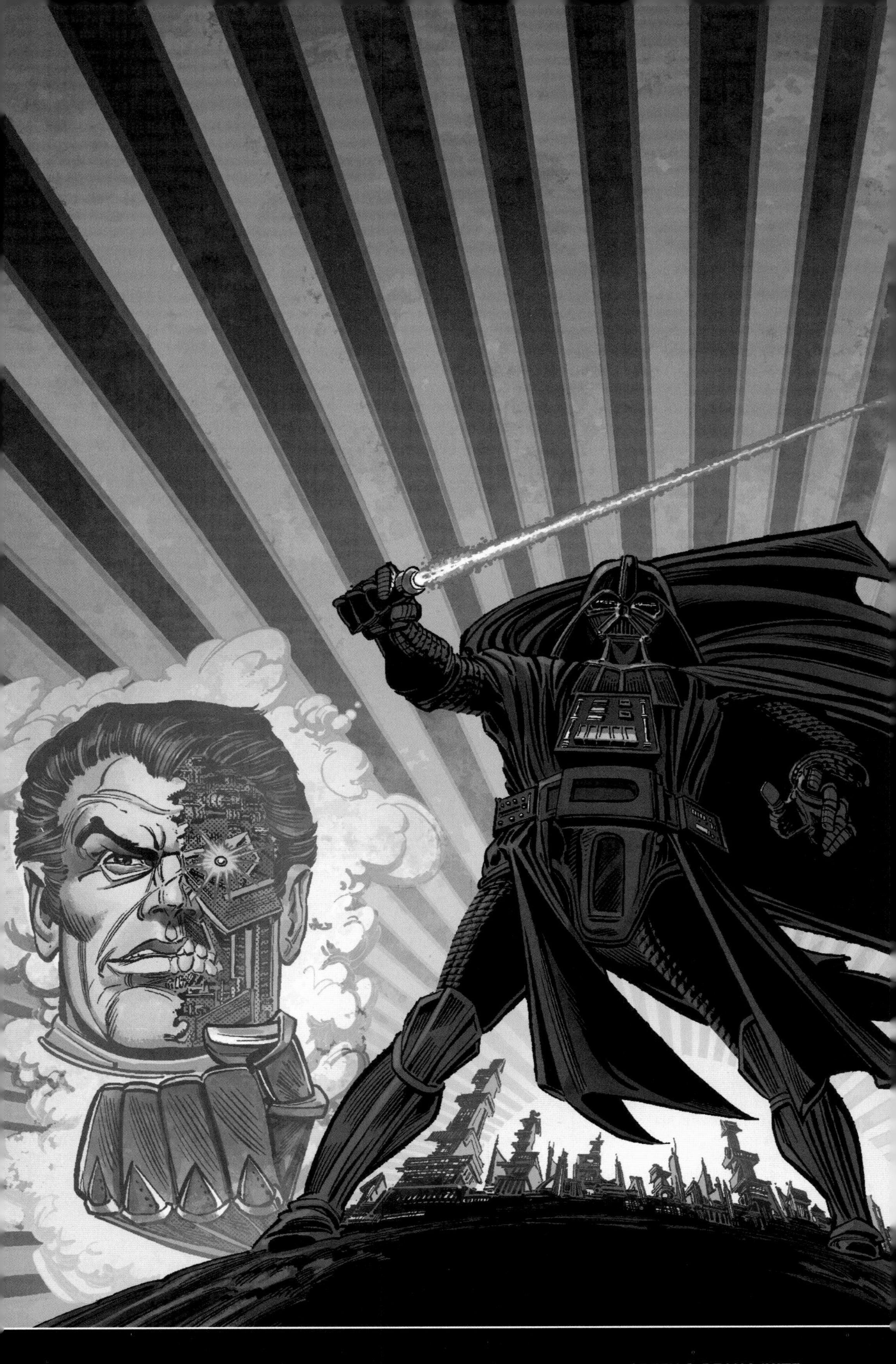

STAR WARS #108 REMASTERED VARIANT BY CARMINE INFANTINO, DAN GREEN & DEAN WHITE

CYNTHIA MARTIN, THE NEW STAR OF STAR WARS™

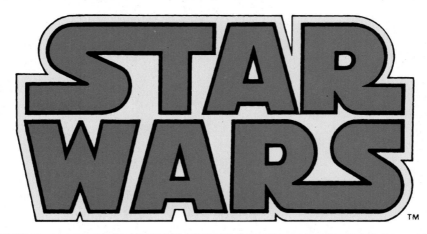

by **Dwight Jon Zimmerman**

ULP!
OH, <YAWN> HAN, IS THAT YOU? IS IT TIME TO FACE THE MUSIC ALREADY?
I FEEL MUCH BETTER.
I THOUGHT YOU WOULD.

Unless you just arrived from another galaxy far, far away you already know about **Luke Skywalker**, **Princess Leia**, **Han Solo** and all the other members of one of the world's most popular science fiction sagas, **STAR WARS**.

But what you may not know is all the excitement that rose from both pros and fans alike when **STAR WARS** editor **Ann Nocenti** announced that newcomer **Cynthia Martin** would be the new regular penciler of everybody's favorite Jedi knight and his friends.

For **STAR WARS** writer **Jo Duffy**, herself, **Ann's** choice was particularly gratifying, because it was **Jo** who discovered **Cynthia** last year at a Creation convention in California.

As **Jo** recalled, "I was at the Marvel table looking at samples from aspiring artists and writers. **Cindy's** boyfriend, **Sean Demine**, was the one who actually showed her art samples to me. **Cindy's** art not only looked very promising, it also looked very exciting. She was rooted in a whole different aesthetic than the people whose work I had already seen. She had a fresh style that the industry could really use. I asked **Sean** to get **Cindy** and bring her over so I could meet her."

It was a momentous meeting that was captured forever on film, for just as the two started talking, the floodlights from a mobile television camera flashed on and **Jo** and **Cynthia** suddenly discovered that they were being interviewed for the nightly news on the local TV station!

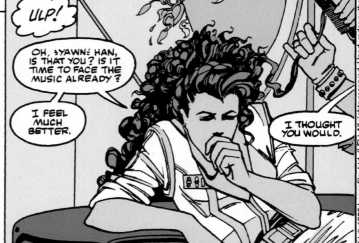

After their moment of television fame had passed, **Jo** gave **Cindy** her card and told her to stay in touch. **Cindy** did, sending more samples of her work as the months passed. Then one day **Cindy** got a phone call from **Ann Nocenti** asking her if she'd like to do a trial issue of **STAR WARS**.

"At first I thought it was a prank," **Cynthia** confessed. "Even though **Jo** said some real nice things about my samples, I really couldn't believe **Ann** was calling me, considering how little experience I have in comics!"

But a prank it wasn't, and with enthusiastic support and pointers from both **Ann** and **Jo**, **Cynthia's** trial issue was so impressive that she was promptly selected as the new regular artist.

"I'm in heaven," **Cynthia** said. "**STAR WARS** is my fave rave. I think I have everything that was ever put out about the movie. And even at this late date I have a hard time believing my incredible luck of now drawing the series."

Oddly enough, **Cynthia** had never been interested in comics, even though her boyfriend is an avid comic book fan. And despite her natural artistic talent, **Cindy** was planning to go to college to become a lawyer. Then **Sean** convinced **Cindy** to read **X-MEN** #173.

"Not only did I read it from cover to cover," **Cindy** said, "it was also the comic that caused me to fall in love with the medium. Right then and there I decided to throw all caution to the wind and become a comic book artist."

For **Cindy**, a self-taught artist who learned her skills by studying art books she borrowed from all the area's libraries, the effort of adapting her style to comics was a challenge.

"It was frustrating for a while," **Cindy** said. "I kept drawing individual pictures. I was not really telling a visual story. I have to hand it to **Sean**, he showed me how to re-orient my thinking. Through him, I began to identify what to look for in a story and how to catch the most significant images on the drawing board. When I did that, the story flowed.

"I'm still learning a lot," **Cindy** quickly added, "but that particular moment of understanding about comic book illustration was my first big step."

Her second step was learning how to work Marvel style, from a plot sent by a writer living on the other side of the continent.

"**Jo** and I talk a lot on the phone," **Cindy** said. "**Jo** has an enormous gift at being able to put ideas into other people's heads. And reading **Jo's** plots is always a lot of fun. She's got a fantastic sense of humor which she uses to great effect in her description of things. **Jo** makes my job so easy because she has so many super ideas and presents them so clearly that I have absolutely no trouble putting the story into pictures."

When she's not busy working on **STAR WARS**, **Cindy** is busy reading the latest Marvel comics. "**The X-MEN** is my life's blood." **Cindy** said. "I'm crazy about that series. And **THE NEW MUTANTS** is so good it makes me want to cry. It's no secret to anyone who knows me that I think **Bill Sienkiewicz's** art is incredible. **DOCTOR STRANGE** is another favorite. I really love **Paul Smith's** work. I'm only sorry

I don't have more time to look at all the comics as much as I'd like."

As for artistic influences, **Cynthia** said, "They're a combination of classic artists and the modern comic book ones. I really had an eclectic education — I studied everybody. And the few times I actually took a formal art course, I found out I hated it. A big influence on me was — and still is — **Leonardo Da Vinci**. He knew more about anatomy than I think I can ever learn."

When asked if she'd like to see anything in particular happen in **STAR WARS**, **Cynthia** said, "What I'd like to see happen is what is happening right now. What **Jo** is doing with the storyline surpasses my wildest fantasy. She is not only remaining true to the spirit of the movies and all the concepts that made the trilogy great, she is giving it new life and blood and not only hanging on to all the old characters, she's adding an incredible group of new ones!"

The most important in the new group is the mysterious **Nagai**. "It is a really ferocious alien civilization that has been watching the on-going fight between the Rebel Alliance and the remaining Imperial forces," **Jo** said. "And they're waiting for the right moment to strike, when they feel the two groups are at their weakest."

And as for **Luke** and his friends, **Jo** said, "They are getting really fed up with the leaders in the Alliance who have been sending them off to all corners of the galaxy on individual missions for what seems to them to be no reason. Also, **Luke**, **Han**, **Leia** and **Lando** have been seeing some pretty obvious developments building up, but no one in the Alliance will take the time to listen to them. Eventually they are going to rebel against the Alliance

leaders and deliberately form their own guerilla band. What happens then is anybody's guess, but you can bet that it will include a lot of hair-raising action."

When asked about anything important happening in the personal lives of the **STAR WARS** heroes, **Jo** said, "The one thing that *won't* be happening is that we will not have **Han** and **Leia** get married. I certainly would if I could, but if that is going to happen, **George Lucas** has to do it first in his movie."

The 100th issue of **STAR WARS** is rapidly approaching. As for any special plans for that issue, **Jo** smiled and said, "Well, it's going to be double-sized, definitely. And **Cynthia** and I are involved right now with a very complex story that is building up to a big shocker of a climax. And it will all happen in that 100th issue. Beyond that, I can't say anything more."

Reader response to their effort has been exciting. "The readers are really involved with the series," **Jo** said. "And it's a great feeling to know that you're reaching an audience that cares about your efforts. A lot of them sense that **Cynthia** and I love these characters as much as they do."

Cynthia added, "I saw the first movie, **STAR WARS**, when I was a kid, and it really is one of those things that stays with you all your life — it made that much of an impact on me. And now to be the artist of the **STAR WARS** comic as well — wow, I mean the idea is just so cosmic as to almost not be believed! It really makes you think that there is a Force out there!"

As **Cynthia** and **Jo** returned to work on their next **STAR WARS** saga, they passed on a special message to all their loyal readers, "May the Force be with you!"

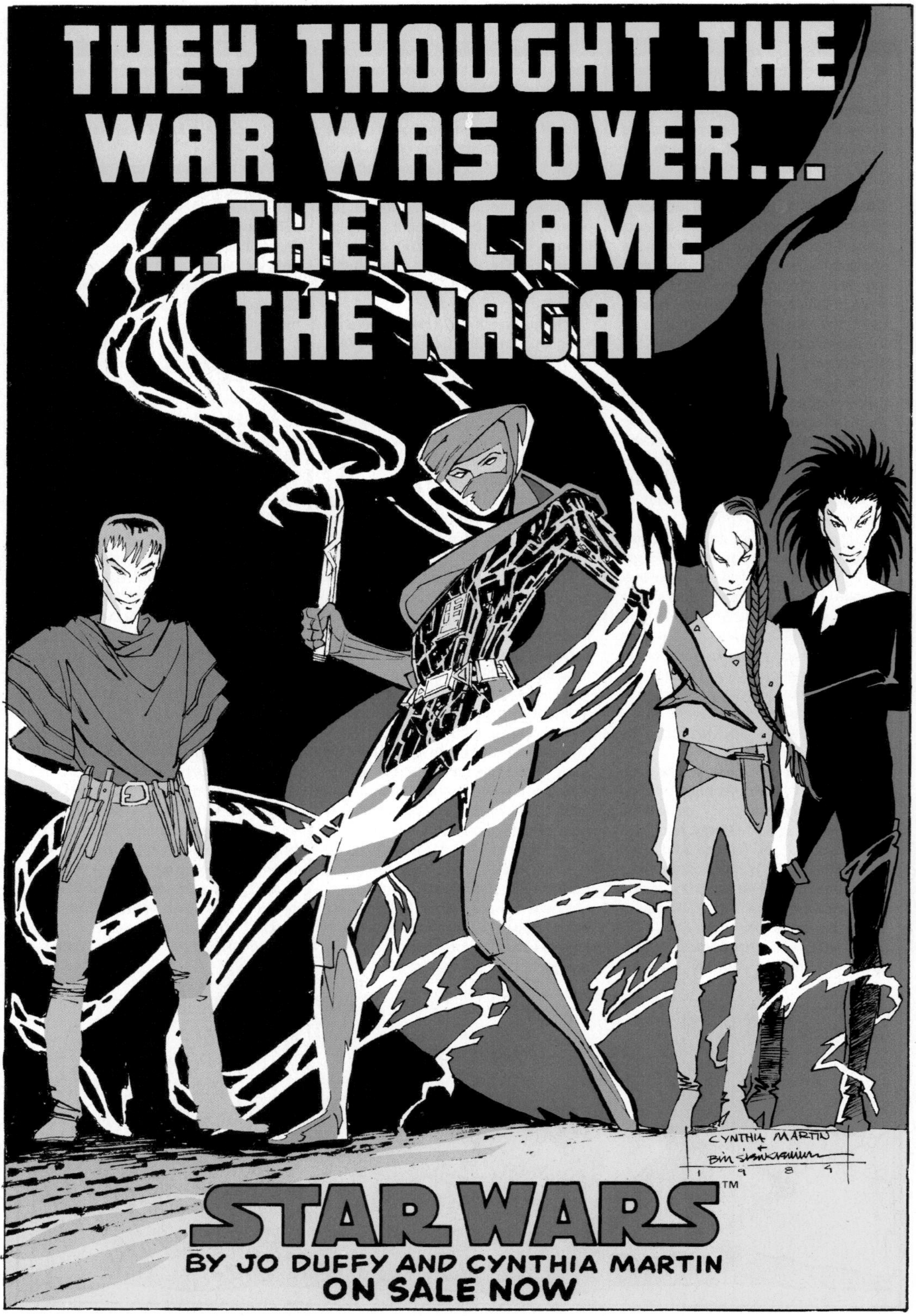
THEY THOUGHT THE WAR WAS OVER...
...THEN CAME THE NAGAI
CYNTHIA MARTIN
1 9 8 4
STAR WARS™
BY JO DUFFY AND CYNTHIA MARTIN
ON SALE NOW

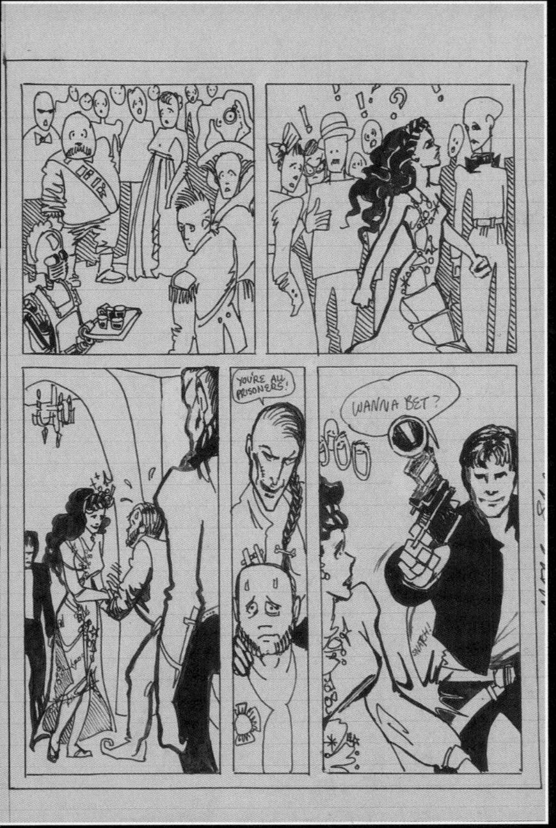
YOU'RE ALL PRISONERS!
WANNA BET?

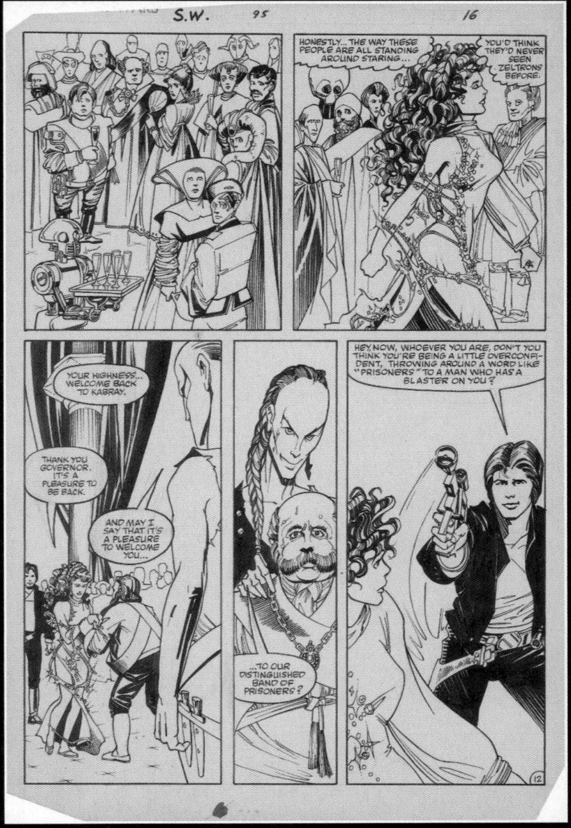
S.W.
95
16
HONESTLY... THE WAY THESE PEOPLE ARE ALL STANDING AROUND STARING...
YOU'D THINK THEY'D NEVER SEEN ZELTRONS BEFORE.
YOUR HIGHNESS... WELCOME BACK TO KABRAY.
THANK YOU GOVERNOR. IT'S A PLEASURE TO BE BACK.
AND MAY I SAY THAT IT'S A PLEASURE TO WELCOME YOU...
...TO OUR DISTINGUISHED BAND OF PRISONERS?
HEY, NOW, WHOEVER YOU ARE, DON'T YOU THINK YOU'RE BEING A LITTLE OVERCONFIDENT, THROWING AROUND A WORD LIKE "PRISONERS" TO A MAN WHO HAS A BLASTER ON YOU?
12

STAR WARS #95, PAGE 12 LAYOUT BY CYNTHIA MARTIN, AND FINISHED ART BY CYNTHIA MARTIN & STEVE LEIALOHA
COURTESY OF HERITAGEAUCTIONS.COM

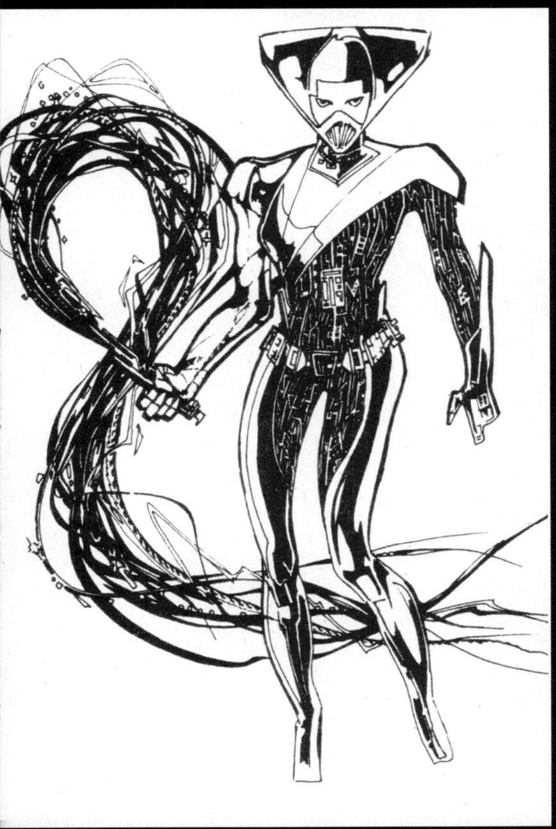

LUMIYA DESIGN SKETCH
BY CYNTHIA MARTIN

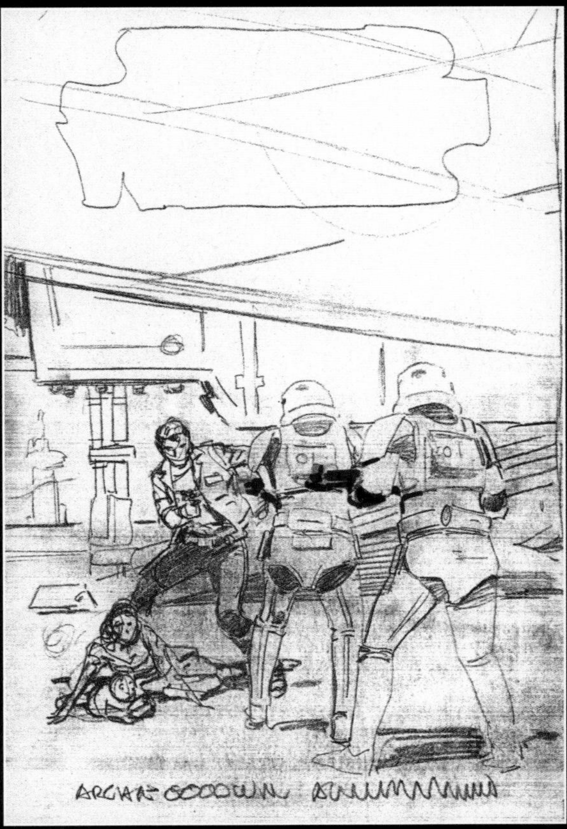
ARGHH-GOOOWN AWWWMMMMMM

CLASSIC STAR WARS: THE VANDELHELM MISSION
COVER SKETCH BY AL WILLIAMSON

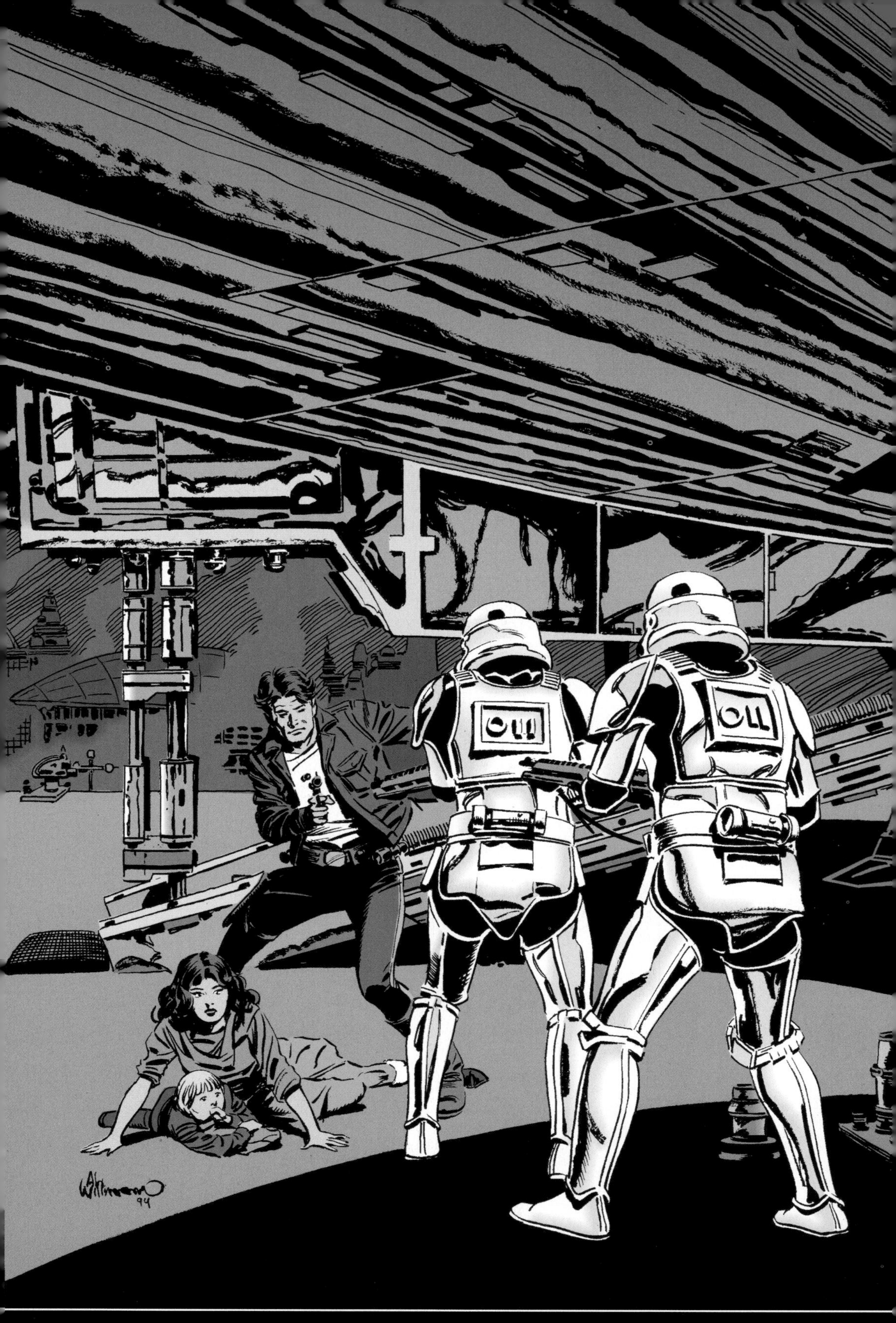

CLASSIC STAR WARS: THE VANDELHELM MISSION (1995) REPRINTED *STAR WARS* #98,
RECOLORED IN MODERN STYLE. COVER BY AL WILLIAMSON & MATT HOLLINGSWORTH.

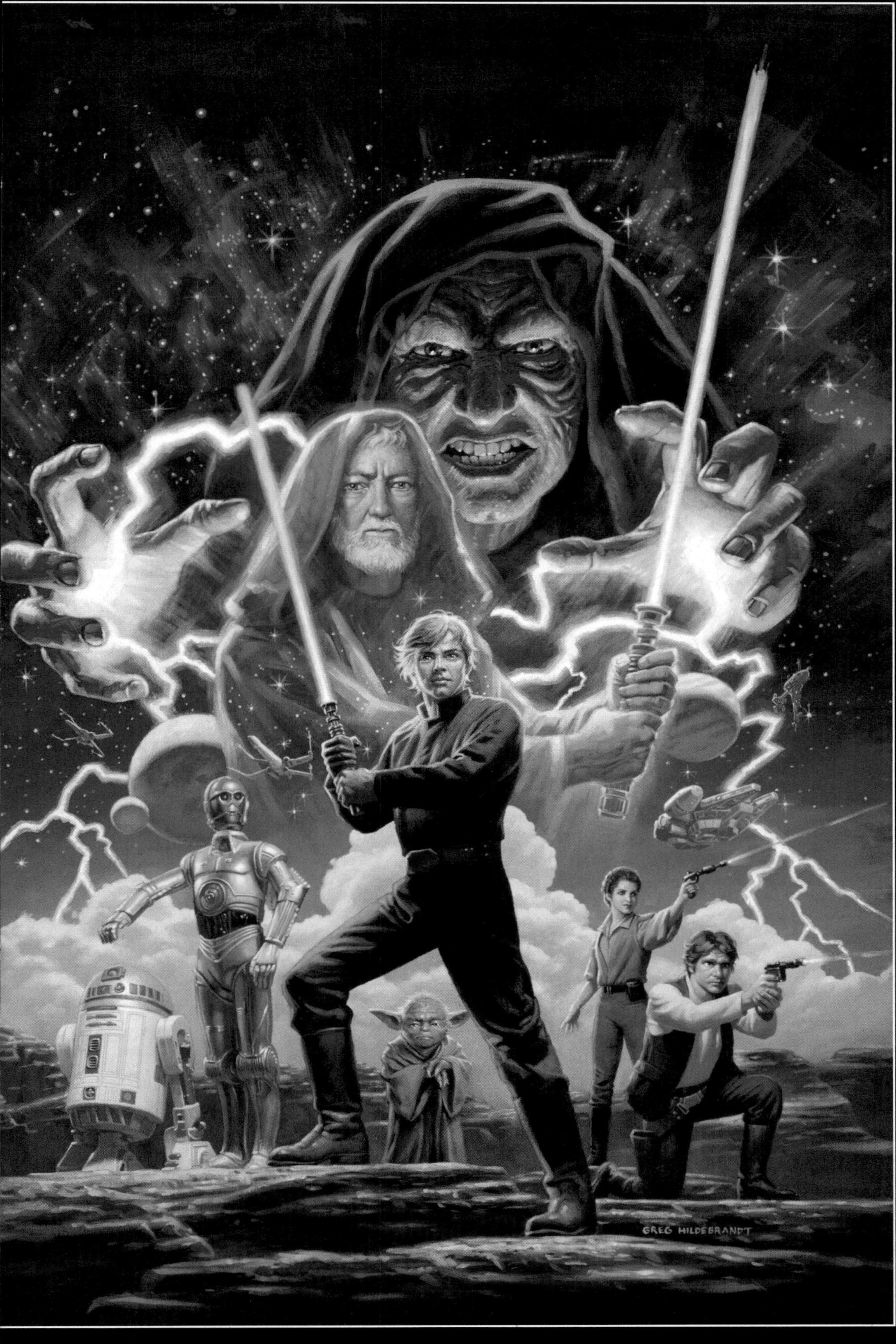
GREG HILDEBRANDT

STAR WARS: THE ORIGINAL MARVEL YEARS OMNIBUS VOL. 3 HC **VARIANT BY GREG HILDEBRANDT**

I could have murdered Chris Claremont.

It was May 25th, 1977, and I could have just killed him.

Maybe not the safest thing to confess…except that this was all several decades ago, the man was and still is a good friend, and to this day he enjoys that same state of happy, clueless, unscathed safety and health as ever, unaware of ever having been in any danger.

But, boy, oh, boy, at the time, I could have just killed him.

Why, you may ask. Why would Jo want to harm her friend, a man whose company and work she has enjoyed for most of her adult life? The man who — in collaboration with some wonderful editors and superbly gifted artists — took the X-Men from "beloved fan-favorite that never really sold well" to "near-universal favorite, unstoppable sales juggernaut and license to print money"?

What did Chris do to deserve it?

I'll tell you what he did.

That dirty, rotten rat saw *Star Wars* — the very first *Star Wars* movie, the one that started it all — a full twelve hours before I could…and he SPOILED it!

I had been looking forward to seeing *Star Wars* for months… mostly because I had read somewhere that Mark Hamill — who had done some truly wonderful work in a variety of films and TV appearances over the past few years and therefore enjoyed a certain crush-worthy cachet among the young women of the day — was working on a big, exciting-sounding science fiction epic.

I loved science fiction, and there was not a lot of it out there at that time in film and television for us to enjoy. *Star Trek*, *The Time Tunnel*, *The Invaders*, *The Outer Limits* all seemed to be over and done; and there was little in the way of cable television yet, and almost no home-video market for revisiting existing treasures like *The Thing* or *Forbidden Planet*.

But heart-throbby Mark Hamill, doing new science fiction, under the direction of the Guy Who Made *American Graffiti*, and working with the Guy Who Built *The Bridge on the River Kwai*, and the voice of the Great White Hope, and the Guy Who Kept Killing Dracula, and one of the guys from *American Graffiti* and *Journey to Shiloh* (I hadn't seen *The Conversation* yet), plus a girl a bunch of my guy friends told me had done good work in a movie called *Shampoo*…well, that was something I could not wait to see.

And when, a few months after finishing college I was fortunate enough to join the staff of Marvel Comics — best job EVER!, by the way — I was delighted to learn that in addition to all of the comic-book adventures of the super heroes I adored, and the barbarians I admired, Marvel was also going to be publishing a comic-book adaptation of *Star Wars*. That Roy Thomas was a friend of a friend of the director, and was writing the comic. Incredible. Marvelous. The Ralph McQuarrie production paintings were being passed around the office. They blew my mind. And Howard Chaykin's story illustrations looked phenomenal. The stills we had on hand made it all look even more real, and so very, very wonderful. So I was very careful about one thing.

I didn't want to know the story. I didn't want to meet the characters or learn the mechanics of the story until I could see the movie. And my older brother, Malachy (who had introduced me to comic books and nurtured my love of science fiction in the first place and who remains my favorite movie-going buddy) and I had plans to see it after work, the day it was due to open.

Back then — in that now hard-to-imagine yesteryear before the existence of social media, before the Internet itself, before *EW*, *TMZ* and the blogosphere — it was still very possible (in fact, it was the norm) to see a movie or TV show without having any but the haziest knowledge of what it was about and what the surprises would be. And since stories and characters were and still are my business, as well as one of my greatest joys, if it looks like something I am going to care about I took and still take the greatest care NOT to be spoiled before I read a book, watch a show or see a movie. I figure it is the simplest courtesy we as audience members owe creators for all of the work and planning and craft they put into thrilling, delighting and scaring us: to let them do their jobs and to enjoy their stories as they are designed to be enjoyed. It a strategy that has paid off, rewarding me with delight and amazement, time and time again. I saw *Citizen Kane* without any advance hint of what made the central character tick. I had no idea, the first time I saw *Psycho*, of just what was up at the Bates Motel, nor of who was really behind it. I had no idea what was coming near the end of *The Wrath of Khan*. And no one gave me a hint of what was really going on in *The Sixth Sense*; meaning that I have had the pure, unspoiled pleasure of having my mind honestly blown by clever, gifted creators, time and time again.

That day, though, I had reckoned without the fact that Chris, a freelance writer, could juggle his schedule so as to catch the very first morning showing of *Star Wars*, while we editors, bullpenners and assistants were all still chained to our desks…and I reckoned without Chris' love of an audience. Before he settled into his groove as a writer, you see, my pal Chris had trained as an actor.

He adored *Star Wars*. He was bubbling over with enthusiasm and he wanted us all to know it. He wanted us to know just what an exciting, original piece of work we all had to look forward to…and he wanted us to know that He Saw It First. So he didn't just burble, he didn't just enthuse, he didn't just give parts of it away… He acted out the whole freaking thing.

Seriously.

He planted himself in the middle of the office where all of our desks were, and minutely described it all, beginning with the titles, the sound, the score, every shot, every detail, every surprise… And I was trapped, like a rat myself, stuck at my desk, trying to work…and — once he got rolling — unable (and no longer really willing) to tear myself away from Chris' enthusiasm, and from how amazing it all sounded, when I was still hours away from being able to see for myself.

I listened. But after months of carefully and deliberately shielding myself from having all of those long-anticipated surprises spoiled, you had better believe I also wanted him dead for it…and I figure, given the nature of the offense, that a jury of my peers (i.e., a dozen or so nerdy fan boys and girls who like to experience their pop culture treats FIRSTHAND first) would not only not convict me, but would e more likely to provide me with an airtight alibi, and hereafter use Chris' sad-but-just fate as a future warning to Those Who Would Spoil.

Luckily, two things intervened to save Chris: One was that someone needed my help right away on something time-sensitive and important in the bullpen, so that I didn't hear any of his re-creation after the trash compactor scene; the second was that before I saw him again, I was able to see *Star Wars* for myself.

And yes, for the first few minutes, I was all, "Yeah, right. This is just the way he described it. If I'd seen it for myself, I'd have just loved this. And he was right about the score, too! Fabulous!" Until, after a very few brief scenes, I was well and truly caught nonetheless, mesmerized, in love with every shot and every character and not caring that I knew much of what was coming, because it was just so superbly, stunningly good.

I did NOT then run out and ruin it for the next unspoiled fan; but in the company of fellow enthusiasts I could not stop talking about it. How smart it was. How well acted. How beautifully the shots were composed, and how amazingly the camera moved. How the effects were above and beyond anything any of us had ever seen before. How Ben Kenobi combined Crazy Old Desert Coot Who Helps Save the Day with elements of Gandalf and Merlin. How Leia moved seamlessly from Acid-Tongued Noblewoman to Fairy Princess in Need of Rescue to Badass Chick with a Blaster. How it was a Western in space. How the tech was not all shiny and new. It was worn. Some of it was dirty. All of it looked used. This was a universe that had clearly been going — and would keep on going — for quite some time. There was drama. There was pathos and tragedy. There was romance and heroism, and weaselly self-interest, and sniping and one-upsmanship among all of the characters, good and bad. There was whimsy and humor, a fat guy named Porkins, for crying out loud, and a robot that acted like a mouse. There were two among the eight main characters who never uttered a single intelligible sound, but whose meanings were always clear, and with whom others carried on long, amusing and informative conversations.

As I have mentioned, this was well in advance of the home-video market, and for that entire summer, I went to the movies every Friday, after work, sitting through back-to-back showings of *Star Wars*, until I had seen it eighteen times.

If I hadn't been able, through the kindness and patience of Archie Goodwin — a good friend, my boss and one of my mentors for much of my early career, who was then writing wonderful *Star Wars* issues himself — to write a couple of *Star Wars* fill-ins of my own, I might have just expired from the stress of loving it so much. Until my friend and colleague Jim Salicrup very kindly pointed out that — since the whole world seemed to be on its way to loving *Star Wars* as much as I did — it was liable to go on as more toys, comics, movies, TV specials and what have you for a long LONG time to come, I might as well calm down and pace myself.

Thank you, Jim. Of course, you were right; but I doubt even you had any inkling then of just how right you would turn out to be.

That decades and decades and decades later, there would be six films done and a seventh on the way. That there would be series after animated series to choose from. Countless toys. Or that I would eventually have had the delight and privilege, for several wonderful years along the way, of being (at that time) the only person in the world writing

new *Star Wars* material. I loved the movies. I adored and admired — and am indebted to — the wonderful work done by my predecessors on the Marvel title — including Archie Roy, Howard, Walter Simonson, Carmine Infantino, David Michelinie... And with many wonderful and talented artists — including the utterly brilliant and delightful Tom Palmer, Cindy Martin and Ron Frenz — I had an utter blast, actually getting paid to do the Best Job Ever...in spades!!!! And in space!

As others have observed, during the films and then after the comics adaptation of *Return of the Jedi* was complete, there were some storytelling challenges inherent in our advancing the narrative of *Star Wars*. We knew going in that George Lucas would be continuing it himself. It was, after all, his baby and his creation, and we owed all of those wonderful movies and all of our own work with those concepts and characters directly to him. But, being big fans of the story, and being writers ourselves with our own ideas, all of us on the book would have loved the chance to write the big stories — to tell the tales of Luke Versus Darth, Ben Versus Darth, Han Loving Leia, the Fall of the Empire, etc. Of course, we couldn't. We didn't own these toys, and we had to be careful not to break them...we simply got to have fun playing with them, as we curated the characters and their universe for the future... and once we had accepted that fact, we each of us, in turn, realized that even without the Big Stories, there were still plenty of other avenues to explore and new characters to introduce, new races to create and new worlds to build.

The universe of *Star Wars* is very roomy indeed, capacious enough to hold and accommodate all of the Jaxxons and Jollis and Hoojibs and Zeltrons and Nagai and Iskalonians and Hiromi we cared to include. I love that, during my own tenure, as long as I didn't mess up or contravene the continuity of potential future movies, and so long as I Put Things Back Where I Found Them by story's end, I could have our heroes spend issue after issue chasing after a block of carbonite that might hold Han, or have the Sarlaac burp up Boba Fett, only to swallow him back down. I love that, in lieu of being able to do stories about the remnants of the Empire, I could have our heroes — who always pretty much wrote themselves, once the structure of the plot was in place — fend off an invasion from A Galaxy Even Farther Away... and then have to face the enemy of their new enemy, from A Galaxy Even Farther Away Than That Last One. I love that we could and did do action. And drama. And pathos. And occasionally some utterly shameless comedy.

I love that nowadays, the Disney Channel continues to take advantage of the size of the *Star Wars* Universe, reinventing the tale of the Rebellion for kids the age of my 8-year-old niece and nephew, by recounting the adventures of an entirely separate band of heroes, whose adventures unfold concurrently with those of Luke, Han and Leia.

I love that *Family Guy* and *Phineas and Ferb* have done affectionate, effective *Star Wars* adaptations of their own. I love knowing that there is a new movie just over the horizon. I love that in the *Yoda Chronicles*, Darth Vader faced off against his old Padawan friends...and Rusty.

And I love that all of you care enough to have picked up this book and read this reminiscence. And even after all these years, I still love to be able to say:

MAY THE FORCE BE WITH YOU!

Jo Duffy
May 201

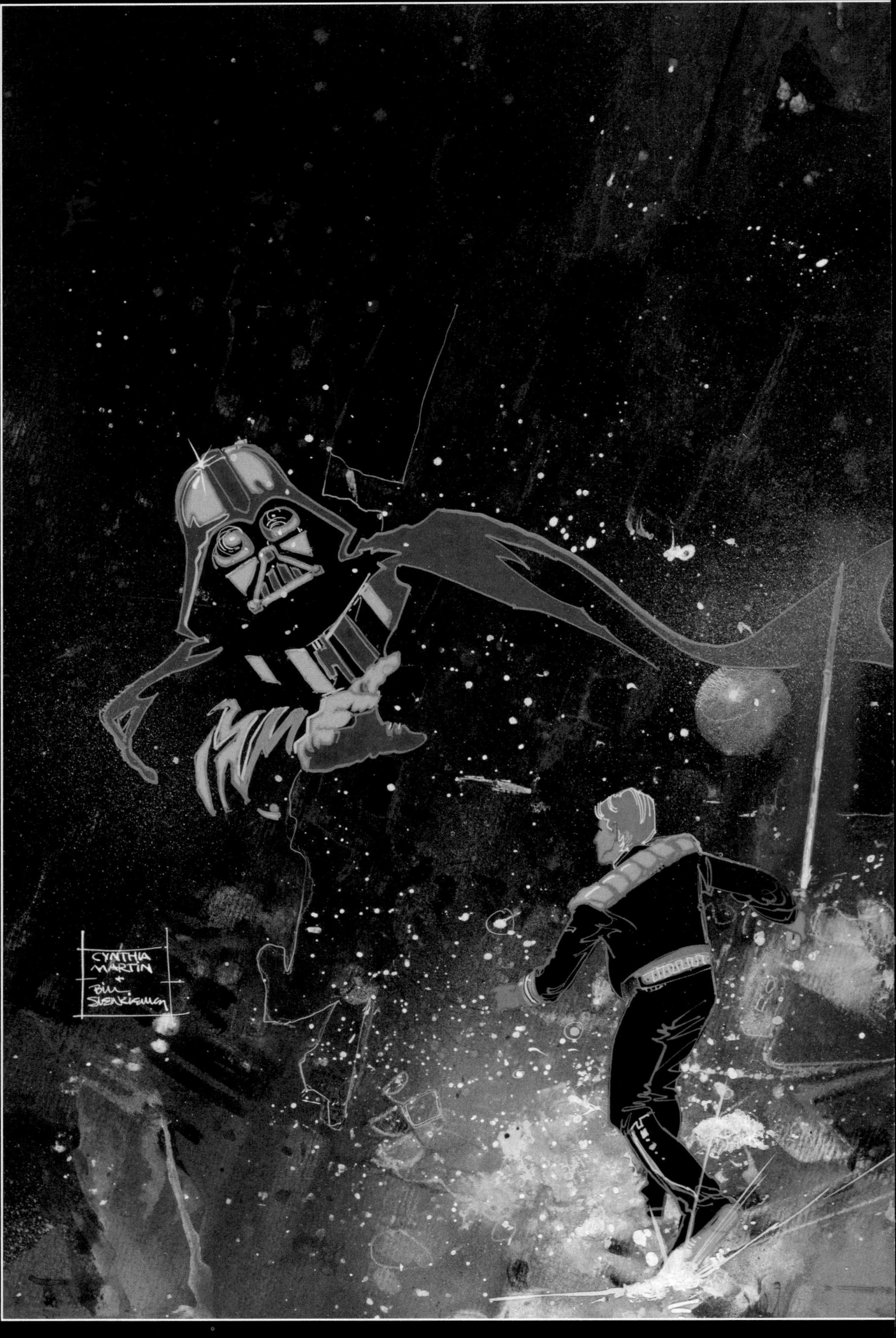
CYNTHIA MARTIN + BILL SIENKIEWICZ

STAR WARS #92 **COVER PAINTING BY CYNTHIA MARTIN & BILL SIENKIEWICZ**

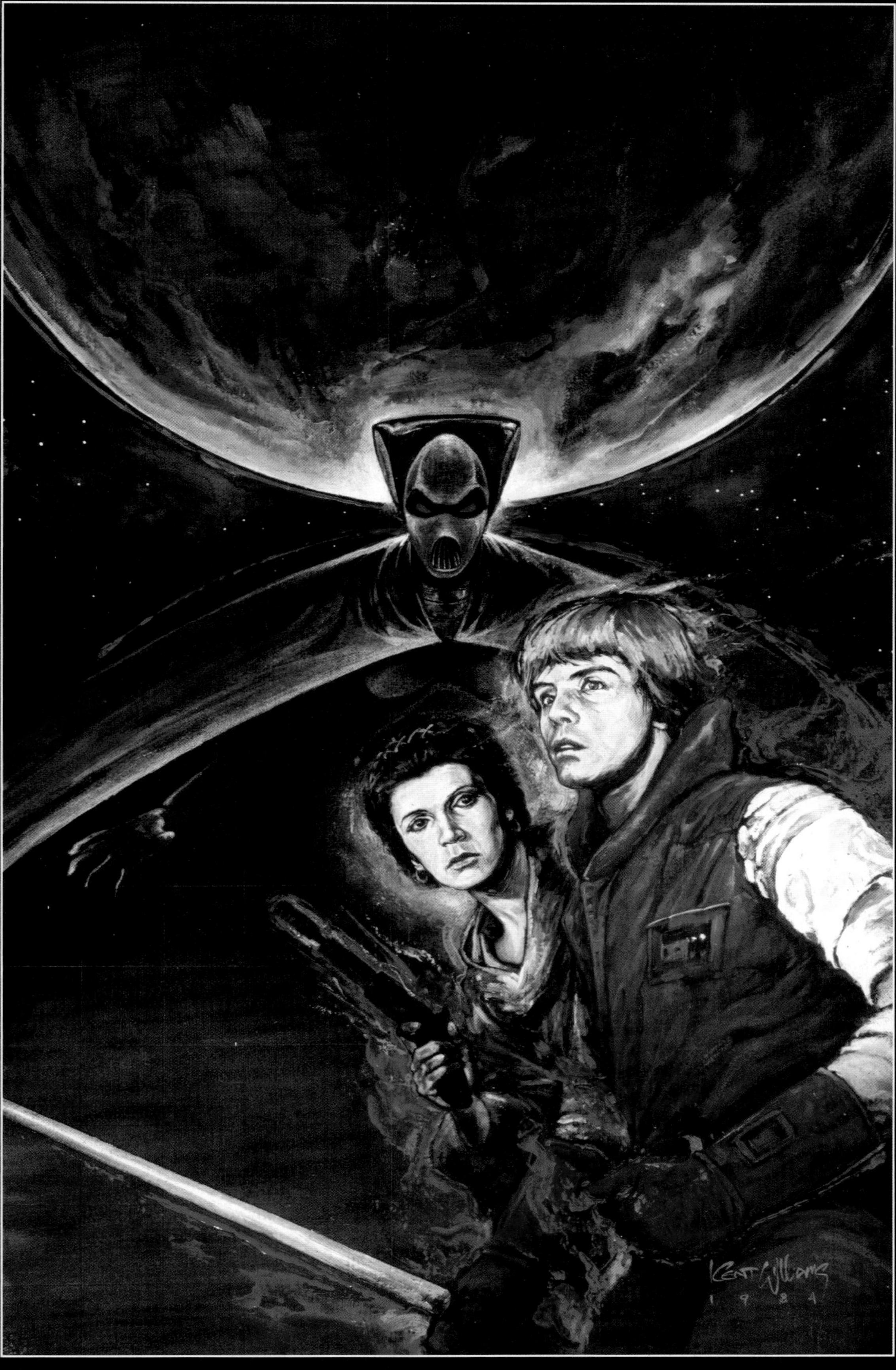

STAR WARS #95 COVER PAINTING BY KENT WILLIAMS

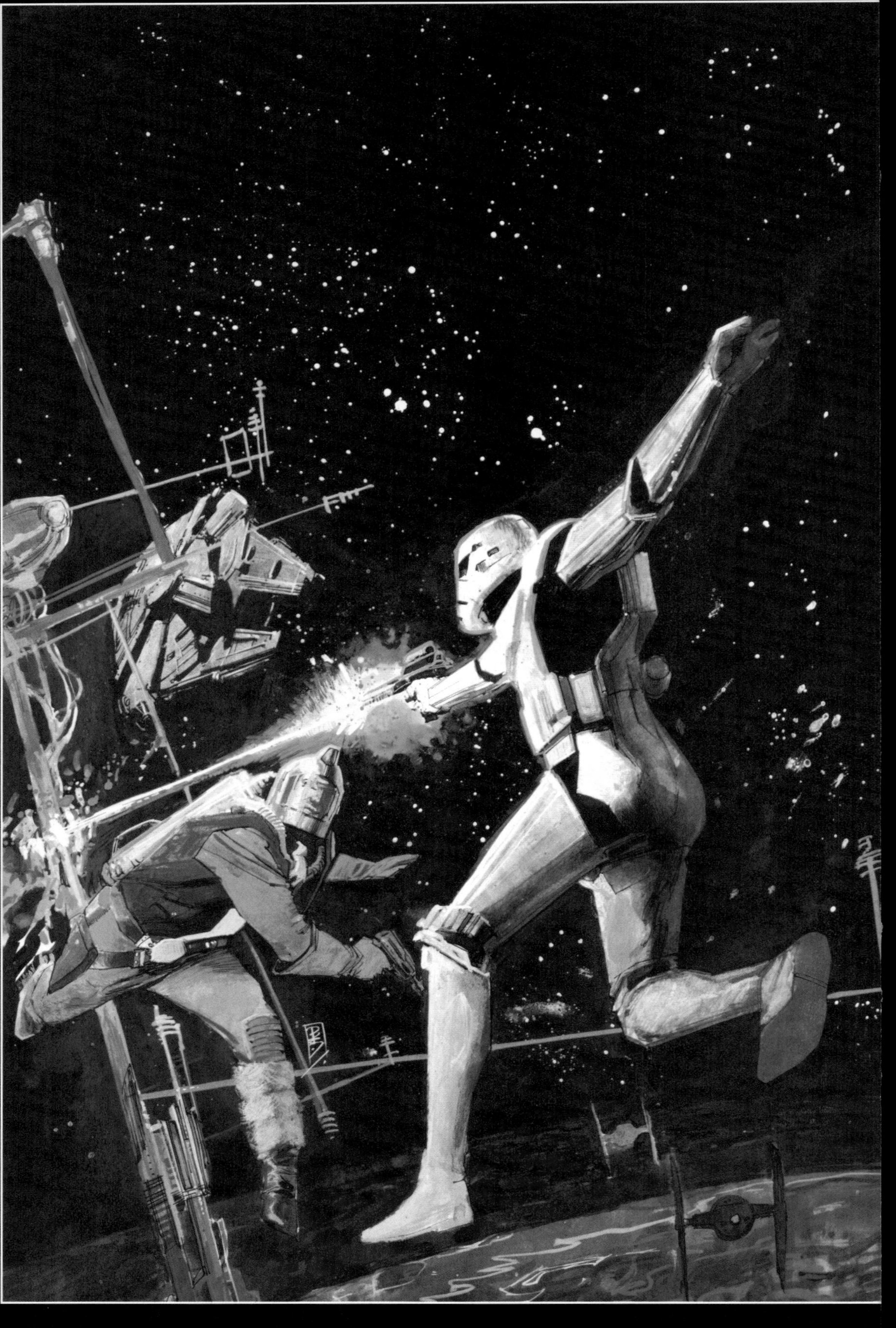

STAR WARS #98 COVER PAINTING BY BILL SIENKIEWICZ

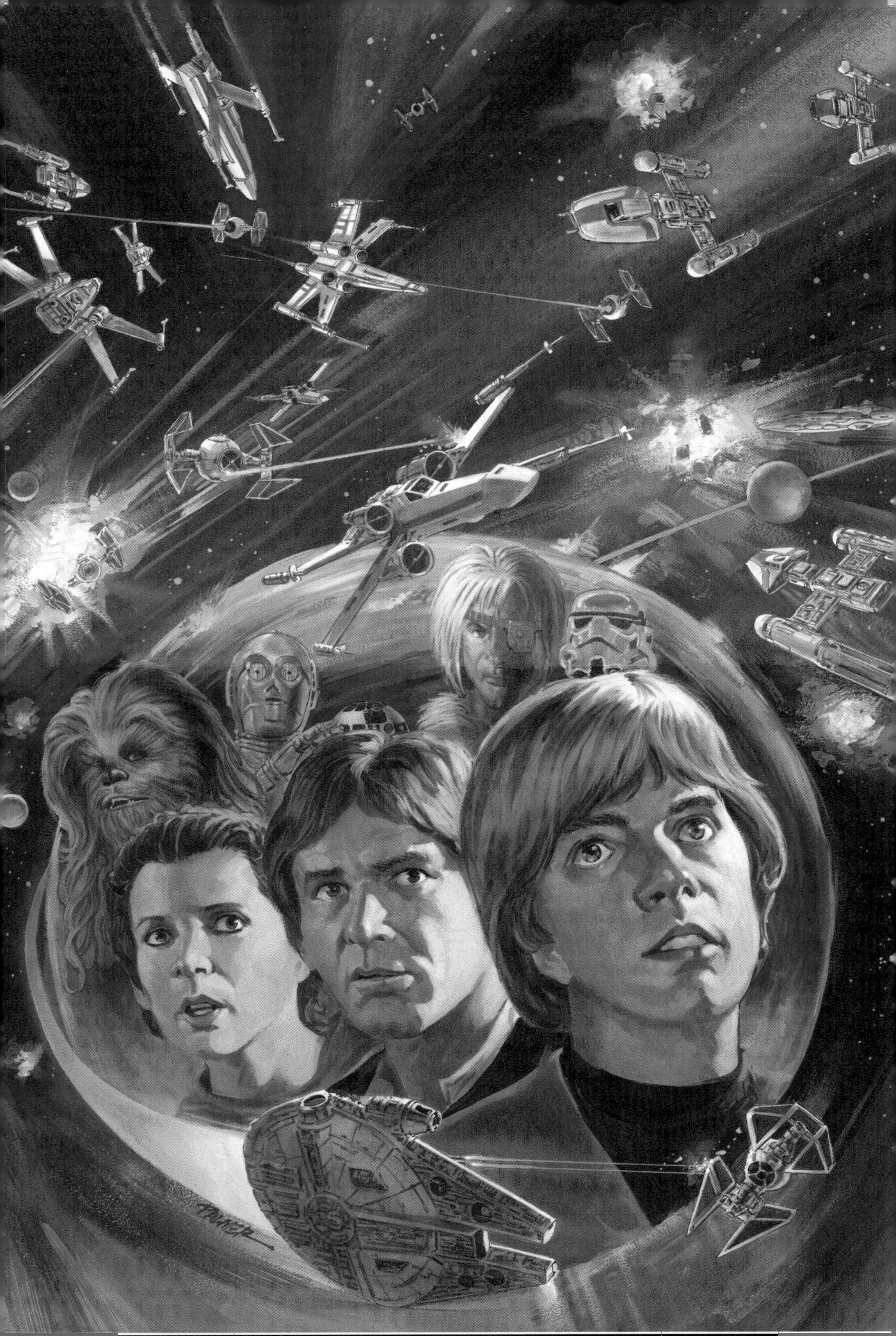

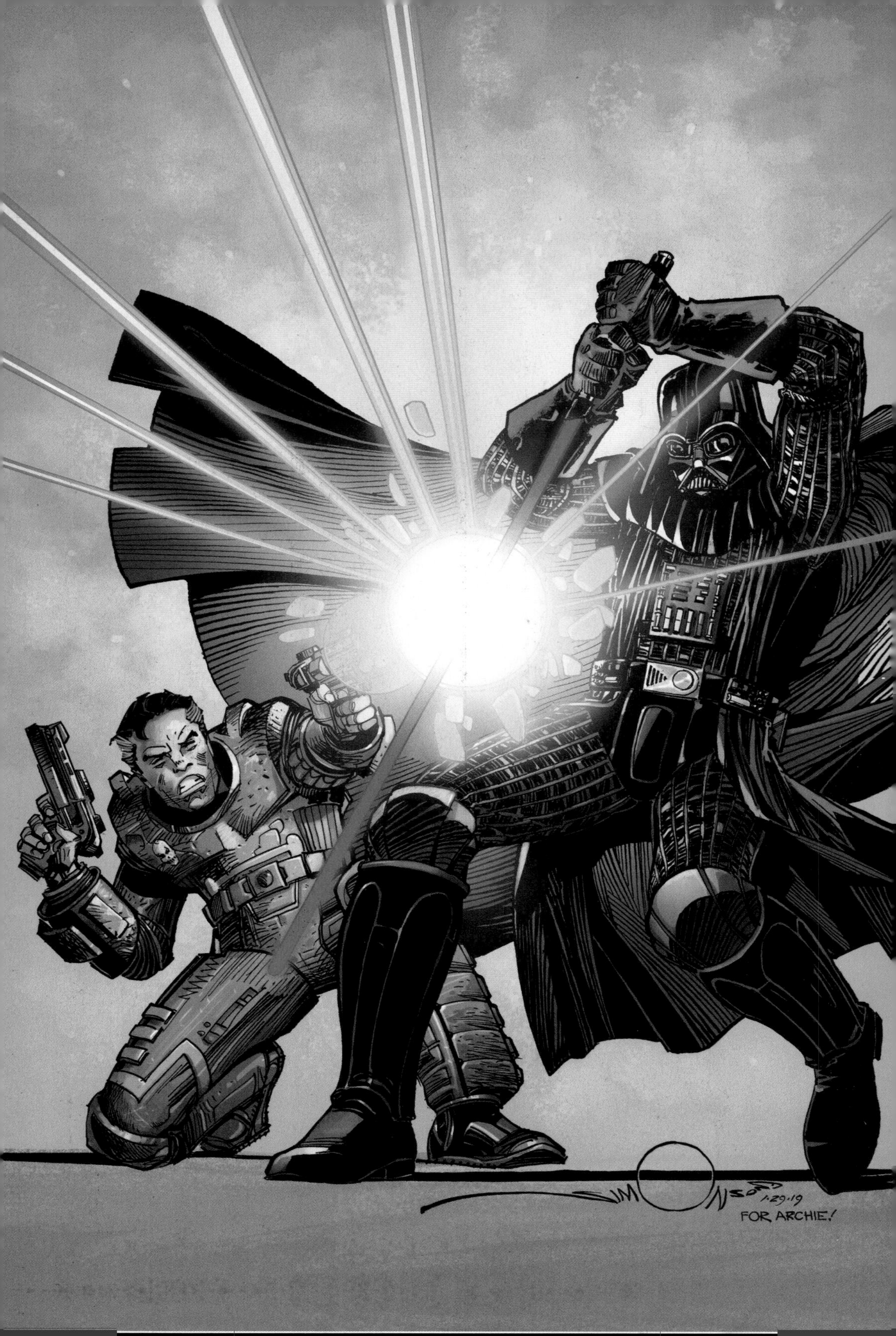
1-29-19
FOR ARCHIE!

STAR FABELA